Sports Illustrated 2014 Almanac

By the Editors of Sports Illustrated

BASEBALL
PRO FOOTBALL
COLLEGE FOOTBALL
PRO BASKETBALL
COLLEGE BASKETBALL
HOCKEY
OLYMPICS
TENNIS
GOLF
SOCCER
MOTOR SPORTS

ISBN 10: 1-60320-976-X
ISBN 13: 978-1-60320-976-2

SPORTS ILLUSTRATED is a registered trademark of Time Inc.

SPORTS ILLUSTRATED 2014 Almanac was prepared by:
Kensington Media Group, Inc.

Editorial Director: Morin Bishop	Art Director: Barbara Chilenskas
Proofreader: Wade Martin	Photo Editor: John Blackmar

Cover photography credits:
PEYTON MANNING: Robert Beck
MIGUEL CABRERA: Robert Beck
LEBRON JAMES: John W. McDonough
ALEX OVECHKIN: Damian Strohmeyer

Back cover photography credits:
PHIL MICKELSON: Andy Lyons/Getty Images
TREY BURKE: David E. Klutho
SERENA WILLIAMS: Bob Martin

Spine photography credit: JOHNNY MANZIEL: Mario Cantu/Cal Sport Media

---

TIME HOME ENTERTAINMENT

Publisher .... Jim Childs
Vice President, Brand & Digital Strategy .... Steven Sandonato
Executive Director, Marketing Services .... Carol Pittard
Executive Director, Retail & Special Sales .... Tom Mifsud
Executive Publishing Director .... Joy Butts
Director, Bookazine Development & Marketing .... Laura Adam
Finance Director .... Glenn Buonocore
Associate Publishing Director .... Megan Pearlman
Associate General Counsel .... Helen Wan
Assistant Director, Special Sales .... Ilene Schreider
Senior Book Production Manager .... Susan Chodakiewicz
Brand Manager .... Michele Bové
Associate Prepress Manager .... Alex Voznesenskiy

Editorial Director .... Stephen Koepp
Copy Chief .... Rina Bander
Design Manager .... Anne-Michelle Gallero

Special thanks: Katherine Barnet, Jeremy Biloon, Dana Campolattaro, Rose Cirrincione, Natalie
Ebel, Assu Etsubneh, Mariana Evans, Christine Font, Susan Hettleman, Hillary Hirsch, David
Kahn, Amy Mangus, Kimberly Marshall, Nina Mistry, Dave Rozzelle, Ricardo Santiago, Gina
Scauzillo, Adriana Tierno, Vanessa Wu.

We welcome your comments and suggestions about Sports Illustrated Books. Please write to us
at: Sports Illustrated, Attention: Book Editors, P.O. Box 11016, Des Moines, IA 50336-1016.
If you would like to order any of our hardcover Collector's Edition books, please call us at
1-800-327-6388 (Monday through Friday, 7 a.m.–8 p.m. Central Time or Saturday, 7 a.m.–6 p.m.
Central Time).

CONTENTS

In compiling the *Sports Illustrated 2014 Almanac*, the editors would like to extend their gratitude to the following organizations for their help in providing information and materials relating to their sports: Major League Baseball; the National Football League; the National Collegiate Athletic Association; the National Basketball Association; the National Hockey League; the Association of Tennis Professionals; the Women's Tennis Association; the U.S. Tennis Association; the U.S. Golf Association; the Ladies Professional Golf Association; the Professional Golfers Association; National Thoroughbred Racing Association; the Breeders' Cup; Churchill Downs; the National Association for Stock Car Auto Racing; Major League Soccer; the Fédération Internationale de Futbol Association; the U.S. Olympic Committee; USA Track & Field; USA Gymnastics.

The following sources were consulted in gathering information:

Baseball mlb.com, worldseries.com, baseballhalloffame.org, baseball-reference.com, *Associated Press* (LCS, WS game recaps)

Pro Football nfl.com, superbowl.com, profootballhof.com, cfl.ca, greycup.cfl.ca, pro-football-reference.com

College Football ncaasports.com, heisman.com, *Official 2013 NCAA Division I-A and I-AA Football Records Book, Official 2013 Division II and III Football Records Book*

Pro Basketball nba.com, hoophall.com

College Basketball ncaasports.com, *Official 20013–14 NCAA Division I Men's Basketball Records Book, Official 2013–14 NCAA Division I Women's Basketball Records Book, Official 2013–14 NCAA Division II and III Men's Basketball Records Book,* sports-reference.com

Hockey nhl.com, hhof.com, ushockeyhall.com

Tennis atptennis.com, sonyericssonwtatour.com, usopen.org, australianopen.com, wimbledon.org, rolandgarros.com, masters-cup.com, daviscup.com, fedcup.com, tennisfame.com

Golf pgatour.com, masters.org, usopen.org, usga.org, opengolf.com, pga.com, lpga.com, knc.com, ussenioropen.com, usamateur.org, rydercup.com, walkercup.org, curtiscup.org, pinggolf.com

Boxing boxrec.com, wbaonline.com, wbcboxing.com, ibf-usba-boxing.com, ibhof.com, thering-online.com, usaboxing.org, olympic.org

Horse Racing ntra.com, equibase.com, bloodhorse.com, kentuckyderby.com, preakness.com, belmontstakes.nyra.com, offtrackbetting.com

Motor Sports nascar.com, formula1.com, indycar.com, americanlemans.com, lemans.org, champcarworldseries.com, indy500.com, daytona24hr.com

Soccer fifa.com, mlsnet.com, ussoccer.com, soccernet.com, uslsoccer.com,

NCAA Sports ncaasports.com

Olympics olympic.org, usoc.org

Track and Field iaaf.org, usatf.org, usoc.org

Miscellaneous Sports letour.fr, usarchery.org, pba.com, fide.com, worldcurling.org, usacurl.org, usacycling.org, iditarod.com, usfigureskating.org, isu.org, fig-gymnastics.com, usa-gymnastics.org, ushandball.org, uscla.com, nll.com, littleleague.org, us-polo.org, prorodeo.org, usrowing.org, usarugby.org, rugbyworldcup.com, amnrl.com, fis-ski.com, asasoftball.com, us-squash.org, ironmanlive.com, usatriathlon.org, fivb.org, usavolleyball.org, themat.com

Multiple Sports espn.go.com, sportsillustrated.cnn.com, sports.yahoo.com

Baseball

DAMIAN STROHMEYER

Boston Very Strong

Led by the unstoppable David Ortiz, the Boston Red Sox rolled past the St. Louis Cardinals, handing the Beantown faithful their third Series title in 10 years

BY MERRELL NODEN

BOSTON STRONG. THAT PHRASE could well have described Red Sox slugger David Ortiz's extraordinary performance in the 2013 World Series, as Ortiz wound up batting .688 to the rest of his team's .169. But BOSTON STRONG was much more than that. It was a cry of defiance following the terror bombing that had disrupted the proud old city's most iconic event, the Boston Marathon. Bostonians love their marathon and their Sox. There could be no more satisfying end to a painful year than watching their Red Sox hammer the St. Louis Cardinals 6–1 in Game 6 to claim the team's third World Series title since 2004, four games to two.

The Cardinals and Red Sox were storied franchises that had each won two Series in the past decade. Boston, however, had fallen on hard times last year. This season, under first-year manager John Farrell, and boosted by the acquisition of seven veteran free agents, Boston had turned its fortunes upside down, going from last in the American League East with 93 losses, to first, with 97 wins. That tied them with the Cardinals, who also led their league with 97.

In a season clouded by major revelations about performance-enhancing drug use, the Red Sox revival was an uplifting story, as were both the superb pitching and wealth of great young players throughout baseball. The talented Dodgers were bumbling along in fourth place in the NL West on May 1, and there was talk of manager Don Mattingly losing his job. That changed with the call up, on June 3, of Yasiel Puig, a muscular 22-year-old who had defected from Cuba in 2012. Puig ignited his new team. Los Angeles went 19–6 in July and finished the season 22 games over .500. It didn't hurt that the Dodgers had a one-two punch of Clayton Kershaw, whose 1.83 ERA was the first under 2.00 by any starter since Pedro Martinez in 2000, and Zack Greinke, who wasn't far behind him (2.63). In New York, Mets fans finally had reason to cheer, with the emergence of Matt Harvey as perhaps the best young arm in baseball behind Kershaw, though the team's followers will have to wait until 2015 to see just how good he can be, as offseason Tommy John surgery will keep Harvey sidelined in 2014.

Another team that struggled was the New York Yankees, who could not recover from a June slump (11–16). These Yankees simply looked old. Derek Jeter played just 17 games all season, with Mark Teixeira (15), Curtis Granderson (61), and Alex Rodriguez (44) joining him for long stints on the disabled list. Only Mariano Rivera performed like his old self, notching 44 saves in a moving

ROBERT BECK

farewell tour of major league stadiums. The greatest reliever in baseball history retires with a career-record 652 saves and career playoff records of 42 saves and a 0.70 ERA.

Hanging over the Yankees was the cloud linking Rodriguez to Biogenesis, the anti-aging clinic in Coral Gables, Fla., that provided drugs to a number of major leaguers. Rodriguez was one of 13 players suspended by Major League Baseball. Ryan Braun of the Brewers accepted his 65-game suspension and sat out the season, but A-Rod refused to do so, hiring a team of lawyers to contest his major league–record 211-game suspension. He later accused the Yankees of mishandling his hip injury, further poisoning his relationship with the baseball world. Things were not pretty in the Bronx.

The best race for the playoffs in either league was the three-way tussle that played out in the National League Central. Two of the contenders, St. Louis and Cincinnati, had reached the playoffs the previous year. The

Ortiz, who recorded an astounding .760 on-base percentage in the World Series, slid home with his team's first run in Boston's Game 4 victory over St. Louis.

third, the Pittsburgh Pirates, hadn't made the playoffs—nor topped .500—since 1992. But this year, led by center fielder and MVP candidate Andrew McCutchen, slugger Pedro Alvarez (who tied Arizona's Paul Goldschmidt for the league lead in homers, with 36), and a strong pitching staff, Pittsburgh contended all season. At the All-Star break they were 56–37, 19 games over .500, and long suffering Pirate fans were speaking openly not just of making playoffs, but even of reaching the Series.

Just getting there would not be enough for the Detroit Tigers, who had reached the ALCS the past two years and lost in the Series last year. Led by Miguel Cabrera, who threatened to win a second straight Triple Crown but had to settle for just the batting title (.348), the Tigers were a powerhouse

JOHN IACONO

You say goodbye, I say hello: Puig's entrance electrified baseball and led to a Dodger renaissance; the great Rivera (below), baseball's finest reliever, exited gracefully.

ROBERT BECK

team. Detroit also had a sensational rotation, starting with the season's only 20-game winner, Max Scherzer (21 wins), not to mention Justin Verlander and Anibel Sanchez, who led the league with an ERA of 2.57.

The Tigers seemed ready for any opponent, but in the ALCS they came up against a Boston rotation that was just as good. Despite the Tiger staff's surrendering only 2.77 earned runs to Boston's 3.06 and holding the Red Sox batting average to a measly .202, the Tigers lost in six games.

Meanwhile, the Cardinals, relying on a balanced lineup that included great pitchers like Adam Wainwright and 22-year-old sensation Michael Wacha (4–0 with a 1.00 ERA to start the playoffs) and veteran power hitters like Carlos Beltran, beat the Dodgers in the NLCS four games to two.

The World Series began as a comedy of errors. No one seemed capable of getting anything right. It wasn't just the 11 errors committed in the first four games. In that same span, baseball fans had witnessed one of the worst blown calls ever, a non-catch on a double play at second base that was quickly corrected by committee; an obstruction call to end Game 3; and a pickoff at first base to end Game 4. As one wag put it, this was not so much the World Series as the Weird Series.

But the Series at last reverted to solid baseball. Ortiz, who got on base 19 of 25 times, was named Series MVP, and the other Red Sox managed to get big hits at the right time. Jonny Gomes batted just .118, but had a game-winning three-run homer in Game 4. Facing Wacha, Shane Victorino hit a three-run double off the Green Monster to put Boston ahead for good in the third inning of Game 6. Unmistakable in the extravagant beards that made them look like a team of Old Testament prophets, this was a team that came together with and drew inspiration from a city that had suffered but recovered.

"I go back to our players understanding their place in the city," mused Red Sox manager John Farrell in his post-Series interview. "They get it. They get that there's a civic responsibility that we have wearing this uniform."

Boston Strong, indeed.

2013 Final Regular Season Standings

National League

EASTERN DIVISION

Team	Won	Lost	Pct	GB	Home	Away
Atlanta	96	66	.593	—	56-25	40-41
Washington	86	76	.531	10	47-34	39-42
NY Mets	74	88	.457	22	33-48	41-40
Philadelphia	73	89	.451	23	43-38	30-51
Miami	62	100	.383	34	36-45	26-55

CENTRAL DIVISION

Team	Won	Lost	Pct	GB	Home	Away
St. Louis	97	65	.599	—	54-27	43-38
†Pittsburgh	94	68	.580	3	50-31	44-37
†Cincinnati	90	72	.556	7	49-31	41-41
Milwaukee	74	88	.457	23	37-44	37-44
Chicago Cubs	66	96	.407	31	31-50	35-46

WESTERN DIVISION

Team	Won	Lost	Pct	GB	Home	Away
LA Dodgers	92	70	.568	—	47-34	45-36
Arizona	81	81	.500	11	45-36	36-45
San Francisco	76	86	.469	16	42-40	34-46
San Diego	76	86	.469	16	45-36	31-50
Colorado	74	88	.457	18	45-36	29-52

†Wild-card teams.

American League

EASTERN DIVISION

Team	Won	Lost	Pct	GB	Home	Away
Boston	97	65	.599	—	53-28	44-37
†Tampa Bay	92	71	.564	5.5	51-30	41-41
NY Yankees	85	77	.525	12	46-35	39-42
Baltimore	85	77	.525	12	46-35	39-42
Toronto	74	88	.457	23	40-41	34-47

CENTRAL DIVISION

Team	Won	Lost	Pct	GB	Home	Away
Detroit	93	69	.574	—	51-30	42-39
†Cleveland	92	70	.568	1	51-30	41-40
Kansas City	86	76	.531	7	44-37	42-39
Minnesota	66	96	.407	27	32-49	34-47
Chi. White Sox	63	99	.389	30	37-44	26-55

WESTERN DIVISION

Team	Won	Lost	Pct	GB	Home	Away
Oakland	96	66	.593	—	52-29	44-37
Texas	91	72	.558	5.5	46-36	45-36
LA Angels	78	84	.481	18	39-42	39-42
Seattle	71	91	.438	25	36-45	35-46
Houston	51	111	.315	45	24-57	27-54

2013 Playoffs

National League wild-card play-in game

Cincinnati 2 at Pittsburgh 6

National League Division Playoffs

Game 1 .... Los Angeles 6 at Atlanta 1
Game 2 .... Los Angeles 3 at Atlanta 4

Game 3 .... Atlanta 6 at Los Angeles 13
Game 4 .... Atlanta 3 at Los Angeles 4

(Los Angeles won series 3–1)

Game 1 .... Pittsburgh 1 at St. Louis 9
Game 2 .... Pittsburgh 7 at St. Louis 1
Game 3 .... St. Louis 3 at Pittsburgh 5

Game 4 .... St. Louis 2 at Pittsburgh 1
Game 5 .... Pittsburgh 1 at St. Louis 6

(St. Louis won series 3–2)

National League Championship Series

Game 1 .... Los Angeles 2 at St. Louis 3 (13)
Game 2 .... Los Angeles 0 at St. Louis 1
Game 3 .... St. Louis 0 at Los Angeles 3

Game 4 .... St. Louis 4 at Los Angeles 2
Game 5 .... St. Louis 4 at Los Angeles 6
Game 6 .... Los Angeles 0 at St. Louis 9

(St. Louis won series 4–2)

GAME 1

															R	H	E
Los Angeles	0	0	2	0	0	0	0	0	0	0	0	0	0		2	9	0
St. Louis	0	0	2	0	0	0	0	0	0	0	0	0	1		3	7	0

W—StL: Lynn. **L**—LA: Withrow. **LOB**—LA: 11; StL: 7. **2B**—LA: Crawford; StL: Beltran. **3B**—LA: Ellis. **RBI**—LA: Uribe (2); StL: Beltran (3). **GIDP**—LA: Uribe, Young. **SAC**—LA: Ellis.

T—4:47. **A**—46,691.

Recap: (AP) Carlos Beltran kept protesting that he's just one player. Albeit a pretty special one in October. "Understand this is not about me," Beltran said. "In order for a team to win a ballgame, a lot of things need to happen right, the right way. We have to pitch, we have to play defense and we have to come through offensively." Beltran had the last two covered like a blanket in Game 1 of the National League Championship Series, giving the St. Louis Cardinals his latest scintillating postseason performance in a 13-inning, 3–2 victory over the Los Angeles Dodgers. Beltran hit a tying, two-run double in the third inning. Then he took charge on defense, calling center fielder Jon Jay off the ball before throwing out a runner at the plate from shallow right field in the 10th to keep it even. Well past midnight at Busch Stadium, Beltran singled into the right-field corner with one out against Kenley Jansen in the 13th inning to finish a game that took 4 hours, 47 minutes.

National League Championship Series *(Cont.)*

GAME 2

Los Angeles	0	0	0	0	0	0	0	0	0	**0**	**5**	**0**
St. Louis	0	0	0	0	1	0	0	x		**1**	**2**	**1**

W—StL: Wacha. **L**—LA: Kershaw. **SV**—StL: Rosenthal. **LOB**—LA: 6; StL: 2. **2B**—StL: Freese; LA: A. Ellis. **3B**—StL: Carpenter. **RBI**—StL: Jay. **SB**—LA: M. Ellis. **SF**—StL: Jay. **GIDP**—LA: Holliday. **PB**—LA: A. Ellis. **E**—StL: Carpenter.

T—2:40. **A**—46,872.

Recap: (AP) Matched against ace Clayton Kershaw, the only thing Michael Wacha lacked was a no-hit watch. Wacha stared down a bases-loaded test in the sixth inning and pitched into the seventh, and the kids in the bullpen also were impervious to October pressure, keeping the Los Angeles Dodgers bats silent for the second straight day and winning 1–0 for a 2–0 lead in the NL Championship Series. The Cardinals managed only two hits off Kershaw and the Dodgers, but Jon Jay's sacrifice fly set up by Freese's double and A.J. Ellis' passed ball in the fifth stood up.

GAME 3

St. Louis	0	0	0	0	0	0	0	0	0	**0**	**4**	**0**
Los Angeles	0	0	0	2	0	0	0	1	x	**3**	**9**	**0**

W—LA: Ryu. **L**—StL: Wainwright. **SV**—LA: Jansen. **LOB**—StL: 4; LA: 5. **2B**—LA: M. Ellis, Gonzalez. **3B**—LA: Puig, A. Ellis. **RBI**—LA: Gonzalez, Puig, Ramirez. **GIDP**—LA: Uribe.

T—2:54. **A**—53,940.

Recap: (AP) Led by a pair of precocious rookies, the Los Angeles Dodgers got themselves right back into the National League Championship Series. Hyun-Jin Ryu outpitched Adam Wainwright with seven innings of three-hit ball, and Yasiel Puig celebrated his RBI triple that helped Los Angeles beat the St. Louis Cardinals 3–0 in Game 3. Adrian Gonzalez's RBI double ended a 1-for-17 drought for the Dodgers with runners in scoring position.

GAME 4

St. Louis	0	0	3	0	0	0	1	0	0	**4**	**6**	**0**
Los Angeles	0	0	0	2	0	0	0	0	0	**2**	**8**	**1**

W—StL: Lynn. **L**—LA: Nolasco. **SV**—StL: Rosenthal. **LOB**—StL: 9; LA: 5. **2B**—StL: Carpenter; LA: Gonzalez, Punto. **HR**—StL: Holliday, Robinson. **RBI**—StL: Carpenter, Holliday (2), Robinson; LA: Puig, A. Ellis. **SAC**—StL: Lynn. **SB**—StL: Carpenter. **PO**—LA: Punto. **GIDP**—StL: Freese; LA: Schumaker, Uribe, Puig. **E**—LA: A. Ellis.

T—3:17. **A**—53,992.

Recap: (AP) Thanks to two big swings and some excellent defense, the St. Louis Cardinals are one win

GAME 4 *(Cont.)*

from the World Series. Matt Holliday and pinch hitter Shane Robinson connected for the first home runs of the National League Championship Series, sending St. Louis past the Los Angeles Dodgers 4-2 for a 3-1 lead in their best-of-seven playoff. In a series starved for offense, the Cardinals scored as many runs as they did in the first three games combined, in which the teams totaled nine.

GAME 5

St. Louis	0	0	2	0	0	0	0	0	2	**4**	**10**	**0**
Los Angeles	0	2	1	0	1	0	1	1	x	**6**	**9**	**0**

W—LA: Greinke. **L**—StL: Kelly. **LOB**—StL: 5; LA: 2. **2B**—StL: Holliday (2). **3B**—StL: Beltran. **HR**—LA: Gonzalez (2), Crawford, A. Ellis. **RBI**—StL: Beltran, Holliday, Adams, Kozma; LA: Uribe, Greinke, Gonzalez (2), Crawford, A. Ellis. **GIDP**—StL: Molina (2); LA: Ramirez.

T—3:10. **A**—53,183.

Recap: (AP) It took the Dodgers five games to hit a home run in the NL Championship Series. Once Adrian Gonzalez powered up for the first one, their dormant offense broke loose. Gonzalez homered twice and Zack Greinke came through with the clutch performance Los Angeles needed in a 6-4 victory against the Cardinals that trimmed St. Louis' lead to 3-2 in the best-of-seven playoff.

GAME 6

Los Angeles	0	0	0	0	0	0	0	0	0	**0**	**2**	**2**
St. Louis	0	0	4	0	5	0	0	x		**9**	**13**	**0**

W—StL: Wacha. **L**—LA: Kershaw. **LOB**—LA: 2; StL: 8. **2B**—LA: A. Ellis; StL: Beltran, Carpenter, Adams. **RBI**—StL: Beltran (2), Molina, Robinson (2), Adams, Wacha, Carpenter. **SF**—StL: Carpenter. **GIDP**—LA: M. Ellis; StL: Robinson. **E**—LA: Puig (2).

T—2:59. **A**—46,899.

Recap: (AP) With the red-clad crowd roaring more loudly with every pitch, Matt Carpenter became more determined to get a hit and help lead the St. Louis Cardinals back to the World Series. On Clayton Kershaw's 11th offering, Carpenter lined a double to right field. It turned out to be the start of something really big. Carlos Beltran followed with another key hit in a four-run third inning that stunned the Dodgers ace. Michael Wacha was again magnificent on the mound and St. Louis advanced to its second World Series in three seasons by roughing up Los Angeles 9-0 in Game 6 of the NL Championship Series. Wacha, 22, was selected MVP of the NLCS after throwing 13⅔ scoreless innings and beating Kershaw twice in the series.

American League wild-card play-in game

Tampa Bay 4 at Cleveland 0

American League Division Playoffs

Game 1 ....Detroit 3 at Oakland 2	Game 4 ....Oakland 6 at Detroit 8
Game 2 ....Detroit 0 at Oakland 1	Game 5 ....Detroit 3 at Oakland 0
Game 3 ....Oakland 6 at Detroit 3	

(Detroit won series 3–2)

Game 1 ....Tampa Bay 2 at Boston 12	Game 3 ....Boston 4 at Tampa Bay 5
Game 2 ....Tampa Bay 4 at Boston 7	Game 4 ....Boston 3 at Tampa Bay 1

(Boston won series 3–1)

American League Championship Series

Game 1 ....Detroit 1 at Boston 0	Game 4 ....Boston 3 at Detroit 7
Game 2 ....Detroit 5 at Boston 6	Game 5 ....Boston 4 at Detroit 3
Game 3 ....Boston 1 at Detroit 0 ·	Game 6 ....Detroit 2 at Boston 5

(Boston won series 4–2)

GAME 1

Detroit	0 0 0 0 0 1 0 0 0	1	9	0
Boston	0 0 0 0 0 0 0 0 0	0	1	1

W—Det: Sanchez. **L**—Bos: Lester. **LOB**—Det: 12; Bos: 8. **2B**—Det: Peralta (2), Hunter. **RBI**—Det: Peralta. **SB**—Bos: Victorino, Berry. **GIDP**—Det: Hunter. **E**—Bos: Victorino. **T**—3:56. **A**—38,210.

Recap: (AP) Lose the war, win the game. That's a trade Anibal Sanchez and the Detroit Tigers were happy to make to take the lead over the Boston Red Sox in the AL Championship Series. Sanchez and four relievers came within two outs of the first combined no-hitter in postseason history, striking out 17 to beat Boston 1–0 in the series opener. Sanchez struck out 12—including a record-tying four in the first inning—but also walked a season-high six. Al Alburquerque, Jose Veras, Drew Smyly and Joaquin Benoit stretched the no-hitter through eight innings. With one out in the ninth, Daniel Nava lined a single to center field off Benoit to end Detroit's bid for the third postseason no-hitter ever. Jhonny Peralta had an RBI single off Jon Lester in the sixth for the game's only run.

GAME 2

Detroit	0 1 0 0 0 0 4 0 0	5	8	1
Boston	0 0 0 0 0 1 0 4 1	6	7	1

W—Bos: Uehara. **L**—Det: Porcello. **LOB**—Det: 6; Bos: 4. **2B**—Det: Martinez, Fielder; Bos: Pedroia, Middlebrooks. **HR**—Det: Cabrera, Avila; Bos: Ortiz. **RBI**—Det: Avila (3), Cabrera, Martinez; Bos: Pedroia, Ortiz (4), Saltalamacchia. **GIDP**—Det: Infante; Bos: Carp. **E**—Det: Iglesias; Bos: Drew. **T**—3:28. **A**—38,029.

Recap: (AP) David Ortiz's line drive sailed just beyond Torii Hunter's reach and into the Boston bullpen, sending the Tigers right fielder flopping headfirst over the wall after it. With one swing, the Red Sox slugger turned everything upside-down. Ortiz's grand slam erased an eighth-inning deficit and ended Detroit's unprecedented run of pitching dominance, and Jonny Gomes scampered around the bases with the game-winning run in the ninth to give Boston a 6–5 victory over Detroit and knot the AL Championship Series at one game apiece.

GAME 3

Boston	0 0 0 0 0 0 1 0 0	1	4	0
Detroit	0 0 0 0 0 0 0 0 0	0	6	1

W—Bos: Lackey. **L**—Det: Verlander. **SV**—Bos: Uehara. **LOB**—Bos: 4; Det: 7. **2B**—Det: Peralta. **HR**—Bos: Napoli. **RBI**—Bos: Napoli. **E**—Det: Hunter.

T—3:20. **A**—42,327.

Recap: (AP) Once again this October, one run was enough. The Boston Red Sox scored it—and now they lead an AL championship series that seemed to be slipping away last weekend. John Lackey edged Justin Verlander in the latest duel of these pitching-rich playoffs, and Boston's bullpen shut down Detroit's big boppers with the game on the line to lift the Red Sox over the Tigers 1–0 for a 2–1 advantage in the ALCS. Mike Napoli homered off Verlander in the seventh inning.

GAME 4

Boston	0 0 0 0 0 1 1 0 1	3	12	0
Detroit	0 5 0 2 0 0 0 0 x	7	9	0

W—Det: Fister. **L**—Bos: Peavy. **LOB**—Bos: 10; Det: 6. **2B**—Bos: Napoli, Ellsbury, Victorino, Bogaerts; Det: Hunter, Infante. **3B**—Bos: Ellsbury. **RBI**—Bos: Saltalamacchia, Victorino, Ellsbury; Det: Jackson (2), Iglesias, Hunter (2), Cabrera (2). **SAC**—Det: Iglesias. **SB**—Det: Jackson, Cabrera. **GIDP**—Det: Hunter, Infante. **T**—3:27. **A**—42,765.

Recap: (AP) A revitalized Austin Jackson delivered in Jim Leyland's revamped lineup as the Tigers built a big lead and held on this time, beating the Boston Red Sox 7–3 to even the ALCS at 2–all. Detroit scored five runs in the second inning, the first coming home on Jackson's walk. Torii Hunter had a two-run double and Miguel Cabrera drove in two runs. Doug Fister allowed a run in six innings, and the Tigers' starting pitchers have yielded only three runs in 27 ALCS innings—and struck out 42.

GAME 5

Boston	0 3 1 0 0 0 0 0 0	4	10	0
Detroit	0 0 0 0 1 1 1 0 0	3	10	1

W—Bos: Lester. **L**—Det: Sanchez. **SV**—Bos: Uehara. **LOB**—Bos: 8; Det: 6. **2B**—Bos: Bogaerts, Ross, Napoli. **HR**—Bos: Napoli. **RBI**—Bos: Napoli, Ross, Ellsbury; Det: Cabrera, Pena. **SB**—Bos: Ellsbury, Pedroia. **SAC**—Bos: Ross. **GIDP**—Bos: Ellsbury. Det: Pena, Jackson, Cabrera. **E**—Det: Cabrera. **PB**—Bos: Ross. **T**—3:47. **A**—42,669.

Recap: (AP) Mike Napoli opened the scoring with another big long ball, Junichi Tazawa again bested Miguel Cabrera in a crucial spot and the Red Sox moved within one win of reaching the World Series by edging the Detroit Tigers 4–3. Napoli opened a three-run second with his homer off Anibal Sanchez. Jon Lester allowed two runs and seven hits in 5⅓ innings. He walked three and struck out three, and the Boston bullpen held on to finish the fourth game of the series to be decided by one run.

GAME 6

Detroit	0 0 0 0 0 2 0 0 0	2	8	1
Boston	0 0 0 0 1 0 4 0 x	5	5	1

W—Bos: Tazawa. **L**—Det: Scherzer. **SV**—Bos: Uehara. **LOB**—Det: 6; Bos: 5. **2B**—Bos: Bogaerts, Gomes. **HR**—Bos: Victorino. **RBI**—Det: Martinez (2); Bos: Ellsbury, Victorino (4). **CS**—Bos: Ellsbury. **PO**—Det: Jackson. **GIDP**—Det: Iglesias; Bos: Pedroia. **E**—Det: Iglesias; Bos: Workman. **T**—3:47. **A**—42,669.

Recap: (AP) Offseason acquisition Shane Victorino brought the Red Sox one big step closer to completing their comeback from a miserable 2012, sending them to the World Series with a seventh-inning grand slam that gave Boston a 5–2 victory over the Detroit Tigers in Game 6 of the AL Championship Series. Detroit took a 2-1 lead in the sixth and 21-game winner Max Scherzer protected it until the seventh, when Boston loaded the bases. Victorino fell behind Jose Veras 0-2 but lofted a hanging curveball over the Green Monster to set off a celebration in the Red Sox dugout and in the Fenway Park stands.

(Boston won series 4–2)

GAME 1

St. Louis	0	0	0	0	0	0	0	0	1	**1**	**7**	**3**
Boston	3	2	0	0	0	0	2	1	x	**8**	**8**	**1**

W—Bos: Lester. **L**—StL: Wainwright. **LOB**—StL: 6; Bos: 4. **2B**—Bos: Napoli, Nava. **HR**—StL: Holliday; Bos: Ortiz. **RBI**—StL: Holliday; Bos: Napoli (3), Pedroia, Ortiz (3), Bogaerts. **SF**—Bos: Ortiz, Bogaerts. **GIDP**—StL: Freese. **E**—StL: Kozma (2), Freese; Bos: Gomes. **T**—3:17. **A**—38,345.

Recap: (AP) Mike Napoli hit a three-run double right after a game-changing call reversal in the first inning, Jon Lester made the early lead stand up and the Red Sox romped past the sloppy St. Louis Cardinals 8–1 for their ninth straight win in a World Series game. A season before Major League Baseball is expected to expand instant replay, fans got to see a preview. The entire six-man crew huddled and flipped a ruling on a forceout at second base—without looking at any video. "I think based on their group conversation, surprisingly, to a certain extent, they overturned it and I think got the call right," Boston manager John Farrell said. David Ortiz was robbed of a grand slam by Carlos Beltran—a catch that sent the star right fielder to a hospital with bruised ribs—but Big Papi later hit a two-run homer after third baseman David Freese's bad throw. The Red Sox also capitalized on two errors by shortstop Pete Kozma.

GAME 2

St. Louis	0	0	0	1	0	0	3	0	0	**4**	**7**	**1**
Boston	0	0	0	0	0	2	0	0	0	**2**	**4**	**2**

W—StL: Wacha. **L**—Bos: Lackey. **SV**—StL: Rosenthal. **LOB**—StL: 6; Bos: 6. **2B**—Bos: Pedroia. **3B**—StL: Holliday. **HR**—Bos: Ortiz. **RBI**—StL: Molina, Carpenter, Beltran; Bos: Ortiz (2). **SF**—StL: Carpenter. **SB**—StL: Kozma, Jay. **GIDP**—Bos: Napoli.

T—3:05. **A**—38,436.

Recap: (AP) Michael Wacha and his Cardinals bullpen provided the power pitching. Carlos Beltran, injected with a painkiller, came through with a huge hit. And this time, it was the Red Sox who were tripped up by fielding failures. Wacha bested John Lackey in a matchup of present and past rookie sensations, and St. Louis beat Boston 4–2 to even the World Series at a game apiece. Matt Holliday tripled and scored on Yadier Molina's fourth-inning grounder, but David Ortiz put Boston ahead 2–1 in the sixth when he pounced on an 85 mph changeup for a two-run homer just over the Green Monster in left field. That ended Wacha's scoreless streak at 18⅔ innings—a rookie record for a single postseason—but it was all he gave up. Lackey faltered in a three-run seventh. St. Louis went ahead when Matt Carpenter hit a sacrifice fly that led to a pair of runs, with the second scoring on errors by catcher Jarrod Saltalamacchia and reliever Craig Breslow—both making their Series debuts.

GAME 3

Boston	0	0	0	0	1	1	0	2	0	**4**	**6**	**2**
St. Louis	2	0	0	0	0	0	2	0	1	**5**	**12**	**0**

W—StL: Rosenthal. **L**—Bos: Workman. **LOB**—Bos: 6; StL: 12. **2B**—StL: Adams, Holliday, Craig.

GAME 3 *(Cont.)*

3B—Bos: Bogaerts. **RBI**—Bos: Carp, Nava (2), Bogaerts; StL: Holliday (3), Molina. **SAC**—StL: Beltran. **SB**—StL: Wong. **GIDP**—Bos: Bogaerts. **E**—Bos: Ellsbury, Middlebrooks. **T**—3:54. **A**—47,432.

Recap: (AP) Who'd ever seen an obstruction call to end a World Series game? No one. In perhaps the wildest finish imaginable, the rare ruling against third baseman Will Middlebrooks allowed Allen Craig to score with two outs in the bottom of the ninth inning and lifted St. Louis over Boston 5-4 for a 2-1 edge. Molina singled with one out in the ninth off losing pitcher Brandon Workman. Craig, just back from a sprained foot, pinch-hit and lined Koji Uehara's first pitch into left field for a double that put runners on second and third. With the infield in, Jon Jay hit a grounder to diving second baseman Dustin Pedroia. He made a sensational stab and threw home to catcher Jarrod Saltalamacchia, who tagged out the sliding Molina. But then Saltalamacchia threw wide of third trying to get Craig. The ball glanced off Middlebrooks' glove and Craig's body, caroming into foul territory down the line. After the ball got by, Middlebrooks, lying on his stomach, raised both legs and tripped Craig, slowing him down as he tried to take off for home. Third base umpire Jim Joyce immediately signaled obstruction. Left fielder Daniel Nava retrieved the ball and made a strong throw home, where Saltalamacchia tagged a sliding Craig in time. But plate umpire Dana DeMuth signaled safe and then pointed to third, making clear that obstruction had been called.

GAME 4

Boston	0	0	0	0	1	3	0	0	0	**4**	**6**	**2**
St. Louis	0	0	1	0	0	0	1	0	0	**2**	**6**	**0**

W—Bos: Doubront. **L**—StL: Lynn. **SV**—Bos: Uehara. **LOB**—Bos: 5; StL: 8. **2B**—Bos: Ortiz; StL: Molina, Robinson. **HR**—Bos: Gomes. **RBI**—Bos: Drew, Gomes (3); StL: Beltran, Carpenter. **SB**—StL: Berry. **PO**—StL: Wong. **GIDP**—Bos: Gomes. **E**—Bos: Ellsbury, Bogaerts. **T**—3:34. **A**—47,469.

Recap: (AP) There's no telling how these wacky World Series games will end. One night after a rare obstruction call, this one finished with a pickoff play—both firsts in postseason history. Oh, and Jonny Gomes hit a decisive, three-run homer when he wasn't even in the original lineup. An entertaining, even goofy World Series is tied at two games apiece after the Boston Red Sox beat the St. Louis Cardinals 4–2, ensuring the title will be decided at Fenway Park in Boston. Inserted into the lineup about 75 minutes before game time after Shane Victorino couldn't shake off a bad back, Gomes hit a tiebreaking shot off reliever Seth Maness in the sixth inning. Felix Doubront and surprise reliever John Lackey, both starters during the regular season, picked up for a gritty Clay Buchholz to help the Red Sox hang on. And of course, another bizarre ending: Koji Uehara picked off rookie pinch-runner Kolten Wong at first base for the final out—with postseason star Carlos Beltran standing at the plate.

GAME 5

Boston	1	0	0	0	0	0	2	0	0	**3**	**9**	**0**
St. Louis	0	0	0	1	0	0	0	0	0	**1**	**4**	**0**

W—Bos: Lester. **L**—StL: Wainwright. **SV**—Bos: Uehara. **LOB**—Bos: 5; StL: 2. **2B**—Bos: Pedroia, Ortiz, Ross; StL: Freese. **HR**—StL: Holliday. **RBI**—Bos: Ortiz, Ross, Ellsbury; StL: Holliday. **SAC**—StL: Kozma. **GIDP**—Bos: Nava; StL: Craig. **T**—2:52. **A**—47,436.

Recap: (AP) Jon Lester bested Adam Wainwright once again, journeyman David Ross hit a tiebreaking double in the seventh inning and the Red Sox downed the St. Louis Cardinals 3–1 to take a 3–2 Series edge. David Ortiz delivered his latest big hit, too, putting Boston in position to capture its third crown in a decade. Not since 1918 have the Red Sox clinched the title at their century-old bandbox. Ortiz enjoyed even more success in Game 5 after moving up from cleanup to the third slot. He is 11-for-15 (.733) in the series with two homers, six RBIs and four walks. Ortiz put Boston ahead with an RBI double in the first, hitting the first pitch after Dustin Pedroia doubled on an 0-2 curve. Ortiz singled the next time up and tied a World Series record by reaching base in nine straight plate appearances.

GAME 6

St. Louis	0	0	0	0	0	0	1	0	0	**1**	**9**	**1**
Boston	0	0	3	3	0	0	0	0	x	**6**	**8**	**1**

W—Bos: Lackey. **L**—StL: Wacha. **LOB**—StL: 9; Bos: 11. **2B**—StL: Carpenter; Bos: Victorino, Ellsbury. **HR**—Bos: Drew. **RBI**—Bos: Victorino (4), Drew, Napoli. **GIDP**—StL: Beltran. **E**—StL: Carpenter; Bos: Pedroia. **T**—3:15. **A**—38,447.

Recap: (AP) David Ortiz and the Boston Red Sox, baseball's bearded wonders, capped their remarkable turnaround by beating the St. Louis Cardinals 6–1 in Game 6 to win their third World Series championship in 10 seasons. And the Red Sox didn't even have to fly the trophy home. For the first time since Babe Ruth's team back in 1918, Boston won the title at Fenway. Shane Victorino, symbolic of these resilient Sox, returned from a stiff back and got Boston rolling with a three-run double off the Green Monster against rookie sensation Michael Wacha. John Lackey became the first pitcher to start and win a Series clincher for two different teams, allowing one run over 6⅔ innings 11 years after his Game 7 victory as an Angels rookie in 2002. Ortiz had himself a Ruthian World Series. He batted .688 (11-for-16) with two homers, six RBIs and eight walks—including four in the finale—for a .760 on-base percentage in 25 plate appearances, the second-highest in Series history. Even slumping Stephen Drew delivered a big hit in Game 6, sending Wacha's first pitch of the fourth into the right-center bullpen for a 4-0 lead. By the time the inning was over, RBI singles by Mike Napoli and Victorino had made it 6-0, and the Red Sox were on their way.

2013 World Series Composite Box Score

ST. LOUIS

BATTING	AB	R	H	HR	RBI	Avg
Matt Carpenter	27	3	8	0	2	.296
Matt Holliday	24	4	6	2	5	.250
Yadier Molina	23	0	7	0	2	.304
Matt Adams	22	0	3	0	0	.136
David Freese	19	0	3	0	0	.158
Jon Jay	18	1	3	0	0	.167
Carlos Beltran	17	1	5	0	3	.294
Allen Craig	16	1	6	0	0	.375
Pete Kozma	10	1	0	0	0	.000
Daniel Descalso	10	2	1	0	0	.100
Shane Robinson	8	1	2	0	0	.250
A. Wainwright	2	0	0	0	0	.000
Lance Lynn	2	0	0	0	0	.000
Joe Kelly	2	0	0	0	0	.000
Kolten Wong	1	0	1	0	0	1.000
Totals	**201**	**14**	**45**	**2**	**12**	**.224**

PITCHING	G	IP	W	L	SV	H	BB	SO	ERA
A. Wainwright	2	12.0	0	2	0	14	2	14	4.50
Michael Wacha	2	9.2	1	1	0	8	8	11	7.45
Carlos Martinez	5	6.0	0	0	0	5	1	5	4.50
Lance Lynn	2	5.2	0	1	0	5	4	5	4.76
Joe Kelly	1	5.1	0	0	0	2	3	6	3.38
T. Rosenthal	4	4.2	1	0	1	1	1	9	0.00
Kevin Siegrist	4	3.1	0	0	0	2	0	2	2.70
John Axford	2	2.1	0	0	0	0	1	5	0.00
Seth Maness	4	2.1	0	0	0	3	0	2	3.86
Randy Choate	4	0.2	0	0	0	1	1	0	0.00
Totals		**52.0**	**2**	**4**	**1**	**41**	**21**	**59**	**3.98**

BOSTON

BATTING	AB	R	H	HR	RBI	Avg
Dustin Pedroia	24	5	5	0	1	.208
Jacoby Ellsbury	24	4	6	0	1	.250
Xander Bogaerts	21	5	5	0	2	.238
Stephen Drew	19	3	3	1	2	.158
Jonny Gomes	17	2	2	1	3	.118
David Ortiz	16	7	11	2	6	.688
David Ross	16	1	3	0	1	.188
Daniel Nava	14	1	2	0	2	.143
Shane Victorino	13	2	2	0	4	.154
Mike Napoli	13	0	2	0	4	.154
J. Saltalamacchia	6	0	0	0	0	.000
Jon Lester	3	0	0	0	0	.000
Mike Carp	2	0	0	0	1	.000
W. Middlebrooks	2	0	0	0	0	.000
Jake Peavy	1	0	0	0	0	.000
Clay Buchholz	1	0	0	0	0	.000
Felix Doubront	1	0	0	0	0	.000
Brandon Workman	1	0	0	0	0	.000
Totals	**194**	**27**	**41**	**4**	**27**	**.211**

PITCHING	G	IP	W	L	SV	H	BB	SO	ERA
Jon Lester	2	15.1	2	0	0	9	1	15	0.59
John Lackey	3	14.0	1	1	0	14	3	11	2.57
Felix Doubront	2	4.2	1	0	0	2	1	3	1.93
Koji Uehara	5	4.2	0	0	2	2	0	3	0.00
Jake Peavy	1	4.0	0	0	0	6	1	4	4.50
Clay Buchholz	1	4.0	0	0	0	3	3	2	0.00
B. Workman	3	3.1	0	1	0	3	1	1	0.00
Junichi Tazawa	5	2.1	0	0	0	1	1	3	0.00
Ryan Dempster	1	1.0	0	0	0	2	0	1	9.00
Craig Breslow	3	0.1	0	0	0	3	2	0	54.00
Totals		**53.2**	**4**	**2**	**2**	**45**	**13**	**43**	**1.84**

National League Batting

BATTING AVERAGE

Michael Cuddyer, Col .... .331
Chris Johnson, Atl .... .321
Freddie Freeman, Atl .... .319
Yadier Molina, StL .... .319
Jayson Werth, Wash .... .318
Matt Carpenter, StL .... .318
Andrew McCutchen, Pit .... .317
Allen Craig, StL .... .315
Troy Tulowitzki, Col .... .312
Joey Votto, Cin .... .305

HITS

Matt Carpenter, StL 199
Daniel Murphy, NYM...............188
Andrew McCutchen, Pit...........185
Paul Goldschmidt, Ari.............182
Hunter Pence, SF...................178
Joey Votto, Cin......................177
Freddie Freeman, Atl..............176
Jean Segura, Mil.....................173
Martin Prado, Ari....................172
Norichika Aoki, Mil..................171
Adrian Gonzalez, LAD............171

DOUBLES

Matt Carpenter, StL 55
Yadier Molina, StL...................44
Jay Bruce, Cin 43
Gerardo Parra, Ari 43
Anthony Rizzo, Chi 40
Brandon Belt, SF......................39
Ian Desmond, Wash................38
Andrew McCutchen, Pit............38
Daniel Murphy, NYM................38

Three tied with 36.

TRIPLES

Denard Span, Wash 11
Carlos Gomez, Mil 10
Starling Marte, Pit 10
Jean Segura, Mil......................10

STOLEN BASES

Eric Young Jr., Col/NYM...........46
Jean Segura, Mil......................44
Starling Marte, Pit 41
Carlos Gomez, Mil 40
Everth Cabrera, SD..................37
Andrew McCutchen, Pit............27
Daniel Murphy, NYM.................23
Juan Pierre, Mia......................23

Six tied with 22.

HOME RUNS

Pedro Alvarez, Pit....................36
Paul Goldschmidt, Ari..............36
Jay Bruce, Cin 30
Domonic Brown, Phi 27
Hunter Pence, SF.....................27
Justin Upton, Atl 27
Carlos Gonzalez, Col...............26
Ryan Zimmerman, Wash 26
Troy Tulowitzki, Col..................25
Jayson Werth, Wash 25

RUNS SCORED

Matt Carpenter, StL 126
Shin-Soo Choo, Cin 107
Paul Goldschmidt, Ari..............103
Matt Holliday, StL....................103
Joey Votto, Cin.......................101
Andrew McCutchen, Pit............97
Justin Upton, Atl 94
Daniel Murphy, NYM.................92
Hunter Pence, SF.....................91
Jay Bruce, Cin 89
Freddie Freeman, Atl................89

RUNS BATTED IN

Paul Goldschmidt, Ari.............125
Jay Bruce, Cin 109
Freddie Freeman, Atl 109
Brandon Phillips, Cin 103
Pedro Alvarez, Pit 100
Adrian Gonzalez, LAD.............100
Hunter Pence, SF.....................99
Allen Craig, StL........................97
Matt Holliday, StL.....................94
Marlon Byrd, Pit/NYM 88

ON-BASE PERCENTAGE

Joey Votto, Cin...................... .435
Shin-Soo Choo, Cin .... .423
Andrew McCutchen, Pit.......... .404
Paul Goldschmidt, Ari........... .401
Jayson Werth, Wash.............. .398
Freddie Freeman, Atl.............. .396
Matt Carpenter, StL .... .392
Troy Tulowitzki, Col................ .391
Michael Cuddyer, Col............. .389
Matt Holliday, StL................... .389

SLUGGING PERCENTAGE

Paul Goldschmidt, Ari........... .551
Troy Tulowitzki, Col............... .540
Jayson Werth, Wash .... .532
Michael Cuddyer, Col............ .530
Marlon Byrd, Pit/NYM .... .511
Andrew McCutchen, Pit......... .508
Carlos Gomez, Mil .... .506
Freddie Freeman, Atl............. .501
Domonic Brown, Phi .... .494
Carlos Beltran, StL................ .491
Joey Votto, Cin..................... .491

BASES ON BALLS

Joey Votto, Cin.......................135
Shin-Soo Choo, Cin 112
Paul Goldschmidt, Ari.............99
Andrew McCutchen, Pit...........78
Dan Uggla, Atl 77

National League Pitching

WINS

Adam Wainwright, StL 19
Jordan Zimmermann, Wash 19
Jorge De La Rosa, Col 16
Clayton Kershaw, LAD.............16
Francisco Liriano, Pit 16
Zack Greinke, LAD 15
Lance Lynn, StL.......................15
Kris Medlen, Atl 15
Shelby Miller, StL.....................15

Eight tied with 14.

GAMES PITCHED

Brad Ziegler, Ari 78
Ronald Belisario, LAD...............77
Paco Rodriguez, LAD................76

Six tied with 75.

SHUTOUTS

Clayton Kershaw, LAD................2
Adam Wainwright, StL 2
Jordan Zimmermann, Wash 2

EARNED RUN AVERAGE

Clayton Kershaw, LAD..........1.83
Jose Fernandez, Mia 2.19
Matt Harvey, NYM..................2.27
Zack Greinke, LAD 2.63
Madison Bumgarner, SF 2.77
Cliff Lee, Phi..........................2.87
Adam Wainwright, StL 2.94
Stephen Strasburg, Wash......3.00
Hyun-Jin Ryu, LAD 3.00
Shelby Miller, StL 3.06

SAVES

Craig Kimbrel, Atl 50
Rafael Soriano, Wash 43
Aroldis Chapman, Cin 38
Sergio Romo, SF......................38
Edward Mujica, StL...................37
Steve Cishek, Mia 34
Kevin Gregg, Chi......................33
Jason Grilli, Pit........................33
Huston Street, SD 33
Jonathan Papelbon, Phi............29

INNINGS PITCHED

Adam Wainwright, StL 241.2
Clayton Kershaw, LAD.........236.0
Cliff Lee, Phi.........................222.2
Cole Hamels, Phi...................220.0
Jeff Samardzija, Chi.............213.2

STRIKEOUTS

Clayton Kershaw, LAD...........232
Cliff Lee, Phi..........................222
Adam Wainwright, StL 219
Jeff Samardzija, Chi................214
A.J. Burnett, Pit......................209

COMPLETE GAMES

Adam Wainwright, StL 5
Jordan Zimmermann, Wash 4
Patrick Corbin, Ari.....................3
Clayton Kershaw, LAD...............3

12 tied with 2.

American League Batting

BATTING AVERAGE

Miguel Cabrera, Det .... .348
Joe Mauer, Min .... .324
Mike Trout, LAA .... .323
Adrian Beltre, Tex .... .315
Robinson Cano, NYY .... .314
David Ortiz, Bos .... .309
Torii Hunter, Det .... .304
Daniel Nava, Bos .... .303
Eric Hosmer, KC .... .302

Three tied at .301.

HITS

Adrian Beltre, Tex 199
Miguel Cabrera, Det 193
Dustin Pedroia, Bos 193
Robinson Cano, NYY 190
Mike Trout, LAA 190
Manny Machado, Bal 189
Eric Hosmer, KC 188
Adam Jones, Bal 186
Torii Hunter, Det 184
Victor Martinez, Det 182

DOUBLES

Manny Machado, Bal 51
Jed Lowrie, Oak 45
Chris Davis, Bal 42
Dustin Pedroia, Bos 42
Robinson Cano, NYY 41
Jarrod Saltalamacchia, Bos 40
Evan Longoria, TB 39
Alexei Ramirez, Chi 39
Carlos Santana, Cle 39
Mike Trout, LAA 39

TRIPLES

Brett Gardner, NYY 10
Mike Trout, LAA 9
Stephen Drew, Bos 8
Jacoby Ellsbury, Bos 8

STOLEN BASES

Jacoby Ellsbury, Bos 52
Rajai Davis, Tor 45
Elvis Andrus, Tex 42
Alex Rios, Tex/Chi 42
Leonys Martin, Tex 36
Jose Altuve, Hou 35
Jarrod Dyson, KC 34
Mike Trout, LAA 33

Three tied at 30.

HOME RUNS

Chris Davis, Bal 53
Miguel Cabrera, Det 44
Edwin Encarnacion, Tor 36
Adam Dunn, Chi 34
Mark Trumbo, LAA 34
Adam Jones, Bal 33
Evan Longoria, TB 32
Adrian Beltre, Tex 30
Brandon Moss, Oak 30
David Ortiz, Bos 30

RUNS SCORED

Mike Trout, LAA 109
Miguel Cabrera, Det 103
Chris Davis, Bal 103
Adam Jones, Bal 100
Austin Jackson, Det 99
Coco Crisp, Oak 93
Jacoby Ellsbury, Bos 92
Elvis Andrus, Tex 91
Evan Longoria, TB 91
Dustin Pedroia, Bos 91

RUNS BATTED IN

Chris Davis, Bal 138
Miguel Cabrera, Det 137
Adam Jones, Bal 108
Robinson Cano, NYY 107
Prince Fielder, Det 106

RUNS BATTED IN (CONT.)

Edwin Encarnacion, Tor 104
David Ortiz, Bos 103
Mark Trumbo, LAA 100
Mike Trout, LAA 97
Josh Donaldson, Oak 93

ON-BASE PERCENTAGE

Miguel Cabrera, Det .... .442
Mike Trout, LAA .... .432
Joe Mauer, Min .... .404
David Ortiz, Bos .... .395
Daniel Nava, Bos .... .385
Josh Donaldson, Oak .... .384
Robinson Cano, NYY .... .383
Carlos Santana, Cle .... .377
Billy Butler, KC .... .374
Dustin Pedroia, Bos .... .372

SLUGGING PERCENTAGE

Miguel Cabrera, Det .... .636
Chris Davis, Bal .... .634
David Ortiz, Bos .... .564
Mike Trout, LAA .... .557
Edwin Encarnacion, Tor .... .534
Brandon Moss, Oak .... .522
Robinson Cano, NYY .... .516
Adrian Beltre, Tex .... .509
Josh Donaldson, Oak .... .499

Two tied at .498

BASES ON BALLS

Mike Trout, LAA 110
Carlos Santana, Cle 93
Miguel Cabrera, Det 90
Edwin Encarnacion, Tor 82
Billy Butler, KC 79
Nick Swisher, Cle 77
Josh Donaldson, Oak 76
Adam Dunn, Chi 76
Jason Kipnis, Cle 76
David Ortiz, Bos 76

American League Pitching

EARNED RUN AVERAGE

Anibal Sanchez, Det 2.57
Bartolo Colon, Oak 2.65
Hisashi Iwakuma, Sea 2.66
Yu Darvish, Tex 2.83
Max Scherzer, Det 2.90
Felix Hernandez, Sea 3.04
Chris Sale, Chi 3.07
James Shields, KC 3.15
Ervin Santana, KC 3.24
Ubaldo Jimenez, Cle 3.30

SAVES

Jim Johnson, Bal 50
Greg Holland, KC 47
Mariano Rivera, NYY 44
Joe Nathan, Tex 43
Addison Reed, Chi 40
Grant Balfour, Oak 38
Fernando Rodney, TB 37
Ernesto Frieri, LAA 37
Glen Perkins, Min 36
Casey Janssen, Tor 34

WINS

Max Scherzer, Det 21
Bartolo Colon, Oak 18
Matt Moore, TB 17
C.J. Wilson, LAA 17
Chris Tillman, Bal 16
Jeremy Guthrie, KC 15
Jon Lester, Bos 15

Seven tied at 14.

GAMES PITCHED

Joel Peralta, TB 80
Cody Allen, Cle 77
Matt Lindstrom, Chi 76
Tanner Scheppers, Tex 76
Dane De La Rosa, LAA 75

SHUTOUTS

Bartolo Colon, Oak 3
Justin Masterson, Cle 3

Six tied with 2.

INNINGS PITCHED

James Shields, KC 228.2
R.A. Dickey, Tor 224.2
Hisashi Iwakuma, Sea 219.2
Justin Verlander, Det 218.1
Max Scherzer, Det 214.1
Chris Sale, Chi 214.1

STRIKEOUTS

Yu Darvish, Tex 277
Max Scherzer, Det 240
Chris Sale, Chi 226
Justin Verlander, Det 217
Felix Hernandez, Sea 216

COMPLETE GAMES

David Price, TB 4
Chris Sale, Chi 4

Six tied with 3.

National League

TEAM BATTING	G	AB	R	H	2B	3B	HR	TB	RBI	OBP	SLG	OPS	BAVG
Colorado Rockies......162		5599	706	1511	283	36	159	2343	673	.323	.418	.741	.270
St. Louis Cardinals 162		5557	783	1494	322	20	125	2231	745	.332	.401	.733	.269
Los Angeles Dodgers...162		5491	649	1447	281	17	138	2176	618	.326	.396	.722	.264
San Francisco Giants...162		5552	629	1446	280	35	107	2117	596	.320	.381	.702	.260
Arizona Diamondbacks..162		5676	685	1468	302	31	130	2222	647	.323	.391	.715	.259
Milwaukee Brewers ...162		5474	640	1381	238	43	157	2176	610	.311	.398	.708	.252
Washington Nationals ..162		5436	656	1365	259	27	161	2161	621	.313	.398	.710	.251
Cincinnati Reds.........162		5499	698	1370	274	20	155	2149	664	.327	.391	.718	.249
Atlanta Braves...........162		5441	688	1354	247	21	181	2186	656	.321	.402	.723	.249
Philadelphia Phillies ..162		5456	610	1355	255	32	140	2094	578	.306	.384	.690	.248
Pittsburgh Pirates......162		5486	634	1346	273	35	161	2172	603	.313	.396	.709	.245
San Diego Padres.....162		5517	618	1349	246	26	146	2085	578	.308	.378	.686	.245
Chicago Cubs 162		5498	602	1307	297	18	172	2156	576	.300	.392	.693	.238
New York Mets..........162		5559	619	1318	263	32	130	2035	593	.306	.366	.672	.237
Miami Marlins 162		5449	513	1257	219	31	95	1823	485	.293	.335	.627	.231

TEAM PITCHING	GP	W	L	SV	SVO	CG	SHO	IP	H	ER	BB	Ks	ERA
Atlanta Braves..............162		96	66	53	69	1	12	1450.1	1326	512	409	1232	3.18
Los Angeles Dodgers ...162		92	70	46	65	7	22	1450.1	1321	524	460	1292	3.25
Pittsburgh Pirates.........162		94	68	55	70	3	16	1470.2	1299	533	435	1261	3.26
Cincinnati Reds............162		90	72	43	59	5	17	1473.2	1294	554	435	1296	3.38
St. Louis Cardinals.......162		97	65	44	64	7	15	1459.2	1366	555	451	1254	3.42
Washington Nationals..162		86	76	47	68	6	13	1445.2	1367	576	405	1236	3.59
Miami Marlins 162		62	100	36	53	2	13	1460.0	1376	602	526	1209	3.71
New York Mets.............162		74	88	40	58	4	10	1476.2	1442	618	458	1125	3.77
Milwaukee Brewers......162		74	88	40	63	4	15	1442.2	1401	615	466	1218	3.84
Arizona Diamondbacks...162		81	81	38	67	6	7	1495.0	1460	651	485	1171	3.92
San Diego Padres........162		76	86	40	53	3	6	1455.0	1407	643	525	1184	3.98
Chicago Cubs..............162		66	96	39	65	3	6	1448.0	1332	643	540	1256	4.00
San Francisco Giants ..162		76	86	41	54	2	13	1447.1	1380	643	521	1199	4.00
Philadelphia Phillies 162		73	89	32	48	6	3	1436.1	1465	689	506	1199	4.32
Colorado Rockies 162		74	88	35	53	1	5	1436.0	1545	708	517	1064	4.44

American League

TEAM BATTING

TEAM BATTING	G	AB	R	H	2B	3B	HR	TB	RBI	OBP	SLG	OPS	BAVG
Detroit Tigers.............162	162	5735	796	1625	292	23	176	2491	767	.346	.434	.780	.283
Boston Red Sox 162	162	5651	853	1566	363	29	178	2521	819	.349	.446	.795	.277
Los Angeles Angels...162	162	5588	733	1476	270	39	164	2316	696	.329	.414	.743	.264
Texas Rangers 163	163	5585	730	1465	262	23	176	2301	691	.323	.412	.735	.262
Kansas City Royals ...162	162	5549	648	1443	254	34	112	2101	620	.315	.379	.694	.260
Baltimore Orioles.......162	162	5620	745	1460	298	14	212	2422	719	.313	.431	.744	.260
Tampa Bay Rays.......163	163	5538	700	1421	296	23	165	2258	670	.329	.408	.737	.257
Cleveland Indians 162	162	5465	745	1391	290	23	171	2240	711	.327	.410	.737	.255
Oakland Athletics......162	162	5521	767	1403	301	25	186	2312	725	.327	.419	.745	.254
Toronto Blue Jays 162	162	5537	712	1398	273	24	185	2274	669	.318	.411	.729	.252
Chicago White Sox....162	162	5563	598	1385	237	19	148	2104	574	.302	.378	.680	.249
New York Yankees 162	162	5449	650	1321	247	24	144	2048	614	.307	.376	.683	.242
Minnesota Twins........162	162	5564	614	1346	285	15	151	2114	590	.312	.380	.692	.242
Houston Astros..........162	162	5457	610	1307	266	16	148	2049	566	.299	.375	.674	.240
Seattle Mariners 162	162	5558	624	1318	249	17	188	2165	597	.306	.390	.695	.237

TEAM PITCHING

TEAM PITCHING	GP	W	L	SV	SVO	CG	SHO	IP	H	ER	BB	Ks	ERA
Kansas City Royals 162	162	86	76	52	73	5	12	1448.1	1366	555	469	1208	3.45
Oakland Athletics 162	162	96	66	46	67	6	13	1452.0	1339	574	428	1183	3.56
Detroit Tigers..................162	162	93	69	39	55	3	12	1462.2	1369	587	462	1428	3.61
Texas Rangers.................163	163	91	72	46	57	4	10	1463.1	1370	589	498	1309	3.62
Tampa Bay Rays..............163	163	92	71	42	60	9	17	1464.0	1315	608	482	1310	3.74
Boston Red Sox...............162	162	97	65	33	57	5	8	1454.0	1366	613	524	1294	3.79
Cleveland Indians............162	162	92	70	38	60	3	16	1441.1	1359	611	554	1379	3.82
New York Yankees 162	162	85	77	49	62	7	10	1447.1	1452	633	437	1233	3.94
Chicago White Sox 162	162	63	99	40	60	5	5	1455.0	1424	643	509	1249	3.98
Baltimore Orioles 162	162	85	77	57	84	2	6	1453.0	1438	678	473	1169	4.20
Los Angeles Angels.......162	162	78	84	41	58	4	12	1457.2	1475	685	533	1200	4.23
Toronto Blue Jays...........162	162	74	88	39	58	4	11	1452.0	1451	685	500	1208	4.25
Seattle Mariners..............162	162	71	91	43	66	4	14	1465.0	1467	702	478	1297	4.31
Minnesota Twins.............162	162	66	96	40	58	1	7	1450.1	1591	733	458	985	4.55
Houston Astros 162	162	51	111	32	61	2	5	1440.0	1530	766	616	1084	4.79

Arizona Diamondbacks

BATTING	G	AB	R	H	2B	3B	HR	RBI	TB	BB	SO	SB	OBP	SLG	BAVG
Martin Prado	155	609	70	172	36	2	14	82	254	47	53	3	.333	.417	.282
Paul Goldschmidt	160	602	103	182	36	3	36	125	332	99	145	15	.401	.551	.302
Gerardo Parra	156	601	79	161	43	4	10	48	242	48	100	10	.323	.403	.268
A.J. Pollock	137	443	64	119	28	5	8	38	181	33	82	12	.322	.409	.269
Miguel Montero	116	413	44	95	14	0	11	42	142	51	110	0	.318	.344	.230
Didi Gregorius	103	357	47	90	16	3	7	28	133	37	65	0	.332	.373	.252
Aaron Hill	87	327	45	95	21	1	11	41	151	29	48	1	.356	.462	.291
Cody Ross	94	317	33	88	17	1	8	38	131	25	50	3	.331	.413	.278
Cliff Pennington	96	269	25	65	13	1	1	18	83	26	54	2	.310	.309	.242
Adam Eaton	66	250	40	63	10	4	3	22	90	17	44	5	.314	.360	.252
*Jason Kubel	89	241	21	53	8	1	5	32	78	24	82	0	.288	.324	.220
Eric Chavez	80	228	28	64	14	2	9	44	109	19	45	1	.332	.478	.281
Wil Nieves	71	195	16	58	11	0	1	22	72	8	32	0	.320	.369	.297
Willie Bloomquist	48	139	16	44	5	1	0	14	51	8	11	0	.360	.367	.317

PITCHING	GP	GS	IP	W-L	SV	HLD	H	ER	HR	BB	SO	ERA
Patrick Corbin	32	32	208.1	14-8	0	0	189	79	19	54	178	3.41
Wade Miley	33	33	202.2	10-10	0	0	201	80	21	66	147	3.55
Trevor Cahill	26	25	146.2	8-10	0	0	143	65	13	65	102	3.99
Brandon McCarthy	22	22	135.0	5-11	0	0	161	68	13	21	76	4.53
*Ian Kennedy	21	21	124.0	3-8	0	0	128	72	18	48	108	5.23
Randall Delgado	20	19	116.1	5-7	0	0	116	55	24	23	79	4.26
Josh Collmenter	49	0	92.0	5-5	0	5	79	32	8	33	85	3.13
Brad Ziegler	78	0	73.0	8-1	13	11	61	18	3	22	44	2.22
Heath Bell	69	0	65.2	5-2	15	8	74	30	12	16	72	4.11
David Hernandez	62	0	62.1	5-6	2	15	50	31	10	24	66	4.48
Will Harris	61	0	52.2	4-1	0	4	50	17	3	15	53	2.91
Tyler Skaggs	7	7	38.2	2-3	0	0	38	22	7	15	36	5.12
Tony Sipp	56	0	37.2	3-2	0	3	35	20	6	22	42	4.78
J.J. Putz	40	0	34.1	3-1	6	6	26	9	4	17	38	2.36
Matt Reynolds	30	0	27.1	0-2	2	5	25	6	2	5	23	1.98

Atlanta Braves

BATTING	G	AB	R	H	2B	3B	HR	RBI	TB	BB	SO	SB	OBP	SLG	BAVG
Andrelton Simmons	157	606	76	150	27	6	17	59	240	40	55	6	.296	.396	.248
Justin Upton	149	558	94	147	27	2	27	70	259	75	161	8	.354	.464	.263
Freddie Freeman	147	551	89	176	27	2	23	109	276	66	121	1	.396	.501	.319
Chris Johnson	142	514	54	165	34	0	12	68	235	29	116	0	.358	.457	.321
Dan Uggla	136	448	60	80	10	3	22	55	162	77	171	2	.309	.362	.179
B.J. Upton	126	391	30	72	14	0	9	26	113	44	151	12	.268	.289	.184
Jason Heyward	104	382	67	97	22	1	14	38	163	48	73	2	.349	.427	.254
Brian McCann	102	356	43	91	13	0	20	57	164	39	66	0	.336	.461	.256
Evan Gattis	105	354	44	86	21	0	21	65	170	21	81	0	.291	.480	.243
Jordan Schafer	94	231	32	57	8	3	3	21	80	29	73	22	.331	.346	.247
Reed Johnson	74	123	13	30	7	1	1	11	42	6	32	0	.311	.341	.244
Gerald Laird	47	121	12	34	8	0	1	13	45	14	23	1	.367	.372	.281
*Juan Francisco	35	108	10	26	2	0	5	16	43	7	43	0	.287	.398	.241
Ramiro Pena	50	97	14	27	5	1	3	12	43	8	18	0	.330	.443	.278
*Elliot Johnson	32	92	8	24	5	2	0	10	33	8	18	8	.317	.359	.261

PITCHING	GP	GS	IP	W-L	SV	HLD	H	ER	HR	BB	SO	ERA
Mike Minor	32	32	204.2	13-9	0	0	177	73	22	46	181	3.21
Kris Medlen	32	31	197.0	15-12	0	0	194	68	18	47	157	3.11
Julio Teheran	30	30	185.2	14-8	0	0	173	66	22	45	170	3.20
Paul Maholm	26	26	153.0	10-11	0	0	169	75	17	47	105	4.41
Tim Hudson	21	21	131.1	8-7	0	0	120	58	10	36	95	3.97
Alex Wood	31	11	77.2	3-3	0	1	76	27	3	27	77	3.13
Anthony Varvaro	62	0	73.1	3-1	1	6	68	23	3	25	43	2.82
Craig Kimbrel	68	0	67.0	4-3	50	0	39	9	4	20	98	1.21
David Carpenter	56	0	65.2	4-1	0	12	45	13	5	20	74	1.78
Luis Avilan	75	0	65.0	5-0	0	27	40	11	1	22	38	1.52
Jordan Walden	50	0	47.0	4-3	1	14	39	18	4	14	54	3.45
*Luis Ayala	37	0	31.0	1-1	0	10	34	10	1	13	20	2.90
Cory Gearrin	37	0	31.0	2-1	1	1	30	13	2	16	23	3.77
Brandon Beachy	5	5	30.0	2-1	0	0	27	15	5	4	23	4.50
*Freddy Garcia	6	3	27.1	1-2	0	0	23	5	2	5	20	1.65

*Mid-season trade.

Chicago Cubs

BATTING

	G	AB	R	H	2B	3B	HR	RBI	TB	BB	SO	SB	OBP	SLG	BAVG
Starlin Castro	161	666	59	163	34	2	10	44	231	30	129	9	.284	.347	.245
Anthony Rizzo	160	606	71	141	40	2	23	80	254	76	127	6	.323	.419	.233
Darwin Barney	141	501	49	104	25	1	7	41	152	36	64	4	.266	.303	.208
Nate Schierholtz	137	462	56	116	32	3	21	68	217	29	94	6	.301	.470	.251
Welington Castillo	113	380	41	104	23	0	8	32	151	34	97	2	.349	.397	.274
*Alfonso Soriano	93	362	47	92	24	1	17	51	169	15	89	10	.287	.467	.254
Luis Valbuena	108	331	34	72	15	1	12	37	125	53	63	1	.331	.378	.218
*David DeJesus	84	284	39	71	19	3	6	27	114	29	55	3	.330	.401	.250
Dioner Navarro	89	240	31	72	7	0	13	34	118	23	36	0	.365	.492	.300
Junior Lake	64	236	26	67	16	0	6	16	101	13	68	4	.332	.428	.284
Ryan Sweeney	70	192	19	51	13	2	6	19	86	17	31	1	.324	.488	.266
*Cody Ransom	57	158	21	32	10	1	9	20	71	22	57	0	.304	.449	.203
Donnie Murphy	46	149	23	38	8	0	11	23	79	8	48	2	.319	.530	.255
Brian Bogusevic	47	143	18	39	7	1	6	16	66	10	35	2	.323	.462	.273
*Julio Borbon	72	104	10	21	3	1	1	3	29	12	22	7	.284	.279	.202
*Scott Hairston	52	99	13	17	2	0	8	19	43	7	25	2	.232	.434	.172

PITCHING

	GP	GS	IP	W-L	SV	HLD	H	ER	HR	BB	SO	ERA
Jeff Samardzija	33	33	213.2	8-13	0	0	210	103	25	78	214	4.34
Travis Wood	32	32	200.0	9-12	0	0	163	69	18	66	144	3.11
Edwin Jackson	31	31	175.1	8-18	0	0	197	97	16	59	135	4.98
Carlos Villanueva	47	15	128.2	7-8	0	2	117	58	14	40	103	4.06
*Scott Feldman	15	15	91.0	7-6	0	0	79	35	10	25	67	3.46
*Matt Garza	11	11	71.0	6-1	0	0	61	25	8	20	62	3.17
Chris Rusin	13	13	66.1	2-6	0	0	66	29	8	24	36	3.93
Kevin Gregg	62	0	62.0	2-6	33	0	53	24	6	32	56	3.48
Hector Rondon	45	0	54.2	2-1	0	2	52	29	6	25	44	4.77
James Russell	74	0	52.2	1-6	0	19	46	21	7	18	37	3.59
*Jake Arrieta	9	9	51.2	4-2	0	0	34	21	7	24	37	3.66
Blake Parker	49	0	46.1	1-2	1	7	39	14	4	15	55	2.72
Michael Bowden	34	0	37.2	1-3	0	0	32	18	3	15	23	4.30
*Pedro Strop	37	0	35.0	2-2	1	14	22	11	1	11	42	2.83
*Carlos Marmol	31	0	27.2	2-4	2	5	26	18	6	21	32	5.86

Cincinnati Reds

BATTING

	G	AB	R	H	2B	3B	HR	RBI	TB	BB	SO	SB	OBP	SLG	BAVG
Jay Bruce	160	626	89	164	43	1	30	109	299	63	185	7	.329	.478	.262
Brandon Phillips	151	606	80	158	24	2	18	103	240	39	98	5	.310	.396	.261
Joey Votto	162	581	101	177	30	3	24	73	285	135	138	6	.435	.491	.305
Shin-Soo Choo	154	569	107	162	34	2	21	54	263	112	133	20	.423	.462	.285
Zack Cozart	151	567	74	144	30	3	12	63	216	26	102	0	.284	.381	.254
Todd Frazier	150	531	63	124	29	3	19	73	216	50	125	6	.314	.407	.234
Devin Mesoraco	103	323	31	77	13	0	9	42	117	24	61	0	.287	.362	.238
Chris Heisey	87	224	29	53	11	1	9	23	93	9	51	3	.279	.415	.237
Ryan Hanigan	75	222	17	44	8	0	2	21	58	29	27	0	.306	.261	.198
Xavier Paul	97	209	24	51	12	0	7	32	84	27	53	0	.339	.402	.244
Derrick Robinson	102	192	21	49	7	3	0	8	62	18	44	4	.322	.323	.255
Jack Hannahan	83	139	12	30	5	1	1	14	40	19	38	0	.317	.288	.216
Cesar Izturis	63	129	6	27	8	0	0	11	35	9	13	0	.259	.271	.209
Ryan Ludwick	38	129	7	31	5	0	2	12	42	10	29	0	.293	.326	.240

PITCHING

	GP	GS	IP	W-L	SV	HLD	H	ER	HR	BB	SO	ERA
Mat Latos	32	32	210.2	14-7	0	0	197	74	14	58	187	3.16
Homer Bailey	32	32	209.0	11-12	0	0	181	81	20	54	199	3.49
Bronson Arroyo	32	32	202.0	14-12	0	0	199	85	32	34	124	3.79
Mike Leake	31	31	192.1	14-7	0	0	193	72	21	48	122	3.37
Tony Cingrani	23	18	104.2	7-4	0	1	72	34	14	43	120	2.92
Alfredo Simon	63	0	87.2	6-4	1	6	68	28	8	26	63	2.87
J.J. Hoover	69	0	66.0	5-5	3	13	47	21	6	26	67	2.86
Aroldis Chapman	68	0	63.2	4-5	38	0	37	18	7	29	112	2.54
Sam LeCure	63	0	61.0	2-1	1	17	50	18	4	24	66	2.66
Johnny Cueto	11	11	60.2	5-2	0	0	46	19	7	18	51	2.82
Logan Ondrusek	52	0	55.0	3-1	0	6	53	25	8	16	53	4.09
Manny Parra	57	0	46.0	2-3	0	16	40	17	5	15	56	3.33
Jonathan Broxton	34	0	30.2	2-2	0	12	27	14	4	12	25	4.11
Greg Reynolds	6	5	29.1	1-3	0	0	38	18	5	6	13	5.52

*Mid-season trade.

Colorado Rockies

BATTING	G	AB	R	H	2B	3B	HR	RBI	TB	BB	SO	SB	OBP	SLG	BAVG
Michael Cuddyer	130	489	74	162	31	3	20	84	259	46	100	10	.389	.530	.331
Nolan Arenado	133	486	49	130	29	4	10	52	197	23	72	2	.301	.405	.267
Wilin Rosario	121	449	63	131	22	1	21	79	218	15	109	4	.315	.486	.292
Troy Tulowitzki	126	446	72	139	27	0	25	82	241	57	85	1	.391	.540	.312
Dexter Fowler	119	415	71	109	18	3	12	42	169	65	105	19	.369	.407	.263
DJ LeMahieu	109	404	39	113	21	3	2	28	146	19	67	18	.311	.361	.280
Todd Helton	124	397	41	99	22	1	15	61	168	40	87	0	.314	.423	.249
Carlos Gonzalez	110	391	72	118	23	6	26	70	231	41	118	21	.367	.591	.302
Josh Rutledge	88	285	45	67	6	1	7	19	96	22	62	12	.294	.337	.235
Jordan Pacheco	95	247	23	59	15	0	1	22	77	10	38	0	.276	.312	.239
Charlie Blackmon	82	246	35	76	17	2	6	22	115	7	49	7	.336	.467	.309
Jonathan Herrera	81	195	16	57	7	2	1	16	71	14	24	3	.336	.364	.292
Corey Dickerson	69	194	32	51	13	5	5	17	89	16	41	2	.316	.459	.263
Yorvit Torrealba	61	179	10	43	8	0	0	16	51	13	24	0	.295	.285	.240
*Eric Young Jr.	57	165	22	40	9	3	1	6	58	11	33	8	.290	.352	.242

PITCHING	GP	GS	IP	W-L	SV	HLD	H	ER	HR	BB	SO	ERA
Jhoulys Chacin	31	31	197.1	14-10	0	0	188	76	11	61	126	3.47
Jorge De La Rosa	30	30	167.2	16-6	0	0	170	65	11	62	112	3.49
Juan Nicasio	31	31	157.2	9-9	0	0	168	90	17	64	119	5.14
Tyler Chatwood	20	20	111.1	8-5	0	0	118	39	5	41	66	3.15
Adam Ottavino	51	0	78.1	1-3	0	8	73	23	5	31	78	2.64
Wilton Lopez	75	0	75.1	3-4	0	8	88	34	6	18	48	4.06
Matt Belisle	72	0	73.0	5-7	0	24	76	35	6	15	62	4.32
Jeff Francis	23	12	70.1	3-5	0	0	89	49	12	24	63	6.27
Jon Garland	12	12	68.0	4-6	0	0	85	44	9	23	32	5.82
Rex Brothers	72	0	67.1	2-1	19	12	51	13	5	36	76	1.74
Josh Outman	61	0	54.0	3-0	0	13	56	26	3	23	53	4.33
Edgmer Escalona	37	0	46.0	1-4	0	7	52	29	8	14	34	5.67
Chad Bettis	16	8	44.2	1-3	0	3	55	28	6	20	30	5.64
Manny Corpas	31	0	41.2	1-2	0	3	40	21	5	16	30	4.54
Rob Scahill	23	0	33.1	1-0	0	1	40	19	5	9	20	5.13
Roy Oswalt	9	6	32.1	0-6	0	1	49	31	3	9	34	8.63

Los Angeles Dodgers

BATTING	G	AB	R	H	2B	3B	HR	RBI	TB	BB	SO	SB	OBP	SLG	BAVG
Adrian Gonzalez	157	583	69	171	32	0	22	100	269	47	98	1	.342	.461	.293
Andre Ethier	142	482	54	131	33	2	12	52	204	61	95	4	.360	.423	.272
Carl Crawford	116	435	62	123	30	3	6	31	177	28	66	15	.329	.407	.283
Mark Ellis	126	433	46	117	13	2	6	48	152	26	74	4	.323	.351	.270
A.J. Ellis	115	390	43	93	17	1	10	52	142	45	78	0	.318	.364	.238
Juan Uribe	132	388	47	108	22	2	12	50	170	30	81	5	.331	.438	.278
Yasiel Puig	104	382	66	122	21	2	19	42	204	36	97	11	.391	.534	.319
Skip Schumaker	125	319	31	84	16	0	2	30	106	28	54	2	.332	.332	.263
Hanley Ramirez	86	304	62	105	25	2	20	57	194	27	52	10	.402	.638	.345
Nick Punto	116	294	34	75	15	0	2	21	96	33	67	3	.328	.327	.255
Matt Kemp	73	263	35	71	15	0	6	33	104	22	76	9	.328	.395	.270
Jerry Hairston Jr.	96	204	17	43	7	0	2	22	56	14	22	0	.265	.275	.211
Tim Federowicz	56	160	12	37	8	0	4	16	57	10	56	0	.275	.356	.231
Scott Van Slyke	53	129	13	31	8	0	7	19	60	20	37	1	.342	.465	.240
*Luis Cruz	45	118	12	15	2	0	1	6	20	5	20	0	.175	.169	.127
Dee Gordon	38	94	9	22	1	1	1	6	28	10	21	10	.314	.298	.234

PITCHING	GP	GS	IP	W-L	SV	HLD	H	ER	HR	BB	SO	ERA
Clayton Kershaw	33	33	236.0	16-9	0	0	164	48	11	52	232	1.83
Hyun-Jin Ryu	30	30	192.0	14-8	0	0	182	64	15	49	154	3.00
Zack Greinke	28	28	177.2	15-4	0	0	152	52	13	46	148	2.63
Chris Capuano	24	20	105.2	4-7	0	0	125	50	11	24	81	4.26
*Ricky Nolasco	16	15	87.0	8-3	0	0	83	34	6	21	75	3.52
Kenley Jansen	75	0	76.2	4-3	28	16	48	16	6	18	111	1.88
Ronald Belisario	77	0	68.0	5-7	1	21	72	30	3	28	49	3.97
J.P. Howell	67	0	62.0	4-1	0	11	42	14	2	23	54	2.03
Stephen Fife	12	10	58.1	4-4	0	0	69	25	7	20	45	3.86
Paco Rodriguez	76	0	54.1	3-4	2	20	30	14	5	19	63	2.32
Brandon League	58	0	54.1	6-4	14	2	69	32	8	15	28	5.30
Josh Beckett	8	8	43.1	0-5	0	0	50	25	8	15	41	5.19
Chris Withrow	26	0	34.2	3-0	1	4	20	10	5	13	43	2.60
*Matt Guerrier	34	0	30.0	2-3	0	3	32	16	3	12	21	4.80

*Mid-season trade.

Miami Marlins

BATTING	G	AB	R	H	2B	3B	HR	RBI	TB	BB	SO	SB	OBP	SLG	BAVG
Adeiny Hechavarria	148	543	30	123	14	8	3	42	162	30	96	11	.267	.298	.227
Giancarlo Stanton	116	425	62	106	26	0	24	62	204	74	140	1	.365	.480	.249
Justin Ruggiano	128	424	49	94	18	1	18	50	168	41	114	15	.298	.396	.222
Placido Polanco	118	377	33	98	13	0	1	23	114	23	31	2	.315	.302	.260
Donovan Solano	102	361	33	90	13	1	3	34	114	23	57	3	.305	.316	.249
Ed Lucas	94	351	43	90	14	1	4	28	118	26	78	1	.311	.336	.256
Juan Pierre	113	308	36	76	11	2	1	8	94	13	27	23	.284	.305	.247
Logan Morrison	85	293	32	71	13	4	6	36	110	38	56	0	.333	.375	.242
Marcell Ozuna	70	275	31	73	17	4	3	32	107	13	57	5	.303	.389	.265
Christian Yelich	62	240	34	69	12	1	4	16	95	31	66	10	.370	.396	.288
Greg Dobbs	114	237	21	54	11	0	2	22	71	22	40	1	.303	.300	.228
Jeff Mathis	73	232	14	42	7	1	5	29	66	21	76	0	.251	.284	.181
Rob Brantly	67	223	11	47	9	0	1	18	59	15	53	0	.263	.265	.211
Derek Dietrich	57	215	32	46	10	2	9	23	87	11	56	1	.275	.405	.214
Chris Coghlan	70	195	10	50	10	3	1	10	69	17	43	2	.318	.354	.256
Jake Marisnick	40	109	6	20	2	1	1	5	27	6	27	3	.231	.248	.183

PITCHING	GP	GS	IP	W-L	SV	HLD	H	ER	HR	BB	SO	ERA
Tom Koehler	29	23	143.0	5-10	0	0	140	70	14	54	92	4.41
Jacob Turner	20	20	118.0	3-8	0	0	116	49	11	54	77	3.74
*Ricky Nolasco	18	18	112.1	5-8	0	0	112	48	11	25	90	3.85
Nate Eovaldi	18	18	106.1	4-6	0	0	100	40	7	40	78	3.39
Henderson Alvarez	17	17	102.2	5-6	0	0	90	41	2	27	57	3.59
Kevin Slowey	20	14	92.0	3-6	0	0	106	42	12	18	76	4.11
Ryan Webb	66	0	80.1	2-6	0	5	70	26	5	27	54	2.91
A.J. Ramos	68	0	80.0	3-4	0	11	58	28	4	43	86	3.15
Steve Cishek	69	0	69.2	4-6	34	1	53	18	3	22	74	2.33
Mike Dunn	75	0	67.2	3-4	2	18	53	20	5	28	72	2.66
Chad Qualls	66	0	62.0	5-2	0	15	57	18	4	19	49	2.61
Alex Sanabia	10	10	55.1	3-7	0	0	69	30	10	25	31	4.88
*Wade LeBlanc	13	7	48.2	1-5	0	0	63	28	6	15	31	5.18
Dan Jennings	47	0	40.2	2-4	0	1	39	17	1	16	38	3.76

Milwaukee Brewers

BATTING	G	AB	R	H	2B	3B	HR	RBI	TB	BB	SO	SB	OBP	SLG	BAVG
Norichika Aoki	155	597	80	171	20	3	8	37	221	55	40	20	.356	.370	.286
Jean Segura	146	588	74	173	20	10	12	49	249	25	84	44	.329	.423	.294
Carlos Gomez	147	536	80	152	27	10	24	73	271	37	146	40	.338	.506	.284
Jonathan Lucroy	147	521	59	146	25	6	18	82	237	46	69	9	.340	.455	.280
Yuniesky Betancourt	137	391	35	83	15	1	13	46	139	14	71	0	.240	.355	.212
Rickie Weeks	104	350	40	73	20	1	10	24	125	40	105	7	.306	.357	.209
Aramis Ramirez	92	304	43	86	18	0	12	49	140	36	55	0	.370	.461	.283
Logan Schafer	134	298	29	63	15	3	4	33	96	25	60	7	.279	.322	.211
*Juan Francisco	89	240	26	53	10	1	13	32	104	25	95	0	.300	.433	.221
Jeff Bianchi	100	236	22	56	8	1	1	25	69	11	46	4	.272	.292	.237
Ryan Braun	61	225	30	67	14	2	9	38	112	27	56	4	.372	.498	.298
Scooter Gennett	213	229	69	11	2	6	21	102	10	42	2	.356	.479	.324
Martin Maldonado	67	183	13	31	7	1	4	22	52	13	53	0	.236	.284	.169
Khris Davis	56	136	27	38	10	0	11	27	81	11	34	3	.353	.596	.279
Caleb Gindl	57	132	17	32	7	2	5	14	58	20	25	2	.340	.439	.242
Alex Gonzalez	41	113	14	20	3	0	1	8	26	3	26	0	.203	.230	.177
Sean Halton	42	101	9	24	4	0	4	17	40	5	31	0	.291	.396	.238

PITCHING	GP	GS	IP	W-L	SV	HLD	H	ER	HR	BB	SO	ERA
Kyle Lohse	32	32	198.2	11-10	0	0	196	74	26	36	125	3.35
Wily Peralta	32	32	183.1	11-15	0	0	187	89	19	73	129	4.37
Yovani Gallardo	31	31	180.2	12-10	0	0	180	84	18	66	144	4.18
Marco Estrada	21	21	128.0	7-4	0	0	109	55	19	29	118	3.87
Tom Gorzelanny	43	10	85.1	3-6	0	6	77	37	11	31	83	3.90
Brandon Kintzler	71	0	77.0	3-3	0	27	66	23	2	16	58	2.69
Alfredo Figaro	33	5	74.0	3-3	1	0	77	34	15	15	54	4.14
Donovan Hand	31	7	68.1	1-5	0	2	71	28	10	21	37	3.69
Tyler Thornburg	18	7	66.2	3-1	0	0	53	15	1	26	48	2.03
Burke Badenhop	63	0	62.1	2-3	1	5	62	24	6	12	42	3.47
Jim Henderson	61	0	60.0	5-5	28	5	44	18	8	24	75	2.70
*John Axford	62	0	54.2	6-7	0	19	62	27	10	23	54	4.45
Mike Gonzalez	75	0	50.0	0-3	0	11	58	26	10	25	60	4.68

*Mid-season trade.

New York Mets

BATTING	G	AB	R	H	2B	3B	HR	RBI	TB	BB	SO	SB	OBP	SLG	BAVG
Daniel Murphy	161	658	92	188	38	4	13	78	273	32	95	23	.319	.415	.286
David Wright	112	430	63	132	23	6	18	58	221	55	79	17	.390	.514	.307
*Marlon Byrd	117	425	61	121	26	5	21	71	220	25	124	2	.330	.518	.285
Juan Lagares	121	392	35	95	21	5	4	34	138	20	96	6	.281	.352	.242
*Eric Young Jr.	91	374	48	94	18	4	1	26	123	35	67	38	.318	.329	.251
*John Buck	101	368	38	79	11	0	15	60	135	29	99	2	.285	.367	.215
Lucas Duda	100	318	42	71	16	0	15	33	132	55	102	0	.352	.415	.223
Ike Davis	103	317	37	65	14	0	9	33	106	57	101	4	.326	.334	.205
Omar Quintanilla	95	315	28	70	9	2	2	21	89	38	70	2	.306	.283	.222
Ruben Tejada	57	208	20	42	12	0	0	10	54	15	24	2	.259	.260	.202
Justin Turner	86	200	12	56	13	1	2	16	77	11	34	0	.319	.385	.280
Josh Satin	75	190	23	53	15	0	3	17	77	30	56	1	.376	.405	.279
Andrew Brown	68	150	16	34	5	0	7	24	60	13	44	1	.288	.400	.227
Anthony Recker	50	135	17	29	7	0	6	19	54	13	49	0	.280	.400	.215
Jordany Valdespin	66	133	16	25	3	1	4	16	42	8	28	4	.250	.316	.188
Mike Baxter	74	132	14	25	6	1	0	4	33	17	28	5	.303	.250	.189
Travis d'Arnaud	31	99	4	20	3	0	1	5	26	12	21	0	.286	.263	.202

PITCHING	GP	GS	IP	W–L	SV	HLD	H	ER	HR	BB	SO	ERA
Dillon Gee	32	32	199.0	12-11	0	0	208	80	24	47	142	3.62
Matt Harvey	26	26	178.1	9-5	0	0	135	45	7	31	191	2.27
Jonathon Niese	24	24	143.0	8-8	0	0	158	59	10	48	105	3.71
Jeremy Hefner	24	23	130.2	4-8	0	0	132	63	20	37	99	4.34
Zack Wheeler	17	17	100.0	7-5	0	0	90	38	10	46	84	3.42
Carlos Torres	33	9	86.1	4-6	0	3	79	33	15	17	75	3.44
Shaun Marcum	14	12	78.1	1-10	0	0	85	46	7	21	60	5.29
LaTroy Hawkins	72	0	70.2	3-2	13	12	71	23	6	10	55	2.93
Scott Rice	73	0	51.0	4-5	0	17	42	21	1	27	41	3.71
Bobby Parnell	49	0	50.0	5-5	22	0	38	12	1	12	44	2.16
Scott Atchison	50	0	45.1	3-3	0	10	45	22	4	12	28	4.37
David Aardsma	43	0	39.2	2-2	0	4	39	19	7	19	36	4.31
Daisuke Matsuzaka	7	7	38.2	3-3	0	0	32	19	4	16	33	4.42
Brandon Lyon	37	0	34.1	2-2	0	8	43	19	3	13	23	4.98
Gonzalez Germen	29	0	34.1	1-2	1	1	32	15	1	16	33	3.93

Philadelphia Phillies

BATTING	G	AB	R	H	2B	3B	HR	RBI	TB	BB	SO	SB	OBP	SLG	BAVG
Jimmy Rollins	160	600	65	151	36	2	6	39	209	59	93	22	.318	.348	.252
Domonic Brown	139	496	65	135	21	4	27	83	245	39	97	8	.324	.494	.272
Chase Utley	131	476	73	135	25	6	18	69	226	45	79	8	.348	.475	.284
*Michael Young	126	468	49	129	24	4	8	42	185	42	78	1	.336	.395	.276
John Mayberry Jr.	134	353	47	80	23	1	11	39	138	27	90	5	.227	.391	.286
Ben Revere	88	315	37	96	9	3	0	17	111	16	36	22	.338	.352	.305
Carlos Ruiz	92	310	30	83	16	0	5	37	114	18	39	1	.320	.368	.268
Ryan Howard	80	286	34	76	20	2	11	43	133	23	95	0	.319	.465	.266
*Delmon Young	80	272	22	71	13	0	8	31	108	14	69	0	.302	.397	.261
Kevin Frandsen	119	252	27	59	10	1	5	26	86	12	29	1	.296	.341	.234
Darin Ruf	73	251	36	62	11	0	14	30	115	33	91	0	.348	.458	.247
Freddy Galvis	70	205	13	48	5	4	6	19	79	13	45	1	.283	.385	.234
Erik Kratz	68	197	21	42	7	0	9	26	76	18	45	0	.280	.386	.213
Cody Asche	50	162	18	38	8	1	5	22	63	15	43	1	.302	.389	.235
Laynce Nix	81	128	11	23	4	0	2	7	33	8	44	1	.228	.258	.180
Cesar Hernandez	34	121	17	35	5	0	0	10	40	9	26	0	.344	.331	.289

PITCHING	GP	GS	IP	W–L	SV	HLD	H	ER	HR	BB	SO	ERA
Cliff Lee	31	31	222.2	14-8	0	0	193	71	22	32	222	2.87
Cole Hamels	33	33	220.0	8-14	0	0	205	88	21	50	202	3.60
Kyle Kendrick	30	30	182.0	10-13	0	0	207	95	18	47	110	4.70
Jonathan Pettibone	18	18	100.1	5-4	0	0	109	45	9	38	66	4.04
John Lannan	14	14	74.1	3-6	0	0	86	44	6	27	38	5.33
Roy Halladay	13	13	62.0	4-5	0	0	55	47	12	36	51	6.82
Jonathan Papelbon	61	0	61.2	5-1	29	0	59	20	6	11	57	2.92
Tyler Cloyd	13	11	60.1	2-7	0	0	83	44	7	25	41	6.56
Justin De Fratus	58	0	46.2	3-3	0	9	45	20	3	25	42	3.86
Antonio Bastardo	48	0	42.2	3-2	2	14	33	11	2	21	47	2.32
Ethan Martin	15	8	40.0	2-5	0	0	42	27	9	26	47	6.08
Jacob Diekman	45	0	38.1	1-4	0	11	34	11	1	16	41	2.58
Raul Valdes	17	1	35.0	1-1	0	0	42	29	7	8	37	7.46
Luis Garcia	24	0	31.1	1-1	0	1	27	13	3	23	23	3.73

*Mid-season trade.

Pittsburgh Pirates

BATTING	G	AB	R	H	2B	3B	HR	RBI	TB	BB	SO	SB	OBP	SLG	BAVG
Andrew McCutchen	157	583	97	185	38	5	21	84	296	78	101	27	.404	.508	.317
Pedro Alvarez	152	558	70	130	22	2	36	100	264	48	186	2	.296	.473	.233
Starling Marte	135	510	83	143	26	10	12	35	225	25	138	41	.343	.441	.280
Neil Walker	133	478	62	120	24	4	16	53	200	50	85	1	.339	.418	.251
Russell Martin	127	438	51	99	21	0	15	55	165	58	108	9	.327	.377	.226
Garrett Jones	144	403	41	94	26	2	15	51	169	31	101	2	.289	.419	.233
Jordy Mercer	103	333	33	95	22	2	8	27	145	22	62	3	.336	.435	.285
Jose Tabata	106	308	35	87	17	5	6	33	132	23	45	3	.342	.429	.282
Clint Barmes	108	304	22	64	15	0	5	23	94	14	70	0	.249	.309	.211
Gaby Sanchez	136	264	29	67	18	0	7	36	106	44	51	1	.361	.402	.254
Travis Snider	111	261	28	56	12	2	5	25	87	24	75	2	.281	.333	.215
Michael McKenry	41	115	9	25	6	0	3	14	40	5	24	0	.262	.348	.217
*Marlon Byrd	30	107	14	34	9	0	3	17	52	6	20	0	.357	.486	.318
Brandon Inge	50	105	5	19	3	0	1	7	25	2	32	0	.204	.238	.181

PITCHING	GP	GS	IP	W–L	SV	HLD	H	ER	HR	BB	SO	ERA
A.J. Burnett	30	30	191.0	10-11	0	0	165	70	11	67	209	3.30
Jeff Locke	30	30	166.1	10-7	0	0	146	65	11	84	125	3.52
Francisco Liriano	26	26	161.0	16-8	0	0	134	54	9	63	163	3.02
Gerrit Cole	19	19	117.1	10-7	0	0	109	42	7	28	100	3.22
Charlie Morton	20	20	116.0	7-4	0	0	113	42	6	36	85	3.26
Jeanmar Gomez	34	8	80.2	3-0	0	3	65	30	6	28	53	3.35
Justin Wilson	58	0	73.2	6-1	0	14	50	17	4	28	59	2.08
Vin Mazzaro	57	0	73.2	8-2	1	6	68	23	3	21	46	2.81
Tony Watson	67	0	71.2	3-1	2	22	51	19	5	12	54	2.39
Mark Melancon	72	0	71.0	3-2	16	26	60	11	1	8	70	1.39
Bryan Morris	55	0	65.0	5-7	0	7	57	25	8	28	37	3.46
Wandy Rodriguez	12	12	62.2	6-4	0	0	58	25	10	12	46	3.59
Jason Grilli	54	0	50.0	0-2	33	2	40	15	4	13	74	2.70
Jared Hughes	29	0	32.0	2-3	0	3	37	17	2	16	23	4.78
Brandon Cumpton	6	5	30.2	2-1	0	0	26	7	1	5	22	2.05

St. Louis Cardinals

BATTING	G	AB	R	H	2B	3B	HR	RBI	TB	BB	SO	SB	OBP	SLG	BAVG
Matt Carpenter	157	626	126	199	55	7	11	78	301	72	98	3	.392	.481	.318
Carlos Beltran	145	554	79	164	30	3	24	84	272	38	90	2	.339	.491	.296
Jon Jay	157	548	75	151	27	2	7	67	203	52	103	10	.351	.370	.276
Matt Holliday	141	520	103	156	31	1	22	94	255	69	86	6	.389	.490	.300
Allen Craig	134	508	71	160	29	2	13	97	232	40	100	2	.373	.457	.315
Yadier Molina	136	505	68	161	44	0	12	80	241	30	55	3	.359	.477	.319
David Freese	138	462	53	121	26	1	9	60	176	47	106	1	.340	.381	.262
Pete Kozma	143	410	44	89	20	0	1	35	112	34	91	3	.275	.273	.217
Daniel Descalso	123	328	43	78	25	1	5	43	120	22	56	6	.290	.366	.238
Matt Adams	108	296	46	84	14	0	17	51	149	23	80	0	.335	.503	.284
Shane Robinson	99	144	22	36	2	1	2	16	46	23	17	5	.345	.319	.250
Tony Cruz	51	123	13	25	6	1	1	13	36	4	25	0	.240	.293	.203

PITCHING	GP	GS	IP	W–L	SV	HLD	H	ER	HR	BB	SO	ERA
Adam Wainwright	34	34	241.2	19-9	0	0	223	79	15	35	219	2.94
Lance Lynn	33	33	201.2	15-10	0	0	189	89	14	76	198	3.97
Shelby Miller	31	31	173.1	15-9	0	0	152	59	20	57	169	3.06
Joe Kelly	37	15	124.0	10-5	0	2	124	37	10	44	79	2.69
Jake Westbrook	21	19	116.2	7-8	0	0	132	60	7	50	44	4.63
Trevor Rosenthal	74	0	75.1	2-4	3	29	63	22	4	20	108	2.63
Edward Mujica	65	0	64.2	2-1	37	5	60	20	9	5	46	2.78
Michael Wacha	15	9	64.2	4-1	0	0	52	20	5	19	65	2.78
Seth Maness	66	0	62.0	5-2	1	15	65	16	4	13	35	2.32
Jaime Garcia	9	9	55.1	5-2	0	0	57	22	6	15	43	3.58
Tyler Lyons	12	8	53.0	2-4	0	0	49	28	5	16	43	4.75
Kevin Siegrist	45	0	39.2	3-1	0	11	17	2	1	18	50	0.45
Randy Choate	64	0	35.1	2-1	0	15	26	9	0	11	28	2.29

*Mid-season trade.

San Diego Padres

BATTING	G	AB	R	H	2B	3B	HR	RBI	TB	BB	SO	SB	OBP	SLG	BAVG
Chase Headley	141	520	59	130	35	2	13	50	208	67	142	8	.347	.400	.250
Jedd Gyorko	125	486	62	121	26	0	23	63	216	33	123	1	.301	.444	.249
Will Venable	151	481	64	129	22	8	22	53	233	29	118	22	.312	.484	.268
Chris Denorfia	144	473	67	132	21	2	10	47	187	42	84	11	.337	.395	.279
Everth Cabrera	95	381	54	108	15	5	4	31	145	41	69	37	.355	.381	.283
Nick Hundley	114	373	35	87	19	0	13	44	145	26	98	1	.290	.389	.233
Alexi Amarista	146	368	35	87	14	4	5	32	124	22	57	4	.282	.337	.236
Yonder Alonso	97	334	34	94	11	0	6	45	123	32	47	6	.341	.368	.281
Jesus Guzman	126	288	33	65	17	0	9	35	109	27	79	3	.297	.378	.226
Kyle Blanks	88	280	31	68	14	0	8	35	106	21	85	1	.305	.379	.243
Carlos Quentin	82	276	42	76	21	0	13	44	136	31	55	0	.363	.493	.275
Logan Forsythe	75	220	22	47	6	1	6	19	73	19	54	6	.281	.332	.214
Mark Kotsay	104	155	8	30	2	0	1	12	35	13	25	0	.253	.226	.194
*Ronny Cedeno	38	123	12	33	2	2	2	9	45	8	31	3	.318	.366	.268

PITCHING	GP	GS	IP	W-L	SV	HLD	H	ER	HR	BB	SO	ERA
Eric Stults	33	33	203.2	11-13	0	0	219	89	18	40	131	3.93
Andrew Cashner	31	26	175.0	10-9	0	1	151	60	12	47	128	3.09
*Edinson Volquez	27	27	142.1	9-10	0	0	168	95	14	69	116	6.01
Tyson Ross	35	16	125.0	3-8	0	0	100	44	8	44	119	3.17
Jason Marquis	20	20	117.2	9-5	0	0	111	53	18	68	72	4.05
Tim Stauffer	43	0	69.2	3-1	0	7	59	29	7	20	64	3.75
Luke Gregerson	73	0	66.1	6-8	4	25	49	20	3	18	64	2.71
Dale Thayer	69	0	65.0	3-5	1	18	59	24	8	22	64	3.32
*Ian Kennedy	10	10	57.1	4-2	0	0	52	27	9	25	55	4.24
Huston Street	58	0	56.2	2-5	33	0	44	17	12	14	46	2.70
Robbie Erlin	11	9	54.2	3-3	0	0	53	25	6	15	40	4.12
Clayton Richard	12	11	52.2	2-5	0	0	65	41	13	21	24	7.01
Nick Vincent	45	0	46.1	6-3	1	10	33	11	1	11	49	2.14
Anthony Bass	24	0	42.0	0-0	0	0	51	25	4	20	31	5.36
Burch Smith	10	7	36.1	1-3	0	0	39	26	9	21	46	6.44
Brad Brach	33	0	31.0	1-0	0	2	36	11	3	19	31	3.19
*Joe Thatcher	50	0	30.0	3-1	0	11	28	7	3	4	29	2.10

San Francisco Giants

BATTING	G	AB	R	H	2B	3B	HR	RBI	TB	BB	SO	SB	OBP	SLG	BAVG
Hunter Pence	162	629	91	178	35	5	27	99	304	52	115	22	.339	.483	.283
Pablo Sandoval	141	525	52	146	27	2	14	79	219	47	79	0	.341	.417	.278
Buster Posey	148	520	61	153	34	1	15	72	234	60	70	2	.371	.450	.294
Brandon Belt	150	509	76	147	39	4	17	67	245	52	125	5	.360	.481	.289
Brandon Crawford	149	499	52	124	24	3	9	43	181	42	96	1	.311	.363	.248
Marco Scutaro	127	488	57	145	23	3	2	31	180	45	34	2	.357	.369	.297
Gregor Blanco	141	452	50	120	17	6	3	41	158	52	95	14	.341	.350	.265
Angel Pagan	71	280	44	79	16	3	5	30	116	23	36	9	.334	.414	.282
Andres Torres	103	272	33	68	17	1	2	21	93	22	61	4	.302	.342	.250
Joaquin Arias	102	225	17	61	9	2	1	19	77	4	33	1	.284	.342	.271
Tony Abreu	53	138	21	37	12	3	2	14	61	6	33	0	.301	.442	.268
Hector Sanchez	63	129	8	32	4	0	3	19	45	7	29	0	.300	.349	.248
Nick Noonan	62	105	12	23	2	0	0	5	25	6	24	0	.261	.238	.219

PITCHING	GP	GS	IP	W-L	SV	HLD	H	ER	HR	BB	SO	ERA
Madison Bumgarner	31	31	201.1	13-9	0	0	146	62	15	62	199	2.77
Tim Lincecum	32	32	197.2	10-14	0	0	184	96	21	76	193	4.37
Matt Cain	30	30	184.1	8-10	0	0	158	82	23	55	158	4.00
Barry Zito	30	25	133.1	5-11	0	0	173	85	19	54	86	5.74
Ryan Vogelsong	19	19	103.2	4-6	0	0	124	66	15	38	67	5.73
Chad Gaudin	30	12	97.0	5-2	0	2	81	33	6	40	88	3.06
Sergio Romo	65	0	60.1	5-8	38	0	53	17	5	12	58	2.54
George Kontos	52	0	55.1	2-2	0	5	60	27	7	18	47	4.39
Jean Machi	51	0	53.0	3-1	0	11	46	14	2	12	51	2.38
Santiago Casilla	57	0	50.0	7-2	2	23	39	12	2	25	38	2.16
Jose Mijares	60	0	49.0	0-3	0	6	67	23	3	20	54	4.22
Yusmeiro Petit	8	7	48.0	4-1	0	0	46	19	4	11	47	3.56
Sandy Rosario	43	0	41.2	3-2	0	7	38	14	1	20	24	3.02
Javier Lopez	69	0	39.1	4-2	1	15	30	8	1	12	37	1.83
Jeremy Affeldt	39	0	33.2	1-5	0	11	27	14	2	17	21	3.74
Guillermo Moscoso	13	2	30.0	2-2	0	0	20	17	5	21	31	5.10

*Mid-season trade.

Washington Nationals

BATTING	G	AB	R	H	2B	3B	HR	RBI	TB	BB	SO	SB	OBP	SLG	BAVG
Denard Span	153	610	75	170	28	11	4	47	232	42	77	20	.327	.380	.279
Ian Desmond	158	600	77	168	38	3	20	80	272	43	145	21	.331	.453	.280
Ryan Zimmerman	147	568	84	156	26	2	26	79	264	60	133	6	.344	.465	.275
Adam LaRoche	152	511	70	121	19	3	20	62	206	72	131	4	.332	.403	.237
Jayson Werth	129	462	84	147	24	0	25	82	246	60	101	10	.398	.532	.318
Bryce Harper	118	424	71	116	24	3	20	58	206	61	94	11	.368	.486	.274
Anthony Rendon	98	351	40	93	23	1	7	35	139	31	69	1	.329	.396	.265
Stephen Lombardozzi	118	290	25	75	15	1	2	22	98	8	34	4	.278	.338	.259
Wilson Ramos	78	287	29	78	9	0	16	59	135	15	42	0	.307	.470	.272
*Kurt Suzuki	79	252	19	56	11	1	3	25	78	20	32	2	.283	.310	.222
Tyler Moore	63	167	16	37	9	0	4	21	58	8	58	0	.260	.347	.222
Danny Espinosa	44	158	11	25	9	0	3	12	43	4	47	1	.193	.272	.158
*Roger Bernadina	85	152	18	27	6	1	2	6	41	12	44	3	.247	.270	.178
Chad Tracy	92	129	6	26	4	0	4	11	42	7	25	0	.243	.326	.202

PITCHING	GP	GS	IP	W-L	SV	HLD	H	ER	HR	BB	SO	ERA
Jordan Zimmermann	32	32	213.1	19-9	0	0	192	77	19	40	161	3.25
Gio Gonzalez	32	32	195.2	11-8	0	0	169	73	17	76	192	3.36
Stephen Strasburg	30	30	183.0	8-9	0	0	136	61	16	56	191	3.00
Dan Haren	31	30	169.2	10-14	1	0	179	88	28	31	151	4.67
Craig Stammen	55	0	81.2	7-6	0	7	78	25	4	27	79	2.76
Ross Detwiler	13	13	71.1	2-7	0	0	92	32	5	14	39	4.04
Tyler Clippard	72	0	71.0	6-3	0	33	37	19	9	24	73	2.41
Rafael Soriano	68	0	66.2	3-3	43	0	65	23	7	17	51	3.11
Drew Storen	68	0	61.2	4-2	3	24	65	31	7	19	58	4.52
Ross Ohlendorf	16	7	60.1	4-1	0	1	56	22	8	14	45	3.28
Tanner Roark	14	5	53.2	7-1	0	1	38	9	1	11	40	1.51
Taylor Jordan	9	9	51.2	1-3	0	0	59	21	3	11	29	3.66
Fernando Abad	39	0	37.2	0-3	0	2	42	14	3	10	32	3.35
Ryan Mattheus	37	0	35.1	0-2	0	6	52	25	1	15	22	6.37

American League Team-by-Team Statistical Leaders

Baltimore Orioles

BATTING	G	AB	R	H	2B	3B	HR	RBI	TB	BB	SO	SB	OBP	SLG	BAVG
Manny Machado	156	667	88	189	51	3	14	71	288	29	113	6	.314	.432	.283
Adam Jones	160	653	100	186	35	1	33	108	322	25	136	14	.318	.493	.285
Nick Markakis	160	634	89	172	24	0	10	59	226	55	76	1	.329	.356	.271
J.J. Hardy	159	601	66	158	27	0	25	76	260	38	73	2	.306	.433	.263
Chris Davis	160	584	103	167	42	1	53	138	370	72	199	4	.370	.634	.286
Nate McLouth	146	531	76	137	31	4	12	36	212	53	86	30	.329	.399	.258
Matt Wieters	148	523	59	123	29	0	22	79	218	43	104	2	.287	.417	.235
Brian Roberts	77	265	33	66	12	1	8	39	104	26	44	3	.312	.392	.249
Ryan Flaherty	85	246	28	55	11	0	10	27	96	19	62	2	.293	.390	.224
Danny Valencia	52	161	20	49	14	1	8	23	89	8	33	0	.335	.553	.304
Nolan Reimold	40	128	17	25	3	0	5	12	43	10	41	0	.250	.336	.195
Steve Pearce	44	119	14	31	7	0	4	13	50	15	25	1	.362	.420	.261
Alexi Casilla	62	112	15	24	4	1	1	10	33	9	20	9	.268	.295	.214
Chris Dickerson	56	105	17	25	5	0	4	13	42	4	36	5	.266	.400	.238

PITCHING	GP	GS	IP	W-L	SV	HLD	H	ER	HR	BB	SO	ERA
Chris Tillman	33	33	206.1	16-7	0	0	184	85	33	68	179	3.71
Miguel Gonzalez	30	28	171.1	11-8	0	0	157	72	24	53	120	3.78
Jason Hammel	26	23	139.1	7-8	1	1	155	77	22	48	96	4.97
Wei-Yin Chen	23	23	137.0	7-7	0	0	142	62	17	39	104	4.07
*Scott Feldman	15	15	90.2	5-6	0	0	80	43	9	31	65	4.27
Tommy Hunter	68	0	86.1	6-5	4	21	71	27	11	14	68	2.81
T.J. McFarland	38	1	74.2	4-1	0	0	83	35	7	28	58	4.22
Jim Johnson	74	0	70.1	3-8	50	0	72	23	5	18	56	2.94
Darren O'Day	68	0	62.0	5-3	2	20	47	15	7	15	59	2.18
Troy Patton	56	0	56.0	2-0	0	8	57	23	8	16	42	3.70
*Freddy Garcia	11	10	53.0	3-5	0	0	60	34	16	12	26	5.77
Brian Matusz	65	0	51.0	2-1	0	18	43	20	3	16	50	3.53
*Bud Norris	11	11	50.2	4-3	0	0	61	27	6	24	57	4.80
Kevin Gausman	20	5	47.2	3-5	0	2	51	30	8	13	49	5.66
Zach Britton	8	7	40.0	2-3	0	0	52	22	4	17	18	4.95

*Mid-season trade.

Boston Red Sox

BATTING	G	AB	R	H	2B	3B	HR	RBI	TB	BB	SO	SB	OBP	SLG	BAVG
Dustin Pedroia	160	641	91	193	42	2	9	84	266	73	75	17	.372	.415	.301
Jacoby Ellsbury	134	577	92	172	31	8	9	53	246	47	92	52	.355	.426	.298
David Ortiz	137	518	84	160	38	2	30	103	292	76	88	4	.395	.564	.309
Mike Napoli	139	498	79	129	38	2	23	92	240	73	187	1	.360	.482	.259
Shane Victorino	122	477	82	140	26	2	15	61	215	25	75	21	.351	.451	.294
Daniel Nava	134	458	77	139	29	0	12	66	204	51	93	0	.385	.445	.303
Stephen Drew	124	442	57	112	29	8	13	67	196	54	124	6	.333	.443	.253
Jarrod Saltalamacchia	121	425	68	116	40	0	14	65	198	43	139	4	.338	.466	.273
Will Middlebrooks	94	348	41	79	18	0	17	49	148	20	98	3	.271	.425	.227
Jonny Gomes	116	312	49	77	17	0	13	52	133	43	89	1	.344	.426	.247
Mike Carp	86	216	34	64	18	2	9	43	113	22	67	1	.362	.523	.296
*Jose Iglesias	63	215	27	71	10	2	1	19	88	11	30	3	.376	.409	.330
David Ross	36	102	11	22	5	0	4	10	39	11	42	1	.298	.382	.216
Jackie Bradley Jr.	37	95	18	18	5	0	3	10	32	10	31	2	.280	.337	.189

PITCHING	GP	GS	IP	W-L	SV	HLD	H	ER	HR	BB	SO	ERA
Jon Lester	33	33	213.1	15-8	0	0	209	89	19	67	177	3.75
John Lackey	29	29	189.1	10-13	0	0	179	74	26	40	161	3.52
Ryan Dempster	32	29	171.1	8-9	0	0	170	87	26	79	157	4.57
Felix Doubront	29	27	162.1	11-6	0	0	161	78	13	71	139	4.32
Clay Buchholz	16	16	108.1	12-1	0	0	75	21	4	36	96	1.74
Koji Uehara	73	0	74.1	4-1	21	13	33	9	5	9	101	1.09
Junichi Tazawa	71	0	68.1	5-4	0	26	70	24	9	12	72	3.16
*Jake Peavy	10	10	64.2	4-1	0	0	56	29	6	19	45	4.04
Craig Breslow	61	0	59.2	5-2	0	14	49	12	3	18	33	1.81
Brandon Workman	20	3	41.2	6-3	0	1	44	23	5	15	47	4.97
Alfredo Aceves	11	6	37.0	4-1	0	0	42	20	8	22	24	4.86
Andrew Miller	37	0	30.2	1-2	0	6	25	9	3	17	48	2.64
Allen Webster	8	7	30.1	1-2	0	0	37	29	7	18	23	8.60
Clayton Mortensen	24	0	30.1	1-2	0	0	32	18	3	16	21	5.34

Chicago White Sox

BATTING	G	AB	R	H	2B	3B	HR	RBI	TB	BB	SO	SB	OBP	SLG	BAVG
Alexei Ramirez	158	637	68	181	39	2	6	48	242	26	68	30	.313	.380	.284
Alejandro De Aza	153	607	84	160	27	4	17	62	246	50	147	20	.323	.405	.264
Adam Dunn	149	525	60	115	15	0	34	86	232	76	189	1	.320	.442	.219
Paul Konerko	126	467	41	114	16	0	12	54	166	45	74	0	.313	.355	.244
Dayan Viciedo	124	441	43	117	23	3	14	56	188	24	98	0	.304	.426	.265
*Alex Rios	109	430	57	119	22	2	12	55	181	32	78	26	.328	.421	.277
Jeff Keppinger	117	423	38	107	13	1	4	40	134	20	41	0	.283	.317	.253
Conor Gillaspie	134	408	46	100	14	3	13	40	159	37	79	0	.305	.390	.245
Gordon Beckham	103	371	46	99	22	1	5	24	138	28	56	5	.322	.372	.267
Tyler Flowers	84	256	24	50	11	0	10	24	91	14	94	0	.247	.355	.195
Josh Phegley	65	204	14	42	7	0	4	22	61	5	41	2	.223	.299	.206
*Avisail Garcia	42	161	19	49	4	2	5	21	72	5	38	3	.327	.447	.304
Jordan Danks	79	160	15	37	7	0	5	12	59	18	57	7	.313	.369	.231

PITCHING	GP	GS	IP	W-L	SV	HLD	H	ER	HR	BB	SO	ERA
Chris Sale	30	30	214.1	11-14	0	0	184	73	23	46	226	3.07
Jose Quintana	33	33	200.0	9-7	0	0	188	78	23	56	164	3.51
Hector Santiago	34	23	149.0	4-9	0	0	137	59	17	72	137	3.56
John Danks	22	22	138.1	4-14	0	0	151	73	28	27	89	4.75
Dylan Axelrod	30	20	128.1	4-11	0	0	170	81	24	43	73	5.68
*Jake Peavy	13	13	80.0	8-4	0	0	74	38	14	17	76	4.28
Nate Jones	70	0	78.0	4-5	0	16	69	36	5	26	89	4.15
Addison Reed	68	0	71.1	5-4	40	0	56	30	6	23	72	3.79
Matt Lindstrom	76	0	60.2	2-4	0	20	64	21	2	23	46	3.12
Andre Rienzo	10	0	56.0	2-3	0	0	55	30	11	28	38	4.82
Jesse Crain	38	0	36.2	2-3	0	19	31	3	0	11	46	0.74
Ramon Troncoso	29	0	30.0	1-4	0	1	30	15	4	16	18	4.50

*Mid-season trade.

Cleveland Indians

BATTING	G	AB	R	H	2B	3B	HR	RBI	TB	BB	SO	SB	OBP	SLG	BAVG
Jason Kipnis	149	564	86	160	36	4	17	84	255	76	143	30	.366	.452	.284
Michael Brantley	151	556	66	158	26	3	10	73	220	40	67	17	.332	.396	.284
Nick Swisher	145	549	74	135	27	2	22	63	232	77	138	1	.341	.423	.246
Carlos Santana	154	541	75	145	39	1	20	74	246	93	110	3	.377	.455	.268
Michael Bourn	130	525	75	138	21	6	6	50	189	40	132	23	.316	.360	.263
Asdrubal Cabrera	136	508	66	123	35	2	14	64	204	35	114	9	.299	.402	.242
Drew Stubbs	146	430	59	100	21	2	10	45	155	44	141	17	.305	.360	.233
Mike Aviles	124	361	54	91	15	0	9	46	133	15	41	8	.282	.368	.252
*Mark Reynolds	99	335	40	72	8	0	15	48	125	43	123	3	.307	.373	.215
Yan Gomes	88	293	45	86	18	2	11	38	141	18	67	2	.345	.481	.294
Lonnie Chisenhall	94	289	30	65	17	0	11	36	115	16	56	1	.270	.398	.225
Ryan Raburn	87	243	40	66	18	0	16	55	132	29	67	0	.357	.543	.272
Jason Giambi	71	186	21	34	8	0	9	31	69	23	56	0	.282	.371	.183

PITCHING	GP	GS	IP	W–L	SV	HLD	H	ER	HR	BB	SO	ERA
Justin Masterson	32	29	193.0	14-10	0	0	156	74	13	76	195	3.45
Ubaldo Jimenez	32	32	182.2	13-9	0	0	163	67	16	80	194	3.30
Scott Kazmir	29	29	158.0	10-9	0	0	162	71	19	47	162	4.04
Corey Kluber	26	24	147.1	11-5	0	0	153	63	15	33	136	3.85
Zach McAllister	24	24	134.1	9-9	0	0	134	56	13	49	101	3.75
Bryan Shaw	70	0	75.0	7-3	1	12	60	27	4	28	73	3.24
Cody Allen	77	0	70.1	6-1	2	11	62	19	7	26	88	2.43
Joe Smith	70	0	63.0	6-2	3	25	54	16	5	23	54	2.29
Matt Albers	56	0	63.0	3-1	0	1	57	22	2	23	35	3.14
Chris Perez	54	0	54.0	5-3	25	1	56	26	11	21	54	4.33
Danny Salazar	10	10	52.0	2-3	0	0	44	18	7	15	65	3.12
Carlos Carrasco	15	7	46.2	1-4	0	0	64	35	4	18	30	6.75
Rich Hill	63	0	38.2	1-2	0	13	38	27	3	29	51	6.28
Vinnie Pestano	37	0	35.1	1-2	6	6	37	16	6	21	37	4.08
Nick Hagadone	36	0	31.1	0-1	0	2	24	19	4	21	30	5.46

Detroit Tigers

BATTING	G	AB	R	H	2B	3B	HR	RBI	TB	BB	SO	SB	OBP	SLG	BAVG
Prince Fielder	162	624	82	174	36	0	25	106	285	75	117	1	.362	.457	.279
Torii Hunter	144	606	90	184	37	5	17	84	282	26	113	3	.334	.465	.304
Victor Martinez	159	605	68	182	36	0	14	83	260	54	62	0	.355	.430	.301
Miguel Cabrera	148	555	103	193	26	1	44	137	353	90	94	3	.442	.636	.348
Austin Jackson	129	552	99	150	30	7	12	49	230	52	129	8	.337	.417	.272
Omar Infante	118	453	54	144	24	3	10	51	204	20	44	5	.345	.450	.318
Andy Dirks	131	438	60	112	16	2	9	37	159	42	84	7	.323	.363	.256
Jhonny Peralta	107	409	50	124	30	0	11	55	187	35	98	3	.358	.457	.303
Alex Avila	102	330	39	75	14	1	11	47	124	44	112	0	.317	.376	.227
Brayan Pena	71	229	19	68	11	0	4	22	91	6	26	0	.315	.397	.297
Don Kelly	112	216	33	48	6	1	6	23	74	27	28	2	.309	.343	.222
Ramon Santiago	80	205	27	46	8	1	1	14	59	21	32	0	.298	.288	.224
Matt Tuiasosopo	81	164	26	40	7	0	7	30	68	25	57	0	.351	.415	.244
*Jose Iglesias	46	135	12	35	6	0	2	10	47	4	30	2	.306	.348	.259

PITCHING	GP	GS	IP	W–L	SV	HLD	H	ER	HR	BB	SO	ERA
Justin Verlander	34	34	218.1	13-12	0	0	212	84	19	75	217	3.46
Max Scherzer	32	32	214.1	21-3	0	0	152	69	18	56	240	2.90
Doug Fister	33	32	208.2	14-9	0	0	229	85	14	44	159	3.67
Anibal Sanchez	29	29	182.0	14-8	0	0	156	52	9	54	202	2.57
Rick Porcello	32	29	177.0	13-8	0	0	185	85	18	42	142	4.32
Drew Smyly	63	0	76.0	6-0	2	21	62	20	4	17	81	2.37
Joaquin Benoit	66	0	67.0	4-1	24	9	47	15	5	22	73	2.01
Al Alburquerque	53	0	49.0	4-3	0	10	39	25	5	34	70	4.59
Jose Alvarez	14	6	38.2	1-5	0	0	42	25	7	16	31	5.82
Phil Coke	49	0	38.1	0-5	1	4	43	23	3	21	30	5.40
Darin Downs	29	0	35.1	0-2	0	4	36	19	4	11	37	4.84

*Mid-season trade.

Houston Astros

BATTING	G	AB	R	H	2B	3B	HR	RBI	TB	BB	SO	SB	OBP	SLG	BAVG
Jose Altuve	152	626	64	177	31	2	5	52	227	32	85	35	.316	.363	.283
Matt Dominguez	152	543	56	131	25	0	21	77	219	30	96	0	.286	.403	.241
Chris Carter	148	506	64	113	24	2	29	82	228	70	212	2	.320	.451	.223
Jason Castro	120	435	63	120	35	1	18	56	211	50	130	2	.350	.485	.276
Brandon Barnes	136	408	46	98	17	1	8	41	141	21	127	11	.289	.346	.240
J.D. Martinez	86	296	24	74	17	0	7	36	112	10	82	2	.272	.378	.250
*Carlos Pena	85	277	38	58	13	1	8	25	97	43	89	1	.324	.350	.209
Brett Wallace	79	262	35	58	14	1	13	36	113	18	104	1	.284	.431	.221
Robbie Grossman	63	257	29	69	14	0	4	21	95	23	70	6	.332	.370	.268
Jonathan Villar	58	210	26	51	9	2	1	8	67	24	71	18	.321	.319	.243
Marwin Gonzalez	72	204	22	45	8	0	4	14	65	9	37	6	.252	.319	.221
Carlos Corporan	64	191	16	43	5	0	7	20	69	10	60	0	.287	.361	.225
*L.J. Hoes	46	167	24	48	7	2	1	10	62	12	34	7	.337	.371	.287
Trevor Crowe	60	165	18	36	7	1	1	13	48	16	39	6	.287	.291	.218
*Ronny Cedeno	51	141	12	31	6	1	1	12	42	6	42	2	.260	.298	.220
*Justin Maxwell	40	137	21	33	10	2	2	8	53	12	43	4	.311	.387	.241
Marc Krauss	52	134	11	28	9	0	4	13	49	10	45	2	.267	.366	.209
Jimmy Paredes	48	125	8	24	4	0	1	10	31	6	44	4	.231	.248	.192

PITCHING	GP	GS	IP	W-L	SV	HLD	H	ER	HR	BB	SO	ERA
Lucas Harrell	36	22	153.2	6-17	0	0	174	100	20	88	89	5.86
Dallas Keuchel	31	22	153.2	6-10	0	2	184	88	20	52	123	5.15
Erik Bedard	32	26	151.0	4-12	1	0	149	77	18	75	138	4.59
Jordan Lyles	27	25	141.2	7-9	1	1	165	88	17	49	93	5.59
*Bud Norris	21	21	126.0	6-9	0	0	135	55	11	43	90	3.93
Brad Peacock	18	14	83.1	5-6	0	2	78	48	15	37	77	5.18
Paul Clemens	35	5	73.1	4-7	0	0	82	44	16	26	49	5.40
Brett Oberholtzer	13	10	71.2	4-5	0	0	66	22	7	13	45	2.76
Jarred Cosart	10	10	60.0	1-1	0	0	46	13	3	35	33	1.95
Philip Humber	17	7	54.2	0-8	0	0	75	48	9	20	36	7.90
Jose Cisnero	28	0	43.2	2-2	0	5	49	20	5	22	41	4.12
*Jose Veras	42	0	43.0	0-4	19	0	29	14	4	14	44	2.93

Kansas City Royals

BATTING	G	AB	R	H	2B	3B	HR	RBI	TB	BB	SO	SB	OBP	SLG	BAVG
Alex Gordon	156	633	90	168	27	6	20	81	267	52	141	11	.327	.422	.265
Eric Hosmer	159	623	86	188	34	3	17	79	279	51	100	11	.353	.448	.302
Alcides Escobar	158	607	57	142	20	4	4	52	182	19	84	22	.234	.300	.259
Billy Butler	162	582	62	168	27	0	15	82	240	79	102	0	.374	.412	.289
Salvador Perez	138	496	48	145	25	3	13	79	215	21	63	0	.323	.433	.292
Mike Moustakas	136	472	42	110	26	0	12	42	172	32	83	2	.287	.364	.233
Lorenzo Cain	115	399	54	100	21	3	4	46	139	33	90	14	.310	.348	.251
David Lough	96	315	35	90	17	4	5	33	130	10	52	5	.311	.413	.286
Jarrod Dyson	87	213	30	55	9	4	2	17	78	21	45	34	.326	.366	.258
Chris Getz	78	209	29	46	6	1	1	18	57	20	24	16	.288	.273	.220
*Jeff Francoeur	59	183	19	38	8	2	3	13	59	8	49	2	.249	.322	.208
*Elliot Johnson	79	162	19	29	2	1	2	9	39	8	49	14	.218	.241	.179
*Emilio Bonifacio	42	158	21	45	6	2	0	11	55	17	37	16	.352	.348	.285
Miguel Tejada	53	156	15	45	5	0	3	20	59	6	25	1	.317	.378	.288
George Kottaras	46	100	13	18	4	0	5	12	37	24	42	1	.349	.370	.180
*Justin Maxwell	35	97	14	26	6	1	5	17	49	11	35	2	.351	.505	.268

PITCHING	GP	GS	IP	W-L	SV	HLD	H	ER	HR	BB	SO	ERA
James Shields	34	34	228.2	13-9	0	0	215	80	20	68	196	3.15
Jeremy Guthrie	33	33	211.2	15-12	0	0	236	95	30	59	111	4.04
Ervin Santana	32	32	211.0	9-10	0	0	190	76	26	51	161	3.24
Wade Davis	31	24	135.1	8-11	0	0	169	80	15	58	114	5.32
Bruce Chen	34	15	121.0	9-4	0	2	107	44	13	36	78	3.27
Luis Mendoza	22	15	94.0	2-6	0	0	106	56	10	43	54	5.36
Luke Hochevar	58	0	70.1	5-2	2	9	41	15	8	17	82	1.92
Greg Holland	68	0	67.0	2-1	47	1	40	9	3	18	103	1.21
Kelvin Herrera	59	0	58.1	5-7	2	20	48	25	9	21	74	3.86
Tim Collins	66	0	53.1	3-6	0	21	49	21	3	28	52	3.54
Aaron Crow	57	0	48.0	7-5	1	19	49	18	6	22	44	3.38
Will Smith	19	1	33.1	2-1	0	6	24	12	6	7	43	3.24

*Mid-season trade.

Los Angeles Angels

BATTING	G	AB	R	H	2B	3B	HR	RBI	TB	BB	SO	SB	OBP	SLG	BAVG
Mark Trumbo	159	620	85	145	30	2	34	100	281	54	184	5	.294	.453	.234
Mike Trout	157	589	109	190	39	9	27	97	328	110	136	33	.432	.557	.323
Josh Hamilton	151	576	73	144	32	5	21	79	249	47	158	4	.307	.432	.250
Erick Aybar	138	550	68	149	33	5	6	54	210	23	59	12	.301	.382	.271
Howie Kendrick	122	478	55	142	21	4	13	54	210	23	89	6	.335	.439	.297
J.B. Shuck	129	437	60	128	20	3	2	39	160	27	54	8	.331	.366	.293
Albert Pujols	99	391	49	101	19	0	17	64	171	40	55	1	.330	.437	.258
Chris Iannetta	115	325	40	73	15	0	11	39	121	68	100	0	.358	.372	.225
*Alberto Callaspo	86	294	32	74	13	0	5	36	102	34	22	0	.324	.347	.252
Hank Conger	92	233	23	58	13	1	7	21	94	17	61	0	.310	.403	.249
Kole Calhoun	58	195	29	55	7	2	8	32	90	21	41	2	.347	.462	.282
Peter Bourjos	55	175	26	48	3	3	3	12	66	10	43	6	.333	.377	.274
*Grant Green	40	125	16	35	8	1	1	16	48	10	38	0	.336	.384	.280
*Chris Nelson	33	109	10	24	1	2	3	18	38	8	36	2	.277	.349	.220
Andrew Romine	47	108	9	28	3	0	0	10	31	7	24	1	.308	.287	.259
Brendan Harris	44	107	14	22	4	0	4	9	38	6	29	0	.252	.355	.206
Luis Jimenez	34	104	15	27	6	0	0	5	33	2	28	0	.260	.317	.291
*Collin Cowgill	50	91	11	21	3	2	2	8	34	5	27	1	.271	.374	.231

PITCHING	GP	GS	IP	W–L	SV	HLD	H	ER	HR	BB	SO	ERA
C.J. Wilson	33	33	212.1	17-7	0	0	200	80	15	85	188	3.39
Jerome Williams	37	25	169.1	9-10	0	0	181	86	23	55	107	4.57
Jered Weaver	24	24	154.1	11-8	0	0	139	56	17	37	117	3.27
Jason Vargas	24	24	150.0	9-8	0	0	162	67	17	46	109	4.02
Garrett Richards	47	17	145.0	7-8	1	5	151	67	12	44	101	4.16
Joe Blanton	28	20	132.2	2-14	0	0	180	89	29	34	108	6.04
Tommy Hanson	15	13	73.0	4-3	0	0	83	44	10	30	56	5.42
Dane De La Rosa	75	0	72.1	6-1	2	20	56	23	3	28	65	2.86
Ernesto Frieri	67	0	68.2	2-4	37	2	55	29	11	30	98	3.80
Michael Kohn	63	0	53.0	1-4	0	8	42	22	7	28	52	3.74
Kevin Jepsen	45	0	36.0	1-3	0	8	41	18	3	14	36	4.50

Minnesota Twins

BATTING	G	AB	R	H	2B	3B	HR	RBI	TB	BB	SO	SB	OBP	SLG	BAVG
Brian Dozier	147	558	72	136	33	4	18	66	231	51	120	14	.312	.414	.244
*Justin Morneau	127	495	56	128	32	0	17	74	211	37	98	0	.315	.426	.259
Ryan Doumit	135	485	49	120	28	1	14	55	192	48	99	1	.314	.396	.247
Trevor Plouffe	129	477	44	121	22	1	14	52	187	34	112	2	.309	.392	.254
Joe Mauer	113	445	62	144	35	0	11	47	212	61	89	0	.404	.476	.324
Pedro Florimon	134	403	44	89	17	0	9	44	133	33	115	15	.281	.330	.221
Josh Willingham	111	389	42	81	20	0	14	48	143	66	128	1	.342	.368	.208
Oswaldo Arcia	97	351	34	88	17	2	14	43	151	23	117	1	.304	.430	.251
Chris Parmelee	101	294	21	67	13	0	8	24	104	33	81	1	.309	.354	.228
Clete Thomas	92	290	39	62	15	0	4	13	89	30	92	1	.290	.307	.214
Aaron Hicks	81	281	37	54	11	3	8	27	95	24	84	9	.259	.338	.192
*Jamey Carroll	59	191	21	44	6	0	0	9	50	13	35	2	.283	.262	.230
Eduardo Escobar	66	165	23	39	5	2	3	10	57	11	34	0	.282	.345	.236
Chris Colabello	55	160	14	31	3	0	7	17	55	20	58	0	.287	.344	.194
Chris Herrmann	57	157	16	32	7	0	4	18	51	18	49	0	.286	.325	.204
*Alex Presley	28	113	9	32	4	1	1	11	41	8	21	1	.336	.363	.283

PITCHING	GP	GS	IP	W–L	SV	HLD	H	ER	HR	BB	SO	ERA
Kevin Correia	31	31	185.1	9-13	0	0	218	86	24	45	101	4.18
Mike Pelfrey	29	29	152.2	5-13	0	0	184	88	13	53	101	5.19
Scott Diamond	24	24	131.0	6-13	0	0	163	79	21	36	52	5.43
Samuel Deduno	18	18	108.0	8-8	0	0	105	46	7	41	67	3.83
Anthony Swarzak	48	0	96.0	3-2	0	3	89	31	7	22	69	2.91
Ryan Pressly	49	0	76.2	3-3	0	1	71	33	5	27	49	3.87
Jared Burton	71	0	66.0	2-9	2	27	61	28	6	22	61	3.82
Glen Perkins	61	0	62.2	2-0	36	0	43	16	5	15	77	2.30
Casey Fien	73	0	62.0	5-2	0	17	51	27	9	12	73	3.92
Josh Roenicke	63	0	62.0	3-1	1	12	63	30	6	36	45	4.35
Brian Duensing	73	0	61.0	6-2	1	15	68	27	4	22	56	3.98
Andrew Albers	10	10	60.0	2-5	0	0	64	27	6	7	25	4.05
Pedro Hernandez	14	12	56.2	3-3	0	0	80	43	10	23	29	6.83
Kyle Gibson	10	10	51.0	2-4	0	0	69	37	7	20	29	6.53
Vance Worley	10	10	48.2	1-5	0	0	82	39	9	15	25	7.21
Liam Hendriks	10	8	47.1	1-3	0	0	67	36	10	14	34	6.85
Caleb Thielbar	49	0	46.0	3-2	0	1	24	9	4	14	39	1.76

*Mid-season trade.

New York Yankees

BATTING	G	AB	R	H	2B	3B	HR	RBI	TB	BB	SO	SB	OBP	SLG	BAVG
Robinson Cano	160	605	81	190	41	0	27	107	312	65	85	7	.383	.516	.314
Brett Gardner	145	539	81	147	33	10	8	52	224	52	127	24	.344	.416	.273
Ichiro Suzuki	150	520	57	136	15	3	7	35	178	26	63	20	.297	.342	.262
Lyle Overbay	142	445	43	107	24	1	14	59	175	36	111	2	.295	.393	.240
Vernon Wells	130	424	45	99	16	0	11	50	148	30	73	7	.282	.349	.233
Eduardo Nunez	90	304	38	79	17	4	3	28	113	20	51	10	.307	.372	.260
Chris Stewart	109	294	28	62	6	0	4	25	80	30	49	4	.293	.272	.211
Jayson Nix	87	267	32	63	9	1	3	24	83	24	80	13	.308	.311	.236
Travis Hafner	82	262	31	53	8	1	12	37	99	32	79	2	.301	.378	.202
*Alfonso Soriano	58	219	37	56	8	0	17	50	115	21	67	8	.325	.525	.256
Curtis Granderson	61	214	31	49	13	2	7	15	87	27	69	8	.317	.407	.229
Alex Rodriguez	44	156	21	38	7	0	7	19	66	23	43	4	.348	.423	.244
David Adams	43	140	10	27	5	1	2	13	40	9	43	0	.252	.286	.193
Austin Romine	60	135	15	28	9	0	1	10	40	8	37	1	.255	.296	.207
*Mark Reynolds	36	110	15	26	6	0	6	19	50	8	31	0	.300	.455	.236
Zoilo Almonte	34	106	9	25	4	0	1	9	32	6	19	3	.274	.302	.236
Kevin Youkilis	28	105	12	23	7	0	2	8	36	8	31	0	.305	.343	.219
Derek Jeter	17	63	8	12	1	0	1	7	16	8	10	0	.288	.254	.190

PITCHING	GP	GS	IP	W–L	SV	HLD	H	ER	HR	BB	SO	ERA
CC Sabathia	32	32	211.0	14-13	0	0	224	112	28	65	175	4.78
Hiroki Kuroda	32	32	201.1	11-13	0	0	191	74	20	43	150	3.31
Andy Pettitte	30	30	185.1	11-11	0	0	198	77	17	48	128	3.74
Phil Hughes	30	29	145.2	4-14	0	0	170	84	24	42	121	5.19
Ivan Nova	23	20	139.1	9-6	0	0	135	48	9	44	116	3.10
David Phelps	22	12	86.2	6-5	0	1	88	48	8	35	79	4.98
Adam Warren	34	2	77.0	3-2	1	1	80	29	10	30	64	3.39
David Robertson	70	0	66.1	5-1	3	33	51	15	5	18	77	2.04
Mariano Rivera	64	0	64.0	6-2	44	0	58	15	6	9	54	2.11
Shawn Kelley	57	0	53.1	4-2	0	11	47	26	8	23	71	4.39
Preston Claiborne	44	0	50.1	0-2	0	4	51	23	7	14	42	4.11
Joba Chamberlain	45	0	42.0	2-1	1	5	47	23	8	26	38	4.93
Boone Logan	61	0	39.0	5-2	0	11	33	14	7	13	50	3.23
*David Huff	11	2	34.2	3-1	0	0	26	18	7	8	26	4.67

Oakland Athletics

BATTING	G	AB	R	H	2B	3B	HR	RBI	TB	BB	SO	SB	OBP	SLG	BAVG
Jed Lowrie	154	603	80	175	45	2	15	75	269	50	91	1	.344	.446	.290
Josh Donaldson	158	579	89	174	37	3	24	93	289	76	110	5	.384	.499	.301
Yoenis Cespedes	135	529	74	127	21	4	26	80	234	37	137	7	.294	.442	.240
Coco Crisp	131	513	93	134	22	3	22	66	228	61	65	21	.335	.444	.261
Brandon Moss	145	446	73	114	23	4	30	87	233	50	140	4	.337	.522	.256
Josh Reddick	114	385	54	87	19	2	12	56	146	46	86	9	.307	.379	.226
Eric Sogard	130	368	45	98	24	3	2	35	134	27	51	10	.322	.364	.266
Seth Smith	117	368	49	93	27	0	8	40	144	39	94	0	.329	.391	.253
Chris Young	107	335	46	67	18	3	12	40	127	36	93	10	.280	.379	.200
Derek Norris	98	264	41	65	16	0	9	30	108	37	71	5	.345	.409	.246
John Jaso	70	207	31	56	12	0	3	21	77	38	45	2	.387	.372	.271
Nate Freiman	80	190	10	52	8	1	4	24	74	14	31	0	.327	.389	.274
*Alberto Callaspo	50	159	20	43	7	0	5	22	65	19	25	0	.350	.409	.270
*Adam Rosales	51	136	11	26	5	0	4	8	43	10	31	0	.267	.316	.191
Stephen Vogt	47	135	18	34	6	1	4	16	54	9	28	0	.295	.400	.252
Daric Barton	37	104	15	28	2	0	3	16	39	13	18	0	.350	.375	.269

PITCHING	GP	GS	IP	W–L	SV	HLD	H	ER	HR	BB	SO	ERA
A.J. Griffin	32	32	200.0	14-10	0	0	171	85	36	54	171	3.83
Jarrod Parker	32	32	197.0	12-8	0	0	178	87	25	63	134	3.97
Bartolo Colon	30	30	190.1	18-6	0	0	193	56	14	29	117	2.65
Tommy Milone	28	26	156.1	12-9	0	0	160	72	25	39	126	4.14
Dan Straily	27	27	152.1	10-8	0	0	132	67	16	57	124	3.96
Sean Doolittle	70	0	69.0	5-5	2	26	53	24	4	13	60	3.13
Ryan Cook	71	0	67.1	6-4	2	23	62	19	2	25	67	2.54
Sonny Gray	12	10	64.0	5-3	0	0	51	19	4	20	67	2.67
Grant Balfour	65	0	62.2	1-3	38	0	48	18	7	27	72	2.59
Jerry Blevins	67	0	60.0	5-0	0	4	47	21	7	17	52	3.15
Jesse Chavez	35	0	57.1	2-4	1	1	50	25	3	20	55	3.92
Brett Anderson	16	5	44.2	1-4	3	1	51	30	5	21	46	6.04
Pat Neshek	45	0	40.1	2-1	0	1	40	15	6	15	29	3.35
Dan Otero	33	0	39.0	2-0	0	8	42	6	0	6	27	1.38

*Mid-season trade.

Seattle Mariners

BATTING	G	AB	R	H	2B	3B	HR	RBI	TB	BB	SO	SB	OBP	SLG	BAVG
Kyle Seager..............160	615	79	160	32	2	22	69	262	68	122	9	.338	.426	.260
Kendrys Morales......156	602	64	167	34	0	23	80	270	49	114	0	.336	.449	.277
Raul Ibanez............124	454	54	110	20	2	29	65	221	42	128	0	.306	.487	.242
Justin Smoak...........131	454	53	108	19	0	20	50	187	64	119	0	.334	.412	.238
Michael Saunders 132	406	59	96	23	3	12	46	161	54	118	13	.323	.397	.236
Dustin Ackley...........113	384	40	97	18	2	4	31	131	37	72	2	.319	.341	.253
Nick Franklin 102	369	38	83	20	1	12	45	141	42	113	6	.303	.382	.225
Brad Miller...............76	306	41	81	11	6	8	36	128	24	52	5	.318	.418	.265
*Michael Morse.........76	283	31	64	13	0	13	27	116	20	80	0	.283	.410	.226
Endy Chavez.............97	266	22	71	10	0	2	14	87	9	31	1	.290	.327	.267
*Brendan Ryan..........87	260	23	50	10	0	3	21	69	21	60	4	.254	.265	.192
Jason Bay...............68	206	30	42	6	0	11	20	81	26	62	3	.298	.393	.204
Mike Zunino...............52	173	22	37	5	0	5	14	57	16	49	1	.290	.329	.214
Franklin Gutierrez.......41	145	18	36	7	0	10	24	73	5	43	3	.273	.503	.248
*Kelly Shoppach.......35	107	11	21	7	0	3	9	37	12	45	0	.293	.346	.196
Jesus Montero............29	101	6	21	1	1	3	9	33	8	21	0	.264	.327	.208
*Henry Blanco............35	96	8	12	2	0	3	14	23	10	26	0	.215	.240	.125

PITCHING	GP	GS	IP	W–L	SV	HLD	H	ER	HR	BB	SO	ERA
Hisashi Iwakuma 33	33	219.2	14-6	0	0	179	65	25	42	185	2.66
Felix Hernandez 31	31	204.1	12-10	0	0	185	69	15	46	216	3.04
Joe Saunders 32	32	183.0	11-16	0	0	232	107	25	61	107	5.26
*Aaron Harang 22	22	120.1	5-11	0	0	133	77	21	28	87	5.76
Brandon Maurer 22	14	90.0	5-8	0	0	114	63	16	27	70	6.30
Erasmo Ramirez..............14	13	72.1	5-3	0	0	79	40	12	26	57	4.98
Yoervis Medina............63	0	68.0	4-6	1	19	49	22	5	40	71	2.91
Charlie Furbush..............71	0	65.0	2-6	0	20	48	27	5	29	80	3.74
Carter Capps..................53	0	59.0	3-3	0	9	73	36	12	23	66	5.49
Tom Wilhelmsen.............59	0	59.0	0-3	24	2	45	27	2	33	45	4.12
Danny Farquhar 46	0	55.2	0-3	16	2	44	26	2	22	79	4.20
Oliver Perez....................61	0	53.0	3-3	2	8	50	22	6	26	74	3.74
Blake Beavan 12	2	39.2	0-2	0	0	46	27	8	8	27	6.13
*Jeremy Bonderman.........7	7	38.1	1-3	0	0	40	21	4	17	16	4.93
Lucas Luetge 35	0	37.0	1-3	0	1	42	20	2	16	27	4.86

Tampa Bay Rays

BATTING	G	AB	R	H	2B	3B	HR	RBI	TB	BB	SO	SB	OBP	SLG	BAVG
Evan Longoria..........160	614	91	165	39	3	32	88	306	70	162	1	.343	.498	.269
Ben Zobrist...............157	612	77	168	36	3	12	71	246	72	91	11	.354	.402	.275
James Loney............158	549	54	164	33	0	13	75	236	44	77	3	.348	.430	.299
Desmond Jennings ..139	527	82	133	31	6	14	54	218	64	115	20	.334	.414	.252
Yunel Escobar.........153	508	61	130	27	1	9	56	186	57	73	4	.332	.366	.256
Matt Joyce...............140	413	61	97	22	0	18	47	173	59	87	7	.328	.419	.235
Kelly Johnson...........118	366	41	86	12	2	16	52	150	35	99	7	.305	.410	.235
Wil Myers...............88	335	50	98	23	0	13	53	160	33	91	5	.354	.478	.293
Jose Molina 99	283	26	66	14	0	2	18	86	22	63	2	.290	.304	.233
Jose Lobaton 100	277	38	69	15	2	7	32	109	30	65	0	.320	.394	.249
Luke Scott...............91	253	27	61	13	2	9	40	105	30	63	1	.326	.415	.241
Sean Rodriguez 96	195	21	48	10	1	5	23	75	17	59	1	.320	.385	.246
Sam Fuld 119	176	25	35	0	3	2	17	47	17	28	8	.270	.267	.199
Ryan Roberts.............60	162	15	40	6	0	5	17	61	11	39	0	.295	.377	.247
*David DeJesus 35	104	13	27	10	0	2	11	43	10	23	2	.328	.413	.260

PITCHING	GP	GS	IP	W–L	SV	HLD	H	ER	HR	BB	SO	ERA
David Price....................27	27	186.2	10-8	0	0	178	69	16	27	151	3.33
Jeremy Hellickson 32	31	174.0	12-10	0	0	185	100	24	50	135	5.17
Roberto Hernandez........32	24	151.0	6-13	1	0	164	82	24	38	113	4.89
Matt Moore 27	27	150.1	17-4	0	0	119	55	14	76	143	3.29
Alex Cobb 22	22	143.1	11-3	0	0	120	44	13	45	134	2.76
Chris Archer 23	23	128.2	9-7	0	0	107	46	15	38	101	3.22
Joel Peralta....................80	0	71.1	3-8	1	41	47	27	7	34	74	3.41
Jamey Wright................66	1	70.0	2-2	0	6	61	24	4	23	65	3.09
Cesar Ramos..................48	0	67.1	2-2	1	1	66	31	6	22	53	4.14
Fernando Rodney...........68	0	66.2	5-4	37	0	53	25	3	36	82	3.38
Jake McGee.................71	0	62.2	5-3	1	28	52	28	8	22	75	4.02
Alex Torres 39	0	58.0	4-2	0	5	32	11	1	20	62	1.71

*Mid-season trade.

Texas Rangers

BATTING	G	AB	R	H	2B	3B	HR	RBI	TB	BB	SO	SB	OBP	SLG	BAVG
Adrian Beltre	161	631	88	199	32	0	30	92	321	50	78	1	.371	.509	.315
Elvis Andrus	156	620	91	168	17	4	4	67	205	52	97	42	.328	.331	.271
Ian Kinsler	136	545	85	151	31	2	13	72	225	51	59	15	.344	.413	.277
A.J. Pierzynski	134	503	48	137	24	1	17	70	214	11	76	1	.297	.425	.272
Mitch Moreland	147	462	60	107	24	1	23	60	202	45	117	0	.299	.437	.232
Leonys Martin	147	457	66	119	21	6	8	49	176	28	104	36	.313	.385	.260
David Murphy	142	436	51	96	26	1	13	45	163	37	59	1	.282	.374	.220
Nelson Cruz	109	413	49	110	18	0	27	76	209	35	109	5	.327	.506	.266
Jurickson Profar	85	286	30	67	11	0	6	26	96	26	63	2	.308	.336	.234
Lance Berkman	73	256	27	62	10	1	6	34	92	38	52	0	.340	.359	.242
Craig Gentry	106	246	39	69	12	4	2	22	95	29	46	24	.373	.386	.280
*Alex Rios	47	186	26	52	11	2	6	26	85	9	30	16	.315	.457	.280
Geovany Soto	54	163	20	40	9	0	9	22	76	20	60	1	.328	.466	.245
Jeff Baker	74	154	21	43	8	0	11	21	84	18	48	1	.360	.545	.279

PITCHING	GP	GS	IP	W-L	SV	HLD	H	ER	HR	BB	SO	ERA
Derek Holland	33	33	213.0	10-9	0	0	210	81	20	64	189	3.42
Yu Darvish	32	32	209.2	13-9	0	0	145	66	26	80	277	2.83
Martin Perez	20	20	124.1	10-6	0	0	129	50	15	37	84	3.62
Alexi Ogando	23	18	104.1	7-4	0	0	87	36	11	41	72	3.11
Nick Tepesch	19	17	93.0	4-6	0	0	100	50	12	27	76	4.84
*Justin Grimm	17	17	89.0	7-7	0	0	116	63	15	31	68	6.37
*Matt Garza	13	13	84.1	4-5	0	0	89	41	12	22	74	4.38
Tanner Scheppers	76	0	76.2	6-2	1	27	58	16	6	24	59	1.88
Joe Nathan	67	0	64.2	6-2	43	0	36	10	2	22	73	1.39
Robbie Ross	65	0	62.1	4-2	0	16	63	21	4	19	58	3.03
Neal Cotts	58	0	57.0	8-3	1	11	36	7	2	18	65	1.11
Jason Frasor	61	0	49.0	4-3	0	10	36	14	4	20	48	2.57
Ross Wolf	22	3	47.2	1-3	0	1	58	22	5	15	21	4.15
Joe Ortiz	32	0	44.2	2-2	0	2	46	21	5	10	27	4.23
Josh Lindblom	8	5	31.1	1-3	0	0	35	19	4	11	21	5.46

Toronto Blue Jays

BATTING	G	AB	R	H	2B	3B	HR	RBI	TB	BB	SO	SB	OBP	SLG	BAVG
Edwin Encarnacion	142	530	90	144	29	1	36	104	283	82	62	7	.370	.534	.272
J.P. Arencibia	138	474	45	92	18	0	21	55	173	18	148	0	.227	.365	.194
Adam Lind	143	465	67	134	26	1	23	67	231	51	103	1	.357	.497	.288
Jose Bautista	118	452	82	117	24	0	28	73	225	69	84	7	.358	.498	.259
Colby Rasmus	118	417	57	115	26	1	22	66	209	37	135	0	.338	.501	.276
Brett Lawrie	107	401	41	102	18	3	11	46	159	30	68	9	.315	.397	.254
Jose Reyes	93	382	58	113	20	0	10	37	163	34	47	15	.353	.427	.296
Maicer Izturis	107	365	33	86	12	0	5	32	113	27	38	1	.288	.310	.236
Melky Cabrera	88	344	39	96	15	2	3	30	124	23	47	2	.322	.360	.279
Rajai Davis	108	331	49	86	16	2	6	24	124	21	67	45	.312	.375	.260
*Emilio Bonifacio	94	262	33	57	16	1	3	20	84	13	66	12	.258	.321	.218
Munenori Kawasaki	96	240	27	55	6	5	1	24	74	32	41	7	.326	.308	.229
Mark DeRosa	88	204	23	48	12	1	7	36	83	28	49	0	.326	.407	.235
Anthony Gose	52	147	15	38	6	5	2	12	60	5	37	4	.283	.408	.259
Josh Thole	45	120	11	21	3	1	1	8	29	12	25	0	.256	.242	.175
Ryan Goins	34	119	11	30	5	0	2	8	41	2	28	0	.264	.345	.252
Moises Sierra	35	107	11	31	13	1	1	13	49	14	29	1	.369	.458	.290
Kevin Pillar	36	102	11	21	4	0	3	13	34	4	29	0	.250	.333	.206

PITCHING	GP	GS	IP	W-L	SV	HLD	H	ER	HR	BB	SO	ERA
R.A. Dickey	34	34	224.2	14-13	0	0	207	105	35	71	177	4.21
Mark Buehrle	33	33	203.2	12-10	0	0	223	94	24	51	139	4.15
Esmil Rogers	44	20	137.2	5-9	0	4	152	73	21	44	96	4.77
J.A. Happ	18	18	92.2	5-7	0	0	91	47	10	45	77	4.56
Josh Johnson	16	16	81.1	2-8	0	0	105	56	15	30	83	6.20
Todd Redmond	17	14	77.0	4-3	0	0	70	37	13	23	76	4.32
Aaron Loup	64	0	69.1	4-6	2	8	66	19	5	13	53	2.47
Brett Cecil	60	0	60.2	5-1	1	11	44	19	4	23	70	2.82
Steve Delabar	55	0	58.2	5-5	1	6	50	21	4	29	82	3.22
Brandon Morrow	10	10	54.1	2-3	0	0	63	34	12	18	42	5.63
Casey Janssen	56	0	52.2	4-1	34	1	39	15	3	13	50	2.56
Darren Oliver	50	0	49.0	3-4	0	8	47	21	6	15	40	3.86
Neil Wagner	36	0	38.0	2-4	0	10	39	16	5	13	33	3.79
Chad Jenkins	10	3	33.1	1-0	0	0	31	10	3	6	15	2.70

*Mid-season trade.

FOR THE RECORD • Year by Year

Results

1903...............Boston (A) 5, Pittsburgh (N) 3	1959...............Los Angeles (N) 4, Chicago (A) 2
1904...............No series	1960...............Pittsburgh (N) 4, New York (A) 3
1905...............New York (N) 4, Philadelphia (A) 1	1961...............New York (A) 4, Cincinnati (N) 1
1906...............Chicago (A) 4, Chicago (N) 2	1962...............New York (A) 4, San Francisco (N) 3
1907...............Chicago (N) 4, Detroit (A) 0; 1 tie	1963...............Los Angeles (N) 4, New York (A) 0
1908...............Chicago (N) 4, Detroit (A) 1	1964...............St. Louis (N) 4, New York (A) 3
1909...............Pittsburgh (N) 4, Detroit (A) 3	1965...............Los Angeles (N) 4, Minnesota (A) 3
1910...............Philadelphia (A) 4, Chicago (N) 1	1966...............Baltimore (A) 4, Los Angeles (N) 0
1911...............Philadelphia (A) 4, New York (N) 2	1967...............St. Louis (N) 4, Boston (A) 3
1912...............Boston (A) 4, New York (N) 3; 1 tie	1968...............Detroit (A) 4, St. Louis (N) 3
1913...............Philadelphia (A) 4, New York (N) 1	1969...............New York (N) 4, Baltimore (A) 1
1914...............Boston (N) 4, Philadelphia (A) 0	1970...............Baltimore (A) 4, Cincinnati (N) 1
1915...............Boston (A) 4, Philadelphia (N) 1	1971...............Pittsburgh (N) 4, Baltimore (A) 3
1916...............Boston (A) 4, Brooklyn (N) 1	1972...............Oakland (A) 4, Cincinnati (N) 3
1917...............Chicago (A) 4, New York (N) 2	1973...............Oakland (A) 4, New York (N) 3
1918...............Boston (A) 4, Chicago (N) 2	1974...............Oakland (A) 4, Los Angeles (N) 1
1919...............Cincinnati (N) 5, Chicago (A) 3	1975...............Cincinnati (N) 4, Boston (A) 3
1920...............Cleveland (A) 5, Brooklyn (N) 2	1976...............Cincinnati (N) 4, New York (A) 0
1921...............New York (N) 5, New York (A) 3	1977...............New York (A) 4, Los Angeles (N) 2
1922...............New York (N) 4, New York (A) 0; 1 tie	1978...............New York (A) 4, Los Angeles (N) 2
1923...............New York (A) 4, New York (N) 2	1979...............Pittsburgh (N) 4, Baltimore (A) 3
1924...............Washington (A) 4, New York (N) 3	1980...............Philadelphia (N) 4, Kansas City (A) 2
1925...............Pittsburgh (N) 4, Washington (A) 3	1981...............Los Angeles (N) 4, New York (A) 2
1926...............St. Louis (N) 4, New York (A) 3	1982...............St. Louis (N) 4, Milwaukee (A) 3
1927...............New York (A) 4, Pittsburgh (N) 0	1983...............Baltimore (A) 4, Philadelphia (N) 1
1928...............New York (A) 4, St. Louis (N) 0	1984...............Detroit (A) 4, San Diego (N) 1
1929...............Philadelphia (A) 4, Chicago (N) 1	1985...............Kansas City (A) 4, St. Louis (N) 3
1930...............Philadelphia (A) 4, St. Louis (N) 2	1986...............New York (N) 4, Boston (A) 3
1931...............St. Louis (N) 4, Philadelphia (A) 3	1987...............Minnesota (A) 4, St. Louis (N) 3
1932...............New York (A) 4, Chicago (N) 0	1988...............Los Angeles (N) 4, Oakland (A) 1
1933...............New York (N) 4, Washington (A) 1	1989...............Oakland (A) 4, San Francisco (N) 0
1934...............St. Louis (N) 4, Detroit (A) 3	1990...............Cincinnati (N) 4, Oakland (A) 0
1935...............Detroit (A) 4, Chicago (N) 2	1991...............Minnesota (A) 4, Atlanta (N) 3
1936...............New York (A) 4, New York (N) 2	1992...............Toronto (A) 4, Atlanta (N) 2
1937...............New York (A) 4, New York (N) 1	1993...............Toronto (A) 4, Philadelphia (N) 2
1938...............New York (A) 4, Chicago (N) 0	1994...............Series canceled due to players' strike.
1939...............New York (A) 4, Cincinnati (N) 0	1995...............Atlanta (N) 4, Cleveland (A) 2
1940...............Cincinnati (N) 4, Detroit (A) 3	1996...............New York (A) 4, Atlanta (N) 2
1941...............New York (A) 4, Brooklyn (N) 1	1997...............Florida (N) 4, Cleveland (A) 3
1942...............St. Louis (N) 4, New York (A) 1	1998...............New York (A) 4, San Diego (N) 0
1943...............New York (A) 4, St. Louis (N) 1	1999...............New York (A) 4, Atlanta (N) 0
1944...............St. Louis (N) 4, St. Louis (A) 2	2000...............New York (A) 4, New York (N) 1
1945...............Detroit (A) 4, Chicago (N) 3	2001...............Arizona (N) 4, New York (A) 3
1946...............St. Louis (N) 4, Boston (A) 3	2002...............Anaheim (A) 4, San Francisco (N) 3
1947...............New York (A) 4, Brooklyn (N) 3	2003...............Florida (N) 4, New York (A) 2
1948...............Cleveland (A) 4, Boston (N) 2	2004...............Boston (A) 4, St. Louis (N) 0
1949...............New York (A) 4, Brooklyn (N) 1	2005...............Chicago (A) 4, Houston (N) 0
1950...............New York (A) 4, Philadelphia (N) 0	2006...............St. Louis (N) 4, Detroit (A) 1
1951...............New York (A) 4, New York (N) 2	2007...............Boston (A) 4, Colorado (N) 0
1952...............New York (A) 4, Brooklyn (N) 3	2008...............Philadelphia (N) 4, Tampa Bay (A) 1
1953...............New York (A) 4, Brooklyn (N) 2	2009...............New York (A) 4, Philadelphia (N) 2
1954...............New York (N) 4, Cleveland (A) 0	2010...............San Francisco (N) 4, Texas (A) 1
1955...............Brooklyn (N) 4, New York (A) 3	2011...............St. Louis (N) 4, Texas (A) 3
1956...............New York (A) 4, Brooklyn (N) 3	2012...............San Francisco (N) 4, Detroit (A) 0
1957...............Milwaukee (N) 4, New York (A) 3	2013...............Boston (A) 4, St. Louis (N) 2
1958...............New York (A) 4, Milwaukee (N) 3	

Most Valuable Players

1955 ....Johnny Podres, Bklyn	1960 ....Bobby Richardson, NY (A)
1956 ....Don Larsen, NY (A)	1961 ....Whitey Ford, NY (A)
1957 ....Lew Burdette, Mil	1962 ....Ralph Terry, NY (A)
1958 ....Bob Turley, NY (A)	1963 ....Sandy Koufax, LA
1959 ....Larry Sherry, LA	1964 ....Bob Gibson, StL

Most Valuable Players *(Cont.)*

1965 ....Sandy Koufax, LA	1990 ....Jose Rijo, Cin
1966 ....Frank Robinson, Balt	1991 ....Jack Morris, Minn
1967 ....Bob Gibson, StL	1992 ....Pat Borders, Tor
1968 ....Mickey Lolich, Det	1993 ....Paul Molitor, Tor
1969 ....Donn Clendenon, NY (N)	1994 ....Series canceled due to strike.
1970 ....Brooks Robinson, Balt	1995 ....Tom Glavine, Atl
1971 ....Roberto Clemente, Pitt	1996 ....John Wetteland, NY (A)
1972 ....Gene Tenace, Oak	1997 ....Livan Hernandez, Fla
1973 ....Reggie Jackson, Oak	1998 ....Scott Brosius, NY (A)
1974 ....Rollie Fingers, Oak	1999 ....Mariano Rivera, NY (A)
1975 ....Pete Rose, Cin	2000 ....Derek Jeter, NY (A)
1976 ....Johnny Bench, Cin	2001 ....Randy Johnson, Ariz
1977 ....Reggie Jackson, NY (A)	Curt Schilling, Ariz
1978 ....Bucky Dent, NY (A)	2002 ....Troy Glaus, Ana
1979 ....Willie Stargell, Pitt	2003 ....Josh Beckett, Fla
1980 ....Mike Schmidt, Phil	2004 ....Manny Ramirez, Bos
1981.............................Ron Cey, LA; Steve Yeager, LA;	2005 ....Jermaine Dye, Chi (A)
Pedro Guerrero, LA	2006 ....David Eckstein, StL
1982 ....Darrell Porter, StL	2007 ....Mike Lowell, Bos
1983 ....Rick Dempsey, Balt	2008 ....Cole Hamels, Phi
1984 ....Alan Trammell, Det	2009 ....Hideki Matsui, NY (A)
1985 ....Bret Saberhagen, KC	2010 ....Edgar Renteria, SF
1986 ....Ray Knight, NY (N)	2011 ....David Freese, StL
1987 ....Frank Viola, Minn	2012 ....Pablo Sandoval, SF
1988 ....Orel Hershiser, LA	2013 ....David Ortiz, Bos
1989 ....Dave Stewart, Oak	

Career Batting Leaders (Minimum 40 at bats)

GAMES

Yogi Berra	75
Mickey Mantle	65
Elston Howard	54
Hank Bauer	53
Gil McDougald	53
Phil Rizzuto	52
Joe DiMaggio	51
Frankie Frisch	50
Pee Wee Reese	44
Roger Maris	41
Babe Ruth	41

AT BATS

Yogi Berra	259
Mickey Mantle	230
Joe DiMaggio	199
Frankie Frisch	197
Gil McDougald	190
Hank Bauer	188
Phil Rizzuto	183
Elston Howard	171
Pee Wee Reese	169
Derek Jeter	156
Roger Maris	152

BATTING AVERAGE

David Ortiz	.455
Bobby Brown	.439
Pepper Martin	.418
Paul Molitor	.418
Hal McRae	.400
Lou Brock	.391
Marquis Grissom	.390
George Brett	.373
Thurman Munson	.373
Pat Borders	.372

TOTAL BASES

Mickey Mantle	123
Yogi Berra	117
Babe Ruth	96
Lou Gehrig	87
Joe DiMaggio	84
Duke Snider	79
Hank Bauer	75
Frankie Frisch	74
Reggie Jackson	74
Gil McDougald	72

HOME RUNS

Mickey Mantle	18
Babe Ruth	15
Yogi Berra	12
Duke Snider	11
Reggie Jackson	10
Lou Gehrig	10
Joe DiMaggio	8
Frank Robinson	8
Bill Skowron	8
Hank Bauer	7
Goose Goslin	7
Gil McDougald	7
Chase Utley	7

RUNS

Mickey Mantle	42
Yogi Berra	41
Babe Ruth	37
Derek Jeter	32
Lou Gehrig	30
Joe DiMaggio	27
Roger Maris	26
Elston Howard	25
Gil McDougald	23
Jackie Robinson	22

RUNS BATTED IN

Mickey Mantle	40
Yogi Berra	39
Lou Gehrig	35
Babe Ruth	33
Joe DiMaggio	30
Bill Skowron	29
Duke Snider	26
Hank Bauer	24
Bill Dickey	24
Reggie Jackson	24
Gil McDougald	24

HITS

Yogi Berra	71
Mickey Mantle	59
Frankie Frisch	58
Joe DiMaggio	54
Derek Jeter	50
Hank Bauer	46
Pee Wee Reese	46
Gil McDougald	45
Phil Rizzuto	45
Lou Gehrig	43
Eddie Collins	42
Elston Howard	42
Babe Ruth	42

STOLEN BASES

Lou Brock	14
Eddie Collins	14
Frank Chance	10
Davey Lopes	10
Phil Rizzuto	10
Frankie Frisch	9
Kenny Lofton	9
Honus Wagner	9

Career Batting Leaders *(Cont.)*

STOLEN BASES (CONT.)

Johnny Evers 8
Roberto Alomar 7
Rickey Henderson 7
Pepper Martin.........................7
Joe Morgan 7
Joe Tinker 7

SLUGGING AVERAGE

David Ortiz...............................795
Reggie Jackson................ .755
Babe Ruth 744
Lou Gehrig 731
Bobby Brown.......................707
Lenny Dykstra 700
Al Simmons.........................658
Lou Brock 655
Pepper Martin 636
Paul Molitor.........................636

STRIKEOUTS

Mickey Mantle 54
Derek Jeter 39
Elston Howard 37
Duke Snider..........................33
Jorge Posada........................31
David Justice 30
Babe Ruth.............................30
Gil McDougald 29
Bill Skowron 26
Bernie Williams.....................26
Hank Bauer...........................25

Career Pitching Leaders

GAMES

Mariano Rivera 24
Whitey Ford 22
Mike Stanton.........................19
Rollie Fingers 16
Jeff Nelson............................16
Allie Reynolds 15
Bob Turley 15
Clay Carroll...........................14
Clem Labine 13
Andy Pettitte 13
Mark Wohlers.........................13

LOSSES

Whitey Ford 8
Eddie Plank 5
Schoolboy Rowe 5
Joe Bush 5
Rube Marquard 5
Christy Mathewson 5

COMPLETE GAMES

Christy Mathewson 10
Chief Bender 9
Bob Gibson 8
Whitey Ford 7
Red Ruffing 7
Waite Hoyt 6
Art Nehf 6
George Mullin 6
Eddie Plank 6

INNINGS PITCHED

Whitey Ford 146.0
Christy Mathewson 101.2
Red Ruffing.........................85.2
Chief Bender.......................85.0
Waite Hoyt 83.2
Bob Gibson 81.0
Art Nehf 79.0
Andy Pettitte 77.2
Allie Reynolds.....................77.0

SAVES

Mariano Rivera 11
Rollie Fingers 6
Allie Reynolds 4
Johnny Murphy........................4
John Wetteland.......................4
Robb Nen 4

*EARNED RUN AVERAGE

Jack Billingham 0.36
Harry Brecheen 0.83
Babe Ruth 0.87
Sherry Smith 0.89
Sandy Koufax 0.95
Mariano Rivera 0.99
Hippo Vaughn 1.00
Monte Pearson 1.01
Christy Mathewson 1.06
Babe Adams......................1.29

STRIKEOUTS

Whitey Ford 94
Bob Gibson 92
Allie Reynolds.......................62
Sandy Koufax 61
Red Ruffing...........................61
Chief Bender 59
George Earnshaw...................56
Andy Pettitte.........................56
John Smoltz..........................52
Roger Clemens......................49
Waite Hoyt 49
Christy Mathewson 48

WINS

Whitey Ford 10
Bob Gibson 7
Allie Reynolds 7
Red Ruffing.............................7
Chief Bender 6
Lefty Gomez 6
Waite Hoyt 6
Three Finger Brown.................5
Jack Coombs 5
Catfish Hunter 5
Christy Mathewson 5
Herb Pennock.........................5
Andy Pettitte 5
Vic Raschi..............................5

*Minimum 25 innings pitched.

SHUTOUTS

Christy Mathewson 4
Three Finger Brown.................3
Whitey Ford 3
Lew Burdette 2
Bill Dinneen 2
Bill Hallahan...........................2
Bob Gibson 2
Art Nehf 2
Allie Reynolds.........................2
Sandy Koufax 2

BASES ON BALLS

Whitey Ford 34
Art Nehf 32
Allie Reynolds 32
Jim Palmer............................31
Bob Turley 29
Paul Derringer 27
Red Ruffing 27
Burleigh Grimes.....................26
Don Gullett 26
Andy Pettitte 26
Vic Raschi.............................25

Alltime Team Rankings, by Championships

Team	W	L	Appearances	Pct.	Most Recent App.	Last Championship
New York Yankees......................27	13	40	.675		2009	2009
St. Louis Cardinals........................11	8	19	.579		2013	2011
Phila./K.C./Oakland Athletics..........9	5	14	.643		1990	1989
Boston Red Sox 8	5	13	.615		2013	2013
New York/San Francisco Giants.....7	12	19	.368		2012	2012
Brooklyn/Los Angeles Dodgers......6	12	18	.333		1988	1988
Pittsburgh Pirates 5	2	7	.714		1979	1979
Cincinnati Reds 5	4	9	.556		1990	1990
Detroit Tigers 4	7	11	.364		2012	1984
Chicago White Sox 3	2	5	.600		2005	2005
Wash. Senators/Minnesota Twins....3	3	6	.500		1991	1991
St. Louis Browns/Baltimore Orioles..3	4	7	.429		1983	1983
Boston/Milwaukee/Atlanta Braves...3	6	9	.333		1999	1995
Florida Marlins 2	0	2	1.000		2003	2003

Alltime Team Rankings, by Championships *(Cont.)*

Team	W	L	Appearances	Pct.	Most Recent App.	Last Championship
Toronto Blue Jays	2	0	2	1.000	1993	1993
New York Mets	2	2	4	.500	2000	1986
Cleveland Indians	2	3	5	.400	1997	1948
Philadelphia Phillies	2	5	7	.286	2009	2008
Chicago Cubs	2	8	10	.200	1945	1908
California/Anaheim/L.A. Angels	1	0	1	1.000	2002	2002
Arizona Diamondbacks	1	0	1	1.000	2001	2001
Kansas City Royals	1	1	2	.500	1985	1985
Tampa Bay Rays	0	1	1	.000	2008	—
Colorado Rockies	0	1	1	.000	2007	—
Houston Astros	0	1	1	.000	2005	—
Seattle Pilots/Milwaukee Brewers	0	1	1	.000	1982	—
Texas Rangers	0	2	2	.000	2011	—
San Diego Padres	0	2	2	.000	1998	—

League Pennant Winners

National League

Year	Team	Manager	W	L	Pct	GA
1900	Brooklyn	Ned Hanlon	82	54	.603	4½
1901	Pittsburgh	Fred Clarke	90	49	.647	7½
1902	Pittsburgh	Fred Clarke	103	36	.741	27½
1903	Pittsburgh	Fred Clarke	91	49	.650	6½
1904	New York	John McGraw	106	47	.693	13
1905	New York	John McGraw	105	48	.686	9
1906	Chicago	Frank Chance	116	36	.763	20
1907	Chicago	Frank Chance	107	45	.704	17
1908	Chicago	Frank Chance	99	55	.643	1
1909	Pittsburgh	Fred Clarke	110	42	.724	6½
1910	Chicago	Frank Chance	104	50	.675	13
1911	New York	John McGraw	99	54	.647	7½
1912	New York	John McGraw	103	48	.682	10
1913	New York	John McGraw	101	51	.664	12½
1914	Boston	George Stallings	94	59	.614	10½
1915	Philadelphia	Pat Moran	90	62	.592	7
1916	Brooklyn	Wilbert Robinson	94	60	.610	2½
1917	New York	John McGraw	98	56	.636	10
1918	Chicago	Fred Mitchell	84	45	.651	10½
1919	Cincinnati	Pat Moran	96	44	.686	9
1920	Brooklyn	Wilbert Robinson	93	61	.604	7
1921	New York	John McGraw	94	59	.614	4
1922	New York	John McGraw	93	61	.604	7
1923	New York	John McGraw	95	58	.621	4½
1924	New York	John McGraw	93	60	.608	1½
1925	Pittsburgh	Bill McKechnie	95	58	.621	8½
1926	St. Louis	Rogers Hornsby	89	65	.578	2
1927	Pittsburgh	Donie Bush	94	60	.610	1½
1928	St. Louis	Bill McKechnie	95	59	.617	2
1929	Chicago	Joe McCarthy	98	54	.645	10½
1930	St. Louis	Gabby Street	92	62	.597	2
1931	St. Louis	Gabby Street	101	53	.656	13
1932	Chicago	Charlie Grimm	90	64	.584	4
1933	New York	Bill Terry	91	61	.599	5
1934	St. Louis	Frankie Frisch	95	58	.621	2
1935	Chicago	Charlie Grimm	100	54	.649	4
1936	New York	Bill Terry	92	62	.597	5
1937	New York	Bill Terry	95	57	.625	3
1938	Chicago	Gabby Hartnett	89	63	.586	2
1939	Cincinnati	Bill McKechnie	97	57	.630	4½
1940	Cincinnati	Bill McKechnie	100	53	.654	12
1941	Brooklyn	Leo Durocher	100	54	.649	2½
1942	St. Louis	Billy Southworth	106	48	.688	2
1943	St. Louis	Billy Southworth	105	49	.682	18
1944	St. Louis	Billy Southworth	105	49	.682	14½
1945	Chicago	Charlie Grimm	98	56	.636	3
1946	St. Louis*	Eddie Dyer	98	58	.628	2
1947	Brooklyn	Burt Shotton	94	60	.610	5

National League *(Cont.)*

Year	Team	Manager	W	L	Pct	GA
1948	Boston	Billy Southworth	91	62	.595	6½
1949	Brooklyn	Burt Shotton	97	57	.630	1
1950	Philadelphia	Eddie Sawyer	91	63	.591	2
1951	New York†	Leo Durocher	98	59	.624	1
1952	Brooklyn	Chuck Dressen	96	57	.627	4½
1953	Brooklyn	Chuck Dressen	105	49	.682	13
1954	New York	Leo Durocher	97	57	.630	5
1955	Brooklyn	Walter Alston	98	55	.641	13½
1956	Brooklyn	Walter Alston	93	61	.604	1
1957	Milwaukee	Fred Haney	95	59	.617	8
1958	Milwaukee	Fred Haney	92	62	.597	8
1959	Los Angeles‡	Walter Alston	88	68	.564	2
1960	Pittsburgh	Danny Murtaugh	95	59	.617	7
1961	Cincinnati	Fred Hutchinson	93	61	.604	4
1962	San Francisco#	Al Dark	103	62	.624	1
1963	Los Angeles	Walter Alston	99	63	.611	6
1964	St. Louis	Johnny Keane	93	69	.574	1
1965	Los Angeles	Walter Alston	97	65	.599	2
1966	Los Angeles	Walter Alston	95	67	.586	1½
1967	St. Louis	Red Schoendienst	101	60	.627	10½
1968	St. Louis	Red Schoendienst	97	65	.599	9
1969	New York (E)††	Gil Hodges	100	62	.617	8
1970	Cincinnati (W)††	Sparky Anderson	102	60	.630	14½
1971	Pittsburgh (E)††	Danny Murtaugh	97	65	.599	7
1972	Cincinnati (W)††	Sparky Anderson	95	59	.617	10½
1973	New York (E)††	Yogi Berra	82	79	.509	1½
1974	Los Angeles (W)††	Walter Alston	102	60	.630	4
1975	Cincinnati (W)††	Sparky Anderson	108	54	.667	20
1976	Cincinnati (W)††	Sparky Anderson	102	60	.630	10
1977	Los Angeles (W)††	Tommy Lasorda	98	64	.605	10
1978	Los Angeles (W)††	Tommy Lasorda	95	67	.586	2½
1979	Pittsburgh (E)††	Chuck Tanner	98	64	.605	2
1980	Philadelphia (E)††	Dallas Green	91	71	.562	1
1981	Los Angeles (W)††	Tommy Lasorda	63	47	.573	**
1982	St. Louis (E)††	Whitey Herzog	92	70	.568	3
1983	Philadelphia (E)††	Pat Corrales/Paul Owens	90	72	.556	6
1984	San Diego (W)††	Dick Williams	92	70	.568	12
1985	St. Louis (E)††	Whitey Herzog	101	61	.623	3
1986	New York (E)††	Davey Johnson	108	54	.667	21½
1987	St. Louis (E)††	Whitey Herzog	95	67	.586	3
1988	Los Angeles (W)††	Tommy Lasorda	94	67	.584	7
1989	San Francisco (W)††	Roger Craig	92	70	.568	3
1990	Cincinnati (W)††	Lou Piniella	91	71	.562	5
1991	Atlanta (W)††	Bobby Cox	94	68	.580	1
1992	Atlanta (W)††	Bobby Cox	98	64	.605	8
1993	Philadelphia (E)††	Jim Fregosi	97	65	.599	3
1994	Season ended Aug. 11 due to players' strike.					
1995	Atlanta (E)††	Bobby Cox	90	54	.625	21
1996	Atlanta (E)††	Bobby Cox	96	66	.593	8
1997	Florida (wc)††	Jim Leyland	92	70	.568	-9
1998	San Diego (W)††	Bruce Bochy	98	64	.605	9½
1999	Atlanta (E)††	Bobby Cox	103	59	.636	6½
2000	New York (wc)††	Bobby Valentine	94	68	.580	-6½
2001	Arizona (W)††	Bob Brenly	92	70	.568	2
2002	San Francisco (wc)††	Dusty Baker	95	66	.590	-2½
2003	Florida (wc)††	Jack McKeon	91	71	.562	-10
2004	St. Louis (C)††	Tony LaRussa	105	57	.648	13
2005	Houston (wc)††	Phil Garner	89	73	.549	-11
2006	St. Louis (C)††	Tony LaRussa	83	78	.516	1½
2007	Colorado (wc)††§	Clint Hurdle	89	73	.549	-1
2008	Philadelphia (E)††	Charlie Manuel	92	70	.568	3
2009	Philadelphia (E)††	Charlie Manuel	93	69	.574	6
2010	San Francisco (W)††	Bruce Bochy	92	70	.568	2
2011	St. Louis (wc)††	Tony LaRussa	90	72	.556	-6
2012	San Francisco (W)††	Bruce Bochy	94	68	.580	8
2013	St. Louis (C)††	Mike Matheny	97	65	.599	3

*Defeated Brooklyn, two games to none, in playoff for pennant. †Defeated Brooklyn, two games to one, in playoff for pennant. ‡Defeated Milwaukee, two games to none, in playoff for pennant. #Defeated Los Angeles, two games to one, in playoff for pennant. § Defeated San Diego in one-game playoff for wild card. ††Won Championship Series. **First half 36–21; second half 27–26, in season split by strike; defeated Houston in playoff for Western Division title.

American League

Year	Team	Manager	W	L	Pct	GA
1901	Chicago	Clark Griffith	83	53	.610	4
1902	Philadelphia	Connie Mack	83	53	.610	5
1903	Boston	Jimmy Collins	91	47	.659	14½
1904	Boston	Jimmy Collins	95	59	.617	1½
1905	Philadelphia	Connie Mack	92	56	.622	2
1906	Chicago	Fielder Jones	93	58	.616	3
1907	Detroit	Hughie Jennings	92	58	.613	1½
1908	Detroit	Hughie Jennings	90	63	.588	½
1909	Detroit	Hughie Jennings	98	54	.645	3½
1910	Philadelphia	Connie Mack	102	48	.680	14½
1911	Philadelphia	Connie Mack	101	50	.669	13½
1912	Boston	Jake Stahl	105	47	.691	14
1913	Philadelphia	Connie Mack	96	57	.627	6½
1914	Philadelphia	Connie Mack	99	53	.651	8½
1915	Boston	Bill Carrigan	101	50	.669	2½
1916	Boston	Bill Carrigan	91	63	.591	2
1917	Chicago	Pants Rowland	100	54	.649	9
1918	Boston	Ed Barrow	75	51	.595	2½
1919	Chicago	Kid Gleason	88	52	.629	3½
1920	Cleveland	Tris Speaker	98	56	.636	2
1921	New York	Miller Huggins	98	55	.641	4½
1922	New York	Miller Huggins	94	60	.610	1
1923	New York	Miller Huggins	98	54	.645	16
1924	Washington	Bucky Harris	92	62	.597	2
1925	Washington	Bucky Harris	96	55	.636	8½
1926	New York	Miller Huggins	91	63	.591	3
1927	New York	Miller Huggins	110	44	.714	19
1928	New York	Miller Huggins	101	53	.656	2½
1929	Philadelphia	Connie Mack	104	46	.693	18
1930	Philadelphia	Connie Mack	102	52	.662	8
1931	Philadelphia	Connie Mack	107	45	.704	13½
1932	New York	Joe McCarthy	107	47	.695	13
1933	Washington	Joe Cronin	99	53	.651	7
1934	Detroit	Mickey Cochrane	101	53	.656	7
1935	Detroit	Mickey Cochrane	93	58	.616	3
1936	New York	Joe McCarthy	102	51	.667	19½
1937	New York	Joe McCarthy	102	52	.662	13
1938	New York	Joe McCarthy	99	53	.651	9½
1939	New York	Joe McCarthy	106	45	.702	17
1940	Detroit	Del Baker	90	64	.584	1
1941	New York	Joe McCarthy	101	53	.656	17
1942	New York	Joe McCarthy	103	51	.669	9
1943	New York	Joe McCarthy	98	56	.636	13½
1944	St. Louis	Luke Sewell	89	65	.578	1
1945	Detroit	Steve O'Neill	88	65	.575	1½
1946	Boston	Joe Cronin	104	50	.675	12
1947	New York	Bucky Harris	97	57	.630	12
1948	Cleveland†	Lou Boudreau	97	58	.626	1
1949	New York	Casey Stengel	97	57	.630	1
1950	New York	Casey Stengel	98	56	.636	3
1951	New York	Casey Stengel	98	56	.636	5
1952	New York	Casey Stengel	95	59	.617	2
1953	New York	Casey Stengel	99	52	.656	8½
1954	Cleveland	Al Lopez	111	43	.721	8
1955	New York	Casey Stengel	96	58	.623	3
1956	New York	Casey Stengel	97	57	.630	9
1957	New York	Casey Stengel	98	56	.636	8
1958	New York	Casey Stengel	92	62	.597	10
1959	Chicago	Al Lopez	94	60	.610	5
1960	New York	Casey Stengel	97	57	.630	8
1961	New York	Ralph Houk	109	53	.673	8
1962	New York	Ralph Houk	96	66	.593	5
1963	New York	Ralph Houk	104	57	.646	10½
1964	New York	Yogi Berra	99	63	.611	1
1965	Minnesota	Sam Mele	102	60	.630	7
1966	Baltimore	Hank Bauer	97	63	.606	9
1967	Boston	Dick Williams	92	70	.568	1
1968	Detroit	Mayo Smith	103	59	.636	12

†Defeated Boston in one-game playoff.

American League *(Cont.)*

Year	Team	Manager	W	L	Pct	GA
1969	Baltimore (E)‡	Earl Weaver	109	53	.673	19
1970	Baltimore (E)‡	Earl Weaver	108	54	.667	15
1971	Baltimore (E)‡	Earl Weaver	101	57	.639	12
1972	Oakland (W)‡	Dick Williams	93	62	.600	5½
1973	Oakland (W)‡	Dick Williams	94	68	.580	6
1974	Oakland (W)‡	Alvin Dark	90	72	.556	5
1975	Boston (E)‡	Darrell Johnson	95	65	.594	4½
1976	New York (E)‡	Billy Martin	97	62	.610	10½
1977	New York (E)‡	Billy Martin	100	62	.617	2½
1978	New York (E)†‡	Billy Martin/Bob Lemon	100	63	.613	1
1979	Baltimore (E)‡	Earl Weaver	102	57	.642	8
1980	Kansas City (W)‡	Jim Frey	97	65	.599	14
1981	New York (E)‡	Gene Michael/Bob Lemon	59	48	.551	#
1982	Milwaukee (E)‡	Buck Rodgers/ Harvey Kuenn	95	67	.586	1
1983	Baltimore (E)‡	Joe Altobelli	98	64	.605	6
1984	Detroit (E)‡	Sparky Anderson	104	58	.642	15
1985	Kansas City (W)‡	Dick Howser	91	71	.562	1
1986	Boston (E)‡	John McNamara	95	66	.590	5½
1987	Minnesota (W)‡	Tom Kelly	85	77	.525	2
1988	Oakland (W)‡	Tony LaRussa	104	58	.642	13
1989	Oakland (W)‡	Tony LaRussa	99	63	.611	7
1990	Oakland (W)‡	Tony LaRussa	103	59	.636	9
1991	Minnesota (W)‡	Tom Kelly	95	67	.586	8
1992	Toronto (E)‡	Cito Gaston	96	66	.593	4
1993	Toronto (E)‡	Cito Gaston	95	67	.586	7
1994	Season ended Aug. 11 due to players' strike.					
1995	Cleveland (C)‡	Mike Hargrove	100	44	.694	30
1996	New York (E)‡	Joe Torre	92	70	.568	4
1997	Cleveland (C)‡	Mike Hargrove	86	75	.534	6
1998	New York (E)‡	Joe Torre	114	48	.704	22
1999	New York (E)‡	Joe Torre	98	64	.605	4
2000	New York (E)‡	Joe Torre	87	74	.540	2½
2001	New York (E)‡	Joe Torre	95	65	.594	13½
2002	Anaheim (wc)‡	Mike Scioscia	99	63	.611	-4
2003	New York (E)‡	Joe Torre	101	61	.623	6
2004	Boston (wc)‡	Terry Francona	98	64	.605	-3
2005	Chicago (C)‡	Ozzie Guillen	99	63	.611	6
2006	Detroit (wc)‡	Jim Leyland	95	67	.586	-1
2007	Boston (E)‡	Terry Francona	96	66	.593	2
2008	Tampa Bay (E)‡	Joe Maddon	97	65	.599	2
2009	New York (E)‡	Joe Girardi	103	59	.636	8
2010	Texas (W)‡	Ron Washington	90	72	.556	9
2011	Texas (W)‡	Ron Washington	96	66	.593	5
2012	Detroit (C)‡	Jim Leyland	88	74	.543	3
2013	Boston (E)‡	John Farrell	97	65	.599	5½

‡Won championship series. †Defeated Boston in one-game playoff.

League Championship Series

National League

1969	New York (E) 3, Atlanta (W) 0
1970	Cincinnati (W) 3, Pittsburgh (E) 0
1971	Pittsburgh (E) 3, San Francisco (W) 1
1972	Cincinnati (W) 3, Pittsburgh (E) 2
1973	New York (E) 3, Cincinnati (W) 2
1974	Los Angeles (W) 3, Pittsburgh (E) 1
1975	Cincinnati (W) 3, Pittsburgh (E) 0
1976	Cincinnati (W) 3, Philadelphia (E) 0
1977	Los Angeles (W) 3, Philadelphia (E) 1
1978	Los Angeles (W) 3, Philadelphia (E) 1
1979	Pittsburgh (E) 3, Cincinnati (W) 0
1980	Philadelphia (E) 3, Houston (W) 2
1981	Los Angeles (W) 3, Montreal (E) 2
1982	St. Louis (E) 3, Atlanta (W) 0
1983	Philadelphia (E) 3, Los Angeles (W) 1

American League

1969	Baltimore (E) 3, Minnesota (W) 0
1970	Baltimore (E) 3, Minnesota (W) 0
1971	Baltimore (E) 3, Oakland (W) 0
1972	Oakland (W) 3, Detroit (E) 2
1973	Oakland (W) 3, Baltimore (E) 2
1974	Oakland (W) 3, Baltimore (E) 1
1975	Boston (E) 3, Oakland (W) 0
1976	New York (E) 3, Kansas City (W) 2
1977	New York (E) 3, Kansas City (W) 2
1978	New York (E) 3, Kansas City (W) 1
1979	Baltimore (E) 3, California (W) 1
1980	Kansas City (W) 3, New York (E) 0
1981	New York (E) 3, Oakland (W) 0
1982	Milwaukee (E) 3, California (W) 2
1983	Baltimore (E) 3, Chicago (W) 1

National League *(Cont.)*

1984	San Diego (W) 3, Chicago (E) 2
1985	St. Louis (E) 4, Los Angeles (W) 2
1986	New York (E) 4, Houston (W) 2
1987	St. Louis (E) 4, San Francisco (W) 3
1988	Los Angeles (W) 4, New York (E) 3
1989	San Francisco (W) 4, Chicago (E) 1
1990	Cincinnati (W) 4, Pittsburgh (E) 2
1991	Atlanta (W) 4, Pittsburgh (E) 3
1992	Atlanta (W) 4, Pittsburgh (E) 3
1993	Philadelphia (E) 4, Atlanta (W) 2
1994	Playoffs canceled due to players' strike.
1995	Atlanta (E) 4, Cincinnati (C) 0
1996	Atlanta (E) 4, St. Louis (C) 3
1997	Florida (wc) 4, Atlanta (E) 2
1998	San Diego (W) 4, Atlanta (E) 2
1999	Atlanta (E) 4, New York (wc) 2
2000	New York (wc) 4, St. Louis (C) 1
2001	Arizona (W) 4, Atlanta (E) 1
2002	San Francisco (wc) 4, St. Louis (C) 1
2003	Florida (wc) 4, Chicago (C) 3
2004	St. Louis (C) 4, Houston (wc) 3
2005	Houston (wc) 4, St. Louis (C) 2
2006	St. Louis (C) 4, New York (E) 3
2007	Colorado (wc) 4, Arizona (W) 0
2008	Philadelphia (E) 4, Los Angeles (W) 1
2009	Philadelphia (E) 4, Los Angeles (W) 1
2010	San Francisco (W) 4, Philadelphia (E) 2
2011	St. Louis (wc) 4, Milwaukee (C) 2
2012	San Francisco (W) 4, St. Louis (wc) 3
2013	St. Louis (C) 4, Los Angeles (W) 2

American League *(Cont.)*

1984	Detroit (E) 3, Kansas City (W) 0
1985	Kansas City (W) 4, Toronto (E) 3
1986	Boston (E) 4, California (W) 3
1987	Minnesota (W) 4, Detroit (E) 1
1988	Oakland (W) 4, Boston (E) 0
1989	Oakland (W) 4, Toronto (E) 1
1990	Oakland (W) 4, Boston (E) 0
1991	Minnesota (W) 4, Toronto (E) 1
1992	Toronto (E) 4, Oakland (W) 2
1993	Toronto (E) 4, Chicago (W) 2
1994	Playoffs canceled due to players' strike.
1995	Cleveland (C) 4, Seattle (W) 2
1996	New York (E) 4, Baltimore (wc) 1
1997	Cleveland (C) 4, Baltimore (E) 2
1998	New York (E) 4, Cleveland (C) 2
1999	New York (E) 4, Boston (wc) 1
2000	New York (E) 4, Seattle (wc) 2
2001	New York (E) 4, Seattle (W) 1
2002	Anaheim (wc) 4, Minnesota (C) 1
2003	New York (E) 4, Boston (wc) 3
2004	Boston (wc) 4, New York (E) 3
2005	Chicago (C) 4, Los Angeles (W) 1
2006	Detroit (wc) 4, Oakland (W) 0
2007	Boston (E) 4, Cleveland (C) 3
2008	Tampa Bay (E) 4, Boston (wc) 3
2009	New York (E) 4, Los Angeles (W) 2
2010	Texas (W) 4, New York (E) 2
2011	Texas (W) 4, Detroit (C) 2
2012	Detroit (C) 4, New York (E) 0
2013	Boston (E) 4, Detroit (C) 2

NLCS Most Valuable Player

1977	Dusty Baker, LA
1978	Steve Garvey, LA
1979	Willie Stargell, Pitt
1980	Manny Trillo, Phi
1981	Burt Hooton, LA
1982	Darrell Porter, StL
1983	Gary Matthews, Phi
1984	Steve Garvey, SD
1985	Ozzie Smith, StL
1986	Mike Scott, Hou
1987	Jeffrey Leonard, SF
1988	Orel Hershiser, LA
1989	Will Clark, SF
1990	R. Myers/R. Dibble, Cin
1991	Steve Avery, Atl
1992	John Smoltz, Atl
1993	Curt Schilling, Phi
1994	Playoffs canceled
1995	Mike Devereaux, Atl
1996	Javier Lopez, Atl
1997	Livan Hernandez, Fla
1998	Sterling Hitchcock, SD
1999	Eddie Perez, Atl
2000	Mike Hampton, NY
2001	Craig Counsell, Ariz
2002	Benito Santiago, SF
2003	Ivan Rodriguez, Fla
2004	Albert Pujols, StL
2005	Roy Oswalt, Hou
2006	Jeff Suppan, StL
2007	Matt Holliday, Col
2008	Cole Hamels, Phi
2009	Ryan Howard, Phi
2010	Cody Ross, SF
2011	David Freese, StL
2012	Marco Scutaro, SF
2013	Michael Wacha, StL

ALCS Most Valuable Player

1980	Frank White, KC
1981	Graig Nettles, NY
1982	Fred Lynn, Calif
1983	Mike Boddicker, Balt
1984	Kirk Gibson, Det
1985	George Brett, KC
1986	Marty Barrett, Bos
1987	Gary Gaetti, Minn
1988	Dennis Eckersley, Oak
1989	Rickey Henderson, Oak
1990	Dave Stewart, Oak
1991	Kirby Puckett, Minn
1992	Roberto Alomar, Tor
1993	Dave Stewart, Tor
1994	Playoffs canceled
1995	Orel Hershiser, Clev
1996	Bernie Williams, NY
1997	Marquis Grissom, Clev
1998	David Wells, NY
1999	Orlando Hernandez, NY
2000	David Justice, NY
2001	Andy Pettitte, NY
2002	Adam Kennedy, Ana
2003	Mariano Rivera, NY
2004	David Ortiz, Bos
2005	Paul Konerko, Chi
2006	Placido Polanco, Det
2007	Josh Beckett, Bos
2008	Matt Garza, TB
2009	CC Sabathia, NY
2010	Josh Hamilton, Tex
2011	Nelson Cruz, Tex
2012	Delmon Young, Det
2013	Koji Uehara, Bos

Divisional Playoffs

National League

1995	Atlanta (E) 3, Colorado (wc) 1
	Cincinnati (C) 3, Los Angeles (W) 0
1996	St. Louis (C) 3, San Diego (W) 0
	Atlanta (E) 3, Los Angeles (wc) 0
1997	Atlanta (E) 3, Houston (C) 0
	Florida (wc) 3, San Francisco (W) 0
1998	San Diego (W) 3, Houston (C) 1
	Atlanta (E) 3, Chicago (wc) 0

American League

1995	Cleveland (C) 3, Boston (E) 0
	Seattle (W) 3, New York (wc) 2
1996	Baltimore (wc) 3, Cleveland (C) 1
	New York (E) 3, Texas (W) 1
1997	Baltimore (wc) 3, Seattle (W) 1
	Cleveland (C) 3, New York (wc) 2
1998	New York (E) 3, Texas (W) 0
	Cleveland (C) 3, Boston (wc) 1

National League *(Cont.)*	American League *(Cont.)*

1999 ....Atlanta (E) 3, Houston (C) 1
New York (wc) 3, Arizona (W) 1
2000 ....St. Louis (C) 3, Atlanta (E) 0
New York (wc) 3, San Francisco (W) 1
2001 ....Atlanta (E) 3, Houston (C) 0
Arizona (W) 3, St. Louis (wc) 2
2002 ....St. Louis (C) 3, Arizona (W) 0
San Francisco (wc) 3, Atlanta (E) 2
2003 ....Chicago (C) 3, Atlanta (E) 2
Florida (wc) 3, San Francisco (W) 1
2004 ....St. Louis (C) 3, Los Angeles (W) 1
Houston (wc) 3, Atlanta (E) 2
2005 ....Houston (wc) 3, Atlanta (E) 1
St. Louis (C) 3, San Diego (W) 1
2006 ....St. Louis (C) 3, San Diego (W) 1
New York (E) 3, Los Angeles (wc) 0
2007 ....Colorado (wc) 3, Philadelphia (E) 0
Arizona (W) 3, Chicago (C) 0
2008 ....Los Angeles (W) 3, Chicago (C) 0
Philadelphia (E) 3, Milwaukee (wc) 1
2009 ....Los Angeles (W) 3, St. Louis, (C) 0
Philadelphia (E) 3, Colorado (wc) 1
2010 ....San Francisco (W) 3, Atlanta, (wc) 1
Philadelphia (E) 3, Cincinnati (C) 0
2011 ....Milwaukee (C) 3, Arizona (W) 2
St. Louis (wc) 3, Philadelphia (E) 2
2012 ....San Francisco (W) 3, Cincinnati (C) 2
St. Louis (C) 3, Washington (E) 2
2013 ....Los Angeles (W) 3, Atlanta (E) 1
St. Louis (C) 3, Pittsburgh (wc) 2

1999 ....New York (E) 3, Texas (W) 1
Boston (wc) 3, Cleveland (C) 2
2000 ....New York (E) 3, Oakland (W) 2
Seattle (wc) 3, Chicago (C) 0
2001 ....Seattle (W) 3, Cleveland (C) 2
New York (E) 3, Oakland (wc) 2
2002 ....Minnesota (C) 3, Oakland (W) 2
Anaheim (wc) 3, New York (E) 1
2003 ....New York (E) 3, Minnesota (C) 1
Boston (wc) 3, Oakland (W) 2
2004 ....New York (E) 3, Minnesota (C) 1
Boston (wc) 3 Anaheim (W) 0
2005 ....Los Angeles (W) 3, New York (E) 2
Chicago (C) 3, Boston (wc) 0
2006 ....Oakland (W) 3, Minnesota (C) 0
Detroit (wc) 3, New York (E) 1
2007 ....Boston (E) 3, Los Angeles (W) 0
Cleveland (C) 3, New York (wc) 1
2008 ....Boston (wc) 3, Los Angeles (W) 1
Tampa Bay (E) 3, Chicago (C) 1
2009 ....Los Angeles (W) 3, Boston (wc) 0
New York (E) 3, Minnesota (C) 0
2010 ....Texas (W) 3, Tampa Bay (E) 2
New York (wc) 3, Minnesota (C) 0
2011 ....Detroit (C) 3, New York (E) 2
Texas (W) 3, Tampa Bay (wc) 1
2012 ....New York (E) 3, Baltimore (wc) 2
Detroit (C) 3, Oakland (W) 2
2013 ....Detroit (C) 3, Oakland (W) 2
Boston (E) 3, Tampa Bay (wc) 1

The All-Star Game

Date	Winner	Score	Site	Date	Winner	Score	Site
7-6-33	American	4–2	Comiskey Park, Chi	7-30-62	American	9–4	Wrigley Field, Chi
7-10-34	American	9–7	Polo Grounds, NY	7-9-63	National	5–3	Municipal Stadium, Clev
7-8-35	American	4–1	Municipal Stadium, Clev	7-7-64	National	7–4	Shea Stadium, NY
7-7-36	National	4–3	Braves Field, Bos	7-13-65	National	6–5	Metro. Stadium, Minn
7-7-37	American	8–3	Griffith Stadium, Wash	7-12-66	National	2–1	Busch Stadium, StL
7-6-38	National	4–1	Crosley Field, Cin	7-11-67	National	2–1	Anaheim Stadium, Cal
7-11-39	American	3–1	Yankee Stadium, NY	7-9-68	National	1–0	Astrodome, Hou
7-10-40	National	4–0	Sportsman's Park, StL	7-23-69	National	9–3	R.F.K. Stadium, Wash.
7-8-41	American	7–5	Briggs Stadium, Det	7-14-70	National	5–4	Riverfront Stadium, Cin
7-6-42	American	3–1	Polo Grounds, NY	7-13-71	American	6–4	Tiger Stadium, Det
7-13-43	American	5–3	Shibe Park, Phi	7-25-72	National	4–3	Atlanta Stadium, Atl
7-11-44	National	7–1	Forbes Field, Pitt	7-24-73	National	7–1	Royals Stadium, KC
1945	No game due to wartime travel restrictions.			7-23-74	National	7–2	Three Rivers Stadium, Pitt
7-9-46	American	12–0	Fenway Park, Bos	7-15-75	National	6–3	County Stadium, Mil
7-8-47	American	2–1	Wrigley Field, Chi	7-13-76	National	7–1	Veterans Stadium, Phi
7-13-48	American	5–2	Sportsman's Park, StL	7-19-77	National	7–5	Yankee Stadium, NY
7-12-49	American	11–7	Ebbets Field, Bklyn	7-11-78	National	7–3	Jack Murphy Stadium, SD
7-11-50	National	4–3	Comiskey Park, Chi	7-17-79	National	7–6	Kingdome, Sea
7-10-51	National	8–3	Briggs Stadium, Det	7-8-80	National	4–2	Dodger Stadium, LA
7-8-52	National	3–2	Shibe Park, Phi	8-9-81	National	5–4	Municipal Stadium, Clev
7-14-53	National	5–1	Crosley Field, Cin	7-13-82	National	4–1	Olympic Stadium, Mtl
7-13-54	American	11–9	Municipal Stadium, Clev	7-6-83	American	13–3	Comiskey Park, Chi
7-12-55	National	6–5	County Stadium, Mil	7-10-84	National	3–1	Candlestick Park, SF
7-10-56	National	7–3	Griffith Stadium, Wash	7-16-85	National	6–1	Metrodome, Minn
7-9-57	American	6–5	Busch Stadium, StL	7-15-86	American	3–2	Astrodome, Hou
7-8-58	American	4–3	Memorial Stadium, Balt	7-14-87	National	2–0	Oakland Coliseum, Oak
7-7-59	National	5–4	Forbes Field, Pitt	7-12-88	American	2–1	Riverfront Stadium, Cin
8-3-59	American	5–3	Memorial Coliseum, LA	7-11-89	American	5–3	Anaheim Stadium, Cal
7-11-60	National	5–3	Municipal Stadium, KC	7-10-90	American	2–0	Wrigley Field, Chi
7-13-60	National	6–0	Yankee Stadium, NY	7-9-91	American	4–2	SkyDome, Tor
7-11-61	National	5–4	Candlestick Park, SF	7-14-92	American	13–6	Jack Murphy Stadium, SD
7-31-61	Tie*	1–1	Fenway Park, Bos	7-13-93	National	9–3	Camden Yards, Balt
7-10-62	National	3–1	D.C. Stadium, Wash	7-12-94	National	8–7	Three Rivers Stadium, Pitt
				7-11-95	National	3–2	Ballpark in Arlington, Tex
				7-9-96	National	6–0	Veterans Stadium, Phi
				7-8-97	American	3–1	Jacobs Field, Cle

*Game called because of rain after nine innings.

Date	Winner	Score	Site
7-7-98	American	13–8	Coors Field, Col
7-13-99	American	4–1	Fenway Park, Bos
7-11-00	American	6–3	Turner Field, Atl
7-10-01	American	4–1	Safeco Field, Sea
7-9-02	Tie (11 inn)	7–7	Miller Park, Mil
7-15-03	American	7–6	Comiskey Park, Chi
7-13-04	American	9–4	Minute Maid Park, Hou
7-12-05	American	7–5	Comerica Park, Det

Date	Winner	Score	Site
7-11-06	American	3–2	PNC Park, Pitt
7-10-07	American	5–4	AT&T Park, SF
7-15-08	American	4–3	Yankee Stadium, NY
7-14-09	American	4–3	Busch Stadium, StL
7-13-10	National	3–1	Angel Stadium, LA
7-12-11	National	5–1	Chase Field, Ari
7-10-12	National	8–0	Kauffman Stadium, KC
7-16-13	American	3–0	Citi Field, NY

Most Valuable Players

1962...Maury Wills, LA NL	1978...Steve Garvey, LA NL	1996...Mike Piazza, LA NL
Leon Wagner, LA AL	1979...Dave Parker, Pitt NL	1997...Sandy Alomar, Clev AL
1963...Willie Mays, SF NL	1980...Ken Griffey, Cin NL	1998...Roberto Alomar, Balt AL
1964...Johnny Callison, Phi NL	1981...Gary Carter, Mtl NL	1999...Pedro Martinez, Bos AL
1965...Juan Marichal, SF NL	1982...Dave Concepcion, Cin NL	2000...Derek Jeter, NY AL
1966...Brooks Robinson, Balt AL	1983...Fred Lynn, Calif AL	2001...Cal Ripken Jr., Balt AL
1967...Tony Perez, Cin NL	1984...Gary Carter, Mtl NL	2002...None selected
1968...Willie Mays, SF NL	1985...LaMarr Hoyt, SD NL	2003...Garret Anderson, Ana AL
1969...Willie McCovey, SF NL	1986...Roger Clemens, Bos AL	2004...Alfonso Soriano, Tex AL
1970...Carl Yastrzemski, Bos AL	1987...Tim Raines, Mtl NL	2005...Miguel Tejada, Balt AL
1971...Frank Robinson, Balt AL	1988...Terry Steinbach, Oak AL	2006...Michael Young, Tex AL
1972...Joe Morgan, Cin NL	1989...Bo Jackson, KC AL	2007...Ichiro Suzuki, Sea AL
1973...Bobby Bonds, SF NL	1990...Julio Franco, Tex AL	2008...J.D. Drew, Bos AL
1974...Steve Garvey, LA NL	1991...Cal Ripken Jr., Balt AL	2009...Carl Crawford, TB AL
1975...Bill Madlock, Chi NL	1992...Ken Griffey Jr., Sea AL	2010...Brian McCann, Atl NL
Jon Matlack, NY NL	1993...Kirby Puckett, Minn AL	2011...Prince Fielder, Mil NL
1976...George Foster, Cin NL	1994...Fred McGriff, Atl NL	2012...Melky Cabrera, SF NL
1977...Don Sutton, LA NL	1995...Jeff Conine, Fla NL	2013...Mariano Rivera, NY AL

The Regular Season

Most Valuable Players
NATIONAL LEAGUE

Year	Name and Team	Position	Noteworthy
1911	Wildfire Schulte, Chi	Outfield	21 HR†, 121 RBI†, .300
1912	*Larry Doyle, NY	Second base	10 HR, 90 RBI, .330
1913	Jake Daubert, Bklyn	First base	52 RBI, .350†
1914	*Johnny Evers, Bos	Second base	FA .976†, .279
1915–23	No selection		
1924	Dazzy Vance, Bklyn	Pitcher	28†–6, 2.16 ERA†, 262 K†
1925	Rogers Hornsby, StL	Second base, Manager	39 HR†, 143 RBI†, .403†
1926	*Bob O'Farrell, StL	Catcher	7 HR, 68 RBI, .293
1927	*Paul Waner, Pitt	Outfield	237 hits†, 131 RBI†, .380†
1928	*Jim Bottomley, StL	First base	31 HR†, 136 RBI†, .325
1929	*Rogers Hornsby, Chi	Second base	39 HR, 149 RBI, 156 runs†, .380
1930	No selection		
1931	*Frankie Frisch, StL	Second base	4 HR, 82 RBI, 28 SB†, .311
1932	Chuck Klein, Phi	Outfield	38 HR†, 137 RBI, 226 hits†, .348
1933	*Carl Hubbell, NY	Pitcher	23†–12, 1.66 ERA†, 10 SO†
1934	*Dizzy Dean, StL	Pitcher	30†–7, 2.66 ERA, 195 K†
1935	*Gabby Hartnett, Chi	Catcher	13 HR, 91 RBI, .344
1936	*Carl Hubbell, NY	Pitcher	26†–6, 2.31 ERA†
1937	Joe Medwick, StL	Outfield	31 HR‡, 154 RBI†, 111 runs†, .374†
1938	Ernie Lombardi, Cin	Catcher	19 HR, 95 RBI, .342†
1939	*Bucky Walters, Cin	Pitcher	27†–11, 2.29 ERA†, 137 K‡
1940	*Frank McCormick, Cin	First base	19 HR, 127 RBI, 191 hits†, .309
1941	*Dolph Camilli, Bklyn	First base	34 HR†, 120 RBI†, .285
1942	*Mort Cooper, StL	Pitcher	22†–7, 1.78 ERA†, 10 SO†
1943	*Stan Musial, StL	Outfield	13 HR, 81 RBI, 220 hits†, .357†
1944	Marty Marion, StL	Shortstop	FA .972†, 63 RBI
1945	*Phil Cavarretta, Chi	First base	6 HR, 97 RBI, .355†
1946	*Stan Musial, StL	First base, Outfield	103 RBI, 124 runs†, 228 hits†, .365†
1947	Bob Elliott, Bos	Third base	22 HR, 113 RBI, .317
1948	Stan Musial, StL	Outfield	39 HR, 131 RBI†, .376†
1949	*Jackie Robinson, Bklyn	Second base	16 HR, 124 RBI, 37 SB†, .342†
1950	*Jim Konstanty, Phi	Pitcher	16–7, 22 saves†, 2.66 ERA

*Played for pennant or, after 1968, division winner. †Led league. ‡Tied for league lead.

Most Valuable Players *(Cont.)*
NATIONAL LEAGUE *(Cont.)*

Year	Name and Team	Position	Noteworthy
1951	Roy Campanella, Bklyn	Catcher	33 HR, 108 RBI, .325
1952	Hank Sauer, Chi	Outfield	37 HR‡, 121 RBI†, .270
1953	*Roy Campanella, Bklyn	Catcher	41 HR, 142 RBI†, .312
1954	*Willie Mays, NY	Outfield	41 HR, 110 RBI, 13 3B†, .345†
1955	*Roy Campanella, Bklyn	Catcher	32 HR, 107 RBI, .318
1956	*Don Newcombe, Bklyn	Pitcher	27†–7, 3.06 ERA
1957	*Hank Aaron, Mil	Outfield	44 HR†, 132 RBI†, .322
1958	Ernie Banks, Chi	Shortstop	47 HR†, 129 RBI†, .313
1959	Ernie Banks, Chi	Shortstop	45 HR, 143 RBI†, .304
1960	*Dick Groat, Pitt	Shortstop	2 HR, 50 RBI, .325†
1961	*Frank Robinson, Cin	Outfield	37 HR, 124 RBI, .323
1962	Maury Wills, LA	Shortstop	104 SB†, 208 hits, .299, GG
1963	*Sandy Koufax, LA	Pitcher	25‡–5, 1.88 ERA†, 306 K†
1964	*Ken Boyer, StL	Third Base	24 HR, 119 RBI†, .295
1965	Willie Mays, SF	Outfield	52 HR†, 112 RBI, .317, GG
1966	Roberto Clemente, Pitt	Outfield	29 HR, 119 RBI, 202 hits, .317, GG
1967	*Orlando Cepeda, StL	First base	25 HR, 111 RBI†, .325
1968	*Bob Gibson, StL	Pitcher	22–9, 1.12 ERA†, 268 K†, 13 SO†, GG
1969	Willie McCovey, SF	First base	45 HR†, 126 RBI†, .320
1970	*Johnny Bench, Cin	Catcher	45 HR†, 148 RBI†, .293, GG
1971	Joe Torre, StL	Third base	24 HR, 137 RBI†, .363†
1972	*Johnny Bench, Cin	Catcher	40 HR†, 125 RBI†, .270, GG
1973	*Pete Rose, Cin	Outfield	5 HR, 64 RBI, .338†, 230 hits†
1974	*Steve Garvey, LA	First base	21 HR, 111 RBI, 200 hits, .312, GG
1975	*Joe Morgan, Cin	Second base	17 HR, 94 RBI, 67 SB, .327, GG
1976	*Joe Morgan, Cin	Second base	27 HR, 111 RBI, 60 SB, .320, GG
1977	George Foster, Cin	Outfield	52 HR†, 149 RBI†, .320
1978	Dave Parker, Pitt	Outfield	30 HR, 117 RBI, .334†, GG
1979	Keith Hernandez, StL	First base	11 HR, 105 RBI, 210 hits, .344†, GG
	*Willie Stargell, Pitt	First base	32 HR, 82 RBI, .281
1980	*Mike Schmidt, Phi	Third base	48 HR†, 121 RBI†, .286, GG
1981	Mike Schmidt, Phi	Third base	31 HR†, 91 RBI†, 78 runs†, .316, GG
1982	*Dale Murphy, Atl	Outfield	36 HR, 109 RBI†, .281, GG
1983	Dale Murphy, Atl	Outfield	36 HR, 121 RBI†, .302, GG
1984	*Ryne Sandberg, Chi	Second base	19 HR, 84 RBI, 114 runs†, .314, GG
1985	*Willie McGee, StL	Outfield	10 HR, 82 RBI, 18 3B†, .353†, GG
1986	Mike Schmidt, Phi	Third base	37 HR†, 119 RBI†, .290, GG
1987	Andre Dawson, Chi	Outfield	49 HR†, 137 RBI†, .287, GG
1988	*Kirk Gibson, LA	Outfield	25 HR, 76 RBI, 106 runs, .290
1989	*Kevin Mitchell, SF	Outfield	47 HR†, 125 RBI†, .291
1990	*Barry Bonds, Pitt	Outfield	33 HR, 114 RBI, .301
1991	*Terry Pendleton, Atl	Third base	23 HR, 86 RBI, .319†
1992	Barry Bonds, Pitt	Outfield	34 HR, 103 RBI, .311
1993	Barry Bonds, SF	Outfield	46 HR†, 123 RBI†, .336
1994	Jeff Bagwell, Hou	First base	39 HR, 116 RBI†, .368
1995	*Barry Larkin, Cin	Shortstop	15 HR, 66 RBI, 51 SB, .319
1996	*Ken Caminiti, SD	Third base	40 HR, 130 RBI, .326
1997	Larry Walker, Col	Outfield	49 HR†, 130 RBI, .452 OBP†, .366, GG
1998	Sammy Sosa, Chi	Outfield	66 HR, 158 RBI†, 134 runs†, 416 TB†, .308
1999	*Chipper Jones, Atl	Third Base	45 HR, 110 RBI, 116 runs, .319
2000	*Jeff Kent, SF	Second Base	33 HR, 125 RBI, 114 runs, .334
2001	Barry Bonds, SF	Outfield	73 HR†, 137 RBI, 177 BB†, .328, .863 SLG†
2002	*Barry Bonds, SF	Outfield	46 HR, 110 RBI, .582 OBP, 198 BB†, .370
2003	*Barry Bonds, SF	Outfield	45 HR, .341, .529 OBP†, .749 SLG†
2004	Barry Bonds, SF	Outfield	45 HR, 101 RBI, .609 OBP, .812 SLG
2005	*Albert Pujols, StL	First Base	41 HR, 117 RBI, .330, .430 OBP†, .609 SLG†
2006	Ryan Howard, Phi	First Base	58 HR†, 149 RBI†, .313, .425 OBP, .659 SLG
2007	*Jimmy Rollins, Phi	Shortstop	30 HR, 94 RBI, .296, 139 runs†, 41 SB, GG
2008	Albert Pujols, StL	First Base	37 HR, 116 RBI, 100 runs, .357, .653 SLG†
2009	*Albert Pujols, StL	First Base	47 HR†, 135 RBI, 124 runs†, .327, .658 SLG†
2010	*Joey Votto, Cin	First Base	37 HR, 113 RBI, 106 runs, .324, .600 SLG†
2011	*Ryan Braun, Mil	Outfield	33 HR, 111 RBI, 109 runs, .332, .597 SLG†
2012	Buster Posey, SF	Catcher	24 HR, 103 RBI, .336†, .408 OBP, .549 SLG

*Played for pennant or, after 1968, division winner. †Led league. ‡Tied for league lead. Notes: 2B=doubles; 3B=triples; FA=fielding average; GG=won Gold Glove, award begun in 1957; K=strikeouts; SO=shutouts; SB=stolen bases; TB=total bases; SLG=slugging average; OBP=on-base percentage.

Most Valuable Players *(Cont.)*

AMERICAN LEAGUE

Year	Name and Team	Position	Noteworthy
1911	Ty Cobb, Det	Outfield	8 HR, 144 RBI†, 24 3B†, .420†
1912	*Tris Speaker, Bos	Outfield	10 HR‡, 98 RBI, 53 2B†, .383
1913	Walter Johnson, Wash	Pitcher	36†–7, 1.09 ERA†, 11 SO†, 243 K†
1914	*Eddie Collins, Phi	Second base	2 HR, 85 RBI, 122 runs†, .344
1915–21	No selection		
1922	George Sisler, StL	First base	8 HR, 105 RBI, 246 hits†, .420†
1923	*Babe Ruth, NY	Outfield	41 HR†, 131 RBI†, .393
1924	*Walter Johnson, Wash	Pitcher	23†–7, 2.72 ERA†, 158 K†
1925	*Roger Peckinpaugh, Wash	Shortstop	4 HR, 64 RBI, .294
1926	George Burns, Clev	First base	114 RBI, 216 hits‡, 64 2B†, .358
1927	*Lou Gehrig, NY	First base	47 HR, 175 RBI†, 52 2B†, .373
1928	Mickey Cochrane, Phi	Catcher	10 HR, 57 RBI, .293
1929–30	No selection		
1931	*Lefty Grove, Phi	Pitcher	31†–4, 2.06 ERA†, 175 K†
1932	Jimmie Foxx, Phi	First base	58 HR†, 169 RBI†, 151 runs†, .364
1933	Jimmie Foxx, Phi	First base	48 HR†, 163 RBI†, .356†
1934	*Mickey Cochrane, Det	Catcher	2 HR, 76 RBI, .320
1935	*Hank Greenberg, Det	First base	36 HR†, 170 RBI†, 203 hits, .328
1936	*Lou Gehrig, NY	First base	49 HR†, 152 RBI, 167 runs†, .354
1937	Charlie Gehringer, Det	Second base	14 HR, 96 RBI, 133 runs, .371†
1938	Jimmie Foxx, Bos	First base	50 HR, 175 RBI†, .349†
1939	*Joe DiMaggio, NY	Outfield	30 HR, 126 RBI, .381†
1940	*Hank Greenberg, Det	Outfield	41 HR†, 150 RBI†, 50 2B†, .340
1941	*Joe DiMaggio, NY	Outfield	30 HR, 125 RBI†, .357
1942	*Joe Gordon, NY	Second base	18 HR, 103 RBI, .322
1943	*Spud Chandler, NY	Pitcher	20†–4, 1.64 ERA†, 5 SO‡
1944	Hal Newhouser, Det	Pitcher	29†–9, 2.22 ERA†, 187 K†
1945	*Hal Newhouser, Det	Pitcher	25†–9, 1.81 ERA†, 8 SO†, 212 K†
1946	*Ted Williams, Bos	Outfield	38 HR, 123 RBI, 142 runs†, .342
1947	*Joe DiMaggio, NY	Outfield	20 HR, 97 RBI, .315
1948	*Lou Boudreau, Clev	Shortstop	18 HR, 106 RBI, .355
1949	Ted Williams, Bos	Outfield	43 HR†, 159 RBI‡, 150 runs†, .343
1950	*Phil Rizzuto, NY	Shortstop	125 runs, 200 hits, .324
1951	*Yogi Berra, NY	Catcher	27 HR, 88 RBI, .294
1952	Bobby Shantz, Phi	Pitcher	24†–7, 2.48 ERA
1953	Al Rosen, Clev	Third base	43 HR†, 145 RBI†, 115 runs†, .336
1954	Yogi Berra, NY	Catcher	22 HR, 125 RBI, .307
1955	Yogi Berra, NY	Catcher	27 HR, 108 RBI, .272
1956	*Mickey Mantle, NY	Outfield	52 HR†, 130 RBI†, 132 runs†, .353†
1957	*Mickey Mantle, NY	Outfield	34 HR, 94 RBI, 121 runs†, .365
1958	Jackie Jensen, Bos	Outfield	35 HR, 122 RBI†, .286
1959	*Nellie Fox, Chi	Second base	2 HR, 70 RBI, .306, GG
1960	*Roger Maris, NY	Outfield	39 HR, 112 RBI†, .283, GG
1961	*Roger Maris, NY	Outfield	61 HR†, 142 RBI†, .269
1962	*Mickey Mantle, NY	Outfield	30 HR, 89 RBI, .321, GG
1963	*Elston Howard, NY	Catcher	28 HR, 85 RBI, .287, GG
1964	Brooks Robinson, Balt	Third base	28 HR, 118 RBI†, .317, GG
1965	*Zoilo Versalles, Minn	Shortstop	126 runs†, 45 2B‡, 12 3B‡, GG
1966	*Frank Robinson, Balt	Outfield	49 HR†, 122 RBI†, 122 runs†, .316†
1967	*Carl Yastrzemski, Bos	Outfield	44 HR‡, 121 RBI†, 112 runs†, .326†, GG
1968	*Denny McLain, Det	Pitcher	31†–6, 1.96 ERA, 280 K
1969	*Harmon Killebrew, Minn	Third base, First base	49 HR†, 140 RBI†, .276
1970	*Boog Powell, Balt	First base	35 HR, 114 RBI, .297
1971	*Vida Blue, Oak	Pitcher	24–8, 1.82 ERA†, 8 SO†, 301 K
1972	Dick Allen, Chi	First base	37 HR†, 113 RBI†, .308
1973	*Reggie Jackson, Oak	Outfield	32 HR†, 117 RBI†, 99 runs†, .293
1974	Jeff Burroughs, Tex	Outfield	25 HR, 118 RBI†, .301
1975	*Fred Lynn, Bos	Outfield	21 HR, 105 RBI, 103 runs†, .331, GG
1976	*Thurman Munson, NY	Catcher	17 HR, 105 RBI, .302
1977	Rod Carew, Minn	First base	100 RBI, 128 runs†, 239 hits†, .388†
1978	Jim Rice, Bos	Outfield, DH	46 HR†, 139 RBI†, 213 hits†, .315
1979	*Don Baylor, Calif	Outfield, DH	36 HR, 139 RBI†, 120 runs†, .296
1980	*George Brett, KC	Third base	24 HR, 118 RBI, .390†
1981	*Rollie Fingers, Mil	Pitcher	6–3, 28 saves†, 1.04 ERA
1982	*Robin Yount, Mil	Shortstop	29 HR, 114 RBI, 210 hits†, .331, GG
1983	*Cal Ripken Jr., Balt	Shortstop	27 HR, 102 RBI, 121 runs†, 211 hits†, .318
1984	*Willie Hernandez, Det	Pitcher	9–3, 32 saves, 1.92 ERA

Most Valuable Players (Cont.)

AMERICAN LEAGUE (Cont.)

Year	Name and Team	Position	Noteworthy
1985	Don Mattingly, NY	First base	35 HR, 145 RBI†, 48 2B†, .324, GG
1986	*Roger Clemens, Bos	Pitcher	24†–4, 2.48 ERA†, 238 K
1987	George Bell, Tor	Outfield	47 HR, 134 RBI†, .308
1988	*Jose Canseco, Oak	Outfield	42 HR†, 124 RBI†, 40 SB, .307
1989	Robin Yount, Mil	Outfield	21 HR, 103 RBI, 101 runs, .318
1990	*Rickey Henderson, Oak	Outfield	28 HR, 119 runs†, 65 SB†, .325
1991	Cal Ripken Jr., Balt	Shortstop	34 HR, 114 RBI, .323
1992	Dennis Eckersley, Oak	Pitcher	7–1, 1.91 ERA, 51 saves
1993	Frank Thomas, Chi	First base	41 HR, 128 RBI, .317
1994	Frank Thomas, Chi	First base	38 HR, 101 RBI, .353
1995	*Mo Vaughn, Bos	First base	39 HR, 126 RBI, .300
1996	*Juan Gonzalez, Tex	Outfield	47 HR, 144 RBI, .314
1997	*Ken Griffey Jr., Sea	Outfield	56 HR†, 125 runs†, 393 TB†, 147 RBI†, .304
1998	*Juan Gonzalez, Tex	Outfield	45 HR, 157 RBI†, 50 2B†, .318
1999	*Ivan Rodriguez, Tex	Catcher	35 HR, 113 RBI, 116 runs, .332, GG
2000	*Jason Giambi, Oak	First Base	43 HR, 137 RBI, .333
2001	*Ichiro Suzuki, Sea	Outfield	.350†, 242 hits†, 127 runs, 56 SB†, GG
2002	*Miguel Tejada, Oak	Shortstop	34 HR, 131 RBI, .308
2003	Alex Rodriguez, Tex	Shortstop	47 HR†, 118 RBI, .600 SLG†, GG
2004	*Vladimir Guerrero, Ana	Outfield	39 HR, 126 RBI, .338 SLG
2005	*Alex Rodriguez, NY	Third Base	48 HR†, 130 RBI, .610 SLG†
2006	*Justin Morneau, Min	First Base	30 HR, 130 RBI, .321, 190 hits
2007	Alex Rodriguez, NY	Third Base	54 HR, 156 RBI, .314, 183 hits, 24 SB
2008	Dustin Pedroia, Bos	Second Base	17 HR, 118 runs, 213 hits, .326, 20 SB, GG
2009	*Joe Mauer, Min	Catcher	28 HR, 94 runs, 96 RBIs, 191 hits, .365, GG
2010	*Josh Hamilton, Tex	Outfield	32 HR, 100 RBI, 95 runs, .359†, .633 SLG†
2011	*Justin Verlander, Detroit	Pitcher	24 W†, 2.40 ERA†, 250 SO†, 251.0 IP†
2012	*Miguel Cabrera, Detroit	Third Base	44 HR†, 139 RBI†, .330†, .606 SLG†

*Played for pennant or, after 1968, division winner. †Led league. ‡Tied for league lead. Notes: 2B=doubles; 3B=triples; FA=fielding average; GG=won Gold Glove, award begun in 1957; K=strikeouts; SO=shutouts; SB=stolen bases; TB=total bases; SLG=slugging average; OBP=on-base percentage.

Rookies of the Year

NATIONAL LEAGUE	AMERICAN LEAGUE
1947* Jackie Robinson, Bklyn (1B)	1949 Roy Sievers, StL (OF)
1948* Alvin Dark, Bos (SS)	1950 Walt Dropo, Bos (1B)
1949 Don Newcombe, Bklyn (P)	1951 Gil McDougald, NY (3B)
1950 Sam Jethroe, Bos (OF)	1952 Harry Byrd, Phi (P)
1951 Willie Mays, NY (OF)	1953 Harvey Kuenn, Det (SS)
1952 Joe Black, Bklyn (P)	1954 Bob Grim, NY (P)
1953 Junior Gilliam, Bklyn (2B)	1955 Herb Score, Clev (P)
1954 Wally Moon, StL (OF)	1956 Luis Aparicio, Chi (SS)
1955 Bill Virdon, StL (OF)	1957 Tony Kubek, NY (OF, SS)
1956 Frank Robinson, Cin (OF)	1958 Albie Pearson, Wash (OF)
1957 Jack Sanford, Phi (P)	1959 Bob Allison, Wash (OF)
1958 Orlando Cepeda, SF (1B)	1960 Ron Hansen, Balt (SS)
1959 Willie McCovey, SF (1B)	1961 Don Schwall, Bos (P)
1960 Frank Howard, LA (OF)	1962 Tom Tresh, NY (SS)
1961 Billy Williams, Chi (OF)	1963 Gary Peters, Chi (P)
1962 Ken Hubbs, Chi (2B)	1964 Tony Oliva, Minn (OF)
1963 Pete Rose, Cin (2B)	1965 Curt Blefary, Balt (OF)
1964 Dick Allen, Phi (3B)	1966 Tommie Agee, Chi (OF)
1965 Jim Lefebvre, LA (2B)	1967 Rod Carew, Minn (2B)
1966 Tommy Helms, Cin (2B)	1968 Stan Bahnsen, NY (P)
1967 Tom Seaver, NY (P)	1969 Lou Piniella, KC (OF)
1968 Johnny Bench, Cin (C)	1970 Thurman Munson, NY (C)
1969 Ted Sizemore, LA (2B)	1971 Chris Chambliss, Clev (1B)
1970 Carl Morton, Mtl (P)	1972 Carlton Fisk, Bos (C)
1971 Earl Williams, Atl (C)	1973 Al Bumbry, Balt (OF)
1972 Jon Matlack, NY (P)	1974 Mike Hargrove, Tex (1B)
1973 Gary Matthews, SF (OF)	1975 Fred Lynn, Bos (OF)
1974 Bake McBride, StL (OF)	1976 Mark Fidrych, Det (P)
1975 John Montefusco, SF (P)	1977 Eddie Murray, Balt (DH)
1976 Pat Zachry, Cin (P)	1978 Lou Whitaker, Det (2B)
Butch Metzger, SD (P)	1979 Alfredo Griffin, Tor (SS)
1977 Andre Dawson, Mtl (OF)	John Castino, Minn (3B)
1978 Bob Horner, Atl (3B)	1980 Joe Charboneau, Clev (OF)

*Just one selection for both leagues.

Rookies of the Year *(Cont.)*

NATIONAL LEAGUE *(Cont.)*

1979	Rick Sutcliffe, LA (P)
1980	Steve Howe, LA (P)
1981	Fernando Valenzuela, LA (P)
1982	Steve Sax, LA (2B)
1983	Darryl Strawberry, NY (OF)
1984	Dwight Gooden, NY (P)
1985	Vince Coleman, StL (OF)
1986	Todd Worrell, StL (P)
1987	Benito Santiago, SD (C)
1988	Chris Sabo, Cin (3B)
1989	Jerome Walton, Chi (OF)
1990	David Justice, Atl (OF)
1991	Jeff Bagwell, Hou (3B)
1992	Eric Karros, LA (1B)
1993	Mike Piazza, LA (C)
1994	Raul Mondesi, LA (OF)
1995	Hideo Nomo, LA (P)
1996	Todd Hollandsworth, LA (OF)
1997	Scott Rolen, Phi (3B)
1998	Kerry Wood, Chi (P)
1999	Scott Williamson, Cin (P)
2000	Rafael Furcal, Atl (SS)
2001	Albert Pujols, StL (OF)
2002	Jason Jennings, Col (P)
2003	Dontrelle Willis, Fla (P)
2004	Jason Bay, Pit (OF)
2005	Ryan Howard, Phi (1B)
2006	Hanley Ramirez, Fla (SS)
2007	Ryan Braun, Mil (OF)
2008	Geovany Soto, Chi (C)
2009	Chris Coghlan, Fla (OF)
2010	Buster Posey, SF (C)
2011	Craig Kimbrel, Atl (P)
2012	Bryce Harper, Wash (OF)

AMERICAN LEAGUE *(Cont.)*

1981	Dave Righetti, NY (P)
1982	Cal Ripken Jr., Balt (SS)
1983	Ron Kittle, Chi (OF)
1984	Alvin Davis, Sea (1B)
1985	Ozzie Guillen, Chi (SS)
1986	Jose Canseco, Oak (OF)
1987	Mark McGwire, Oak (1B)
1988	Walt Weiss, Oak (SS)
1989	Gregg Olson, Balt (P)
1990	Sandy Alomar Jr, Clev (C)
1991	Chuck Knoblauch, Minn (2B)
1992	Pat Listach, Mil (SS)
1993	Tim Salmon, Calif (OF)
1994	Bob Hamelin, KC (DH)
1995	Marty Cordova, Minn (OF)
1996	Derek Jeter, NY (SS)
1997	Nomar Garciaparra, Bos (SS)
1998	Ben Grieve, Oak (OF)
1999	Carlos Beltran, KC (OF)
2000	Kazuhiro Sasaki, Sea (P)
2001	Ichiro Suzuki, Sea (OF)
2002	Eric Hinske, Tor (3B)
2003	Angel Berroa, KC (SS)
2004	Bobby Crosby, Oak (SS)
2005	Huston Street, Oak (P)
2006	Justin Verlander, Det (P)
2007	Dustin Pedroia, Bos (2B)
2008	Evan Longoria, TB (3B)
2009	Andrew Bailey, Oak (P)
2010	Neftali Feliz, Tex (P)
2011	Jeremy Hellickson, TB (P)
2012	Mike Trout, LA (OF)

2012 Gold Glove winners

NATIONAL LEAGUE

C	Yadier Molina, StL (5)
P	Mark Buehrle, Mia (4)
1B	Adam LaRoche, Wash
2B	Darwin Barney, Chi
SS	Jimmy Rollins, Phi (4)
3B	Chase Headley, SD
OF	Carlos Gonzalez, Col (2)
OF	Andrew McCutchen, Pit
OF	Jason Heyward, Atl

Note: Number in parentheses indicates career totals.

AMERICAN LEAGUE

C	Matt Wieters, Bal (2)
P	Jeremy Hellickson, TB
	Jake Peavy, Chi
1B	Mark Teixeira, NY (5)
2B	Robinson Cano, NY (2)
SS	J.J. Hardy, Bal
3B	Adrian Beltre, Tex (4)
OF	Alex Gordon, KC (2)
OF	Adam Jones, Bal (2)
OF	Josh Reddick, Oak

2012 Silver Slugger winners

NATIONAL LEAGUE

C	Buster Posey, SF
P	Stephen Strasburg, Wash
1B	Adam LaRoche, Wash
2B	Aaron Hill, Ari (2)
SS	Ian Desmond, Wash
3B	Chase Headley, SD
OF	Andrew McCutchen, Pit
OF	Ryan Braun, Mil (5)
OF	Jay Bruce, Cin

Note: Number in parentheses indicates career totals.

AMERICAN LEAGUE

C	A.J. Pierzynski, Chi
DH	Billy Butler, KC
1B	Prince Fielder, Det (3)
2B	Robinson Cano, NY (4)
SS	Derek Jeter, NY (5)
3B	Miguel Cabrera, Det (2)
OF	Mike Trout, LA
OF	Josh Willingham, Min
OF	Josh Hamilton, Tex (3)

Cy Young Award

Year	W–L	Sv	ERA	Year	W–L	Sv	ERA
1956....*Don Newcombe, Bklyn (NL)	27–7	0	3.06	1962....Don Drysdale, LA (NL)	25–9	1	2.83
1957....Warren Spahn, Mil (NL)	21–11	3	2.69	1963....*Sandy Koufax, LA (NL)	25–5	0	1.88
1958....Bob Turley, NY (AL)	21–7	1	2.97	1964....Dean Chance, LA (AL)	20–9	4	1.65
1959....Early Wynn, Chi (AL)	22–10	0	3.17	1965....Sandy Koufax, LA (NL)	26–8	2	2.04
1960....Vernon Law, Pitt (NL)	20–9	0	3.08	1966....Sandy Koufax, LA (NL)	27–9	0	1.73
1961....Whitey Ford, NY (AL)	25–4	0	3.21				

NATIONAL LEAGUE

Year	W–L	Sv	ERA
1967.....Mike McCormick, SF	22–10	0	2.85
1968.....*Bob Gibson, StL	22–9	0	1.12
1969.....Tom Seaver, NY	25–7	0	2.21
1970.....Bob Gibson, StL	23–7	0	3.12
1971.....Ferguson Jenkins, Chi	24–13	0	2.77
1972.....Steve Carlton, Phi	27–10	0	1.97
1973.....Tom Seaver, NY	19–10	0	2.08
1974.....Mike Marshall, LA	15–12	21	2.42
1975.....Tom Seaver, NY	22–9	0	2.38
1976.....Randy Jones, SD	22–14	0	2.74
1977.....Steve Carlton, Phi	23–10	0	2.64
1978.....Gaylord Perry, SD	21–6	0	2.72
1979.....Bruce Sutter, Chi	6–6	37	2.23
1980.....Steve Carlton, Phi	24–9	0	2.34
1981.....Fernando Valenzuela, LA	13–7	0	2.48
1982.....Steve Carlton, Phi	23–11	0	3.10
1983.....John Denny, Phi	19–6	0	2.37
1984.....†Rick Sutcliffe, Chi	16–1	0	2.69
1985.....Dwight Gooden, NY	24–4	0	1.53
1986.....Mike Scott, Hou	18–10	0	2.22
1987.....Steve Bedrosian, Phi	5–3	40	2.83
1988.....Orel Hershiser, LA	23–8	1	2.26
1989.....Mark Davis, SD	4–3	44	1.85
1990.....Doug Drabek, Pitt	22–6	0	2.76
1991.....Tom Glavine, Atl	20–11	0	2.55
1992.....Greg Maddux, Chi	20–11	0	2.18
1993.....Greg Maddux, Atl	20–10	0	2.36
1994.....Greg Maddux, Atl	16–6	0	1.56
1995.....Greg Maddux, Atl	19–2	0	1.63
1996.....John Smoltz, Atl	24–8	0	2.94
1997.....Pedro Martinez, Mtl	17–8	0	1.90
1998.....Tom Glavine, Atl	20–6	0	2.47
1999.....Randy Johnson, Ari	17–9	0	2.48
2000.....Randy Johnson, Ari	19–7	0	2.64
2001.....Randy Johnson, Ari	21–6	0	2.49
2002.....Randy Johnson, Ari	24–5	0	2.32
2003.....Eric Gagne, LA	2–3	55	1.20
2004.....Roger Clemens, Hou	18–4	0	2.98
2005.....Chris Carpenter, StL	21–5	0	2.83
2006.....Brandon Webb, Ari	16–8	0	3.10
2007.....Jake Peavy, SD	19–6	0	2.54
2008.....Tim Lincecum, SF	18–5	0	2.62
2009.....Tim Lincecum, SF	15–7	0	2.48
2010.....Roy Halladay, Phi	21–10	0	2.44
2011.....Clayton Kershaw, LA	21–5	0	2.28
2012.....R.A. Dickey, NY	20–6	0	2.73

AMERICAN LEAGUE

Year	W–L	Sv	ERA
1967.....Jim Lonborg, Bos	22–9	0	3.16
1968.....*Denny McLain, Det	31–6	0	1.96
1969.....Denny McLain, Det	24–9	0	2.80
Mike Cuellar, Balt	23–11	0	2.38
1970.....Jim Perry, Minn	24–12	0	3.03
1971.....*Vida Blue, Oak	24–8	0	1.82
1972.....Gaylord Perry, Clev	24–16	1	1.92
1973.....Jim Palmer, Balt	22–9	1	2.40
1974.....Catfish Hunter, Oak	25–12	0	2.49
1975.....Jim Palmer, Balt	23–11	1	2.09
1976.....Jim Palmer, Balt	22–13	0	2.51
1977.....Sparky Lyle, NY	13–5	26	2.17
1978.....Ron Guidry, NY	25–3	0	1.74
1979.....Mike Flanagan, Balt	23–9	0	3.08
1980.....Steve Stone, Balt	25–7	0	3.23
1981.....*Rollie Fingers, Mil	6–3	28	1.04
1982.....Pete Vuckovich, Mil	18–6	0	3.34
1983.....LaMarr Hoyt, Chi	24–10	0	3.66
1984.....*Willie Hernandez, Det	9–3	32	1.92
1985.....Bret Saberhagen, KC	20–6	0	2.87
1986.....*Roger Clemens, Bos	24–4	0	2.48
1987.....Roger Clemens, Bos	20–9	0	2.97
1988.....Frank Viola, Minn	24–7	0	2.64
1989.....Bret Saberhagen, KC	23–6	0	2.16
1990.....Bob Welch, Oak	27–6	0	2.95
1991.....Roger Clemens, Bos	18–10	0	2.62
1992.....*Dennis Eckersley, Oak	7–1	51	1.91
1993.....Jack McDowell, Chi	22–10	0	3.37
1994.....David Cone, KC	16–4	0	2.94
1995.....Randy Johnson, Sea	18–2	0	2.48
1996.....Pat Hentgen, Tor	20–10	0	3.22
1997.....Roger Clemens, Tor	21–7	0	2.05
1998.....Roger Clemens, Tor	20–6	0	2.65
1999.....Pedro Martinez, Bos	23–4	0	1.55
2000.....Pedro Martinez, Bos	18–6	0	1.74
2001.....Roger Clemens, NY	20–3	0	3.51
2002.....Barry Zito, Oak	23–5	0	2.75
2003.....Roy Halladay, Tor	22–7	0	3.25
2004.....Johan Santana, Min	20–6	0	2.61
2005.....Bartolo Colon, LA	21–8	0	3.48
2006.....Johan Santana, Min	19–6	0	2.77
2007.....CC Sabathia, Cle	19–7	0	3.21
2008.....Cliff Lee, Cle	22–3	0	2.54
2009.....Zack Greinke, KC	16–8	0	2.16
2010.....Felix Hernandez, Sea	13–12	0	2.27
2011.....*Justin Verlander, Det	24–5	0	2.40
2012.....David Price, TB	20–5	0	2.56

*Won the MVP and Cy Young awards in the same season.
†NL games only. Sutcliffe pitched 15 games with Cleveland before being traded to the Cubs.

Career Individual Batting

GAMES

Pete Rose	3562
Carl Yastrzemski	3308
Hank Aaron	3298
Rickey Henderson	3081
Ty Cobb	3034
Eddie Murray	3026
Stan Musial	3026
Cal Ripken Jr.	3001
Willie Mays	2992
Barry Bonds	2986
Dave Winfield	2973
Omar Vizquel	2968
Rusty Staub	2951
Brooks Robinson	2896
Robin Yount	2856
Craig Biggio	2850
Al Kaline	2834
Rafael Palmeiro	2831
Harold Baines	2830
Eddie Collins	2826
Reggie Jackson	2820
Frank Robinson	2808
Honus Wagner	2792

AT BATS

Pete Rose	14053
Hank Aaron	12364
Carl Yastrzemski	11988
Cal Ripken Jr.	11551
Ty Cobb	11434
Eddie Murray	11336
Robin Yount	11008
Dave Winfield	11003
Stan Musial	10972
Rickey Henderson	10961
Willie Mays	10881
Craig Biggio	10876
Paul Molitor	10835
Brooks Robinson	10654
*Derek Jeter	10614
Omar Vizquel	10586
Rafael Palmeiro	10472
Honus Wagner	10430
George Brett	10349

RUNS

Rickey Henderson	2295
Ty Cobb	2246
Barry Bonds	2227
Hank Aaron	2174
Babe Ruth	2174
Pete Rose	2165
Willie Mays	2062
Cap Anson	1996
Stan Musial	1949
*Alex Rodriguez	1919
Lou Gehrig	1888
Tris Speaker	1882
*Derek Jeter	1876
Mel Ott	1859
Craig Biggio	1834
Frank Robinson	1829
Eddie Collins	1821
Carl Yastrzemski	1816
Ted Williams	1798
Paul Molitor	1782

BATTING AVERAGE (5,000 AB)

Ty Cobb	.367
Rogers Hornsby	.358
Ed Delahanty	.346
Tris Speaker	.345
Billy Hamilton	.344
Ted Williams	.344
Dan Brouthers	.342
Harry Heilmann	.342
Babe Ruth	.342
Willie Keeler	.341
Bill Terry	.341
Lou Gehrig	.340
George Sisler	.340
Jesse Burkett	.338
Tony Gwynn	.338
Nap Lajoie	.338
Al Simmons	.334
Cap Anson	.333
Eddie Collins	.333
Paul Waner	.333
Sam Thompson	.331
Heinie Manush	.330
Wade Boggs	.328
Rod Carew	.328
Honus Wagner	.327

HOME RUNS

Barry Bonds	762
Hank Aaron	755
Babe Ruth	714
Willie Mays	660
*Alex Rodriguez	654
Ken Griffey Jr.	630
Jim Thome	612
Sammy Sosa	609
Frank Robinson	586
Mark McGwire	583
Harmon Killebrew	573
Rafael Palmeiro	569
Reggie Jackson	563
Manny Ramirez	555
Mike Schmidt	548
Mickey Mantle	536
Jimmie Foxx	534
Willie McCovey	521
Frank Thomas	521
Ted Williams	521
Ernie Banks	512
Eddie Mathews	512
Mel Ott	511
Gary Sheffield	509
Eddie Murray	504
Lou Gehrig	493
Fred McGriff	493
*Albert Pujols	492
Stan Musial	475
Willie Stargell	475

RUNS BATTED IN

Hank Aaron	2297
Babe Ruth	2213
Cap Anson	2076
Barry Bonds	1996
Lou Gehrig	1995
*Alex Rodriguez	1969
Stan Musial	1951
Ty Cobb	1937
Jimmie Foxx	1922
Eddie Murray	1917
Willie Mays	1903
Mel Ott	1860
Carl Yastrzemski	1844
Ted Williams	1839
Ken Griffey Jr.	1836
Rafael Palmeiro	1835
Dave Winfield	1833
Manny Ramirez	1831
Al Simmons	1827
Frank Robinson	1812
Honus Wagner	1732
Frank Thomas	1704
Reggie Jackson	1702
Jim Thome	1699
Cal Ripken Jr.	1695
Gary Sheffield	1676

HITS

Pete Rose	4256
Ty Cobb	4191
Hank Aaron	3771
Stan Musial	3630
Tris Speaker	3515
Carl Yastrzemski	3419
Cap Anson	3418
Honus Wagner	3415
Paul Molitor	3319
*Derek Jeter	3316
Eddie Collins	3313
Willie Mays	3283
Eddie Murray	3255
Nap Lajoie	3251
Cal Ripken Jr.	3184
George Brett	3154
Paul Waner	3152
Robin Yount	3142
Tony Gwynn	3141
Dave Winfield	3110
Craig Biggio	3060
Rickey Henderson	3055
Rod Carew	3053
Lou Brock	3023
Rafael Palmeiro	3020
Wade Boggs	3010
Al Kaline	3007
Roberto Clemente	3000

* Active in 2013.

Career Individual Batting *(Cont.)*

DOUBLES

Tris Speaker	792
Pete Rose	746
Stan Musial	725
Ty Cobb	724
Craig Biggio	668
George Brett	665
Nap Lajoie	657
Carl Yastrzemski	646
Honus Wagner	640
Hank Aaron	624
Paul Molitor	605
Paul Waner	605
Cal Ripken Jr.	603
Barry Bonds	601
Luis Gonzalez	596
Todd Helton	592
Rafael Palmeiro	585
Robin Yount	583
Cap Anson	581
Wade Boggs	578

TRIPLES

Sam Crawford	309
Ty Cobb	295
Honus Wagner	252
Jake Beckley	243
Roger Connor	233
Tris Speaker	222
Fred Clarke	220
Dan Brouthers	205
Joe Kelley	194
Paul Waner	191
Bid McPhee	188
Eddie Collins	187
Ed Delahanty	185
Sam Rice	184
Jesse Burkett	182
Ed Konetchy	182
Edd Roush	182
Buck Ewing	178
Rabbit Maranville	177
Stan Musial	177

BASES ON BALLS

Barry Bonds	2558
Rickey Henderson	2190
Babe Ruth	2062
Ted Williams	2021
Joe Morgan	1865
Carl Yastrzemski	1845
Jim Thome	1747
Mickey Mantle	1733
Mel Ott	1708
Frank Thomas	1667
Eddie Yost	1614
Darrell Evans	1605
Stan Musial	1599
Pete Rose	1566
Harmon Killebrew	1559
Chipper Jones	1512
Lou Gehrig	1508
Mike Schmidt	1507
Eddie Collins	1499
Gary Sheffield	1475
Willie Mays	1464
Bobby Abreu	1456
Jimmie Foxx	1452

* Active in 2013.

SLUGGING AVERAGE (5,000 AB)

Babe Ruth	.690
Ted Williams	.634
Lou Gehrig	.632
Jimmie Foxx	.609
Barry Bonds	.607
Hank Greenberg	.605
*Albert Pujols	.599
Mark McGwire	.588
Manny Ramirez	.585
Joe Dimaggio	.579
Rogers Hornsby	.577
*Miguel Cabrera	.568
Larry Walker	.565
Albert Belle	.564
Johnny Mize	.562
Juan Gonzalez	.561
Stan Musial	.559
*Alex Rodriguez	.558
Willie Mays	.557
Mickey Mantle	.557

STOLEN BASES

Rickey Henderson	1406
Lou Brock	938
Billy Hamilton	912
Ty Cobb	892
Tim Raines	808
Vince Coleman	752
Eddie Collins	745
Max Carey	738
Honus Wagner	722
Joe Morgan	689
Willie Wilson	668
Bert Campaneris	649
Kenny Lofton	622
Otis Nixon	620
George Davis	616
Tom Brown	615
*Juan Pierre	614
Dummy Hoy	594
Maury Wills	586
George Van Haltren	583

ON-BASE PERCENTAGE (5,000 AB)

Ted Williams	.482
Babe Ruth	.474
Billy Hamilton	.455
Lou Gehrig	.447
Barry Bonds	.444
Rogers Hornsby	.434
Ty Cobb	.433
Jimmie Foxx	.428
Tris Speaker	.428
Eddie Collins	.424
Mickey Mantle	.421
Dan Brouthers	.420
Mickey Cochrane	.419
Frank Thomas	.419
Edgar Martinez	.418
Stan Musial	.417
Ed Delahanty	.417
Clarence Childs	.416
Jesse Burkett	.415
Wade Boggs	.415
*Todd Helton	.414
Mel Ott	.414

TOTAL BASES

Hank Aaron	6856
Stan Musial	6134
Willie Mays	6066
Barry Bonds	5976
Ty Cobb	5859
Babe Ruth	5793
Pete Rose	5752
Carl Yastrzemski	5539
*Alex Rodriguez	5480
Eddie Murray	5397
Rafael Palmeiro	5388
Frank Robinson	5373
Ken Griffey Jr.	5271
Dave Winfield	5221
Cal Ripken Jr.	5168
Tris Speaker	5101
Lou Gehrig	5060
George Brett	5044
Mel Ott	5041
Jimmie Foxx	4956
Ted Williams	4884

STRIKEOUTS

Reggie Jackson	2597
Jim Thome	2548
Sammy Sosa	2306
*Adam Dunn	2220
*Alex Rodriguez	2075
Andres Galarraga	2003
Jose Canseco	1942
Willie Stargell	1936
Mike Cameron	1901
Mike Schmidt	1883
Fred McGriff	1882
Tony Perez	1867
Bobby Abreu	1819
Dave Kingman	1816
Manny Ramirez	1813
Ken Griffey Jr.	1779
Bobby Bonds	1757
Craig Biggio	1753
*Derek Jeter	1753
Andruw Jones	1748
Dale Murphy	1748
Carlos Delgado	1745
Alfonso Soriano	1732
Lou Brock	1730
Jim Edmonds	1729

The 30–30 Club (minimum of 30 HR and 30 SB in single season)

Year		HR	SB	Year		HR	SB
1922	Kenny Williams, StL	39	37	1997	Jeff Bagwell, Hou	43	31
1956	Willie Mays, NYG	36	40	1997	Raul Mondesi, LA	30	32
1957	Willie Mays, NYG	35	38	1997	Barry Bonds, SF	40	37
1963	Hank Aaron, Mil	44	31	1998	Alex Rodriguez, Sea	42	46
1969	Bobby Bonds, SF	32	45	1998	Shawn Green, Tor	35	35
1970	Tommy Harper, Mil	31	38	1999	Jeff Bagwell, Hou	42	30
1973	Bobby Bonds, SF	39	43	1999	Raul Mondesi, LA	33	36
1975	Bobby Bonds, NYY	32	30	2000	Preston Wilson, Fla	31	36
1977	Bobby Bonds, Cal	37	41	2001	Vladimir Guerrero, Mtl	34	37
1978	Bobby Bonds, Chi/Tex	31	43	2001	Jose Cruz Jr., Tor	34	32
1983	Dale Murphy, Atl	36	30	2001	Bobby Abreu, Phi	31	36
1987	Joe Carter, Clev	32	31	2002	Alfonso Soriano, NYY	39	41
1987	Eric Davis, Cin	37	50	2002	Vladimir Guerrero, Mtl	39	40
1987	Darryl Strawberry, NYM	39	36	2003	Alfonso Soriano, NYY	38	35
1987	Howard Johnson, NYM	36	32	2004	Carlos Beltran, KC/Hou	38	42
1988	Jose Canseco, Oak	42	40	2004	Bobby Abreu, Phi	30	40
1989	Howard Johnson, NYM	36	41	2005	Alfonso Soriano, Tex	36	30
1990	Ron Gant, Atl	32	33	2006	Alfonso Soriano, Wash	46	41
1990	Barry Bonds, Pitt	33	52	2007	Brandon Phillips, Cin	30	32
1991	Ron Gant, Atl	32	34	2007	Jimmy Rollins, Phi	30	41
1991	Howard Johnson, NYM	38	30	2007	David Wright, NYM	30	34
1992	Barry Bonds, Pitt	34	39	2008	Grady Sizemore, Cle	33	38
1993	Sammy Sosa, ChiC	33	36	2008	Hanley Ramirez, Fla	33	35
1995	Barry Bonds, SF	33	31	2009	Ian Kinsler, Tex	31	31
1995	Sammy Sosa, ChiC	36	34	2011	Matt Kemp, LA	39	40
1996	Barry Bonds, SF	42	40	2011	Ryan Braun, Mil	33	33
1996	Ellis Burks, Col	40	32	2011	Jacoby Ellsbury, Bos	32	39
1996	Barry Larkin, Cin	33	36	2011	Ian Kinsler, Tex	32	30
1996	Dante Bichette, Col	31	31	2012	Mike Trout, LAA	30	49
1997	Larry Walker, Col	49	33	2012	Ryan Braun, Mil	41	30

Career Individual Pitching

GAMES

Jesse Orosco	1251
Mike Stanton	1178
John Franco	1119
*Mariano Rivera	1115
Dennis Eckersley	1071
Hoyt Wilhelm	1070
Dan Plesac	1064
Mike Timlin	1058
Kent Tekulve	1050
Trevor Hoffman	1035
Jose Mesa	1022
Lee Smith	1022
Roberto Hernandez	1010
Mike Jackson	1005
Goose Gossage	1002
Lindy McDaniel	987
Todd Jones	982
David Weathers	964
Rollie Fingers	944
LaTroy Hawkins	943
Gene Garber	931
Eddie Guardado	908
Cy Young	906
Arthur Rhodes	900
Sparky Lyle	899
Jim Kaat	898

INNINGS PITCHED

Cy Young	7356.0
Pud Galvin	6003.1
Walter Johnson	5914.1
Phil Niekro	5404.1
Nolan Ryan	5386.0
Gaylord Perry	5350.1
Don Sutton	5282.1
Warren Spahn	5243.1
Steve Carlton	5217.1
Grover Alexander	5190.0
Kid Nichols	5056.1
Tim Keefe	5049.2
Greg Maddux	5008.1
Bert Blyleven	4970.0
Bobby Mathews	4956.0
Roger Clemens	4916.2
Mickey Welch	4802.0
Tom Seaver	4782.2
Christy Mathewson	4780.2
Tommy John	4710.1
Robin Roberts	4688.2
Early Wynn	4564.0
John Clarkson	4536.1
Charley Radbourn	4535.1
Tony Mullane	4531.1
Jim Kaat	4530.1

WINS

Cy Young	511
Walter Johnson	417
Grover Alexander	373
Christy Mathewson	373
Pud Galvin	365
Warren Spahn	363
Kid Nichols	361
Greg Maddux	355
Roger Clemens	354
Tim Keefe	342
Steve Carlton	329
John Clarkson	328
Eddie Plank	326
Nolan Ryan	324
Don Sutton	324
Phil Niekro	318
Gaylord Perry	314
Tom Seaver	311
Charley Radbourn	309
Mickey Welch	307
Tom Glavine	305
Randy Johnson	303
Lefty Grove	300
Early Wynn	300
Bobby Matthews	297
Tommy John	288

LOSSES

Cy Young	316
Pud Galvin	310
Nolan Ryan	292
Walter Johnson	279
Phil Niekro	274
Gaylord Perry	265
Don Sutton	256
Jack Powell	254
Eppa Rixey	251
Bert Blyleven	250
Bobby Mathews	248
Robin Roberts	245
Warren Spahn	245
Steve Carlton	244
Early Wynn	244
Jim Kaat	237
Frank Tanana	236
Gus Weyhing	232
Tommy John	231
Bob Friend	230
Ted Lyons	230
Greg Maddux	227
Ferguson Jenkins	226
Tim Keefe	225
Red Ruffing	225
Bob Newsom	222

WINNING PERCENTAGE**

Al Spalding	.795
Spud Chandler	.717
Whitey Ford	.690
Dave Foutz	.690
Bob Caruthers	.688
Pedro Martinez	.687
Don Gullett	.686
Lefty Grove	.680
Joe Wood	.672
Vic Raschi	.667
Larry Corcoran	.665
Christy Mathewson	.665
Sam Leever	.660
*Roy Halladay	.659
Roger Clemens	.658
Sal Maglie	.657
Dick McBride	.656
Sandy Koufax	.655
Johnny Allen	.654
*Jered Weaver	.653
Ron Guidry	.651
Lefty Gomez	.649
*Tim Hudson	.649
John Clarkson	.648

SAVES

*Mariano Rivera	652
Trevor Hoffman	601
Lee Smith	478
John Franco	424
Billy Wagner	422
Dennis Eckersley	390
Jeff Reardon	367
Troy Percival	358
Randy Myers	347
Rollie Fingers	341
*Joe Nathan	341
John Wetteland	330
Francisco Cordero	329
Roberto Hernandez	326
Jose Mesa	321
Todd Jones	319
Rick Aguilera	318
Robb Nen	314
Tom Henke	311
Goose Gossage	310
Jeff Montgomery	304
*Francisco Rodriguez	304
Doug Jones	303
Jason Isringhausen	300
Bruce Sutter	300

* Active in 2013. ** Minumum 100 victories.

Career Individual Pitching *(Cont.)*

EARNED RUN AVERAGE**

Ed Walsh	1.82
Addie Joss	1.89
Al Spalding	2.04
Three Finger Brown	2.06
John Ward	2.10
Christy Mathewson	2.13
Tommy Bond	2.14
Rube Waddell	2.16
Walter Johnson	2.17
Ed Reulbach	2.28
Will White	2.28
Eddie Plank	2.35
Larry Corcoran	2.36
Eddie Cicotte	2.38
Candy Cummings	2.39
Doc White	2.39
Nap Rucker	2.42
George Bradley	2.43
Jim McCormick	2.43
Chief Bender	2.46

COMPLETE GAMES

Cy Young	749
Pud Galvin	639
Tim Keefe	554
Walter Johnson	531
Kid Nichols	531
Mickey Welch	525
Bobby Mathews	525
Charley Radbourn	489
John Clarkson	485
Tony Mullane	468
Jim McCormick	466
Gus Weyhing	448
Grover Alexander	437
Christy Mathewson	434
Jack Powell	422
Eddie Plank	410
Will White	394
Amos Rusie	392
Vic Willis	388
Tommy Bond	386

BASES ON BALLS

Nolan Ryan	2795
Steve Carlton	1833
Phil Niekro	1809
Early Wynn	1775
Bob Feller	1764
Bobo Newsom	1732
Amos Rusie	1707
Charlie Hough	1665
Roger Clemens	1580
Gus Weyhing	1566
Red Ruffing	1541
Tom Glavine	1500
Randy Johnson	1497
Bump Hadley	1442
Warren Spahn	1434
Earl Whitehill	1431
Tony Mullane	1408
Sad Sam Jones	1396
Jack Morris	1390
Tom Seaver	1390
Gaylord Perry	1379

SHUTOUTS

Walter Johnson	110
Grover Alexander	90
Christy Mathewson	79
Cy Young	76
Eddie Plank	69
Warren Spahn	63
Nolan Ryan	61
Tom Seaver	61
Bert Blyleven	60
Don Sutton	58
Pud Galvin	57
Ed Walsh	57
Bob Gibson	56
Three Finger Brown	55
Steve Carlton	55
Jim Palmer	53
Gaylord Perry	53
Juan Marichal	52
Rube Waddell	50
Vic Willis	50

STRIKEOUTS

Nolan Ryan	5714
Randy Johnson	4875
Roger Clemens	4672
Steve Carlton	4136
Bert Blyleven	3701
Tom Seaver	3640
Don Sutton	3574
Gaylord Perry	3534
Walter Johnson	3509
Greg Maddux	3371
Phil Niekro	3342
Ferguson Jenkins	3192
Pedro Martinez	3154
Bob Gibson	3117
Curt Schilling	3116
John Smoltz	3084
Jim Bunning	2855
Mickey Lolich	2832
Mike Mussina	2813
Cy Young	2803

Alltime Winningest Managers

CAREER

	W	L	Pct	Yrs		W	L	Pct	Yrs
Connie Mack	3755	3967	.486	53	Casey Stengel	1942	1868	.510	25
John McGraw	2810	1987	.586	33	Gene Mauch	1907	2044	.483	26
Tony LaRussa	2796	2419	.536	33	Bill McKechnie	1904	1737	.523	25
Bobby Cox	2571	2068	.554	29	Lou Piniella	1858	1737	.517	23
Joe Torre	2406	2051	.540	29	*Jim Leyland	1813	1767	.506	22
Sparky Anderson	2238	1855	.547	26	*Dusty Baker	1690	1530	.525	20
Bucky Harris	2168	2228	.493	29	Ralph Houk	1627	1539	.514	20
Joe McCarthy	2155	1346	.616	24	Fred Clarke	1609	1189	.575	19
Walter Alston	2063	1634	.558	23	Dick Williams	1592	1474	.519	21
Leo Durocher	2015	1717	.540	24	Tommy Lasorda	1589	1434	.526	20

REGULAR SEASON

	W	L	Pct	Yrs		W	L	Pct	Yrs
Connie Mack	3731	3948	.486	53	Casey Stengel	1905	1842	.508	25
John McGraw	2763	1948	.586	33	Gene Mauch	1902	2037	.483	26
Tony LaRussa	2728	2365	.536	33	Bill McKechnie	1896	1723	.524	25
Bobby Cox	2504	2001	.556	29	Lou Piniella	1835	1713	.517	23
Joe Torre	2326	1997	.538	29	*Jim Leyland	1769	1728	.506	22
Sparky Anderson	2194	1834	.545	26	*Dusty Baker	1671	1504	.526	20
Bucky Harris	2157	2218	.493	29	Ralph Houk	1619	1531	.514	20
Joe McCarthy	2125	1333	.615	24	Fred Clarke	1602	1181	.576	19
Walter Alston	2040	1613	.558	23	Tommy Lasorda	1599	1439	.526	21
Leo Durocher	2008	1709	.540	24	Dick Williams	1571	1451	.520	21

WORLD SERIES

	W	L	T	Pct	App	WS		W	L	T	Pct	App	WS
Casey Stengel	37	26	0	.587	10	7	Bucky Harris	11	10	0	.524	3	2
Joe McCarthy	30	13	0	.698	9	7	Billy Southworth	11	11	0	.500	4	2
John McGraw	26	28	2	.482	9	2	Earl Weaver	11	13	0	.458	4	1
Connie Mack	24	19	0	.558	8	5	Bobby Cox	11	18	0	.379	5	1
Joe Torre	21	11	0	.657	6	4	Whitey Herzog	10	11	0	.476	3	1
Walter Alston	20	20	0	.500	7	4	Terry Francona	8	0	0	1.000	2	2
Miller Huggins	18	15	1	.544	6	3	Bill Carrigan	8	2	0	.800	2	2
Sparky Anderson	16	12	0	.571	5	3	Cito Gaston	8	4	0	.667	2	2
Tony LaRussa	13	16	0	.448	6	3	*Bruce Bochy	8	5	0	.615	3	2
Tommy Lasorda	12	11	0	.522	4	2	Danny Murtaugh	8	6	0	.571	2	2
Dick Williams	12	14	0	.462	4	2	Tom Kelly	8	6	0	.571	2	2
Frank Chance	11	9	1	.548	4	2	Ralph Houk	8	8	0	.500	3	2

* Active in 2013.

Individual Batting Records (Single Season)

HITS

Ichiro Suzuki, 2004	262
George Sisler, 1920	257
Lefty O'Doul, 1929	254
Bill Terry, 1930	254
Al Simmons, 1925	253
Rogers Hornsby, 1922	250
Chuck Klein, 1930	250
Ty Cobb, 1911	248
George Sisler, 1922	246
Ichiro Suzuki, 2001	242

BATTING AVERAGE

Levi Meyerle, 1871	.492
Hugh Duffy, 1894	.440
Tip O'Neill, 1887	.435
Ross Barnes, 1872	.432
Cal McVey, 1871	.431
Ross Barnes, 1876	.429
Nap Lajoie, 1901	.426
Ross Barnes, 1873	.425
Willie Keeler, 1897	.424
Rogers Hornsby, 1924	.424

DOUBLES

Earl Webb, 1931	67
George Burns, 1926	64
Joe Medwick, 1936	64
Hank Greenberg, 1934	63
Paul Waner, 1932	62
Charlie Gehringer, 1936	60
Tris Speaker, 1923	59
Chuck Klein, 1930	59
Todd Helton, 2000	59
Billy Herman, 1935	57
Billy Herman, 1936	57
Carlos Delgado, 2000	57

TOTAL BASES

Babe Ruth, 1921	457
Rogers Hornsby, 1922	450
Lou Gehrig, 1927	447
Chuck Klein, 1930	445
Jimmie Foxx, 1932	438
Stan Musial, 1948	429
Sammy Sosa, 2001	425
Hack Wilson, 1930	423
Chuck Klein, 1932	420
Lou Gehrig, 1930	419
Luis Gonzalez, 2001	419

TRIPLES

Chief Wilson, 1912	36
Dave Orr, 1886	31
Heinie Reitz, 1894	31
Perry Werden, 1893	29
Harry Davis, 1897	28
George Davis, 1893	27
Sam Thompson, 1894	27
Jimmy Williams, 1899	27
John Reilly, 1890	26
George Treadway, 1894	26
Sam Crawford, 1914	26
Joe Jackson, 1912	26
Kiki Cuyler, 1925	26

HOME RUNS

Barry Bonds, 2001	73
Mark McGwire, 1998	70
Sammy Sosa, 1998	66
Mark McGwire, 1999	65
Sammy Sosa, 2001	64
Sammy Sosa, 1999	63
Roger Maris, 1961	61
Babe Ruth, 1927	60
Babe Ruth, 1921	59
Jimmie Foxx, 1932	58
Hank Greenberg, 1938	58
Mark McGwire, 1997	58
Ryan Howard, 2006	58

RUNS BATTED IN

Hack Wilson, 1930	191
Lou Gehrig, 1931	184
Hank Greenberg, 1937	183
Lou Gehrig, 1927	175
Jimmie Foxx, 1938	175
Lou Gehrig, 1930	174
Babe Ruth, 1921	171
Chuck Klein, 1930	170
Hank Greenberg, 1935	170
Jimmie Foxx, 1932	169

STRIKEOUTS

Mark Reynolds, 2009	223
Adam Dunn, 2012	222
Chris Carter, 2013	212
Mark Reynolds, 2010	211
Drew Stubbs, 2011	205
Mark Reynolds, 2008	204
Ryan Howard, 2007	199
Ryan Howard, 2008	199
Adam Dunn, 2010	199
Chris Davis, 2013	199

RUNS

Billy Hamilton, 1894	192
Tom Brown, 1891	177
Babe Ruth, 1921	177
Tip O'Neill, 1887	167
Lou Gehrig, 1936	167
Billy Hamilton, 1895	166
Willie Keeler, 1894	165
Joe Kelley, 1894	165
Arlie Latham, 1887	163
Babe Ruth, 1928	163
Lou Gehrig, 1931	163

STOLEN BASES

Hugh Nicol, 1887	138
Rickey Henderson, 1982	130
Arlie Latham, 1887	129
Lou Brock, 1974	118
Charlie Comiskey, 1887	117
John Ward, 1887	111
Billy Hamilton, 1889	111
Billy Hamilton, 1891	111
Vince Coleman, 1985	110
Arlie Latham, 1888	109
Vince Coleman, 1987	109

BASES ON BALLS

Barry Bonds, 2004	232
Barry Bonds, 2002	198
Barry Bonds, 2001	177
Babe Ruth, 1923	170
Ted Williams, 1947	162
Ted Williams, 1949	162
Mark McGwire, 1998	162
Ted Williams, 1946	156
Eddie Yost, 1956	151
Barry Bonds, 1996	151
Babe Ruth, 1920	150

SLUGGING AVERAGE

Barry Bonds, 2001	.863
Babe Ruth, 1920	.847
Babe Ruth, 1921	.846
Barry Bonds, 2004	.812
Barry Bonds, 2002	.799
Babe Ruth, 1927	.772
Lou Gehrig, 1927	.765
Babe Ruth, 1923	.764
Rogers Hornsby, 1925	.756
Mark McGwire, 1998	.752

Individual Pitching Records (Single Season)

GAME APPEARANCES

Mike Marshall, 1974	106
Kent Tekulve, 1979	94
Salomon Torres, 2006	94
Mike Marshall, 1973	92
Pedro Feliciano, 2010	92
Kent Tekulve, 1978	91
Wayne Granger, 1969	90
Mike Marshall, 1979	90
Kent Tekulve, 1987	90
Mark Eichhorn, 1987	89
Steve Kline, 2001	89
Paul Quantrill, 2003	89
Jim Brower, 2004	89
Julian Tavarez, 2009	89

GAMES STARTED

Will White, 1879	75
Pud Galvin, 1883	75
Jim McCormick, 1880	74
Guy Hecker, 1884	73
Charley Radbourn, 1884	73
Jim Galvin, 1884	72
John Clarkson, 1889	72
Bobby Mathews, 1875	70
John Clarkson, 1885	70
Bill Hutchison, 1892	70

INNINGS PITCHED

Will White, 1878	680.0
Charley Radbourn, 1884	678.2
Guy Hecker, 1884	670.2
Jim McCormick, 1880	657.2
Jim Galvin, 1883	656.1
Jim Galvin, 1884	636.1
Charley Radbourn, 1883	632.1
Bill Hutchison, 1892	627.0
Bobby Mathews, 1875	626.2

WINS

Charley Radbourn, 1884	59
Al Spalding, 1875	55
John Clarkson, 1885	53
Al Spalding, 1874	52
Guy Hecker, 1884	52
John Clarkson, 1889	49
Charley Radbourn, 1883	48
Charlie Buffinton, 1884	48
Al Spalding, 1876	47
John Ward, 1879	47

LOSSES

John Coleman, 1883	48
Will White, 1880	42
Larry McKeon, 1884	41
George Bradley, 1879	40
Jim McCormick, 1879	40
Bobby Mathews, 1875	38
Henry Porter, 1888	37
Kid Carsey, 1891	37
George Cobb, 1892	37

WINNING PERCENTAGE

Roy Face, 1959	.947
Johnny Allen, 1937	.938
Greg Maddux, 1995	.905
Randy Johnson, 1995	.900
Ron Guidry, 1978	.893
Freddie Fitzsimmons, 1940	.889
Lefty Grove, 1931	.886
Bob Stanley, 1978	.882
Preacher Roe, 1951	.880
Cliff Lee, 2008	.880
Tom Seaver, 1981	.875
Maz Scherzer, 2013	.875

SAVES

Francisco Rodriguez, 2008	62
Bobby Thigpen, 1990	57
John Smoltz, 2002	55
Eric Gagne, 2003	55
Randy Myers, 1993	53
Trevor Hoffman, 1998	53
Mariano Rivera, 2004	53
Eric Gagne, 2002	52
Dennis Eckersley, 1992	51
Rod Beck, 1998	51
Jim Johnson, 2012	51

EARNED RUN AVERAGE

Tim Keefe, 1880	0.86
Dutch Leonard, 1914	0.96
Three Finger Brown, 1906	1.04
Bob Gibson, 1968	1.12
Christy Mathewson, 1909	1.14
Walter Johnson, 1913	1.14
Jack Pfiester, 1907	1.15
Addie Joss, 1908	1.16
Carl Lundgren, 1907	1.17
Denny Driscoll, 1882	1.21

SHUTOUTS

George Bradley, 1876	16
Grover Alexander, 1916	16
Jack Coombs, 1910	13
Bob Gibson, 1968	13
Jim Galvin, 1884	12
Ed Morris, 1886	12
Grover Alexander, 1915	12
Tommy Bond, 1879	11
Charles Radbourn, 1884	11
Dave Foutz, 1886	11
Christy Mathewson, 1908	11
Ed Walsh, 1908	11
Walter Johnson, 1913	11
Sandy Koufax, 1963	11
Dean Chance, 1964	11

COMPLETE GAMES

Will White, 1879	75
Charley Radbourn, 1884	73
Jim McCormick, 1880	72
Pud Galvin, 1883	72
Guy Hecker, 1884	72
Pud Galvin, 1884	71
Bobby Mathews, 1875	69
John Clarkson, 1885	68
John Clarkson, 1889	68

STRIKEOUTS

Matt Kilroy, 1886	513
Toad Ramsey, 1886	499
Hugh Daily, 1884	483
Dupee Shaw, 1884	451
Charley Radbourn, 1884	441
Charlie Buffinton, 1884	417
Guy Hecker, 1884	385
Nolan Ryan, 1973	383
Sandy Koufax, 1965	382

BASES ON BALLS

Amos Rusie, 1890	289
Mark Baldwin, 1889	274
Amos Rusie, 1892	267
Amos Rusie, 1891	262
Mark Baldwin, 1890	249
Jack Stivetts, 1891	232
Mark Baldwin, 1891	227
Phil Knell, 1891	226
Bob Barr, 1890	219

Manager of the Year

NATIONAL LEAGUE

1983	Tommy Lasorda, LA
1984	Jim Frey, Chi
1985	Whitey Herzog, StL
1986	Hal Lanier, Hou
1987	Buck Rodgers, Mtl
1988	Tommy Lasorda, LA
1989	Don Zimmer, Chi
1990	Jim Leyland, Pitt
1991	Bobby Cox, Atl
1992	Jim Leyland, Pitt
1993	Dusty Baker, SF
1994	Felipe Alou, Mtl
1995	Don Baylor, Col
1996	Bruce Bochy, SD
1997	Dusty Baker, SF
1998	Larry Dierker, Hou
1999	Jack McKeon, Cin

AMERICAN LEAGUE

1983	Tony LaRussa, Chi
1984	Sparky Anderson, Det
1985	Bobby Cox, Tor
1986	John McNamara, Bos
1987	Sparky Anderson, Det
1988	Tony LaRussa, Oak
1989	Frank Robinson, Balt
1990	Jeff Torborg, Chi
1991	Tom Kelly, Minn
1992	Tony LaRussa, Oak
1993	Gene Lamont, Chi
1994	Buck Showalter, NY
1995	Lou Piniella, Sea
1996	Joe Torre, NY/Johnny Oates, Tex
1997	Davey Johnson, Balt
1998	Joe Torre, NY
1999	Jimy Williams, Bos

Manager of the Year (Cont.)

NATIONAL LEAGUE

2000	Dusty Baker, SF
2001	Larry Bowa, Phi
2002	Tony LaRussa, StL
2003	Jack McKeon, Fla
2004	Bobby Cox, Atl
2005	Bobby Cox, Atl
2006	Joe Girardi, Fla
2007	Bob Melvin, Ari
2008	Lou Piniella, Chi
2009	Jim Tracy, Col
2010	Bud Black, SD
2011	Kirk Gibson, Ari
2012	Davey Johnson, Wash

AMERICAN LEAGUE

2000	Jerry Manuel, Chi
2001	Lou Piniella, Sea
2002	Mike Scioscia, Ana
2003	Tony Pena, KC
2004	Buck Showalter, Tex
2005	Ozzie Guillen, Chi
2006	Jim Leyland, Det
2007	Eric Wedge, Cle
2008	Joe Maddon, TB
2009	Mike Scioscia, LA
2010	Ron Gardenhire, Min
2011	Joe Maddon, TB
2012	Bob Melvin, Oak

Individual Batting Records (Single Game)

MOST HITS

7	Wilbert Robinson, Balt	June 10, 1892
	Rennie Stennett, Pitt	Sept 16, 1975

MOST HOME RUNS

4	Bobby Lowe, Bos (N)	May 30, 1894
	Ed Delahanty, Phi	July 13, 1896
	Lou Gehrig, NY (A)	June 3, 1932
	Chuck Klein, Phi (N)	July 10, 1936
	Pat Seerey, Chi (A)	July 18, 1948
	Gil Hodges, Bklyn	Aug 31, 1950
	Joe Adcock, Mil	July 31, 1954
	Rocky Colavito, Clev	June 10, 1959
	Willie Mays, SF	April 30, 1961
	Mike Schmidt, Phi	April 17, 1976
	Bob Horner, Atl	July 6, 1986
	Mark Whiten, StL	Sept 7, 1993
	Mike Cameron, Sea	May 2, 2002
	Shawn Green, LA	May 23, 2002
	Carlos Delgado, Tor	Sept 25, 2003
	Josh Hamilton, Tex	May 8, 2012

MOST GRAND SLAMS

2	Tony Lazzeri, NY (A)	May 24, 1936
	Jim Tabor, Bos (A)	July 4, 1939
	Rudy York, Bos (A)	July 27, 1946
	Jim Gentile, Balt	May 9, 1961
	Tony Cloninger, Atl	July 3, 1966
	Jim Northrup, Det	June 24, 1968
	Frank Robinson, Balt	June 26, 1970
	Robin Ventura, Chi (A)	Sept 4, 1995
	Chris Hoiles, Balt	Aug 14, 1998
	Fernando Tatis, StL	Apr 23, 1999
	N. Garciaparra, Bos	May 10, 1999
	Bill Mueller, Bos	July 29, 2003
	Josh Willingham, Wash	July 27, 2009

MOST RUNS

7	Guy Hecker, Lou	Aug 15, 1886

MOST RBIs

12	Jim Bottomley, StL	Sept 16, 1924
	Mark Whiten, StL	Sept 7, 1993

Note: All single-game hitting records for a nine-inning game.

Individual Batting Records (Single Inning)

MOST RUNS

3	Tommy Burns, Chi (N)	Sept 6, 1883, 7th inning
	Ned Williamson, Chi (N)	Sept 6, 1883, 7th inning
	Sammy White, Bos (A)	June 18, 1953, 7th inning

MOST HITS

3	Tommy Burns, Chi (N)	Sept 6, 1883, 7th inning
	Fred Pfeiffer, Chi (N)	Sept 6, 1883, 7th inning

MOST HITS (CONT.)

Ned Williamson, Chi (N)	Sept 6, 1883, 7th inning
Gene Stephens, Bos (A)	June 18, 1953, 7th inning
Johnny Damon, Bos (A)	June 27, 2003, 1st inning

MOST RBIs

8	Fernando Tatis, StL	Apr 23, 1999, 3rd inning

Individual Pitching Records (Single Game)

MOST INNINGS PITCHED

26	Leon Cadore, Bklyn	May 1, 1920, tie 1–1
	Joe Oeschger, Bos (N)	May 1, 1920, tie 1–1

MOST RUNS ALLOWED

24	Al Travers, Det	May 18, 1912

MOST HITS ALLOWED

36	Jack Wadsworth, Lou	Aug 17, 1894

MOST STRIKEOUTS (9 INNINGS)

20	Roger Clemens, Bos	April 29, 1986
20	Roger Clemens, Bos	Sept 18, 1996
20	Kerry Wood, Chi (N)	May 6, 1998
20	Randy Johnson, Ariz	May 8, 2001

MOST WALKS ALLOWED

16	Bill George, NY (N)	May 30, 1887
	George Van Haltren, Chi (N)	June 27, 1887
	Henry Gruber, Clev	Apr 19, 1890
	Bruno Haas, Phi (A)	June 2, 1915

MOST WILD PITCHES

6	J.R. Richard, Hou	April 10, 1979
	Phil Niekro, Atl	Aug 14, 1979
	Bill Gullickson, Mtl	April 10, 1982

Individual Pitching Records (Single Inning)

MOST RUNS ALLOWED

13 .....Lefty O'Doul, Bos (A)   July 7, 1923

MOST WILD PITCHES

4 ....Walter Johnson, Wash	Sept 21, 1914
Phil Niekro, Atl	Aug 14, 1979
Kevin Gregg, Ana	July 25, 2004
Ryan Madson, Phi	July 25, 2006

MOST WALKS ALLOWED

8 ....Dolly Gray, Wash   Aug 28, 1909

Miscellaneous Records

LONGEST GAME, BY INNINGS

26 .....Brooklyn 1, Boston 1   May 1, 1920

LONGEST NINE-INNING GAME, BY TIME

4:45...New York (A) 14, Boston 11   Aug 18, 2006

Baseball Hall of Fame

Players

	Position	Career	Selected		Position	Career	Selected
Hank Aaron	OF	1954–76	1982	Joe Cronin	SS	1926–45	1956
Grover Alexander	P	1911–30	1938	Candy Cummings	P	1872–77	1939
Roberto Alomar	2B	1988–2004	2011	Kiki Cuyler	OF	1921–38	1968
Cap Anson	1B	1876–97	1939	Ray Dandridge*	3B		1987
Luis Aparicio	SS	1956–73	1984	George Davis	SS	1890–1909	1998
Luke Appling	SS	1930–50	1964	Andre Dawson	OF	1976–96	2010
Richie Ashburn	OF	1948–62	1995	Leon Day*	P		1995
Earl Averill	OF	1929–41	1975	Dizzy Dean	P	1930–47	1953
Jose Mendez Baez*	P	1908–26	2006	Ed Delahanty	OF	1888–1903	1945
Frank Baker	3B	1908–22	1955	Bill Dickey	C	1928–46	1954
Dave Bancroft	SS	1915–30	1971	Martin Dihigo*	P-OF		1977
Ernie Banks	SS-1B	1953–71	1977	Joe DiMaggio	OF	1936–51	1955
Jake Beckley	1B	1888–1907	1971	Larry Doby	OF	1947–59	1998
Cool Papa Bell*	OF		1974	Bobby Doerr	2B	1937–51	1986
Johnny Bench	C	1967–83	1989	Don Drysdale	P	1956–69	1984
Chief Bender	P	1903–25	1953	Hugh Duffy	OF	1888–1906	1945
Yogi Berra	C	1946–65	1972	Dennis Eckersley	P	1975–98	2004
Bert Blyleven	P	1970–90; '92	2011	Johnny Evers	2B	1902–29	1939
Wade Boggs	3B	1982-99	2005	Buck Ewing	C	1880–97	1946
Jim Bottomley	1B	1922–37	1974	Red Faber	P	1914–33	1964
Lou Boudreau	SS	1938–52	1970	Bob Feller	P	1936–56	1962
Roger Bresnahan	C	1897–1915	1945	Rick Ferrell	C	1929–47	1984
George Brett	3B	1973–93	1999	Rollie Fingers	P	1968–85	1992
Lou Brock	OF	1961–79	1985	Carlton Fisk	C	1969–93	2000
Dan Brouthers	1B	1879–1904	1945	Elmer Flick	OF	1898–1910	1963
Ray Brown*	P	1930–48	2006	Whitey Ford	P	1950–67	1974
Three Finger Brown	P	1903–16	1949	Bill Foster*	P		1996
Willard Jesse Brown*	OF	1935–58	2006	Nellie Fox	2B	1947–65	1997
Jim Bunning	P	1955–71	1996	Jimmie Foxx	1B	1925–45	1951
Jesse Burkett	OF	1890–1905	1946	Frankie Frisch	2B	1919–37	1947
Roy Campanella	C	1948–57	1969	Pud Galvin	P	1879–92	1965
Rod Carew	1B-2B	1967–85	1991	Lou Gehrig	1B	1923–39	1939
Max Carey	OF	1910–29	1961	Charlie Gehringer	2B	1924–42	1949
Steve Carlton	P	1965–88	1994	Bob Gibson	P	1959–75	1981
Gary Carter	C	1974–92	2003	Josh Gibson*	C		1972
Orlando Cepeda	1B	1958–74	1999	Lefty Gomez	P	1930–43	1972
Frank Chance	1B	1898–1914	1946	Joe Gordon	2B	1938–43/46-50	2009
Oscar Charleston*	OF		1976	Goose Goslin	OF	1921–38	1968
Jack Chesbro	P	1899–1909	1946	Rich "Goose" Gossage	P	1972-94	2008
Fred Clarke	OF	1894–1915	1945	Ulysses F. Grant*	2B	1886–1903	2006
John Clarkson	P	1882–94	1963	Hank Greenberg	1B	1930–47	1956
Roberto Clemente	OF	1955–72	1973	Burleigh Grimes	P	1916–34	1964
Ty Cobb	OF	1905–28	1936	Lefty Grove	P	1925–41	1947
Mickey Cochrane	C	1925–37	1947	Tony Gwynn	OF	1982–2001	2007
Eddie Collins	2B	1906–30	1939	Chick Hafey	OF	1924–37	1971
Jimmy Collins	3B	1895–1908	1945	Jesse Haines	P	1918–37	1970
Earle Combs	OF	1924–35	1970	Billy Hamilton	OF	1888–1901	1961
Roger Connor	1B	1880–97	1976	Gabby Hartnett	C	1922–41	1955
Andrew Cooper*	P	1920–41	2006	Harry Heilmann	OF	1914–32	1952
Stan Coveleski	P	1912–28	1969	Rickey Henderson	OF	1979–2003	2009
Sam Crawford	OF	1899–1917	1957	Billy Herman	2B	1931–47	1975

Note: Career dates indicate first and last appearances in the majors. *Elected on the basis of their career in the Negro leagues.

Players *(Cont.)*

	Position	Career	Selected
Joseph Hill*	OF	1899–1925	2006
Harry Hooper	OF	1909–25	1971
Rogers Hornsby	2B	1915–37	1942
Waite Hoyt	P	1918–38	1969
Carl Hubbell	P	1928–43	1947
Catfish Hunter	P	1965–79	1987
Monte Irvin*	OF	1949–56	1973
Reggie Jackson	OF	1967–87	1993
Travis Jackson	SS	1922–36	1982
Ferguson Jenkins	P	1965–83	1991
Hugh Jennings	SS	1891–1918	1945
Judy Johnson*	3B		1975
Walter Johnson	P	1907–27	1936
Addie Joss	P	1902–10	1978
Al Kaline	OF	1953–74	1980
Tim Keefe	P	1880–93	1964
Willie Keeler	OF	1892–1910	1939
George Kell	3B	1943–57	1983
Joe Kelley	OF	1891–1908	1971
George Kelly	1B	1915–32	1973
King Kelly	C	1878–93	1945
Harmon Killebrew	1B-3B	1954–75	1984
Ralph Kiner	OF	1946–55	1975
Chuck Klein	OF	1928–44	1980
Sandy Koufax	P	1955–66	1972
Nap Lajoie	2B	1896–1916	1937
Barry Larkin	SS	1986–2004	2012
Tony Lazzeri	2B	1926–39	1991
Bob Lemon	P	1941–58	1976
Buck Leonard*	1B		1977
Fred Lindstrom	3B	1924–36	1976
Pop Lloyd*	SS-1B		1977
Ernie Lombardi	C	1931–47	1986
Ted Lyons	P	1923–46	1955
James Mackey*	C	1920–47	2006
Mickey Mantle	OF	1951–68	1974
Heinie Manush	OF	1923–39	1964
Rabbit Maranville	SS-2B	1912–35	1954
Juan Marichal	P	1960–75	1983
Rube Marquard	P	1908–25	1971
Eddie Mathews	3B	1952–68	1978
Christy Mathewson	P	1900–16	1936
Willie Mays	OF	1951–73	1979
Bill Mazeroski	2B	1956–72	2001
Tommy McCarthy	OF	1884–96	1946
Willie McCovey	1B	1959–80	1986
Joe McGinnity	P	1899–1908	1946
Bid McPhee	2B	1882–99	2000
Joe Medwick	OF	1932–48	1968
Johnny Mize	1B	1936–53	1981
Paul Molitor	3B	1978–98	2004
Joe Morgan	2B	1963–84	1990
Eddie Murray	1B	1977–97	2003
Stan Musial	OF-1B	1941–63	1969
Hal Newhouser	P	1939–55	1992
Kid Nichols	P	1890–1906	1949
Phil Niekro	P	1964–87	1997
Jim O'Rourke	OF	1876–1904	1945
Mel Ott	OF	1926–47	1951
Satchel Paige*	P	1948–65	1971
Jim Palmer	P	1965–84	1990
Herb Pennock	P	1912–34	1948
Tony Perez	1B	1964–86	2000
Gaylord Perry	P	1962–83	1991
Eddie Plank	P	1901–17	1946
Kirby Puckett	OF	1984–95	2001
Charley Radbourn	P	1880–91	1939
Pee Wee Reese	SS	1940–58	1984
Jim Rice	OF	1974–89	2009
Sam Rice	OF	1915–35	1963
Cal Ripken Jr.	SS	1981–2001	2007
Eppa Rixey	P	1912–33	1963
Phil Rizzuto	SS	1941–56	1994
Robin Roberts	P	1948–66	1976
Brooks Robinson	3B	1955–77	1983
Frank Robinson	OF	1956–76	1982
Jackie Robinson	2B	1947–56	1962
Joe (Bullet) Rogan*	P		1998
Edd Roush	OF	1913–31	1962
Red Ruffing	P	1924–47	1967
Amos Rusie	P	1889–1901	1977
Babe Ruth	OF	1914–35	1936
Nolan Ryan	P	1966–93	1999
Ryne Sandberg	2B	1981–97	2005
Ron Santo	3B	1960–74	2012
Louis Santop*	C	1909–26	2006
Ray Schalk	C	1912–29	1955
Mike Schmidt	3B	1972–89	1995
Red Schoendienst	2B	1945–63	1989
Tom Seaver	P	1967–86	1992
Joe Sewell	SS	1920–33	1977
Al Simmons	OF	1924–44	1953
George Sisler	1B	1915–30	1939
Enos Slaughter	OF	1938–59	1985
Hilton Smith*	P		2001
Ozzie Smith	SS	1978–96	2002
Duke Snider	OF	1947–64	1980
Warren Spahn	P	1942–65	1973
Al Spalding	P	1871–78	1939
Tris Speaker	OF	1907–28	1937
Willie Stargell	OF-1B	1962–82	1988
Turkey Stearns*	CF		2000
Don Sutton	P	1966–88	1998
Bruce Sutter	P	1976–88	2006
George Suttles*	C	1923–44	2006
Benjamin Harrison Taylor*	P-1B	1908–29	2006
Bill Terry	1B	1923–36	1954
Sam Thompson	OF	1885–1906	1974
Joe Tinker	SS	1902–16	1946
Cristóbal Torriente*	OF	1913–32	2006
Pie Traynor	3B	1920–37	1948
Dazzy Vance	P	1915–35	1955
Arky Vaughan	SS	1932–48	1985
Rube Waddell	P	1897–1910	1946
Honus Wagner	SS	1897–1917	1936
Bobby Wallace	SS	1894–1918	1953
Ed Walsh	P	1904–17	1946
Lloyd Waner	OF	1927–45	1967
Paul Waner	OF	1926–45	1952
John Ward	2B-P	1878–94	1964
Mickey Welch	P	1880–92	1973
Willie Wells*	SS	1924–49	1997
Zach Wheat	OF	1909–27	1959
Hoyt Wilhelm	P	1952–72	1985
Billy Williams	OF	1959–76	1987
Ted Williams	OF	1939–60	1966
Vic Willis	P	1898–1910	1995
Ernest Judson Wilson*	3B	1922–45	2006
Hack Wilson	OF	1923–34	1979
Dave Winfield	OF	1973–95	2001
Early Wynn	P	1939–63	1972
Carl Yastrzemski	OF	1961–83	1989
Cy Young	P	1890–1911	1937
Ross Youngs	OF	1917–26	1972
Robin Yount	SS	1974–93	1999

*Elected on the basis of their career in the Negro leagues.

Pioneers/Executives

	Selected
Ed Barrow (manager-executive)	1953
Morgan Bulkeley (executive)	1937
Alexander Cartwright (executive)	1938
Henry Chadwick (writer-executive)	1938
Happy Chandler (commissioner)	1982
Charles Comiskey (manager-executive)	1939
Barney Dreyfuss (executive)	2008
Ford Frick (commissioner-executive)	1970
Warren Giles (executive)	1979
Pat Gillick (executive)	2011
Clark Griffith (executive)	1946
Will Harridge (executive)	1972
William Hulbert (executive)	1995
Ban Johnson (executive)	1937
Bowie Kuhn (commissioner)	2008
Kenesaw M. Landis (commissioner)	1944
Larry MacPhail Sr. (executive)	1978
Lee MacPhail Jr. (executive)	1998
Effa Manley (executive)	2006
Walter O'Malley (executive)	2008
Alex Pompez (executive)	2006
Cum Posey (player-manager-owner)	2006
Branch Rickey (manager-executive)	1967
Al Spalding (player-executive)	1939
Bill Veeck Jr. (owner)	1991
George Weiss (executive)	1971
Sol White (player-manager)	2006
J.L. Wilkinson (executive)	2006
George Wright (player-manager)	1937
Harry Wright (player-manager-executive)	1953
Tom Yawkey (executive)	1980

Managers

	Managed	Selected
Walter Alston	1954–76	1983
Sparky Anderson	1970–94	2000
Leo Durocher	1939–73	1994
Rube Foster	1907–26	1981
Ned Hanlon	1899–1907	1996
Bucky Harris	1924–56	1975
Miller Huggins	1913–29	1964
Tommy Lasorda	1977–96	1997
Al Lopez	1951–69	1977
Connie Mack	1894–1950	1937
Joe McCarthy	1926–50	1957
John McGraw	1899–1932	1937
Bill McKechnie	1915–46	1962
Wilbert Robinson	1902–31	1945
Frank Selee	1890–1905	1999
Billy Southworth	1929, 1940–51	2008
Casey Stengel	1934–65	1966
Earl Weaver	1968–82, 85–86	1996
Dick Williams	1967–69, 71–88	2008
Whitey Herzog	1973–90	2010

Umpires

	Selected
Al Barlick	1989
Nestor Chylak	1999
Jocko Conlan	1974
Tom Connolly	1953
Billy Evans	1973
Doug Harvey	2010
Cal Hubbard	1976
Bill Klem	1953
Bill McGowan	1992

Notable Achievements

No-Hit Games, Nine Innings or More

NATIONAL LEAGUE

Date	Pitcher and Game
1876......July 15	George Bradley, StL vs Hart 2–0
1880......June 12	John Richmond, Wor vs Clev 1–0 (perfect game)
June 17	Monte Ward, Prov vs Buff 5–0 (perfect game)
Aug 19	Larry Corcoran, Chi vs Bos 6–0
Aug 20	Pud Galvin, Buff vs Wor 1–0
1882......Sept 20	Larry Corcoran, Chi vs Wor 5–0
Sept 22	Tim Lovett, Bklyn vs NY 4–0
1883......July 25	Hoss Radbourn, Prov vs Clev 8–0
Sept 13	Hugh Daily, Clev vs Phi 1–0
1884......June 27	Larry Corcoran, Chi vs Prov 6–0
Aug 4	Pud Galvin, Buff vs Det 18–0
1885......July 27	John Clarkson, Chi vs Prov 4–0
Aug 29	Charles Ferguson, Phi vs Prov 1–0
1891......June 22	Tom Lovett, Bklyn vs NY 4–0
July 31	Amos Rusie, NY vs Bklyn 6–0
1892......Aug 6	Jack Stivetts, Bos vs Bklyn 11–0
Aug 22	Alex Sanders, Lou vs Balt 6–2
Oct 15	Bumpus Jones, Cin vs Pitt 7–1 (Jones' first major league game)
1893......Aug 16	Bill Hawke, Balt vs Wash 5–0
1897......Sept 18	Cy Young, Clev vs Cin 6–0
1898......Apr 22	Ted Breitenstein, Cin vs Pitt 11–0
Apr 22	Jim Hughes, Balt vs Bos 8–0
July 8	Frank Donahue, Phi vs Bos 5–0
Aug 21	Walter Thornton, Chi vs Bklyn 2–0
1899......May 25	Deacon Phillippe, Lou vs NY 7–0
Aug 7	Vic Willis, Bos vs Wash 7–1
1900......July 12	Noodles Hahn, Cin vs Phi 4–0
1901......July 15	Christy Mathewson, NY vs StL 5–0
1903......Sept 18	Chick Fraser, Phi vs Chi 10–0
1904......June 11	Bob Wicker, Chi at NY 1–0 (hit in 10th; won in 12th)
1905......June 13	Christy Mathewson, NY vs Chi 1–0
1906......May 1	John Lush, Phi vs Bklyn 6–0
July 20	Mal Eason, Bklyn vs StL 2–0
Aug 1	Harry McIntire, Bklyn vs Pitt 0–1 (hit in 11th; lost in 13th)
1907......May 8	Frank Pfeffer, Bos vs Cin 6–0
Sept 20	Nick Maddox, Pitt vs Bklyn 2–1
1908......July 4	George Wiltse, NY vs Phi 1–0 (10 innings)
Sept 5	Nap Rucker, Bklyn vs Bos 6–0
1909......Apr 15	Leon Ames, NY vs Bklyn 0–3 (hit in 10th; lost in 13th)
1912......Sept 6	Jeff Tesreau, NY vs Phi 3–0
1914......Sept 9	George Davis, Bos vs Phi 7–0
1915......Apr 15	Rube Marquard, NY vs Bklyn 2–0
Aug 31	Jimmy Lavender, Chi vs NY 2–0
1916......June 16	Tom Hughes, Bos vs Pitt 2–0
1917......May 2	Jim Vaughn, Chi vs Cin 0–1 (hit in 10th; lost in 10th)
May 2	Fred Toney, Cin vs Chi 1–0 (10 innings)

No-Hit Games, Nine Innings or More *(Cont.)*

NATIONAL LEAGUE *(Cont.)*

Date	Pitcher and Game	Date	Pitcher and Game
1919......May 11	Hod Eller, Cin vs StL 6–0	1973......Aug 5	Phil Niekro, Atl vs SD 9–0
1922......May 7	Jesse Barnes, NY vs Phi 6–0	1975......Aug 24	Ed Halicki, SF vs NY 6–0
1924......July 17	Jesse Haines, StL vs Bos 5–0	1976......July 9	Larry Dierker, Hou vs Mtl 6–0
1925......Sept 13	Dazzy Vance, Bklyn vs Phi 10–1	Aug 9	John Candelaria, Pitt vs LA 2–0
1929......May 8	Carl Hubbell, NY vs Pitt 11–0	Sept 29	John Montefusco, SF vs Atl 9–0
1934......Sept 21	Paul Dean, StL vs Bklyn 3–0	1978......Apr 16	Bob Forsch, StL vs Phi 5–0
1938......June 11	Johnny Vander Meer, Cin vs Bos 3–0	June 16	Tom Seaver, Cin vs StL 4–0
June 15	Johnny Vander Meer, Cin vs Bklyn 6–0	1979......Apr 7	Ken Forsch, Hou vs Atl 6–0
1940......Apr 30	Tex Carleton, Bklyn vs Cin, 3–0	1980......June 27	Jerry Reuss, LA vs SF 8–0
1941......Aug 30	Lon Warneke, StL vs Cin 2–0	1981......May 10	Charlie Lea, Mtl vs SF 4–0
1944......Apr 27	Jim Tobin, Bos vs Bklyn 2–0	Sept 26	Nolan Ryan, Hou vs LA 5–0
May 15	Clyde Shoun, Cin vs Bos 1–0	1983......Sept 26	Bob Forsch, StL vs Mtl 3–0
1946......Apr 23	Ed Head, Bklyn vs Bos 5–0	1986......Sept 25	Mike Scott, Hou vs SF 2–0
1947......June 18	Ewell Blackwell, Cin vs Bos 6–0	1988......Sept 16	Tom Browning, Cin vs LA 1–0
1948......Sept 9	Rex Barney, Bklyn vs NY 2–0		(perfect game)
1950......Aug 11	Vern Bickford, Bos vs Bklyn 7–0	1990......June 29	Fernando Valenzuela, LA vs StL 6–0
1951......May 6	Cliff Chambers, Pitt vs Bos 3–0	Aug 15	Terry Mulholland, Phi vs SF 6–0
1952......June 19	Carl Erskine, Bklyn vs Chi 5–0	1991......May 23	Tommy Greene, Phi vs Mtl 2–0
1954......June 12	Jim Wilson, Mil vs Phi 2–0	July 26	Mark Gardner, Mtl vs LA 0–1
1955......May 12	Sam Jones, Chi vs Pitt 4–0		(hit in 10th, lost in 10th)
1956......May 12	Carl Erskine, Bklyn vs NY 3–0	July 28	Dennis Martinez, Mtl vs LA 2–0
Sept 25	Sal Maglie, Bklyn vs Phi 5–0		(perfect game)
1959......May 26	Harvey Haddix, Pitt vs Mil 0–1	Sept 11	Kent Mercker (6), Mark Wohlers (2),
	(hit in 13th; lost in 13th)		and Alejandro Pena (1), Atl vs SD 1–0
1960......May 15	Don Cardwell, Chi vs StL 4–0	1992......Aug 17	Kevin Gross, LA vs SF 2–0
Aug 18	Lew Burdette, Mil vs Phi 1–0	1993......Sept 8	Darryl Kile, Hou vs NY 7–1
Sept 16	Warren Spahn, Mil vs Phi 4–0	1994......Apr 8	Kent Mercker, Atl vs LA 6–0
1961......Apr 28	Warren Spahn, Mil vs SF 1–0	1995......June 3	Pedro Martinez, Mtl vs SD 1–0
1962......June 30	Sandy Koufax, LA vs NY 5–0		(perfect through nine, hit in 10th)
1963......May 11	Sandy Koufax, LA vs SF 8–0	July 14	Ramon Martinez, LA vs Fla 7–0
May 17	Don Nottebart, Hou vs Phi 4–1	1996......May 11	Al Leiter, Fla vs Col 11–0
June 15	Juan Marichal, SF vs Hou 1–0	Sept 17	Hideo Nomo, LA vs Col 9–0
1964......Apr 23	Ken Johnson, Hou vs Cin 0–1	1997......June 10	Kevin Brown, Fla vs SF 9–0
June 4	Sandy Koufax, LA vs Phi 3–0	July 12	Francisco Cordova (9) and
June 21	Jim Bunning, Phi vs NY 6–0		Ricardo Rincon (1), Pitt vs Col 3–0
	(perfect game)	1999......June 25	Jose Jimenez, StL vs Ariz 1–0
1965......June 14	Jim Maloney, Cin vs NY 0–1	2001......May 12	A.J. Burnett, Fla vs SD 3–0
	(hit in 11th; lost in 11th)	Sept 3	Bud Smith, StL vs SD 4–0
Aug 19	Jim Maloney, Cin vs Chi 1–0	2003......April 27	Kevin Millwood, Phi vs SF 1–0
	(10 innings)	June 11	‡R. Oswalt (1), P. Munro (2.2), K.
Sept 9	Sandy Koufax, LA vs Chi 1–0		Saarloos (1.1), B. Lidge (2), O. Dotel
	(perfect game)		(1), B. Wagner (1), Hou vs NYY 8–0
1967......June 18	Don Wilson, Hou vs Atl 2–0	2004......May 18	Randy Johnson, Ariz vs Atl 2–0
1968......July 29	George Culver, Cin vs Phi 6–1		(perfect game)
Sept 17	Gaylord Perry, SF vs StL 1–0	2006......Sept 6	Anibal Sanchez, Fla vs Ariz 2–0
Sept 18	Ray Washburn, StL vs SF 2–0	2008......Sept 14	†Carlos Zambrano, Chi vs Hou 5–0
1969......Apr 17	Bill Stoneman, Mtl vs Phi 7–0	2009......July 10	Jonathan Sanchez, SF vs SD 8–0
Apr 30	Jim Maloney, Cin vs Hou 10–0	2010......Apr 17	Ubaldo Jimenez, Col vs Atl 4–0
May 1	Don Wilson, Hou vs Cin 4–0	May 29	Roy Halladay, Phi vs Fla 1–0
Aug 19	Ken Holtzman, Chi vs Atl 3–0		(perfect game)
Sept 20	Bob Moose, Pitt vs NY 4–0	June 26	‡Edwin Jackson, Ariz vs TB 1–0
1970......June 12	Dock Ellis, Pitt vs SD 2–0	Oct 6	Roy Halladay, Phi vs Cin 4–0
July 20	Bill Singer, LA vs Phi 5–0		(NLDS)
1971......June 3	Ken Holtzman, Chi vs Cin 1–0	2012......June 1	Johan Santana, NY vs. StL 8–0
June 23	Rick Wise, Phi vs Cin 4–0	June 13	Matt Cain, SF vs. Hou 10–0
Aug 14	Bob Gibson, StL vs Pitt 11–0	Sept 28	Homer Bailey, Cin vs. Pit 1–0
1972......Apr 16	Burt Hooton, Chi vs Phi 4–0	2013......July 2	Homer Bailey, Cin vs. SF 3–0
Sept 2	Milt Pappas, Chi vs SD 8–0	July 13	Tim Lincecum, SF vs SD 9–0
Oct 2	Bill Stoneman, Mtl vs NY 7–0	Sept 29	‡Henderson Alvarez, Mia vs Det 1–0

Note: Includes the games struck from the official record book on Sept. 4, 1991, when baseball's committee on statistical accuracy voted to define no-hitters as games of nine innings or more that end with a team getting no hits.

†Game played in Milwaukee due to weather-related closure of Houston's home field.

‡Interleague game.

No-Hit Games, Nine Innings or More *(Cont.)*

AMERICAN LEAGUE

Date	Pitcher and Game
1901......May 9	Earl Moore, Clev vs Chi 2–4 (hit in 10th; lost in 10th)
1902......Sept 20	Jimmy Callahan, Chi vs Det 3–0
1904......May 5	Cy Young, Bos vs Phi 3–0 (perfect game)
Aug 17	Jesse Tannehill, Bos vs Chi 6–0
1905......July 22	Weldon Henley, Phi vs StL 6–0
Sept 6	Frank Smith, Chi vs Det 15–0
Sept 27	Bill Dinneen, Bos vs Chi 2–0
1908......June 30	Cy Young, Bos vs NY 8–0
Sept 18	Bob Rhoades, Clev vs Bos 2–1
Sept 20	Frank Smith, Chi vs Phi 1–0
Oct 2	Addie Joss, Clev vs Chi 1–0 (perfect game)
1910......Apr 20	Addie Joss, Clev vs Chi 1–0
May 12	Chief Bender, Phi vs Clev 4–0
Aug 30	Tom Hughes, NY vs Clev 0–5 (hit in 10th; lost in 11th)
1911......July 29	Joe Wood, Bos vs StL 5–0
Aug 27	Ed Walsh, Chi vs Bos 5–0
1912......July 4	George Mullin, Det vs StL 7–0
Aug 30	Earl Hamilton, StL vs Det 5–1
1914......May 14	Jim Scott, Chi vs Wash 0–1 (hit in 10th; lost in 10th)
May 31	Joe Benz, Chi vs Clev 6–1
1916......June 21	George Foster, Bos vs NY 2–0
Aug 26	Joe Bush, Phi vs Clev 5–0
Aug 30	Dutch Leonard, Bos vs StL 4–0
1917......Apr 14	Ed Cicotte, Chi vs StL 11–0
Apr 24	George Mogridge, NY vs Bos 2–1
May 5	Ernie Koob, StL vs Chi 1–0
May 6	Bob Groom, StL vs Chi 3–0
June 23	Ernie Shore, Bos vs Wash 4–0 (perfect game)
1918......June 3	Dutch Leonard, Bos vs Det 5–0
1919......Sept 10	Ray Caldwell, Clev vs NY 3–0
1920......July 1	Walter Johnson, Wash vs Bos 1–0
1922......Apr 30	Charlie Robertson, Chi vs Det 2–0 (perfect game)
1923......Sept 4	Sam Jones, NY vs Phi 2–0
Sept 7	Howard Ehmke, Bos vs Phi 4–0
1926......Aug 21	Ted Lyons, Chi vs Bos 6–0
1931......Apr 29	Wes Ferrell, Clev vs StL 9–0
Aug 8	Bob Burke, Wash vs Bos 5–0
1934......Sept 18	Bobo Newsom, StL vs Bos 1–2 (hit in 10th; lost in 10th)
1935......Aug 31	Vern Kennedy, Chi vs Clev 5–0
1937......June 1	Bill Dietrich, Chi vs StL 8–0
1938......Aug 27	Monte Pearson, NY vs Clev 13–0
1940......Apr 16	Bob Feller, Clev vs Chi 1–0 (opening day)
1945......Sept 9	Dick Fowler, Phi vs StL 1–0
1946......Apr 30	Bob Feller, Clev vs NY 1–0
1947......July 10	Don Black, Clev vs Phi 3–0
Sep 3	Bill McCahan, Phi vs Wash 3–0
1948......June 30	Bob Lemon, Clev vs Det 2–0
1951......July 1	Bob Feller, Clev vs Det 2–1
July 12	Allie Reynolds, NY vs Clev 1–0
Sept 28	Allie Reynolds, NY vs Bos 8–0
1952......May 15	Virgil Trucks, Det vs Wash 1–0
Aug 25	Virgil Trucks, Det vs NY 1–0
1953......May 6	Bobo Holloman, StL vs Phi 6–0 (first major league start)
1956......July 14	Mel Parnell, Bos vs Chi 4–0
Oct 8	Don Larsen, NY (A) vs Bklyn (N) 2–0 (World Series) (perfect game)

Date	Pitcher and Game
1957......Aug 20	Bob Keegan, Chi vs Wash 6–0
1958......July 20	Jim Bunning, Det vs Bos 3–0
Sept 20	Hoyt Wilhelm, Balt vs NY 1–0
1962......May 5	Bo Belinsky, LA vs Balt 2–0
June 26	Earl Wilson, Bos vs LA 2–0
Aug 1	Bill Monbouquette, Bos vs Chi 1–0
Aug 26	Jack Kralick, Minn vs KC 1–0
1965......Sept 16	Dave Morehead, Bos vs Clev 2–0
1966......June 10	Sonny Siebert, Clev vs Wash 2–0
1967......Apr 30	Steve Barber (8⅔) and Stu Miller (⅓), Balt vs Det 1–2
Aug 25	Dean Chance, Minn vs Clev 2–1
Sept 10	Joel Horlen, Chi vs Det 6–0
1968......Apr 27	Tom Phoebus, Balt vs Bos 6–0
May 8	Jim (Catfish) Hunter, Oak vs Minn 4–0 (perfect game)
1969......Aug 13	Jim Palmer, Balt vs Oak 8–0
1970......July 3	Clyde Wright, Cal vs Oak 4–0
Sept 21	Vida Blue, Oak vs Minn 6–0
1973......Apr 27	Steve Busby, KC vs Det 3–0
May 15	Nolan Ryan, Cal vs KC 3–0
July 15	Nolan Ryan, Cal vs Det 6–0
July 30	Jim Bibby, Tex vs Oak 6–0
1974......June 19	Steve Busby, KC vs Mil 2–0
July 19	Dick Bosman, Clev vs Oak 4–0
Sept 28	Nolan Ryan, Cal vs Minn 4–0
1975......June 1	Nolan Ryan, Cal vs Balt 1–0
Sept 28	Vida Blue (5), Glenn Abbott (1), Paul Lindblad (1), Rollie Fingers (2), Oak vs Cal 5–0
1976......July 28	John Odom (5) and Francisco Barrios (4), Chi vs Oak 2–1
1977......May 14	Jim Colborn, KC vs Tex 6–0
May 30	Dennis Eckersley, Clev vs Cal 1–0
Sept 22	Bert Blyleven, Tex vs Cal 6–0
1981......May 15	Len Barker, Clev vs Tor 3–0 (perfect game)
1983......July 4	Dave Righetti, NY vs Bos 4–0
Sept 29	Mike Warren, Oak vs Chi 3–0
1984......Apr 7	Jack Morris, Det vs Chi 4–0
Sept 30	Mike Witt, Cal vs Tex 1–0 (perfect game)
1986......Sept 19	Joe Cowley, Chi vs Cal 7–1
1987......Apr 15	Juan Nieves, Mil vs Balt 7–0
1990......Apr 11	Mark Langston (7), Mike Witt (2), Cal vs Sea 1–0
June 2	Randy Johnson, Sea vs Det 2–0
June 11	Nolan Ryan, Tex vs Oak 5–0
June 29	Dave Stewart, Oak vs Tor 5–0
July 1	Andy Hawkins, NY vs Chi 0–4 (eight no-hit innings in loss)
Sept 2	Dave Stieb, Tor vs Clev 3–0
1991......May 1	Nolan Ryan, Tex vs Tor 3–0
July 13	Bob Milacki (6), Mike Flanagan (1), Mark Williamson (1), and Gregg Olson (1), Balt vs Oak 2–0
Aug 11	Wilson Alvarez, Chi vs Balt 7–0
Aug 26	Bret Saberhagen, KC vs Chi 7–0
1993......Apr 22	Chris Bosio, Sea vs Bos 7–0
Sept 4	Jim Abbott, NY vs Clev 4–0
1994......Apr 27	Scott Erickson, Minn vs Mil 6–0
July 28	Kenny Rogers, Texas vs Cal 4–0 (perfect game)
1996......May 14	Dwight Gooden, NY vs Sea 2–0

No-Hit Games, Nine Innings or More *(Cont.)*

AMERICAN LEAGUE *(Cont.)*

Date	Pitcher and Game	Date	Pitcher and Game
1998......May 17	David Wells, NY vs Minn 4–0 (perfect game)	2009......July 23	Mark Buehrle, Chi vs TB 5–0 (perfect game)
1999......July 18	David Cone, NY vs Mtl 6–0 (perfect game)	2010......May 9	Dallas Braden, Oak vs TB 4–0 (perfect game)
Sept 11	Eric Milton, Minn vs Ana 7–0	July 26	Matt Garza, TB vs Det 5–0
2001......Apr 4	Hideo Nomo, Bos vs Balt 3–0	2011......May 3	Francisco Liriano, Min vs Chi 1–0
2002......Apr 27	Derek Lowe, Bos vs TB 10–0	May 7	Justin Verlander, Det vs Tor 9–0
2007......Apr 19	Mark Buehrle, Chi vs Tex, 6–0	July 27	Ervin Santana, LA vs Cle 3–1
June 12	Justin Verlander, Det vs Mil 4–0	2012......April 21	Philip Humber, Chi vs. Sea 4–0
Sep 1	Clay Buchholz, Bos vs Balt 10–0	May 2	Jered Weaver, LA vs. Min 9–0
2008......May 19	Jon Lester, Bos vs KC 7–0		

Longest Hitting Streaks

NATIONAL LEAGUE

Player and Team	Year	G
Willie Keeler, Balt	1897	44
Pete Rose, Cin	1978	44
Bill Dahlen, Chi	1894	42
Tommy Holmes, Bos	1945	37
Billy Hamilton, Phi	1894	36
Jimmy Rollins, Phi	2005–06	36
Fred Clarke, Lou	1895	35
Luis Castillo, Fla	2002	35
Chase Utley, Phi	2006	35
Benito Santiago, SD	1987	34
George Davis, NY	1893	33
Rogers Hornsby, StL	1922	33
Dan Uggla, Atl	2011	33

AMERICAN LEAGUE

Player and Team	Year	G
Joe DiMaggio, NY	1941	56
George Sisler, StL	1922	41
Ty Cobb, Det	1911	40
Paul Molitor, Mil	1987	39
Ty Cobb, Det	1917	35
George Sisler, StL	1925	34
George McQuinn, StL	1938	34
Dom DiMaggio, Bos	1949	34
Hal Chase, NY	1907	33
Heinie Manush, Wash	1933	33

Triple Crown Hitters

NATIONAL LEAGUE

Player and Team	Year	HR	RBI	BA
Paul Hines, Prov	1878	4	50	.358
Hugh Duffy, Bos	1894	18	145	.438
Heinie Zimmerman*, Chi	1912	14	103	.372
Rogers Hornsby, StL	1922	42	152	.401
	1925	39	143	.403
Chuck Klein, Phi	1933	28	120	.368
Joe Medwick, StL	1937	31	154	.374

*Zimmerman ranked first in RBIs as calculated by Ernie Lanigan, but only third as calculated by Information Concepts Inc.

AMERICAN LEAGUE

Player and Team	Year	HR	RBI	BA
Nap Lajoie, Phi	1901	14	125	.422
Ty Cobb, Det	1909	9	115	.377
Jimmie Foxx, Phi	1933	48	163	.356
Lou Gehrig, NY	1934	49	165	.363
Ted Williams, Bos	1942	36	137	.356
	1947	32	114	.343
Mickey Mantle, NY	1956	52	130	.353
Frank Robinson, Balt	1966	49	122	.316
Carl Yastrzemski, Bos	1967	44	121	.326
Miguel Cabrera, Det	2012	44	139	.330

Triple Crown Pitchers

NATIONAL LEAGUE

Player and Team	Year	W	L	SO	ERA
Tommy Bond, Bos	1877	40	17	170	2.11
Hoss Radbourn, Prov	1884	60	12	441	1.38
Tim Keefe, NY	1888	35	12	333	1.74
John Clarkson, Bos	1889	49	19	284	2.73
Amos Rusie, NY	1894	36	13	195	2.78
Christy Mathewson, NY	1905	31	8	206	1.27
	1908	37	11	259	1.43
Grover Alexander, Phi	1915	31	10	241	1.22
	1916	33	12	167	1.55
	1917	30	13	201	1.86
Hippo Vaughn, Chi	1918	22	10	148	1.74
Dazzy Vance, Bklyn	1924	28	6	262	2.16
Bucky Walters, Cin	1939	27	11	137	2.29
Sandy Koufax, LA	1963	25	5	306	1.88
	1965	26	8	382	2.04
	1966	27	9	317	1.73
Steve Carlton, Phi	1972	27	10	310	1.97
Dwight Gooden, NY	1985	24	4	268	1.53
Randy Johnson, Ariz	2002	24	5	334	2.32
*Clayton Kershaw, LA	2011	21	5	248	2.28

AMERICAN LEAGUE

Player and Team	Year	W	L	SO	ERA
Cy Young, Bos	1901	33	10	158	1.62
Rube Waddell, Phi	1905	26	11	287	1.48
Walter Johnson, Wash	1913	36	7	303	1.09
	1918	23	13	162	1.27
	1924	23	7	158	2.72
Lefty Grove, Phi	1930	28	5	209	2.54
	1931	31	4	175	2.06
Lefty Gomez, NY	1934	26	5	158	2.33
	1937	21	11	194	2.33
Hal Newhouser, Det	1945	25	9	212	1.81
Roger Clemens, Tor	1997	21	7	292	2.05
	1998	20	6	271	2.64
Pedro Martinez, Bos	1999	23	4	313	2.07
*Johan Santana, Minn	2006	19	6	245	2.77
Justin Verlander, Det	2011	24	5	250	2.40

*Tied with another pitcher for most wins.

Consecutive Games Played,
500 or More Games

Cal Ripken Jr.	2,632	Sandy Alomar Sr.	648
Lou Gehrig	2,130	Eddie Brown	618
Everett Scott	1,307	Roy McMillan	585
Steve Garvey	1,207	George Pinckney	577
*Miguel Tejada	1,152	Steve Brodie	574
Billy Williams	1,117	Aaron Ward	565
Joe Sewell	1,103	Alex Rodriguez	546
Stan Musial	895	Candy LaChance	540
Eddie Yost	829	Buck Freeman	535
Gus Suhr	822	Fred Luderus	533
Nellie Fox	798	Hideki Matsui	518
Pete Rose	745	Clyde Milan	511
Dale Murphy	740	Charlie Gehringer	511
Richie Ashburn	730	Vada Pinson	508
Ernie Banks	717	*Prince Fielder	505
Pete Rose	678	Tony Cuccinello	504
Earl Averill	673	Charlie Gehringer	504
Frank McCormick	652		

*Active player in 2013.

Unassisted Triple Plays

Player and Team	Date	Pos	Opp	Opp Batter
Neal Ball, Clev	7-19-09	SS	Bos	Amby McConnell
Bill Wambsganss, Clev	10-10-20	2B	Bklyn	Clarence Mitchell
George Burns, Bos	9-14-23	1B	Clev	Frank Brower
Ernie Padgett, Bos	10-6-23	SS	Phi	Walter Holke
Glenn Wright, Pitt	5-7-25	SS	StL	Jim Bottomley
Jimmy Cooney, Chi	5-30-27	SS	Pitt	Paul Waner
Johnny Neun, Det	5-31-27	1B	Clev	Homer Summa
Ron Hansen, Wash	7-30-68	SS	Clev	Joe Azcue
Mickey Morandini, Phi	9-20-92	2B	Pitt	Jeff King
John Valentin, Bos	7-15-94	SS	Minn	Marc Newfield
Randy Velarde, Oak	5-29-00	2B	NYY	Shane Spencer
Rafael Furcal, Atl	8-10-03	SS	StL	Woody Williams
Troy Tulowitzki, Col	4-29-07	SS	Atl	Chipper Jones
Asdrubal Cabrera, Cle	5-12-08	2B	Tor	Lyle Overbay
Eric Bruntlett, Phi	8-23-09	2B	NYM	Jeff Francoeur

Year-by-Year Leaders

NATIONAL LEAGUE
Leading Batsmen

Year	Player and Team	BA	Year	Player and Team	BA
1900	Honus Wagner, Pitt	.381	1923	Rogers Hornsby, StL	.384
1901	Jesse Burkett, StL	.382	1924	Rogers Hornsby, StL	.424
1902	Ginger Beaumtl, Pitt	.357	1925	Rogers Hornsby, StL	.403
1903	Honus Wagner, Pitt	.355	1926	Bubbles Hargrave, Cin	.353
1904	Honus Wagner, Pitt	.349	1927	Paul Waner, Pitt	.380
1905	Cy Seymour, Cin	.377	1928	Rogers Hornsby, Bos	.387
1906	Honus Wagner, Pitt	.339	1929	Lefty O'Doul, Phi	.398
1907	Honus Wagner, Pitt	.350	1930	Bill Terry, NY	.401
1908	Honus Wagner, Pitt	.354	1931	Chick Hafey, StL	.349
1909	Honus Wagner, Pitt	.339	1932	Lefty O'Doul, Bklyn	.368
1910	Sherry Magee, Phi	.331	1933	Chuck Klein, Phi	.368
1911	Honus Wagner, Pitt	.334	1934	Paul Waner, Pitt	.362
1912	Heinie Zimmerman, Chi	.372	1935	Arky Vaughan, Pitt	.385
1913	Jake Daubert, Bklyn	.350	1936	Paul Waner, Pitt	.373
1914	Jake Daubert, Bklyn	.329	1937	Joe Medwick, StL	.374
1915	Larry Doyle, NY	.320	1938	Ernie Lombardi, Cin	.342
1916	Hal Chase, Cin	.339	1939	Johnny Mize, StL	.349
1917	Edd Roush, Cin	.341	1940	Debs Garms, Pitt	.355
1918	Zach Wheat, Bklyn	.335	1941	Pete Reiser, Bklyn	.343
1919	Edd Roush, Cin	.321	1942	Ernie Lombardi, Bos	.330
1920	Rogers Hornsby, StL	.370	1943	Stan Musial, StL	.357
1921	Rogers Hornsby, StL	.397	1944	Dixie Walker, Bklyn	.357
1922	Rogers Hornsby, StL	.401	1945	Phil Cavarretta, Chi	.355

NATIONAL LEAGUE *(Cont.)*
Leading Batsmen *(Cont.)*

Year	Player and Team	BA	Year	Player and Team	BA
1946	Stan Musial, St	.365	1981	Bill Madlock, Pitt	.341
1947	Harry Walker, StL-Phi	.363	1982	Al Oliver, Mtl	.331
1948	Stan Musial, StL	.376	1983	Bill Madlock, Pitt	.323
1949	Jackie Robinson, Bklyn	.342	1984	Tony Gwynn, SD	.351
1950	Stan Musial, StL	.346	1985	Willie McGee, StL	.353
1951	Stan Musial, StL	.355	1986	Tim Raines, Mtl	.334
1952	Stan Musial, StL	.336	1987	Tony Gwynn, SD	.370
1953	Carl Furillo, Bklyn	.344	1988	Tony Gwynn, SD	.313
1954	Willie Mays, NY	.345	1989	Tony Gwynn, SD	.336
1955	Richie Ashburn, Phi	.338	1990	Willie McGee, StL	.335
1956	Hank Aaron, Mil	.328	1991	Terry Pendleton, Atl	.319
1957	Stan Musial, StL	.351	1992	Gary Sheffield, SD	.330
1958	Richie Ashburn, Phi	.350	1993	Andres Galarraga, Col	.370
1959	Hank Aaron, Mil	.355	1994	Tony Gwynn, SD	.394
1960	Dick Groat, Pitt	.325	1995	Tony Gwynn, SD	.368
1961	Roberto Clemente, Pitt	.351	1996	Tony Gwynn, SD	.353
1962	Tommy Davis, LA	.346	1997	Tony Gwynn, SD	.372
1963	Tommy Davis, LA	.326	1998	Larry Walker, Col	.363
1964	Roberto Clemente, Pitt	.339	1999	Larry Walker, Col	.379
1965	Roberto Clemente, Pitt	.329	2000	Todd Helton, Col	.372
1966	Matty Alou, Pitt	.342	2001	Larry Walker, Col	.350
1967	Roberto Clemente, Pitt	.357	2002	Barry Bonds, SF	.370
1968	Pete Rose, Cin	.335	2003	Albert Pujols, StL	.359
1969	Pete Rose, Cin	.348	2004	Barry Bonds, SF	.362
1970	Rico Carty, Atl	.366	2005	Derrek Lee, Chi	.335
1971	Joe Torre, StL	.363	2006	Freddy Sanchez, Pitt	.334
1972	Billy Williams, Chi	.333	2007	Matt Holliday, Col	.340*
1973	Pete Rose, Cin	.338	2008	Chipper Jones, Atl	.364
1974	Ralph Garr, Atl	.353	2009	Hanley Ramirez, Fla	.342
1975	Bill Madlock, Chi	.354	2010	Carlos Gonzalez, Col	.336
1976	Bill Madlock, Chi	.339	2011	Jose Reyes, NY	.337
1977	Dave Parker, Pitt	.338	2012	Buster Posey, SF	.336
1978	Dave Parker, Pitt	.334	2013	Michael Cuddyer, Col	.331
1979	Keith Hernandez, StL	.344			
1980	Bill Buckner, Chi	.324			

*Includes one-game NL Wild Card tiebreaker.

Leaders in Runs Scored

Year	Player and Team	Runs	Year	Player and Team	Runs
1900	Roy Thomas, Phi	131	1925	Kiki Cuyler, Pitt	144
1901	Jesse Burkett, StL	139	1926	Kiki Cuyler, Pitt	113
1902	Honus Wagner, Pitt	105	1927	Lloyd Waner, Pitt	133
1903	Ginger Beaumont, Pitt	137		Rogers Hornsby, NY	133
1904	George Browne, NY	99	1928	Paul Waner, Pitt	142
1905	Mike Donlin, NY	124	1929	Rogers Hornsby, Chi	156
1906	Honus Wagner, Pitt	103	1930	Chuck Klein, Phi	158
	Frank Chance, Chi	103	1931	Bill Terry, NY	121
1907	Spike Shannon, NY	104		Chuck Klein, Phi	121
1908	Fred Tenney, NY	101	1932	Chuck Klein, Phi	152
1909	Tommy Leach, Pitt	126	1933	Pepper Martin, StL	122
1910	Sherry Magee, Phi	110	1934	Paul Waner, Pitt	122
1911	Jimmy Sheckard, Chi	121	1935	Augie Galan, Chi	133
1912	Bob Bescher, Cin	120	1936	Arky Vaughan, Pitt	122
1913	Tommy Leach, Chi	99	1937	Joe Medwick, StL	111
	Max Carey, Pitt	99	1938	Mel Ott, NY	116
1914	George Burns, NY	100	1939	Billy Werber, Cin	115
1915	Gavvy Cravath, Phi	89	1940	Arky Vaughan, Pitt	113
1916	George Burns, NY	105	1941	Pete Reiser, Bklyn	117
1917	George Burns, NY	103	1942	Mel Ott, NY	118
1918	Heinie Groh, Cin	88	1943	Arky Vaughan, Bklyn	112
1919	George Burns, NY	86	1944	Bill Nicholson, Chi	116
1920	George Burns, NY	115	1945	Eddie Stanky, Bklyn	128
1921	Rogers Hornsby, StL	131	1946	Stan Musial, StL	124
1922	Rogers Hornsby, StL	141	1947	Johnny Mize, NY	137
1923	Ross Youngs, NY	121	1948	Stan Musial, StL	135
1924	Frankie Frisch, NY	121	1949	Pee Wee Reese, Bklyn	132
	Rogers Hornsby, StL	121	1950	Earl Torgeson, Bos	120

NATIONAL LEAGUE (Cont.)
Leaders in Runs Scored (Cont.)

Year	Player and Team	Runs	Year	Player and Team	Runs
1951	Ralph Kiner, Pitt	124	1982	Lonnie Smith, StL	120
	Stan Musial, StL	124	1983	Tim Raines, Mtl	133
1952	Solly Hemus, StL	105	1984	Ryne Sandberg, Chi	114
	Stan Musial, StL	105	1985	Dale Murphy, Atl	118
1953	Duke Snider, Bklyn	132	1986	Von Hayes, Phi	107
1954	Stan Musial, StL	120		Tony Gwynn, SD	107
	Duke Snider, Bklyn	120	1987	Tim Raines, Mtl	123
1955	Duke Snider, Bklyn	126	1988	Brett Butler, SF	109
1956	Frank Robinson, Cin	122	1989	Will Clark, SF	104
1957	Hank Aaron, Mil	118		Howard Johnson, NY	104
1958	Willie Mays, SF	121		Ryne Sandberg, Chi	104
1959	Vada Pinson, Cin	131	1990	Ryne Sandberg, Chi	116
1960	Bill Bruton, Mil	112	1991	Brett Butler, LA	112
1961	Willie Mays, SF	129	1992	Barry Bonds, Pitt	109
1962	Frank Robinson, Cin	134	1993	Lenny Dykstra, Phi	143
1963	Hank Aaron, Mil	121	1994	Jeff Bagwell, Hou	104
1964	Dick Allen, Phi	125	1995	Craig Biggio, Hou	123
1965	Tommy Harper, Cin	126	1996	Ellis Burks, Col	142
1966	Felipe Alou, Atl	122	1997	Craig Biggio, Hou	146
1967	Hank Aaron, Atl	113	1998	Sammy Sosa, Chi	134
	Lou Brock, StL	113	1999	Jeff Bagwell, Hou	143
1968	Glenn Beckert, Chi	98	2000	Jeff Bagwell, Hou	152
1969	Bobby Bonds, SF	120	2001	Sammy Sosa, Chi	146
	Pete Rose, Cin	120	2002	Sammy Sosa, Chi	122
1970	Billy Williams, Chi	137	2003	Albert Pujols, StL	137
1971	Lou Brock, StL	126	2004	Albert Pujols, StL	133
1972	Joe Morgan, Cin	122	2005	Albert Pujols, StL	129
1973	Bobby Bonds, SF	131	2006	Chase Utley, Phi	131
1974	Pete Rose, Cin	110	2007	Jimmy Rollins, Phi	139
1975	Pete Rose, Cin	112	2008	Hanley Ramirez, Fla	125
1976	Pete Rose, Cin	130	2009	Albert Pujols, StL	124
1977	George Foster, Cin	124	2010	Albert Pujols, StL	115
1978	Ivan DeJesus, Chi	104	2011	Matt Kemp, LA	115
1979	Keith Hernandez, StL	116	2012	Ryan Braun, Mil	108
1980	Keith Hernandez, StL	111	2013	Matt Carpenter, StL	126
1981	Mike Schmidt, Phi	78			

Leaders in Hits

Year	Player and Team	Hits	Year	Player and Team	Hits
1900	Willie Keeler, Bklyn	208	1927	Paul Waner, Pitt	237
1901	Jesse Burkett, StL	228	1928	Freddy Lindstrom, NY	231
1902	Ginger Beaumont, Pitt	194	1929	Lefty O'Doul, Phi	254
1903	Ginger Beaumont, Pitt	209	1930	Bill Terry, NY	254
1904	Ginger Beaumont, Pitt	185	1931	Lloyd Waner, Pitt	214
1905	Cy Seymour, Cin	219	1932	Chuck Klein, Phi	226
1906	Harry Steinfeldt, Chi	176	1933	Chuck Klein, Phi	223
1907	Ginger Beaumont, Bos	187	1934	Paul Waner, Pitt	217
1908	Honus Wagner, Pitt	201	1935	Billy Herman, Chi	227
1909	Larry Doyle, NY	172	1936	Joe Medwick, StL	223
1910	Bobby Byrne, Pitt	178	1937	Joe Medwick, StL	237
	Honus Wagner, Pitt	178	1938	Frank McCormick, Cin	209
1911	Doc Miller, Bos	192	1939	Frank McCormick, Cin	209
1912	Heinie Zimmerman, Chi	207	1940	Stan Hack, Chi	191
1913	Gavvy Cravath, Phi	179		Frank McCormick, Cin	191
1914	Sherry Magee, Phi	171	1941	Stan Hack, Chi	186
1915	Larry Doyle, NY	189	1942	Enos Slaughter, StL	188
1916	Hal Chase, Cin	184	1943	Stan Musial, StL	220
1917	Heinie Groh, Cin	182	1944	Phil Cavarretta, Chi	197
1918	Charlie Hollocher, Chi	161		Stan Musial, StL	197
1919	Ivy Olson, Bklyn	164	1945	Tommy Holmes, Bos	224
1920	Rogers Hornsby, StL	218	1946	Stan Musial, StL	228
1921	Rogers Hornsby, StL	235	1947	Tommy Holmes, Bos	191
1922	Rogers Hornsby, StL	250	1948	Stan Musial, StL	230
1923	Frankie Frisch, NY	223	1949	Stan Musial, StL	207
1924	Rogers Hornsby, StL	227	1950	Duke Snider, Bklyn	199
1925	Jim Bottomley, StL	227	1951	Richie Ashburn, Phi	221
1926	Eddie Brown, Bos	201	1952	Stan Musial, StL	194

NATIONAL LEAGUE *(Cont.)*
Leaders in Hits *(Cont.)*

Year	Player and Team	Hits	Year	Player and Team	Hits
1953	Richie Ashburn, Phi	205	1984	Tony Gwynn, SD	213
1954	Don Mueller, NY	212	1985	Willie McGee, StL	216
1955	Ted Kluszewski, Cin	192	1986	Tony Gwynn, SD	211
1956	Hank Aaron, Mil	200	1987	Tony Gwynn, SD	218
1957	Red Schoendienst, NY-Mil	200	1988	Andres Galarraga, Mtl	184
1958	Richie Ashburn, Phi	215	1989	Tony Gwynn, SD	203
1959	Hank Aaron, Mil	223	1990	Brett Butler, SF	192
1960	Willie Mays, SF	190		Lenny Dykstra, Phi	192
1961	Vada Pinson, Cin	208	1991	Terry Pendleton, Atl	187
1962	Tommy Davis, LA	230	1992	Terry Pendleton, Atl	199
1963	Vada Pinson, Cin	204		Andy Van Slyke, Pitt	199
1964	Roberto Clemente, Pitt	211	1993	Lenny Dykstra, Phi	194
	Curt Flood, StL	211	1994	Tony Gwynn, SD	165
1965	Pete Rose, Cin	209	1995	Dante Bichette, Col	197
1966	Felipe Alou, Atl	218		Tony Gwynn, SD	197
1967	Roberto Clemente, Pitt	209	1996	Lance Johnson, NY	227
1968	Felipe Alou, Atl	210	1997	Tony Gwynn, SD	220
	Pete Rose, Cin	210	1998	Dante Bichette, Col	219
1969	Matty Alou, Pitt	231	1999	Luis Gonzalez, Ariz	206
1970	Pete Rose, Cin	205	2000	Todd Helton, Col	216
	Billy Williams, Chi	205	2001	Rich Aurilia, SF	206
1971	Joe Torre, StL	230	2002	Vladimir Guerrero, Mon	206
1972	Pete Rose, Cin	198	2003	Albert Pujols, StL	212
1973	Pete Rose, Cin	230	2004	Juan Pierre, Fla	221
1974	Ralph Garr, Atl	214	2005	Derrek Lee, Chi	199
1975	Dave Cash, Phi	213	2006	Juan Pierre, Chi	204
1976	Pete Rose, Cin	215	2007	Matt Holliday, Col	216*
1977	Dave Parker, Pitt	215	2008	Jose Reyes, NY	204
1978	Steve Garvey, LA	202	2009	Ryan Braun, Mil	203
1979	Garry Templeton, StL	211	2010	Carlos Gonzalez, Col	197
1980	Steve Garvey, LA	200	2011	Starlin Castro, Chi	207
1981	Pete Rose, Phi	140	2012	Andrew McCutchen, Pitt	194
1982	Al Oliver, Mtl	204	2013	Matt Carpenter, StL	199
1983	Jose Cruz, Hou	189			
	Andre Dawson, Mtl	189	*Includes one-game NL Wild Card tiebreaker.		

Home Run Leaders

Year	Player and Team	HR	Year	Player and Team	HR
1900	Herman Long, Bos	12	1924	Jack Fournier, Bklyn	27
1901	Sam Crawford, Cin	16	1925	Rogers Hornsby, StL	39
1902	Tommy Leach, Pitt	6	1926	Hack Wilson, Chi	21
1903	Jimmy Sheckard, Bklyn	9	1927	Cy Williams, Phi	30
1904	Harry Lumley, Bklyn	9		Hack Wilson, Chi	30
1905	Fred Odwell, Cin	9	1928	Jim Bottomley, StL	31
1906	Tim Jordan, Bklyn	12		Hack Wilson, Chi	31
1907	Dave Brain, Bos	10	1929	Chuck Klein, Phi	43
1908	Tim Jordan, Bklyn	12	1930	Hack Wilson, Chi	56
1909	Red Murray, NY	7	1931	Chuck Klein, Phi	31
1910	Fred Beck, Bos	10	1932	Chuck Klein, Phi	38
	Wildfire Schulte, Chi	10		Mel Ott, NY	38
1911	Wildfire Schulte, Chi	21	1933	Chuck Klein, Phi	28
1912	Heinie Zimmerman, Chi	14	1934	Ripper Collins, StL	35
1913	Gavvy Cravath, Phi	19		Mel Ott, NY	35
1914	Gavvy Cravath, Phi	19	1935	Wally Berger, Bos	34
1915	Gavvy Cravath, Phi	24	1936	Mel Ott, NY	33
1916	Dave Robertson, NY	12	1937	Joe Medwick, StL	31
	Cy Williams, Chi	12		Mel Ott, NY	31
1917	Gavvy Cravath, Phi	12	1938	Mel Ott, NY	36
	Dave Robertson, NY	12	1939	Johnny Mize, StL	28
1918	Gavvy Cravath, Phi	8	1940	Johnny Mize, StL	43
1919	Gavvy Cravath, Phi	12	1941	Dolph Camilli, Bklyn	34
1920	Cy Williams, Phi	15	1942	Mel Ott, NY	30
1921	George Kelly, NY	23	1943	Bill Nicholson, Chi	29
1922	Rogers Hornsby, StL	42	1944	Bill Nicholson, Chi	33
1923	Cy Williams, Phi	41	1945	Tommy Holmes, Bos	28

NATIONAL LEAGUE *(Cont.)*
Home Run Leaders *(Cont.)*

Year	Player and Team	HR	Year	Player and Team	HR
1946	Ralph Kiner, Pitt	23	1979	Dave Kingman, Chi	48
1947	Ralph Kiner, Pitt	51	1980	Mike Schmidt, Phi	48
	Johnny Mize, NY	51	1981	Mike Schmidt, Phi	31
1948	Ralph Kiner, Pitt	40	1982	Dave Kingman, NY	37
	Johnny Mize, NY	40	1983	Mike Schmidt, Phi	40
1949	Ralph Kiner, Pitt	54	1984	Dale Murphy, Atl	36
1950	Ralph Kiner, Pitt	47		Mike Schmidt, Phi	36
1951	Ralph Kiner, Pitt	42	1985	Dale Murphy, Atl	37
1952	Ralph Kiner, Pitt	37	1986	Mike Schmidt, Phi	37
	Hank Sauer, Chi	37	1987	Andre Dawson, Chi	49
1953	Eddie Mathews, Mil	47	1988	Darryl Strawberry, NY	39
1954	Ted Kluszewski, Cin	49	1989	Kevin Mitchell, SF	47
1955	Willie Mays, NY	51	1990	Ryne Sandberg, Chi	40
1956	Duke Snider, Bklyn	43	1991	Howard Johnson, NY	38
1957	Hank Aaron, Mil	44	1992	Fred McGriff, SD	35
1958	Ernie Banks, Chi	47	1993	Barry Bonds, SF	46
1959	Eddie Mathews, Mil	46	1994	Matt Williams, SF	43
1960	Ernie Banks, Chi	41	1995	Dante Bichette, Col	40
1961	Orlando Cepeda, SF	46	1996	Andres Galarraga, Col	47
1962	Willie Mays, SF	49	1997	Larry Walker, Col	49
1963	Hank Aaron, Mil	44	1998	Mark McGwire, StL	70
	Willie McCovey, SF	44	1999	Mark McGwire, StL	65
1964	Willie Mays, SF	47	2000	Sammy Sosa, Chi	50
1965	Willie Mays, SF	52	2001	Barry Bonds, SF	73
1966	Hank Aaron, Atl	44	2002	Sammy Sosa, Chi	49
1967	Hank Aaron, Atl	39	2003	Jim Thome, Phi	47
1968	Willie McCovey, SF	36	2004	Adrian Beltre, LA	48
1969	Willie McCovey, SF	45	2005	Andruw Jones, Atl	51
1970	Johnny Bench, Cin	45	2006	Ryan Howard, Phi	58
1971	Willie Stargell, Pitt	48	2007	Prince Fielder, Mil	50
1972	Johnny Bench, Cin	40	2008	Ryan Howard, Phi	48
1973	Willie Stargell, Pitt	44	2009	Albert Pujols, StL	47
1974	Mike Schmidt, Phi	36	2010	Albert Pujols, StL	42
1975	Mike Schmidt, Phi	38	2011	Matt Kemp, LA	39
1976	Mike Schmidt, Phi	38	2012	Ryan Braun, Mil	41
1977	George Foster, Cin	52	2013	Pedro Alvarez, Pitt	36
1978	George Foster, Cin	40			

Runs Batted In Leaders

Year	Player and Team	RBI	Year	Player and Team	RBI
1900	Elmer Flick, Phi	110	1924	George Kelly, NY	136
1901	Honus Wagner, Pitt	126	1925	Rogers Hornsby, StL	143
1902	Honus Wagner, Pitt	91	1926	Jim Bottomley, StL	120
1903	Sam Mertes, NY	104	1927	Paul Waner, Pitt	131
1904	Bill Dahlen, NY	80	1928	Jim Bottomley, StL	136
1905	Cy Seymour, Cin	121	1929	Hack Wilson, Chi	159
1906	Jim Nealon, Pitt	83	1930	Hack Wilson, Chi	190
	Harry Steinfeldt, Chi	83	1931	Chuck Klein, Phi	121
1907	Sherry Magee, Phi	85	1932	Don Hurst, Phi	143
1908	Honus Wagner, Pitt	109	1933	Chuck Klein, Phi	120
1909	Honus Wagner, Pitt	100	1934	Mel Ott, NY	135
1910	Sherry Magee, Phi	123	1935	Wally Berger, Bos	130
1911	Wildfire Schulte, Chi	121	1936	Joe Medwick, StL	138
1912	Heinie Zimmerman, Chi	103	1937	Joe Medwick, StL	154
1913	Gavvy Cravath, Phi	128	1938	Joe Medwick, StL	122
1914	Sherry Magee, Phi	103	1939	Frank McCormick, Cin	128
1915	Gavvy Cravath, Phi	115	1940	Johnny Mize, StL	137
1916	Heinie Zimmerman, Chi-NY	83	1941	Dolph Camilli, Bklyn	120
1917	Heinie Zimmerman, NY	102	1942	Johnny Mize, NY	110
1918	Sherry Magee, Phi	76	1943	Bill Nicholson, Chi	128
1919	Hi Myers, Bklyn	73	1944	Bill Nicholson, Chi	122
1920	Rogers Hornsby, StL	94	1945	Dixie Walker, Bklyn	124
	George Kelly, NY	94	1946	Enos Slaughter, StL	130
1921	Rogers Hornsby, StL	126	1947	Johnny Mize, NY	138
1922	Rogers Hornsby, StL	152	1948	Stan Musial, StL	131
1923	Irish Meusel, NY	125	1949	Ralph Kiner, Pitt	127

NATIONAL LEAGUE (Cont.)
Runs Batted In Leaders (Cont.)

Year	Player and Team	RBI	Year	Player and Team	RBI
1950	Del Ennis, Phi	126	1983	Dale Murphy, Atl	121
1951	Monte Irvin, NY	121	1984	Gary Carter, Mtl	106
1952	Hank Sauer, Chi	121		Mike Schmidt, Phi	106
1953	Roy Campanella, Bklyn	142	1985	Dave Parker, Cin	125
1954	Ted Kluszewski, Cin	141	1986	Mike Schmidt, Phi	119
1955	Duke Snider, Bklyn	136	1987	Andre Dawson, Chi	137
1956	Stan Musial, StL	109	1988	Will Clark, SF	109
1957	Hank Aaron, Mil	132	1989	Kevin Mitchell, SF	125
1958	Ernie Banks, Chi	129	1990	Matt Williams, SF	122
1959	Ernie Banks, Chi	143	1991	Howard Johnson, NY	117
1960	Hank Aaron, Mil	126	1992	Darren Daulton, Phi	109
1961	Orlando Cepeda, SF	142	1993	Barry Bonds, SF	123
1962	Tommy Davis, LA	153	1994	Jeff Bagwell, Hou	116
1963	Hank Aaron, Mil	130	1995	Dante Bichette, Col	128
1964	Ken Boyer, StL	119	1996	Andres Galarraga, Col	150
1965	Deron Johnson, Cin	130	1997	Andres Galarraga, Col	140
1966	Hank Aaron, Atl	127	1998	Sammy Sosa, Chi	158
1967	Orlando Cepeda, StL	111	1999	Mark McGwire, StL	147
1968	Willie McCovey, SF	105	2000	Todd Helton, Col	147
1969	Willie McCovey, SF	126	2001	Sammy Sosa, Chi	160
1970	Johnny Bench, Cin	148	2002	Lance Berkman, Hou	128
1971	Joe Torre, StL	137	2003	Preston Wilson, Col	141
1972	Johnny Bench, Cin	125	2004	Vinny Castilla, Col	131
1973	Willie Stargell, Pitt	119	2005	Andruw Jones, Atl	128
1974	Johnny Bench, Cin	129	2006	Ryan Howard, Phi	149
1975	Greg Luzinski, Phi	120	2007	Matt Holliday, Col	137*
1976	George Foster, Cin	121	2008	Ryan Howard, Phi	146
1977	George Foster, Cin	149	2009	Prince Fielder, Mil	141
1978	George Foster, Cin	120		Ryan Howard, Phi	141
1979	Dave Winfield, SD	118	2010	Albert Pujols, StL	118
1980	Mike Schmidt, Phi	121	2011	Matt Kemp, LA	126
1981	Mike Schmidt, Phi	91	2012	Chase Headley, SD	115
1982	Dale Murphy, Atl	109	2013	Paul Goldschmidt, Ari	125
	Al Oliver, Mtl	109			

*Includes one-game NL Wild Card tiebreaker.

Leading Base Stealers

Year	Player and Team	SB	Year	Player and Team	SB
1900	Patsy Donovan, StL	45	1925	Max Carey, Pitt	46
	George Van Haltren, NY	45	1926	Kiki Cuyler, Pitt	35
1901	Honus Wagner, Pitt	48	1927	Frankie Frisch, StL	48
1902	Honus Wagner, Pitt	43	1928	Kiki Cuyler, Chi	37
1903	Frank Chance, Chi	67	1929	Kiki Cuyler, Chi	43
	Jimmy Sheckard, Bklyn	67	1930	Kiki Cuyler, Chi	37
1904	Honus Wagner, Pitt	53	1931	Frankie Frisch, StL	28
1905	Art Devlin, NY	59	1932	Chuck Klein, Phi	20
	Billy Maloney, Chi	59	1933	Pepper Martin, StL	26
1906	Frank Chance, Chi	57	1934	Pepper Martin, StL	23
1907	Honus Wagner, Pitt	61	1935	Augie Galan, Chi	22
1908	Honus Wagner, Pitt	53	1936	Pepper Martin, StL	23
1909	Bob Bescher, Cin	54	1937	Augie Galan, Chi	23
1910	Bob Bescher, Cin	70	1938	Stan Hack, Chi	16
1911	Bob Bescher, Cin	80	1939	Stan Hack, Chi	17
1912	Bob Bescher, Cin	67		Lee Handley, Pitt	17
1913	Max Carey, Pitt	61	1940	Lonny Frey, Cin	22
1914	George Burns, NY	62	1941	Danny Murtaugh, Phi	18
1915	Max Carey, Pitt	36	1942	Pete Reiser, Bklyn	20
1916	Max Carey, Pitt	63	1943	Arky Vaughan, Bklyn	20
1917	Max Carey, Pitt	46	1944	Johnny Barrett, Pitt	28
1918	Max Carey, Pitt	58	1945	Red Schoendienst, StL	26
1919	George Burns, NY	40	1946	Pete Reiser, Bklyn	34
1920	Max Carey, Pitt	52	1947	Jackie Robinson, Bklyn	29
1921	Frankie Frisch, NY	49	1948	Richie Ashburn, Phi	32
1922	Max Carey, Pitt	51	1949	Jackie Robinson, Bklyn	37
1923	Max Carey, Pitt	51	1950	Sam Jethroe, Bos	35
1924	Max Carey, Pitt	49	1951	Sam Jethroe, Bos	35

NATIONAL LEAGUE *(Cont.)*
Leading Base Stealers *(Cont.)*

Year	Player and Team	SB	Year	Player and Team	SB
1952	Pee Wee Reese, Bklyn	30	1983	Tim Raines, Mtl	90
1953	Bill Bruton, Mil	26	1984	Tim Raines, Mtl	75
1954	Bill Bruton, Mil	34	1985	Vince Coleman, StL	110
1955	Bill Bruton, Mil	35	1986	Vince Coleman, StL	107
1956	Willie Mays, NY	40	1987	Vince Coleman, StL	109
1957	Willie Mays, NY	38	1988	Vince Coleman, StL	81
1958	Willie Mays, SF	31	1989	Vince Coleman, StL	65
1959	Willie Mays, SF	27	1990	Vince Coleman, StL	77
1960	Maury Wills, LA	50	1991	Marquis Grissom, Mtl	76
1961	Maury Wills, LA	35	1992	Marquis Grissom, Mtl	78
1962	Maury Wills, LA	104	1993	Chuck Carr, Fla	58
1963	Maury Wills, LA	40	1994	Craig Biggio, Hou	39
1964	Maury Wills, LA	53	1995	Quilvio Veras, Fla	56
1965	Maury Wills, LA	94	1996	Eric Young, Col	53
1966	Lou Brock, StL	74	1997	Tony Womack, Pitt	60
1967	Lou Brock, StL	52	1998	Tony Womack, Pitt	58
1968	Lou Brock, StL	62	1999	Tony Womack, Ariz	72
1969	Lou Brock, StL	53	2000	Luis Castillo, Fla	62
1970	Bobby Tolan, Cin	57	2001	Juan Pierre, Col	46
1971	Lou Brock, StL	64	2002	Luis Castillo, Fla	48
1972	Lou Brock, StL	63	2003	Juan Pierre, Fla	65
1973	Lou Brock, StL	70	2004	Scott Podsednik, Mil	70
1974	Lou Brock, StL	118	2005	Jose Reyes, NY	60
1975	Davey Lopes, LA	77	2006	Jose Reyes, NY	64
1976	Davey Lopes, LA	63	2007	Jose Reyes, NY	78
1977	Frank Taveras, Pitt	70	2008	Willy Taveras, Hou	68
1978	Omar Moreno, Pitt	71	2009	Michael Bourn, Hou	61
1979	Omar Moreno, Pitt	77	2010	Michael Bourn, Hou	52
1980	Ron LeFlore, Mtl	97	2011	Micheal Bourn, Hou/Atl	61
1981	Tim Raines, Mtl	71	2012	Everth Cabrera, SD	44
1982	Tim Raines, Mtl	78	2013	Eric Young, NY	46

Leading Pitchers—Winning Percentage

Year	Pitcher and Team	W	L	Pct	Year	Pitcher and Team	W	L	Pct
1900	Jesse Tannehill, Pitt	20	6	.769	1930	Freddie Fitzsimmons, NY	19	7	.731
1901	Jack Chesbro, Pitt	21	10	.677	1931	Paul Derringer, StL	18	8	.692
1902	Jack Chesbro, Pitt	28	6	.824	1932	Lon Warneke, Chi	22	6	.786
1903	Sam Leever, Pitt	25	7	.781	1933	Ben Cantwell, Bos	20	10	.667
1904	Joe McGinnity, NY	35	8	.814	1934	Dizzy Dean, StL	30	7	.811
1905	Sam Leever, Pitt	20	5	.800	1935	Bill Lee, Chi	20	6	.769
1906	Ed Reulbach, Chi	19	4	.826	1936	Carl Hubbell, NY	26	6	.813
1907	Ed Reulbach, Chi	17	4	.810	1937	Carl Hubbell, NY	22	8	.733
1908	Ed Reulbach, Chi	24	7	.774	1938	Bill Lee, Chi	22	9	.710
1909	Howie Camnitz, Pitt	25	6	.806	1939	Paul Derringer, Cin	25	7	.781
	Christy Mathewson, NY	25	6	.806	1940	Freddie Fitzsimmons, Bklyn	16	2	.889
1910	King Cole, Chi	20	4	.833	1941	Elmer Riddle, Cin	19	4	.826
1911	Rube Marquard, NY	24	7	.774	1942	Larry French, Bklyn	15	4	.789
1912	Claude Hendrix, Pitt	24	9	.727	1943	Mort Cooper, StL	21	8	.724
1913	Bert Humphries, Chi	16	4	.800	1944	Ted Wilks, StL	17	4	.810
1914	Bill James, Bos	26	7	.788	1945	Harry Brecheen, StL	15	4	.789
1915	Grover Alexander, Phi	31	10	.756	1946	Murray Dickson, StL	15	6	.714
1916	Tom Hughes, Bos	16	3	.842	1947	Larry Jansen, NY	21	5	.808
1917	Ferdie Schupp, NY	21	7	.750	1948	Harry Brecheen, StL	20	7	.741
1918	Claude Hendrix, Chi	19	7	.731	1949	Preacher Roe, Bklyn	15	6	.714
1919	Dutch Ruether, Cin	19	6	.760	1950	Sal Maglie, NY	18	4	.818
1920	Burleigh Grimes, Bklyn	23	11	.676	1951	Preacher Roe, Bklyn	22	3	.880
1921	Bill Doak, StL	15	6	.714	1952	Hoyt Wilhelm, NY	15	3	.833
1922	Pete Donohue, Cin	18	9	.667	1953	Carl Erskine, Bklyn	20	6	.769
1923	Dolf Luque, Cin	27	8	.771	1954	Johnny Antonelli, NY	21	7	.750
1924	Emil Yde, Pitt	16	3	.842	1955	Don Newcombe, Bklyn	20	5	.800
1925	Bill Sherdel, StL	15	6	.714	1956	Don Newcombe, Bklyn	27	7	.794
1926	Ray Kremer, Pitt	20	6	.769	1957	Bob Buhl, Mil	18	7	.720
1927	Larry Benton, Bos-NY	17	7	.708	1958	Lew Burdette, Mil	20	10	.667
1928	Larry Benton, NY	25	9	.735		Warren Spahn, Mil	22	11	.667
1929	Charlie Root, Chi	19	6	.760	1959	Roy Face, Pitt	18	1	.947

Note: Percentages based on 15 or more victories.

NATIONAL LEAGUE *(Cont.)*
Leading Pitchers—Winning Percentage *(Cont.)*

Year	Pitcher and Team	W	L	Pct	Year	Pitcher and Team	W	L	Pct
1960	Ernie Broglio, StL	21	9	.700	1988	David Cone, NY	20	3	.870
1961	Johnny Podres, LA	18	5	.783	1989	Mike Bielecki, Chi	18	7	.720
1962	Bob Purkey, Cin	23	5	.821	1990	Doug Drabeck, Pitt	22	6	.786
1963	Ron Perranoski, LA	16	3	.842 ~	1991	John Smiley, Pitt	20	8	.714
1964	Sandy Koufax, LA	19	5	.792		Jose Rijo, Cin	15	6	.714
1965	Sandy Koufax, LA	26	8	.765	1992	Bob Tewksbury, StL	16	5	.762
1966	Juan Marichal, SF	25	6	.806	1993	Tom Glavine, Atl	22	6	.786
1967	Dick Hughes, StL	16	6	.727	1994	Ken Hill, Mtl	16	5	.762
1968	Steve Blass, Pitt	18	6	.750	1995	Greg Maddux, Atl	19	2	.905
1969	Tom Seaver, NY	25	7	.781	1996	John Smoltz, Atl	24	8	.750
1970	Bob Gibson, StL	23	7	.767	1997	Denny Neagle, Atl	20	5	.800
1971	Don Gullett, Cin	16	6	.727	1998	John Smoltz, Atl	17	3	.850
1972	Gary Nolan, Cin	15	5	.750	1999	Mike Hampton, Hou	22	4	.846
1973	Tommy John, LA	16	7	.696	2000	Randy Johnson, Ariz	19	7	.730
1974	Andy Messersmith, LA	20	6	.769	2001	Curt Schilling, Ariz	22	6	.786
1975	Don Gullett, Cin	15	4	.789	2002	Randy Johnson, Ariz	24	5	.828
1976	Steve Carlton, Phi	20	7	.741	2003	Jason Schmidt, SF	17	5	.773
1977	John Candelaria, Pitt	20	5	.800	2004	Roger Clemens, Hou	18	4	.818
1978	Gaylord Perry, SD	21	6	.778	2005	Chris Carpenter, StL	21	5	.808
1979	Tom Seaver, Cin	16	6	.727	2006	Carlos Zambrano, Chi	16	7	.695
1980	Jim Bibby, Pitt	19	6	.760	2007	Brad Penny, LA	16	4	.800
1981*	Tom Seaver, Cin	14	2	.875	2008	Tim Lincecum, SF	18	5	.783
1982	Phil Niekro, Atl	17	4	.810	2009	Chris Carpenter, StL	17	4	.810
1983	John Denny, Phi	19	6	.760	2010	Ubaldo Jimenez, Col	19	8	.704
1984	Rick Sutcliffe, Chi	16	1	.941	2011	Ian Kennedy, Ari	21	4	.840
1985	Orel Hershiser, LA	19	3	.864	2012	Kyle Lohse, StL	16	3	.842
1986	Bob Ojeda, NY	18	5	.783	2013	Zack Greinke, LA	15	4	.789
1987	Dwight Gooden, NY	15	7	.682					

*1981 percentages based on 10 or more victories. All other years, percentages based on 15 or more victories.

Leading Pitchers—Earned Run Average

Year	Player and Team	ERA	Year	Player and Team	ERA
1900	Rube Waddell, Pitt	2.37	1932	Lon Warneke, Chi	2.37
1901	Jesse Tannehill, Pitt	2.18	1933	Carl Hubbell, NY	1.66
1902	Jack Taylor, Chi	1.33	1934	Carl Hubbell, NY	2.30
1903	Sam Leever, Pitt	2.06	1935	Cy Blanton, Pitt	2.59
1904	Joe McGinnity, NY	1.61	1936	Carl Hubbell, NY	2.31
1905	Christy Mathewson, NY	1.27	1937	Jim Turner, Bos	2.38
1906	Three Finger Brown, Chi	1.04	1938	Bill Lee, Chi	2.66
1907	Jack Pfiester, Chi	1.15	1939	Bucky Walters, Cin	2.29
1908	Christy Mathewson, NY	1.43	1940	Bucky Walters, Cin	2.48
1909	Christy Mathewson, NY	1.14	1941	Elmer Riddle, Cin	2.24
1910	George McQuillan, Phi	1.60	1942	Mort Cooper, StL	1.77
1911	Christy Mathewson, NY	1.99	1943	Howie Pollet, StL	1.75
1912	Jeff Tesreau, NY	1.96	1944	Ed Heusser, Cin	2.38
1913	Christy Mathewson, NY	2.06	1945	Hank Borowy, Chi	2.14
1914	Bill Doak, StL	1.72	1946	Howie Pollet, StL	2.10
1915	Grover Alexander, Phi	1.22	1947	Warren Spahn, Bos	2.33
1916	Grover Alexander, Phi	1.55	1948	Harry Brecheen, StL	2.24
1917	Grover Alexander, Phi	1.83	1949	Dave Koslo, NY	2.50
1918	Hippo Vaughn, Chi	1.74	1950	Jim Hearn, StL-NY	2.49
1919	Grover Alexander, Chi	1.72	1951	Chet Nichols, Bos	2.88
1920	Grover Alexander, Chi	1.91	1952	Hoyt Wilhelm, NY	2.43
1921	Bill Doak, StL	2.58	1953	Warren Spahn, Mil	2.10
1922	Rosy Ryan, NY	3.00	1954	Johnny Antonelli, NY	2.29
1923	Dolf Luque, Cin	1.93	1955	Bob Friend, Pitt	2.84
1924	Dazzy Vance, Bklyn	2.16	1956	Lew Burdette, Mil	2.71
1925	Dolf Luque, Cin	2.63	1957	Johnny Podres, Bklyn	2.66
1926	Ray Kremer, Pitt	2.61	1958	Stu Miller, SF	2.47
1927	Ray Kremer, Pitt	2.47	1959	Sam Jones, SF	2.82
1928	Dazzy Vance, Bklyn	2.09	1960	Mike McCormick, SF	2.70
1929	Bill Walker, NY	3.08	1961	Warren Spahn, Mil	3.01
1930	Dazzy Vance, Bklyn	2.61	1962	Sandy Koufax, LA	2.54
1931	Bill Walker, NY	2.26	1963	Sandy Koufax, LA	1.88

Note: Based on 10 complete games through 1950, then 154 innings until National League expanded in 1962, when it became 162 innings. In strike-shortened 1981, one inning per game required.

NATIONAL LEAGUE *(Cont.)*

Leading Pitchers—Earned Run Average *(Cont.)*

Year	Player and Team	ERA	Year	Player and Team	ERA
1964	Sandy Koufax, LA	1.74	1990	Danny Darwin, Hou	2.21
1965	Sandy Koufax, LA	2.04	1991	Dennis Martinez, Mtl	2.39
1966	Sandy Koufax, LA	1.73	1992	Bill Swift, SF	2.08
1967	Phil Niekro, Atl	1.87	1993	Greg Maddux, Atl	2.36
1968	Bob Gibson, StL	1.12	1994	Greg Maddux, Atl	1.56
1969	Juan Marichal, SF	2.10	1995	Greg Maddux, Atl	1.63
1970	Tom Seaver, NY	2.81	1996	Kevin Brown, Fla	1.89
1971	Tom Seaver, NY	1.76	1997	Pedro Martinez, Mtl	1.90
1972	Steve Carlton, Phi	1.98	1998	Greg Maddux, Atl	1.98
1973	Tom Seaver, NY	2.08	1999	Randy Johnson, Ariz	2.48
1974	Buzz Capra, Atl	2.28	2000	Kevin Brown, LA	2.58
1975	Randy Jones, SD	2.24	2001	Randy Johnson, Ariz	2.49
1976	John Denny, StL	2.52	2002	Randy Johnson, Ariz	2.32
1977	John Candelaria, Pitt	2.34	2003	Jason Schmidt, SF	2.34
1978	Craig Swan, NY	2.43	2004	Jake Peavy, SD	2.27
1979	J.R. Richard, Hou	2.71	2005	Roger Clemens, Hou	1.87
1980	Don Sutton, LA	2.21	2006	Roy Oswalt, Hou	2.98
1981	Nolan Ryan, Hou	1.69	2007	Jake Peavy, SD	2.54*
1982	Steve Rogers, Mtl	2.40	2008	Johan Santana, NYM	2.53
1983	Atlee Hammaker, SF	2.25	2009	Chris Carpenter, StL	2.24
1984	Alejandro Pena, LA	2.48	2010	Josh Johnson, Fla	2.30
1985	Dwight Gooden, NY	1.53	2011	Clayton Kershaw, LA	2.28
1986	Mike Scott, Hou	2.22	2012	Clayton Kershaw, LA	2.53
1987	Nolan Ryan, Hou	2.76	2013	Clayton Kershaw, LA	1.83
1988	Joe Magrane, StL	2.18			
1989	Scott Garrelts, SF	2.28			

*Includes one-game NL Wild Card tiebreaker.

Leading Pitchers—Strikeouts

Year	Player and Team	SO	Year	Player and Team	SO
1900	Rube Waddell, Pitt	133	1937	Carl Hubbell, NY	159
1901	Noodles Hahn, Cin	233	1938	Clay Bryant, Chi	135
1902	Vic Willis, Bos	226	1939	Claude Passeau, Phi-Chi	137
1903	Christy Mathewson, NY	267		Bucky Walters, Cin	137
1904	Christy Mathewson, NY	212	1940	Kirby Higbe, Phi	137
1905	Christy Mathewson, NY	206	1941	Johnny Vander Meer, Cin	202
1906	Fred Beebe, Chi-StL	171	1942	Johnny Vander Meer, Cin	186
1907	Christy Mathewson, NY	178	1943	Johnny Vander Meer, Cin	174
1908	Christy Mathewson, NY	259	1944	Bill Voiselle, NY	161
1909	Orval Overall, Chi	205	1945	Preacher Roe, Pitt	148
1910	Christy Mathewson, NY	190	1946	Johnny Schmitz, Chi	135
1911	Rube Marquard, NY	237	1947	Ewell Blackwell, Cin	193
1912	Grover Alexander, Phi	195	1948	Harry Brecheen, StL	149
1913	Tom Seaton, Phi	168	1949	Warren Spahn, Bos	151
1914	Grover Alexander, Phi	214	1950	Warren Spahn, Bos	191
1915	Grover Alexander, Phi	241	1951	Don Newcombe, Bklyn	164
1916	Grover Alexander, Phi	167		Warren Spahn, Bos	164
1917	Grover Alexander, Phi	200	1952	Warren Spahn, Bos	183
1918	Hippo Vaughn, Chi	148	1953	Robin Roberts, Phi	198
1919	Hippo Vaughn, Chi	141	1954	Robin Roberts, Phi	185
1920	Grover Alexander, Chi	173	1955	Sam Jones, Chi	198
1921	Burleigh Grimes, Bklyn	136	1956	Sam Jones, Chi	176
1922	Dazzy Vance, Bklyn	134	1957	Jack Sanford, Phi	188
1923	Dazzy Vance, Bklyn	197	1958	Sam Jones, StL	225
1924	Dazzy Vance, Bklyn	262	1959	Don Drysdale, LA	242
1925	Dazzy Vance, Bklyn	221	1960	Don Drysdale, LA	246
1926	Dazzy Vance, Bklyn	140	1961	Sandy Koufax, LA	269
1927	Dazzy Vance, Bklyn	184	1962	Don Drysdale, LA	232
1928	Dazzy Vance, Bklyn	200	1963	Sandy Koufax, LA	306
1929	Pat Malone, Chi	166	1964	Bob Veale, Pitt	250
1930	Bill Hallahan, StL	177	1965	Sandy Koufax, LA	382
1931	Bill Hallahan, StL	159	1966	Sandy Koufax, LA	317
1932	Dizzy Dean, StL	191	1967	Jim Bunning, Phi	253
1933	Dizzy Dean, StL	199	1968	Bob Gibson, StL	268
1934	Dizzy Dean, StL	195	1969	Ferguson Jenkins, Chi	273
1935	Dizzy Dean, StL	182	1970	Tom Seaver, NY	283
1936	Van Lingle Mungo, Bklyn	238	1971	Tom Seaver, NY	289

NATIONAL LEAGUE *(Cont.)*
Leading Pitchers—Strikeouts *(Cont.)*

Year	Player and Team	SO	Year	Player and Team	SO
1972	Steve Carlton, Phi	310	1994	Andy Benes, SD	189
1973	Tom Seaver, NY	251	1995	Hideo Nomo, LA	236
1974	Steve Carlton, Phi	240	1996	John Smoltz, Atl	276
1975	Tom Seaver, NY	243	1997	Curt Schilling, Phi	319
1976	Tom Seaver, NY	235	1998	Curt Schilling, Phi	300
1977	Phil Niekro, Atl	262	1999	Randy Johnson, Ariz	364
1978	J.R. Richard, Hou	303	2000	Randy Johnson, Ariz	347
1979	J.R. Richard, Hou	313	2001	Randy Johnson, Ariz	372
1980	Steve Carlton, Phi	286	2002	Randy Johnson, Ariz	334
1981	Fernando Valenzuela, LA	180	2003	Kerry Wood, Chi	266
1982	Steve Carlton, Phi	286	2004	Randy Johnson, Ariz	290
1983	Steve Carlton, Phi	275	2005	Jake Peavy, SD	216
1984	Dwight Gooden, NY	276	2006	Aaron Harang, Cin	216
1985	Dwight Gooden, NY	268	2007	Jake Peavy, SD	240*
1986	Mike Scott, Hou	306	2008	Tim Lincecum, SF	265
1987	Nolan Ryan, Hou	270	2009	Tim Lincecum, SF	261
1988	Nolan Ryan, Hou	228	2010	Tim Lincecum, SF	231
1989	Jose DeLeon, StL	201	2011	Clayton Kershaw, LA	248
1990	David Cone, NY	233	2012	R.A. Dickey, NY	230
1991	David Cone, NY	241	2013	Clayton Kershaw, LA	232
1992	John Smoltz, Atl	215			
1993	Jose Rijo, Cin	227			

*Includes one-game NL Wild Card tiebreaker.

Leading Pitchers—Saves

Year	Player and Team	SV	Year	Player and Team	SV
1947	Hugh Casey, Bklyn	18	1981	Bruce Sutter, StL	25
1948	Harry Gumpert, Cin	17	1982	Bruce Sutter, StL	36
1949	Ted Wilks, StL	9	1983	Lee Smith, Chi	29
1950	Jim Konstanty, Phi	22	1984	Bruce Sutter, StL	45
1951	Ted Wilks, StL, Pitt	13	1985	Jeff Reardon, Mtl	41
1952	Al Brazle, StL	16	1986	Todd Worrell, StL	36
1953	Al Brazle, StL	18	1987	Steve Bedrosian, Phi	40
1954	Jim Hughes, Bklyn	24	1988	John Franco, Cin	39
1955	Jack Meyer, Phi	16	1989	Mark Davis, SD	44
1956	Clem Labine, Bklyn	19	1990	John Franco, NY	33
1957	Clem Labine, Bklyn	17	1991	Lee Smith, StL	47
1958	Roy Face, Pitt	20	1992	Lee Smith, StL	42
1959	Lindy McDaniel, StL	15	1993	Randy Myers, Chi	53
	Don McMahon, Mil	15	1994	John Franco, NY	30
1960	Lindy McDaniel, StL	26	1995	Randy Myers, Chi	38
1961	Roy Face, Pitt	17	1996	Jeff Brantley, Cin	44
	Stu Miller, SF	17		Todd Worrell, LA	44
1962	Roy Face, Pitt	28	1997	Jeff Shaw, Cin	42
1963	Lindy McDaniel, Chi	22	1998	Trevor Hoffman, SD	53
1964	Hal Woodeshick, Hou	23	1999	Ugueth Urbina, Mtl	41
1965	Ted Abernathy, Chi	31	2000	Antonio Alfonseca, Fla	45
1966	Phil Regan, LA	21	2001	Robb Nen, SF	45
1967	Ted Abernathy, Cin	28	2002	John Smoltz, Atl	55
1968	Phil Regan, Chi-LA	25	2003	Eric Gagne, LA	55
1969	Fred Gladding, Hou	29	2004	Armando Benitez, Fla	47
1970	Wayne Granger, Cin	35		Jason Isringhausen, StL	47
1971	Dave Giusti, Pitt	30	2005	Chad Cordero, Wash	47
1972	Clay Carroll, Cin	37	2006	Trevor Hoffman, SD	46
1973	Mike Marshall, Mtl	13	2007	Jose Valverde, Ariz	47
1974	Mike Marshall, LA	21	2008	Jose Valverde, Hou	44
1975	Rawly Eastwick, Cin	22	2009	Heath Bell, SD	42
	Al Hrabosky, StL	22	2010	Brian Wilson, SF	48
1976	Rawly Eastwick, Cin	26	2011	John Axford, Mil	46
1977	Rollie Fingers, SD	35		Craig Kimbrel, Atl	46
1978	Rollie Fingers, SD	37	2012	Craig Kimbrel, Atl	42
1979	Bruce Sutter, Chi	37		Jason Motte, StL	42
1980	Bruce Sutter, Chi	28	2013	Craig Kimbrel, Atl	50

AMERICAN LEAGUE
Leading Batsmen

Year	Player and Team	BA	Year	Player and Team	BA
1901	Nap Lajoie, Phi	.422	1958	Ted Williams, Bos	.328
1902	Ed Delahanty, Wash	.376	1959	Harvey Kuenn, Det	.353
1903	Nap Lajoie, Clev	.355	1960	Pete Runnels, Bos	.320
1904	Nap Lajoie, Clev	.381	1961	Norm Cash, Det	.361
1905	Elmer Flick, Clev	.306	1962	Pete Runnels, Bos	.326
1906	George Stone, StL	.358	1963	Carl Yastrzemski, Bos	.321
1907	Ty Cobb, Det	.350	1964	Tony Oliva, Minn	.323
1908	Ty Cobb, Det	.324	1965	Tony Oliva, Minn	.321
1909	Ty Cobb, Det	.377	1966	Frank Robinson, Balt	.316
1910	Nap Lajoie, Clev†	.383	1967	Carl Yastrzemski, Bos	.326
1911	Ty Cobb, Det	.420	1968	Carl Yastrzemski, Bos	.301
1912	Ty Cobb, Det	.410	1969	Rod Carew, Minn	.332
1913	Ty Cobb, Det	.390	1970	Alex Johnson, Cal	.329
1914	Ty Cobb, Det	.368	1971	Tony Oliva, Minn	.337
1915	Ty Cobb, Det	.369	1972	Rod Carew, Minn	.318
1916	Tris Speaker, Clev	.386	1973	Rod Carew, Minn	.350
1917	Ty Cobb, Det	.383	1974	Rod Carew, Minn	.364
1918	Ty Cobb, Det	.382	1975	Rod Carew, Minn	.359
1919	Ty Cobb, Det	.384	1976	George Brett, KC	.333
1920	George Sisler, StL	.407	1977	Rod Carew, Minn	.388
1921	Harry Heilmann, Det	.394	1978	Rod Carew, Minn	.333
1922	George Sisler, StL	.420	1979	Fred Lynn, Bos	.333
1923	Harry Heilmann, Det	.403	1980	George Brett, KC	.390
1924	Babe Ruth, NY	.378	1981	Carney Lansford, Bos	.336
1925	Harry Heilmann, Det	.393	1982	Willie Wilson, KC	.332
1926	Heinie Manush, Det	.378	1983	Wade Boggs, Bos	.361
1927	Harry Heilmann, Det	.398	1984	Don Mattingly, NY	.343
1928	Goose Goslin, Wash	.379	1985	Wade Boggs, Bos	.368
1929	Lew Fonseca, Clev	.369	1986	Wade Boggs, Bos	.357
1930	Al Simmons, Phi	.381	1987	Wade Boggs, Bos	.363
1931	Al Simmons, Phi	.390	1988	Wade Boggs, Bos	.366
1932	Dale Alexander, Det-Bos	.367	1989	Kirby Puckett, Minn	.339
1933	Jimmie Foxx, Phi	.356	1990	George Brett, KC	.329
1934	Lou Gehrig, NY	.363	1991	Julio Franco, Tex	.341
1935	Buddy Myer, Wash	.349	1992	Edgar Martinez, Sea	.343
1936	Luke Appling, Chi	.388	1993	John Olerud, Tor	.363
1937	Charlie Gehringer, Det	.371	1994	Paul O'Neill, NY	.359
1938	Jimmie Foxx, Bos	.349	1995	Edgar Martinez, Sea	.356
1939	Joe DiMaggio, NY	.381	1996	Alex Rodriguez, Sea	.358
1940	Joe DiMaggio, NY	.352	1997	Frank Thomas, Chi	.347
1941	Ted Williams, Bos	.406	1998	Bernie Williams, NY	.339
1942	Ted Williams, Bos	.356	1999	Nomar Garciaparra, Bos	.357
1943	Luke Appling, Chi	.328	2000	Nomar Garciaparra, Bos	.372
1944	Lou Boudreau, Clev	.327	2001	Ichiro Suzuki, Sea	.350
1945	Snuffy Stirnweiss, NY	.309	2002	Manny Ramirez, Bos	.349
1946	Mickey Vernon, Wash	.353	2003	Bill Mueller, Bos	.326
1947	Ted Williams, Bos	.343	2004	Ichiro Suzuki, Sea	.372
1948	Ted Williams, Bos	.369	2005	Michael Young, Tex	.331
1949	George Kell, Det	.343	2006	Joe Mauer, Minn	.347
1950	Billy Goodman, Bos	.354	2007	Magglio Ordonez, Det	.363
1951	Ferris Fain, Phi	.344	2008	Joe Mauer, Minn	.330
1952	Ferris Fain, Phi	.327	2009	Joe Mauer, Minn	.365*
1953	Mickey Vernon, Wash	.337	2010	Josh Hamilton, Tex	.359
1954	Bobby Avila, Clev	.341	2011	Miguel Cabrera, Det	.344
1955	Al Kaline, Det	.340	2012	Miguel Cabrera, Det	.330
1956	Mickey Mantle, NY	.353	2013	Miguel Cabrera, Det	.348
1957	Ted Williams, Bos	.388			

†League president Ban Johnson declared Ty Cobb batting champion with a .385 average, beating Lajoie's .384. However, subsequent research has led to the revision of Lajoie's average to .383 and Cobb's to .382.
*Includes one-game AL Central playoff tiebreaker.

Leaders in Runs Scored

Year	Player and Team	Runs	Year	Player and Team	Runs
1901	Nap Lajoie, Phi	145	1959	Eddie Yost, Det	115
1902	Dave Fultz, Phi	110	1960	Mickey Mantle, NY	119
1903	Patsy Dougherty, Bos	108	1961	Mickey Mantle, NY	132
1904	Patsy Dougherty, Bos-NY	113		Roger Maris, NY	132
1905	Harry Davis, Phi	92	1962	Albie Pearson, LA	115
1906	Elmer Flick, Clev	98	1963	Bob Allison, Minn	99
1907	Sam Crawford, Det	102	1964	Tony Oliva, Minn	109
1908	Matty McIntyre, Det	105	1965	Zoilo Versalles, Minn	126
1909	Ty Cobb, Det	116	1966	Frank Robinson, Balt	122
1910	Ty Cobb, Det	106	1967	Carl Yastrzemski, Bos	112
1911	Ty Cobb, Det	147	1968	Dick McAuliffe, Det	95
1912	Eddie Collins, Phi	137	1969	Reggie Jackson, Oak	123
1913	Eddie Collins, Phi	125	1970	Carl Yastrzemski, Bos	125
1914	Eddie Collins, Phi	122	1971	Don Buford, Balt	99
1915	Ty Cobb, Det	144	1972	Bobby Murcer, NY	102
1916	Ty Cobb, Det	113	1973	Reggie Jackson, Oak	99
1917	Donie Bush, Det	112	1974	Carl Yastrzemski, Bos	93
1918	Ray Chapman, Clev	84	1975	Fred Lynn, Bos	103
1919	Babe Ruth, Bos	103	1976	Roy White, NY	104
1920	Babe Ruth, NY	158	1977	Rod Carew, Minn	128
1921	Babe Ruth, NY	177	1978	Ron LeFlore, Det	126
1922	George Sisler, StL	134	1979	Don Baylor, Cal	120
1923	Babe Ruth, NY	151	1980	Willie Wilson, KC	133
1924	Babe Ruth, NY	143	1981	Rickey Henderson, Oak	89
1925	Johnny Mostil, Chi	135	1982	Paul Molitor, Mil	136
1926	Babe Ruth, NY	139	1983	Cal Ripken, Balt	121
1927	Babe Ruth, NY	158	1984	Dwight Evans, Bos	121
1928	Babe Ruth, NY	163	1985	Rickey Henderson, NY	146
1929	Charlie Gehringer, Det	131	1986	Rickey Henderson, NY	130
1930	Al Simmons, Phi	152	1987	Paul Molitor, Mil	114
1931	Lou Gehrig, NY	163	1988	Wade Boggs, Bos	128
1932	Jimmie Foxx, Phi	151	1989	Wade Boggs, Bos	113
1933	Lou Gehrig, NY	138		Rickey Henderson, NY-Oak	113
1934	Charlie Gehringer, Det	134	1990	Rickey Henderson, Oak	119
1935	Lou Gehrig, NY	125	1991	Paul Molitor, Mil	133
1936	Lou Gehrig, NY	167	1992	Tony Philips, Det	114
1937	Joe DiMaggio, NY	151	1993	Rafael Palmeiro, Tex	124
1938	Hank Greenberg, Det	144	1994	Frank Thomas, Chi	106
1939	Red Rolfe, NY	139	1995	Albert Belle, Clev	121
1940	Ted Williams, Bos	134		Edgar Martinez, Sea	121
1941	Ted Williams, Bos	135	1996	Alex Rodriguez, Sea	141
1942	Ted Williams, Bos	141	1997	Ken Griffey Jr., Sea	125
1943	George Case, Wash	102	1998	Derek Jeter, NY	127
1944	Snuffy Stirnweiss, NY	125	1999	Roberto Alomar, Clev	138
1945	Snuffy Stirnweiss, NY	107	2000	Johnny Damon, KC	136
1946	Ted Williams, Bos	142	2001	Alex Rodriguez, Tex	133
1947	Ted Williams, Bos	125	2002	Alfonso Soriano, NY	128
1948	Tommy Henrich, NY	138	2003	Alex Rodriguez, Tex	124
1949	Ted Williams, Bos	150	2004	Vladimir Guerrero, Ana	124
1950	Dom DiMaggio, Bos	131	2005	Alex Rodriguez, NY	124
1951	Dom DiMaggio, Bos	113	2006	Grady Sizemore, Clev	134
1952	Larry Doby, Clev	104	2007	Alex Rodriguez, NY	143
1953	Al Rosen, Clev	115	2008	Dustin Pedroia, Bos	118
1954	Mickey Mantle, NY	129	2009	Dustin Pedroia, Bos	115
1955	Al Smith, Clev	123	2010	Mark Teixeira, NY	113
1956	Mickey Mantle, NY	132	2011	Curtis Granderson, NY	136
1957	Mickey Mantle, NY	121	2012	Mike Trout, LA	129
1958	Mickey Mantle, NY	127	2013	Mike Trout, LA	109

AMERICAN LEAGUE (Cont.)
Leaders in Hits

Year	Player and Team	Hits	Year	Player and Team	Hits
1901	Nap Lajoie, Phi	229	1956	Harvey Kuenn, Det	196
1902	Piano Legs Hickman, Bos-Clev	194	1957	Nellie Fox, Chi	196
1903	Patsy Dougherty, Bos	195	1958	Nellie Fox, Chi	187
1904	Nap Lajoie, Clev	211	1959	Harvey Kuenn, Det	198
1905	George Stone, StL	187	1960	Minnie Minoso, Chi	184
1906	Nap Lajoie, Clev	214	1961	Norm Cash, Det	193
1907	Ty Cobb, Det	212	1962	Bobby Richardson, NY	209
1908	Ty Cobb, Det	188	1963	Carl Yastrzemski, Bos	183
1909	Ty Cobb, Det	216	1964	Tony Oliva, Minn	217
1910	Nap Lajoie, Clev	227	1965	Tony Oliva, Minn	185
1911	Ty Cobb, Det	248	1966	Tony Oliva, Minn	191
1912	Ty Cobb, Det	227	1967	Carl Yastrzemski, Bos	189
1913	Joe Jackson, Clev	197	1968	Bert Campaneris, Oak	177
1914	Tris Speaker, Bos	193	1969	Tony Oliva, Minn	197
1915	Ty Cobb, Det	208	1970	Tony Oliva, Minn	204
1916	Tris Speaker, Clev	211	1971	Cesar Tovar, Minn	204
1917	Ty Cobb, Det	225	1972	Joe Rudi, Oak	181
1918	George Burns, Phi	178	1973	Rod Carew, Minn	203
1919	Ty Cobb, Det	191	1974	Rod Carew, Minn	218
	Bobby Veach, Det	191	1975	George Brett, KC	195
1920	George Sisler, StL	257	1976	George Brett, KC	215
1921	Harry Heilmann, Det	237	1977	Rod Carew, Minn	239
1922	George Sisler, StL	246	1978	Jim Rice, Bos	213
1923	Charlie Jamieson, Clev	222	1979	George Brett, KC	212
1924	Sam Rice, Wash	216	1980	Willie Wilson, KC	230
1925	Al Simmons, Phi	253	1981	Rickey Henderson, Oak	135
1926	George Burns, Clev	216	1982	Robin Yount, Mil	210
	Sam Rice, Wash	216	1983	Cal Ripken Jr., Balt	211
1927	Earle Combs, NY	231	1984	Don Mattingly, NY	207
1928	Heinie Manush, StL	241	1985	Wade Boggs, Bos	240
1929	Dale Alexander, Det	215	1986	Don Mattingly, NY	238
	Charlie Gehringer, Det	215	1987	Kirby Puckett, Minn	207
1930	Johnny Hodapp, Clev	225		Kevin Seitzer, KC	207
1931	Lou Gehrig, NY	211	1988	Kirby Puckett, Minn	234
1932	Al Simmons, Phi	216	1989	Kirby Puckett, Minn	215
1933	Heinie Manush, Wash	221	1990	Rafael Palmeiro, Tex	191
1934	Charlie Gehringer, Det	214	1991	Paul Molitor, Mil	216
1935	Joe Vosmik, Clev	216	1992	Kirby Puckett, Minn	210
1936	Earl Averill, Clev	232	1993	Paul Molitor, Tor	211
1937	Beau Bell, StL	218	1994	Kenny Lofton, Clev	160
1938	Joe Vosmik, Bos	201	1995	Lance Johnson, Chi	186
1939	Red Rolfe, NY	213	1996	Paul Molitor, Minn	225
1940	Doc Cramer, Bos	200	1997	Nomar Garciaparra, Bos	209
	Barney McCosky, Det	200	1998	Alex Rodriguez, Sea	213
	Rip Radcliff, StL	200	1999	Derek Jeter, NY	219
1941	Cecil Travis, Wash	218	2000	Darin Erstad, Ana	240
1942	Johnny Pesky, Bos	205	2001	Ichiro Suzuki, Sea	242
1943	Dick Wakefield, Det	200	2002	Alfonso Soriano, NY	209
1944	Snuffy Stirnweiss, NY	205	2003	Vernon Wells, Tor	215
1945	Snuffy Stirnweiss, NY	195	2004	Ichiro Suzuki, Sea	262
1946	Johnny Pesky, Bos	208	2005	Michael Young, Tex	221
1947	Johnny Pesky, Bos	207	2006	Ichiro Suzuki, Sea	224
1948	Bob Dillinger, StL	207	2007	Ichiro Suzuki, Sea	238
1949	Dale Mitchell, Clev	203	2008	Dustin Pedroia, Bos	213
1950	George Kell, Det	218		Ichiro Suzuki, Sea	213
1951	George Kell, Det	191	2009	Ichiro Suzuki, Sea	225
1952	Nellie Fox, Chi	192	2010	Ichiro Suzuki, Sea	214
1953	Harvey Kuenn, Det	209	2011	Adrian Gonzalez, Bos	213
1954	Nellie Fox, Chi	201		Michael Young, Tex	213
	Harvey Kuenn, Det	201	2012	Derek Jeter, NY	216
1955	Al Kaline, Det	200	2013	Adrian Beltre, Tex	199

AMERICAN LEAGUE *(Cont.)*
Home Run Leaders

Year	Player and Team	HR	Year	Player and Team	HR
1901	Nap Lajoie, Phi	13	1960	Mickey Mantle, NY	40
1902	Socks Seybold, Phi	16	1961	Roger Maris, NY	61
1903	Buck Freeman, Bos	13	1962	Harmon Killebrew, Minn	48
1904	Harry Davis, Phi	10	1963	Harmon Killebrew, Minn	45
1905	Harry Davis, Phi	8	1964	Harmon Killebrew, Minn	49
1906	Harry Davis, Phi	12	1965	Tony Conigliaro, Bos	32
1907	Harry Davis, Phi	8	1966	Frank Robinson, Balt	49
1908	Sam Crawford, Det	7	1967	Harmon Killebrew, Minn	44
1909	Ty Cobb, Det	9		Carl Yastrzemski, Bos	44
1910	Jake Stahl, Bos	10	1968	Frank Howard, Wash	44
1911	Frank Baker, Phi	9	1969	Harmon Killebrew, Minn	49
1912	Frank Baker, Phi	10	1970	Frank Howard, Wash	44
	Tris Speaker, Bos	10	1971	Bill Melton, Chi	33
1913	Frank Baker, Phi	13	1972	Dick Allen, Chi	37
1914	Frank Baker, Phi	9	1973	Reggie Jackson, Oak	32
1915	Braggo Roth, Chi-Clev	7	1974	Dick Allen, Chi	32
1916	Wally Pipp, NY	12	1975	Reggie Jackson, Oak	36
1917	Wally Pipp, NY	9		George Scott, Mil	36
1918	Babe Ruth, Bos	11	1976	Graig Nettles, NY	32
	Tilly Walker, Phi	11	1977	Jim Rice, Bos	39
1919	Babe Ruth, Bos	29	1978	Jim Rice, Bos	46
1920	Babe Ruth, NY	54	1979	Gorman Thomas, Mil	45
1921	Babe Ruth, NY	59	1980	Reggie Jackson, NY	41
1922	Ken Williams, StL	39		Ben Oglivie, Mil	41
1923	Babe Ruth, NY	41	1981	Tony Armas, Oak	22
1924	Babe Ruth, NY	46		Dwight Evans, Bos	22
1925	Bob Meusel, NY	33		Bobby Grich, Cal	22
1926	Babe Ruth, NY	47		Eddie Murray, Balt	22
1927	Babe Ruth, NY	60	1982	Reggie Jackson, Cal	39
1928	Babe Ruth, NY	54		Gorman Thomas, Mil	39
1929	Babe Ruth, NY	46	1983	Jim Rice, Bos	39
1930	Babe Ruth, NY	49	1984	Tony Armas, Bos	43
1931	Lou Gehrig, NY	46	1985	Darrell Evans, Det	40
	Babe Ruth, NY	46	1986	Jesse Barfield, Tor	40
1932	Jimmie Foxx, Phi	58	1987	Mark McGwire, Oak	49
1933	Jimmie Foxx, Phi	48	1988	Jose Canseco, Oak	42
1934	Lou Gehrig, NY	49	1989	Fred McGriff, Tor	36
1935	Jimmie Foxx, Phi	36	1990	Cecil Fielder, Det	51
	Hank Greenberg, Det	36	1991	Jose Canseco, Oak	44
1936	Lou Gehrig, NY	49		Cecil Fielder, Det	44
1937	Joe DiMaggio, NY	46	1992	Juan Gonzalez, Tex	43
1938	Hank Greenberg, Det	58	1993	Juan Gonzalez, Tex	46
1939	Jimmie Foxx, Bos	35	1994	Ken Griffey Jr., Sea	40
1940	Hank Greenberg, Det	41	1995	Albert Belle, Clev	50
1941	Ted Williams, Bos	37	1996	Mark McGwire, Oak	52
1942	Ted Williams, Bos	36	1997	Ken Griffey Jr., Sea	56
1943	Rudy York, Det	34	1998	Ken Griffey Jr., Sea	56
1944	Nick Etten, NY	22	1999	Ken Griffey Jr., Sea	48
1945	Vern Stephens, StL	24	2000	Troy Glaus, Ana	47
1946	Hank Greenberg, Det	44	2001	Alex Rodriguez, Tex	52
1947	Ted Williams, Bos	32	2002	Alex Rodriguez, Tex	57
1948	Joe DiMaggio, NY	39	2003	Alex Rodriguez, Tex	47
1949	Ted Williams, Bos	43	2004	Manny Ramirez, Bos	43
1950	Al Rosen, Clev	37	2005	Alex Rodriguez, NY	48
1951	Gus Zernial, Chi-Phi	33	2006	David Ortiz, Bos	54
1952	Larry Doby, Clev	32	2007	Alex Rodriguez, NY	54
1953	Al Rosen, Clev	43	2008	Miguel Cabrera, Det	37
1954	Larry Doby, Clev	32	2009	Carlos Pena, TB	39
1955	Mickey Mantle, NY	37		Mark Teixeira, NY	39
1956	Mickey Mantle, NY	52	2010	Jose Bautista, Tor	54
1957	Roy Sievers, Wash	42	2011	Jose Bautista, Tor	43
1958	Mickey Mantle, NY	42	2012	Miguel Cabrera, Det	44
1959	Rocky Colavito, Clev	42	2013	Chris Davis, Bal	53
	Harmon Killebrew, Wash	42			

AMERICAN LEAGUE (Cont.)
Runs Batted In Leaders

Year	Player and Team	RBI	Year	Player and Team	RBI
1901	Nap Lajoie, Phi	125	1956	Mickey Mantle, NY	130
1902	Buck Freeman, Bos	121	1957	Roy Sievers, Wash	114
1903	Buck Freeman, Bos	104	1958	Jackie Jensen, Bos	122
1904	Nap Lajoie, Clev	102	1959	Jackie Jensen, Bos	112
1905	Harry Davis, Phi	83	1960	Roger Maris, NY	112
1906	Harry Davis, Phi	96	1961	Roger Maris, NY	142
1907	Ty Cobb, Det	116	1962	Harmon Killebrew, Minn	126
1908	Ty Cobb, Det	108	1963	Dick Stuart, Bos	118
1909	Ty Cobb, Det	107	1964	Brooks Robinson, Balt	118
1910	Sam Crawford, Det	120	1965	Rocky Colavito, Clev	108
1911	Ty Cobb, Det	144	1966	Frank Robinson, Balt	122
1912	Frank Baker, Phi	133	1967	Carl Yastrzemski, Bos	121
1913	Frank Baker, Phi	126	1968	Ken Harrelson, Bos	109
1914	Sam Crawford, Det	104	1969	Harmon Killebrew, Minn	140
1915	Sam Crawford, Det	112	1970	Frank Howard, Wash	126
	Bobby Veach, Det	112	1971	Harmon Killebrew, Minn	119
1916	Del Pratt, StL	103	1972	Dick Allen, Chi	113
1917	Bobby Veach, Det	103	1973	Reggie Jackson, Oak	117
1918	Bobby Veach, Det	78	1974	Jeff Burroughs, Tex	118
1919	Babe Ruth, Bos	114	1975	George Scott, Mil	109
1920	Babe Ruth, NY	137	1976	Lee May, Balt	109
1921	Babe Ruth, NY	171	1977	Larry Hisle, Minn	119
1922	Ken Williams, StL	155	1978	Jim Rice, Bos	139
1923	Babe Ruth, NY	131	1979	Don Baylor, Cal	139
1924	Goose Goslin, Wash	129	1980	Cecil Cooper, Mil	122
1925	Bob Meusel, NY	138	1981	Eddie Murray, Balt	78
1926	Babe Ruth, NY	145	1982	Hal McRae, KC	133
1927	Lou Gehrig, NY	175	1983	Cecil Cooper, Mil	126
1928	Lou Gehrig, NY	142		Jim Rice, Bos	126
	Babe Ruth, NY	142	1984	Tony Armas, Bos	123
1929	Al Simmons, Phi	157	1985	Don Mattingly, NY	145
1930	Lou Gehrig, NY	174	1986	Joe Carter, Clev	121
1931	Lou Gehrig, NY	184	1987	George Bell, Tor	134
1932	Jimmie Foxx, Phi	169	1988	Jose Canseco, Oak	124
1933	Jimmie Foxx, Phi	163	1989	Ruben Sierra, Tex	119
1934	Lou Gehrig, NY	165	1990	Cecil Fielder, Det	132
1935	Hank Greenberg, Det	170	1991	Cecil Fielder, Det	133
1936	Hal Trosky, Clev	162	1992	Cecil Fielder, Det	124
1937	Hank Greenberg, Det	183	1993	Albert Belle, Clev	129
1938	Jimmie Foxx, Bos	175	1994	Kirby Puckett, Minn	112
1939	Ted Williams, Bos	145	1995	Albert Belle, Clev	126
1940	Hank Greenberg, Det	150		Mo Vaughn, Bos	126
1941	Joe DiMaggio, NY	125	1996	Albert Belle, Clev	148
1942	Ted Williams, Bos	137	1997	Ken Griffey Jr., Sea	147
1943	Rudy York, Det	118	1998	Juan Gonzales, Tex	157
1944	Vern Stephens, StL	109	1999	Manny Ramirez, Clev	165
1945	Nick Etten, NY	111	2000	Edgar Martinez, Sea	145
1946	Hank Greenberg, Det	127	2001	Bret Boone, Sea	141
1947	Ted Williams, Bos	114	2002	Alex Rodriguez, Tex	142
1948	Joe DiMaggio, NY	155	2003	Carlos Delgado, Tor	145
1949	Vern Stephens, Bos	159	2004	Miguel Tejada, Balt	150
	Ted Williams, Bos	159	2005	David Ortiz, Bos	148
1950	Walt Dropo, Bos	144	2006	David Ortiz, Bos	137
	Vern Stephens, Bos	144	2007	Alex Rodriguez, NY	156
1951	Gus Zernial, Chi-Phi	129	2008	Josh Hamilton, Tex	130
1952	Al Rosen, Clev	105	2009	Mark Teixeira, NY	122
1953	Al Rosen, Clev	145	2010	Miguel Cabrera, Det	126
1954	Larry Doby, Clev	126	2011	Curtis Granderson, NY	119
1955	Ray Boone, Det	116	2012	Miguel Cabrera, Det	139
	Jackie Jensen, Bos	116	2013	Chris Davis, Bal	138

AMERICAN LEAGUE *(Cont.)*
Leading Base Stealers

Year	Player and Team	SB	Year	Player and Team	SB
1901	Frank Isbell, Chi	48	1957	Luis Aparicio, Chi	28
1902	Topsy Hartsel, Phi	54	1958	Luis Aparicio, Chi	29
1903	Harry Bay, Clev	46	1959	Luis Aparicio, Chi	56
1904	Harry Bay, Clev	42	1960	Luis Aparicio, Chi	51
	Elmer Flick, Clev	42	1961	Luis Aparicio, Chi	53
1905	Danny Hoffman, Phi	46	1962	Luis Aparicio, Chi	31
1906	John Anderson, Wash	39	1963	Luis Aparicio, Balt	40
	Elmer Flick, Clev	39	1964	Luis Aparicio, Balt	57
1907	Ty Cobb, Det	49	1965	Bert Campaneris, KC	51
1908	Patsy Dougherty, Chi	47	1966	Bert Campaneris, KC	52
1909	Ty Cobb, Det	76	1967	Bert Campaneris, KC	55
1910	Eddie Collins, Phi	81	1968	Bert Campaneris, Oak	62
1911	Ty Cobb, Det	83	1969	Tommy Harper, Sea	73
1912	Clyde Milan, Wash	88	1970	Bert Campaneris, Oak	42
1913	Clyde Milan, Wash	75	1971	Amos Otis, KC	52
1914	Fritz Maisel, NY	74	1972	Bert Campaneris, Oak	52
1915	Ty Cobb, Det	96	1973	Tommy Harper, Bos	54
1916	Ty Cobb, Det	68	1974	Bill North, Oak	54
1917	Ty Cobb, Det	55	1975	Mickey Rivers, Cal	70
1918	George Sisler, StL	45	1976	Bill North, Oak	75
1919	Eddie Collins, Chi	33	1977	Freddie Patek, KC	53
1920	Sam Rice, Wash	63	1978	Ron LeFlore, Det	68
1921	George Sisler, StL	35	1979	Willie Wilson, KC	83
1922	George Sisler, StL	51	1980	Rickey Henderson, Oak	100
1923	Eddie Collins, Chi	49	1981	Rickey Henderson, Oak	56
1924	Eddie Collins, Chi	42	1982	Rickey Henderson, Oak	130
1925	John Mostil, Chi	43	1983	Rickey Henderson, Oak	108
1926	John Mostil, Chi	35	1984	Rickey Henderson, Oak	66
1927	George Sisler, StL	27	1985	Rickey Henderson, NY	80
1928	Buddy Myer, Bos	30	1986	Rickey Henderson, NY	87
1929	Charlie Gehringer, Det	27	1987	Harold Reynolds, Sea	60
1930	Marty McManus, Det	23	1988	Rickey Henderson, NY	93
1931	Ben Chapman, NY	61	1989	Rickey Henderson, NY-Oak	77
1932	Ben Chapman, NY	38	1990	Rickey Henderson, Oak	65
1933	Ben Chapman, NY	27	1991	Rickey Henderson, Oak	58
1934	Bill Werber, Bos	40	1992	Kenny Lofton, Clev	66
1935	Bill Werber, Bos	29	1993	Kenny Lofton, Clev	70
1936	Lyn Lary, StL	37	1994	Kenny Lofton, Clev	60
1937	Ben Chapman, Wash-Bos	35	1995	Kenny Lofton, Clev	54
	Bill Werber, Phi	35	1996	Kenny Lofton, Clev	75
1938	Frank Crosetti, NY	27	1997	Brian Hunter, Det	74
1939	George Case, Wash	51	1998	Rickey Henderson, Oak	66
1940	George Case, Wash	35	1999	Brian Hunter, Sea	44
1941	George Case, Wash	33	2000	Johnny Damon, KC	46
1942	George Case, Wash	44	2001	Ichiro Suzuki, Sea	56
1943	George Case, Wash	61	2002	Alfonso Soriano, NY	41
1944	Snuffy Stirnweiss, NY	55	2003	Carl Crawford, TB	55
1945	Snuffy Stirnweiss, NY	33	2004	Carl Crawford, TB	59
1946	George Case, Clev	28	2005	Chone Figgins, LA	62
1947	Bob Dillinger, StL	34	2006	Carl Crawford, TB	58
1948	Bob Dillinger, StL	28	2007	Carl Crawford, TB	50
1949	Bob Dillinger, StL	20		Brian Roberts, Balt	50
1950	Dom DiMaggio, Bos	15	2008	Jacoby Ellsbury, Bos	50
1951	Minnie Minoso, Clev-Chi	31	2009	Jacoby Ellsbury, Bos	70
1952	Minnie Minoso, Chi	22	2010	Juan Pierre, Chi	68
1953	Minnie Minoso, Chi	25	2011	Coco Crisp, Oak	49
1954	Jackie Jensen, Bos	22		Brett Gardner, NY	49
1955	Jim Rivera, Chi	25	2012	Mike Trout, LA	49
1956	Luis Aparicio, Chi	21	2013	Jacoby Ellsbury, Bos	52

AMERICAN LEAGUE (Cont.)

Leading Pitchers—Winning Percentage

Year	Pitcher and Team	W	L	Pct	Year	Pitcher and Team	W	L	Pct
1901	Clark Griffith, Chi	24	7	.774	1958	Bob Turley, NY	21	7	.750
1902	Bill Bernhard, Phi-Clev	18	5	.783	1959	Bob Shaw, Chi	18	6	.750
1903	Earl Moore, Clev	22	7	.759	1960	Jim Perry, Clev	18	10	.643
1904	Jack Chesbro, NY	41	12	.774	1961	Whitey Ford, NY	25	4	.862
1905	Jess Tannehill, Bos	22	9	.710	1962	Ray Herbert, Chi	20	9	.690
1906	Eddie Plank, Phi	19	6	.760	1963	Whitey Ford, NY	24	7	.774
1907	Wild Bill Donovan, Det	25	4	.862	1964	Wally Bunker, Balt	19	5	.792
1908	Ed Walsh, Chi	40	15	.727	1965	Mudcat Grant, Minn	21	7	.750
1909	George Mullin, Det	29	8	.784	1966	Sonny Siebert, Clev	16	8	.667
1910	Chief Bender, Phi	23	5	.821	1967	Joel Horlen, Chi	19	7	.731
1911	Chief Bender, Phi	17	5	.773	1968	Denny McLain, Det	31	6	.838
1912	Smoky Joe Wood, Bos	34	5	.872	1969	Jim Palmer, Balt	16	4	.800
1913	Walter Johnson, Wash	36	7	.837	1970	Mike Cuellar, Balt	24	8	.750
1914	Chief Bender, Phi	17	3	.850	1971	Dave McNally, Balt	21	5	.808
1915	Smoky Joe Wood, Bos	15	5	.750	1972	Catfish Hunter, Oak	21	7	.750
1916	Eddie Cicotte, Chi	15	7	.682	1973	Catfish Hunter, Oak	21	5	.808
1917	Reb Russell, Chi	15	5	.750	1974	Mike Cuellar, Balt	22	10	.688
1918	Sad Sam Jones, Bos	16	5	.762	1975	Mike Torrez, Balt	20	9	.690
1919	Eddie Cicotte, Chi	29	7	.806	1976	Bill Campbell, Minn	17	5	.773
1920	Jim Bagby, Clev	31	12	.721	1977	Paul Splittorff, KC	16	6	.727
1921	Carl Mays, NY	27	9	.750	1978	Ron Guidry, NY	25	3	.893
1922	Joe Bush, NY	26	7	.788	1979	Mike Caldwell, Mil	16	6	.727
1923	Herb Pennock, NY	19	6	.760	1980	Steve Stone, Balt	25	7	.781
1924	Walter Johnson, Wash	23	7	.767	1981*	Pete Vuckovich, Mil	14	4	.778
1925	Stan Coveleski, Wash	20	5	.800	1982	Jim Palmer, Balt	15	5	.750
1926	George Uhle, Clev	27	11	.711		Pete Vuckovich, Mil	18	6	.750
1927	Waite Hoyt, NY	22	7	.759	1983	Richard Dotson, Chi	22	7	.759
1928	General Crowder, StL	21	5	.808	1984	Doyle Alexander, Tor	17	6	.739
1929	Lefty Grove, Phi	20	6	.769	1985	Ron Guidry, NY	22	6	.786
1930	Lefty Grove, Phi	28	5	.848	1986	Roger Clemens, Bos	24	4	.857
1931	Lefty Grove, Phi	31	4	.886	1987	Roger Clemens, Bos	20	9	.690
1932	Johnny Allen, NY	17	4	.810	1988	Frank Viola, Minn	24	7	.774
1933	Lefty Grove, Phi	24	8	.750	1989	Bret Saberhagen, KC	23	6	.793
1934	Lefty Gomez, NY	26	5	.839	1990	Bob Welch, Oak	27	6	.818
1935	Eldon Auker, Det	18	7	.720	1991	Scott Erickson, Minn	20	8	.714
1936	Monte Pearson, NY	19	7	.731	1992	Mike Mussina, Balt	18	5	.783
1937	Johnny Allen, Clev	15	1	.938	1993	Jimmy Key, NY	18	6	.750
1938	Red Ruffing, NY	21	7	.750	1994	Jimmy Key, NY	17	4	.810
1939	Lefty Grove, Bos	15	4	.789	1995	Randy Johnson, Sea	18	2	.900
1940	Schoolboy Rowe, Det	16	3	.842	1996	Charles Nagy, Clev	17	5	.773
1941	Lefty Gomez, NY	15	5	.750	1997	Randy Johnson, Sea	20	4	.833
1942	Ernie Bonham, NY	21	5	.808	1998	David Wells, NY	18	4	.818
1943	Spud Chandler, NY	20	4	.833	1999	Pedro Martinez, Bos	23	4	.852
1944	Tex Hughson, Bos	18	5	.783	2000	Tim Hudson, Oak	20	6	.769
1945	Hal Newhouser, Det	25	9	.735	2001	Roger Clemens, NY	20	3	.870
1946	Boo Ferriss, Bos	25	6	.806	2002	Pedro Martinez, Bos	20	4	.833
1947	Allie Reynolds, NY	19	8	.704	2003	Roy Halladay, Tor	22	7	.759
1948	Jack Kramer, Bos	18	5	.783	2004	Curt Schilling, Bos	21	6	.778
1949	Ellis Kinder, Bos	23	6	.793	2005	Cliff Lee, Clev	18	5	.783
1950	Vic Raschi, NY	21	8	.724	2006	Roy Halladay, Tor	16	5	.762
1951	Bob Feller, Clev	22	8	.733	2007	Justin Verlander, Det	18	6	.750
1952	Bobby Shantz, Phi	24	7	.774	2008	Cliff Lee, Clev	22	3	.880
1953	Ed Lopat, NY	16	4	.800	2009	Felix Hernandez, Sea	19	5	.792
1954	Sandy Consuegra, Chi	16	3	.842	2010	David Price, TB	19	6	.760
1955	Tommy Byrne, NY	16	5	.762	2011	Justin Verlander, Det	24	5	.828
1956	Whitey Ford, NY	19	6	.760	2012	David Price, TB	20	5	.800
1957	Dick Donovan, Chi	16	6	.727		Jered Weaver, LA	20	5	.800
	Tom Sturdivant, NY	16	6	.727	2013	Max Scherzer, Det	21	3	.875

*1981 percentages based on 10 or more victories. Note: Percentages based on 15 or more victories in all other years.

AMERICAN LEAGUE *(Cont.)*
Leading Pitchers—Earned Run Average

Year	Player and Team	ERA	Year	Player and Team	ERA
1913	Walter Johnson, Wash	1.14	1964	Dean Chance, LA	1.65
1914	Dutch Leonard, Bos	1.01	1965	Sam McDowell, Clev	2.18
1915	Smoky Joe Wood, Bos	1.49	1966	Gary Peters, Chi	1.98
1916	Babe Ruth, Bos	1.75	1967	Joe Horlen, Chi	2.06
1917	Eddie Cicotte, Chi	1.53	1968	Luis Tiant, Clev	1.60
1918	Walter Johnson, Wash	1.27	1969	Dick Bosman, Wash	2.19
1919	Walter Johnson, Wash	1.49	1970	Diego Segui, Oak	2.56
1920	Bob Shawkey, NY	2.46	1971	Vida Blue, Oak	1.82
1921	Red Faber, Chi	2.47	1972	Luis Tiant, Bos	1.91
1922	Red Faber, Chi	2.80	1973	Jim Palmer, Balt	2.40
1923	Stan Coveleski, Clev	2.76	1974	Catfish Hunter, Oak	2.49
1924	Walter Johnson, Wash	2.72	1975	Jim Palmer, Balt	2.09
1925	Stan Coveleski, Wash	2.84	1976	Mark Fidrych, Det	2.34
1926	Lefty Grove, Phi	2.51	1977	Frank Tanana, Cal	2.54
1927	Wilcy Moore, NY#	2.28	1978	Ron Guidry, NY	1.74
1928	Garland Braxton, Wash	2.52	1979	Ron Guidry, NY	2.78
1929	Lefty Grove, Phi	2.81	1980	Rudy May, NY	2.47
1930	Lefty Grove, Phi	2.54	1981	Steve McCatty, Oak	2.32
1931	Lefty Grove, Phi	2.06	1982	Rick Sutcliffe, Clev	2.96
1932	Lefty Grove, Phi	2.84	1983	Rick Honeycutt, Tex	2.42
1933	Monte Pearson, Clev	2.33	1984	Mike Boddicker, Balt	2.79
1934	Lefty Gomez, NY	2.33	1985	Dave Stieb, Tor	2.48
1935	Lefty Grove, Bos	2.70	1986	Roger Clemens, Bos	2.48
1936	Lefty Grove, Bos	2.81	1987	Jimmy Key, Tor	2.76
1937	Lefty Gomez, NY	2.33	1988	Allan Anderson, Minn	2.45
1938	Lefty Grove, Bos	3.07	1989	Bret Saberhagen, KC	2.16
1939	Lefty Grove, Bos	2.54	1990	Roger Clemens, Bos	1.93
1940	Bob Feller, Clev†	2.62	1991	Roger Clemens, Bos	2.62
1941	Thornton Lee, Chi	2.37	1992	Roger Clemens, Bos	2.41
1942	Ted Lyons, Chi	2.10	1993	Kevin Appier, KC	2.56
1943	Spud Chandler, NY	1.64	1994	Steve Ontiveros, Oak	2.65
1944	Dizzy Trout, Det	2.12	1995	Randy Johnson, Sea	2.48
1945	Hal Newhouser, Det	1.81	1996	Juan Guzman, Tor	2.93
1946	Hal Newhouser, Det	1.94	1997	Roger Clemens, Tor	2.05
1947	Spud Chandler, NY	2.46	1998	Roger Clemens, Tor	2.64
1948	Gene Bearden, Clev	2.43	1999	Pedro Martinez, Bos	2.07
1949	Mel Parnell, Bos	2.78	2000	Pedro Martinez, Bos	1.74
1950	Early Wynn, Clev	3.20	2001	Freddy Garcia, Sea	3.05
1951	Saul Rogovin, Det-Chi	2.78	2002	Pedro Martinez, Bos	2.26
1952	Allie Reynolds, NY	2.07	2003	Pedro Martinez, Bos	2.22
1953	Ed Lopat, NY	2.43	2004	Johan Santana, Minn	2.61
1954	Mike Garcia, Clev	2.64	2005	Kevin Millwood, Clev	2.86
1955	Billy Pierce, Chi	1.97	2006	Johan Santana, Minn	2.77
1956	Whitey Ford, NY	2.47	2007	John Lackey, LA	3.01
1957	Bobby Shantz, NY	2.45	2008	Cliff Lee, Clev	2.54
1958	Whitey Ford, NY	2.01	2009	Zack Greinke, KC	2.16
1959	Hoyt Wilhelm, Balt	2.19	2010	Felix Hernandez, Sea	2.27
1960	Frank Baumann, Chi	2.68	2011	Justin Verlander, Det	2.40
1961	Dick Donovan, Wash	2.40	2012	David Price, TB	2.56
1962	Hank Aguirre, Det	2.21	2013	Anibel Sanchez, Det	2.57
1963	Gary Peters, Chi	2.33			

Note: Based on 10 complete games through 1950, then 154 innings until the American League expanded in 1961, when it became 162 innings. In strike-shortened 1981, one inning per game required. Earned runs not tabulated in American League prior to 1913. #Wilcy Moore pitched only six complete games—he started 12—in 1927 but was recognized as leader because of 213 innings pitched. †Ernie Bonham, New York, had 1.91 ERA and 10 complete games in 1940 but appeared in only 12 games and 99 innings, and Bob Feller was recognized as the leader.

AMERICAN LEAGUE (Cont.)
Leading Pitchers—Strikeouts

Year	Player and Team	SO	Year	Player and Team	SO
1901	Cy Young, Bos	159	1957	Early Wynn, Clev	184
1902	Rube Waddell, Phi	210	1958	Early Wynn, Chi	179
1903	Rube Waddell, Phi	301	1959	Jim Bunning, Det	201
1904	Rube Waddell, Phi	349	1960	Jim Bunning, Det	201
1905	Rube Waddell, Phi	286	1961	Camilo Pascual, Minn	221
1906	Rube Waddell, Phi	203	1962	Camilo Pascual, Minn	206
1907	Rube Waddell, Phi	226	1963	Camilo Pascual, Minn	202
1908	Ed Walsh, Chi	269	1964	Al Downing, NY	217
1909	Frank Smith, Chi	177	1965	Sam McDowell, Clev	325
1910	Walter Johnson, Wash	313	1966	Sam McDowell, Clev	225
1911	Ed Walsh, Chi	255	1967	Jim Lonborg, Bos	246
1912	Walter Johnson, Wash	303	1968	Sam McDowell, Clev	283
1913	Walter Johnson, Wash	243	1969	Sam McDowell, Clev	279
1914	Walter Johnson, Wash	225	1970	Sam McDowell, Clev	304
1915	Walter Johnson, Wash	203	1971	Mickey Lolich, Det	308
1916	Walter Johnson, Wash	228	1972	Nolan Ryan, Cal	329
1917	Walter Johnson, Wash	188	1973	Nolan Ryan, Cal	383
1918	Walter Johnson, Wash	162	1974	Nolan Ryan, Cal	367
1919	Walter Johnson, Wash	147	1975	Frank Tanana, Cal	269
1920	Stan Coveleski, Clev	133	1976	Nolan Ryan, Cal	327
1921	Walter Johnson, Wash	143	1977	Nolan Ryan, Cal	341
1922	Urban Shocker, StL	149	1978	Nolan Ryan, Cal	260
1923	Walter Johnson, Wash	130	1979	Nolan Ryan, Cal	223
1924	Walter Johnson, Wash	158	1980	Len Barker, Clev	187
1925	Lefty Grove, Phi	116	1981	Len Barker, Clev	127
1926	Lefty Grove, Phi	194	1982	Floyd Bannister, Sea	209
1927	Lefty Grove, Phi	174	1983	Jack Morris, Det	232
1928	Lefty Grove, Phi	183	1984	Mark Langston, Sea	204
1929	Lefty Grove, Phi	170	1985	Bert Blyleven, Clev-Minn	206
1930	Lefty Grove, Phi	209	1986	Mark Langston, Sea	245
1931	Lefty Grove, Phi	175	1987	Mark Langston, Sea	262
1932	Red Ruffing, NY	190	1988	Roger Clemens, Bos	291
1933	Lefty Gomez, NY	163	1989	Nolan Ryan, Tex	301
1934	Lefty Gomez, NY	158	1990	Nolan Ryan, Tex	232
1935	Tommy Bridges, Det	163	1991	Roger Clemens, Bos	241
1936	Tommy Bridges, Det	175	1992	Randy Johnson, Sea	241
1937	Lefty Gomez, NY	194	1993	Randy Johnson, Sea	308
1938	Bob Feller, Clev	240	1994	Randy Johnson, Sea	204
1939	Bob Feller, Clev	246	1995	Randy Johnson, Sea	294
1940	Bob Feller, Clev	261	1996	Roger Clemens, Bos	257
1941	Bob Feller, Clev	260	1997	Roger Clemens, Tor	292
1942	Bobo Newsom, Wash	113	1998	Roger Clemens, Tor	271
	Tex Hughson, Bos	113	1999	Pedro Martinez, Bos	313
1943	Allie Reynolds, Clev	151	2000	Pedro Martinez, Bos	284
1944	Hal Newhouser, Det	187	2001	Hideo Nomo, Bos	220
1945	Hal Newhouser, Det	212	2002	Pedro Martinez, Bos	239
1946	Bob Feller, Clev	348	2003	Esteban Loaiza, Chi	207
1947	Bob Feller, Clev	196	2004	Johan Santana, Minn	265
1948	Bob Feller, Clev	164	2005	Johan Santana, Minn	238
1949	Virgil Trucks, Det	153	2006	Johan Santana, Minn	245
1950	Bob Lemon, Clev	170	2007	Scott Kazmir, TB	239
1951	Vic Raschi, NY	164	2008	A.J. Burnett, Tor	231
1952	Allie Reynolds, NY	160	2009	Justin Verlander, Det	269
1953	Billy Pierce, Chi	186	2010	Jered Weaver, LA	233
1954	Bob Turley, Balt	185	2011	Justin Verlander, Det	250
1955	Herb Score, Clev	245	2012	Justin Verlander, Det	239
1956	Herb Score, Clev	263	2013	Yu Darvish, Tex	277

AMERICAN *(Cont.)*
Leading Pitchers—Saves

FYear	Player and Team	SV	Year	Player and Team	SV
1947	Joe Page, NY	17	1981	Rollie Fingers, Mil	28
1948	Russ Christopher, Clev	17	1982	Dan Quisenberry, KC	35
1949	Joe Page, NY	29	1983	Dan Quisenberry, KC	35
1950	Mickey Harris, Wash	15	1984	Dan Quisenberry, KC	44
1951	Ellis Kinder, Bos	14	1985	Dan Quisenberry, KC	37
1952	Harry Dorish, Chi	11	1986	Dave Righetti, NY	46
1953	Ellis Kinder, Bos	27	1987	Tom Henke, Tor	34
1954	Johnny Sain, NY	22	1988	Dennis Eckersley, Oak	45
1955	Ray Narleski, Clev	19	1989	Jeff Russell, Tex	38
1956	George Zuverink, Bal	16	1990	Bobby Thigpen, Chi	57
1957	Bob Grim, NY	19	1991	Bryan Harvey, Cal	46
1958	Ryne Duren, NY	20	1992	Dennis Eckersley, Oak	51
1959	Turk Lown, Chi	15	1993	Jeff Montgomery, KC	45
1960	Mike Fornieles, Bos	14		Duane Ward, Tor	45
	Johnny Klippstein, Clev	14	1994	Lee Smith, Bal	33
1961	Luis Arroyo, NY	29	1995	Jose Mesa, Clev	46
1962	Dick Radatz, Bos	24	1996	John Wetteland, NY	43
1963	Stu Miller, Bal	27	1997	Randy Myers, Balt	45
1964	Dick Radatz, Bos	29	1998	Tom Gordon, Bos	46
1965	Ron Kline, Wash	29	1999	Mariano Rivera, NY	45
1966	Jack Aker, KC	32	2000	Todd Jones, Det	42
1967	Minnie Rojas, Cal	27	2001	Mariano Rivera, NY	50
1968	Al Worthington, Minn	18	2002	Eddie Guardado, Minn	45
1969	Ron Perranoski, Minn	31	2003	Keith Foulke, Oak	43
1970	Ron Perranoski, Minn	34	2004	Mariano Rivera, NY	53
1971	Ken Sanders, Mil	31	2005	Francisco Rodríguez, LA	45
1972	Sparky Lyle, NY	35		Bob Wickman, Clev	45
1973	John Hiller, Det	38	2006	Francisco Rodríguez, LA	47
1974	Terry Forster, Chi	24	2007	Joe Borowski, Clev	45
1975	Goose Gossage, Chi	26	2008	Francisco Rodriguez, LA	62
1976	Sparky Lyle, NY	23	2009	Brian Fuentes, LA	48
1977	Bill Campbell, Bos	31	2010	Rafael Soriano, TB	45
1978	Goose Gossage, NY	27	2011	Jose Valverde, Det	49
1979	Mike Marshall, Minn	32	2012	Jim Johnson, Bal	51
1980	Dan Quisenberry, KC	33	2013	Jim Johnson, Bal	50

The Commissioners of Baseball

Kenesaw Mountain Landis.....Elected Nov. 12, 1920. Served until his death on Nov. 25, 1944.

Happy Chandler......................Elected April 24, 1945. Served until July 15, 1951.

Ford Frick ....Elected Sept. 20, 1951. Served until Nov. 16, 1965.

William Eckert........................Elected Nov. 17, 1965. Served until Dec. 20, 1968.

Bowie Kuhn ....Elected Feb. 8, 1969. Served until Sept. 30, 1984.

Peter Ueberroth......................Elected March 3, 1984. Took office Oct. 1, 1984. Served through March 31, 1989.

A. Bartlett Giamatti.................Elected Sept. 8, 1988. Took office April 1, 1989. Served until his death on Sept. 1, 1989.

Francis Vincent Jr. ....Appointed Acting Commissioner Sept. 2, 1989. Elected Commissioner Sept. 13, 1989. Served through Sept. 7, 1992.

Allan H. (Bud) Selig...............Elected chairman of the executive council and given the powers of interim commissioner on Sept. 9, 1992. Unanimously elected Commissioner July 9, 1998.

Joe Flacco led the Baltmore Ravens to a 34–31 victory over the San Francisco 49ers in Super Bowl XLVII

Pro Football

JOHN BIEVER

Recovering Nicely

Dogged by controversy and scandal early on, the NFL got back on track with a bumper crop of talented rookies and rejuvenated veterans before finishing strong in a competitive and entertaining Super Bowl

BY HANK HERSCH

THE 2012 NFL SEASON THAT began under the cloud of a scandal and the president's indignation ended with bright glimpses of the quarterbacking future and an embrace of fraternal love. The climax occurred on the carpet of the Superdome in New Orleans, after second-year 49ers QB Colin Kaepernick made another electric statement on behalf of the read-option but coming up just short. Then San Francisco coach Jim Harbaugh congratulated his older brother, John, who had just guided the Ravens to a 34–31 victory in Super Bowl XLVII. "The toughest part of all was walking across the field," said John. "There was a great amount of elation and a great amount of devastation and those two feelings went hand-in-hand at that moment."

Tell that to commissioner Roger Goodell. After steering the league toward a new collective bargaining agreement in the summer of 2011, he encountered a new problem in the spring of '12: Bountygate. Revelations that the Saints had been using a slush fund to pay players for injuring opponents prompted Goodell to hand down a raft of penalties, including year-long suspensions for coach Sean Payton, defensive coordinator Gregg Williams and linebacker Jonathan Vilma. (Vilma's suspension was later vacated.)

Then three weeks into the season a crew of replacement referees—working in place of the locked-out officials—bollixed the final play of a 14–12 Seahawks victory over the Packers, ruling what should have been a Green Bay interception in the end zone a 24-yard touchdown catch for receiver Golden Tate. "Terrible," President Obama called the ruling. "I've been saying for months we gotta get our refs back." Two days after the blown call (aka the Fail Mary, aka the Inaccurate Reception), Goodell negotiated a settlement with the referees union.

Lost in the controversy was the mind and arm that launched the fourth-down TD, 5'11" Russell Wilson. A third-round pick out of Wisconsin, he began the season as the starter and quickly justified the wisdom of coach Pete Carroll's decision. Wilson led Seattle to the playoffs, rushing for 489 yards and throwing for 3,118 with a passer rating of 100.0—including 115.2 in December, when the Seahawks went 5–0. That combination of accuracy and precocity hardly made him unique among his draft class.

AL TIELEMANS

Sibling rivalry: Super Bowl XLVII, a.k.a. the Harbowl, featured the Ravens of John (left) versus the 49ers of younger brother, Jim.

Robert Griffin III, chosen second out Baylor, merely set the rookie record for passer rating (102.4) while guiding the Redskins to the postseason for the first time since 2007. And Andrew Luck, the No. 1 pick out of Stanford, took the Colts from 2–14 in 2011 to an 11–5 mark and the playoffs, breaking the first-year standards for passing yardage (4,374) and fourth-quarter comebacks (seven).

Wilson and Griffin wound up meeting in the NFC wild-card round, just the second postseason matchup of rookie QBs. (Seattle won 24–14, while Griffin left after tearing his right ACL and LCL.) "It's the evolution of football," said Carroll, "screaming at us."

Want more? Try a 27-year-old running back who, after suffering a torn ACL *and* MCL the previous December, not only returned in time to start the season opener but also finished with 2,097 yards, just nine

yards short of the league's rushing record. "How is that humanly possible?" Vikings running backs coach James Saxon would wonder after watching his star charge, 6'1", 217-pound Adrian Peterson, make a crazy cut and accelerate past a fleet of fleet defensive backs to the end zone. Peterson was voted the MVP, edging quarterback Peyton Manning, who made his own comeback from spinal fusion surgery, which had sidelined him for the entire 2011 season. The 36-year-old Manning completed a league-high 68.6% of his passes in taking his new team, the Broncos, to an AFC-best 13–3 record.

But in the divisional playoffs, home-field advantage and an 11-game winning streak weren't enough to carry Manning past Baltimore. A 70-yard Joe Flacco pass to Jacoby Jones with 31 seconds left tied the game, then a 47-yard Justin Tucker field goal—set up by a Manning pick—ended it, 38–35 in double overtime. Led by linebacker Ray Lewis, a 13-time Pro Bowler playing in his 17th and final season, the Ravens' D took

Wilson proved adept with both his arm and his feet, throwing for 3,118 yards and rushing for another 489.

up in the NFC title game by rallying San Francisco past the Falcons in the fourth quarter, 28–24.

Amid all the talk in New Orleans of Lewis's last game and Kaepernick's emergence and the Harbowl—what are the odds of brothers turned NFL coaches squaring off for the Lombardi Trophy?—Flacco received relatively scant attention. A drop-back passer and gifted bomb-thrower, he was the winningest QB since he entered the league in 2008, with a postseason victory in every season, but he was widely perceived as Baltimore's weak link when it mattered most. Not that he felt that way: Flacco turned down a lucrative contract extension in the belief that by season's end he would be worth more.

If that showed him to be a gambler, his call on third-and-inches in the fourth quarter confirmed it. After the Ravens had charged to a 28–6 lead—half of the points coming on Jones's 56-yard TD catch and 108-yard kickoff return—a partial power outage at the Superdome delayed play for 34 minutes. Kaepernick then turned on the juice, cutting the lead to 31–29. Baltimore had the ball on its own 45, and Flacco weighed his choices: handoff, sneak or audible to a pass. He took the riskiest option and threw a 15-yard pass to Anquan Boldin. "When you're a quarterback," Flacco said, "you take the play that's there."

That set up Tucker's 38-yard field goal and iced the Ravens' second title in 13 seasons. And Flacco? A few weeks after being named Super Bowl MVP, he signed a six-year, $120 million contract, the richest in the NFL.

over in the AFC championship game, forcing the potent Patriots into turnovers on their final four drives. At halftime of the 28–13 come-from-behind victory, said John Harbaugh, "We calmed down a little bit. We talked to the guys and told them it was going to be about playing persistent, patient and poised."

The other Harbaugh in the playoff bracket was watching one of the season's riskier decisions pay huge dividends. In late November he replaced QB Alex Smith, the No. 1 pick in 2005 who had led the team to the playoffs in '11, with a second-year man from Nevada. "The hot hand," Harbaugh called Kaepernick, a 6' 4", 230-pound second-round pick with blazing speed and a 94 mph fastball. And hot he remained, going 5-2-1 to finish the regular season before a pair of playoff wins. In a 45–31 defeat of the Packers, Kap threw for 263 yards and *rushed* for 181—a record for a QB in any NFL game. He followed that

2012 NFL Final Standings

American Football Conference

EAST DIVISION

	W	L	T	Pct	Pts	OP
New England	12	4	0	.750	557	331
Miami	7	9	0	.438	288	317
NY Jets	6	10	0	.375	281	375
Buffalo	6	10	0	.375	344	435

NORTH DIVISION

	W	L	T	Pct	Pts	OP
Baltimore	10	6	0	.625	398	344
*Cincinnati	10	6	0	.625	391	320
Pittsburgh	8	8	0	.500	336	314
Cleveland	5	11	0	.313	302	368

SOUTH DIVISION

	W	L	T	Pct	Pts	OP
Houston	12	4	0	.750	416	331
*Indianapolis	11	5	0	.688	357	387
Tennessee	6	10	0	.375	330	471
Jacksonville	2	14	0	.125	255	444

WEST DIVISION

	W	L	T	Pct	Pts	OP
Denver	13	3	0	.813	481	289
San Diego	7	9	0	.438	350	350
Oakland	4	12	0	.250	290	443
Kansas City	2	14	0	.125	211	425

National Football Conference

EAST DIVISION

	W	L	T	Pct	Pts	OP
Washington	10	6	0	.625	436	388
NY Giants	9	7	0	.563	429	344
Dallas	8	8	0	.500	376	400
Philadelphia	4	12	0	.250	280	444

NORTH DIVISION

	W	L	T	Pct	Pts	OP
Green Bay	11	5	0	.688	433	336
*Minnesota	10	6	0	.625	379	348
Chicago	10	6	0	.625	375	277
Detroit	4	12	0	.250	372	437

SOUTH DIVISION

	W	L	T	Pct	Pts	OP
Atlanta	13	3	0	.813	419	299
Carolina	7	9	0	.438	357	363
New Orleans	7	9	0	.438	461	454
Tampa Bay	7	9	0	.438	389	394

WEST DIVISION

	W	L	T	Pct	Pts	OP
San Francisco	11	4	1	.719	397	273
*Seattle	11	5	0	.688	412	245
St. Louis	7	8	1	.469	299	348
Arizona	5	11	0	.313	250	357

* Wild-card team.

2012–13 NFL Playoffs

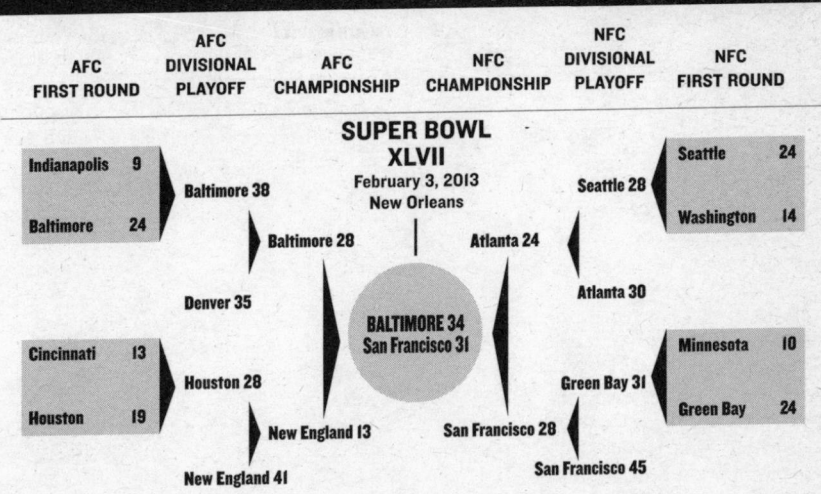

AFC FIRST ROUND	AFC DIVISIONAL PLAYOFF	AFC CHAMPIONSHIP	NFC CHAMPIONSHIP	NFC DIVISIONAL PLAYOFF	NFC FIRST ROUND

SUPER BOWL XLVII
February 3, 2013
New Orleans

BALTIMORE 34
San Francisco 31

Indianapolis 9
Baltimore 24
Baltimore 38
Baltimore 28
Denver 35
Cincinnati 13
Houston 19
Houston 28
New England 13
New England 41

Seattle 24
Washington 14
Seattle 28
Atlanta 24
Atlanta 30
Minnesota 10
Green Bay 24
Green Bay 31
San Francisco 28
San Francisco 45

NFL Playoff Recaps

AFC Wild Card Games

Cincinnati	0	7	3	3—13
Houston	3	6	7	3—19

FIRST QUARTER: Houston: FG Graham 48, 7:49.

SECOND QUARTER: Houston: FG Graham 27, 13:07.

Cincinnati: TD Hall 21 interception return (Brown kick), 9:30.

Houston: FG Graham 22, 2:19.

THIRD QUARTER: Houston: TD Foster 1 run (Graham kick), 10:31.

Cincinnati: FG Brown 34, 7:48.

FOURTH QUARTER: Houston: FG Graham 24, 14:17.

Cincinnati: FG Brown 47, 9:03.

A: 71,738.

Indianapolis	0	6	3	0—9
Baltimore	0	10	7	7—24

SECOND QUARTER: Baltimore: FG Tucker 23, 11:18.

Indianapolis: FG Vinatieri 47, 2:25.

Baltimore: TD Leach 2 run (Tucker kick), :50.

Indianapolis: FG Vinatieri 52, :00.

THIRD QUARTER: Baltimore: TD Pitta 20 pass from Flacco (Tucker kick), 8:26.

Indianapolis: FG Vinatieri 26, :40.

FOURTH QUARTER: Baltimore: TD Boldin 18 pass from Flacco (Tucker kick), 9:14.

A: 71,379.

NFC Wild Card Games

Minnesota	3	0	0	7—10
Green Bay	7	10	7	0—24

FIRST QUARTER: Minnesota: FG Walsh 33, 9:26.

Green Bay: TD Harris 9 run (Crosby kick), :28.

SECOND QUARTER: Green Bay: FG Crosby 20, 3:25.

Green Bay: TD Kuhn 3 run (Crosby kick), :38.

THIRD QUARTER: Green Bay: TD Kuhn 9 pass from Rodgers (Crosby kick), 9:25

FOURTH QUARTER: Minnesota: TD Jenkins 50 pass from Webb (Walsh kick), 3:39.

A: 71,548.

Seattle	0	13	0	11—24
Washington	14	0	0	0—14

FIRST QUARTER: Washington: TD Royster 4 pass from Griffin (Forbath kick), 9:57.

Washington: TD Paulsen 4 pass from Griffin (Forbath kick), 2:26.

SECOND QUARTER: Seattle: FG Hauschka 32, 12:05.

Seattle: TD Robinson 4 pass from Wilson (Hauschka kick), 4:38.

Seattle: FG Hauschka 29, :00.

FOURTH QUARTER: Seattle: TD Lynch 27 run (two-point conversion successful).

Seattle: FG Hauschka 22, 5:32.

A: 84,325.

AFC Divisional Games

Baltimore	14	7	7	7	0	3—38
Denver	14	7	7	7	0	0—35

FIRST QUARTER: Denver: TD Holliday 90 punt return (Prater kick), 12:14.

Baltimore: TD Smith 59 pass from Flacco (Tucker kick), 10:31.

Baltimore: TD Graham 39 interception return (Tucker kick), 9:29.

Denver: TD Stokley 15 pass from Manning (Prater kick), 4:02.

SECOND QUARTER: Denver: TD Moreno 14 pass from Manning (Prater kick), 7:26.

Baltimore: TD Smith 32 pass from Flacco (Tucker kick), :36.

THIRD QUARTER: Denver: Holliday 104-yard kickoff return (Prater kick), 14:47.

Baltimore: Rice 1 run (Tucker kick), :20.

FOURTH QUARTER: Denver: TD Thomas 17 pass from Manning (Prater kick), 7:11.

Baltimore: TD Jones 70 pass from Flacco (Tucker kick), :31.

SECOND OVERTIME: Baltimore: FG Tucker 47, 13:18.

A: 76,732.

Houston	3	10	0	15—28
New England	7	10	14	10—41

FIRST QUARTER: Houston: FG Graham 27, 13:57.

New England: TD Vereen 1 run (Gostkowski kick), 1:28.

SECOND QUARTER: New England: FG Gostkowski 37, 10:16.

New England: TD Vereen 8 pass from Brady (Gostkowski kick), 3:38.

Houston: TD Foster 1 run (Graham kick), 1:15.

Houston: FG Graham 55, :00.

THIRD QUARTER: New England: TD Ridley 8 run (Gostkowski kick), 11:30.

New England: TD Lloyd 5 pass from Brady (Gostkowski kick), 1:21.

FOURTH QUARTER: New England: TD Vereen 33 pass from Brady (Gostkowski kick), 13:07.

Houston: TD Posey 25 pass from Schaub (Graham kick), 11:35.

Houston: TD Foster 1 pass from Schaub (two-point conversion successful), 5:11.

New England: FG Gostkowski 38, 1:14.

A: 68,756.

NFC Divisional Games

Green Bay	14	7	3	7—31
San Francisco	7	17	7	14—45

FIRST QUARTER: Green Bay: TD Shields 52 interception return (Crosby kick), 12:48.

San Francisco: TD Kaepernick 20 run (Akers kick), 9:01.

Green Bay: TD Harris 18 run (Crosby kick), :29.

SECOND QUARTER: San Francisco: TD Crabtree 12 pass from Kaepernick (Akers kick), 10:59.

San Francisco: TD Crabtree 20 pass from Kaepernick (Akers kick), 5:26.

Green Bay: TD Jones 20 pass from Rodgers (Crosby kick), 2:33.

San Francisco: FG Akers 36, :00.

THIRD QUARTER: Green Bay: FG Crosby 31, 8:25.

San Francisco: TD Kaepernick 56 run (Akers kick), 7:07.

FOURTH QUARTER: San Francisco: TD Gore 2 run (Akers kick), 14:57.

San Francisco: TD Dixon 2 run (Akers kick), 3:34.

Green Bay: TD Jennings 3 pass from Rodgers (Crosby kick), :57.

A: 69,732.

Seattle	0	0	7	21—28
Atlanta	10	10	7	3—30

FIRST QUARTER: Atlanta: FG Bryant 39, 9:40.

Atlanta: TD Gonzalez 1 pass from Ryan (Bryant kick), 3:10.

SECOND QUARTER: Atlanta: FG Bryant 37, 9:13.

Atlanta: TD White 47 pass from Ryan (Bryant kick), 4:16.

THIRD QUARTER: Seattle: Tate 29 pass from Wilson (Longwell kick), 9:47.

Atlanta: TD Snelling 5 pass from Ryan (Bryant kick), 2:11.

FOURTH QUARTER: Seattle: TD Wilson 1 run (Longwell kick), 13:01.

Seattle: TD Miller 3 pass from Wilson (Longwell kick), 9:13.

Seattle: TD Lynch 2 run (Longwell kick), :31.

Atlanta: FG Bryant 49, :08.

A: 70,366.

AFC Championship

Baltimore	0	7	7	14—28
New England	3	10	0	0—13

FIRST QUARTER: New England: FG Gostkowski 31, 6:21.

SECOND QUARTER: Baltimore: TD Rice 2 run (Tucker kick), 9:28.

New England: TD Welker 1 pass from Brady (Gostkowski kick), 4:18.

New England: FG Gostkowski 25, :00.

THIRD QUARTER: Baltimore: TD Pitta 5 pass from Flacco (Tucker kick), 6:14.

FOURTH QUARTER: Baltimore: TD Boldin 3 pass from Flacco (Tucker kick), 14:56.

Baltimore: TD Boldin 11 pass from Flacco (Tucker kick), 11:13.

A: 68,756.

NFC Championship

San Francisco	0	14	7	7—28
Atlanta	10	14	0	0—24

FIRST QUARTER: Atlanta: TD Jones 46 pass from Ryan (Bryant kick), 11:24.

Atlanta: FG Bryant 35, 3:20.

SECOND QUARTER: Atlanta: TD Jones 20 pass from Ryan (Bryant kick), 14:54.

San Francisco: TD James 15 run (Akers kick), 8:08.

San Francisco: TD Davis 4 pass from Kaepernick (Akers kick), 1:55.

Atlanta: TD Gonzalez 10 pass from Ryan (Bryant kick), :25.

THIRD QUARTER: San Francisco: TD Gore 5 run (Akers kick), 10:47.

FOURTH QUARTER: San Francisco: TD Gore 9 run (Akers kick), 8:23.

A: 70,863.

Super Bowl XLVII Recap

Baltimore	7	14	7	6—34
San Francisco	3	3	17	8—31

FIRST QUARTER: Baltimore: TD Boldin 13 pass from Flacco (Tucker kick), 10:36.
Baltimore 7-0.

San Francisco: FG Akers 36, 3:58.
Baltimore 7-3.

SECOND QUARTER: Baltimore: TD Pitta 1 pass from Flacco (Tucker kick), 7:10.
Baltimore 14-3.

Baltimore: TD J.Jones 56 pass from Flacco (Tucker kick), 1:45.
Baltimore 21-3.

San Francisco: FG Akers 27, 0:00.
Baltimore 21-6.

THIRD QUARTER: Baltimore: TD J. Jones 108 kickoff return (Tucker kick), 14:49.
Baltimore 28-6.

San Francisco: TD Crabtree 31 pass from Kaepernick (Akers kick), 7:20.
Baltimore 28-13.

San Francisco: TD Gore 6 run (Akers kick), 4:59.
Baltimore 28-20.

San Francisco: FG Akers 34, 3:10.
Baltimore 28-23.

FOURTH QUARTER: Baltimore: FG Tucker 19, 12:54.
Baltimore 31-23.

San Francisco: TD Kaepernick 15 run (two-point conversion failed), 9:57.
Baltimore 31-29.

Baltimore: FG Tucker 38, 4:19.
Baltimore 34-29.

San Francisco: Safety Koch (ran out of end zone), :04.
Baltimore 34-31.

A: 71,024.

Team Statistics

	Baltimore	San Francisco
FIRST DOWNS	21	23
Rushing	6	9
Passing	13	13
Penalty	2	1
THIRD DOWN EFF	9–16	2–9
FOURTH DOWN EFF	0–2	0–1
TOTAL NET YARDS	367	468
Total plays	70	60
Avg gain	5.2	7.8
NET YARDS RUSHING	93	182
Rushes	35	29
Avg per rush	2.7	6.3
NET YARDS PASSING	274	286
Completed–Att–Int	22–33–0	16–28–1
Yards per pass	8.3	10.2
Sacked–yards lost	2–13	3–16
Had intercepted	0	1
PUNTS–Avg	3–47.0	3–53.0
PENALTIES–Yds	2–20	5–33
FUMBLES–Lost	2–1	1–1
Time of Possession	32:23	27:37

Passing

BALTIMORE

	Comp	Att	Yds	Int	TD	Rtg
Flacco	27	33	287	0	3	124.2

SAN FRANCISCO

	Comp	Att	Yds	Int	TD	Rtg
Kaepernick	16	28	302	1	1	91.7

Rushing

BALTIMORE

	No.	Yds	Lg	TD
Rice	20	59	12	0
Pierce	12	33	8	0
Tucker	1	8	8	0
Leach	1	1	1	0
Koch	1	-8	-8	0

SAN FRANCISCO

	No.	Yds	Lg	TD
Gore	19	110	33	1
Kaepernick	7	62	15	1
James	3	10	9	0

Receiving

BALTIMORE

	No.	Yds	Lg	TD
Boldin	6	104	30	1
J. Jones	1	56	56	1
Dickson	2	37	23	0
Smith	2	35	20	0
Pitta	4	26	9	1
Rice	4	19	7	0
Leach	3	10	8	0

SAN FRANCISCO

	No.	Yds	Lg	TD
Crabtree	5	109	31	1
Davis	6	104	29	0
Walker	3	48	28	0
Moss	2	41	32	0

Defense

BALTIMORE

	Tackles	Solo	Int	Sack
Ellerbe	9	6	0	0
Lewis	7	4	0	0
Graham	6	4	0	0
Reed	5	5	1	0
Upshaw	5	4	0	0
Tyson	4	1	0	0
Kruger	3	3	0	2
Williams	3	3	0	0
A. Jones	2	2	0	1
Ngata	2	2	0	0
Allen	2	2	0	0
B. Pollard	2	2	0	0
Suggs	2	1	0	0
Koch	1	1	0	0
Bynes	1	1	0	0
McClellan	1	1	0	0
Smith	1	1	0	0
Pitta	1	1	0	0
Ihedigbo	1	1	0	0
Kemoeatu	1	1	0	0
Cody	1	0	0	0

SAN FRANCISCO

	Tackles	Solo	Int	Sack
Willis	10	8	0	0
Bowman	9	7	0	0
Goldson	9	6	0	0
Whitner	8	7	0	0
Brooks	5	5	0	1
Walker	4	4	0	0
Culliver	4	4	0	0
Sopoaga	4	3	0	0
J. Smith	3	3	0	0
Rogers	3	3	0	0
McDonald	3	2	0	1
Brown	3	2	0	0
Jean Francois	2	1	0	0
A. Smith	2	1	0	0
Gooden	1	1	0	0
Davis	1	1	0	0
Wilhoite	1	1	0	0
Dixon	1	1	0	0
McBath	1	1	0	0

2012 *Associated Press* All-Pro Team

First Team
OFFENSE

Peyton Manning, Denver	Quarterback
Adrian Peterson, Minnesota	Running back
Marshawn Lynch, Seattle	Running back
Vonta Leach, Baltimore	Fullback
Tony Gonzalez, Atlanta	Tight end
Calvin Johnson, Detroit	Wide receiver
Brandon Marshall, Chicago	Wide receiver
Duane Brown, Houston	Tackle
Ryan Clady, Denver	Tackle
Mike Iupati, San Francisco	Guard
Jahri Evans, New Orleans	Guard
Max Unger, Seattle	Center

DEFENSE

J.J. Watt, Houston	Defensive end
Cameron Wake, Miami	Defensive end
Geno Atkins, Cincinnati	Defensive tackle
Vince Wilfork, New England	Defensive tackle
Von Miller, Denver	Outside linebacker
Aldon Smith, San Francisco	Outside linebacker
Patrick Willis, San Francisco	Inside linebacker
NaVorro Bowman, San Francisco	Inside linebacker
Richard Sherman, Seattle	Cornerback
Charles Tillman, Chicago	Cornerback
Earl Thomas, Seattle	Safety
Dashon Goldson, San Francisco	Safety

SPECIALISTS

Blair Walsh, Minnesota	Kicker
Jacoby Jones, Baltimore	Kick Returner
Andy Lee, San Francisco	Punter

Second Team
OFFENSE

Aaron Rodgers, Green Bay	Quarterback
Alfred Morris, Washington	Running back
Jamaal Charles, Kansas City	Running back
Jerome Felton, Minnesota	Fullback
Jason Witten, Dallas	Tight end
A.J. Green, Cincinnati	Wide receiver
Andre Johnson, Houston	Wide receiver
Joe Thomas, Cleveland	Tackle
Joe Staley, San Francisco	Tackle
Marshal Yanda, Baltimore	Guard
Logan Mankins, New England	Guard
Maurkice Pouncey, Pittsburgh	Center

DEFENSE

Justin Smith, San Francisco	Defensive end
Julius Peppers, Chicago	Defensive end
Justin Smith, San Francisco	Defensive tackle
Ndamukong Suh, Detroit	Defensive tackle
Haloti Ngata, Baltimore	Defensive tackle
Chad Greenway, Minnesota	Outside linebacker
Ahmad Brooks, San Francisco	Outside linebacker
Clay Matthews, Green Bay	Outside linebacker
DeMarcus Ware, Dallas	Outside linebacker
Daryl Washington, Arizona	Inside linebacker
London Fletcher, Washington	Inside linebacker
Champ Bailey, Denver	Cornerback
Tim Jennings, Chicago	Cornerback
Eric Weddle, San Diego	Safety
Jairus Byrd, Buffalo	Safety

SPECIALISTS

Phil Dawson, Cleveland	Kicker
David Wilson, NY Giants	Kick Returner
Thomas Morstead, New Orleans	Punter

BALTIMORE RAVENS (10-6)

44	CINCINNATI	13
23	at Philadelphia	24
31	NEW ENGLAND	30
23	CLEVELAND	16
9	at Kansas City	6
31	DALLAS	29
13	at Houston	43
25	at Cleveland	15
55	OAKLAND	20
13	at Pittsburgh	10
16	at San Diego	13*
20	PITTSBURGH	23
28	at Washington	31*
17	DENVER	34
33	NY GIANTS	14
17	at Cincinnati	23
398		344

BUFFALO BILLS (6-10)

28	at NY Jets	48
35	KANSAS CITY	17
24	at Cleveland	14
28	NEW ENGLAND	52
3	at San Francisco	45
19	at Arizona	16*
34	TENNESSEE	35
9	at Houston	21
31	at New England	37
19	MIAMI	14
13	at Indianapolis	20
34	JACKSONVILLE	18
12	ST. LOUIS	15
17	SEATTLE	50
10	at Miami	24
28	NY JETS	9
344		435

CINCINNATI BENGALS (10-6)

13	at Baltimore	44
34	CLEVELAND	27
38	at Washington	31
27	at Jacksonville	10
13	MIAMI	17
24	at Cleveland	34
17	PITTSBURGH	24
23	DENVER	31
31	NY GIANTS	13
28	at Kansas City	6
34	OAKLAND	10
20	at San Diego	13
19	DALLAS	20
34	at Philadelphia	13
13	at Pittsburgh	10
23	BALTIMORE	17
391		320

CLEVELAND BROWNS (5-11)

16	PHILADELPHIA	17
27	at Cincinnati	34
14	BUFFALO	24
16	at Baltimore	23
27	at NY Giants	41
34	CINCINNATI	24
13	at Indianapolis	17
7	SAN DIEGO	6
15	BALTIMORE	25
20	at Dallas	23*
20	PITTSBURGH	14
20	at Oakland	17
30	KANSAS CITY	7
21	WASHINGTON	38
12	at Denver	34
10	at Pittsburgh	24
302		368

DENVER BRONCOS (13-3)

31	PITTSBURGH	19
21	at Atlanta	27
25	HOUSTON	31
37	OAKLAND	6
21	at New England	31
35	at San Diego	24
34	NEW ORLEANS	14
31	at Cincinnati	23
36	at Carolina	14
30	SAN DIEGO	23
17	at Kansas City	9
31	TAMPA BAY	23
26	at Oakland	13
34	at Baltimore	17
34	CLEVELAND	12
38	KANSAS CITY	3
481		289

HOUSTON TEXANS (12-4)

30	MIAMI	10
27	at Jacksonville	7
31	at Denver	25
38	TENNESSEE	14
23	at NY Jets	17
24	GREEN BAY	42
43	BALTIMORE	13
21	BUFFALO	9
13	at Chicago	6
43	JACKSONVILLE	37*
34	at Detroit	31*
24	at Tennessee	10
14	at New England	42
29	INDIANAPOLIS	17
6	MINNESOTA	23
16	at Indianapolis	28
416		331

INDIANAPOLIS COLTS (11-5)

21	at Chicago	41
23	MINNESOTA	20
17	JACKSONVILLE	22
30	GREEN BAY	27
9	at NY Jets	35
17	CLEVELAND	13
19	at Tennessee	13*
23	MIAMI	20
27	at Jacksonville	10
24	at New England	59
20	BUFFALO	13
35	at Detroit	33
27	TENNESSEE	23
17	at Houston	29
20	at Kansas City	13
28	HOUSTON	16
357		387

JACKSONVILLE JAGUARS (2-14)

23	at Minnesota	26*
7	HOUSTON	27
22	at Indianapolis	17
10	CINCINNATI	27
3	CHICAGO	41
23	at Oakland	26*
15	at Green Bay	24
14	DETROIT	31
10	INDIANAPOLIS	27
37	at Houston	43*
24	TENNESSEE	19
18	at Buffalo	34
10	NY JETS	17
3	at Miami	24
16	NEW ENGLAND	23
20	at Tennessee	38
255		444

KANSAS CITY CHIEFS (2-14)

24	ATLANTA	40
17	at Buffalo	35
27	at New Orleans	24*
20	SAN DIEGO	37
6	BALTIMORE	9
10	at Tampa Bay	38
16	OAKLAND	26
13	at San Diego	31
13	at Pittsburgh	16*
6	CINCINNATI	28
9	DENVER	17
27	CAROLINA	21
7	at Cleveland	30
0	at Oakland	15
13	INDIANAPOLIS	20
3	at Denver	38
211		425

MIAMI DOLPHINS (7-9)

10	at Houston	30	14	at Buffalo	19
35	OAKLAND	13	24	SEATTLE	21
20	NY JETS	23*	16	NEW ENGLAND	23
21	at Arizona	24*	13	at San Francisco	27
17	at Cincinnati	13	24	JACKSONVILLE	3
17	ST. LOUIS	14	24	BUFFALO	10
30	at NY Jets	9	0	at New England	28
20	at Indianapolis	23	288		317
3	TENNESSEE	37			

*Overtime game

NEW ENGLAND PATRIOTS (12-4)

34	at Tennessee	13
18	ARIZONA	20
30	at Baltimore	31
52	at Buffalo	28
31	DENVER	21
23	at Seattle	24
29	NY JETS	26*
45	at St. Louis	7
37	BUFFALO	31
59	INDIANAPOLIS	24
49	at NY Jets	19
23	at Miami	16
42	HOUSTON	14
34	SAN FRANCISCO	41
23	at Jacksonville	16
28	MIAMI	0
557		331

NEW YORK JETS (6-10)

48	BUFFALO	28
10	at Pittsburgh	27
23	at Miami	20*
0	SAN FRANCISCO	34
17	HOUSTON	23
35	INDIANAPOLIS	9
26	at New England	29*
9	MIAMI	30
7	at Seattle	28
27	at St. Louis	13
19	NEW ENGLAND	49
7	ARIZONA	6
17	at Jacksonville	10
10	at Tennessee	14
17	SAN DIEGO	27
9	at Buffalo	28
281		375

OAKLAND RAIDERS (4-12)

14	SAN DIEGO	22
13	at Miami	35
34	PITTSBURGH	31
6	at Denver	37
20	at Atlanta	23
26	JACKSONVILLE	23*
26	at Kansas City	16
32	TAMPA BAY	42
20	at Baltimore	55
17	NEW ORLEANS	38
10	at Cincinnati	34
17	CLEVELAND	20
13	DENVER	26
15	KANSAS CITY	0
6	at Carolina	17
21	at San Diego	24
290		443

PITTSBURGH STEELERS (8-8)

19	at Denver	31
27	NY JETS	10
31	at Oakland	34
16	PHILADELPHIA	14
23	at Tennessee	26
24	at Cincinnati	17
27	WASHINGTON	12
24	at NY Giants	20
16	KANSAS CITY	13*
10	BALTIMORE	13
14	at Cleveland	20
23	at Baltimore	20
24	SAN DIEGO	34
24	at Dallas	27*
10	CINCINNATI	13
24	CLEVELAND	10
336		314

SAN DIEGO CHARGERS (7-9)

22	at Oakland	14
38	TENNESSEE	10
3	ATLANTA	27
37	at Kansas City	20
24	at New Orleans	31
24	DENVER	35
6	at Cleveland	7
31	KANSAS CITY	13
24	at Tampa Bay	34
23	at Denver	30
13	BALTIMORE	16*
13	CINCINNATI	20
34	at Pittsburgh	24
7	CAROLINA	31
27	at NY Jets	17
24	OAKLAND	21
350		350

TENNESSEE TITANS (6-10)

13	NEW ENGLAND	34
10	at San Diego	38
44	DETROIT	41*
14	at Houston	38
7	at Minnesota	30
26	PITTSBURGH	23
35	at Buffalo	34
13	INDIANAPOLIS	19*
20	CHICAGO	51
37	at Miami	3
19	at Jacksonville	24
10	HOUSTON	24
23	at Indianapolis	27
14	NY JETS	10
7	at Green Bay	55
38	JACKSONVILLE	20
330		471

2012 NFC Team-by-Team Results

ARIZONA CARDINALS (5-11)

20	SEATTLE	16
20	at New England	18
27	PHILADELPHIA	6
24	MIAMI	21*
3	at St. Louis	17
16	BUFFALO	19*
14	at Minnesota	21
3	SAN FRANCISCO	24
17	at Green Bay	31
19	at Atlanta	23
17	ST. LOUIS	31
6	at NY Jets	7
0	at Seattle	58
38	DETROIT	10
13	CHICAGO	28
13	at San Francisco	27
250		357

ATLANTA FALCONS (13-3)

40	at Kansas City	24
27	DENVER	21
27	at San Diego	3
30	CAROLINA	28
24	at Washington	17
23	OAKLAND	20
30	at Philadelphia	17
19	DALLAS	13
27	at New Orleans	31
23	ARIZONA	19
24	at Tampa Bay	23
23	NEW ORLEANS	13
20	at Carolina	30
34	NY GIANTS	0
31	at Detroit	18
17	TAMPA BAY	22
419		299

CAROLINA PANTHERS (7-9)

10	at Tampa Bay	16
35	NEW ORLEANS	27
7	NY GIANTS	36
28	at Atlanta	30
12	SEATTLE	16
14	DALLAS	19
22	at Chicago	23
21	at Washington	13
14	DENVER	36
21	TAMPA BAY	27*
30	at Philadelphia	22
21	at Kansas City	27
30	ATLANTA	20
31	at San Diego	7
17	OAKLAND	6
44	at New Orleans	38
357		363

*Overtime game

CHICAGO BEARS (10-6)

41	INDIANAPOLIS	21
10	at Green Bay	23
23	ST. LOUIS	6
34	at Dallas	18
41	at Jacksonville	3
13	DETROIT	7
23	CAROLINA	22
51	at Tennessee	20
6	HOUSTON	13
7	at San Francisco	32
28	MINNESOTA	10
17	SEATTLE	23*
14	at Minnesota	21
13	GREEN BAY	21
28	at Arizona	13
26	at Detroit	24
375		**277**

DALLAS COWBOYS (8-8)

24	at NY Giants	17
7	at Seattle	22
16	TAMPA BAY	10
18	CHICAGO	34
29	at Baltimore	31
19	at Carolina	14
24	NY GIANTS	29
13	at Atlanta	19
38	at Philadelphia	23
23	CLEVELAND	20*
31	WASHINGTON	38
38	PHILADELPHIA	33
20	at Cincinnati	19
27	PITTSBURGH	24*
31	NEW ORLEANS	34*
18	at Washington	28
376		**400**

DETROIT LIONS (4-12)

27	ST. LOUIS	23
19	at San Francisco	27
41	at Tennessee	44*
13	MINNESOTA	20
26	at Philadelphia	23*
7	at Chicago	13
28	SEATTLE	24
31	at Jacksonville	14
24	at Minnesota	34
20	GREEN BAY	24
31	HOUSTON	34*
33	INDIANAPOLIS	35
20	at Green Bay	27
10	at Arizona	38
18	ATLANTA	31
24	CHICAGO	26
372		**437**

GREEN BAY PACKERS (11-5)

22	SAN FRANCISCO	30
23	CHICAGO	10
12	at Seattle	14
28	NEW ORLEANS	27
27	at Indianapolis	30
42	at Houston	24
30	at St. Louis	20
24	JACKSONVILLE	15
31	ARIZONA	17
24	at Detroit	20
10	at NY Giants	38
23	MINNESOTA	14
27	DETROIT	20
21	at Chicago	13
55	TENNESSEE	7
34	at Minnesota	37
433		**336**

MINNESOTA VIKINGS (10-6)

26	JACKSONVILLE	23*
20	at Indianapolis	23
24	SAN FRANCISCO	13
20	at Detroit	13
30	TENNESSEE	7
26	at Washington	38
21	ARIZONA	14
17	TAMPA BAY	36
20	at Seattle	30
34	DETROIT	24
10	at Chicago	28
14	at Green Bay	23
21	CHICAGO	14
36	at St. Louis	22
23	at Houston	6
37	GREEN BAY	34
379		**348**

NEW ORLEANS SAINTS (7-9)

32	WASHINGTON	40
27	at Carolina	35
24	KANSAS CITY	27*
27	at Green Bay	28
31	SAN DIEGO	24
35	at Tampa Bay	28
14	at Denver	34
28	PHILADELPHIA	13
31	ATLANTA	27
38	at Oakland	17
21	SAN FRANCISCO	31
13	at Atlanta	23
27	at NY Giants	52
41	TAMPA BAY	0
34	at Dallas	31*
38	CAROLINA	44
461		**454**

NEW YORK GIANTS (9-7)

17	DALLAS	24
41	TAMPA BAY	34
36	at Carolina	7
17	at Philadelphia	19
41	CLEVELAND	27
26	at San Francisco	3
27	WASHINGTON	23
29	at Dallas	24
20	PITTSBURGH	24
13	at Cincinnati	31
38	GREEN BAY	10
16	at Washington	17
52	NEW ORLEANS	27
0	at Atlanta	34
14	at Baltimore	33
42	PHILADELPHIA	7
429		**344**

PHILADELPHIA EAGLES (4-12)

17	at Cleveland	16
24	BALTIMORE	23
6	at Arizona	27
19	NY GIANTS	17
14	at Pittsburgh	16
23	DETROIT	26*
17	ATLANTA	30
13	at New Orleans	28
23	DALLAS	38
6	at Washington	31
22	CAROLINA	30
33	at Dallas	38
23	at Tampa Bay	21
13	CINCINNATI	34
20	WASHINGTON	27
7	at NY Giants	42
280		**444**

SAN FRANCISCO 49ERS (11-4-1)

30	at Green Bay	22
27	DETROIT	19
13	at Minnesota	24
34	at NY Jets	0
45	BUFFALO	3
3	NY GIANTS	26
13	SEATTLE	6
24	at Arizona	3
24	ST. LOUIS	24*
32	CHICAGO	7
31	at New Orleans	21
13	at St. Louis	16*
27	MIAMI	13
41	at New England	34
13	at Seattle	42
27	ARIZONA	13
397		**273**

*Overtime game

SEATTLE SEAHAWKS (11-5)

16	at Arizona	20
27	DALLAS	7
14	GREEN BAY	12
13	at St. Louis	19
16	at Carolina	12
24	NEW ENGLAND	23
6	at San Francisco	13
24	at Detroit	28
30	MINNESOTA	20
28	NY JETS	7
21	at Miami	24
23	at Chicago	17*
58	ARIZONA	0
50	at Buffalo	17
42	SAN FRANCISCO	13
20	ST. LOUIS	13
412		245

ST. LOUIS RAMS (7-8-1)

23	at Detroit	27
31	WASHINGTON	28
6	at Chicago	23
19	SEATTLE	13
17	ARIZONA	3
14	at Miami	17
20	GREEN BAY	30
7	NEW ENGLAND	45
24	at San Francisco	24*
13	NY JETS	27
31	at Arizona	17
16	SAN FRANCISCO	13*
15	at Buffalo	12
22	MINNESOTA	36
28	at Tampa Bay	13
13	at Seattle	20
299		348

TAMPA BAY BUCCANEERS (7-9)

16	CAROLINA	10
34	at NY Giants	41
10	at Dallas	16
22	WASHINGTON	24
38	KANSAS CITY	10
28	NEW ORLEANS	35
36	at Minnesota	17
42	at Oakland	32
34	SAN DIEGO	24
27	at Carolina	21*
23	ATLANTA	24
23	at Denver	31
21	PHILADELPHIA	23
0	at New Orleans	41
13	ST. LOUIS	28
22	at Atlanta	17
389		394

WASHINGTON REDSKINS (10-6)

40	at New Orleans	32		13	CAROLINA	21
28	at St. Louis	31		31	PHILADELPHIA	6
31	CINCINNATI	38		38	at Dallas	31
24	at Tampa Bay	22		17	NY GIANTS	16
17	ATLANTA	24		31	BALTIMORE	28*
38	MINNESOTA	26		38	at Cleveland	21
23	at NY Giants	27		27	at Philadelphia	20
12	at Pittsburgh	27		28	DALLAS	18
				436		388

*Overtime game

2012 NFL Individual Leaders

American Football Conference

Scoring

TOUCHDOWNS	TD	Rush	Rec	Ret	2PT	Pts	KICKING	FG	PAT	Pts
A. Foster, Hou	17	15	2	0	0	102	S. Gostkowski, NE	29	66	153
E. Decker, Den	13	0	13	0	0	78	S. Graham, Hou	31	45	138
S. Ridley, NE	12	12	0	0	0	72	M. Prater, Den	26	55	133
T. Richardson, Cle	12	11	1	0	0	72	J. Tucker, Bal	30	42	132
R. Gronkowski, NE	11	0	11	0	0	66	S. Janikowski, Oak	31	25	118
A.J. Green, Cin	11	0	11	0	0	66	S. Suisham, Pit	28	34	118
R. Rice, Bal	10	9	1	0	0	60	P. Dawson, Cle	29	29	116
D. Thomas, Den	10	0	10	0	0	60	A. Vinatieri, Ind	26	37	115
H. Miller, Pit	8	0	8	0	1	50	R. Bironas, Ten	25	35	110
Six tied at 48.							R. Lindell, Buf	21	39	102

Passing

	Att	Comp	Pct	Yds	Yds/Att	Lg	TD	Int	Rating Pts
Peyton Manning, Den	583	400	68.6	4,659	7.99	71	37	11	105.8
Tom Brady, NE	637	401	63.0	4,827	7.58	83	34	8	98.7
Ben Roethlisberger, Pit	449	284	63.3	3,265	7.27	82	26	8	97.0
Matt Schaub, Hou	544	350	64.3	4,008	7.37	60	22	12	90.7
Philip Rivers, SD	527	338	64.1	3,606	6.84	80	26	15	88.6
Joe Flacco, Bal	531	317	59.7	3,817	7.19	61	22	10	87.7
Andy Dalton, Cin	528	329	62.3	3,669	6.95	59	27	16	87.4
Carson Palmer, Oak	565	345	61.1	4,018	7.11	64	22	14	85.3
Ryan Fitzpatrick, Buf	505	306	60.6	3,400	6.73	68	24	16	83.3
Blaine Gabbert, Jac	278	162	58.3	1,662	5.98	80	9	6	77.4
Andrew Luck, Ind	627	339	54.1	4,374	6.98	70	23	18	76.5

American Football Conference *(Cont.)*

Pass Receiving

RECEPTIONS	No.	Yds	Avg	Lg	TD	YARDS	Yds	No.	Avg	Lg	TD
Wes Welker, NE	118	1,354	11.5	59	6	Andre Johnson, Hou	1,598	112	14.3	60T	4
Andre Johnson, Hou	112	1,598	14.3	60T	4	D. Thomas, Den	1,434	94	15.3	71T	10
Reggie Wayne, Ind	106	1,355	12.8	33	5	Reggie Wayne, Ind	1,355	106	12.8	33	5
A.J. Green, Cin	97	1,350	13.9	73T	11	Wes Welker, NE	1,354	118	11.5	59	6
D. Thomas, Den	94	1,434	15.3	71T	10	A.J. Green, Cin	1,350	97	13.9	73T	11
Eric Decker, Den	85	1,064	12.5	55	13	Brian Hartline, Mia	1,083	74	14.6	80T	1
Steve Johnson, Buf	79	1,046	13.2	63	6	Eric Decker, Den	1,064	85	12.5	55	13
Brandon Myers, Oak	79	806	10.2	29	4	Steve Johnson, Buf	1,046	79	13.2	63	6
Brian Hartline, Mia	74	1,083	14.6	80T	1	Cecil Shorts, Jax	979	55	17.8	80	7
Brandon Lloyd, NE	74	911	12.3	53	4	Anquan Boldin, Bal	921	65	14.2	43	4

Rushing

	Att	Yds	Avg	Lg	TD
Jamaal Charles, KC	285	1,509	5.3	91	5
Arian Foster, Hou	351	1,424	4.1	46	15
Stevan Ridley, NE	290	1,263	4.4	41	12
C.J. Spiller, Buf	207	1,244	6.0	62	6
Chris Johnson, Ten	276	1,243	4.5	94	6
Ray Rice, Bal	257	1,143	4.4	46	9
B. Green-Ellis, Cin	278	1,094	3.9	48	6
Shonn Greene, NYJ	276	1,063	3.9	36	8
Reggie Bush, Mia	227	986	4.3	65	6
Trent Richardson, Cle	267	950	3.6	32	11

Interceptions

	No.	Yds	Lg	TD
Jairus Byrd, Buf	5	81	45	0
Devin McCourty, NE	5	53	34	0
10 tied with 4.				

Sacks

J.J. Watt, Hou	20.5
Von Miller, Den	18.5
Cameron Wake, Mia	15.0
Geno Atkins, Cin	12.5
Michael Johnson, Cin	11.5
Elvis Dumervil, Den	11.0
Mario Williams, Buf	10.5
Justin Houston, KC	10.0
Shaun Phillips, SD	9.5
Tamba Hali, KC	9.0
Paul Kruger, Bal	9.0

Punting

	No.	Yds	Lng	Avg	Net Avg	Blk	In 20	TB	Ret	Ret Avg
Bryan Anger, Jax	91	4353	73	47.8	40.8	1	31	5	40	12.4
Donnie Jones, Hou	88	4150	66	47.2	40.5	0	28	5	48	10.1
Mike Scifres, SD	81	3914	66	48.3	40.6	3	30	7	40	9.1
Sam Koch, Bal	83	3911	60	47.1	40.8	0	28	7	49	7.8
Dustin Colquitt, KC	83	3887	71	46.8	40.8	0	45	7	27	13.4

Punt Returns

	No.	Yds	Avg	Lg	TD
Leodis McKelvin, Buf	23	431	18.7	88	2
Darius Reynaud, Ten	31	410	13.2	81	2
Marcus Thigpen, Mia	26	316	12.2	72	1
Keshawn Martin, Hou	22	267	12.1	71	0
Josh Cribbs, Cle	38	457	12.0	60	0

Kickoff Returns

	No.	Yds	Avg	Lg	TD
Jacoby Jones, Bal	38	1167	30.7	108	2
Joe McKnight, NYJ	39	1072	27.5	100	1
Josh Cribbs, Cle	43	1178	27.4	74	0
Marcus Thigpen, Mia	38	1040	27.4	96	1
Chris Rainey, Pit	39	1035	26.5	68	0

National Football Conference

Scoring

TOUCHDOWNS	TD	Rush	Rec	Ret	2PT	Pts	KICKING	FG	PAT	Pts
J. Jones, GB	14	0	14	0	0	84	Lawrence Tynes, NYG	33	46	145
A. Peterson, Min	13	12	1	0	1	80	Matt Bryant, Atl	33	44	143
A. Morris, Was	13	13	0	0	0	78	Blair Walsh, Min	35	36	141
D. Bryant, Dal	12	0	12	0	1	74	Jason Hanson, Det	32	38	134
M. Lynch, Sea	12	11	1	0	0	72	David Akers, SF	29	44	131
D. Martin, TB	12	11	1	0	0	72	Dan Bailey, Dal	29	37	124
M. Turner, Atl	11	10	1	0	0	66	Connor Barth, TB	28	39	123
B. Marshall, Chi	11	0	11	0	0	66	Steven Hauschka, Sea	24	46	118
F. Gore, SF	10	8	1	1	0	60	Mason Crosby, GB	21	50	113
M. Colston, NO	10	0	10	0	0	60	Garrett Hartley, NO	18	57	111
V. Cruz, NYG	10	0	10	0	0	60				
J. Jones, Atl	10	0	10	0	0	60				

National Football Conference (Cont.)

Passing

	Att	Comp	Pct	Yds	Yds/Att	Lg	TD	Int	Rating Pts
Aaron Rodgers, GB	552	371	67.2	4,295	7.78	73	39	8	108.0
Robert Griffin III, Wash	393	258	65.6	3,200	8.14	88	20	5	102.4
Russell Wilson, Sea	393	252	64.1	3,118	7.93	67	26	10	100.0
Matt Ryan, Atl	615	422	68.6	4,719	7.67	80	32	14	99.1
Drew Brees, NO	670	422	63.0	5,177	7.73	80	43	19	96.3
Tony Romo, Dal	648	425	65.6	4,903	7.57	85	28	19	90.5
Eli Manning, NYG	536	321	59.9	3,948	7.37	80	26	15	87.2
Cam Newton, Car	485	280	57.7	3,869	7.98	82	19	12	86.2
Sam Bradford, StL	551	328	59.5	3,702	6.72	80	21	13	82.6
Josh Freeman, TB	558	306	54.8	4,065	7.29	95	27	17	81.6

Pass Receiving

RECEPTIONS	No.	Yds	Avg	Lg	TD	YARDS	Yds	No.	Avg	Lg	TD
Calvin Johnson, Det	122	1,964	16.1	53	5	Calvin Johnson, Det	1,964	122	16.1	53	5
B. Marshall, Chi	118	1,508	12.8	56	11	B. Marshall, Chi	1,508	118	12.8	56	11
Jason Witten, Dal	110	1,039	9.4	36	3	V. Jackson, TB	1,384	72	19.2	95	8
Tony Gonzalez, Atl	93	930	10.0	25	8	Dez Bryant, Dal	1,382	92	15.0	85T	12
Dez Bryant, Dal	92	1,382	15.0	85T	12	Roddy White, Atl	1,351	92	14.7	59	7
Roddy White, Atl	92	1,351	14.7	59	7	Julio Jones, Atl	1,198	79	15.2	80T	10
Victor Cruz, NYG	86	1,092	12.7	80T	10	Steve Smith, Car	1,174	73	16.1	66	4
M. Crabtree, SF	85	1,105	13.0	49T	9	M. Colston, NO	1,154	83	13.9	60	10
Jimmy Graham, NO	85	982	11.6	46	9	M. Crabtree, SF	1,105	85	13.0	49T	9
M. Colston, NO	83	1,154	13.9	60	10	Victor Cruz, NYG	1,092	86	12.7	80T	10

Rushing

	Att	Yds	Avg	Lg	TD
Adrian Peterson, Min	348	2,097	6.0	82	12
Alfred Morris, Was	335	1,613	4.8	39	13
Marshawn Lynch, Sea	315	1,590	5.0	77	11
Doug Martin, TB	319	1,454	4.6	70	11
Frank Gore, SF	258	1,214	4.7	37	8
Matt Forte Chi	248	1,094	4.4	46	5
Steven Jackson, StL	257	1,042	4.1	46	4
Ahmad Bradshaw, NYG	221	1,015	4.6	37	6
LeSean McCoy, Phi	200	840	4.2	34	2
Robert Griffin III, Was	120	815	6.8	76	7

Sacks

Jared Allen, Min	22.0
Aldon Smith, SF	19.5
Clay Matthews, GB	13.0
Charles Johnson, Car	12.5
Jared Allen, Min	12.0
Julius Peppers, Chi	11.5
Chris Clemons, Sea	11.5
DeMarcus Ware, Dal	11.5
Chris Long, StL	11.5
Anthony Spencer, Dal	11.0
Greg Hardy, Car	11.0

Interceptions

	No.	Yds	Lg	TD
Tim Jennings, Chi	9	105	31	1
Stevie Brown, NYG	8	307	70	0
Richard Sherman, Sea	8	57	29	1
Patrick Peterson, Ari	7	64	31	0
Thomas DeCoud, Atl	6	42	24	0
Casey Hayward, GB	6	81	24	0

Punting

	No.	Yds	Lng	Avg	Net Avg	Blk	In 20	TB	Ret	Ret Avg
Dave Zastudil, Ari	112	5209	70	46.5	41.4	0	46	8	48	8.6
Johnny Hekker, StL	82	3756	68	45.8	39.9	0	22	4	41	9.8
Thomas Morstead, NO	74	3707	70	50.1	43.2	0	20	6	31	12.6
Michael Koenen, TB	76	3440	64	45.3	37.4	1	22	6	40	11.0
Adam Podlesh, Chi	81	3399	64	42.0	39.4	0	34	6	25	3.4

Punt Returns

	No.	Yds	Avg	Lg	TD
Dwayne Harris, Dal	22	354	16.1	78	1
Damaris Johnson, Phi	26	291	11.2	98	1
Ted Ginn, SF	32	326	10.2	38	0
Roscoe Parrish, TB	30	298	9.9	39	0
Randall Cobb, GB	31	292	9.4	75	1

Kickoff Returns

	No.	Yds	Avg	Lg	TD
Leon Washington, Sea	27	784	29.0	98	1
David Wilson, NYG	57	1533	26.9	97	1
Travaris Cadet, NO	26	690	26.5	75	0
Devin Hester, Chi	24	621	25.9	40	0
Jacquizz Rodgers, ATL	23	592	25.7	77	0

AFC Total Offense

	Total Plays	Yds/ Game	Pts/ Game	1st Dwns/ Game	Time of Poss
New England	1,191	427.9	34.8	27.8	30:56
Denver	1,090	397.9	30.1	23.8	31:16
Houston	1,090	372.1	26.0	21.3	33:46
Indianapolis	1,109	362.4	22.3	22.5	30:46
Baltimore	1,042	352.5	24.9	19.6	28:40
Oakland	1,032	344.0	18.1	18.8	29:30
Buffalo	983	342.9	21.5	18.8	30:11
Pittsburgh	1,023	332.8	21.0	19.2	32:11
Cincinnati	1,016	332.7	24.4	18.2	30:26
Kansas City	1,015	319.2	13.2	17.9	30:20
Cleveland	998	314.2	18.9	17.4	28:14
Tennessee	957	313.1	20.6	16.2	27:41
Miami	981	311.5	18.0	18.0	28:60
Jacksonville	994	299.2	15.9	16.8	28:03
NY Jets	1,034	299.2	17.6	18.7	30:26
San Diego	988	297.2	21.9	18.3	31:37

AFC Total Defense

	Opp Total Plays	Opp Yds/ Game	Opp Yds/ Play	Opp Pts/ Game
Pittsburgh	951	275.8	4.6	19.6
Denver	1,015	290.8	4.6	18.1
Cincinnati	1,034	319.7	4.9	20.0
Houston	1,015	323.2	5.1	20.7
NY Jets	1,019	323.4	5.1	23.4
San Diego	1,012	326.4	5.2	21.9
Baltimore	1,086	350.9	5.2	21.5
Oakland	995	354.5	5.7	27.7
Kansas City	973	356.5	5.9	26.6
Miami	1,073	356.8	5.3	19.8
Buffalo	1,042	362.9	5.6	27.2
Cleveland	1,095	363.8	5.3	23.0
New England	1,046	373.2	5.7	20.7
Indianapolis	995	374.2	6.0	24.2
Tennessee	1,086	374.9	5.5	29.4
Jacksonville	1,100	380.5	5.5	27.8

NFC Total Offense

	Total Plays	Yds/ Game	Pts/ Game	1st Dwns/ Game	Time of Poss
New Orleans	1,067	410.9	28.8	22.0	28:59
Detroit	1,160	408.8	23.2	23.9	32:05
Washington	994	383.2	27.2	21.3	31:12
Dallas	1,049	374.6	23.5	21.1	31:01
Atlanta	1,021	369.1	26.2	21.4	30:52
Tampa Bay	1,008	363.8	24.3	18.8	30:19
San Francisco	969	361.8	24.8	20.1	31:46
Carolina	988	360.7	22.3	20.5	29:51
Green Bay	1,042	359.4	27.1	21.3	30:26
NY Giants	968	355.4	26.8	20.4	29:10
Philadelphia	1,079	354.1	17.5	20.8	29:44
Seattle	974	350.6	25.8	19.4	31:50
Minnesota	1,001	336.6	23.7	19.1	28:44
St. Louis	1,002	329.0	18.7	17.9	29:47
Chicago	999	310.6	23.4	18.2	31:48
Arizona	1,018	263.1	15.6	15.4	29:19

NFC Total Defense

	Opp Total Plays	Opp Yds/ Game	Opp Yds/ Play	Opp Pts/ Game
San Francisco	1,012	294.4	4.7	17.1
Seattle	968	306.2	5.1	15.3
Chicago	1,021	315.6	4.9	17.3
Carolina	1,010	333.1	5.3	22.7
Green Bay	1,033	336.8	5.2	21.0
Arizona	1,041	337.8	5.2	22.3
Detroit	998	341.1	5.5	27.3
St. Louis	1,041	342.6	5.3	21.8
Philadelphia	994	343.2	5.5	27.8
Minnesota	1,083	350.0	5.2	21.8
Dallas	986	355.4	5.8	25.0
Atlanta	991	365.6	5.9	18.7
Washington	1,031	377.7	5.9	24.2
Tampa Bay	1,031	379.9	5.9	24.6
NY Giants	1,016	383.4	6.0	21.5
New Orleans	1,089	440.1	6.5	28.4

Takeaways/Giveaways

American Football Conference

	Takeaways			Giveaways			Net
	Int	Fum	Total	Int	Fum	Total	Diff
New England	20	21	41	9	7	16	25
Houston	15	14	29	13	4	17	12
Baltimore	13	12	25	11	5	16	9
Cincinnati	14	16	30	16	10	26	4
Cleveland	17	12	29	18	8	26	3
San Diego	14	14	28	15	11	26	2
Denver	16	8	24	11	14	25	-1
Jacksonville	12	11	23	17	9	26	-3
Tennessee	19	5	24	16	12	28	-4
Oakland	11	8	19	16	10	26	-7
Miami	10	6	16	13	13	26	-10
Pittsburgh	10	10	20	14	16	30	-10
Indianapolis	12	3	15	18	9	27	-12
Buffalo	12	9	21	17	17	34	-13
NY Jets	11	12	23	19	18	37	-14
Kansas City	7	6	13	20	17	37	-24

National Football Conference

	Takeaways			Giveaways			Net
	Int	Fum	Total	Int	Fum	Total	Diff
Chicago	24	20	44	16	8	24	20
Washington	21	10	31	8	6	14	17
NY Giants	21	14	35	15	6	21	14
Atlanta	20	11	31	14	4	18	13
Seattle	18	13	31	10	8	18	13
San Francisco	14	11	25	8	8	16	9
Green Bay	18	5	23	8	8	16	7
Tampa Bay	18	8	26	17	6	23	3
New Orleans	15	11	26	19	5	24	2
Carolina	11	12	23	12	10	22	1
Arizona	22	11	33	21	13	34	-1
St. Louis	17	4	21	14	8	22	-1
Minnesota	10	12	22	12	11	23	-1
Dallas	7	9	16	19	10	29	-13
Detroit	11	6	17	17	16	33	-16
Philadelphia	8	5	13	15	22	37	-24

Baltimore Ravens

SCORING

| | TD | | | | | | |
SCORING	Rush	Rec	Ret	FG	PAT	2PT	Pts
Justin Tucker	0	0	0	30	42	0	132
Ray Rice	9	1	0	0	0	0	60
Torrey Smith	0	8	0	0	0	0	48
Dennis Pitta	0	7	0	0	0	0	42
Anquan Boldin	0	4	0	0	0	1	26
Jacoby Jones	0	1	3	0	0	0	24
Joe Flacco	3	0	0	0	0	0	18

RUSHING

RUSHING	No.	Yds	Avg	Lg	TD
Ray Rice	257	1143	4.4	46	9
Bernard Pierce	108	532	4.9	78	1
Tyrod Taylor	14	73	5.2	28	1

PASSING

PASSING	Att	Comp	Pct Comp	Yds	Avg Gain	TD	Int	Rating Pts
J. Flacco	531	317	59.7	3817	7.2	22	10	87.7

RECEIVING

RECEIVING	No.	Yds	Avg	TD	Lg
Anquan Boldin	65	921	14.2	4	43
Torrey Smith	49	855	17.4	8	54
Dennis Pitta	61	669	11.0	7	61
Ray Rice	61	478	7.8	1	43
Jacoby Jones	30	406	13.5	1	47
Ed Dickson	21	225	10.7	0	40
Vonta Leach	21	143	6.8	0	18

INTERCEPTIONS: Cary Williams, Ed Reed, 4

PUNTING	No.	Yds	Avg	Net Avg	Blk	In 20	TB	Lg
S. Koch	83	3911	47.1	40.8	0	28	7	60

SACKS: Paul Kruger, 9.0

Buffalo Bills

SCORING

| | TD | | | | | | |
SCORING	Rush	Rec	Ret	FG	PAT	2PT	Pts
Rian Lindell	0	0	0	21	39	0	102
C.J. Spiller	6	2	0	0	0	0	48
Scott Chandler	0	6	0	0	0	0	36
Steve Johnson	0	6	0	0	0	0	36
Brad Smith	1	2	1	0	0	0	24
Fred Jackson	3	1	0	0	0	0	24
Donald Jones	0	4	0	0	0	0	24

RUSHING

RUSHING	No.	Yds	Avg	Lg	TD
C.J. Spiller	207	1244	6.0	62	6
Fred Jackson	115	437	3.8	15	3
Ryan Fitzpatrick	48	197	4.1	20	1
Tashard Choice	47	193	4.1	22	1

PASSING

PASSING	Att	Comp	Pct Comp	Yds	Avg Gain	TD	Int	Rating Pts
R. Fitzpatrick	505	306	60.6	3400	6.7	24	16	83.3

RECEIVING

RECEIVING	No.	Yds	Avg	TD	Lg
Steve Johnson	79	1046	13.2	6	63
Scott Chandler	43	571	13.3	6	43
C.J. Spiller	43	459	10.7	2	66
Donald Jones	41	443	10.8	4	68
T.J. Graham	31	322	10.4	1	51
Fred Jackson	34	217	6.4	1	34
Brad Smith	14	152	10.9	2	35

INTERCEPTIONS: Jairus Byrd, 5

PUNTING	No.	Yds	Avg	Net Avg	Blk	In 20	TB	Lg
S. Powell	65	2860	44.0	38.1	0	23	2	62

SACKS: Mario Williams, 10.5

Cincinnati Bengals

SCORING

| | TD | | | | | | |
SCORING	Rush	Rec	Ret	FG	PAT	2PT	Pts
Mike Nugent	0	0	0	19	35	0	92
A.J. Green	0	11	0	0	0	0	66
Josh Brown	0	0	0	11	8	0	41
B. Green-Ellis	6	0	0	0	0	0	36
J. Gresham	0	5	0	0	0	0	30
Andrew Hawkins	0	4	0	0	0	0	24
Andy Dalton	4	0	0	0	0	0	24
Mohamed Sanu	0	4	0	0	0	0	24

RUSHING

RUSHING	No.	Yds	Avg	Lg	TD
B. Green-Ellis	278	1094	3.9	48	6
Cedric Peerman	36	258	7.2	48	1
Andy Dalton	47	120	2.6	17	4
Brian Leonard	33	106	3.2	11	0

PASSING

PASSING	Att	Comp	Pct Comp	Yds	Avg Gain	TD	Int	Rating Pts
A. Dalton	528	329	62.3	3669	6.9	27	16	87.4

RECEIVING

RECEIVING	No.	Yds	Avg	TD	Lg
A.J. Green	97	1350	13.9	11	73
Jermaine Gresham	64	737	11.5	5	55
Andrew Hawkins	51	533	10.5	4	59
Brandon Tate	13	211	16.2	1	44
Armon Binns	18	210	11.7	1	48
Marvin Jones	18	201	11.2	1	23

INTERCEPTIONS: Reggie Nelson, Chris Crocker, 3

PUNTING	No.	Yds	Avg	Net Avg	Blk	In 20	TB	Lg
K Huber	76	3540	46.6	42.0	0	33	7	69

SACKS: Geno Atkins, 12.5

Cleveland Browns

SCORING

| | TD | | | | | | |
SCORING	Rush	Rec	Ret	FG	PAT	2PT	Pts
Phil Dawson	0	0	0	29	29	0	116
Trent Richardson	11	1	0	0	0	0	72
Josh Gordon	0	5	0	0	0	0	30
Greg Little	0	4	0	0	0	0	24
Benjamin Watson	0	3	0	0	0	0	18
Travis Benjamin	0	2	1	0	0	0	18

RUSHING

RUSHING	No.	Yds	Avg	Lg	TD
Trent Richardson	267	950	3.6	32	11
Montario Hardesty	65	271	4.2	25	1
Brandon Weeden	27	111	4.1	25	0

PASSING

PASSING	Att	Comp	Pct Comp	Yds	Avg Gain	TD	Int	Rating Pts
B. Weeden	517	297	57.4	3385	6.5	14	17	72.6

RECEIVING

RECEIVING	No.	Yds	Avg	TD	Lg
Josh Gordon	50	805	16.1	5	71
Greg Little	53	647	12.2	4	43
Benjamin Watson	49	501	10.2	3	27
Trent Richardson	51	367	7.2	1	27
Travis Benjamin	18	298	16.6	2	69
M. Massaquoi	17	254	14.9	0	35
Jordan Cameron	20	226	11.3	1	28
Chris Ogbonnaya	24	187	7.8	0	38

INTERCEPTIONS: S. Brown, U. Young, J. Haden, 3

PUNTING	No.	Yds	Avg	Net Avg	Blk	In 20	TB	Lg
R. Hodges	90	3766	41.8	37.1	0	29	4	58

SACKS: Jabaal Sheard, 7.0

Denver Broncos

SCORING

SCORING	Rush	Rec	Ret	FG	PAT	2PT	Pts
Matt Prater 0	0	0	26	55	0	133
Eric Decker 0	13	0	0	0	0	78
D. Thomas.............0	10	0	0	0	0	60
Brandon Stokley...0	5	0	0	0	0	30
Joel Dreessen 0	5	0	0	0	0	30
Willis McGahee 4	0	0	0	0	1	26
K. Moreno 4	0	0	0	0	0	24

RUSHING

RUSHING	No.	Yds	Avg	Lg	TD
Willis McGahee 167	731	4.4	31	4
Knowshon Moreno ...138	525	3.8	20	4
Ronnie Hillman 85	330	3.9	31	1
Lance Ball 42	158	3.8	22	1

PASSING

PASSING	Att	Comp	Pct Comp	Yds	Avg Gain	TD	Int	Rating Pts
P. Manning...583	400	68.6	4659	8.0	37	11	105.8

RECEIVING

RECEIVING	No.	Yds	Avg	TD	Lg
Demaryius Thomas...94	1434	15.3	10	71
Eric Decker 85	1064	12.5	13	55
Jacob Tamme 52	555	10.7	2	36
Brandon Stokley 45	544	12.1	5	38
Joel Dreessen 41	356	8.7	5	30
Willis McGahee 26	221	8.5	0	31
Knowshon Moreno ...21	167	8.0	0	26

INTERCEPTIONS: Wesley Woodyard, Chris Harris, 3

PUNTING

PUNTING	No.	Yds	Avg	Net Avg	Blk	In 20	TB	Lg
B. Colquitt...67	3099	46.3	42.1	0	27	4	67

SACKS: Von Miller, 18.5

Houston Texans

SCORING

SCORING	Rush	Rec	Ret	FG	PAT	2PT	Pts
Shayne Graham...0	0	0	31	45	0	138
Arian Foster........15	2	0	0	0	0	102
Owen Daniels......0	6	0	0	0	0	36
Andre Johnson.....0	4	0	0	0	0	24
James Casey 0	3	0	0	0	0	18
Garrett Graham....0	3	0	0	0	0	18

RUSHING

RUSHING	No.	Yds	Avg	Lg	TD
Arian Foster 351	1424	4.1	46	15
Justin Forsett 63	374	5.9	81	1
Ben Tate 65	279	4.3	25	2

PASSING

PASSING	Att	Comp	Pct Comp	Yds	Avg Gain	TD	Int	Rating Pts
M. Schaub544	350	64.3	4008	7.4	22	12	90.7

RECEIVING

RECEIVING	No.	Yds	Avg	TD	Lg
Andre Johnson.......112	1598	14.3	4	60
Owen Daniels..........62	716	11.5	6	39
Kevin Walter 41	518	12.6	2	52
James Casey 34	330	9.7	3	30
Garrett Graham........28	263	9.4	3	30
Arian Foster..............40	217	5.4	2	23

INTERCEPTIONS: Kareem Jackson, 4

PUNTING

PUNTING	No.	Yds	Avg	Net Avg	Blk	In 20	TB	Lg
D. Jones 88	4150	47.2	40.5	0	28	5	66

SACKS: J.J. Watt, 20.5

Indianapolis Colts

SCORING

SCORING	Rush	Rec	Ret	FG	PAT	2PT	Pts
Adam Vinatieri......0	0	0	26	37	0	115
T.Y. Hilton 0	7	1	0	0	0	48
Reggie Wayne 0	5	0	0	0	0	30
Andrew Luck........5	0	0	0	0	0	30
Donnie Avery 0	3	0	0	0	0	18
Delone Carter.......3	0	0	0	0	0	18
Vick Ballard..........2	1	0	0	0	0	18
Dwayne Allen.......0	3	0	0	0	0	18

RUSHING

RUSHING	No.	Yds	Avg	Lg	TD
Vick Ballard 211	814	3.9	26	2
Donald Brown...........108	417	3.9	19	1
Andrew Luck 62	255	4.1	19	5
Delone Carter 32	122	3.8	20	3

PASSING

PASSING	Att	Comp	Pct Comp	Yds	Avg Gain	TD	Int	Rating Pts
A. Luck.....627	339	54.1	4374	7.0	23	18	76.5

RECEIVING

RECEIVING	No.	Yds	Avg	TD	Lg
Reggie Wayne........106	1355	12.8	5	33
T.Y. Hilton 50	861	17.2	7	70
Donnie Avery 60	781	13.0	3	48
Dwayne Allen 45	521	11.6	3	40
Coby Fleener 26	281	10.8	2	26

INTERCEPTIONS: Darius Butler, 4

PUNTING

PUNTING	No.	Yds	Avg	Net Avg	Blk	In 20	TB	Lg
P. McAfee ...73	3520	48.2	40.3	1	26	8	64

SACKS: Robert Mathis, 8.0

Jacksonville Jaguars

SCORING

SCORING	Rush	Rec	Ret	FG	PAT	2PT	Pts
Josh Scobee 0	0	0	25	18	0	93
Cecil Shorts 0	7	0	0	0	0	42
Justin Blackmon...0	5	0	0	0	1	32
Marcedes Lewis...0	4	0	0	0	0	24
Rashad Jennings .2	0	0	0	0	1	14

RUSHING

RUSHING	No.	Yds	Avg	Lg	TD
Maurice Jones-Drew ..86	414	4.8	59	1
Rashad Jennings 101	283	2.8	21	2
Montell Owens 42	209	5.0	32	1

PASSING

PASSING	Att	Comp	Pct Comp	Yds	Avg Gain	TD	Int	Rating Pts
C. Henne 308	166	53.9	2084	6.8	11	11	72.2
B. Gabbert...278	162	58.3	1662	6.0	9	6	77.4

RECEIVING

RECEIVING	No.	Yds	Avg	TD	Lg
Cecil Shorts..............55	979	17.8	7	80
Justin Blackmon.......64	865	13.5	5	81
Marcedes Lewis......52	540	10.4	4	26
Laurent Robinson....24	252	10.5	0	32
Jordan Shipley 23	244	10.6	1	36

INTERCEPTIONS: Derek Cox, 4

PUNTING

PUNTING	No.	Yds	Avg	Net Avg	Blk	In 20	TB	Lg
B. Anger 91	4353	47.8	40.8	1	31	5	73

SACKS: Tyson Alualu, 3.5

Kansas City Chiefs

SCORING

		TD					
SCORING	Rush	Rec	Ret	FG	PAT	2PT	Pts
Ryan Succop 0	0	0	28	17	0	101
Jamaal Charles 5	1	0	0	0	0	36
Dwayne Bowe 0	3	0	0	0	0	18
Shaun Draughn....2	0	0	0	0	0	12

RUSHING

RUSHING	No.	Yds	Avg	Lg	TD
Jamaal Charles 285	1509	5.3	91	5
Peyton Hillis................85	309	3.6	18	1
Shaun Draughn..........59	233	3.9	25	2
Matt Cassel................27	145	5.4	21	1

PASSING

PASSING	Att	Comp	Pct Comp	Yds	Avg Gain	TD	Int	Rating Pts
M. Cassel...277	161	58.1	1796	6.5	6	12	66.7
B. Quinn....197	112	56.9	1141	5.8	2	8	60.1

RECEIVING

RECEIVING	No.	Yds	Avg	TD	Lg
Dwayne Bowe 59	801	13.6	3	47
Tony Moeaki 33	453	13.7	1	38
Dexter McCluster 52	452	8.7	1	31
Jon Baldwin 20	325	16.3	1	57
Jamaal Charles 35	236	6.7	1	22
Shaun Draughn........24	158	6.6	0	23

INTERCEPTIONS: Brandon Flowers, 3

PUNTING

PUNTING	No.	Yds	Avg	Net Avg	Blk	In 20	TB	Lg
D. Colquitt...83	3887	46.8	40.8	0	45	7	71

SACKS: Justin Houston, 10.0

New England Patriots

SCORING

		TD					
SCORING	Rush	Rec	Ret	FG	PAT	2PT	Pts
S. Gostkowski 0	0	0	29	66	0	153
Stevan Ridley 12	0	0	0	0	0	72
Rob Gronkowski...0	11	0	0	0	0	66
Danny Woodhead 4	3	0	0	0	0	42
Wes Welker 0	6	0	0	0	0	36
Brandon Lloyd 0	4	1	0	0	0	30
Julian Edelman ...0	3	2	0	0	0	30
Aaron Hernandez...0	5	0	0	0	0	30
Tom Brady 4	0	0	0	0	0	24
Shane Vereen.......3	1	0	0	0	0	24

RUSHING

RUSHING	No.	Yds	Avg	Lg	TD
Stevan Ridley 290	1263	4.4	41	12
Danny Woodhead 76	301	4.0	19	4
Brandon Bolden 56	274	4.9	27	2
Shane Vereen 62	251	4.0	16	3

PASSING

PASSING	Att	Comp	Pct Comp	Yds	Avg Gain	TD	Int	Rating Pts
T. Brady 637	401	63.0	4827	7.6	34	8	98.7

RECEIVING

RECEIVING	No.	Yds	Avg	TD	Lg
Wes Welker 118	1354	11.5	6	59
Brandon Lloyd 74	911	12.3	4	53
Rob Gronkowski.......55	790	14.4	11	41
Aaron Hernandez.....51	483	9.5	5	31
Danny Woodhead 40	446	11.2	4	25
Julian Edelman 21	235	11.2	3	56

INTERCEPTIONS: Devin McCourty, 5

PUNTING

PUNTING	No.	Yds	Avg	Net Avg	Blk	In 20	TB	Lg
Z. Mesko.....60	2585	43.1	37.9	1	28	6	62

SACKS: Rob Ninkovich, 8.0

Miami Dolphins

SCORING

		TD					
SCORING	Rush	Rec	Ret	FG	PAT	2PT	Pts
Dan Carpenter 0	0	0	22	26	0	92
Reggie Bush 6	2	0	0	0	0	48
Anthony Fasano ...0	5	0	0	0	1	32
Daniel Thomas.....4	0	0	0	0	0	24
Jorvorskie Lane....2	1	0	0	0	1	20

RUSHING

RUSHING	No.	Yds	Avg	Lg	TD
Reggie Bush 227	986	4.3	65	6
Daniel Thomas..........91	325	3.6	20	4
Lamar Miller 51	250	4.9	28	1
Ryan Tannehill 49	211	4.3	31	2

PASSING

PASSING	Att	Comp	Pct Comp	Yds	Avg Gain	TD	Int	Rating Pts
R. Tannehill...484	282	58.3	3294	6.8	12	13	76.1

RECEIVING

RECEIVING	No.	Yds	Avg	TD	Lg
Brian Hartline 74	1083	14.6	1	80
Davone Bess 61	778	12.8	1	39
Anthony Fasano 41	332	8.1	5	22
Reggie Bush 35	292	8.3	2	25
Charles Clay 18	212	11.8	2	31

INTERCEPTIONS: Reshad Jones, 4

PUNTING

PUNTING	No.	Yds	Avg	Net Avg	Blk	In 20	TB	Lg
B. Fields......74	3715	50.2	41.2	0	29	9	67

SACKS: Cameron Wake, 15.0

New York Jets

SCORING

		TD					
SCORING	Rush	Rec	Ret	FG	PAT	2PT	Pts
Nick Folk 0	0	0	21	30	0	93
Shonn Greene........8	0	0	0	0	0	48
Bilal Powell...........4	0	0	0	0	0	24
Jeff Cumberland...0	3	0	0	0	0	18
Jeremy Kerley......0	2	1	0	0	0	18
Stephen Hill..........0	3	0	0	0	0	18

RUSHING

RUSHING	No.	Yds	Avg	Lg	TD
Shonn Greene 276	1063	3.9	36	8
Bilal Powell 110	437	4.0	18	4
Joe McKnight 30	179	6.0	61	0
Tim Tebow 32	102	3.2	22	0

PASSING

PASSING	Att	Comp	Pct Comp	Yds	Avg Gain	TD	Int	Rating Pts
M. Sanchez...453	246	54.3	2883	6.4	13	18	66.9

RECEIVING

RECEIVING	No.	Yds	Avg	TD	Lg
Jeremy Kerley 56	827	14.8	2	66
Jeff Cumberland 29	359	12.4	3	39
Dustin Keller.............28	317	11.3	2	32
Chaz Schilens 28	289	10.3	2	25
Santonio Holmes......20	272	13.6	1	38
Stephen Hill..............21	252	12.0	3	33

INTERCEPTIONS: Antonio Cromartie, 3

PUNTING

PUNTING	No.	Yds	Avg	Net Avg	Blk	In 20	TB	Lg
R. Malone ...84	3848	45.8	38.5	2	27	8	61

SACKS: Quinton Coples, 5.5

Oakland Raiders

SCORING	Rush	Rec	Ret	FG	PAT	2PT	Pts
S. Janikowski 0	0	0	0	31	25	0	118
Denarius Moore ...0	7	0	0	0	0	0	42
D. Heyward-Bey...0	5	0	0	0	0	0	30
Brandon Myers 0	4	0	0	0	0	0	24
Rod Streater.........0	3	0	0	0	0	1	20
D. McFadden 2	1	0	0	0	0	0	18

RUSHING	No.	Yds	Avg	Lg	TD
Darren McFadden 216	707	3.3	64	2
Marcel Reece 59	271	4.6	17	0
Mike Goodson 35	221	6.3	43	0

PASSING	Att	Comp	Pct Comp	Yds	Avg Gain	TD	Int	Rating Pts
C. Palmer...565	345	61.1	4018	7.1	22	14	85.3

RECEIVING	No.	Yds	Avg	TD	Lg
Brandon Myers 79	806	10.2	4	29
Denarius Moore........51	741	14.5	7	58
D. Heyward-Bey........41	606	14.8	5	59
Rod Streater 39	584	15.0	3	64
Marcel Reece 52	496	9.5	1	56
Derek Hagan 20	259	13.0	0	38
Darren McFadden 42	258	6.1	1	20

INTERCEPTIONS: Joselio Hanson, Michael Huff, Matt Giordano, Phillip Adams, 2

PUNTING	No.	Yds	Avg	Net Avg	Blk	In 20	TB	Lg
S. Lechler ...81	3826	47.2	39.0	1	21	9	68

SACKS: Lamarr Houston, 4.5

San Diego Chargers

SCORING	Rush	Rec	Ret	FG	PAT	2PT	Pts
Nick Novak...........0	0	0	0	18	33	0	87
Antonio Gates 0	7	0	0	0	0	0	42
D. Alexander........0	7	0	0	0	0	0	42
Malcom Floyd 0	5	0	0	0	0	0	30
Nate Kaeding.......0	0	0	0	7	6	0	27
Jackie Battle 3	1	0	0	0	0	0	24
Dante Rosario 0	3	0	0	0	0	0	18

RUSHING	No.	Yds	Avg	Lg	TD
Ryan Mathews...........184	707	3.8	31	1
Jackie Battle................95	311	3.3	52	3
Ronnie Brown..............46	220	4.8	21	0
Curtis Brinkley 39	115	2.9	13	0

PASSING	Att	Comp	Pct Comp	Yds	Avg Gain	TD	Int	Rating Pts
P. Rivers......527	338	64.1	3606	6.8	26	15	88.6

RECEIVING	No.	Yds	Avg	TD	Lg
Malcom Floyd 56	814	14.5	5	39
Danario Alexander ...37	658	17.8	7	80
Antonio Gates 49	538	11.0	7	34
Ronnie Brown...........49	371	7.6	0	25
Ryan Mathews 39	252	6.5	0	24
Eddie Royal..............23	234	10.2	1	31

INTERCEPTIONS: Eric Weddle, Quentin Jammer, 3

PUNTING	No.	Yds	Avg	Net Avg	Blk	In 20	TB	Lg
M. Scifres....81	3914	48.3	40.6	3	30	7	66

SACKS: Shaun Phillips, 9.5

Pittsburgh Steelers

SCORING	Rush	Rec	Ret	FG	PAT	2PT	Pts
Shaun Suisham ...0	0	0	0	28	34	0	118
Heath Miller..........0	8	0	0	0	0	1	50
Mike Wallace........0	8	0	0	0	0	0	48
Antonio Brown......0	5	0	0	0	0	0	30

RUSHING	No.	Yds	Avg	Lg	TD
Jonathan Dwyer 156	623	4.0	34	2
Isaac Redman..........110	410	3.7	28	2
Rashard Mendenhall..51	182	3.6	20	0

PASSING	Att	Comp	Pct Comp	Yds	Avg Gain	TD	Int	Rating Pts
Roethlisberger449	284	63.3	3265	7.3	26	8	97.0
Charlie Batch...70	45	64.3	475	6.8	1	4	64.9
Byron Leftwich..53	25	47.2	272	5.1	0	1	54.9

RECEIVING	No.	Yds	Avg	TD	Lg
Mike Wallace............64	836	13.1	8	82
Heath Miller...............71	816	11.5	8	43
Antonio Brown..........66	787	11.9	5	60
Emmanuel Sanders..44	626	14.2	1	37
Isaac Redman...........19	244	12.8	0	55

INTERCEPTIONS: Lawrence Timmons, 3

PUNTING	No.	Yds	Avg	Net Avg	Blk	In 20	TB	Lg
D. Butler......77	3374	43.8	37.8	1	26	6	79

SACKS: James Harrison, Lawrence Timmons, 6.0

Tennessee Titans

SCORING	Rush	Rec	Ret	FG	PAT	2PT	Pts
Rob Bironas 0	0	0	0	25	35	0	110
Chris Johnson 6	0	0	0	0	0	0	36
Kenny Britt 0	4	0	0	0	0	1	26
Nate Washington .0	4	0	0	0	0	0	24
Jared Cook 0	4	0	0	0	0	0	24
Kendall Wright 0	4	0	0	0	0	0	24
Darius Reynaud ...0	0	3	0	0	0	0	18
Jamie Harper 3	0	0	0	0	0	0	18

RUSHING	No.	Yds	Avg	Lg	TD
Chris Johnson 276	1243	4.5	94	6
Jake Locker................41	291	7.1	32	1

PASSING	Att	Comp	Pct Comp	Yds	Avg Gain	TD	Int	Rating Pts
J. Locker......314	177	56.4	2176	6.9	10	11	74.0
M.Hasselbeck...221	138	62.4	1367	6.2	7	5	81.0

RECEIVING	No.	Yds	Avg	TD	Lg
Nate Washington......46	746	16.2	4	71
Kendall Wright..........64	626	9.8	4	38
Kenny Britt 45	589	13.1	4	46
Jared Cook...............44	523	11.9	4	61
Damian Williams 30	324	10.8	0	27
Craig Stevens 23	275	12.0	1	46
Chris Johnson 36	232	6.4	0	22

INTERCEPTIONS: Michael Griffin, Jason McCourty, 4

PUNTING	No.	Yds	Avg	Net Avg	Blk	In 20	TB	Lg
B. Kern........81	3855	47.6	40.4	2	30	5	71

SACKS: Derrick Morgan, 6.5

Arizona Cardinals

SCORING

	TD						
	Rush	Rec	Ret	FG	PAT	2PT	Pts
Jay Feely	0	0	0	25	25	0	100
Beanie Wells	5	0	0	0	0	0	30
Andre Roberts	0	5	0	0	0	0	30
Larry Fitzgerald	0	4	0	0	0	0	24
L. Stephens-Howling	4	0	0	0	0	0	24

RUSHING

	No.	Yds	Avg	Lg	TD
L Stephens-Howling	111	357	3.2	52	4
Beanie Wells	88	234	2.7	31	5
William Powell	59	216	3.7	17	0
Ryan Williams	58	164	2.8	25	0

PASSING

	Att	Comp	Pct Comp	Yds	Avg Gain	TD	Int	Rating Pts
K. Kolb	183	109	59.6	1169	6.4	8	3	86.1
J. Skelton	201	109	54.2	1132	5.6	2	9	55.4
R. Lindley	171	89	52.0	752	4.4	0	7	46.7

RECEIVING

	No.	Yds	Avg	TD	Lg
Larry Fitzgerald	71	798	11.2	4	37
Andre Roberts	64	759	11.9	5	46
Michael Floyd	45	562	12.5	2	53
Rob Housler	45	417	9.3	0	33
Early Doucet	28	207	7.4	0	18
William Powell	19	132	6.9	0	25

INTERCEPTIONS: Patrick Peterson, 7

PUNTING

	No.	Yds	Avg	Net Avg	Blk	In 20	TB	Lg
D. Zastudil	112	5209	46.5	41.4	0	46	8	70

SACKS: Daryl Washington, 9.0

Atlanta Falcons

SCORING

	TD						
	Rush	Rec	Ret	FG	PAT	2PT	Pts
Matt Bryant	0	0	0	33	44	0	143
Michael Turner	10	1	0	0	0	0	66
Julio Jones	0	10	0	0	0	0	60
Tony Gonzalez	0	8	0	0	0	0	48
Roddy White	0	7	0	0	0	0	42

RUSHING

	No.	Yds	Avg	Lg	TD
Michael Turner	222	800	3.6	43	10
Jacquizz Rodgers	94	362	3.9	43	1
Matt Ryan	34	141	4.1	16	1

PASSING

	Att	Comp	Pct Comp	Yds	Avg Gain	TD	Int	Rating Pts
M. Ryan	615	422	68.6	4719	7.7	32	14	99.1

RECEIVING

	No.	Yds	Avg	TD	LG
Roddy White	92	1351	14.7	7	59
Julio Jones	79	1198	15.2	10	80
Tony Gonzalez	93	930	10.0	8	25
Jacquizz Rodgers	53	402	7.6	1	32
Harry Douglas	38	396	10.4	1	37
Jason Snelling	31	203	6.5	1	16
Michael Turner	19	128	6.7	1	60

INTERCEPTIONS: Thomas DeCoud, 6

PUNTING

	No.	Yds	Avg	Net Avg	Blk	In 20	TB	Lg
M. Bosher	60	2847	47.5	40.7	1	22	4	63

SACKS: Abraham, 10.0

Carolina Panthers

SCORING

	TD						
	Rush	Rec	Ret	FG	PAT	2PT	Pts
Cam Newton	8	0	0	0	0	0	48
Graham Gano	0	0	0	9	20	0	47
Justin Medlock	0	0	0	7	23	0	44
D. Williams	5	2	0	0	0	0	42
Mike Tolbert	7	0	0	0	0	0	42
Greg Olsen	0	5	0	0	0	0	30
Steve Smith	0	4	0	0	0	0	24
Brandon LaFell	0	4	0	0	0	0	24

RUSHING

	No.	Yds	Avg	Lg	TD
Cam Newton	127	741	5.8	72	8
DeAngelo Williams	173	737	4.3	65	5
Jonathan Stewart	93	336	3.6	21	1
Mike Tolbert	54	183	3.4	13	7

PASSING

	Att	Comp	Pct Comp	Yds	Avg Gain	TD	Int	Rating Pts
C. Newton	485	280	57.7	3869	8.0	19	12	86.2

RECEIVING

	No.	Yds	Avg	TD	Lg
Steve Smith	73	1174	16.1	4	66
Greg Olsen	69	843	12.2	5	47
Brandon LaFell	44	677	15.4	4	62
Louis Murphy	25	336	13.4	1	55
Mike Tolbert	27	268	9.9	0	26

INTERCEPTIONS: Luke Kuechly, Charles Godfrey, Captain Munnerlyn, Haruki Nakamura, 2

PUNTING

	No.	Yds	Avg	Net Avg	Blk	In 20	TB	Lg
B. Norman	76	3267	43.0	36.5	1	20	7	63

SACKS: Charles Johnson, 12.5

Chicago Bears

SCORING

	TD						
	Rush	Rec	Ret	FG	PAT	2PT	Pts
Robbie Gould	0	0	0	21	33	0	96
Brandon Marshall	0	11	0	0	0	0	66
Matt Forte	5	1	0	0	0	0	36
Michael Bush	5	0	0	0	0	0	30
Olindo Mare	0	0	0	6	7	0	25
Charles Tillman	0	0	3	0	0	0	18
Alshon Jeffery	0	3	0	0	0	0	18

RUSHING

	No.	Yds	Avg	Lg	TD
Matt Forte	248	1094	4.4	46	5
Michael Bush	114	411	3.6	20	5
Jay Cutler	41	233	5.7	24	0
Armando Allen	27	124	4.6	46	1

PASSING

	Att	Comp	Pct Comp	Yds	Avg Gain	TD	Int	Rating Pts
J. Cutler	434	255	58.8	3033	7.0	19	14	81.3
J. Campbell	51	32	62.7	265	5.2	2	2	72.8

RECEIVING

	No.	Yds	Avg	TD	Lg
Brandon Marshall	118	1508	12.8	11	56
Earl Bennett	29	375	12.9	2	60
Alshon Jeffery	24	367	15.3	3	55
Matt Forte	44	340	7.7	1	47
Devin Hester	23	242	10.5	1	39
Kellen Davis	19	229	12.1	2	25

INTERCEPTIONS: Tim Jennings, 9

PUNTING

	No.	Yds	Avg	Net Avg	Blk	In 20	TB	Lg
A. Podlesh	81	3399	42.0	39.4	0	34	6	64

SACKS: Julius Peppers, 11.5

Dallas Cowboys

SCORING	Rush	Rec	Ret	FG	PAT	2PT	Pts
			TD				
Dan Bailey............	0	0	0	29	37	0	124
Dez Bryant............	0	12	0	0	0	1	74
Miles Austin.........	0	6	0	0	0	0	36
Felix Jones...........	3	2	0	0	0	0	30
Kevin Ogletree.....	0	4	0	0	0	0	24
DeMarco Murray..4		0	0	0	0	0	24
Jason Witten	0	3	0	0	0	0	18

RUSHING	No.	Yds	Avg	Lg	TD
D. Murray	161	663	4.1	48	4
Felix Jones	111	402	3.6	22	3

PASSING	Att	Comp	Pct Comp	Yds	Avg Gain	TD	Int	Rating Pts
T. Romo......	648	425	65.6	4903	7.6	28	19	90.5

RECEIVING	No.	Yds	Avg	TD	Lg
Dez Bryant	92	1382	15.0	12	85
Jason Witten	110	1039	9.4	3	36
Miles Austin............	66	943	14.3	6	49
Kevin Ogletree	32	436	13.6	4	65
Felix Jones	25	262	10.5	2	39
DeMarco Murray	35	251	7.2	0	22

INTERCEPTIONS: Brandon Carr, 3

PUNTING	No.	Yds	Avg	Net Avg	Blk	In 20	TB	Lg
B. Moorman...	56	2497	44.6	38.9	0	22	3	64
C. Jones.........	12	542	45.2	40.0	1	6	0	60

SACKS: DeMarcus Ware, 11.5

Green Bay Packers

SCORING	Rush	Rec	Ret	FG	PAT	2PT	Pts
			TD				
Mason Crosby......	0	0	0	21	50	0	113
James Jones........	0	14	0	0	0	0	84
Randall Cobb........	0	8	1	0	0	0	54
Jordy Nelson........	0	7	0	0	0	1	44
Greg Jennings	0	4	0	0	0	0	24
Tom Crabtree	0	3	0	0	0	0	18

RUSHING	No.	Yds	Avg	Lg	TD
Alex Green	135	464	3.4	41	0
Aaron Rodgers...........	54	259	4.8	27	2
James Starks...........	71	255	3.6	22	1
Cedric Benson	71	248	3.5	11	1

PASSING	Att	Comp	Pct Comp	Yds	Avg Gain	TD	Int	Rating Pts
A. Rodgers...	552	371	67.2	4295	7.8	39	8	108.0

RECEIVING	No.	Yds	Avg	TD	Lg
Randall Cobb...........	80	954	11.9	8	39
James Jones...........	64	784	12.3	14	49
Jordy Nelson.............	49	745	15.2	7	73
Jermichael Finley	61	667	10.9	2	40
Greg Jennings	36	366	10.2	4	45

INTERCEPTIONS: Casey Hayward, 6

PUNTING	No.	Yds	Avg	Net Avg	Blk	In 20	TB	Lg
T. Masthay ...	70	3043	43.5	38.9	1	30	5	65

SACKS: Clay Matthews, 13.0

Detroit Lions

SCORING	Rush	Rec	Ret	FG	PAT	2PT	Pts
			TD				
Jason Hanson......	0	0	0	32	38	0	134
Mikel Leshoure.....	9	0	0	0	0	0	54
Calvin Johnson ...	0	5	0	0	0	0	30
Matthew Stafford..4		0	0	0	0	0	24
Titus Young	0	4	0	0	0	0	24
Brandon Pettigrew	0	3	0	0	0	0	18
Joique Bell	3	0	0	0	0	0	18

RUSHING	No.	Yds	Avg	Lg	TD
Mikel Leshoure	215	798	3.7	16	9
Joique Bell	82	414	5.0	67	3

PASSING	Att	Comp	Pct Comp	Yds	Avg Gain	TD	Int	Rating Pts
M. Stafford...	727	435	59.8	4967	6.8	20	17	79.8

RECEIVING	No.	Yds	Avg	TD	Lg
Calvin Johnson	122	1964	16.1	5	53
Brandon Pettigrew ...	59	567	9.6	3	24
Tony Scheffler	42	504	12.0	1	57
Joique Bell	52	485	9.3	0	50
Titus Young	33	383	11.6	4	49
Ryan Broyles............	22	310	14.1	2	40
Nate Burleson	27	240	8.9	2	26

INTERCEPTIONS: Chris Houston, Don Carey, 2

PUNTING	No.	Yds	Avg	Net Avg	Blk	In 20	TB	Lg
N. Harris......	67	2783	41.5	37.6	0	21	1	58

SACKS: Cliff Avril, 9.5

Minnesota Vikings

SCORING	Rush	Rec	Ret	FG	PAT	2PT	Pts
			TD				
Blair Walsh	0	0	0	35	36	0	141
Adrian Peterson...12		1	0	0	0	1	80
Kyle Rudolph	0	9	0	0	0	1	56
Percy Harvin	1	3	1	0	0	0	30

RUSHING	No.	Yds	Avg	Lg	TD
Adrian Peterson	348	2097	6.0	82	12
Christian Ponder	60	253	4.2	29	2
Toby Gerhart	50	169	3.4	22	1
Percy Harvin...............	22	96	4.4	20	1

PASSING	Att	Comp	Pct Comp	Yds	Avg Gain	TD	Int	Rating Pts
C. Ponder ...	483	300	62.1	2935	6.1	18	12	81.2

RECEIVING	No.	Yds	Avg	TD	Lg
Percy Harvin.............	62	677	10.9	3	45
Kyle Rudolph	53	493	9.3	9	29
Michael Jenkins	40	449	11.2	2	32
Jarius Wright	22	310	14.1	2	65
Jerome Simpson	26	274	10.5	0	33
Adrian Peterson	40	217	5.4	1	20
Devin Aromashodu ..11		182	16.5	0	31
Toby Gerhart	20	155	7.8	0	21

INTERCEPTIONS: Harrison Smith, Antoine Winfield, 3

PUNTING	No.	Yds	Avg	Net Avg	Blk	In 20	TB	Lg
C. Kluwe	72	3237	45.0	39.7	0	18	2	59

SACKS: Jared Allen, 12.0

New Orleans Saints

SCORING	Rush	Rec	Ret	FG	PAT	2PT	Pts
Garrett Hartley 0	0	0		18	57	0	111
Marques Colston..0	10	0		0	0	0	60
Jimmy Graham....0	9	0		0	0	0	54
Darren Sproles.....1	7	0		0	0	1	50
Lance Moore........0	6	0		0	0	0	36
Mark Ingram.......5	0	0		0	0	0	30
David Thomas......0	4	0		0	0	0	24
Joe Morgan.........0	3	0		0	0	0	18

RUSHING	No.	Yds	Avg	Lg	TD
Mark Ingram.............156		602	3.9	31	5
Pierre Thomas 105		473	4.5	48	1
Darren Sproles 48		244	5.1	47	1
Chris Ivory 40		217	5.4	56	2

PASSING	Att	Comp	Pct Comp	Yds	Avg Gain	TD	Int	Rating Pts
D. Brees......670	422	63.0		5177	7.7	43	19	96.3

RECEIVING	No.	Yds	Avg	TD	Lg
Marques Colston......83		1154	13.9	10	60
Lance Moore............65		1041	16.0	6	51
Jimmy Graham........85		982	11.6	9	46
Darren Sproles 75		667	8.9	7	44
Joe Morgan..............10		379	37.9	3	80
Pierre Thomas 39		354	9.1	1	36
Devery Henderson...22		316	14.4	1	41

INTERCEPTIONS: Patrick Robinson, Jabari Greer, 3

PUNTING	No.	Yds	Avg	Net Avg	Blk	In 20	TB	Lg
T. Morstead...74	3707	50.1		43.2	0	20	6	70

SACKS: Cameron Jordan, 8.0

Philadelphia Eagles

SCORING	Rush	Rec	Ret	FG	PAT	2PT	Pts
Alex Henery 0	0	0		27	25	0	106
Jeremy Maclin.....0	7	0		0	0	0	42
LeSean McCoy 2	3	0		0	0	0	30
Bryce Brown 4	0	0		0	0	0	24
Riley Cooper 0	3	0		0	0	0	18

RUSHING	No.	Yds	Avg	Lg	TD
LeSean McCoy.........200		840	4.2	34	2
Bryce Brown.............115		564	4.9	65	4
Michael Vick...............62		332	5.4	20	1

PASSING	Att	Comp	Pct Comp	Yds	Avg Gain	TD	Int	Rating Pts
M. Vick........351	204	58.1		2362	6.7	12	10	78.1
N. Foles 265	161	60.8		1699	6.4	6	5	79.1

RECEIVING	No.	Yds	Avg	TD	Lg
Jeremy Maclin..........69		857	12.4	7	70
DeSean Jackson......45		700	15.6	2	77
Brent Celek 57		684	12.0	1	34
Jason Avant 53		648	12.2	0	39
LeSean McCoy 54		373	6.9	3	36
Damaris Johnson....19		256	13.5	0	32
Riley Cooper 23		248	10.8	3	23
Clay Harbor..............25		186	7.4	2	19

INTERCEPTIONS: Dominique Rodgers-Cromartie, 3

PUNTING	No.	Yds	Avg	Net Avg	Blk	In 20	TB	Lg
M. McBriar ...55	2560	46.5		36.5	1	13	7	66

SACKS: Fletcher Cox, Brandon Graham, Jason Babin, 5.5

New York Giants

SCORING	Rush	Rec	Ret	FG	PAT	2PT	Pts
Lawrence Tynes...0	0	0		33	46	0	145
Victor Cruz 0	10	0		0	0	0	60
Andre Brown 8	0	0		0	0	1	50
Ahmad Bradshaw...6	0	0		0	0	0	36
David Wilson 4	1	1		0	0	0	36
Martellus Bennett...0	5	0		0	0	0	30

RUSHING	No.	Yds	Avg	Lg	TD
Ahmad Bradshaw....221		1015	4.6	37	6
Andre Brown 73		385	5.3	31	8
David Wilson 71		358	5.0	52	4

PASSING	Att	Comp	Pct Comp	Yds	Avg Gain	TD	Int	Rating Pts
E. Manning...536	321	59.9		3948	7.4	26	15	87.2

RECEIVING	No.	Yds	Avg	TD	Lg
Victor Cruz 86		1092	12.7	10	80
Hakeem Nicks...........53		692	13.1	3	50
Martellus Bennett 55		626	11.4	5	33
Domenik Hixon.........39		567	14.5	2	41
Rueben Randle 19		298	15.7	3	56
Ahmad Bradshaw....23		245	10.7	0	59
Ramses Barden 14		220	15.7	0	31

INTERCEPTIONS: Stevie Brown, 8

PUNTING	No.	Yds	Avg	Net Avg	Blk	In 20	TB	Lg
S. Weatherford...58	2757	47.5		39.4	0	22	6	68

SACKS: Jason Pierre-Paul, 6.5

St. Louis Rams

SCORING	Rush	Rec	Ret	FG	PAT	2PT	Pts
Greg Zuerlein.......0	0	0		23	26	0	95
Brandon Gibson...0	5	0		0	0	0	30
Steven Jackson....4	0	0		0	0	1	26
Lance Kendricks ..0	4	0		0	0	1	26
Austin Pettis 0	4	0		0	0	0	24
Janoris Jenkins 0	0	4		0	0	0	24
Danny Amendola .0	3	0		0	0	1	20
Chris Givens 0	3	0		0	0	1	20

RUSHING	No.	Yds	Avg	Lg	TD
Steven Jackson........257		1042	4.1	46	4
Daryl Richardson 98		475	4.8	53	0
Sam Bradford.............37		127	3.4	21	1

PASSING	Att	Comp	Pct Comp	Yds	Avg Gain	TD	Int	Rating Pts
S. Bradford...551	328	59.5		3702	6.7	21	13	82.6

RECEIVING	No.	Yds	Avg	TD	Lg
Chris Givens 42		698	16.6	3	65
Brandon Gibson......51		691	13.5	5	34
Danny Amendola 63		666	10.6	3	56
Lance Kendricks 42		519	12.4	4	80
Steven Jackson.......38		321	8.4	0	22
Austin Pettis 30		261	8.7	4	36
Daryl Richardson 24		163	6.8	0	26

INTERCEPTIONS: Janoris Jenkins, 4

PUNTING	No.	Yds	Avg	Net Avg	Blk	In 20	TB	Lg
J. Hekker...82	3756	45.8		39.9	0	22	4	68

SACKS: Chris Long, 11.5

San Francisco 49ers

SCORING

| | | TD | | | | | |
SCORING	Rush	Rec	Ret	FG	PAT	2PT	Pts
David Akers	0	0	0	29	44	0	131
Frank Gore	8	1	1	0	0	0	60
Michael Crabtree	0	9	0	0	0	0	54
Vernon Davis	0	5	0	0	0	0	30
Colin Kaepernick	5	0	0	0	0	0	30
Randy Moss	0	3	0	0	0	0	18
Delanie Walker	0	3	0	0	0	0	18

RUSHING

RUSHING	No.	Yds	Avg	Lg	TD
Frank Gore	258	1214	4.7	37	8
Colin Kaepernick	63	415	6.6	50	5
Kendall Hunter	72	371	5.2	26	2

PASSING

PASSING	Att	Comp	Pct Comp	Yds	Avg Gain	TD	Int	Rating Pts
C. Kaepernick	218	136	62.4	1814	8.3	10	3	98.3
A. Smith	218	153	70.2	1737	8.0	13	5	104.1

RECEIVING

RECEIVING	No.	Yds	Avg	TD	Lg
Michael Crabtree	85	1105	13.0	9	49
Vernon Davis	41	548	13.4	5	53
Mario Manningham	42	449	10.7	1	40
Randy Moss	28	434	15.5	3	55
Delanie Walker	21	344	16.4	3	45
Frank Gore	28	234	8.4	1	26

INTERCEPTIONS: Dashon Goldson, 3

PUNTING	No.	Yds	Avg	Net Avg	Blk	In 20	TB	Lg
A. Lee	67	3226	48.1	43.2	0	36	4	66

SACKS: Aldon Smith, 19.5

Tampa Bay Buccaneers

SCORING

| | | TD | | | | | |
SCORING	Rush	Rec	Ret	FG	PAT	2PT	Pts
Connor Barth	0	0	0	28	39	0	123
Doug Martin	11	1	0	0	0	0	72
Mike Williams	0	9	0	0	0	0	54
Vincent Jackson	0	8	0	0	0	1	50
Dallas Clark	0	4	0	0	0	0	24

RUSHING

RUSHING	No.	Yds	Avg	Lg	TD
Doug Martin	319	1454	4.6	70	11
LeGarrette Blount	41	151	3.7	35	2

PASSING

PASSING	Att	Comp	Pct Comp	Yds	Avg Gain	TD	Int	Rating Pts
J. Freeman	558	306	54.8	4065	7.3	27	17	81.6

RECEIVING

RECEIVING	No.	Yds	Avg	TD	Lg
Vincent Jackson	72	1384	19.2	8	95
Mike Williams	63	996	15.8	9	65
Doug Martin	49	472	9.6	1	64
Dallas Clark	47	435	9.3	4	33
Tiquan Underwood	28	425	15.2	2	62

INTERCEPTIONS: Ronde Barber, 4

PUNTING	No.	Yds	Avg	Net Avg	Blk	In 20	TB	Lg
M. Koenen	76	3440	45.3	37.4	1	22	6	64

SACKS: Michael Bennett, 9.0

Seattle Seahawks

SCORING

| | | TD | | | | | |
SCORING	Rush	Rec	Ret	FG	PAT	2PT	Pts
Steven Hauschka	0	0	0	24	46	0	118
Marshawn Lynch	11	1	0	0	0	0	72
Sidney Rice	0	7	0	0	0	0	42
Golden Tate	0	7	0	0	0	0	42
Russell Wilson	4	0	0	0	0	0	24
Zach Miller	0	3	0	0	0	0	18
Anthony McCoy	0	3	0	0	0	0	18
Doug Baldwin	0	3	0	0	0	0	18

RUSHING

RUSHING	No.	Yds	Avg	Lg	TD
Marshawn Lynch	315	1590	5.0	77	11
Russell Wilson	94	489	5.2	25	4
Robert Turbin	80	354	4.4	26	0

PASSING

PASSING	Att	Comp	Pct Comp	Yds	Avg Gain	TD	Int	Rating Pts
R. Wilson	393	252	64.1	3118	7.9	26	10	100.0

RECEIVING

RECEIVING	No.	Yds	Avg	TD	Lg
Sidney Rice	50	748	15.0	7	46
Golden Tate	45	688	15.3	7	51
Zach Miller	38	396	10.4	3	30
Doug Baldwin	29	366	12.6	3	50
Anthony McCoy	18	291	16.2	3	67
Marshawn Lynch	23	196	8.5	1	27
Robert Turbin	19	181	9.5	0	20

INTERCEPTIONS: Richard Sherman, 8

PUNTING	No.	Yds	Avg	Net Avg	Blk	In 20	TB	Lg
J. Ryan	65	2963	45.6	40.8	0	30	3	73

SACKS: Chris Clemons, 11.5

Washington Redskins

SCORING

| | | TD | | | | | |
SCORING	Rush	Rec	Ret	FG	PAT	2PT	Pts
Kai Forbath	0	0	0	17	33	0	84
Alfred Morris	13	0	0	0	0	0	78
Santana Moss	0	8	0	0	0	0	48
Robert Griffin III	7	0	0	0	0	0	42
Billy Cundiff	0	0	0	7	17	0	38
Pierre Garcon	0	4	1	0	0	0	30
Josh Morgan	0	2	1	0	0	0	18
L. Hankerson	0	3	0	0	0	0	18
Aldrick Robinson	0	3	0	0	0	0	18

RUSHING

RUSHING	No.	Yds	Avg	Lg	TD
Alfred Morris	335	1613	4.8	39	13
Robert Griffin III	120	815	6.8	76	7

PASSING

PASSING	Att	Comp	Pct Comp	Yds	Avg Gain	TD	Int	Rating Pts
R. Griffin III	393	258	65.6	3200	8.1	20	5	102.4
K. Cousins	48	33	68.8	466	9.7	4	3	101.6

RECEIVING

RECEIVING	No.	Yds	Avg	TD	Lg
Pierre Garcon	44	633	14.4	4	88
Santana Moss	41	573	14.0	8	77
Leonard Hankerson	38	543	14.3	3	68
Josh Morgan	48	510	10.6	2	32
Fred Davis	24	325	13.5	0	29
Logan Paulsen	25	308	12.3	1	31

INTERCEPTIONS: London Fletcher, 5

PUNTING	No.	Yds	Avg	Net Avg	Blk	In 20	TB	Lg
S. Rocca	68	2984	43.9	37.2	2	22	3	61

SACKS: Ryan Kerrigan, 8.5

First two rounds of the 78th annual NFL Draft, held April 25, 2013 in New York City.

First Round

Team	Selection	Position
1 ....Kansas City Chiefs	Eric Fisher, Central Michigan	OT
2 ....Jacksonville Jaguars	Luke Joeckel, Texas A&M	OT
3 ....Miami Dolphins (from Oakland)	Dion Jordan, Oregon	DE
4 ....Philadelphia Eagles	Lane Johnson, Oklahoma	OT
5 ....Detroit Lions	Ziggy Ansah, BYU	DE
6 ....Cleveland Browns	Barkevious Mingo, LSU	DE
7 ....Arizona Cardinals	Jonathan Cooper, North Carolina	OG
8 ....St. Louis Rams (from Buffalo)	Tavon Austin, West Virginia	WR
9 ....NY Jets	Dee Milliner, Alabama	CB
10 ....Tennessee Titans	Chance Warmack, Alabama	OG
11 ....San Diego Chargers	D.J. Fluker, Alabama	OT
12 ....Oakland Raiders (from Miami)	D.J. Hayden, Houston	CB
13 ....NY Jets (from Tampa Bay)	Sheldon Richardson, Missouri	DT
14 ....Carolina Panthers	Lotulelei, Star, Utah	DT
15 ....New Orleans Saints	Kenny Vaccaro, Texas	SS
16 ....Buffalo Bills (from St. Louis)	EJ Manuel, Florida St	QB
17 ....Pittsburgh Steelers	Jarvis Jones, Georgia	OLB
18 ....San Francisco 49ers (from Dallas)	Eric Reid, LSU	FS
19 ....NY Giants	Justin Pugh, Syracuse	OT
20 ....Chicago Bears	Kyle Long, Oregon	OG
21 ....Cincinnati Bengals	Tyler Eifert, Notre Dame	TE
22 ....Atlanta Falcons (from Wash through StL)	Desmond Trufant, Washington	CB
23 ....Minnesota Vikings	Sharrif Floyd, Florida	DT
24 ....Indianapolis Colts	Bjoern Werner, Florida St	DE
25 ....Minnesota Vikings (from Seattle)	Xavier Rhodes, Florida St	CB
26 ....Green Bay Packers	Datone Jones, UCLA	DE
27 ....Houston Texans	DeAndre Hopkins, Clemson	WR
28 ....Denver Broncos	Sylvester Williams, North Carolina	DT
29 ....Minnesota Vikings (from New England)	Cordarrelle Patterson, Tennessee	WR
30 ....St. Louis Rams (from Atlanta)	Alec Ogletree, Georgia	ILB
31 ....Dallas Cowboys (from San Francisco)	Travis Frederick, Wisconsin	C
32 ....Baltimore Ravens	Matt Elam, Florida	FS

Second Round

Team	Selection	Position
33 ....Jacksonville Jaguars	John Cyprien, Florida International	FS
34 ....Tennessee Titans (from KC through SF)	Justin Hunter, Tennessee	WR
35 ....Philadelphia Eagles	Zach Ertz, Stanford	TE
36 ....Detroit Lions	Darius Slay, Mississippi St	CB
37 ....Cincinnati Bengals (from Oakland)	Giovani Bernard, North Carolina	RB
38 ....San Diego Chargers (from Arizona)	Manti Te'o, Notre Dame	ILB
39 ....New York Jets	Geno Smith, West Virginia	QB
40 ....San Francisco 49ers (from Tennessee)	Cornellius Carradine, Florida St	DE
41 ....Buffalo Bills	Robert Woods, USC	WR
42 ....Oakland Raiders (from Miami)	Menelik Watson, Florida St	OT
43 ....Tampa Bay Buccaneers	Johnthan Banks, Mississippi St	CB
44 ....Carolina Panthers	Kawann Short, Purdue	DT
45 ....Arizona Cardinals (from San Diego)	Kevin Minter, LSU	ILB
46 ....Buffalo Bills (from St. Louis)	Kiko Alonso, Oregon	ILB
47 ....Dallas Cowboys	Gavin Escobar, San Diego St	TE
48 ....Pittsburgh Steelers	Le'Veon Bell, Michigan St	RB
49 ....New York Giants	Johnathan Hankins, Ohio St	DT
50 ....Chicago Bears	Jon Bostic, Florida	ILB
51 ....Washington Redskins	David Amerson, N.C. State	CB
52 ....New England Patriots (from Minnesota)	Jamie Collins, Southern Miss	OLB
53 ....Cincinnati Bengals	Margus Hunt, SMU	DE
54 ....Miami Dolphins (from Indianapolis)	Jamar Taylor, Boise St	CB
55 ....San Francisco 49ers (from Green Bay)	Vance McDonald, Rice	TE
56 ....Baltimore Ravens (from Seattle)	Arthur Brown, Kansas St	ILB
57 ....Houston Texans	D.J. Swearinger, South Carolina	SS
58 ....Denver Broncos	Montee Ball, Wisconsin	RB
59 ....New England Patriots	Aaron Dobson, Marshall	WR
60 ....Atlanta Falcons	Robert Alford, Southeastern Louisiana	CB
61 ....Green Bay Packers (from San Francisco)	Eddie Lacy, Alabama	RB
62 ....Seattle Seahawks (from Baltimore)	Christine Michael, Texas A&M	RB

Regular Season Results

WEST DIVISION	W	L	T	Pts	PF	PA
†British Columbia	13	5	0	26	479	354
*Calgary	12	6	0	24	535	430
*Saskatchewan	8	10	0	16	457	409
*Edmonton	7	11	0	14	422	450

EAST DIVISION	W	L	T	Pts	PF	PA
†Montreal	11	7	0	22	478	489
*Toronto	9	9	0	18	445	491
Winnipeg	6	12	0	12	376	531
Hamilton	6	12	0	12	538	576

†Clinched division title.

*Clinched playoff berth.

Playoff Results

DIVISION SEMI-FINALS

Nov. 11, 2012

TORONTO 42, Edmonton 26
CALGARY 36, Saskatchewan 30

DIVISION FINALS

Nov. 18, 2012

Toronto 27, MONTREAL 20
Calgary 34, BRITISH COLUMBIA 29
Home team in caps.

2012 Grey Cup Championship

Nov. 25, 2012, Toronto

Calgary	3	3	5	11—22
Toronto	7	17	3	8—35

FIRST QUARTER: Toronto: TD Owens 5 pass from Ray (Waters convert), 7:32.

Calgary: FG Paredes 40, 4:09.

SECOND QUARTER: Toronto: TD Home 25 interception return (Waters convert), 14:46.

Toronto: FG Waters 16, 9:25.

Calgary: FG Paredes 18, 2:33.

Toronto: TD Inman 1 pass from Jackson (Waters convert), :22.

THIRD QUARTER: Calgary: FG Paredes 27, 6:29.

Toronto: FG Waters 30, 3:01.

Calgary: Safety :04.

FOURTH QUARTER: Calgary: FG Paredes 19, 9:58.

Toronto: TD Durie 7 pass from Ray (Waters convert), 5:56.

Toronto: Single Prefonaine punt 53, 1:42.

Calgary: TD Price 12 pass from Mitchell (2-pt conversion), :20.

A: 53,208.

Season-by-Season NFL Final Standings

1920*

	W	L	T	Pct	Pts	OP
Akron Pros	8	0	3	1.000	151	7
Decatur Staleys	10	1	2	.909	164	21
Buffalo All-Americans	9	1	1	.900	258	32
Chicago Cardinals	6	2	1	.750	101	29
Rock Island Independents	6	2	2	.750	201	49
Dayton Triangles	5	2	2	.714	150	54
Rochester Jeffersons	6	3	2	.667	156	57
Canton Bulldogs	7	4	2	.636	208	57
Detroit Heralds	2	3	3	.400	53	82
Cleveland Tigers	2	4	2	.333	28	46
Chicago Tigers	2	5	1	.286	49	63
Hammond Pros	2	5	0	.286	41	154
Columbus Panhandles	2	6	2	.250	41	121
Muncie Flyers	0	1	0	.000	0	45

*no official standings kept

1921

	W	L	T	Pct	Pts	OP
Buffalo All-Americans	9	1	2	.900	211	29
Chicago Staleys	9	1	1	.900	128	53
Akron Pros	8	3	1	.727	148	31
Canton Bulldogs	5	2	3	.714	106	55
Rock Island Independents	4	2	1	.667	65	30
Evansville Crimson Giants	3	2	0	.600	89	46
Green Bay Packers	3	2	1	.600	70	55
Chicago Cardinals	3	3	2	.500	54	53
Dayton Triangles	4	4	1	.500	96	67
Rochester Jeffersons	2	3	0	.400	85	76
Cleveland Tigers	3	5	0	.375	95	58
Washington Senators	1	2	0	.333	21	43
Cincinnati Celts	1	3	0	.250	14	117
Hammond Pros	1	3	1	.250	17	45
Minneapolis Marines	1	3	0	.250	37	41
Detroit Tigers	1	5	1	.167	19	109
Columbus Panhandles	1	8	0	.111	47	222
Muncie Flyers	0	2	0	.000	0	28
Louisville Brecks	0	2	0	.000	0	27
New York Giants	0	2	0	.000	0	72
Tonawanda Kardex	0	1	0	.000	0	45

1922

	W	L	T	Pct	Pts	OP
Canton Bulldogs	10	0	2	1.000	184	15
Chicago Bears	9	3	0	.750	123	44
Chicago Cardinals	8	3	0	.727	96	50
Toledo Maroons	5	2	2	.714	94	59
Rock Island Independents	4	2	1	.667	154	27
Racine Legion	6	4	1	.600	122	56
Dayton Triangles	4	3	1	.571	80	62
Green Bay Packers	4	3	3	.571	70	54
Buffalo All-Americans	5	4	1	.556	87	41
Akron Pros	3	5	2	.375	146	95
Milwaukee Badgers	2	4	3	.333	51	71
Oorang Indians	3	6	0	.333	69	190
Minneapolis Marines	1	3	0	.250	19	40
Louisville Brecks	1	3	0	.250	13	140
Evansville Crimson Giants	0	3	0	.000	6	88
Rochester Jeffersons	0	4	1	.000	13	76
Hammond Pros	0	5	1	.000	0	69
Columbus Panhandles	0	8	0	.000	24	174

1923

	W	L	T	Pct	Pts	OP
Canton Bulldogs	11	0	1	1.000	246	19
Chicago Bears	9	2	1	.818	123	35
Green Bay Packers	7	2	1	.778	85	34
Milwaukee Badgers	7	2	3	.778	100	49
Cleveland Indians	3	1	3	.750	52	49
Chicago Cardinals	8	4	0	.667	139	37
Duluth Kelleys	4	3	0	.571	35	33
Buffalo All-Americans	5	4	3	.556	94	43
Columbus Tigers	5	4	1	.556	119	35
Racine Legion	4	4	2	.500	86	76
Toledo Maroons	3	3	2	.500	35	66
Rock Island Independents	2	3	3	.400	83	62
Minneapolis Marines	2	5	2	.286	48	80
St. Louis All-Stars	1	4	2	.200	14	32
Hammond Pros	1	5	1	.167	14	59
Dayton Triangles	1	6	1	.143	16	95
Akron Pros	1	6	0	.143	25	74
Oorang Indians	1	10	0	.091	24	235
Louisville Brecks	0	3	0	.000	0	90
Rochester Jeffersons	0	4	0	.000	6	141

1924

	W	L	T	Pct	Pts	OP
Cleveland Bulldogs	7	1	1	.875	229	60
Chicago Bears	6	1	4	.857	136	55
Frankfort Yellow Jackets	11	2	1	.846	326	109
Duluth Kelleys	5	1	0	.833	56	16
Rock Island Independents	5	2	2	.714	81	15
Green Bay Packers	7	4	0	.636	108	38
Racine Legion	4	3	3	.571	69	47
Chicago Cardinals	5	4	1	.556	90	67
Buffalo Bisons	6	5	0	.545	120	140
Columbus Tigers	4	4	0	.500	91	68
Hammond Pros	2	2	1	.500	18	45
Milwaukee Badgers	5	8	0	.385	142	188
Akron Pros	2	6	0	.250	59	132
Dayton Triangles	2	6	0	.250	45	148
Kansas City Blues	2	7	0	.222	46	124
Kenosha Maroons	0	4	1	.000	12	117
Minneapolis Marines	0	6	0	.000	14	108
Rochester Jeffersons	0	7	0	.000	14	179

1925

	W	L	T	Pct	Pts	OP
Chicago Cardinals	11	2	1	.846	230	65
Pottsville Maroons	10	2	0	.833	280	45
Detroit Panthers	8	2	2	.800	118	42
New York Giants	8	4	0	.667	122	67
Akron Pros	4	2	2	.650	65	51
Frankfort Yellow Jackets	13	7	0	.643	196	189
Chicago Bears	9	5	3	.625	158	96
Rock Island Independents	5	3	3	.615	99	58
Green Bay Packers	8	5	0	.545	151	120
Providence Steam Roller	6	5	1	.500	131	108
Canton Bulldogs	4	4	0	.385	50	73
Cleveland Bulldogs	5	8	1	.286	75	134
Kansas City Cowboys	2	5	1	.200	68	106
Hammond Pros	1	4	0	.143	23	87

1925 *(Cont.)*

	W	L	T	Pct	Pts	OP
Buffalo Bisons	1	6	2	.143	33	113
Duluth Kelleys	0	3	0	.000	6	25
Rochester Jeffersons	0	6	1	.000	26	91
Milwaukee Badgers	0	6	0	.000	7	191
Dayton Triangles	0	7	1	.000	3	84
Columbus Tigers	0	9	0	.000	28	124

1926

	W	L	T	Pct	Pts	OP
Frankfort Yellow Jackets	14	1	2	.765	223	43
Chicago Bears	12	1	3	.844	216	63
Pottsville Maroons	10	2	2	.714	155	29
Kansas City Cowboys	8	3	0	.727	76	54
Green Bay Packers	7	3	3	.462	144	68
Los Angeles Buccaneers	6	3	1	.600	67	57
NY Giants	8	4	1	.583	140	45
Duluth Eskimos	6	5	3	.429	114	81
Buffalo Rangers	4	4	2	.400	53	62
Chicago Cardinals	5	6	1	.417	67	86
Providence Steam Roller	5	7	1	.417	94	96
Detroit Panthers	4	6	2	.500	115	52
Hartford Blues	3	7	0	.300	57	99
Brooklyn Lions	3	8	0	.273	60	150
Milwaukee Badgers	2	7	0	.222	41	66
Akron Indians	1	4	3	.125	23	89
Dayton Triangles	1	4	1	.167	15	82
Racine Tornadoes	1	4	0	.200	8	92
Columbus Tigers	1	6	0	.143	26	93
Canton Bulldogs	1	9	3	.077	46	172
Hammond Pros	0	4	0	.000	3	56
Louisville Colonels	0	4	0	.000	0	108

1927

	W	L	T	Pct	Pts	OP
NY Giants	11	1	1	.917	197	20
Green Bay Packers	7	2	1	.778	113	43
Chicago Bears	9	3	2	.750	149	98
Cleveland Bulldogs	8	4	1	.667	209	107
Providence Steam Roller	8	5	1	.615	105	88
New York Yankees	7	8	1	.467	142	174
Frankfort Yellow Jackets	6	9	3	.400	152	166
Pottsville Maroons	5	8	0	.385	80	163
Chicago Cardinals	3	7	1	.300	69	134
Dayton Triangles	1	6	1	.143	15	57
Duluth Eskimos	1	8	0	.111	68	134
Buffalo Bisons	0	5	0	.000	8	123

1928

	W	L	T	Pct	Pts	OP
Providence Steam Roller	8	1	1	.889	128	36
Frankfort Yellow Jackets	11	3	1	.786	169	84
Detroit Wolverines	7	2	1	.778	189	76
Green Bay Packers	6	4	3	.600	120	92
Chicago Bears	7	5	1	.583	182	85
NY Giants	4	7	2	.364	79	137
NY Yankees	4	8	1	.333	104	179
Pottsville Maroons	2	8	0	.200	74	134
Chicago Cardinals	1	5	0	.167	7	107
Dayton Triangles	0	7	0	.000	9	131

1929

	W	L	T	Pct	Pts	OP
Green Bay Packers	12	0	1	1.000	198	22
NY Giants	13	1	1	.929	312	86
Frankfort Yellow Jackets	10	4	5	.714	139	128
Chicago Cardinals	6	6	1	.500	154	83
Boston Bulldogs	4	4	0	.500	98	73
Staten Island Stapletons	3	6	3	.429	89	62
Providence Steam Roller	4	5	2	.400	107	117
Orange Tornadoes	3	6	4	.375	32	90
Chicago Bears	4	9	2	.308	119	227
Buffalo Bisons	1	7	1	.125	48	142
Minneapolis Red Jackets	1	9	0	.100	48	185
Dayton Triangles	0	6	0	.000	7	136

1930

	W	L	T	Pct	Pts	OP
Green Bay Packers	10	3	1	.769	234	111
NY Giants	13	4	0	.765	308	98
Chicago Bears	9	4	1	.692	169	71
Brooklyn Dodgers	7	4	1	.636	154	59
Providence Steam Roller	6	4	1	.600	90	125
Staten Island Stapletons	5	5	2	.500	95	112
Chicago Cardinals	5	6	2	.455	128	132
Portsmouth Spartans	5	6	3	.455	176	161
Frankfort Yellow Jackets	4	13	1	.222	113	321
Minneapolis Red Jackets	1	7	1	.125	27	165
Newark Tornadoes	1	10	1	.091	51	190

1931

	W	L	T	Pct	Pts	OP
Green Bay Packers	12	2	0	.857	318	94
Portsmouth Spartans	11	3	0	.786	161	77
Chicago Bears	8	5	0	.615	145	92
Chicago Cardinals	5	4	0	.556	120	128
NY Giants	7	6	1	.538	161	127
Providence Steam Roller	4	4	3	.500	78	127
Staten Island Stapletons	4	6	1	.400	79	118
Cleveland Indians	2	8	0	.200	45	137
Brooklyn Dodgers	2	12	0	.143	64	199
Frankfort Yellow Jackets	1	6	1	.143	13	85

1932

	W	L	T	Pct	Pts	OP
Chicago Bears	7	1	6	.875	160	44
Green Bay Packers	10	3	1	.769	152	63
Portsmouth Spartans	6	2	4	.750	116	71
Boston Braves	4	4	2	.500	55	79
NY Giants	4	6	2	.400	93	113
Brooklyn Dodgers	3	9	0	.250	63	131
Chiago Cardinals	2	6	2	.250	72	114
Staten Island Stapletons	2	7	3	.222	77	173

1933

EAST	W	L	T	Pct	Pts	OP
NY Giants	11	3	0	.786	244	101
Brooklyn Dodgers	5	4	1	.556	93	54
Boston Redskins	5	5	2	.500	103	97
Philadelphia Eagles	3	5	1	.375	77	158
Pittsburgh Pirates	3	6	2	.333	67	208

1933 *(Cont.)*

WEST	W	L	T	Pct	Pts	OP
Chicago Bears	10	2	1	.833	133	82
Portsmouth Spartans	6	5	0	.545	128	87
Green Bay Packers	5	7	1	.417	170	107
Cincinnati Reds	3	6	1	.333	38	110
Chicago Cardinals	1	9	1	.100	52	101

1934

EAST	W	L	T	Pct	Pts	OP
NY Giants	8	5	0	.615	147	107
Boston Redskins	6	6	0	.500	107	93
Brooklyn Dodgers	4	7	0	.364	60	153
Philadelphia Eagles	4	7	0	.364	127	85
Pittsburgh Pirates	2	10	0	.167	51	206

WEST	W	L	T	Pct	Pts	OP
Chicago Bears	13	0	0	1.000	286	86
Detroit Lions	10	3	0	.769	238	59
Green Bay Packers	7	6	0	.538	156	112
Chicago Cardinals	5	6	0	.455	80	84
St. Louis Gunners	1	2	0	.333	27	61
Cincinnati Reds	0	8	0	.000	10	243

1935

EAST	W	L	T	Pct	Pts	OP
NY Giants	9	3	0	.750	180	96
Brooklyn Dodgers	5	6	1	.455	90	141
Pittsburgh Pirates	4	8	0	.333	99	209
Boston Redskins	2	8	1	.200	65	123
Philadelphia Eagles	2	9	0	.182	60	179

WEST	W	L	T	Pct	Pts	OP
Detroit Lions	7	3	2	.700	191	111
Green Bay Packers	8	4	0	.667	181	96
Chicago Bears	6	4	2	.600	192	106
Chicago Cardinals	6	4	2	.600	99	97

1936

EAST	W	L	T	Pct	Pts	OP
Boston Redskins	7	5	0	.583	149	110
Pittsburgh Pirates	6	6	0	.500	98	187
NY Giants	5	6	1	.455	115	163
Brooklyn Dodgers	3	8	1	.273	92	161
Philadelphia Eagles	1	11	0	.083	51	206

WEST	W	L	T	Pct	Pts	OP
Green Bay	10	1	1	.909	248	118
Chicago Bears	9	3	0	.750	222	94
Detroit Lions	8	4	0	.667	235	102
Chicago Cardinals	3	8	1	.273	74	143

1937

EAST	W	L	T	Pct	Pts	OP
Washington Redskins	8	3	0	.727	195	120
NY Giants	6	3	2	.667	128	109
Pittsburgh Pirates	4	7	0	.364	122	145
Brooklyn Dodgers	3	7	1	.300	82	174
Philadelphia Eagles	2	8	1	.200	86	177

1937 *(Cont.)*

WEST	W	L	T	Pct	Pts	OP
Chicago Bears	9	1	1	.900	201	100
Green Bay Packers	7	4	0	.636	220	122
Detroit Lions	7	4	0	.636	180	105
Chicago Cardinals	5	5	1	.500	135	165
Cleveland Rams	1	10	0	.091	75	207

1938

EAST	W	L	T	Pct	Pts	OP
NY Giants	8	2	1	.800	194	79
Washington Redskins	6	3	2	.667	148	154
Brooklyn Dodgers	4	4	3	.500	131	161
Philadelphia Eagles	5	6	0	.455	154	164
Pittsburgh Pirates	2	9	0	.182	79	169

WEST	W	L	T	Pct	Pts	OP
Green Bay Packers	8	3	0	.727	223	118
Detroit Lions	7	4	0	.636	119	108
Chicago Bears	6	5	0	.545	194	148
Cleveland Rams	4	7	0	.364	131	215
Chicago Cardinals	2	9	0	.182	111	168

1939

EAST	W	L	T	Pct	Pts	OP
NY Giants	9	1	1	.168	168	85
Washington Redskins	8	2	1	.242	242	94
Brooklyn Dodgers	4	6	1	.108	108	219
Philadelphia Eagles	1	9	1	.105	105	200
Pittsburgh Pirates	1	9	1	.114	114	216

WEST	W	L	T	Pct	Pts	OP
Green Bay Packers	9	2	0	.818	233	153
Chicago Bears	8	3	0	.727	298	157
Detroit Lions	6	5	0	.545	145	150
Cleveland Rams	5	5	1	.195	195	164
Chicago Cardinals	1	10	0	.091	84	254

1940

EAST	W	L	T	Pct	Pts	OP
Washington Redskins	9	2	0	.818	245	142
Brooklyn Dodgers	8	2	0	.800	179	110
NY Giants	6	4	1	.545	131	133
Pittsburgh Pirates	2	7	2	.182	67	174
Philadelphia Eagles	1	10	0	.091	121	200

WEST	W	L	T	Pct	Pts	OP
Chicago Bears	8	3	0	.727	238	152
Green Bay Packers	6	4	1	.600	238	155
Detroit Lions	5	5	1	.500	120	177
Cleveland Rams	4	6	1	.400	181	191
Chicago Cardinals	2	7	2	.222	139	222

1941

EAST	W	L	T	Pct	Pts	OP
NY Giants	8	3	0	.727	238	114
Brooklyn	7	4	0	.636	158	127
Washington	6	5	0	.545	176	174
Philadelphia	2	8	1	.200	119	218
Pittsburgh	1	9	1	.100	103	276

1941 *(Cont.)*

WEST

	W	L	T	Pct	Pts	OP
Green Bay	10	1	0	.909	258	120
Chicago Bears	10	1	0	.909	396	147
Detroit	4	6	1	.400	121	195
Chicago Cardinals	3	7	1	.300	127	197
Cleveland	2	9	0	.182	116	244

1942

EAST

	W	L	T	Pct	Pts	OP
Washington	10	1	0	.909	227	102
Pittsburgh	7	4	0	.636	167	119
NY Giants	5	5	1	.500	155	139
Brooklyn	3	8	0	.273	100	168
Philadelphia	2	9	0	.182	134	239

WEST

	W	L	T	Pct	Pts	OP
Chicago Bears	11	0	0	1.000	376	84
Green Bay	8	2	1	.800	300	215
Cleveland	5	6	0	.455	150	207
Chicago Cardinals	3	8	0	.273	98	209
Detroit	0	11	0	.000	38	263

1943

EAST

	W	L	T	Pct	Pts	OP
Washington	6	3	1	.667	229	137
NY Giants	6	3	1	.667	197	170
Phi/Pitt Eagles/Steelers	5	4	1	.556	225	230
Brooklyn	2	8	0	.200	65	234

WEST

	W	L	T	Pct	Pts	OP
Chicago Bears	8	1	1	.889	303	157
Green Bay	7	2	1	.778	264	172
Detroit	3	6	1	.333	178	218
Chicago Cardinals	0	10	0	.000	95	238

1944

EAST

	W	L	T	Pct	Pts	OP
NY Giants	8	1	1	.889	206	75
Philadelphia	7	1	2	.875	267	131
Washington	6	3	1	.667	169	180
Boston	2	8	0	.200	82	233
Brooklyn Tigers	0	10	0	.000	69	166

WEST

	W	L	T	Pct	Pts	OP
Green Bay	8	2	0	.800	238	141
Chicago Bears	6	3	1	.667	258	172
Detroit	6	3	1	.667	216	151
Cleveland	4	6	0	.400	188	224
Chi/Pitt Cards/Steelers	0	10	0	.000	116	336

1945

EAST

	W	L	T	Pct	Pts	OP
Washington	8	2	0	.800	209	121
Philadelphia	7	3	0	.700	272	133
NY Giants	3	6	1	.333	179	198
Bos/Bkn Yanks/Tigers	3	6	1	.333	123	211
Pittsburgh	2	8	0	.200	79	220

WEST

	W	L	T	Pct	Pts	OP
Cleveland	9	1	0	.900	244	136
Detroit	7	3	0	.700	195	194
Green Bay	6	4	0	.600	258	173
Chicago Bears	3	7	0	.300	192	235
Chicago Cardinals	1	9	0	.100	98	228

1946

EAST

	W	L	T	Pct	Pts	OP
NY Giants	7	3	1	.700	236	162
Philadelphia	6	5	0	.545	231	220
Washington	5	5	1	.500	171	191
Pittsburgh	5	5	1	.500	136	117
Boston	2	8	1	.200	189	273

WEST

	W	L	T	Pct	Pts	OP
Chicago Bears	8	2	1	.800	289	193
Los Angeles	6	4	1	.600	277	257
Chicago Cardinals	6	5	0	.545	260	198
Green Bay	6	5	0	.545	148	158
Detroit	1	10	0	.091	142	310

1947

EAST

	W	L	T	Pct	Pts	OP
Pittsburgh	8	4	0	.667	240	259
Philadelphia	8	4	0	.667	308	242
Boston	4	7	1	.364	168	256
Washington	4	8	0	.333	295	367
NY Giants	2	8	2	.200	190	309

WEST

	W	L	T	Pct	Pts	OP
Chicago Cardinals	9	3	0	.750	306	231
Chicago Bears	8	4	0	.667	363	241
Green Bay	6	5	1	.542	274	210
Los Angeles	6	6	0	.500	259	214
Detroit	3	9	0	.250	231	305

1948

EAST

	W	L	T	Pct	Pts	OP
Philadelphia	9	2	1	.818	376	156
Washington	7	5	0	.583	291	287
Pittsburgh	4	8	0	.333	200	243
NY Giants	4	8	0	.333	297	388
Boston	3	9	0	.250	174	372

WEST

	W	L	T	Pct	Pts	OP
Chicago Cardinals	11	1	0	.917	395	226
Chicago Bears	10	2	0	.833	375	151
Los Angeles	6	5	1	.545	327	269
Green Bay	3	9	0	.250	154	290
Detroit	2	10	0	.167	200	407

1949

EAST

	W	L	T	Pct	Pts	OP
Philadelphia	11	1	0	.917	364	134
Pittsburgh	6	5	1	.545	224	214
NY Giants	6	6	0	.500	287	298
Washington	4	7	1	.364	268	339
NY Bulldogs	1	10	1	.091	153	368

WEST

	W	L	T	Pct	Pts	OP
Los Angeles	8	2	2	.800	360	239
Chicago Bears	9	3	0	.750	332	218
Chicago Cardinals	6	5	1	.545	360	301
Detroit	4	8	0	.333	237	259
Green Bay	2	10	0	.167	114	329

1950

EAST

	W	L	T	Pct	Pts	OP
Cleveland	10	2	0	.833	310	144
NY Giants	10	2	0	.833	268	150
Philadelphia	6	6	0	.500	254	141
Pittsburgh	6	6	0	.500	180	195
Chicago Cardinals	5	7	0	.417	233	287
Washington	3	9	0	.250	232	326

WEST

	W	L	T	Pct	Pts	OP
Chicago Bears	9	3	0	.750	279	207
Los Angeles	9	3	0	.750	466	309
NY Yanks	7	5	0	.583	366	367
Detroit	6	6	0	.500	321	285
San Francisco	3	9	0	.250	213	300
Green Bay	3	9	0	.250	244	406
Baltimore	1	11	0	.067	213	462

1951

AMERICAN

	W	L	T	Pct	Pts	OP
Cleveland	11	1	0	.917	331	152
NY Giants	9	2	1	.818	254	161
Washington	5	7	0	.417	183	296
Pittsburgh	4	7	1	.364	183	235
Philadelphia	4	8	0	.333	234	264
Chicago Cardinals	3	9	0	.250	210	287

NATIONAL

	W	L	T	Pct	Pts	OP
Los Angeles	8	4	0	.667	392	261
Detroit	7	4	1	.636	336	259
San Francisco	7	4	1	.636	255	205
Chicago Bears	7	5	0	.583	286	282
Green Bay	3	9	0	.250	254	375
NY Yanks	1	9	2	.100	241	382

1952

AMERICAN

	W	L	T	Pct	Pts	OP
Cleveland	8	4	0	.667	310	213
Philadelphia	7	5	0	.583	252	271
NY Giants	7	5	0	.583	234	231
Pittsburgh	5	7	0	.417	300	273
Washington	4	8	0	.333	240	287
Chicago Cardinals	4	8	0	.333	172	221

NATIONAL

	W	L	T	Pct	Pts	OP
Detroit	9	3	0	.750	344	192
Los Angeles	9	3	0	.750	349	234
San Francisco	7	5	0	.583	285	221
Green Bay	6	6	0	.500	295	312
Chicago Bears	5	7	0	.417	245	326
Dallas	1	11	0	.083	182	427

1953

EAST

	W	L	T	Pct	Pts	OP
Cleveland	11	1	0	.917	348	162
Philadelphia	7	4	1	.636	352	215
Washington	6	5	1	.545	208	215
Pittsburgh	5	7	0	.417	211	272
NY Giants	4	8	0	.333	188	277
Chicago Cardinals	1	10	1	.091	190	337

1953 *(Cont.)*

WEST

	W	L	T	Pct	Pts	OP
Detroit	10	2	0	.833	271	205
San Francisco	9	3	0	.750	372	237
Los Angeles	8	3	1	.727	366	236
Chicago Bears	3	8	1	.273	218	262
Baltimore	3	9	0	.250	182	350
Green Bay	2	9	1	.182	200	338

1954

EAST

	W	L	T	Pct	Pts	OP
Cleveland	9	3	0	.750	336	162
Philadelphia	7	4	1	.636	284	230
NY Giants	7	5	0	.583	293	184
Pittsburgh	5	7	0	.417	219	263
Washington	3	9	0	.250	207	432
Chicago Cardinals	2	10	0	.167	183	347

WEST

	W	L	T	Pct	Pts	OP
Detroit	9	2	1	.818	337	189
Chicago Bears	8	4	0	.667	301	279
San Francisco	7	4	1	.636	313	251
Los Angeles	6	5	1	.545	314	285
Green Bay	4	8	0	.333	234	251
Baltimore	3	9	0	.250	131	279

1955

EAST

	W	L	T	Pct	Pts	OP
Cleveland	9	2	1	.818	349	218
Washington	8	4	0	.667	246	222
NY Giants	6	5	1	.545	267	223
Philadelphia	4	7	1	.364	248	231
Chicago Cardinals	4	7	1	.364	224	252
Pittsburgh	4	8	0	.333	195	285

WEST

	W	L	T	Pct	Pts	OP
Los Angeles	8	3	1	.727	260	231
Chicago Bears	8	4	0	.667	294	251
Green Bay	6	6	0	.500	258	276
Baltimore	5	6	1	.455	214	239
San Francisco	4	8	0	.333	216	298
Detroit	3	9	0	.250	230	275

1956

EAST

	W	L	T	Pct	Pts	OP
NY Giants	8	3	1	.727	264	197
Chicago Cardinals	7	5	0	.583	240	182
Washington	6	6	0	.500	183	225
Pittsburgh	5	7	0	.417	217	250
Cleveland	5	7	0	.417	167	177
Philadelphia	3	8	1	.273	143	215

WEST

	W	L	T	Pct	Pts	OP
Chicago Bears	9	2	1	.818	269	169
Detroit	9	3	0	.750	300	188
San Francisco	5	6	1	.455	233	284
Baltimore	5	7	0	.417	270	322
Green Bay	4	8	0	.333	264	342
Los Angeles	4	8	0	.333	291	307

1957

EAST

	W	L	T	Pct	Pts	OP
Cleveland	9	2	1	.818	269	169
NY Giants	7	5	0	.583	251	211
Pittsburgh	6	6	0	.500	155	178
Washington	5	6	1	.455	251	230
Philadelphia	4	8	0	.333	173	224
Chicago Cardinals	3	9	0	.250	200	299

WEST

	W	L	T	Pct	Pts	OP
San Francisco	8	4	0	.667	260	264
Detroit	8	4	0	.667	251	231
Baltimore	7	5	0	.583	303	235
Los Angeles	6	6	0	.500	307	278
Chicago Bears	5	7	0	.417	203	211
Green Bay	3	9	0	.250	218	311

1958

EAST

	W	L	T	Pct	Pts	OP
Cleveland	9	3	0	.750	302	217
NY Giants	9	3	0	.750	246	183
Pittsburgh	7	4	1	.636	261	230
Washington	4	7	1	.364	214	268
Chicago Cardinals	2	9	1	.182	261	356
Philadelphia	2	9	1	.182	235	306

WEST

	W	L	T	Pct	Pts	OP
Baltimore	9	3	0	.750	381	203
Los Angeles	8	4	0	.667	344	278
Chicago Bears	8	4	0	.667	298	230
San Francisco	6	6	0	.500	257	324
Detroit	4	7	1	.364	261	276
Green Bay	1	10	1	.091	193	382

1959

EAST

	W	L	T	Pct	Pts	OP
NY Giants	10	2	0	.833	284	167
Philadelphia	7	5	0	.583	268	278
Cleveland	7	5	0	.583	270	214
Pittsburgh	6	5	1	.545	257	216
Washington	3	9	0	.250	185	350
Chicago Cardinals	2	10	0	.167	231	324

WEST

	W	L	T	Pct	Pts	OP
Baltimore	9	3	0	.750	374	251
Chicago Bears	8	4	0	.667	246	196
Green Bay	7	5	0	.583	248	240
San Francisco	7	5	0	.583	255	237
Detroit	3	8	1	.273	203	275
Los Angeles	2	10	0	.167	242	315

1960

NFL EAST

	W	L	T	Pct	Pts	OP
Philadelphia	10	2	0	.833	321	246
Cleveland	8	3	1	.727	362	217
NY Giants	6	4	2	.600	271	261
St. Louis	6	5	1	.545	288	230
Pittsburgh	5	6	1	.455	240	275
Washington	1	9	2	.100	178	309

1960 *(Cont.)*

NFL WEST

	W	L	T	Pct	Pts	OP
Green Bay	8	4	0	.667	332	209
Detroit	7	5	0	.583	239	212
San Francisco	7	5	0	.583	208	205
Baltimore	6	6	0	.500	288	234
Chicago	5	6	1	.455	194	299
LA Rams	4	7	1	.364	265	297
Dallas Cowboys	0	11	1	.000	177	369

AFL EAST

	W	L	T	Pct	Pts	OP
Houston	10	4	0	.714	379	285
NY Titans	7	7	0	.500	382	399
Buffalo	5	8	1	.385	296	303
Boston	5	9	0	.357	286	349

AFL WEST

	W	L	T	Pct	Pts	OP
LA Chargers	10	4	0	.714	373	336
Dallas Texans	8	6	0	.571	361	253
Oakland	6	8	0	.429	319	388
Denver	4	9	1	.308	309	393

1961

NFL EAST

	W	L	T	Pct	Pts	OP
NY Giants	10	3	1	.769	368	220
Philadelphia	10	4	0	.714	361	297
Cleveland	8	5	1	.615	319	270
St. Louis	7	7	0	.500	279	267
Pittsburgh	6	8	0	.429	295	287
Dallas Cowboys	4	9	1	.308	236	380
Washington	1	12	1	.077	174	392

NFL WEST

	W	L	T	Pct	Pts	OP
Green Bay	11	3	0	.786	391	223
Detroit	8	5	1	.615	270	258
Baltimore	8	6	0	.571	302	307
Chicago	8	6	0	.571	326	302
San Francisco	7	6	1	.538	346	272
Los Angeles	4	10	0	.286	263	407
Minnesota	3	11	0	.214	285	407

AFL EAST

	W	L	T	Pct	Pts	OP
Houston	10	3	1	.769	513	242
Boston	9	4	1	.692	413	313
NY Titans	7	7	0	.500	301	390
Buffalo	6	8	0	.429	294	342

AFL WEST

	W	L	T	Pct	Pts	OP
San Diego Chargers	12	2	0	.857	396	219
Dallas Texans	6	8	0	.429	334	343
Denver	3	11	0	.214	251	432
Oakland	2	12	0	.143	237	458

1962

NFL EAST

	W	L	T	Pct	Pts	OP
NY Giants	12	2	0	.857	398	283
Pittsburgh	9	5	0	.642	312	363
Cleveland	7	6	1	.538	291	257
Washington	5	7	2	.417	305	376
Dallas Cowboys	5	8	1	.385	398	402
St. Louis	4	9	1	.308	287	361
Philadelphia	3	10	1	.231	282	356

1962 *(Cont.)*

NFL WEST	W	L	T	Pct	Pts	OP
Green Bay	13	1	0	.929	415	148
Detroit	11	3	0	.786	315	177
Chicago	9	5	0	.643	321	287
Baltimore	7	7	0	.500	293	288
San Francisco	6	8	0	.429	282	331
Minnesota	2	11	1	.154	254	410
Los Angeles	1	12	1	.077	220	334

AFL EAST	W	L	T	Pct	Pts	OP
Houston	11	3	0	.786	387	270
Boston	9	4	1	.692	346	295
Buffalo	7	6	1	.538	309	272
NY Titans	5	9	0	.357	278	423

AFL WEST	W	L	T	Pct	Pts	OP
Dallas Texans	11	3	0	.786	389	233
Denver	6	7	0	.462	323	313
San Diego	4	9	0	.308	293	362
Oakland	1	13	0	.071	213	370

1963

NFL EAST	W	L	T	Pct	Pts	OP
NY Giants	11	3	0	.786	448	280
Cleveland	10	4	0	.714	343	262
St. Louis	9	5	0	.643	341	283
Pittsburgh	7	4	3	.636	321	295
Dallas	4	10	0	.286	305	378
Washington	3	11	0	.214	279	398
Philadelphia	2	10	2	.214	242	381

NFL WEST	W	L	T	Pct	Pts	OP
Chicago	11	1	2	.917	301	144
Green Bay	11	2	1	.846	369	206
Baltimore	8	6	0	.571	316	285
Minnesota	5	8	1	.385	309	390
Detroit	5	8	1	.385	32	265
Los Angeles	5	9	0	.357	210	350
San Francisco	2	12	0	.143	198	391

AFL EAST	W	L	T	Pct	Pts	OP
Boston	7	6	1	.538	327	257
Buffalo	7	6	1	.538	304	291
Houston	6	8	0	.429	302	372
NY Jets	5	8	1	.385	249	399

AFL WEST	W	L	T	Pct	Pts	OP
San Diego	11	3	0	.786	399	255
Oakland	10	4	0	.714	363	282
Kansas City	5	7	2	.417	347	263
Denver	2	11	1	.154	301	473

1964

NFL EAST	W	L	T	Pct	Pts	OP
Cleveland	10	3	1	.769	415	293
St. Louis	9	3	2	.750	357	331
Philadelphia	6	8	0	.429	312	313
Washington	6	8	0	.429	307	305
Dallas	5	8	1	.385	250	289
Pittsburgh	5	9	0	.357	253	315
NY Giants	2	10	2	.167	241	399

1964 *(Cont.)*

NFL WEST	W	L	T	Pct	Pts	OP
Baltimore	12	2	0	.857	428	225
Green Bay	8	5	1	.615	342	245
Minnesota	8	5	1	.615	355	296
Detroit	7	5	2	.583	280	260
Los Angeles	5	7	2	.417	283	339
Chicago	5	9	0	.357	260	379
San Francisco	4	10	0	.286	236	330

AFL EAST	W	L	T	Pct	Pts	OP
Buffalo	12	2	0	.857	400	242
Boston	10	3	1	.769	365	297
NY Jets	5	8	1	.385	278	315
Houston	4	10	0	.286	310	355

AFL WEST	W	L	T	Pct	Pts	OP
San Diego	8	5	1	.615	341	300
Kansas City	7	7	0	.500	366	306
Oakland	5	7	2	.417	303	350
Denver	2	11	1	.154	240	438

1965

NFL EAST	W	L	T	Pct	Pts	OP
Cleveland	11	3	0	.786	363	325
NY Giants	7	7	0	.500	270	338
Dallas	7	7	0	.500	325	280
Washington	6	8	0	.429	257	301
St. Louis	5	9	0	.357	296	309
Philadelphia	5	9	0	.357	363	359
Pittsburgh	2	12	0	.143	202	397

NFL WEST	W	L	T	Pct	Pts	OP
Green Bay	10	3	1	.769	316	224
Baltimore	9	3	1	.769	389	263
Chicago	9	5	0	.643	409	275
San Francisco	7	6	1	.538	421	402
Minnesota	7	6	0	.500	383	362
Detroit	6	7	1	.462	257	295
Los Angeles	4	10	0	.286	269	328

AFL EAST	W	L	T	Pct	Pts	OP
Buffalo	10	3	1	.769	313	226
NY Jets	5	8	1	.385	285	303
Boston	4	8	2	.333	244	302
Houston	4	10	0	.286	298	429

AFL WEST	W	L	T	Pct	Pts	OP
San Diego	9	2	3	.818	340	227
Oakland	8	5	1	.615	298	239
Kansas City	7	5	2	.583	322	285
Denver	4	10	0	.286	303	392

1966

NFL EAST	W	L	T	Pct	Pts	OP
Dallas	10	3	1	.769	445	239
Cleveland	9	5	0	.643	403	259
Philadelphia	9	5	0	.643	326	340
St. Louis	8	5	1	.625	264	265
Washington	7	7	0	.500	351	355
Pittsburgh	5	8	1	.385	316	347
Atlanta	3	11	0	.214	204	437
NY Giants	1	12	1	.077	263	501

1966 *(Cont.)*

NFL WEST	W	L	T	Pct	Pts	OP
Green Bay	12	2	0	.857	335	163
Baltimore	9	5	0	.643	314	226
Los Angeles	8	6	0	.571	289	212
San Francisco	6	6	2	.500	320	325
Chicago	5	7	2	.417	234	272
Detroit	4	9	1	.308	206	317
Minnesota	4	9	1	.308	292	304

AFL EAST	W	L	T	Pct	Pts	OP
Buffalo	9	4	1	.692	358	255
Boston	8	4	2	.677	315	283
NY Jets	6	6	2	.500	322	312
Houston	3	11	0	.214	335	396
Miami	3	11	0	.214	213	362

AFL WEST	W	L	T	Pct	Pts	OP
Kansas City	11	2	1	.846	448	276
Oakland	8	5	1	.615	315	288
San Diego	7	6	1	.538	335	284
Denver	4	10	0	.286	196	381

1967

NFL CAPITOL	W	L	T	Pct	Pts	OP
Dallas	9	5	0	.643	342	268
Philadelphia	6	7	1	.462	351	409
Washington	5	6	3	.455	347	353
New Orleans	3	11	0	.214	233	379

NFL CENTURY	W	L	T	Pct	Pts	OP
Cleveland	9	5	0	.643	334	297
NY Giants	7	7	0	.500	369	379
St. Louis	6	7	1	.462	333	356
Pittsburgh	4	9	1	.308	281	320

NFL COASTAL	W	L	T	Pct	Pts	OP
Los Angeles	11	1	2	.917	398	196
Baltimore	11	1	2	.917	394	198
San Francisco	7	7	0	.500	273	337
Atlanta	1	12	1	.077	175	422

NFL CENTRAL	W	L	T	Pct	Pts	OP
Green Bay	9	4	1	.692	332	209
Chicago	7	6	1	.538	239	218
Detroit	5	7	2	.417	260	259
Minnesota	3	8	3	.273	233	294

AFL EAST	W	L	T	Pct	Pts	OP
Houston	9	4	1	.692	258	199
NY Jets	8	5	1	.615	371	329
Buffalo	4	10	0	.286	237	285
Miami	4	10	0	.286	219	407
Boston	3	10	1	.231	280	389

AFL WEST	W	L	T	Pct	Pts	OP
Oakland	13	1	0	.929	468	233
Kansas City	9	5	0	.643	408	254
San Diego	8	5	1	.615	360	352
Denver	3	11	0	.214	256	409

1968

NFL CAPITOL	W	L	T	Pct	Pts	OP
Dallas	12	2	0	.857	431	186
NY Giants	7	7	0	.500	294	325
Washington	5	9	0	.357	249	358
Philadelphia	2	12	0	.143	202	351

1968 *(Cont.)*

NFL CENTURY	W	L	T	Pct	Pts	OP
Cleveland	10	4	0	.714	394	273
St. Louis	9	4	1	.692	325	289
New Orleans	4	9	1	.308	246	327
Pittsburgh	2	11	1	.154	244	397

NFL COASTAL	W	L	T	Pct	Pts	OP
Baltimore	13	1	0	.929	402	144
Los Angeles	10	3	1	.769	312	200
San Francisco	7	6	1	.538	303	310
Atlanta	2	12	0	.143	202	351

NFL CENTRAL	W	L	T	Pct	Pts	OP
Minnesota	8	6	0	.571	282	242
Chicago	7	7	0	.500	250	333
Green Bay	6	7	1	.462	281	227
Detroit	4	8	2	.333	207	241

AFL EAST	W	L	T	Pct	Pts	OP
NY Jets	11	3	0	.786	419	280
Houston	7	7	0	.500	303	248
Miami	5	8	1	.385	276	355
Boston	4	10	0	.286	229	406
Buffalo	1	12	1	.077	199	367

AFL WEST	W	L	T	Pct	Pts	OP
Oakland	12	2	0	.857	453	233
Kansas City	12	2	0	.857	371	170
San Diego	9	5	0	.643	382	310
Denver	5	9	0	.357	255	404
Cincinnati	3	11	0	.214	215	329

1969

NFL CAPITOL	W	L	T	Pct	Pts	OP
Dallas	11	2	1	.846	369	223
Washington	7	5	2	.583	307	319
New Orleans	5	9	0	.357	311	393
Philadelphia	4	9	1	.308	279	377

NFL CENTURY	W	L	T	Pct	Pts	OP
Cleveland	10	3	1	.769	351	300
NY Giants	6	8	0	.429	264	298
St. Louis	4	9	1	.308	314	389
Pittsburgh	1	13	0	.071	218	404

NFL COASTAL	W	L	T	Pct	Pts	OP
Los Angeles	11	3	0	.786	320	243
Baltimore	8	5	1	.615	279	268
Atlanta	6	8	0	.429	276	268
San Francisco	4	8	2	.333	277	319

NFL CENTRAL	W	L	T	Pct	Pts	OP
Minnesota	12	2	0	.857	379	133
Detroit	9	4	1	.692	259	188
Green Bay	8	6	0	.571	269	221
Chicago	1	13	0	.071	210	339

AFL EAST	W	L	T	Pct	Pts	OP
NY Jets	10	4	0	.714	353	269
Houston	6	6	2	.500	278	279
Buffalo	4	10	0	.286	230	359
Boston	4	10	0	.286	266	316
Miami	3	10	1	.231	233	332

1969 *(Cont.)*

AFL WEST

	W	L	T	Pct	Pts	OP
Oakland	12	1	1	.923	377	242
Kansas City	11	3	0	.786	359	177
San Diego	8	6	0	.571	288	276
Denver	5	8	1	.385	297	344
Cincinnati	4	9	1	.308	280	367

1970

AFC EAST

	W	L	T	Pct	Pts	OP
Baltimore	11	2	1	.846	321	234
Miami	10	4	0	.714	297	228
NY Jets	4	10	0	.286	255	286
Buffalo	3	10	1	.231	204	337
Boston	2	12	0	.143	149	361

AFC CENTRAL

	W	L	T	Pct	Pts	OP
Cincinnati	8	6	0	.571	312	255
Cleveland	7	7	0	.500	286	265
Pittsburgh	5	9	0	.357	210	272
Houston	3	10	1	.231	217	352

AFC WEST

	W	L	T	Pct	Pts	OP
Oakland	8	4	2	.667	300	293
Kansas City	7	5	2	.583	272	244
San Diego	5	6	3	.455	282	278
Denver	5	8	1	.385	253	264

NFC EAST

	W	L	T	Pct	Pts	OP
Dallas	10	4	0	.714	299	221
NY Giants	9	5	0	.643	301	270
St. Louis	8	5	1	.615	325	228
Washington	6	8	0	.429	297	314
Philadelphia	3	10	1	.231	241	332

NFC CENTRAL

	W	L	T	Pct	Pts	OP
Minnesota	12	2	0	.857	335	143
Detroit	10	4	0	.714	347	202
Green Bay	6	8	0	.429	196	293
Chicago	6	8	0	.429	256	261

NFC WEST

	W	L	T	Pct	Pts	OP
San Francisco	10	3	1	.769	352	267
LA Rams	9	4	1	.692	325	202
Atlanta	4	8	2	.333	206	261
New Orleans	2	11	1	.154	172	347

1971

AFC EAST

	W	L	T	Pct	Pts	OP
Miami	10	3	1	.769	315	174
Baltimore	10	4	0	.714	313	140
New England	6	8	0	.429	238	325
NY Jets	6	8	0	.429	212	299
Buffalo	1	13	0	.071	184	394

AFC CENTRAL

	W	L	T	Pct	Pts	OP
Cleveland	9	5	0	.643	285	273
Pittsburgh	6	8	0	.429	246	292
Houston	4	9	1	.308	251	330
Cincinnati	4	10	0	.286	284	265

AFC WEST

	W	L	T	Pct	Pts	OP
Kansas City	10	3	1	.769	302	208
Oakland	8	4	2	.667	344	278
San Diego	6	8	0	.429	311	341
Denver	4	9	1	.308	203	275

1971 *(Cont.)*

NFC EAST

	W	L	T	Pct	Pts	OP
Dallas	11	3	0	.786	406	222
Washington	9	4	1	.692	276	190
Philadelphia	6	7	1	.462	221	302
St. Louis	4	9	1	.308	231	279
NY Giants	4	10	0	.286	228	362

NFC CENTRAL

	W	L	T	Pct	Pts	OP
Minnesota	11	3	0	.786	245	139
Detroit	7	6	1	.538	341	286
Chicago	6	8	0	.429	185	276
Green Bay	4	8	2	.333	274	298

NFC WEST

	W	L	T	Pct	Pts	OP
San Francisco	9	5	0	.643	300	216
Los Angeles	8	5	1	.615	313	260
Atlanta	7	6	1	.538	274	277
New Orleans	4	8	2	.333	266	347

1972

AFC EAST

	W	L	T	Pct	Pts	OP
Miami	14	0	0	1.000	385	171
NY Jets	7	7	0	.500	367	324
Baltimore	5	9	0	.357	235	252
Buffalo	4	9	1	.321	257	377
New England	3	11	0	.214	192	446

AFC CENTRAL

	W	L	T	Pct	Pts	OP
Pittsburgh	11	3	0	.786	343	175
Cleveland	10	4	0	.714	268	249
Cincinnati	8	6	0	.571	299	229
Houston	1	13	0	.071	164	380

AFC WEST

	W	L	T	Pct	Pts	OP
Oakland	10	3	1	.750	365	248
Kansas City	8	6	0	.571	287	254
Denver	5	9	0	.357	325	350
San Diego	4	9	1	.321	264	344

NFC EAST

	W	L	T	Pct	Pts	OP
Washington	11	3	0	.786	336	218
Dallas	10	4	0	.286	319	240
NY Giants	8	6	0	.571	331	247
St. Louis	4	9	1	.321	193	303
Philadelphia	2	11	1	.179	145	352

NFC CENTRAL

	W	L	T	Pct	Pts	OP
Green Bay	10	4	0	.714	304	226
Detroit	8	5	1	.607	339	290
Minnesota	7	7	0	.500	301	252
Chicago	4	9	1	.321	225	275

NFC WEST

	W	L	T	Pct	Pts	OP
San Francisco	8	5	1	.607	353	249
Atlanta	7	7	0	.500	269	274
Los Angeles	6	7	1	.464	291	286
New Orleans	2	11	1	.179	215	361

1973

AFC EAST

	W	L	T	Pct	Pts	OP
Miami	12	2	0	.857	343	150
Buffalo	9	5	0	.643	259	230
New England	5	9	0	.357	258	300
Baltimore	4	10	0	.286	226	341
NY Jets	4	10	0	.286	240	306

1973 *(Cont.)*

AFC CENTRAL

	W	L	T	Pct	Pts	OP
Pittsburgh	10	4	0	.714	347	210
Cincinnati	10	4	0	.714	286	231
Cleveland	7	5	2	.571	234	255
Houston	1	13	0	.071	199	447

AFC WEST

	W	L	T	Pct	Pts	OP
Oakland	9	4	1	.679	292	175
Kansas City	7	5	2	.571	231	192
Denver	7	5	2	.571	354	296
San Diego	2	11	1	.179	188	386

NFC EAST

	W	L	T	Pct	Pts	OP
Washington	10	4	0	.714	325	198
Dallas	10	4	0	.714	325	198
Philadelphia	5	8	1	.393	310	393
St. Louis	4	9	1	.321	286	365
NY Giants	2	11	1	.179	226	362

NFC CENTRAL

	W	L	T	Pct	Pts	OP
Minnesota	12	2	0	.857	296	168
Detroit	6	7	1	.464	271	247
Green Bay	5	7	2	.429	202	259
Chicago	3	11	0	.214	195	334

NFC WEST

	W	L	T	Pct	Pts	OP
Los Angeles	12	2	0	.857	388	178
Atlanta	9	5	0	.643	318	224
New Orleans	5	9	0	.357	163	312
San Francisco	5	9	0	.357	262	319

1974

AFC EAST

	W	L	T	Pct	Pts	OP
Miami	11	3	0	.786	327	216
Buffalo	9	5	0	.643	264	244
NY Jets	7	7	0	.500	279	300
New England	7	7	0	.500	348	289
Baltimore	2	12	0	.143	190	329

AFC CENTRAL

	W	L	T	Pct	Pts	OP
Pittsburgh	10	3	1	.750	305	189
Houston	7	7	0	.500	236	282
Cincinnati	7	7	0	.500	283	259
Cleveland	4	10	0	.283	251	344

AFC WEST

	W	L	T	Pct	Pts	OP
Oakland	12	2	0	.857	355	228
Denver	7	6	1	.536	302	294
Kansas City	5	9	0	.357	233	293
San Diego	5	9	0	.357	212	285

NFC EAST

	W	L	T	Pct	Pts	OP
Washington	10	4	0	.714	320	196
St. Louis	10	4	0	.714	285	218
Dallas	8	6	0	.571	297	235
Philadelphia	7	7	0	.500	242	217
NY Giants	2	12	0	.143	195	299

NFC CENTRAL

	W	L	T	Pct	Pts	OP
Minnesota	10	4	0	.714	310	195
Detroit	7	7	0	.500	256	270
Green Bay	6	8	0	.429	210	206
Chicago	4	10	0	.286	152	279

1974 *(Cont.)*

NFC WEST

	W	L	T	Pct	Pts	OP
Los Angeles	10	4	0	.714	263	181
San Francisco	6	8	0	.429	226	236
New Orleans	5	9	0	.357	166	263
Atlanta	3	11	0	.214	111	271

1975

AFC EAST

	W	L	T	Pct	Pts	OP
Miami	10	4	0	.714	357	222
Baltimore	10	4	0	.714	395	269
Buffalo	8	6	0	.571	420	355
NY Jets	3	11	0	.214	258	433
New England	3	11	0	.214	258	358

AFC CENTRAL

	W	L	T	Pct	Pts	OP
Pittsburgh	12	2	0	.857	373	162
Cincinnati	11	3	0	.786	340	246
Houston	10	4	0	.714	293	226
Cleveland	3	11	0	.214	218	372

AFC WEST

	W	L	T	Pct	Pts	OP
Oakland	11	3	0	.786	375	255
Denver	6	8	0	.429	254	307
Kansas City	5	9	0	.357	282	341
San Diego	2	12	0	.143	189	345

NFC EAST

	W	L	T	Pct	Pts	OP
St. Louis	11	3	0	.786	356	276
Dallas	10	4	0	.714	350	268
Washington	8	6	0	.571	325	276
NY Giants	5	9	0	.357	216	306
Philadelphia	4	10	0	.286	225	302

NFC CENTRAL

	W	L	T	Pct	Pts	OP
Minnesota	12	2	0	.857	377	180
Detroit	7	7	0	.500	245	262
Green Bay	4	10	0	.286	226	285
Chicago	4	10	0	.286	191	379

NFC WEST

	W	L	T	Pct	Pts	OP
Los Angeles	12	2	0	.857	312	135
San Francisco	5	9	0	.357	255	286
Atlanta	4	10	0	.286	240	289
New Orleans	2	12	0	.143	165	360

1976

AFC EAST

	W	L	T	Pct	Pts	OP
Baltimore	11	3	0	.786	417	246
New England	11	3	0	.786	376	236
Miami	6	8	0	.429	263	264
NY Jets	3	11	0	.214	169	383
Buffalo	2	12	0	.143	246	363

AFC CENTRAL

	W	L	T	Pct	Pts	OP
Cincinnati	10	4	0	.714	335	210
Pittsburgh	10	4	0	.714	342	138
Cleveland	9	5	0	.643	267	287
Houston	5	9	0	.357	222	273

AFC WEST

	W	L	T	Pct	Pts	OP
Oakland	13	1	0	.929	350	237
Denver	9	5	0	.643	315	206
San Diego	6	8	0	.429	248	285
Kansas City	5	9	0	.357	290	376
Tampa Bay	0	14	0	.000	125	412

1976 (Cont.)

NFC EAST

	W	L	T	Pct	Pts	OP
Dallas	11	3	0	.786	296	194
Washington	10	4	0	.714	291	217
St. Louis	10	4	0	.714	309	267
Philadelphia	4	10	0	.286	165	286
NY Giants	3	11	0	.214	170	250

NFC CENTRAL

	W	L	T	Pct	Pts	OP
Minnesota	11	2	1	.821	305	176
Chicago	7	7	0	.500	253	216
Detroit	6	8	0	.429	262	220
Green Bay	5	9	0	.357	218	299

NFC WEST

	W	L	T	Pct	Pts	OP
Los Angeles	10	3	1	.750	351	190
San Francisco	8	6	0	.571	270	190
Atlanta	4	10	0	.286	172	312
New Orleans	4	10	0	.286	253	346
Seattle	2	12	0	.143	229	429

1977

AFC EAST

	W	L	T	Pct	Pts	OP
Miami	10	4	0	.714	313	197
Baltimore	10	4	0	.714	295	221
New England	9	5	0	.643	279	217
Buffalo	3	11	0	.214	160	313
NY Jets	3	11	0	.214	191	300

AFC CENTRAL

	W	L	T	Pct	Pts	OP
Pittsburgh	9	5	0	.643	283	243
Houston	8	6	0	.571	299	230
Cincinnati	8	6	0	.571	238	235
Cleveland	6	8	0	.429	269	267

AFC WEST

	W	L	T	Pct	Pts	OP
Denver	12	2	0	.857	274	148
Oakland	11	3	0	.786	351	230
San Diego	7	7	0	.500	222	205
Seattle	5	9	0	.357	282	373
Kansas City	2	12	0	.143	225	349

NFC EAST

	W	L	T	Pct	Pts	OP
Dallas	12	2	0	.857	345	212
Washington	9	5	0	.643	196	189
St. Louis	7	7	0	.500	272	287
NY Giants	5	9	0	.357	181	265
Philadelphia	5	9	0	.357	220	207

NFC CENTRAL

	W	L	T	Pct	Pts	OP
Chicago	9	5	0	.643	255	253
Minnesota	9	5	0	.643	231	227
Detroit	6	8	0	.429	183	252
Green Bay	4	10	0	.286	134	219
Tampa Bay	2	12	0	.143	103	223

NFC WEST

	W	L	T	Pct	Pts	OP
Los Angeles	10	4	0	.714	302	146
Atlanta	7	7	0	.500	179	129
San Francisco	5	9	0	.357	220	260
New Orleans	3	11	0	.214	232	336

1978

AFC EAST

	W	L	T	Pct	Pts	OP
New England	11	5	0	.688	358	286
Miami	11	5	0	.688	372	254
NY Jets	8	8	0	.500	359	364
Buffalo	5	11	0	.313	302	354
Baltimore	5	11	0	.313	239	421

AFC CENTRAL

	W	L	T	Pct	Pts	OP
Pittsburgh	14	2	0	.875	356	195
Houston	10	6	0	.625	283	298
Cleveland	8	8	0	.500	334	356
Cincinnati	4	12	0	.250	252	284

AFC WEST

	W	L	T	Pct	Pts	OP
Denver	10	6	0	.625	282	198
Seattle	9	7	0	.563	345	358
Oakland	9	7	0	.563	311	283
San Diego	9	7	0	.563	355	309
Kansas City	4	12	0	.250	243	327

NFC EAST

	W	L	T	Pct	Pts	OP
Dallas	12	4	0	.750	384	208
Philadelphia	9	7	0	.563	270	250
Washington	8	8	0	.500	273	283
St. Louis	6	10	0	.375	248	296
NY Giants	6	10	0	.375	264	298

NFC CENTRAL

	W	L	T	Pct	Pts	OP
Green Bay	8	7	1	.531	249	269
Minnesota	8	7	1	.531	294	306
Detroit	7	9	0	.438	290	300
Chicago	7	9	0	.438	253	274
Tampa Bay	5	11	0	.313	241	259

NFC WEST

	W	L	T	Pct	Pts	OP
Los Angeles	12	4	0	.750	316	245
Atlanta	9	7	0	.563	240	290
New Orleans	7	9	0	.438	281	298
San Francisco	2	14	0	.125	219	350

1979

AFC EAST

	W	L	T	Pct	Pts	OP
Miami	10	6	0	.625	341	257
New England	9	7	0	.563	411	326
NY Jets	8	8	0	.500	337	383
Buffalo	7	9	0	.438	268	279
Baltimore	5	11	0	.313	271	351

AFC CENTRAL

	W	L	T	Pct	Pts	OP
Pittsburgh	12	4	0	.750	416	262
Houston	11	5	0	.688	362	331
Cleveland	9	7	0	.563	359	352
Cincinnati	4	12	0	.250	337	421

AFC WEST

	W	L	T	Pct	Pts	OP
San Diego	12	4	0	.750	411	246
Denver	10	6	0	.625	289	262
Seattle	9	7	0	.563	378	372
Oakland	9	7	0	.563	365	337
Kansas City	7	9	0	.438	238	262

NFC EAST

	W	L	T	Pct	Pts	OP
Dallas	11	5	0	.688	371	313
Philadelphia	11	5	0	.688	339	282
Washington	10	6	0	.625	348	295
NY Giants	6	10	0	.375	237	323
St. Louis	5	11	0	.313	307	358

1979 *(Cont.)*

NFC CENTRAL	W	L	T	Pct	Pts	OP
Chicago	10	6	0	.625	306	249
Tampa Bay	10	6	0	.625	273	237
Minnesota	7	9	0	.438	259	337
Green Bay	5	11	0	.313	246	316
Detroit	2	14	0	.125	219	365

NFC WEST	W	L	T	Pct	Pts	OP
Los Angeles	9	7	0	.563	323	309
New Orleans	8	8	0	.500	370	360
Atlanta	6	10	0	.375	300	388
San Francisco	2	14	0	.125	308	416

1980

AFC EAST	W	L	T	Pct	Pts	OP
Buffalo	11	5	0	.688	320	260
New England	10	6	0	.625	441	325
Miami	8	8	0	.500	266	305
Baltimore	7	9	0	.438	355	387
NY Jets	4	12	0	.250	302	395

AFC CENTRAL	W	L	T	Pct	Pts	OP
Cleveland	11	5	0	.688	357	310
Houston	11	5	0	.688	295	251
Pittsburgh	9	7	0	.563	352	313
Cincinnati	6	10	0	.375	244	312

AFC WEST	W	L	T	Pct	Pts	OP
San Diego	11	5	0	.688	418	327
Oakland	11	5	0	.688	364	306
Denver	8	8	0	.500	310	323
Kansas City	8	8	0	.500	319	336
Seattle	4	12	0	.250	291	408

NFC EAST	W	L	T	Pct	Pts	OP
Dallas	12	4	0	.750	454	311
Philadelphia	12	4	0	.750	384	222
Washington	6	10	0	.375	261	293
St. Louis	5	11	0	.313	299	350
NY Giants	4	12	0	.250	249	425

NFC CENTRAL	W	L	T	Pct	Pts	OP
Detroit	9	7	0	.563	334	272
Minnesota	9	7	0	.563	317	308
Chicago	7	9	0	.438	304	264
Tampa Bay	5	10	1	.344	271	341
Green Bay	5	10	1	.344	231	371

NFC WEST	W	L	T	Pct	Pts	OP
Atlanta	12	4	0	.750	405	272
Los Angeles	11	5	0	.688	424	289
San Francisco	6	10	0	.375	320	415
New Orleans	1	15	0	.063	291	487

1981

AFC EAST	W	L	T	Pct	Pts	OP
Miami	11	4	1	.719	345	275
NY Jets	10	5	1	.656	355	287
Buffalo	10	6	0	.625	311	276
Baltimore	2	14	0	.125	259	533
New England	2	14	0	.125	322	370

AFC CENTRAL	W	L	T	Pct	Pts	OP
Cincinnati	12	4	0	.750	421	304
Pittsburgh	8	8	0	.500	356	297
Houston	7	9	0	.438	281	355
Cleveland	5	11	0	.313	276	375

1981 *(Cont.)*

AFC WEST	W	L	T	Pct	Pts	OP
Denver	10	6	0	.625	321	289
San Diego	10	6	0	.625	478	390
Kansas City	9	7	0	.563	343	290
Oakland	7	9	0	.438	273	343
Seattle	6	10	0	.375	322	388

NFC EAST	W	L	T	Pct	Pts	OP
Dallas	12	4	0	.750	367	277
Philadelphia	10	6	0	.625	368	221
NY Giants	9	7	0	.563	295	257
Washington	8	8	0	.500	347	349
St. Louis	7	9	0	.438	315	407

NFC CENTRAL	W	L	T	Pct	Pts	OP
Tampa Bay	9	7	0	.563	315	268
Detroit	8	8	0	.500	397	322
Green Bay	8	8	0	.500	324	361
Minnesota	7	9	0	.438	325	369
Chicago	6	10	0	.375	253	324

NFC WEST	W	L	T	Pct	Pts	OP
San Francisco	13	3	0	.813	357	250
Atlanta	7	9	0	.438	426	355
Los Angeles	6	10	0	.375	303	351
New Orleans	4	12	0	.250	207	378

1982 (strike-shortened)

AFC EAST	W	L	T	Pct	Pts	OP
Miami	7	2	0	.778	198	131
NY Jets	6	3	0	.667	245	166
New England	5	4	0	.556	143	157
Buffalo	4	5	0	.444	150	154
Baltimore	0	8	1	.056	113	236

AFC CENTRAL	W	L	T	Pct	Pts	OP
Cincinnati	7	2	0	.778	232	177
Pittsburgh	6	3	0	.667	204	146
Cleveland	4	5	0	.444	140	182
Houston	1	8	0	.111	136	245

AFC WEST	W	L	T	Pct	Pts	OP
LA Raiders	8	1	0	.889	260	200
San Diego	6	3	0	.667	288	221
Seattle	4	5	0	.444	127	147
Kansas City	3	6	0	.333	176	184
Denver	2	7	0	.222	148	226

NFC EAST	W	L	T	Pct	Pts	OP
Washington	8	1	0	.889	190	128
Dallas	6	3	0	.667	226	145
St. Louis	5	4	0	.556	135	170
NY Giants	4	5	0	.444	164	160
Philadelphia	3	6	0	.333	191	195

NFC CENTRAL	W	L	T	Pct	Pts	OP
Green Bay	5	3	1	.611	226	169
Tampa Bay	5	4	0	.556	158	178
Minnesota	5	4	0	.556	187	198
Detroit	4	5	0	.444	181	176
Chicago	3	6	0	.333	141	174

NFC WEST	W	L	T	Pct	Pts	OP
Atlanta	5	4	0	.556	183	199
New Orleans	4	5	0	.444	129	160
San Francisco	3	6	0	.333	209	206
LA Rams	2	7	0	.222	200	250

1983

AFC EAST	W	L	T	Pct	Pts	OP
Miami	12	4	0	.750	389	250
Buffalo	8	8	0	.500	283	351
New England	8	8	0	.500	274	289
Baltimore	7	9	0	.438	264	354
NY Jets	7	9	0	.438	313	331

AFC CENTRAL	W	L	T	Pct	Pts	OP
Pittsburgh	10	6	0	.625	355	303
Cleveland	9	7	0	.563	356	342
Cincinnati	7	9	0	.438	346	302
Houston	2	14	0	.125	288	460

AFC WEST	W	L	T	Pct	Pts	OP
LA Raiders	12	4	0	.750	442	338
Seattle	9	7	0	.563	403	397
Denver	9	7	0	.563	302	327
San Diego	6	10	0	.375	358	462
Kansas City	6	10	0	.375	386	367

NFC EAST	W	L	T	Pct	Pts	OP
Washington	14	2	0	.875	541	332
Dallas	12	4	0	.750	479	360
St. Louis	8	7	1	.531	374	428
Philadelphia	5	11	0	.313	233	322
NY Giants	3	12	1	.219	267	347

NFC CENTRAL	W	L	T	Pct	Pts	OP
Detroit	9	7	0	.563	347	286
Minnesota	8	8	0	.500	316	348
Chicago	8	8	0	.500	311	301
Green Bay	8	8	0	.500	429	439
Tampa Bay	2	14	0	.125	241	380

NFC WEST	W	L	T	Pct	Pts	OP
San Francisco	10	6	0	.625	432	293
LA Rams	9	7	0	.563	361	344
New Orleans	8	8	0	.500	319	337
Atlanta	7	9	0	.438	370	389

1984

AFC EAST	W	L	T	Pct	Pts	OP
Miami	14	2	0	.875	513	298
New England	9	7	0	.563	362	352
NY Jets	7	9	0	.438	332	364
Indianapolis Colts	4	12	0	.250	239	414
Buffalo	2	14	0	.125	250	454

AFC CENTRAL	W	L	T	Pct	Pts	OP
Pittsburgh	9	7	0	.563	387	310
Cincinnati	8	8	0	.500	339	339
Cleveland	5	11	0	.313	250	297
Houston	3	13	0	.188	240	437

AFC WEST	W	L	T	Pct	Pts	OP
Denver	13	3	0	.813	353	241
Seattle	12	4	0	.750	418	282
LA Raiders	11	5	0	.313	368	278
Kansas City	8	8	0	.500	314	324
San Diego	7	9	0	.438	394	413

NFC EAST	W	L	T	Pct	Pts	OP
Washington	11	5	0	.688	426	310
NY Giants	9	7	0	.563	299	301
Dallas	9	7	0	.563	308	308
St. Louis	9	7	0	.563	423	345
Philadelphia	6	9	1	.406	278	320

1984 *(Cont.)*

NFC CENTRAL	W	L	T	Pct	Pts	OP
Chicago	10	6	0	.625	325	248
Green Bay	8	8	0	.500	390	309
Tampa Bay	6	10	0	.375	335	380
Detroit	4	11	1	.281	283	408
Minnesota	3	13	0	.188	276	484

NFC WEST	W	L	T	Pct	Pts	OP
San Francisco	15	1	0	.938	475	227
LA Rams	10	6	0	.625	346	316
New Orleans	7	9	0	.438	298	361
Atlanta	4	12	0	.250	281	382

1985

AFC EAST	W	L	T	Pct	Pts	OP
Miami	12	4	0	.750	428	320
New England	11	5	0	.688	362	290
NY Jets	11	5	0	.688	393	264
Indianapolis	5	11	0	.313	320	386
Buffalo	2	14	0	.125	200	381

AFC CENTRAL	W	L	T	Pct	Pts	OP
Cleveland	8	8	0	.500	287	294
Cincinnati	7	9	0	.438	441	437
Pittsburgh	7	9	0	.438	379	355
Houston	5	11	0	.313	284	412

AFC WEST	W	L	T	Pct	Pts	OP
LA Raiders	12	4	0	.750	354	308
Denver	11	5	0	.688	380	329
Seattle	8	8	0	.500	349	303
San Diego	8	8	0	.500	467	435
Kansas City	6	10	0	.375	317	360

NFC EAST	W	L	T	Pct	Pts	OP
Washington	10	6	0	.625	297	312
NY Giants	10	6	0	.625	399	283
Dallas	10	6	0	.625	357	333
Philadelphia	7	9	0	.438	286	310
St. Louis	5	11	0	.313	278	414

NFC CENTRAL	W	L	T	Pct	Pts	OP
Chicago	15	1	0	.938	456	198
Green Bay	8	8	0	.500	337	355
Detroit	7	9	0	.438	307	366
Minnesota	7	9	0	.438	346	359
Tampa Bay	2	14	0	.125	294	448

NFC WEST	W	L	T	Pct	Pts	OP
LA Rams	11	5	0	.688	340	277
San Francisco	10	6	0	.625	411	263
New Orleans	5	11	0	.313	294	401
Atlanta	4	12	0	.250	282	452

1986

AFC EAST	W	L	T	Pct	Pts	OP
New England	11	5	0	.688	412	307
NY Jets	10	6	0	.625	364	386
Miami	8	8	0	.500	430	405
Buffalo	4	12	0	.250	287	348
Indianapolis	3	13	0	.188	299	400

AFC CENTRAL	W	L	T	Pct	Pts	OP
Cleveland	12	4	0	.750	391	310
Cincinnati	10	6	0	.625	409	394
Pittsburgh	6	10	0	.375	307	336
Houston	5	11	0	.313	274	329

1986 (*Cont.*)

AFC WEST

	W	L	T	Pct	Pts	OP
Denver	11	5	0	.688	378	327
Kansas City	10	6	0	.625	358	326
Seattle	10	6	0	.625	366	293
LA Raiders	8	8	0	.500	323	346
San Diego	4	12	0	.250	335	396

NFC EAST

	W	L	T	Pct	Pts	OP
NY Giants	14	2	0	.875	371	236
Washington	12	4	0	.750	368	296
Dallas	7	9	0	.438	346	337
Philadelphia	5	10	1	.344	256	312
St. Louis	4	11	1	.281	218	351

NFC CENTRAL

	W	L	T	Pct	Pts	OP
Chicago	14	2	0	.875	352	187
Minnesota	9	7	0	.563	398	273
Detroit	5	11	0	.313	277	326
Green Bay	4	12	0	.250	254	418
Tampa Bay	2	14	0	.125	239	473

NFC WEST

	W	L	T	Pct	Pts	OP
San Francisco	10	5	1	.656	374	247
LA Rams	10	6	0	.625	309	267
Atlanta	7	8	1	.469	280	280
New Orleans	7	9	0	.438	288	287

1987 (strike-shortened)

AFC EAST

	W	L	T	Pct	Pts	OP
Indianapolis	9	6	0	.643	300	238
Miami	8	7	0	.533	362	335
New England	8	7	0	.533	320	293
Buffalo	7	8	0	.467	320	293
NY Jets	6	9	0	.400	334	360

AFC CENTRAL

	W	L	T	Pct	Pts	OP
Cleveland	10	5	0	.700	390	239
Houston	9	6	0	.600	345	349
Pittsburgh	8	7	0	.533	285	299
Cincinnati	4	11	0	.267	285	370

AFC WEST

	W	L	T	Pct	Pts	OP
Denver	10	4	1	.667	379	288
Seattle	9	6	0	.600	371	314
San Diego	8	7	0	.563	253	317
LA Raiders	5	10	0	.333	301	289
Kansas City	4	11	0	.267	276	388

NFC EAST

	W	L	T	Pct	Pts	OP
Washington	11	4	0	.733	379	285
Dallas	7	8	0	.467	340	348
St. Louis	7	8	0	.467	362	368
Philadelphia	7	8	0	.467	337	380
NY Giants	6	9	0	.400	280	312

NFC CENTRAL

	W	L	T	Pct	Pts	OP
Chicago	11	4	0	.733	356	282
Minnesota	8	7	0	.533	336	335
Green Bay	5	9	1	.367	255	300
Tampa Bay	4	11	0	.267	286	360
Detroit	4	11	0	.267	269	384

NFC WEST

	W	L	T	Pct	Pts	OP
San Francisco	13	2	0	.867	459	253
New Orleans	12	3	0	.800	422	283
LA Rams	6	9	0	.400	317	361
Atlanta	3	12	0	.200	205	436

1988

AFC EAST

	W	L	T	Pct	Pts	OP
Buffalo	12	4	0	.750	329	237
New England	9	7	0	.563	250	284
Indianapolis	9	7	0	.563	354	315
NY Jets	8	7	1	.531	372	354
Miami	6	10	0	.375	319	380

AFC CENTRAL

	W	L	T	Pct	Pts	OP
Cincinnati	12	4	0	.750	448	329
Cleveland	10	6	0	.625	304	288
Houston	10	6	0	.625	424	365
Pittsburgh	5	1	0	.313	336	421

AFC WEST

	W	L	T	Pct	Pts	OP
Seattle	9	7	0	.563	339	329
Denver	8	8	0	.500	327	352
LA Raiders	7	9	0	.438	325	369
San Diego	6	10	0	.375	231	332
Kansas City	4	11	1	.281	254	320

NFC EAST

	W	L	T	Pct	Pts	OP
NY Giants	10	6	0	.625	359	304
Philadelphia	10	6	0	.625	379	319
Phoenix Cardinals	7	9	0	.438	344	398
Washington	7	9	0	.438	345	387
Dallas	3	13	0	.188	265	381

NFC CENTRAL

	W	L	T	Pct	Pts	OP
Chicago	12	4	0	.750	312	215
Minnesota	11	5	0	.688	406	233
Tampa Bay	5	11	0	.313	261	350
Detroit	4	12	0	.250	220	313
Green Bay	4	12	0	.250	240	315

NFC WEST

	W	L	T	Pct	Pts	OP
New Orleans	10	6	0	.625	312	283
San Francisco	10	6	0	.625	369	294
LA Rams	10	6	0	.625	407	293
Atlanta	5	11	0	.313	244	315

1989

AFC EAST

	W	L	T	Pct	Pts	OP
Buffalo	9	7	0	.563	407	317
Miami	8	8	0	.500	331	379
Indianapolis	8	8	0	.500	298	301
New England	5	11	0	.313	297	391
NY Jets	4	12	0	.250	253	411

AFC CENTRAL

	W	L	T	Pct	Pts	OP
Cleveland	9	6	1	.594	334	254
Houston	9	7	0	.563	365	412
Pittsburgh	9	7	0	.563	265	326
Cincinnati	8	8	0	.500	404	285

AFC WEST

	W	L	T	Pct	Pts	OP
Denver	11	5	0	.688	362	226
Kansas City	8	7	1	.531	318	286
LA Raiders	8	8	0	.500	315	297
Seattle	7	9	0	.438	241	327
San Diego	6	10	0	.375	266	290

NFC EAST

	W	L	T	Pct	Pts	OP
NY Giants	12	4	0	.750	348	252
Philadelphia	11	5	0	.688	342	274
Washington	10	6	0	.625	386	308
Phoenix	5	11	0	.313	258	377
Dallas	1	15	0	.063	204	393

1989 *(Cont.)*

NFC CENTRAL	W	L	T	Pct	Pts	OP
Green Bay	10	6	0	.625	362	356
Minnesota	10	6	0	.625	351	275
Detroit	7	9	0	.438	312	364
Chicago	6	10	0	.375	358	377
Tampa Bay	5	11	0	.313	320	419

NFC WEST	W	L	T	Pct	Pts	OP
San Francisco	14	2	0	.875	442	253
LA Rams	11	5	0	.688	426	344
New Orleans	9	7	0	.563	386	301
Atlanta	3	13	0	.188	279	437

1990

AFC EAST	W	L	T	Pct	Pts	OP
Buffalo	13	3	0	.813	428	263
Miami	12	4	0	.750	336	242
Indianapolis	7	9	0	.438	281	353
NY Jets	6	10	0	.375	295	345
New England	1	15	0	.063	181	446

AFC CENTRAL	W	L	T	Pct	Pts	OP
Pittsburgh	9	7	0	.563	292	240
Cincinnati	9	7	0	.563	360	352
Houston	9	7	0	.563	405	307
Cleveland	3	13	0	.188	228	462

AFC WEST	W	L	T	Pct	Pts	OP
LA Raiders	12	4	0	.750	337	268
Kansas City	11	5	0	.688	369	257
Seattle	9	7	0	.563	306	286
San Diego	6	10	0	.375	315	281
Denver	5	11	0	.313	331	374

NFC EAST	W	L	T	Pct	Pts	OP
NY Giants	13	3	0	.813	335	211
Washington	10	6	0	.625	381	301
Philadelphia	10	6	0	.625	396	299
Dallas	7	9	0	.438	244	308
Phoenix	5	11	0	.313	268	396

NFC CENTRAL	W	L	T	Pct	Pts	OP
Chicago	11	5	0	.688	348	280
Green Bay	6	10	0	.375	271	347
Minnesota	6	10	0	.375	351	326
Detroit	6	10	0	.375	373	413
Tampa Bay	6	10	0	.375	264	367

NFC WEST	W	L	T	Pct	Pts	OP
San Francisco	14	2	0	.875	353	239
New Orleans	8	8	0	.500	274	275
LA Rams	5	11	0	.313	345	412
Atlanta	5	11	0	.313	348	365

1991

AFC EAST	W	L	T	Pct	Pts	OP
Buffalo	13	3	0	.813	458	318
Miami	8	8	0	.500	343	349
NY Jets	8	8	0	.500	314	293
New England	6	10	0	.375	211	305
Indianapolis	1	15	0	.063	143	381

AFC CENTRAL	W	L	T	Pct	Pts	OP
Houston	11	5	0	.688	386	251
Pittsburgh	7	9	0	.438	292	344
Cleveland	6	10	0	.375	293	298
Cincinnati	3	13	0	.188	263	435

1991 *(Cont.)*

AFC WEST	W	L	T	Pct	Pts	OP
Denver	12	4	0	.750	304	235
Kansas City	10	6	0	.625	322	252
LA Raiders	9	7	0	.563	298	297
Seattle	7	9	0	.438	276	261
San Diego	4	12	0	.250	274	342

NFC EAST	W	L	T	Pct	Pts	OP
Washington	14	2	0	.875	485	224
Dallas	11	5	0	.688	342	310
Philadelphia	10	6	0	.625	285	244
NY Giants	8	8	0	.500	281	297
Phoenix	4	12	0	.250	196	344

NFC CENTRAL	W	L	T	Pct	Pts	OP
Detroit	12	4	0	.750	339	295
Chicago	11	5	0	.688	299	269
Minnesota	8	8	0	.500	301	306
Green Bay	4	12	0	.250	273	313
Tampa Bay	3	13	0	.188	199	365

NFC WEST	W	L	T	Pct	Pts	OP
New Orleans	11	5	0	.688	341	211
Atlanta	10	6	0	.625	361	338
San Francisco	10	6	0	.625	393	239
LA Rams	3	13	0	.188	234	390

1992

AFC EAST	W	L	T	Pct	Pts	OP
Buffalo	11	5	0	.688	381	283
Miami	11	5	0	.688	340	281
Indianapolis	9	7	0	.563	216	302
NY Jets	4	12	0	.250	220	315
New England	2	14	0	.125	205	363

AFC CENTRAL	W	L	T	Pct	Pts	OP
Pittsburgh	11	5	0	.688	299	225
Houston	10	6	0	.625	352	258
Cleveland	7	9	0	.438	272	275
Cincinnati	5	11	0	.313	274	364

AFC WEST	W	L	T	Pct	Pts	OP
San Diego	11	5	0	.688	335	241
Kansas City	10	6	0	.625	348	282
Denver	8	8	0	.500	262	329
LA Raiders	7	9	0	.438	249	281
Seattle	2	14	0	.125	140	312

NFC EAST	W	L	T	Pct	Pts	OP
Dallas	13	3	0	.813	409	243
Philadelphia	11	5	0	.688	354	245
Washington	9	7	0	.563	300	255
NY Giants	6	10	0	.375	306	367
Phoenix	4	12	0	.250	243	332

NFC CENTRAL	W	L	T	Pct	Pts	OP
Minnesota	11	5	0	.688	374	249
Green Bay	9	7	0	.563	276	296
Tampa Bay	5	11	0	.313	267	365
Detroit	5	11	0	.313	273	332
Chicago	5	11	0	.313	295	361

NFC WEST	W	L	T	Pct	Pts	OP
San Francisco	14	2	0	.875	431	236
New Orleans	12	4	0	.750	330	202
Atlanta	6	10	0	.375	327	414
LA Rams	6	10	0	.375	313	383

1993

AFC EAST	W	L	T	Pct	Pts	OP
Buffalo	12	4	0	.750	329	242
Miami	9	7	0	.563	349	351
NY Jets	8	8	0	.500	270	247
New England	5	11	0	.313	238	286
Indianapolis	4	12	0	.250	189	378

AFC CENTRAL	W	L	T	Pct	Pts	OP
Houston	12	4	0	.750	368	238
Pittsburgh	9	7	0	.563	308	281
Cleveland	7	9	0	.438	304	307
Cincinnati	3	13	0	.188	187	319

AFC WEST	W	L	T	Pct	Pts	OP
Kansas City	11	5	0	.688	328	291
LA Raiders	10	6	0	.625	306	326
Denver	9	7	0	.563	373	284
San Diego	8	8	0	.500	322	290
Seattle	6	10	0	.375	280	314

NFC EAST	W	L	T	Pct	Pts	OP
Dallas	12	4	0	.750	376	229
NY Giants	11	5	0	.688	288	205
Philadelphia	8	8	0	.500	293	315
Phoenix	7	9	0	.438	326	269
Washington	4	12	0	.250	230	345

NFC CENTRAL	W	L	T	Pct	Pts	OP
Detroit	10	6	0	.625	298	292
Green Bay	9	7	0	.563	340	282
Minnesota	9	7	0	.563	277	290
Chicago	7	9	0	.438	234	230
Tampa Bay	5	11	0	.313	237	375

NFC WEST	W	L	T	Pct	Pts	OP
San Francisco	10	6	0	.625	473	295
New Orleans	8	8	0	.500	317	343
Atlanta	6	10	0	.375	316	385
LA Rams	5	11	0	.313	221	367

1994

AFC EAST	W	L	T	Pct	Pts	OP
Miami	10	6	0	.625	389	327
New England	10	6	0	.625	351	312
Indianapolis	8	8	0	.500	307	320
Buffalo	7	9	0	.438	340	356
NY Jets	6	10	0	.375	264	320

AFC CENTRAL	W	L	T	Pct	Pts	OP
Pittsburgh	12	4	0	.750	316	234
Cleveland	11	5	0	.688	340	204
Cincinnati	3	13	0	.188	276	406
Houston	2	14	0	.125	226	352

AFC WEST	W	L	T	Pct	Pts	OP
San Diego	11	5	0	.688	384	306
LA Raiders	9	7	0	.563	303	327
Kansas City	9	7	0	.563	319	298
Denver	7	9	0	.438	347	396
Seattle	6	10	0	.375	287	323

1994 *(Cont.)*

NFC EAST	W	L	T	Pct	Pts	OP
Dallas	12	4	0	.750	414	248
NY Giants	9	7	0	.563	279	305
Arizona Cardinals	8	8	0	.500	235	267
Philadelphia	7	9	0	.438	308	308
Washington	3	13	0	.188	320	412

NFC CENTRAL	W	L	T	Pct	Pts	OP
Minnesota	10	6	0	.625	356	314
Green Bay	9	7	0	.563	382	287
Detroit	9	7	0	.563	357	342
Chicago	9	7	0	.563	271	307
Tampa Bay	6	10	0	.375	251	351

NFC WEST	W	L	T	Pct	Pts	OP
San Francisco	13	3	0	.813	505	296
New Orleans	7	9	0	.438	348	407
Atlanta	7	9	0	.438	317	385
LA Rams	4	12	0	.250	286	365

1995

AFC EAST	W	L	T	Pct	Pts	OP
Buffalo	10	6	0	.625	350	335
Miami	9	7	0	.563	398	332
Indianapolis	9	7	0	.563	331	316
New England	6	10	0	.375	294	377
NY Jets	3	13	0	.188	233	384

AFC CENTRAL	W	L	T	Pct	Pts	OP
Pittsburgh	11	5	0	.688	407	327
Houston	7	9	0	.438	348	324
Cincinnati	7	9	0	.438	349	374
Cleveland	5	11	0	.313	289	356
Jacksonville Jaguars	4	12	0	.250	275	404

AFC WEST	W	L	T	Pct	Pts	OP
Kansas City	13	3	0	.813	358	241
San Diego	9	7	0	.563	321	323
Oakland Raiders	8	8	0	.500	348	332
Denver	8	8	0	.500	388	345
Seattle	8	8	0	.500	363	366

NFC EAST	W	L	T	Pct	Pts	OP
Dallas	12	4	0	.750	435	291
Philadelphia	10	6	0	.625	318	338
Washington	6	10	0	.375	326	359
NY Giants	5	11	0	.313	290	340
Arizona	4	12	0	.250	275	422

NFC CENTRAL	W	L	T	Pct	Pts	OP
Green Bay	11	5	0	.688	404	314
Detroit	10	6	0	.625	436	336
Chicago	9	7	0	.563	392	360
Minnesota	8	8	0	.500	412	385
Tampa Bay	7	9	0	.438	238	335

NFC WEST	W	L	T	Pct	Pts	OP
San Francisco	11	5	0	.688	457	258
Atlanta	9	7	0	.563	362	349
St. Louis Rams	7	9	0	.438	309	418
Carolina Panthers	7	9	0	.438	289	325
New Orleans	7	9	0	.438	319	348

1996

AFC EAST
	W	L	T	Pct	Pts	OP
New England	11	5	0	.688	418	313
Buffalo	10	6	0	.625	319	266
Indianapolis	9	7	0	.563	317	334
Miami	8	8	0	.500	339	325
NY Jets	1	15	0	.063	279	454

AFC CENTRAL
	W	L	T	Pct	Pts	OP
Pittsburgh	10	6	0	.625	344	257
Jacksonville	9	7	0	.563	325	334
Houston	8	8	0	.500	345	319
Cincinnati	8	8	0	.500	372	369
Baltimore Ravens	4	12	0	.250	371	441

AFC WEST
	W	L	T	Pct	Pts	OP
Denver	13	3	0	.813	391	275
Kansas City	9	7	0	.563	297	300
San Diego	8	8	0	.500	310	376
Seattle	7	9	0	.438	317	375
Oakland	7	9	0	.438	340	293

NFC EAST
	W	L	T	Pct	Pts	OP
Dallas	10	6	0	.625	286	250
Philadelphia	10	6	0	.625	363	341
Washington	9	7	0	.563	364	312
Arizona	7	9	0	.438	300	397
NY Giants	6	10	0	.375	242	297

NFC CENTRAL
	W	L	T	Pct	Pts	OP
Green Bay	13	3	0	.813	456	210
Minnesota	9	7	0	.563	298	315
Chicago	7	9	0	.438	283	305
Tampa Bay	6	10	0	.375	221	293
Detroit	5	11	0	.313	302	368

NFC WEST
	W	L	T	Pct	Pts	OP
San Francisco	12	4	0	.750	398	257
Carolina	12	4	0	.750	367	218
St. Louis	6	10	0	.375	303	409
New Orleans	3	13	0	.188	229	339
Atlanta	3	13	0	.188	309	461

1997

AFC EAST
	W	L	T	Pct	Pts	OP
New England	10	6	0	.625	369	289
Miami	9	7	0	.563	339	327
NY Jets	9	7	0	.563	348	287
Buffalo	6	10	0	.375	255	367
Indianapolis	3	13	0	.188	313	401

AFC CENTRAL
	W	L	T	Pct	Pts	OP
Jacksonville	11	5	0	.688	394	318
Pittsburgh	11	5	0	.688	372	307
Tennessee Oilers	8	8	0	.500	333	310
Cincinnati	7	9	0	.438	355	405
Baltimore	6	9	1	.375	326	345

AFC WEST
	W	L	T	Pct	Pts	OP
Kansas City	13	3	0	.813	375	232
Denver	12	4	0	.750	472	287
Seattle	8	8	0	.500	365	362
Oakland	4	12	0	.250	324	419
San Diego	4	12	0	.250	266	425

1997 (Cont.)

NFC EAST
	W	L	T	Pct	Pts	OP
NY Giants	10	5	1	.656	307	265
Washington	8	7	1	.531	327	289
Philadelphia	6	9	1	.406	317	372
Dallas	6	10	0	.375	304	314
Arizona	4	12	0	.250	283	379

NFC CENTRAL
	W	L	T	Pct	Pts	OP
Green Bay	13	3	0	.813	422	282
Tampa Bay	10	6	0	.625	299	263
Detroit	9	7	0	.563	379	306
Minnesota	9	7	0	.563	354	359
Chicago	4	12	0	.250	263	421

NFC WEST
	W	L	T	Pct	Pts	OP
San Francisco	13	3	0	.813	375	265
Carolina	7	9	0	.438	265	314
Atlanta	7	9	0	.438	320	361
New Orleans	6	10	0	.375	237	327
St. Louis	5	11	0	.313	299	359

1998

AFC EAST
	W	L	T	Pct	Pts	OP
NY Jets	12	4	0	.750	416	266
Miami	10	6	0	.625	321	265
Buffalo	10	6	0	.625	400	333
New England	9	7	0	.563	337	329
Indianapolis	3	13	0	.188	310	444

AFC CENTRAL
	W	L	T	Pct	Pts	OP
Jacksonville	11	5	0	.688	392	338
Tennessee	8	8	0	.500	330	320
Pittsburgh	7	9	0	.438	263	303
Baltimore	6	10	0	.375	269	335
Cincinnati	3	13	0	.188	268	452

AFC WEST
	W	L	T	Pct	Pts	OP
Denver	14	2	0	.875	501	309
Oakland	8	8	0	.500	288	356
Seattle	8	8	0	.500	372	310
Kansas City	7	9	0	.438	327	363
San Diego	5	11	0	.313	241	342

NFC EAST
	W	L	T	Pct	Pts	OP
Dallas	10	6	0	.625	381	275
Arizona	9	7	0	.563	325	378
NY Giants	8	8	0	.500	287	309
Washington	6	10	0	.375	319	421
Philadelphia	3	13	0	.188	161	344

NFC CENTRAL
	W	L	T	Pct	Pts	OP
Minnesota	15	1	0	.938	556	296
Green Bay	11	5	0	.688	408	319
Tampa Bay	8	8	0	.500	314	295
Detroit	5	11	0	.313	306	378
Chicago	4	12	0	.250	276	368

NFC WEST
	W	L	T	Pct	Pts	OP
Atlanta	14	2	0	.875	442	289
San Francisco	12	4	0	.750	479	328
New Orleans	6	10	0	.375	305	359
Carolina	4	12	0	.250	336	413
St. Louis	4	12	0	.250	285	378

1999

AFC EAST	W	L	T	Pct	Pts	OP
Indianapolis	13	3	0	.813	423	333
Buffalo	11	5	0	.688	320	229
Miami	9	7	0	.563	326	336
NY Jets	8	8	0	.500	309	309
New England	8	8	0	.500	299	284

AFC CENTRAL	W	L	T	Pct	Pts	OP
Jacksonville	14	2	0	.875	396	217
Tennessee Titans	13	3	0	.813	392	324
Baltimore	8	8	0	.500	324	277
Pittsburgh	6	10	0	.375	317	320
Cincinnati	4	12	0	.250	283	460
Cleveland Browns	2	14	0	.125	217	437

AFC WEST	W	L	T	Pct	Pts	OP
Seattle	9	7	0	.563	338	298
Kansas City	9	7	0	.563	390	322
Oakland	8	8	0	.500	390	329
San Diego	8	8	0	.500	269	316
Denver	6	10	0	.375	314	318

NFC EAST	W	L	T	Pct	Pts	OP
Washington	10	6	0	.625	443	377
Dallas	8	8	0	.500	352	276
NY Giants	7	9	0	.438	299	358
Arizona	6	10	0	.375	245	382
Philadelphia	5	11	0	.313	272	357

NFC CENTRAL	W	L	T	Pct	Pts	OP
Tampa Bay	11	5	0	.688	270	235
Minnesota	10	6	0	.625	399	335
Green Bay	8	8	0	.500	357	341
Detroit	8	8	0	.500	322	323
Chicago	6	10	0	.375	272	341

NFC WEST	W	L	T	Pct	Pts	OP
St. Louis	13	3	0	.813	526	242
Carolina	8	8	0	.500	421	381
Atlanta	5	11	0	.313	285	380
San Francisco	4	12	0	.250	295	453
New Orleans	3	13	0	.188	260	434

2000

AFC EAST	W	L	T	Pct	Pts	OP
Miami	11	5	0	.688	323	226
Indianapolis	10	6	0	.625	429	326
NY Jets	9	7	0	.563	321	321
Buffalo	8	8	0	.500	315	350
New England	5	11	0	.313	276	338

AFC CENTRAL	W	L	T	Pct	Pts	OP
Tennessee	13	3	0	.813	346	191
Baltimore	12	4	0	.750	333	165
Pittsburgh	9	7	0	.563	321	255
Jacksonville	7	9	0	.438	367	327
Cincinnati	4	12	0	.250	185	359
Cleveland	3	13	0	.188	161	419

AFC WEST	W	L	T	Pct	Pts	OP
Oakland	12	4	0	.750	479	299
Denver	11	5	0	.688	485	369
Kansas City	7	9	0	.438	355	354
Seattle	6	10	0	.375	320	405
San Diego	1	15	0	.063	269	440

2000 *(Cont.)*

NFC EAST	W	L	T	Pct	Pts	OP
NY Giants	12	4	0	.750	328	246
Philadelphia	11	5	0	.688	351	245
Washington	8	8	0	.500	281	269
Dallas	5	11	0	.313	294	361
Arizona	3	13	0	.188	210	443

NFC CENTRAL	W	L	T	Pct	Pts	OP
Minnesota	11	5	0	.688	397	371
Tampa Bay	10	6	0	.625	388	269
Green Bay	9	7	0	.563	353	323
Detroit	9	7	0	.563	307	307
Chicago	5	11	0	.313	216	355

NFC WEST	W	L	T	Pct	Pts	OP
New Orleans	10	6	0	.625	354	306
St. Louis	10	6	0	.625	540	471
Carolina	7	9	0	.438	310	310
San Francisco	6	10	0	.375	388	422
Atlanta	4	12	0	.250	252	413

2001

AFC EAST	W	L	T	Pct	Pts	OP
New England	11	5	0	.688	371	272
Miami	11	5	0	.688	344	290
NY Jets	10	6	0	.625	308	295
Indianapolis	6	10	0	.375	413	486
Buffalo	3	13	0	.188	265	420

AFC CENTRAL	W	L	T	Pct	Pts	OP
Pittsburgh	13	3	0	.813	352	212
Baltimore	10	6	0	.625	303	265
Cleveland	7	9	0	.438	285	319
Tennessee	7	9	0	.438	336	388
Jacksonville	6	10	0	.375	294	286
Cincinnati	6	10	0	.375	226	309

AFC WEST	W	L	T	Pct	Pts	OP
Oakland	10	6	0	.625	399	327
Seattle	9	7	0	.563	301	324
Denver	8	8	0	.500	340	339
Kansas City	6	10	0	.375	320	344
San Diego	5	11	0	.313	332	321

NFC EAST	W	L	T	Pct	Pts	OP
Philadelphia	11	5	0	.688	343	208
Washington	8	8	0	.500	256	303
NY Giants	7	9	0	.438	294	321
Arizona	7	9	0	.438	295	343
Dallas	5	11	0	.313	246	338

NFC CENTRAL	W	L	T	Pct	Pts	OP
Chicago	13	3	0	.813	338	203
Green Bay	12	4	0	.750	390	266
Tampa Bay	9	7	0	.563	324	280
Minnesota	5	11	0	.313	290	390
Detroit	2	14	0	.125	270	424

NFC WEST	W	L	T	Pct	Pts	OP
St. Louis	14	2	0	.875	503	273
San Francisco	12	4	0	.750	409	282
Atlanta	7	9	0	.438	291	377
New Orleans	7	9	0	.438	333	409
Carolina	1	15	0	.938	253	410

2002

AFC EAST
	W	L	T	Pct	Pts	OP
New England	9	7	0	.563	384	346
Miami	9	7	0	.563	378	301
NY Jets	9	7	0	.563	359	336
Buffalo	8	8	0	.500	379	397

AFC NORTH
	W	L	T	Pct	Pts	OP
Pittsburgh	10	5	1	.656	390	345
Cleveland	9	7	0	.563	344	320
Baltimore	7	9	0	.438	316	354
Cincinnati	2	14	0	.125	279	456

AFC SOUTH
	W	L	T	Pct	Pts	OP
Tennessee	11	5	0	.688	367	324
Indianapolis	10	6	0	.625	349	313
Jacksonville	6	10	0	.375	328	315
Houston Texans	4	12	0	.250	213	356

AFC WEST
	W	L	T	Pct	Pts	OP
Oakland	11	5	0	.688	450	304
Denver	9	7	0	.563	392	344
Kansas City	8	8	0	.500	467	399
San Diego	8	8	0	.500	333	367

NFC EAST
	W	L	T	Pct	Pts	OP
Philadelphia	12	4	0	.750	415	241
NY Giants	10	6	0	.625	320	279
Washington	7	9	0	.438	307	365
Dallas	5	11	0	.313	217	329

NFC NORTH
	W	L	T	Pct	Pts	OP
Green Bay	12	4	0	.750	398	328
Minnesota	6	10	0	.375	390	442
Chicago	4	12	0	.250	281	379
Detroit	3	13	0	.188	306	451

NFC SOUTH
	W	L	T	Pct	Pts	OP
Tampa Bay	12	4	0	.750	346	196
Atlanta	9	6	1	.594	402	314
New Orleans	9	7	0	.563	432	388
Carolina	7	9	0	.438	258	302

NFC WEST
	W	L	T	Pct	Pts	OP
San Francisco	10	6	0	.625	367	351
St. Louis	7	9	0	.438	316	367
Seattle	7	9	0	.438	355	369
Arizona	5	11	0	.313	262	417

2003

AFC EAST
	W	L	T	Pct	Pts	OP
New England	14	2	0	.875	348	238
Miami	10	6	0	.625	311	261
Buffalo	6	10	0	.375	243	279
NY Jets	6	10	0	.375	283	299

AFC NORTH
	W	L	T	Pct	Pts	OP
Baltimore	10	6	0	.625	391	281
Cincinnati	8	8	0	.500	346	384
Pittsburgh	6	10	0	.375	300	327
Cleveland	5	11	0	.313	254	322

AFC SOUTH
	W	L	T	Pct	Pts	OP
Indianapolis	12	4	0	.750	447	336
Tennessee	12	4	0	.750	435	324
Houston	5	11	0	.313	255	380
Jacksonville	5	11	0	.313	276	331

2003 *(Cont.)*

AFC WEST
	W	L	T	Pct	Pts	OP
Kansas City	13	3	0	.813	484	332
Denver	10	6	0	.625	381	301
Oakland	4	12	0	.250	270	379
San Diego	4	12	0	.250	313	441

NFC EAST
	W	L	T	Pct	Pts	OP
Philadelphia	12	4	0	.750	374	287
Dallas	10	6	0	.625	289	260
Washington	5	11	0	.313	287	372
NY Giants	4	12	0	.250	243	387

NFC NORTH
	W	L	T	Pct	Pts	OP
Green Bay	10	6	0	.625	442	307
Minnesota	9	7	0	.563	416	353
Chicago	7	9	0	.438	283	346
Detroit	5	11	0	.313	270	379

NFC SOUTH
	W	L	T	Pct	Pts	OP
Carolina	11	5	0	.688	325	304
New Orleans	8	8	0	.500	340	326
Tampa Bay	7	9	0	.438	301	264
Atlanta	5	11	0	.313	299	422

NFC WEST
	W	L	T	Pct	Pts	OP
St. Louis	12	4	0	.750	447	328
Seattle	10	6	0	.625	404	327
San Francisco	7	9	0	.438	384	337
Arizona	4	12	0	.250	225	452

2004

AFC EAST
	W	L	T	Pct	Pts	OP
New England	14	2	0	.875	437	260
NY Jets	10	6	0	.625	333	261
Buffalo	9	7	0	.562	395	284
Miami	4	12	0	.250	275	354

AFC NORTH
	W	L	T	Pct	Pts	OP
Pittsburgh	15	1	0	.938	372	251
Baltimore	9	7	0	.562	317	268
Cincinnati	8	8	0	.500	374	372
Cleveland	4	12	0	.250	275	354

AFC SOUTH
	W	L	T	Pct	Pts	OP
Indianapolis	12	4	0	.750	522	351
Jacksonville	9	7	0	.562	261	280
Houston	7	9	0	.438	309	339
Tennessee	5	11	0	.312	344	439

AFC WEST
	W	L	T	Pct	Pts	OP
San Diego	12	4	0	.750	446	313
Denver	10	6	0	.625	381	304
Kansas City	7	9	0	.438	483	435
Oakland	5	11	0	.312	320	442

NFC EAST
	W	L	T	Pct	Pts	OP
Philadelphia	13	3	0	.812	386	260
NY Giants	6	10	0	.375	303	347
Dallas	6	10	0	.375	293	405
Washington	6	10	0	.375	240	265

NFC NORTH
	W	L	T	Pct	Pts	OP
Green Bay	10	6	0	.625	424	380
Minnesota	8	8	0	.500	405	395
Detroit	6	10	0	.375	296	350
Chicago	5	11	0	.312	231	331

2004 *(Cont.)*

NFC SOUTH

	W	L	T	Pct	Pts	OP
Atlanta	11	5	0	.688	340	337
New Orleans	8	8	0	.500	348	405
Carolina	7	9	0	.438	355	339
Tampa Bay	5	11	0	.312	301	304

NFC WEST

	W	L	T	Pct	Pts	OP
Seattle	9	7	0	.562	371	373
St. Louis	8	8	0	.500	319	392
Arizona	6	10	0	.375	284	322
San Francisco	2	14	0	.125	259	452

2005

AFC EAST

	W	L	T	Pct	Pts	OP
New England	10	6	0	.625	379	338
Miami	9	7	0	.562	318	317
Buffalo	5	11	0	.312	271	367
NY Jets	4	12	0	.250	240	355

AFC NORTH

	W	L	T	Pct	Pts	OP
Cincinnati	11	5	0	.688	421	350
Pittsburgh	11	5	0	.688	389	258
Cleveland	6	10	0	.375	232	301
Baltimore	6	10	0	.375	265	299

AFC SOUTH

	W	L	T	Pct	Pts	OP
Indianapolis	14	2	0	.875	439	247
Jacksonville	12	4	0	.750	361	269
Tennessee	4	12	0	.250	299	421
Houston	2	14	0	.125	260	431

AFC WEST

	W	L	T	Pct	Pts	OP
Denver	13	3	0	.812	395	258
Kansas City	10	6	0	.625	403	325
San Diego	9	7	0	.562	418	312
Oakland	4	12	0	.250	290	383

NFC EAST

	W	L	T	Pct	Pts	OP
NY Giants	11	5	0	.688	422	314
Washington	10	6	0	.625	359	293
Dallas	9	7	0	.562	325	308
Philadelphia	6	10	0	.375	310	388

NFC NORTH

	W	L	T	Pct	Pts	OP
Chicago	11	5	0	.688	260	202
Minnesota	9	7	0	.562	306	344
Detroit	5	11	0	.312	254	345
Green Bay	4	12	0	.250	298	344

NFC SOUTH

	W	L	T	Pct	Pts	OP
Carolina	11	5	0	.688	391	259
Tampa Bay	11	5	0	.688	300	274
Atlanta	8	8	0	.500	351	341
New Orleans	3	13	0	.188	235	398

NFC WEST

	W	L	T	Pct	Pts	OP
Seattle	13	3	0	.812	452	271
St. Louis	6	10	0	.375	363	429
Arizona	5	11	0	.312	311	387
San Francisco	4	12	0	.250	239	428

2006

AFC EAST

	W	L	T	Pct	Pts	OP
New England	12	4	0	.750	385	237
NY Jets	10	6	0	.625	316	295
Buffalo	7	9	0	.438	300	311
Miami	6	10	0	.375	260	283

2006 *(Cont.)*

AFC NORTH

	W	L	T	Pct	Pts	OP
Baltimore	13	3	0	.812	353	201
Cincinnati	8	8	0	.500	373	331
Pittsburgh	8	8	0	.500	353	315
Cleveland	4	12	0	.250	238	356

AFC SOUTH

	W	L	T	Pct	Pts	OP
Indianapolis	12	4	0	.750	427	360
Tennessee	8	8	0	.500	324	400
Jacksonville	8	8	0	.500	371	274
Houston	6	10	0	.375	267	366

AFC WEST

	W	L	T	Pct	Pts	OP
San Diego	14	2	0	.875	492	303
Kansas City	9	7	0	.562	331	315
Denver	9	7	0	.562	319	305
Oakland	2	14	0	.125	168	332

NFC EAST

	W	L	T	Pct	Pts	OP
Philadelphia	10	6	0	.625	398	328
Dallas	9	7	0	.562	425	350
NY Giants	8	8	0	.500	355	362
Washington	5	11	0	.312	307	376

NFC NORTH

	W	L	T	Pct	Pts	OP
Chicago	13	3	0	.812	427	255
Green Bay	8	8	0	.500	301	366
Minnesota	6	10	0	.375	282	327
Detroit	3	13	0	.188	305	398

NFC SOUTH

	W	L	T	Pct	Pts	OP
New Orleans	10	6	0	.625	413	322
Carolina	8	8	0	.500	270	305
Atlanta	7	9	0	.438	292	328
Tampa Bay	4	12	0	.250	211	353

NFC WEST

	W	L	T	Pct	Pts	OP
Seattle	9	7	0	.562	335	341
St. Louis	8	8	0	.500	367	381
San Francisco	7	9	0	.438	298	412
Arizona	5	11	0	.312	314	389

2007

AFC EAST

	W	L	T	Pct	Pts	OP
New England	16	0	0	1.000	589	274
Buffalo	7	9	0	.438	252	354
NY Jets	4	12	0	.250	268	355
Miami	1	15	0	.063	267	437

AFC NORTH

	W	L	T	Pct	Pts	OP
Pittsburgh	10	6	0	.625	393	269
Cleveland	10	6	0	.625	402	382
Cincinnati	7	9	0	.438	380	385
Baltimore	5	11	0	.313	275	384

AFC SOUTH

	W	L	T	Pct	Pts	OP
Indianapolis	13	3	0	.813	450	262
Jacksonville	11	5	0	.688	411	304
Tennessee	10	6	0	.625	301	297
Houston	8	8	0	.500	379	384

AFC WEST

	W	L	T	Pct	Pts	OP
San Diego	11	5	0	.688	412	284
Denver	7	9	0	.438	320	409
Kansas City	4	12	0	.250	226	335
Oakland	4	12	0	.250	286	398

2007 *(Cont.)*

NFC EAST

	W	L	T	Pct	Pts	OP
Dallas	13	3	0	.813	455	325
NY Giants	10	6	0	.625	373	351
Washington	9	7	0	.563	334	310
Philadelphia	8	8	0	.500	336	300

NFC NORTH

	W	L	T	Pct	Pts	OP
Green Bay	13	3	0	.813	435	291
Minnesota	8	8	0	.500	365	311
Detroit	7	9	0	.438	346	444
Chicago	7	9	0	.438	334	348

NFC SOUTH

	W	L	T	Pct	Pts	OP
Tampa Bay	9	7	0	.563	334	270
Carolina	7	9	0	.438	267	347
New Orleans	7	9	0	.438	379	388
Atlanta	4	12	0	.250	259	414

NFC WEST

	W	L	T	Pct	Pts	OP
Seattle	10	6	0	.625	393	291
Arizona	8	8	0	.500	404	399
San Francisco	5	11	0	.313	219	364
St. Louis	3	13	0	.188	263	438

2008

AFC EAST

	W	L	T	Pct	Pts	OP
Miami	11	5	0	.688	345	317
New England	11	5	0	.688	410	309
NY Jets	9	7	0	.563	405	356
Buffalo	7	9	0	.438	336	342

AFC NORTH

	W	L	T	Pct	Pts	OP
Pittsburgh	12	4	0	.750	347	223
Baltimore	11	5	0	.688	385	244
Cincinnati	4	11	1	.281	204	364
Cleveland	4	12	0	.250	232	350

AFC SOUTH

	W	L	T	Pct	Pts	OP
Tennessee	13	3	0	.813	375	234
Indianapolis	12	4	0	.750	377	298
Houston	8	8	0	.500	366	394
Jacksonville	5	11	0	.313	302	367

AFC WEST

	W	L	T	Pct	Pts	OP
San Diego	8	8	0	.500	439	347
Denver	8	8	0	.500	370	448
Oakland	5	11	0	.313	263	388
Kansas City	2	14	0	.125	291	440

NFC EAST

	W	L	T	Pct	Pts	OP
NY Giants	12	4	0	.750	427	294
Philadelphia	9	6	1	.594	416	289
Dallas	9	7	0	.563	362	365
Washington	8	8	0	.500	265	296

NFC NORTH

	W	L	T	Pct	Pts	OP
Minnesota	10	6	0	.625	379	333
Chicago	9	7	0	.563	375	350
Green Bay	6	10	0	.375	419	380
Detroit	0	16	0	.000	268	517

NFC SOUTH

	W	L	T	Pct	Pts	OP
Carolina	12	4	0	.750	414	329
Atlanta	11	5	0	.688	391	325
Tampa Bay	9	7	0	.563	361	323
New Orleans	8	8	0	.500	463	393

2008 *(Cont.)*

NFC WEST

	W	L	T	Pct	Pts	OP
Arizona	9	7	0	.563	427	426
San Francisco	7	9	0	.438	339	381
Seattle	4	12	0	.250	294	392
St. Louis	2	14	0	.125	232	465

2009

AFC EAST

	W	L	T	Pct	Pts	OP
New England	10	6	0	.625	427	285
NY Jets	9	7	0	.563	348	236
Miami	7	9	0	.438	360	390
Buffalo	6	10	0	.375	258	326

AFC NORTH

	W	L	T	Pct	Pts	OP
Cincinnati	10	6	0	.625	305	291
Baltimore	9	7	0	.563	391	261
Pittsburgh	9	7	0	.563	368	324
Cleveland	5	11	0	.313	245	375

AFC SOUTH

	W	L	T	Pct	Pts	OP
Indianapolis	14	2	0	.875	416	307
Houston	9	7	0	.563	388	333
Tennessee	8	8	0	.500	354	402
Jacksonville	7	9	0	.438	290	380

AFC WEST

	W	L	T	Pct	Pts	OP
San Diego	13	3	0	.813	454	320
Denver	8	8	0	.500	326	324
Oakland	5	11	0	.313	197	379
Kansas City	4	12	0	.250	294	424

NFC EAST

	W	L	T	Pct	Pts	OP
Dallas	11	5	0	.688	361	250
Philadelphia	11	5	0	.688	429	337
NY Giants	8	8	0	.500	402	427
Washington	4	12	0	.250	266	336

NFC NORTH

	W	L	T	Pct	Pts	OP
Minnesota	12	4	0	.750	470	312
Green Bay	11	5	0	.688	461	297
Chicago	7	9	0	.438	327	375
Detroit	2	14	0	.125	262	494

NFC SOUTH

	W	L	T	Pct	Pts	OP
New Orleans	13	3	0	.813	510	341
Atlanta	9	7	0	.563	363	325
Carolina	8	8	0	.500	315	308
Tampa Bay	3	13	0	.188	244	400

NFC WEST

	W	L	T	Pct	Pts	OP
Arizona	10	6	0	.625	375	325
San Francisco	8	8	0	.500	330	281
Seattle	5	11	0	.313	280	390
St. Louis	1	15	0	.063	175	436

2010

AFC EAST

	W	L	T	Pct	Pts	OP
New England	14	2	0	.875	518	313
NY Jets	11	5	0	.688	367	304
Miami	7	9	0	.438	273	333
Buffalo	4	12	0	.250	283	425

AFC NORTH

	W	L	T	Pct	Pts	OP
Pittsburgh	12	4	0	.750	375	232
Baltimore	12	4	0	.750	357	270
Cincinnati	5	11	0	.313	271	332
Cleveland	4	12	0	.250	322	395

2010 *(Cont.)*

AFC SOUTH

	W	L	T	Pct	Pts	OP
Indianapolis	10	6	0	.625	435	388
Jacksonville	8	8	0	.500	353	419
Houston	6	10	0	.375	390	427
Tennessee	6	10	0	.375	356	336

AFC WEST

	W	L	T	Pct	Pts	OP
Kansas City	10	6	0	.625	366	326
San Diego	9	7	0	.563	441	322
Oakland	8	8	0	.500	410	371
Denver	4	12	0	.250	344	471

NFC EAST

	W	L	T	Pct	Pts	OP
Philadelphia	10	6	0	.625	439	377
NY Giants	10	6	0	.625	394	347
Dallas	6	10	0	.375	394	436
Washington	6	10	0	.375	302	377

NFC NORTH

	W	L	T	Pct	Pts	OP
Chicago	11	5	0	.688	334	286
Green Bay	10	6	0	.625	388	240
Detroit	6	10	0	.375	362	369
Minnesota	6	10	0	.375	281	348

NFC SOUTH

	W	L	T	Pct	Pts	OP
Atlanta	13	3	0	.813	414	288
New Orleans	11	5	0	.688	384	307
Tampa Bay	10	6	0	.625	341	318
Carolina	2	14	0	.125	196	408

NFC WEST

	W	L	T	Pct	Pts	OP
Seattle	7	9	0	.438	310	407
St. Louis	7	9	0	.438	289	328
San Francisco	6	10	0	.375	305	346
Arizona	5	11	0	.313	289	434

2011

AFC EAST

	W	L	T	Pct	Pts	OP
New England	13	3	0	.813	513	342
NY Jets	8	8	0	.500	377	363
Miami	6	10	0	.375	329	313
Buffalo	6	10	0	.375	372	434

AFC NORTH

	W	L	T	Pct	Pts	OP
Baltimore	12	4	0	.750	378	266
Pittsburgh	12	4	0	.750	325	227
Cincinnati	9	7	0	.563	344	323
Cleveland	4	12	0	.250	218	307

AFC SOUTH

	W	L	T	Pct	Pts	OP
Houston	10	6	0	.625	381	278
Tennessee	9	7	0	.563	325	317
Jacksonville	5	11	0	.313	243	329
Indianapolis	2	14	0	.125	243	430

AFC WEST

	W	L	T	Pct	Pts	OP
Denver	8	8	0	.500	309	390
San Diego	8	8	0	.500	406	377
Oakland	8	8	0	.500	359	433
Kansas City	7	9	0	.438	212	338

NFC EAST

	W	L	T	Pct	Pts	OP
NY Giants	9	7	0	.563	394	400
Philadelphia	8	8	0	.500	396	328
Dallas	8	8	0	.500	369	347
Washington	5	11	0	.313	288	367

2011 *(Cont.)*

NFC NORTH

	W	L	T	Pct	Pts	OP
Green Bay	15	1	0	.938	560	359
Detroit	10	6	0	.625	474	387
Chicago	8	8	0	.500	353	341
Minnesota	3	13	0	.188	340	449

NFC SOUTH

	W	L	T	Pct	Pts	OP
New Orleans	13	3	0	.813	547	339
Atlanta	10	6	0	.625	402	350
Carolina	6	10	0	.375	406	429
Tampa Bay	4	12	0	.250	287	494

NFC WEST

	W	L	T	Pct	Pts	OP
San Francisco	13	3	0	.813	380	229
Arizona	8	8	0	.500	312	348
Seattle	7	9	0	.438	321	315
St. Louis	2	14	0	.125	193	407

2012

AFC EAST

	W	L	T	Pct	Pts	OP
New England	12	4	0	.750	557	331
Miami	7	9	0	.438	288	317
NY Jets	6	10	0	.375	281	375
Buffalo	6	10	0	.375	344	435

AFC NORTH

	W	L	T	Pct	Pts	OP
Baltimore	10	6	0	.625	398	344
Cincinnati	10	6	0	.625	391	320
Pittsburgh	8	8	0	.500	336	314
Cleveland	5	11	0	.313	302	368

AFC SOUTH

	W	L	T	Pct	Pts	OP
Houston	12	4	0	.750	416	331
Indianapolis	11	5	0	.688	357	387
Tennessee	6	10	0	.375	330	471
Jacksonville	2	14	0	.125	255	444

AFC WEST

	W	L	T	Pct	Pts	OP
Denver	13	3	0	.813	481	289
San Diego	7	9	0	.438	350	350
Oakland	4	12	0	.250	290	443
Kansas City	2	14	0	.125	211	425

NFC EAST

	W	L	T	Pct	Pts	OP
Washington	10	6	0	.625	436	388
NY Giants	9	7	0	.563	429	344
Dallas	8	8	0	.500	376	400
Philadelphia	4	12	0	.250	280	444

NFC NORTH

	W	L	T	Pct	Pts	OP
Green Bay	11	5	0	.688	433	336
Minnesota	10	6	0	.625	379	348
Chicago	10	6	0	.625	375	277
Detroit	4	12	0	.250	372	437

NFC SOUTH

	W	L	T	Pct	Pts	OP
Atlanta	13	3	0	.813	419	299
Carolina	7	9	0	.438	357	363
New Orleans	7	9	0	.438	461	454
Tampa Bay	7	9	0	.438	389	394

NFC WEST

	W	L	T	Pct	Pts	OP
San Francisco	11	4	1	.719	397	273
Seattle	11	5	0	.688	412	245
St. Louis	7	8	1	.469	299	348
Arizona	5	11	0	.313	250	357

Results

	Date	Winner (Share)	Loser (Share)	Score	Site (Attendance)
I	1-15-67	Green Bay ($15,000)	Kansas City ($7,500)	35–10	Los Angeles (61,946)
II	1-14-68	Green Bay ($15,000)	Oakland ($7,500)	33–14	Miami (75,546)
III	1-12-69	NY Jets ($15,000)	Baltimore ($7,500)	16–7	Miami (75,389)
IV	1-11-70	Kansas City ($15,000)	Minnesota ($7,500)	23–7	New Orleans (80,562)
V	1-17-71	Baltimore ($15,000)	Dallas ($7,500)	16–13	Miami (79,204)
VI	1-16-72	Dallas ($15,000)	Miami ($7,500)	24–3	New Orleans (81,023)
VII	1-14-73	Miami ($15,000)	Washington ($7,500)	14–7	Los Angeles (90,182)
VIII	1-13-74	Miami ($15,000)	Minnesota ($7,500)	24–7	Houston (71,882)
IX	1-12-75	Pittsburgh ($15,000)	Minnesota ($7,500)	16–6	New Orleans (80,997)
X	1-18-76	Pittsburgh ($15,000)	Dallas ($7,500)	21–17	Miami (80,187)
XI	1-9-77	Oakland ($15,000)	Minnesota ($7,500)	32–14	Pasadena (103,438)
XII	1-15-78	Dallas ($18,000)	Denver ($9,000)	27–10	New Orleans (76,400)
XIII	1-21-79	Pittsburgh ($18,000)	Dallas ($9,000)	35–31	Miami (79,484)
XIV	1-20-80	Pittsburgh ($18,000)	Los Angeles ($9,000)	31–19	Pasadena (103,985)
XV	1-25-81	Oakland ($18,000)	Philadelphia ($9,000)	27–10	New Orleans (76,135)
XVI	1-24-82	San Francisco ($18,000)	Cincinnati ($9,000)	26–21	Pontiac, Mich. (81,270)
XVII	1-30-83	Washington ($36,000)	Miami ($18,000)	27–17	Pasadena (103,667)
XVIII	1-22-84	LA Raiders ($36,000)	Washington ($18,000)	38–9	Tampa (72,920)
XIX	1-20-85	San Francisco ($36,000)	Miami ($18,000)	38–16	Stanford, Calif. (84,059)
XX	1-26-86	Chicago ($36,000)	New England ($18,000)	46–10	New Orleans (73,818)
XXI	1-25-87	NY Giants ($36,000)	Denver ($18,000)	39–20	Pasadena (101,063)
XXII	1-31-88	Washington ($36,000)	Denver ($18,000)	42–10	San Diego (73,302)
XXIII	1-22-89	San Francisco ($36,000)	Cincinnati ($18,000)	20–16	Miami (75,129)
XXIV	1-28-90	San Francisco ($36,000)	Denver ($18,000)	55–10	New Orleans (72,919)
XXV	1-27-91	NY Giants ($36,000)	Buffalo ($18,000)	20–19	Tampa (73,813)
XXVI	1-26-92	Washington ($36,000)	Buffalo ($18,000)	37–24	Minneapolis (63,130)
XXVII	1-31-93	Dallas ($36,000)	Buffalo ($18,000)	52–17	Pasadena (98,374)
XXVIII	1-30-94	Dallas ($38,000)	Buffalo ($23,500)	30–13	Atlanta (72,817)
XXIX	1-29-95	San Francisco ($42,000)	San Diego ($26,000)	49–26	Miami (74,107)
XXX	1-28-96	Dallas ($42,000)	Pittsburgh ($27,000)	27–17	Tempe, Ariz. (76,347)
XXXI	1-26-97	Green Bay ($48,000)	New England ($29,000)	35–21	New Orleans (72,301)
XXXII	1-25-98	Denver ($48,000)	Green Bay ($29,000)	31–24	San Diego (68,912)
XXXIII	1-31-99	Denver ($53,000)	Atlanta ($32,500)	34–19	Miami (74,803)
XXXIV	1-30-00	St. Louis ($58,000)	Tennessee ($33,000)	23–16	Atlanta (72,625)
XXXV	1-28-01	Baltimore ($58,000)	NY Giants ($34,500)	34–7	Tampa (71,921)
XXXVI	2-3-02	New England ($63,000)	St. Louis ($34,500)	20–17	New Orleans (72,922)
XXXVII	1-26-03	Tampa Bay ($64,000)	Oakland ($35,000)	48–21	San Diego (67,603)
XXXVIII	2-1-04	New England ($64,000)	Carolina ($35,000)	32–29	Houston (71,525)
XXXIX	2-6-05	New England ($68,000)	Philadelphia ($36,500)	24–21	Jacksonville (78,125)
XL	2-5-06	Pittsburgh ($73,000)	Seattle ($38,000)	21–10	Detroit (68,206)
XLI	2-4-07	Indianapolis ($78,000)	Chicago ($40,000)	29–17	Miami (74,512)
XLII	2-3-08	NY Giants ($78,000)	New England ($40,000)	17–14	Glendale, Ariz. (71,101)
XLIII	2-1-09	Pittsburgh ($78,000)	Arizona ($40,000)	27–23	Tampa (70,774)
XLIV	2-7-10	New Orleans ($83,000)	Indianapolis ($42,000)	31–17	Miami (74,059)
XLV	2-6-11	Green Bay ($83,000)	Pittsburgh ($42,000)	31–25	Arlington, Tex. (103,219)
XLVI	2-5-12	NY Giants ($88,000)	New England ($44,000)	21–17	Indianapolis (68,658)
XLVVII	2-3-13	Baltimore Ravens ($88,000)	San Francisco ($44,000)	34–31	New Orleans (71,024)

Most Valuable Players

Super Bowl	Player/ Team	Position	Super Bowl	Player/ Team	Position
I	Bart Starr, GB	QB	XXI	Phil Simms, NYG	QB
II	Bart Starr, GB	QB	XXII	Doug Williams, Wash	QB
III	Joe Namath, NYJ	QB	XXIII	Jerry Rice, SF	WR
IV	Len Dawson, KC	QB	XXIV	Joe Montana, SF	QB
V	Chuck Howley, Dal	LB	XXV	Ottis Anderson, NYG	RB
VI	Roger Staubach, Dal	QB	XXVI	Mark Rypien, Wash	QB
VII	Jake Scott, Mia	S	XXVII	Troy Aikman, Dal	QB
VIII	Larry Csonka, Mia	RB	XXVIII	Emmitt Smith, Dal	RB
IX	Franco Harris, Pit	RB	XXIX	Steve Young, SF	QB
X	Lynn Swann, Pit	WR	XXX	Larry Brown, Dal	CB
XI	Fred Biletnikoff, Oak	WR	XXXI	Desmond Howard, GB	KR
XII	Randy White/Harvey Martin, Dal	DT/DE	XXXII	Terrell Davis, Den	RB
XIII, XIV	Terry Bradshaw, Pit	QB	XXXIII	John Elway, Den	QB
XV	Jim Plunkett, Oak	QB	XXXIV	Kurt Warner, StL	QB
XVI	Joe Montana, SF	QB	XXXV	Ray Lewis, Balt	LB
XVII	John Riggins, Wash	RB	XXXVI	Tom Brady, NE	QB
XVIII	Marcus Allen, LA Raiders	RB	XXXVII	Dexter Jackson, TB	S
XIX	Joe Montana, SF	QB	XXXVIII	Tom Brady, NE	QB
XX	Richard Dent, Chi	DE	XXXIX	Deion Branch, NE	WR

Most Valuable Players *(Cont.)*

Super Bowl	Player/ Team	Position	Super Bowl	Player/ Team	Position
XL	Hines Ward, Pit	WR	XLIV	Drew Brees, NO	QB
XLI	Peyton Manning, Ind	QB	XLV	Aaron Rodgers, GB	QB
XLII	Eli Manning, NYG	QB	XLVI	Eli Manning, NYG	QB
XLIII	Santonio Holmes, Pit	WR	XLVII	Joe Flacco, Bal	QB

Composite Standings, by Wins

	W	L	Pct	Pts	Opp Pts
Pittsburgh Steelers	6	2	.750	193	164
San Francisco 49ers	5	1	.833	219	123
Dallas Cowboys	5	3	.625	221	132
Green Bay Packers	4	1	.800	158	101
New York Giants	4	1	.800	104	104
Oakland/LA Raiders	3	2	.600	132	114
Washington Redskins	3	2	.600	122	103
New England Patriots	3	4	.429	138	186
Baltimore Ravens	2	0	1.000	68	38
Baltimore/Indianapolis Colts	2	2	.500	69	77
Miami Dolphins	2	3	.400	74	103
Denver Broncos	2	4	.333	115	206
Tampa Bay Buccaneers	1	0	1.000	48	21
New Orleans Saints	1	0	1.000	34	17
New York Jets	1	0	1.000	16	7
Chicago Bears	1	1	.500	63	39
Kansas City Chiefs	1	1	.500	33	42
Los Angeles/St. Louis Rams	1	2	.333	59	67
Carolina Panthers	0	1	.000	29	32
San Diego Chargers	0	1	.000	26	49
Arizona Cardinals	0	1	.000	23	27
Atlanta Falcons	0	1	.000	19	34
Tennessee Titans	0	1	.000	16	23
Seattle Seahawks	0	1	.000	10	21
Cincinnati Bengals	0	2	.000	37	46
Philadelphia Eagles	0	2	.000	31	51
Buffalo Bills	0	4	.000	73	139
Minnesota Vikings	0	4	.000	34	95

Career Leaders

Passing

	GP	Att	Comp	Pct Comp	Yds	Avg Gain/ Att	TD	Pct TD	Int	Pct Int	Lg	Rating Pts
Joe Montana, SF	4	122	83	68.0	1142	9.36	11	9.0	0	0.0	44	127.8
Jim Plunkett, Oak/LA Rai	2	46	29	63.0	433	9.41	4	8.7	0	0.0	t80	122.8
Terry Bradshaw, Pit	4	84	49	58.3	932	11.10	9	10.7	4	4.8	t75	112.8
Troy Aikman, Dal	3	80	56	70.0	689	8.61	5	6.3	1	1.3	t56	111.9
Bart Starr, GB	2	47	29	61.7	452	9.62	3	6.4	1	2.1	t62	106.0
Brett Favre, GB	2	69	39	56.5	502	7.28	5	7.2	1	1.4	t81	97.6
Roger Staubach, Dal	4	97	61	62.9	734	7.57	8	8.2	4	4.1	t45	96.3
Eli Manning, NY Giants	2	74	49	66.2	551	7.45	3	4.1	1	1.4	45	96.2
Kurt Warner, StL, Ari	3	133	83	62.4	1156	8.69	6	4.5	3	2.3	t73	95.9
Tom Brady, NE	5	197	127	64.5	1277	6.48	9	4.6	2	1.0	52	93.8
Peyton Manning, Ind	2	83	58	67.5	580	6.99	2	2.4	2	2.4	t53	85.4

Note: Minimum 40 attempts.

Rushing Yards

	GP	Yds	Att	Avg	Lg	TD
Franco Harris, Pit	4	354	101	3.5	25	4
Larry Csonka, Mia	3	297	57	5.2	49	2
Emmitt Smith, Dal	3	289	70	4.1	38	5
Terrell Davis, Den	2	259	55	4.7	27	3
John Riggins, Was	2	230	64	3.6	43	2
Timmy Smith, Was	1	204	22	9.3	58	2
Thurman Thomas, Buf	4	204	52	3.9	31	4
Roger Craig, SF	3	201	52	3.9	18	2
Marcus Allen, LA Rai	1	191	20	9.6	t74	2
Antowain Smith, NE	2	175	44	4.0	17	1

t-scored touchdown

Receptions

	GP	No.	Yds	Avg	Lg	TD
Jerry Rice, SF	4	33	589	17.9	t48	8
Andre Reed, Buf	4	27	323	12.0	40	0
Deion Branch, NE	3	24	321	13.4	52	1
Roger Craig, SF	3	20	212	10.6	40	2
Thurman Thomas, Buf	4	20	144	7.2	24	0
Wes Welker, NE	2	18	163	9.1	19	0
Jay Novacek, Dal	3	17	148	8.7	23	2
Joseph Addai, Ind	2	17	124	7.3	17	0
Lynn Swann, Pit	4	16	364	22.8	t74	3
Michael Irvin, Dal	3	16	256	16.0	25	2
Troy Brown, NE	3	16	182	11.4	23	0

Single-Game Leaders

Scoring

	Pts

Terrell Davis: XXXII, Denver vs Green Bay (3 rec)..18
Ricky Watters: XXIX, San Francisco vs San Diego
(1 rush, 2 rec) 18
Jerry Rice: XXIX, San Francisco vs San Diego (3
rec); XXIV, San Francisco vs Denver (3 rec) 18
Roger Craig: XIX, San Francisco vs Miami
(1 rush, 2 rec) 18

Rushing Yards

	Yds

Timmy Smith: XXII, Washington vs Denver...........204
Marcus Allen: XVIII, LA Raiders vs Washington....191
John Riggins: XVII, Washington vs Miami 166
Franco Harris: IX, Pittsburgh vs Minnesota 158
Terrell Davis: XXXII, Denver vs Green Bay.............157
Larry Csonka: VIII, Miami vs Minnesota 145
Clarence Davis: XI, Oakland vs Minnesota 137
Thurman Thomas: XXV, Buffalo vs NY Giants 135
Emmitt Smith: XXVIII, Dallas vs Buffalo 132
Michael Pittman: XXXVII, Tampa Bay vs Oakland 124

Receptions

	No.

Wes Welker: XLII, New England vs NY Giants 11
Deion Branch: XXXIX, New England vs Phila. 11
Jerry Rice: XXIII, San Francisco vs Cincinnati........11
Dan Ross: XVI, Cincinnati vs San Francisco 11
Hakeem Nicks, XLVI, NY Giants vs. New England .10
Joseph Addai: XLI, Indianapolis vs Chicago...........10
Deion Branch: XXXVIII, New England vs Carolina ..10
Andre Hastings: XXX, Pittsburgh vs Dallas 10
Jerry Rice: XXIX, San Francisco vs San Diego........10
Tony Nathan: XIX, Miami vs San Francisco.............10

Touchdown Passes

	No.

Steve Young: XXIX, San Francisco vs San Diego 6
Joe Montana: XXIV, San Francisco vs Denver 5
Troy Aikman: XXVII, Dallas vs Buffalo 4
Doug Williams: XXII, Washington vs Denver 4
Terry Bradshaw: XIII, Pittsburgh vs Dallas 4
Nine tied with three.

Passing Yards

	Yds

Kurt Warner: XXXIV, St. Louis vs Tennessee.........414
Kurt Warner: XLIII, Arizona vs Pittsburgh 377
Kurt Warner: XXXVI, St. Louis vs New England.....365
Donovan McNabb, XXXIX, Phila. vs. New England..357
Joe Montana: XXIII, San Francisco vs Cincinnati..357
Tom Brady: XXXVIII, New England vs Carolina.....354
Doug Williams: XXII, Washington vs Denver 340
John Elway: XXXIII, Denver vs Atlanta...................336
Peyton Manning: XLIV, Indianapolis vs New Orl'ns .333
Joe Montana: XIX, San Francisco vs Miami...........331
Steve Young: XXIX, San Francisco vs San Diego .325
Jake Delhomme: XXXVIII Carolina vs New England..323
Dan Marino: XIX, Miami vs San Francisco..............318
Terry Bradshaw: XIII, Pittsburgh vs Dallas 318

Receiving Yards

	Yds

Jerry Rice: XXIII, San Francisco vs Cincinnati.......215
Ricky Sanders: XXII, Washington vs Denver 193
Isaac Bruce: XXXIV, St. Louis vs Tennessee.........162
Lynn Swann: X, Pittsburgh vs Dallas 161
Andre Reed: XXVII, Buffalo vs Dallas 152
Rod Smith: XXXIII, Denver vs Atlanta 152
Jerry Rice: XXIX, San Francisco vs San Diego 149
Jerry Rice: XXIV, San Francisco vs Denver...........148
Deion Branch: XXXVIII, New England vs Carolina ..143

Super Bowl History Recaps*

I - 1967

Green Bay	7	7	14	7—35
Kansas City	0	10	0	0—10

FIRST QUARTER: GB: McGee 37 pass from Starr
(Chandler kick), 8:56. **Green Bay 7–0.**
SECOND QUARTER: KC: McClinton 7 pass from Dawson
(Mercer kick), 4:20. **7-7.**
GB: Taylor 14 run (Chandler kick), 10:23. **Green Bay
14–7.**
KC: FG Mercer 31, 14:06. **Green Bay 14–10.**
THIRD QUARTER: GB: Pitts 5 run (Chandler kick), 2:27.
Green Bay 21–10.
GB: McGee 13 pass from Starr (Chandler kick),
14:09. **Green Bay 28–10.**
FOURTH QUARTER: GB: Pitts 1 run (Chandler kick), 8:25.
Green Bay 35–10.
A: 61,946.

II - 1968

Green Bay	3	13	10	7—33
Oakland	0	7	0	7—14

FIRST QUARTER: GB: FG Chandler 39 5:07.
Green Bay 3–0.
SECOND QUARTER: GB: FG Chandler, 20, 3:08.
Green Bay 6–0.
GB: Dowler 62 pass from Starr (Chandler kick), 4:10.
Green Bay 13–0.
Oak: Miller 23 pass from Lamonica (Blanda kick),
8:45. **Green Bay 13–7.**
GB: FG Chandler 43, 14:59. **Green Bay 16–7.**
THIRD QUARTER: GB: Anderson 2 run (Chandler kick),
9:06. **Green Bay 23–7.**
GB: FG Chandler 31, 14:58. **Green Bay 26–7.**
FOURTH QUARTER:
GB: Adderley 60 int return (Chandler kick), 3:57.
Green Bay 33–7.
Oak: Miller 23 pass from Lamonica (Blanda kick),
5:47. **Green Bay 33–14.**
A: 75,546.

*From 1967 to 1999, Super Bowl scoring times indicate the time elapsed in each quarter. Starting in 2000, times
listed give the time remaining in each quarter.

III - 1969

NY Jets	0	7	6	3—16
Baltimore	0	0	0	7—7

SECOND QUARTER: Jets: Snell 4 run (Turner kick), 5:57. **Jets: 7-0.**

THIRD QUARTER: Jets: FG Turner 32, 4:52. **Jets: 10-0.** Jets: FG Turner 30, 11:02. **Jets: 13-0.**

FOURTH QUARTER: Jets: FG Turner 9, 1:34. **Jets: 16-0.** Balt: Hill 1 run (Michaels kick), 11:41. **Jets: 16-7.** A: 75,389.

IV - 1970

Kansas City	3	13	7	0—23
Minnesota	0	0	7	0—7

FIRST QUARTER: KC: FG Stenerud 48, 8:08. **Kansas City 3-0.**

SECOND QUARTER: KC: FG Stenerud 32, 1:40. **Kansas City 6-0.** KC: FG Stenerud 25, 7:08. **Kansas City 9-0.** KC: Garrett 5 run (Stenerud kick), 9:26. **Kansas City 16-0.**

THIRD QUARTER: Minn: Osborn 4 run (Cox kick), 10:28. **Kansas City 16-7.** KC: Taylor 46 pass from Dawson (Stenerud kick), 13:38. **Kansas City 23-7.** A: 80,562.

V - 1971

Baltimore	0	6	0	10—16
Dallas	3	10	0	0—13

FIRST QUARTER: Dal: FG Clark 14, 9:28. **Dallas 3-0.**

SECOND QUARTER: Dal: FG Clark 30, 0:08. **Dallas 6-0.** Balt: Mackey 75 pass from Unitas (kick blocked). 0:50. **6-6.** Dal: Thomas 7 pass from Morton (Clark kick), 7:07. **Dallas 13-6.**

FOURTH QUARTER: Balt: Nowatzke 2 run (O'Brien kick), 7:25. **13-13.** Balt: FG O'Brien 32, 14:55. **Baltimore 16-13.** A: 79,204.

VI - 1972

Dallas	3	7	7	7—24
Miami	0	3	0	0—3

FIRST QUARTER: Dal: FG Clark 9, 13:37. **Dallas 3-0.**

SECOND QUARTER: Dal: Alworth 7 pass from Staubach (Clark kick), 13:45. **Dallas 10-0.** Mia: FG Yepremian, 31, 14:56. **Dallas 10-3.**

THIRD QUARTER: Dal: D. Thomas 3 run (Clark kick), 5:17. **Dallas 17-3.**

FOURTH QUARTER: Dal: Ditka 7 pass from Staubach (Clark kick), 3:18. **Dallas 24-3.** A: 81,023.

VII - 1973

Miami	7	7	0	0—14
Washington	0	0	0	7—7

FIRST QUARTER: Mia: Twilley 28 pass from Griese (Yepremian kick), 14:59. **Miami 7-0.**

SECOND QUARTER: Mia: Kiick 1 run (Yepremian kick), 14:42. **Miami 14-0.**

FOURTH QUARTER: Wash: Bass 49 fumble recovery return (Knight kick), 12:53. **Miami 14-7.** A: 90,182.

VIII - 1974

Miami	14	3	7	0—24
Minnesota	0	0	0	7—7

FIRST QUARTER: Mia: Csonka 5 run (Yepremian kick), 5:27. **Miami 7-0.** Mia: Kiick 1 run (Yepremian kick), 13:38. **Miami 14-0.**

SECOND QUARTER: Mia: FG Yepremian 28, 8:58. **Miami 17-0.**

THIRD QUARTER: Mia: Csonka 2 run (Yepremian kick), 6:16. **Miami 24-0.**

FOURTH QUARTER: Minn: Tarkenton 4 run (Cox kick), 1:35. **Miami 24-7.** A: 71,882.

IX - 1975

Pittsburgh	0	2	7	7—16
Minnesota	0	0	0	6—6

SECOND QUARTER: Pit: White tackled Tarkenton for safety, 7:49. **Pittsburgh 2-0.**

THIRD QUARTER: Pit: Harris 9 run (Gerela kick), 1:35. **Pittsburgh 9-0.**

FOURTH QUARTER: Minn: T. Brown recovered blocked punt in end zone (kick failed), 4:27. **Pittsburgh 9-6.** Pit: L. Brown 4 pass from Bradshaw (Gerela kick), 11:29. **Pittsburgh 16-6.** A: 80,997.

X - 1976

Pittsburgh	7	0	0	14—21
Dallas	7	3	0	7—17

FIRST QUARTER: Dal: D. Pearson 29 pass from Staubach (Fritsch kick), 4:36. **Dallas 7-0.** Pit: Grossman 7 pass from Bradshaw (Gerela kick), 9:03. **7-7.**

SECOND QUARTER: Dal: FG Fritsch 36, 0:15. **Dallas 10-7.**

FOURTH QUARTER: Pit: Harrison blocked Hoopes's punt for safety, 3:32. **Dallas 10-9.** Pit: FG Gerela 36, 6:19. **Pittsburgh 12-10.** Pit: FG Gerela 18, 8:32. **Pittsburgh 15-10.** Pit: Swann 64 pass from Bradshaw (kick failed), 11:58. **Pittsburgh 21-10.** Dal: P. Howard 34 pass from Staubach (Fritsch kick), 13:12. **Pittsburgh 21-17.** A: 80,187.

XI - 1977

Oakland	0	16	3	13—32
Minnesota	0	0	7	7—14

SECOND QUARTER: Oak: FG Mann, 24, 0:48. **Oakland 3-0.** Oak: Casper 1 pass from Stabler (Mann kick), 7:50. **Oakland 10-0.** Oak: Banaszak 1 run (kick failed), 11:27. **Oakland 16-0.**

THIRD QUARTER: Oak: FG Mann, 40, 9:44. **Oakland 19-0.** Min: S. White 8 pass from Tarkenton (Cox kick), 14:13. **Oakland 19-7.**

FOURTH QUARTER: Oak: Banaszak 2 run (Mann kick), 7:21. **Oakland 26-7.** Oak: Brown 75 int return (kick failed), 9:17. **Oakland 32-7.** Min: Voigt 13 pass from Lee (Cox kick), 14:35. **Oakland 32-14.** A: 103,438.

XII - 1978

Dallas	10	3	7	7—27
Denver	0	0	10	0—10

FIRST QUARTER: Dal: Dorsett 3 run (Herrera kick), 10:31. **Dallas 7-0.**
Dal: FG Herrera 35, 13:29. **Dallas 10-0.**

SECOND QUARTER: Dal: FG Herrera 43, 3:44. **Dallas 13-0.**

THIRD QUARTER: Den: FG Turner 47, 2:28. **Dallas 13-3.**
Dal: Johnson 45 pass from Staubach (Herrera kick), 8:01. **Dallas 20-3.**
Den: Lytle 1 run (Turner kick), 9:21. **Dallas 20-10.**

FOURTH QUARTER: Dal: Richards 29 pass from Newhouse (Herrera kick), 7:56. **Dallas 27-10.**
A: 76,400.

XIII - 1979

Pittsburgh	7	14	0	14—35
Dallas	7	7	3	14—31

FIRST QUARTER: Pit: Stallworth 28 pass from Bradshaw (Gerela kick), 5:13. **Pittsburgh 7-0.**
Dal: Hill 39 pass from Staubach (Septien kick), 15:00. **7-7.**

SECOND QUARTER: Dal: Hegman 37 fumble recovery return (Septien kick), 2:52. **Dallas 14-7.**
Pit: Stallworth 75 pass from Bradshaw (Gerela kick), 4:35. **14-14.**
Pit: Bleier 7 pass from Bradshaw (Gerela kick), 14:34. **Pittsburgh 21-14.**

THIRD QUARTER: Dal: FG Septien 27, 12:24. **Pittsburgh 21-17.**

FOURTH QUARTER: Pit: Harris 22 run (Gerela kick), 7:50. **Pittsburgh 28-17.**
Pit: Swann 18 pass from Bradshaw (Gerela kick), 8:09. **Pittsburgh 35-17.**
Dal: DuPree 7 pass from Staubach (Septien kick), 12:33. **Pittsburgh 35-24.**
Dal: B. Johnson 4 pass from Staubach (Septien kick), 14:38. **Pittsburgh 35-31.**
A: 79,484.

XIV - 1980

Pittsburgh	3	7	7	14—31
LA Rams	7	6	6	0—19

FIRST QUARTER: Pit: FG Bahr, 41, 7:29. **Pittsburgh 3-0.**
LA: Bryant 1 run (Corral kick), 12:16. **LA Rams 7-3.**

SECOND QUARTER: Pit: Harris 1 run (Bahr kick), 2:08. **Pittsburgh 10-7.**
LA: FG Corral 31, 7:39. **10-10.**
LA: FG Corral 45, 14:46. **LA Rams 13-10.**

THIRD QUARTER: Pit: Swann 47 pass from Bradshaw (Bahr kick), 2:48. **Pittsburgh 17-13.**
LA: Smith 24 pass from McCutcheon (kick failed), 4:45. **LA Rams 19-17.**

FOURTH QUARTER: Pit: Stallworth 73 pass from Bradshaw (Bahr kick), 2:56. **Pittsburgh 24-19.**
Pit: Harris 1 run (Bahr kick), 13:11. **Pittsburgh 31-19.**
A: 103,985.

XV - 1981

Oakland	14	0	10	3—27
Philadelphia	0	3	0	7—10

FIRST QUARTER: Oak: Branch 2 pass from Plunkett (Bahr kick), 6:04. **Oakland 7-0.**
Oak: King 80 pass from Plunkett (Bahr kick), 14:51. **Oakland 14-0.**

SECOND QUARTER: Phi: FG Franklin 30, 4:32. **Oakland 14-3.**

THIRD QUARTER: Oak: Branch 29 pass from Plunkett (Bahr kick), 2:36. **Oakland 21-3.**
Oak: FG Bahr 46, 10:25. **Oakland 24-3.**

FOURTH QUARTER: Phi: Krepfle 8 pass from Jaworski (Franklin kick), 1:01. **Oakland 24-10.**
Oak: FG Bahr, 35, 6:31. **Oakland 27-10.**
A: 76,135.

XVI - 1982

San Francisco	7	13	0	6—26
Cincinnati	0	0	7	14—21

FIRST QUARTER: SF: Montana 1 run (Wersching kick), 9:08. **San Francisco 7-0.**

SECOND QUARTER: SF: E. Cooper 11 pass from Montana (Wersching kick), 8:07. **San Francisco 14-0.**
SF: FG Wersching 22, 14:45. **San Francisco 17-0.**
SF: FG Wersching 26, 14:58. **San Francisco 20-0.**

THIRD QUARTER: Cin: Anderson 5 run (Breech kick), 3:35. **San Francisco 20-7.**

FOURTH QUARTER: Cin: Ross 4 pass from Anderson (Breech kick), 4:54. **San Francisco 20-14.**
SF: FG Wersching 40, 9:35. **San Francisco 23-14.**
SF: FG Wersching 23, 13:03. **San Francisco 26-14.**
Cin: Ross 3 pass from Anderson (Breech kick), 14:44. **San Francisco 26-21.**
A: 81,270.

XVII - 1983

Washington	0	10	3	14—27
Miami	7	10	0	0—17

FIRST QUARTER: Mia: Cefalo 76 pass from Woodley (Von Schamann kick), 6:49. **Miami 7-0.**

SECOND QUARTER: Wash: FG Moseley 31, 0:21. **Miami 7-3.**
Mia: FG Von Schamann 20, 9:00. **Miami 10-3.**
Wash: Garrett 4 pass from Theismann (Moseley kick), 13:09. **10-10.**
Mia: Walker 98 kick return (Von Schamann kick), 13:22. **Miami 17-10.**

THIRD QUARTER: Wash: FG Moseley 20, 6:51. **Miami 17-13.**

FOURTH QUARTER: Wash: Riggins 43 run (Moseley kick), 4:59. **Washington 20-17.**
Wash: Brown 6 pass from Theismann (Moseley kick), 13:05. **Washington 27-17.**
A: 103,667.

XVIII - 1984

LA Raiders	7	14	14	3—38
Washington	0	3	6	0—9

FIRST QUARTER: LA: Jensen 0 blocked punt return (Bahr kick), 4:52. **LA Raiders 7-0.**

SECOND QUARTER: LA: Branch 12 pass from Plunkett (Bahr kick), 5:46. **LA Raiders 14-0.**
Wash: FG Moseley 24, 11:55. **LA Raiders 14-3.**
LA: Squirek 5 int return (Bahr kick), 14:53.
LA Raiders 21-3.

THIRD QUARTER: Wash: Riggins 1 run (kick blocked), 4:08. **LA Raiders 21-9.**
LA: Allen 5 run (Bahr kick), 7:54. **LA Raiders 28-9.**
LA: Allen 74 run (Bahr kick), 15:00. **LA Raiders 35-9.**

FOURTH QUARTER: LA: FG Bahr 21, 12:36.
LA Raiders 38-9.
A: 72,920.

XIX - 1985

San Francisco	7	21	10	0—38
Miami	10	6	0	0—16

FIRST QUARTER: Mia: FG Von Schamann 37, 7:36.
Miami 3-0.
SF: Monroe 33 pass from Montana (Wersching kick), 11:48. **San Francisco 7-3.**
Mia: D. Johnson 2 pass from Marino (Von Schamann kick), 14:15. **Miami 10-7.**

SECOND QUARTER: SF: Craig 8 pass from Montana (Wersching kick), 3:26. **San Francisco 14-10.**
SF: Montana 6 run (Wersching kick), 8:02.
San Francisco 21-10.
SF: Craig 2 run (Wersching kick), 12:55.
San Francisco 28-10.
Mia: FG Von Schamann 31, 14:48.
San Francisco 28-13.
Mia: FG Von Schamann 30, 15:00.
San Francisco 28-16.

THIRD QUARTER: SF: FG Wersching 27, 4:48.
San Francisco 31-16.
SF: Craig 16 pass from Montana (Wersching kick), 8:42. **San Francisco 38-16.**
A: 84,059.

XX - 1986

Chicago	13	10	21	2—46
New England	3	0	0	7—10

FIRST QUARTER: NE: FG Franklin 36, 1:19.
New England 3-0.
Chi: FG Butler 28, 5:40. **3-3.**
Chi: FG Butler 24, 13:34. **Chicago 6-3.**
Chi: Suhey 11 run (Butler kick), 14:37. **Chicago 13-3.**

SECOND QUARTER: Chi: McMahon 2 run (Butler kick), 7:36. **Chicago 20-3.**
Chi: FG Butler 24, 15:00. **Chicago 23-3.**

THIRD QUARTER: Chi: McMahon 1 run (Butler kick), 7:38.
Chicago 30-3.
Chi: Phillips 28 int return (Butler kick), 8:44. **Chicago 37-3.**
Chi: Perry 1 run (Butler kick), 11:38. **Chicago 44-3.**

FOURTH QUARTER: NE: Fryar 8 pass from Grogan (Franklin kick), 1:46. **Chicago 44-10.**
Chi: Waechter safety, 9:24. **Chicago 46-10.**
A: 73,818.

XXI - 1987

NY Giants	7	2	17	13—39
Denver	10	0	0	10—20

FIRST QUARTER: Den: FG Karlis 48, 4:09. **Denver 3-0.**
NYG: Mowatt 6 pass from Simms (Allegre kick), 9:33.
NY Giants 7-3.
Den: Elway 4 run (Karlis kick), 12:54. **Denver 10-7.**

SECOND QUARTER: NYG: Martin safety, 12:14.
Denver 10-9.

THIRD QUARTER: NYG: Bavaro 13 pass from Simms (Allegre kick), 4:52. **NY Giants 16-10.**
NYG: FG Allegre 21, 11:06. **NY Giants 19-10.**
NYG: Morris 1 run (Allegre kick), 14:36.
NY Giants 26-10.

FOURTH QUARTER: NYG: McConkey 6 pass from Simms (Allegre kick), 4:04. **NY Giants 33-10.**
Den: FG Karlis 28, 8:59. **NY Giants 33-13.**
NYG: Anderson 2 run (kick failed), 11:42.
NY Giants 39-13.
Den: Johnson 47 pass from Elway (Karlis kick), 12:54. **NY Giants 39-20.**
A: 101,063.

XXII - 1988

Washington	0	35	0	7—42
Denver	10	0	0	0—10

FIRST QUARTER: Den: Nattiel 56 pass from Elway (Karlis kick), 1:57. **Denver 7-0.**
Den: FG Karlis 24, 5:51. **Denver 10-0.**

SECOND QUARTER: Wash: Sanders 80 pass from D. Williams (Haji-Sheikh kick), 0:53. **Denver 10-7.**
Wash: Clark 27 pass from D. Williams (Haji-Sheikh kick), 4:45. **Washington 14-10.**
Wash: Smith 58 run (Haji-Sheikh kick), 8:33.
Washington 21-10.
Wash: Sanders 50 pass from D. Williams (Haji-Sheikh kick), 11:18. **Washington 28-10.**
Wash: Didier 8 pass from D. Williams (Haji-Sheikh kick), 13:56. **Washington 35-10.**

FOURTH QUARTER: Wash: Smith 4 run (Haji-Sheikh kick), 1:51. **Washington 42-10.**

A: 73,302.

XXIII - 1989

San Francisco	3	0	3	14—20
Cincinnati	0	3	10	3—16

FIRST QUARTER: SF: FG Cofer 41, 11:46.
San Francisco 3-0.

SECOND QUARTER: Cin: FG Breech 34, 13:41. **3-3.**

THIRD QUARTER: Cin: FG Breech 43, 9:15.
Cincinnati 6-3.
SF: FG Cofer 32, 14:10. **6-6.**
Cin: Jennings 93 kick return (Breech kick), 14:26.
Cincinnati 13-6.

FOURTH QUARTER: SF: Rice 14 pass from Montana (Cofer kick), 0:57. **13-13.**
Cin: FG Breech 40, 11:40. **Cincinnati 16-13.**
SF: Taylor 10 pass from Montana (Cofer kick), 14:26.
San Francisco 20-16.
A: 75,129.

XXIV - 1990

San Francisco	13	14	14	14—55
Denver	3	0	7	0—10

FIRST QUARTER: SF: Rice 20 pass from Montana (Cofer kick), 4:54. **San Francisco 7-0.**
Den: FG Treadwell 42, 8:13. **San Francisco 7-3.**
SF: Jones 7 pass from Montana (kick failed), 14:57. **San Francisco 13-3.**

SECOND QUARTER: SF: Rathman 1 run (Cofer kick), 7:45. **San Francisco 20-3.**
SF: Rice 38 pass from Montana (Cofer kick), 14:26. **San Francisco 27-3.**

THIRD QUARTER: SF: Rice 28 pass from Montana (Cofer kick), 2:12. **San Francisco 34-3.**
SF: Taylor 35 pass from Montana (Cofer kick), 5:16. **San Francisco 41-3.**
Den: Elway 3 run (Treadwell kick), 8:07. **San Francisco 41-10.**

FOURTH QUARTER: SF: Rathman 3 run (Cofer kick), 0:03. **San Francisco 48-10.**
SF: Craig 1 run (Cofer kick), 1:13. **San Francisco 55-10.**
A: 72,919.

XXV - 1991

NY Giants	3	7	7	3—20
Buffalo	3	9	0	7—19

FIRST QUARTER: NYG: FG Bahr 28, 7:46. **NY Giants 3-0.**
Buff: FG Norwood 23, 9:09. **3-3.**

SECOND QUARTER: Buff: D. Smith 1 run (Norwood kick), 2:30. **Buffalo 10-3.**
Buff: B. Smith safety 0, 6:33. **Buffalo 12-3.**
NYG: Baker 14 pass from Hostetler (Bahr kick), 14:35. **Buffalo 12-10.**

THIRD QUARTER: NYG: Anderson 1 run (Bahr kick), 9:29. **NY Giants 17-12.**

FOURTH QUARTER: Buff: Thomas 31 run (Norwood kick), 0:08. **Buffalo 19-17.**
NYG: FG Bahr 21, 7:40. **NY Giants 20-19.**
A: 73,813.

XXVI - 1992

Washington	0	17	14	6—37
Buffalo	0	0	10	14—24

SECOND QUARTER: Wash: FG Lohmiller 34, 1:58. **Washington 3-0.**
Wash: Byner 10 pass from Rypien (Lohmiller kick), 5:06. **Washington 10-0.**
Wash: Riggs 1 run (Lohmiller kick), 7:43. **Washington 17-0.**

THIRD QUARTER: Wash: Riggs 2 run (Lohmiller kick), 0:16. **Washington 24-0.**
Buff: FG Norwood 21, 3:01. **Washington 24-3.**
Buff: Thomas 1 run (Norwood kick), 9:02. **Washington 24-10.**
Wash: Clark 30 pass from Rypien (Lohmiller kick), 13:36. **Washington 31-10.**

FOURTH QUARTER: Wash: FG Lohmiller 25, 0:06. **Washington 34-10.**
Wash: FG Lohmiller 39, 3:24. **Washington 37-10.**
Buff: Metzelaars 2 pass from Kelly (Norwood kick), 9:01. **Washington 37-17.**
Buff: Beebe 4 pass from Kelly (Norwood kick), 11:05. **Washington 37-24.**
A: 63,130.

XXVII - 1993

Dallas	14	14	3	21—52
Buffalo	7	3	7	0—17

FIRST QUARTER: Buff: Thomas 2 run (Christie kick), 5:00. **Buffalo 7-0.**
Dal: Novacek 23 pass from Aikman (Elliott kick), 13:24. **7-7.**
Dal: J.Jones 2 fumble return (Elliott kick), 13:39. **Dallas 14-7.**

SECOND QUARTER: Buff: FG Christie 21, 11:36. **Dallas 14-10.**
Dal: Irvin 19 pass from Aikman (Elliott kick), 13:06. **Dallas 21-10.**
Dal: Irvin 18 pass from Aikman (Elliott kick), 13:24. **Dallas 28-10.**

THIRD QUARTER: Dal: FG Elliott 20, 6:39. **Dallas 31-10.**
Buff: Beebe 40 pass from Reich (Christie kick), 15:00. **Dallas 31-17.**

FOURTH QUARTER: Dal: Harper 45 pass from Aikman (Elliott kick), 4:56. **Dallas 38-17.**
Dal: E. Smith 10 run (Elliott kick), 6:48. **Dallas 45-17.**
Dal: Norton 9 fumble return (Elliott kick), 7:29. **Dallas 52-17.**
A: 98,374.

XXVIII - 1994

Dallas	6	0	14	10—30
Buffalo	3	10	0	0—13

FIRST QUARTER: Dal: FG Murray 41, 2:19. **Dallas 3-0.**
Buff: FG Christie 54: 4:41. **3-3.**
Dal: FG Murray 24, 11:05. **Dallas 6-3.**

SECOND QUARTER: Buff: Thomas 4 run (Christie kick), 2:34. **Buffalo 10-6.**
Buff: FG Christie 28, 15:00. **Buffalo 13-6.**

THIRD QUARTER: Dal: Washington fumble return (Murray kick), 0:55. **13-13.**
Dal: Smith15 run (Murray kick), 0:55. **Dallas 20-13.**

FOURTH QUARTER: Dal: Smith1 run (Murray kick), 5:10. **Dallas 27-13.**
Dal: FG Murray 20, 12:10. **Dallas 30-13.**
A: 72,817.

XXIX - 1995

San Francisco	14	14	14	7—49
San Diego	7	3	8	8—26

FIRST QUARTER: SF: Rice 44 pass from Young (Brien kick), 1:24. **San Francisco 7-0.**
SF: Watters 51 pass from Young (Brien kick, 4:55. **San Francisco 14-0.**
SD: Means 1 run (Carney kick), 12:16. **San Francisco 14-7.**

SECOND QUARTER: SF: Floyd 5 pass from Young (Brien kick), 1:58. **San Francisco 21-7.**
SF: Watters 8 pass from Young (Brien kick), 10:16. **San Francisco 28-7.**
SD: FG Carney 31, 13:16. **San Francisco 28-10.**

THIRD QUARTER: SF: Watters 9 run (Brien kick), 5:25. **San Francisco 35-10.**
SF: Rice 15 pass from Young (Brien kick), 11:42. **San Francisco 42-10.**

XXIX - 1995 *(Cont.)*

THIRD QUARTER *(CONT.)*: SD: Coleman 98 kickoff return (Humphries 2-pt conv pass to Seay), 11:59. **San Francisco 42–18.**
FOURTH QUARTER: SF: Rice 7 pass from Young (Brien kick), 1:11. **San Francisco 49–18.**
SD: Martin 30 pass from Humphries (Humphries 2-pt conv pass to Pupunu), 12:35. **San Francisco 49–26.**
A: 74,107.

XXX - 1996

Dallas	10	3	7	7—27
Pittsburgh	0	7	0	10—17

FIRST QUARTER: Dal: FG Boniol 42, 2:55. **Dallas 3–0.**
Dal: Novacek 3 pass from Aikman (Boniol kick), 9:37. **Dallas 10–0.**

SECOND QUARTER: Dal: FG Boniol 35, 8:57. **Dallas 13–0.**
Pit: Thigpen 6 pass from O'Donnell (N. Johnson kick), 14:47. **Dallas 13–7.**

THIRD QUARTER: Dal: E. Smith 1 run (Boniol kick), 8:18. **Dallas 20–7.**
FOURTH QUARTER: Pit: FG N. Johnson 46, 3:40. **Dallas 20–10.**
Pit: Morris 1 run (N. Johnson kick), 8:24. **Dallas 20–17.**
Dal: E. Smith 4 run (Boniol kick), 11:17. **Dallas 27–17.**
A: 76,347.

XXXI - 1997

Green Bay	10	17	8	0—35
New England	14	0	7	0—21

FIRST QUARTER: GB: Rison 54 pass from Favre (Jacke kick), 3:32. **Green Bay 7–0.**
GB: FG Jacke 37, 6:18. **Green Bay 10–0.**
NE: Byars 1 pass from Bledsoe (Vinatieri kick), 8:25. **Green Bay 10–7.**
NE: Coates 4 pass from Bledsoe (Vinatieri kick), 12:27. **New England 14–10.**

SECOND QUARTER: GB: Freeman 81 pass from Favre (Jacke kick), 0:56. **Green Bay 17–14.**
GB: FG Jacke 31, 6:45. **Green Bay 20–14.**
GB: Favre 2 run (Jacke kick), 13:49. **Green Bay 27–14.**

THIRD QUARTER: NE: Martin 18 run (Vinatieri kick), 11:33. **Green Bay 27–21.**
GB: Howard 99 kickoff return (Favre 2 pt conv pass to Chmura), 11:50. **Green Bay 35–21.**
A: 72,301.

XXXII - 1998

Denver	7	10	7	7—31
Green Bay	7	7	3	7—24

FIRST QUARTER: GB: Freeman 22 pass from Favre (Longwell kick), 4:02. **Green Bay 7–0.**
Den: Davis 1 run (Elam kick), 9:21. **7–7.**

SECOND QUARTER: Den: Elway 1 run (Elam kick), 0:05. **Denver 14–7.**
Den: FG Elam 51, 2:39. **Denver 17–7.**
GB: Chmura 6 pass from Favre (Longwell kick), 14:48. **Denver 17–14.**

XXXII - 1998 *(Cont.)*

THIRD QUARTER: GB: FG Longwell 27, 3:01. **17–17.**
Den: Davis 1 run (Elam kick), 14:26. **Denver 24–17.**
FOURTH QUARTER: GB: Freeman 13 pass from Favre (Longwell kick), 1:28. **24–24.**
Den: Davis 1 run (Elam kick), 13:15. **Denver 31–24.**
A: 68,912.

XXXIII - 1999

Denver	7	10	0	17—34
Atlanta	3	3	0	13—19

FIRST QUARTER: Atl: FG Andersen 32, 5:25. **Atlanta 3–0.**
Den: Griffith 1 run (Elam kick), 11:05. **Denver 7–3.**

SECOND QUARTER: Den: FG Elam 26, 5:43. **Denver 10–3.**
Den: Smith 80 pass from Elway (Elam kick), 10:06. **Denver 17–3.**
Atl: FG Andersen 28, 12:35. **Denver 17–6.**

FOURTH QUARTER: Den: Griffith 1 run (Elam kick), 0:04. **Denver 24–6.**
Den: Elway 3 run (Elam kick), 3:40. **Denver 31–6.**
Atl: Dwight 94 kickoff return (Andersen kick), 3:59. **Denver 31–13.**
Den: FG Elam 37, 7:52. **Denver 34–13.**
Atl: Mathis 3 pass from Chandler (2-pt conv failed), 12:56. **Denver 34–19.**
A: 74,803.

XXXIV - 2000

St. Louis	3	6	7	7—23
Tennessee	0	0	6	10—16

FIRST QUARTER: StL: FG Wilkins 27, 3:00. **St. Louis 3–0.**

SECOND QUARTER: StL: FG Wilkins 29, 4:16. **St. Louis 6–0.**
StL: FG Wilkins 28, 0:15. **St. Louis 9–0.**

THIRD QUARTER: StL: Holt 9 pass from Warner (Wilkins kick), 7:20. **St. Louis 16–0.**
Tenn: George 1 run (2-pt conv failed), 0:14. **St. Louis 16–6.**

FOURTH QUARTER: Tenn: George 2 run (Del Greco kick), 7:21. **St. Louis 16–13.**
Tenn: FG Del Greco 43, 2:15. **16–16.**
StL: Bruce 73 pass from Warner, 1:54. **St. Louis 23–16.**
A: 72,265.

XXXV - 2001

Baltimore	7	3	14	10—34
NY Giants	0	0	7	0—7

FIRST QUARTER: Balt: Stokely 38 pass from Dilfer (Stover kick), 6:50. **Baltimore 7–0.**

SECOND QUARTER: Balt: FG Stover 47, 1:41. **Baltimore 10–0.**

THIRD QUARTER: Balt: Starks 49 int return (Stover kick), 3:49. **Baltimore 17–0.**
NYG: Dixon 97 kickoff return (Daluiso kick), 3:31. **Baltimore 17–7.**
Balt: Je. Lewis 84 kickoff return (Stover kick), 3:13. **Baltimore 24–7.**

XXXV - 2001 *(Cont.)*

FOURTH QUARTER: Balt: Ja. Lewis 3 run (Stover kick), 8:45. **Baltimore 31-7.**
Balt: FG Stover 34, 5:28. **Baltimore 34-7.**
A: 71,921.

XXXVI - 2002

New England	0	14	3	3—20
St. Louis	3	0	0	14—17

FIRST QUARTER: StL: FG Wilkins 50, 3:50. **St. Louis 3-0.**
SECOND QUARTER: NE: Law 47 int return (Vinatieri kick), 8:49. **New England 7-3.**
NE: Patten 8 pass from Brady (Vinatieri kick), 0:31. **New England 14-3.**
THIRD QUARTER: NE: FG Vinatieri 37, 1:18. **New Eng. 17-3.**
FOURTH QUARTER: StL: Warner 2 run (Wilkins kick), 9:31. **New England 17-10.**
StL: Proehl 26 pass from Warner (Wilkins kick), 1:30. **17-17.**
NE: FG Vinatieri 48, 0:00. **New England 20-17.**
A: 72,922.

XXXVII - 2003

Tampa Bay	3	17	14	14—48
Oakland	3	0	6	12—21

FIRST QUARTER: Oak: FG Janikowski 40, 10:20. **Oakland 3-0.**
TB: FG Gramatica 31, 7:51. **3-3.**
SECOND QUARTER: TB: FG Gramatica 43, 11:16. **Tampa Bay 6-3.**
TB: Alstott 2 run (Gramatica kick), 6:24. **Tampa Bay 13-3.**
TB: McCardell 5 pass from B. Johnson (Gramatica kick), 0:30. **Tampa Bay 20-3.**
THIRD QUARTER: TB: McCardell 8 pass from B. Johnson (Gramatica kick), 5:30. **Tampa Bay 27-3.**
TB: Smith 44 int. return (Gramatica kick), 4:47. **Tampa Bay 34-3.**
Oak: Porter 39 pass from Gannon (2-pt conv failed), 2:14. **Tampa Bay 34-9.**
FOURTH QUARTER: Oak: Johnson 13 return of blocked punt (2-pt. conversion failed), 14:14. **Tampa Bay 34-15.**
Oak: Rice 48 pass from Gannon (2-pt conv failed), 6:06. **Tampa Bay 34-21.**
TB: Brooks 44 int. return (Gramatica kick), 1:18. **Tampa Bay 41-21.**
TB: Smith 50 int. return (Gramatica kick), 0:02. **Tampa Bay 48-21.**
A: 67,603.

XXXVIII - 2004

New England	0	14	0	18—32
Carolina	0	10	0	19—29

SECOND QUARTER: NE: Branch 5 pass from Brady (Vinatieri kick), 3:11. **New England 7-0.**
Car: Smith 39 pass from Delhomme (Kasay kick), 1:17. **7-7.**
NE: Givens 5 pass from Brady (Vinatieri kick), 0:28. **New England 14-7.**
Car: FG Kasay 50, 0:00. **New England 14-10.**
FOURTH QUARTER: NE: Smith 2 run (Vinatieri kick), 14:49. **New England 21-10.**
Car: Foster 33 run (2-pt conv failed), 12:49. **New England 21-16.**

XXXVIII - 2004 *(Cont.)*

Car: Muhammad 85 pass from Delhomme (2-pt conv failed), 7:13. **Carolina 22-21.**
NE: Vrabel 1 pass from Brady (Faulk ran for 2-pt conv), 2:51. **New England 29-22.**
Car: Proehl 12 pass from Delhomme (Kasay kick), 1:18. **29-29.**
NE: FG Vinatieri 41, 0:04. **New England 32-29.**
A: 71,525.

XXXIX - 2005

New England	0	7	7	10—24
Philadelphia	0	7	7	7—21

SECOND QUARTER: Phil: Smith 6 pass from McNabb (Akers kick), 10:05. **Philadelphia 7-0.**
NE: Givens 4 pass from Brady (Vinatieri kick), 1:10. **7-7.**
THIRD QUARTER: NE: Vrabel 2 pass from Brady (Vinatieri kick), 11:04. **New England 14-7.**
Phil: Westbrook 10 pass from McNabb (Akers kick), 3:35. **14-14.**
FOURTH QUARTER: NE: Dillon 2 run (Vinatieri kick), 13:44. **New England 21-14.**
NE: FG Vinatieri 22, 8:40. **New England 24-14.**
Phil: Lewis 30 pass from McNabb (Akers kick), 1:48. **New England 24-21.**
A: 78,125.

XL - 2006

Pittsburgh	0	7	7	7—21
Seattle	3	0	7	0—10

FIRST QUARTER: Sea: FG Brown 47, 0:22. **Seattle 3-0.**
SECOND QUARTER: Pit: Roethlisberger 1 run (Reed kick), 1:55. **Pittsburgh 7-3.**
THIRD QUARTER: Pit: Parker 75 run (Reed kick) , 14:38. **Pittsburgh 14-3.**
Sea: Stevens 16 pass from Hasselbeck (Brown kick), 6:45. **Pittsburgh 14-10.**
FOURTH QUARTER: Pit: Ward 43 pass from Randle El (Reed kick), 8:56. **Pittsburgh 21-10.**
A: 68,206.

XLI - 2007

Indianapolis	6	10	6	7—29
Chicago	14	0	3	0—17

FIRST QUARTER: Chi: TD Hester 92 kick return (Gould kick) 14:46. **Chicago 7-0.**
Ind: TD Wayne 53 pass from Manning, 6:50 (Vinatieri kick failed). **Chicago 7-6.**
Chi: TD Muhammad 4 pass from Grossman (Gould kick), 4:34. **Chicago 14-6.**
SECOND QUARTER: Ind: FG Vinatieri 29, 11:17. **Chicago 14-9.**
Ind: TD Rhodes 1 run (Vinatieri kick), 6:09. **Indianapolis 16-14.**
THIRD QUARTER: Indi FG Vinatieri 24, 7:26. **Indianapolis 19-14.**
Ind: FG Vinatieri 20, 3:16. **Indianapolis 22-14.**
Chi: FG Gould 44, 1:14. **Indianapolis 22-17.**
FOURTH QUARTER: Ind: TD Hayden 56 interception return (Vinatieri kick) 11:44. **Indianapolis 29-17.**
A: 74,512.

XLII - 2008

NY Giants	3	0	0	14—17
New England	0	7	0	7—14

FIRST QUARTER: NYG: FG Tynes 32, 5:01. **NY Giants 3-0.**

SECOND QUARTER: NE: TD Maroney 1 run (Gostkowski kick), 14:57. **New England 7-3.**

FOURTH QUARTER: NYG: TD Tyree 5 pass from Manning (Tynes kick), 11:05. **NY Giants 10-7.**
NE: TD Moss 6 pass from Brady (Gostkowski kick), 2:42. **New England 14-10.**
NYG: TD Burress 13 pass from Manning (Tynes kick), 0:35. **NY Giants 17-14.**
A: 71,101.

XLIII - 2009

Pittsburgh	3	14	3	7—27
Arizona	0	7	0	16—23

FIRST QUARTER: Pit: FG Reed 18, 9:45. **Pittsburgh 3-0.**

SECOND QUARTER: Pit: Russell 1 run (Reed kick), 14:01. **Pittsburgh 10-0.**
Ari: Patrick 1 pass from Warner (Rackers kick), 8:34. **Pittsburgh 10-7.**
Pit: Harrison 100 Int return (Rackers kick), 0:00. **Pittsburgh 17-7.**

THIRD QUARTER: Pit: FG Reed 21, 2:11. **Pittsburgh 20-7.**

FOURTH QUARTER: Ari: Fitzgerald 1 pass from Warner (Rackers kick), 7:33. **Pittsburgh 20-14.**
Ari: Safety (Hartwig offensive holding penalty in end zone), 2:58. **Pittsburgh 20-16.**
Ari: Fitzgerald 64 pass from Warner (Rackers kick), 2:37. **Arizona 23-20.**
Pit: Holmes 6 pass from Roethlisberger (Reed kick), 0:35. **Pittsburgh 27-23.**
A: 70,774.

XLIV - 2010

New Orleans	0	6	10	15—31
Indianapolis	10	0	7	0—17

FIRST QUARTER: Ind: FG Stover 38, 7:29. **Indianapolis 3-0.**
Ind: TD Garcon 19 pass from Manning (Stover kick), 0:36. **Indianapolis 10-0.**

SECOND QUARTER: NO: FG Hartley 46, 9:34. **Indianapolis 10-3.**
NO: FG Hartley 44, 0:00. **Indianapolis 10-6.**

THIRD QUARTER: NO: TD Thomas 16 pass from Brees (Hartley kick), 11:41. **New Orleans 13-10.**
Ind: TD Addai 4 run (Stover kick), 6:15. **Indianapolis 17-13.**
NO: FG Hartley 47, 2:01. **Indianapolis 17-16.**

FOURTH QUARTER: NO: TD Shockey 2 pass from Brees (Moore 2 pass from Brees for 2-pt. conv), 5:42. **New Orleans 24-17.**
NO: TD Porter 74 interception return (Hartley kick), 3:12. **New Orleans 31-17.**
A: 74,059.

XLV - 2011

Pittsburgh	0	10	7	8—25
Green Bay	14	7	0	10—31

FIRST QUARTER: GB: TD Nelson 29 pass from Rodgers (Crosby kick), 3:44. **Green Bay 7-0.**
GB TD Collins 37 interception return (Crosby kick), 3:20. **Green Bay 14-0.**

XLV - 2011 *(Cont.)*

SECOND QUARTER: Pit: FG Suisham 33, 11:08. **Green Bay 14-3.**
GB: TD Jennings 21 pass from Rodgers (Crosby kick), 2:24. **Green Bay 21-3.**
Pit: TD Ward 8 pass from Roethlisberger (Suisham kick), 0:39. **Green Bay 21-10.**

THIRD QUARTER: Pit: TD Mendenhall 8 run (Suisham kick), 10:19. **Green Bay 21-17.**

FOURTH QUARTER: GB: TD Jennings 8 pass from Rodgers (Crosby kick), 11:57. **Green Bay 28-17.**
Pit: TD Wallace 25 pass from Roethlisberger (Randle El 2 run for 2-pt. conv), 7:34. **Green Bay 28-25.**
GB: FG Crosby 23, 2:07. **Green Bay 31-25.**
A: 103,219.

XLVI - 2012

New England	0	10	7	0—17
NY Giants	9	0	6	6—21

FIRST QUARTER: NYG: Safety (Brady called for intentional grounding in end zone), 8:52. **NY Giants 2-0.**
NYG: TD Cruz 2 pass from Manning (Tynes kick), 3:24. **NY Giants 9-0.**

SECOND QUARTER: NE FG Gostkowski 29, 13:48. **NY Giants 9-3.**
NE: TD Woodhead 4 pass from Brady (Gostkowski kick), 0:08. **New England 10-9.**

THIRD QUARTER: NE: TD Hernandez 12 pass from Brady (Gostkowski kick), 11:20. **New England 17-9.**
NYG: FG Tynes 38, 6:43. **New England 17-12.**
NYG: FG Tynes 33, 0:35. **New England 17-15.**

FOURTH QUARTER: NYG: TD Bradshaw 6 run (2-pt conv failed), 0:57. **NY Giants 21-17.**
A: 68,658.

XLVII - 2013

Baltimore	7	14	7	6—34
San Francisco	3	3	17	8—31

FIRST QUARTER: Bal: TD Boldin 13 pass from Flacco (Tucker kick), 10:36. **Baltimore 7-0.**
SF: FG Akers 36, 3:58. **Baltimore 7-3.**

SECOND QUARTER: Bal: TD Pitta 1 pass from Flacco (Tucker kick), 7:10. **Baltimore 14-3.**
Bal: TD J. Jones 56 pass from Flacco (Tucker kick), 1:45. **Baltimore 21-3.**
SF: FG Akers 27, 0:00. **Baltimore 21-6.**

THIRD QUARTER: Bal: TD J. Jones 108 kickoff return (Tucker kick), 14:49. **Baltimore 28-6.**
SF: TD Crabtree 31 pass from Kaepernick (Akers kick), 7:20. **Baltimore 28-13.**
SF: TD Gore 6 run (Akers kick), 4:59. **Baltimore 28-20.**
SF: FG Akers 34, 3:10. **Baltimore 28-23.**

FOURTH QUARTER: Bal: FG Tucker 19, 12:54. **Baltimore 31-23.**
SF: TD Kaepernick 15 run (two-point conversion failed), 9:57. **Baltimore 31-29.**
Bal: FG Tucker 38, 4:19. **Baltimore 34-29.**
SF: Safety Koch (ran out of end zone), 0:04. **Baltimore 34-31.**

A: 71,024.

1933
NFL championship Chicago Bears 23, NY Giants 21
1934
NFL championship NY Giants 30, Chicago Bears 13
1935
NFL championship Detroit 26, NY Giants 7
1936
NFL championship Green Bay 21, Boston 6
1937
NFL championship Washington 28, Chicago Bears 21
1938
NFL championship NY Giants 23, Green Bay 17
1939
NFL championship Green Bay 27, NY Giants 0
1940
NFL championship Chicago Bears 73, Washington 0
1941
W. div. playoff Chicago Bears 33, Green Bay 14
NFL championship Chicago Bears 37, NY Giants 9
1942
NFL championship Washington 14, Chicago Bears 6
1943
E. div. playoff Washington 28, NY Giants 0
NFL championship Chicago Bears 41, Washington 21
1944
NFL championship Green Bay 14, NY Giants 7
1945
NFL championship Cleveland 15, Washington 14
1946
NFL championship Chicago Bears 24, NY Giants 14
1947
E. div. playoff Philadelphia 21, Pittsburgh 0
NFL championship Chi Cardinals 28, Philadelphia 21
1948
NFL championship Philadelphia 7, Chi Cardinals 0
1949
NFL championship Philadelphia 14, Los Angeles 0
1950
Am. Conf. playoff Cleveland 8, NY Giants 3
Nat. Conf. playoff Los Angeles 24, Chicago Bears 14
NFL championship Cleveland 30, Los Angeles 28
1951
NFL championship Los Angeles 24, Cleveland 17
1952
Nat. Conf. playoff Detroit 31, Los Angeles 21
NFL championship Detroit 17, Cleveland 7
1953
NFL championship Detroit 17, Cleveland 16
1954
NFL championship Cleveland 56, Detroit 10
1955
NFL championship Cleveland 38, Los Angeles 14
1956
NFL championship NY Giants 47, Chicago Bears 7
1957
W. Conf. playoff Detroit 31, San Francisco 27
NFL championship Detroit 59, Cleveland 14
1958
E. Conf. playoff NY Giants 10, Cleveland 0
NFL championship Baltimore 23, NY Giants 17
1959
NFL championship Baltimore 31, NY Giants 16

1960
NFL championship Philadelphia 17, Green Bay 13
AFL championship Houston 24, LA Chargers 16
1961
NFL championship Green Bay 37, NY Giants 0
AFL championship Houston 10, San Diego 3
1962
NFL championship Green Bay 16, NY Giants 7
AFL championship Dallas Texans 20, Houston 17
1963
NFL championship Chicago 14, NY Giants 10
AFL E. div. playoff Boston 26, Buffalo 8
AFL championship San Diego 51, Boston 10
1964
NFL championship Cleveland 27, Baltimore 0
AFL championship Buffalo 20, San Diego 7
1965
NFL W. Conf. Green Bay 13, Baltimore 10
playoff
NFL championship Green Bay 23, Cleveland 12
AFL championship Buffalo 23, San Diego 0
1966
NFL championship Green Bay 34, Dallas 27
AFL championship Kansas City 31, Buffalo 7
1967
NFL E. Conf. Dallas 52, Cleveland 14
championship
NFL W. Conf. Green Bay 28, Los Angeles 7
championship
NFL championship Green Bay 21, Dallas 17
AFL championship Oakland 40, Houston 7
1968
NFL E. Conf. Cleveland 31, Dallas 20
championship
NFL W. Conf. Baltimore 24, Minnesota 14
championship
NFL championship Baltimore 34, Cleveland 0
AFL W. div. playoff Oakland 41, Kansas City 6
AFL championship NY Jets 27, Oakland 23
1969
NFL E. Conf. Cleveland 38, Dallas 14
championship
NFL W. Conf. Minnesota 23, Los Angeles 20
championship
NFL championship Minnesota 27, Cleveland 7
AFL div. playoffs Kansas City 13, NY Jets 6
Oakland 56, Houston 7
AFL championship Kansas City 17, Oakland 7
1970
AFC div. playoffs Baltimore 17, Cincinnati 0
Oakland 21, Miami 14
AFC championship Baltimore 27, Oakland 17
NFC div. playoffs Dallas 5, Detroit 0
San Francisco 17, Minnesota 14
NFC championship Dallas 17, San Francisco 10
1971
AFC div. playoffs Miami 27, Kansas City 24
Baltimore 20, Cleveland 3
AFC championship Miami 21, Baltimore 0
NFC div. playoffs Dallas 20, Minnesota 12
San Francisco 24, Washington 20
NFC championship Dallas 14, San Francisco 3
1972
AFC div. playoffs Pittsburgh 13, Oakland 7
Miami 20, Cleveland 14
AFC championship Miami 21, Pittsburgh 17

1972 *(Cont.)*

NFC div. playoffs	Dallas 30, San Francisco 28
	Washington 16, Green Bay 3
NFC championship	Washington 26, Dallas 3

1973

AFC div. playoffs	Oakland 33, Pittsburgh 14
	Miami 34, Cincinnati 16
AFC championship	Miami 27, Oakland 10
NFC div. playoffs	Minnesota 27, Washington 20
	Dallas 27, Los Angeles 16
NFC championship	Minnesota 27, Dallas 10

1974

AFC div. playoffs	Oakland 28, Miami 26
	Pittsburgh 32, Buffalo 14
AFC championship	Pittsburgh 24, Oakland 13
NFC div. playoffs	Minnesota 30, St Louis 14
	Los Angeles 19, Washington 10
NFC championship	Minnesota 14, Los Angeles 10

1975

AFC div. playoffs	Pittsburgh 28, Baltimore 10
	Oakland 31, Cincinnati 28
AFC championship	Pittsburgh 16, Oakland 10
NFC div. playoffs	Los Angeles 35, St Louis 23
	Dallas 17, Minnesota 14
NFC championship	Dallas 37, Los Angeles 7

1976

AFC div. playoffs	Oakland 24, New England 21
	Pittsburgh 40, Baltimore 14
AFC championship	Oakland 24, Pittsburgh 7
NFC div. playoffs	Minnesota 35, Washington 20
	Los Angeles 14, Dallas 12
NFC championship	Minnesota 24, Los Angeles 13

1977

AFC div. playoffs	Denver 34, Pittsburgh 21
	Oakland 37, Baltimore 31
AFC championship	Denver 20, Oakland 17
NFC div. playoffs	Dallas 37, Chicago 7
	Minnesota 14, Los Angeles 7
NFC championship	Dallas 23, Minnesota 6

1978

AFC 1st-rd. playoff	Houston 17, Miami 9
AFC div. playoffs	Houston 31, New England 14
	Pittsburgh 33, Denver 10
AFC championship	Pittsburgh 34, Houston 5
NFC 1st-rd. playoff	Atlanta 14, Philadelphia 13
NFC div. playoffs	Dallas 27, Atlanta 20
	Los Angeles 34, Minnesota 10
NFC championship	Dallas 28, Los Angeles 0

1979

AFC 1st-rd. playoff	Houston 13, Denver 7
AFC div. playoffs	Houston 17, San Diego 14
	Pittsburgh 34, Miami 14
AFC championship	Pittsburgh 27, Houston 13
NFC 1st-rd. playoff	Philadelphia 27, Chicago 17
NFC div. playoffs	Tampa Bay 24, Philadelphia 17
	Los Angeles 21, Dallas 19
NFC championship	Los Angeles 9, Tampa Bay 0

1980

AFC 1st-rd. playoff	Oakland 27, Houston 7
AFC div. playoffs	San Diego 20, Buffalo 14
	Oakland 14, Cleveland 12
AFC championship	Oakland 34, San Diego 27
NFC 1st-rd. playoff	Dallas 34, Los Angeles 13
NFC div. playoffs	Philadelphia 31, Minnesota 16
	Dallas 30, Atlanta 27
NFC championship	Philadelphia 20, Dallas 7

1981

AFC 1st-rd. playoff	Buffalo 31, NY Jets 27
AFC div. playoffs	San Diego 41, Miami 38
	Cincinnati 28, Buffalo 21
AFC championship	Cincinnati 27, San Diego 7
NFC 1st-rd. playoff	NY Giants 27, Philadelphia 21
NFC div. playoffs	Dallas 38, Tampa Bay 0
	San Francisco 38, NY Giants 24
NFC championship	San Francisco 28, Dallas 27

1982

AFC 1st-rd. playoffs	Miami 28, New England 13
	LA Raiders 27, Cleveland 10
	NY Jets 44, Cincinnati 17
	San Diego 31, Pittsburgh 28
AFC div. playoffs	NY Jets 17, LA Raiders 14
	Miami 34, San Diego 13
AFC championship	Miami 14, NY Jets 0
NFC 1st-rd. playoffs	Washington 31, Detroit 7
	Green Bay 41, St Louis 16
	Minnesota 30, Atlanta 24
	Dallas 30, Tampa Bay 17
NFC div. playoffs	Washington 21, Minnesota 7
	Dallas 37, Green Bay 26
NFC championship	Washington 31, Dallas 17

1983

AFC 1st-rd. playoff	Seattle 31, Denver 7
AFC div. playoffs	Seattle 27, Miami 20
	LA Raiders 38, Pittsburgh 10
AFC championship	LA Raiders 30, Seattle 14
NFC 1st-rd. playoff	LA Rams 24, Dallas 17
NFC div. playoffs	San Francisco 24, Detroit 23
	Washington 51, LA Rams 7
NFC championship	Washington 24, San Francisco 21

1984

AFC 1st-rd. playoff	Seattle 13, LA Raiders 7
AFC div. playoffs	Miami 31, Seattle 10
	Pittsburgh 24, Denver 17
AFC championship	Miami 45, Pittsburgh 28
NFC 1st-rd. playoff	NY Giants 16, LA Rams 13
NFC div. playoffs	San Francisco 21, NY Giants 10
	Chicago 23, Washington 19
NFC championship	San Francisco 23, Chicago 0

1985

AFC 1st-rd. playoff	New England 26, NY Jets 14
AFC div. playoffs	Miami 24, Cleveland 21
	New England 27, LA Raiders 20
AFC championship	New England 31, Miami 14
NFC 1st-rd. playoff	NY Giants 17, San Francisco 3
NFC div. playoffs	LA Rams 20, Dallas 0
	Chicago 21, NY Giants 0
NFC championship	Chicago 24, LA Rams 0

1986

AFC 1st-rd. playoff	NY Jets 35, Kansas City 15
AFC div. playoffs	Cleveland 23, NY Jets 20
	Denver 22, New England 17
AFC championship	Denver 23, Cleveland 20
NFC 1st-rd. playoff	Washington 19, LA Rams 7
NFC div playoffs	Washington 27, Chicago 13
	NY Giants 49, San Francisco 3
NFC championship	NY Giants 17, Washington 0

1987

AFC 1st-rd. playoff	Houston 23, Seattle 20
AFC div. playoffs	Cleveland 38, Indianapolis 21
	Denver 34, Houston 10
AFC championship	Denver 38, Cleveland 33
NFC 1st-rd. playoff	Minnesota 44, New Orleans 10
NFC div playoffs	Minnesota 36, San Francisco 24
	Washington 21, Chicago 17
NFC championship	Washington 17, Minnesota 10

1988

AFC 1st-rd. playoff   Houston 24, Cleveland 23
AFC div. playoffs   Cincinnati 21, Seattle 13
                      Buffalo 17, Houston 10
AFC championship   Cincinnati 21, Buffalo 10
NFC 1st-rd. playoff   Minnesota 28, LA Rams 17
NFC div. playoffs   Chicago 20, Philadelphia 12
                      San Francisco 34, Minnesota 9
NFC championship   San Francisco 28, Chicago 3

1989

AFC 1st-rd. playoff   Pittsburgh 26, Houston 23
AFC div. playoffs   Cleveland 34, Buffalo 30
                      Denver 24, Pittsburgh 23
AFC championship   Denver 37, Cleveland 21
NFC 1st-rd. playoff   LA Rams 21, Philadelphia 7
NFC div. playoffs   LA Rams 19, NY Giants 13
                      San Francisco 41, Minnesota 13
NFC championship   San Francisco 30, LA Rams 3

1990

AFC 1st-rd. playoffs Miami 17, Kansas City 16
                      Cincinnati 41, Houston 14
AFC div. playoffs   Buffalo 44, Miami 34
                      LA Raiders 20, Cincinnati 10
AFC championship   Buffalo 51, LA Raiders 3
NFC 1st-rd. playoffs Chicago 16, New Orleans 6
                      Washington 20, Philadelphia 6
NFC div. playoffs   NY Giants 31, Chicago 3
                      San Francisco 28, Washington 10
NFC championship   NY Giants 15, San Francisco 13

1991

AFC 1st-rd. playoffs Houston 17, NY Jets 10
                      Kansas City 10, LA Raiders 6
AFC div. playoffs   Denver 26, Houston 24
                      Buffalo 37, Kansas City 14
AFC championship   Buffalo 10, Denver 7
NFC 1st-rd. playoffs Atlanta 27, New Orleans 20
                      Dallas 17, Chicago 13
NFC div. playoffs   Washington 24, Atlanta 7
                      Detroit 38, Dallas 6
NFC championship   Washington 41, Detroit 10

1992

AFC 1st-rd. playoffs San Diego 17, Kansas City 0
                      Buffalo 41, Houston 38 (OT)
AFC div. playoffs   Buffalo 24, Pittsburgh 3
                      Miami 31, San Diego 0
AFC championship   Buffalo 29, Miami 10
NFC 1st-rd. playoffs Washington 24, Minnesota 7
                      Philadelphia 36, New Orleans 20
NFC div. playoffs   San Francisco 20, Washington 13
                      Dallas 34, Philadelphia 10
NFC championship   Dallas 30, San Francisco 20

1993

AFC 1st-rd. playoffs LA Raiders 42, Denver 24
                      Kansas City 27, Pittsburgh 24 (OT)
AFC div. playoffs   Buffalo 29, LA Raiders 23
                      Kansas City 28, Houston 20
AFC championship   Buffalo 30, Kansas City 13
NFC 1st-rd. playoffs NY Giants 17, Minnesota 10
                      Green Bay 28, Detroit 24
NFC div. playoffs   San Francisco 44, NY Giants 3
                      Dallas 27, Green Bay 17
NFC championship   Dallas 38, San Francisco 21

1994

AFC 1st-rd. playoffs Miami 27, Kansas City 17
                      Cleveland 20, New England 13
AFC div. playoffs   San Diego 22, Miami 21
                      Pittsburgh 29, Cleveland 9
AFC championship   San Diego 17, Pittsburgh 13
NFC 1st-rd. playoffs Green Bay 16, Detroit 12
                      Chicago 35, Minnesota 18

1994 *(Cont.)*

NFC div. playoffs   Dallas 35, Green Bay 9
                      San Francisco 44, Chicago 15
NFC championship   San Francisco 38, Dallas 28

1995

AFC 1st-rd. playoffs Buffalo 37, Miami 22
                      Indianapolis 35, San Diego 20
AFC div. playoffs   Pittsburgh 40, Buffalo 21
                      Indianapolis 10, Kansas City 7
AFC championship   Pittsburgh 20, Indianapolis 16
NFC 1st-rd. playoffs Philadelphia 58, Detroit 37
                      Green Bay 37, Atlanta 20
NFC div. playoffs   Dallas 30, Philadelphia 11
                      Green Bay 27, San Francisco 17
NFC championship   Dallas 38, Green Bay 27

1996

AFC 1st-rd. playoffs Jacksonville 30, Buffalo 27
                      Pittsburgh 42, Indianapolis 14
AFC div. playoffs   Jacksonville 30, Denver 27
                      New England 28, Pittsburgh 3
AFC championship   New England 20, Jacksonville 6
NFC 1st-rd. playoffs Dallas 40, Minnesota 15
                      San Francisco 14, Philadelphia 0
NFC div. playoffs   Green Bay 35, San Francisco 14
                      Carolina 26, Dallas 17
NFC championship   Green Bay 30, Carolina 13

1997

AFC 1st-rd. playoffs Denver 42, Jacksonville 17
                      New England 17, Miami 3
AFC div. playoffs   Denver 14, Kansas City 10
                      Pittsburgh 7, New England 6
AFC championship   Denver 24, Pittsburgh 21
NFC 1st-rd. playoffs Minnesota 23, NY Giants 22
                      Tampa Bay 20, Detroit 10
NFC div. playoffs   Green Bay 21, Tampa Bay 7
                      San Francisco 38, Minnesota 22
NFC championship   Green Bay 23, San Francisco 10

1998

AFC 1st-rd. playoffs Miami 24, Buffalo 17
                      Jacksonville 25, New England 10
AFC div. playoffs   Denver 38, Miami 3
                      NY Jets 34, Jacksonville 24
AFC championship   Denver 23, NY Jets 10
NFC 1st-rd. playoffs Arizona 20, Dallas 7
                      San Francisco 30, Green Bay 27
NFC div. playoffs   Atlanta 20, San Francisco 18
                      Minnesota 41, Arizona 21
NFC championship   Atlanta 30, Minnesota 27 (OT)

1999

AFC 1st-rd. playoffs Tennessee 22, Buffalo 16
                      Miami 20, Seattle 17
AFC div. playoffs   Jacksonville 62, Miami 7
                      Tennessee 19, Indianapolis 16
AFC championship   Tennessee 33, Jacksonville 14
NFC 1st-rd. playoffs Washington 27, Detroit 13
                      Minnesota 27, Dallas 10
NFC div. playoffs   Tampa Bay 14, Washington 13
                      St. Louis 49, Minnesota 37
NFC championship   St. Louis 11, Tampa Bay 6

2000

AFC 1st-rd. playoffs Baltimore 21, Denver 3
                      Miami 23, Indianapolis 17 (OT)
AFC div. playoffs   Baltimore 24, Tennessee 10
                      Oakland 27, Miami 0
AFC championship   Baltimore 16, Oakland 3
NFC 1st-rd. playoffs New Orleans 31, St. Louis 28
                      Philadelphia 21, Tampa Bay 3
NFC div. playoffs   NY Giants 20, Philadelphia 10
                      Minnesota 34, New Orleans 16
NFC championship   NY Giants 41, Minnesota 0

2001

AFC 1st-rd. playoffs	Oakland 38, NY Jets 24
	Baltimore 20, Miami 3
AFC div. playoffs	New England 16, Oakland 13 (OT)
	Pittsburgh 27, Baltimore 10
AFC championship	New England 24, Pittsburgh 17
NFC 1st-rd. playoffs	Philadelphia 31, Tampa Bay 9
	Green Bay 25, San Francisco 15
NFC div. playoffs	Philadelphia 33, Chicago 19
	St. Louis 45, Green Bay 17
NFC championship	St. Louis 29, Philadelphia 24

2002

AFC 1st-rd. playoffs	NY Jets 41, Indianapolis 0
	Pittsburgh 36, Cleveland 33
AFC div. playoffs	Tennessee 34, Pittsburgh 31 (OT)
	Oakland 30, NY Jets 10
AFC championship	Oakland 41, Tennessee 24
NFC 1st-rd. playoffs	Atlanta 27, Green Bay 7
	San Francisco 39, NY Giants 38
NFC div. playoffs	Philadelphia 20, Atlanta 6
	Tampa Bay 31, San Francisco 6
NFC championship	Tampa Bay 27, Philadelphia 10

2003

AFC 1st-rd. playoffs	Tennessee 20, Baltimore 17
	Indianapolis 41, Denver 10
AFC div. playoffs	New England 17, Tennessee 14
	Indianapolis 38, Kansas City 31
AFC championship	New England 24, Indianapolis 14
NFC 1st-rd. playoffs	Carolina 29, Dallas 10
	Green Bay 37, Seattle 31 (OT)
NFC div. playoffs	Carolina 29, St. Louis 23
	Philadelphia 20, Green Bay 17 (OT)
NFC championship	Carolina 14, Philadelphia 3

2004

AFC 1st-rd. playoffs	Indianapolis 49, Denver 24
	NY Jets 20, San Diego 17
AFC div. playoffs	New England 20, Indianapolis 3
	Pittsburgh 20, NY Jets 17
AFC championship	New England 41, Pittsburgh 27
NFC 1st-rd. playoffs	Minnesota 31, Green Bay 17
	St. Louis 27, Seattle 20
NFC div. playoffs	Atlanta 47, St. Louis 17
	Philadelphia 27, Minnesota 14
NFC championship	Philadelphia 27, Atlanta 10

2005

AFC 1st-rd. playoffs	Pittsburgh 31, Cincinnati 17
	New England 28, Jacksonville 3
AFC div. playoffs	Pittsburgh 21, Indianapolis 18
	Denver 27, New England 13
AFC championship	Pittsburgh 34, Denver 17
NFC 1st-rd. playoffs	Washington 17, Tampa Bay 10
	Carolina 23, NY Giants 0
NFC div. playoffs	Seattle 20, Washington 10
	Carolina 29, Chicago 21
NFC championship	Seattle 34, Carolina 14

2006

AFC 1st-rd. playoffs	Indianapolis 23, Kansas City 8
	New England 37, NY Jets 16
AFC div. playoffs	Indianapolis 15, Baltimore 6
	New England 24, San Diego 21
AFC championship	Indianapolis 38, New England 34
NFC 1st-rd. playoffs	Seattle 21, Dallas 20
	Philadelphia 23, NY Giants 20
NFC div. playoffs	Chicago 27, Seattle 24
	New Orleans 27, Philadelphia 24
NFC championship	Chicago 39, New Orleans 14

2007

AFC 1st-rd. playoffs	Jacksonville 31, Pittsburgh 29
	San Diego 17, Tennessee 6
AFC div. playoffs	New England 31, Jacksonville 20
	San Diego 28, Indianapolis 24
AFC championship	New England 21, San Diego 12
NFC 1st-rd. playoffs	Seattle 35, Washington 14
	NY Giants 24, Tampa Bay 14
NFC div. playoffs	NY Giants 21, Dallas 17
	Green Bay 42, Seattle 20
NFC championship	NY Giants 23, Green Bay 20 (OT)

2008

AFC 1st-rd. playoffs	Baltimore 27, Miami 9
	San Diego 23, Indianapolis 17 (OT)
AFC div. playoffs	Baltimore 13, Tennessee 10
	Pittsburgh 35, San Diego 24
AFC championship	Pittsburgh 23, Baltimore 14
NFC 1st-rd. playoffs	Philadelphia 26, Minnesota 14
	Arizona 30, Atlanta 24
NFC div. playoffs	Philadelphia 23, NY Giants 11
	Arizona 33, Carolina 13
NFC championship	Arizona 32, Philadelphia 25

2009

AFC 1st-rd. playoffs	NY Jets 24, Cincinnati 14
	Baltimore 33, New England 14
AFC div. playoffs	NY Jets 17, San Diego 14
	Indianapolis 20, Baltimore 3
AFC championship	Indianapolis 30, NY Jets 17
NFC 1st-rd. playoffs	Dallas 34, Philadelphia 14
	Arizona 51, Green Bay 45 (OT)
NFC div. playoffs	Minnesota 34, Dallas 3
	New Orleans 45, Arizona 14
NFC championship	New Orleans 31, Minnesota 28 (OT)

2010

AFC 1st-rd. playoffs	NY Jets 17, Indianapolis 16
	Baltimore 30, Kansas City 17
AFC div. playoffs	NY Jets 28, New England 21
	Pittsburgh 31, Baltimore 24
AFC championship	Pittsburgh 24, NY Jets 19
NFC 1st-rd. playoffs	Seattle 41, New Orleans 36
	Green Bay 21, Philadelphia 16
NFC div. playoffs	Chicago 35, Seattle 24
	Green Bay 48, Atlanta 21
NFC championship	Green Bay 21, Chicago 14

2011

AFC 1st-rd. playoffs	Houston 31, Cincinnati 10
	Denver 29, Pittsburgh 23
AFC div. playoffs	New England 45, Denver 10
	Baltimore 20, Houston 13
AFC championship	New England 23, Baltimore 20
NFC 1st-rd. playoffs	New Orleans 45, Detroit 28
	NY Giants 24, Atlanta 2
NFC div. playoffs	San Francisco 36, New Orleans 32
	NY Giants 37, Green Bay 20
NFC championship	NY Giants 20, San Francisco 17

2012

AFC 1st-rd. playoffs	Baltimore 24, Indianapolis 9
	Houston 19, Cincinnati 13
AFC div. playoffs	Baltimore 38, Denver 35
	New England 41, Houston 28
AFC championship	Baltimore 28, New England 13
NFC 1st-rd. playoffs	Seattle 24, Washington 14
	Green Bay 24, Minnesota 10
NFC div. playoffs	Atlanta 30, Seattle 28
	San Francisco 45, Green Bay 31
NFC championship	San Francisco 28, Atlanta 24

Career Leaders

Scoring

	Yrs	TD	FG	PAT	Pts
Morten Andersen	25	0	565	849	2,544
Gary Anderson	23	0	538	820	2,434
†Jason Hanson	21	0	495	665	2,150
John Carney	23	0	478	628	2,062
Matt Stover	20	0	471	591	2,004
George Blanda	26	9	335	943	2,002
Jason Elam	17	0	436	675	1,983
John Kasay	20	0	461	587	1,970
†Adam Vinatieri	17	0	413	626	1,867
Norm Johnson	18	0	366	638	1,736
Nick Lowery	18	0	383	562	1,711
Jan Stenerud	19	0	373	580	1,699
†Ryan Longwell	15	0	361	604	1,687
†David Akers	15	0	367	521	1,622
Lou Groza	21	1	264	810	1,608
Eddie Murray	19	0	352	538	1,594
Al Del Greco	17	0	347	543	1,584
†Olindo Mare	15	0	356	487	1,555
Steve Christie	15	0	336	468	1,476
Pat Leahy	18	0	304	558	1,470

Note: Adam Vinatieri completed one two-point conversion in 1998.

Rushing

	Yrs	Att	Yds	Avg	Lg	TD
Emmitt Smith	15	4,409	18,355	4.2	75	164
Walter Payton	13	3,838	16,726	4.4	76	110
Barry Sanders	10	3,062	15,269	5.0	85	99
Curtis Martin	11	3,518	14,101	4.0	70	90
LaD. Tomlinson	11	3,174	13,684	4.3	85	144
Jerome Bettis	13	3,479	13,662	3.9	71	91
Eric Dickerson	11	2,996	13,259	4.4	85	90
Tony Dorsett	12	2,936	12,739	4.3	99	77
Jim Brown	9	2,359	12,312	5.2	80	106
Marshall Faulk	12	2,836	12,279	4.3	71	100
Edgerrin James	11	3,028	12,246	4.0	72	80
Marcus Allen	16	3,022	12,243	4.1	61	123
Franco Harris	13	2,949	12,120	4.1	75	91
Thurman Thomas	13	2,877	12,074	4.2	80	66
Fred Taylor	13	2,534	11,695	4.6	80	66
John Riggins	14	2,916	11,352	3.9	66	104
Corey Dillon	10	2,618	11,241	4.3	96	82
O.J. Simpson	11	2,404	11,236	4.7	94	61
Warrick Dunn	12	2,669	10,967	4.1	90	49
Ricky Watters	10	2,622	10,643	4.1	57	78

Touchdowns

	Yrs	Rush	Rec	Ret	Total TD
Jerry Rice	20	10	197	1	208
Emmitt Smith	15	164	11	0	175
LaDainian Tomlinson	11	145	17	0	162
†Randy Moss	14	0	156	1	157
Terrell Owens	15	3	153	0	156
Marcus Allen	16	123	21	1	145
Marshall Faulk	12	100	36	0	136
Cris Carter	16	0	130	1	131
Marvin Harrison	13	0	128	0	128
Jim Brown	9	106	20	0	126

	Yrs	Rush	Rec	Ret	Total TD
Walter Payton	13	110	15	0	125
John Riggins	14	104	12	0	116
Lenny Moore	12	63	48	2	113
Shaun Alexander	9	100	12	0	112
Barry Sanders	10	99	10	0	109
Tim Brown	17	1	100	4	105
Don Hutson	11	3	99	3	105
†Tony Gonzalez	16	0	103	0	103
Steve Largent	14	1	100	0	101
Franco Harris	13	91	9	0	100
Curtis Martin	12	90	10	0	100

Combined Yards Gained

	Yrs	Total	Rush	Rec	Int Ret	Punt Ret	Kickoff Ret	Fum Ret
Jerry Rice	20	23,546	645	22,895	0	0	6	0
Brian Mitchell	14	23,330	1,967	2,336	0	4,999	14,014	14
Walter Payton	13	21,803	16,726	4,538	0	0	539	0
Emmitt Smith	15	21,583	18,355	3,224	0	0	0	4
Tim Brown	17	19,682	190	14,934	0	3,320	1,235	3
Marshall Faulk	12	19,190	12,279	6,875	0	0	18	18
LaDainian Tomlinson	11	18,456	13,684	4,772	0	0	0	0
Barry Sanders	10	18,308	15,269	2,921	0	0	118	0
Herschel Walker	12	18,168	8,225	4,859	0	0	5,084	0
Marcus Allen	16	17,654	12,243	5,411	0	0	0	0
Curtis Martin	11	17,430	14,101	3,329	0	0	0	0
Tiki Barber	10	17,359	10,449	5,183	0	1,181	544	2
Eric Metcalf	13	17,230	2,392	5,572	0	3,453	5,813	0
Derrick Mason	15	17,150	3	12,061	0	1,590	3,496	0
Thurman Thomas	13	16,532	12,074	4,458	0	0	0	0
Tony Dorsett	12	16,293	12,739	3,554	0	0	0	0
Terrell Owens	15	16,263	251	15,934	0	0	78	0
†Steve Smith	12	15,869	387	11,452	0	1,652	2,371	7
Henry Ellard	16	15,718	50	13,777	0	1,527	364	0
Warrick Dunn	12	15,664	10,967	4,339	0	48	310	0

†Active in 2012.

Career Leaders (Cont.)

Passing

PASSER RATING*

	Yrs	Att	Comp	Pct Comp	Yds	Avg Gain	TD	Pct TD	Int	Pct Int	Rating Pts
†Aaron Rodgers	8	2,665	1,752	65.7	21,661	8.1	171	6.4	46	1.7	104.9
Steve Young	15	4,149	2,667	64.3	33,124	8.0	232	5.6	107	2.6	96.8
†Tom Brady	13	5,958	3,798	63.7	44,806	7.5	334	5.6	123	2.1	96.6
†Peyton Manning	14	7,793	5,082	65.2	59,487	7.6	436	5.6	209	2.7	95.7
†Tony Romo	9	3,240	2,097	64.7	25,737	7.9	177	5.5	91	2.9	95.6
†Philip Rivers	9	3,564	2,268	63.6	27,891	7.8	189	5.3	93	2.6	94.5
†Drew Brees	12	6,149	4,035	65.6	45,919	7.5	324	5.3	165	2.7	94.3
Kurt Warner	12	4,070	2,666	65.5	32,344	7.9	208	5.1	128	3.1	93.7
†Ben Roethlisberger	9	3,762	2,374	63.1	29,844	7.9	191	5.1	108	2.9	92.7
Joe Montana	15	5,391	3,409	63.2	40,551	7.5	273	5.2	139	2.6	92.3
†Matt Schaub	9	2,823	1,816	64.3	21,944	7.8	120	4.3	70	2.5	91.9
†Matt Ryan	5	2,637	1,654	62.7	18,957	7.2	127	4.8	60	2.3	90.9
Chad Pennington	11	2,471	1,632	66.0	17,823	7.2	102	4.1	64	2.6	90.1
Daunte Culpepper	11	3,199	2,016	63.0	24,123	7.6	149	4.7	106	3.3	87.8
Jeff Garcia	11	3,676	2,264	61.6	25,537	6.9	161	4.4	83	2.3	87.5
Otto Graham	10	2,626	1,464	55.8	23,584	9.0	174	6.6	135	5.1	86.6
Dan Marino	17	8,358	4,967	59.4	61,361	7.3	420	5.0	252	3.0	86.4
†Joe Flacco	5	2,489	1,507	60.5	17,633	7.1	102	4.1	56	2.2	86.3
†Carson Palmer	9	4,110	2,568	62.5	29,465	7.2	189	4.6	130	3.2	86.2
Brett Favre	20	10,169	6,300	62.0	71,838	7.1	508	5.0	336	3.3	86.0
Trent Green	11	3,740	2,266	60.6	28,475	7.6	162	4.3	114	3.0	86.0
David Garrard	9	2,281	1,406	61.6	16,003	7.0	89	3.9	54	2.4	85.8
Donovan McNabb	13	5,374	3,170	59.0	37,276	6.9	234	4.4	117	2.2	85.6
Rich Gannon	18	4,206	2,533	60.2	28,743	6.8	180	4.3	104	2.3	84.7
Marc Bulger	8	3,171	1,969	62.1	22,814	7.2	122	3.8	93	2.9	84.4
Jim Kelly	11	4,779	2,874	60.1	35,467	7.4	237	5.0	175	3.7	84.4

*1,500 or more attempts. The passer ratings are based on performance standards established for completion percentage, interception percentage, touchdown percentage and average gain. Passers are allocated points according to how their marks compare with those standards.

PASSING YARDS

	Yrs	Att	Comp	Pct Comp	Yds		Yrs	Att	Comp	Pct Comp	Yds
Brett Favre	20	10,169	6,300	62.0	71,838	Johnny Unitas	18	5,186	2,830	54.6	40,239
Dan Marino	17	8,358	4,967	59.4	61,361	Dave Krieg	19	5,311	3,105	58.5	38,147
†Peyton Manning	14	7,793	5,082	65.2	59,487	Boomer Esiason	14	5,205	2,969	57.0	37,920
John Elway	16	7,250	4,123	56.9	51,475	Donovan McNabb	13	5,374	3,170	59.0	37,276
Warren Moon	17	6,823	3,988	58.5	49,325	Jim Kelly	11	4,779	2,874	60.1	35,467
Fran Tarkenton	18	6,467	3,686	57.0	47,003	Jim Everett	12	4,923	2,841	57.7	34,837
Vinny Testaverde	21	6,701	3,787	56.5	46,233	Jim Hart	19	5,076	2,593	51.1	34,665
†Drew Brees	12	6,149	4,035	65.6	45,919	†Matt Hasselback	14	5,018	3,029	60.4	34,517
†Tom Brady	13	5,958	3,798	63.7	44,806	Steve DeBerg	17	4,746	2,924	61.6	34,241
Drew Bledsoe	14	6,717	3,839	57.2	44,611	John Hadl	16	4,687	2,363	50.4	33,503
Dan Fouts	15	5,604	3,297	58.8	43,040	Phil Simms	14	4,647	2,576	55.4	33,462
Kerry Collins	17	6,261	3,487	55.7	40,922	Steve Young	15	4,149	2,667	64.3	33,124
Joe Montana	15	5,391	3,409	63.2	40,551						

PASSING TOUCHDOWNS

	No.		No.		No.
Brett Favre	508	Dave Krieg	261	Steve Young	232
†Peyton Manning	436	Sonny Jurgensen	255	John Brodie	214
Dan Marino	420	Dan Fouts	254	Terry Bradshaw	212
Fran Tarkenton	342	Drew Bledsoe	251	†Eli Manning	211
†Tom Brady	334	Boomer Esiason	247	Jim Hart	209
†Drew Brees	324	John Hadl	244	Kerry Collins	208
John Elway	300	*Y.A. Tittle	242	Kurt Warner	208
Warren Moon	291	Len Dawson	239	Randall Cunningham	207
Johnny Unitas	290	Jim Kelly	237	Jim Everett	203
Vinny Testaverde	275	George Blanda	236	Roman Gabriel	201
Joe Montana	273	Donovan McNabb	234	†Matt Hasselback	201

* Includes 30 TDs with Baltimore Colts (1948–49) in All-American Football Conference.

† Active in 2012.

Career Leaders (Cont.)

Receiving

RECEPTIONS

	Yrs	No.	Yds	Avg	Lg	TD		Yrs	No.	Yds	Avg	Lg	TD
Jerry Rice	20	1,549	22,895	14.8	96	197	Jimmy Smith	13	862	12,287	14.3	75	67
†Tony Gonzalez	16	1,242	14,268	11.5	73	103	Muhsin Muhammad	14	860	11,438	13.3	72	62
Marvin Harrison	12	1,102	14,580	13.2	80	128	Irving Fryar	17	851	12,785	15.0	80	84
Cris Carter	16	1,101	13,899	12.6	80	130	Rod Smith	12	849	11,389	13.4	85	68
Tim Brown	17	1,094	14,934	13.7	80	100	Larry Centers	14	827	6,797	8.2	54	28
Terrell Owens	15	1,078	15,934	14.8	98	153	Steve Largent	14	819	13,089	16.0	74	100
Isaac Bruce	16	1,024	15,208	14.9	80	91	Andre Johnson	10	818	11,254	13.8	77	56
Hines Ward	14	1,000	12,083	12.1	85	85	Shannon Sharpe	14	815	10,060	12.3	82	62
†Randy Moss	14	982	15,292	15.6	82	156	Henry Ellard	16	814	13,777	16.9	81	65
†Reggie Wayne	12	968	13,063	13.5	71	78	Keyshawn Johnson	11	814	10,571	13.0	76	64
Andre Reed	16	951	13,198	13.9	83	87	†Jason Witten	10	806	8,948	11.1	69	44
Derrick Mason	15	943	12,061	12.8	79	66	†Steve Smith	12	772	11,452	14.8	80	63
Art Monk	16	940	12,721	13.5	79	68	†Anquan Boldin	10	772	10,165	13.2	79	58
Torry Holt	11	920	13,382	14.5	85	74	†Wes Welker	9	768	8,580	11.2	99	38
Keenan McCardell	17	883	11,373	12.9	76	63	Marshall Faulk	11	767	6,875	9.0	85	36

YARDS

Jerry Rice	22,895	Henry Ellard	13,777	Charlie Joiner	12,146
Terrell Owens	15,934	Torry Holt	13,382	Hines Ward	12,083
†Randy Moss	15,292	Andre Reed	13,198	Derrick Mason	12,061
Isaac Bruce	15,208	Steve Largent	13,089	Michael Irvin	11,904
Tim Brown	14,934	†Reggie Wayne	13,063	Don Maynard	11,834
Marvin Harrison	14,580	Irving Fryar	12,785	†Steve Smith	11,452
†Tony Gonzalez	14,268	Art Monk	12,721	Muhsin Muhammad	11,438
James Lofton	14,004	Jimmy Smith	12,287	Rod Smith	11,389
Cris Carter	13,899				

Sacks

Bruce Smith	200.0	Jason Taylor	139.5
Reggie White	198.0	John Randle	137.5
Kevin Greene	160.0	Richard Dent	137.5
Chris Doleman	150.5	Leslie O'Neal	132.5
Michael Strahan	141.5	Lawrence Taylor	132.5

Note: Stat officially compiled since 1982.

Interceptions

	Yrs	No.	Yds	Avg	Lg	TD
Paul Krause	16	81	1,185	14.6	81	3
Emlen Tunnell	14	79	1,282	16.2	55	4
Rod Woodson	17	71	1,483	20.9	98	12
Dick (Night Train) Lane	14	68	1,207	17.8	80	5
Ken Riley	15	65	596	9.2	66	5
Ronnie Lott	14	63	730	8.5	66	5
Darren Sharper	14	63	1,412	22.4	99	11
Dick LeBeau	14	62	762	12.3	70	3
Dave Brown	15	62	698	11.3	90	5
†Ed Reed	11	61	1,541	25.2	107	7

Punting

	Yrs	No.	Yds	Avg	Lg	Blk
†Shane Lechler	13	1,014	48,215	47.5	80	4
†Brandon Fields	6	450	20,893	46.4	71	2
†Britton Colquitt	3	254	11,717	46.1	67	0
†Andy Lee	9	790	36,295	45.9	82	3
†Donnie Jones	9	736	33,529	45.6	80	3
†Pat McAfee	4	290	13,170	45.4	66	2
†Mat McBriar	9	549	24,929	45.4	75	4
†Mike Scifres	10	573	25,958	45.3	71	8
Sammy Baugh	16	338	15,245	45.1	85	9
†Brett Kern	5	354	15,964	45.1	71	2
†Jon Ryan	7	548	24,676	45.0	77	3

Note: 250 or more punts.

Punt Returns

	Yrs	No.	Yds	Avg	Lg	TD
George McAfee	8	112	1,431	12.8	74	2
Jack Christiansen	8	85	1,084	12.8	89	8
Claude Gibson	5	110	1,381	12.6	85	3
Bill Dudley	9	124	1,515	12.2	96	3
†Devin Hester	7	246	2,985	12.1	89	12
Rick Upchurch	9	248	3,008	12.1	92	8
Desmond Howard	11	244	2,895	11.9	95	8
†Patrick Peterson	2	95	1,125	11.8	99	4
Billy Johnson	14	282	3,317	11.8	87	6
Mack Herron	3	84	982	11.7	66	0

Note: 75 or more returns.

Kickoff Returns

	Yrs	No.	Yds	Avg	Lg	TD
Gale Sayers	7	91	2,781	30.6	103	6
Lynn Chandnois	7	92	2,720	29.6	93	3
†Joe McKnight	3	76	2,205	29.0	107	2
Abe Woodson	9	193	5,538	28.7	105	5
Claude (Buddy) Young	6	90	2,514	27.9	104	2
†Percy Harvin	4	114	3,183	27.9	105	5
Travis Williams	5	102	2,801	27.5	105	6
Joe Arenas	7	139	3,798	27.3	96	1
Clifton Smith	3	75	2,038	27.2	97	1
Clarence Davis	7	79	2,140	27.1	76	0

Note: 75 or more returns.

† Active in 2012.

Single-Season Leaders

Scoring

POINTS

	Year	TD	PAT	FG	Pts
LaDainian Tomlinson, SD	2006	31	0	0	186
Paul Hornung, GB	1960	15	41	15	176
Shaun Alexander, Sea	2005	28	0	0	168
†David Akers, SF	2011	0	34	44	166
Gary Anderson, Min	1998	0	59	35	164
Jeff Wilkins, StL	2003	0	46	39	163
Priest Holmes, KC	2003	27	0	0	162
Mark Moseley, Was	1983	0	62	33	161
Marshall Faulk, StL	2000	26	2	0	160
Mike Vanderjagt, Ind	2003	0	46	37	157
Gino Cappelletti, Bos	1964	7	37	25	155
†Stephen Gostkowski, NE	2012	0	29	66	153
Emmitt Smith, Dal	1995	25	0	0	150
Chip Lohmiller, Was	1991	0	56	31	149
†Stephen Gostkowski, NE	2008	0	40	36	148
†Jay Feely, NYG	2005	0	43	35	148

Note: Faulk's and Cappelletti's totals include two-point conversions.

TOUCHDOWNS

	Year	Rush	Rec	Ret	Total
LaDainian Tomlinson, SD	2006	28	3	0	31
Shaun Alexander, Sea	2005	27	1	0	28
Priest Holmes, KC	2003	27	0	0	27
Marshall Faulk, StL	2000	18	8	0	26
Emmitt Smith, Dal	1995	25	0	0	25
Priest Holmes, KC	2002	21	3	0	24
John Riggins, Was	1983	24	0	0	24
†Randy Moss, NE	2007	0	23	0	23
Terrell Davis, Den	1998	21	2	0	23
Jerry Rice, SF	1987	1	22	0	23
O.J. Simpson, Buf	1975	16	7	0	23

FIELD GOALS

	Year	FGA	FGM
†David Akers	2011	52	44
†Neil Rackers, Ari	2005	42	40
Jeff Wilkins, StL	2003	42	39
†Olindo Mare, Mia	1999	46	39
Mike Vanderjagt, Ind	2003	37	37
†John Kasay, Car	1996	45	37
†Stephen Gostkowski, NE	2008	40	36
Al Del Greco, Ten	1998	39	36
Cary Blanchard, Ind	1996	40	36

Rushing

YARDS GAINED

	Year	Att	Yds	Avg
Eric Dickerson, LA Rams	1984	379	2,105	5.6
†Adrian Peterson, Min	2012	348	2,097	6.0
Jamal Lewis, Bal	2003	387	2,066	5.3
Barry Sanders, Det	1997	335	2,053	6.1
Terrell Davis, Den	1998	392	2,008	5.1
†Chris Johnson, Ten	2009	358	2,006	5.6
O.J. Simpson, Buf	1973	332	2,003	6.0
Earl Campbell, Hou	1980	373	1,934	5.2
Ahman Green, GB	2003	355	1,883	5.3
Barry Sanders, Det	1994	331	1,883	5.7
Shaun Alexander, Sea	2005	370	1,880	5.1
Jim Brown, Cle	1963	291	1,863	6.4
Tiki Barber, NYG	2005	357	1,860	5.2
Ricky Williams, Mia	2002	383	1,853	4.8
Walter Payton, Chi	1977	339	1,852	5.5

AVERAGE GAIN

	Year	Avg
†Michael Vick, Atl	2006	8.45
Beattie Feathers, Chi	1934	8.44
Randall Cunningham, Phi	1990	7.98
†Michael Vick, Atl	2004	7.50
†Michael Vick, Atl	2002	6.88

Minimum 100 attempts.

TOUCHDOWNS

	Year	No.
LaDainian Tomlinson, SD	2006	28
Shaun Alexander, Sea	2005	27
Priest Holmes, KC	2003	27
Emmitt Smith, Dal	1995	25
John Riggins, Was	1983	24

Passing

YARDS GAINED

	Year	Att	Comp	Pct	Yds
†Drew Brees, NO	2011	657	468	71.2	5,476
†Tom Brady, NE	2011	611	401	65.6	5,235
†Drew Brees, NO	2012	670	422	63.0	5,177
Dan Marino, Mia	1984	564	362	64.2	5,084
†Drew Brees, NO	2008	635	413	65.0	5,069
†Matthew Stafford, Det	2011	663	421	63.5	5,038
†Matthew Stafford, Det	2012	727	435	59.8	4,967
†Eli Manning, NYG	2011	589	359	61.0	4,933
†Tony Romo, Dal	2012	648	425	65.6	4,903
Kurt Warner, StL	2001	546	375	68.7	4,830
†Tom Brady, NE	2012	637	401	63.0	4,827
†Tom Brady, NE	2007	578	398	68.9	4,806
Dan Fouts, SD	1981	609	360	59.1	4,802
†Matt Schaub, Hou	2009	583	396	67.9	4,770
Dan Marino, Mia	1986	623	378	60.7	4,746

PASSER RATING

	Year	Rat.
†Aaron Rodgers, GB	2011	122.5
†Peyton Manning, Ind	2004	121.1
†Tom Brady, NE	2007	117.2
Steve Young, SF	1994	112.8
Joe Montana, SF	1989	112.4
†Tom Brady, NE	2010	111.0
Daunte Culpepper, Min	2004	110.9

TOUCHDOWNS

	Year	No.
†Tom Brady, NE	2007	50
†Peyton Manning, Ind	2004	49
Dan Marino, Mia	1984	48
†Drew Brees, NO,	2011	46
†Aaron Rodgers, GB	2011	45
Dan Marino, Mia	1986	44
†Drew Brees, NO	2012	43
†Matthew Stafford, Det	2011	41
Kurt Warner, StL	1999	41
†Aaron Rodgers, GB	2012	39
†Tom Brady, NE	2011	39
Daunte Culpepper, Min	2004	39
Brett Favre, GB	1996	39

† Active in 2012.

Single-Season Leaders (Cont.)

Receiving

RECEPTIONS

	Year	No.	Yds
Marvin Harrison, Ind	2002	143	1,722
Herman Moore, Det	1995	123	1,686
†Wes Welker, NE	2009	123	1,348
Cris Carter, Min	1994	122	1,256
Cris Carter, Min	1995	122	1,371
†Calvin Johnson, Det	2012	122	1,964
Jerry Rice, SF	1995	122	1,848
†Wes Welker, NE	2011	122	1,569
Isaac Bruce, StL	1995	119	1,781
†Brandon Marshall, Chi	2012	118	1,508
†Wes Welker, NE	2012	118	1,354
Torry Holt, StL	2003	117	1,696
Jimmy Smith, Jac	1999	116	1,636

YARDS GAINED

	Year	Yds
†Calvin Johnson, Det	2012	1,964
Jerry Rice, SF	1995	1,848
Isaac Bruce, StL	1995	1,781
Charley Hennigan, Hou	1961	1,746
Marvin Harrison, Ind	2002	1,722
Torry Holt, StL	2003	1,696

TOUCHDOWNS

	Year	No.
†Randy Moss, NE	2007	23
Jerry Rice, SF	1987	22
Mark Clayton, Mia	1984	18
Sterling Sharpe, GB	1994	18
Nine players tied with 17.		

All-Purpose Yards

	Year	Run	Rec	Ret	Ttl Yds
†Darren Sproles, NO	2011	603	710	1,383	2,696
Derrick Mason, Ten	2000	1	895	1,794	2,690
Michael Lewis, NO	2002	15	200	2,432	2,647
†Fred Jackson, Buf	2009	1,062	371	1,083	2,516
†Josh Cribbs, Cle	2009	381	135	1,994	2,510
†Chris Johnson, Ten	2009	2,006	503	0	2,509
Lionel James, SD	1985	516	1,027	992	2,535
Brian Mitchell, Was	1994	311	236	1,930	2,477
Dante Hall, KC	2003	73	423	1,950	2,446
Mack Herron, NE	1974	824	474	1,146	2,444
Gale Sayers, Chi	1966	1,231	447	762	2,440
Terry Metcalf, StL Cards	1975	816	378	1,245	2,439
Marshall Faulk, StL	1999	1,381	1,048	0	2,429
Timmy Brown, Phi	1963	841	487	1,097	2,425
MarTay Jenkins, Ari	2000	-4	219	2,187	2,402

Interceptions

	Year	No.
Dick (Night Train) Lane, LA Rams	1952	14
Lester Hayes, Oak	1980	13
Spec Sanders, NY Yanks	1950	13
Dan Sandifer, Was	1948	13
Nine tied with 12.		

Punt Returns

	Year	Avg
Jack Christiansen, Det	1952	21.5
Red Cochran, Chi Cards	1949	20.9
Jerry Davis, Chi Cards	1948	20.9
Bob Hayes, Dal	1968	20.8
Billy Grimes, GB	1950	19.1
Jack Christiansen, Det	1951	19.1
Minimum of 15 returns.		

Punting

	Year	No.	Yds	Avg
Sammy Baugh, Was	1940	35	1,799	51.4
†Shane Lechler, Oak	2009	96	4,909	51.1
†Andy Lee, SF	2011	78	3,970	50.9
†Shane Lechler, Oak	2011	78	3,960	50.8
†Brandon Fields, Mia	2012	73	3,666	50.2
†Thomas Morstead, NO	2012	74	3,707	50.1
†Donnie Jones, StL	2008	82	4,100	50.0
†Shane Lechler, Oak	2007	73	3,585	49.1
†Mat McBriar, Dal	2008	24	1,175	49.0
Yale Lary, Det	1963	35	1,713	48.9

Sacks

	Year	No.
Michael Strahan, NYG	2001	22.5
Mark Gastineau, NYJ	1984	22.0
†Jared Allen, Min	2011	22.0
Chris Doleman, Min	1989	21.0
Reggie White, Phi	1987	21.0
Lawrence Taylor, NYG	1986	20.5
†J.J. Watt, Hou	2012	20.5
†DeMarcus Ware, Dal	2008	20.0
Derrick Thomas, KC	1990	20.0
Tim Harris, GB	1989	19.5
†Aldon Smith, SF	2012	19.5
†DeMarcus Ware, Dal	2011	19.5

Kickoff Returns

	Year	Avg
Travis Williams, GB	1967	41.1
Gale Sayers, Chi	1967	37.7
†Percy Harvin, Min	2012	35.9
Ollie Matson, Chi Cards	1958	35.5
Jim Duncan, Balt Colts	1970	35.4
Minimum of 14 returns.		

Single-Game Leaders

Scoring

POINTS

	Date	Pts
Ernie Nevers, Chi Cards vs Chi	11-28-29	40
Gale Sayers, Chi vs SF	12-12-65	36
Dub Jones, Clev vs Chi	11-25-51	36
Paul Hornung, GB vs Balt Colts	10-8-61	33

On Thanksgiving Day, 1929, Nevers scored all the Cardinals' points on six rushing TDs and four PATs. The Cards defeated Red Grange and the Bears, 40–6. Jones and Sayers each rushed for four touchdowns and scored two more on returns in their teams' victories. Hornung scored four touchdowns and kicked 6 PATs and a field goal in a 45-7 win over the Colts.

FIELD GOALS

	Date	No.
†Rob Bironas, Ten vs Hou	10-21-07	8
†Shayne Graham, Cin vs Balt	11-11-07	7
†Billy Cundiff, Dal vs NYG (OT)	9-15-03	7
Chris Boniol, Dal vs GB	11-18-96	7
Rich Karlis, Min vs LA Rams (OT)	11-5-89	7
Jim Bakken, StL Cards vs Pit	9-24-67	7

Bironas was 8 for 8.

Bakken was 7 for 9; Cundiff was 7 for 8; and Karlis, Boniol, and Graham went 7 for 7.

† Active in 2012.

Single-Game Leaders *(Cont.)*
Scoring *(Cont.)*

TOUCHDOWNS

	Date	No.
Gale Sayers, Chi vs SF	12-12-65	6
Dub Jones, Clev vs Chi	11-25-51	6
Ernie Nevers, Chi Cards vs Chi	11-28-29	6
Clinton Portis, Den vs KC	12-07-03	5
Shaun Alexander, Sea vs Min	9-29-02	5
James Stewart, Jac vs Phil	10-12-97	5
Ricky Watters, SF vs NY Giants	1-15-94	5
Jerry Rice, SF vs Atl	10-14-90	5
Kellen Winslow, SD vs Oak	11-22-81	5
Paul Hornung, GB vs Balt Colts	12-12-65	5
Jim Brown, Clev vs Balt Colts	11-1-59	5
Bob Shaw, Chi Cards vs Balt Colts	10-2-50	5

Rushing

YARDS GAINED

	Date	Yds
†Adrian Peterson, Min vs SD	11-4-07	296
Jamal Lewis, Balt vs Cle	9-14-03	295
Jerome Harrison, Cle vs KC	12-20-09	286
Corey Dillon, Cin vs Den	10-22-00	278
Walter Payton, Chi vs Min	11-20-77	275
O.J. Simpson, Buf vs Det	11-25-76	273

TOUCHDOWNS

	Date	No.
Ernie Nevers, Chi Cards vs Chi	11-28-29	6
Clinton Portis, Den vs KC	12-7-03	5
James Stewart, Jac vs Phil	10-12-97	5
Ricky Watters, SF vs. NY Giants	1-15-94	5
Jim Brown, Clev vs Balt Colts	11-1-59	5
Jimmie Conzelman, RI vs Evansville	10-15-22	5

CARRIES

	Date	No.
Jamie Morris, Wash vs Cin	12-17-88	45
Rudi Johnson, Cin vs Hou	11-9-03	43
James Wilder, TB vs GB	9-30-84	43
Butch Woolfolk, NYG vs Phil	11-20-83	43
Ricky Williams, Mia vs Buf	9-21-03	42
Terrell Davis, Den vs Buf (OT)	10-26-97	42
James Wilder, TB vs Pit	10-30-83	42

Passing

YARDS GAINED

	Date	Yds
N. Van Brocklin, Rams vs NY Yanks	9-28-51	554
†Matt Schaub, Hou	11-18-12	527
Warren Moon, Hou vs KC	12-16-90	527
Boomer Esiason, Ariz vs Wash	11-10-96	522
Dan Marino, Mia vs NYJ	10-23-88	521
†Matthew Stafford, Det vs. GB	1-1-12	520

TOUCHDOWNS

	Date	No.
Joe Kapp, Min vs Balt Colts	9-28-69	7
Y.A. Tittle, NYG vs Wash	10-28-62	7
Adrian Burk, Phil vs Wash	10-17-54	7
Sid Luckman, Chi vs NYG	11-14-43	7

Twenty-five tied at 6.

COMPLETIONS

	Date	No.
Drew Bledsoe, NE vs Min	11-13-94	45
†Matt Schaub, Hou vs Jax	11-18-12	43
Rich Gannon, Oak vs Pit	9-15-02	43
Vinny Testaverde, NYJ vs Sea	12-6-98	42
Richard Todd, NYJ vs SF	9-21-80	42
†Tony Romo, Dal vs NYG	12-06-09	41
Warren Moon, Hou vs Dal	11-10-91	41

Nine tied at 40.

Receiving

YARDS GAINED

	Date	Yds
Flipper Anderson, LA Rams vs NO	11-26-89	336
Stephone Paige, KC vs SD	12-22-85	309
Jim Benton, Clev vs Det	11-22-45	303
Cloyce Box, Det vs Balt Colts	12-3-50	302
Jimmy Smith, Jax vs Balt Ravens	9-10-00	291

RECEPTIONS

	Date	No.
†Brandon Marshall, Den vs Ind	12-13-09	21
Terrell Owens, SF vs Chi	12-17-00	20
†Jason Witten, Dal vs NYG	10-28-12	18
†Brandon Marshall, Den vs SD	9-14-08	18
Tom Fears, Rams vs GB	12-3-50	18
Clark Gaines, NYJ vs SF	9-21-80	17
†Wes Welker, NE vs. Buf	9-25-11	16
Troy Brown, NE vs KC	9-22-02	16
Keenan McCardell, Jax vs Rams	10-20-96	16
Jerry Rice, SF vs Rams	11-20-94	16
Sonny Randle, StL Cards vs NYG	11-4-62	16

† Active in 2012.

Single-Game Leaders (Cont.)

Receiving (Cont.)
TOUCHDOWNS

	Date	No.
Jerry Rice, SF vs Atl	10-14-90	5
Kellen Winslow, SD vs Oak	11-22-81	5
Bob Shaw, Chi Cards vs Balt Colts	10-2-50	5

All-Purpose Yards

	Date	Yds
Glyn Milburn, Den vs Sea	12-10-95	404
†Adrian Peterson, Minn vs. Chi	10-14-07	361
Michael Lewis, NO vs. Wash	10-13-02	356
Ed Podolak, KC vs Mia	12-25-71	350
Tyrone Hughes, NO vs. LA Rams	10-23-94	347
Lionel James, SD vs LA Rai	11-10-85	345

Longest Plays

RUSHING	Opponent	Year	Yds
Tony Dorsett, Dal	Min	1983	99
Ahman Green, GB	Den	2003	98
Bob Gage, Pit	Chi	1949	97
Andy Uram, GB	Chi Cards	1939	97
Corey Dillon, Cin	Det	2001	96
Garrison Hearst, SF	NYJ	1998	96
Jim Spavital, Balt Colts	GB	1950	96
Bob Hoernschemeyer, Det	NY Yanks	1950	96

PASSING	Opponent	Year	Yds
†Eli Manning to Victor Cruz, NYG	NYJ	2011	99
†Tom Brady to Wes Welker, NE	Mia	2011	99
Gus Frerotte to Bernard Berrian, Min	Chi	2008	99
Jeff Garcia to Andre Davis, Clev	Cin	2004	99
Trent Green to Marc Boerigter, KC	SD	2002	99
Brett Favre to Robert Brooks, GB	Chi	1995	99
Stan Humphries to Tony Martin, SD	Sea	1994	99
Ron Jaworski to Mike Quick, Phil	Atl	1985	99
Jim Plunkett to Cliff Branch, LA Raiders	Wash	1983	99
Sonny Jurgensen to Gerry Allen, Wash	Chi	1968	99
Karl Sweetan to Pat Studstill, Det	Balt Colts	1966	99
George Izo to Bobby Mitchell, Wash	Clev	1963	99
Frank Filchock to Andy Farkas, Wash	Pit	1939	99

FIELD GOALS	Opponent	Year	Yds
†David Akers, SF	GB	2012	63
†Sebastian Janikowski, Oak	Den	2011	63
Tom Dempsey, NO	Det	1970	63
Jason Elam, Den	Jac	1998	63
†Matt Bryant, TB	Phi	2006	62

PUNTS	Opponent	Year	Yds
Steve O'Neal, NYJ	Den	1969	98
Joe Lintzenich, Chi	NYG	1931	94
Shawn McCarthy, NE	Buf	1991	93
Randall Cunningham, Phil	NYG	1989	91

INTERCEPTION RETURNS	Opponent	Year	Yds
†Ed Reed, Balt	Phi	2008	107
†Ed Reed, Balt	Clev	2004	106
Louis Oliver, Mia	Buf	1992	103
Vencie Glenn, SD	Den	1987	103

FUMBLE RETURNS	Opponent	Year	Yds
Aeneas Williams, Ari	Was	2000	104
Jack Tatum, Oak	GB	1972	104
Travis Davis, Pit	Car	1999	102
Chris Martin, KC	Mia	1991	100

KICKOFF RETURNS	Opponent	Year	Yds
†Jacoby Jones, Bal	SF	2013	108
†Randall Cobb, GB	NO	2011	108
Ellis Hobbs, NE	NYJ	2007	108
†Joe McKnight, NYJ	Bal	2011	107
†Brad Smith, NYJ	Ind	2009	106
Roy Green, StL Cards	Dal	1979	106
Noland Smith, NYJ	Den	1967	106
Al Carmichael, GB	Chi	1956	106
Twelve players tied at 105.			

PUNT RETURNS	Opponent	Year	Yds
Robert Bailey, LA Rams	NO	1994	103
†Patrick Peterson, Ari	StL	2011	99
†Damaris Johnson, Phi	Dal	2012	98
Gil LeFebvre, Cin	Brooklyn	1933	98
Charlie West, Min	Wash	1968	98
Dennis Morgan, Dal	StL Cards	1974	98
Terance Mathis, NYJ	Dal	1990	98
Greg Pruitt, LA Raiders	Was	1983	97
†Bryan McCann, Dal	Det	2010	97

MISSED FIELD GOAL RETURNS	Opponent	Year	Yds
†Antonio Cromartie, SD	Min	2007	109
†Devin Hester, Chi	NYG	2006	108
†Nathan Vasher, Chi	SF	2005	108
Chris McAlister, Balt	Den	2002	107
Aaron Glenn, NYJ	Ind	1998	104

† Active in 2012.

Rushing

Year	Player, Team	Att	Yards	Avg	TD
1932	Cliff Battles, Bos	148	576	3.9	3
1933	Jim Musick, Bos	173	809	4.7	5
1934	Beattie Feathers, Chi	119	1,004	8.4	8
1935	Doug Russell, Chi Cards	140	499	3.6	0
1936	Alphonse Leemans, NY	206	830	4.0	2
1937	Cliff Battles, Wash	216	874	4.0	5
1938	Byron White, Pit	152	567	3.7	4
1939	Bill Osmanski, Chi	121	699	5.8	7
1940	Byron White, Det	146	514	3.5	5
1941	Clarence Manders, Bklyn	111	486	4.4	5
1942	Bill Dudley, Pit	162	696	4.3	5
1943	Bill Paschal, NY	147	572	3.9	10
1944	Bill Paschal, NY	196	737	3.8	9
1945	Steve Van Buren, Phil	143	832	5.8	15
1946	Bill Dudley, Pit	146	604	4.1	3
1947	Steve Van Buren, Phil	217	1,008	4.6	13
1948	Steve Van Buren, Phil	201	945	4.7	10
1949	Steve Van Buren, Phil	263	1,146	4.4	11
1950	Marion Motley, Clev	140	810	5.8	3
1951	Eddie Price, NY	271	971	3.6	7
1952	Dan Towler, LA	156	894	5.7	10
1953	Joe Perry, SF	192	1,018	5.3	10
1954	Joe Perry, SF	173	1,049	6.1	8
1955	Alan Ameche, Balt	213	961	4.5	9
1956	Rick Casares, Chi	234	1,126	4.8	12
1957	Jim Brown, Clev	202	942	4.7	9
1958	Jim Brown, Clev	257	1,527	5.9	17
1959	Jim Brown, Clev	290	1,329	4.6	14
1960	Jim Brown, Clev, NFL	215	1,257	5.8	9
	Abner Haynes, Dallas Texans, AFL	156	875	5.6	9
1961	Jim Brown, Clev, NFL	305	1,408	4.6	8
	Billy Cannon, Hou, AFL	200	948	4.7	6
1962	Jim Taylor, GB, NFL	272	1,474	5.4	19
	Cookie Gilchrist, Buf, AFL	214	1,096	5.1	13
1963	Jim Brown, Clev, NFL	291	1,863	6.4	12
	Clem Daniels, Oak, AFL	215	1,099	5.1	3
1964	Jim Brown, Clev, NFL	280	1,446	5.2	7
	Cookie Gilchrist, Buf, AFL	230	981	4.3	6
1965	Jim Brown, Clev, NFL	289	1,544	5.3	17
	Paul Lowe, SD, AFL	222	1,121	5.0	7
1966	Jim Nance, Bos, AFL	299	1,458	4.9	11
	Gale Sayers, Chi, NFL	229	1,231	5.4	8
1967	Jim Nance, Bos, AFL	269	1,216	4.5	7
	Leroy Kelly, Clev, NFL	235	1,205	5.1	11
1968	Leroy Kelly, Clev, NFL	248	1,239	5.0	16
	Paul Robinson, Cin, AFL	238	1,023	4.3	8
1969	Gale Sayers, Chi, NFL	236	1,032	4.4	8
	Dickie Post, SD, AFL	182	873	4.8	6
1970	Larry Brown, Wash, NFC	237	1,125	4.7	5
	Floyd Little, Den, AFC	209	901	4.3	3
1971	Floyd Little, Den, AFC	284	1,133	4.0	6
	John Brockington, GB, NFC	216	1,105	5.1	4
1972	O.J. Simpson, Buf, AFC	292	1,251	4.3	6
	Larry Brown, Wash, NFC	285	1,216	4.3	8
1973	O.J. Simpson, Buf, AFC	332	2,003	6.0	12
	John Brockington, GB, NFC	265	1,144	4.3	3
1974	Otis Armstrong, Den, AFC	263	1,407	5.3	9
	Lawrence McCutcheon, LA, NFC	236	1,109	4.7	3
1975	O.J. Simpson, Buf, AFC	329	1,817	5.5	16
	Jim Otis, StL, NFC	269	1,076	4.0	5
1976	O.J. Simpson, Buf, AFC	290	1,503	5.2	8
	Walter Payton, Chi, NFC	311	1,390	4.5	13
1977	Walter Payton, Chi, NFC	339	1,852	5.5	14
	Mark van Eeghen, Oak, AFC	324	1,273	3.9	7
1978	Earl Campbell, Hou, AFC	302	1,450	4.8	13
	Walter Payton, Chi, NFC	333	1,395	4.2	11
1979	Earl Campbell, Hou, AFC	368	1,697	4.6	19
	Walter Payton, Chi, NFC	369	1,610	4.4	14
1980	Earl Campbell, Hou, AFC	373	1,934	5.2	13
	Walter Payton, Chi, NFC	317	1,460	4.6	6
1981	George Rogers, NO, NFC	378	1,674	4.4	13
	Earl Campbell, Hou, AFC	361	1,376	3.8	10
1982	Freeman McNeil, NYJ, AFC	151	786	5.2	6
	Tony Dorsett, Dal, NFC	177	745	4.2	5
1983	Eric Dickerson, LA, NFC	390	1,808	4.6	18
	Curt Warner, Sea, AFC	335	1,449	4.3	13
1984	Eric Dickerson, LA, NFC	379	2,105	5.6	14
	Earnest Jackson, SD, AFC	296	1,179	4.0	8
1985	Marcus Allen, LA, AFC	380	1,759	4.6	11
	Gerald Riggs, Atl, NFC	397	1,719	4.3	10
1986	Eric Dickerson, LA, NFC	404	1,821	4.5	11
	Curt Warner, Sea, AFC	319	1,481	4.6	13
1987	Charles White, LA, NFC	324	1,374	4.2	11
	Eric Dickerson, Ind, AFC	223	1,011	4.5	5
1988	Eric Dickerson, Ind, AFC	388	1,659	4.3	14
	Herschel Walker, Dal, NFC	361	1,514	4.2	5
1989	Christian Okoye, KC, AFC	370	1,480	4.0	12
	Barry Sanders, Det, NFC	280	1,470	5.3	14
1990	Barry Sanders, Det, NFC	255	1,304	5.1	13
	Thurman Thomas, Buf, AFC	271	1,297	4.8	11
1991	Emmitt Smith, Dal, NFC	365	1,563	4.3	12
	Thurman Thomas, Buf, AFC	288	1,407	4.9	7
1992	Emmitt Smith, Dal, NFC	373	1,713	4.6	18
	Barry Foster, Pit, AFC	390	1,690	4.3	11
1993	Emmitt Smith, Dal, NFC	283	1,486	5.3	9
	Thurman Thomas, Buf, AFC	355	1,315	3.7	6
1994	Barry Sanders, Det, NFC	331	1,883	5.7	7
	Chris Warren, Sea, AFC	333	1,545	4.6	9
1995	Emmitt Smith, Dal, NFC	377	1,773	4.7	25
	Curtis Martin, NE, AFC	368	1,487	4.0	14
1996	Barry Sanders, Det, NFC	307	1,553	5.1	11
	Terrell Davis, Den, AFC	345	1,538	4.5	13
1997	Barry Sanders, Det, NFC	335	2,053	6.1	11
	Terrell Davis, Den, AFC	369	1,750	4.7	15
1998	Terrell Davis, Den, AFC	392	2,008	5.1	21
	Jamal Anderson, Atl, NFC	410	1,846	4.5	14
1999	Edgerrin James, Ind, AFC	369	1,553	4.2	13
	Stephen Davis, Wash, NFC	290	1,405	4.8	17
2000	Edgerrin James, Ind, AFC	387	1,709	4.4	13
	Robert Smith, Min, NFC	295	1,521	5.2	7
2001	Priest Holmes, Kan, AFC	327	1,555	4.8	8
	Stephen Davis, Wash, NFC	356	1,432	4.0	5
2002	Ricky Williams, Mia, AFC	383	1,853	4.8	16
	Deuce McAllister, NO, NFC	325	1,388	4.3	13

Rushing *(Cont.)*

Year	Player, Team	Att	Yards	Avg	TD
2003	Jamal Lewis, Balt, AFC	387	2,066	5.3	14
	Ahman Green, GB, NFC	355	1,883	5.3	15
2004	Curtis Martin				
	NY Jets, AFC	371	1,697	4.6	12
	Shaun Alexander,				
	Sea, NFC	353	1,696	4.8	16
2005	Shaun Alexander,				
	Sea, NFC	370	1,880	5.1	27
	Larry Johnson, KC, AFC	336	1,750	5.2	20
2006	LaDainian Tomlinson,				
	SD, AFC	348	1,815	5.2	28
	Frank Gore, SF, NFC	312	1,695	5.4	8
2007	LaDainian Tomlinson,				
	SD, AFC	315	1,474	4.7	15
	Adrian Peterson,				
	Min, NFC	238	1,341	5.6	12

Year	Player, Team	Att	Yards	Avg	TD
2008	Adrian Peterson,				
	Min, NFC	363	1,760	4.8	10
	Thomas Jones, NYJ, AFC	290	1,312	4.5	13
2009	Chris Johnson, Ten, AFC	358	2,006	5.6	14
	Steven Jackson,				
	StL, NFC	324	1,416	4.4	4
2010	Arian Foster, Hou, AFC	327	1,616	4.9	16
	Michael Turner, Atl, NFC	334	1,371	4.1	12
2011	M. Jones-Drew, Jax, AFC	343	1,606	4.7	8
	Michael Turner, Atl, NFC	301	1,340	4.5	11
2012	Adrian Peterson,				
	Min, NFC	348	2,097	6.0	12
	Jamaal Charles, KC, AFC	285	1,509	5.3	5

Passing

Year	Player, Team	Att	Comp	Yards	TD	Int
1932	Arnie Herber, GB	101	37	639	9	9
1933	Harry Newman, NYG	136	53	973	11	17
1934	Arnie Herber, GB	115	42	799	8	12
1935	Ed Danowski, NYG	113	57	794	10	9
1936	Arnie Herber, GB	173	77	1,239	11	13
1937	Sammy Baugh, Wash	171	81	1,127	8	14
1938	Ed Danowski, NYG	129	70	848	7	8
1939	Parker Hall, Clev	208	106	1,227	9	13
1940	Sammy Baugh, Wash	177	111	1,367	12	10
1941	Cecil Isbell, GB	206	117	1,479	15	11
1942	Cecil Isbell, GB	268	146	2,021	24	14
1943	Sammy Baugh, Wash	239	133	1,754	23	19
1944	Frank Filchock, Wash	147	84	1,139	13	9
1945	Sid Luckman, Chi	217	117	1,725	14	10
1946	Bob Waterfield, LA	251	127	1,747	18	17
1947	Sammy Baugh, Wash	354	210	2,938	25	15
1948	Tommy Thompson, Phil	246	141	1,965	25	11
1949	Sammy Baugh, Wash	255	145	1,903	18	14
1950	Norm Van Brocklin, LA	233	127	2,061	18	14
1951	Bob Waterfield, LA	176	88	1,566	13	10
1952	Norm Van Brocklin, LA	205	113	1,736	14	17
1953	Otto Graham, Clev	258	167	2,722	11	9
1954	Norm Van Brocklin, LA	260	139	2,637	13	21
1955	Otto Graham, Clev	185	98	1,721	15	8
1956	Ed Brown, Chi	168	96	1,667	11	12
1957	Tommy O'Connell, Clev	110	63	1,229	9	8
1958	Eddie LeBaron, Wash	145	79	1,365	11	10
1959	Charlie Conerly, NYG	194	113	1,706	14	4
1960	Jack Kemp, LA, AFL	406	211	3,018	20	25
	Milt Plum, Clev, NFL	250	151	2,297	21	5
1961	George Blanda,					
	Hou, AFL	362	187	3,330	36	22
	Milt Plum, Clev, NFL	302	177	2,416	18	10
1962	Len Dawson, Dal, AFL	310	189	2,759	29	17
	Bart Starr, GB, NFL	285	178	2,438	12	9
1963	Y.A. Tittle, NY, NFL	367	221	3,145	36	14
	Tobin Rote, SD, AFL	286	170	2,510	20	17

Year	Player, Team	Att	Comp	Yards	TD	Int
1964	Len Dawson, KC, AFL	354	199	2,879	30	18
	Bart Starr, GB, NFL	272	163	2,144	15	4
1965	John Hadl, SD, AFL	348	174	2,798	20	21
	Rudy Bukich, Chi, NFL	312	176	2,641	20	9
1966	Len Dawson, KC, AFL	284	159	2,527	26	10
	Bart Starr, GB, NFL	251	156	2,257	14	3
1967	Sonny Jurgensen,					
	Wash, NFL	508	288	3,747	31	16
	Daryle Lamonica,					
	Oak, AFL	425	220	3,228	30	20
1968	Earl Morrall, Balt, NFL	317	182	2,909	26	17
	Len Dawson, KC, AFL	224	131	2,109	17	9
1969	S. Jurgensen, Wash, NFL	442	274	3,102	22	15
	Greg Cook, Cin, AFL	197	106	1,854	15	11
1970	John Brodie, SF, NFC	378	223	2,941	24	10
	Daryle Lamonica,					
	Oak, AFC	356	179	2,516	22	15
1971	Bob Griese, Mia, AFC	263	145	2,089	19	9
	Roger Staubach,					
	Dal, NFC	211	126	1,882	15	4
1972	Norm Snead, NY, NFC	325	196	2,307	17	12
	Earl Morrall, Mia, AFC	150	83	1,360	11	7
#1973	Roger Staubach,					
	Dal, NFC	62.6	2,428	23	15	94.6
	Ken Stabler,					
	Oak, AFC	62.7	1,997	14	10	88.3
1974	Ken Anderson,					
	Cin, AFC	64.9	2,667	18	10	95.7
	Sonny Jurgensen,					
	Wash, NFC	64.1	1,185	11	5	94.5
1975	Ken Anderson,					
	Cin, AFC	60.5	3,169	21	11	93.9
	Fran Tarkenton,					
	Min, NFC	64.2	2,994	25	13	91.8
1976	Ken Stabler,					
	Oak, AFC	66.7	2,737	27	17	103.4
	James Harris,					
	LA, NFC	57.6	1,460	8	6	89.6

#Since 1973, the annual passing NFL leaders have been determined by a passer rating system that compares individual performances to a fixed performance standard. Before 1973, total passing yards gained was used.

Passing* *(Cont.)*

Year	Player, Team	Comp%	Yds	TD	Int	Rating	Year	Player, Team	Comp%	Yds	TD	Int	Rating
1977	Bob Griese, Mia, AFC	58.6	2,252	22	13	87.8	1992	Steve Young, SF, NFC	66.7	3,465	25	7	107.0
	Roger Staubach, Dal, NFC	58.2	2,620	18	9	87.0		Warren Moon, Hou, AFC	64.7	2,521	18	12	89.3
1978	Roger Staubach, Dal, NFC	55.9	3,190	25	16	84.9	1993	Steve Young, SF, NFC	68.0	4,023	29	16	101.5
	Terry Bradshaw, Pit, AFC	56.3	2,915	28	20	84.7		John Elway Den, AFC	63.2	4,030	25	10	92.8
1979	Roger Staubach, Dal, NFC	57.9	3,586	27	11	92.3	1994	Steve Young, SF, NFC	70.3	3,969	35	10	112.8
	Dan Fouts, SD, AFC	62.6	4,082	24	24	82.6		Dan Marino, Mia, AFC	62.0	4,453	30	17	89.2
1980	Brian Sipe, Clev, AFC	60.8	4,132	30	14	91.4	1995	Jim Harbaugh, Ind, AFC	61.2	2,575	17	5	100.7
	Ron Jaworski, Phi, NFC	57.0	3,529	27	12	91.0		Brett Favre, GB, NFC	62.9	4,413	38	13	99.5
1981	Ken Anderson, Cin, AFC	62.6	3,754	29	10	98.4	1996	Steve Young, SF, NFC	67.7	2,410	14	6	97.2
	Joe Montana, SF, NFC	63.7	3,565	19	12	88.4		John Elway, Den, AFC	61.6	3,328	26	14	89.2
1982	Ken Anderson, Cin, AFC	70.6	2,495	12	9	95.3	1997	Steve Young, SF, NFC	67.7	3,029	19	6	104.7
	Joe Theismann, Wash, NFC	63.9	2,033	13	9	91.3		Mark Brunell, Jax, AFC	60.7	3,281	18	7	91.2
1983	Steve Bartkowski, Atl, NFC	63.4	3,167	22	5	97.6	1998	Randall Cunningham, Min, NFC	60.9	3,704	34	10	106.0
	Dan Marino, Mia AFC	58.4	2,210	20	6	96.0		Vinny Testaverde, NYJ, AFC	61.5	3,256	29	7	101.6
1984	Dan Marino, Mia, AFC	64.2	5,084	48	17	108.9	1999	Kurt Warner, StL, NFC	65.1	4,353	41	13	109.2
	Joe Montana, SF, NFC	64.6	3,630	28	10	102.9		Peyton Manning, Ind, AFC	62.1	4,135	26	15	90.7
1985	Ken O'Brien, NY, AFC	60.9	3,888	25	8	96.2	2000	Brian Griese, Den, AFC	64.3	2,688	19	4	102.9
	Joe Montana, SF, NFC	61.3	3,653	27	13	91.3		Trent Green, StL, NFC	60.4	2,063	16	5	101.8
1986	Tommy Kramer, Min, NFC	55.9	3,000	24	10	92.6	2001	Kurt Warner, StL, NFC	68.7	4,830	36	22	101.4
	Dan Marino, Mia, AFC	60.7	4,746	44	23	92.5		Rich Gannon, Oak, AFC	65.8	3,828	27	9	95.5
1987	Joe Montana, SF, NFC	66.8	3,054	31	13	102.1	2002	Brad Johnson, TB, NFC	62.3	3,049	22	6	92.9
	Bernie Kosar, Clev, AFC	61.9	3,033	22	9	95.4		Chad Pennington, NY, AFC	68.9	3,120	22	6	104.2
1988	Boomer Esiason, Cin, AFC	57.5	3,572	28	14	97.4	2003	Steve McNair, Ten, AFC	62.5	3,215	24	7	100.4
	Wade Wilson, Min, NFC	61.4	2,746	15	9	91.5		Daunte Culpepper, Min, NFC	65.0	3,479	25	11	96.4
1989	Joe Montana, SF, NFC	70.2	3,521	26	8	112.4	2004	Peyton Manning, Ind, AFC	67.6	4,557	49	10	121.1
	Boomer Esiason, Cin, AFC	56.7	3,525	28	11	92.1		Daunte Culpepper, Min, NFC	69.2	4,717	39	11	110.9
1990	Jim Kelly, Buf, AFC	63.3	2,829	24	9	101.2	2005	Peyton Manning, Ind, AFC	67.3	3,747	28	10	104.1
	Phil Simms, NY, NFC	59.2	2,284	15	4	92.7		Matt Hasselbeck, GB, NFC	65.5	3,459	24	9	98.2
1991	Steve Young, SF, NFC	64.5	2,517	17	8	101.8	2006	Peyton Manning, Ind, AFC	65.0	4,397	31	9	101.0
	Jim Kelly, Buf, AFC	64.1	3,844	33	17	97.6		Drew Brees, NO, NFC	64.3	4,418	26	11	96.2

Passing *(Cont.)*

Year	Player, Team	Comp%	Yds	TD	Int	Rating	Year	Player, Team	Comp%	Yds	TD	Int	Rating
2007	Tom Brady, NE, AFC	68.9	4,806	50	8	117.2	2010	Tom Brady, NE, AFC	65.9	3,900	36	4	111.0
	Tony Romo, Dal, NFC	64.4	4,211	36	19	97.4		Aaron Rodgers, GB, NFC	65.7	3,922	28	11	101.2
2008	Philip Rivers, SD, AFC	65.3	4,009	34	11	105.5	2011	Aaron Rodgers, GB, NFC	68.3	4,643	45	6	122.5
	Kurt Warner, Ari, NFC	67.1	4,583	30	14	96.9		Tom Brady, NE, AFC	65.6	5,235	39	12	105.6
2009	Drew Brees, NO, NFC	70.6	4,388	34	11	109.6	2012	Aaron Rodgers GB, NFC	67.2	4,295	39	8	108.0
	Philip Rivers, SD, AFC	65.2	4,254	28	9	104.4		Peyton Manning Den, AFC	68.6	4,659	37	11	105.8

Pass Receiving†

Year	Player, Team	No.	Yds	Avg	TD	Year	Player, Team	No.	Yds	Avg	TD
1932	Ray Flaherty, NY	21	350	16.7	3	1965	Lionel Taylor, Den, AFL	85	1,131	13.3	6
1933	John Kelly, Brooklyn	22	246	11.2	3		Dave Parks, SF, NFL	80	1,344	16.8	12
1934	Joe Carter, Phil	16	238	14.9	4	1966	Lance Alworth, SD, AFL	73	1,383	18.9	13
	Morris Badgro, NY	16	206	12.9	1		Charley Taylor, Wash, NFL	72	1,119	15.5	12
1935	Tod Goodwin, NY	26	432	16.6	4	1967	George Sauer, NY, AFL	75	1,189	15.9	6
1936	Don Hutson, GB	34	536	15.8	8		Charley Taylor, Wash, NFL	70	990	14.1	9
1937	Don Hutson, GB	41	552	13.5	7	1968	Clifton McNeil, SF, NFL	71	994	14.0	7
1938	Gaynell Tinsley, Chi Cards	41	516	12.6	1		Lance Alworth, SD, AFL	68	1,312	19.3	10
1939	Don Hutson, GB	34	846	24.9	6	1969	Dan Abramowicz, NO, NFL	73	1,015	13.9	7
1940	Don Looney, Phil	58	707	12.2	4		Lance Alworth, SD, AFL	64	1,003	15.7	4
1941	Don Hutson, GB	58	738	12.7	10	1970	Dick Gordon, Chi, NFC	71	1,026	14.5	13
1942	Don Hutson, GB	74	1,211	16.4	17		Marlin Briscoe, Buf, AFC	57	1,036	18.2	8
1943	Don Hutson, GB	47	776	16.5	11	1971	Fred Biletnikoff, Oak, AFC	61	929	15.2	9
1944	Don Hutson, GB	58	866	14.9	9		Bob Tucker, NY, NFC	59	791	13.4	4
1945	Don Hutson, GB	47	834	17.7	9	1972	Harold Jackson, Phil, NFL	62	1,048	16.9	4
1946	Jim Benton, LA	63	981	15.6	6		Fred Biletnikoff, Oak, AFC	58	802	13.8	7
1947	Jim Keane, Chi	64	910	14.2	10	1973	Harold Carmichael, Phil, NFC	67	1,116	16.7	9
1948	Tom Fears, LA	51	698	13.7	4		Fred Willis, Hou, AFC	57	371	6.5	1
1949	Tom Fears, LA	77	1,013	13.2	9	1974	Lydell Mitchell, Balt, AFC	72	544	7.6	2
1950	Tom Fears, LA	84	1,116	13.3	7		Charles Young, Phil, NFC	63	696	11.0	3
1951	Elroy Hirsch, LA	66	1,495	22.7	17	1975	Chuck Foreman, Min, NFC	73	691	9.5	9
1952	Mac Speedie, Clev	62	911	14.7	5		Reggie Rucker, Clev, AFC	60	770	12.8	3
1953	Pete Pihos, Phil	63	1,049	16.7	10		Lydell Mitchell, Balt, AFC	60	544	9.1	4
1954	Pete Pihos, Phil	60	872	14.5	10	1976	MacArthur Lane, KC, AFC	66	686	10.4	1
	Billy Wilson, SF	60	830	13.8	5		Drew Pearson, Dal, NFC	58	806	13.9	6
1955	Pete Pihos, Phil	62	864	13.9	7	1977	Lydell Mitchell, Balt, AFC	71	620	8.7	4
1956	Billy Wilson, SF	60	889	14.8	5		Ahmad Rashad, Min, NFC	51	681	13.4	2
1957	Billy Wilson, SF	52	757	14.6	6	1978	Rickey Young, Min, NFC	88	704	8.0	5
1958	Raymond Berry, Balt	56	794	14.2	9		Steve Largent, Sea, AFC	71	1,168	16.5	8
	Pete Retzlaff, Phil	56	766	13.7	2	1979	Joe Washington, Balt, AFC	82	750	9.1	3
1959	Raymond Berry, Balt	66	959	14.5	14		Ahmad Rashad, Min, NFC	80	1,156	14.5	9
1960	Lionel Taylor, Den, AFL	92	1,235	13.4	12	1980	Kellen Winslow, SD, AFC	89	1,290	14.5	9
	Raymond Berry, Balt, NFL	74	1,298	17.5	10		Earl Cooper, SF, NFC	83	567	6.8	4
1961	Lionel Taylor, Den, AFL	100	1,176	11.8	4	1981	Kellen Winslow, SD, AFC	88	1,075	12.2	10
	Jim Phillips, LA, NFL	78	1,092	14.0	5		Dwight Clark, SF, NFC	85	1,105	13.0	4
1962	Lionel Taylor, Den, AFL	77	908	11.8	4						
	Bobby Mitchell, Wash, NFL	72	1,384	19.2	11						
1963	Lionel Taylor, Den, AFL	78	1,101	14.1	10						
	Bobby Joe Conrad, StL, NFL	73	967	13.2	10						
1964	Charley Hennigan, Hou, AFL	101	1,546	15.3	8						
	Johnny Morris, Chi, NFL	93	1,200	12.9	10						

†Most catches.

Pass Receiving† *(Cont.)*

Year	Player, Team	No.	Yds	Avg	TD
1982	Dwight Clark, SF, NFC	60	913	15.2	5
	Kellen Winslow, SD, AFC	54	721	13.4	6
1983	Todd Christensen,				
	LA Raiders, AFC	92	1,247	13.6	12
	Roy Green, StL, NFC	78	1,227	15.7	14
	Charlie Brown, Wash, NFC	78	1,225	15.7	8
	Earnest Gray, NY, NFC	78	1,139	14.6	5
1984	Art Monk, Wash, NFC	106	1,372	12.9	7
	Ozzie Newsome,				
	Clev, AFC	89	1,001	11.2	5
1985	Roger Craig, SF, NFC	92	1,016	11.0	6
	Lionel James, SD, AFC	86	1,027	11.9	6
1986	Todd Christensen,				
	LA Raiders, AFC	95	1,153	12.1	8
	Jerry Rice, SF, NFC	86	1,570	18.3	15
1987	J.T. Smith, StL Card, NFC	91	1,117	12.3	8
	Al Toon, NY, AFC	68	976	14.4	5
1988	Al Toon, NY, AFC	93	1,067	11.5	5
	Henry Ellard,				
	LA, NFC	86	1,414	16.4	10
1989	Sterling Sharpe, GB, NFC	90	1,423	15.8	12
	Andre Reed, Buf, AFC	88	1,312	14.9	9
1990	Jerry Rice, SF, NFC	100	1,502	15.0	13
	Haywood Jeffires,				
	Hou, AFC	74	1,048	14.2	8
	Drew Hill, Hou, AFC	74	1,019	13.8	5
1991	Haywood Jeffires,				
	Hou, AFC	100	1,181	11.8	7
	Michael Irvin, Dal, NFC	93	1,523	16.4	8
1992	Sterling Sharpe,				
	GB, NFC	108	1,461	13.5	13
	Haywood Jeffires,				
	Hou, AFC	90	913	10.1	9
1993	Sterling Sharpe,				
	GB, NFC	112	1,274	11.4	11
	Reggie Langhorne,				
	Ind, AFC	85	1,038	12.2	3
1994	Cris Carter, Min, NFC	122	1,256	10.3	7
	Ben Coates, NE, AFC	96	1,174	12.2	7
1995	Herman Moore,				
	Det, NFC	123	1,686	13.7	14
	Carl Pickens, Cin, AFC	99	1,234	12.5	17
1996	Jerry Rice, SF, NFC	108	1,254	11.6	8
	Carl Pickens, Cin, AFC	100	1,180	11.8	12
1997	Herman Moore, Det, NFC	104	1,293	12.4	8
	Tim Brown, Oak, AFC	104	1,408	13.5	5
1998	O.J. McDuffie, Mia, AFC	90	1,050	11.7	7
	Frank Sanders,				
	Ariz, NFC	89	1,145	12.9	3
1999	Jimmy Smith, Jax, AFC	116	1,636	14.1	6
	Muhsin Muhammad,				
	Car, NFC	96	1,253	13.1	8
2000	Muhsin Muhammad,				
	Car, NFC	102	1,183	11.6	6
	Marvin Harrison, Ind, AFC	102	1,413	13.9	14
2001	Rod Smith, Den, AFC	113	1,343	11.9	11
	Keyshawn Johnson,				
	TB, NFC	106	1,266	11.9	1
2002	Marvin Harrison, Ind, AFC	143	1,722	12.0	11
	Randy Moss, Min, NFC	106	1,347	12.7	7
2003	Torry Holt, StL, NFC	117	1,696	14.5	12
	LaDainian Tomlinson,				
	SD, AFC	100	725	7.3	4
2004	Tony Gonzalez, KC, AFC	102	1,258	12.3	7
	Joe Horn, NO, NFC	94	1,399	14.9	11
2005	Steve Smith, Car, NFC	103	1,563	15.2	12
	Chad Johnson, Cin, AFC	97	1,432	14.8	9
2006	Chad Johnson, Cin, AFC	87	1,369	15.7	7
	Roy Williams, Det, NFC	82	1,310	16.0	7
2007	Reggie Wayne, Ind, AFC	104	1,510	14.5	10
	Larry Fitzgerald, Ari, NFC	100	1,409	14.1	10
2008	Andre Johnson, Hou, AFC	115	1,575	13.7	8
	Larry Fitzgerald, Ari, NFC	96	1,431	14.9	12
2009	Wes Welker, NE, AFC	123	1,348	11.0	4
	Steve Smith, NYG, NFC	107	1,220	11.4	7
2010	Roddy White, Atl, NFC	115	1,389	12.1	10
	Reggie Wayne, Ind, AFC	111	1,355	12.2	6
2011	Wes Welker, NE, AFC	122	1,569	12.9	9
	Rod White, Atl, NFC	100	1,296	13.0	8
2012	Calvin Johnson, Det, NFC	122	1,964	16.1	5
	Wes Welker, NE, AFC	118	1,354	11.5	6

†Most catches.

Scoring

Year	Player, Team	TD	FG	PAT	TP
1932	Earl Clark, Portsmouth	6	3	10	55
1933	Ken Strong, NY	6	5	13	64
	Glenn Presnell, Ports	6	6	10	64
1934	Jack Manders, Chi	3	10	31	79
1935	Earl Clark, Det	6	1	16	55
1936	Earl Clark, Det	7	4	19	73
1937	Jack Manders, Chi	5	18	15	69
1938	Clarke Hinkle, GB	7	3	7	58
1939	Andy Farkas, Wash	11	0	2	68
1940	Don Hutson, GB	7	0	15	57
1941	Don Hutson, GB	12	1	20	95
1942	Don Hutson, GB	17	1	33	138
1943	Don Hutson, GB	12	3	36	117
1944	Don Hutson, GB	9	0	31	85
1945	Steve Van Buren, Phil	18	0	2	110
1946	Ted Fritsch, GB	10	9	13	100
1947	Pat Harder, Chicago Cards	7	7	39	102
1948	Pat Harder, Chicago Cards	6	7	53	110
1949	Pat Harder, Chicago Cards	8	3	45	102
	Gene Roberts, NY	17	0	0	102
1950	Doak Walker, Det	11	8	38	128
1951	Elroy Hirsch, LA	17	0	0	102
1952	Gordy Soltau, SF	7	6	34	94
1953	Gordy Soltau, SF	6	10	48	114
1954	Bobby Walston, Phi	11	4	36	114
1955	Doak Walker, Det	7	9	27	96
1956	Bobby Layne, Det	5	12	33	99
1957	Sam Baker, Was	1	14	29	77
	Lou Groza, Cle	0	15	32	77
1958	Jim Brown, Cle	18	0	0	108

Scoring (Cont.)

Year	Player, Team	TD	FG	PAT	TP
1959	Paul Hornung, GB	7	7	31	94
1960	Paul Hornung, GB, NFL	15	15	41	176
	Gene Mingo, Den, AFL	6	18	33	123
1961	Gino Cappelletti, Bos, AFL	8	17	48	147
	Paul Hornung, GB, NFL	10	15	41	146
1962	Gene Mingo, Den, AFL	4	27	32	137
	Jim Taylor, GB, NFL	19	0	0	114
1963	Gino Cappelletti, Bos, AFL	2	22	35	113
	Don Chandler, NY, NFL	0	18	52	106
1964	Gino Cappelletti, Bos, AFL	7	25	36	155
	Lenny Moore, Balt, NFL	20	0	0	120
1965	Gale Sayers, Chi, NFL	22	0	0	132
	Gino Cappelletti, Bos, AFL	9	17	27	132
1966	Gino Cappelletti, Bos, AFL	6	16	35	119
	Bruce Gossett, LA, NFL	0	28	29	113
1967	Jim Bakken, StL, NFL	0	27	36	117
	George Blanda, Oak, AFL	0	20	56	116
1968	Jim Turner, NY, AFL	0	34	43	145
	Leroy Kelly, Clev, NFL	20	0	0	120
1969	Jim Turner, NY, AFL	0	32	33	129
	Fred Cox, Min, NFL	0	26	43	121
1970	Fred Cox, Min, NFC	0	30	35	125
	Jan Stenerud, KC, AFC	0	30	26	116
1971	Garo Yepremian, Mia, AFC	0	28	33	117
	Curt Knight, Was, NFC	0	29	27	114
1972	Chester Marcol, GB, NFC	0	33	29	128
	Bobby Howfield, NY AFC	0	27	40	121
1973	David Ray, LA, NFC	0	30	40	130
	Roy Gerela, Pit, AFC	0	29	36	123
1974	Chester Marcol, GB, NFC	0	25	19	94
	Roy Gerela, Pit, AFC	0	20	33	93
1975	O.J. Simpson, Buf, AFC	23	0	0	138
	Chuck Foreman, Min, NFC	22	0	0	132
1976	Toni Linhart, Balt, AFC	0	20	49	109
	Mark Moseley, Wash, NFC	0	22	31	97
1977	Errol Mann, Oak, AFC	0	20	39	99
	Walter Payton, Chi, NFC	16	0	0	96
1978	Frank Corral, LA, NFC	0	29	31	118
	Pat Leahy, NY, AFC	0	22	41	107
1979	John Smith, NE, AFC	0	23	46	115
	Mark Moseley, Was, NFC	0	25	39	114
1980	John Smith, NE, AFC	0	26	51	129
	Ed Murray, Det, NFC	0	27	35	116
1981	Ed Murray, Det, NFC	0	25	46	121
	Rafael Septien, Dal, NFC	0	27	40	121
	Jim Breech, Cin, AFC	0	22	49	115
	Nick Lowery, KC, AFC	0	26	37	115
1982	Marcus Allen, LA, AFC	14	0	0	84
	Wendell Tyler, LA, NFC	13	0	0	78
1983	Mark Moseley, Was, NFC	0	33	62	161
	Gary Anderson, Pit, AFC	0	27	38	119
1984	Ray Wersching, SF, NFC	0	25	56	131
	Gary Anderson, Pit, AFC	0	24	45	117
1985	Kevin Butler, Chi, NFC	0	31	51	144
	Gary Anderson, Pit, AFC	0	33	40	139
1986	Tony Franklin, NE, AFC	0	32	44	140
	Kevin Butler, Chi, NFC	0	28	36	120
1987	Jerry Rice, SF, NFC	23	0	0	138
	Jim Breech, Cin, AFC	0	24	25	97
1988	Scott Norwood, Buf, AFC	0	32	33	129
	Mike Cofer, SF, NFC	0	27	40	121
1989	Mike Cofer, SF, NFC	0	29	49	136
	David Treadwell, Den, AFC	0	27	39	120
1990	Nick Lowery, KC, AFC	0	34	37	139
	Chip Lohmiller, Was, NFC	0	30	41	131
1991	Chip Lohmiller, Was, NFC	0	31	56	149
	Pete Stoyanovich, Mia, AFC	0	31	28	121
1992	Pete Stoyanovich, Mia, AFC	0	30	34	124
	Morten Anderson, NO, NFC	0	29	33	120
	Chip Lohmiller, Was, NFC	0	30	30	120
1993	Jeff Jaeger, Rai, AFC	0	35	27	132
	Jason Hanson, Det, NFC	0	34	28	130
1994	John Carney, SD, AFC	0	34	33	135
	Fuad Reveiz, Min, NFC	0	34	30	132
	Emmitt Smith, Dal, NFC	22	0	0	132
1995	Emmitt Smith, Dal, NFC	25	0	0	150
	Norm Johnson, Pit, AFC	0	34	39	141
1996	John Kasay, Car, NFC	0	37	34	145
	Cary Blanchard, Ind, AFC	0	36	27	135
1997	Mike Hollis, Jax, AFC	0	41	31	134
	Richie Cunningham, Dal, NFC	0	34	24	126
1998	Gary Anderson, Min, NFC	0	35	59	164
	Steve Christie, Buf, AFC	0	33	41	140
1999	Mike Vanderjagt, Ind, AFC	0	34	43	145
	Jeff Wilkins, StL, NFC	0	20	64	124
2000	Marshall Faulk, StL, NFC	26	0	0	160
	Matt Stover, Balt, AFC	0	35	30	135
2001	Marshall Faulk, StL, NFC	21	0	0	128
	Mike Vanderjagt, Ind, AFC	0	28	41	125
2002	Priest Holmes, KC, AFC	24	0	0	144
	Jay Feely, Atl, NFC	0	32	42	138
2003	Jeff Wilkins StL, NFC	0	39	46	163
	Priest Holmes, KC, AFC	27	0	0	162
2004	Adam Vinatieri, NE, AFC	0	31	48	141
	David Akers, Phi, NFC	0	27	41	122
2005	Shaun Alexander, Sea, NFC	28	0	0	168
	Shayne Graham, Cin, AFC	0	28	47	131
2006	LaDainian Tomlinson, SD, AFC	31	0	0	186
	Robbie Gould, Chi, NFC	0	32	47	143
2007	Mason Crosby, GB, NFC	0	31	48	141
	Randy Moss, NE, AFC	23	0	0	138
2008	Stephen Gostkowski, NE, AFC	0	36	40	148
	David Akers, Phi, NFC	0	33	45	144
2009	Nate Kaeding, SD, AFC	0	32	50	146
	David Akers, Phi, NFC	0	32	43	139
2010	David Akers, Phi, NFC	0	32	47	143
	Sebastian Janikowski, Oak, AFC	0	33	43	142
2011	David Akers, SF, NFC	0	44	34	166
	Stephen Gostkowski, NE, AFC	0	28	59	143
2012	Stephen Gostkowski, NE, AFC	0	29	66	153
	Lawrence Tynes, NYG, NFC	0	33	46	145

Interceptions

Year	Player, Team	Int	Yds	Year	Player, Team	Int	Yds
1940	Clarence Parker, Brooklyn	6	146	1975	Mel Blount, Pit, AFC	11	121
	Kent Ryan, Det	6	65		Paul Krause, Min, NFC	10	201
	Don Hutson, GB	6	24	1976	Monte Jackson, LA, NFC	10	173
1941	Marshall Goldberg, Chicago Cards	7	54		Ken Riley, Cin, AFC	9	141
	Art Jones, Pit	7	35	1977	Lyle Blackwood, Balt, AFC	10	163
1942	Clyde Turner, Chicago Bears	8	96		Rolland Lawrence, Atl, NFC	7	138
1943	Sammy Baugh, Wash	11	112	1978	Thom Darden, Clev, AFC	10	200
1944	Howard Livingston, NYG	9	172		Ken Stone, StL, NFC	9	139
1945	Ray Zimmerman, Phil	7	90		Willie Buchanon, GB, NFC	9	93
1946	Bill Dudley, Pittsburgh	10	242	1979	Mike Reinfeldt, Hou, AFC	12	205
1947	Frank Reagan, NYG	10	203		Lemar Parrish, Wash, NFC	9	65
	Frank Seno, Bos	10	100	1980	Lester Hayes, Oak, AFC	13	273
1948	Dan Sandifier, Wash	13	258		Nolan Cromwell, LA, NFC	8	140
1949	Bob Nussbaumer, Chicago Cards	12	157	1981	Everson Walls, Dal, NFC	11	133
1950	Orban Sanders, NY Yanks	13	199		John Harris, Sea, AFC	10	155
1951	Otto Schnellbacher, NYG	11	194	1982	Everson Walls, Dal, NFC	7	61
1952	Dick Lane, LA	14	298		Ken Riley, Cin, AFC	5	88
1953	Jack Christiansen, Det	12	238		Bobby Jackson, NYJ, AFC	5	84
1954	Dick Lane, Chicago Cards	10	181		Dwayne Woodruff, Pit, AFC	5	53
1955	Will Sherman, LA	11	101		Donnie Shell, Pit, AFC	5	27
1956	Lindon Crow, Chicago Cards	11	170	1983	Mark Murphy, Wash, NFC	9	127
1957	Milt Davis, Balt	10	219		Ken Riley, Cin, AFC	8	89
	Jack Christiansen, Det	10	137		Vann McElroy, LA, AFC	8	68
	Jack Butler, Pit	10	85	1984	Ken Easley, Sea, AFC	10	126
1958	Jim Patton, NYG	11	183		Tom Flynn, GB, NFC	9	106
1959	Dean Derby, Pit	7	127	1985	Everson Walls, Dal, NFC	9	31
	Milt Davis, Balt	7	119		Albert Lewis, KC, AFC	8	59
	Don Shinnick, Balt	7	70		Eugene Daniel, Ind, AFC	8	53
1960	Goose Gonsoulin, Den, AFL	11	98	1986	Ronnie Lott, SF, NFC	10	134
	Dave Baker, SF, NFL	10	96		Deron Cherry, KC, AFC	9	150
	Jerry Norton, StL, NFL	10	96	1987	Barry Wilburn, Wash, NFC	9	135
1961	Billy Atkins, Buf, AFL	10	158		Mike Prior, Ind, AFC	6	57
	Dick Lynch, NYG, NFL	9	60		Mark Kelso, Buf, AFC	6	25
1962	Lee Riley, NY Titans, AFL	11	122		Keith Bostic, Hou, AFC	6	-14
	Willie Wood, GB, NFL	9	132	1988	Scott Case, Atl, NFC	10	47
1963	Fred Glick, Hous, AFL	12	180		Erik McMillan, NYJ, AFC	8	168
	Dick Lynch, NYG, NFL	9	251	1989	Felix Wright, Clev, AFC	9	91
	Roosevelt Taylor, Chi, NFL	9	172		Eric Allen, Phil, NFC	8	38
1964	Dainard Paulson, NYJ, AFL	12	157	1990	Mark Carrier, Chi, NFC	10	39
	Paul Krause, Wash, NFL	12	140		Richard Johnson, Hou, AFC	8	100
1965	W. K. Hicks, Hous, AFL	9	156	1991	Ronnie Lott, LA, AFC	8	52
	Bobby Boyd, Balt, NFL	9	78		Ray Crockett, Det, NFC	6	141
1966	Larry Wilson, StL, NFL	10	180		Deion Sanders, Atl, NFC	6	119
	Johnny Robinson, KC, AFL	10	136		Aeneas Williams, Pho, NFC	6	60
	Bobby Hunt, KC, AFL	10	113		Tim McKyer, Atl, NFC	6	24
1967	Lem Barney, Det, NFL	10	232	1992	Henry Jones, Buf, AFC	8	263
	Dave Whitsell, NO, NFL	10	178		Audray McMillian, Min, NFC	8	157
	Miller Farr, Hous, AFL	10	264	1993	Eugene Robinson, Sea, AFC	9	80
	Tom Janik, Buf, AFL	10	222		Nate Odomes, Buf, AFC	9	65
	Dick Westmoreland, Mia, AFL	10	127		Deion Sanders, Atl, NFC	7	91
1968	Dave Grayson, Oak, AFL	10	195	1994	Eric Turner, Clev, AFC	9	199
	Willie Williams, NYG, NFL	10	103		Aeneas Williams, Ariz, NFC	9	89
1969	Mel Renfro, Dal, NFL	10	118	1995	Orlando Thomas, Min, NFC	9	108
	Emmitt Thomas, KC, AFL	9	146		Willie Williams, Pit, AFC	7	122
1970	Johnny Robinson, KC, AFC	10	155	1996	Tyrone Braxton, Den, AFC	9	128
	Dick LeBeau, Det, NFC	9	96		Keith Lyle, StL, NFC	9	152
1971	Bill Bradley, Phil, NFC	11	248	1997	Ryan McNeil, StL, NFC	9	127
	Ken Houston, Hou, AFC	9	220		Mark McMillian, KC, AFC	8	274
1972	Bill Bradley, Phil, NFC	9	73		Darryl Williams, Sea, AFC	8	172
	Mike Sensibaugh, KC, AFC	8	65	1998	Ty Law, NE, AFC	9	133
1973	Dick Anderson, Mia, AFC	8	163		Kwamie Lassiter, Ariz, NFC	9	80
	Mike Wagner, Pit, AFC	8	134	1999	Rod Woodson, Balt, AFC	7	195
	Bobby Bryant, Min, NFC	7	105		Sam Madison, Mia, AFC	7	164
1974	Emmitt Thomas, KC, AFC	12	214		James Hasty, KC, AFC	7	98
	Ray Brown, Atl, NFC	8	164		Donnie Abraham, TB, NFC	7	115
					Troy Vincent, Phil, NFC	7	91

Interceptions *(Cont.)*

Year	Player, Team	Int	Yds	Year	Player, Team	Int	Yds
2000	Darren Sharper, GB, NFC	9	109	2007	Antonio Cromartie, SD, AFC	10	144
	Samari Rolle, Ten, AFC	7	140		O.J. Atogwe, StL, NFC	8	125
	Brian Walker, Mia, AFC	7	80	2008	Ed Reed, Balt, AFC	9	264
2001	Ronde Barber, TB, NFC	10	86		Nick Collins, GB, NFC	7	295
	Anthony Henry, Clev, AFC	10	177		Charles Woodson, GB, NFC	7	169
2002	Rod Woodson, Oak, AFC	8	225	2009	Darren Sharper, NO, NFC	9	376
	Brian Kelly, TB, NFC	8	68		Charles Woodson, GB, NFC	9	179
2003	Brian Russell, Min, NFC	9	185		Asante Samuel, Phi, NFC	9	117
	Tony Parrish, SF, NFC	9	202		Jairus Byrd, Buf, AFC	9	118
	Patrick Surtain, Mia, AFC	7	59	2010	Ed Reed, Bal, AFC	8	183
	Ed Reed, Balt, AFC	7	132		Asante Samuel, Phi, NFC	7	70
	Marcus Coleman, Hou, AFC	7	95	2011	Eric Weddle, SD, AFC	7	89
2004	Ed Reed, Balt, AFC	9	358		Charles Woodson, GB, NFC	7	63
	Chris Gamble, Car, NFC	6	15	2012	Tim Jennings, Chi, NFC	9	105
	Ken Lucas, Sea, NFC	6	46		Jairus Byrd, Buf, AFC	5	81
2005	Ty Law, NYJ, AFC	10	195		Devin McCourty, NE, AFC	5	53
	Deltha O'Neal, Cin, AFC	10	103				
	Darren Sharper, Min, NFC	9	276				
2006	Champ Bailey, Den, AFC	10	162				
	Asante Samuel, NE, AFC	10	120				
	Walt Harris, SF, NFC	8	84				
	Charles Woodson, GB, NFC	8	61				

Sacks*

Year	Player, Team	Sacks	Year	Player, Team	Sacks
1982	Doug Martin, Min, NFC	11.5	1997	John Randle, Min, NFC	15.5
	Jesse Baker, Hou, AFC	7.5		Bruce Smith, Buf, AFC	14.0
1983	Mark Gastineau, NYJ, AFC	19.0	1998	Michael Sinclair, Sea, AFC	16.5
	Fred Dean, SF, NFC	17.5		Reggie White, GB, NFC	16.0
1984	Mark Gastineau, NYJ, AFC	22.0	1999	Kevin Carter, StL, NFC	17.0
	Richard Dent, Chi, NFC	17.5		Jevon Kearse, Ten, AFC	14.5
1985	Richard Dent, Chi, NFC	17.0	2000	La'Roi Glover, NO, NFC	17.0
	Andre Tippett, NE, AFC	16.5		Trace Armstrong, Mia, AFC	16.5
1986	Lawrence Taylor, NYG, NFC	20.5	2001	Michael Strahan, NYG, NFC	22.5
	Sean Jones, LA, AFC	15.5		Peter Boulware, Balt, AFC	15.0
1987	Reggie White, Phil, NFC	21.0	2002	Jason Taylor, Mia, AFC	18.5
	Andre Tippett, NE, AFC	12.5		Simeon Rice, TB, NFC	15.5
1988	Reggie White, Phil, NFC	18.0	2003	Michael Strahan, NYG, NFC	18.5
	G. Townsend, LA, AFC	11.5		Adewale Ogunleye, Mia, AFC	15.0
1989	Chris Doleman, Min, NFC	21.0	2004	Dwight Freeney, Ind, AFC	16.0
	Lee Williams, SD, AFC	14.0		Bertrand Berry, Ariz, NFC	14.5
1990	Derrick Thomas, KC, AFC	20.0	2005	Derrick Burgess, Oak, AFC	16.0
	Charles Haley, SF, NFC	16.0		Osi Umenyiora, NYG, NFC	14.5
1991	Pat Swilling, NO, NFC	17.0	2006	Shawne Merriman, SD, AFC	17.0
	William Fuller, Hou, AFC	15.0		Aaron Kampman, GB, NFC	15.5
1992	Clyde Simmons, Phil, NFC	19.0	2007	Jared Allen, KC, AFC	15.5
	Leslie O'Neal, SD, AFC	17.0		Patrick Kerney, Sea, NFC	14.5
1993	Neil Smith, KC, AFC	15.0	2008	DeMarcus Ware, Dal, NFC	20.0
	Renaldo Turnbull, NO, NFC	13.0		Joey Porter, Mia, AFC	17.5
	Reggie White, GB, NFC	13.0	2009	Elvis Dumervil, Den, AFC	17.0
1994	Kevin Greene, Pit, AFC	14.0		Jared Allen, Min, NFC	14.5
	Ken Harvey, Wash, NFC	13.5	2010	DeMarcus Ware, Dal, NFC	15.5
	John Randle, Min, NFC	13.5		Tamba Hali, KC, AFC	14.5
1995	Bryce Paup, Buf, AFC	17.5	2011	Jared Allen, Min, NFC	22.0
	William Fuller, Phil, NFC	13.0		Terrell Suggs, Bal, AFC	14.0
	Wayne Martin, NO, NFC	13.0	2012	J.J. Watt, Hou, AFC	20.5
1996	Kevin Greene, Car, NFC	14.5		Aldon Smith, SF, NFC	19.5
	Michael McCrary, Sea, AFC	13.5			
	Bruce Smith, Buf, AFC	13.5			

*Sacks were not kept as an official NFL statistic until 1982.

Pro Bowl Alltime Results

Date	Result	Date	Result	Date	Result
1-15-39	NY Giants 13, Pro All-Stars 10	1-16-65	AFL West 38, East 14	2-1-87	AFC 10, NFC 6
1-14-40	Green Bay 16, NFL All-Stars 7	1-15-66	AFL All-Stars 30, Buffalo 19	2-7-88	AFC 15, NFC 6
12-29-40	Chi Bears 28, NFL All-Stars 14	1-15-66	NFL East 36, West 7	1-29-89	NFC 34, AFC 3
1-4-42	Chi Bears 35, NFL All-Stars 24	1-21-67	AFL East 30, West 23	2-4-90	NFC 27, AFC 21
12-27-42	NFL All-Stars 17, Washington 14	1-22-67	NFL East 20, West 10	2-3-91	AFC 23, NFC 21
1-14-51	A. Conf. 28, N. Conf. 27	1-21-68	AFL East 25, West 24	2-2-92	NFC 21, AFC 15
1-12-52	N. Conf. 30, A. Conf. 13	1-21-68	NFL West 38, East 20	2-7-93	AFC 23, NFC 20
1-10-53	N. Conf. 27, A. Conf. 7	1-19-69	AFL West 38, East 25	2-6-94	NFC 17, AFC 3
1-17-54	East 20, West 9	1-19-69	NFL West 10, East 7	2-5-95	AFC 41, NFC 13
1-16-55	West 26, East 19	1-17-70	AFL West 26, East 3	2-4-96	NFC 20, AFC 13
1-15-56	East 31, West 30	1-18-70	NFL West 16, East 13	2-2-97	AFC 26, NFC 23
1-13-57	West 19, East 10	1-24-71	NFC 27, AFC 6	2-1-98	AFC 29, NFC 24
1-12-58	West 26, East 7	1-23-72	AFC 26, NFC 13	2-7-99	AFC 23, NFC 10
1-11-59	East 28, West 21	1-21-73	AFC 33, NFC 28	2-6-00	NFC 51, AFC 31
1-17-60	West 38, East 21	1-20-74	AFC 15, NFC 13	2-4-01	AFC 38, NFC 17
1-15-61	West 35, East 31	1-20-75	NFC 17, AFC 10	2-10-02	AFC 38, NFC 30
1-7-62	AFL West 47, East 27	1-26-76	NFC 23, AFC 20	2-2-03	AFC 45, NFC 20
1-14-62	NFL West 31, East 30	1-17-77	AFC 24, NFC 14	2-8-04	NFC 55, AFC 52
1-13-63	AFL West 21, East 14	1-23-78	NFC 14, AFC 13	2-13-05	AFC 38, NFC 27
1-13-63	NFL East 30, West 20	1-29-79	NFC 13, AFC 7	2-12-06	NFC 23, AFC 17
1-12-64	NFL West 31, East 17	1-27-80	NFC 37, AFC 27	2-10-07	AFC 31, NFC 28
1-19-64	AFL West 27, East 24	2-1-81	NFC 21, AFC 7	2-10-08	NFC 42, AFC 30
1-10-65	NFL West 34, East 14	1-31-82	AFC 16, NFC 13	2-8-09	NFC 30, AFC 21
		2-6-83	NFC 20, AFC 19	1-31-10	AFC 41, NFC 34
		1-29-84	NFC 45, AFC 3	1-30-11	NFC 55, AFC 41
		1-27-85	AFC 22, NFC 14	1-29-12	AFC 59, NFC 41
		2-2-86	NFC 28, AFC 24	1-27-13	NFC 62, AFC 35

Chicago All-Star Game* Results

Date	Result (Attendance)	Date	Result (Attendance)
8-31-34	Chi Bears 0, All-Stars 0 (79,432)	8-12-55	All-Stars 30, Cleveland 27 (75,000)
8-29-35	Chi Bears 5, All-Stars 0 (77,450)	8-10-56	Cleveland 26, All-Stars 0 (75,000)
9-2-36	All-Stars 7, Detroit 7 (76,000)	8-9-57	NY Giants 22, All-Stars 12 (75,000)
9-1-37	All-Stars 6, Green Bay 0 (84,560)	8-15-58	All-Stars 35, Detroit 19 (70,000)
8-31-38	All-Stars 28, Washington 16 (74,250)	8-14-59	Baltimore 29, All-Stars 0 (70,000)
8-30-39	NY Giants 9, All-Stars 0 (81,456)	8-12-60	Baltimore 32, All-Stars 7 (70,000)
8-29-40	Green Bay 45, All-Stars 28 (84,567)	8-4-61	Philadelphia 28, All-Stars 14 (66,000)
8-28-41	Chi Bears 37, All-Stars 13 (98,203)	8-3-62	Green Bay 42, All-Stars 20 (65,000)
8-28-42	Chi Bears 21, All-Stars 0 (101,100)	8-2-63	All-Stars 20, Green Bay 17 (65,000)
8-25-43	All-Stars 27, Washington 7 (48,471)	8-7-64	Chicago 28, All-Stars 17 (65,000)
8-30-44	Chi Bears 24, All-Stars 21 (48,769)	8-6-65	Cleveland 24, All-Stars 16 (68,000)
8-30-45	Green Bay 19, All-Stars 7 (92,753)	8-5-66	Green Bay 38, All-Stars 0 (72,000)
8-23-46	All-Stars 16, Los Angeles 0 (97,380)	8-4-67	Green Bay 27, All-Stars 0 (70,934)
8-22-47	All-Stars 16, Chi Bears 0 (105,840)	8-2-68	Green Bay 34, All-Stars 17 (69,917)
8-20-48	Chi Cardinals 28, All-Stars 0 (101,220)	8-1-69	NY Jets 26, All-Stars 24 (74,208)
8-12-49	Philadelphia 38, All-Stars 0 (93,780)	7-31-70	Kansas City 24, All-Stars 3 (69,940)
8-11-50	All-Stars 17, Philadelphia 7 (88,885)	7-30-71	Baltimore 24, All-Stars 17 (52,289)
8-17-51	Cleveland 33, All-Stars 0 (92,180)	7-28-72	Dallas 20, All-Stars 7 (54,162)
8-15-52	Los Angeles 10, All-Stars 7 (88,316)	7-27-73	Miami 14, All-Stars 3 (54,103)
8-14-53	Detroit 24, All-Stars 10 (93,818)	1974	No game
8-13-54	Detroit 31, All-Stars 6 (93,470)	8-1-75	Pittsburgh 21, All-Stars 14 (54,562)
		7-23-76	Pittsburgh 24, All-Stars 0 (52,895)

*Discontinued.

Alltime Winningest NFL Head Coaches

Most Career Wins

Coach	Yrs	Teams	Regular Season				Career			
			W	L	T	Pct	W	L	T	Pct
Don Shula 33		Balt Colts, Dolphins	328	156	6	.676	347	173	6	.665
George Halas..........40		Bears	318	148	31	.671	324	151	31	.671
Tom Landry.............29		Cowboys	250	162	6	.605	270	178	6	.601
Curly Lambeau 33		Packers, Chi Cards, Redskins	226	132	22	.624	229	134	22	.623
*Paul Brown 25		Browns, Bengals	213	104	9	.672	222	112	9	.660
Chuck Noll 23		Steelers	193	148	1	.566	209	156	1	.572
M. Schottenheimer.....20		Browns, Chiefs, Redskins, Chargers	200	126	1	.613	205	139	1	.596
Dan Reeves 23		Broncos, NY Giants, Falcons	190	165	2	.535	201	174	2	.536
†Bill Belichick..........18		Browns, Patriots	187	101	0	.649	205	109	0	.653
Chuck Knox 22		LA Rams, Bills, Seahawks	186	147	1	.558	193	158	1	.550
Bill Parcells 18		NY Giants, Patriots, NY Jets, Cowboys	172	130	1	.569	183	138	1	.570
†Mike Shanahan 19		Raiders, Broncos, Redskins	167	125	0	.572	175	131	0	.572
Mike Holmgren........17		Packers, Seahawks	161	111	0	.592	174	122	0	.588
Joe Gibbs 15		Redskins	154	94	0	.621	171	101	0	.629
Bud Grant 18		Vikings	158	96	5	.620	168	108	5	.607
†Tom Coughlin.........16		Jaguars, NY Giants	151	121	0	.555	162	128	0	.559
Bill Cowher..............14		Steelers	149	90	1	.623	161	99	1	.619
Marv Levy 17		Chiefs, Bills	143	112	0	.561	154	120	0	.562
†Jeff Fisher 18		Hou/Tenn Oilers, Tenn Titans	149	129	0	.536	154	135	0	.533
Steve Owen.............23		NY Giants	151	100	17	.595	153	108	17	.581
Tony Dungy.............13		Buccaneers, Ind Colts	139	69	0	.668	148	79	0	.652
Hank Stram 17		Chiefs, Saints	131	97	10	.571	136	100	10	.573

Top Winning Percentages

	W	L	T	Pct		W	L	T	Pct
Vince Lombardi..............105	35	6	.740		*Paul Brown....................222	112	9	.660	
John Madden 112	39	7	.731		†Bill Belichick.................205	109	0	.653	
George Allen 118	54	5	.681		Tony Dungy....................148	79	0	.652	
George Halas.................324	151	31	.671		George Seifert................124	67	0	.650	
Don Shula......................347	173	6	.665		Joe Gibbs......................171	101	0	.629	

Note: Minimum 100 victories.

†Active in 2012. *Includes a 52–4–3 (5–0 playoff) record with Browns in AAFC and a 7–20–1 record with Bengals in AFL.

Pro Football Most Valuable Players

Year	Player/ Team	Position	Year	Player/ Team	Position
1938	Mel Hein, NYG (NFL)	C	1955	Lou Groza, Clev (TSN)	OT/K
1939	Parker Hall, Clev (NFL)	HB		Otto Graham, Clev (UP, TSN)	QB
1940	Ace Parker, Brooklyn (NFL)	QB		Harlon Hill, Chi Bears (NEA)	E
1941	Don Hutson, GB (NFL)	E	1956	Frank Gifford, NYG (UP, NEA, TSN)	HB
1942	Don Hutson, GB (NFL)	E	1957	Y.A. Tittle, SF (UP)	QB
1943	Sid Luckman, Chi Bears (NFL)	QB		Jim Brown, Clev (AP, TSN)	FB
1944	Frank Sinkwich, Det (NFL)	HB		John Unitas, Balt (NEA)	QB
1945	Bob Waterfield, Clev (NFL)	QB	1958	Jim Brown, Clev (UP, AP, NEA, TSN)	FB
1946	Bill Dudley, Pit (NFL)	HB	1959	John Unitas, Balt (UP, MCP, TSN)	QB
	Glenn Dobbs, Brooklyn (AAFC)	HB		Charley Conerly, NYG (AP, NEA)	QB
1947	No Selection (NFL)		1960	Norm Van Brocklin, Phil, NFL (UP, AP, NEA, TSN, MCP)	QB
	Otto Graham, Clev (AAFC)	QB		Joe Schmidt, Det, NFL (UP- tie)	LB
1948	No Selection (NFL)			Abner Haynes, Dal Texans, AFL (UP, TSN)	HB
	Otto Graham, Clev (AAFC-tie)	QB	1961	Paul Hornung, GB, NFL (UP, AP, TSN, MCP)	HB
	Frankie Albert, SF (AAFC-tie)	QB		Y.A. Tittle, NYG (NEA)	QB
1949	No Selection (NFL)			George Blanda, Hous, AFL (UP, TSN)	QB
1950	No Selection (NFL)		1962	Y.A. Tittle, NYG, NFL (UP, TSN)	QB
1951	Otto Graham, Clev (UP)	QB		Jim Taylor, GB, NFL (AP, NEA)	FB
1952	No Selection (NFL)			Andy Robustelli, NYG, NFL (MCP)	DE
1953	Otto Graham, Clev (UP)	QB		Cookie Gilchrist, Buf, AFL (UP)	FB
1954	Joe Perry, SF (UP)	FB		Len Dawson, Dal Texans, AFL (TSN)	QB
			1963	Jim Brown, Clev, NFL (UP, NEA (tie), MCP)	FB
				Y.A. Tittle, NYG, NFL (AP, NEA (tie), TSN)	QB
				Lance Alworth, SD, AFL (UP)	WR

Year	Player/ Team	Position
	Clem Daniels, Oak, AFL (TSN)	HB
1964	Johnny Unitas, Balt,	QB
	NFL (UP, AP, TSN, MCP)	
	Lenny Moore, Balt, NFL (NEA)	HB
	Gino Cappelletti, Boston, AFL (UP, TSN)	WR
1965	Jim Brown, Clev, NFL (UP, AP, TSN, NEA)	FB
	Pete Retzlaff, Phil, NFL (MCP)	TE
	Jack Kemp, Buf, AFL (UP)	QB
	Paul Lowe, SD, AFL (TSN)	RB
1966	Bart Starr, GB, NFL (UP, AP, NEA, TSN)	QB
	Don Meredith, Dal, NFL (MCP)	QB
	Jim Nance, Boston, AFL (UP, AP, TSN)	FB
1967	Johnny Unitas, Balt,	QB
	NFL (UP, AP, NEA, TSN, MCP)	
	Daryl Lamonica, Oak, AFL (UP, TSN)	QB
1968	Earl Morrall, Balt,	QB
	NFL (UP, AP, NEA, TSN, PFW)	
	Leroy Kelly, Clev, AFL (MCP)	HB
	Joe Namath, NYJ, AFL (UP, TSN, PFW)	QB
1969	Roman Gabriel, LA Rams, NFL (UP, AP,	
	NEA, MCP, TSN, PFW)	QB
	Daryle Lamonica, Oak, AFL (UP, TSN, PFW)	QB
	Joe Namath, NYJ, AFL (AP)	QB
1970	John Brodie, SF (AP, NEA)	QB
	George Blanda, Oak (MCP)	QB/K
1971	Alan Page, Min (AP)	DT
	Bob Griese, Miami (NEA)	QB
	Roger Staubach, Dal (MCP)	QB
1972	Larry Brown, Wash (AP, NEA, MCP)	RB
1973	O.J. Simpson, Buf (AP, NEA, MCP)	RB
1974	Ken Stabler, Oak (AP, NEA)	QB
	Merlin Olsen, LA Rams (MCP)	DT
1975	Fran Tarkenton, Min	QB
	(PFWA, AP, NEA, MCP)	
1976	Bert Jones, Balt (PFWA, AP, NEA)	QB
	Ken Stabler, Oak (MCP)	QB
1977	Walter Payton, Chi (PFWA, AP, NEA)	RB
	Bob Griese, Miami (MCP)	QB
1978	Earl Campbell, Hous (PFWA, NEA)	RB
	Terry Bradshaw, Pit (AP, MCP)	QB
1979	Earl Campbell, Hou	RB
	(PFWA, AP, NEA, MCP)	
1980	Brian Sipe, Clev (PFWA, AP, TSN)	QB
	Earl Campbell, Hou (NEA)	RB
	Ron Jaworski, Phil (MCP)	QB
1981	Ken Anderson, Cin	QB
	(PFWA, AP, NEA, TSN, MCP)	
1982	Dan Fouts, SD (PFWA, NEA)	QB
	Mark Moseley, Wash (AP, TSN)	K
	Joe Theismann, Wash (MCP)	QB
1983	Joe Theismann, Wash	QB

Year	Player/ Team	Position
	(PFWAA, AP, NEA)	
	Eric Dickerson, LA Rams (TSN)	RB
	John Riggins, Wash (MCP)	RB
1984	Dan Marino, Miami	QB
	(PFWAA, AP, NEA, MCP, TSN)	
1985	Marcus Allen, LA Raiders	RB
	(PFWAA, AP, TSN)	
	Walter Payton, Chi (NEA, MCP)	RB
1986	Lawrence Taylor, NYG	LB
	(PFWAA, AP, MCP, TSN)	
	Phil Simms, NYG (NEA)	QB
1987	Jerry Rice, SF (PFWAA, NEA, MCP, TSN)	WR
	John Elway, Den (AP)	QB
1988	Boomer Esiason, Cin (PFWAA, AP, TSN)	QB
	Roger Craig, SF (NEA)	RB
	Randall Cunningham, Phil (MCP)	QB
1989	Joe Montana, SF	QB
	(PFWAA, AP, NEA, MCP, TSN)	
1990	Randall Cunningham, Phil (PFWAA)	QB
	Joe Montana, SF (AP)	QB
	Jerry Rice, SF (TSN)	WR
1991	Thurman Thomas, Buf (PFWAA, AP, TSN)	RB
	Barry Sanders, Det (MCP)	RB
1992	Steve Young, SF (PFWAA, AP, MCP, TSN)	QB
1993	Emmitt Smith, Dal (PFWAA, AP, MCP, TSN)	RB
1994	Steve Young, SF (PFWAA, AP, MCP, TSN)	QB
1995	Brett Favre, GB (PFWAA, AP, MCP, TSN)	QB
1996	Brett Favre, GB (PFWAA, AP, MCP, TSN)	QB
1997	Brett Favre, GB (AP – tie)	QB
	Barry Sanders, Det	RB
	(PFWAA, AP (tie), MCP, TSN)	
1998	Terrell Davis, Den (PFWAA, AP, TSN)	RB
	Randall Cunningham, Min (MCP)	QB
1999	Kurt Warner, StL (AP, PFWAA, MCP)	QB
2000	Marshall Faulk, StL (AP, PFWAA)	RB
	Rich Gannon, Oak (MCP)	QB
2001	Kurt Warner, StL (AP)	QB
	Marshall Faulk, StL (PFWAA, MCP, TSN)	RB
2002	Rich Gannon, Oak (AP)	QB
2003	Peyton Manning, Ind (AP - tie)	QB
	Steve McNair, Ten (AP - tie)	QB
2004	Peyton Manning, Ind (AP)	QB
2005	Shaun Alexander, Sea (AP)	RB
2006	LaDainian Tomlinson, SD (AP)	RB
2007	Tom Brady, NE (AP)	QB
2008	Peyton Manning, Ind (AP)	QB
2009	Peyton Manning, Ind (AP)	QB
2010	Tom Brady, NE (AP)	QB
2011	Aaron Rodgers, GB (AP)	QB
2012	Adrian Peterson, Min (AP)	RB

NOTE: AP-Associated Press; UP-United Press; PFW-*Pro Football Weekly*; TSN-*The Sporting News*; PFWAA-Pro Football Writers Association of America; PFWA-Pro Football Writers of America; MCP-Maxwell Club of Philadelphia; NEA-Newspaper Enterprise Association.

The NFL began awarding its MVP award, the Joe F. Carr Trophy (Carr was league president from 1921-39), in 1938, and continued to do so until 1946. Since that time, the NFL's Most Valuable Players and Players of the Year have been named by a variety of sources, among them, the United Press, the Associated Press, the Maxwell Club of Philadelphia, and the Pro Football Writers Association of America, as well as magazines such as *Pro Football Weekly* and *The Sporting News*.

Pro Football Rookies of the Year

Year	Player/ Team	Position
1955	Alan Ameche, Balt (UP, TSN)	FB
1956	Lenny Moore, Balt (UP)	HB
	J.C. Caroline, Chi Bears (TSN)	DB
1957	Jim Brown, Clev (UP, AP, TSN)	FB
1958	Jimmy Orr, Pit (UP, AP)	OE
	Bobby Mitchell, Cle (TSN)	HB
1959	Nick Pietrosante, Det (AP, TSN)	FB
	Boyd Dowler, GB (UP)	OE
1960	Gail Cogdill, Det, NFL (AP, UP, TSN)	OE
	Abner Haynes, Dal Texans, AFL (UP, TSN)	HB
1961	Mike Ditka, Chi Bears, NFL (AP, UP, TSN)	OE
	Earl Faison, SD, AFL (UP, TSN)	DE
1962	Ronnie Bull, Chi Bears, NFL (AP, UP, TSN)	HB
	Curtis McClinton, Dal, AFL (UP, TSN)	FB
1963	Paul Flatley, Min, NFL (AP, UP, TSN)	OE
	Billy Joe, Den, AFL (UP, TSN)	FB
1964	Charley Taylor, Wash, NFL (AP, UP, TSN, NEA)	HB
	Matt Snell, NYJ, AFL (UP, TSN)	FB
1965	Gale Sayers, Chi, NFL (AP, UP, TSN, NEA)	HB
	Joe Namath, NYJ, AFL (UP, TSN)	QB
1966	Johnny Roland, StL, NFL (UP)	HB
	Tommy Nobis, Atl, NFL (AP, TSN, NEA)	LB
	Bobby Burnett, Buf, AFL (UP, TSN)	HB
1967	Mel Farr, Det, NFL (AP-Off, UP, TSN, NEA)	HB
	Lem Barney, Det NFL (AP-Def)	CB
	George Webster, Hous, AFL (UP)	LB
	Dickie Post, SD, AFL (TSN)	HB
1968	Earl McCullouch, Det, NFL (AP-Off, UP, TSN, NEA)	OE
	Claude Humphrey, Atl, NFL (AP-Def)	DE
	Paul Robinson, Cin, AFL (UP, TSN)	HB
1969	Calvin Hill, Dal, NFL (AP-Off, UP, TSN, NEA)	HB
	Joe Greene, Pit, NFL (AP-Def)	DT
	Greg Cook, Cin, AFL (UP)	QB
	Carl Garrett, Boston, AFL (TSN)	HB
1970	Raymond Chester, Oak (NEA)	TE
	Dennis Shaw, Buf (AP-Off, UP-AFC)	QB
	Bruce Taylor, SF (AP-Def, UP-NFC)	DB
1971	Jim Plunkett, NE (UP-AFC)	QB
	John Brockington, GB (AP-Off, UP-NFC)	RB
	Isiah Robertson, SF (AP-Def)	LB
1972	Franco Harris, Pit (AP-Off, PFW, UP-AFC)	RB
	Chester Marcol, GB (UP-NFC)	PK
	Willie Buchanan, GB (AP-Def)	CB
1973	Chuck Foreman, Min (AP-Off, PFW)	RB
	Wally Chambers, Chi (AP-Def)	DT
	Bobbie Clark, Cin (UP-AFC)	RB
	Charle Young, Phil (UP-NFC)	TE
1974	Don Woods, SD (AP-Off, PFW, UP-AFC)	RB
	John Hicks, NYG (UP-NFC)	G
	Jack Lambert, Pit (AP-Def)	LB
1975	Steve Bartkowski, Atl (PFW)	QB
	Robert Brazile, Hous (AP-Def, UP-AFC)	LB
	Mike Thomas, Wash (AP-Off, UP-NFC)	RB
1976	Mike Haynes, NE (AP-Def, UP-AFC)	DB
	Sammy White, Min (AP-Off, UP-NFC)	WR
1977	Tony Dorsett, Dal (NEA, AP-Off, UP-NFC)	RB
	A.J. Duhe, Mia (AP-Def, UP-AFC)	DE
1978	Earl Campbell, Hou (NEA, PFWA, AP-Off, UP-AFC)	RB
	Al "Bubba" Baker, Det (AP-Def, UP-NFC)	DE
1979	Ottis Anderson, StL (NEA, PFWA, AP-Off, UP-NFC)	RB
	Jerry Butler, Buf (UP-AFC)	WR
	Jim Haslett, Buf (AP-Def)	LB
1980	Billy Sims, Det (NEA, TSN, PFWA, AP-Off, UP-NFC)	RB
	Joe Cribbs, Buf (UP-AFC)	RB
	Buddy Curry, Atl (AP-Def tie)	LB
	Al Richardson, Atl (AP-Def tie)	LB
1981	Lawrence Taylor, NYG (NEA, AP-Def)	LB
	George Rogers, NO (TSN, PFWA, AP-Off, UP-NFC)	RB
	Joe Delaney, KC (UP-AFC)	RB
1982	Marcus Allen, LA Raiders (NEA, TSN, PFWA, AP-Off, UP-AFC)	RB
	Jim McMahon, Chi (UP-NFC)	QB
	Chip Banks, Cle (AP-Def)	LB
1983	Eric Dickerson, LA Rams (NEA, PFWA, AP-Off, UP-NFC)	RB
	Dan Marino, Mia (TSN)	QB
	Curt Warner, Sea (UP-AFC)	RB
	Vernon Maxwell, Balt (AP-Def)	LB
1984	Louis Lipps, Pit (NEA, TSN, PFWA, AP-Off, UP-NFC)	WR
	Paul McFadden, Phil (UP-NFC)	PK
	Bill Maas, KC (AP-Def)	DT
1985	Eddie Brown, Cin (NEA, TSN, AP-Off, PFWA)	WR
	Kevin Mack, Clev (UP-AFC)	RB
	Jerry Rice, SF (UP-NFC)	WR
	Duane Bickett, Ind (AP-Def)	LB
1986	Reuben Mayes, NO (NEA, TSN, PFWA, AP-Off, UP-NFC)	RB
	Leslie O'Neal, SD (AP-Def, UP-AFC)	DE
1987	Shane Conlan, Buf (PFWA, AP-Def, UP-AFC)	LB
	Bo Jackson, LA Raiders (NEA)	RB
	Robert Awalt, StL (TSN, UP-NFC)	TE
	Troy Stradford, Mia (AP-Off)	RB
1988	John Stephens, NE (NEA, AP-Off, PFWA)	RB
	Keith Jackson, Phil (TSN, UP-NFC)	TE
	Eric McMillan, NYJ (AP-Def)	S
1989	Barry Sanders, Det (NEA, TSN, PFWA, AP-Off, UP-NFC)	RB
	Derrick Thomas, KC (AP-Def, UP-AFC)	LB
1990	Mark Carrier, Chi (PFWA, UP-NFC, AP-Def)	S
	Emmitt Smith, Dal (AP-Off)	RB
	Richmond Webb, Mia (TSN, UP-AFC)	OT
1991	Mike Croel, Den (PFWA, TSN, AP-Def, UP-AFC)	LB
	Lawrence Dawsey, TB (UP-NFC)	WR
	Leonard Russell, NE (AP-Off)	RB
1992	Dale Carter, KC (PFWA, AP-Def, UP-AFC)	CB
	Carl Pickens, Cin (AP-Off)	WR
	Santana Dotson, TB (TSN)	DE
	Robert Jones, Dal (UP-NFC)	LB
1993	Jerome Bettis, LA Rams (PFWA, TSN, AP-Off, UP-NFC)	RB
	Rick Mirer, Sea (UP-AFC)	QB
	Dana Stubblefield, SF (AP-Def)	DT
1994	Marshall Faulk, Ind (PFWA, TSN, AP-Off, UP-AFC)	RB
	Bryant Young, SF (UP-NFC)	DT
	Tim Bowens, Mia (AP-Def)	DT
1995	Curtis Martin, NE (PFWA, TSN, AP-Off, UP-AFC)	RB
	Rashaan Salaam, Chi (UP-NFC)	RB
	Hugh Douglas, NYJ (AP-Def)	DE

Year	Player/ Team	Position
1996	Eddie George, Ten (AP, PFWA, AP-Off, TSN)	RB
	Terry Glenn, NE (UP-AFC)	WR
	Simeon Rice, Ariz (AP-Def, UP-NFC)	DE
1997	Warrick Dunn, TB (PFWA, AP-Off, TSN)	RB
	Peter Boulware, Balt (AP-Def)	LB
1998	Randy Moss, Min (PFWA, AP-Off, TSN)	WR
	Charles Woodson, LA Raiders (AP-Def)	CB
1999	Edgerrin James, Ind (AP-Off, TSN)	RB
	Jevon Kearse, Ten (AP-Def)	DE
2000	Mike Anderson, Den (AP-Off, TSN)	RB
	Brian Urlacher, Chi (AP-Def)	LB
2001	Anthony Thomas, Chi (AP-Off)	RB
	Kendrell Bell, Pit (AP-Def)	LB
2002	Clinton Ports, Den (AP-Off)	RB
	Julius Peppers, Car (AP-Def)	DE
2003	Ânquan Boldin, Ariz (AP-Off)	WR
	Terrell Suggs, Bal (AP-Def)	LB

Year	Player/ Team	Position
2004	Ben Roethlisberger, Pit (AP-Off)	QB
	Jonathan Vilma, NYJ (AP-Def)	LB
2005	Carnell Williams, TB (AP-Off)	RB
	Shawne Merriman, SD (AP-Def)	LB
2006	Vince Young, Ten (AP-Off)	QB
	DeMeco Ryans, Hou (AP-Def)	LB
2007	Adrian Peterson, Min (AP-Off)	RB
	Patrick Willis, SF (AP-Def)	LB
2008	Matt Ryan, Atl (AP-Off)	QB
	Jerod Mayo, NE (AP-Def)	LB
2009	Percy Harvin, Min (AP-Off)	WR
	Brian Cushing, Hou (AP-Def)	LB
2010	Sam Bradford, StL (AP-Off)	QB
	Ndamukong Suh, Det (AP-Def)	DT
2011	Cam Newton, Car (AP-Off)	QB
	Von Miller, Den (AP-Def)	LB
2012	Robert Griffin III, Was (AP-Off)	QB
	Luke Kuechly, Car (AP-Def)	LB

NOTE: AP-Associated Press, UP-United Press, PFW-*Pro Football Weekly*, TSN-*The Sporting News*, PFWAA-Pro Football Writers Association of America, PFWA-Pro Football Writers of America, MCP-Maxwell Club of Philadelphia, NEA-Newspaper Enterprise Association. Starting in 1960, the United Press annually awarded two Rookie of the Year awards, one to an AFL player and one to a NFL player. After the AFL-NFL merger, the UP kept the two-award format for the AFC and NFC. The UP stopped awarding RoY awards after the 1996 season. Starting in 1967, the Associated Press began announcing two annual Rookie of the Year awards as well. One went to the best offensive rookie in the NFL, the other to the best defensive rookie.

Alltime Number-One Draft Choices

Year	Team	Selection	Position
1936	Philadelphia	Jay Berwanger, Chicago	HB
1937	Philadelphia	Sam Francis, Nebraska	FB
1938	Cleveland	Corbett Davis, Indiana	FB
1939	Chicago Cardinals	Ki Aldrich, Texas Christian	C
1940	Chicago Cardinals	George Cafego, Tennessee	HB
1941	Chicago Bears	Tom Harmon, Michigan	HB
1942	Pittsburgh	Bill Dudley, Virginia	HB
1943	Detroit	Frank Sinkwich, Georgia	HB
1944	Boston	Angelo Bertelli, Notre Dame	QB
1945	Chicago Cardinals	Charley Trippi, Georgia	HB
1946	Boston	Frank Dancewicz, Notre Dame	QB
1947	Chicago Bears	Bob Fenimore, Oklahoma A&M	HB
1948	Washington	Harry Gilmer, Alabama	QB
1949	Philadelphia	Chuck Bednarik, Pennsylvania	C
1950	Detroit	Leon Hart, Notre Dame	E
1951	New York Giants	Kyle Rote, SMU	HB
1952	Los Angeles	Bill Wade, Vanderbilt	QB
1953	San Francisco	Harry Babcock, Georgia	E
1954	Cleveland	Bobby Garrett, Stanford	QB
1955	Baltimore	George Shaw, Oregon	QB
1956	Pittsburgh	Gary Glick, Colorado A&M	DB
1957	Green Bay	Paul Hornung, Notre Dame	HB
1958	Chicago Cardinals	King Hill, Rice	QB
1959	Green Bay	Randy Duncan, Iowa	QB
1960	Los Angeles	Billy Cannon, LSU	RB
1961	Minnesota	Tommy Mason, Tulane	RB
	Buffalo (AFL)	Ken Rice, Auburn	G
1962	Washington	Ernie Davis, Syracuse	RB
	Oakland (AFL)	Roman Gabriel, North Carolina St	QB
1963	LA Rams	Terry Baker, Oregon St	QB
	Kansas City (AFL)	Buck Buchanan, Grambling	DT
1964	San Francisco	Dave Parks, Texas Tech	E
	Boston (AFL)	Jack Concannon, Boston College	QB
1965	NY Giants	Tucker Frederickson, Auburn	RB
	Houston (AFL)	Lawrence Elkins, Baylor	E
1966	Atlanta	Tommy Nobis, Texas	LB
	Miami (AFL)	Jim Grabowski, Illinois	RB
1967	Baltimore	Bubba Smith, Michigan St	DT

Year	Team	Selection	Position
1968	Minnesota	Ron Yary, USC	T
1969	Buffalo (AFL)	O.J. Simpson, USC	RB
1970	Pittsburgh	Terry Bradshaw, Louisiana Tech	QB
1971	New England	Jim Plunkett, Stanford	QB
1972	Buffalo	Walt Patulski, Notre Dame	DE
1973	Houston	John Matuszak, Tampa	DE
1974	Dallas	Ed Jones, Tennessee St	DE
1975	Atlanta	Steve Bartkowski, California	QB
1976	Tampa Bay	Lee Roy Selmon, Oklahoma	DE
1977	Tampa Bay	Ricky Bell, USC	RB
1978	Houston	Earl Campbell, Texas	RB
1979	Buffalo	Tom Cousineau, Ohio St	LB
1980	Detroit	Billy Sims, Oklahoma	RB
1981	New Orleans	George Rogers, South Carolina	RB
1982	New England	Kenneth Sims, Texas	DT
1983	Baltimore	John Elway, Stanford	QB
1984	New England	Irving Fryar, Nebraska	WR
1985	Buffalo	Bruce Smith, Virginia Tech	DE
1986	Tampa Bay	Bo Jackson, Auburn	RB
1987	Tampa Bay	Vinny Testaverde, Miami (Fla.)	QB
1988	Atlanta	Aundray Bruce, Auburn	LB
1989	Dallas	Troy Aikman, UCLA	QB
1990	Indianapolis	Jeff George, Illinois	QB
1991	Dallas	Russell Maryland, Miami (Fla.)	DT
1992	Indianapolis	Steve Emtman, Washington	DT
1993	New England	Drew Bledsoe, Washington St	QB
1994	Cincinnati	Dan Wilkinson, Ohio St	DT
1995	Cincinnati	Ki-Jana Carter, Penn St	RB
1996	New York Jets	Keyshawn Johnson, USC	WR
1997	St. Louis	Orlando Pace, Ohio St	OT
1998	Indianapolis	Peyton Manning, Tennessee	QB
1999	Cleveland	Tim Couch, Kentucky	QB
2000	Cleveland	Courtney Brown, Penn St	DE
2001	Atlanta	Michael Vick, Virginia Tech	QB
2002	Houston	David Carr, Fresno St	QB
2003	Cincinnati	Carson Palmer, USC	QB
2004	San Diego	Eli Manning, Mississippi	QB
2005	San Francisco	Alex Smith, Utah	QB
2006	Houston	Mario Williams, North Carolina St	DE
2007	Oakland	JaMarcus Russell, LSU	QB
2008	Miami	Jake Long, Michigan	OT
2009	Detroit	Matthew Stafford, Georgia	QB
2010	St. Louis	Sam Bradford, Oklahoma	QB
2011	Carolina	Cam Newton, Auburn	QB
2012	Indianapolis	Andrew Luck, Stanford	QB
2013	Kansas City	Eric Fisher, Central Michigan	OT

From 1947 through 1958, the first selection in the draft was a bonus pick, awarded to the winner of a random draw. That club, in turn, forfeited its last-round draft choice. The winner of the bonus choice was eliminated from future draws. The system was abolished after 1958, by which time all clubs had received a bonus choice.

Members of the Pro Football Hall of Fame

Herb Adderley	Bobby Bell	Junious (Buck) Buchanan	George Connor
Troy Aikman	Raymond Berry	Nick Buoniconti	Jimmy Conzelman
George Allen	Elvin Bethea	Dick Butkus	Lou Creekmur
Larry Allen	Charles W. Bidwill Sr.	Jack Butler	Larry Csonka
Marcus Allen	Fred Biletnikoff	Earl Campbell	Curley Culp
Lance Alworth	George Blanda	Tony Canadeo	Al Davis
Doug Atkins	Mel Blount	Joe Carr	Willie Davis
Morris (Red) Badgro	Terry Bradshaw	Harry Carson	Dermontti Dawson
Lem Barney	Bob (the Boomer) Brown	Cris Carter	Len Dawson
Cliff Battles	Jim Brown	Dave Casper	Fred Dean
Sammy Baugh	Paul Brown	Guy Chamberlin	Joe DeLamielleure
Chuck Bednarik	Roosevelt Brown	Jack Christiansen	Richard Dent
Bert Bell	Willie Brown	Earl (Dutch) Clark	Eric Dickerson

Dan Dierdorf
Mike Ditka
Chris Doleman
Art Donovan
Tony Dorsett
John (Paddy) Driscoll
Bill Dudley
Albert Glen (Turk) Edwards
Carl Eller
John Elway
Weeb Ewbank
Marshall Faulk
Tom Fears
Jim Finks
Ray Flaherty
Len Ford
Dan Fortmann
Dan Fouts
Benny Friedman
Frank Gatski
Bill George
Joe Gibbs
Frank Gifford
Sid Gillman
Otto Graham
Harold (Red) Grange
Bud Grant
Darrell Green
Joe Greene
Forrest Gregg
Bob Griese
Russ Grimm
Lou Groza
Joe Guyon
George Halas
Jack Ham
Dan Hampton
Chris Hanburger
John Hannah
Franco Harris
Bob Hayes
Mike Haynes
Ed Healey
Mel Hein
Ted Hendricks
Wilbur (Pete) Henry
Arnie Herber
Bill Hewitt
Gene Hickerson
Clarke Hinkle
Elroy (Crazylegs) Hirsch
Paul Hornung
Ken Houston
Robert (Cal) Hubbard
Sam Huff
Lamar Hunt
Don Hutson
Michael Irvin
Rickey Jackson
Jimmy Johnson
John Henry Johnson
Charlie Joiner
David (Deacon) Jones
Stan Jones
Henry Jordan

Sonny Jurgensen
Jim Kelly
Leroy Kelly
Cortez Kennedy
Walt Kiesling
Frank (Bruiser) Kinard
Paul Krause
Earl (Curly) Lambeau
Jack Lambert
Tom Landry
Dick (Night Train) Lane
Jim Langer
Willie Lanier
Steve Largent
Yale Lary
Dante Lavelli
Bobby Layne
Dick LeBeau
Alphonse (Tuffy) Leemans
Marv Levy
Bob Lilly
Floyd Little
Larry Little
James Lofton
Vince Lombardi
Howie Long
Ronnie Lott
Sid Luckman
William Roy (Link) Lyman
Tom Mack
John Mackey
John Madden
Tim Mara
Wellington Mara
Gino Marchetti
Dan Marino
George Preston Marshall
Curtis Martin
Ollie Matson
Bruce Matthews
Don Maynard
George McAfee
Mike McCormack
Randall McDaniel
Tommy McDonald
Hugh McElhenny
John (Blood) McNally
Mike Michalske
Wayne Millner
Bobby Mitchell
Ron Mix
Art Monk
Joe Montana
Warren Moon
Lenny Moore
Marion Motley
Mike Munchak
Anthony Munoz
George Musso
Bronko Nagurski
Joe Namath
Earle (Greasy) Neale
Ernie Nevers
Ozzie Newsome
Ray Nitschke

Chuck Noll
Leo Nomellini
Jonathan Ogden
Merlin Olsen
Jim Otto
Steve Owen
Alan Page
Bill Parcells
Clarence (Ace) Parker
Jim Parker
Walter Payton
Joe Perry
Pete Pihos
Fritz Pollard
John Randle
Hugh (Shorty) Ray
Dan Reeves
Mel Renfro
Jerry Rice
Les Richter
John Riggins
Jim Ringo
Willie Roaf
Dave Robinson
Andy Robustelli
Art Rooney
Dan Rooney
Pete Rozelle
Bob St. Clair
Ed Sabol
Barry Sanders
Charlie Sanders
Deion Sanders
Warren Sapp
Gale Sayers
Joe Schmidt
Tex Schramm
Lee Roy Selmon
Shannon Sharpe
Billy Shaw
Art Shell
Don Shula
O.J. Simpson
Mike Singletary
Jackie Slater
Bruce Smith
Emmitt Smith
Jackie Smith
John Stallworth
Bart Starr
Roger Staubach
Ernie Stautner
Jan Stenerud
Dwight Stephenson
Hank Stram
Ken Strong
Joe Stydahar
Lynn Swann
Fran Tarkenton
Charley Taylor
Jim Taylor
Lawrence Taylor
Derrick Thomas
Emmitt Thomas
Thurman Thomas

Jim Thorpe
Andre Tippett
Y.A. Tittle
George Trafton
Charley Trippi
Emlen Tunnell
Clyde (Bulldog) Turner
Johnny Unitas
Gene Upshaw
Norm Van Brocklin
Steve Van Buren
Doak Walker
Bill Walsh
Paul Warfield
Bob Waterfield
Mike Webster
Roger Wehrli
Arnie Weinmeister
Randy White
Reggie White
Dave Wilcox
Bill Willis
Larry Wilson
Ralph Wilson
Kellen Winslow
Alex Wojciechowicz
Willie Wood
Rod Woodson
Rayfield Wright
Ron Yary
Steve Young
Jack Youngblood
Gary Zimmerman

Canadian Football League Grey Cup

Year	Results	Site	Attendance
1909	U of Toronto 26, Parkdale 6	Toronto	3,807
1910	U of Toronto 16, Hamilton Tigers 7	Hamilton	12,000
1911	U of Toronto 14, Toronto 7	Toronto	13,687
1912	Hamilton Alerts 11, Toronto 4	Hamilton	5,337
1913	Hamilton Tigers 44, Parkdale 2	Hamilton	2,100
1914	Toronto 14, U of Toronto 2	Toronto	10,500
1915	Hamilton Tigers 13, Toronto RAA 7	Toronto	2,808
1916–19	No game	—	—
1920	U of Toronto 16, Toronto 3	Toronto	10,088
1921	Toronto 23, Edmonton 0	Toronto	9,558
1922	Queen's U 13, Edmonton 1	Kingston	4,700
1923	Queen's U 54, Regina 0	Toronto	8,629
1924	Queen's U 11, Balmy Beach 3	Toronto	5,978
1925	Ottawa Senators 24, Winnipeg 1	Ottawa	6,900
1926	Ottawa Senators 10, Toronto U 7	Toronto	8,276
1927	Balmy Beach 9, Hamilton Tigers 6	Toronto	13,676
1928	Hamilton Tigers 30, Regina 0	Hamilton	4,767
1929	Hamilton Tigers 14, Regina 3	Hamilton	1,906
1930	Balmy Beach 11, Regina 6	Toronto	3,914
1931	Montreal AAA 22, Regina 0	Montreal	5,112
1932	Hamilton Tigers 25, Regina 6	Hamilton	4,806
1933	Toronto 4, Sarnia 3	Sarnia	2,751
1934	Sarnia 20, Regina 12	Toronto	8,900
1935	Winnipeg 18, Hamilton Tigers 12	Hamilton	6,405
1936	Sarnia 26, Ottawa RR 20	Toronto	5,883
1937	Toronto 4, Winnipeg 3	Toronto	11,522
1938	Toronto 30, Winnipeg 7	Toronto	18,778
1939	Winnipeg 8, Ottawa 7	Ottawa	11,738
1940	Ottawa 8, Balmy Beach 2	Toronto	4,998
1940	Ottawa 12, Balmy Beach 5	Ottawa	1,700
1941	Winnipeg 18, Ottawa 16	Toronto	19,065
1942	Toronto RCAF 8, Winnipeg RCAF 5	Toronto	12,455
1943	Hamilton F Wild 23, Winnipeg RCAF 14	Toronto	16,423
1944	Montreal St H-D Navy 7, Hamilton F Wild 6	Hamilton	3,871
1945	Toronto 35, Winnipeg 0	Toronto	18,660
1946	Toronto 28, Winnipeg 6	Toronto	18,960
1947	Toronto 10, Winnipeg 9	Toronto	18,885
1948	Calgary 12, Ottawa 7	Toronto	20,013
1949	Montreal Als 28, Calgary 15	Toronto	20,087
1950	Toronto 13, Winnipeg 0	Toronto	27,101
1951	Ottawa 21, Saskatchewan 14	Toronto	27,341
1952	Toronto 21, Edmonton 11	Toronto	27,391
1953	Hamilton Ticats 12, Winnipeg 6	Toronto	27,313
1954	Edmonton 26, Montreal 25	Toronto	27,321
1955	Edmonton 34, Montreal 19	Vancouver	39,417
1956	Edmonton 50, Montreal 27	Toronto	27,425
1957	Hamilton 32, Winnipeg 7	Toronto	27,051
1958	Winnipeg 35, Hamilton 28	Vancouver	36,567
1959	Winnipeg 21, Hamilton 7	Toronto	33,133
1960	Ottawa 16, Edmonton 6	Vancouver	38,102
1961	Winnipeg 21, Hamilton 14	Toronto	32,651
1962	Winnipeg 28, Hamilton 27	Toronto	32,655
1963	Hamilton 21, British Columbia 10	Vancouver	36,545
1964	British Columbia 34, Hamilton 24	Toronto	32,655
1965	Hamilton 22, Winnipeg 16	Toronto	32,655
1966	Saskatchewan 29, Ottawa 14	Vancouver	36,553
1967	Hamilton 24, Saskatchewan 1	Ottawa	31,358
1968	Ottawa 24, Calgary 21	Toronto	32,655
1969	Ottawa 29, Saskatchewan 11	Montreal	33,172
1970	Montreal 23, Calgary 10	Toronto	32,669
1971	Calgary 14, Toronto 11	Vancouver	34,484
1972	Hamilton 13, Saskatchewan 10	Hamilton	33,993
1973	Ottawa 22, Edmonton 18	Toronto	36,653
1974	Montreal 20, Edmonton 7	Vancouver	34,450
1975	Edmonton 9, Montreal 8	Calgary	32,454
1976	Ottawa 23, Saskatchewan 20	Toronto	53,467
1977	Montreal 41, Edmonton 6	Montreal	68,318
1978	Edmonton 20, Montreal 13	Toronto	54,695

Canadian Football League Grey Cup (Cont.)

Year	Results	Site	Attendance
1979	Edmonton 17, Montreal 9	Montreal	65,113
1980	Edmonton 48, Hamilton 10	Toronto	54,661
1981	Edmonton 26, Ottawa 23	Montreal	52,478
1982	Edmonton 32, Toronto 16	Toronto	54,741
1983	Toronto 18, British Columbia 17	Vancouver	59,345
1984	Winnipeg 47, Hamilton 17	Edmonton	60,081
1985	British Columbia 37, Hamilton 24	Montreal	56,723
1986	Hamilton 39, Edmonton 15	Vancouver	59,621
1987	Edmonton 38, Toronto 36	Vancouver	59,478
1988	Winnipeg 22, British Columbia 21	Ottawa	50,604
1989	Saskatchewan 43, Hamilton 40	Toronto	54,088
1990	Winnipeg 50, Edmonton 11	Vancouver	46,968
1991	Toronto 36, Calgary 21	Winnipeg	51,985
1992	Calgary 24, Winnipeg 10	Toronto	45,863
1993	Edmonton 33, Winnipeg 23	Calgary	50,035
1994	British Columbia 26, Baltimore 23	Vancouver	55,097
1995	Baltimore 37, Calgary 20	Regina, Saskatchewan	52,564
1996	Toronto 43, Edmonton 37	Hamilton, Ontario	38,595
1997	Toronto 47, Saskatchewan 23	Edmonton	60,431
1998	Calgary 26, Hamilton 24	Winnipeg	34,157
1999	Hamilton 32, Calgary 21	Vancouver	45,118
2000	British Columbia 28, Montreal 26	Calgary	43,822
2001	Calgary 27, Winnipeg 19	Montreal	65,255
2002	Montreal 25, Edmonton 16	Edmonton	62,531
2003	Edmonton 34, Montreal 22	Regina, Saskatchewan	50,909
2004	Toronto 27, British Columbia 19	Ottawa	51,242
2005	Edmonton 38, Montreal 35 (OT)	Vancouver	59,157
2006	British Columbia 25, Montreal 14	Winnipeg	44,786
2007	Saskatchewan 23, Winnipeg 19	Toronto	52,230
2008	Calgary 22, Montreal 14	Montreal	66,308
2009	Montreal 28, Saskatchewan 27	Calgary	46,020
2010	Montreal 21, Saskatchewan 18	Edmonton	63,317
2011	British Columbia 34, Winnipeg 23	Vancouver	54,313
2012	Toronto 35, Calgary 22	Toronto	53,208

In 1909, Earl Grey, the Governor-General of Canada, donated a trophy for the Rugby Football Championship of Canada. The trophy, which subsequently became known as the Grey Cup, was originally open only to teams registered with the Canada Rugby Union. Since 1954, it has been awarded to the winner of the Canadian Football League's championship game.

AMERICAN FOOTBALL LEAGUE I

Year	Champion	Record
1926	Philadelphia Quakers	7-2

AMERICAN FOOTBALL LEAGUE II

Year	Champion	Record
1936	Boston Shamrocks	8-3
1937	LA Bulldogs	8-0

AMERICAN FOOTBALL LEAGUE III

Year	Champion	Record
1940	Columbus Bullies	8-1-1
1941	Columbus Bullies	5-1-2

ALL-AMERICAN FOOTBALL CONFERENCE

Year	Championship Game
1946	Cleveland 14, NY Yankees 9
1947	Cleveland 14, NY Yankees 3
1948	Cleveland 49, Buffalo 7
1949	Cleveland 21, San Francisco 7

WORLD FOOTBALL LEAGUE

Year	World Bowl Championship
1974	Birmingham 22, Florida 21
1975	Disbanded midseason

UNITED STATES FOOTBALL LEAGUE

Year	Championship Game
1983	Michigan 24, Philadelphia 22
1984	Philadelphia 23, Arizona 3
1985	Baltimore 28, Oakland 24

X FOOTBALL LEAGUE

Year	Championship Game
2001	Los Angeles 38, San Francisco 6

NFL EUROPE*

Year	Champion	Record
1991	London	9-1-0
1992	Sacramento	8-2-0
1995	Frankfurt	6-4-0
1996	Scotland	7-3-0
1997	Barcelona	5-5-0
1998	Rhein	7-3-0
1999	Frankfurt	6-4-0
2000	Rhein	7-3-0
2001	Berlin	6-4-0
2002	Berlin	6-4-0
2003	Frankfurt	6-4-0
2004	Berlin	9-1-0
2005	Amsterdam	6-4-0
2006	Frankfurt	7-3-0
2007	Hamburg	7-3-0

*Known as the World League of American Football until 1998. League folded after the 2007 season.

UNITED FOOTBALL LEAGUE†

Year	Championship Game
2009	Las Vegas 20, Florida 17
2010	Las Vegas 23, Florida 20
2011	Virginia 17, Las Vegas 3

†The league ceased operations in October 2012.

College Football

AJ McCarron and Alabama dominated Notre Dame en route to the BCS national championship

Unstoppable Tide

With three championships in the last four seasons, Alabama coach Nick Saban is doing what many thought impossible: creating a dynasty in college football

BY B.J. SCHECTER

COLLEGE FOOTBALL HAS grown in popularity over the last decade, captivating the nation with its passion, pageantry and, yes, even the arcane and controversial BCS. Turn on the television on any given Saturday in the fall and you're sure to find at least a half dozen games or more available for viewing. But the devotion and fanaticism for the sport has always remained at a fever pitch in the Southeast. Football is a religion, a way of life in the South, and as the SEC has continued to dominate college football by winning seven straight national titles, it has become clear that nobody does it better.

The epicenter of the SEC dominance has been Alabama, where the Crimson Tide has won back-to-back national titles and three of the last four championships. Florida, Texas and California may produce more top players, but nowhere is the passion and history more prevalent than in Tuscaloosa, Ala. The entire state still reveres legendary coach Bear Bryant, who won six national titles, and the houndstooth hat Bryant wore on the sidelines is as synonymous with the Crimson Tide today as it was in the 1960s and '70s. Current Alabama coach Nick Saban has brought back the glory days and

is as close to an icon as there is in college football today. Saban continues to win in every facet of the game—recruiting, on the field, on the balance sheet (Alabama continues to be one of the most profitable athletic departments in the country)—and in this part of the country he is affectionately known as St. Nick. After demolishing Notre Dame 42–14 in the national championship game, Saban is on the verge of establishing a dynasty.

The term dynasty has virtually disappeared from the college sports lexicon. With scholarship restrictions, increased television exposure and more talent from coast to coast, it is extremely difficult for one program to sustain success. But Saban has somehow been able to do it in the most football-mad region in the country.

"There's a *Sports Illustrated* cover hanging in my room—because I'm on it—from 2010," said Alabama senior All-America offensive lineman Barrett Jones. "It says, DYNASTY. CAN ANYONE STOP ALABAMA? I'll never forget looking at that thing and wondering if we could really be a dynasty. Three out of four. I'm no dynasty expert, but that seems like a dynasty to me."

Alabama's dynasty-in-the-making almost came to a screeching halt in 2012. When the

Heisman winner Manziel staked his claim to the nation's attention in November, throwing for 253 yards and rushing for another 92 in Texas A&M's upset of Alabama.

Crimson Tide lost to Heisman Trophy winner Johnny Manziel and Texas A&M at home on Nov. 10, Alabama's title chances appeared to be over. But the following week two of the teams ahead of the Crimson Tide, Kansas State and Oregon, lost within a few hours of one another, vaulting Notre Dame to No. 1 and Alabama to No. 2.

The Crimson Tide caught a break, but everything nearly fell apart in the SEC title game in Atlanta on Dec. 1. In the Georgia Dome, Alabama faced a biting Georgia Bulldogs team looking to prove it belonged among the nation's elite. Alabama trailed 21–10 with 6:31 remaining in the third quarter before the mounting a furious comeback. The fourth quarter produced

the best and most intense football of the season as both teams slugged it out and clawed for every yard. In the end, Bama quarterback AJ McCarron came through with a beautifully executed 45-yard touchdown pass to Amari Cooper, and the Crimson Tide defense tackled Georgia's Chris Conley on the Alabama five-yard line as time expired to preserve a thrilling 32–28 victory.

Alabama manhandled Notre Dame in the BCS Championship game from the opening kickoff, and early in the first quarter it was clear that the Crimson Tide was in a different league. But though the Irish were embarrassed by Alabama, it didn't diminish what Notre Dame had accomplished in going 12-0 during the regular season. The Irish woke up the echoes, and under the deft direction of coach Brian Kelly regained its relevance. Love them or hate them, college football is better when Notre Dame is

The bizarre tale surrounding T'eo's alleged girlfriend ultimately overwhelmed his substantial on-field accomplishments.

good. The Irish strike a cord with fans in much the same way as the New York Yankees in baseball and the Dallas Cowboys in professional football.

Still, Notre Dame was far from dominant in the regular season and the championship game debacle left many feeling like the Irish were a fraud. The week after getting embarrassed on the field they were embarrassed off of it when the sports gossip website Deadspin.com broke a story that Notre Dame star Manti Te'o's girlfriend never existed and her death early in the season was a hoax. Whether Te'o was in on the scam or was duped as he claimed to be, the scandal created a huge firestorm because Te'o's story—he claimed that his girlfriend died just days after his grandmother had passed in September and received an overwhelming amount of support and attention—was a large factor in Te'o finishing second to Texas A&M's Johnny Manziel in the Heisman Trophy voting. (By season's end Manziel had electrified the nation with his quick feet, accurate arm and flair for the dramatic.)

The fact that one of the biggest college football stars in the nation claimed to have a girlfriend he had never met was dubious at best, but Te'o's parents, teammates and the national media bought the story initially and Te'o said the lie had grown out of control. Even more baffling was the fact that Te'o answered questions about the death of his fake girlfriend during a title game press conference, more than a week after he came clean to Notre Dame officials that he never actually met this girlfriend and that he had been told that she never existed. The hoax clearly weighed on Te'o in the championship game as one of the nation's best defensive players looked lost against Alabama's powerful offense.

Under Saban a lot of teams have looked lost against the Crimson Tide. After winning his third title, the comparisons to Bryant came immediately but this time Saban embraced them. "I read his book, I heard a lot of stories," said Saban of Bryant. "From what I understand, he was a very good fundamental coach. But what he really did well was create intangibles like toughness and discipline and give great effort and executing your job.... What you have to admire most about Coach Bryant is that he could do it for such a long time at such a high level. Because people think there is a continuum of success. There is no continuum of success. It starts over with every team."

That may be true, but Alabama has a good head start on the rest of the nation. Some might call that a continuum of success. Others would call it a dynasty.

Final Polls

Associated Press

		Record	Pts	Head Coach	SI Preseason Rank
1	Alabama (59)	13-1	1,475	Nick Saban	1
2	Oregon	12-1	1,358	Chip Kelly	4
3	Ohio State	12-0	1,302	Urban Meyer	22
4	Notre Dame	12-1	1,288	Brian Kelly	*
5 (tie)	Georgia	12-2	1,230	Mark Richt	9
5 (tie)	Texas A&M	11-2	1,230	Kevin Sumlin	*
7	Stanford	12-2	1,169	David Shaw	17
8	South Carolina	11-2	1,038	Steve Spurrier	7
9	Florida	11-2	933	Will Muschamp	*
10	Florida State	12-2	922	Jimbo Fisher	11
11	Clemson	11-2	889	Dabo Swinney	14
12	Kansas State	11-2	871	Bill Snyder	16
13	Louisville	11-2	781	Charlie Strong	*
14	LSU	10-3	756	Les Miles	3
15	Oklahoma	10-3	615	Mike Stoops	5
16	Utah State	11-2	456	Matt Wells	*
17	Northwestern	10-3	443	Pat Fitzgerald	*
18	Boise State	11-2	419	Chris Petersen	23
19	Texas	9-4	358	Mack Brown	15
20	Oregon State	9-4	303	Mike Riley	*
21	San Jose State	11-2	243	Ron Caragher	*
22	Northern Illinois	12-2	227	Rod Carey	*
23	Vanderbilt	9-4	180	James Franklin	*
24	Michigan	8-5	147	Brady Hoke	13
25	Nebraska	10-4	119	Bo Pelini	19

60 sportswriters and broadcasters following bowl games (first-place votes in parentheses). *Not ranked in preseason top 25.

USA Today/Coaches

		Pts	SI Preseason Rank			Pts	SI Preseason Rank
1	Alabama (56)	1400	1	14	Boise State	633	23
2	Oregon	1322	4	15	Oklahoma	600	5
3	Notre Dame	1253	*	16	Northwestern	580	*
4	Georgia	1213	9	17	Utah State	444	*
5	Texas A&M	1171	*	18	Texas	398	15
6	Stanford	1167	17	19	Oregon State	366	*
7	South Carolina	1064	7	20	Vanderbilt	248	*
8	Florida State	942	11	21	San Jose State	244	*
9	Clemson	916	14	22	Cincinnati	186	*
10	Florida	886	*	23	Nebraska	175	19
11	Kansas State	841	16	24	Northern Illinois	156	*
12	LSU	775	3	25	Tulsa	110	*
13	Louisville	772	*				

Note: Voted by a panel of 59 FBS (I-A) head coaches; 25 points for 1st, 24 for 2nd, etc. (first-place votes in parentheses). *Not ranked in preseason top 25.

Bowls and Playoffs

NCAA Football Bowl Subdivision (I-A) Bowl Results

Date	Bowl	Result	Payout/Team ($)	Attendance
12-15-12	New Mexico	Arizona 49, Nevada 48	456,250	24,610
12-15-12	Famous Idaho Potato	Utah St 41, Toledo 15	325,000	29,243
12-20-12	Poinsettia	BYU 23, San Diego St 6	500,000	35,442
12-21-12	St. Petersburg	Central Florida 38, Ball St 17	537,500	21,759
12-22-12	New Orleans	LA-Lafayette 43, East Carolina 34	500,000	48,828
12-22-12	Las Vegas	Boise St 28, Washington 26	1.1 million	33,217
12-24-12	Hawaii	Southern Methodist 43, Fresno St 10	650,000	30,024
12-26-12	Little Caesars	Central Michigan 24, Western Kentucky 21	750,000	23,310
12-27-12	Military	San Jose St 29, Bowling Green 20	1 million	17,835
12-27-12	Belk	Cincinnati 48, Duke 34	1.7 million	48,128
12-27-12	Holiday	Baylor 49, UCLA 26	2.075 million	55,507
12-28-12	Independence	Ohio 45, LA-Monroe 14	1.15 million	41,853
12-28-12	Russell Athletic	Virginia Tech 13, Rutgers 10	2.275 million	48,127

NCAA Football Bowl Subdivision (I-A) Bowl Results *(Cont.)*

Date	Bowl	Result	Payout/Team($)	Attendance
12-28-12	Meineke Car Care	Texas Tech 34, Minnesota 31	1.7 million	50,386
12-29-12	Armed Forces	Rice 33, Air Force 14	600,000	40,754
12-29-12	Pinstripe	Syracuse 38, West Virginia 14	1.8 million	39,098
12-29-12	Fight Hunger	Arizona St 62, Navy 28	837,500	34,172
12-29-12	Alamo	Texas 31, Oregon St 27	3.175 million	65,277
12-29-12	Buffalo Wild Wings	Michigan St 17, TCU 16	3.35 million	44,617
12-31-12	Music City	Vanderbilt 38, NC State 24	1.8375 million	55,801
12-31-12	Sun	Georgia Tech 21, USC 7	2 million	47,922
12-31-12	Liberty	Tulsa 31, Iowa St 17	1.4375 million	53,687
12-31-12	Chick-fil-A	Clemson 25, LSU 24	3.967 million (ACC) 2.932 million (SEC)	68,027
01-01-13	Gator	Northwestern 34, Mississippi St 20	3.5 million	48,612
01-01-12	Heart of Dallas	Oklahoma 58, Purdue 14	1.1 million	48,313
01-01-13	Outback	South Carolina 33, Michigan 28	3.5 million	54,527
01-01-13	Capital One	Georgia 45, Nebraska 31	4.55 million	59,712
01-01-13	Rose	Stanford 20, Wisconsin 14	17 million	93,359
01-01-13	Orange	Florida St 31, Northern Illinois 10	17 million	72,073
01-02-13	Sugar	Louisville 33, Florida 23	17 million	54,178
01-03-13	Fiesta	Oregon 35, Kansas St 17	17 million	70,242
01-04-13	Cotton	Texas A&M 41, Oklahoma 13	3.625 million	87,025
01-05-13	Compass	Mississippi 38, Pittsburgh 17	1 million (SEC) 900,000 (Big East)	59,135
01-06-13	GoDaddy.com	Arkansas St 17, Kent St 13	750,000	37,913
01-07-13	BCS Championship	Alabama 42, Notre Dame 14	18 million	80,120

NCAA FCS (I-AA) Championship Box Score

North Dakota St	3	7	15	14—39
Sam Houston St	0	10	0	3—13

FIRST QUARTER

North Dakota St: FG Keller 32, 3:49.

SECOND QUARTER

Sam Houston St: FG Antonio 38, 14:18.
North Dakota St: TD Jensen 20 run (Keller kick), 3:09.
Sam Houston St: TD Williams 1 pass from Bell (Antonio kick), :33.

THIRD QUARTER

North Dakota St: TD Jensen 1 run (Keller kick), 8:30.
North Dakota St: TD Ojuri 2 run (2-pt conversion successful)

FOURTH QUARTER

Sam Houston St: FG Antonio 32, 13:20.
North Dakota St: TD Jensen 1 run (Keller kick), 10:13.
North Dakota St: TD Ojuri 11 run (Keller kick), 6:00.

	NORTH DAKOTA ST	SAM HOUSTON ST
First downs	22	23
Rushes-net yards	45-300	38-116
Net passing yards	141	275
Comp/Att/Int	10-17-0	20-35-4
Punts/total yards	4-168	10-442
Fumbles-lost	0-0	0-0
Penalties-yards	4-38	7-80
Time of possession	30:13	29:47

1-5-13, Frisco, Texas; Att: 21,411.

Small College Championship Summaries

NCAA DIVISION II

First round: Shippensburg 58, Bloomsburg 20; Indiana (PA) 27, Shepherd 17; Indianapolis 31, Midwestern St 14; West Texas A&M 38, Chadron St 30; Missouri Western St 57, Minnesota Duluth 55; Northwest Missouri St 35, Harding 0; Lenoir-Rhyne 21, Fort Valley St 6; West Alabama 41, Miles 7.
Second Round: Winston-Salem 37, Shippensburg 14; Indiana (PA) 17, New Haven 14; Colorado St-Pueblo 28, Indianapolis 7; West Texas A&M 33, Ashland 28; Missouri Western St 45, Henderson St 21; Minnesota St-Mankato 38, Northwest Missouri St 35; Carson-Newman 38, Lenoir-Rhyne 35; Valdosta St 49, West Alabama 21.
Quarterfinals: Winston-Salem 21, Indiana (PA) 17; West Texas A&M 34, Colorado St-Pueblo 13; Minnesota St-Mankato 17, Missouri Western St 10; Valdosta St 48, Carson-Newman 26.
Semifinals: Winston-Salem 41, West Texas A&M 18; Valdosta St 35, Minnesota St-Mankato 19.

NCAA DIVISION II

Championship: 12-15-12, Florence, Ala., Att: 7,525.				
Valdosta St	14	7	0	14—35
Winston-Salem	0	0	7	0—7

NCAA DIVISION III

First round: Linfield 27, Pacific Lutheran 24; North Central (IL) 41, Cal Lutheran 21; Bethel (MN) 24, Conc-Chicago 23; Wisconsin-Oshkosh 55, St. Scholastica 10; Hobart 38, Washington & Lee 20; Wittenberg 52, Heidelberg 38; Elmhurst 27, Coe 24; St. Thomas (MN) 48, St. Norbert 17; Mount Union 72, Christopher Newport 14; Johns Hopkins 42, Washington & Jefferson 10; Salisbury 17, Rowan 9; Widener 44, Bridgewater St 14; Wesley 73, Mount Ida 14; SUNY Cortland 20, Framingham St 19; Franklin 42, Adrian 10; Mary Hardin-Baylor 59, Louisiana College 20.

NCAA DIVISION III *(CONT.)*

Second Round: Linfield 30, North Central (IL) 14; Wisconsin-Oshkosh 37, Bethel (MN) 14; Hobart 35, Wittenberg 10; St. Thomas (MN) 24, Elmhurst 17; Mount Union 55, Johns Hopkins 13; Widener 28, Salisbury 7; Wesley 56, SUNY Cortland 6; Mary Hardin-Baylor 63, Franklin 17.
Quarterfinals:Wisconsin-Oshkosh 31, Linfield 24; St. Thomas (MN) 47, Hobart 7; Mount Union 72, Widener 17; Mary Hardin-Baylor 32, Wesley 20.
Semifinals: St. Thomas (MN) 28, Wisconsin-Oshkosh 14; Mount Union 48, Mary Hardin-Baylor 35.

NCAA DIVISION III

Championship: 12-14-12, Salem, Va., Att: 6,027

St. Thomas (MN)	0	7	3	0—10
Mount Union	14	0	7	7—28

NAIA CHAMPIONSHIP

Championship: 12-13-12, Rome, Ga., Att: 5,263

Marian (IN)	7	3	0	17	3—30
Morningside (IA)	14	0	6	7	0—27

Awards

Heisman Memorial Trophy

Player, School	Class	Pos	1st	2nd	3rd	Total
Johnny Manziel, Texas A&M	Fr.	QB	474	252	103	2,029
Manti Te'o, Notre Dame	Sr.	LB	321	309	125	1,706
Collin Klein, Kansas State	Sr.	QB	60	197	320	894
Marquise Lee, Southern Cal	Jr.	WR	19	33	84	207

Note: Former Heisman winners and the media vote, with ballots allowing for three names (3 points for 1st, 2 for 2nd, 1 for 3rd).

Other Awards

Maxwell Award (Player)	Manti Te'o, Notre Dame, LB
Sporting News Player of the Year	Johnny Manziel, Texas A&M, QB
Walter Camp Player of the Year	Manti Te'o, Notre Dame, LB
Chuck Bednarik Award (Defense)	Manti Te'o, Notre Dame, LB
Vince Lombardi/Rotary Award (Lineman/LB)	Manti Te'o, Notre Dame, LB
Outland Trophy (Interior Lineman)	Luke Joeckel, Texas A&M, OT
Davey O'Brien Award (QB)	Johnny Manziel, Texas A&M, QB
Unitas Golden Arm Award (Senior QB)	Collin Klein, Kansas State, QB
Doak Walker Award (RB)	Montee Ball, Wisconsin, RB
Biletnikoff Award (WR)	Marquise Lee, Southern Cal, WR
Butkus Award (Linebacker)	Manti Te'o, Notre Dame, LB
Jim Thorpe Award (Defensive Back)	Johnthan Banks, Mississippi St, CB
Associated Press Player of the Year	Johnny Manziel, Texas A&M, QB
Walter Payton Award (FCS Player)	Taylor Heinicke, Old Dominion, QB
Harlon Hill Trophy (Div. II Player)	Zach Zulli, Shippensburg, QB
Gagliardi Trophy (Div. III Player)	Scottie Williams, Elmhurst (IL), RB

Coaches' Awards

Home Depot Award	Brian Kelly, Notre Dame
Eddie Robinson Award (FCS)	Craig Bohl, North Dakota State
Bobby Dodd Award	Bill Snyder, Kansas State
Bear Bryant Award	Bill O'Brien, Penn St

AFCA Coaches of the Year

FBS (Division I-A)	Brian Kelly, Notre Dame
FCS (Division I-AA)	Craig Bohl, North Dakota State
Division II	David Dean, Valdosta St
Division III	Glenn Caruso, St. Thomas (MN)
NAIA	Steve Ryan, Morningside College

Associated Press First Team All-America

OFFENSE

QB	Johnny Manziel, Texas A&M
RB	Montee Ball, Wisconsin
RB	Ka'Deem Carey, Arizona
WR	Marqise Lee, USC
WR	Terrance Williams, Baylor
TE	Zach Ertz, Stanford
OT	Luke Joeckel, Texas A&M
OT	Taylor Lewan, Michigan
OG	Chance Warmack, Alabama
OG	Jonathan Cooper, North Carolina
C	Barrett Jones, Alabama
K	Cairo Santos, Tulane
All-P	Tavon Austin, West Virginia

DEFENSE

DE	Jadeveon Clowney, South Carolina
DE	Bjoern Werner, Florida State
DT	Star Lotulelei, Utah
DT	Will Sutton, Arizona State
LB	Manti Te'o, Notre Dame
LB	Jarvis Jones, Georgia
LB	C.J. Mosley, Alabama
CB	Dee Milliner, Alabama
CB	Jordan Poyer, Oregon State
S	Phillip Thomas, Fresno State
S	Matt Elam, Florida
P	Ryan Allen, Louisiana Tech

Football Bowl Subdivision (I-A)

ATLANTIC COAST CONFERENCE

ATLANTIC	Conference W	L	Full Season W	L	Pct
Florida State	7	1	12	2	.857
Clemson	7	1	11	2	.846
North Carolina State	4	4	7	6	.538
Wake Forest	3	5	5	7	.417
Maryland	2	6	4	8	.333
Boston College	1	7	2	10	.167

COASTAL	W	L	W	L	Pct
Georgia Tech	5	3	7	7	.500
North Carolina	5	3	8	4	.667
Miami (FL)	5	3	7	5	.583
Virginia Tech	4	4	7	6	.538
Duke	3	5	6	7	.462
Virginia	2	6	4	8	.333

BIG EAST CONFERENCE

	Conference W	L	Full Season W	L	Pct
Louisville	5	2	11	2	.846
Rutgers	5	2	9	4	.692
Cincinnati	5	2	10	3	.769
Syracuse	5	2	8	5	.615
Pittsburgh	3	4	6	7	.462
Temple	2	5	4	7	.364
Connecticut	2	5	5	7	.417
South Florida	1	6	3	9	.250

BIG TEN CONFERENCE

LEGENDS	Conference W	L	Full Season W	L	Pct
Nebraska	7	1	10	4	.714
Michigan	6	2	8	5	.615
Northwestern	5	3	10	3	.769
Michigan State	3	5	7	6	.538
Iowa	2	6	4	8	.333
Minnesota	2	6	6	7	.462

LEADERS	W	L	W	L	Pct
*Ohio State	8	0	12	0	1.000
Penn State	6	2	8	4	.667
Wisconsin	4	4	8	6	.571
Purdue	3	5	6	7	.462
Indiana	2	6	4	8	.333
Illinois	0	8	2	10	.167

BIG 12 CONFERENCE

	Conference W	L	Full Season W	L	Pct
Kansas State	8	1	11	2	.846
Oklahoma	8	1	10	3	.769
Texas	5	4	9	4	.692
Oklahoma State	5	4	8	5	.615
Baylor	4	5	8	5	.615
Texas Tech	4	5	8	5	.615
TCU	4	5	7	6	.538
West Virginia	4	5	7	6	.538
Iowa State	3	6	6	7	.462
Kansas	0	9	1	11	.083

Football Bowl Subdivision (I-A) *(Cont.)*

CONFERENCE USA

EAST	Conference W	L	Full Season W	L	Pct
UCF	7	1	10	4	.714
East Carolina	7	1	8	5	.615
Marshall	4	4	5	7	.417
Memphis	4	4	4	8	.333
UAB	2	6	3	9	.250
Southern Miss	0	8	0	12	.000

WEST	W	L	W	L	Pct
Tulsa	7	1	11	3	.786
Southern Methodist	5	3	7	6	.538
Rice	4	4	7	6	.538
Houston	4	4	5	7	.417
UTEP	2	6	3	9	.250
Tulane	2	6	2	10	.167

MID-AMERICAN ATHLETIC CONFERENCE

EAST	Conference W	L	Full Season W	L	Pct
Kent State	8	0	11	3	.786
Bowling Green	6	2	8	5	.615
Ohio	4	4	9	4	.692
Buffalo	3	5	4	8	.333
Miami (OH)	3	5	4	8	.333
Massachusetts	1	7	1	11	.083
Akron	0	8	1	11	.083

WEST	W	L	W	L	Pct
Northern Illinois	8	0	12	2	.857
Ball State	6	2	9	4	.692
Toledo	6	2	9	4	.692
Central Michigan	4	4	7	6	.538
Western Michigan	2	6	4	8	.333
Eastern Michigan	1	7	2	10	.167

MOUNTAIN WEST CONFERENCE

	Conference W	L	Full Season W	L	Pct
San Diego State	7	1	9	4	.692
Boise State	7	1	11	2	.846
Fresno State	7	1	9	4	.692
Air Force	5	3	6	7	.462
Nevada	4	4	7	6	.538
Wyoming	3	5	4	8	.333
Colorado State	3	5	4	8	.333
UNLV	2	6	2	11	.182
New Mexico	1	7	4	9	.308
Hawaii	1	7	3	9	.250

PACIFIC 12 CONFERENCE

NORTH	Conference W	L	Full Season W	L	Pct
Stanford	8	1	12	2	.857
Oregon	8	1	12	1	.923
Oregon State	6	3	9	4	.692
Washington	5	4	7	6	.538
California	2	7	3	9	.250
Washington State	1	8	3	9	.250

SOUTH	W	L	W	L	Pct
UCLA	6	3	9	5	.643
*USC	5	4	7	6	.538
Arizona State	5	4	8	5	.615
Arizona	4	5	8	5	.615
Utah	3	6	5	7	.417
Colorado	1	8	1	11	.083

*Barred from bowl eligibility by the NCAA for rules violations.

Football Bowl Subdivision (I-A) *(Cont.)*

SOUTHEASTERN CONFERENCE

	Conference		Full Season		
EAST	**W**	**L**	**W**	**L**	**Pct**
Georgia	7	1	12	2	.857
Florida	7	1	11	2	.846
South Carolina	6	2	11	2	.846
Vanderbilt	5	3	9	4	.692
Missouri	2	6	5	7	.417
Tennessee	1	7	5	7	.417
Kentucky	0	8	2	10	.167
WEST					
Alabama	7	1	13	1	.929
LSU	6	2	10	3	.769
Texas A&M	6	2	11	2	.846
Mississippi State	4	4	8	5	.615
Mississippi	3	5	7	6	.538
Arkansas	2	6	4	8	.333
Auburn	0	8	3	9	.250

SUN BELT CONFERENCE

	Conference		Full Season		
	W	**L**	**W**	**L**	**Pct**
Arkansas State	7	1	10	3	.769
Louisiana-Lafayette	6	2	9	4	.692
Louisiana-Monroe	6	2	8	5	.615
Middle Tennessee	6	2	8	4	.667
Western Kentucky	4	4	7	6	.539
Troy	3	5	5	7	.417
North Texas	3	5	4	8	.333
FIU	2	6	3	9	.250
Florida Atlantic	2	6	3	9	.250
South Alabama	1	7	2	11	.182

WESTERN ATHLETIC CONFERENCE

	Conference		Full Season		
	W	**L**	**W**	**L**	**Pct**
Utah State	6	0	11	2	.846
San Jose State	5	1	11	2	.846
Louisiana Tech	4	2	9	3	.750
Texas-San Antonio	3	3	8	4	.667
Texas State	2	4	4	8	.333
Idaho	1	5	1	11	.083
New Mexico State	0	6	1	11	.083

INDEPENDENTS

	Full Season		
	W	**L**	**Pct**
Notre Dame	12	1	.923
Brigham Young	8	5	.615
Navy	8	5	.615
Army	2	10	.167

Football Championship Subdivision (I-AA)

BIG SKY CONFERENCE

	Conference		Full Season		
	W	**L**	**W**	**L**	**Pct**
Eastern Washington	7	1	11	3	.786
Montana State	7	1	11	2	.846
Cal Poly	7	1	9	3	.750
Northern Arizona	6	2	8	3	.727
Sacramento State	4	4	6	5	.545
Northern Colorado	4	4	5	6	.455
Southern Utah	4	4	5	6	.455
North Dakota	3	5	5	6	.455
UC Davis	3	5	4	7	.364
Montana	3	5	5	6	.455
Portland State	2	6	3	8	.273
Weber State	2	6	2	9	.182
Idaho State	0	8	1	10	.091

BIG SOUTH CONFERENCE

	Conference		Full Season		
	W	**L**	**W**	**L**	**Pct**
Coastal Carolina	5	1	8	5	.615
Liberty	5	1	6	5	.545
Stony Brook	5	1	10	3	.769
Charleston Southern	3	3	5	6	.455
Gardner-Webb	2	4	3	8	.273
Virginia Military	1	5	2	9	.182
Presbyterian	0	6	2	9	.182

COLONIAL CONFERENCE

	Conference		Full Season		
	W	**L**	**W**	**L**	**Pct**
Old Dominion	7	1	11	2	.846
Villanova	6	2	8	4	.667
Towson	6	2	7	4	.374
New Hampshire	6	2	8	4	.667
Richmond	6	2	8	3	.727
James Madison	5	3	7	4	.364
Maine	4	4	5	6	.455
Delaware	2	6	5	6	.455
William & Mary	1	7	2	9	.182
Georgia State	1	7	1	10	.091
Rhode Island	0	8	0	11	.000

IVY LEAGUE

	Conference		Full Season		
	W	**L**	**W**	**L**	**Pct**
Pennsylvania	6	1	6	4	.600
Harvard	5	2	8	2	.800
Brown	4	3	7	3	.700
Dartmouth	4	3	6	4	.600
Princeton	4	3	5	5	.500
Columbia	2	5	3	7	.300
Cornell	2	5	4	6	.400
Yale	1	6	2	8	.200

Football Champ. Subdivision (I-AA) *(Cont.)*

MID-EASTERN ATHLETIC CONFERENCE

	Conference		Full Season		
	W	L	W	L	Pct
Bethune-Cookman	8	0	9	3	.750
Howard	6	2	7	4	.636
North Carolina A&T	5	3	7	4	.636
North Carolina Central	5	3	6	5	.545
Delaware State	5	3	6	5	.545
South Carolina State	4	4	5	6	.455
Florida A&M	4	4	4	7	.364
Hampton	3	5	3	7	.300
Norfolk State	2	6	4	7	.364
Morgan State	2	6	3	8	.273
Savannah State	0	8	1	10	.091

MISSOURI VALLEY CONFERENCE

	Conference		Full Season		
	W	L	W	L	Pct
North Dakota State	7	1	14	1	.933
South Dakota State	6	2	9	4	.692
Illinois State	5	3	9	4	.692
Indiana State	5	3	7	4	.636
Southern Illinois	5	3	6	5	.545
Youngstown State	4	4	7	4	.636
Northern Iowa	4	4	5	6	.455
Missouri State	3	5	3	8	.273
Western Illinois	1	7	3	8	.273
South Dakota	0	8	1	10	.091

NORTHEAST CONFERENCE

	Conference		Full Season		
	W	L	W	L	Pct
Wagner	7	1	9	4	.692
Albany	7	1	9	2	.818
Monmouth	4	3	5	5	.500
St. Francis (PA)	4	4	5	6	.455
Bryant	4	4	4	7	.364
Robert Morris	3	5	4	7	.364
Duquesne	3	5	5	6	.455
Central Connecticut St	2	5	2	8	.200
Sacred Heart	1	7	2	9	.182

OHIO VALLEY CONFERENCE

	Conference		Full Season		
	W	L	W	L	Pct
Eastern Illinois	6	1	7	5	.583
Eastern Kentucky	6	2	8	3	.727
Tennessee-Martin	6	2	8	3	.727
Jacksonville State	5	3	6	5	.545
Tennessee State	4	3	8	3	.727
Murray State	4	4	5	6	.455
Southeast Missouri St	2	6	3	8	.273
Austin Peay	1	7	2	9	.182
Tennessee Tech	1	7	3	8	.273

PATRIOT LEAGUE

	Conference		Full Season		
	W	L	W	L	Pct
Colgate	6	0	8	4	.667
Lehigh	5	1	10	1	.909
Fordham	3	3	6	5	.545
Lafayette	2	4	5	6	.455
Georgetown	2	4	5	6	.455
Holy Cross	2	4	2	9	.182
Bucknell	1	5	3	8	.273

Football Champ. Subdivision (I-AA) *(Cont.)*

PIONEER LEAGUE

	Conference		Full Season		
	W	L	W	L	Pct
Drake	7	1	8	3	.727
San Diego	7	1	8	3	.727
Butler	7	1	8	3	.727
Jacksonville	5	3	7	4	.636
Dayton	5	3	6	5	.545
Morehead State	3	5	4	7	.364
Marist	3	5	4	7	.364
Davidson	2	6	2	9	.182
Valparaiso	1	7	1	10	.091
Campbell	0	8	1	10	.091

SOUTHERN CONFERENCE

	Conference		Full Season		
	W	L	W	L	Pct
Georgia Southern	6	2	10	4	.714
Wofford	6	2	9	4	.692
Appalachian State	6	2	8	4	.667
Chattanooga	5	3	6	5	.545
Samford	5	3	7	4	.636
Citadel	5	3	7	4	.636
Furman	2	6	3	8	.273
Elon	1	7	3	8	.273
Western Carolina	0	8	1	10	.091

SOUTHLAND CONFERENCE

	Conference		Full Season		
	W	L	W	L	Pct
Central Arkansas	6	1	9	3	.750
Sam Houston State	6	1	11	4	.733
SE Louisiana	5	2	5	6	.455
McNeese State	4	3	7	4	.636
Stephen F. Austin	4	3	5	6	.455
Northwestern State	2	5	4	7	.364
Lamar	1	6	4	8	.333
Nicholls	0	7	1	10	.091

SOUTHWESTERN ATHLETIC CONFERENCE

	Conference		Full Season		
EAST	W	L	W	L	Pct
Jackson State	7	2	7	5	.583
Alabama State	7	2	7	4	.636
Alabama A&M	6	3	7	4	.636
Mississippi Valley St	5	4	5	6	.455
Alcorn State	4	5	4	7	.364
WEST					
Arkansas-Pine Bluff	8	1	10	2	.833
Prairie View A&M	3	6	3	8	.273
Southern University	3	6	4	7	.364
Texas Southern	2	7	2	9	.182
Grambling State	0	9	1	10	.091

INDEPENDENTS

	Full Season		
	W	L	Pct
Abilene Christian	7	4	.636
Monmouth	5	5	.500
Incarnate Word	2	9	.182

Football Bowl Subdivision (I-A)

SCORING

	Class	GP	TD	XP	FG	Pts	Pts/Game
Kenneth Dixon, Louisiana Tech	Fr.	12	28	0	0	168	14.00
Quinn Sharp, Oklahoma St.	Sr.	13	0	72	28	156	12.00
Stedman Bailey, West Virginia	Jr.	13	25	0	0	150	11.54
Stefphon Jefferson, Nevada	Jr.	13	25	0	0	150	11.54
Giovani Bernard, North Carolina	So.	10	19	0	0	114	11.40
Ka'Deem Carey, Arizona	So.	13	24	0	0	144	11.08
Alex Singleton, Tulsa	Sr.	14	25	0	0	150	10.71
Kenjon Barner, Oregon	Sr.	13	23	0	0	138	10.62
Collin Klein, Kansas St.	Sr.	13	23	0	0	138	10.62
Latavius Murray, UCF	Sr.	11	19	0	0	114	10.36

FIELD GOALS

	Class	GP	FGA	FG	Pct	FG/Game
Quinn Sharp, Oklahoma St.	Sr.	13	34	28	.824	2.15
Steven Schott, Ball St.	Sr.	13	32	25	.781	1.92
Caleb Sturgis, Florida	Sr.	13	28	24	.857	1.85
Jeremiah Detmer, Toledo	So.	13	29	24	.828	1.85
Dustin Hopkins, Florida St.	Sr.	14	30	25	.833	1.79
Chris Boswell, Rice	Jr.	13	29	23	.793	1.77
Matt Weller, Ohio	Sr.	13	31	23	.742	1.77
Kyle Brindza, Notre Dame	So.	13	31	23	.742	1.77
Dan Conroy, Michigan St.	Sr.	13	32	23	.719	1.77
Cairo Santos, Tulane	Jr.	12	21	21	1.000	1.75

TOTAL OFFENSE

			Rushing		Passing			Total Offense	
	Class	GP	Car	Net	Att	Yds	Tot. Yds	Yds/Play	Yds/Game
Johnny Manziel, Texas A&M	Fr.	13	201	1410	434	3706	5116	8.06	393.54
Nick Florence, Baylor	Sr.	13	139	568	464	4309	4877	8.09	375.15
Colby Cameron, Louisiana Tech	Sr.	12	61	177	522	4147	4324	7.42	360.33
Jordan Lynch, Northern Ill.	Jr.	14	294	1815	394	3138	4953	7.20	353.79
Rakeem Cato, Marshall	So.	12	57	31	584	4201	4232	6.60	352.67
Matt Scott, Arizona	Sr.	12	113	506	499	3620	4126	6.74	343.83
Tajh Boyd, Clemson	Jr.	13	186	514	427	3896	4410	7.19	339.23
Geno Smith, West Virginia	Sr.	13	66	151	518	4205	4356	7.46	335.08
Seth Doege, Texas Tech	Sr.	13	48	59	541	4205	4264	7.24	328.00
Cody Fajardo, Nevada	So.	12	190	1121	367	2786	3907	7.01	325.58

RUSHING

	Class	GP	Car	Yds	TD	Avg	Yds/Game
Ka'Deem Carey, Arizona	So.	13	303	1929	23	6.37	148.38
Stefphon Jefferson, Nevada	Jr.	13	375	1883	24	5.02	144.85
Le'Veon Bell, Michigan St.	Jr.	13	382	1793	12	4.69	137.92
Kenjon Barner, Oregon	Sr.	13	278	1767	21	6.36	135.92
Antonio Andrews, Western Ky.	Jr.	13	304	1728	11	5.68	132.92
Montee Ball, Wisconsin	Sr.	14	356	1830	22	5.14	130.71
Jordan Lynch, Northern Ill.	Jr.	14	294	1815	19	6.17	129.64
David Fluellen, Toledo	Jr.	12	259	1498	13	5.78	124.83
Johnathan Franklin, UCLA	Sr.	14	282	1734	13	6.15	123.86
Beau Blankenship, Ohio	Jr.	13	312	1604	15	5.14	123.38

PASSING EFFICIENCY

	Class	GP	Att	Comp	Pct Comp	Yds	Yds/Att	TD	Int	Rating Pts
A.J. McCarron, Alabama	Jr.	14	314	211	67.20	2933	9.34	30	3	175.28
Aaron Murray, Georgia	Jr.	14	386	249	64.51	3893	10.09	36	10	174.82
David Fales, San Jose St.	Jr.	13	451	327	72.51	4193	9.30	33	9	170.76
J.W. Walsh, Oklahoma St.	Fr.	10	163	109	66.87	1564	9.60	13	3	170.11
Tajh Boyd, Clemson	Jr.	13	427	287	67.21	3896	9.12	36	13	165.59
Geno Smith, West Virginia	Sr.	13	518	369	71.24	4205	8.12	42	6	163.86
Marcus Mariota, Oregon	Fr.	13	336	230	68.45	2677	7.97	32	6	163.23
Teddy Bridgewater, Louisville	So.	13	419	287	68.50	3718	8.87	27	8	160.48
Taylor Kelly, Arizona St.	So.	13	359	241	67.13	3039	8.47	29	9	159.88
Connor Shaw, South Carolina	Jr.	11	228	154	67.54	1956	8.58	17	7	158.07

Note: Minimum 15 attempts per game.

Football Bowl Subdivision (I-A) *(Cont.)*

RECEPTIONS PER GAME

	Class	GP	No.	Yds	TD	Rec/G
Jordan White, Western Mich.	Sr.	13	140	1911	17	10.77
Tommy Shuler, Marshall	So.	12	110	1138	6	9.17
Marqise Lee, Southern California	So.	13	118	1721	14	9.08
Stedman Bailey, West Virginia	Jr.	13	114	1622	25	8.77
Tavon Austin, West Virginia	Sr.	13	114	1289	12	8.77
Quinton Patton, Louisiana Tech	Sr.	12	104	1392	13	8.67

RECEIVING YARDS PER GAME

	Class	GP	No.	Yds	TD	Yds/Game
Terrance Williams, Baylor	Sr.	13	97	1832	12	140.92
Marqise Lee, Southern California	So.	13	118	1721	14	132.38
Stedman Bailey, West Virginia	Jr.	13	114	1622	25	124.77
Quinton Patton, Louisiana Tech	Sr.	12	104	1392	13	116.00
Cobi Hamilton, Arkansas	Sr.	12	90	1335	5	111.25

ALL-PURPOSE RUNNING

	Class	GP	Rush	Rec	PR	KOR	Total Yds	Yds/Game
Antonio Andrews, Western Kentucky	Jr.	13	1728	432	234	767	3161	243.10
Tavon Austin, West Virginia	Sr.	13	643	1289	165	813	2910	223.85
Marqise Lee, Southern California	So.	13	106	1721	0	856	2683	206.38
Giovani Bernard, North Carolina	So.	10	1228	490	263	0	1981	198.10
Dri Archer, Kent St.	Jr.	14	1429	561	-4	591	2577	184.07

INTERCEPTIONS

	Class	GP	No.	Int/Game
Phillip Thomas, Fresno St	Sr.	13	8	.62
Jordan Poyer, Oregon St	Sr.	12	7	.58
Bene Benwikere, San Jose St	Jr.	13	7	.54
Manti Te'o, Notre Dame	Sr.	13	7	.54

Five tied with 6.

PUNTING

	Class	No.	Avg Y/Pt
Ryan Allen, Louisiana Tech	Sr.	45	48.04
Josh Hubner, Arizona St	Sr.	52	47.13
P. Kontodiakos, Colorado St	Sr.	59	46.47
Alex Dunnachie, Hawaii	Sr.	49	46.16
Kyle Christy, Florida	So.	66	45.80

Note: Minimum of 3.6 punts per game.

PUNT RETURNS

	Class	No.	Yds	TD	Avg
Tramaine Thompson, Kansas St	Jr.	16	316	1	19.75
Giovani Bernard, North Carolina	So.	16	263	2	16.44
Rashad Greene, Florida St	So.	20	307	2	15.35
Ace Sanders, South Carolina	Jr.	28	429	2	15.32
Khalid Wooten, Nevada	Sr.	16	242	0	15.13

Note: Minimum 1.2 punt returns per game.

KICKOFF RETURNS

	Class	No.	Yds	TD	Avg
Quincy McDuffie, UCF	Sr.	17	582	3	34.24
Duke Johnson, Miami (FL)	Fr.	27	892	2	33.04
Tyler Lockett, Kansas St.	So.	21	688	2	32.76
Reggie Whatley, Middle Tenn.	So.	25	762	1	30.48
Chase Clayton, New Mexico	So.	20	608	2	30.40

Note: Minimum of 1.2 kickoff returns per game.

Football Championship Subdivision (I-AA)

SCORING

	Class	GP	TD	XP	FG	Pts	Pts/Game
Gavin McCarney, Colgate	Jr.	12	23	0	0	140*	11.67
Jordan McCord, Colgate	Sr.	12	23	0	0	138	11.50
Drew Smith, Albany (NY)	Sr.	10	19	0	0	114	11.40
Miguel Maysonet, Stony Brook	Sr.	13	23	0	0	138	10.62
David Johnson, Northern Iowa	So.	11	18	0	0	108	9.82
Aaron Mellette, Elon	Sr.	11	18	0	0	108	9.82

*Includes one two-point conversion.

FIELD GOALS

	Class	GP	FGA	FG	Pct	FG/Game
Patrick Murray, Fordham	Sr.	11	30	25	.833	2.27
Colton Cook, Southern Utah	Jr.	11	22	19	.864	1.73
Sean Baner, Delaware	Jr.	11	23	18	.783	1.64
Jamin Godfrey, Tennessee St.	Jr.	11	20	16	.800	1.45
Ernie Collins, San Diego	Sr.	11	22	16	.727	1.45
Adam Shreiner, Elon	Sr.	11	22	16	.727	1.45

TOTAL OFFENSE

			Rushing		Passing			Total Offense	
	Class	GP	Car	Net	Att	Yds	Total Yds	Yds/Play	Yds/Game
Taylor Heinicke, Old Dominion	So.	13	126	470	579	5076	5546	7.87	426.62
Casey Brockman, Murray St	Sr.	11	102	73	517	3729	3802	6.14	345.64
Jeff Mathews, Cornell	Jr.	9	57	-150	405	3196	3046	6.59	338.44
Kevin Yost, Idaho St	Sr.	11	63	-69	553	3690	3621	5.88	329.18
Michael Colvin, Lehigh	Sr.	11	106	479	369	3114	3593	7.56	326.64

RUSHING

	Class	GP	Car	Yds	Avg	TD	Yds/Game
Zach Zenner, South Dakota St.	So.	13	300	2044	6.81	13	157.23
Eric Breitenstein, Wofford	Sr.	13	290	2035	7.02	19	156.54
Miguel Maysonet, Stony Brook	Sr.	13	267	1964	7.36	21	151.08
Carlton Koonce, Fordham	Sr.	11	300	1596	5.32	13	145.09
Jordan McCord, Colgate	Sr.	12	322	1708	5.30	23	142.33

PASSING EFFICIENCY

					Pct					Rating
	Class	GP	Att	Comp	Comp	Yds	Yds/Att	TD	Int	Pts
Kyle Essington, Stony Brook	Sr.	12	205	120	58.54	2032	9.91	23	8	171.02
Taylor Heinicke, Old Dominion	So.	13	579	398	68.74	5076	8.77	44	14	162.62
Colton Chapple, Harvard	Sr.	10	294	194	65.99	2567	8.73	24	7	161.51
Vernon Adams, Eastern Wash.	Fr.	12	215	131	60.93	1956	9.10	20	8	160.61
Chuckie Looney, Marist	Jr.	10	248	150	60.48	2315	9.33	18	8	156.40

Note: Minimum 15 attempts per game.

RECEPTIONS PER GAME

	Class	GP	No.	Yds	TD	Rec/G
Erik Lora, Eastern Illinois	Jr.	12	136	1664	12	11.33
Aaron Mellette, Elon	Sr.	11	97	1398	18	8.82
Cordell Roberson, Stephen F. Austin	Sr.	9	77	1006	10	8.56
Walter Powell, Murray St	Jr.	11	94	1213	10	8.55
Rodrick Rumble, Idaho St	Sr.	9	74	1006	6	8.22

RECEIVING YARDS PER GAME

	Class	GP	No.	Yds	TD	Yds/Game
Erik Lora, Eastern Illinois	Jr.	12	136	1664	12	138.67
Brandon Kaufman, Eastern Washington	Jr.	14	93	1850	16	132.14
Aaron Mellette, Elon	Sr.	11	97	1398	18	127.09
Jordan Harris, Bryant	Jr.	10	61	1243	15	124.30
Luke Tasker, Cornell	Sr.	10	75	1207	8	120.70

ALL-PURPOSE RUNNING

	Class	GP	Rush	Rec	PR	KOR	Total Yds	Yds/Game
Tyler Varga, Yale	Fr.	8	935	100	0	519	1554	194.25
Walter Powell, Murray St.	Jr.	11	5	1213	301	604	2123	193.00
Fabian Truss, Samford	Jr.	11	1063	291	0	624	1978	179.82
Miguel Maysonet, Stony Brook	Sr.	13	1964	43	0	309	2316	178.15
Jerodis Williams, Furman	Sr.	11	1170	171	0	574	1915	174.09

Football Championship Subdivision (I-AA) (Cont.)

INTERCEPTIONS

	Class	GP	No.	Yds	TD	Int/G
S. Godbolt, Tennessee St	So.	10	6	67	0	.60
Matthew Steinbeck, Bucknell	So.	11	6	158	0	.55
Brooklyn Fox, Eastern Ky	Sr.	11	6	138	0	.55
Ben Ericksen, Illinois St	Sr.	13	7	56	0	.54
Four tied with .50						

PUNTING

	Class	No.	Avg
Andy Wilder, Northern Arizona	Jr.	61	46.33
Patrick Murray, Fordham	Sr.	52	45.96
Sam Martin, Appalachian St	Sr.	60	45.92
Bobby Wenzig, Alabama St	Jr.	61	45.57
Chad Zinchini, Tennessee Tech	Jr.	65	44.77

Division II

SCORING

	Class	GP	TD	XP	FG	Pts	Pts/Game
Monterae Williams, Findlay	Sr.	10	21	0	0	126	12.60
Franklyn Quiteh, Bloomsburg	Jr.	12	25	0	0	150	12.50
Keidrick Jackson, Midwestern St	Jr.	11	21	0	0	126	11.45
Jordan Roberts, Charleston (WV)	Sr.	11	20	0	0	122	11.09
Rayon Simmons, Winona St	Sr.	12	21	0	0	126	10.50

Note: McNeill's total includes one two-point conversion.

FIELD GOALS

	Class	GP	FGA	FG	Pct	FG/Game
Blake Barnes, Tarleton St.	Fr.	10	20	18	.900	1.80
David Van Voris, Adams St.	Sr.	11	23	18	.783	1.64
Sam Brockshus, Minn St-Mankato	Jr.	14	27	21	.778	1.50
Taylor Groff, East Stroudsburg	Jr.	10	23	15	.652	1.50
Braden Wieking, Sioux Falls	Sr.	11	19	16	.842	1.45
Zach Tapia, N.M. Highlands	So.	11	25	16	.640	1.45

TOTAL OFFENSE

			Rushing		Passing		Total Offense		
	Class	GP	Car	Net	Att	Yds	Total Yds	Yds/Play	Yds/Game
Joe Clancy, Merrimack	Sr.	10	60	49	510	3945	3994	7.01	399.40
Emmanuel Lewis, N.M. Highlands	Jr.	10	92	262	472	3664	3926	6.96	392.60
Zach Zulli, Shippensburg	Jr.	13	102	224	544	4747	4971	7.70	382.38
Kevin Rodgers, Henderson St	So.	11	27	27	409	4002	4029	9.24	366.27
Matt Brown, Colorado Mines	So.	11	104	154	596	3859	4013	5.73	364.82

RUSHING

	Class	GP	Car	Yds	TD	Yds/Game
Franklyn Quiteh, Bloomsburg	Jr.	12	287	2121	24	176.75
Michael Hill, Missouri Western St	Sr.	14	311	2168	16	154.86
Rayon Simmons, Winona St.	Sr.	12	309	1774	19	147.83
Nick Ricciardulli, Humboldt St	Jr.	11	281	1579	12	143.55
Jordan Roberts, Charleston (WV)	Sr.	11	238	1572	18	142.91

PASSING EFFICIENCY

	Class	GP	Att	Comp	Pct Comp	Yds	TD	Int	Rating Pts
Isiah Grimes, Grand Valley St	So.	10	203	119	58.62	2213	22	8	178.07
Kevin Rodgers, Henderson St	So.	11	409	271	66.26	4002	41	12	175.66
Kameron Smith, Winston-Salem	Sr.	14	360	214	59.44	3312	43	11	170.03
Taylor Housewright, Ashland	Sr.	12	358	241	67.32	3071	32	4	166.64
Zach Zulli, Shippensburg	Jr.	13	544	342	62.87	4747	54	10	165.25

Note: Minimum 15 attempts per game.

RECEPTIONS PER GAME

	Class	GP	No.	Yds	TD	Rec/Game
Isaiah Voegeli, Merrimack	Sr.	10	108	1500	14	10.80
Jeff Janis, Saginaw Valley	Jr.	11	106	1635	17	9.64
Chris Bowden, Wingate	Sr.	11	106	1359	9	9.64
Justin Bernard, St. Anselm	Jr.	11	97	1110	15	8.82
Julian Walker, St. Joseph's (IN)	Jr.	11	94	1082	11	8.55

RECEIVING YARDS PER GAME

	Class	GP	No.	Yds	TD	Yds/Game
Isaiah Voegeli, Merrimack	Sr.	10	108	1500	14	150.00
Jeff Janis, Saginaw Valley	Jr.	11	106	1635	17	148.64
Chris Bowden, Wingate	Sr.	11	106	1359	9	123.55
Lemar Durant, Simon Fraser	So.	11	91	1318	17	119.82
Joe Webb, Urbana	Jr.	9	63	1074	5	119.33

Division II (Cont.)

INTERCEPTIONS

	Class	GP	No.	Yds	Int/Game
Jack Moro, St. Cloud St.	Jr.	11	11	64	1.00
Markell Rice, American Int'l.	Sr.	10	8	120	.80
Dexter Moody, Albany St. (GA)	Jr.	10	7	154	.70
Trelan Taylor, Chadron St.	Sr.	12	8	107	.67

Three tied with .64

PUNTING

	Class	No.	Avg
Taylor Accardi, Colorado Mines.	Sr.	49	51.12
Brandon Kliesen, Colorado St-Pueblo	Jr.	48	45.60
Randy Weich, Wayne St (NE).	Sr.	56	44.84
Kyle Goodburn, Northwest Mo. St.	So.	51	44.27
Justin Rosenbaum, Fort Valley St.	Sr.	67	43.96

Note: Minimum 3.6 punts per game.

Division III

SCORING

	Class	GP	TD	XP	FG	Pts	Pts/Game
Dominique Carson, Sul Ross St.	Sr.	9	28	0	0	168	18.67
Luke Heinsohn, Washington & Lee	Sr.	11	22	48	2	188*	17.09
Lamont Williams, Carroll (WI)	So.	9	24	0	0	144	16.00
Trevor Manuel, Huntingdon	Sr.	9	21	0	0	126	14.00
James Clay, Mt. St. Joseph	Sr.	10	23	0	0	138	13.80

*Heinsohn's total includes one two-point conversion.

FIELD GOALS

	Class	GP	FGA	FG	Pct	FG/Game
Miles Mackenzie, Ohio Wesleyan	So.	10	29	18	.621	1.80
Eric Kindler, Wisconsin-Whitewater	Jr.	10	25	17	.680	1.70
Allen Cain, Texas Lutheran	Sr.	10	27	17	.630	1.70
Kevin Grady, Redlands	Jr.	9	18	14	.778	1.56
Mike DeBole, SUNY Cortland	Jr.	11	22	16	.727	1.45

TOTAL OFFENSE

			Rushing		Passing		Total Offense		
	Class	GP	Car	Net	Att	Yds	Total Yds	Yds/Play	Yds/Game
Logan Turner, Hardin-Simmons	Sr.	10	16	-71	431	4116	4045	9.05	404.50
A.J. Springer, Sul Ross St	Sr.	10	114	616	361	3192	3808	8.02	380.80
Ayrton Scott, Augsburg	Fr.	10	209	1436	283	2245	3681	7.48	368.10
McCallum Foote, Middlebury	Jr.	8	24	31	402	2897	2928	6.87	366.00
Shane Brozowski, Castleton	Sr.	9	52	-74	399	3294	3220	7.14	357.78

RUSHING

	Class	GP	Car	Yds	TD	Yds/Game
James Clay, Mount St. Joseph	Sr.	10	307	2124	21	212.40
Scottie Williams, Elmhurst	Sr.	12	329	2046	22	170.50
Evan Bunker, Trinity (CT)	Jr.	8	207	1275	11	159.38
Matthew Biggers, La Verne	Jr.	9	244	1397	11	155.22
Melikke Van Alstyne, Framingham St.	Jr.	12	311	1790	18	149.17

PASSING EFFICIENCY

	Class	GP	Att	Comp	Pct Comp	Yds	TD	Int	Rating Pts
Kevin Burke, Mount Union	So.	15	359	249	69.36	3772	38	7	188.65
Lidarral Bailey, Mary Hardin-Baylor	Sr.	14	276	195	70.65	2642	30	3	184.76
Zach Shultis, Cal Lutheran	Sr.	9	213	148	69.48	1866	24	3	177.44
Jimmy Stainback, Birmingham-So.	Sr.	10	155	95	61.29	1698	15	7	176.21
Jordan Roberts, Wheaton (IL)	Jr.	10	286	201	70.28	2500	29	5	173.67

Note: Minimum 15 attempts per game.

RECEPTIONS PER GAME

	Class	GP	No.	Yds	TD	Rec/Game
Matthew Tuckness, Occidental	Sr.	8	84	1028	8	10.50
Zach Driscoll, Middlebury	Sr.	8	83	1134	15	10.38
James Gladstone, Westminster (MO)	Sr.	10	96	1246	14	9.60
Rob Bambini, Curry	Sr.	8	74	908	14	9.25
Eric Rogers, Cal Lutheran	Sr.	10	91	1298	18	9.10

RECEIVING YARDS PER GAME

	Class	GP	No.	Yds	TD	Yds/Game
Zach Driscoll, Middlebury	Sr.	8	83	1134	15	141.75
Brandon Boyle, Castleton	Jr.	11	96	1533	18	139.36
Eric Rogers, Cal Lutheran	Sr.	10	91	1298	18	129.80
Matthew Tuckness, Occidental	Sr.	8	84	1028	8	128.50
Antwan Thorpe, Greensboro	Sr.	10	81	1270	11	127.00

Division III *(Cont.)*

INTERCEPTIONS	Class	GP	No.	Yds	Int/G
Zach Autenreib, Thomas More	Sr.	8	8	200	1.00
Alex Miller, Western New England	Sr.	10	8	125	.80
Donnie Cimino, Wesleyan (CT)	So.	8	6	59	.75
Andrew Kukesh, Bates	Jr.	8	6	39	.75

Seven tied with .70

PUNTING	Class	No.	Avg
Christian Hallingstad, WI-La Crosse	Sr.	79	44.38
Brandon Abbott, Hardin-Simmons	Jr.	37	42.38
Jeff Sauer, Chicago	Sr.	42	42.24
Kyle Hamby, Salisbury	So.	52	42.23
Michael Parks, Franklin	Jr.	47	41.74

Note: Minimum 3.6 per game.

2012 NCAA FBS (I-A) Team Leaders

Offense

SCORING

	GP	Pts	Avg
Louisiana Tech	12	618	51.50
Oregon	13	644	49.54
Oklahoma St.	13	594	45.69
Baylor	13	578	44.46
Texas A&M	13	578	44.46
Clemson	13	533	41.00
Marshall	12	491	40.92
North Carolina	12	487	40.58
West Virginia	13	513	39.46
Florida St.	14	550	39.29

RUSHING

	GP	Car	Yds	Avg	TD	Yds/Game
Army	12	806	4438	5.51	32	369.83
Air Force	13	804	4111	5.11	39	316.23
Oregon	13	685	4098	5.98	48	315.23
Georgia Tech	14	808	4357	5.39	48	311.21
New Mexico	13	688	3917	5.69	34	301.31
Navy	13	700	3620	5.17	28	278.46
Nevada	13	674	3523	5.23	41	271.00
Nebraska	14	662	3547	5.36	33	253.36
Tulsa	14	689	3440	4.99	41	245.71
Ohio St.	12	559	2907	5.20	37	242.25

PASSING

	GP	Att	Comp	Int	Pct Comp	Yds	Yds/Gm	TD
Marshall	12	607	424	12	69.85	4381	365.08	39
Texas Tech	13	594	418	16	70.37	4627	355.92	44
Louisiana Tech	12	533	365	5	68.48	4209	350.75	33
Baylor	13	475	294	13	61.89	4427	340.54	34
Oklahoma	13	571	376	11	65.85	4374	336.46	30
San Jose St.	13	468	336	9	71.79	4325	332.69	35
Oklahoma St.	13	495	312	16	63.03	4312	331.69	34
Troy	12	509	337	12	66.21	3978	331.50	22
Washington St.	12	624	363	21	58.17	3965	330.42	23
West Virginia	13	537	378	7	70.39	4292	330.15	44

TOTAL OFFENSE

	GP	Plays	Yds	Avg	TD	Yds/Game
Louisiana Tech	12	1054	6935	6.58	84	577.92
Baylor	13	1072	7439	6.94	76	572.23
Texas A&M	13	1025	7261	7.08	78	558.54
Oklahoma St.	13	1014	7111	7.01	73	547.00
Oregon	13	1058	6986	6.60	89	537.38
Marshall	12	1087	6411	5.90	65	534.25
Arizona	13	1082	6840	6.32	65	526.15
Nevada	13	1080	6693	6.20	66	514.85
Clemson	13	1062	6665	6.28	68	512.69
West Virginia	13	998	6526	6.54	69	502.00

Defense

OPPONENTS' SCORING

	GP	Pts	Avg
Alabama	14	153	10.93
Notre Dame	13	166	12.77
BYU	13	182	14.00
Rutgers	13	184	14.15
Florida	13	188	14.46
Florida St.	14	206	14.71
Utah St.	13	200	15.38
Boise St.	13	205	15.77
Michigan St.	13	212	16.31
Bowling Green	13	218	16.77

TOTAL DEFENSE

	GP	Plays	Yds	Avg Y/Play	Avg Y/G
Alabama	14	837	3500	4.18	250.00
Florida St.	14	922	3558	3.86	254.14
BYU	13	790	3459	4.38	266.08
Michigan St.	13	816	3567	4.37	274.38
Florida	13	857	3737	4.36	287.46
Bowling Green	13	824	3856	4.68	296.62
Notre Dame	13	830	3971	4.78	305.46
LSU	13	897	3999	4.46	307.62
Connecticut	12	811	3719	4.59	309.92
Rutgers	13	882	4051	4.59	311.62

OPPONENTS' RUSHING

	GP	Car	Yds	Avg	TD	Yds/G
Alabama	14	440	1069	2.43	10	76.36
BYU	13	412	1130	2.74	5	86.92
Florida St.	14	469	1292	2.75	10	92.29
Florida	13	413	1234	2.99	12	94.92
Stanford	14	446	1358	3.04	15	97.00
Rutgers	13	460	1263	2.75	6	97.15
Connecticut	12	430	1175	2.73	10	97.92
Michigan St.	13	391	1282	3.28	6	98.62
LSU	13	440	1321	3.00	14	101.62
TCU	13	422	1370	3.25	11	105.38

TURNOVER MARGIN

		Turnovers Gained			Turnovers Lost			
	GP	Fum	Int	Total	Fum	Int	Total	Mar/G
Oregon	13	14	26	40	10	9	19	1.62
Boise St.	13	18	18	36	9	7	16	1.54
Kansas St.	13	13	18	31	3	9	12	1.46
Kent St.	14	15	23	38	7	11	18	1.43
LSU	13	15	18	33	10	7	17	1.23
Mississippi St.	13	14	19	33	7	10	17	1.23
Florida	13	10	20	30	10	5	15	1.15
Fresno St.	13	13	22	35	12	8	20	1.15
Ohio	13	12	13	25	5	5	10	1.15
Louisiana Tech	12	16	10	26	8	5	13	1.08
Northwestern	13	16	13	29	8	7	15	1.08
SMU	13	16	21	37	8	15	23	1.08

OPPONENTS' PASSING EFFICIENCY

	GP	Att	Comp	Pct Comp	Int	Pct Int	Yds	Yds/Att	TD	Pct TD	Rating Pts
Florida St.	14	453	221	48.79	11	2.43	2266	5.00	13	2.87	95.42
Florida	13	444	231	52.03	20	4.50	2503	5.64	7	1.58	95.57
Michigan St.	13	425	223	52.47	14	3.29	2285	5.38	10	2.35	98.81
Fresno St.	13	381	196	51.44	22	5.77	2173	5.70	15	3.94	100.80
Boise St.	13	376	219	58.24	18	4.79	2203	5.86	4	1.06	101.40
Vanderbilt	13	432	232	53.70	11	2.55	2493	5.77	7	1.62	102.43
Alabama	14	397	217	54.66	18	4.53	2431	6.12	8	2.02	103.68
Utah St.	13	475	257	54.11	14	2.95	2708	5.70	12	2.53	104.44
Nebraska	14	397	187	47.10	13	3.27	2354	5.93	18	4.53	105.32
Arizona St.	13	394	198	50.25	21	5.33	2183	5.54	23	5.84	105.40

FOR THE RECORD•Year by Year

NCAA Football Bowl Subdivision* National Champions

Year	Champion	Record	Bowl Game	Head Coach
1883	Yale	8-0-0	No bowl	Ray Tompkins (Captain)
1884	Yale	9-0-0	No bowl	Eugene L. Richards (Captain)
1885	Princeton	9-0-0	No bowl	Charles DeCamp (Captain)
1886	Yale	9-0-1	No bowl	Robert N. Corwin (Captain)
1887	Yale	9-0-0	No bowl	Harry W. Beecher (Captain)
1888	Yale	13-0-0	No bowl	Walter Camp
1889	Princeton	10-0-0	No bowl	Edgar Poe (Captain)
1890	Harvard	11-0-0	No bowl	George A. Stewart/George C. Adams
1891	Yale	13-0-0	No bowl	Walter Camp
1892	Yale	13-0-0	No bowl	Walter Camp
1893	Princeton	11-0-0	No bowl	Tom Trenchard (Captain)
1894	Yale	16-0-0	No bowl	William C. Rhodes
1895	Pennsylvania	14-0-0	No bowl	George Woodruff
1896	Princeton	10-0-1	No bowl	Garrett Cochran
1897	Pennsylvania	15-0-0	No bowl	George Woodruff
1898	Harvard	11-0-0	No bowl	W. Cameron Forbes
1899	Harvard	10-0-1	No bowl	Benjamin H. Dibblee
1900	Yale	12-0-0	No bowl	Malcolm McBride
1901	Michigan	11-0-0	Won Rose	Fielding Yost
1902	Michigan	11-0-0	No bowl	Fielding Yost
1903	Princeton	11-0-0	No bowl	Art Hillebrand
1904	Pennsylvania	12-0-0	No bowl	Carl Williams
1905	Chicago	11-0-0	No bowl	Amos Alonzo Stagg
1906	Princeton	9-0-1	No bowl	Bill Roper
1907	Yale	9-0-1	No bowl	Bill Knox
1908	Pennsylvania	11-0-1	No bowl	Sol Metzger
1909	Yale	10-0-0	No bowl	Howard Jones
1910	Harvard	8-0-1	No bowl	Percy Houghton
1911	Princeton	8-0-2	No bowl	Bill Roper
1912	Harvard	9-0-0	No bowl	Percy Houghton
1913	Harvard	9-0-0	No bowl	Percy Houghton
1914	Army	9-0-0	No bowl	Charley Daly
1915	Cornell	9-0-0	No bowl	Al Sharpe
1916	Pittsburgh	8-0-0	No bowl	Pop Warner
1917	Georgia Tech	9-0-0	No bowl	John Heisman
1918	Pittsburgh	4-1-0	No bowl	Pop Warner
1919	Harvard	9-0-1	Won Rose	Bob Fisher
1920	California	9-0-0	Won Rose	Andy Smith
1921	Cornell	8-0-0	No bowl	Gil Dobie
1922	Cornell	8-0-0	No bowl	Gil Dobie
1923	Illinois	8-0-0	No bowl	Bob Zuppke
1924	Notre Dame	10-0-0	Won Rose	Knute Rockne
1925	Alabama (H)	10-0-0	Won Rose	Wallace Wade
	Dartmouth (D)	8-0-0	No bowl	Jesse Hawley
1926	Alabama (H)	9-0-1	Tied Rose	Wallace Wade
	Stanford (D)(H)	10-0-1	Tied Rose	Pop Warner
1927	Illinois	7-0-1	No bowl	Bob Zuppke
1928	Georgia Tech (H)	10-0-0	Won Rose	Bill Alexander
	USC (D)	9-0-1	No bowl	Howard Jones
1929	Notre Dame	9-0-0	No bowl	Knute Rockne
1930	Notre Dame	10-0-0	No bowl	Knute Rockne
1931	USC	10-1-0	Won Rose	Howard Jones
1932	USC (H)	10-0-0	Won Rose	Howard Jones
	Michigan (D)	8-0-0	No bowl	Harry Kipke
1933	Michigan	7-0-1	No bowl	Harry Kipke
1934	Minnesota	8-0-0	No bowl	Bernie Bierman
1935	Minnesota (H)	8-0-0	No bowl	Bernie Bierman
	SMU (D)	12-1-0	Lost Rose	Matty Bell
1936	Minnesota	7-1-0	No bowl	Bernie Bierman
1937	Pittsburgh	9-0-1	No bowl	Jock Sutherland
1938	TCU (AP)	11-0-0	Won Sugar	Dutch Meyer
	Notre Dame (D)	8-1-0	No bowl	Elmer Layden
1939	USC (D)	8-0-2	Won Rose	Howard Jones
	Texas A&M (AP)	11-0-0	Won Sugar	Homer Norton

*In 2007, the NCAA renamed Division I-A as the "Football Bowl Subdivision" and Division I-AA as the "Football Championship Subdivision."

Year	Champion	Record	Bowl Game	Head Coach
1940	Minnesota	8-0-0	No bowl	Bernie Bierman
1941	Minnesota	8-0-0	No bowl	Bernie Bierman
1942	Ohio St	9-1-0	No bowl	Paul Brown
1943	Notre Dame	9-1-0	No bowl	Frank Leahy
1944	Army	9-0-0	No bowl	Red Blaik
1945	Army	9-0-0	No bowl	Red Blaik
1946	Notre Dame	8-0-1	No bowl	Frank Leahy
1947	Notre Dame	9-0-0	No bowl	Frank Leahy
	Michigan*	10-0-0	Won Rose	Fritz Crisler
1948	Michigan	9-0-0	No bowl	Bennie Oosterbaan
1949	Notre Dame	10-0-0	No bowl	Frank Leahy
1950	Oklahoma	10-1-0	Lost Sugar	Bud Wilkinson
1951	Tennessee	10-1-0	Lost Sugar	Bob Neyland
1952	Michigan St	9-0-0	No bowl	Biggie Munn
1953	Maryland	10-1-0	Lost Orange	Jim Tatum
1954	Ohio St	10-0-0	Won Rose	Woody Hayes
	UCLA (UPI)	9-0-0	No bowl	Red Sanders
1955	Oklahoma	11-0-0	Won Orange	Bud Wilkinson
1956	Oklahoma	10-0-0	No bowl	Bud Wilkinson
1957	Auburn	10-0-0	No bowl	Shug Jordan
	Ohio St (UPI)	9-1-0	Won Rose	Woody Hayes
1958	LSU	11-0-0	Won Sugar	Paul Dietzel
1959	Syracuse	11-0-0	Won Cotton	Ben Schwartzwalder
1960	Minnesota	8-2-0	Lost Rose	Murray Warmath
1961	Alabama	11-0-0	Won Sugar	Bear Bryant
1962	USC	11-0-0	Won Rose	John McKay
1963	Texas	11-0-0	Won Cotton	Darrell Royal
1964	Alabama	10-1-0	Lost Orange	Bear Bryant
1965	Alabama	9-1-1	Won Orange	Bear Bryant
	Michigan St (UPI)	10-1-0	Lost Rose	Duffy Daugherty
1966	Notre Dame	9-0-1	No bowl	Ara Parseghian
1967	USC	10-1-0	Won Rose	John McKay
1968	Ohio St	10-0-0	Won Rose	Woody Hayes
1969	Texas	11-0-0	Won Cotton	Darrell Royal
1970	Nebraska	11-0-1	Won Orange	Bob Devaney
	Texas (UPI)	10-1-0	Lost Cotton	Darrell Royal
1971	Nebraska	13-0-0	Won Orange	Bob Devaney
1972	USC	12-0-0	Won Rose	John McKay
1973	Notre Dame	11-0-0	Won Sugar	Ara Parseghian
	Alabama (UPI)	11-1-0	Lost Sugar	Bear Bryant
1974	Oklahoma	11-0-0	No bowl	Barry Switzer
	USC (UPI)	10-1-1	Won Rose	John McKay
1975	Oklahoma	11-1-0	Won Orange	Barry Switzer
1976	Pittsburgh	12-0-0	Won Sugar	Johnny Majors
1977	Notre Dame	11-1-0	Won Cotton	Dan Devine
1978	Alabama	11-1-0	Won Sugar	Bear Bryant
	USC (UPI)	12-1-0	Won Rose	John Robinson
1979	Alabama	12-0-0	Won Sugar	Bear Bryant
1980	Georgia	12-0-0	Won Sugar	Vince Dooley
1981	Clemson	12-0-0	Won Orange	Danny Ford
1982	Penn St	11-1-0	Won Sugar	Joe Paterno
1983	Miami (Fla.)	11-1-0	Won Orange	Howard Schnellenberger
1984	BYU	13-0-0	Won Holiday	LaVell Edwards
1985	Oklahoma	11-1-0	Won Orange	Barry Switzer
1986	Penn St	12-0-0	Won Fiesta	Joe Paterno
1987	Miami (Fla.)	12-0-0	Won Orange	Jimmy Johnson
1988	Notre Dame	12-0-0	Won Fiesta	Lou Holtz
1989	Miami (Fla.)	11-1-0	Won Sugar	Dennis Erickson
1990	Colorado	11-1-1	Won Orange	Bill McCartney
	Georgia Tech (UPI)	11-0-1	Won Citrus	Bobby Ross
1991	Miami (Fla.)	12-0-0	Won Orange	Dennis Erickson
	Washington (CNN)	12-0-0	Won Rose	Don James
1992	Alabama	13-0-0	Won Sugar	Gene Stallings
1993	Florida St	12-1-0	Won Orange	Bobby Bowden
1994	Nebraska	13-0-0	Won Orange	Tom Osborne
1995	Nebraska	12-0-0	Won Fiesta	Tom Osborne
†1996	Florida	12–1	Won Sugar	Steve Spurrier
1997	Michigan	12–0	Won Rose	Lloyd Carr
	Nebraska (ESPN)	13–0	Won Orange	Tom Osborne

NCAA FBS (Div. I-A) National Champions *(Cont.)*

Year	Champion	Record	Bowl Game	Head Coach
1998	Tennessee	13–0	Won Fiesta	Phillip Fulmer
1999	Florida St	12–0	Won Sugar	Bobby Bowden
2000	Oklahoma	13–0	Won Orange	Bob Stoops
2001	Miami (Fla.)	12–0	Won Rose	Larry Coker
2002	Ohio St	14–0	Won Fiesta	Jim Tressel
2003	LSU	13–1	Won Sugar	Nick Saban
	USC	12–1	Won Rose	Pete Carroll
§2004	Vacated			
2005	Texas	13–0	Won Rose	Mack Brown
‡2006	Florida	13–1	Won BCS Nat'l Championship	Urban Meyer
2007	LSU	12–2	Won BCS Nat'l Championship	Les Miles
2008	Florida	13–1	Won BCS Nat'l Championship	Urban Meyer
2009	Alabama	14–0	Won BCS Nat'l Championship	Nick Saban
2010	Auburn	14–0	Won BCS Nat'l Championship	Gene Chizik
2011	Alabama	12–1	Won BCS Nat'l Championship	Nick Saban
2012	Alabama	13–1	Won BCS Nat'l Championship	Nick Saban

*The AP, which had voted Notre Dame No. 1, took a second vote, giving the national title to Michigan after its 49–0 win over USC in the Rose Bowl. Note: Selectors: Helms Athletic Foundation (H) 1883–1935, The Dickinson System (D) 1924–40, The Associated Press (AP) 1936–2005, United Press International (UPI) 1958–90, *USA Today*/CNN (CNN) 1991–96, and *USA Today*/ESPN (ESPN) 1997–2005. †In 1996 the NCAA introduced overtime to break ties. ‡In 2006, the BCS established a separate national championship game in addition to its existing four-bowl structure. §USC's 2005 Orange Bowl victory and 2004 national championship were vacated in 2010 due to rules violations.

Results of Major Bowl Games

Rose Bowl

1-1-02	Michigan 49, Stanford 0		1-1-59	Iowa 38, California 12
1-1-16	Washington St 14, Brown 0		1-1-60	Washington 44, Wisconsin 8
1-1-17	Oregon 14, Pennsylvania 0		1-2-61	Washington 17, Minnesota 7
1-1-18	Mare Island 19, Camp Lewis 7		1-1-62	Minnesota 21, UCLA 3
1-1-19	Great Lakes 17, Mare Island 0		1-1-63	USC 42, Wisconsin 37
1-1-20	Harvard 7, Oregon 6		1-1-64	Illinois 17, Washington 7
1-1-21	California 28, Ohio St 0		1-1-65	Michigan 34, Oregon St 7
1-2-22	Washington & Jefferson 0, California 0		1-1-66	UCLA 14, Michigan St 12
1-1-23	USC 14, Penn St 3		1-2-67	Purdue 14, USC 13
1-1-24	Navy 14, Washington 14		1-1-68	USC 14, Indiana 3
1-1-25	Notre Dame 27, Stanford 10		1-1-69	Ohio St 27, USC 16
1-1-26	Alabama 20, Washington 19		1-1-70	USC 10, Michigan 3
1-1-27	Alabama 7, Stanford 7		1-1-71	Stanford 27, Ohio St 17
1-2-28	Stanford 7, Pittsburgh 6		1-1-72	Stanford 13, Michigan 12
1-1-29	Georgia Tech 8, California 7		1-1-73	USC 42, Ohio St 17
1-1-30	USC 47, Pittsburgh 14		1-1-74	Ohio St 42, USC 21
1-1-31	Alabama 24, Washington St 0		1-1-75	USC 18, Ohio St 17
1-1-32	USC 21, Tulane 12		1-1-76	UCLA 23, Ohio St 10
1-2-33	USC 35, Pittsburgh 0		1-1-77	USC 14, Michigan 6
1-1-34	Columbia 7, Stanford 0		1-2-78	Washington 27, Michigan 20
1-1-35	Alabama 29, Stanford 13		1-1-79	USC 17, Michigan 10
1-1-36	Stanford 7, Southern Methodist 0		1-1-80	USC 17, Ohio St 16
1-1-37	Pittsburgh 21, Washington 0		1-1-81	Michigan 23, Washington 6
1-1-38	California 13, Alabama 0		1-1-82	Washington 28, Iowa 0
1-2-39	USC 7, Duke 3		1-1-83	UCLA 24, Michigan 14
1-1-40	USC 14, Tennessee 0		1-2-84	UCLA 45, Illinois 9
1-1-41	Stanford 21, Nebraska 13		1-1-85	USC 20, Ohio St 17
1-1-42	Oregon St 20, Duke 16		1-1-86	UCLA 45, Iowa 28
1-1-43	Georgia 9, UCLA 0		1-1-87	Arizona St 22, Michigan 15
1-1-44	USC 29, Washington 0		1-1-88	Michigan St 20, USC 17
1-1-45	USC 25, Tennessee 0		1-2-89	Michigan 22, USC 14
1-1-46	Alabama 34, USC 14		1-1-90	USC 17, Michigan 10
1-1-47	Illinois 45, UCLA 14		1-1-91	Washington 46, Iowa 34
1-1-48	Michigan 49, USC 0		1-1-92	Washington 34, Michigan 14
1-1-49	Northwestern 20, California 14		1-1-93	Michigan 38, Washington 31
1-2-50	Ohio St 17, California 14		1-1-94	Wisconsin 21, UCLA 16
1-1-51	Michigan 14, California 6		1-2-95	Penn St 38, Oregon 20
1-1-52	Illinois 40, Stanford 7		1-1-96	USC 41, Northwestern 32
1-1-53	USC 7, Wisconsin 0		1-1-97	Ohio St 20, Arizona St 17
1-1-54	Michigan St 28, UCLA 20		1-1-98	Michigan 21, Washington St 16
1-1-55	Ohio St 20, USC 7		1-1-99	Wisconsin 38, UCLA 31
1-2-56	Michigan St 17, UCLA 14		1-1-00	Wisconsin 17, Stanford 9
1-1-57	Iowa 35, Oregon St 19		1-1-01	Washington 34, Purdue 24
1-1-58	Ohio St 10, Oregon 7		1-3-02	Miami 37, Nebraska 14

Rose Bowl *(Cont.)*

1-1-03 ....Oklahoma 34, Washington St 14
1-1-04 ....USC 28, Michigan 14
1-1-05 ....Texas 38, Michigan 37
1-4-06 ....Texas 41, USC 38
1-1-07 ....USC 32, Michigan 18
1-1-08 ....USC 49, Illinois 17
1-1-09 ....USC 38, Penn St 24
1-1-10 ....Ohio St 26, Oregon 17
1-1-11 ....TCU 21, Wisconsin 19
1-2-12 ....Oregon 45, Wisconsin 38
1-1-13 ....Stanford 20, Wisconsin 14

City: Pasadena. Stadium: Rose Bowl, capacity 96,576.
Playing Sites: Tournament Park (1902, 1916–22), Rose Bowl
(1923–41, since 1943), Duke Stadium, Durham, NC (1942).

Orange Bowl

1-1-35 ....Bucknell 26, Miami (Fla.) 0
1-1-36 ....Catholic 20, Mississippi 19
1-1-37 ....Duquesne 13, Mississippi St 12
1-1-38 ....Auburn 6, Michigan St 0
1-2-39 ....Tennessee 17, Oklahoma 0
1-1-40 ....Georgia Tech 21, Missouri 7
1-1-41 ....Mississippi St 14, Georgetown 7
1-1-42 ....Georgia 40, TCU 26
1-1-43 ....Alabama 37, Boston College 21
1-1-44 ....LSU 19, Texas A&M 14
1-1-45 ....Tulsa 26, Georgia Tech 12
1-1-46 ....Miami (Fla.) 13, Holy Cross 6
1-1-47 ....Rice 8, Tennessee 0
1-1-48 ....Georgia Tech 20, Kansas 14
1-1-49 ....Texas 41, Georgia 28
1-2-50 ....Santa Clara 21, Kentucky 13
1-1-51 ....Clemson 15, Miami (Fla.) 14
1-1-52 ....Georgia Tech 17, Baylor 14
1-1-53 ....Alabama 61, Syracuse 6
1-1-54 ....Oklahoma 7, Maryland 0
1-1-55 ....Duke 34, Nebraska 7
1-2-56 ....Oklahoma 20, Maryland 6
1-1-57 ....Colorado 27, Clemson 21
1-1-58 ....Oklahoma 48, Duke 21
1-1-59 ....Oklahoma 21, Syracuse 6
1-1-60 ....Georgia 14, Missouri 0
1-2-61 ....Missouri 21, Navy 14
1-1-62 ....LSU 25, Colorado 7
1-1-63 ....Alabama 17, Oklahoma 0
1-1-64 ....Nebraska 13, Auburn 7
1-1-65 ....Texas 21, Alabama 17
1-1-66 ....Alabama 39, Nebraska 28
1-2-67 ....Florida 27, Georgia Tech 12
1-1-68 ....Oklahoma 26, Tennessee 24
1-1-69 ....Penn St 15, Kansas 14
1-1-70 ....Penn St 10, Missouri 3
1-1-71 ....Nebraska 17, LSU 12
1-1-72 ....Nebraska 38, Alabama 6
1-1-73 ....Nebraska 40, Notre Dame 6
1-1-74 ....Penn St 16, LSU 9
1-1-75 ....Notre Dame 13, Alabama 11
1-1-76 ....Oklahoma 14, Michigan 6
1-1-77 ....Ohio St 27, Colorado 10
1-2-78 ....Arkansas 31, Oklahoma 6
1-1-79 ....Oklahoma 31, Nebraska 24
1-1-80 ....Oklahoma 24, Florida St 7
1-1-81 ....Oklahoma 18, Florida St 17
1-1-82 ....Clemson 22, Nebraska 15
1-1-83 ....Nebraska 21, LSU 20
1-2-84 ....Miami (Fla.) 31, Nebraska 30
1-1-85 ....Washington 28, Oklahoma 17
1-1-86 ....Oklahoma 25, Penn St 10
1-1-87 ....Oklahoma 42, Arkansas 8

Orange Bowl *(Cont.)*

1-1-88 ....Miami (Fla.) 20, Oklahoma 14
1-2-89 ....Miami (Fla.) 23, Nebraska 3
1-1-90 ....Notre Dame 21, Colorado 6
1-1-91 ....Colorado 10, Notre Dame 9
1-1-92 ....Miami (Fla.) 22, Nebraska 0
1-1-93 ....Florida St 27, Nebraska 14
1-1-94 ....Florida St 18, Nebraska 16
1-1-95 ....Nebraska 24, Miami (Fla.) 17
1-1-96 ....Florida St 31, Notre Dame 26
12-31-96 ....Nebraska 41, Virginia Tech 21
1-2-98 ....Nebraska 42, Tennessee 17
1-2-99 ....Florida 31, Syracuse 10
1-1-00 ....Michigan 35, Alabama 34 (OT)
1-3-01 ....Oklahoma 13, Florida St 2
1-2-02 ....Florida 56, Maryland 23
1-2-03 ....USC 38, Iowa 17
1-1-04 ....Miami (Fla.) 16, Florida St 15
1-4-05 ....*Vacated
1-3-06 ....Penn State 26, Florida State 23 (3OT)
1-2-07 ....Louisville 24, Wake Forest 13
1-3-08 ....Kansas 24, Virginia Tech 21
1-1-09 ....Virginia Tech 20, Cincinnati 7
1-5-10 ....Iowa 24, Georgia Tech 14
1-3-11 ....Stanford 40, Virginia Tech 12
1-4-12 ....West Virginia 70, Clemson 33
1-1-13 ....Florida State 31, Northern Illinois 10

City: Miami. Stadium: Pro Player Stadium, capacity 75,192.
Playing Sites: Orange Bowl (1935–96), Pro Player Stadium
(1996–2005), Dolphin(s) Stadium (2005–09), Land Shark
Stadium (2010). *USC's 2005 Orange Bowl victory was
vacated in 2010 due to rules violations.

Sugar Bowl

1-1-35 ....Tulane 20, Temple 14
1-1-36 ....TCU 3, LSU 2
1-1-37 ....Santa Clara 21, LSU 14
1-1-38 ....Santa Clara 6, LSU 0
1-2-39 ....TCU 15, Carnegie Tech 7
1-1-40 ....Texas A&M 14, Tulane 13
1-1-41 ....Boston Col 19, Tennessee 13
1-1-42 ....Fordham 2, Missouri 0
1-1-43 ....Tennessee 14, Tulsa 7
1-1-44 ....Georgia Tech 20, Tulsa 18
1-1-45 ....Duke 29, Alabama 26
1-1-46 ....Oklahoma St 33, St. Mary's (Calif.) 13
1-1-47 ....Georgia 20, North Carolina 10
1-1-48 ....Texas 27, Alabama 7
1-1-49 ....Oklahoma 14, North Carolina 6
1-2-50 ....Oklahoma 35, LSU 0
1-1-51 ....Kentucky 13, Oklahoma 7
1-1-52 ....Maryland 28, Tennessee 13
1-1-53 ....Georgia Tech 24, Mississippi 7
1-1-54 ....Georgia Tech 42, W Virginia 19
1-1-55 ....Navy 21, Mississippi 0
1-2-56 ....Georgia Tech 7, Pittsburgh 0
1-1-57 ....Baylor 13, Tennessee 7
1-1-58 ....Mississippi 39, Texas 7
1-1-59 ....LSU 7, Clemson 0
1-1-60 ....Mississippi 21, LSU 0
1-2-61 ....Mississippi 14, Rice 6
1-1-62 ....Alabama 10, Arkansas 3
1-1-63 ....Mississippi 17, Arkansas 13
1-1-64 ....Alabama 12, Mississippi 7
1-1-65 ....LSU 13, Syracuse 10
1-1-66 ....Missouri 20, Florida 18
1-2-67 ....Alabama 34, Nebraska 7
1-1-68 ....LSU 20, Wyoming 13
1-1-69 ....Arkansas 16, Georgia 2
1-1-70 ....Mississippi 27, Arkansas 22
1-1-71 ....Tennessee 34, Air Force 13

Sugar Bowl *(Cont.)*

1-1-72..............Oklahoma 40, Auburn 22
12-31-72..........Oklahoma 14, Penn St 0
12-31-73..........Notre Dame 24, Alabama 23
12-31-74..........Nebraska 13, Florida 10
12-31-75..........Alabama 13, Penn St 6
1-1-77..............Pittsburgh 27, Georgia 3
1-2-78..............Alabama 35, Ohio St 6
1-1-79..............Alabama 14, Penn St 7
1-1-80..............Alabama 24, Arkansas 9
1-1-81..............Georgia 17, Notre Dame 10
1-1-82..............Pittsburgh 24, Georgia 20
1-1-83..............Penn St 27, Georgia 23
1-2-84..............Auburn 9, Michigan 7
1-1-85..............Nebraska 28, LSU 10
1-1-86..............Tennessee 35, Miami (Fla.) 7
1-1-87..............Nebraska 30, LSU 15
1-1-88..............Syracuse 16, Auburn 16
1-2-89..............Florida St 13, Auburn 7
1-1-90..............Miami (Fla.) 33, Alabama 25
1-1-91..............Tennessee 23, Virginia 22
1-1-92..............Notre Dame 39, Florida 28
1-1-93..............Alabama 34, Miami (Fla.) 13
1-1-94..............Florida 41, West Virginia 7
1-2-95..............Florida St 23, Florida 17
12-31-95..........Virginia Tech 28, Texas 10
1-2-97..............Florida 52, Florida St 20
1-1-98..............Florida St 31, Ohio St 14
1-1-99..............Ohio St 24, Texas A&M 14
1-4-00..............Florida St 46, Virginia Tech 29
1-2-01..............Miami (Fla.) 37, Florida 20
1-1-02..............LSU 47, Illinois 34
1-1-03 ....Georgia 26, Florida St 13
1-4-04..............LSU 21, Oklahoma 14
1-3-05..............Auburn 16, Virginia Tech 13
1-2-06 ....West Virginia 38, Georgia 35
1-3-07..............LSU 41, Notre Dame 14
1-1-08..............Georgia 41, Hawaii 10
1-2-09 ....Utah 31, Alabama 17
1-1-10 ....Florida 51, Cincinnati 24
1-4-11..............Vacated
1-3-12 ....Michigan 23, Virginia Tech 20
1-2-13..............Louisville 33, Florida 23

City: New Orleans. Stadium: Louisiana Superdome, capacity 76,791. Playing Sites: Tulane Stadium (1935–74), Louisiana Superdome (since 1975). Due to Hurricane Katrina, 2006 Sugar Bowl played in Atlanta's Georgia Dome.

Cotton Bowl

1-1-37..............TCU 16, Marquette 6
1-1-38..............Rice 28, Colorado 14
1-2-39..............St. Mary's (Calif.) 20, Texas Tech 13
1-1-40..............Clemson 6, Boston Col 3
1-1-41..............Texas A&M 13, Fordham 12
1-1-42..............Alabama 29, Texas A&M 21
1-1-43..............Texas 14, Georgia Tech 7
1-1-44..............Texas 7, Randolph Field 7
1-1-45..............Oklahoma St 34, TCU 0
1-1-46..............Texas 40, Missouri 27
1-1-47..............Arkansas 0, LSU 0
1-1-48..............Southern Methodist 13, Penn St 13
1-1-49..............Southern Methodist 21, Oregon 13
1-2-50..............Rice 27, North Carolina 13
1-1-51..............Tennessee 20, Texas 14
1-1-52..............Kentucky 20, TCU 7
1-1-53..............Texas 16, Tennessee 0
1-1-54..............Rice 28, Alabama 6
1-1-55..............Georgia Tech 14, Arkansas 6
1-2-56..............Mississippi 14, TCU 13
1-1-57..............TCU 28, Syracuse 27
1-1-58..............Navy 20, Rice 7

Cotton Bowl *(Cont.)*

1-1-59..............TCU 0, Air Force 0
1-1-60..............Syracuse 23, Texas 14
1-2-61..............Duke 7, Arkansas 6
1-1-62..............Texas 12, Mississippi 7
1-1-63..............LSU 13, Texas 0
1-1-64..............Texas 28, Navy 6
1-1-65..............Arkansas 10, Nebraska 7
1-1-66..............LSU 14, Arkansas 7
12-31-66..........Georgia 24, Southern Methodist 9
1-1-68..............Texas A&M 20, Alabama 16
1-1-69..............Texas 36, Tennessee 13
1-1-70..............Texas 21, Notre Dame 17
1-1-71..............Notre Dame 24, Texas 11
1-1-72..............Penn St 30, Texas 6
1-1-73..............Texas 17, Alabama 13
1-1-74..............Nebraska 19, Texas 3
1-1-75..............Penn St 41, Baylor 20
1-1-76..............Arkansas 31, Georgia 10
1-1-77..............Houston 30, Maryland 21
1-2-78..............Notre Dame 38, Texas 10
1-1-79..............Notre Dame 35, Houston 34
1-1-80..............Houston 17, Nebraska 14
1-1-81..............Alabama 30, Baylor 2
1-1-82..............Texas 14, Alabama 12
1-1-83..............SMU 7, Pittsburgh 3
1-2-84..............Georgia 10, Texas 9
1-1-85..............Boston Col 45, Houston 28
1-1-86..............Texas A&M 36, Auburn 16
1-1-87..............Ohio St 28, Texas A&M 12
1-1-88..............Texas A&M 35, Notre Dame 10
1-2-89..............UCLA 17, Arkansas 3
1-1-90..............Tennessee 31, Arkansas 27
1-1-91..............Miami (Fla.) 46, Texas 3
1-1-92..............Florida St 10, Texas A&M 2
1-1-93..............Notre Dame 28, Texas A&M 3
1-1-94..............Notre Dame 24, Texas A&M 21
1-2-95..............USC 55, Texas Tech 14
1-1-96..............Colorado 38, Oregon 6
1-1-97..............BYU 19, Kansas St 15
1-1-98..............UCLA 29, Texas A&M 23
1-1-99..............Texas 38, Mississippi St 11
1-1-00..............Arkansas 27, Texas 6
1-1-01..............Kansas St 35, Tennessee 21
1-1-02..............Oklahoma 10, Arkansas 3
1-1-03..............Texas 35, LSU 20
1-2-04..............Mississippi 31, Oklahoma St 28
1-1-05..............Tennessee 38, Texas A&M 7
1-2-06..............Alabama 13, Texas Tech 10
1-1-07..............Auburn 17, Nebraska 14
1-1-08..............Missouri 38, Arkansas 7
1-2-09..............Mississippi 47, Texas Tech 34
1-2-10..............Mississippi 21, Oklahoma St 7
1-7-11..............LSU 41, Texas A&M 24
1-6-12..............Arkansas 29, Kansas State 16
1-4-13..............Texas A&M 41, Oklahoma 13

City: Dallas. Stadium: Cotton Bowl (1937–2009), capacity 88,175. Cowboys Stadium (2010–), capacity 71,167.

Sun Bowl

1-1-36..............Hardin-Simmons 14, New Mexico St 14
1-1-37..............Hardin-Simmons 34, UTEP 6
1-1-38..............W Virginia 7, Texas Tech 6
1-2-39..............Utah 26, New Mexico 0
1-1-40..............Catholic 0, Arizona St 0
1-1-41..............Case Reserve 26, Arizona St 13
1-1-42..............Tulsa 6, Texas Tech 0
1-1-43..............2nd Air Force 13, Hardin-Simmons 7
1-1-44..............Southwestern (Tex.) 7, New Mexico 0
1-1-45..............Southwestern (Tex.) 35, New Mexico 0
1-1-46..............New Mexico 34, Denver 24

Sun Bowl *(Cont.)*

1-1-47 ....Cincinnati 18, Virginia Tech 6
1-1-48 ....Miami (Ohio) 13, Texas Tech 12
1-1-49 ....W Virginia 21, UTEP 12
1-2-50 ....UTEP 33, Georgetown 20
1-1-51 ....W Texas St 14, Cincinnati 13
1-1-52 ....Texas Tech 25, Pacific 14
1-1-53 ....Pacific 26, Southern Miss 7
1-1-54 ....UTEP 37, Southern Miss 14
1-1-55 ....UTEP 47, Florida St 20
1-2-56 ....Wyoming 21, Texas Tech 14
1-1-57 ....George Washington 13, UTEP 0
1-1-58 ....Louisville 34, Drake 20
12-31-58 ....Wyoming 14, Hardin-Simmons 6
12-31-59 ....New Mexico St 28, N Texas 8
12-31-60 ....New Mexico St 20, Utah St 13
12-30-61 ....Villanova 17, Wichita St 9
12-31-62 ....W Texas St 15, Ohio 14
12-31-63 ....Oregon 21, Southern Methodist 14
12-26-64 ....Georgia 7, Texas Tech 0
12-31-65 ....UTEP 13, TCU 12
12-24-66 ....Wyoming 28, Florida St 20
12-30-67 ....UTEP 14, Mississippi 7
12-28-68 ....Auburn 34, Arizona 10
12-20-69 ....Nebraska 45, Georgia 6
12-19-70 ....Georgia 17, Texas Tech 9
12-18-71 ....LSU 33, Iowa St 15
12-30-72 ....North Carolina 32, Texas Tech 28
12-29-73 ....Missouri 34, Auburn 17
12-28-74 ....Mississippi St 26, North Carolina 24
12-26-75 ....Pittsburgh 33, Kansas 19
1-2-77 ....Texas A&M 37, Florida 14
12-31-77 ....Stanford 24, LSU 14
12-23-78 ....Texas 42, Maryland 0
12-22-79 ....Washington 14, Texas 7
12-27-80 ....Nebraska 31, Mississippi St 17
12-26-81 ....Oklahoma 40, Houston 14
12-25-82 ....North Carolina 26, Texas 10
12-24-83 ....Alabama 28, Southern Methodist 7
12-22-84 ....Maryland 28, Tennessee 27
12-28-85 ....Georgia 13, Arizona 13
12-25-86 ....Alabama 28, Washington 6
12-25-87 ....Oklahoma St 35, W Virginia 33
12-24-88 ....Alabama 29, Army 28
12-30-89 ....Pittsburgh 31, Texas A&M 28
12-31-90 ....Michigan St 17, USC 16
12-31-91 ....UCLA 6, Illinois 3
12-31-92 ....Baylor 20, Arizona 15
12-24-93 ....Oklahoma 41, Texas Tech 10
12-30-94 ....Texas 35, North Carolina 31
12-29-95 ....Iowa 38, Washington 18
12-31-96 ....Stanford 38, Michigan St 0
12-31-97 ....Arizona St 17, Iowa 7
12-31-98 ....TCU 28, USC 19
12-31-99 ....Oregon 24, Minnesota 20
12-29-00 ....Wisconsin 21, UCLA 20
12-31-01 ....Washington St 33, Purdue 27
12-31-02 ....Purdue 34, Washington 24
12-31-03 ....Minnesota 31, Oregon 30
12-31-04 ....Arizona St 27, Purdue 23
12-30-05 ....UCLA 50, Northwestern 39
12-29-06 ....Oregon State 39, Missouri 38
12-31-07 ....Oregon 56, South Florida 21
12-31-08 ....Oregon St 3, Pittsburgh 0
12-31-09 ....Oklahoma 31, Stanford 27
12-31-10 ....Notre Dame 33, Miami (Fla.) 17
12-31-11 ....Utah 30, Georgia Tech 27
12-31-12 ....Georgia Tech 21, USC 7

City: El Paso. Stadium: Sun Bowl, capacity 51,200.
Name Changes: Sun Bowl (1936–86; 94–), John Hancock
Sun Bowl (1987–88), John Hancock Bowl (1989–93).
Playing Sites: Kidd Field (1936–62), Sun Bowl (since 1963).

Gator Bowl

1-1-46 ....Wake Forest 26, South Carolina 14
1-1-47 ....Oklahoma 34, North Carolina St 13
1-1-48 ....Maryland 20, Georgia 20
1-1-49 ....Clemson 24, Missouri 23
1-2-50 ....Maryland 20, Missouri 7
1-1-51 ....Wyoming 20, Washington & Lee 7
1-1-52 ....Miami (Fla.) 14, Clemson 0
1-1-53 ....Florida 14, Tulsa 13
1-1-54 ....Texas Tech 35, Auburn 13
12-31-54 ....Auburn 33, Baylor 13
12-31-55 ....Vanderbilt 25, Auburn 13
12-29-56 ....Georgia Tech 21, Pittsburgh 14
12-28-57 ....Tennessee 3, Texas A&M 0
12-27-58 ....Mississippi 7, Florida 3
1-2-60 ....Arkansas 14, Georgia Tech 7
12-31-60 ....Florida 13, Baylor 12
12-30-61 ....Penn St 30, Georgia Tech 15
12-29-62 ....Florida 17, Penn St 7
12-28-63 ....North Carolina 35, Air Force 0
1-2-65 ....Florida St 36, Oklahoma 19
12-31-65 ....Georgia Tech 31, Texas Tech 21
12-31-66 ....Tennessee 18, Syracuse 12
12-30-67 ....Penn St 17, Florida St 17
12-28-68 ....Missouri 35, Alabama 10
12-27-69 ....Florida 14, Tennessee 13
1-2-71 ....Auburn 35, Mississippi 28
12-31-71 ....Georgia 7, North Carolina 3
12-30-72 ....Auburn 24, Colorado 3
12-29-73 ....Texas Tech 28, Tennessee 19
12-30-74 ....Auburn 27, Texas 3
12-29-75 ....Maryland 13, Florida 0
12-27-76 ....Notre Dame 20, Penn St 9
12-30-77 ....Pittsburgh 34, Clemson 3
12-29-78 ....Clemson 17, Ohio St 15
12-28-79 ....North Carolina 17, Michigan 15
12-29-80 ....Pittsburgh 37, South Carolina 9
12-28-81 ....North Carolina 31, Arkansas 27
12-30-82 ....Florida St 31, W Virginia 12
12-30-83 ....Florida 14, Iowa 6
12-28-84 ....Oklahoma St 21, South Carolina 14
12-30-85 ....Florida St 34, Oklahoma St 23
12-27-86 ....Clemson 27, Stanford 21
12-31-87 ....LSU 30, South Carolina 13
1-1-89 ....Georgia 34, Michigan St 27
12-30-89 ....Clemson 27, W Virginia 7
1-1-91 ....Michigan 35, Mississippi 3
12-29-91 ....Oklahoma 48, Virginia 14
12-31-92 ....Florida 27, North Carolina St 10
12-31-93 ....Alabama 24, North Carolina 10
12-30-94 ....Tennessee 45, Virginia Tech 23
1-1-96 ....Syracuse 41, Clemson 0
1-1-97 ....North Carolina 20, W Virginia 13
1-1-98 ....North Carolina 42, Virginia Tech 13
1-1-99 ....Georgia Tech 35, Notre Dame 28
1-1-00 ....Miami 27, Georgia Tech 13
1-1-01 ....Virginia Tech 41, Clemson 20
1-1-02 ....Florida St 30, Virginia Tech 17
1-1-03 ....North Carolina St 28, Notre Dame 6
1-1-04 ....Maryland 41, W Virginia 7
1-1-05 ....Florida State 30, W Virginia 18
1-2-06 ....Virginia Tech 35, Louisville 24
1-1-07 ....W Virginia 38, Georgia Tech 35
1-1-08 ....Texas Tech 31, Virginia 28
1-1-09 ....Nebraska 26, Clemson 21
1-1-10 ....Florida St 33, W Virginia 21
1-1-11 ....Mississippi St 52, Michigan 14

Gator Bowl *(Cont.)*

1-2-12..............Florida 24, Ohio State 17
1-1-13..............Northwestern 34, Mississippi St 20

City: Jacksonville, FL. Stadium: Gator Bowl Stadium (1946-1993); Ben Hill Griffin Stadium (1994); Alltel Stadium (1997–2007), Jacksonville Municipal Stadium (1995–96, 2008–), capacity 76,976.

Capital One Bowl

1-1-47..............Catawba 31, Maryville (Tenn.) 6
1-1-48..............Catawba 7, Marshall 0
1-1-49..............Murray St 21, Sul Ross St 21
1-2-50..............St. Vincent 7, Emory & Henry 6
1-1-51..............Morris Harvey 35, Emory & Henry 14
1-1-52..............Stetson 35, Arkansas St 20
1-1-53..............E Texas St 33, Tennessee Tech 0
1-1-54..............E Texas St 7, Arkansas St 7
1-1-55..............NE-Omaha 7, Eastern Kentucky 6
1-2-56..............Juniata 6, Missouri Valley 6
1-1-57..............W Texas St 20, Southern Miss 13
1-1-58..............E Texas St 10, Southern Miss 9
12-27-58..........E Texas St 26, Missouri Valley 7
1-1-60..............Middle Tennessee St 21, Presbyterian 12
12-30-60..........Citadel 27, Tennessee Tech 0
12-29-61..........Lamar 21, Middle Tennessee St 14
12-22-62..........Houston 49, Miami (Ohio) 21
12-28-63..........Western Kentucky 27, Coast Guard 0
12-12-64..........E Carolina 14, Massachusetts 13
12-11-65..........E Carolina 31, Maine 0
12-10-66..........Morgan St 14, W Chester 6
12-16-67..........TN-Martin 25, W Chester 8
12-27-68..........Richmond 49, Ohio 42
12-26-69..........Toledo 56, Davidson 33
12-28-70..........Toledo 40, William & Mary 12
12-28-71..........Toledo 28, Richmond 3
12-29-72..........Tampa 21, Kent St 18
12-22-73..........Miami (Ohio) 16, Florida 7
12-21-74..........Miami (Ohio) 21, Georgia 10
12-20-75..........Miami (Ohio) 20, South Carolina 7
12-18-76..........Oklahoma St 49, BYU 21
12-23-77..........Florida St 40, Texas Tech 17
12-23-78..........North Carolina St 30, Pittsburgh 17
12-22-79..........LSU 34, Wake Forest 10
12-20-80..........Florida 35, Maryland 20
12-19-81..........Missouri 19, Southern Miss 17
12-18-82..........Auburn 33, Boston Col 26
12-17-83..........Tennessee 30, Maryland 23
12-22-84..........Georgia 17, Florida St 17
12-28-85..........Ohio St 10, BYU 7
1-1-87..............Auburn 16, USC 7
1-1-88..............Clemson 35, Penn St 10
1-2-89..............Clemson 13, Oklahoma 6
1-1-90..............Illinois 31, Virginia 21
1-1-91..............Georgia Tech 45, Nebraska 21
1-1-92..............California 37, Clemson 13
1-1-93..............Georgia 21, Ohio State 14
1-1-94..............Penn State 31, Tennessee 13
1-2-95..............Alabama 24, Ohio St 17
1-1-96..............Tennessee 20, Ohio St 14
1-1-97..............Tennessee 48, Northwestern 28
1-1-98..............Florida 21, Penn St 6
1-1-99..............Michigan 45, Arkansas 31
1-1-00..............Michigan St 37, Florida 34
1-1-01..............Michigan 31, Auburn 28
1-1-02..............Tennessee 45, Michigan 17
1-1-03..............Auburn 13, Penn St 9
1-1-04..............Georgia 34, Purdue 27 (OT)
1-1-05..............Iowa 30, LSU 25
1-2-06..............Wisconsin 24, Auburn 10
1-1-07..............Wisconsin 17, Arkansas 14
1-1-08..............Michigan 41, Florida 35

Capital One Bowl *(Cont.)*

1-1-09..............Georgia 24, Michigan St 12
1-1-10..............Penn St 19, LSU 17
1-1-11..............Alabama 49, Michigan St 7
1-2-12..............South Carolina 30, Nebraska 13
1-1-13..............Georgia 45, Nebraska 31

City: Orlando, FL. Stadium: Florida Citrus Bowl, capacity 70,000. Name Change: Tangerine Bowl (1947–82). Florida Citrus Bowl (1983–2007). Playing Sites: Tangerine Bowl (1947–72, 1974–82); Florida Field, Gainesville (1973); Orlando Stadium/Florida Citrus Bowl-Orlando (1983–2007).

Liberty Bowl

12-19-59..........Penn St 7, Alabama 0
12-17-60..........Penn St 41, Oregon 12
12-16-61..........Syracuse 15, Miami (Fla.) 14
12-15-62..........Oregon St 6, Villanova 0
12-21-63..........Mississippi St 16, North Carolina St 12
12-19-64..........Utah 32, W Virginia 6
12-18-65..........Mississippi 13, Auburn 7
12-10-66..........Miami (Fla.) 14, Virginia Tech 7
12-16-67..........North Carolina St 14, Georgia 7
12-14-68..........Mississippi 34, Virginia Tech 17
12-13-69..........Colorado 47, Alabama 33
12-12-70..........Tulane 17, Colorado 3
12-20-71..........Tennessee 14, Arkansas 13
12-18-72..........Georgia Tech 31, Iowa St 30
12-17-73..........North Carolina St 31, Kansas 18
12-16-74..........Tennessee 7, Maryland 3
12-22-75..........USC 20, Texas A&M 0
12-20-76..........Alabama 36, UCLA 6
12-19-77..........Nebraska 21, North Carolina 17
12-23-78..........Missouri 20, LSU 15
12-22-79..........Penn St 9, Tulane 6
12-27-80..........Purdue 28, Missouri 25
12-30-81..........Ohio St 31, Navy 28
12-29-82..........Alabama 21, Illinois 15
12-29-83..........Notre Dame 19, Boston Col 18
12-27-84..........Auburn 21, Arkansas 15
12-27-85..........Baylor 21, LSU 7
12-29-86..........Tennessee 21, Minnesota 14
12-29-87..........Georgia 20, Arkansas 17
12-28-88..........Indiana 34, South Carolina 10
12-28-89..........Mississippi 42, Air Force 29
12-27-90..........Air Force 23, Ohio St 11
12-29-91..........Air Force 38, Mississippi St 15
12-31-92..........Mississippi 13, Air Force 0
12-28-93..........Louisville 18, Michigan St 7
12-31-94..........Illinois 30, E Carolina 0
12-30-95..........East Carolina 19, Stanford 13
12-27-96..........Syracuse 30, Houston 17
12-31-97..........Southern Miss 41, Pittsburgh 7
12-31-98..........Tulane 41, BYU 27
12-31-99..........Southern Miss 23, Colorado St 17
12-29-01..........Colorado St 22, Louisville 17
12-31-01..........Louisville 28, BYU 10
12-31-02..........TCU 17, Colorado St 3
12-31-03..........Utah 17, Southern Mississippi 0
12-31-04..........Louisville 44, Boise State 40
12-31-05..........Tulsa 31, Fresno State 24
12-29-06..........South Carolina 44, Houston 36
12-29-07..........Mississippi St 10, Central Florida 3
1-2-09..............Kentucky 25, East Carolina 19
1-2-10..............Arkansas 20, East Carolina 17
12-31-10..........Central Florida 10, Georgia 6
12-31-11..........Cincinnati 31, Vanderbilt 24
12-31-12..........Iowa St 31, Iowa State 17

City: Memphis (since 1965). Stadium: Liberty Bowl Memorial Stadium, capacity 62,921.
Playing Sites: Philadelphia (Municipal Stadium, 1959–63), Atlantic City (Convention Center, 1964).

Bluebonnet Bowl

12-19-59..........Clemson 23, TCU 7
12-17-60..........Texas 3, Alabama 3
12-16-61..........Kansas 33, Rice 7
12-22-62..........Missouri 14, Georgia Tech 10
12-21-63..........Baylor 14, LSU 7
12-19-64..........Tulsa 14, Mississippi 7
12-18-65..........Tennessee 27, Tulsa 6
12-17-66..........Texas 19, Mississippi 0
12-23-67..........Colorado 31, Miami (Fla.) 21
12-31-68..........Southern Methodist 28, Oklahoma 27
12-31-69..........Houston 36, Auburn 7
12-31-70..........Alabama 24, Oklahoma 24
12-31-71..........Colorado 29, Houston 17
12-30-72..........Tennessee 24, LSU 17
12-29-73..........Houston 47, Tulane 7
12-23-74..........North Carolina St 31, Houston 31
12-27-75..........Texas 38, Colorado 21
12-31-76..........Nebraska 27, Texas Tech 24
12-31-77..........USC 47, Texas A&M 28
12-31-78..........Stanford 25, Georgia 22
12-31-79..........Purdue 27, Tennessee 22
12-31-80..........North Carolina 16, Texas 7
12-31-81..........Michigan 33, UCLA 14
12-31-82..........Arkansas 28, Florida 24
12-31-83..........Oklahoma St 24, Baylor 14
12-31-84..........West Virginia 31, TCU 14
12-31-85..........Air Force 24, Texas 16
12-31-86..........Baylor 21, Colorado 9
12-31-87..........Texas 32, Pittsburgh 27

City: Houston. Playing sites: Rice Stadium (1959–67;
1985–86), Astrodome (1968–84, 1987).
Name change: Astro-Bluebonnet Bowl (1968–84). Bowl
was discontinued after 1987.

Chick-fil-A Bowl

12-3-68............LSU 31, Florida St 27
12-30-69..........W Virginia 14, South Carolina 3
12-30-70..........Arizona St 48, North Carolina 26
12-30-71..........Mississippi 41, Georgia Tech 18
12-29-72..........North Carolina St 49, W Virginia 13
12-28-73..........Georgia 17, Maryland 16
12-28-74..........Vanderbilt 6, Texas Tech 6
12-31-75..........W Virginia 13, North Carolina St 10
12-31-76..........Kentucky 21, North Carolina 0
12-31-77..........North Carolina St 24, Iowa St 14
12-25-78..........Purdue 41, Georgia Tech 21
12-31-79..........Baylor 24, Clemson 18
1-2-81............Miami (Fla.) 20, Virginia Tech 10
12-31-81..........W Virginia 26, Florida 6
12-31-82..........Iowa 28, Tennessee 22
12-30-83..........Florida St 28, North Carolina 3
12-31-84..........Virginia 27, Purdue 24
12-31-85..........Army 31, Illinois 29
12-31-86..........Virginia Tech 25, North Carolina St 24
1-2-88............Tennessee 27, Indiana 22
12-31-88..........North Carolina St 28, Iowa 23
12-30-89..........Syracuse 19, Georgia 18
12-29-90..........Auburn 27, Indiana 23
1-1-92............E. Carolina 37, North Carolina St 34
1-2-93............North Carolina 21, Mississippi St 17
12-31-93..........Clemson 14, Kentucky 13
1-1-95............North Carolina St 28, Mississippi St 24
12-30-95..........Virginia 34, Georgia 27
12-28-96..........LSU 10, Clemson 7
1-2-98............Auburn 21, Clemson 17
12-31-98..........Georgia 35, Virginia 33
12-30-99..........Mississippi St 17, Clemson 7
12-29-00..........LSU 28, Georgia Tech 14
12-31-01..........North Carolina 16, Auburn 10

Chick-fil-A Bowl *(Cont.)*

12-31-02..........Maryland 30, Tennessee 3
1-2-04............Clemson 27, Tennessee 14
12-31-04..........Miami (Fla.) 27, Florida 10
12-30-05..........LSU 40, Miami (Fla.) 3
12-30-06..........Georgia 31, Virginia Tech 24
12-31-07..........Auburn 23, Clemson 20 (OT)
12-31-08..........LSU 38, Georgia Tech 3
12-31-09..........Virginia Tech 37, Tennessee 14
12-31-10..........Florida St 26, South Carolina 17
12-31-11..........Auburn 43, Virginia 24
12-31-12..........Clemson 25, LSU 24

City: Atlanta. Stadium: Georgia Dome, capacity 71,500.
Name change: Peach Bowl (1968–2005). Playing Sites:
Grant Field (1968–70), Atlanta–Fulton County Stadium
(1971–92), Georgia Dome (1993–).

Fiesta Bowl

12-27-71..........Arizona St 45, Florida St 38
12-23-72..........Arizona St 49, Missouri 35
12-21-73..........Arizona St 28, Pittsburgh 7
12-28-74..........Oklahoma St 16, BYU 6
12-26-75..........Arizona St 17, Nebraska 14
12-25-76..........Oklahoma 41, Wyoming 7
12-25-77..........Penn St 42, Arizona St 30
12-25-78..........Arkansas 10, UCLA 10
12-25-79..........Pittsburgh 16, Arizona 10
12-26-80..........Penn St 31, Ohio St 19
1-1-82............Penn St 26, USC 10
1-1-83............Arizona St 32, Oklahoma 21
1-2-84............Ohio St 28, Pittsburgh 23
1-1-85............UCLA 39, Miami (Fla.) 37
1-1-86............Michigan 27, Nebraska 23
1-2-87............Penn St 14, Miami (Fla.) 10
1-1-88............Florida St 31, Nebraska 28
1-2-89............Notre Dame 34, W Virginia 21
1-1-90............Florida St 41, Nebraska 17
1-1-91............Louisville 34, Alabama 7
1-1-92............Penn St 42, Tennessee 17
1-1-93............Syracuse 26, Colorado 22
1-1-94............Arizona 29, Miami (Fla.) 0
1-2-95............Colorado 41, Notre Dame 24
1-2-96............Nebraska 62, Florida 24
1-1-97............Penn St 38, Texas 15
12-31-97..........Kansas St 35, Syracuse 18
1-4-99............Tennessee 23, Florida St 16
1-2-00............Nebraska 31, Tennessee 21
1-1-01............Oregon St 41, Notre Dame 9
1-1-02............Oregon 38, Colorado 16
1-3-03............Ohio St 31, Miami (Fla.) 24 (2 OT)
1-2-04............Ohio St 35, Kansas St 28
1-1-05............Utah 35, Pittsburgh 7
1-2-06............Ohio St 34, Notre Dame 20
1-1-07............Boise St 43, Oklahoma 42
1-2-08............West Virginia 48, Oklahoma 28
1-5-09............Texas 24, Ohio St 21
1-4-10............Boise St 17, TCU 10
1-1-11............Oklahoma 48, Connecticut 20
1-2-12............Oklahoma St 41, Stanford 38
1-3-13............Oregon 35, Kansas State 17

Stadium: Sun Devil Stadium, Tempe, Ariz. (1971–2006),
capacity 73,471. University of Phoenix Stadium,
Glendale, Ariz. (2007–), capacity 72,200.

Independence Bowl

12-13-76..........McNeese St 20, Tulsa 16
12-17-77..........Louisiana Tech 24, Louisville 14
12-16-78..........E Carolina 35, Louisiana Tech 13
12-15-79..........Syracuse 31, McNeese St 7
12-13-80..........Southern Miss 16, McNeese St 14
12-12-81..........Texas A&M 33, Oklahoma St 16
12-11-82..........Wisconsin 14, Kansas St 3
12-10-83..........Air Force 9, Mississippi 3
12-15-84..........Air Force 23, Virginia Tech 7
12-21-85..........Minnesota 20, Clemson 13
12-20-86..........Mississippi 20, Texas Tech 17
12-19-87..........Washington 24, Tulane 12
12-23-88..........Southern Miss 38, UTEP 18
12-16-89..........Oregon 27, Tulsa 24
12-15-90..........Louisiana Tech 34, Maryland 34
12-29-91..........Georgia 24, Arkansas 15
12-31-92..........Wake Forest 39, Oregon 35
12-31-93..........Virginia Tech 45, Indiana 20
12-28-94..........Virginia 20, TCU 10
12-29-95..........LSU 45, Michigan St 26
12-31-96..........Auburn 32, Army 29
12-28-97..........LSU 27, Notre Dame 9
12-31-98..........Mississippi 35, Texas Tech 18
12-31-99..........Mississippi 27, Oklahoma 25
12-31-00..........Mississippi St 43, Texas A&M 41
12-27-01..........Alabama 14, Iowa St 13
12-27-02..........Mississippi 27, Nebraska 23
12-31-03..........Arkansas 27, Missouri 14
12-28-04..........Iowa State 17, Miami (Ohio) 13
12-30-05..........Missouri 38, South Carolina 31
12-28-06..........Oklahoma State 34, Alabama 31
12-30-07..........Alabama 30, Colorado 24
12-28-08..........Louisiana Tech 17, Northern Ill. 10
12-28-09..........Georgia 44, Texas A&M 20
12-27-10..........Air Force 14, Georgia Tech 7
12-26-11..........Missouri 41, North Carolina 24
12-28-12..........Ohio 45, LA-Monroe 14

City: Shreveport, LA. Stadium: Independence Stadium, capacity 50,459.

All-American Bowl

12-22-77..........Maryland 17, Minnesota 7
12-20-78..........Texas A&M 28, Iowa St 12
12-29-79..........Missouri 24, South Carolina 14
12-27-80..........Arkansas 34, Tulane 15
12-31-81..........Mississippi St 10, Kansas 0
12-31-82..........Air Force 36, Vanderbilt 28
12-22-83..........W Virginia 20, Kentucky 16
12-29-84..........Kentucky 20, Wisconsin 19
12-31-85..........Georgia Tech 17, Michigan St 14
12-31-86..........Florida St 27, Indiana 13
12-22-87..........Virginia 22, BYU 16
12-29-88..........Florida 14, Illinois 10
12-28-89..........Texas Tech 49, Duke 21
12-28-90..........North Carolina St 31, Southern Miss 27

City: Birmingham, AL. Stadium: Legion Field.
Name Change: Hall of Fame Classic (1977–84). Bowl
was discontinued after 1990.

Holiday Bowl

12-22-78..........Navy 23, BYU 16
12-21-79..........Indiana 38, BYU 37
12-19-80..........BYU 46, SMU 45
12-18-81..........BYU 38, Washington St 36
12-17-82..........Ohio St 47, BYU 17
12-23-83..........BYU 21, Missouri 17
12-21-84..........BYU 24, Michigan 17
12-22-85..........Arkansas 18, Arizona St 17
12-30-86..........Iowa 39, San Diego St 38
12-30-87..........Iowa 20, Wyoming 19

Holiday Bowl *(Cont.)*

12-30-88..........Oklahoma St 62, Wyoming 14
12-29-89..........Penn St 50, BYU 39
12-29-90..........Texas A&M 65, BYU 14
12-30-91..........Iowa 13, BYU 13
12-30-92..........Hawaii 27, Illinois 17
12-30-93..........Ohio St 28, BYU 21
12-30-94..........Michigan 24, Colorado St 14
12-29-95..........Kansas St 54, Colorado St 21
12-30-96..........Colorado 33, Washington 21
12-29-97..........Colorado St 35, Missouri 24
12-30-98..........Arizona 23, Nebraska 20
12-29-99..........Kansas St 24, Washington 20
12-29-00..........Oregon 35, Texas 30
12-28-01..........Texas 47, Washington 43
12-27-02..........Kansas St 34, Arizona St 27
12-30-03..........Washington St 28, Texas 20
12-30-04..........Texas Tech 45, California 31
12-29-05..........Oklahoma 17, Oregon 14
12-28-06..........California 45, Texas A&M 10
12-27-07..........Texas 52, Arizona St 34
12-30-08..........Oregon 42, Oklahoma St 31
12-30-09..........Nebraska 33, Arizona 0
12-30-11..........Washington 19, Nebraska 7
12-28-11..........Texas 21, California 10
12-27-12..........Baylor 49, UCLA 26

City: San Diego. Stadium: Qualcomm Stadium,
capacity 70,000.

Las Vegas Bowl

12-19-81..........Toledo 27, San Jose St 25
12-18-82..........Fresno St 29, Bowling Green 28
12-17-83..........Northern Illinois 20,
                       Cal St–Fullerton 13
12-15-84..........UNLV 30, Toledo 13*
12-14-85..........Fresno St 51, Bowling Green 7
12-13-86..........San Jose St 37, Miami (Ohio) 7
12-12-87..........Eastern Michigan 30, San Jose St 27
12-10-88..........Fresno St 35, Western Michigan 30
12-9-90............Fresno St 27, Ball St 6
12-8-90............San Jose St 48, Central Michigan 24
12-14-91..........Bowling Green 28, Fresno St 21
12-18-92..........Bowling Green 35, Nevada 34
12-17-93..........Utah St 42, Ball St 33
12-15-94..........UNLV 52, Central Michigan 24
12-14-95..........Toledo 40, Nevada 37
12-19-96..........Nevada 18, Ball St 15
12-19-97..........Oregon 41, Air Force 13
12-19-98..........North Carolina 20, San Diego St 13
12-18-99..........Utah 17, Fresno St 16
12-21-00..........UNLV 31, Arkansas 14
12-25-01..........Utah 10, USC 6
12-25-02..........UCLA 27, New Mexico 13
12-24-03..........Oregon St 55, New Mexico 14
12-23-04..........Wyoming 24, UCLA, 21
12-22-05..........California 35, BYU 28
12-21-06..........BYU 38, Oregon 8
12-22-07..........BYU 17, UCLA 16
12-20-08..........Arizona 31, BYU 21
12-22-09..........BYU 44, Oregon St 20
12-22-10..........Boise State 26, Utah 3
12-22-11..........Boise State 56, Arizona St 24
12-22-12..........Boise State 28, Washington 26

* Toledo won later by forfeit. City: Las Vegas (since
1992). Stadium: Sam Boyd Silver Bowl Stadium,
capacity 40,000. Name change: California Bowl
(1981–91). Playing sites: Fresno, CA (Bulldog Stadium,
1981–91), Las Vegas.

Aloha Bowl

12-25-82 ....Washington 21, Maryland 20
12-26-83 ....Penn St 13, Washington 10
12-29-84 ....Southern Methodist 27, Notre Dame 20
12-28-85 ....Alabama 24, USC 3
12-27-86 ....Arizona 30, North Carolina 21
12-25-87 ....UCLA 20, Florida 16
12-25-88 ....Washington St 24, Houston 22
12-25-89 ....Michigan St 33, Hawaii 13
12-25-90 ....Syracuse 28, Arizona 0
12-25-91 ....Georgia Tech 18, Stanford 17
12-25-92 ....Kansas 23, BYU 20
12-25-93 ....Colorado 41, Fresno St 30
12-25-94 ....Boston College 12, Kansas St 7
12-25-95 ....Kansas 51, UCLA 30
12-25-96 ....Navy 42, California 38
12-25-97 ....Washington 51, Michigan St 23
12-25-98 ....Colorado 51, Oregon 43
12-25-99 ....Wake Forest 23, Arizona St 3
12-25-00 ....Boston College 31, Arizona St 17

City: Honolulu. Stadium: Aloha Stadium. Bowl was discontinued after 2000.

Freedom Bowl

12-16-84 ....Iowa 55, Texas 17
12-30-85 ....Washington 20, Colorado 17
12-30-86 ....UCLA 31, BYU 10
12-30-87 ....Arizona St 33, Air Force 28
12-29-88 ....BYU 20, Colorado 17
12-30-89 ....Washington 34, Florida 7
12-29-90 ....Colorado St 32, Oregon 31
12-30-91 ....Tulsa 28, San Diego St 17
12-29-92 ....Fresno St 24, USC 7
12-30-93 ....USC 28, Utah 21
12-29-94 ....Utah 16, Arizona 13

City: Anaheim. Stadium: Anaheim Stadium. Bowl was discontinued after 1994.

Outback Bowl

12-23-86 ....Boston College 27, Georgia 24
1-2-88 ....Michigan 28, Alabama 24
1-2-89 ....Syracuse 23, LSU 10
1-1-90 ....Auburn 31, Ohio St 14
1-1-91 ....Clemson 30, Illinois 0
1-1-92 ....Syracuse 24, Ohio St 17
1-1-93 ....Tennessee 38, Boston College 23
1-1-94 ....Michigan 42, North Carolina St 7
1-2-95 ....Wisconsin 34, Duke 20
1-1-96 ....Penn St 43, Auburn 14
1-1-97 ....Alabama 17, Michigan 14
1-1-98 ....Georgia 33, Wisconsin 6
1-1-99 ....Penn St 26, Kentucky 14
1-1-00 ....Georgia 28, Purdue 25
1-1-01 ....South Carolina 24, Ohio St 7
1-1-02 ....South Carolina 31, Ohio St 28
1-1-03 ....Michigan 38, Florida 30
1-1-04 ....Iowa 37, Florida 17
1-1-05 ....Georgia 24, Wisconsin 21
1-2-06 ....Florida 31, Iowa 24
1-1-07 ....Penn State 20, Tennessee 10
1-1-08 ....Tennessee 21, Wisconsin 17
1-1-09 ....Iowa 31, South Carolina 10
1-1-10 ....Auburn 38, Northwestern 35
1-1-11 ....Florida 37, Penn St 24
1-2-12 ....Michigan St 33, Georgia 30
1-1-13 ....South Carolina 33, Michigan 28

City: Tampa. Stadium: Raymond James Stadium, capacity 75,000. Name change: Hall of Fame Bowl (1986–95).

Buffalo Wild Wings Bowl

12-31-89 ....Arizona 17, North Carolina St 10
12-31-90 ....California 17, Wyoming 15
12-31-91 ....Indiana 24, Baylor 0
12-29-92 ....Washington St 31, Utah 28
12-29-93 ....Kansas St 52, Wyoming 17
12-29-94 ....BYU 31, Oklahoma 6
12-27-95 ....Texas Tech 55, Air Force 41
12-27-96 ....Wisconsin 38, Utah 10
12-27-97 ....Arizona 20, New Mexico 14
12-26-98 ....Missouri 34, W Virginia 31
12-31-99 ....Colorado 62, Boston College 28
12-28-00 ....Iowa St 37, Pittsburgh 29
12-29-01 ....Syracuse 26, Kansas St 3
12-26-02 ....Pittsburgh 38, Oregon St 13
12-26-03 ....California 52, Virginia Tech 49
12-28-04 ....Oregon State 38, Notre Dame 21
12-27-05 ....Arizona State 45, Rutgers 40
12-29-06 ....Texas Tech 44, Minnesota 41
12-31-07 ....Oklahoma St 49, Indiana 33
12-31-08 ....Kansas 42, Minnesota 21
12-31-09 ....Iowa St 14, Minnesota 13
12-28-10 ....Iowa 27, Missouri 24
12-30-11 ....Oklahoma 31, Iowa 14
12-29-12 ....Michigan State 17, TCU 16

City: Tucson. Stadium: Arizona Stadium, capacity 55,883. Name change: Copper Bowl (1989–97), Insight.com Bowl (1998–2000), Insight Bowl (2001–2011).

Tangerine Bowl

12-28-90 ....Florida St 24, Penn St 17
12-28-91 ....Alabama 30, Colorado 25
1-1-93 ....Stanford 24, Penn St 3
1-1-94 ....Boston College 31, Virginia 13
1-2-95 ....South Carolina 24, W Virginia 21
12-30-95 ....North Carolina 20, Arkansas 10
12-27-96 ....Miami (Fla.) 31, Virginia 21
12-29-97 ....Georgia Tech 35, W Virginia 30
12-29-98 ....Miami (Fla.) 46, North Carolina St 23
12-30-99 ....Illinois 62, Virginia 21
12-28-00 ....North Carolina St 38, Minnesota 30
12-20-01 ....Pittsburgh 34, North Carolina St 19
12-23-02 ....Texas Tech 55, Clemson 15
12-22-03 ....North Carolina St 56, Kansas 26

City: Miami. Stadium: Pro Player Stadium, capacity 75,192. Name change: Blockbuster Bowl (1990–93), Carquest Bowl (1994–97), Micron PC Bowl (1998–2001). Bowl was discontinued after 2003.

Alamo Bowl

12-31-93 ....California 37, Iowa 3
12-31-94 ....Washington St 10, Baylor 3
12-28-95 ....Texas A&M 22, Michigan 20
12-29-96 ....Iowa 27, Texas Tech 0
12-30-97 ....Purdue 33, Oklahoma St 20
12-29-98 ....Purdue 37, Kansas St 34
12-28-99 ....Penn St 24, Texas A&M 0
12-30-00 ....Nebraska 66, Northwestern 17
12-29-01 ....Iowa 19, Texas Tech 16
12-28-02 ....Wisconsin 31, Colorado 28 (OT)
12-29-03 ....Nebraska 17, Michigan St 3
12-29-04 ....Ohio State 33, Oklahoma State 7
12-28-05 ....Nebraska 32, Michigan 28
12-30-06 ....Texas 26, Iowa 24
12-29-07 ....Penn St 24, Texas A&M 17
12-29-08 ....Missouri 30, Northwestern 23
1-2-10 ....Texas Tech 41, Michigan St 31
12-29-10 ....Oklahoma 36, Arizona 10
12-29-11 ....Baylor 67, Washington 56
12-29-12 ....Texas 31, Oregon State 27

City: San Antonio, TX. Stadium: Alamodome, capaciity 67,000.

1936

		Record	Coach
1.	Minnesota	7-1-0	Bernie Bierman
2.	LSU	9-0-1	Bernie Moore
3.	Pittsburgh	7-1-1	Jock Sutherland
4.	Alabama	8-0-1	Frank Thomas
5.	Washington	7-1-1	Jimmy Phelan
6.	Santa Clara	7-1-0	Buck Shaw
7.	Northwestern	7-1-0	Pappy Waldorf
8.	Notre Dame	6-2-1	Elmer Layden
9.	Nebraska	7-2-0	Dana X. Bible
10.	Pennsylvania	7-1-0	Harvey Harman
11.	Duke	9-1-0	Wallace Wade
12.	Yale	7-1-0	Ducky Pond
13.	Dartmouth	7-1-1	Red Blaik
14.	Duquesne	7-2-0	John Smith
15.	Fordham	5-1-2	Jim Crowley
16.	TCU	8-2-2	Dutch Meyer
17.	Tennessee	6-2-2	Bob Neyland
18.	Arkansas	7-3-0	Fred Thomsen
19.	Navy	6-3-0	Tom Hamilton
20.	Marquette	7-1-0	Frank Murray

1937

		Record	Coach
1.	Pittsburgh	9-0-1	Jock Sutherland
2.	California	9-0-1	Stub Allison
3.	Fordham	7-0-1	Jim Crowley
4.	Alabama	9-0-0	Frank Thomas
5.	Minnesota	6-2-0	Bernie Bierman
6.	Villanova	8-0-1	Clipper Smith
7.	Dartmouth	7-0-2	Red Blaik
8.	LSU	9-1-0	Bernie Moore
9.	Notre Dame	6-2-1	Elmer Layden
	Santa Clara	8-0-0	Buck Shaw
11.	Nebraska	6-1-2	Biff Jones
12.	Yale	6-1-1	Ducky Pond
13.	Ohio St	6-2-0	Francis Schmidt
14.	Holy Cross	8-0-2	Eddie Anderson
	Arkansas	6-2-2	Fred Thomsen
16.	TCU	4-2-2	Dutch Meyer
17.	Colorado	8-0-0	Bunnie Oakes
18.	Rice	5-3-2	Jimmy Kitts
19.	North Carolina	7-1-1	Ray Wolf
20.	Duke	7-2-1	Wallace Wade

1938

		Record	Coach
1.	TCU	10-0-0	Dutch Meyer
2.	Tennessee	10-0-0	Bob Neyland
3.	Duke	9-0-0	Wallace Wade
4.	Oklahoma	10-0-0	Tom Stidham
5.	#Notre Dame	8-1-0	Elmer Layden
6.	Carnegie Tech	7-1-0	Bill Kern
7.	USC	8-2-0	Howard Jones
8.	Pittsburgh	8-2-0	Jock Sutherland
9.	Holy Cross	8-1-0	Eddie Anderson
10.	Minnesota	6-2-0	Bernie Bierman
11.	Texas Tech	10-0-0	Pete Cawthon
12.	Cornell	5-1-1	Carl Snavely
13.	Alabama	7-1-1	Frank Thomas
14.	California	10-1-0	Stub Allison
15.	Fordham	6-1-2	Jim Crowley
16.	Michigan	6-1-1	Fritz Crisler
17.	Northwestern	4-2-2	Pappy Waldorf

1938 (Cont.)

		Record	Coach
18.	Villanova	8-0-1	Clipper Smith
19.	Tulane	7-2-1	Red Dawson
20.	Dartmouth	7-2-0	Red Blaik

#Selected No. 1 by the Dickinson System.

1939

		Record	Coach
1.	Texas A&M	10-0-0	Homer Norton
2.	Tennessee	10-0-0	Bob Neyland
3.	#USC	7-0-2	Howard Jones
4.	Cornell	8-0-0	Carl Snavely
5.	Tulane	8-0-1	Red Dawson
6.	Missouri	8-1-0	Don Faurot
7.	UCLA	6-0-4	Babe Horrell
8.	Duke	8-1-0	Wallace Wade
9.	Iowa	6-1-1	Eddie Anderson
10.	Duquesne	8-0-1	Buff Donelli
11.	Boston College	9-1-0	Frank Leahy
12.	Clemson	8-1-0	Jess Neely
13.	Notre Dame	7-2-0	Elmer Layden
14.	Santa Clara	5-1-3	Buck Shaw
15.	Ohio St	6-2-0	Francis Schmidt
16.	Georgia Tech	7-2-0	Bill Alexander
17.	Fordham	6-2-0	Jim Crowley
18.	Nebraska	7-1-1	Biff Jones
19.	Oklahoma	6-2-1	Tom Stidham
20.	Michigan	6-2-0	Fritz Crisler

#Selected No. 1 by the Dickinson System.

1940

		Record	Coach
1.	Minnesota	8-0-0	Bernie Bierman
2.	Stanford	9-0-0	C. Shaughnessy
3.	Michigan	7-1-0	Fritz Crisler
4.	Tennessee	10-0-0	Bob Neyland
5.	Boston College	10-0-0	Frank Leahy
6.	Texas A&M	8-1-0	Homer Norton
7.	Nebraska	8-1-0	Biff Jones
8.	Northwestern	6-2-0	Pappy Waldorf
9.	Mississippi St	9-0-1	Allyn McKeen
10.	Washington	7-2-0	Jimmy Phelan
11.	Santa Clara	6-1-1	Buck Shaw
12.	Fordham	7-1-0	Jim Crowley
13.	Georgetown	8-1-0	Jack Hagerty
14.	Pennsylvania	6-1-1	George Munger
15.	Cornell	6-2-0	Carl Snavely
16.	SMU	8-1-1	Matty Bell
17.	Hard.-Simmons	9-0-0	Abe Woodson
18.	Duke	7-2-0	Wallace Wade
19.	Lafayette	9-0-0	Hooks Mylin
20.	—		

Only 19 teams selected.

1941

		Record	Coach
1.	Minnesota	8-0-0	Bernie Bierman
2.	Duke	9-0-0	Wallace Wade
3.	Notre Dame	8-0-1	Frank Leahy
4.	Texas	8-1-1	Dana X. Bible
5.	Michigan	6-1-1	Fritz Crisler
6.	Fordham	7-1-0	Jim Crowley
7.	Missouri	8-1-0	Don Faurot
8.	Duquesne	8-0-0	Buff Donelli

Note: Except where indicated with an asterisk, the polls from 1936 through 1964 were taken before the bowl games and those from 1965 through the present were taken after the bowl games.

1941 (*Cont.*)

		Record	Coach
9.	Texas A&M	9-1-0	Homer Norton
10.	Navy	7-1-1	Swede Larson
11.	Northwestern	5-3-0	Pappy Waldorf
12.	Oregon St	7-2-0	Lon Stiner
13.	Ohio St	6-1-1	Paul Brown
14.	Georgia	8-1-1	Wally Butts
15.	Pennsylvania	7-1-1	George Munger
16.	Mississippi St	8-1-1	Allyn McKeen
17.	Mississippi	6-2-1	Harry Mehre
18.	Tennessee	8-2-0	John Barnhill
19.	Washington St	6-4-0	Babe Hollingbery
20.	Alabama	8-2-0	Frank Thomas

1942

		Record	Coach
1.	Ohio St	9-1-0	Paul Brown
2.	Georgia	10-1-0	Wally Butts
3.	Wisconsin	8-1-1	H. Stuhldreher
4.	Tulsa	10-0-0	Henry Frnka
5.	Georgia Tech	9-1-0	Bill Alexander
6.	Notre Dame	7-2-2	Frank Leahy
7.	Tennessee	8-1-1	John Barnhill
8.	Boston College	8-1-0	Denny Myers
9.	Michigan	7-3-0	Fritz Crisler
10.	Alabama	7-3-0	Frank Thomas
11.	Texas	8-2-0	Dana X. Bible
12.	Stanford	6-4-0	Marchie Schwartz
13.	UCLA	7-3-0	Babe Horrell
14.	William & Mary	9-1-1	Carl Voyles
15.	Santa Clara	7-2-0	Buck Shaw
16.	Auburn	6-4-1	Jack Meagher
17.	Washington St	6-2-2	Babe Hollingbery
18.	Mississippi St	8-1-1	Allyn McKeen
19.	Minnesota	5-4-0	George Hauser
	Holy Cross	5-4-1	Ank Scanlon
	Penn St	6-1-1	Bob Higgins

1943

		Record	Coach
1.	Notre Dame	9-1-0	Frank Leahy
2.	Iowa Pre-Flight	9-1-0	Don Faurot
3.	Michigan	8-1-0	Fritz Crisler
4.	Navy	8-1-0	Billick Whelchel
5.	Purdue	9-0-0	Elmer Burnham
6.	Great Lakes	10-2-0	Tony Hinkle
7.	Duke	8-1-0	Eddie Cameron
8.	Del Monte P-F	7-1-0	Bill Kern
9.	Northwestern	6-2-0	Pappy Waldorf
10.	March Field	9-1-0	Paul Schissler
11.	Army	7-2-1	Red Blaik
12.	Washington	4-0-0	Ralph Welch
13.	Georgia Tech	7-3-0	Bill Alexander
14.	Texas	7-1-0	Dana X. Bible
15.	Tulsa	6-0-1	Henry Frnka
16.	Dartmouth	6-1-0	Earl Brown
17.	Bainbridge NTS	7-0-0	Joe Maniaci
18.	Colorado College	7-0-0	Hal White
19.	Pacific	7-2-0	Amos A. Stagg
20.	Pennsylvania	6-2-1	George Munger

1944

		Record	Coach
1.	Army	9-0-0	Red Blaik
2.	Ohio St	9-0-0	Carroll Widdoes
3.	Randolph Field	11-0-0	Frank Tritico
4.	Navy	6-3-0	Oscar Hagberg
5.	Bainbridge NTS	9-0-0	Joe Maniaci
6.	Iowa Pre-Flight	10-1-0	Jack Meagher

1944 (*Cont.*)

		Record	Coach
7.	USC	7-0-2	Jeff Cravath
8.	Michigan	8-2-0	Fritz Crisler
9.	Notre Dame	8-2-0	Ed McKeever
10.	March Field	7-1-2	Paul Schissler
11.	Duke	5-4-0	Eddie Cameron
12.	Tennessee	8-0-1	John Barnhill
13.	Georgia Tech	8-2-0	Bill Alexander
	Norman P-F	6-0-0	John Gregg
15.	Illinois	5-4-1	Ray Eliot
16.	El Toro Marines	8-1-0	Dick Hanley
17.	Great Lakes	9-2-1	Paul Brown
18.	Fort Pierce	9-0-0	Hamp Pool
19.	St. Mary's P-F	4-4-0	Jules Sikes
20.	2nd Air Force	7-2-1	Bill Reese

1945

		Record	Coach
1.	Army	9-0-0	Red Blaik
2.	Alabama	9-0-0	Frank Thomas
3.	Navy	7-1-1	Oscar Hagberg
4.	Indiana	9-0-1	Bo McMillan
5.	Oklahoma A&M	8-0-0	Jim Lookabaugh
6.	Michigan	7-3-0	Fritz Crisler
7.	St. Mary's (CA)	7-1-0	Jimmy Phelan
8.	Pennsylvania	6-2-0	George Munger
9.	Notre Dame	7-2-1	Hugh Devore
10.	Texas	9-1-0	Dana X. Bible
11.	USC	7-3-0	Jeff Cravath
12.	Ohio St	7-2-0	Carroll Widdoes
13.	Duke	6-2-0	Eddie Cameron
14.	Tennessee	8-1-0	John Barnhill
15.	LSU	7-2-0	Bernie Moore
16.	Holy Cross	8-1-0	John DeGrosa
17.	Tulsa	8-2-0	Henry Frnka
18.	Georgia	8-2-0	Wally Butts
19.	Wake Forest	4-3-1	Peahead Walker
20.	Columbia	8-1-0	Lou Little

1946

		Record	Coach
1.	Notre Dame	8-0-1	Frank Leahy
2.	Army	9-0-1	Red Blaik
3.	Georgia	10-0-0	Wally Butts
4.	UCLA	10-0-0	B. LaBrucherie
5.	Illinois	7-2-0	Ray Eliot
6.	Michigan	6-2-1	Fritz Crisler
7.	Tennessee	9-1-0	Bob Neyland
8.	LSU	9-1-0	Bernie Moore
9.	North Carolina	8-1-1	Carl Snavely
10.	Rice	8-2-0	Jess Neely
11.	Georgia Tech	8-2-0	Bobby Dodd
12.	Yale	7-1-1	Howard Odell
13.	Pennsylvania	6-2-0	George Munger
14.	Oklahoma	7-3-0	Jim Tatum
15.	Texas	8-2-0	Dana X. Bible
16.	Arkansas	6-3-1	John Barnhill
17.	Tulsa	9-1-0	J.O. Brothers
18.	North Carolina St	8-2-0	Beattie Feathers
19.	Delaware	9-0-0	Bill Murray
20.	Indiana	6-3-0	Bo McMillan

1947

		Record	Coach
1.	Notre Dame	9-0-0	Frank Leahy
2.	#Michigan	9-0-0	Fritz Crisler
3.	SMU	9-0-1	Matty Bell
4.	Penn St	9-0-0	Bob Higgins
5.	Texas	9-1-0	Blair Cherry

Annual Associated Press Top 20 *(Cont.)*

1947 *(Cont.)*

		Record	Coach
6.	Alabama	8-2-0	Red Drew
7.	Pennsylvania	7-0-1	George Munger
8.	USC	7-1-1	Jeff Cravath
9.	North Carolina	8-2-0	Carl Snavely
10.	Georgia Tech	9-1-0	Bobby Dodd
11.	Army	5-2-2	Red Blaik
12.	Kansas	8-0-2	George Sauer
13.	Mississippi	8-2-0	Johnny Vaught
14.	William & Mary	9-1-0	Rube McCray
15.	California	9-1-0	Pappy Waldorf
16.	Oklahoma	7-2-1	Bud Wilkinson
17.	North Carolina St	5-3-1	Beattie Feathers
18.	Rice	6-3-1	Jess Neely
19.	Duke	4-3-2	Wallace Wade
20.	Columbia	7-2-0	Lou Little

#The AP, which had voted Notre Dame No. 1 before the bowl games, took a second vote, giving the title to Michigan after its 49–0 win over USC in the Rose Bowl.

1948

		Record	Coach
1.	Michigan	9-0-0	Bennie Oosterbaan
2.	Notre Dame	9-0-1	Frank Leahy
3.	North Carolina	9-0-1	Carl Snavely
4.	California	10-0-0	Pappy Waldorf
5.	Oklahoma	9-1-0	Bud Wilkinson
6.	Army	8-0-1	Red Blaik
7.	Northwestern	7-2-0	Bob Voigts
8.	Georgia	9-1-0	Wally Butts
9.	Oregon	9-1-0	Jim Aiken
10.	SMU	8-1-1	Matty Bell
11.	Clemson	10-0-0	Frank Howard
12.	Vanderbilt	8-2-1	Red Sanders
13.	Tulane	9-1-0	Henry Frnka
14.	Michigan St	6-2-2	Biggie Munn
15.	Mississippi	8-1-0	Johnny Vaught
16.	Minnesota	7-2-0	Bernie Bierman
17.	William & Mary	6-2-2	Rube McCray
18.	Penn St	7-1-1	Bob Higgins
19.	Cornell	8-1-0	Lefty James
20.	Wake Forest	6-3-0	Peahead Walker

1949

		Record	Coach
1.	Notre Dame	10-0-0	Frank Leahy
2.	Oklahoma	10-0-0	Bud Wilkinson
3.	California	10-0-0	Pappy Waldorf
4.	Army	9-0-0	Red Blaik
5.	Rice	9-1-0	Jess Neely
6.	Ohio St	6-1-2	Wes Fesler
7.	Michigan	6-2-1	Bennie Oosterbaan
8.	Minnesota	7-2-0	Bernie Bierman
9.	LSU	8-2-0	Gaynell Tinsley
10.	Pacific	11-0-0	Larry Siemering
11.	Kentucky	9-2-0	Bear Bryant
12.	Cornell	8-1-0	Lefty James
13.	Villanova	8-1-0	Jim Leonard
14.	Maryland	8-1-0	Jim Tatum
15.	Santa Clara	7-2-1	Len Casanova
16.	North Carolina	7-3-0	Carl Snavely
17.	Tennessee	7-2-1	Bob Neyland
18.	Princeton	6-3-0	Charlie Caldwell
19.	Michigan St	6-3-0	Biggie Munn
20.	Missouri	7-3-0	Don Faurot
	Baylor	8-2-0	Bob Woodruff

1950

		Record	Coach
1.	Oklahoma	10-0-0	Bud Wilkinson
2.	Army	8-1-0	Red Blaik
3.	Texas	9-1-0	Blair Cherry
4.	Tennessee	10-1-0	Bob Neyland
5.	California	9-0-1	Pappy Waldorf
6.	Princeton	9-0-0	Charlie Caldwell
7.	Kentucky	10-1-0	Bear Bryant
8.	Michigan St	8-1-0	Biggie Munn
9.	Michigan	5-3-1	Bennie Oosterhaan
10.	Clemson	8-0-1	Frank Howard
11.	Washington	8-2-0	Howard Odell
12.	Wyoming	9-0-0	Bowden Wyatt
13.	Illinois	7-2-0	Ray Eliot
14.	Ohio St	6-3-0	Wes Fesler
15.	Miami (Fla.)	9-0-1	Andy Gustafson
16.	Alabama	9-2-0	Red Drew
17.	Nebraska	6-2-1	Bill Glassford
18.	Washington & Lee	8-2-0	George Barclay
19.	Tulsa	9-1-1	J.O. Brothers
20.	Tulane	6-2-1	Henry Frnka

1951

		Record	Coach
1.	Tennessee	10-0-0	Bob Neyland
2.	Michigan St	9-0-0	Biggie Munn
3.	Maryland	9-0-0	Jim Tatum
4.	Illinois	8-0-1	Ray Eliot
5.	Georgia Tech	10-0-1	Bobby Dodd
6.	Princeton	9-0-0	Charlie Caldwell
7.	Stanford	9-1-0	Chuck Taylor
8.	Wisconsin	7-1-1	Ivy Williamson
9.	Baylor	8-1-1	George Sauer
10.	Oklahoma	8-2-0	Bud Wilkinson
11.	TCU	6-4-0	Dutch Meyer
12.	California	8-2-0	Pappy Waldorf
13.	Virginia	8-1-0	Art Guepe
14.	San Francisco	9-0-0	Joe Kuharich
15.	Kentucky	7-4-0	Bear Bryant
16.	Boston University	6-4-0	Buff Donelli
17.	UCLA	5-3-1	Red Sanders
18.	Washington St	7-3-0	Forest Evashevski
19.	Holy Cross	8-2-0	Eddie Anderson
20.	Clemson	7-2-0	Frank Howard

1952

		Record	Coach
1.	Michigan St	9-0-0	Biggie Munn
2.	Georgia Tech	11-0-0	Bobby Dodd
3.	Notre Dame	7-2-1	Frank Leahy
4.	Oklahoma	8-1-1	Bud Wilkinson
5.	USC	9-1-0	Jess Hill
6.	UCLA	8-1-0	Red Sanders
7.	Mississippi	8-0-2	Johnny Vaught
8.	Tennessee	8-1-1	Bob Neyland
9.	Alabama	9-2-0	Red Drew
10.	Texas	8-2-0	Ed Price
11.	Wisconsin	6-2-1	Ivy Williamson
12.	Tulsa	8-1-1	J.O. Brothers
13.	Maryland	7-2-0	Jim Tatum
14.	Syracuse	7-2-0	Ben Schwartzwalder
15.	Florida	7-3-0	Bob Woodruff
16.	Duke	8-2-0	Bill Murray
17.	Ohio St	6-3-0	Woody Hayes
18.	Purdue	4-3-2	Stu Holcomb
19.	Princeton	8-1-0	Charlie Caldwell
20.	Kentucky	5-4-2	Bear Bryant

1953

		Record	Coach
1.	Maryland	10-0-0	Jim Tatum
2.	Notre Dame	9-0-1	Frank Leahy
3.	Michigan St	8-1-0	Biggie Munn
4.	Oklahoma	8-1-1	Bud Wilkinson
5.	UCLA	8-1-0	Red Sanders
6.	Rice	8-2-0	Jess Neely
7.	Illinois	7-1-1	Ray Eliot
8.	Georgia Tech	8-2-1	Bobby Dodd
9.	Iowa	5-3-1	Forest Evashevski
10.	W Virginia	8-1-0	Art Lewis
11.	Texas	7-3-0	Ed Price
12.	Texas Tech	10-1-0	DeWitt Weaver
13.	Alabama	6-2-3	Red Drew
14.	Army	7-1-1	Red Blaik
15.	Wisconsin	6-2-1	Ivy Williamson
16.	Kentucky	7-2-1	Bear Bryant
17.	Auburn	7-2-1	Shug Jordan
18.	Duke	7-2-1	Bill Murray
19.	Stanford	6-3-1	Chuck Taylor
20.	Michigan	6-3-0	Bennie Oosterbaan

1954

		Record	Coach
1.	Ohio St	9-0-0	Woody Hayes
2.	#UCLA	9-0-0	Red Sanders
3.	Oklahoma	10-0-0	Bud Wilkinson
4.	Notre Dame	9-1-0	Terry Brennan
5.	Navy	7-2-0	Eddie Erdelatz
6.	Mississippi	9-1-0	Johnny Vaught
7.	Army	7-2-0	Red Blaik
8.	Maryland	7-2-1	Jim Tatum
9.	Wisconsin	7-2-0	Ivy Williamson
10.	Arkansas	8-2-0	Bowden Wyatt
11.	Miami (Fla.)	8-1-0	Andy Gustafson
12.	W Virginia	8-1-0	Art Lewis
13.	Auburn	7-3-0	Shug Jordan
14.	Duke	7-2-1	Bill Murray
15.	Michigan	6-3-0	Bennie Oosterbaan
16.	Virginia Tech	8-0-1	Frank Moseley
17.	USC	8-3-0	Jess Hill
18.	Baylor	7-3-0	George Sauer
19.	Rice	7-3-0	Jess Neely
20.	Penn St	7-2-0	Rip Engle

#Selected No. 1 by UPI.

1955

		Record	Coach
1.	Oklahoma	10-0-0	Bud Wilkinson
2.	Michigan St	8-1-0	Duffy Daugherty
3.	Maryland	10-0-0	Jim Tatum
4.	UCLA	9-1-0	Red Sanders
5.	Ohio St	7-2-0	Woody Hayes
6.	TCU	9-1-0	Abe Martin
7.	Georgia Tech	8-1-1	Bobby Dodd
8.	Auburn	8-1-1	Shug Jordan
9.	Notre Dame	8-2-0	Terry Brennan
10.	Mississippi	9-1-0	Johnny Vaught
11.	Pittsburgh	7-3-0	John Michelosen
12.	Michigan	7-2-0	Bennie Oosterbaan
13.	USC	6-4-0	Jess Hill
14.	Miami (Fla.)	6-3-0	Andy Gustafson
15.	Miami (Ohio)	9-0-0	Ara Parseghian
16.	Stanford	6-3-1	Chuck Taylor
17.	Texas A&M	7-2-1	Bear Bryant
18.	Navy	6-2-1	Eddie Erdelatz
19.	W Virginia	8-2-0	Art Lewis
20.	Army	6-3-0	Red Blaik

1956

		Record	Coach
1.	Oklahoma	10-0-0	Bud Wilkinson
2.	Tennessee	10-0-0	Bowden Wyatt
3.	Iowa	8-1-0	Forest Evashevski
4.	Georgia Tech	9-1-0	Bobby Dodd
5.	Texas A&M	9-0-1	Bear Bryant
6.	Miami (Fla.)	8-1-1	Andy Gustafson
7.	Michigan	7-2-0	Bennie Oosterbaan
8.	Syracuse	7-1-0	Ben Schwartzwalder
9.	Michigan St	7-2-0	Duffy Daugherty
10.	Oregon St	7-2-1	Tommy Prothro
11.	Baylor	8-2-0	Sam Boyd
12.	Minnesota	6-1-2	Murray Warmath
13.	Pittsburgh	7-2-1	John Michelosen
14.	TCU	7-3-0	Abe Martin
15.	Ohio St	6-3-0	Woody Hayes
16.	Navy	6-1-2	Eddie Erdelatz
17.	Geo Washington	7-1-1	Gene Sherman
18.	USC	8-2-0	Jess Hill
19.	Clemson	7-1-2	Frank Howard
20.	Colorado	7-2-1	Dallas Ward
	Penn St	6-2-1	Rip Engle

1957

		Record	Coach
1.	Auburn	10-0-0	Shug Jordan
2.	#Ohio St	8-1-0	Woody Hayes
3.	Michigan St	8-1-0	Duffy Daugherty
4.	Oklahoma	9-1-0	Bud Wilkinson
5.	Navy	8-1-1	Eddie Erdelatz
6.	Iowa	7-1-1	Forest Evashevski
7.	Mississippi	8-1-1	Johnny Vaught
8.	Rice	7-3-0	Jess Neely
9.	Texas A&M	8-2-0	Bear Bryant
10.	Notre Dame	7-3-0	Terry Brennan
11.	Texas	6-3-1	Darrell Royal
12.	Arizona St	10-0-0	Dan Devine
13.	Tennessee	7-3-0	Bowden Wyatt
14.	Mississippi St	6-2-1	Wade Walker
15.	North Carolina St	7-1-2	Earle Edwards
16.	Duke	6-2-2	Bill Murray
17.	Florida	6-2-1	Bob Woodruff
18.	Army	7-2-0	Red Blaik
19.	Wisconsin	6-3-0	Milt Brunt
20.	VMI	9-0-1	John McKenna

#Selected No. 1 by UPI.

1958

		Record	Coach
1.	LSU	10-0-0	Paul Dietzel
2.	Iowa	7-1-1	Forest Evashevski
3.	Army	8-0-1	Red Blaik
4.	Auburn	9-0-1	Shug Jordan
5.	Oklahoma	9-1-0	Bud Wilkinson
6.	Air Force	9-0-1	Ben Martin
7.	Wisconsin	7-1-1	Milt Bruhn
8.	Ohio St	6-1-2	Woody Hayes
9.	Syracuse	8-1-0	Ben Schwartzwalder
10.	TCU	8-2-0	Abe Martin
11.	Mississippi	8-2-0	Johnny Vaught
12.	Clemson	8-2-0	Frank Howard
13.	Purdue	6-1-2	Jack Mollenkopf
14.	Florida	6-3-1	Bob Woodruff
15.	South Carolina	7-3-0	Warren Giese

1958 *(Cont.)*

		Record	Coach
16.	California	7-3-0	Pete Elliott
17.	Notre Dame	6-4-0	Terry Brennan
18.	SMU	6-4-0	Bill Meek
19.	Oklahoma St	7-3-0	Cliff Speegle
20.	Rutgers	8-1-0	John Stiegman

1959

		Record	Coach
1.	Syracuse	10-0-0	Ben Schwartzwalder
2.	Mississippi	9-1-0	Johnny Vaught
3.	LSU	9-1-0	Paul Dietzel
4.	Texas	9-1-0	Darrell Royal
5.	Georgia	9-1-0	Wally Butts
6.	Wisconsin	7-2-0	Milt Bruhn
7.	TCU	8-2-0	Abe Martin
8.	Washington	9-1-0	Jim Owens
9.	Arkansas	8-2-0	Frank Broyles
10.	Alabama	7-1-2	Bear Bryant
11.	Clemson	8-2-0	Frank Howard
12.	Penn St	8-2-0	Rip Engle
13.	Illinois	5-3-1	Ray Eliot
14.	USC	8-2-0	Don Clark
15.	Oklahoma	7-3-0	Bud Wilkinson
16.	Wyoming	9-1-0	Bob Devaney
17.	Notre Dame	5-5-0	Joe Kuharich
18.	Missouri	6-4-0	Dan Devine
19.	Florida	5-4-1	Bob Woodruff
20.	Pittsburgh	6-4-0	John Michelosen

1960

		Record	Coach
1.	Minnesota	8-1-0	Murray Warmath
2.	Mississippi	9-0-1	Johnny Vaught
3.	Iowa	8-1-0	Forest Evashevski
4.	Navy	9-1-0	Wayne Hardin
5.	Missouri	9-1-0	Dan Devine
6.	Washington	9-1-0	Jim Owens
7.	Arkansas	8-2-0	Frank Broyles
8.	Ohio St	7-2-0	Woody Hayes
9.	Alabama	8-1-1	Bear Bryant
10.	Duke	7-3-0	Bill Murray
11.	Kansas	7-2-1	Jack Mitchell
12.	Baylor	8-2-0	John Bridgers
13.	Auburn	8-2-0	Shug Jordan
14.	Yale	9-0-0	Jordan Oliver
15.	Michigan St	6-2-1	Duffy Daugherty
16.	Penn St	6-3-0	Rip Engle
17.	New Mexico St	10-0-0	Warren Woodson
18.	Florida	8-2-0	Ray Graves
19.	Syracuse	7-2-0	Ben Schwartzwalder
	Purdue	4-4-1	Jack Mollenkopf

1961

		Record	Coach
1.	Alabama	10-0-0	Bear Bryant
2.	Ohio St	8-0-1	Woody Hayes
3.	Texas	9-1-0	Darrell Royal
4.	LSU	9-1-0	Paul Dietzel
5.	Mississippi	9-1-0	Johnny Vaught
6.	Minnesota	7-2-0	Murray Warmath
7.	Colorado	9-1-0	Sonny Grandelius
8.	Michigan St	7-2-0	Duffy Daugherty
9.	Arkansas	8-2-0	Frank Broyles
10.	Utah St	9-0-1	John Ralston
11.	Missouri	7-2-1	Dan Devine
12.	Purdue	6-3-0	Jack Mollenkopf

1961 *(Cont.)*

		Record	Coach
13.	Georgia Tech	7-3-0	Bobby Dodd
14.	Syracuse	7-3-0	Ben Schwartzwalder
15.	Rutgers	9-0-0	John Bateman
16.	UCLA	7-3-0	Bill Barnes
17.	Rice	7-3-0	Jess Neely
	Penn St	7-3-0	Rip Engle
	Arizona	8-1-1	Jim LaRue
20.	Duke	7-3-0	Bill Murray

1962

		Record	Coach
1.	USC	10-0-0	John McKay
2.	Wisconsin	8-1-0	Milt Bruhn
3.	Mississippi	9-0-0	Johnny Vaught
4.	Texas	9-0-1	Darrell Royal
5.	Alabama	9-1-0	Bear Bryant
6.	Arkansas	9-1-0	Frank Broyles
7.	LSU	8-1-1	Charlie McClendon
8.	Oklahoma	8-2-0	Bud Wilkinson
9.	Penn St	9-1-0	Rip Engle
10.	Minnesota	6-2-1	Murray Warmath
11–20: UPI			
11.	Georgia Tech	7-2-1	Bobby Dodd
12.	Missouri	7-1-2	Dan Devine
13.	Ohio St	6-3-0	Woody Hayes
14.	Duke	8-2-0	Bill Murray
	Washington	7-1-2	Jim Owens
16.	Northwestern	7-2-0	Ara Parseghian
	Oregon St	8-2-0	Tommy Prothro
18.	Arizona St	7-2-1	Frank Kush
	Miami (Fla.)	7-3-0	Andy Gustafson
	Illinois	2-7-0	Pete Elliott

1963

		Record	Coach
1.	Texas	10-0-0	Darrell Royal
2.	Navy	9-1-0	Wayne Hardin
3.	Illinois	7-1-1	Pete Elliott
4.	Pittsburgh	9-1-0	John Michelosen
5.	Auburn	9-1-0	Shug Jordan
6.	Nebraska	9-1-0	Bob Devaney
7.	Mississippi	7-0-2	Johnny Vaught
8.	Alabama	8-2-0	Bear Bryant
9.	Oklahoma	8-2-0	Bud Wilkinson
10.	Michigan St	6-2-1	Duffy Daugherty
11–20: UPI			
11.	Mississippi St	6-2-2	Paul Davis
12.	Syracuse	8-2-0	Ben Schwartzwalder
13.	Arizona St	8-1-0	Frank Kush
14.	Memphis St	9-0-1	Billy J. Murphy
15.	Washington	6-4-0	Jim Owens
16.	Penn St	7-3-0	Rip Engle
	USC	7-3-0	John McKay
	Missouri	7-3-0	Dan Devine
19.	North Carolina	8-2-0	Jim Hickey
20.	Baylor	7-3-0	John Bridgers

1964

		Record	Coach
1.	Alabama	10-0-0	Bear Bryant
2.	Arkansas	10-0-0	Frank Broyles
3.	Notre Dame	9-1-0	Ara Parseghian
4.	Michigan	8-1-0	Bump Elliott
5.	Texas	9-1-0	Darrell Royal
6.	Nebraska	9-1-0	Bob Devaney
7.	LSU	7-2-1	Charlie McClendon

1964 *(Cont.)*

		Record	Coach
8.	Oregon St	8-2-0	Tommy Prothro
9.	Ohio St	7-2-0	Woody Hayes
10.	USC	7-3-0	John McKay
11–20: UPI			
11.	Florida St	8-1-1	Bill Peterson
12.	Syracuse	7-3-0	Ben Schwartzwalder
13.	Princeton	9-0-0	Dick Colman
14.	Penn St	6-4-0	Rip Engle
	Utah	8-2-0	Ray Nagel
16.	Illinois	6-3-0	Pete Elliott
	New Mexico	9-2-0	Bill Weeks
18.	Tulsa	8-2-0	Glenn Dobbs
19.	Missouri	6-3-1	Dan Devine
20.	Mississippi	5-4-1	Johnny Vaught
	Michigan St	4-5-1	Duffy Daugherty

1965

		Record	Coach
1.	Alabama	9-1-1	Bear Bryant
2.	#Michigan St	10-1-0	Duffy Daugherty
3.	Arkansas	10-1-0	Frank Broyles
4.	UCLA	8-2-1	Tommy Prothro
5.	Nebraska	10-1-0	Bob Devaney
6.	Missouri	8-2-1	Dan Devine
7.	Tennessee	8-1-2	Doug Dickey
8.	LSU	8-3-0	Charlie McClendon
9.	Notre Dame	7-2-1	Ara Parseghian
10.	USC	7-2-1	John McKay
11–20: UPI			
11.	Texas Tech	8-2-0	J.T. King
12.	Ohio St	7-2-0	Woody Hayes
13.	Florida	7-3-0	Ray Graves
14.	Purdue	7-2-1	Jack Mollenkopf
15.	Georgia	6-4-0	Vince Dooley
16.	Tulsa	8-2-0	Glenn Dobbs
17.	Mississippi	6-4-0	Johnny Vaught
18.	Kentucky	6-4-0	Charlie Bradshaw
19	Syracuse	7-3-0	Ben Schwartzwalder
20.	Colorado	6-2-2	Eddie Crowder

#Selected No. 1 by UPI.

1966

		Record	Coach
1.	Notre Dame	9-0-1	Ara Parseghian
2.	Michigan St	9-0-1	Duffy Daugherty
3.	Alabama	10-0-0	Bear Bryant
4.	Georgia	9-1-0	Vince Dooley
5.	UCLA	9-1-0	Tommy Prothro
6.	Nebraska	9-1-0	Bob Devaney
7.	Purdue	8-2-0	Jack Mollenkopf
8.	Georgia Tech	9-1-0	Bobby Dodd
9.	Miami (Fla.)	7-2-1	Charlie Tate
10.	SMU	8-2-0	Hayden Fry
11–20: UPI			
11.	Florida	8-2-0	Ray Graves
12.	Mississippi	8-2-0	Johnny Vaught
13.	Arkansas	8-2-0	Frank Broyles
14.	Tennessee	7-3-0	Doug Dickey
15.	Wyoming	9-1-0	Lloyd Eaton
16.	Syracuse	8-2-0	Ben Schwartzwalder
17.	Houston	8-2-0	Bill Yeoman
18.	USC	7-3-0	John McKay
19.	Oregon St	7-3-0	Dee Andros
20.	Virginia Tech	8-1-1	Jerry Claiborne

1967

		Record	Coach
1.	USC	9-1-0	John McKay
2.	Tennessee	9-1-0	Doug Dickey
3.	Oklahoma	9-1-0	Chuck Fairbanks
4.	Indiana	9-1-0	John Pont
5.	Notre Dame	8-2-0	Ara Parseghian
6.	Wyoming	10-0-0	Lloyd Eaton
7.	Oregon St	7-2-1	Dee Andros
8.	Alabama	8-1-1	Bear Bryant
9.	Purdue	8-2-0	Jack Mollenkopf
10.	Penn St	8-2-0	Joe Paterno
11–20: UPI†			
11.	UCLA	7-2-1	Tommy Prothro
12.	Syracuse	8-2-0	Ben Schwartzwalder
13.	Colorado	8-2-0	Eddie Crowder
14.	Minnesota	8-2-0	Murray Warmath
15.	Florida St	7-2-1	Bill Peterson
16.	Miami (Fla.)	7-3-0	Charlie Tate
17.	North Carolina St	8-2-0	Earle Edwards
18.	Georgia	7-3-0	Vince Dooley
19.	Houston	9-2-0	Bill Yeoman
20.	Arizona St	8-2-0	Frank Kush

†UPI ranked Penn St 11th and did not rank Alabama, which was on probation.

1968

		Record	Coach
1.	Ohio St	10-0-0	Woody Hayes
2.	Penn St	11-0-0	Joe Paterno
3.	Texas	9-1-1	Darrell Royal
4.	USC	9-1-1	John McKay
5.	Notre Dame	7-2-1	Ara Parseghian
6.	Arkansas	10-1-0	Frank Broyles
7.	Kansas	9-2-0	Pepper Rodgers
8.	Georgia	8-1-2	Vince Dooley
9.	Missouri	8-3-0	Dan Devine
10.	Purdue	8-2-0	Jack Mollenkopf
11.	Oklahoma	7-4-0	Chuck Fairbanks
12.	Michigan	8-2-0	Bump Elliott
13.	Tennessee	8-2-1	Doug Dickey
14.	SMU	8-3-0	Hayden Fry
15.	Oregon St	7-3-0	Dee Andros
16.	Auburn	7-4-0	Shug Jordan
17.	Alabama	8-3-0	Bear Bryant
18.	Houston	6-2-2	Bill Yeoman
19.	LSU	8-3-0	Charlie McClendon
20.	Ohio	10-1-0	Bill Hess

1969

		Record	Coach
1.	Texas	11-0-0	Darrell Royal
2.	Penn St	11-0-0	Joe Paterno
3.	USC	10-0-1	John McKay
4.	Ohio St	8-1-0	Woody Hayes
5.	Notre Dame	8-2-1	Ara Parseghian
6.	Missouri	9-2-0	Dan Devine
7.	Arkansas	9-2-0	Frank Broyles
8.	Mississippi	8-3-0	Johnny Vaught
9.	Michigan	8-3-0	Bo Schembechler
10.	LSU	9-1-0	Charlie McClendon
11.	Nebraska	9-2-0	Bob Devaney
12.	Houston	9-2-0	Bill Yeoman
13.	UCLA	8-1-1	Tommy Prothro
14.	Florida	9-1-1	Ray Graves
15.	Tennessee	9-2-0	Doug Dickey
16.	Colorado	8-3-0	Eddie Crowder

1969 (Cont.)

		Record	Coach
17.	W Virginia	10-0-1	Jim Carlen
18.	Purdue	8-2-0	Jack Mollenkopf
19.	Stanford	7-2-1	John Ralston
20.	Auburn	8-3-0	Shug Jordan

1970

		Record	Coach
1.	Nebraska	11-0-1	Bob Devaney
2.	Notre Dame	10-1-0	Ara Parseghian
3.	#Texas	10-1-0	Darrell Royal
4.	Tennessee	11-0-1	Bill Battle
5.	Ohio St	9-1-0	Woody Hayes
6.	Arizona St	11-0-0	Frank Kush
7.	LSU	9-3-0	Charlie McClendon
8.	Stanford	9-3-0	John Ralston
9.	Michigan	9-1-0	Bo Schembechler
10.	Auburn	9-2-0	Shug Jordan
11.	Arkansas	9-2-0	Frank Broyles
12.	Toledo	12-0-0	Frank Lauterbur
13.	Georgia Tech	9-3-0	Bud Carson
14.	Dartmouth	9-0-0	Bob Blackman
15.	USC	6-4-1	John McKay
16.	Air Force	9-3-0	Ben Martin
17.	Tulane	8-4-0	Jim Pittman
18.	Penn St	7-3-0	Joe Paterno
19.	Houston	8-3-0	Bill Yeoman
20.	Oklahoma	7-4-1	Chuck Fairbanks
	Mississippi	7-4-0	Johnny Vaught

#Selected No. 1 by UPI.

1971

		Record	Coach
1.	Nebraska	13-0-0	Bob Devaney
2.	Oklahoma	11-1-0	Chuck Fairbanks
3.	Colorado	10-2-0	Eddie Crowder
4.	Alabama	11-1-0	Bear Bryant
5.	Penn St	11-1-0	Joe Paterno
6.	Michigan	11-1-0	Bo Schembechler
7.	Georgia	11-1-0	Vince Dooley
8.	Arizona St	11-1-0	Frank Kush
9.	Tennessee	10-2-0	Bill Battle
10.	Stanford	9-3-0	John Ralston
11.	LSU	9-3-0	Charlie McClendon
12.	Auburn	9-2-0	Shug Jordan
13.	Notre Dame	8-2-0	Ara Parseghian
14.	Toledo	12-0-0	John Murphy
15.	Mississippi	10-2-0	Billy Kinard
16.	Arkansas	8-3-1	Frank Broyles
17.	Houston	9-3-0	Bill Yeoman
18.	Texas	8-3-0	Darrell Royal
19.	Washington	8-3-0	Jim Owens
20.	USC	6-4-1	John McKay

1972

		Record	Coach
1.	USC	12-0-0	John McKay
2.	Oklahoma	11-1-0	Chuck Fairbanks
3.	Texas	10-1-0	Darrell Royal
4.	Nebraska	9-2-1	Bob Devaney
5.	Auburn	10-1-0	Shug Jordan
6.	Michigan	10-1-0	Bo Schembechler
7.	Alabama	10-2-0	Bear Bryant
8.	Tennessee	10-2-0	Bill Battle
9.	Ohio St	9-2-0	Woody Hayes
10.	Penn St	10-2-0	Joe Paterno

1972 (Cont.)

		Record	Coach
11.	LSU	9-2-1	Charlie McClendon
12.	North Carolina	11-1-0	Bill Dooley
13.	Arizona St	10-2-0	Frank Kush
14.	Notre Dame	8-3-0	Ara Parseghian
15.	UCLA	8-3-0	Pepper Rodgers
16.	Colorado	8-4-0	Eddie Crowder
17.	North Carolina St	8-3-1	Lou Holtz
18.	Louisville	9-1-0	Lee Corso
19.	Washington St	7-4-0	Jim Sweeney
20.	Georgia Tech	7-4-1	Bill Fulch

1973

		Record	Coach
1.	Notre Dame	11-0-0	Ara Parseghian
2.	Ohio St	10-0-1	Woody Hayes
3.	Oklahoma	10-0-1	Barry Switzer
4.	#Alabama	11-1-0	Bear Bryant
5.	Penn St	12-0-0	Joe Paterno
6.	Michigan	10-0-1	Bo Schembechler
7.	Nebraska	9-2-1	Tom Osborne
8.	USC	9-2-1	John McKay
9.	Arizona St	11-1-0	Frank Kush
	Houston	11-1-0	Bill Yeoman
11.	Texas Tech	11-1-0	Jim Carlen
12.	UCLA	9-2-0	Pepper Rodgers
13.	LSU	9-3-0	Charlie McClendon
14.	Texas	8-3-0	Darrell Royal
15.	Miami (Ohio)	11-0-0	Bill Mallory
16.	North Carolina St	9-3-0	Lou Holtz
17.	Missouri	8-4-0	Al Onofrio
18.	Kansas	7-4-1	Don Fambrough
19.	Tennessee	8-4-0	Bill Battle
20.	Maryland	8-4-0	Jerry Claiborne
	Tulane	9-3-0	Bennie Ellender

#Selected No. 1 by UPI.

1974

		Record	Coach
1.	Oklahoma	11-0-0	Barry Switzer
2.	#USC	10-1-1	John McKay
3.	Michigan	10-1-0	Bo Schembechler
4.	Ohio St	10-2-0	Woody Hayes
5.	Alabama	11-1-0	Bear Bryant
6.	Notre Dame	10-2-0	Ara Parseghian
7.	Penn St	10-2-0	Joe Paterno
8.	Auburn	10-2-0	Shug Jordan
9.	Nebraska	9-3-0	Tom Osborne
10.	Miami (Ohio)	10-0-1	Dick Crum
11.	North Carolina St	9-2-1	Lou Holtz
12.	Michigan St	7-3-1	Denny Stolz
13.	Maryland	8-4-0	Jerry Claiborne
14.	Baylor	8-4-0	Grant Teaff
15.	Florida	8-4-0	Doug Dickey
16.	Texas A&M	8-3-0	Emory Ballard
17.	Mississippi St	9-3-0	Bob Tyler
	Texas	8-4-0	Darrell Royal
19.	Houston	8-3-1	Bill Yeoman
20.	Tennessee	7-3-2	Bill Battle

#Selected No. 1 by UPI

1975

		Record	Coach
1.	Oklahoma	11-1-0	Barry Switzer
2.	Arizona St	12-0-0	Frank Kush
3.	Alabama	11-1-0	Bear Bryant
4.	Ohio St	11-1-0	Woody Hayes

1975 *(Cont.)*

		Record	Coach
5.	UCLA	9-2-1	Dick Vermeil
6.	Texas	10-2-0	Darrell Royal
7.	Arkansas	10-2-0	Frank Broyles
8.	Michigan	8-2-2	Bo Schembechler
9.	Nebraska	10-2-0	Tom Osborne
10.	Penn St	9-3-0	Joe Paterno
11.	Texas A&M	10-2-0	Emory Bellard
12.	Miami (Ohio)	11-1-0	Dick Crum
13.	Maryland	9-2-1	Jerry Claiborne
14.	California	8-3-0	Mike White
15.	Pittsburgh	8-4-0	Johnny Majors
16.	Colorado	9-3-0	Bill Mallory
17.	USC	8-4-0	John McKay
18.	Arizona	9-2-0	Jim Young
19.	Georgia	9-3-1	Vince Dooley
20.	W Virginia	9-3-0	Bobby Bowden

1976

		Record	Coach
1.	Pittsburgh	12-0-0	Johnny Majors
2.	USC	11-1-0	John Robinson
3.	Michigan	10-2-0	Bo Schembechler
4.	Houston	10-2-0	Bill Yeoman
5.	Oklahoma	9-2-1	Barry Switzer
6.	Ohio St	9-2-1	Woody Hayes
7.	Texas A&M	10-2-0	Emory Bellard
8.	Maryland	11-1-0	Jerry Claiborne
9.	Nebraska	9-3-1	Tom Osborne
10.	Georgia	10-2-0	Vince Dooley
11.	Alabama	9-3-0	Bear Bryant
12.	Notre Dame	9-3-0	Dan Devine
13.	Texas Tech	10-2-0	Steve Sloan
14.	Oklahoma St	9-3-0	Jim Stanley
15.	UCLA	9-2-1	Terry Donahue
16.	Colorado	8-4-0	Bill Mallory
17.	Rutgers	11-0-0	Frank Burns
18.	Kentucky	9-3-0	Fran Curci
19.	Iowa St	8-3-0	Earle Bruce
20.	Mississippi St	9-2-0	Bob Tyler

1977

		Record	Coach
1.	Notre Dame	11-1-0	Dan Devine
2.	Alabama	11-1-0	Bear Bryant
3.	Arkansas	11-1-0	Lou Holtz
4.	Texas	11-1-0	Fred Akers
5.	Penn St	11-1-0	Joe Paterno
6.	Kentucky	10-1-0	Fran Curci
7.	Oklahoma	10-2-0	Barry Switzer
8.	Pittsburgh	9-2-1	Jackie Sherrill
9.	Michigan	10-2-0	Bo Schembechler
10.	Washington	10-2-0	Don James
11.	Ohio St	9-3-0	Woody Hayes
12.	Nebraska	9-3-0	Tom Osborne
13.	USC	8-4-0	John Robinson
14.	Florida St	10-2-0	Bobby Bowden
15.	Stanford	9-3-0	Bill Walsh
16.	San Diego St	10-1-0	Claude Gilbert
17.	North Carolina	8-3-1	Bill Dooley
18.	Arizona St	9-3-0	Frank Kush
19.	Clemson	8-3-1	Charley Pell
20.	BYU	9-2-0	LaVell Edwards

1978

		Record	Coach
1.	Alabama	11-1-0	Bear Bryant
2.	#USC	12-1-0	John Robinson
3.	Oklahoma	11-1-0	Barry Switzer

1978 *(Cont.)*

		Record	Coach
4.	Penn St	11-1-0	Joe Paterno
5.	Michigan	10-2-0	Bo Schembechler
6.	Clemson	11-1-0	Charley Pell
7.	Notre Dame	9-3-0	Dan Devine
8.	Nebraska	9-3-0	Tom Osborne
9.	Texas	9-3-0	Fred Akers
10.	Houston	9-3-0	Bill Yeoman
11.	Arkansas	9-2-1	Lou Holtz
12.	Michigan St	8-3-0	Darryl Rogers
13.	Purdue	9-2-1	Jim Young
14.	UCLA	8-3-1	Terry Donahue
15.	Missouri	8-4-0	Warren Powers
16.	Georgia	9-2-1	Vince Dooley
17.	Stanford	8-4-0	Bill Walsh
18.	North Carolina St	9-3-0	Bo Rein
19.	Texas A&M	8-4-0	Emory Bellard/ Tom Wilson
20.	Maryland	9-3-0	Jerry Claiborne

#Selected No. 1 by UPI.

1979

		Record	Coach
1.	Alabama	12-0-0	Bear Bryant
2.	USC	11-0-1	John Robinson
3.	Oklahoma	11-1-0	Barry Switzer
4.	Ohio St	11-1-0	Earle Bruce
5.	Houston	11-1-0	Bill Yeoman
6.	Florida St	11-1-0	Bobby Bowden
7.	Pittsburgh	11-1-0	Jackie Sherrill
8.	Arkansas	10-2-0	Lou Holtz
9.	Nebraska	10-2-0	Tom Osborne
10.	Purdue	10-2-0	Jim Young
11.	Washington	10-1-0	Don James
12.	Texas	9-3-0	Fred Akers
13.	BYU	11-1-0	LaVell Edwards
14.	Baylor	8-4-0	Grant Teaff
15.	North Carolina	8-3-1	Dick Crum
16.	Auburn	8-3-0	Doug Barfield
17.	Temple	10-2-0	Wayne Hardin
18.	Michigan	8-4-0	Bo Schembechler
19.	Indiana	8-4-0	Lee Corso
20.	Penn St	8-4-0	Joe Paterno

1980

		Record	Coach
1.	Georgia	12-0-0	Vince Dooley
2.	Pittsburgh	11-1-0	Jackie Sherrill
3.	Oklahoma	10-2-0	Barry Switzer
4.	Michigan	10-2-0	Bo Schembechler
5.	Florida St	10-2-0	Bobby Bowden
6.	Alabama	10-2-0	Bear Bryant
7.	Nebraska	10-2-0	Tom Osborne
8.	Penn St	10-2-0	Joe Paterno
9.	Notre Dame	9-2-1	Dan Devine
10.	North Carolina	11-1-0	Dick Crum
11.	USC	8-2-1	John Robinson
12.	BYU	12-1-0	LaVell Edwards
13.	UCLA	9-2-0	Terry Donahue
14.	Baylor	10-2-0	Grant Teaff
15.	Ohio St	9-3-0	Earle Bruce
16.	Washington	9-3-0	Don James
17.	Purdue	9-3-0	Jim Young
18.	Miami (Fla.)	9-3-0	H. Schnellenberger
19.	Mississippi St	9-3-0	Emory Bellard
20.	SMU	8-4-0	Ron Meyer

1981

		Record	Coach
1.	Clemson	12-0-0	Danny Ford
2.	Texas	10-1-1	Fred Akers
3.	Penn St	10-2-0	Joe Paterno
4.	Pittsburgh	11-1-0	Jackie Sherrill
5.	SMU	10-1-0	Ron Meyer
6.	Georgia	10-2-0	Vince Dooley
7.	Alabama	9-2-1	Bear Bryant
8.	Miami (Fla.)	9-2-0	H. Schnellenberger
9.	North Carolina	10-2-0	Dick Crum
10.	Washington	10-2-0	Don James
11.	Nebraska	9-3-0	Tom Osborne
12.	Michigan	9-3-0	Bo Schembechler
13.	BYU	11-2-0	LaVell Edwards
14.	USC	9-3-0	John Robinson
15.	Ohio St	9-3-0	Earle Bruce
16.	Arizona St	9-2-0	Darryl Rogers
17.	W Virginia	9-3-0	Don Nehlen
18.	Iowa	8-4-0	Hayden Fry
19.	Missouri	8-4-0	Warren Powers
20.	Oklahoma	7-4-1	Barry Switzer

1982

		Record	Coach
1.	Penn St	11-1-0	Joe Paterno
2.	SMU	11-0-1	Bobby Collins
3.	Nebraska	12-1-0	Tom Osborne
4.	Georgia	11-1-0	Vince Dooley
5.	UCLA	10-1-1	Terry Donahue
6.	Arizona St	10-2-0	Darryl Rogers
7.	Washington	10-2-0	Don James
8.	Clemson	9-1-1	Danny Ford
9.	Arkansas	9-2-1	Lou Holtz
10.	Pittsburgh	9-3-0	Foge Fazio
11.	LSU	8-3-1	Jerry Stovall
12.	Ohio St	9-3-0	Earle Bruce
13.	Florida St	9-3-0	Bobby Bowden
14.	Auburn	9-3-0	Pat Dye
15.	USC	8-3-0	John Robinson
16.	Oklahoma	8-4-0	Barry Switzer
17.	Texas	9-3-0	Fred Akers
18.	North Carolina	8-4-0	Dick Crum
19.	W Virginia	9-3-0	Don Nehlen
20.	Maryland	8-4-0	Bobby Ross

1983

		Record	Coach
1.	Miami (Fla.)	11-1-0	H. Schnellenberger
2.	Nebraska	12-1-0	Tom Osborne
3.	Auburn	11-1-0	Pat Dye
4.	Georgia	10-1-1	Vince Dooley
5.	Texas	11-1-0	Fred Akers
6.	Florida	9-2-1	Charlie Pell
7.	BYU	11-1-0	LaVell Edwards
8.	Michigan	9-3-0	Bo Schembechler
9.	Ohio St	9-3-0	Earle Bruce
10.	Illinois	10-2-0	Mike White
11.	Clemson	9-1-1	Danny Ford
12.	SMU	10-2-0	Bobby Collins
13.	Air Force	10-2-0	Ken Hatfield
14.	Iowa	9-3-0	Hayden Fry
15.	Alabama	8-4-0	Ray Perkins
16.	W Virginia	9-3-0	Don Nehlen
17.	UCLA	7-4-1	Terry Donahue
18.	Pittsburgh	8-3-1	Foge Fazio
19.	Boston College	9-3-0	Jack Bicknell
20.	E Carolina	8-3-0	Ed Emory

1984

		Record	Coach
1.	BYU	13-0-0	LaVell Edwards
2.	Washington	11-1-0	Don James
3.	Florida	9-1-1	Chas Pell (0-1-1)
			Galen Hall (9-0)
4.	Nebraska	10-2-0	Tom Osborne
5.	Boston College	10-2-0	Jack Bicknell
6.	Oklahoma	9-2-1	Barry Switzer
7.	Oklahoma St	10-2-0	Pat Jones
8.	SMU	10-2-0	Bobby Collins
9.	UCLA	9-3-0	Terry Donahue
10.	USC	10-3-0	Ted Tollner
11.	South Carolina	10-2-0	Joe Morrison
12.	Maryland	9-3-0	Bobby Ross
13.	Ohio St	9-3-0	Earle Bruce
14.	Auburn	9-4-0	Pat Dye
15.	LSU	8-3-1	Bill Arnsparger
16.	Iowa	8-4-1	Hayden Fry
17.	Florida St	7-3-2	Bobby Bowden
18.	Miami (Fla.)	8-5-0	Jimmy Johnson
19.	Kentucky	9-3-0	Jerry Claiborne
20.	Virginia	8-2-2	George Welsh

1985

		Record	Coach
1.	Oklahoma	11-1-0	Barry Switzer
2.	Michigan	10-1-1	Bo Schembechler
3.	Penn St	11-1-0	Joe Paterno
4.	Tennessee	9-1-2	Johnny Majors
5.	Florida	9-1-1	Galen Hall
6.	Texas A&M	10-2-0	Jackie Sherrill
7.	UCLA	9-2-1	Terry Donahue
8.	Air Force	12-1-0	Fisher DeBerry
9.	Miami (Fla.)	10-2-0	Jimmy Johnson
10.	Iowa	10-2-0	Hayden Fry
11.	Nebraska	9-3-0	Tom Osborne
12.	Arkansas	10-2-0	Ken Hatfield
13.	Alabama	9-2-1	Ray Perkins
14.	Ohio St	9-3-0	Earle Bruce
15.	Florida St	9-3-0	Bobby Bowden
16.	BYU	11-3-0	LaVell Edwards
17.	Baylor	9-3-0	Grant Teaff
18.	Maryland	9-3-0	Bobby Ross
19.	Georgia Tech	9-2-1	Bill Curry
20.	LSU	9-2-1	Bill Arnsparger

1986

		Record	Coach
1.	Penn St	12-0-0	Joe Paterno
2.	Miami (Fla.)	11-1-0	Jimmy Johnson
3.	Oklahoma	11-1-0	Barry Switzer
4.	Arizona St	10-1-1	John Cooper
5.	Nebraska	10-2-0	Tom Osborne
6.	Auburn	10-2-0	Pat Dye
7.	Ohio St	10-3-0	Earle Bruce
8.	Michigan	11-2-0	Bo Schembechler
9.	Alabama	10-3-0	Ray Perkins
10.	LSU	9-3-0	Bill Arnsparger
11.	Arizona	9-3-0	Larry Smith
12.	Baylor	9-3-0	Grant Teaff
13.	Texas A&M	9-3-0	Jackie Sherrill
14.	UCLA	8-3-1	Terry Donahue
15.	Arkansas	9-3-0	Ken Hatfield
16.	Iowa	9-3-0	Hayden Fry
17.	Clemson	8-2-2	Danny Ford
18.	Washington	8-3-1	Don James
19.	Boston College	9-3-0	Jack Bicknell
20.	Virginia Tech	9-2-1	Bill Dooley

1987

		Record	Coach
1.	Miami (Fla.)	12-0-0	Jimmy Johnson
2.	Florida St.	11-1-0	Bobby Bowden
3.	Oklahoma	11-1-0	Barry Switzer
4.	Syracuse	11-0-1	Dick MacPherson
5.	LSU	10-1-1	Mike Archer
6.	Nebraska	10-2-0	Tom Osborne
7.	Auburn	9-1-2	Pat Dye
8.	Michigan St.	9-2-1	George Perles
9.	UCLA	10-2-0	Terry Donahue
10.	Texas A&M	10-2-0	Jackie Sherrill
11.	Oklahoma St.	10-2-0	Pat Jones
12.	Clemson	10-2-0	Danny Ford
13.	Georgia	9-3-0	Vince Dooley
14.	Tennessee	10-2-1	Johnny Majors
15.	South Carolina	8-4-0	Joe Morrison
16.	Iowa	10-3-0	Hayden Fry
17.	Notre Dame	8-4-0	Lou Holtz
18.	USC	8-4-0	Larry Smith
19.	Michigan	8-4-0	Bo Schembechler
20.	Arizona St	7-4-1	John Cooper

1988

		Record	Coach
1.	Notre Dame	12-0-0	Lou Holtz
2.	Miami (Fla.)	11-1-0	Jimmy Johnson
3.	Florida St.	11-1-0	Bobby Bowden
4.	Michigan	9-2-1	Bo Schembechler
5.	West Virginia	11-1-0	Don Nehlen
6.	UCLA	10-2-0	Terry Donahue
7.	USC	10-2-0	Larry Smith
8.	Auburn	10-2-0	Pat Dye
9.	Clemson	10-2-0	Danny Ford
10.	Nebraska	11-2-0	Tom Osborne
11.	Oklahoma St.	10-2-0	Pat Jones
12.	Arkansas	10-2-0	Ken Hatfield
13.	Syracuse	10-2-0	Dick MacPherson
14.	Oklahoma	9-3-0	Barry Switzer
15.	Georgia	9-3-0	Vince Dooley
16.	Washington St.	9-3-0	Dennis Erickson
17.	Alabama	9-3-0	Bill Curry
18.	Houston	9-3-0	Jack Pardee
19.	LSU	8-4-0	Mike Archer
20.	Indiana	8-3-1	Bill Mallor

†1989

		Record	Coach
1.	Miami (Fla.)	11-1-0	Dennis Erickson
2.	Notre Dame	12-1-0	Lou Holtz
3.	Florida St.	10-2-0	Bobby Bowden
4.	Colorado	11-1-0	Bill McCartney
5.	Tennessee	11-1-0	Johnny Majors
6.	Auburn	10-2-0	Pat Dye
7.	Michigan	10-2-0	Bo Schembechler
8.	USC	9-2-1	Larry Smith
9.	Alabama	10-2-0	Bill Curry
10.	Illinois	10-2-0	John Mackovic
11.	Nebraska	10-2-0	Tom Osborne
12.	Clemson	10-2-0	Danny Ford
13.	Arkansas	10-2-0	Ken Hatfield
14.	Houston	9-2-0	Jack Pardee
15.	Penn St	8-3-1	Joe Paterno
16.	Michigan St.	8-4-0	George Perles
17.	Pittsburgh	8-3-1	Mike Gottfried
18.	Virginia	10-3-0	George Welsh
19.	Texas Tech	9-3-0	Spike Dykes

†In 1989 the AP expanded its final poll to 25 teams.

1989 *(Cont.)*

		Record	Coach
20.	Texas A&M	8-4-0	R.C. Slocum
21.	W Virginia	8-3-1	Don Nehlen
22.	BYU	10-3-0	LaVell Edwards
23.	Washington	8-4-0	Don James
24.	Ohio St	8-4-0	John Cooper
25.	Arizona	8-4-0	Dick Tomey

1990

		Record	Coach
1.	Colorado	11-1-1	Bill McCartney
2.	#Ga. Tech	11-0-1	Bobby Ross
3.	Miami (Fla.)	10-2-0	Dennis Erickson
4.	Florida St.	10-2-0	Bobby Bowden
5.	Washington	10-2-0	Don James
6.	Notre Dame	9-3-0	Lou Holtz
7.	Michigan	9-3-0	Gary Moeller
8.	Tennessee	9-2-2	Johnny Majors
9.	Clemson	10-2-0	Ken Hatfield
10.	Houston	10-1-0	John Jenkins
11.	Penn St	9-3-0	Joe Paterno
12.	Texas	10-2-0	David McWilliams
13.	Florida	9-2-0	Steve Spurrier
14.	Louisville	10-1-1	H. Schnellenberger
15.	Texas A&M	9-3-1	R.C. Slocum
16.	Michigan St.	8-3-1	George Perles
17.	Oklahoma	8-3-0	Gary Gibbs
18.	Iowa	8-4-0	Hayden Fry
19.	Auburn	8-3-1	Pat Dye
20.	USC	8-4-1	Larry Smith
21.	Mississippi	9-3-0	Billy Brewer
22.	BYU	10-3-0	LaVell Edwards
23.	Virginia	8-4-0	George Wells
24.	Nebraska	9-3-0	Tom Osborne
25.	Illinois	8-4-0	John Mackovic

#Selected No. 1 by *UPI*.

1991

		Record	Coach
1.	Miami (Fla.)	12-0-0	Dennis Erickson
2.	#Washington	12-0-0	Don James
3.	Penn St	11-2-0	Joe Paterno
4.	Florida St.	11-2-0	Bobby Bowden
5.	Alabama	11-1-0	Gene Stallings
6.	Michigan	10-2-0	Gary Moeller
7.	Florida	10-2-0	Steve Spurrier
8.	California	10-2-0	Bruce Snyder
9.	E Carolina	11-1-0	Bill Lewis
10.	Iowa	10-1-1	Hayden Fry
11.	Syracuse	10-2-0	Paul Pasqualoni
12.	Texas A&M	10-2-0	R.C. Slocum
13.	Notre Dame	10-3-0	Lou Holtz
14.	Tennessee	9-3-0	Johnny Majors
15.	Nebraska	9-2-1	Tom Osborne
16.	Oklahoma	9-3-0	Gary Gibbs
17.	Georgia	9-3-0	Ray Goff
18.	Clemson	9-2-1	Ken Hatfield
19.	UCLA	9-3-0	Terry Donahue
20.	Colorado	8-3-1	Bill McCartney
21.	Tulsa	10-2-0	David Rader
22.	Stanford	8-4-0	Dennis Green
23.	BYU	8-3-2	LaVell Edwards
24.	North Carolina St	9-3-0	Dick Sheridan
25.	Air Force	10-3-0	Fisher DeBerry

#Selected No. 1 by *USA Today*/CNN.

1992

		Record	Coach
1.	Alabama	13-0-0	Gene Stallings
2.	Florida St	11-1-0	Bobby Bowden
3.	Miami (Fla.)	11-1-0	Dennis Erickson
4.	Notre Dame	10-1-1	Lou Holtz
5.	Michigan	9-0-3	Gary Moeller
6.	Syracuse	10-2-0	Paul Pasqualoni
7.	Texas A&M	12-1-0	R.C. Slocum
8.	Georgia	10-2-0	Ray Goff
9.	Stanford	10-3-0	Bill Walsh
10.	Florida	9-4-0	Steve Spurrier
11.	Washington	9-3-0	Don James
12.	Tennessee	9-3-0	Johnny Majors
13.	Colorado	9-2-1	Bill McCartney
14.	Nebraska	9-3-0	Tom Osborne
15.	Washington St	9-3-0	Mike Price
16.	Mississippi	9-3-0	Billy Brewer
17.	North Carolina St	9-3-1	Dick Sheridan
18.	Ohio St	8-3-1	John Cooper
19.	North Carolina	9-3-0	Mack Brown
20.	Hawaii	11-2-0	Bob Wagner
21.	Boston College	8-3-1	Tom Coughlin
22.	Kansas	8-4-0	Glen Mason
23.	Mississippi St	7-5-0	Jackie Sherrill
24.	Fresno St	9-4-0	Jim Sweeney
25.	Wake Forest	8-4-0	Bill Dooley

1993

		Record	Coach
1.	Florida St	12-1-0	Bobby Bowden
2.	Notre Dame	11-1-0	Lou Holtz
3.	Nebraska	11-1-0	Tom Osborne
4.	Auburn	11-0-0	Terry Bowden
5.	Florida	11-2-0	Steve Spurrier
6.	Wisconsin	10-1-1	Barry Alvarez
7.	W Virginia	11-1-0	Don Nehlen
8.	Penn St	10-2-0	Joe Paterno
9.	Texas A&M	10-2-0	R.C. Slocum
10.	Arizona	10-2-0	Dick Tomey
11.	Ohio St	10-1-1	John Cooper
12.	Tennessee	9-2-1	Phil Fulmer
13.	Boston College	9-3-0	Tom Coughlin
14.	Alabama	9-3-1	Gene Stallings
15.	Miami (Fla.)	9-3-0	Dennis Erickson
16.	Colorado	8-3-1	Bill McCartney
17.	Oklahoma	9-3-0	Gary Gibbs
18.	UCLA	8-4-0	Terry Donahue
19.	North Carolina	10-3-0	Mack Brown
20.	Kansas St	9-2-1	Bill Snyder
21.	Michigan	8-4-0	Gary Moeller
22.	Virginia Tech	9-3-0	Frank Beamer
23.	Clemson	9-3-0	Ken Hatfield
24.	Louisville	9-3-0	H. Schnellenberger
25.	California	9-4-0	Keith Gilbertson

1994

		Record	Coach
1.	Nebraska	13-0-0	Tom Osborne
2.	Penn St	12-0-0	Joe Paterno
3.	Colorado	11-1-0	Bill McCartney
4.	Florida St	10-1-1	Bobby Bowden
5.	Alabama	12-1-0	Gene Stallings
6.	Miami (Fla.)	10-2-0	Dennis Erickson
7.	Florida	10-2-0	Steve Spurrier
8.	Texas A&M	10-0-1	R.C. Slocum
9.	Auburn	9-1-1	Terry Bowden

1994 *(Cont.)*

		Record	Coach
10.	Utah	10-2-0	Ron McBride
11.	Oregon	9-4-0	Rich Brooks
12.	Michigan	8-4-0	Gary Moeller
13.	USC	8-3-1	John Robinson
14.	Ohio St	9-4-0	John Cooper
15.	Virginia	9-3-0	George Welsh
16.	Colorado St	10-2-0	Sonny Lubick
17.	North Carolina St	9-3-0	Mike O'Cain
18.	BYU	10-3-0	LaVell Edwards
19.	Kansas St	9-3-0	Bill Snyder
20.	Arizona	8-4-0	Dick Tomey
21.	Washington St	8-4-0	Mike Price
22.	Tennessee	8-4-0	Phillip Fulmer
23.	Boston College	7-4-1	Dan Henning
24.	Mississippi St	8-4-0	Jackie Sherrill
25.	Texas	8-4-0	John Mackovic

1995

		Record	Coach
1.	Nebraska	12-0-0	Tom Osborne
2.	Florida	12-1-0	Steve Spurrier
3.	Tennessee	11-1-0	Phillip Fulmer
4.	Florida St	10-2-0	Bobby Bowden
5.	Colorado	10-2-0	Rick Neuheisel
6.	Ohio St	11-2-0	John Cooper
7.	Kansas St	10-2-0	Bill Snyder
8.	Northwestern	10-2-0	Gary Barnett
9.	Kansas	10-2-0	Glen Mason
10.	Virginia Tech	10-2-0	Frank Beamer
11.	Notre Dame	9-3-0	Lou Holtz
12.	USC	9-2-1	John Robinson
13.	Penn St	9-3-0	Joe Paterno
14.	Texas	10-2-1	John Mackovic
15.	Texas A&M	9-3-0	R.C. Slocum
16.	Virginia	9-4-0	George Welsh
17.	Michigan	9-4-0	Lloyd Carr
18.	Oregon	9-3-0	Mike Bellotti
19.	Syracuse	9-3-0	Paul Pasqualoni
20.	Miami (Fla.)	8-3-0	Butch Davis
21.	Alabama	8-3-0	Gene Stallings
22.	Auburn	8-4-0	Terry Bowden
23.	Texas Tech	9-3-0	Spike Dykes
24.	Toledo	11-0-1	Gary Pinkel
25.	Iowa	8-4-0	Hayden Fry

*1996

		Record	Coach
1.	Florida	12-1	Steve Spurrier
2.	Ohio St	11-1	John Cooper
3.	Florida St	11-1	Bobby Bowden
4.	Arizona St	11-1	Bruce Snyder
5.	BYU	14-1	LaVell Edwards
6.	Nebraska	11-2	Tom Osborne
7.	Penn St	11-2	Joe Paterno
8.	Colorado	10-2	Rick Neuheisel
9.	Tennessee	10-2	Phillip Fulmer
10.	North Carolina	10-2	Mack Brown
11.	Alabama	10-3	Gene Stallings
12.	LSU	10-2	Gerry DiNardo
13.	Virginia Tech	10-2	Frank Beamer
14.	Miami (Fla.)	9-3	Butch Davis
15.	Northwestern	9-3	Gary Barnett
16.	Washington	9-3	Jim Lambright
17.	Kansas St	9-3	Bill Snyder
18.	Iowa	9-3	Hayden Fry

†In 1989 the AP expanded its final poll to 25 teams.

*In 1996 the NCAA introduced overtime to break ties.

1996 *(Cont.)*

		Record	Coach
19.	Notre Dame	8–3	Lou Holtz
20.	Michigan	8–4	Lloyd Carr
21.	Syracuse	9–3	Paul Pasqualoni
22.	Wyoming	10–2	Joe Tiller
23.	Texas	8–5	John Mackovic
24.	Auburn	8–4	Terry Bowden
25.	Army	10–2	Bob Sutton

1997

		Record	Coach
1.	Michigan	12–0	Lloyd Carr
#2.	Nebraska	13–0	Tom Osborne
3.	Florida St	11–1	Bobby Bowden
4.	Florida	10–2	Steve Spurrier
5.	UCLA	10–2	Bob Toledo
6.	North Carolina	11–1	Mack Brown
7.	Tennessee	11–2	Phillip Fulmer
8.	Kansas St	11–1	Bill Snyder
9.	Washington St	10–2	Mike Price
10.	Georgia	10–2	Jim Donnan
11.	Auburn	10–3	Terry Bowden
12.	Ohio St	10–3	John Cooper
13.	LSU	9–3	Gerry DiNardo
14.	Arizona St	8–3	Bruce Snyder
15.	Purdue	9–3	Joe Tiller
16.	Penn St	9–3	Joe Paterno
17.	Colorado St	11–2	Sonny Lubick
18.	Washington	8–4	Jim Lambright
19.	Southern Mississippi	9–3	Jeff Bower
20.	Texas A&M	9–4	R.C. Slocum
21.	Syracuse	9–4	Paul Pasqualoni
22.	Mississippi	8–4	Tommy Tuberville
23.	Missouri	7–5	Larry Smith
24.	Oklahoma St	8–4	Bob Simmons
25.	Georgia Tech	7–5	George O'Leary

#Selected No. 1 by *USA Today*/CNN.

1998

		Record	Coach
1.	Tennessee	13–0	Phillip Fulmer
2.	Ohio St	11–1	John Cooper
3.	Florida St	11–2	Bobby Bowden
4.	Arizona	12–1	Dick Tomey
5.	Florida	10–2	Steve Spurrier
6.	Wisconsin	11–1	Barry Alvarez
7.	Tulane	12–0	Tommy Bowden
8.	UCLA	10–2	Bob Toledo
9.	Georgia Tech	10–2	George O'Leary
10.	Kansas St	11–2	Bill Snyder
11.	Texas A&M	11–3	R.C. Slocum
12.	Michigan	10–3	Lloyd Carr
13.	Air Force	12–1	Fisher DeBerry
14.	Georgia	9–3	Jim Donnan
15.	Texas	9–3	Mack Brown
16.	Arkansas	9–3	Houston Nutt
17.	Penn St	9–3	Joe Paterno
18.	Virginia	9–3	George Welsh
19.	Nebraska	9–4	Frank Solich
20.	Miami (Fla.)	9–3	Butch Davis
21.	Missouri	8–4	Larry Smith
22.	Notre Dame	9–3	Bob Davie
23.	Virginia Tech	9–3	Frank Beamer
24.	Purdue	9–4	Joe Tiller
25.	Syracuse	8–4	Paul Pasqualoni

1999

		Record	Coach
1.	Florida St	12–0	Bobby Bowden
2.	Virginia Tech	11–1	Frank Beamer
3.	Nebraska	12–1	Frank Solich
4.	Wisconsin	10–2	Barry Alvarez
5.	Michigan	10–2	Lloyd Carr
6.	Kansas St	11–1	Bill Snyder
7.	Michigan St	10–2	Nick Saban
8.	Alabama	10–3	Mike DuBose
9.	Tennessee	9–3	Phillip Fulmer
10.	Marshall	13–0	Bob Pruett
11.	Penn St	10–3	Joe Paterno
12.	Florida	9–4	Steve Spurrier
13.	Mississippi St	10–2	Jackie Sherrill
14.	Southern Miss	9–3	Jeff Bower
15.	Miami (Fla.)	9–4	Butch Davis
16.	Georgia	8–4	Jim Donnan
17.	Arkansas	8–4	Houston Nutt
18.	Minnesota	8–4	Glen Mason
19.	Oregon	9–3	Mike Bellotti
20.	Georgia Tech	8–4	George O'Leary
21.	Texas	9–5	Mack Brown
22.	Mississippi	8–4	David Cutcliffe
23.	Texas A&M	8–4	R.C. Slocum
24.	Illinois	8–4	Ron Turner
25.	Purdue	7–5	Joe Tiller

2000

		Record	Coach
1.	Oklahoma	13–0	Bob Stoops
2.	Miami (Fla.)	11–1	Butch Davis
3.	Washington	11–1	Rick Neuheisel
4.	Oregon St	11–1	Dennis Erickson
5.	Florida St	11–2	Bobby Bowden
6.	Virginia Tech	11–1	Frank Beamer
7.	Oregon	10–2	Mike Belotti
8.	Nebraska	10–2	Frank Solich
9.	Kansas St	11–3	Bill Snyder
10.	Florida	10–3	Steve Spurrier
11.	Michigan	9–3	Lloyd Carr
12.	Texas	9–3	Mack Brown
13.	Purdue	8–4	Joe Tiller
14.	Colorado St	10–2	Sonny Lubick
15.	Notre Dame	9–3	Bob Davie
16.	Clemson	9–3	Tommy Bowden
17.	Georgia Tech	9–3	George O'Leary
18.	Auburn	9–4	Tommy Tuberville
19.	South Carolina	8–4	Lou Holtz
20.	Georgia	8–4	Jim Donnan
21.	TCU	10–2	Dennis Franchione
22.	LSU	8–4	Nick Saban
23.	Wisconsin	9–4	Barry Alvarez
24.	Mississippi St	8–4	Jackie Sherrill
25.	Iowa St	9–3	Dan McCarney

2001

		Record	Coach
1.	Miami (Fla.)	12–0	Larry Coker
2.	Oregon	11–1	Mike Belotti
3.	Florida	10–2	Steve Spurrier
4.	Tennessee	11–2	Phillip Fulmer
5.	Texas	11–2	Mack Brown
6.	Oklahoma	11–2	Bob Stoops
7.	LSU	10–3	Nick Saban
8.	Nebraska	11–2	Frank Solich
9.	Colorado	10–3	Gary Barnett
10.	Washington St	10–2	Mike Price

2001 *(Cont.)*

	Record	Coach
11. Maryland	10–2	Ralph Friedgen
12. Illinois	10–2	Ron Turner
13. South Carolina	9–3	Lou Holtz
14. Syracuse	10–3	Paul Pasqualoni
15. Florida St	8–4	Bobby Bowden
16. Stanford	9–3	Tyrone Willingham
17. Louisville	11–2	John Smith
18. Virginia Tech	8–4	Frank Beamer
19. Washington	8–4	Rick Neuheisel
20. Michigan	8–4	Lloyd Carr
21. Boston College	8–4	Tom O'Brien
22. Georgia	8–4	Mark Richt
23. Toledo	10–2	Tom Amstutz
24. Georgia Tech	9–3	George O'Leary
25. BYU	12–2	Gary Crowton

2002

	Record	Coach
1. Ohio St	14–0	Jim Tressel
2. Miami (Fla.)	12–1	Larry Coker
3. Georgia	13–1	Mark Richt
4. USC	11–2	Pete Carroll
5. Oklahoma	12–2	Bob Stoops
6. Texas	11–2	Mack Brown
7. Kansas St	11–2	Bill Snyder
8. Iowa	11–2	Kirk Ferentz
9. Michigan	10–3	Lloyd Carr
10. Washington St	10–3	Mike Price
11. Alabama	10–3	Dennis Franchione
12. North Carolina St	11–3	Chuck Amato
13. Maryland	11–3	Ralph Friedgen
14. Auburn	9–4	Tommy Tuberville
15. Boise St	12–1	Dan Hawkins
16. Penn St	9–4	Joe Paterno
17. Notre Dame	10–3	Tyrone Willingham
18. Virginia Tech	10–4	Frank Beamer
19. Pittsburgh	9–4	Walt Harris
20. Colorado	9–5	Gary Barnett
21. Florida St	9–5	Bobby Bowden
22. Virginia	9–5	Al Groh
23. TCU	10–2	Gary Patterson
24. Marshall	11–2	Bob Pruett
25. W Virginia	9–4	Rich Rodriguez

2003

	Record	Coach
1. USC	12–1	Pete Carroll
#2. LSU	13–1	Nick Saban
3. Oklahoma	12–2	Bob Stoops
4. Ohio St	11–2	Jim Tressel
5. Miami (Fla.)	11–2	Larry Coker
6. Michigan	10–3	Lloyd Carr
7. Georgia	11–3	Mark Richt
8. Iowa	10–3	Kirk Ferentz
9. Washington St	10–3	Bill Doba
10. Miami (Ohio)	13–1	Terry Hoeppner
11. Florida St	10–3	Bobby Bowden
12. Texas	10–3	Mack Brown
13. Kansas St	11–4	Bill Snyder
Mississippi	10–3	David Cutcliffe
15. Tennessee	10–3	Phillip Fulmer
16. Boise St	13–1	Dan Hawkins
17. Maryland	10–3	Ralph Friedgen
18. Nebraska	10–3	Frank Solich/Bo Pelini
Purdue	9–4	Joe Tiller
20. Minnesota	10–3	Glen Mason
21. Utah	10–2	Urban Meyer

2003 *(Cont.)*

	Record	Coach
22. Clemson	9–4	Tommy Bowden
23. Bowling Green	11–3	Gregg Brandon
24. Florida	8–5	Ron Zook
25. TCU	11–2	Gary Patterson

#Selected No. 1 by *USA Today*/CNN.

2004

	Record	Coach
1. *Vacated		
2. Auburn	13-0	Tommy Tuberville
3. Oklahoma	12-1	Bob Stoops
4. Utah	12-0	Kyle Whittingham
5. Texas	11-1	Mack Brown
6. Louisville	11-1	Bobby Petrino
7. Georgia	10-2	Mark Richt
8. Iowa	10-2	Kirk Ferentz
9. California	10-2	Jeff Tedford
10. Virginia Tech	10-3	Frank Beamer
11. Miami (Fla.)	9-3	Larry Coker
12. Boise St	11–1	Dan Hawkins
13. Tennessee	10-3	Phillip Fulmer
14. Michigan	9-3	Lloyd Carr
15. Florida St	8-5	Bobby Bowden
16. LSU	9-3	Les Miles
17. Wisconsin	9-3	Barry Alvarez
18. Texas Tech	8-4	Mike Leach
19. Arizona St	9-3	Dirk Koetter
20. Ohio St	8-4	Jim Tressel
21. Boston College	9-3	Tom O'Brien
22. Fresno St	9-3	Pat Hill
23. Virginia	8-4	Al Groh
24. Navy	10-2	Paul Johnson
25. Pittsburgh	8-4	Walt Harris

*USC was stripped of its 2004 season victories in 2010.

2005

	Record	Coach
1. Texas	13-0	Mack Brown
2. *Vacated		
3. Penn St	11-1	Joe Paterno
4. Ohio St	10-2	Jim Tressel
5. Texas	11-1	Mack Brown
6. LSU	11-2	Les Miles
7. Virginia Tech	10-3	Frank Beamer
8. Alabama	10-2	Mike Shula
9. Notre Dame	9-3	Charlie Weis
10. Georgia	10-3	Mark Richt
11. TCU	11-1	Gary Patterson
12. Florida	9-3	Urban Meyer
Oregon	10-2	Mike Bellotti
14. Auburn	9-3	Tommy Tuberville
15. Wisconsin	9-3	Barry Alvarez
15. Michigan	9-3	Lloyd Carr
16. UCLA	10-2	Karl Dorrell
17. Miami (Fla.)	9-3	Larry Coker
18. Boston College	9-3	Tom O'Brien
19. Louisville	9-3	Bobby Petrino
20. Texas Tech	9-3	Mike Leach
21. Clemson	8-4	Tommy Bowden
22. Oklahoma	8-4	Bob Stoops
23. Florida St	8-5	Bobby Bowden
24. Nebraska	8-4	Bill Callahan
25. California	8-4	Jeff Tedford

*USC was stripped of its 2005 season victories in 2010.

2006

		Record	Coach
1.	Florida	13-1	Urban Meyer
2.	Ohio St	12-1	Jim Tressel
3.	LSU	11-2	Les Miles
4.	USC	11-2	Pete Carroll
5.	Boise St	13-0	Chris Petersen
6.	Louisville	12-1	Steve Kragthorpe
7.	Wisconsin	12-1	Bret Bielema
8.	Michigan	11-2	Lloyd Carr
9.	Auburn	11-2	Tommy Tuberville
10.	W Virginia	11-2	Rich Rodriguez
11.	Oklahoma	11-3	Bob Stoops
12.	Rutgers	11-2	Greg Schiano
13.	Texas	10-3	Mack Brown
14.	California	10-3	Jeff Tedford
15.	Arkansas	10-4	Houston Nutt
16.	BYU	11-2	Bronco Mendenhall
17.	Notre Dame	10-3	Charlie Weis
18.	Wake Forest	11-3	Jim Grobe
19.	Virginia Tech	10-3	Frank Beamer
20.	Boston College	10-3	Jeff Jagodzinski
21.	Oregon St	10-4	Mike Riley
22.	TCU	11-2	Gary Patterson
23.	Georgia	9-4	Mark Richt
24.	Penn St	9-4	Joe Paterno
25.	Tennessee	9-4	Phillip Fulmer

2007

		Record	Coach
1.	LSU	12-2	Les Miles
2.	Georgia	11-2	Mark Richt
3.	USC	11-2	Pete Carroll
4.	Missouri	12-2	Gary Pinkell
5.	Ohio St	11-2	Jim Tressel
6.	W Virginia	11-2	Rich Rodriguez
7.	Kansas	12-1	Mark Mangino
8.	Oklahoma	11-3	Bob Stoops
9.	Virginia Tech	11-3	Frank Beamer
10.	Texas	10-3	Mack Brown
	Boston College	11-3	Jeff Jagodzinski
12.	Tennessee	10-4	Philip Fulmer
13.	Florida	9-4	Urban Meyer
14.	BYU	11-2	Bronco Mendenhall
15.	Auburn	9-4	Tommy Tuberville
16.	Arizona St	10-3	Dennis Erickson
17.	Cincinnati	10-3	Brian Kelly
18.	Michigan	9-4	Lloyd Carr
19.	Hawaii	12-1	June Jones
20.	Illinois	9-4	Ron Zook
21.	Clemson	9-4	Tommy Bowden
22.	Texas Tech	9-4	Mike Leach
23.	Oregon	9-4	Mike Bellotti
24.	Wisconsin	9-4	Bret Bielema
25.	Oregon St	9-4	Mike Riley

2008

		Record	Coach
1.	Florida	12-1	Urban Meyer
2.	Utah	12-0	Kyle Whittingham
3.	USC	11-1	Pete Carroll
4.	Texas	11-1	Mack Brown
5.	Oklahoma	12-1	Bob Stoops
6.	Alabama	12-2	Nick Saban
7.	TCU	10-2	Gary Patterson
8.	Penn St	11-1	Joe Paterno
9.	Ohio State	10-2	Jim Tressel

2008 *(Cont.)*

		Record	Coach
10.	Oregon	9-3	Mike Bellotti
11.	Boise St	12-0	Chris Petersen
12.	Texas Tech	11-1	Mike Leach
13.	Georgia	9-3	Mike Richt
14.	Mississippi	8-4	Houston Nutt
15.	Virginia Tech	9-4	Frank Beamer
16.	Oklahoma St	9-3	Mike Gundy
17.	Cincinnati	11-2	Brian Kelly
18.	Oregon St	8-4	Mike Riley
19.	Missouri	9-4	Gary Pinkel
20.	Iowa	8-4	Kirk Ferentz
21.	Florida St	8-4	Bobby Bowden
22.	Georgia Tech	9-3	Paul Johnson
23.	W Virginia	8-4	Bill Stewart
24.	Michigan St	9-3	Mark Dantonio
25.	BYU	10-2	Bronco Mendenhall

2009

		Record	Coach
1.	Alabama	14-0	Nick Saban
2.	Texas	13-1	Mack Brown
3.	Florida	13-1	Urban Meyer
4.	Boise St	14-0	Chris Petersen
5.	Ohio St	11-2	Jim Tressel
6.	TCU	12-1	Gary Patterson
7.	Iowa	11-2	Mark Mangino
8.	Cincinnati	12-1	Brian Kelly
9.	Penn St	11-2	Joe Paterno
10.	Virginia Tech	10-3	Frank Beamer
11.	Oregon	10-3	Chip Kelly
12.	BYU	11-2	Bronco Mendenhall
13.	Georgia Tech	11-3	Paul Johnson
14.	Nebraska	10-4	Bo Pelini
15.	Pittsburgh	10-3	Dave Wannstedt
16.	Wisconsin	10-3	Bret Bielema
17.	LSU	9-4	Les Miles
18.	Utah	10-3	Kyle Whittingham
19.	Miami (Fla.)	9-4	Randy Shannon
20.	Mississippi	9-4	Houston Nutt
21.	Texas Tech	9-4	Mike Leach
22.	USC	9-4	Pete Carroll
23.	Central Michigan	12-2	Butch Jones
24.	Clemson	9-5	Dabo Swinney
25.	W Virginia	9-4	Bill Stewart

2010

		Record	Coach
1.	Auburn	14-0	Gene Chizik
2.	TCU	13-0	Gary Patterson
3.	Oregon	12-1	Chip Kelly
4.	Stanford	12-1	Jim Harbaugh
5.	Ohio St	12-1	Jim Tressel
6.	Oklahoma	12-2	Bob Stoops
7.	Wisconsin	11-2	Bret Bielema
8.	LSU	11-2	Les Miles
9.	Boise St	12-1	Chris Petersen
10.	Alabama	10-3	Nick Saban
11.	Nevada	13-1	Chris Ault
12.	Arkansas	10-3	Bobby Petrino
13.	Oklahoma St	11-2	Mike Gundy
14.	Michigan St	11-2	Mark Dantonio
15.	Mississippi St	9-4	Dan Mullen

2010 *(Cont.)*

		Record	Coach
16.	Virginia Tech	11-3	Frank Beamer
17.	Florida St	10-4	Jimbo Fisher
18.	Missouri	10-3	Gary Pinkel
19.	Texas A&M	9-4	Mike Sherman
20.	Nebraska	10-4	Bo Pelini
21.	Central Florida	11-3	George O'Leary
22.	South Carolina	9-5	Steve Spurrier
23.	Maryland	9-4	Ralph Friedgen
24.	Tulsa	10-3	Todd Graham
25.	North Carolina St	9-4	Todd O'Brien

2011

		Record	Coach
1.	Alabama	12-1	Nick Saban
2.	LSU	13-1	Les Miles
3.	Oklahoma State	12-1	Mike Gundy
4.	Oregon	12-2	Chip Kelly
5.	Arkansas	11-2	Bobby Petrino
6.	USC	10-2	Lane Kiffin
7.	Stanford	11-2	David Shaw
8.	Boise State	12-1	Chris Petersen
9.	South Carolina	11-2	Steve Spurrier
10.	Wisconsin	11-3	Bret Bielema
11.	Michigan State	11-3	Mark Dantonio
12.	Michigan	11-2	Brady Hoke
13.	Baylor	10-3	Art Briles
14.	TCU	11-2	Gary Patterson
15.	Kansas State	10-3	Bill Snyder
16.	Oklahoma	10-3	Bob Stoops
17.	W Virginia	10-3	Dana Holgorsen
18.	Houston	13-1	Tony Levine
19.	Georgia	10-4	Mark Richt
20.	Southern Miss	12-2	Larry Fedora
21.	Virginia Tech	11-3	Frank Beamer
22.	Clemson	10-4	Dabo Swinney
23.	Florida State	9-4	Jimbo Fisher
24.	Nebraska	9-4	Bo Pelini
25.	Cincinnati	10-3	Butch Jones

2012

	Record	Coach
1. Alabama	13-1	Nick Saban
2. Oregon	12-1	Chip Kelly
3. Ohio State	12-0	Urban Meyer
4. Notre Dame	12-1	Brian Kelly
5. Georgia	12-2	Mark Richt
5. Texas A&M	11-2	Kevin Sumlin
7. Stanford	12-2	David Shaw
8. South Carolina	11-2	Steve Spurrier
9. Florida	11-2	Will Muschamp
10. Florida State	12-2	Jimbo Fisher
11. Clemson	11-2	Dabo Swinney
12. Kansas State	11-2	Bill Snyder
13. Louisville	11-2	Charlie Strong
14. LSU	10-3	Les Miles
15. Oklahoma	10-3	Mike Stoops
16. Utah State	11-2	Matt Wells
17. Northwestern	10-3	Pat Fitzgerald
18. Boise State	11-2	Chris Petersen
19. Texas	9-4	Mack Brown
20. Oregon State	9-4	Mike Riley
21. San Jose State	11-2	Ron Caragher
22. N Illinois	12-2	Rod Carey
23. Vanderbilt	9-4	James Franklin
24. Michigan	8-5	Brady Hoke
25. Nebraska	10-4	Bo Pelini

Football Championship Subdivision (Div. I-AA)

Year	Winner	Runner-Up	Score
1978	Florida A&M	Massachusetts	35–28
1979	Eastern Kentucky	Lehigh	30–7
1980	Boise St	Eastern Kentucky	31–29
1981	Idaho St	Eastern Kentucky	34–23
1982	Eastern Kentucky	Delaware	17–14
1983	Southern Illinois	Western Carolina	43–7
1984	Montana St	Louisiana Tech	19–6
1985	Georgia Southern	Furman	44–42
1986	Georgia Southern	Arkansas St	48–21
1987	NE Louisiana	Marshall	43–42
1988	Furman	Georgia Southern	17–12
1989	Georgia Southern	Stephen F. Austin St	37–34
1990	Georgia Southern	Nevada-Reno	36–13
1991	Youngstown St	Marshall	25–17
1992	Marshall	Youngstown St	31–28
1993	Youngstown St	Marshall	17–5
1994	Youngstown St	Boise St	28–14
1995	Montana	Marshall	22–20
1996	Marshall	Montana	49–29
1997	Youngstown St	McNesse St	10–9
1998	Massachusetts	Georgia Southern	55–43
1999	Georgia Southern	Youngstown St	59–24
2000	Georgia Southern	Montana	27–25
2001	Montana	Furman	13–6
2002	Western Kentucky	McNeese St	34–14
2003	Delaware	Colgate	40–0
2004	James Madison	Montana	31–21
2005	Appalachian St	Northern Iowa	21–16
2006	Appalachian St	Massachusetts	28–17
2007	Appalachian St	Delaware	49–21
2008	Richmond	Montana	24–7
2009	Villanova	Montana	23–21
2010	Eastern Washington	Delaware	20–19
2011	North Dakota St	Sam Houston St	17-6
2012	North Dakota St	Sam Houston St	39–13

Division II

Year	Winner	Runner-Up	Score
1973	Louisiana Tech	Western Kentucky	34–0
1974	Central Michigan	Delaware	54–14
1975	Northern Michigan	Western Kentucky	16–14
1976	Montana St	Akron	24–13
1977	Lehigh	Jacksonville St	33–0
1978	Eastern Illinois	Delaware	10–9
1979	Delaware	Youngstown St	38–21
1980	Cal Poly SLO	Eastern Illinois	21–13
1981	SW Texas St	North Dakota St	42–13
1982	SW Texas St	UC–Davis	34–9
1983	North Dakota St	Central St (Ohio)	41–21
1984	Troy St	North Dakota St	18–17
1985	North Dakota St	North Alabama	35–7
1986	North Dakota St	South Dakota	27–7
1987	Troy St	Portland St	31–17
1988	North Dakota St	Portland St	35–21
1989	Mississippi College	Jacksonville St	3–0
1990	N Dakota St	Indiana (Pa.)	51–11
1991	Pittsburg St	Jacksonville St	23–6
1992	Jacksonville St	Pittsburg St	17–13
1993	North Alabama	Indiana (Pa.)	41–34
1994	North Alabama	Texas A&M–Kingsville	16–10
1995	North Alabama	Pittsburg St	27–7
1996	Northern Colorado	Carson-Newman	23–14
1997	Northern Colorado	New Haven	51–0
1998	NW Missouri St	Carson-Newman	24–6
1999	NW Missouri St	Carson-Newman	58–52 (OT)
2000	Delta St	Bloomsburg	63–34
2001	Grand Valley St	North Dakota	17–14
2002	Grand Valley St	Valdosta St	31–24

Division II *(Cont.)*

Year	Winner	Runner-Up	Score
2003	Grand Valley St	North Dakota	10–3
2004	Valdosta State	Pittsburg State	36–31
2005	Grand Valley St	NW Missouri St	21–17
2006	Grand Valley St	NW Missouri St	17–14
2007	Valdosta St	NW Missouri St	25–20
2008	Minnesota-Duluth	NW Missouri St	21–14
2009	NW Missouri St	Grand Valley St	30–23
2010	Minnesota-Duluth	Delta St	20–17
2011	Pittsburg St	Wayne St	35–21
2012	Valdosta St	Winston-Salem	35–7

Division III

Year	Winner	Runner-Up	Score
1973	Wittenberg	Juniata	41–0
1974	Central (Iowa)	Ithaca	10–8
1975	Wittenberg	Ithaca	28–0
1976	St. John's (Minn.)	Towson St	31–28
1977	Widener	Wabash	39–36
1978	Baldwin-Wallace	Wittenberg	24–10
1979	Ithaca	Wittenberg	14–10
1980	Dayton	Ithaca	63–0
1981	Widener	Dayton	17–10
1982	West Georgia	Augustana (Ill.)	14–0
1983	Augustana (Ill.)	Union (N.Y.)	21–17
1984	Augustana (Ill.)	Central (Iowa)	21–12
1985	Augustana (Ill.)	Ithaca	20–7
1986	Augustana (Ill.)	Salisbury St	31–3
1987	Wagner	Dayton	19–3
1988	Ithaca	Central (Iowa)	39–24
1989	Dayton	Union (N.Y.)	17–7
1990	Allegheny	Lycoming	21–14 (OT)
1991	Ithaca	Dayton	34–20
1992	UW-LaCrosse	Washington & Jefferson	16–12
1993	Mount Union	Rowan	34–24
1994	Albion	Washington & Jefferson	38–15
1995	UW-LaCrosse	Rowan	36–7
1996	Mount Union	Rowan	56–24
1997	Mount Union	Lycoming	61–12
1998	Mount Union	Rowan	44–24
1999	Pacific Lutheran	Rowan	42–13
2000	Mount Union	St. John's (Minn.)	10–7
2001	Mount Union	Bridgewater	30–27
2002	Mount Union	Trinity (Tex.)	48–7
2003	St. John's (Minn.)	Mount Union	24–6
2004	Linfield	Mary Hardin-Baylor	28–21
2005	Mount Union	UW-Whitewater	35–28
2006	Mount Union	UW-Whitewater	35–16
2007	UW-Whitewater	Mount Union	31–21
2008	Mount Union	UW-Whitewater	31–26
2009	UW-Whitewater	Mount Union	38–28
2010	UW-Whitewater	Mount Union	31–21
2011	UW-Whitewater	Mount Union	13–10
2012	Mount Union	St. Thomas (MN)	28–10

NAIA Divisional Championships

Division I

Year	Winner	Runner-Up	Score
1956	St. Joseph's (Ind.)/Montana St		0–0
1957	Pittsburg St (Kan.)	Hillsdale	27–26
1958	NE Oklahoma	Northern Arizona	19–13
1959	Texas A&I	Lenoir-Rhyne	20–7
1960	Lenoir-Rhyne	Humboldt St	15–14
1961	Pittsburg St (Kan.)	Linfield	12–7
1962	Central St (Okla.)	Lenoir-Rhyne	28–13
1963	St. John's (Minn.)	Prairie View	33–27

Division I (Cont.)

Year	Winner	Runner-Up	Score
1964	Concordia-Moorhead/ Sam Houston St		7–7
1965	St. John's (Minn.)	Linfield	33–0
1966	Waynesburg	UW-Whitewater	42–21
1967	Fairmont St	Eastern Washington	28–21
1968	Troy St (Mich.)	Texas A&I	43–35
1969	Texas A&I	Concordia-Moorhead (Minn.)	32–7
1970	Texas A&I	Wofford	48–7
1971	Livingston (Ala.)	Arkansas Tech	14–12
1972	E Texas St	Carson-Newman	21–18
1973	Abilene Christian	Elon	42–14
1974	Texas A&I	Henderson St	34–23
1975	Texas A&I	Salem (W.V.)	37–0
1976	Texas A&I	Central Arkansas	26–0
1977	Abilene Christian	SW Oklahoma	24–7
1978	Angelo St	Elon	34–14
1979	Texas A&I	Central St (Okla.)	20–14
1980	Elon	NE Oklahoma	17–10
1981	Elon	Pittsburg St	3–0
1982	Central St (Okla.)	Mesa	14–11
1983	Carson-Newman	Mesa	36–28
1984	Carson-Newman/Central Arkansas		19–19
1985	Central Arkansas/Hillsdale		10–10
1986	Carson-Newman	Cameron	17–0
1987	Cameron	Carson-Newman	30–2
1988	Carson-Newman	Adams St (Col.)	56–21
1989	Carson-Newman	Emporia St	34–20
1990	Central St (Ohio)	Mesa St	38–16
1991	Central Arkansas	Central St (Ohio)	19–16
1992	Central St (Ohio)	Gardner-Webb	19–16
1993	East Central (Okla.)	Glenville St	49–35
1994	Northeastern St (Okla.)	Arkansas–Pine Bluff	13–12
1995	Central St (Ohio)	Northeastern St (Okla.)	37–7
1996	SW Oklahoma St	Montana Tech	33–31
1997	Findlay	Willamette	14–7
1998	Azusa Pacific	Olivet Nazarene	17–14
1999	Northwestern Oklahoma St	Georgetown (Ky.)	34–26
2000	Georgetown (Ky.)	Northwestern Oklahoma St	20–0
2001	Georgetown (Ky.)	Sioux Falls (S.D.)	49–27
2002	Carroll (Mont.)	Georgetown (Ky.)	28–7
2003	Carroll (Mont.)	Northwestern Oklahoma St	41–28
2004	Carroll (Mont.)	St. Francis (Ind.)	15–13
2005	Carroll (Mont.)	St. Francis (Ind.)	27–10
2006	Sioux Falls (S.D.)	St. Francis (Ind.)	23–19
2007	Carroll (Mont.)	Sioux Falls (S.D.)	17–9
2008	Sioux Falls (S.D.)	Carroll (Mont.)	23–7
2009	Sioux Falls (S.D.)	Lindenwood	25–22
2010	Carroll (Mont.)	Sioux Falls (S.D.)	10–7
2011	St. Xavier (Ill.)	Carroll (Mont.)	24-20
2012	Marian (Ind.)	Morningside (Iowa)	30–27

Division II†

Year	Winner	Runner-Up	Score
1970	Westminster (Pa.)	Anderson	21–16
1971	California Lutheran	Westminster (Pa.)	30–14
1972	Missouri Southern	Northwestern (Iowa)	21–14
1973	Northwestern (Iowa)	Glenville St	10–3
1974	Texas Lutheran	Missouri Valley	42–0
1975	Texas Lutheran	California Lutheran	34–8
1976	Westminster (Pa.)	Redlands	20–13
1977	Westminster (Pa.)	California Lutheran	17–9
1978	Concordia-Moorhead (Minn.)	Findlay	7–0
1979	Findlay	Northwestern (Iowa)	51–6
1980	Pacific Lutheran	Wilmington (Ohio)	38–10
1981	Austin Coll./Conc.-Moorhead (Minn.)		24–24
1982	Linfield	William Jewell	33–15
1983	Northwestern (Iowa)	Pacific Lutheran	25–21

†In 1997 the NAIA consolidated its two divisions into one.

†Division II *(Cont.)*

Year	Winner	Runner-Up	Score
1984	Linfield	Northwestern (Iowa)	33–22
1985	UW-La Crosse	Pacific Lutheran	24–7
1986	Linfield	Baker	17–0
1987	Pacific Lutheran	UW-Stevens Point*	16–16
1988	Westminster (Pa.)	UW-La Crosse	21–14
1989	Westminster (Pa.)	UW-La Crosse	51–30
1990	Peru St	Westminster (Pa.)	17–7
1991	Georgetown (Ky.)	Pacific Lutheran	28–20
1992	Findlay	Linfield	26–13
1993	Pacific Lutheran	Westminster (Pa.)	50–20
1994	Westminster (Pa.)	Pacific Lutheran	27–7
1995	Findlay	Central Washington	21–21
1996	Sioux Falls (S.D.)	Western Washington	47–25

*Forfeited 1987 season due to use of an ineligible player. †In 1997 the NAIA consolidated its two divisions into one.

Awards

Heisman Memorial Trophy

Awarded to the best college player by the Downtown Athletic Club of New York City. The trophy is named after John W. Heisman, who coached Georgia Tech to the national championship in 1917 and later served as DAC athletic director.

Year	Winner, College, Position	Winner's Season Statistics	Runner-Up, College
1935	Jay Berwanger, Chicago, HB	Rush: 119 Yds: 577 TD: 6	Monk Meyer, Army
1936	Larry Kelley, Yale, E	Rec: 17 Yds: 372 TD: 6	Sam Francis, Nebraska
1937	Clint Frank, Yale, HB	Rush: 157 Yds: 667 TD: 11	Byron White, Colorado
1938	†Davey O'Brien, TCU, QB	Att/Comp: 194/110 Yds: 1733 TD: 19	Marshall Goldberg, Pittsburgh
1939	Nile Kinnick, Iowa, HB	Rush: 106 Yds: 374 TD: 5	Tom Harmon, Michigan
1940	Tom Harmon, Michigan, HB	Rush: 191 Yds: 852 TD: 16	John Kimbrough, Texas A&M
1941	†Bruce Smith, Minnesota, HB	Rush: 98 Yds: 480 TD: 6	Angelo Bertelli, Notre Dame
1942	Frank Sinkwich, Georgia, HB	Att/Comp: 166/84 Yds: 1392 TD: 10	Paul Governali, Columbia
1943	Angelo Bertelli, Notre Dame, QB	Att/Comp: 36/25 Yds: 511 TD: 10	Bob Odell, Pennsylvania
1944	Les Horvath, Ohio State, QB	Rush: 163 Yds: 924 TD: 12	Glenn Davis, Army
1945	*†Doc Blanchard, Army, FB	Rush: 101 Yds: 718 TD: 13	Glenn Davis, Army
1946	Glenn Davis, Army, HB	Rush: 123 Yds: 712 TD: 7	Charley Trippi, Georgia
1947	†John Lujack, Notre Dame, QB	Att/Comp: 109/61 Yds: 777 TD: 9	Bob Chappius, Michigan
1948	*Doak Walker, SMU, HB	Rush: 108 Yds: 532 TD: 8	Charlie Justice, North Carolina
1949	†Leon Hart, Notre Dame, E	Rec: 19 Yds: 257 TD: 5	Charlie Justice, North Carolina
1950	*Vic Janowicz, Ohio St, HB	Att/Comp: 77/32 Yds: 561 TD: 12	Kyle Rote, SMU
1951	Dick Kazmaier, Princeton, HB	Rush: 149 Yds: 861 TD: 9	Hank Lauricella, Tennessee
1952	Billy Vessels, Oklahoma, HB	Rush: 167 Yds: 1072 TD: 17	Jack Scarbath, Maryland
1953	John Lattner, Notre Dame, HB	Rush: 134 Yds: 651 TD: 6	Paul Giel, Minnesota
1954	Alan Ameche, Wisconsin, FB	Rush: 146 Yds: 641 TD: 9	Kurt Burris, Oklahoma
1955	Howard Cassady, Ohio St, HB	Rush: 161 Yds: 958 TD: 15	Jim Swink, TCU
1956	Paul Hornung, Notre Dame, QB	Att/Comp: 111/59 Yds: 917 TD: 3	Johnny Majors, Tennessee
1957	John David Crow, Texas A&M, HB	Rush: 129 Yds: 562 TD: 10	Alex Karras, Iowa
1958	Pete Dawkins, Army, HB	Rush: 78 Yds: 428 TD: 6	Randy Duncan, Iowa
1959	Billy Cannon, LSU, HB	Rush: 139 Yds: 598 TD: 6	Rich Lucas, Penn St
1960	Joe Bellino, Navy, HB	Rush: 168 Yds: 834 TD: 18	Tom Brown, Minnesota
1961	Ernie Davis, Syracuse, HB	Rush: 150 Yds: 823 TD: 15	Bob Ferguson, Ohio St
1962	Terry Baker, Oregon St, QB	Att/Comp: 203/112 Yds: 1738 TD: 15	Jerry Stovall, LSU
1963	*Roger Staubach, Navy, QB	Att/Comp: 161/107 Yds: 1474 TD: 7	Billy Lothridge, Georgia Tech
1964	John Huarte, Notre Dame, QB	Att/Comp: 205/114 Yds: 2062 TD: 16	Jerry Rhome, Tulsa
1965	Mike Garrett, USC, HB	Rush: 267 Yds: 1440 TD: 16	Howard Twilley, Tulsa
1966	Steve Spurrier, Florida, QB	Att/Comp: 291/179 Yds: 2012 TD: 1	Bob Griese, Purdue
1967	Gary Beban, UCLA, QB	Att/Comp: 156/87 Yds: 1359 TD: 8	O.J. Simpson, USC
1968	O.J. Simpson, USC, HB	Rush: 383 Yds: 1880 TD: 23	Leroy Keyes, Purdue

Awards (Cont.)

Heisman Memorial Trophy (Cont.)

Year	Winner, College, Position	Winner's Season Statistics	Runner-Up, College
1969	Steve Owens, Oklahoma, FB	Rush: 358 Yds: 1523 TD: 23	Mike Phipps, Purdue
1970	Jim Plunkett, Stanford, QB	Att/Comp: 358/191 Yds: 2715 TD: 18	Joe Theismann, Notre Dame
1971	Pat Sullivan, Auburn, QB	Att/Comp: 281/162 Yds: 2012; 20 TD	Ed Marinaro, Cornell
1972	Johnny Rodgers, Nebraska, FL	Rec: 55 Yds: 942 TD: 17	Greg Pruitt, Oklahoma
1973	John Cappelletti, Penn St, HB	Rush: 286 Yds: 1522 TD: 17	John Hicks, Ohio St
1974	*Archie Griffin, Ohio St, HB	Rush: 256 Yds: 1695 TD: 12	Anthony Davis, USC
1975	Archie Griffin, Ohio St, HB	Rush: 262 Yds: 1450 TD: 4	Chuck Muncie, California
1976	†Tony Dorsett, Pittsburgh, HB	Rush: 370 Yds: 2150 TD: 23	Ricky Bell, USC
1977	Earl Campbell, Texas, FB	Rush: 267 Yds: 1744 TD: 19	Terry Miller, Oklahoma St
1978	*Billy Sims, Oklahoma, HB	Rush: 231 Yds: 1762 TD: 20	Chuck Fusina, Penn St
1979	Charles White, USC, HB	Rush: 332 Yds: 1803 TD: 19	Billy Sims, Oklahoma
1980	George Rogers, South Carolina, HB	Rush: 324 Yds: 1894 TD: 14	Hugh Green, Pittsburgh
1981	Marcus Allen, USC, HB	Rush: 433 Yds: 2427 TD: 23	Herschel Walker, Georgia
1982	*Herschel Walker, Georgia, HB	Rush: 335 Yds: 1752 TD: 17	John Elway, Stanford
1983	Mike Rozier, Nebraska, HB	Rush: 275 Yds: 2148 TD: 29	Steve Young, BYU
1984	Doug Flutie, Boston College, QB	Att/Comp: 396/233 Yds: 3454 TD: 27	Keith Byars, Ohio St
1985	Bo Jackson, Auburn, HB	Rush: 278 Yds: 1786 TD: 17	Chuck Long, Iowa
1986	Vinny Testaverde, Miami (Fla.), QB	Att/Comp: 276/175 Yds: 2557 TD: 26	Paul Palmer, Temple
1987	Tim Brown, Notre Dame, WR	Rec: 39 Yds: 846 TD: 7	Don McPherson, Syracuse
1988	*Barry Sanders, Oklahoma St, RB	Rush: 344 Yds: 2628 TD: 39	Rodney Peete, USC
1989	*Andre Ware, Houston, QB	Att/Comp: 578/365 Yds: 4699 TD: 46	Anthony Thompson, Indiana
1990	*Ty Detmer, BYU, QB	Att/Comp: 562/361 Yds: 5188 TD: 41	Raghib Ismail, Notre Dame
1991	*Desmond Howard, Michigan, WR	Rec: 61 Yds: 950 TD: 23	Casey Weldon, Florida St
1992	Gino Torretta, Miami (FL), QB	Att/Comp: 402/228 Yds: 3060 TD: 19	Marshall Faulk, San Diego St
1993	†Charlie Ward, Florida St, QB	Att/Comp: 380/264 Yds: 3032 TD: 27	Heath Shuler, Tennessee
1994	Rashaan Salaam, Colorado, RB	Rush: 298 Yds: 2055 TD: 24	Ki-Jana Carter, Penn St
1995	Eddie George, Ohio State, RB	Rush: 303 Yds: 1826 TD: 23	Tommie Frazier, Nebraska
1996	†Danny Wuerffel, Florida, QB	Att/Comp: 360/207 Yds: 3625 TD: 39	Troy Davis, Iowa St
1997	†Charles Woodson, Michigan, CB/WR	7 interceptions; Rec: 11 Yds: 231 TD: 4	Peyton Manning, Tennessee
1998	Ricky Williams, Texas, RB	Rush: 361 Yds: 2124 TD: 28	Michael Bishop, Kansas St
1999	Ron Dayne, Wisconsin, RB	Rush: 303 Yds: 1834 TD: 19	Joe Hamilton, Georgia Tech
2000	Chris Weinke, Florida St, QB	Att/Comp: 431/266 Yds: 4167 TD: 33	Josh Heupel, Oklahoma
2001	Eric Crouch, Nebraska, QB	Att/Comp: 189/105 Yds: 1510 TD: 7; Rush: 1115 Yds, 18 TD	Rex Grossman, Florida
2002	Carson Palmer, USC, QB	Att/Comp: 450/228 Yds: 3639 TD: 32	Brad Banks, Iowa
2003	Jason White, Oklahoma, QB	Pct. Comp: 64; 3744 Yds: TD: 40	Larry Fitzgerald, Pittsburgh
2004	*†Matt Leinart, USC, QB	Att/Comp: 269/412 Yds: 2990 TD: 28	Adrian Peterson, Oklahoma
2005	**Vacated		Vince Young, Texas
2006	Troy Smith, Ohio State, QB	Att/Comp: 311/203 Yds: 2542 TD: 30	Darren McFadden, Arkansas
2007	^Tim Tebow, Florida, QB	Att/Comp: 350/234 Yds: 3286 TD: 32	Darren McFadden, Arkansas
2008	^Sam Bradford, Oklahoma, QB	Att/Comp: 483/328 Yds: 4720 TD: 50	Colt McCoy, Texas
2009	^†Mark Ingram, Alabama, RB	Rush: 249 Yds:1,542 TD: 15	Toby Gerhart, Stanford
2010	*†Cam Newton, Auburn, QB	Att/Comp: 280/185 Yds: 2854 TD: 30 Rush:1473 Yds TD: 20	Andrew Luck, Stanford
2011	Robert Griffin III, Baylor	Att/Comp: 402/291 Yds: 4293 TD: 37 Rush: 699 Yds TD: 10	Andrew Luck, Stanford
2012	#Johnny Manziel, Texas A&M	Att/Comp: 434/295 Yds: 3706 TD: 26 Rush: 1410 Yds TD: 21	Manti Te'o, Notre Dame

*Junior; ^Sophomore; #Freshman (all others seniors). †Winners who played for national championship teams the same year. Note: Former Heisman winners and national media cast votes, with ballots allowing for three names (3 points for first, 2 for second and 1 for third). **In September 2010, Reggie Bush forfeited the 2005 Heisman Trophy he won while at USC.

Maxwell Award

Given to the outstanding college player of the year by the Maxwell Club of Philadelphia.

Year	Player, College, Position	Year	Player, College, Position
1937	Clint Frank, Yale, HB	1975	Archie Griffin, Ohio St, RB
1938	Davey O'Brien, TCU, QB	1976	Tony Dorsett, Pittsburgh, RB
1939	Nile Kinnick, Iowa, HB	1977	Ross Browner, Notre Dame, DE
1940	Tom Harmon, Michigan, HB	1978	Chuck Fusina, Penn St, QB
1941	Bill Dudley, Virginia, HB	1979	Charles White, USC, RB
1942	Paul Governali, Columbia, QB	1980	Hugh Green, Pittsburgh, DE
1943	Bob Odell, Pennsylvania, HB	1981	Marcus Allen, USC, RB
1944	Glenn Davis, Army, HB	1982	Herschel Walker, Georgia, RB
1945	Doc Blanchard, Army, FB	1983	Mike Rozier, Nebraska, RB
1946	Charley Trippi, Georgia, HB	1984	Doug Flutie, Boston College, QB
1947	Doak Walker, SMU, HB	1985	Chuck Long, Iowa, QB
1948	Chuck Bednarik, Pennsylvania, C	1986	Vinny Testaverde, Miami (Fla.), QB
1949	Leon Hart, Notre Dame, E	1987	Don McPherson, Syracuse, QB
1950	Reds Bagnell, Pennsylvania, HB	1988	Barry Sanders, Oklahoma St, RB
1951	Dick Kazmaier, Princeton, HB	1989	Anthony Thompson, Indiana, RB
1952	John Lattner, Notre Dame, HB	1990	Ty Detmer, BYU, QB
1953	John Lattner, Notre Dame, HB	1991	Desmond Howard, Michigan, WR
1954	Ron Beagle, Navy, E	1992	Gino Torretta, Miami (Fla.), QB
1955	Howard Cassady, Ohio St, HB	1993	Charlie Ward, Florida St, QB
1956	Tommy McDonald, Oklahoma, HB	1994	Kerry Collins, Penn St, QB
1957	Bob Reifsnyder, Navy, T	1995	Eddie George, Ohio St, RB
1958	Pete Dawkins, Army, HB	1996	Danny Wuerffel, Florida, QB
1959	Rich Lucas, Penn St, QB	1997	Peyton Manning, Tennessee, QB
1960	Joe Bellino, Navy, HB	1998	Ricky Williams, Texas, RB
1961	Bob Ferguson, Ohio St, FB	1999	Ron Dayne, Wisconsin, RB
1962	Terry Baker, Oregon St, QB	2000	Drew Brees, Purdue, QB
1963	Roger Staubach, Navy, QB	2001	Ken Dorsey, Miami (Fla.), QB
1964	Glenn Ressler, Penn St, C	2002	Larry Johnson, Penn St, RB
1965	Tommy Nobis, Texas, LB	2003	Eli Manning, Mississippi, QB
1966	Jim Lynch, Notre Dame, LB	2004	Jason White, Oklahoma, QB
1967	Gary Beban, UCLA, QB	2005	Vince Young, Texas, QB
1968	O.J. Simpson, USC, RB	2006	Brady Quinn, Notre Dame, QB
1969	Mike Reid, Penn St, DT	2007	Tim Tebow, Florida, QB
1970	Jim Plunkett, Stanford, QB	2008	Tim Tebow, Florida, QB
1971	Ed Marinaro, Cornell, RB	2009	Colt McCoy, Texas, QB
1972	Brad Van Pelt, Michigan St, DB	2010	Cam Newton, Auburn, QB
1973	John Cappelletti, Penn St, RB	2011	Andrew Luck, Stanford, QB
1974	Steve Joachim, Temple, QB	2012	Manti Te'o, Notre Dame

Davey O'Brien National Quarterback Award

Given to the top quarterback in the nation by the Davey O'Brien Educational and Charitable Trust of Fort Worth. Named for TCU Hall of Fame quarterback Davey O'Brien (1936–38).

Year	Player, College	Year	Player, College
1981	Jim McMahon, BYU	1997	Peyton Manning, Tennessee
1982	Todd Blackledge, Penn St	1998	Michael Bishop, Kansas St
1983	Steve Young, BYU	1999	Joe Hamilton, Georgia Tech
1984	Doug Flutie, Boston College	2000	Chris Weinke, Florida St
1985	Chuck Long, Iowa	2001	Eric Crouch, Nebraska
1986	Vinny Testaverde, Miami (Fla.)	2002	Brad Banks, Iowa
1987	Don McPherson, Syracuse	2003	Jason White, Oklahoma
1988	Troy Aikman, UCLA	2004	Jason White, Oklahoma
1989	Andre Ware, Houston	2005	Vince Young, Texas
1990	Ty Detmer, BYU	2006	Troy Smith, Ohio St
1991	Ty Detmer, BYU	2007	Tim Tebow, Florida
1992	Gino Torretta, Miami (Fla.)	2008	Sam Bradford, Oklahoma
1993	Charlie Ward, Florida St	2009	Colt McCoy, Texas
1994	Kerry Collins, Penn St	2010	Cam Newton, Auburn
1995	Danny Wuerffel, Florida	2011	Robert Griffin III, Baylor
1996	Danny Wuerffel, Florida	2012	Johnny Manziel, Texas A&M

Note: Originally honored the outstanding football player in the Southwest as follows: 1977—Earl Campbell, Texas, RB; 1978—Billy Sims, Oklahoma, RB; 1979—Mike Singletary, Baylor, LB; 1980—Mike Singletary, Baylor, LB.

Vince Lombardi/Rotary Award

Given to the outstanding college lineman or linebacker, the award is sponsored by the Rotary Club of Houston.

Year	Player, College, Position	Year	Player, College, Position
1970	Jim Stillwagon, Ohio St, MG	1992	Marvin Jones, Florida St, LB
1971	Walt Patulski, Notre Dame, DE	1993	Aaron Taylor, Notre Dame, OT
1972	Rich Glover, Nebraska, MG	1994	Warren Sapp, Miami (Fla.), DT
1973	John Hicks, Ohio St, OT	1995	Orlando Pace, Ohio St, OT
1974	Randy White, Maryland, DT	1996	Orlando Pace, Ohio St, OT
1975	Lee Roy Selmon, Oklahoma, DT	1997	Grant Wistrom, Nebraska, DE
1976	Wilson Whitley, Houston, DT	1998	Dat Nguyen, Texas A&M, LB
1977	Ross Browner, Notre Dame, DE	1999	Corey Moore, Virginia Tech, DE
1978	Bruce Clark, Penn St, DT	2000	Jamal Reynolds, Florida St, DE
1979	Brad Budde, USC, G	2001	Julius Peppers, North Carolina, DE
1980	Hugh Green, Pittsburgh, DE	2002	Terrell Suggs, Arizona St, DE
1981	Kenneth Sims, Texas, DT	2003	Tommie Harris, Oklahoma, DT
1982	Dave Rimington, Nebraska, C	2004	David Pollack, Georgia, DE
1983	Dean Steinkuhler, Nebraska, G	2005	A.J. Hawk, Ohio St, LB
1984	Tony Degrate, Texas, DT	2006	LaMarr Woodley, Michigan, DE
1985	Tony Casillas, Oklahoma, NG	2007	Glenn Dorsey, LSU, DT
1986	Cornelius Bennett, Alabama, LB	2008	Brian Orakpo, Texas, DE
1987	Chris Spielman, Ohio St, LB	2009	Ndamukong Suh, Nebraska, DT
1988	Tracy Rocker, Auburn, DT	2010	Nick Fairley, Auburn, DT
1989	Percy Snow, Michigan St, LB	2011	Luke Kuechly, Boston College, LB
1990	Chris Zorich, Notre Dame, NG	2012	Manti Te'o, Notre Dame, LB
1991	Steve Emtman, Washington, DT		

Outland Trophy

Given to the outstanding interior lineman, selected by the Football Writers Association of America.

Year	Player, College, Position	Year	Player, College, Position
1946	George Connor, Notre Dame, T	1980	Mark May, Pittsburgh, OT
1947	Joe Steffy, Army, G	1981	Dave Rimington, Nebraska, C
1948	Bill Fischer, Notre Dame, G	1982	Dave Rimington, Nebraska, C
1949	Ed Bagdon, Michigan St, G	1983	Dean Steinkuhler, Nebraska, G
1950	Bob Gain, Kentucky, T	1984	Bruce Smith, Virginia Tech, DT
1951	Jim Weatherall, Oklahoma, T	1985	Mike Ruth, Boston College, NG
1952	Dick Modzelewski, Maryland, T	1986	Jason Buck, BYU, DT
1953	J.D. Roberts, Oklahoma, G	1987	Chad Hennings, Air Force, DT
1954	Bill Brooks, Arkansas, G	1988	Tracy Rocker, Auburn, DT
1955	Calvin Jones, Iowa, G	1989	Mohammed Elewonibi, BYU, G
1956	Jim Parker, Ohio St, G	1990	Russell Maryland, Miami (Fla.), DT
1957	Alex Karras, Iowa, T	1991	Steve Emtman, Washington, DT
1958	Zeke Smith, Auburn, G	1992	Will Shields, Nebraska, G
1959	Mike McGee, Duke, T	1993	Rob Waldrop, Arizona, NG
1960	Tom Brown, Minnesota, G	1994	Zach Wiegert, Nebraska, G
1961	Merlin Olsen, Utah St, T	1995	Jonathan Ogden, UCLA, OT
1962	Bobby Bell, Minnesota, T	1996	Orlando Pace, Ohio St, OT
1963	Scott Appleton, Texas, T	1997	Aaron Taylor, Nebraska, G
1964	Steve DeLong, Tennessee, T	1998	Kris Farris, UCLA, OL
1965	Tommy Nobis, Texas, G	1999	Chris Samuels, Alabama, OL
1966	Loyd Phillips, Arkansas, T	2000	John Henderson, Tennessee, DT
1967	Ron Yary, USC, T	2001	Bryant McKinnie, Miami (Fla.), OT
1968	Bill Stanfill, Georgia, T	2002	Rien Long, Washington St, DL
1969	Mike Reid, Penn St, DT	2003	Robert Gallery, Iowa, OT
1970	Jim Stillwagon, Ohio St, MG	2004	Jammal Brown, Oklahoma, OT
1971	Larry Jacobson, Nebraska, DT	2005	Greg Eslinger, Minnesota, C
1972	Rich Glover, Nebraska, MG	2006	Joe Thomas, Wisconsin, OT
1973	John Hicks, Ohio St, OT	2007	Glenn Dorsey, LSU, DT
1974	Randy White, Maryland, DE	2008	Andre Smith, Alabama, OT
1975	Lee Roy Selmon, Oklahoma, DT	2009	Ndamukong Suh, Nebraska, DT
1976	Ross Browner, Notre Dame, DE	2010	Gabe Carimi, Wisconsin, OT
1977	Brad Shearer, Texas, DT	2011	Barrett Jones, Alabama, OT
1978	Greg Roberts, Oklahoma, G	2012	Luke Joeckel, Texas A&M, OT
1979	Jim Ritcher, North Carolina St, C		

Butkus Award

Given to the top collegiate linebacker, the award was established by the Downtown Athletic Club of Orlando and named for college Hall of Famer Dick Butkus of Illinois.

Year	Player, College
1985	Brian Bosworth, Oklahoma
1986	Brian Bosworth, Oklahoma
1987	Paul McGowan, Florida St
1988	Derrick Thomas, Alabama
1989	Percy Snow, Michigan St
1990	Alfred Williams, Colorado
1991	Erick Anderson, Michigan
1992	Marvin Jones, Florida St
1993	Trev Alberts, Nebraska
1994	Dana Howard, Illinois
1995	Kevin Hardy, Illinois
1996	Matt Russell, Colorado
1997	Andy Katzenmoyer, Ohio St
1998	Chris Claiborne, USC
1999	LaVar Arrington, Penn St
2000	Dan Morgan, Miami (Fla.)
2001	Rocky Calmus, Oklahoma
2002	E.J. Henderson, Maryland
2003	Teddy Lehman, Oklahoma
2004	Derrick Johnson, Texas
2005	Paul Posluszny, Penn State
2006	Patrick Willis, Mississippi
2007	James Laurinaitis, Ohio St
2008	Aaron Curry, Wake Forest
2009	Rolando McClain, Alabama
2010	Von Miller, Texas A&M
2011	Luke Kuechly, Boston College
2012	Manti Te'o, Notre Dame

Jim Thorpe Award

Given to the best defensive back of the year, the award is presented by the Jim Thorpe Athletic Club of Oklahoma City.

Year	Player, College
1986	Thomas Everett, Baylor
1987	Bennie Blades, Miami (Fla.) Rickey Dixon, Oklahoma
1988	Deion Sanders, Florida St
1989	Mark Carrier, USC
1990	Darryl Lewis, Arizona
1991	Terrell Buckley, Florida St
1992	Deon Figures, Colorado
1993	Antonio Langham, Alabama
1994	Chris Hudson, Colorado
1995	Greg Myers, Colorado St
1996	Lawrence Wright, Florida
1997	Charles Woodson, Michigan
1998	Antoine Winfield, Ohio St
1999	Tyrone Carter, Minnesota
2000	Jamar Fletcher, Wisconsin
2001	Roy Williams, Oklahoma
2002	Terence Newman, Kansas St
2003	Derrick Strait, Oklahoma
2004	Carlos Rogers, Auburn
2005	Michael Huff, Texas
2006	Aaron Ross, Texas
2007	Antoine Cason, Arizona
2008	Malcolm Jenkins, Ohio St
2009	Eric Berry, Tennessee
2010	Patrick Peterson, LSU
2011	Morris Claiborne, LSU
2012	Johnthan Banks, Mississippi St

Walter Payton Player of the Year Award

Given to the top FCS (I-AA) player, voted by Div. I-AA sports information directors.

Year	Player, College, Position
1987	Kenny Gamble, Colgate, RB
1988	Dave Meggett, Towson St, RB
1989	John Friesz, Idaho, QB
1990	Walter Dean, Grambling, RB
1991	Jamie Martin, Weber St, QB
1992	Michael Payton, Marshall, QB
1993	Doug Nussmeier, Idaho, QB
1994	Steve McNair, Alcorn St, QB
1995	Dave Dickenson, Montana, QB
1996	Archie Amerson, Northern Arizona, RB
1997	Brian Finneran, Villanova, WR
1998	Jerry Azumah, New Hampshire, RB
1999	Adrian Peterson, Georgia Southern, RB
2000	Louis Ivory, Furman, RB
2001	Brian Westbrook, Villanova, RB
2002	Tony Romo, Eastern Ilinois, QB
2003	Jamaal Branch, Colgate, RB
2004	Lang Campbell, William & Mary, QB
2005	Erik Meyer, Eastern Washington, QB
2006	Ricky Santos, New Hampshire, QB
2007	Jayson Foster, Georgia Southern, QB
2008	Armanti Edwards, Appalachian St, QB
2009	Armanti Edwards, Appalachian St, QB
2010	Jeremy Moses, Stephen F. Austin, QB
2011	Bo Levi Mitchell, Eastern Washington, QB
2012	Taylor Heinicke, Old Dominion, QB

Career

SCORING

Most Points Scored: 500—Montee Ball, Wisconsin, 2009–12

Most Points Scored per Game: 12.1—Marshall Faulk, San Diego St, 1991–93

Most Touchdowns Scored: 83—Montee Ball, Wisconsin, 2009–12 (77 rushing, 6 receiving)

Most Touchdowns Scored per Game: 2.0—Marshall Faulk, San Diego St, 1991–93

Most Touchdowns Scored, Rushing: 77—Montee Ball, Wisconsin, 2009–12

Most Touchdowns Scored, Passing: 155—Case Keenum, Houston, 2007–11; 131—Colt Brennan, Hawaii, 2005–07 (3 years)

Most Touchdowns Scored, Receiving: 60—Jarrett Dillard, Rice, 2005–08

Most Touchdowns Scored, Interception Returns: 5—1996–99; Darrent Williams, Okla St, 2001–04; Ken Thomas, San Jose St, 1979–82; Jackie Walker, Tennessee, 1969–71; Deltha O'Neal, California,

Most Touchdowns Scored, Punt Returns: 8—Wes Welker, Texas Tech, 2000–03; Antonio Perkins, Oklahoma, 2001–04

Most Touchdowns Scored, Kickoff Returns: 7—C.J. Spiller, Clemson, 2006–09

TOTAL OFFENSE

Most Plays: 2,587—Timmy Chang, Hawaii, 2000–04

Most Plays per Game: 50.1—Kliff Kingsbury, Texas Tech, 1999–2002

Most Yards Gained: 20,114—Case Keenum, Houston, 2007-11 (897 rushing, 19,217 passing)

Most Yards Gained per Game: 387.9—Colt Brennan, Hawaii, 2005–07

Most 300+ Yard Games: 40—Case Keenum, Houston, 2007-11

RUSHING

Most Rushes: 1,215—Steve Bartalo, Colorado St, 1983–86 (4,813 yds)

Most Rushes per Game: 34.0—Ed Marinaro, Cornell, 1969–71

Most Yards Gained: 6,397—Ron Dayne, Wisconsin, 1996–99

Most Yards Gained per Game: 174.6—Ed Marinaro, Cornell, 1969–71

Most 100+ Yard Games: 34—DeAngelo Williams, Memphis, 2002–05

Most 200+ Yard Games: 11—Marcus Allen, USC, 1978–81; Ricky Williams, Texas, 1995–98; Ron Dayne, Wisconsin, 1996–99

SPECIAL TEAMS

Highest Punt Return Average: 23.6—Jack Mitchell, Oklahoma, 1946–48

††Highest Kickoff Return Average: 35.1—Anthony Davis, Southern California, 1972-74

Highest Average Yards per Punt: 46.3—Todd Sauerbrun, West Virginia, 1991–93 (150–199 punts). 45.3—Ryan Plackemeier, Wake Forest, 2002–05 (200-250 punts). 45.2—Daniel Sepulveda, Baylor, 2003–06 (250+ punts).

†Minimum 200 receptions.
‡Minimum 275 plays.
††Minimum 1.2 returns per game and 30 returns.

PASSING

Highest Passing Efficiency Rating: 175.6—Sam Bradford, Oklahoma, 2007–09 (min. 325 comp.)

Most Passes Attempted: 2,436—Timmy Chang, Hawaii, 2000–04

Most Passes Attempted per Game: 47.0—Tim Rattay, Louisiana Tech, 1997–99

Most Passes Completed: 1,546—Case Keenum, Houston, 2007–11

Most Passes Completed per Game: 31.2—Graham Harrell, Texas Tech, 2005–08

Highest Completion Percentage: 70.4—Colt Brennan, Hawaii, 2005–07

Most Yards Gained: 19,217—Case Keenum, Houston, 2007–11

Most Yards Gained per Game: 386.2—Tim Rattay, Louisiana Tech, 1997–99 (3 years); 351.0—Graham Harrell, Texas Tech, 2005–08 (4 years)

RECEIVING

Most Passes Caught: 349—Ryan Broyles, Oklahoma, 2008-11 (4,586 yards)

Most Passes Caught per Game: 10.5—Emmanuel Hazard, Houston, 1989–90

Most Yards Gained: 5,005—Trevor Insley, Nevada, 1996–99

Most Yards Gained per Game: 140.9—Alex Van Dyke, Nevada, 1994–95

†Highest Average Gain per Reception: 19.0—Ryan Yarborough, Wyoming, 1990–93

ALL-PURPOSE RUNNING

Most Plays: 1,347—Steve Bartalo, Colorado St, 1983-86 (1,215 rushes, 132 receptions)

Most Yards Gained: 7,796—Damaris Johnson, Tulsa, 2008–10 (1,062 rushing, 2,746 receiving, 3,417 KO returns, 571 punt returns)

Most Yards Gained per Game: 237.8—Ryan Benjamin, Pacific, 1990–92

‡Highest Average Gain per Play: 17.4—Anthony Carter, Michigan, 1979–82

INTERCEPTIONS

Most Passes Intercepted: 29—Al Brosky, Illinois, 1950–52

Most Passes Intercepted per Game: 1.1—Al Brosky, Illinois, 1950–52

Most Yards on Interception Returns: 501—Terrell Buckley, Florida St, 1989–91

Highest Average Gain per Interception: 26.5—Tom Pridemore, West Virginia, 1975–77

Single Season

SCORING

Most Points Scored: 236—Montee Ball, Wisconsin, 2011
Most Points Scored per Game: 21.3—Barry Sanders, Oklahoma St, 1988
Most Touchdowns Scored: 39—Barry Sanders, Oklahoma St, 1988; Montee Ball, Wisconsin, 2011
Most Touchdowns Scored, Rushing: 39—Barry Sanders, Oklahoma St, 1988
Most Touchdowns Scored, Passing: 58—Colt Brennan, Hawaii, 2006
Most Touchdowns Scored, Receiving: 27—Troy Edwards, Louisiana Tech, 1998
Most Touchdowns Scored, Interception Returns: 4—Deltha O'Neal, California, 1999
Most Touchdowns Scored, Punt Returns: 5—Chad Owens, Hawaii, 2004
Most Touchdowns Scored, Kickoff Returns: 5—Ashlan Davis, Tulsa, 2004

TOTAL OFFENSE

Most Plays: 814—Kliff Kingsbury, Texas Tech, 2002
Most Yards Gained: 5,976—B.J. Symons, Texas Tech, 2003
Most Yards Gained per Game: 474.6—David Klingler, Houston, 1990
Most 300+ Yard Games: 14—Colt Brennan, Hawaii, 2006; Paul Smith, Tulsa, 2007

RUSHING

Most Rushes: 450—Kevin Smith, Central Florida, 2007
Most Rushes per Game: 39.6—Ed Marinaro, Cornell, 1971
Most Yards Gained: 2,628—Barry Sanders, Oklahoma St, 1988
Most Yards Gained per Game: 238.9—Barry Sanders, Oklahoma St, 1988
Most 100+ Yard Games: 13—Shonn Greene, Iowa, 2008

PASSING

Highest Passing Efficiency Rating: 191.78—Russell Wilson, Wisconsin, 2011
Most Passes Attempted: 719—B.J. Symons, Texas Tech, 2003
Most Passes Attempted per Game: 58.5—David Klingler, Houston, 1990
Most Passes Completed: 512—Graham Harrell, Texas Tech, 2007

PASSING (Cont.)

Most Passes Completed per Game: 39.4—Graham Harrell, Texas Tech, 2007
Highest Completion Percentage: 76.7—Colt McCoy, Texas, 2008
Most Yards Gained: 5,140—David Klingler, Houston, 1990 (11 games); 5,336—B.J. Symons, Texas Tech, 2003 (12 games); 5,833—B.J. Symons, Texas Tech, 2003 (13-plus games)
Most Yards Gained per Game: 467.3—David Klingler, Houston, 1990

RECEIVING

Most Passes Caught: 155—Freddie Barnes, Bowling Green, 2009
Most Passes Caught per Game: 13.4—Howard Twilley, Tulsa, 1965
Most Yards Gained: 2,060—Trevor Insley, Nevada, 1999
Most Yards Gained per Game: 187.3—Trevor Insley, Nevada, 1999
Highest Average Gain per Reception: 31.9—Brennan Marion, Tulsa, 2007 (min. 30 receptions)

ALL-PURPOSE RUNNING

Most Plays: 432—Marcus Allen, USC, 1981
Most Yards Gained: 3,250—Barry Sanders, Oklahoma St, 1988
Most Yards Gained per Game: 295.5—Barry Sanders, Oklahoma St, 1988
Highest Average Gain per Play: 21.2—Taveon Rogers, New Mexico St, 2011 (min. 100 plays)

INTERCEPTIONS

Most Passes Intercepted: 14—Al Worley, Washington, 1968
Most Yards on Interception Returns: 302—Charles Phillips, USC, 1974
Highest Average Gain per Interception: 51.8—Norm Thompson, Utah, 1969

SPECIAL TEAMS

Highest Punt Return Average: 28.5—Maurice Drew, UCLA, 2005
Highest Kickoff Return Average: 40.1—Paul Allen, BYU, 1961
Highest Average Yards per Punt: 50.3—Chad Kessler, LSU, 1997 (min. 36 punts)

Single Game

SCORING

Most Points Scored: 48—Howard Griffith, Illinois, 1990 (vs Southern Illinois)
Most Field Goals: 7—Dale Klein, Nebraska, 1985 (vs Missouri); Mike Prindle, Western Michigan, 1984 (vs Marshall)
Most Extra Points (Kick): 13—Derek Mahoney, Fresno St, 1991 (vs New Mexico); Terry Leiweke, Houston, 1968 (vs Tulsa)
Most Extra Points (2-Pts): 6—Jim Pilot, New Mexico St, 1961 (vs Hardin-Simmons), all 6 rush

PASSING

Most Passes Completed: 58—Andy Schmitt, Eastern Michigan, 2008 (vs Central Michigan)
Most Yards Gained: 716—David Klingler, Houston, 1990 (vs Arizona St)
Most Touchdown Passes: 11—David Klingler, Houston, 1990 [vs Eastern Washington (I-AA)]

TOTAL OFFENSE

Most Yards Gained: 732—David Klingler, Houston, 1990 (vs Arizona St); (716 pass, 16 rush)

RUSHING

Most Yards Gained: 406—LaDainian Tomlinson, TCU, 1999 (vs UTEP)
Most Touchdowns Rushed: 8—Howard Griffith, Illinois, 1990 (vs Southern Illinois)

RECEIVING

Most Passes Caught: 23—Randy Gatewood, UNLV, 1994 (vs Idaho); Tyler Jones, Eastern Michigan, 2008 (vs Central Michigan)
Most Yards Gained: 405—Troy Edwards, Louisiana Tech, 1998 (vs Nebraska)
Most Touchdown Catches: 7—Rashaun Woods, Oklahoma St, 2003 (vs SMU)

Career

SCORING

Most Points Scored: 544—Brian Westbrook, Villanova, 1997–98, 2000-01
Most Touchdowns Scored: 89—Brian Westbrook, Villanova, 1997–98, 2000-01
Most Touchdowns Scored, Rushing: 84—Adrian Peterson, Georgia Southern, 1998–2001
Most Touchdowns Scored, Passing: 140—Bruce Eugene, Grambling St, 2001–05
Most Touchdowns Scored, Receiving: 58—David Ball, New Hampshire, 2003–06

RUSHING

Most Rushes: 1,240—Jordan Scott, Colgate, 2005–08
Most Rushes per Game: 38.2—Arnold Mickens, Butler, 1994–95
Most Yards Gained: 6,559—Adrian Peterson, Georgia Southern, 1998–2001
Most Yards Gained per Game: 190.7—Arnold Mickens, Butler, 1994–95 (2 years); 164.5—Adrian Peterson, Georgia Southern, 1998–2000 (3 years); 156.2—Adrian Peterson, Georgia Southern, 1998–2001 (4 years)

PASSING

Highest Passing Efficiency Rating: 176.7—Josh Johnson, San Diego, 2004–07
Most Passes Attempted: 1,893—Jeremy Moses, Stephen F. Austin, 2007–10
Most Passes Completed: 1,184—Jeremy Moses, Stephen F. Austin, 2007–10
Most Passes Completed per Game: 26.9—Jeremy Moses, Stephen F. Austin, 2007–10 (min. 1,000 comp.)
Highest Completion Percentage: 69.6—Eric Sanders, Northern Iowa, 2004–07
Most Yards Gained: 14,496—Steve McNair, Alcorn St, 1991–94
Most Yards Gained per Game: 350.0—Neil Lomax, Portland St, 1978–80

RECEIVING

Most Passes Caught: 395—Terrell Hudgins, Elon, 2006–09
Most Yards Gained: 5,250—Terrell Hudgins, Elon, 2006–09
Most Yards Gained per Game: 116.7—Terrell Hudgins, Elon, 2006–09 (min. 3,000 yds)
Highest Average Gain per Reception: 22.0—Dedric Ward, Northern Iowa, 1993–96 (min. 125 rec.)

Single Season

SCORING

Most Points Scored: 234—Omar Cuff, Delaware, 2007
Most Touchdowns Scored: 39—Omar Cuff, Delaware, 2007 (15 games)
Most Touchdowns Scored, Rushing: 35—Omar Cuff, Delaware, 2007
Most Touchdowns Scored, Passing: 56—Willie Totten, Mississippi Valley St, 1984; Bruce Eugene, Grambling St, 2005
Most Touchdowns Scored, Receiving: 27—Jerry Rice, Mississippi Valley St, 1984

RUSHING

Most Rushes: 450—Jamaal Branch, Colgate, 2003
Most Rushes per Game: 40.9—Arnold Mickens, Butler, 1994
Most Yards Gained: 2,326—Jamaal Branch, Colgate, 2003
Most Yards Gained per Game: 225.5—Arnold Mickens, Butler, 1994

PASSING

Highest Passing Efficiency Rating: 204.6—Shawn Knight, William & Mary, 1993
Most Passes Attempted: 598—Jeremy Moses, Stephen F. Austin, 2008
Most Passes Completed: 385—Brett Gordon, Villanova, 2002; Jeremy Moses, Stephen F. Austin, 2009
Most Passes Completed per Game: 32.4—Willie Totten, Mississippi Valley St, 1984
Highest Completion Percentage: 75.2—Eric Sanders, Northern Iowa, 2007
Most Yards Gained: 5,076—Taylor Heinicke, Old Dominion, 2012
Most Yards Gained per Game: 455.7—Willie Totten, Mississippi Valley St, 1984

RECEIVING

Most Passes Caught: 136—Erik Lora, Eastern Illinois, 2012
Most Yards Gained: 1,850—Brandon Kaufman, Eastern Washington, 2012
Most Yards Gained per Game: 168.2—Jerry Rice, Mississippi Valley St, 1984
Highest Average Gain per Reception: 28.9—Mikhael Ricks, Stephen F. Austin, 1997; (min. 35 receptions); 21.0—Kevin Norrell, Stony Brook, 2012 (min. 60 receptions)

Single Game

SCORING

Most Points Scored: 42—Omar Cuff, Delaware, 2007 (vs William & Mary); Jesse Burton, McNeese St, 1998 (vs Southern Utah); Archie Amerson, Northern Arizona, 1996 (vs Weber St)
Most Field Goals: 8—Goran Lingmerth, Northern Arizona, 1986 (vs Idaho)

RUSHING

Most Yards Gained: 437—Maurice Hicks, North Carolina A&T, 2001 (vs Morgan St)
Most Touchdowns Rushed: 7—Archie Amerson, Northern Arizona, 1996 (vs Weber St)

PASSING

Most Passes Completed: 57—Jeremy Moses, Stephen F. Austin, 2008, (vs. Sam Houston St)
Most Yards Gained: 730—Taylor Heinicke, Old Dominion, 2012 (vs New Hampshire)
Most Touchdown Passes: 9—Willie Totten, Mississippi Valley St, 1984 (vs Kentucky St); Drew Hubel, Portland St, 2007 (vs Weber St)

RECEIVING

Most Passes Caught: 24—Chas Gessner, Brown, 2002, (vs Rhode Island); Jerry Rice, Mississippi Valley St, 1983 (vs Southern–Birmingham)
Most Yards Gained: 376—Kassim Osgood, Cal Poly, 2000 (vs Northern Iowa)
Most Touchdown Catches: 6—Cos DeMatteo, Chattanooga, 2000 (vs Mississippi Valley St)

NCAA Division II Individual Records

Career

SCORING

Most Points Scored: 656—Germaine Rice, Pittsburg St, 2003–06
Most Touchdowns Scored: 109—Germaine Rice, Pittsburg St, 2003–06; Danny Woodhead, Chadron St 2004–07
Most Touchdowns Scored, Rushing: 107—Germaine Rice, Pittsburg St, 2003–06
Most Touchdowns Scored, Passing: 148—Jimmy Terwilliger, East Stroudsburg, 2003–06
Most Touchdowns Scored, Receiving: 78—Dallas Mall, Bentley, 2001–04

RUSHING

Most Rushes: 1,271—Xavier Omon, NW Missouri St, 2004–07
Most Rushes per Game: 29.8—Bernie Peeters, Luther, 1968–71
Most Yards Gained: 7,962—Danny Woodhead, Chadron St, 2004–07
Most Yards Gained per Game: 183.4—Anthony Gray, Western New Mexico, 1997–98

PASSING

Highest Passing Efficiency Rating: 170.7—Jimmy Terwilliger, East Stroudsburg, 2003–06 (Min. 750 comps.)
Most Passes Attempted: 1,898—Andrew Webb, Fort Lewis, 2000–03

PASSING *(Cont.)*

Most Passes Completed: 1,119—Steven Gachette, Southwest Baptist, 2007–10
Most Passes Completed per Game: 25.9—Evan Gray, Missouri S&T*, 2003–05
Highest Completion Percentage: 70.2—Troy Weatherhead, Hillsdale, 2006–10 (min. 1,000 att.)
Most Yards Gained: 14,733—Zach Amedro, West Liberty, 2007–10
Most Yards Gained per Game: 334.8—Zach Amedro, West Liberty, 2007–10

RECEIVING

Most Passes Caught: 323—Clarence Coleman, Ferris St, 1998–2001
Most Yards Gained: 4,983—Clarence Coleman, Ferris St, 1998–2001
Most Yards Gained per Game: 160.8—Chris George, Glenville St, 1993–94
Highest Average Gain per Reception: 23.2—Romar Crenshaw, SE Oklahoma, 2000–03 (min. 135 receptions)

*Missouri S&T was formerly known as Missouri-Rolla.

Single Season

SCORING

Most Points Scored: 228—Xavier Odom, Northwest Missouri St, 2007; Danny Woodhead, Chadron St, 2006

Most Touchdowns Scored: 38—Xavier Omon, NW Missouri St, 2007; Danny Woodhead, Chadron St, 2006

Most Touchdowns Scored, Rushing: 37—Xavier Omon, NW Missouri St, 2007

Most Touchdowns Scored, Passing: 54—Dusty Bonner, Valdosta St, 2000; Zach Zulli, Shippensburg, 2012

Most Touchdowns Scored, Receiving: 35—David Kircus, Grand Valley St, 2002

RUSHING

Most Rushes: 385—Joe Gough, Wayne St (Mich.), 1994

Most Rushes per Game: 38.6—Mark Perkins, Hobart, 1968

Most Yards Gained: 2,756—Danny Woodhead, Chadron St, 2006

Most Yards Gained per Game: 222.0—Anthony Gray, Western New Mexico, 1997

PASSING

Highest Passing Efficiency Rating: 221.6—Curt Anes, Grand Valley St, 2001 (min. 100 comp.); 196.5—Dusty Bonner, Valdosta St, 2001 (min. 200 comp.)

Most Passes Attempted: 670—Eric Czerniewski, Central Missouri, 2010

Most Passes Completed: 447—Eric Czerniewski, Central Missouri, 2010

Most Passes Completed per Game: 40.4—J.J. Harp, Eastern New Mexico, 2009

Highest Completion Percentage: 76.9—Troy Weatherhead, Hillsdale, 2010 (min. 250 att.)

Most Yards Gained: 5,207—Eric Czerniewski, Central Missouri, 2010

Most Yards Gained per Game: 437.3—J.J. Harp, Eastern New Mexico, 2009

RECEIVING

Most Passes Caught: 143—Nick Smart, Southwest Baptist, 2007

Most Yards Gained: 1,876—Chris George, Glenville St, 1993

Most Yards Gained per Game: 187.6—Chris George, Glenville St, 1993

Highest Average Gain per Reception: 32.5—Tyrone Johnson, Western St, 1991 (min. 30 receptions)

Single Game

SCORING

Most Points Scored: 48—Paul Zaeske, North Park, 1968 (vs North Central [Ill.]); Junior Wolf, Okla. Panhandle St, 1958 (vs St. Mary [Ks.])

Most Field Goals: 6—Steve Huff, Central Missouri St, 1985 (vs SE Missouri St); Austin Wellock, Ashland, 2002 (vs. Wayne St)

RUSHING

Most Yards Gained: 418—Jarom Freeman, Southern Connecticut St, 2007 (vs Bryant)

Most Touchdowns Rushed: 8—Junior Wolf, Okla. Panhandle St, 1958 (vs St. Mary [Ks.])

PASSING

Most Passes Completed: 64—J.J. Harp, Eastern New Mexico, 2009 (vs SE Oklahoma)

Most Yards Gained: 695—J.J. Harp, Eastern New Mexico, 2009 (vs SE Oklahoma)

Most Touchdowns Passed: 10—Bruce Swanson, North Park, 1968 (vs North Central [Ill.])

RECEIVING

Most Passes Caught: 23—Chris George, Glenville St, 1994 (vs W.V. Wesleyan); Barry Wagner, Alabama A&M, 1989 (vs Clark Atlanta)

Most Yards Gained: 401—Kevin Ingram, West Chester, 1998 (vs Clarion)

Most Touchdown Catches: 8—Paul Zaeske, North Park, 1968 (vs North Central [Ill.])

NCAA Division III Individual Records

Career

SCORING

Most Points Scored: 780—Nate Kmic, Mount Union, 2005–08

Most Touchdowns Scored: 130—Nate Kmic, Mount Union, 2005–08

Most Touchdowns Scored, Rushing: 125—Nate Kmic, Mount Union, 2005–08

Most Touchdowns Scored, Passing: 148—Justin Peery, Westminster (Mo.), 1996–99

Most Touchdowns Scored, Receiving: 75—Scott Pingel, Westminster (Mo.), 1996–99

RUSHING

Most Rushes: 1,324—Levell Coppage, Wis.-Whitewater, 2008-11

Most Rushes per Game: 32.7—Chris Sizemore, Bridgewater (Va.), 1972–74

RUSHING (Cont.)

Most Yards Gained: 8,074—Nate Kmic, Mount Union, 2005–08

Most Yards Gained per Game: 187.1—Tony Sutton, Wooster, 2002–04

PASSING

Highest Passing Efficiency Rating: 194.2—Greg Micheli, Mount Union, 2005–08 (min. 325 comps.)

Most Passes Attempted: 1,982—Josh Vogelbach, Guilford, 2005–08

Most Passes Completed: 1,205—Alex Tanney, Monmouth (Ill.), 2007-11

Most Passes Completed per Game: 29.7—Josh Vogelbach, Guilford, 2005–08

Highest Completion Percentage: 74.1—Greg Micheli, Mount Union, 2005–08 (min. 750 att.)

Career *(Cont.)*

PASSING *(Cont.)*

Most Yards Gained: 14,249—Alex Tanney, Monmouth (Ill.), 2007-11
Most Yards Gained per Game: 358.9—Brett Elliott, Linfield, 2004–05

RECEIVING

Most Passes Caught: 463—Michael Zweifel, Wis.-River Falls/Dubuque, 2007–11
Most Yards Gained: 6,108—Scott Pingel, Westminster (Mo.), 1996–99
Most Yards Gained per Game: 156.6—Scott Pingel, Westminster (Mo.), 1996–99
Highest Average Gain per Reception: 23.4—Michael Coleman, Widener, 1998–2001

Single Season

SCORING

Most Points Scored: 264—Nate Kmic, Mount Union, 2008
Most Points Scored per Game: 20.8—James Regan, Pomona-Pitzer, 1997
Most Touchdowns Scored: 44—Nate Kmic, Mount Union, 2008
Most Touchdowns Scored, Rushing: 43—Nate Kmic, Mount Union, 2008
Most Touchdowns Scored, Passing: 61—Brett Elliott, Linfield, 2004
Most Touchdowns Scored, Receiving: 26—Scott Pingel, Westminster (Mo.), 1998; Jack Phelan, Hartwick, 2008

RUSHING

Most Rushes: 463—Dante Washington, Carthage, 2004
Most Rushes per Game: 38.0—Mike Birosak, Dickinson, 1989
Most Yards Gained: 2,790—Nate Kmic, Mount Union, 2008
Most Yards Gained per Game: 238.5—Dante Brown, Marietta, 1996

PASSING

Highest Passing Efficiency Rating: 225.0—Mike Simpson, Eureka, 1994
Most Passes Attempted: 575—Brett Dietz, Hanover, 2003
Most Passes Completed: 360—Brett Dietz, Hanover, 2003
Most Passes Completed per Game: 32.9—Justin Peery, Westminster (Mo.), 1999
Highest Completion Percentage: 75.0—Greg Micheli, Mount Union, 2008
Most Yards Gained: 4,595—Brett Elliott, Linfield, 2004
Most Yards Gained per Game: 450.1—Justin Peery, Westminster (Mo.), 1998

RECEIVING

Most Passes Caught: 140—Michael Zweifel, Dubuque, 2011
Most Yards Gained: 2,157—Scott Pingel, Westminster, (Mo.), 1998
Most Yards Gained per Game: 215.7—Scott Pingel, Westminster, (Mo.), 1998
Highest Average Gain per Reception: 26.9—Marty Redlawsk, Concordia (Ill.), 1985 (min. 35 receptions)

Single Game

SCORING

Most Points Scored: 48—Carey Bender, Coe, 1994 (vs Beloit)
Most Field Goals: 6—Jim Hever, Rhodes, 1984 (vs Millsaps)

PASSING

Most Passes Completed: 56—Brandon Luczak, Kalamazoo, 2009 (vs Hope)
Most Yards Gained: 731—Zamir Amin, Menlo, 2000 (vs California Lutheran)
Most Touchdown Passes: 9—Joe Zarlinga, Ohio Northern, 1998 (vs Capital)

RUSHING

Most Yards Gained: 441—Dante Brown, Marietta, 1996 (vs Baldwin-Wallace)
Most Touchdowns Rushed: 8—Carey Bender, Coe, 1994 (vs Beloit)

RECEIVING

Most Passes Caught: 25—Daniel Passafiume, Hanover, 2009 (vs Franklin)
Most Yards Gained: 418—Lewis Howes, Principia, 2002 (vs Martin Luther)
Most Touchdown Catches: 7—Matt Perceval, Wesleyan (Conn.), 1998 (vs Middlebury)

Career

Scoring

POINTS (KICKERS)

	Years	Pts
Dustin Hopkins, Florida St	2009–12	466
Kyle Brotzman, Boise St	2007–10	439
Art Carmody, Louisville	2004–07	433
‡Kevin Kelly, Penn St	2005–08	425
Roman Anderson, Houston	1988–91	423

‡includes one TD and one 2-pt. conversion (rush)

POINTS (NON-KICKERS)

	Years	Pts
Montee Ball, Wisconsin	2009–12	500
Travis Prentice, Miami (Ohio)	1996–99	468
Ricky Williams, Texas	1995–98	452
Taurean Henderson, Texas Tech	2002–05	414
Brock Forsey, Boise St	1999–02	408

POINTS PER GAME (NON-KICKERS)

	Years	Pts/Game
Marshall Faulk, San Diego St	1991–93	12.1
Ed Marinaro, Cornell	1969–71	11.8
Bill Burnett, Arkansas	1968–70	11.3
Steve Owens, Oklahoma	1967–69	11.2
Eddie Talboom, Wyoming	1948–50	10.8

Total Offense

YARDS GAINED

	Years	Yds
Case Keenum, Houston	2007–11	20,114
Timmy Chang, Hawaii	2000–04	16,910
Landry Jones, Oklahoma	2009–12	16,271
Dan LeFevour, Central Michigan	2006–09	15,853
Graham Harrell, Texas Tech	2005–08	15,599
Colt McCoy, Texas	2006–09	14,824

YARDS PER GAME

	Years	Yds/Game
Colt Brennan, Hawaii	2005–07	387.9
Tim Rattay, Louisiana Tech	1997–99	382.4
Case Keenum, Houston	2007–11	352.9
Graham Harrell, Texas Tech	2005–08	346.6
Chase Holbrook, New Mexico St	2005–08	321.4

Rushing

YARDS GAINED

	Years	Yds
Ron Dayne, Wisconsin	1996–99	6,397
Ricky Williams, Texas	1995–98	6,279
Tony Dorsett, Pittsburgh	1973–76	6,082
DeAngelo Williams, Memphis	2002–05	6,026
Charles White, USC	1976–79	5,598
Travis Prentice, Miami (Ohio)	1996–99	5,596

YARDS PER GAME

	Years	Yds/Game
Ed Marinaro, Cornell	1969–71	174.6
O.J. Simpson, USC	1967–68	164.4
Herschel Walker, Georgia	1980–82	159.4
Garrett Wolfe, Northern Illinois	2004-06	156.5
LeShon Johnson, Northern Illinois	1992–93	150.6

TOUCHDOWNS RUSHING

	Years	TD
Montee Ball, Wisconsin	2009–12	77
Travis Prentice, Miami (Ohio)	1996–99	73
Ricky Williams, Texas	1995–98	72
Anthony Thompson, Indiana	1986–89	64
Cedric Benson, Texas	2001–04	64
Ron Dayne, Wisconsin	1996–99	63

Passing

PASSING EFFICIENCY

	Years	Rating
Sam Bradford, Oklahoma	2007–09	175.6
Tim Tebow, Florida	2006–09	170.8
Kellen Moore, Boise St	2008–11	169.0
Ryan Dinwiddie, Boise St	2000–03	168.9
Colt Brennan, Hawaii	2005–07	167.7

Note: Minimum 500 completions.

YARDS GAINED

	Years	Yds
Case Keenum, Houston	2007–11	19,217
Timmy Chang, Hawaii	2000–04	17,072
Landry Jones, Oklahoma	2009–12	16,646
Graham Harrell, Texas Tech	2005–08	15,793
Ty Detmer, BYU	1988–91	15,031

COMPLETIONS

	Years	Comp
Case Keenum, Houston	2007–11	1,546
Graham Harrell, Texas Tech	2005–08	1,403
Timmy Chang, Hawaii	2000–04	1,388
Kliff Kingsbury, Texas Tech	1999–02	1,231
Dan LeFevour, Central Michigan	2006–09	1,171

TOUCHDOWNS PASSING

	Years	TD
Case Keenum, Houston	2007–11	155
Kellen Moore, Boise St	2008–11	142
Graham Harrell, Texas Tech	2005–08	134
Colt Brennan, Hawaii	2005–07	131
Landry Jones, Oklahoma	2009–12	123

Receiving

CATCHES

	Years	No.
Ryan Broyles, Oklahoma	2008–11	349
Tyron Carrier, Houston	2008–11	320
Taylor Stubblefield, Purdue	2001–04	316
Josh Davis, Marshall	2001–04	306
Jordan White, W Michigan	2007, 09–11	306
Eric Page, Toledo	2009–11	306

CATCHES PER GAME

	Years	No./Game
Emmanuel Hazard, Houston	1989–90	10.5
Alex Van Dyke, Nevada	1994–95	10.3
Jason Phillips, Houston	1987–88	9.4
Michael Crabtree, Texas Tech	2007–08	8.9
Howard Twilley, Tulsa	1963–65	8.7

YARDS GAINED

	Years	Yds
Trevor Insley, Nevada	1996–99	5,005
Ryan Broyles, Oklahoma	2008-11	4,586
Marcus Harris, Wyoming	1993–96	4,518
Rashaun Woods, Oklahoma St	2000–03	4,414
Ryan Yarborough, Wyoming	1990–93	4,357

TOUCHDOWN CATCHES

	Years	TD
Jarrett Dillard, Rice	2005–08	60
Troy Edwards, Louisiana Tech	1996–98	50
Darius Watts, Marshall	2000–03	47
Ryan Broyles, Oklahoma	2008–11	45
Aaron Turner, Pacific	1989–92	43

Career *(Cont.)*

All-Purpose Running

YARDS GAINED	Years	Yds
Damaris Johnson, Tulsa	2008–10	7,796
Brandon West, Western Michigan	2006–09	7,764
C.J. Spiller, Clemson	2006–09	7,588
DeAngelo Williams, Memphis	2002–05	7,573
T.Y. Hilton, FIU	2008–11	7,498

YARDS PER GAME	Years	Yds/Game
Ryan Benjamin, Pacific	1990–92	237.8
Sheldon Canley, San Jose St	1988–90	205.8
Jeremy Maclin, Missouri	2007–08	200.3
Damaris Johnson, Tulsa	2008–10	194.9
Howard Stevens, Louisville	1971–72	193.7

Interceptions

PLAYER/SCHOOL	Years	Int
Al Brosky, Illinois	1950–52	29
John Provost, Holy Cross	1972–74	27
Martin Bayless, Bowling Green	1980–83	27
Tom Curtis, Michigan	1967–69	25
Tony Thurman, Boston College	1981–84	25
Tracy Saul, Texas Tech	1989–92	25

Punting Average

PLAYER/SCHOOL	Years	Avg
Daniel Sepulveda, Baylor	2003–06	45.24
Shane Lechler, Texas A&M	1996–99	44.69
Bobby Cowan, Idaho	2009–12	44.67
Bill Smith, Mississippi	1983–86	44.33
Jeff Locke, UCLA	2009–12	44.23

Note: Minimum 250 punts.

Punt Return Average

PLAYER/SCHOOL	Years	Avg
Jack Mitchell, Oklahoma	1946–48	23.6
Gene Gibson, Cincinnati	1949–50	20.5
Eddie Macon, Pacific	1949–51	18.9
Jackie Robinson, UCLA	1939–40	18.8
Dan Shelton, Illinois	2001–04	17.9

Note: Minimum 30 returns.

Kickoff Return Average

PLAYER/SCHOOL	Years	Avg
Anthony Davis, USC	1972–74	35.1
Eric Booth, Southern Miss	1994–97	32.4
Overton Curtis, Utah St	1957–58	31.0
Reggie Dunn, Utah	2010–12	30.9
Justin Miller, Clemson	2001–04	30.7
Fred Montgomery, New Mexico St	1991–92	30.5

Note: Minimum 30 returns.

Single Season

Scoring

POINTS	Year	Pts
Montee Ball, Wisconsin	2011	236
Barry Sanders, Oklahoma St	1988	234
Brock Forsey, Boise St	2002	192
Troy Edwards, Louisiana Tech	1998	186
Kevin Smith, Central Florida	2007	180

FIELD GOALS	Year	FG
Billy Bennett, Georgia	2003	31
Leigh Tiffin, Alabama	2009	30
John Lee, UCLA	1984	29
John Sullivan, New Mexico	2007	29
Randy Bullock, Texas A&M	2011	29

All-Purpose Running

YARDS GAINED	Year	Yds
Barry Sanders, Oklahoma St	1988	3,250
*Antonio Andrews, W Kentucky	2012	3,161
Ryan Benjamin, Pacific	1991	2,995
Chris Johnson, East Carolina	2007	2,960
Tavon Austin, W Virginia	2012	2,910

YARDS PER GAME	Year	Yds/Game
Barry Sanders, Oklahoma St	1988	295.5
Ryan Benjamin, Pacific	1991	249.6
Byron (Whizzer) White, Colorado	1937	246.3
Mike Pringle, Fullerton St	1989	244.6
*Antonio Andrews, W Kentucky	2012	243.2

*Active player.

Total Offense

YARDS GAINED	Year	Yds
B.J. Symons, Texas Tech	2003	5,976
Colt Brennan, Hawaii	2006	5,915
Case Keenum, Houston	2009	5,829
Case Keenum, Houston	2011	5,666
Graham Harrell, Texas Tech	2007	5,614

Total Offense *(Cont.)*

YARDS PER GAME	Year	Yds/Game
David Klingler, Houston	1990	474.6
B.J. Symons, Texas Tech	2003	459.7
Graham Harrell, Texas Tech	2007	431.8
Andre Ware, Houston	1989	423.7
Colt Brennan, Hawaii	2006	422.5

Rushing

YARDS GAINED	Year	Yds
Barry Sanders, Oklahoma St	1988	2,628
Kevin Smith, Central Florida	2007	2,567
Marcus Allen, USC	1981	2,342
Troy Davis, Iowa St	1996	2,185
LaDainian Tomlinson, TCU	2000	2,158

YARDS PER GAME	Year	Yds/Game
Barry Sanders, Oklahoma St	1988	238.9
Marcus Allen, USC	1981	212.9
Ed Marinaro, Cornell	1971	209.0
Troy Davis, Iowa St	1996	198.6
LaDainian Tomlinson, TCU	2000	196.2

TOUCHDOWNS RUSHING	Year	TD
Barry Sanders, Oklahoma St	1988	37
Montee Ball, Wisconsin	2011	33
Mike Rozier, Nebraska	1983	29
Kevin Smith, Central Florida	2007	29
Willis McGahee, Miami (Fla.)	2002	28
Toby Gerhart, Stanford	2009	28

Passing

PASSING EFFICIENCY	Year	Rating
Russell Wilson, Wisconsin	2011	191.8
Robert Griffin III, Baylor	2011	189.5
Colt Brennan, Hawaii	2006	186.0
Shaun King, Tulane	1998	183.3
Kellen Moore, Boise St	2010	182.6

Single Season *(Cont.)*

Passing *(Cont.)*

YARDS GAINED	Year	Yds
B.J. Symons, Texas Tech	2003	5,833
Graham Harrell, Texas Tech	2007	5,705
Case Keenum, Houston	2009	5,671
Case Keenum, Houston	2011	5,631
Colt Brennan, Hawaii	2006	5,549

COMPLETIONS	Year	Att	Comp
Graham Harrell, Texas Tech	2007	713	512
Case Keenum, Houston	2009	700	492
Kliff Kingsbury, Texas Tech	2002	712	479
B.J. Symons, Texas Tech	2003	719	470
Graham Harrell, Texas Tech	2008	626	442

TOUCHDOWNS PASSING	Year	TD
Colt Brennan, Hawaii	2006	58
David Klingler, Houston	1990	54
B.J. Symons, Texas Tech	2003	52
Sam Bradford, Oklahoma	2008	50
Graham Harrell, Texas Tech	2007	48
Case Keenum, Houston	2011	48

Receiving

CATCHES	Year	GP	No.
Freddie Barnes, Bowling Green	2009	13	155
Emmanuel Hazard, Houston	1989	11	142
Troy Edwards, Louisiana Tech	1998	12	140
Jordan White, W Michigan	2011	13	140
Nate Burleson, Nevada	2002	12	138

Receiving *(Cont.)*

CATCHES	Year	GP	No.
Howard Twilley, Tulsa	1965	10	134
Trevor Insley, Nevada	1999	11	134
Michael Crabtree, Texas Tech	2008	13	134

CATCHES PER GAME	Year	No.	No./Game
Howard Twilley, Tulsa	1965	134	13.4
Emmanuel Hazard, Houston	1989	142	12.9
Trevor Insley, Nevada	1999	134	12.2
Freddie Barnes, Bowling Green	2009	155	11.9
Alex Van Dyke, Nevada	1995	129	11.7
Troy Edwards, Louisiana Tech	1998	140	11.7

YARDS GAINED	Year	Yds
Trevor Insley, Nevada	1999	2,060
Troy Edwards, Louisiana Tech	1998	1,996
Michael Crabtree, Texas Tech	2007	1,962
Jordan White, W Michigan	2011	1,911
Greg Salas, Hawaii	2010	1,889

TOUCHDOWN CATCHES	Year	TD
Troy Edwards, Louisiana Tech	1998	27
Randy Moss, Marshall	1997	25
Stedman Bailey, West Virginia	2012	25
Emmanuel Hazard, Houston	1989	22
Larry Fitzgerald, Pittsburgh	2003	22
Michael Crabtree, Texas Tech	2007	22

Single Game

Scoring

POINTS	Opponent	Year	Pts
Howard Griffith, Illinois	Southern Illinois	1990	48
Marshall Faulk, San Diego St.	Pacific	1991	44
Jim Brown, Syracuse	Colgate	1956	43
Fred Wendt, UTEP*	New Mexico St	1948	42
Arnold Boykin, Mississippi	Mississippi St	1951	42
Rashaun Woods, Okla. St	SMU	2003	42

*UTEP was Texas Mines in 1948.

FIELD GOALS	Opponent	Year	FG
Dale Klein, Nebraska	Missouri	1985	7
Mike Prindle, Western Michigan	Marshall	1984	7

Note: 20 tied with 6.

Klein's distances were 32-22-43-44-29-43-43.
Prindle's distances were 32-44-42-23-48-41-27.

Total Offense

YARDS GAINED	Opponent	Year	Yds
David Klingler, Houston	Arizona St	1990	732
Matt Vogler, TCU	Houston	1990	696
Geno Smith, W Virginia	Baylor	2012	687
B.J. Symons, Texas Tech	Mississippi	2003	681
Brian Lindgren, Idaho	Middle Tenn St	2001	657
Graham Harrell, Texas Tech	Oklahoma St	2007	643

Passing

YARDS GAINED	Opponent	Year	Yds
David Klingler, Houston	Arizona St	1990	716
Matt Vogler, TCU	Houston	1990	690
B.J. Symons, Texas Tech	Mississippi	2003	661
Geno Smith, W Virginia	Baylor	2012	656
Graham Harrell, Texas Tech	Oklahoma St	2007	646

Passing *(Cont.)*

COMPLETIONS	Opponent	Year	Comp
Andy Schmitt, E. Michigan	Central Mich.	2008	58
Case Keenum, Houston	East Carolina	2009	56
Drew Brees, Purdue	Wisconsin	1998	55
Rusty LaRue, Wake Forest	Duke	1995	55
David Piland, Houston	Lousiana Tech	2012	53
Case Keenum, Houston	UTEP	2009	51

Note: Five tied with 49.

TOUCHDOWNS PASSING	Opponent	Year	TD
David Klingler, Houston	E. Wash	1990	11

Note: Klingler's TD passes were for 5-48-29-7-3-7-40-10-7-8-51 yards, respectively.

Rushing

YARDS GAINED	Opponent	Year	Yds
LaDainian Tomlinson, TCU	UTEP	1999	406
Tony Sands, Kansas	Missouri	1991	396
Marshall Faulk, San Diego St.	Pacific	1991	386
Troy Davis, Iowa St	Missouri	1996	378
Anthony Thompson, Indiana	Wisconsin	1989	377
Robbie Mixon, Cent. Mich.	Eastern Mich	2002	377

TOUCHDOWNS RUSHING	Opponent	Year	TD
Howard Griffith, Illinois	Southern Illinois	1990	8

Note: Griffith's TD runs were for 5-51-7-41-5-18-5-3 yards, respectively.

Single Game *(Cont.)*

Receiving

CATCHES	Opponent	Year	No.
Tyler Jones, E. Michigan. ...Central Mich.		2008	23
Randy Gatewood, UNLV.....Idaho		1994	23
Freddie Barnes, Bowl. Green..Kent St		2009	22
Jay Miller, BYU ....New Mexico		1973	22
Troy Edwards, La. Tech......Nebraska		1998	21
Chris Daniels, Purdue ....Michigan St		1999	21
Quinton Patton, La. Tech ....Texas A&M		2012	21

Receiving (Cont.)

YARDS GAINED	Opponent	Year	Yds
Troy Edwards, Louisiana Tech..Nebraska		1998	405
Randy Gatewood, UNLV.........Idaho		1994	363
Chuck Hughes, UTEP*...........North Texas		1965	349
Donnie Avery, Houston ....Rice		2007	346
Marquise Lee, Southern Cal ...Arizona		2012	345

*UTEP was Texas Western in 1965.

TOUCHDOWN CATCHES	Opponent	Year	TD
Rashaun Woods, Okla. St .....SMU		2003	7
Tim Delaney, San Diego St ...New Mex. St		1969	6

Longest Plays

PASSING (since 1941)	Opponent	Year	Yds
Fred Owens to Jack Ford, Portland...................St. Mary's (Ca.)		1947	99
Bo Burris to Warren McVea, Houston................................Washington St		1966	99
Colin Clapton to Eddie Jenkins, Holy Cross ....Boston Univ.		1970	99
Terry Peel to Robert Ford, Houston.................................Syracuse		1970	99
Terry Peel to Robert Ford, Houston................................San Diego St		1972	99
Cris Collinsworth to Derrick Gaffney, Florida ....Rice		1977	99
Scott Ankrom to James Maness, TCU....................................Rice		1984	99
Gino Toretta to Horace Copeland, Miami (Fla.) ....Arkansas		1991	99
John Paci to Thomas Lewis, Indiana...................................Penn St		1993	99
Troy DeGar to Wes Caswell Tulsa...................................Oklahoma		1996	99
Drew Brees to Vinny Sutherland, Purdue ....Northwestern		1999	99
Dan Urban to Justin McCariens, Northern Illinois....................Ball St		2000	99
Jason Johnson to Brandon Marshall, Arizona..................................Idaho		2001	99
Dondrial Pinkins to Troy Williamson, South Carolina ....Virginia		2003	99
Jim Sorgi to Lee Evans, Wisconsin.............................Akron		2003	99
Giovanni Vizza to Casey Fitzgerald, North Texas ....La.-Monroe		2007	99
Jeff Tuel to Johnny Forzani, Washington St......................Arizona St		2009	99
Sean Renfree to Jamison Crowder Duke.....................................Miami (Fla.)		2012	99

21 tied at 98.

RUSHING (since 1941)	Opponent	Year	Yd
Gale Sayers, Kansas ....Nebraska		1963	99
Max Anderson, Arizona St....Wyoming		1967	99
Ralph Thompson, West Texas St ....Wichita St		1970	99
Kelsey Finch, Tennessee......Florida		1977	99
Eric Vann, Kansas ....Oklahoma		1997	99
Terry Caulley, Connecticut ...Army		2006	99
Broderick Green, Arkansas ..E. Michigan		2009	99
Ronnie Hillman, San Diego St ..Wyoming		2011	99

12 tied at 98 yards.

FIELD GOALS	Opponent	Year	Yds
Steve Little, Arkansas ....Texas		1977	67
Russell Erxleben, Texas.........Rice		1977	67
Joe Williams, Wichita St.........Southern Ill.		1978	67
Tony Franklin, Texas A&M ....Baylor		1976	65
Martin Gramatica, Kansas St...Northern Ill.		1998	65

PUNTS	Opponent	Year	Yds
Pat Brady, Nevada* ....Loyola (Ca.)		1950	99
George O'Brien, Wisconsin ...Iowa		1952	96
Preston-Johnson, SMU ....Pittsburgh		1940	94
Carl Knox, TCU ....Oklahoma St		1947	94
John Hadl, Kansas.................Oklahoma		1959	94

*Nevada was Nevada-Reno in 1950.

FOOTBALL BOWL SUBDIVISION (I-A) WINNINGEST TEAMS

Alltime Winning Percentage

	Yrs	W	L	T	Pct	GP	Bowl Record
Michigan	133	903	315	36	.734	1,254	20-22-0
Notre Dame	124	865	301	42	.733	1,208	15-17-0
Boise St	45	388	148	2	.723	538	9-4-0
Oklahoma	118	831	310	53	.718	1,194	27-18-1
Ohio St	123	837	316	53	.716	1,206	20-23-0
Texas	120	867	334	33	.716	1,234	27-22-2
Alabama	118	827	321	43	.712	1,191	34-22-3
Southern Cal	119	786	319	54	.701	1,159	31-16-0
Nebraska	123	856	353	40	.701	1,249	24-26-0
Tennessee	116	799	354	53	.684	1,206	25-24-0
Florida St	66	485	237	17	.668	739	23-14-2
Penn St	126	723	365	41	.659	1,129	21-14-2
LSU	119	743	393	47	.648	1,183	22-21-1
Georgia	119	759	402	54	.647	1,215	27-18-3
Miami (Fla.)	87	581	331	19	.634	931	18-16-0
Florida	106	680	387	40	.632	1,107	20-20-0
Auburn	120	714	414	47	.628	1,175	22-13-2
Miami (Ohio)	124	668	410	44	.615	1,122	7-3-0
Washington	123	679	424	50	.611	1,152	15-16-1
Arizona St	100	569	361	24	.609	954	13-12-1
Virginia Tech	119	696	441	46	.608	1,183	10-15-0
Central Michigan	112	583	381	36	.601	1,000	3-4-0
West Virginia	120	708	463	45	.601	1,216	14-18-0
Texas A&M	118	692	452	48	.601	1,192	15-19
Arkansas	119	684	460	40	.595	1,184	13-23-3

Note: Includes bowl and playoff games.

Alltime Victories

Michigan 903	LSU 743	Florida 680
Texas 867	Penn St......................723	Washington 679
Notre Dame..................865	Auburn 714	Colorado 675
Nebraska......................856	West Virginia..............708	Miami (Ohio) 668
Ohio St.........................837	Syracuse 699	Clemson.........................668
Oklahoma.....................831	Virginia Tech..............696	Navy...............................664
Alabama.......................827	Georgia Tech..............693	Army...............................654
Tennessee 799	Texas A&M.................692	North Carolina.................654
Southern Cal 786	Arkansas 684	Minnesota.......................652
Georgia........................759	Pittsburgh..................683	Michigan State................645

NUMBER ONE VS NUMBER TWO

The No. 1 and No. 2 teams, according to the Associated Press Poll, have met 47 times, including 15 bowl games, since the poll's inception in 1936. The No. 1 teams have a 27-18-2 record in these matchups. Notre Dame (5-3-2) has played in 10 of the games.

Date	Results	Stadium
10-9-43	No. 1 Notre Dame 35, No. 2 Michigan 12	Michigan (Ann Arbor)
11-20-43	No. 1 Notre Dame 14, No. 2 Iowa Pre-Flight 13	Notre Dame (South Bend)
12-2-44	No. 1 Army 23, No. 2 Navy 7	Municipal (Baltimore)
11-10-45	No. 1 Army 48, No. 2 Notre Dame 0	Yankee (New York)
12-1-45	No. 1 Army 32, No. 2 Navy 13	Municipal (Philadelphia)
11-9-46	No. 1 Army 0, No. 2 Notre Dame 0	Yankee (New York)
1-1-63	No. 1 USC 42, No. 2 Wisconsin 37 (Rose Bowl)	Rose Bowl (Pasadena)
10-12-63	No. 2 Texas 28, No. 1 Oklahoma 7	Cotton Bowl (Dallas)
1-1-64	No. 1 Texas 28, No. 2 Navy 6 (Cotton Bowl)	Cotton Bowl (Dallas)
11-19-66	No. 1 Notre Dame 10, No. 2 Michigan St 10	Spartan (East Lansing)
9-28-68	No. 1 Purdue 37, No. 2 Notre Dame 22	Notre Dame (South Bend)
1-1-69	No. 1 Ohio St 27, No. 2 USC 16 (Rose Bowl)	Rose Bowl (Pasadena)
12-6-69	No. 1 Texas 15, No. 2 Arkansas 14	Razorback (Fayetteville)
11-25-71	No. 1 Nebraska 35, No. 2 Oklahoma 31	Owen Field (Norman)
1-1-72	No. 1 Nebraska 38, No. 2 Alabama 6 (Orange Bowl)	Orange Bowl (Miami)
1-1-79	No. 2 Alabama 14, No. 1 Penn St 7 (Sugar Bowl)	Sugar Bowl (New Orleans)
9-26-81	No. 1 USC 28, No. 2 Oklahoma 24	Coliseum (Los Angeles)
1-1-83	No. 2 Penn St 27, No. 1 Georgia 23 (Sugar Bowl)	Sugar Bowl (New Orleans)
10-19-85	No. 1 Iowa 12, No. 2 Michigan 10	Kinnick (Iowa City)
9-27-86	No. 2 Miami (Fla.) 28, No. 1 Oklahoma 16	Orange Bowl (Miami)
1-2-87	No. 2 Penn St 14, No. 1 Miami (Fla.) 10 (Fiesta Bowl)	Sun Devil (Tempe)
11-21-87	No. 2 Oklahoma 17, No. 1 Nebraska 7	Memorial (Lincoln)

NUMBER ONE VS NUMBER TWO *(Cont.)*

Date	Results	Stadium
1-1-88	No. 2 Miami (Fla.) 20, No. 1 Oklahoma 14 (Orange Bowl)	Orange Bowl (Miami)
11-26-88	No. 1 Notre Dame 27, No. 2 USC 10	Coliseum (Los Angeles)
9-16-89	No. 1 Notre Dame 24, No. 2 Michigan 19	Michigan (Ann Arbor)
11-16-91	No. 2 Miami (Fla.) 17, No. 1 Florida St 16	Doak Campbell (Tallahassee)
1-1-93	No. 2 Alabama 34, No. 1 Miami (Fla.) 13 (Sugar Bowl)	Superdome (New Orleans)
11-13-93	No. 2 Notre Dame 31, No. 1 Florida St 24	Notre Dame (South Bend)
1-1-94	No. 1 Florida St 18, No. 2 Nebraska 16 (Orange Bowl)	Orange Bowl (Miami)
1-2-96	No. 1 Nebraska 62, No. 2 Florida 24 (Fiesta Bowl)	Sun Devil (Tempe)
11-30-96	No. 2 Florida St 24, No. 1 Florida 21	Doak Campbell (Tallahassee)
1-4-99	No. 1 Tennessee 23, No. 2 Florida St 16 (Fiesta Bowl)	Sun Devil (Tempe)
1-4-00	No. 1 Florida St 46, No. 2 Virginia Tech 29 (Sugar Bowl)	Superdome (New Orleans)
1-3-03	No. 2 Ohio St 31, No. 1 Miami (Fla.) 24 [2OT] (Fiesta Bowl)	Sun Devil (Tempe)
1-5-06	No. 2 Texas 41, No. 1 USC 38 (Rose Bowl)	Rose Bowl (Pasadena)
9-9-06	No. 1 Ohio St 24, No. 2 Texas 7	Texas Memorial (Austin)
11-18-06	No. 1 Ohio St 42, No. 2 Michigan 39	Ohio (Columbus)
1-8-07	No. 2 Florida 41, No. 1 Ohio St 14 (BCS Championship)	Univ. of Phoenix (Glendale)
1-7-08	No. 2 LSU 38, No. 1 Ohio St. 24 (BCS Championship)	Superdome (New Orleans)
12-6-08	No. 2 Florida 31, No. 1 Alabama 20 (SEC Championship)	Georgia Dome (Atlanta)
1-8-09	No. 1 Florida 24, No. 2 Oklahoma 14 (BCS Championship)	Dolphins Stadium (Miami)
12-5-09	No. 1 Florida 13, No. 2 Alabama 32 (SEC Championship)	Georgia Dome (Atlanta)
1-7-10	No. 1 Alabama 37, No. 2 Texas 21 (BCS Championship)	Rose Bowl (Pasadena)
1-10-11	No. 1 Auburn 22, No. 2 Oregon 19 (BCS Championship)	Univ. of Phoenix (Glendale)
11-5-11	No. 1 LSU 9, No. 2 Alabama 6	Alabama (Tuscaloosa)
1-9-12	No. 2 Alabama 21, No. 1 LSU 0 (BCS Championship)	Superdome (New Orleans)
1-7-13	No. 2 Alabama 42, No. 1 Notre Dame 14 (BCS Champ.)	Sun Life (Miami)

Note: No. 1 USC's Orange Bowl victory over No. 2 Oklahoma on Jan. 4, 2005 was vacated in 2010 for rules violations.

LONGEST FBS (I-A) WINNING STREAKS

Wins	Team	Yrs	Ended by	Score
47	Oklahoma	1953–57	Notre Dame	7–0
39	Washington	1908–14	Oregon St	0–0
37	Yale	1890–93	Princeton	6–0
37	Yale	1887–89	Princeton	10–0
35	Toledo	1969–71	Tampa	21–0
34	Miami	2000–03	Ohio St	31–24 (2 OT)
34	Pennsylvania	1894–96	Lafayette	6–4
31	Oklahoma	1948–50	Kentucky	13–7
31	Pittsburgh	1914–18	Cleveland Naval Reserve	10–9
31	Pennsylvania	1896–98	Harvard	10–0

LONGEST FBS (I-A) UNBEATEN STREAKS

No.	W	T	Team	Yrs	Ended by	Score
63	59	4	Washington	1907–17	California	27–0
56	55	1	Michigan	1901–05	Chicago	2–0
50	46	4	California	1920–25	Olympic Club	15–0
48	47	1	Oklahoma	1953–57	Notre Dame	7–0
48	47	1	Yale	1885–89	Princeton	10–0
47	42	5	Yale	1879–85	Princeton	6–5
44	42	2	Yale	1894–96	Princeton	24–6
42	39	3	Yale	1904–08	Harvard	4–0
39	37	2	Notre Dame	1946–50	Purdue	28–14
37	36	1	Oklahoma	1972–75	Kansas	23–3
37	37	0	Yale	1890–93	Princeton	6–0
35	35	0	Toledo	1969–71	Tampa	21–0
35	34	1	Minnesota	1903–05	Wisconsin	16–12
34	34	0	Miami (Fla.)	2000–03	Ohio St	31–24 (2 OT)
34	33	1	Nebraska	1912–16	Kansas	7–3
34	34	0	Pennsylvania	1894–96	Lafayette	6–4
34	32	2	Princeton	1884–87	Harvard	12–0
34	29	5	Princeton	1877–82	Harvard	1–0
33	30	3	Tennessee	1926–30	Alabama	18–6
33	31	2	Georgia Tech	1914–18	Pittsburgh	32–0
33	30	3	Harvard	1911–15	Cornell	10–0
32	31	1	Nebraska	1969–71	UCLA	20–17
32	30	2	Army	1944–47	Columbia	21–20
32	31	1	Harvard	1898–1900	Yale	28–0

Note: Includes bowl games.

LONGEST FBS (I-A) LOSING STREAKS

Losses		Seasons	Ended Against	Score
34	Northwestern	1979–82	Northern Illinois	31–6
28	Virginia	1958–61	William & Mary	21–6
28	Kansas St	1945–48	Arkansas St	37–6
27	New Mexico St	1988–90	Cal St–Fullerton	43–9
27	Eastern Michigan	1980–82	Kent St	9–7

MOST-PLAYED FBS (I-A) RIVALRIES

GP	Opponents (Series Leader Listed First)	Record	First Game	GP	Opponents (Series Leader Listed First)	Record	First Game
122	Minnesota–Wisconsin	59-55-8	1890	110	Kansas–Kansas St	65-40-5	1902
120	Missouri–Kansas	56-55-9	1891	109	Michigan–Ohio St	58-45-6	1897
118	Texas–Texas A&M	76-37-5	1894	109	Mississippi–Mississippi St	61-42-6	1901
117	Nebraska–Kansas	91-23-3	1892	108	TCU–Baylor	51-50-7	1899
117	Miami (Ohio)–Cincinnati	59-51-7	1888	108	Tennessee–Kentucky	75-24-9	1893
117	North Carolina–Virginia	60-53-4	1892	107	Georgia–Georgia Tech	63-39-5	1893
116	Auburn–Georgia	54-54-8	1892	107	Texas–Oklahoma	59-43-5	1900
116	Oregon–Oregon St	60-46-10	1894	107	Oklahoma–Oklahoma St	83-17-7	1904
115	Purdue–Indiana	72-37-6	1891	106	Tennessee–Vanderbilt	73-28-5	1888
115	Stanford–California	58-46-11	1892	105	Nebraska–Iowa St	86-17-2	1896
113	Navy–Army	57-49-7	1890	105	N Carolina–Wake Forest	68-35-2	1888
110	Utah–Utah St	77-29-4	1892				
110	Clemson–South Carolina	65-41-4	1896				

NCAA Coaches' Records

ALLTIME WINNINGEST FBS (I-A) COACHES
By Percentage

Coach (Alma Mater)	Colleges Coached	Yrs	W	L	T	Pct
Knute Rockne (Notre Dame '14)†	Notre Dame 1918–30	13	105	12	5	.881
Frank W. Leahy (Notre Dame '31)†	Boston College 1939–40; Notre Dame 1941–43, 1946–53	13	107	13	9	.864
George W. Woodruff (Yale 1889)†	Pennsylvania 1892–01; Illinois 1903; Carlisle 1905	12	142	25	2	.846
Barry Switzer (Arkansas '60)	Oklahoma 1973–88	16	157	29	4	.837
Tom Osborne (Hastings '59)†	Nebraska 1973–97	25	255	49	3	.836
*Urban Meyer (Cincinnati '86)	Bowling Green 2001–02; Utah 2003–04; Florida 2005–10, Ohio St 2012–	11	116	23	0	.835
Fielding Yost (West Virginia 1895)†	Ohio Wesleyan 1897; Nebraska 1898; Kansas 1899; Stanford 1900; Michigan 1901–23, 1925–26	30	198	35	12	.833
Percy D. Haughton (Harvard 1899)†	Cornell 1899–1900; Harvard 1908–16; Columbia 1923–24	13	96	17	6	.832
Bob Neyland (Army '16)†	Tennessee 1926–34, 1936–40, 1946–52	21	173	31	12	.829
Bud Wilkinson (Minnesota '37)†	Oklahoma 1947–63	17	145	29	4	.826
Jock Sutherland (Pittsburgh '18)†	Lafayette 1919–23; Pittsburgh 1924–38	20	144	28	14	.812
Bob Devaney (Alma [Mich] '39)†	Wyoming 1957–61; Nebraska 1962–72	16	136	30	7	.806
*Bob Stoops (Iowa '83)	Oklahoma 1999–	14	149	37	0	.801
Frank W. Thomas (Notre Dame '23)†	Tenn.-Chattanooga 1925–28; Alabama 1931–42, 1944–46	19	141	33	9	.795
Henry L. Williams (Yale 1891)†	Army 1891; Minnesota 1900–21	23	141	34	12	.786
Gil Dobie (Minnesota '02)†	North Dakota St 1906–07; Washington 1908-16; Navy 1917–19; Cornell 1920–35; Boston College 1936–38	33	180	45	15	.781
Paul (Bear) Bryant (Alabama '36)†	Maryland 1945; Kentucky 1946–53; Texas A&M 1954–57; Alabama 1958–82	38	323	85	17	.780
Fred Folsom (Dartmouth 1895)	Colorado 1895–99, 1901–02; Dartmouth 1903–06; Colorado 1908–15	19	106	28	6	.779
Bo Schembechler (Miami [Ohio] '51)	Miami (Ohio) 1963–68; Michigan 1969–89	27	234	65	8	.775
Fritz Crisler (U of Chicago '22)	Minnesota 1930–31; Princeton 1932–37; Michigan 1938–47	18	116	32	9	.768

*Active in 2012. †Hall of Fame member.

Note: Minimum 10 years as head coach at Division I institutions; record at four-year colleges only; bowl games included; ties computed as half won, half lost.

ALLTIME WINNINGEST FBS (I-A) COACHES (Cont.)
By Victories

	Yrs	W	L	T	Pct		Yrs	W	L	T	Pct
Bobby Bowden	44	377	129	4	.743	*Mack Brown	29	236	117	1	.668
Paul (Bear) Bryant	38	323	85	17	.780	Bo Schembechler	27	234	65	8	.775
Glenn (Pop) Warner	44	319	106	32	.733	*Chris Ault	28	233	109	1	.681
Amos Alonzo Stagg	57	314	199	35	.605	Hayden Fry	37	232	178	10	.564
††Joe Paterno	46	298	136	3	.685	†Jim Tressel	25	229	79	2	.742
*Frank Beamer	32	258	127	4	.668	*Steve Spurrier	23	208	77	2	.728
LaVell Edwards	29	257	100	3	.718	Jess Neely	40	207	176	19	.539
Tom Osborne	25	255	49	3	.836	Warren Woodson	31	203	95	14	.673
Lou Holtz	33	249	132	7	.651	Don Nehlen	30	202	128	8	.609
Woody Hayes	33	238	72	10	.759	Vince Dooley	25	201	77	10	.715
						Eddie Anderson	39	201	128	15	.606

*Active in 2012. Record at four-year colleges only. †One bowl win and 11 regular-season victories from Tressel's totals were vacated in 2010. ††Six bowl wins and 105 regular-season victories were vacated in 2012.

Most Bowl Victories

	W	L	T		W	L	T
Bobby Bowden	21	10	1	John Robinson	8	1	0
Joe Paterno	18	12	1	Barry Alvarez	8	3	0
Paul (Bear) Bryant	15	12	2	Terry Donahue	8	4	1
*Mack Brown	13	7	0	Barry Switzer	8	5	0
Lou Holtz	12	8	2	Jackie Sherrill	8	6	0
Tom Osborne	12	13	0	Philip Fulmer	8	7	0
Don James	10	5	0	Darrell Royal	8	7	1
John Vaught	10	8	0	Vince Dooley	8	10	2
Bobby Dodd	9	4	0	*Tom O'Brien	8	2	0
Johnny Majors	9	7	0	*Mark Richt	8	4	0
*Steve Spurrier	9	10	0	*Nick Saban	8	6	0
*Frank Beamer	9	11	0				

WINNINGEST ACTIVE* FBS (I-A) COACHES
By Percentage

Coach, College	Yrs	W	L	T	Pct.	Bowls W	L	T
Chris Petersen, Boise St.	7	84	8	0	.913	5	2	0
Urban Meyer, Ohio St.	11	116	23	0	.835	7	1	0
Bob Stoops, Oklahoma	14	149	37	0	.801	7	7	0
Gary Patterson, TCU	13	116	36	0	.763	7	5	0
Mark Richt, Georgia	12	118	40	0	.747	8	4	0
Brian Kelly, Notre Dame	23	199	68	2	.743	3	3	0
Bobby Petrino, W Kentucky	8	75	26	0	.743	4	3	0
Larry Coker, UTSA	8	72	25	0	.742	4	2	0
Bret Bielema, Wisconsin	7	68	24	0	.739	2	4	0
Nick Saban, Alabama	17	154	55	1	.736	8	6	0
Les Miles, LSU	12	113	42	0	.729	6	5	0
Steve Spurrier, South Carolina	23	208	77	2	.728	9	10	0
Bronco Mendenhall, BYU	8	74	29	0	.718	6	2	0
Bo Pelini, Nebraska	6	49	20	0	.710	3	3	0
Kevin Sumlin, Texas A&M	5	46	19	0	.708	2	1	0
Paul Johnson, Georgia Tech	16	147	65	0	.693	3	6	0
Kyle Whittingham, Utah	9	71	32	0	.689	7	1	0
Frank Beamer, Virginia Tech	32	258	127	4	.668	9	11	0
Mack Brown, Texas	29	236	117	1	.668	13	7	0
Bill Snyder, Kansas St	21	170	85	1	.666	6	8	0

#Bowl games included. Ties computed as half win, half loss. Note: Minimum five years as Div. I-A head coach at four-year colleges only.

By Victories

*Active in 2012.

WINNINGEST ACTIVE* FCS (I-AA) COACHES
By Percentage

Coach, College	Yrs	W	L	T	Pct
Chris Creighton, Drake	16	133	41	0	.764
Al Bagnoli, Penn	31	233	80	0	.744
Craig Bohl, North Dakota St	10	89	32	0	.736
Chris Hatcher, Murray St	13	112	42	0	.727
Beau Baldwin, Eastern Wash	6	53	21	0	.716
Rick Chamberlin, Dayton	5	40	16	0	.714
Dale Lennon, Southern Ill.	16	137	56	0	.710
Rod Broadway, N.C. A&T	10	80	33	0	.708
Danny Rocco, Richmond	7	55	23	0	.705
Mark Farley, U. of Northern Iowa	12	104	46	0	.693
Buddy Pough, South Carolina St.	11	88	39	0	.693
Matt Viator, McNeese St	7	52	24	0	.684
Dick Biddle, Colgate	17	133	65	0	.672
Chuck Priore, Stony Brook	13	86	43	0	.667
Rick Comegy, Jackson St.	21	156	82	0	.655

By Victories

Bob Ford, Albany (N.Y.)	264	Rick Comegy, Jackson St.	156
Al Bagnoli, Penn	233	Tim Walsh, Cal Poly	143
Rob Ash, Montana St	226	Dale Lennon, Southern Ill.	137
Andy Talley, Villanova	225	Chris Creighton, Drake	133
Jimmye Laycock, William & Mary	215	Dick Biddle, Colgate	133
Walt Hameline, Wagner	213	Terry Allen, Missouri St	123
Mike Ayers, Wofford	182	Watson Brown, Tennessee Tech	122
Tim Murphy, Harvard	160		

WINNINGEST ACTIVE* DIVISION II COACHES
By Percentage

Coach, College	Yrs	W	L	T	Pct
Willie J. Slater, Tuskegee	7	63	15	0	.808
Ken Sparks, Carson-Newman	33	308	83	2	.786
David Dean, Valdosta St	6	54	17	0	.761
Danny Hale, Bloomsburg	25	213	69	1	.754
John Wristen, Colorado St–Pueblo	5	43	14	0	.754
Tom Sawyer, Winona St	17	140	56	0	.714
Bill Maskill, Midwestern St	13	101	42	0	.706
Bill Zwaan, West Chester	16	131	56	0	.701
Mike White, Albany St (Ga.)	13	99	44	0	.692
Scott Underwood, St. Cloud St	5	40	18	0	.690
Todd Hoffner, Minnesota St–Mankato	12	89	42	0	.679
Bryan Collins, LIU Post	15	110	54	0	.671
Darrell Morris, Neb.-Kearney	13	95	47	0	.669
Pete Shinnick, UNC Pembroke	13	75	38	0	.664
Monte Cater, Shepherd	32	219	111	2	.663

Ties computed as half win, half loss. Playoff games included.

Note: Minimum five years as a college head coach; record at four-year colleges only.

By Victories

Ken Sparks, Carson-Newman	308	Rob Smith, Humboldt St	140
Dennis Douds, East Stroudsburg	237	Bobby Wallace, North Alabama	132
Monte Cater, Shepherd	219	Bill Zwaan, West Chester	131
Danny Hale, Bloomsburg	213	Keith Otterbein, Hillsdale	131
Joe Glenn, South Dakota	188	Jerry Partridge, Mo. Western St	124
George Mihalik, Slippery Rock	167	Don Carthel, West Tex. A&M	124
Richard Cavanaugh, Southern Conn. St	166	Art Wilkins, American	119
Tom Sawyer, Winona St	140		

*Active in 2012.

WINNINGEST ACTIVE* DIVISION III COACHES
By Percentage

Coach, College	Yrs	W	L	T	Pct
Lance Leipold, Wis.-Whitewater	6	79	6	0	.929
Jeff Devanney, Trinity (Conn.)	7	49	7	0	.875
Mike Sirianni, Wash. & Jeff.	10	93	21	0	.816
Joe Fincham, Wittenberg	17	154	35	0	.815
Pete Fredenburg, Mary Hardin-Baylor	15	146	34	0	.811
Joe Smith, Linfield	7	60	14	0	.811
Rick Willis, Wartburg	14	119	31	0	.793
John Thorne, North Central (Ill.)	11	97	27	0	.782
Mike Drass, Wesley	20	176	49	1	.781
Mike Swider, Wheaton (Ill.)	17	140	41	0	.773
Jim Purtill, St. Norbert	15	122	36	1	.770
Jeff McMartin, Central (Iowa)	9	73	23	0	.760
Glenn Caruso, St. Thomas (Minn.)	7	63	20	0	.759
Ben McEnroe, Cal Lutheran	6	44	14	0	.759
Jim Hilvert, Thomas More	6	50	16	0	.758

Ties computed as half won, half lost. Playoff games included.
Note: Minimum five years as a college head coach; record at four-year colleges only.

By Victories

Rick Giancola, Montclair St.	214	Barry H. Streeter, Gettysburg	174
Eric Hamilton, TCNJ	212	Steve Johnson, Bethel (Minn)	173
Michael DeLong, Springfield	185	Norm Eash, Ill. Wesleyan	164
Rich Lackner, Carnegie Mellon	181	Mike Maynard, Redlands	157
Steve Mohr, Trinity (Texas)	181	Jim Margraff, Johns Hopkins	157
Larry Kindbom, Washington-St. Louis	176	Brien Cullen, Worcester St	156
Vic Wallace, Rockford	176	John Audino, Union	155
Mike Drass, Wesley	176		

NAIA Coaches' Records

WINNINGEST ACTIVE* NAIA COACHES
By Percentage

Coach, College	Yrs	W	L	T	Pct
Mike Van Diest, Carroll (Mont.)	14	164	26	0	.863
Bill Cronin, Georgetown (Ky.)	16	155	36	0	.812
Steve Ryan, Morningside (Iowa)	11	98	31	0	.760
Mike Feminis, St. Xavier (Ill.)	14	127	43	0	.747
John Bland, Cumberlands (Ky.)	7	57	20	0	.740
Paul Troth, Missouri Valley	16	127	52	0	.709
Hank Biesiot, Dickinson St (N.D.)	37	257	111	1	.698
Kevin Donly, St. Francis (Ind.)	34	264	120	1	.687
Mike Magistrelli, St. Ambrose (Iowa)	6	43	21	0	.672
Monty Lewis, Friends (Kan.)	20	129	65	0	.665
Larry Wilcox, Benedictine (Kan.)	34	236	130	0	.645
Mike Gardner, Tabor (Kan.)	9	60	36	0	.625
Kent Kessinger, Ottawa (Kan.)	9	58	38	0	.604
Todd Hafner, William Penn (Iowa)	9	61	40	0	.604
Dennis McCulloch, Valley City St (N.D.)	16	94	70	0	.573

Playoff games included.
Note: Minimum five years as a collegiate head coach and includes record against four-year institutions only.

By Victories

Kevin Donley, St. Francis (Ind.)	264	Mike Feminis, St. Xavier (Ill.)	127
Hank Biesiot, Dickinson St (N.D.)	257	Paul Troth, Missouri Valley	127
Larry Wilcox, Benedictine (Kan.)	236	Steve Ryan, Morningside (Iowa)	98
Mike Van Diest, Carroll (Mont.)	164	Brian Keller, Nebraska Wesleyan	94
Bill Cronin, Georgetown (Ky.)	155	Dennis McCulloch, Valley City State (N.D.)	94
Monty Lewis, Friends (Kan.)	129	Andy Lambert, Sterling (Kan.)	81
Dave Dallas, Kansas Wesleyan	128	Todd Hafner, William Penn (Iowa)	61
		Mike Gardner, Tabor (Kan.)	60

*Active in 2012.

LeBron James savored the championship trophy after his dominant performance in Game 7 of the NBA Finals

Pro Basketball

Debut of a Dynasty

With two titles in two seasons, the Miami Heat established themselves as the dominant team of the decade, a position they aren't likely to relinquish soon

BY CHRIS MANNIX

THE YEAR STARTED LIKE SO many others in San Antonio: with criticism and doubt. The Spurs won 50 games in the lockout-shortened 2011–2012 season and were up 2–0 on Oklahoma City in the Western Conference Finals before collapsing and losing in six. Yet despite returning the steady Tim Duncan, despite the presence of All-Star playmaker Tony Parker and despite a roster loaded with young talent—the "old Spurs" tag has always been a little misleading—San Antonio was far from a trendy pick to come out of the Western Conference at the start of the season. "If we can become a good defensive team," said Spurs coach Gregg Popovich in October, embracing the team's underdog status, "I'll be happy with our season."

Of course, who came out of the West didn't seem to matter, not with Miami likely waiting for them. After stumbling through an uneven first season together, the Heat's Big Three—LeBron James, Dwyane Wade and Chris Bosh—got it together in Year Two, submitting a 46-win regular season and a five-game demolition of Oklahoma City in the NBA Finals. Wade turned the

team over to James, Bosh accepted his reduced role and the supporting parts (Mario Chalmers, Udonis Haslem and Shane Battier, among others) found their niche. The Heat returned all its key pieces in 2012–13, added Boston defector Ray Allen and looked poised to pick up right where the team left off.

Besides, who in the East could challenge them? Chicago? Without Derrick Rose, out for the season with a torn ACL, the Bulls were no threat. New York? The Knicks had Carmelo Anthony, Tyson Chandler and a collection of shooters, but as always their playoff fate would be tied to the health of Amar'e Stoudemire, whose knee problems had become chronic. Boston? The aging, depleted Celtics had heart and a healthy hatred for the Heat, but Boston blew a chance to close out Miami at home in the '11 conference finals and proceeded to lose two straight and bow out.

Indeed, Miami looked like a team ready to roll through the regular season, and it would, winning an NBA-best 66 games, making much of the season anticlimactic. James picked up his second straight MVP (remember when moving to Miami meant

With Miami's season on the line in Games 6 and 7 of the Finals, James took charge, averaging 34.5 points and 11 rebounds in the two critical games.

JOHN W. McDONOUGH

he wasn't supposed to win any more of them?), Wade and Bosh were All-Stars, and the ageless Allen, reinvented as a sixth man, averaged 10.9 points and made 41.9% of his three pointers.

The real drama was in the West. After failing to come to terms with supersub James Harden, the Thunder stunned everyone when they shipped Harden to Houston for a package headlined by Kevin Martin. Losing Harden—the offensive option when Kevin Durant wasn't in the game, the playmaker when he was—appeared crippling. Right up until it wasn't. With Harden gone, Durant and Russell Westbrook picked up their games, powering Oklahoma City to a conference-best 60-win season.

The team that was supposed to challenge the Thunder for conference supremacy—the Lakers— had real problems. Last summer, Los Angeles acquired the biggest fish on the trading block, Dwight Howard. Howard was supposed to be the second star Kobe Bryant needed to win another title, supposed to form a fearsome front line with Pau Gasol, supposed to be the man to transition the Lakers from Bryant's team to his. He wasn't. The lingering effects of offseason back surgery plagued Howard early in the season, and a fractured relationship with Bryant and head coach Mike D'Antoni— who took over after Mike Brown was fired five (five!) games into the season—detonated the Lakers title hopes. L.A. snuck into the postseason as the No. 7 seed and without Bryant, who went down with a torn left Achilles tendon in April, the Lakers were swept out of the first round by San Antonio.

It was another injury though that shook up the postseason. In the second

GREG NELSON

Aging but still effective, Duncan led the Spurs past L.A., Golden State and Memphis in the West before the magic ran out—just barely—against Miami in the Finals.

Heat nemesis Rajon Rondo sidelined with a torn ACL, Miami's first challenge didn't come until the conference finals against a bruising Indiana team. The Pacers—emboldened by last season's second round scrap against Miami—came out physical, pounding the Heat on the inside with Roy Hibbert and David West. After James rescued Miami from a Game 1 loss with a buzzer-beating layup, Indiana rallied in Game 2, stunning the Heat in Miami with a decisive 97–93 win. The teams traded wins the rest of the way, forcing a Game 7, where once again James strapped the team to his back, pumping in 32 points in a 99–76 blowout. "We understand that it's hard to get to the Finals," Wade said. "We knew this was going to be tough."

In truth, the Heat needed to be tested. In many ways, San Antonio was the perfect foil. The Spurs play a disciplined, low turnover offense (unlike Indiana), have a dynamic point guard in Parker (ditto), a 7-foot(ish) front line in Duncan and Tiago Splitter and a defensive weapon in small forward Kawhi Leonard. Those advantages were on display in Game 1: Behind a flawless 21-point, six-assist, zero-turnover night from Parker, San Antonio stole the opener in Miami. They built a 3–2 series lead at home, pushing a bewildered Heat team to the brink of elimination with the series shifting back to South Beach. There, James once again took over. In Game 6, James posted 32 points, ten rebounds and 11 assists while Allen's three-pointer with 5.2 seconds left forced overtime, salvaging the Heat's season.

James was even better in Game 7, submitting 37 points and 12 rebounds, pushing the Heat past a weary Spurs team for its second straight championship. As the confetti rained down on James, washing away any lingering criticism, all in attendance acknowledged the obvious: A dynasty had been born.

quarter of Game 2 of Oklahoma City's first round series against the Rockets, Westbrook, the Thunder's dynamic point guard, collided knees with Houston's Patrick Beverly. The collision caused Westbrook to tear the lateral meniscus of his right knee, ending his season. With Westbrook down—and the Thunder eliminated in the second round—the Spurs took advantage, sweeping Memphis in the conference finals to advance to the franchise's fifth Finals since 1999.

The Eastern Conference playoffs went according to script, at least early. With Rose down, Stoudemire (surprise!) hurt and

FOR THE RECORD • 2012—2013

NBA Final Standings

Western Conference

NORTHWEST DIVISION

Team	W	L	Pct	GB
‡Oklahoma City	60	22	.732	—
*Denver	57	25	.695	3
Utah	43	39	.524	17
Portland	33	49	.402	27
Minnesota	31	51	.378	29

PACIFIC DIVISION

Team	W	L	Pct	GB
†LA Clippers	56	26	.683	—
*Golden State	47	35	.573	9
*LA Lakers	45	37	.549	11
Sacramento	28	54	.341	28
Phoenix	25	57	.305	31

SOUTHWEST DIVISION

Team	W	L	Pct	GB
†San Antonio	58	24	.707	—
*Memphis	56	26	.683	2
*Houston	45	37	.549	13
Dallas	41	41	.500	17
New Orleans	27	55	.329	31

Eastern Conference

ATLANTIC DIVISION

Team	W	L	Pct	GB
†New York	54	28	.659	—
*Brooklyn	49	33	.598	5
*Boston	41	40	.506	12½
Philadelphia	34	48	.415	20
Toronto	34	48	.415	20

CENTRAL DIVISION

Team	W	L	Pct	GB
†Indiana	49	32	.605	—
*Chicago	45	37	.549	4½
*Milwaukee	38	44	.463	11½
Detroit	29	53	.354	20½
Cleveland	24	58	.293	25½

SOUTHEAST DIVISION

Team	W	L	Pct	GB
‡Miami	66	16	.805	—
*Atlanta	44	38	.537	22
Washington	29	53	.354	37
Charlotte	21	61	.256	45
Orlando	20	62	.244	46

†Clinched division title.   *Clinched playoff berth.   ‡Clinched conference title.

2013 NBA Playoffs

Eastern Conference First Round

Game 1	Boston	78	at New York	85			
Game 2	Boston	71	at New York	87			
Game 3	New York	90	at Boston	76			
Game 4	New York	90	at Boston	97*			
Game 5	Boston	92	at New York	86			
Game 6	New York	88	at Boston	80			

New York won series 4–2.

Game 1	Atlanta	90	at Indiana	107
Game 2	Atlanta	98	at Indiana	113
Game 3	Indiana	69	at Atlanta	90
Game 4	Indiana	91	at Atlanta	102
Game 5	Atlanta	83	at Indiana	106
Game 6	Indiana	81	at Atlanta	73

Indiana won series 4–2.

Game 1	Milwaukee	87	at Miami	110
Game 2	Milwaukee	86	at Miami	98
Game 3	Miami	104	at Milwaukee	91
Game 4	Miami	88	at Milwaukee	77

Miami won series 4–0.

Game 1	Chicago	89	at Brooklyn	106
Game 2	Chicago	90	at Brooklyn	82
Game 3	Brooklyn	76	at Chicago	79
Game 4	Brooklyn	134	at Chicago	142***
Game 5	Chicago	91	at Brooklyn	110
Game 6	Brooklyn	95	at Chicago	92
Game 7	Chicago	99	at Brooklyn	93

Chicago won series 4–3.

Western Conference First Round

Game 1	LA Lakers	79	at San Antonio	91
Game 2	LA Lakers	91	at San Antonio	102
Game 3	San Antonio	120	at LA Lakers	89
Game 4	San Antonio	103	at LA Lakers	82

San Antonio won series 4–0.

Game 1	Golden State	95	at Denver	97
Game 2	Golden State	131	at Denver	117
Game 3	Denver	108	at Golden State	110
Game 4	Denver	101	at Golden State	115
Game 5	Golden State	100	at Denver	107
Game 6	Denver	88	at Golden State	92

Golden State won series 4–2.

Game 1	Memphis	91	at LA Clippers	112
Game 2	Memphis	91	at LA Clippers	93
Game 3	LA Clippers	82	at Memphis	94
Game 4	LA Clippers	83	at Memphis	104
Game 5	Memphis	103	at LA Clippers	93
Game 6	LA Clippers	105	at Memphis	118

Memphis won series 4–2.

Game 1	Houston	91	at Okla. City	120
Game 2	Houston	102	at Okla. Cty	105
Game 3	Okla. City	104	at Houston	101
Game 4	Okla. City	103	at Houston	105
Game 5	Houston	107	Okla. City	100
Game 6	Okla. City	103	Houston	94

Oklahoma City won series 4–2.

Eastern Conference Semifinals

Game 1	Indiana	102	at New York	95
Game 2	Indiana	79	at New York	105
Game 3	New York	71	at Indiana	82
Game 4	New York	82	at Indiana	93
Game 5	Indiana	75	at New York	85
Game 6	New York	99	at Indiana	106

Indiana won series 4–2.

Game 1	Chicago	93	at Miami	86
Game 2	Chicago	78	at Miami	115
Game 3	Miami	104	at Chicago	94
Game 4	Miami	88	at Chicago	65
Game 5	Chicago	91	at Miami	94

Miami won series 4–1.

Western Conference Semifinals

Game 1	Memphis	91	at Okla. City	93
Game 2	Memphis	99	at Okla. City	93
Game 3	Okla. State	81	at Memphis	87
Game 4	Okla. State	97	at Memphis	103*
Game 5	Memphis	88	at Okla. City	84

Memphis won series 4–1.

Game 1	Golden State	127	at San Antonio	129**
Game 2	Golden State	100	at San Antonio	91
Game 3	San Antonio	102	at Golden State	92
Game 4	San Antonio	87	at Golden State	97*
Game 5	Golden State	91	at San Antonio	109
Game 6	San Antonio	94	at Golden State	82

San Antonio won series 4–2.

Eastern Conference Finals

Game 1	Indiana	102	at Miami	103*
Game 2	Indiana	97	at Miami	93
Game 3	Miami	114	at Indiana	96
Game 4	Miami	92	at Indiana	99
Game 5	Indiana	79	at Miami	90
Game 6	Miami	77	at Indiana	91
Game 7	Indiana	76	at Miami	99

Miami won series 4–3.

Western Conference Finals

Game 1	Memphis	83	at San Antonio	105
Game 2	Memphis	89	at San Antonio	93*
Game 3	San Antonio	104	at Memphis	93*
Game 4	San Antonio	93	at Memphis	10986

San Antonio won series 4–0.

NBA Finals

Game 1	San Antonio	92	at Miami	88
Game 2	San Antonio	84	at Miami	103
Game 3	Miami	77	at San Antonio	113
Game 4	Miami	109	at San Antonio	93
Game 5	Miami	104	at San Antonio	114
Game 6	San Antonio	100	at Miami	103*
Game 7	San Antonio	88	at Miami	95

Miami won series 4–3.

*Overtime game. **Double Overtime. ***Triple Overtime.

NBA Finals Composite Box Score

MIAMI HEAT

Player	GP	Mpg	FG%	3FG%	FT%	Off.	Reb./per game Total	Apg	Spg	Bpg	TOpg	Ppg
LeBron James	7	43.0	.447	.353	.795	2.4	10.9	7.0	2.3	0.9	2.6	25.3
Dwyane Wade	7	36.4	.476	.000	.773	1.3	4.0	4.6	1.9	1.3	2.3	19.6
Chris Bosh	7	34.3	.462	.000	.733	2.9	8.9	2.1	1.9	1.6	1.0	11.9
Ray Allen	7	27.6	.543	.545	.923	0.3	2.3	1.6	0.1	0.0	1.3	10.6
Mario Chalmers	7	31.6	.388	.406	.692	0.1	2.7	2.1	0.7	0.3	3.8	10.6
Shane Battier	7	12.4	.444	.444	1.000	0.3	1.6	0.9	0.1	0.3	0.0	5.6
Mike Miller	7	21.7	.591	.611	.000	0.3	2.7	0.9	0.6	0.3	0.3	5.3
Chris Andersen	5	14.2	.727	.000	.600	1.2	3.0	0.0	0.8	0.6	0.8	4.4
Norris Cole	5	16.4	.273	.333	.500	0.2	1.0	2.4	0.8	0.2	1.0	3.0
Udonis Haslem	6	10.7	.444	.000	1.000	0.7	2.8	0.0	0.0	0.2	0.2	1.5
James Jones	3	4.0	.400	.667	.000	0.0	0.3	0.0	0.0	0.3	0.3	2.0
Rashard Lewis	3	4.0	.333	.000	.000	0.3	0.7	0.7	0.0	0.0	0.7	1.3
Joel Anthony	4	3.8	.500	.000	.000	1.0	1.8	0.0	0.0	0.0	0.0	0.5
Avg/Total	**7**	**243.6**	**.459**	**.432**	**.771**	**9.9**	**39.7**	**21.1**	**8.7**	**5.17**	**11.9**	**97.0**

SAN ANTONIO SPURS

Player	GP	Mpg	FG%	3FG%	FT%	Off.	Reb./per game Total	Apg	Spg	Bpg	TOpg	Ppg
Kevin Durant	5	42.6	.548	.394	.839	1.2	6.0	2.2	1.4	1.0	3.8	30.6
Tim Duncan	7	36.3	.490	.000	.821	3.7	12.1	1.4	0.9	1.4	2.3	18.9
Tony Parker	7	35.1	.412	.286	.727	0.4	1.9	6.4	1.0	0.1	2.1	15.7
Kawhi Leonard	7	36.4	.513	.348	.706	3.0	11.1	0.9	2.0	0.4	1.0	14.6
Danny Green	7	35.4	.444	.551	.875	0.9	4.1	0.7	1.0	1.6	1.1	14.0
Manu Ginobili	7	28.4	.433	.250	.786	0.1	2.1	4.3	0.7	0.0	3.1	11.6
Gary Neal	7	24.4	.414	.467	1.000	0.1	2.4	0.9	0.0	0.0	1.1	9.4
Tiago Splitter	7	15.3	.448	.000	.800	0.9	2.0	0.4	0.7	.4	1.3	4.9
Boris Diaw	6	15.7	.500	.500	.750	0.8	2.5	1.7	0.0	0.2	0.8	4.0
DeJuan Blair	3	5.7	.455	.000	.333	0.7	2.7	0.3	0.7	0.0	0.0	3.7
Matt Bonner	6	6.0	.400	.250	1.000	0.0	1.2	0.2	0.2	0.0	0.0	1.8
Cory Joseph	6	7.2	.444	.000	.500	0.5	1.0	1.0	0.3	0.0	0.8	1.8
Patrick Mills	2	6.5	.400	.000	.000	0.0	0.5	0.0	0.0	0.0	0.0	2.0
Nando De Colo	2	2.5	.000	.000	.000	0.0	0.5	0.5	0.0	0.0	0.0	0.0
Tracy McGrady	2	7.0	.000	.000	.000	0.0	2.0	2.5	0.0	0.5	0.0	0.0
Avg/Total	**7**	**243.1**	**.451**	**.407**	**.766**	**10.6**	**41.9**	**18.4**	**7.0**	**4.35**	**13.6**	**97.7**

NBA Finals Game Box Scores

Game 1

SAN ANTONIO 92

Player	Min	FG M-A	FT M-A	Reb O-T	A	PF	S	TO	TP
K. Leonard	35	3-9	4-4	2-10	1	2	1	0	10
T. Duncan	37	8-19	4-4	3-14	4	4	1	2	20
T. Splitter	25	3-6	1-2	1-2	0	0	0	1	7
D. Green	34	4-9	0-0	0-5	0	3	1	0	12
T. Parker	40	9-18	3-4	0-0	6	1	1	0	21
M. Ginobili	30	4-11	3-4	0-0	3	2	2	1	13
B. Diaw	9	1-1	0-0	0-1	1	0	0	0	2
C. Joseph	2	0-1	0-0	0-0	0	0	0	0	0
G. Neal	22	3-9	0-0	0-2	1	0	0	0	7
M. Bonner	7	0-1	0-0	0-3	0	0	0	0	0
Totals	240	35-84	15-18	6-37	16	12	6	4	92

Percentages: FG—.417, FT—.838. 3-pt goals: 7–23, .304 (Leonard 0–4, Green 4–9, Ginobili 2–5, Neal 1–5). Blocked shots: 5 (Duncan 3, Splitter, Green).

A: 19,775. Officials: T. Brothers, M. McCutchen, J. Phillips.

MIAMI 88

Player	Min	FG M-A	FT M-A	Reb O-T	A	PF	S	TO	TP
L. James	42	7-16	3-4	2-18	10	0	0	2	18
U. Haslem	17	1-1	0-0	0-4	0	2	0	0	2
C. Bosh	35	6-16	1-2	1-5	1	4	3	1	13
D. Wade	36	7-15	3-4	2-2	2	0	1	1	17
M. Chalmers	27	3-10	0-0	0-1	2	0	0	1	8
R. Allen	24	3-4	4-5	1-3	0	1	0	1	13
M. Miller	20	2-3	0-0	0-4	0	0	0	1	5
C. Andersen	13	3-5	1-2	1-3	0	3	0	1	7
N. Cole	17	2-4	0-0	0-2	4	1	0	0	5
S. Battier	6	0-3	0-0	0-1	1	1	0	0	0
J. Anthony	3	0-1	0-0	2-3	0	0	0	0	0
Totals	240	34-78	12-17	9-46	20	12	4	8	88

Percentages: FG—.436, FT—.706. 3-pt goals: 8–25, .320 (James 1–5, Bosh 0–4, Chalmers 2–6, Allen 3–4, Miller 1–2, Cole 1–1, Battier 0–3). Blocked shots: 2 (Bosh, Battier).

Game 2

SAN ANTONIO 84

Player	Min	FG M-A	FT M-A	Reb O-T	A	PF	S	TO	TP
K. Leonard	33	4-12	0-1	8-14	2	2	1	1	9
T. Duncan	30	3-13	3-4	3-11	1	1	0	1	9
T. Splitter	23	2-5	0-0	0-1	1	0	1	0	4
D. Green	30	6-6	0-0	0-1	1	4	0	1	17
T. Parker	33	5-14	3-4	1-3	5	0	0	5	13
M. Ginobili	18	2-6	0-0	0-2	1	3	1	3	5
B. Diaw	11	0-0	0-0	0-0	2	1	0	0	0
G. Neal	22	3-7	2-2	0-2	0	2	0	3	10
C. Joseph	9	3-3	2-3	2-3	1	0	0	1	8
T. McGrady	8	0-1	0-0	0-2	2	0	0	0	0
P. Mills	8	1-3	0-0	0-0	0	0	0	2	2
M. Bonner	8	2-4	0-0	0-1	0	0	0	0	5
D. Blair	8	1-4	0-0	1-4	0	0	1	0	2
Totals	240	32-78	10-14	15-44	16	14	3	16	84

Percentages: FG—.410, FT—.714. 3-pt goals: 10–20, .500 (Leonard 1–3, Green 5–6, Parker 0–1, Ginobili 1–4, Neal 2–3, Mills 0–2, Bonner 1–2). Blocked shots: 4 (Splitter, Green, Parker, McGrady).

MIAMI 103

Player	Min	FG M-A	FT M-A	Reb O-T	A	PF	S	TO	TP
L. James	41	7-17	2-2	1-8	7	2	3	2	17
U. Haslem	16	2-4	1-1	2-2	0	2	0	0	5
C. Bosh	31	6-10	0-0	4-10	4	1	3	0	12
D. Wade	30	5-13	0-2	0-2	6	1	0	2	10
M. Chalmers	35	6-12	5-5	0-4	2	1	1	0	19
M. Miller	16	3-3	0-0	0-0	1	2	1	0	9
R. Allen	25	5-8	0-0	0-1	0	0	0	0	13
C. Andersen	14	3-3	3-4	1-4	0	5	1	1	9
N. Cole	13	1-5	0-0	1-2	1	2	0	0	2
R. Lewis	5	2-3	0-0	0-1	1	0	0	1	4
J. Anthony	5	0-0	0-0	0-1	0	0	0	0	0
S. Battier	5	1-3	0-0	0-1	0	0	0	0	3
J. Jones	5	0-2	0-0	0-0	0	1	0	0	0
Totals	240	41-83	11-14	9-36	22	17	9	6	103

Percentages: FG—.494, FT—.786. 3-pt goals: 10–19, .526 (James 1–3, Chalmers 2–4, Miller 3–3, Allen 3–5, Cole 0–1, Battier 1–3). Blocked shots: 6 (James 3, Bosh, Wade, Andersen).

A: 19,900. Officials: Joe Crawford, E. Malloy, K. Mauer.

Game 3

MIAMI 77

Player	Min	FG M-A	FT M-A	Reb O-T	A	PF	S	TO	TP
L. James	39	7-21	0-0	1-11	5	0	2	2	15
U. Haslem	10	0-2	0-0	2-3	0	2	0	0	0
C. Bosh	32	4-10	4-6	2-10	4	2	1	1	12
D. Wade	34	7-15	2-2	0-0	5	0	4	2	16
M. Chalmers	20	0-5	0-0	1-2	1	4	0	4	0
M. Miller	22	5-5	0-0	0-0	0	1	0	1	15
C. Andersen	11	1-1	0-0	0-0	0	2	0	1	2
N. Cole	27	3-8	1-2	0-1	3	3	2	3	8
R. Allen	19	2-2	0-0	1-2	3	0	2	4	4
S. Battier	8	0-2	0-0	0-3	0	2	0	0	0
J. Jones	6	1-2	0-0	0-1	0	1	0	1	3
J. Anthony	6	1-1	0-0	2-3	1	0	0	2	2
R. Lewis	6	0-2	0-0	0-0	1	0	0	0	0
Totals	240	31-76	7-10	9-36	21	17	9	16	77

Percentages: FG—.408, FT—.700. 3-pt goals: 8–18, .444 (James 1–5, Bosh 0–1, Chalmers 0–1, Miller 5–5, Cole 1–2, Battier 0–2, Jones 1–2). Blocked shots: 8 (Bosh 3, Haslem, Wade, Andersen, Cole, Jones).

SAN ANTONIO 113

Player	Min	FG M-A	FT M-A	Reb O-T	A	PF	S	TO	TP
K. Leonard	29	6-10	0-0	3-12	2	2	4	1	14
T. Duncan	29	5-11	2-4	7-14	1	2	0	4	12
T. Splitter	24	3-7	2-2	4-5	1	2	2	0	8
D. Green	31	9-15	2-2	3-4	0	1	2	0	27
T. Parker	27	2-5	1-3	0-2	8	2	0	2	6
M. Ginobili	23	3-7	1-2	0-2	6	2	0	2	7
M. Bonner	12	0-3	2-2	0-2	1	1	0	0	2
C. Joseph	20	1-4	0-1	1-2	4	0	2	3	2
G. Neal	25	9-17	0-0	0-4	3	0	0	0	24
T. McGrady	7	0-2	0-0	0-2	3	0	0	0	0
P. Mills	6	1-2	0-0	0-1	0	0	0	2	2
D. Blair	6	4-5	1-3	1-2	0	1	0	0	9
Totals	240	43-88	11-19	19-52	29	13	10	12	113

Percentages: FG—.489, FT—.579. 3-pt goals: 16–32, .500 (Leonard 2–3, Green 7–9, Parker 1–1, Ginobili 0–4, Bonner 0–2, Joseph 0–1, Neal 6–10, McGrady 0–1, Mills 0–1). Blocked shots: 4 (Duncan 2, Green 2).

A: 18,581. Officials: J. Capers, D. Crawford, M. Davis.

Game 4

MIAMI 109

Player	Min	FG M-A	FT M-A	Reb O-T	A	PF	S	TO	TP
L. James	41	15-25	2-4	3-11	4	2	2	1	33
M. Miller	21	0-1	0-0	0-1	2	3	0	0	0
C. Bosh	38	8-14	4-4	2-13	1	3	2	1	20
D. Wade	40	14-25	4-4	2-6	4	4	6	0	32
M. Chalmers	29	2-4	0-0	0-4	5	3	1	4	6
N. Cole	19	0-4	0-0	0-2	4	2	1	0	0
R. Allen	33	5-10	3-3	0-1	2	3	0	1	14
U. Haslem	10	1-1	0-0	0-5	0	5	0	1	2
S. Battier	9	0-1	2-2	0-0	1	1	0	0	2
Totals	240	45-85	15-17	7-41	23	26	13	9	109

Percentages: FG—.529, FT—.882. 3-pt goals: 4–12, .333 (James 1–2, Miller 0–1, Chalmers 2–3, Cole 0–1, Allen 1–4, Battier 0–1). Blocked shots: 7 (James 2, Miller, Bosh 2, Wade, Battier).

A: 18,581. Officials: M. Callahan, S. Foster, B. Kennedy.

SAN ANTONIO 93

Player	Min	FG M-A	FT M-A	Reb O-T	A	PF	S	TO	TP
K. Leonard	33	5-10	1-2	1-7	0	2	1	1	12
T. Duncan	33	6-10	8-10	1-5	1	2	0	3	20
T. Splitter	14	0-3	4-4	1-3	1	1	1	3	4
D. Green	36	3-8	1-2	0-4	4	5	1	2	10
T. Parker	32	7-16	1-3	1-4	9	0	1	3	15
G. Neal	31	4-7	2-2	0-3	0	2	0	2	13
M. Ginobili	26	1-5	3-4	0-2	2	4	0	1	5
C. Joseph	9	0-1	1-2	0-1	1	0	0	1	1
M. Bonner	7	2-2	0-0	0-1	0	1	0	0	0
B. Diaw	11	3-6	2-2	1-3	1	1	0	2	9
D. Blair	4	0-2	0-0	0-0	1	0	1	0	0
N. De Colo	4	0-0	0-0	0-0	1	0	0	0	0
Totals	240	31-70	23-31	5-36	21	18	5	18	93

Percentages: FG—.443, FT—.742. 3-pt goals: 8–16, .500. (Leonard 1–2, Green 3–5, Parker 0–1, Neal 3–4, Ginobili 0–3, Diaw 1–1). Blocked shots: 4 (Leonard 2, Duncan, Green).

Game 5

MIAMI 104

Player	Min	FG M-A	FT M-A	Reb O-T	A	PF	S	TO	TP
L. James	44	8-22	7-9	3-6	8	1	4	3	25
C. Bosh	38	7-11	2-2	5-6	1	4	1	1	16
M. Chalmers	27	2-10	1-2	0-4	1	5	1	2	7
M. Miller	25	0-1	0-0	1-5	1	4	1	1	0
D. Wade	40	10-22	5-6	2-4	10	1	1	4	25
U. Haslem	9	0-1	0-0	0-3	0	2	0	0	0
R. Lewis, PF	1	0-1	0-0	1-1	0	0	0	1	0
J. Jones	1	1-1	0-0	0-0	0	0	0	0	3
S Battier	18	2-6	1-1	0-1	3	2	0	0	7
J. Anthony	1	0-0	0-0	0-0	0	0	0	0	0
N. Cole	7	0-1	0-0	0-0	0	1	0	1	0
R. Allen	30	7-10	3-3	0-4	1	4	0	0	21
Totals	240	37-86	19-23	12-34	25	24	8	13	104

Percentages: FG—.430, FT—.826. 3-pt goals: 11–23, .478 (James 2–4, Chalmers 2–6, Miller 0–1, Jones 1–1, Battier 2–6, Cole 0–1, Allen 4–4). Blocked shots: 3 (Wade 2, Bosh).

SAN ANTONIO 114

Player	Min	FG M-A	FT M-A	Reb O-T	A	PF	S	TO	TP
T. Duncan	38	7-10	3-4	3-12	1	1	0	1	17
K. Leonard	33	6-8	2-2	1-8	1	3	3	2	16
T. Parker	36	10-14	6-8	0-1	5	2	0	3	26
M. Ginobili	33	8-14	7-8	0-2	10	4	1	3	24
D. Green	39	8-15	2-2	0-6	0	4	0	2	24
M. Bonner	1	0-0	0-0	0-0	0	0	1	0	0
B. Diaw	27	0-1	1-2	1-4	3	2	0	3	1
T. Splitter	10	2-4	0-0	0-2	0	3	0	3	4
G. Neal	21	1-4	0-0	0-1	1	2	0	1	2
C. Joseph	1	0-0	0-0	0-0	0	0	0	0	0
N. de Colo	1	0-0	0-0	0-0	0	0	0	0	0
Totals	240	42-70	21-26	5-36	21	21	5	18	114

Percentages: FG—.600, FT—.808. 3-pt goals: 9–22, .409 (Leonard 2–4, Parker 0–1, Ginobili 1–4, Green 6–10, Diaw 0–1, Neal 0–2). Blocked shots: 8 (Duncan 3, Green 3, Diaw, Splitter).
A: 18,581. Officials: M. McCutchen, T. Brothers, E. Malloy.

Game 6

SAN ANTONIO 100

Player	Min	FG M-A	FT M-A	Reb O-T	A	PF	S	TO	TP
K. Leonard	46	9-14	3-4	2-11	0	3	3	0	22
M. Ginobili	35	2-5	4-6	1-4	3	4	1	8	9
T. Duncan	44	13-21	4-5	5-17	0	2	1	2	30
D. Green	41	1-7	0-0	2-4	0	4	1	1	3
T. Parker	43	6-23	6-7	1-3	8	1	2	0	19
G. Neal	24	2-7	0-0	0-1	0	2	0	1	5
B. Diaw	23	2-6	3-4	1-4	2	2	0	0	7
T. Splitter	8	2-2	1-2	0-1	0	3	0	1	5
M. Bonner	10	0-0	0-0	0-0	0	0	0	0	0
Totals	265	37-85	21-28	12-45	13	21	8	13	100

Percentages: FG—.435, FT—.750. 3-pt goals: 5–18, .278 (Leonard 1–3, Ginobili 1–3, Green 1–5, Parker 1–3, Diaw 0–1, Neal 1–3). Blocked shots: 2 (Green 2).

MIAMI 103

Player	Min	FG M-A	FT M-A	Reb O-T	A	PF	S	TO	TP
L. James	50	11-26	9-12	4-10	11	3	3	6	32
M. Miller	30	3-4	0-0	1-7	2	5	0	0	8
C. Bosh	39	5-12	0-1	3-11	2	0	3	1	10
D. Wade	37	6-15	2-2	2-4	4	4	0	3	14
M. Chalmers	43	7-11	2-2	0-4	2	2	0	3	20
R. Allen	41	3-8	2-2	0-1	2	5	1	2	9
S. Battier	13	3-4	0-0	1-1	0	3	0	0	9
C. Andersen	14	0-1	1-2	1-4	0	4	3	0	1
Totals	265	38-81	16-21	12-42	23	26	10	15	103

Percentages: FG—.469, FT—.762. 3-pt goals: 11–19, .579 (James 1–5, Miller 2–2, Chalmers 4–5, Allen 1–3, Battier 3–4). Blocked shots: 6 (James, Miller, Wade 2, Bosh 2).
A: 19,900. Officials: M. Callahan, J. Crawford, K. Mauer.

Game 7

SAN ANTONIO 88

Player	Min	FG M-A	FT M-A	Reb O-T	A	PF	S	TO	TP
K. Leonard	45	8-17	2-4	4-16	0	2	1	2	19
M. Ginobili	35	6-12	4-4	0-3	5	4	0	4	18
T. Duncan	43	8-18	8-8	4-12	2	4	4	3	24
D. Green	36	1-12	2-2	1-5	0	3	2	2	5
T. Parker	37	3-12	4-4	0-0	4	1	3	2	10
G. Neal	26	2-7	0-0	1-4	1	2	0	1	5
B. Diaw	13	2-2	0-0	2-3	1	2	0	0	5
T. Splitter	4	1-2	0-0	0-0	0	1	2	0	2
C. Joseph	0:22	0-0	0-0	0-0	0	0	0	0	0
Totals	240	31-82	20-22	12-43	13	19	12	14	88

Percentages: FG—.378, FT—.909. 3-pt goals: 6–19, .316 (Leonard 1–4, Ginobili 2–5, Green 1–6, Diaw 1–1, Neal 1–3). Blocked shots: 3 (Leonard, Duncan, Green).

MIAMI 95

Player	Min	FG M-A	FT M-A	Reb O-T	A	PF	S	TO	TP
L. James	45	12-23	8-8	3-12	4	2	2	2	37
M. Miller	19	0-5	0-0	0-2	0	2	2	0	0
C. Bosh	28	0-5	0-0	3-7	2	5	0	2	0
D. Wade	39	11-21	1-2	1-10	1	0	1	4	23
M. Chalmers	40	6-15	1-4	0-0	2	3	2	4	14
R. Allen	20	0-4	0-0	0-4	4	2	0	3	0
S. Battier	29	6-8	0-0	1-4	1	1	1	0	18
C. Andersen	19	1-1	1-2	3-4	0	2	0	1	3
U. Haslem	2	0-0	0-0	0-0	0	2	0	0	0
Totals	240	36-82	11-16	11-43	14	19	8	16	95

Percentages: FG—.439, FT—.688. 3-pt goals: 12–32, .375 (James 5–10, Miller 0–4, Bosh 0–1, Chalmers 1–7, Allen 0–2, Battier 6–8). Blocked shots: 4 (Bosh, Wade 2, Andersen).
A: 19,900. Officials: D. Crawford, S. Foster, M. McCutchen.

2012-13 All-NBA Teams

FIRST TEAM	SECOND TEAM	THIRD TEAM
F LeBron James, Mia	F Carmelo Anthony, NYK	F David Lee, GS
F Kevin Durant, OKC	F Blake Griffin, LAC	F Paul George, Ind
C Tim Duncan, SA	C Marc Gasol, Mem	C Dwight Howard, LAL
G Kobe Bryant, LAL	G Tony Parker, SA	G Dwyane Wade, Mia
G Chris Paul, LAC	G Russell Westbrook, OKC	G James Harden, Hou

All-Rookie Teams

FIRST TEAM	SECOND TEAM
Damian Lillard, Por	Andre Drummond, Det
Bradley Beal, Wash	Jonas Valanciunas, Tor
Anthony Davis, NO	Michael Kidd-Gilchrist, Cha
Dion Walters, Cle	Kyle Singler, Det
Harrison Barnes, GS	Tyler Zeller, Cle

All-Defensive Teams

FIRST TEAM	SECOND TEAM
F LeBron James, Mia	F Tim Duncan, SA
F Serge Ibaka, OKC	F Paul George, Ind
C Tyson Chandler, NYK	C Marc Gasol, Mem
C Joakim Noah, Chi	G Avery Bradley, Bos
G Tony Allen, Mem	G Mike Conley, Mem
G Chris Paul, LAC	

2012-13 NBA Regular Season Individual Leaders

Scoring

	GP	Pts	Avg
Carmelo Anthony, NY	67	1920	28.7
Kevin Durant, OKC	81	2280	28.1
Kobe Bryant, LAL	78	2133	27.3
LeBron James, Mia	76	2036	26.8
James Harden, Hou	78	2023	25.9
Russell Westbrook, OKC	82	1903	23.2
Stephen Curry, GS	78	1786	22.9
Dwyane Wade, Mia	69	1463	21.2
LaMarcus Aldridge, Por	74	1560	21.1
Brook Lopez, Bkn	74	1437	19.4

Rebounds

	GP	Reb	Avg
Dwight Howard, LAL	76	945	12.4
Nikola Vucevic, Orl	77	917	11.9
Omer Asik, Hou	82	956	11.7
Zach Randolph, Mem	76	854	11.2
David Lee, GS	79	886	11.2
Reggie Evans, Bkn	80	888	11.1
J.J. Hickson, Por	80	828	10.4
Al Horford, Atl	74	757	10.2
DeMarcus Cousins, Sac	75	746	9.9
Carlos Boozer, Chi	79	771	9.8

Assists

	GP	Ast	Avg
Rajon Rondo, Bos	38	420	11.1
Chris Paul, LAC	70	678	9.7
Greivis Vasquez, NO	78	704	9.0
Jrue Holiday, Phi	78	625	8.0
Deron Williams, Bkn	78	604	7.7
Tony Parker, SA	66	499	7.6
Russell Westbrook, OKC	82	607	7.4
Goran Dragic, Phx	77	569	7.4
Jameer Nelson, Orl	56	413	7.4
Ricky Rubio, Minn	57	418	7.3
LeBron James, Mia	76	551	7.3

Field-Goal Percentage

	FGM	FGA	Pct
DeAndre Jordan, LAC	314	488	.643
Dwight Howard, LAL	470	813	.578
JaVale McGee, Den	303	527	.575
Serge Ibaka, OKC	446	778	.573
LeBron James, Mia	765	1354	.565
J.J. Hickson, Por	418	744	.562
Tiago Splitter, SA	315	563	.560
Amir Johnson, Tor	336	606	.554
Kenneth Faried, Den	380	689	.552
Al Horford, Atl	576	1060	.543

Free-Throw Percentage

	FTM	FTA	Pct
Kevin Durant, OKC	679	750	.905
Stephen Curry, GS	262	291	.900
J.J. Redick, Mil/Orl	171	190	.900
Kevin Martin, OKC	219	246	.890
Ray Allen, Mia	140	158	.886
Chris Paul, LAC	286	323	.885
Isaiah Thomas, Sac	253	287	.882
Jeff Teague, Atl	199	226	.881
Darren Collison, Dal	242	275	.880
Jamal Crawford, LAC	216	248	.871

Three-Point Field-Goal Percentage

	3FGM	3FGA	Pct
Jose Calderon, Det/Tor	130	282	.461
Kyle Korver, Atl	189	414	.457
Stephen Curry, GS	272	600	.453
Ersan Ilyasova, Mil	95	214	.444
Steve Nash, LAL	57	130	.438
Shane Battier, Mia	136	316	.430
Danny Green, SA	177	413	.429
Mike Dunleavy, Mil	128	299	.428
Willie Green, LAC	71	166	.428
Kevin Martin, OKC	158	371	.426

Steals

	GP	Steals	Avg
Chris Paul, LAC	70	169	2.41
Ricky Rubio, Minn	57	137	2.40
Mike Conley, Mem	80	174	2.18
Monta Ellis, Mil	82	169	2.06
Kemba Walker, Cha	82	160	1.95
Dwyane Wade, Mia	69	128	1.86
James Harden, Hou	78	142	1.82
Paul George, Ind	79	143	1.81
Russell Westbrook, OKC	82	145	1.77
Thaddeus Young, Phi	76	133	1.75

Blocked Shots

	GP	BS	Avg
Serge Ibaka, OKC	80	242	3.03
Larry Sanders, Mil	71	201	2.83
Tim Duncan, SA	69	183	2.65
Roy Hibbert, Ind	79	206	2.61
Dwight Howard, LAL	76	186	2.45
Joakim Noah, Chi	66	141	2.14
Brook Lopez, Bkn	74	154	2.08
JaVale McGee, Den	79	157	1.99
Josh Smith, Atl	76	136	1.79
Bismack Biyombo, Cha	80	143	1.79

Offense

Team	FG Pct	3FG Pct	FT Pct	Rebound Avg Off	Total	A	TO	Stl	Scoring Avg
Denver Nuggets	47.8	34.3	70.1	13.3	45.0	24.4	14.7	9.3	106.1
Houston Rockets	46.1	36.6	75.4	11.1	43.4	23.2	15.8	8.3	106.0
Oklahoma City Thunder	48.1	37.7	82.8	10.4	43.6	21.4	14.6	8.3	105.7
San Antonio Spurs	48.1	37.6	79.1	8.1	41.3	25.1	14.1	8.5	103.0
Miami Heat	49.6	39.6	75.4	8.2	38.6	23.0	13.3	8.7	102.9
Los Angeles Lakers	45.8	35.5	69.2	11.5	44.8	22.2	14.6	7.0	102.2
Golden State Warriors	45.8	40.3	79.0	10.8	45.0	22.5	14.8	6.9	101.2
Los Angeles Clippers	47.8	35.8	71.1	11.4	41.6	23.9	13.8	9.6	101.1
Dallas Mavericks	46.2	37.2	79.3	9.4	41.9	23.2	13.5	7.9	101.1
Sacramento Kings	44.7	36.3	76.9	11.5	40.6	20.8	14.0	8.2	100.2
New York Knicks	44.8	37.6	75.9	10.9	40.6	19.3	11.6	8.2	100.0
Milwaukee Bucks	43.5	36.0	73.6	13.0	44.0	22.9	13.6	8.4	98.9
Atlanta Hawks	46.4	37.1	71.5	9.2	40.9	24.5	14.3	8.1	98.0
Utah Jazz	45.4	36.6	76.4	12.1	42.0	22.7	14.2	8.4	98.0
Portland Trail Blazers	44.8	35.3	77.6	10.7	40.8	21.8	14.2	6.6	97.5
Toronto Raptors	44.6	34.3	78.8	10.6	40.2	21.5	13.2	7.3	97.2
Brooklyn Nets	45.0	35.7	73.1	12.8	42.8	20.3	13.9	7.3	96.9
Boston Celtics	46.5	35.8	77.6	8.1	39.3	22.8	13.9	8.2	96.5
Cleveland Cavaliers	43.4	34.6	75.6	12.2	41.0	20.7	13.4	7.9	96.5
Minnesota Timberwolves	43.9	30.5	74.2	11.9	42.0	22.4	14.1	8.5	95.7
Phoenix Suns	44.3	33.0	74.4	11.7	41.6	22.6	15.0	8.0	95.2
Detroit Pistons	44.9	35.6	69.9	12.1	42.1	21.2	14.6	7.0	94.9
Indiana Pacers	43.6	34.7	74.6	12.9	45.9	20.3	14.5	7.2	94.7
New Orleans Hornets	44.8	36.3	77.6	12.0	41.6	21.0	13.7	6.3	94.1
Orlando Magic	44.8	32.9	75.5	10.9	42.7	22.8	14.0	6.4	94.1
Memphis Grizzlies	44.4	34.5	77.3	12.9	42.7	20.9	13.2	8.6	93.4
Charlotte Bobcats	42.5	33.5	75.0	11.2	40.3	19.4	13.1	7.2	93.4
Washington Wizards	43.5	36.5	73.3	10.8	43.2	21.6	14.6	7.3	93.2
Chicago Bulls	43.7	35.3	77.3	12.5	43.2	23.0	13.7	7.2	93.2
Philadelphia 76ers	44.4	36.0	72.9	10.9	41.3	22.8	12.6	7.4	93.2

Defense (Opponents' Statistics)

Team	FG Pct	3FG Pct	FT Pct	Rebound Avg. Off	Total	A	TO	Stl	Scoring Avg
Memphis Grizzlies	43.5	33.8	74.8	10.3	39.1	19.5	14.7	7.3	89.3
Indiana Pacers	42.0	32.7	76.0	11.2	40.9	19.2	13.0	7.5	90.7
Chicago Bulls	44.3	34.6	73.9	11.0	41.1	18.8	13.1	7.3	92.9
Los Angeles Clippers	44.3	37.3	74.9	10.9	39.1	22.1	15.4	7.4	94.6
Miami Heat	44.0	35.0	76.6	11.2	40.1	20.2	14.7	7.9	95.0
Brooklyn Nets	46.4	36.6	73.1	10.7	39.2	21.4	13.0	7.5	95.1
New York Knicks	45.8	35.7	75.7	10.0	41.6	19.3	14.5	6.4	95.7
Washington Wizards	44.0	34.9	73.8	11.0	44.2	21.5	13.9	7.8	95.8
Philadelphia 76ers	45.4	34.9	76.0	11.0	44.0	22.8	13.8	7.2	96.5
Oklahoma City Thunder	42.5	34.6	77.4	12.0	40.7	20.5	14.2	8.2	96.5
San Antonio Spurs	44.2	35.3	76.0	11.1	42.5	21.4	14.3	8.2	96.6
Boston Celtics	44.1	34.2	74.0	11.4	43.6	21.6	14.4	7.8	96.7
Atlanta Hawks	48.4	37.9	71.5	11.3	43.7	22.3	14.6	8.4	97.5
New Orleans Hornets	47.1	37.4	75.9	10.2	39.3	23.4	12.7	7.9	97.9
Utah Jazz	45.8	37.0	75.7	11.0	40.8	20.6	14.1	7.8	98.1
Minnesota Timberwolves	46.8	36.9	75.2	10.6	42.1	22.3	15.3	8.1	98.1
Toronto Raptors	45.8	36.1	74.7	10.7	41.7	21.9	13.7	7.0	98.7
Detroit Pistons	45.9	36.0	76.2	11.1	41.8	22.4	13.1	8.4	98.8
Golden State Warriors	43.9	34.7	74.8	11.1	42.7	23.5	12.9	8.2	100.3
Milwaukee Bucks	45.4	34.8	75.9	12.4	46.0	23.1	15.3	8.0	100.4
Portland Trail Blazers	47.4	34.0	76.1	11.0	42.4	23.7	12.7	8.4	100.7
Los Angeles Lakers	45.3	35.7	73.2	11.5	42.7	23.4	12.4	8.5	101.0
Orlando Magic	46.3	35.9	73.8	10.8	42.8	23.7	12.1	7.2	101.1
Denver Nuggets	44.4	36.3	73.1	12.4	41.6	23.6	15.2	8.0	101.1
Cleveland Cavaliers	47.6	37.2	73.9	10.8	42.1	23.9	14.7	7.6	101.2
Phoenix Suns	47.0	38.8	75.7	11.7	43.4	22.8	14.8	8.4	101.6
Dallas Mavericks	44.5	35.9	75.3	12.0	45.6	22.0	14.0	8.5	101.7
Houston Rockets	45.4	38.8	77.6	10.7	41.6	22.7	14.2	8.5	102.5
Charlotte Bobcats	47.1	38.8	74.7	11.8	44.1	25.3	13.6	6.9	102.7
Sacramento Kings	47.2	35.5	78.3	11.9	43.6	25.1	14.1	7.6	105.1

NBA Team-by-Team Statistical Leaders

Atlanta Hawks

Player	GP	MPG	FG%	3Pt%	FT%	OFF	DEF	Total	APG	SPG	BPG	TOPG	PFPG	PPG
Josh Smith	76	35.3	.465	.303	.517	1.8	6.7	8.40	4.2	1.24	1.79	2.97	2.30	17.5
Al Horford	74	37.2	.543	.500	.644	2.6	7.6	10.2	3.2	1.05	1.05	1.99	2.20	17.4
Jeff Teague	80	32.9	.451	.359	.881	0.3	1.9	2.3	7.2	1.46	0.35	2.88	2.26	14.6
Louis Williams	39	28.7	.422	.367	.868	0.2	1.8	2.1	3.6	1.13	0.26	1.90	1.41	14.1
Kyle Korver	74	30.5	.461	.457	.859	0.3	3.6	4.0	2.0	0.95	0.50	0.95	2.30	10.9
Devin Harris	58	24.5	.438	.335	.727	0.1	1.9	2.0	3.4	1.10	0.22	1.52	1.78	9.9
Ivan Johnson	69	15.0	.520	.077	.618	1.1	2.8	3.9	0.7	0.81	0.20	1.03	1.90	6.6
John Jenkins	61	14.8	.446	.384	.843	0.3	1.3	1.5	0.9	0.20	0.16	0.66	0.61	6.1
Zaza Pachulia	52	21.8	.473	.000	.757	2.5	3.9	6.5	1.5	0.67	0.23	1.35	2.46	5.9
Shelvin Mack	20	13.4	.488	.400	.571	0.0	1.2	1.2	2.2	0.45	0.00	1.20	1.40	5.2
Mack (TOT)	31	13.4	.460	.367	.563	0.1	1.2	1.3	2.2	0.48	0.00	1.10	0.00	4.6
D. Stevenson	56	20.7	.374	.364	.522	0.3	1.9	2.2	0.9	0.52	0.11	0.41	1.23	5.1
Mike Scott	40	9.4	.476	.000	.768	1.0	1.8	2.8	0.3	0.10	0.05	0.53	0.80	4.6
Anthony Tolliver	62	15.5	.380	.338	.863	0.5	2.0	2.5	0.5	0.24	0.19	0.58	1.06	4.1
Johan Petro	31	11.4	.436	.250	.917	1.1	2.5	3.6	0.5	0.32	0.29	0.77	1.55	3.5
Dahntay Jones	28	13.6	.390	.250	.677	0.4	0.7	1.1	0.7	0.43	0.04	0.57	1.64	3.1
Jones (TOT)	78	13.0	.369	.224	.770	0.3	1.0	1.3	0.6	0.28	0.08	0.49	0.00	3.4
Hawks	82	242.1	.464	.371	.715	9.24	31.62	40.87	24.5	8.10	4.50	14.87	17.96	98.0
Opponents	82	242.1	.450	.379	.763	11.32	32.43	43.74	22.3	8.40	4.27	15.23	18.82	97.5

Boston Celtics

Player	GP	MPG	FG%	3Pt%	FT%	OFF	DEF	Total	APG	SPG	BPG	TOPG	PFPG	PPG
Paul Pierce	77	33.4	.436	.380	.776	0.6	5.7	6.3	4.8	1.09	0.39	2.78	2.73	18.6
Kevin Garnett	68	29.7	.496	.125	.786	1.1	6.7	7.8	2.3	1.15	0.91	1.62	2.26	14.8
Rajon Rondo	38	37.4	.484	.240	.645	1.1	4.4	5.6	11.1	1.84	0.24	3.89	2.53	13.7
Jeff Green	81	27.8	.467	.385	.808	0.7	3.2	3.9	1.6	0.69	0.84	1.63	2.16	12.8
Jason Terry	79	26.9	.434	.372	.870	0.2	1.8	2.0	2.5	0.84	0.14	1.29	1.39	10.1
Avery Bradley	50	28.7	.402	.317	.755	0.6	1.6	2.2	2.1	1.28	0.38	1.44	2.58	9.2
Jordan Crawford	27	21.6	.415	.320	.792	0.5	2.3	2.7	2.5	0.44	0.07	1.63	1.67	9.1
Crawford (TOT)	70	24.4	.415	.337	.811	0.6	2.4	3.0	3.2	0.56	0.10	2.01	0.00	11.6
Brandon Bass	81	27.6	.486	.000	.860	1.6	3.7	5.2	1.0	0.54	0.79	0.99	2.32	8.7
Courtney Lee	78	24.9	.464	.372	.861	0.4	2.0	2.4	1.8	1.14	0.27	1.08	1.78	7.8
Jared Sullinger	45	19.8	.493	.200	.746	2.0	3.8	5.9	0.8	0.49	0.49	0.64	3.42	6.0
Terrence Williams	24	13.3	.495	.333	.429	0.2	1.7	1.8	1.6	0.46	0.08	0.92	0.54	4.6
Chris Wilcox	61	13.6	.719	.000	.672	0.9	2.0	3.0	0.4	0.52	0.46	0.56	2.05	4.2
Shavlik Randolph	16	12.4	.583	.000	.407	1.8	2.6	4.4	0.3	0.50	0.44	0.63	2.38	4.2
D.J. White	12	7.2	.522	.000	.556	0.3	0.8	1.1	0.3	0.08	0.50	0.17	0.42	2.4
Fab Melo	6	6.0	.500	.000	.556	0.0	0.5	0.5	0.0	0.33	0.33	0.17	1.17	1.2
Celtics	81	244.9	.465	.358	.776	8.07	31.27	39.35	22.8	8.24	4.51	14.58	21.20	96.5
Opponents	81	244.9	.441	.342	.740	11.42	32.14	43.56	21.6	7.83	4.67	15.30	19.43	96.7

Brooklyn Nets

Player	GP	MPG	FG%	3Pt%	FT%	OFF	DEF	Total	APG	SPG	BPG	TOPG	PFPG	PPG
Brook Lopez	74	30.4	.521	.000	.758	2.8	4.1	6.9	0.9	0.45	2.08	1.77	2.05	19.4
Deron Williams	78	36.4	.440	.378	.859	0.4	2.6	3.0	7.7	0.96	0.38	2.79	2.49	18.9
Joe Johnson	72	36.7	.423	.375	.820	0.7	2.3	3.0	3.5	0.68	0.19	1.71	1.38	16.3
Andray Blatche	82	19.0	.512	.136	.685	2.0	3.1	5.1	1.0	1.05	0.66	1.50	1.99	10.3
Gerald Wallace	69	30.1	.397	.282	.637	1.0	3.6	4.6	2.6	1.41	0.67	1.59	1.71	7.7
C.J. Watson	80	19.0	.418	.411	.780	0.5	1.3	1.8	2.0	0.82	0.15	0.86	1.54	6.8
Kris Humphries	65	18.3	.448	.000	.789	1.9	3.7	5.6	0.5	0.25	0.51	0.88	1.95	5.8
MarShon Brooks	73	12.5	.463	.273	.734	0.4	1.0	1.4	1.0	0.47	0.22	0.95	1.27	5.4
Jerry Stackhouse	37	14.7	.384	.337	.870	0.1	0.8	0.9	0.9	0.19	0.11	0.65	0.84	4.9
Reggie Evans	80	24.6	.479	.000	.509	3.3	7.8	11.1	0.5	0.93	0.16	1.39	2.49	4.5
Keith Bogans	74	19.0	.380	.343	.647	0.2	1.4	1.6	1.0	0.38	0.05	0.66	1.46	4.2
Mirza Teletovic	53	9.4	.384	.343	.818	0.6	1.2	1.8	0.4	0.25	0.15	0.38	1.00	3.5
Tyshawn Taylor	38	5.8	.368	.462	.556	0.1	0.4	0.5	0.6	0.34	0.00	0.66	0.66	2.2
Tornike Shengelia	19	4.9	.435	.500	.563	0.5	0.7	1.2	0.2	0.16	0.05	0.58	0.58	1.6
Kris Joseph	4	7.5	.000	.000	.500	0.0	0.5	0.5	0.0	0.75	0.00	0.00	0.25	0.5
Joseph (TOT)	10	5.4	.143	.000	.625	0.1	0.6	0.7	0.1	0.30	0.00	0.20	0.00	0.9
Nets	82	242.1	.450	.357	.731	12.77	30.00	42.77	20.3	7.31	4.77	14.71	18.29	96.9
Opponents	82	242.1	.464	.366	.731	10.71	28.49	39.20	21.4	7.49	4.76	13.44	21.35	95.1

Charlotte Bobcats

Player	GP	MPG	FG%	3Pt%	FT%	OFF	DEF	Total	APG	SPG	BPG	TOPG	PFPG	PPG
Kemba Walker	82	34.9	.423	.322	.798	0.7	2.7	3.5	5.7	2.0	0.4	2.4	1.9	17.7
Gerald Henderson	68	31.4	.447	.330	.824	0.8	2.9	3.7	2.6	1.0	0.5	1.6	2.2	15.5
Ramon Sessions	61	27.1	.408	.308	.839	0.4	2.3	2.8	3.8	0.8	0.1	1.7	1.5	14.4
Ben Gordon	75	20.8	.408	.387	.843	0.2	1.5	1.7	1.9	0.5	0.2	1.8	1.8	11.2
Byron Mullens	53	26.9	.385	.317	.646	1.3	5.0	6.4	1.5	0.6	0.6	1.4	2.1	10.6
M. Kidd-Gilchrist	78	26.0	.458	.222	.749	1.7	4.2	5.8	1.5	0.7	0.9	1.3	2.1	9.0
Jannero Pargo	32	15.8	.368	.336	.923	0.3	0.8	1.1	2.1	0.6	0.1	1.3	1.3	6.5
Jeff Taylor	77	19.6	.431	.344	.728	0.7	1.3	1.9	0.8	0.6	0.2	0.6	1.8	6.1
Josh McRoberts	67	22.2	.455	.286	.765	1.4	3.5	4.9	2.1	0.5	0.4	1.0	2.0	6.0
Tyrus Thomas	26	13.8	.353	.375	.839	0.6	1.7	2.3	0.7	0.5	0.6	0.7	2.0	4.8
Bismack Biyombo	80	27.3	.451	.000	.521	2.4	4.8	7.3	0.4	0.4	1.8	1.0	2.4	4.8
Jeff Adrien	52	13.7	.429	.000	.650	1.3	2.5	3.8	0.7	0.3	0.5	0.6	1.5	4.0
Reggie Williams	40	9.5	.432	.306	.476	0.2	1.1	1.3	1.0	0.3	0.0	0.5	0.5	3.6
Brendan Haywood	61	19.0	.431	.000	.455	2.0	2.7	4.8	0.5	0.3	0.8	0.8	2.0	3.5
Cory Higgins	6	5.3	.316	.200	.500	0.2	0.3	0.5	0.8	0.5	0.0	0.0	0.8	2.3
DeSagana Diop	22	10.3	.296	.000	.000	0.5	1.9	2.3	0.6	0.2	0.7	0.4	0.9	0.7
Bobcats	**82**	**241.5**	**.425**	**.335**	**.750**	**11.2**	**29.1**	**40.3**	**19.4**	**7.2**	**5.8**	**14.1**	**19.0**	**93.4**
Opponents	**82**	**241.5**	**.471**	**.388**	**.747**	**11.8**	**32.3**	**44.1**	**25.3**	**6.9**	**6.9**	**14.0**	**21.3**	**102.7**

Chicago Bulls

Player	GP	MPG	FG%	3Pt%	FT%	OFF	DEF	Total	APG	SPG	BPG	TOPG	PFPG	PPG
Luol Deng	75	38.7	.426	.322	.816	2.2	4.2	6.3	3.0	1.1	0.4	1.9	1.4	16.5
Carlos Boozer	79	32.2	.477	.000	.731	2.2	7.5	9.8	2.3	0.8	0.4	2.2	3.0	16.2
Nate Robinson	82	25.4	.433	.405	.799	0.4	1.9	2.2	4.4	1.0	0.1	1.8	2.5	13.1
Joakim Noah	66	36.8	.481	.000	.751	3.9	7.2	11.1	4.0	1.2	2.1	2.7	2.8	11.9
Richard Hamilton	50	21.8	.429	.308	.857	0.3	1.3	1.7	2.4	0.5	0.1	1.7	1.9	9.8
Marco Belinelli	73	25.8	.395	.357	.839	0.2	1.7	1.9	2.0	0.6	0.1	1.1	1.9	9.6
Jimmy Butler	82	26.0	.467	.381	.803	1.7	2.3	4.0	1.4	1.0	0.4	0.8	1.2	8.6
Taj Gibson	65	22.4	.485	.000	.679	1.9	3.4	5.3	0.9	0.4	1.4	1.2	2.6	8.0
Kirk Hinrich	60	29.4	.377	.390	.714	0.3	2.4	2.6	5.2	1.0	0.4	1.6	3.2	7.6
Daequan Cook	49	9.0	.305	.286	.750	0.1	1.1	1.2	0.4	0.2	0.1	0.3	0.5	2.8
Nazr Mohammed	63	11.0	.367	.000	.723	1.2	1.9	3.1	0.4	0.3	0.5	0.4	1.5	2.6
Marquis Teague	48	8.2	.381	.174	.562	0.1	0.8	0.9	1.3	0.2	0.1	0.7	1.0	2.1
V. Radmanovic	25	5.8	.302	.185	.667	0.4	0.7	1.1	0.3	0.3	0.2	0.3	1.2	1.3
Malcolm Thomas	12	4.8	.500	.000	.625	0.4	0.9	1.3	0.3	0.2	0.2	0.2	0.7	1.2
Bulls	**82**	**241.8**	**.437**	**.353**	**.773**	**12.5**	**30.7**	**43.2**	**23.0**	**7.2**	**5.1**	**14.3**	**19.7**	**93.2**
Opponents	**82**	**241.8**	**.443**	**.346**	**.739**	**11.0**	**30.1**	**41.1**	**18.8**	**7.3**	**5.8**	**13.7**	**19.6**	**92.9**

Cleveland Cavaliers

Player	GP	MPG	FG%	3Pt%	FT%	OFF	DEF	Total	APG	SPG	BPG	TOPG	PFPG	PPG
Kyrie Irving	59	34.7	.452	.391	.855	0.6	3.1	3.7	5.9	1.51	0.36	3.24	2.47	22.5
Dion Waiters	61	28.8	.412	.310	.746	0.4	2.1	2.4	3.0	0.97	0.26	1.98	1.85	14.7
Anderson Varejao	25	36.0	.478	.000	.755	5.5	8.9	14.4	3.4	1.48	0.56	1.76	2.72	14.1
Tristan Thompson	82	31.3	.488	.000	.608	3.7	5.7	9.4	1.3	0.73	0.87	1.50	2.85	11.7
C.J. Miles	65	21.0	.415	.384	.869	0.4	2.3	2.7	1.0	0.75	0.26	1.06	2.12	11.2
Wayne Ellington	38	25.9	.439	.371	.898	0.5	2.5	3.0	1.6	0.76	0.05	0.87	1.13	10.4
Ellington (TOT)	78	21.3	.427	.392	.907	0.3	1.8	2.1	1.3	0.58	0.04	0.73	0.00	7.9
Alonzo Gee	82	31.0	.410	.315	.795	0.9	3.0	3.9	1.6	1.30	0.35	1.61	2.43	10.3
Marreese Speights	39	18.5	.457	.200	.806	1.8	3.3	5.1	0.7	0.36	0.67	1.15	2.28	10.2
Speights (TOT)	79	16.5	.445	.300	.771	1.8	3.0	4.9	0.6	0.30	0.67	1.01	0.00	8.3
Tyler Zeller	77	26.4	.438	.000	.764	2.1	3.6	5.7	1.2	0.45	0.91	1.23	3.26	7.9
Shaun Livingston	49	23.2	.507	.000	.843	0.6	1.9	2.5	3.6	0.76	0.59	1.20	2.14	7.2
Livingston (TOT)	66	22.0	.480	.000	.867	0.5	1.9	2.4	3.3	0.73	0.47	1.15	0.00	6.3
Daniel Gibson	46	17.1	.340	.344	.703	0.1	1.2	1.3	1.8	0.65	0.09	0.67	1.94	5.4
Omri Casspi	43	11.7	.394	.329	.537	0.5	2.2	2.7	0.7	0.58	0.28	0.51	1.05	4.0
Luke Walton	50	17.1	.392	.299	.500	0.8	2.1	2.9	3.3	0.84	0.26	1.20	1.96	3.4
Kevin Jones	32	10.4	.402	.000	.600	1.2	1.3	2.4	0.3	0.28	0.16	0.25	0.78	3.0
Chris Quinn	7	11.1	.250	.000	1.000	0.1	0.1	0.3	1.3	0.43	0.00	0.86	0.57	1.4
Cavaliers	**82**	**240.6**	**.434**	**.346**	**.756**	**12.24**	**28.77**	**41.01**	**20.7**	**7.89**	**4.07**	**14.01**	**21.18**	**96.5**
Opponents	**82**	**240.6**	**.476**	**.372**	**.739**	**10.84**	**31.26**	**42.10**	**23.9**	**7.61**	**6.83**	**15.23**	**19.70**	**101.2**

Dallas Mavericks

Player	GP	MPG	FG%	3Pt%	FT%	OFF	DEF	Total	APG	SPG	BPG	TOPG	PFPG	PPG
Dirk Nowitzki	53	31.3	.471	.414	.860	0.7	6.2	6.8	2.5	0.72	0.70	1.32	1.75	17.3
O.J. Mayo	82	35.5	.449	.407	.820	0.4	3.1	3.5	4.4	1.13	0.28	2.56	2.38	15.3
Vince Carter	81	25.8	.435	.406	.816	0.7	3.4	4.1	2.4	0.93	0.54	1.31	2.79	13.4
Shawn Marion	67	30.0	.514	.315	.782	2.2	5.7	7.8	2.4	1.10	0.70	1.54	1.66	12.1
Darren Collison	81	29.3	.471	.353	.880	0.4	2.3	2.7	5.1	1.23	0.10	2.14	1.72	12.0
Chris Kaman	66	20.7	.507	.000	.788	1.5	4.2	5.6	0.8	0.44	0.79	1.56	2.14	10.5
Brandan Wright	64	18.0	.597	.000	.615	1.3	2.7	4.1	0.6	0.41	1.19	0.53	1.22	8.5
Elton Brand	72	21.2	.473	.000	.710	1.8	4.2	6.0	1.0	0.69	1.25	0.79	2.67	7.2
Mike James	45	19.2	.373	.384	.793	0.2	1.4	1.6	3.1	0.58	0.07	1.22	2.11	6.1
Jae Crowder	78	17.3	.384	.328	.644	0.4	1.9	2.4	1.2	0.81	0.22	0.63	1.64	5.0
R. Beaubois	45	12.2	.369	.292	.789	0.2	1.1	1.3	1.9	0.42	0.09	0.73	1.20	4.0
Bernard James	46	9.9	.515	.000	.610	1.1	1.7	2.8	0.1	0.26	0.83	0.39	1.39	2.8
Josh Akognon	2	3.0	.500	.500	.000	0.0	0.0	0.0	0.5	0.00	0.00	0.00	1.50	2.5
Anthony Morrow	17	4.8	.500	.200	1.000	0.1	0.2	0.2	0.2	0.06	0.00	0.24	0.59	2.3
Morrow (TOT)	41	9.3	.441	.372	.909	0.3	0.5	0.7	0.3	0.32	0.02	0.20	0.90	4.0
Jared Cunningham	8	3.3	.429	.667	1.000	0.1	0.3	0.4	0.1	0.13	0.00	0.25	0.38	2.0
Mavericks	82	243.7	.462	.372	.793	9.35	32.56	41.92	23.2	7.90	5.54	13.95	20.71	101.1
Opponents	82	243.7	.445	.359	.753	12.01	33.56	45.57	22.0	8.51	4.15	14.66	18.87	101.7

Denver Nuggets

Player	GP	MPG	FG%	3Pt%	FT%	OFF	DEF	Total	APG	SPG	BPG	TOPG	PFPG	PPG
Ty Lawson	73	34.4	.461	.366	.756	0.5	2.2	2.7	6.9	1.47	0.11	2.49	1.85	16.7
Danilo Gallinari	71	32.5	.418	.373	.822	0.9	4.3	5.2	2.5	0.90	0.41	1.56	1.83	16.2
Andre Iguodala	80	34.7	.451	.317	.574	1.0	4.3	5.3	5.4	1.74	0.65	2.58	1.59	13.0
Wilson Chandler	43	25.1	.462	.413	.793	1.0	4.0	5.1	1.3	1.05	0.28	1.40	2.77	13.0
Corey Brewer	82	24.4	.425	.296	.690	0.7	2.2	2.9	1.5	1.44	0.28	1.24	1.88	12.1
Kenneth Faried	80	28.1	.552	.000	.613	3.3	5.9	9.2	1.0	1.01	1.04	1.41	2.93	11.5
Andre Miller	82	26.2	.479	.266	.840	0.7	2.2	2.9	5.9	0.89	0.13	2.10	1.94	9.6
JaVale McGee	79	18.1	.575	.000	.591	2.0	2.8	4.8	0.3	0.38	1.99	1.14	2.33	9.1
Kosta Koufos	81	22.4	.581	.000	.558	2.6	4.3	6.9	0.4	0.54	1.27	0.65	3.04	8.0
Evan Fournier	38	11.3	.493	.407	.769	0.2	0.8	0.9	1.2	0.50	0.03	0.84	1.71	5.3
Jordan Hamilton	40	9.9	.418	.370	.500	0.8	1.6	2.4	0.6	0.38	0.20	0.47	0.60	5.2
Anthony Randolph	39	8.4	.491	.000	.689	0.7	1.7	2.4	0.3	0.49	0.54	0.95	1.05	3.7
Timofey Mozgov	41	8.9	.506	.000	.769	1.2	1.4	2.6	0.2	0.15	0.44	0.61	1.39	2.6
Julyan Stone	4	7.0	1.000	.000	.750	0.5	0.3	0.8	0.5	0.25	0.00	0.50	1.00	1.8
Quincy Miller	7	3.7	.333	.000	.500	0.1	0.1	0.3	0.4	0.14	0.00	0.14	0.43	1.3
Nuggets	82	242.7	.478	.343	.701	13.32	31.72	45.04	24.4	9.29	6.50	15.28	20.51	106.1
Opponents	82	242.7	.444	.363	.731	12.44	29.16	41.60	23.6	8.02	6.76	15.92	21.65	101.1

Detroit Pistons

Player	GP	MPG	FG%	3Pt%	FT%	OFF	DEF	Total	APG	SPG	BPG	TOPG	PFPG	PPG
Greg Monroe	81	33.2	.486	.000	.689	2.9	6.7	9.6	3.5	1.30	0.68	2.89	2.35	16.0
Brandon Knight	75	31.5	.407	.367	.733	0.7	2.6	3.3	4.0	0.77	0.11	2.73	2.09	13.3
Jose Calderon	28	31.7	.527	.520	.893	0.2	2.3	2.5	6.6	1.07	0.07	1.82	1.46	11.6
Calderon (TOT)	73	29.6	.491	.461	.900	0.3	2.1	2.4	7.1	0.79	0.11	1.73	0.00	11.3
Rodney Stuckey	76	28.6	.406	.302	.783	0.6	2.2	2.8	3.6	0.67	0.22	1.76	1.67	11.5
Will Bynum	65	18.8	.469	.316	.809	0.4	1.1	1.5	3.6	0.69	0.08	1.92	1.97	9.8
Kyle Singler	82	28.0	.428	.350	.806	1.3	2.7	4.0	0.9	0.70	0.45	1.20	2.65	8.8
Andre Drummond	60	20.7	.608	.500	.371	2.8	4.8	7.6	0.5	0.98	1.58	0.95	2.40	7.9
Jonas Jerebko	49	18.2	.449	.301	.773	1.4	2.4	3.8	0.9	0.78	0.16	0.86	1.84	7.7
Jason Maxiell	72	24.8	.446	.000	.621	1.9	3.8	5.7	0.8	0.44	1.32	1.13	2.39	6.9
Charlie Villanueva	69	15.8	.377	.347	.551	0.7	2.8	3.5	0.8	0.45	0.57	0.57	1.39	6.8
Khris Middleton	27	17.6	.440	.311	.844	0.1	1.7	1.9	1.0	0.56	0.15	0.41	1.96	6.1
Corey Maggette	18	14.3	.355	.238	.750	0.3	1.1	1.4	1.1	0.33	0.11	0.94	2.33	5.3
V. Kravtsov	25	9.0	.717	.000	.297	1.0	0.8	1.8	0.4	0.20	0.36	0.56	1.28	3.1
Kim English	41	9.9	.375	.280	.724	0.2	0.6	0.9	0.6	0.39	0.07	0.46	1.12	2.9
Pistons	82	241.5	.449	.356	.699	12.09	30.04	42.12	21.2	7.00	4.88	15.13	19.79	94.9
Opponents	82	241.5	.459	.360	.762	11.11	30.66	41.77	22.4	8.43	5.76	13.73	19.88	98.8

Golden State Warriors

Player	GP	MPG	FG%	3Pt%	FT%	OFF	DEF	Total	APG	SPG	BPG	TOPG	PFPG	PPG
			Field Goals			**Rebounds Per Game**								
Stephen Curry	78	38.2	.451	.453	.900	0.8	3.3	4.0	6.9	1.6	0.2	3.1	2.5	22.9
David Lee	79	36.8	.519	.000	.797	2.8	8.5	11.2	3.5	0.8	0.3	2.6	3.1	18.5
Klay Thompson	82	35.8	.422	.401	.841	0.4	3.3	3.7	2.2	1.0	0.5	1.9	2.9	16.6
Jarrett Jack	79	29.7	.452	.404	.843	0.3	2.8	3.1	5.6	0.8	0.1	2.0	1.7	12.9
Carl Landry	81	23.2	.540	.333	.817	2.2	3.7	6.0	0.8	0.4	0.4	1.4	2.3	10.8
Harrison Barnes	81	25.4	.439	.359	.758	0.7	3.5	4.1	1.2	0.6	0.2	1.2	1.7	9.2
Brandon Rush	2	12.5	.667	.000	.667	0.0	0.5	0.5	1.0	0.0	0.0	1.5	2.5	7.0
Andrew Bogut	32	24.6	.451	1.000	.500	2.1	5.5	7.7	2.1	0.6	1.7	1.1	2.7	5.8
Richard Jefferson	56	10.1	.456	.311	.717	0.1	1.4	1.5	0.6	0.2	0.1	0.4	0.8	3.1
Draymond Green	79	13.4	.327	.209	.818	0.7	2.6	3.3	0.7	0.5	0.3	0.6	2.0	2.9
Festus Ezeli	78	14.4	.438	.000	.531	1.8	2.2	4.0	0.3	0.3	0.9	0.8	2.0	2.4
Kent Bazemore	61	4.4	.371	.294	.614	0.1	0.3	0.4	0.4	0.3	0.1	0.3	0.4	2.0
Scott Machado	6	3.5	.500	.000	1.000	0.0	0.2	0.2	1.0	0.3	0.0	1.3	0.0	1.3
Andris Biedrins	53	9.3	.476	.000	.308	0.2	2.2	2.9	0.3	0.3	0.8	0.3	1.9	0.5
Warriors	**82**	**241.5**	**45.8**	**40.3**	**79.0**	**10.8**	**34.2**	**45.0**	**22.5**	**6.9**	**4.2**	**15.1**	**21.4**	**101.2**
Opponents	**82**	**241.5**	**43.9**	**34.7**	**74.8**	**11.1**	**31.7**	**42.7**	**23.5**	**8.2**	**4.9**	**13.5**	**19.2**	**100.3**

Houston Rockets

Player	GP	MPG	FG%	3Pt%	FT%	OFF	DEF	Total	APG	SPG	BPG	TOPG	PFPG	PPG
			Field Goals			**Rebounds Per Game**								
James Harden	78	38.3	.438	.368	.851	0.8	4.1	4.9	5.8	1.82	0.49	3.78	2.28	25.9
Chandler Parsons	76	36.3	.486	.385	.729	1.0	4.3	5.3	3.5	0.99	0.42	1.93	1.95	15.5
Jeremy Lin	82	32.2	.441	.339	.785	0.4	2.6	3.0	6.1	1.63	0.35	2.88	2.50	13.4
Carlos Delfino	67	25.2	.405	.375	.857	0.3	3.0	3.3	2.0	1.01	0.13	1.07	1.70	10.6
Omer Asik	82	30.0	.541	.000	.562	3.4	8.3	11.7	0.9	0.56	1.06	2.11	2.72	10.1
Francisco Garcia	18	17.7	.432	.386	.857	0.1	1.2	1.3	1.1	0.78	0.39	0.67	1.22	6.4
Garcia (TOT)	58	17.7	.393	.374	.857	0.1	1.4	1.6	1.1	0.79	0.66	0.55	0.00	5.5
Greg Smith	70	15.9	.620	.000	.623	1.6	3.0	4.6	0.4	0.26	0.57	0.59	2.50	6.0
D. Motiejunas	44	12.2	.455	.289	.627	0.8	1.3	2.1	0.7	0.16	0.33	0.84	1.66	5.7
Patrick Beverley	41	17.4	.418	.375	.829	1.1	1.6	2.7	2.9	0.90	0.51	1.07	2.02	5.6
Terrence Jones	19	14.5	.457	.263	.765	1.5	1.9	3.4	0.8	0.63	1.00	0.68	1.11	5.5
Thomas Robinson	19	13.0	.449	.000	.421	1.6	2.5	4.1	0.5	0.84	0.26	1.21	1.53	4.5
Robinson (TOT)	70	15.1	.430	.000	.523	1.7	2.8	4.5	0.7	0.59	0.37	1.26	0.00	4.8
James Anderson	29	10.6	.406	.327	.895	0.5	1.5	2.0	1.1	0.41	0.10	0.62	0.62	4.0
Anderson (TOT)	39	10.3	.413	.350	.857	0.5	1.4	1.8	1.1	0.38	0.13	0.64	0.00	3.8
Aaron Brooks	7	5.4	.308	.286	.000	0.1	0.1	0.3	0.9	0.14	0.43	0.57	0.71	1.4
Brooks (TOT)	53	18.8	.453	.373	.769	0.2	1.3	1.5	2.2	0.57	0.19	1.26	0.00	7.1
Tim Ohlbrecht	3	4.0	.333	.000	1.000	0.0	0.3	0.3	0.3	0.33	0.00	1.33	0.33	1.0
Rockets	**82**	**240.5**	**.461**	**.366**	**.754**	**11.09**	**32.34**	**43.43**	**23.2**	**8.28**	**4.38**	**16.44**	**20.27**	**106.0**
Opponents	**82**	**241.1**	**.454**	**.368**	**.776**	**10.68**	**30.96**	**41.65**	**22.7**	**8.45**	**6.07**	**14.76**	**20.41**	**102.5**

Indiana Pacers

Player	GP	MPG	FG%	3Pt%	FT%	OFF	DEF	Total	APG	SPG	BPG	TOPG	PFPG	PPG
			Field Goals			**Rebounds Per Game**								
Paul George	79	37.6	.419	.362	.807	1.1	6.5	7.6	4.1	1.8	0.6	2.9	2.9	17.4
David West	73	33.4	.498	.211	.768	2.0	5.7	7.7	2.9	1.0	0.9	2.2	2.0	17.1
George Hill	76	34.5	.443	.368	.817	0.6	3.1	3.7	4.7	1.1	0.3	1.5	1.8	14.2
Roy Hibbert	79	28.7	.448	.250	.741	3.7	4.6	8.3	1.4	0.5	2.6	2.1	3.5	11.9
L. Stephenson	78	29.2	.460	.330	.652	0.6	3.3	3.9	2.9	1.0	0.2	1.4	2.1	8.8
Tyler Hansbrough	81	16.9	.432	.000	.720	2.0	2.6	4.6	0.4	0.4	0.2	1.0	1.9	7.0
Gerald Green	60	18.0	.366	.314	.800	0.5	1.8	2.4	0.8	0.3	0.4	0.9	1.1	7.0
Danny Granger	5	14.8	.286	.200	.625	0.6	1.2	1.8	0.6	0.4	0.2	0.8	1.2	5.4
Ian Mahinmi	80	16.5	.453	.000	.608	1.4	2.4	3.9	0.3	0.5	0.8	1.2	2.5	5.0
D.J. Augustin	76	16.1	.350	.353	.838	0.3	0.9	1.2	2.2	0.4	0.0	0.9	0.8	4.7
Orlando Johnson	51	12.1	.400	.383	.719	0.4	1.8	2.2	0.9	0.2	0.2	0.6	1.0	4.0
Jeff Pendergraph	37	10.0	.484	.500	.913	0.8	2.0	2.8	0.4	0.2	0.3	0.6	1.2	3.9
Sam Young	56	12.4	.392	.308	.535	0.5	1.7	2.2	0.8	0.3	0.1	0.6	1.1	2.8
Ben Hansbrough	28	7.1	.333	.261	.778	0.1	0.6	0.6	0.8	0.2	0.1	0.6	0.8	2.0
Dominic McGuire	26	14.9	.429	.000	.300	0.7	2.3	3.0	0.8	0.5	0.4	0.5	1.5	2.0
Miles Plumlee	14	3.9	.238	.000	.750	0.9	0.7	1.6	0.1	0.0	0.2	0.2	0.4	0.9
Pacers	**81**	**241.9**	**.436**	**.347**	**.746**	**12.9**	**33.0**	**45.9**	**20.3**	**7.2**	**6.3**	**15.1**	**20.0**	**94.7**
Opponents	**81**	**241.9**	**.420**	**.327**	**.760**	**11.2**	**29.6**	**40.9**	**19.2**	**7.5**	**5.7**	**13.5**	**21.9**	**90.7**

Los Angeles Clippers

Player	GP	MPG	FG%	3Pt%	FT%	OFF	DEF	Total	APG	SPG	BPG	TOPG	PFPG	PPG
			Field Goals			**Rebounds Per Game**								
Blake Griffin	80	32.5	.538	.179	.660	2.3	6.0	8.3	3.7	1.21	0.63	2.31	2.89	18.0
Chris Paul	70	33.4	.481	.328	.885	0.8	3.0	3.7	9.7	2.41	0.14	2.27	2.04	16.9
Jamal Crawford	76	29.3	.438	.376	.871	0.3	1.4	1.7	2.5	1.04	0.17	1.92	0.93	16.5
Caron Butler	78	24.1	.424	.388	.833	0.5	2.3	2.9	1.0	0.65	0.14	0.92	1.78	10.4
Matt Barnes	80	25.7	.462	.342	.744	1.4	3.2	4.6	1.5	1.02	0.79	1.13	2.91	10.3
DeAndre Jordan	82	24.5	.643	.000	.386	2.6	4.7	7.2	0.3	0.59	1.37	1.22	2.34	8.8
Eric Bledsoe	76	20.4	.445	.397	.791	1.0	1.9	3.0	3.1	1.43	0.72	1.80	1.47	8.5
Chauncey Billups	22	19.0	.402	.367	.938	0.1	1.4	1.5	2.2	0.55	0.05	1.18	1.14	8.4
Willie Green	72	16.5	.461	.428	.719	0.2	1.1	1.3	0.8	0.40	0.17	0.43	1.33	6.3
Lamar Odom	82	19.7	.399	.200	.476	1.4	4.4	5.9	1.7	0.84	0.71	1.05	2.61	4.0
Ryan Hollins	60	11.1	.614	.000	.750	0.8	1.5	2.3	0.2	0.10	0.57	0.73	2.22	3.4
Maalik Wayns	6	6.2	.438	.333	1.000	0.0	0.3	0.3	1.2	0.50	0.00	0.33	1.33	3.3
Wayns (TOT)	27	7.5	.295	.226	.895	0.0	0.2	0.3	1.0	0.22	0.00	0.56	0.00	2.8
Grant Hill	29	15.1	.388	.273	.583	0.2	1.5	1.7	0.9	0.38	0.24	0.86	1.34	3.2
Ronny Turiaf	65	10.8	.505	.000	.365	0.7	1.6	2.3	0.5	0.29	0.54	0.45	1.23	1.9
DaJuan Summers	2	3.5	.250	.000	.000	0.0	1.0	1.0	0.5	0.00	0.00	0.00	0.00	1.0
Clippers	82	240.6	.478	.358	.711	11.44	30.18	41.62	23.9	9.56	5.62	14.60	20.93	101.1
Opponents	82	240.6	.443	.373	.749	10.87	28.23	39.10	22.1	7.39	4.09	16.09	20.88	94.6

Los Angeles Lakers

Player	GP	MPG	FG%	3Pt%	FT%	OFF	DEF	Total	APG	SPG	BPG	TOPG	PFPG	PPG
			Field Goals			**Rebounds Per Game**								
Kobe Bryant	78	38.6	.463	.324	.839	0.8	4.7	5.6	6.0	1.4	0.3	3.7	2.2	27.3
Dwight Howard	76	35.8	.578	.167	.492	3.3	9.1	12.4	1.4	1.1	2.4	3.0	3.8	17.1
Pau Gasol	49	33.8	.466	.286	.702	2.3	6.3	8.6	4.1	0.5	1.2	2.1	1.9	13.7
Steve Nash	50	32.5	.497	.438	.922	0.5	2.3	2.8	6.7	0.6	0.1	2.5	1.4	12.7
Metta World Peace	75	33.7	.403	.342	.734	1.3	3.6	5.0	1.5	1.6	0.6	1.3	2.6	12.4
Antawn Jamison	76	21.5	.464	.361	.691	1.4	3.3	4.8	0.7	0.4	0.3	0.7	1.6	9.4
Jodie Meeks	78	21.3	.387	.357	.896	0.5	1.7	2.2	0.9	0.7	0.1	0.7	1.3	7.9
Steve Blake	45	26.1	.422	.421	.771	0.5	2.5	2.9	3.8	0.8	0.1	1.4	1.8	7.3
Earl Clark	59	23.1	.440	.337	.697	1.4	4.1	5.5	1.1	0.6	0.7	1.1	1.7	7.3
Jordan Hill	29	15.8	.497	.000	.656	2.8	2.9	5.7	0.4	0.3	0.7	0.9	1.9	6.7
Darius Morris	48	14.2	.388	.364	.649	0.5	0.7	1.2	1.6	0.4	0.0	0.9	1.2	4.0
Devin Ebanks	19	10.4	.329	.273	.786	0.5	1.6	2.2	0.5	0.2	0.1	0.6	1.2	3.4
Chris Duhon	46	17.8	.382	.363	.462	0.2	1.2	1.5	2.9	0.4	0.0	0.9	1.2	2.9
Robert Sacre	32	6.3	.375	.000	.636	0.3	0.8	1.1	0.2	0.0	0.3	0.3	1.2	1.3
A. Goudelock	1	6.0	.000	.000	.000	1.0	0.0	1.0	0.0	0.0	0.0	0.0	0.0	0.0
D. Johnson-Odom	4	1.5	.000	.000	.000	0.2	0.8	1.0	0.2	0.0	0.0	0.0	0.0	0.0
Lakers	82	240.9	.458	.355	.692	11.5	33.3	44.8	22.2	7.0	5.2	15.0	17.9	102.2
Opponents	82	240.9	.453	.357	.732	11.5	31.1	42.7	23.4	8.5	4.8	12.9	23.1	101.0

Memphis Grizzlies

Player	GP	MPG	FG%	3Pt%	FT%	OFF	DEF	Total	APG	SPG	BPG	TOPG	PFPG	PPG
			Field Goals			**Rebounds Per Game**								
Zach Randolph	76	34.3	.460	.087	.750	4.1	7.2	11.2	1.4	0.80	0.41	1.97	2.37	15.4
Mike Conley	80	34.5	.440	.362	.830	0.5	2.3	2.8	6.1	2.17	0.30	2.36	2.14	14.6
Marc Gasol	80	35.0	.494	.071	.848	2.3	5.5	7.8	4.0	1.00	1.74	1.96	3.19	14.1
Tony Allen	79	26.7	.445	.125	.717	1.5	3.1	4.6	1.2	1.51	0.56	1.19	2.67	8.9
Tayshaun Prince	37	31.7	.429	.366	.595	0.8	3.4	4.2	2.3	0.73	0.32	0.95	1.11	8.8
Prince (TOT)	82	32.1	.438	.404	.738	0.9	3.6	4.4	2.4	0.59	0.30	1.09	0.00	10.4
Jerryd Bayless	80	22.1	.419	.353	.836	0.3	1.9	2.2	3.3	0.74	0.21	1.50	2.10	8.7
Quincy Pondexter	59	21.1	.428	.395	.787	0.7	1.5	2.2	1.0	0.59	0.10	0.71	1.61	6.4
Darrell Arthur	59	16.4	.451	.278	.717	1.2	1.7	2.9	0.6	0.41	0.56	0.73	2.14	6.1
Ed Davis	36	15.1	.517	.000	.569	1.6	2.9	4.4	0.2	0.36	1.31	0.50	2.22	5.1
Davis (TOT)	81	20.1	.539	.000	.617	1.9	3.8	5.7	0.8	0.47	1.05	0.78	0.00	7.7
Keyon Dooling	7	11.7	.476	.417	.857	0.0	0.1	0.1	1.1	0.14	0.00	0.71	1.14	4.4
Austin Daye	31	10.6	.423	.345	.688	0.2	1.7	1.9	0.7	0.29	0.45	0.52	1.26	4.0
Daye (TOT)	55	12.3	.433	.418	.765	0.3	1.9	2.2	0.8	0.25	0.40	0.53	0.00	4.5
Tony Wroten	35	7.8	.384	.250	.724	0.4	0.4	0.8	1.2	0.23	0.11	0.83	0.97	2.6
Jon Leuer	19	5.1	.625	.000	.571	0.4	0.8	1.3	0.2	0.21	0.00	0.16	0.53	1.8
Leuer (TOT)	28	6.7	.481	.000	.462	0.5	0.9	1.3	0.3	0.21	0.00	0.29	0.00	2.0
Grizzlies	82	241.5	.444	.345	.773	12.92	29.82	42.73	20.9	8.57	5.32	13.95	20.24	93.4
Opponents	82	241.5	.435	.338	.748	10.31	28.77	39.07	19.5	7.32	5.49	15.46	20.04	89.3

Miami Heat

Player	GP	MPG	FG%	3Pt%	FT%	OFF	DEF	Total	APG	SPG	BPG	TOPG	PFPG	PPG
			Field Goals			Rebounds Per Game								
LeBron James......76		37.9	.565	.406	.753	1.3	6.8	8.0	7.2	1.7	0.9	3.0	1.4	26.8
Dwyane Wade......69		34.7	.521	.258	.725	1.2	3.7	5.0	5.1	1.9	0.8	2.8	2.0	21.2
Chris Bosh 74		33.2	.535	.284	.798	1.8	5.0	6.8	1.7	0.9	1.4	1.7	2.3	16.6
Ray Allen...:.......79		25.8	.449	.419	.886	0.5	2.2	2.7	1.7	0.8	0.2	1.3	1.6	10.9
Mario Chalmers...77		26.9	.429	.409	.795	0.2	2.0	2.2	3.5	1.5	0.2	1.5	2.5	8.6
Shane Battier 72		24.8	.420	.430	.842	0.5	1.8	2.3	1.0	0.6	0.8	0.5	2.1	6.6
Norris Cole 80		19.9	.421	.357	.650	0.2	1.4	1.6	2.0	0.7	0.1	1.3	1.9	5.6
Rashard Lewis 55		14.4	.414	.389	.622	0.3	1.9	2.2	0.5	0.4	0.3	0.6	1.2	5.2
Chris Andersen 42		14.9	.577	.667	.677	1.4	2.7	4.1	0.4	0.4	1.0	0.6	2.1	4.9
Mike Miller 59		15.3	.433	.417	.727	0.3	2.4	2.7	1.7	0.4	0.1	0.6	1.1	4.8
Udonis Haslem 75		18.9	.514	.000	.711	1.3	4.1	5.4	0.5	0.4	0.2	0.6	2.3	3.9
Juwan Howard 7		7.3	.526	.000	1.000	0.0	1.1	1.1	0.9	0.0	0.0	0.6	1.3	3.0
Josh Harrellson 6		5.2	.444	.200	.500	0.5	0.7	1.2	0.0	0.2	0.2	0.5	0.7	1.7
James Jones........38		5.8	.344	.302	.500	0.0	0.6	0.6	0.3	0.1	0.2	0.1	0.4	1.6
Joel Anthony 62		9.1	.515	.000	.607	0.7	1.1	1.9	0.2	0.2	0.7	0.4	0.8	1.4
Jarvis Varnado 13		4.5	.429	.000	.500	0.2	0.5	0.7	0.2	0.1	0.2	0.5	0.8	0.6
Heat 82		242.4	.496	.396	.754	8.2	30.4	38.6	23.0	8.7	5.4	13.9	18.7	102.9
Opponents 82		242.4	.440	.350	.766	11.2	28.9	40.1	20.2	7.9	3.2	15.6	20.4	95.0

Milwaukee Bucks

Player	GP	MPG	FG%	3Pt%	FT%	OFF	DEF	Total	APG	SPG	BPG	TOPG	PFPG	PPG
			Field Goals			Rebounds Per Game								
Monta Ellis 82		37.5	.416	.287	.773	0.5	3.3	3.9	6.0	2.06	0.44	3.10	2.00	19.2
Brandon Jennings ..80		36.2	.399	.375	.819	0.7	2.3	3.1	6.5	1.56	0.13	2.54	1.94	17.5
Ersan Ilyasova 73		27.6	.462	.444	.796	2.1	5.0	7.1	1.6	0.93	0.49	1.03	2.53	13.2
J.J. Redick 28		28.7	.403	.318	.918	0.3	1.6	1.9	2.7	0.32	0.14	1.18	1.68	12.3
J.J. Redick (TOT)....78		30.5	.434	.366	.900	0.2	2.0	2.2	3.8	0.49	0.12	1.77	0.00	14.1
Mike Dunleavy 75		25.9	.442	.428	.820	0.4	3.5	3.9	1.9	0.52	0.47	1.20	1.80	10.5
Larry Sanders 71		27.3	.506	.000	.618	3.2	6.3	9.5	1.2	0.75	2.83	1.23	3.28	9.8
Luc Mbah a Moute ..58		22.9	.401	.351	.571	1.5	2.9	4.4	0.9	0.72	0.24	1.21	1.41	6.7
Samuel Dalembert...47		16.3	.542	1.000	.691	2.2	3.6	5.9	0.4	0.36	1.13	1.09	1.91	6.7
John Henson..........63		13.1	.482	.000	.533	1.8	2.9	4.7	0.5	0.30	0.67	0.75	1.32	6.0
Marquis Daniels 59		18.4	.376	.278	.741	0.8	1.7	2.5	1.1	0.86	0.17	0.76	1.31	5.5
Gustavo Ayon 12		13.6	.595	.000	.083	1.7	3.3	4.9	1.0	0.75	0.33	0.75	2.00	4.3
Ayon (TOT) 55		13.4	.551	.000	.400	1.1	2.5	3.6	1.3	0.40	0.31	0.85	0.00	3.7
Ekpe Udoh 76		17.3	.435	.000	.748	1.5	1.8	3.3	0.6	0.51	1.12	0.57	1.83	4.3
Drew Gooden 16		9.4	.328	.200	.688	0.8	1.1	1.9	0.4	0.31	0.38	0.56	1.31	3.3
Ish Smith.................16		8.6	.395	.400	.000	0.1	0.9	0.9	1.9	0.50	0.19	0.63	0.75	2.4
Smith (TOT)...........52		9.9	.352	.296	.429	0.2	0.9	1.2	1.7	0.40	0.17	0.71	0.00	2.4
Joel Przybilla 12		5.7	.250	.000	.000	0.4	1.3	1.8	0.3	0.08	0.17	0.33	0.83	0.2
Bucks.........................82		241.8	.435	.360	.736	13.02	30.94	43.96	22.9	8.35	6.71	14.10	18.95	98.9
Opponents.....................82		241.8	.454	.348	.759	12.43	33.62	46.05	23.1	8.02	4.42	15.98	19.11	100.7

Minnesota Timberwolves

Player	GP	MPG	FG%	3Pt%	FT%	OFF	DEF	Total	APG	SPG	BPG	TOPG	PFPG	PPG
			Field Goals			Rebounds Per Game								
Kevin Love............18		34.3	.352	.217	.704	3.6	10.4	14.0	2.3	0.72	0.50	2.17	1.89	18.3
Nikola Pekovic 62		31.6	.520	.000	.744	3.7	5.1	8.8	0.9	0.69	0.81	1.63	2.31	16.3
Andrei Kirilenko 64		31.8	.507	.292	.752	1.6	4.1	5.5	2.8	1.50	0.97	1.86	1.28	12.4
Derrick Williams....78		24.6	.430	.332	.706	1.2	4.3	5.5	0.6	0.56	0.47	1.29	1.63	12.0
Luke Ridnour 82		30.2	.453	.311	.848	0.5	2.0	2.5	3.8	1.00	0.18	1.59	2.28	11.5
Jose Barea 74		23.1	.417	.346	.784	0.5	2.3	2.8	4.0	0.43	0.00	1.96	1.77	11.3
Ricky Rubio 57		29.7	.360	.293	.799	0.8	3.2	4.0	7.3	2.40	0.09	3.02	2.51	10.7
Chase Budinger ...23		22.1	.414	.321	.762	0.7	2.4	3.1	1.1	0.61	0.30	1.00	1.26	9.4
D. Cunningham ...80		25.1	.468	.000	.650	1.8	3.3	5.1	0.8	1.05	0.47	0.70	1.91	8.7
Alexey Shved.......77		23.9	.372	.295	.720	0.5	1.7	2.3	3.7	0.70	0.35	1.91	1.52	8.6
Brandon Roy...........5		24.4	.314	.000	.700	0.6	2.2	2.8	4.6	0.60	0.00	1.40	1.00	5.8
Mickael Gelabale...36		17.9	.518	.308	.875	0.9	1.9	2.8	0.7	0.44	0.11	0.44	1.31	5.0
Malcolm Lee 16		18.1	.382	.333	.600	0.9	1.5	2.4	1.3	0.75	0.38	0.63	1.88	4.9
Greg Stiemsma.....76		15.9	.457	.000	.768	0.8	2.6	3.4	0.4	0.58	1.18	0.78	2.42	4.0
Chris Johnson.......30		9.5	.640	.000	.618	0.7	1.3	2.0	0.3	0.23	0.93	0.43	1.63	3.9
Timberwolves............82		240.6	.439	.305	.742	11.87	30.16	42.02	22.4	8.54	4.72	14.81	18.40	95.7
Opponents 82		240.6	.468	.369	.752	10.62	31.50	42.12	22.3	8.06	5.87	15.88	22.52	98.1

New Orleans Hornets

Player	GP	MPG	FG%	3Pt%	FT%	OFF	DEF	Total	APG	SPG	BPG	TOPG	PFPG	PPG
			Field Goals			Rebounds Per Game								
Eric Gordon	42	30.1	.402	.324	.842	0.2	1.6	1.8	3.3	1.07	0.19	2.79	1.79	17.0
Ryan Anderson	81	30.9	.423	.382	.844	2.4	4.0	6.4	1.2	0.52	0.38	1.20	2.21	16.2
Greivis Vasquez	78	34.4	.433	.342	.805	0.6	3.8	4.3	9.0	0.85	0.08	3.17	2.44	13.9
Anthony Davis	64	28.8	.516	.000	.751	2.6	5.6	8.2	1.0	1.17	1.75	1.39	2.47	13.5
Robin Lopez	82	26.0	.534	.000	.778	2.8	2.9	5.6	0.8	0.39	1.56	1.34	2.04	11.3
Jason Smith	51	17.2	.490	.000	.843	1.3	2.4	3.6	0.7	0.29	0.88	1.08	2.41	8.2
Al-Farouq Aminu	76	27.2	.475	.211	.737	1.8	5.9	7.7	1.4	1.21	0.67	1.53	2.01	7.3
Brian Roberts	78	17.0	.417	.386	.909	0.2	1.0	1.2	2.8	0.47	0.04	0.91	1.38	7.1
Austin Rivers	61	23.2	.372	.326	.546	0.3	1.5	1.8	2.1	0.43	0.15	1.21	2.00	6.2
Roger Mason Jr.	69	17.7	.433	.415	.907	0.2	1.8	1.9	1.1	0.38	0.16	0.74	1.51	5.3
Xavier Henry	50	12.5	.410	.364	.630	0.4	1.4	1.8	0.3	0.32	0.10	0.62	1.44	3.9
Lance Thomas	59	10.9	.500	.000	.729	0.7	1.2	1.9	0.3	0.19	0.12	0.24	1.32	2.5
Lou Amundson	18	11.6	.429	.000	.500	1.3	1.9	3.2	0.4	0.50	0.33	0.44	1.50	2.4
Amundson (TOT)	39	9.5	.395	.000	.333	1.2	1.5	2.7	0.3	0.41	0.31	0.49	0.00	1.9
Darius Miller	52	13.3	.407	.393	1.000	0.2	1.3	1.5	0.8	0.33	0.23	0.44	1.71	2.3
Terrel Harris	13	8.3	.105	.000	.500	0.0	1.3	1.3	0.5	0.15	0.23	1.00	1.08	0.4
Harris (TOT)	20	6.8	.148	.000	.700	0.2	1.1	1.3	0.5	0.10	0.15	0.85	0.00	0.8
Hornets	82	241.2	.448	.363	.776	12.05	29.59	41.63	21.0	6.34	5.37	14.55	20.40	94.1
Opponents	82	241.2	.471	.374	.759	10.18	29.16	39.34	23.4	7.90	6.00	13.24	18.71	97.9

New York Knicks

Player	GP	MPG	FG%	3Pt%	FT%	OFF	DEF	Total	APG	SPG	BPG	TOPG	PFPG	PPG
			Field Goals			Rebounds Per Game								
Carmelo Anthony	67	37.0	.449	.379	.830	2.0	4.9	6.9	2.6	0.78	0.48	2.61	3.06	28.7
J.R. Smith	80	33.5	.422	.356	.762	0.8	4.5	5.3	2.7	1.25	0.30	1.68	2.83	18.1
Amar'e Stoudemire	29	23.5	.577	.000	.808	2.1	2.9	5.0	0.4	0.34	0.72	1.72	3.07	14.2
Raymond Felton	68	34.0	.427	.360	.789	0.8	2.1	2.9	5.5	1.38	0.21	2.28	1.91	13.9
Earl Barron	1	37.0	.357	.000	.500	6.0	12.0	18.0	2.0	0.00	1.00	1.00	1.00	11.0
Barron (TOT)	12	13.2	.353	.000	.429	1.8	3.3	5.1	0.4	0.42	0.50	0.92	0.00	3.3
Tyson Chandler	66	32.8	.637	.000	.694	4.1	6.6	10.7	0.9	0.64	1.14	1.32	2.85	10.4
Chris Copeland	56	15.4	.479	.421	.759	0.6	1.5	2.1	0.5	0.29	0.21	0.89	1.86	8.7
Kenyon Martin	18	23.9	.602	.000	.425	1.9	3.4	5.3	0.4	0.89	0.94	0.89	3.56	7.2
Iman Shumpert	45	22.1	.396	.402	.766	0.7	2.3	3.0	1.7	0.96	0.16	0.82	2.20	6.8
Steve Novak	81	20.3	.414	.425	.909	0.2	1.7	1.9	0.4	0.35	0.10	0.15	1.20	6.6
Jason Kidd	76	26.9	.372	.351	.833	0.7	3.6	4.3	3.3	1.64	0.33	1.00	1.64	6.0
Quentin Richardson	1	29.0	.091	.250	1.000	5.0	5.0	10.0	1.0	0.00	0.00	2.00	1.00	5.0
Pablo Prigioni	78	16.2	.455	.396	.880	0.5	1.3	1.8	3.0	0.88	0.03	1.10	1.63	3.5
James White	57	7.6	.431	.341	.579	0.1	0.8	0.8	0.5	0.23	0.07	0.30	0.77	2.2
Marcus Camby	24	10.4	.321	.000	.421	1.0	2.3	3.3	0.6	0.29	0.58	0.63	1.17	1.8
Knicks	82	240.6	.448	.376	.759	10.85	29.71	40.56	19.3	8.20	3.59	12.05	20.12	100.0
Opponents	82	240.6	.458	.357	.757	10.05	31.60	41.65	19.3	6.38	3.99	15.15	19.22	95.7

Oklahoma City Thunder

Player	GP	MPG	FG%	3Pt%	FT%	OFF	DEF	Total	APG	SPG	BPG	TOPG	PFPG	PPG
			Field Goals			Rebounds Per Game								
Kevin Durant	81	38.5	.510	.416	.905	0.6	7.3	7.9	4.6	1.4	1.3	3.5	1.8	28.1
Russell Westbrook	82	34.9	.438	.323	.800	1.4	3.9	5.2	7.4	1.8	0.3	3.3	2.3	23.2
Kevin Martin	77	27.7	.450	.426	.890	0.4	1.9	2.3	1.4	0.9	0.1	1.3	1.8	14.0
Serge Ibaka	80	31.1	.573	.351	.749	2.8	4.9	7.7	0.5	0.4	3.0	1.6	2.7	13.2
Thabo Sefolosha	81	27.5	.481	.419	.826	0.7	3.2	3.9	1.5	1.3	0.5	0.8	2.2	7.6
Derek Fisher	33	17.4	.342	.375	.921	0.1	1.1	1.1	1.4	0.6	0.1	0.9	1.7	5.3
Reggie Jackson	70	14.2	.458	.231	.839	0.3	2.1	2.4	1.7	0.4	0.2	0.8	1.2	5.3
Nick Collison	81	19.5	.595	.000	.769	1.5	2.6	4.1	1.5	0.6	0.4	0.9	2.4	5.1
Kendrick Perkins	78	25.1	.457	.000	.611	1.4	4.6	6.0	1.4	0.6	1.1	1.4	2.9	4.2
Jeremy Lamb	23	6.4	.353	.300	1.000	0.2	0.6	0.6	0.8	0.2	0.1	0.3	0.6	3.1
Ronnie Brewer	60	14.2	.354	.303	.410	0.7	1.6	2.3	0.8	0.7	0.1	0.3	0.6	3.0
Daniel Orton	13	8.0	.462	.000	.529	1.0	1.0	2.0	0.3	0.3	0.2	0.3	1.0	2.5
H. Thabeet	66	11.7	.604	.000	.604	1.0	1.9	3.0	0.2	0.5	0.9	0.6	2.2	2.4
Perry Jones	38	7.4	.394	.000	.667	0.3	1.3	1.6	0.3	0.1	0.2	0.4	0.6	2.3
DeAndre Liggins	39	7.4	.447	.368	.500	0.3	1.0	1.4	0.4	0.5	0.1	0.4	0.8	1.5
Thunder	82	241.8	.481	.377	.828	10.4	33.2	43.6	21.4	8.3	7.6	15.3	20.2	105.7
Opponents	82	241.8	.425	.346	.774	12.0	28.7	40.7	20.5	8.2	3.9	14.8	20.7	96.5

Orlando Magic

Player	GP	MPG	FG%	3Pt%	FT%	OFF	DEF	Total	APG	SPG	BPG	TOPG	PFPG	PPG
Tobias Harris	27	36.1	.453	.310	.721	2.1	6.4	8.5	2.1	0.89	1.37	1.78	3.30	17.3
Harris (TOT)	55	23.6	.455	.315	.752	1.3	3.9	5.2	1.3	0.58	0.80	1.20	0.00	11.0
Arron Afflalo	64	36.0	.439	.300	.857	0.5	3.3	3.7	3.2	0.63	0.17	2.16	2.14	16.5
Glen Davis	34	31.3	.448	.000	.718	1.6	5.6	7.2	2.1	0.94	0.62	1.88	2.59	15.1
Jameer Nelson	56	35.3	.392	.341	.873	0.4	3.3	3.7	7.4	1.27	0.11	2.75	2.88	14.7
Nikola Vucevic	77	33.2	.519	.000	.683	3.5	8.4	11.9	1.9	0.79	1.03	1.83	2.83	13.1
Beno Udrih	27	27.3	.408	.396	.857	0.6	1.7	2.3	6.1	0.93	0.04	2.04	1.89	10.2
Udrih (TOT)	66	22.1	.441	.333	.816	0.5	1.6	2.1	4.6	0.62	0.05	1.64	0.00	8.2
Maurice Harkless	76	26.0	.461	.274	.570	1.6	2.8	4.4	0.7	1.16	0.82	0.91	1.89	8.2
Andrew Nicholson	75	16.7	.527	.000	.798	0.9	2.5	3.4	0.6	0.32	0.43	1.05	1.77	7.8
E'Twaun Moore	75	22.4	.396	.340	.797	0.6	1.6	2.2	2.7	0.68	0.31	1.40	1.63	7.8
Al Harrington	10	11.9	.351	.267	.750	0.6	2.1	2.7	1.0	0.40	0.10	0.70	1.80	5.1
Kyle O'Quinn	57	11.2	.513	.000	.667	1.1	2.5	3.7	0.9	0.19	0.46	0.65	1.88	4.1
DeQuan Jones	63	12.7	.436	.257	.667	0.3	1.4	1.7	0.3	0.30	0.35	0.48	0.87	3.7
Doron Lamb	24	12.4	.397	.476	.632	0.2	1.0	1.2	0.5	0.25	0.00	0.42	1.04	3.2
Lamb (TOT)	47	12.3	.368	.378	.588	0.2	0.8	1.0	0.7	0.28	0.00	0.55	0.00	3.3
Hedo Turkoglu	11	17.2	.264	.042	.500	0.4	2.0	2.4	2.1	0.64	0.09	1.09	1.00	2.9
Magic	82	241.2	.448	.329	.755	10.85	31.85	42.71	22.8	6.44	4.37	14.52	19.40	94.1
Opponents	82	241.2	.463	.359	.738	10.83	31.93	42.76	23.7	7.22	5.24	12.44	16.50	101.1

Philadelphia 76ers

Player	GP	MPG	FG%	3Pt%	FT%	OFF	DEF	Total	APG	SPG	BPG	TOPG	PFPG	PPG
Jrue Holiday	78	37.5	.431	.368	.752	1.1	3.1	4.2	8.0	1.58	0.41	3.74	2.18	17.7
Thaddeus Young	76	34.6	.531	.125	.574	2.4	5.1	7.5	1.6	1.75	0.72	1.18	2.51	14.8
Evan Turner	82	35.3	.419	.365	.740	0.7	5.6	6.3	4.3	0.87	0.21	2.28	2.40	13.3
Spencer Hawes	82	27.2	.464	.356	.777	2.1	5.1	7.2	2.2	0.29	1.38	1.60	2.84	11.0
Nick Young	59	23.9	.413	.357	.820	0.4	1.8	2.2	1.4	0.61	0.24	0.85	1.42	10.6
Jason Richardson	33	28.4	.402	.341	.606	0.6	3.3	3.8	1.5	1.21	0.45	0.79	1.73	10.5
Dorell Wright	79	22.6	.396	.374	.851	0.5	3.3	3.8	1.9	0.78	0.44	0.81	1.24	9.2
Damien Wilkins	61	18.0	.459	.333	.743	0.5	1.2	1.7	1.5	0.61	0.30	0.80	1.61	6.4
Lavoy Allen	79	21.1	.454	.000	.717	2.0	3.0	5.0	0.9	0.30	0.70	0.70	2.28	5.8
Justin Holiday	9	15.8	.333	.250	.750	0.0	1.6	1.6	1.7	0.33	0.67	1.00	0.78	4.7
Arnett Moultrie	47	11.5	.582	.000	.643	1.6	1.5	3.1	0.2	0.36	0.21	0.40	0.91	3.7
Royal Ivey	53	13.2	.431	.420	.563	0.3	0.8	1.1	0.6	0.43	0.06	0.38	1.38	3.2
Charles Jenkins	12	12.5	.368	.000	.500	0.3	0.7	0.9	1.3	0.50	0.08	0.17	0.33	2.5
Jenkins (TOT)	59	7.5	.405	.500	.545	0.1	0.4	0.5	0.7	0.25	0.03	0.36	0.00	1.9
Kwame Brown	22	12.2	.459	.000	.368	1.0	2.3	3.4	0.4	0.27	0.45	0.36	1.68	1.9
Sixers	82	240.9	.444	.360	.729	10.93	30.40	41.33	22.8	7.43	4.68	13.05	18.35	93.2
Opponents	82	240.9	.454	.349	.760	11.01	32.98	43.99	22.8	7.20	4.83	14.33	16.23	96.5

Phoenix Suns

Player	GP	MPG	FG%	3Pt%	FT%	OFF	DEF	Total	APG	SPG	BPG	TOPG	PFPG	PPG
Goran Dragic	77	33.5	.443	.319	.748	0.8	2.3	3.10	7.4	1.61	0.34	2.75	2.78	14.7
Luis Scola	82	26.6	.473	.188	.787	1.9	4.7	6.60	2.2	0.82	0.43	1.55	3.13	12.8
Marcin Gortat	61	30.8	.521	.000	.652	2.1	6.4	8.50	1.2	0.66	1.61	1.62	2.08	11.1
Jared Dudley	79	27.5	.468	.391	.796	1.0	2.1	3.10	2.6	0.95	0.10	1.28	1.62	10.9
Shannon Brown	59	23.8	.420	.277	.784	0.7	1.8	2.50	1.8	1.00	0.25	1.25	1.56	10.5
Michael Beasley	75	20.7	.405	.313	.746	0.7	3.1	3.80	1.5	0.41	0.45	1.92	1.43	10.1
Jermaine O'Neal	55	18.7	.482	.000	.835	1.5	3.8	5.30	0.8	0.35	1.42	1.33	2.29	8.3
Markieff Morris	82	22.4	.407	.336	.732	1.6	3.2	4.80	1.3	0.94	0.78	1.27	2.55	8.2
Wesley Johnson	50	19.1	.407	.323	.771	0.4	2.0	2.50	0.7	0.44	0.36	0.96	1.12	8.0
P.J. Tucker	79	24.2	.473	.314	.744	1.7	2.8	4.40	1.4	0.78	0.24	0.85	1.84	6.4
Marcus Morris	23	16.1	.405	.308	.405	0.7	1.8	2.50	0.7	0.78	0.17	1.04	1.74	5.7
Morris (TOT)	77	19.8	.422	.369	.564	1.0	2.6	3.60	0.8	0.58	0.26	1.00	0.00	7.7
Hamed Haddadi	17	13.8	.459	.000	.500	1.9	3.2	5.10	0.5	0.29	1.24	1.59	2.65	4.1
Haddadi (TOT)	30	10.7	.427	.000	.519	1.4	2.3	3.70	0.4	0.20	0.90	1.03	0.00	2.8
Kendall Marshall	48	14.6	.371	.315	.571	0.1	0.8	0.90	3.0	0.46	0.08	1.19	1.00	3.0
Diante Garrett	19	7.8	.327	.200	.500	0.3	0.5	0.80	1.6	0.53	0.00	0.84	0.26	2.1
Suns	82	241.5	.443	.330	.744	11.70	29.93	41.62	22.6	8.04	5.29	15.60	20.59	95.2
Opponents	82	241.5	.470	.388	.757	11.68	31.67	43.35	22.8	8.35	5.12	15.34	18.43	101.6

Portland Trail Blazers

Player	GP	MPG	FG%	3Pt%	FT%	OFF	DEF	Total	APG	SPG	BPG	TOPG	PFPG	PPG
			Field Goals			Rebounds Per Game								
LaMarcus Aldridge	74	37.7	.484	.143	.810	2.4	6.7	9.1	2.6	0.84	1.23	1.93	2.53	21.1
Damian Lillard	82	38.6	.429	.368	.844	0.5	2.6	3.1	6.5	0.90	0.23	2.96	2.10	19.0
Wesley Matthews	69	34.8	.436	.398	.797	0.5	2.3	2.8	2.5	1.30	0.26	1.58	2.49	14.8
Nicolas Batum	73	38.5	.423	.372	.848	1.3	4.3	5.6	4.9	1.25	1.14	2.60	1.90	14.3
J.J. Hickson	80	29.0	.562	.000	.679	3.3	7.0	10.3	1.1	0.60	0.64	1.81	2.00	12.7
Eric Maynor	27	21.2	.422	.380	.683	0.1	0.9	1.0	4.0	0.44	0.04	1.78	1.33	6.9
Maynor (TOT)	64	15.0	.377	.354	.726	0.1	0.6	0.7	2.8	0.34	0.02	1.23	0.00	4.5
Meyers Leonard	69	17.5	.545	.429	.809	1.2	2.5	3.7	0.5	0.16	0.55	0.71	2.43	5.5
Will Barton	73	12.2	.382	.138	.769	0.5	1.5	2.0	0.8	0.47	0.12	0.82	0.77	4.0
Luke Babbitt	62	11.8	.368	.348	.769	0.2	2.0	2.2	0.5	0.23	0.08	0.35	1.32	3.9
Victor Claver	49	16.6	.392	.287	.467	0.6	1.8	2.4	0.9	0.53	0.24	0.88	1.53	3.8
Nolan Smith	40	7.2	.368	.214	.714	0.2	0.5	0.7	0.9	0.17	0.03	0.72	0.65	2.8
A. Pavlovic	39	13.5	.353	.300	.167	0.2	1.3	1.4	0.8	0.62	0.13	0.36	1.51	2.6
Joel Freeland	51	9.4	.408	.000	.667	0.8	1.5	2.3	0.3	0.25	0.22	0.37	1.31	2.6
Jared Jeffries	38	9.2	.296	.000	.522	0.7	0.9	1.6	0.4	0.16	0.16	0.45	1.53	1.2
Trail Blazers	82	242.1	.448	.353	.776	10.66	30.17	40.83	21.8	6.56	4.31	14.67	18.51	97.5
Opponents	82	242.1	.474	.340	.761	10.99	31.44	42.43	23.7	8.43	4.38	13.10	18.74	100.7

Sacramento Kings

Player	GP	MPG	FG%	3Pt%	FT%	OFF	DEF	Total	APG	SPG	BPG	TOPG	PFPG	PPG
			Field Goals			Rebounds Per Game								
DeMarcus Cousins	75	30.5	.465	.182	.738	3.0	7.0	9.9	2.7	1.44	0.73	3.00	3.59	17.1
Tyreke Evans	65	31.0	.478	.338	.775	0.9	3.6	4.4	3.5	1.38	0.42	1.97	2.05	15.2
Isaiah Thomas	79	26.9	.440	.358	.882	0.4	1.7	2.0	4.0	0.85	0.04	1.77	2.11	13.9
Marcus Thornton	74	24.0	.429	.372	.881	0.7	1.8	2.5	1.3	0.85	0.06	0.94	1.46	12.7
Jason Thompson	82	27.9	.502	.000	.694	2.1	4.6	6.7	1.0	0.59	0.74	1.23	2.77	10.9
John Salmons	76	30.0	.399	.371	.773	0.4	2.3	2.7	3.0	0.67	0.33	1.12	1.88	8.8
Patrick Patterson	24	23.2	.494	.444	.786	1.7	3.2	4.8	1.3	0.54	0.54	0.79	2.00	8.0
Patterson (TOT)	41	25.0	.512	.386	.762	1.6	3.2	4.7	1.1	0.44	0.56	0.86	0.00	10.4
Jimmer Fredette	69	14.0	.421	.417	.859	0.3	0.8	1.0	1.3	0.45	0.04	0.99	0.93	7.2
Toney Douglas	22	17.1	.430	.389	1.000	0.5	1.7	2.2	2.6	1.41	0.05	1.14	1.91	6.1
Douglas (TOT)	71	18.1	.403	.380	.905	0.5	1.5	1.9	2.1	1.00	0.04	1.14	0.00	7.5
Travis Outlaw	38	11.7	.418	.280	.731	0.4	1.2	1.6	0.6	0.29	0.21	0.50	0.92	5.3
James Johnson	54	16.3	.413	.095	.597	0.9	1.8	2.7	1.1	0.76	0.93	1.26	1.83	5.1
Cole Aldrich	15	11.7	.568	.000	.727	1.2	3.0	4.2	0.2	0.13	0.93	0.60	1.27	3.3
Aldrich (TOT)	45	8.6	.550	.000	.600	0.7	2.0	2.7	0.2	0.11	0.51	0.51	0.00	2.2
Chuck Hayes	74	16.3	.442	.000	.625	1.5	2.5	4.0	1.5	0.42	0.24	0.59	1.54	2.7
Kings	82	241.8	.447	.363	.769	11.50	29.09	40.59	20.8	8.18	4.17	14.62	20.94	100.2
Opponents	82	241.8	.472	.355	.783	11.87	31.72	43.59	25.1	7.61	6.31	14.73	19.95	105.1

San Antonio Spurs

Player	GP	MPG	FG%	3Pt%	FT%	OFF	DEF	Total	APG	SPG	BPG	TOPG	PFPG	PPG
			Field Goals			Rebounds Per Game								
Tony Parker	66	32.9	.522	.353	.845	0.3	2.7	3.0	7.6	0.82	0.09	2.58	1.39	20.3
Tim Duncan	69	30.1	.502	.286	.817	1.8	8.1	9.9	2.7	0.72	2.65	2.13	1.70	17.8
Kawhi Leonard	58	31.2	.494	.374	.825	1.1	4.9	6.0	1.6	1.67	0.55	1.07	1.71	11.9
Manu Ginobili	60	23.2	.425	.353	.796	0.5	2.9	3.4	4.6	1.33	0.22	2.20	1.90	11.8
Danny Green	80	27.5	.448	.429	.848	0.5	2.6	3.0	1.8	1.15	0.68	1.18	1.55	10.5
Tiago Splitter	81	24.7	.560	.000	.730	1.8	4.6	6.4	1.6	0.78	0.79	1.23	1.99	10.3
Gary Neal	68	21.8	.412	.355	.865	0.2	1.9	2.1	1.9	0.44	0.03	1.01	1.37	9.5
Boris Diaw	75	22.8	.539	.385	.723	0.9	2.5	3.4	2.4	0.69	0.36	1.12	1.91	5.8
DeJuan Blair	61	14.0	.524	.000	.629	1.1	2.7	3.8	0.7	0.61	0.16	0.80	1.84	5.4
Patty Mills	58	11.3	.469	.400	.842	0.2	0.7	0.9	1.1	0.45	0.07	0.67	0.95	5.1
Cory Joseph	28	13.9	.464	.286	.857	0.4	1.4	1.9	1.9	0.54	0.14	0.75	0.89	4.5
Matt Bonner	68	13.4	.487	.442	.733	0.4	1.5	1.9	0.5	0.25	0.28	0.24	1.26	4.2
Nando De Colo	72	12.8	.436	.378	.795	0.3	1.6	1.9	1.9	0.57	0.08	1.13	1.21	3.8
Aron Baynes	16	8.8	.500	.000	.583	0.8	1.3	2.0	0.3	0.06	0.38	0.69	1.44	2.7
Spurs	82	242.4	.481	.376	.791	8.12	33.18	41.31	25.1	8.48	5.44	14.71	17.40	103.0
Opponents	82	242.4	.442	.353	.760	11.12	31.43	42.55	21.4	8.23	4.94	14.89	19.09	96.6

Toronto Raptors

Player	GP	MPG	FG%	3Pt%	FT%	OFF	DEF	Total	APG	SPG	BPG	TOPG	PFPG	PPG
			Field Goals			Rebounds Per Game								
Rudy Gay	33	34.7	.425	.336	.856	1.3	5.1	6.4	2.8	1.73	0.67	2.85	2.88	19.5
Gay (TOT)	75	35.8	.416	.323	.814	1.3	4.8	6.1	2.7	1.51	0.71	2.64	0.00	18.2
DeMar DeRozan	82	36.7	.445	.283	.831	0.6	3.3	3.9	2.5	0.93	0.29	1.84	2.11	18.1
Andrea Bargnani	35	28.7	.399	.309	.844	0.7	2.9	3.7	1.1	0.60	0.66	1.54	1.83	12.7
Kyle Lowry	68	29.7	.401	.362	.795	0.8	3.9	4.7	6.4	1.38	0.35	2.31	3.21	11.6
Alan Anderson	65	23.0	.383	.333	.857	0.5	1.8	2.3	1.6	0.74	0.11	1.23	2.02	10.7
Amir Johnson	81	28.7	.554	.385	.727	2.8	4.7	7.5	1.5	1.00	1.36	1.44	3.72	10.0
Jonas Valanciunas	62	23.9	.557	.000	.789	2.0	4.0	6.0	0.7	0.27	1.26	1.52	3.03	8.9
Linas Kleiza	20	18.8	.333	.303	.842	0.5	2.1	2.6	0.8	0.20	0.10	0.70	2.25	7.4
Terrence Ross	73	17.0	.407	.332	.714	0.5	1.5	2.0	0.7	0.59	0.19	0.66	1.67	6.4
Mickael Pietrus	19	20.3	.347	.313	.667	0.3	1.6	1.9	0.5	0.63	0.32	0.84	1.74	5.3
John Lucas III	63	13.1	.386	.377	.720	0.1	0.9	1.0	1.7	0.37	0.02	0.41	0.79	5.3
Landry Fields	51	20.3	.457	.143	.642	1.2	2.9	4.1	1.2	0.63	0.16	0.82	1.24	4.7
Sebastian Telfair	13	14.2	.290	.270	.833	0.1	1.2	1.2	3.0	0.69	0.08	0.85	1.54	4.3
Telfair (TOT)	59	16.6	.362	.353	.783	0.2	1.2	1.4	2.6	0.63	0.19	1.08	0.00	5.6
Quincy Acy	29	11.8	.560	.500	.816	1.0	1.6	2.7	0.4	0.45	0.52	0.59	1.83	4.0
Aaron Gray	42	12.2	.533	.000	.523	1.1	2.0	3.2	0.8	0.17	0.12	0.86	2.02	2.8
Raptors	**82**	**243.7**	**.446**	**.343**	**.788**	**10.62**	**29.59**	**40.21**	**21.5**	**7.26**	**4.78**	**13.71**	**22.39**	**97.2**
Opponents	**82**	**243.7**	**.458**	**.361**	**.747**	**10.70**	**31.02**	**41.72**	**21.9**	**7.05**	**4.72**	**14.26**	**20.12**	**98.7**

Utah Jazz

Player	GP	MPG	FG%	3Pt%	FT%	OFF	DEF	Total	APG	SPG	BPG	TOPG	PFPG	PPG
			Field Goals			Rebounds Per Game								
Al Jefferson	78	33.1	.494	.118	.770	2.0	7.2	9.2	2.1	1.03	1.14	1.35	2.18	17.8
Paul Millsap	78	30.4	.490	.333	.742	2.3	4.8	7.1	2.6	1.31	1.03	1.77	2.97	14.6
Gordon Hayward	72	29.2	.435	.415	.827	0.7	2.4	3.1	3.0	0.81	0.53	1.67	1.74	14.1
Mo Williams	46	30.8	.430	.383	.882	0.5	1.9	2.4	6.2	1.00	0.20	2.72	2.28	12.9
Randy Foye	82	27.4	.397	.410	.819	0.2	1.3	1.5	2.0	0.80	0.33	1.12	2.32	10.8
Derrick Favors	77	23.2	.482	.000	.688	2.4	4.7	7.1	1.0	0.87	1.69	1.68	3.21	9.4
Enes Kanter	70	15.4	.544	1.000	.795	1.9	2.4	4.3	0.4	0.40	0.46	1.44	1.66	7.2
Marvin Williams	73	23.7	.423	.325	.778	0.8	2.8	3.6	1.1	0.51	0.52	0.82	1.34	7.2
Alec Burks	64	17.8	.420	.359	.713	0.6	1.7	2.3	1.4	0.55	0.20	1.16	1.78	7.0
DeMarre Carroll	66	16.8	.460	.286	.765	1.3	1.5	2.8	0.9	0.88	0.36	0.52	1.80	6.0
Jamaal Tinsley	66	18.5	.368	.307	.692	0.3	1.5	1.7	4.4	0.97	0.21	1.61	1.61	3.5
Jeremy Evans	37	5.8	.614	.000	.636	0.7	0.9	1.6	0.3	0.22	0.35	0.22	0.81	2.0
Earl Watson	48	17.3	.308	.179	.680	0.5	1.3	1.8	4.0	0.83	0.17	1.44	1.96	2.0
Kevin Murphy	17	3.1	.250	.200	.000	0.0	0.2	0.2	0.1	0.06	0.00	0.18	0.24	0.9
Jazz	**82**	**242.4**	**.454**	**.366**	**.764**	**12.06**	**29.96**	**42.02**	**22.7**	**8.42**	**6.28**	**14.76**	**21.34**	**98.0**
Opponents	**82**	**242.4**	**.458**	**.370**	**.757**	**10.99**	**29.83**	**40.82**	**20.6**	**7.81**	**5.85**	**14.71**	**20.37**	**98.1**

Washington Wizards

Player	GP	MPG	FG%	3Pt%	FT%	OFF	DEF	Total	APG	SPG	BPG	TOPG	PFPG	PPG
			Field Goals			Rebounds Per Game								
John Wall	49	32.7	.441	.267	.804	0.7	3.3	4.0	7.6	1.31	0.76	3.20	2.39	18.5
Bradley Beal	56	31.2	.410	.386	.786	0.8	3.0	3.8	2.4	0.89	0.52	1.61	2.02	13.9
Nene	61	27.2	.480	.000	.729	1.7	5.0	6.7	2.9	0.90	0.61	2.28	2.80	12.6
Martell Webster	76	28.9	.442	.422	.848	0.7	3.2	3.9	1.9	0.66	0.22	1.18	2.18	11.4
Emeka Okafor	79	26.0	.477	.000	.571	2.5	6.2	8.8	1.2	0.57	0.97	1.35	1.84	9.7
Trevor Ariza	56	26.3	.417	.364	.821	0.8	4.0	4.8	2.0	1.29	0.36	1.50	1.29	9.5
Kevin Seraphin	79	21.8	.461	.000	.693	1.4	3.0	4.4	0.7	0.30	0.75	1.65	2.67	9.1
A.J. Price	57	22.4	.390	.350	.790	0.4	1.6	2.0	3.6	0.58	0.05	1.12	1.28	7.7
Cartier Martin	41	16.9	.381	.397	.714	0.3	2.2	2.4	0.5	0.46	0.15	0.78	1.41	6.6
Trevor Booker	48	18.5	.491	.000	.556	2.0	2.9	5.0	0.8	0.67	0.33	0.65	1.98	5.3
Garrett Temple	51	22.7	.407	.325	.703	0.6	1.8	2.4	2.3	0.98	0.33	1.20	1.84	5.1
Chris Singleton	57	16.2	.382	.194	.571	0.9	2.3	3.2	0.6	0.67	0.42	0.79	2.18	4.1
Jan Vesely	51	11.8	.500	.000	.308	0.8	1.5	2.4	0.5	0.29	0.33	0.53	2.10	2.5
Jason Collins	6	9.0	.167	.000	1.000	0.2	1.2	1.3	0.3	0.33	0.67	0.33	1.83	0.7
Collins (TOT)	38	10.1	.310	.000	.719	0.6	1.0	1.6	0.2	0.32	0.26	0.47	0.00	1.1
Wizards	**82**	**242.1**	**.435**	**.365**	**.733**	**10.82**	**32.34**	**43.16**	**21.6**	**7.29**	**4.59**	**15.10**	**20.50**	**93.2**
Opponents	**82**	**242.1**	**.440**	**.349**	**.738**	**11.01**	**33.16**	**44.17**	**21.5**	**7.79**	**4.37**	**14.55**	**19.13**	**95.8**

2013 NBA Draft

The 2013 NBA Draft was held on June 27, 2013 in Brooklyn, New York.

First Round

1. CLE—Anthony Bennett, UNLV
2. ORL—Victor Oladipo, Indiana
3. WAS—Otto Porter, Georgetown
4. CHA—Cody Zeller, Indiana
5. PHO—Alex Len, Maryland
6. NO—Nerlens Noel, Kentucky (traded to PHI)
7. SAC—Ben McLemore, Kansas
8. DET—Kentavious Caldwell-Pope, Georgia
9. MIN—Trey Burke, Michigan (traded to Utah)
10. POR—C.J. McCollum, Lehigh
11. PHI—Michael Carter-Williams, Syracuse
12. OKC—Steven Adams, Pittsburgh
13. DAL—Kelly Olynyk, Gonzaga (traded to BOS)
14. UTAH—Shabazz Muhammad, UCLA (traded to MIN)
15. MIL—Giannis Adetokunbo, Greece
16. BOS—Lucas Nogueira, Brazil (traded to ATL)
17. ATL—Dennis Schroeder, Germany
18. ATL—Shane Larkin, Miami (traded to DAL)
19. CLE—Sergey Karasev, Russia
20. CHI—Tony Snell, New Mexico
21. UTAH—Gorgui Dieng, Louisville (traded to MIN)

First Round (Cont.)

22. BRO—Mason Plumlee, Duke
23. IND—Solomon Hill, Arizona
24. NY—Tim Hardaway Jr., Michigan
25. LAC—Reggie Bullock, North Carolina
26. MIN—Andre Roberson, Colorado (traded to OKC via GS and HOU)
27. DEN—Rudy Gobert, France (traded to Utah)
28. SA—Livio Jean-Charles, France
29. OKC—Archie Goodwin, Kentucky (traded to PHO via GS)
30. PHO—Nemanja Nedovic, Serbia (traded to GS)

Second Round

31. CLE—Allen Crabbe, Cal
32. OKC—Alex Abrines, Spain
33. CLE—Caririck Felix, Arizona St
34. HOU—Isaiah Canaan, Murray St
35. PHI—Glen Rice Jr., Rio Grande Valley Vipers (traded to WAS)
36. SAC—Ray McCallum, Detroit
37. DET—Tony Mitchell, UNT
38. WAS—Nate Wolters, South Dakota State (traded to MIL)
39. POR—Jeff Withey, Kansas
40. POR—Grant Jarrett, Arizona
41. MEM—Jamaal Franklin, San Diego State

Second Round (Cont.)

42. PHI—Pierre Jackson, Baylor (traded to NO)
43. MIL—Ricky Ledo, Providence (traded to DAL)
44. DAL—Mike Muscala, Bucknell (traded to ATL)
45. POR—Marko Todorovic, Spain
46. UTAH—Erick Green, Virginia Tech (traded to DEN)
47. ATL—Raul Neto, Brazil
48. LAL—Ryan Kelly, Duke
49. CHI—Erik Murphy, Florida
50. ATL—James Ennis, Long Beach St (traded to MIA)
51. ORL—Romero Osby, Oklahoma
52. MIN—Lorenzo Brown, NC State
53. IND—Colton Iverson, Colorado State (traded to BOS)
54. WAS—Arsalan Kazemi, Oregon
55. MEM—Joffrey Lauvergne, France
56. DET—Peyton Siva, Louisville
57. PHO—Alex Oriakhi, Missouri
58. SA—Deshaun Thomas, Ohio St
59. MIN—Bojan Dubljevic, Serbia
60. MEM—Janis Timma, Latvia

Women's National Basketball Association

2013 Final Regular Season Standings

WESTERN CONFERENCE

Team	W	L	Pct	GB
†Minnesota	26	8	.765	—
*Los Angeles	24	10	.706	2.0
*Phoenix	19	15	.559	7.0
*Seattle	17	17	.500	9.0
San Antonio	12	22	.353	14.0
Tulsa	11	23	.324	15.0

EASTERN CONFERENCE

Team	W	L	Pct	GB
†Chicago	24	10	.706	—
*Atlanta	17	17	.500	7.0
*Washington	17	17	.500	7.0
*Indiana	16	18	.471	8.0
New York	11	23	.324	13.0
Connecticut	10	26	.294	14.0

†Clinched conference title.   *Clinched playoff berth.

2013 Playoffs

WESTERN CONFERENCE SEMI-FINALS

Game 1......Seattle 64   at Minnesota 80
Game 2......Minnesota 58   at Seattle 55
Minneapolis won series 2–0.

Game 1......Phoenix 86   at Los Angeles 75
Game 2......Los Angeles 82   at Phoenix 73
Game 3......Phoenix 78   at Los Angeles 77
Phoenix won series 2–1

WESTERN CONFERENCE FINALS

Game 1.....Phoenix 62   at Minnesota 85
Game 2......Minnesota 72   at Phoenix 65
Minnesota won series 2–0.

EASTERN CONFERENCE SEMI-FINALS

Game 1......Indiana 85   at Chicago 72
Game 2......Chicago 57   at Indiana 79
Indiana won series 2–0.

Game 1......Washington 71   at Atlanta 56
Game 2......Atlanta 63   at Washington 45
Game 3......Washington 72   at Atlanta 80
Atlanta won series 2–1.

EASTERN CONFERENCE FINALS

Game 1......Indiana 79   at Atlanta 84
Game 2......Atlanta 67   at Indiana 53
Atlanta won series 2–0.

WNBA FINALS

Game 1 ....Atlanta 59   at Minnesota 84
Game 2 ....Atlanta 63   at Minnesota 88
Game 3 ....Minnesota 86   at Atlanta 77
Minnesota won series 3–0.

2013 WNBA Finals MVP: Maya Moore, Minnesota

NBA Champions

Season	Winner	Series	Runner-Up	Winning Coach	Finals MVP
1946–47	Philadelphia	4–1	Chicago	Eddie Gottlieb	—
1947–48	Baltimore	4–2	Philadelphia	Buddy Jeannette	—
1948–49	Minneapolis	4–2	Washington	John Kundla	—
1949–50	Minneapolis	4–2	Syracuse	John Kundla	—
1950–51	Rochester	4–3	New York	Les Harrison	—
1951–52	Minneapolis	4–3	New York	John Kundla	—
1952–53	Minneapolis	4–1	New York	John Kundla	—
1953–54	Minneapolis	4–3	Syracuse	John Kundla	—
1954–55	Syracuse	4–3	Ft Wayne	Al Cervi	—
1955–56	Philadelphia	4–1	Ft Wayne	George Senesky	—
1956–57	Boston	4–3	St Louis	Red Auerbach	—
1957–58	St Louis	4–2	Boston	Alex Hannum	—
1958–59	Boston	4–0	Minneapolis	Red Auerbach	—
1959–60	Boston	4–3	St Louis	Red Auerbach	—
1960–61	Boston	4–1	St Louis	Red Auerbach	—
1961–62	Boston	4–3	LA Lakers	Red Auerbach	—
1962–63	Boston	4–2	LA Lakers	Red Auerbach	—
1963–64	Boston	4–1	San Francisco	Red Auerbach	—
1964–65	Boston	4–1	LA Lakers	Red Auerbach	—
1965–66	Boston	4–3	LA Lakers	Red Auerbach	—
1966–67	Philadelphia	4–2	San Francisco	Alex Hannum	—
1967–68	Boston	4–2	LA Lakers	Bill Russell	—
1968–69	Boston	4–3	LA Lakers	Bill Russell	Jerry West, LA
1969–70	New York	4–3	LA Lakers	Red Holzman	Willis Reed, NY
1970–71	Milwaukee	4–0	Baltimore	Larry Costello	Kareem Abdul-Jabbar, Mil
1971–72	LA Lakers	4–1	New York	Bill Sharman	Wilt Chamberlain, LA
1972–73	New York	4–1	LA Lakers	Red Holzman	Willis Reed, NY
1973–74	Boston	4–3	Milwaukee	Tommy Heinsohn	John Havlicek, Bos
1974–75	Golden State	4–0	Washington	Al Attles	Rick Barry, GS
1975–76	Boston	4–2	Phoenix	Tommy Heinsohn	JoJo White, Bos
1976–77	Portland	4–2	Philadelphia	Jack Ramsay	Bill Walton, Port
1977–78	Washington	4–3	Seattle	Dick Motta	Wes Unseld, Wash
1978–79	Seattle	4–1	Washington	Lenny Wilkens	Dennis Johnson, Sea
1979–80	LA Lakers	4–2	Philadelphia	Paul Westhead	Magic Johnson, LA
1980–81	Boston	4–2	Houston	Bill Fitch	Cedric Maxwell, Bos
1981–82	LA Lakers	4–2	Philadelphia	Pat Riley	Magic Johnson, LA
1982–83	Philadelphia	4–0	LA Lakers	Billy Cunningham	Moses Malone, Phil
1983–84	Boston	4–3	LA Lakers	K.C. Jones	Larry Bird, Bos
1984–85	LA Lakers	4–2	Boston	Pat Riley	Kareem Abdul-Jabbar, LA
1985–86	Boston	4–2	Houston	K.C. Jones	Larry Bird, Bos
1986–87	LA Lakers	4–2	Boston	Pat Riley	Magic Johnson, LA
1987–88	LA Lakers	4–3	Detroit	Pat Riley	James Worthy, LA
1988–89	Detroit	4–0	LA Lakers	Chuck Daly	Joe Dumars, Det
1989–90	Detroit	4–1	Portland	Chuck Daly	Isiah Thomas, Det
1990–91	Chicago	4–1	LA Lakers	Phil Jackson	Michael Jordan, Chi
1991–92	Chicago	4–2	Portland	Phil Jackson	Michael Jordan, Chi
1992–93	Chicago	4–2	Phoenix	Phil Jackson	Michael Jordan, Chi
1993–94	Houston	4–3	New York	Rudy Tomjanovich	Hakeem Olajuwon, Hou
1994–95	Houston	4–0	Orlando	Rudy Tomjanovich	Hakeem Olajuwon, Hou
1995–96	Chicago	4–2	Seattle	Phil Jackson	Michael Jordan, Chi
1996–97	Chicago	4–2	Utah	Phil Jackson	Michael Jordan, Chi
1997–98	Chicago	4–2	Utah	Phil Jackson	Michael Jordan, Chi
1998–99	San Antonio	4–1	New York	Gregg Popovich	Tim Duncan, SA
1999–00	LA Lakers	4–2	Indiana	Phil Jackson	Shaquille O'Neal, LA
2000–01	LA Lakers	4–1	Philadelphia	Phil Jackson	Shaquille O'Neal, LA
2001–02	LA Lakers	4–0	New Jersey	Phil Jackson	Shaquille O'Neal, LA
2002–03	San Antonio	4–2	New Jersey	Gregg Popovich	Tim Duncan, SA
2003–04	Detroit	4–1	LA Lakers	Larry Brown	Chauncey Billups, Det
2004–05	San Antonio	4–3	Detroit	Gregg Popovich	Tim Duncan, SA
2005–06	Miami	4–2	Dallas	Pat Riley	Dwyane Wade, Mia
2006–07	San Antonio	4–0	Cleveland	Gregg Popovich	Tony Parker, SA
2007–08	Boston	4–2	LA Lakers	Doc Rivers	Paul Pierce, Bos
2008–09	LA Lakers	4–2	Orlando	Phil Jackson	Kobe Bryant, LA
2009–10	LA Lakers	4–3	Boston	Phil Jackson	Kobe Bryant, LA
2010–11	Dallas	4–2	Miami	Rick Carlisle	Dirk Nowitzki, Dal
2011–12	Miami	4–1	Oklahoma City	Erik Spoelstra	LeBron James, Mia
2012–13	Miami	4–3	San Antonio	Erik Spoelstra	LeBron James, Mia

Regular Season Most Valuable Player: Maurice Podoloff Trophy

Season	Player, Team	GP	Field Goals FGM	Pct	3-Pt FG FGM	Pct	Free Throws FTM	Pct	Rebounds Off	Total	A	Stl	BS	Avg
1955–56	Bob Pettit, StL	72	646	42.9	–	–	557	73.6	–	1,164	189	–	–	25.7
1956–57	Bob Cousy, Bos	64	478	37.8	–	–	363	82.1	–	309	478	–	–	20.6
1957–58	Bill Russell, Bos	69	456	44.2	–	–	230	51.9	–	1,564	202	–	–	16.6
1958–59	Bob Pettit, StL	72	719	43.8	–	–	667	75.9	–	1,182	221	–	–	29.2
1959–60	Wilt Chamberlain, Phil	72	1,065	46.1	–	–	577	58.2	–	1,941	168	–	–	37.6
1960–61	Bill Russell, Bos	78	532	42.6	–	–	258	55.0	–	1,868	264	–	–	16.9
1961–62	Bill Russell, Bos	76	575	45.7	–	–	286	59.5	–	1,891	341	–	–	18.9
1962–63	Bill Russell, Bos	78	511	43.2	–	–	287	55.5	–	1,843	348	–	–	16.8
1963–64	Oscar Robertson, Cin	79	840	48.3	–	–	800	85.3	–	783	868	–	–	31.4
1964–65	Bill Russell, Bos	78	429	43.8	–	–	244	57.3	–	1,878	410	–	–	14.1
1965–66	Wilt Chamberlain, Phil	79	1,074	54.0	–	–	501	51.3	–	1,943	414	–	–	33.5
1966–67	Wilt Chamberlain, Phil	81	785	68.3	–	–	386	44.1	–	1,957	630	–	–	24.1
1967–68	Wilt Chamberlain, Phil	82	819	59.5	–	–	354	38.0	–	1,952	702	–	–	24.3
1968–69	Wes Unseld, Balt	82	427	47.6	–	–	277	60.5	–	1,491	213	–	–	13.8
1969–70	Willis Reed, NY	81	702	50.7	–	–	351	75.6	–	1,126	161	–	–	21.7
1970–71	Lew Alcindor*, Mil	82	1,063	57.7	–	–	470	69.0	–	1,311	272	–	–	31.7
1971–72	Kareem Abdul-Jabbar, Mil	81	1,159	57.4	–	–	504	68.9	–	1,346	370	–	–	34.8
1972–73	Dave Cowens, Bos	82	740	45.2	–	–	204	77.9	–	1,329	333	–	–	20.5
1973–74	Kareem Abdul-Jabbar, Mil	81	948	53.9	–	–	295	70.2	287	1,178	386	112	283	27.0
1974–75	Bob McAdoo, Buff	82	1,095	51.2	–	–	641	80.5	307	1,155	179	92	174	34.5
1975–76	Kareem Abdul-Jabbar, LAL	82	914	52.9	–	–	447	70.3	272	1,383	413	119	338	27.7
1976–77	Kareem Abdul-Jabbar, LAL	82	888	57.9	–	–	376	70.1	266	1,090	319	101	261	26.2
1977–78	Bill Walton, Port	58	460	52.2	–	–	177	72.0	118	766	291	60	146	18.9
1978–79	Moses Malone, Hou	82	716	54.0	–	–	599	73.9	587	1,444	147	79	119	24.8
1979–80	Kareem Abdul-Jabbar, LAL	82	835	60.4	0	00.0	364	76.5	190	886	371	81	280	24.8
1980–81	Julius Erving, Phil	82	794	52.1	4	22.2	422	78.7	244	657	364	173	147	24.6
1981–82	Moses Malone, Hou	81	945	51.9	0	00.0	630	76.2	558	1,188	142	76	125	31.1
1982–83	Moses Malone, Phil	78	654	50.1	0	00.0	600	76.1	445	1,194	101	89	157	24.5
1983–84	Larry Bird, Bos	79	758	49.2	18	24.7	374	88.8	181	796	520	144	69	24.2
1984–85	Larry Bird, Bos	80	918	52.2	56	42.7	403	88.2	164	842	531	129	98	28.7
1985–86	Larry Bird, Bos	82	796	49.6	82	42.3	441	89.6	190	805	557	166	51	25.8
1986–87	Magic Johnson, LAL	80	683	52.2	8	20.5	535	84.8	122	504	977	138	36	23.9
1987–88	Michael Jordan, Chi	82	1,069	53.5	7	13.2	723	84.1	139	449	485	259	131	35.0
1988–89	Magic Johnson, LAL	77	579	50.9	59	31.4	513	91.1	111	607	988	138	22	22.5
1989–90	Magic Johnson, LAL	79	546	48.0	106	38.4	567	89.0	128	522	907	132	34	22.3
1990–91	Michael Jordan, Chi	82	990	53.9	29	31.2	571	85.1	118	492	453	223	83	31.5
1991–92	Michael Jordan, Chi	80	943	51.9	27	27.0	491	83.2	91	511	489	182	75	30.1
1992–93	Charles Barkley, Phx	76	716	52.0	67	30.5	445	76.5	237	928	385	119	74	25.6
1993–94	Hakeem Olajuwon, Hou	80	894	52.8	8	42.1	388	71.6	229	955	287	128	297	27.3
1994–95	David Robinson, SA	81	788	53.0	6	30.0	656	77.4	234	877	236	134	262	27.6
1995–96	Michael Jordan, Chi	82	916	49.5	111	42.7	548	83.4	148	543	352	180	42	30.4
1996–97	Karl Malone, Utah	82	864	55.0	0	00.0	521	75.5	193	809	368	113	48	27.4
1997–98	Michael Jordan, Chi	82	881	46.5	30	23.8	565	78.4	130	475	283	141	45	28.7
1998–99	Karl Malone, Utah	49	393	49.3	0	00.0	378	78.8	107	463	201	62	28	23.8
1999–00	Shaquille O'Neal, LAL	79	956	57.4	0	00.0	432	52.4	336	1078	299	36	239	29.7
2000–01	Allen Iverson, Phil	71	762	42.0	98	32.0	585	81.4	50	273	325	78	20	31.1
2001–02	Tim Duncan, SA	82	764	50.8	1	10.0	560	79.9	268	1042	307	61	203	25.5
2002–03	Tim Duncan, SA	81	714	51.3	6	27.3	450	71.0	260	1045	316	55	237	23.3
2003–04	Kevin Garnett, Minn	82	804	49.9	11	25.6	368	79.1	245	1139	409	120	178	24.2
2004–05	Steve Nash, Phx	75	430	50.2	94	43.1	211	88.7	80	330	861	74	6	26.0
2005–06	Steve Nash, Phx	79	541	51.2	150	43.9	257	92.1	47	333	826	61	12	18.8
2006–07	Dirk Nowitzki, Dal	78	673	50.2	72	41.6	498	90.4	122	693	263	52	62	24.6
2007–08	Kobe Bryant, LAL	82	775	45.9	150	36.1	623	84.0	94	517	441	151	40	28.3
2008–09	LeBron James, Cle	81	789	48.9	132	34.4	594	78.0	106	613	587	137	93	28.4
2009–10	LeBron James, Cle	76	768	50.3	129	33.3	756	76.7	71	554	651	125	77	29.7
2010–11	Derrick Rose, Chi	81	711	44.5	128	33.2	476	85.8	81	330	623	85	51	25.0
2011–12	LeBron James, Mia	62	621	53.1	54	36.2	387	77.1	94	492	387	115	50	27.1
2012–13	LeBron James, Mia	76	765	56.5	103	40.6	403	75.3	97	610	551	129	67	26.8

*Alcindor changed his name to Kareem Abdul-Jabbar after the 1970–71 season.

Coach of the Year: Arnold (Red) Auerbach Trophy

1962–63...Harry Gallatin, StL
1963–64...Alex Hannum, SF
1964–65...Red Auerbach, Bos
1965–66...Dolph Schayes, Phil
1966–67...Johnny Kerr, Chi
1967–68...Richie Guerin, StL
1968–69...Gene Shue, Balt
1969–70...Red Holzman, NY
1970–71...Dick Motta, Chi
1971–72...Bill Sharman, LA
1972–73...Tom Heinsohn, Bos
1973–74...Ray Scott, Det
1974–75...Phil Johnson, KC-Oma
1975–76...Bill Fitch, Clev
1976–77...Tom Nissalke, Hou
1977–78...Hubie Brown, Atl
1978–79...Cotton Fitzsimmons, KC

1979–80...Bill Fitch, Bos
1980–81...Jack McKinney, Ind
1981–82...Gene Shue, Wash
1982–83...Don Nelson, Mil
1983–84...Frank Layden, Utah
1984–85...Don Nelson, Mil
1985–86...Mike Fratello, Atl
1986–87...Mike Schuler, Port
1987–88...Doug Moe, Den
1988–89...Cotton Fitzsimmons, Phx
1989–90...Pat Riley, LAL
1990–91...Don Chaney, Hou
1991–92...Don Nelson, GS
1992–93...Pat Riley, NY
1993–94...Lenny Wilkens, Atl
1994–95...Del Harris, LAL
1995–96...Phil Jackson, Chi

1996–97...Pat Riley, Mia
1997–98...Larry Bird, Ind
1998–99...Mike Dunleavy, Port
1999–00...Glenn (Doc) Rivers, Orl
2000–01...Larry Brown, Phil
2001–02...Rick Carlisle, Det
2002–03...Gregg Popovich, SA
2003–04...Hubie Brown, Mem
2004–05...Mike D'Antoni, Phx
2005–06...Avery Johnson, Dal
2006–07...Sam Mitchell, Tor
2007–08...Byron Scott, NO
2008–09...Mike Brown, Cle
2009–10...Scott Brooks, OKC
2010–11...Tom Thibodeau, Chi
2011–12...Gregg Popovich, SA
2012–13...George Karl, Den

Note: Award named after Auerbach in 1986.

Rookie of the Year: Eddie Gottlieb Trophy

1952–53...Don Meineke, FW
1953–54...Ray Felix, Balt
1954–55...Bob Pettit, Mil
1955–56...Maurice Stokes, Roch
1956–57...Tom Heinsohn, Bos
1957–58...Woody Sauldsberry, Phi
1958–59...Elgin Baylor, Minn
1959–60...Wilt Chamberlain, Phil
1960–61...Oscar Robertson, Cin
1961–62...Walt Bellamy, Chi
1962–63...Terry Dischinger, Chi
1963–64...Jerry Lucas, Cin
1964–65...Willis Reed, NY
1965–66...Rick Barry, SF
1966–67...Dave Bing, Det
1967–68...Earl Monroe, Balt
1968–69...Wes Unseld, Balt
1969–70...K. Abdul-Jabbar, Mil
1970–71...Dave Cowens, Bos
          Geoff Petrie, Port
1971–72...Sidney Wicks, Port
1972–73...Bob McAdoo, Buf

1973–74...Ernie DiGregorio, Buf
1974–75...Keith Wilkes, GS
1975–76...Alvan Adams, Phx
1976–77...Adrian Dantley, Buf
1977–78...Walter Davis, Phx
1978–79...Phil Ford, KC
1979–80...Larry Bird, Bos
1980–81...Darrell Griffith, Utah
1981–82...Buck Williams, NJ
1982–83...Terry Cummings, SD
1983–84...Ralph Sampson, Hou
1984–85...Michael Jordan, Chi
1985–86...Patrick Ewing, NY
1986–87...Chuck Person, Ind
1987–88...Mark Jackson, NY
1988–89...Mitch Richmond, GS
1989–90...David Robinson, SA
1990–91...Derrick Coleman, NJ
1991–92...Larry Johnson, Cha
1992–93...Shaquille O'Neal, Orl
1993–94...Chris Webber, GS

1994–95...Grant Hill, Det
          Jason Kidd, Dal
1995–96...Damon Stoudamire, Tor
1996–97...Allen Iverson, Phil
1997–98...Tim Duncan, SA
1998–99...Vince Carter, Tor
1999–00...Elton Brand, Chi
          Steve Francis, Hou
2000–01..Mike Miller, Orl
2001–02..Pau Gasol, Mem
2002–03..Amare Stoudemire, Phx
2003–04..LeBron James, Clev
2004–05..Emeka Okafor, Cha
2005–06...Chris Paul, NO
2006–07...Brandon Roy, Por
2007–08...Kevin Durant, Sea
2008–09...Derrick Rose, Chi
2009–10...Tyreke Evans, Sac
2010–11...Blake Griffin, LAC
2011–12...Kyrie Irving, Cle
2012–13...Damian Lillard, Port

Defensive Player of the Year

1982–83...Sidney Moncrief, Mil
1983–84...Sidney Moncrief, Mil
1984–85...Mark Eaton, Utah
1985–86...Alvin Robertson, SA
1986–87...Michael Cooper, LAL
1987–88...Michael Jordan, Chi
1988–89...Mark Eaton, Utah
1989–90...Dennis Rodman, Det
1990–91...Dennis Rodman, Det
1991–92...David Robinson, SA
1992–93...Hakeem Olajuwon, Hou

1993–94...Hakeem Olajuwon, Hou
1994–95...Dikembe Mutombo, Den
1995–96...Gary Payton, Sea
1996–97...Dikembe Mutombo, Atl
1997–98...Dikembe Mutombo, Atl
1998–99...Alonzo Mourning, Mia
1999–00...Alonzo Mourning, Mia
2000–01...Dikembe Mutombo, Phil/Atl
2001–02...Ben Wallace, Det
2002–03...Ben Wallace, Det
2003–04...Ron Artest, Ind

2004–05...Ben Wallace, Det
2005–06...Ben Wallace, Det
2006–07...Marcus Camby, Den
2007–08...Kevin Garnett, Bos
2008–09...Dwight Howard, Orl
2009–10...Dwight Howard, Orl
2010–11...Dwight Howard, Orl
2011–12...Tyson Chandler, NY
2012–13...Marc Gasol, Mem

Sixth Man Award

1982–83...Bobby Jones, Phil
1983–84...Kevin McHale, Bos
1984–85...Kevin McHale, Bos
1985–86...Bill Walton, Bos
1986–87...Ricky Pierce, Mil
1987–88...Roy Tarpley, Dal
1988–89...Eddie Johnson, Phx
1989–90...Ricky Pierce, Mil
1990–91...Detlef Schrempf, Ind
1991–92...Detlef Schrempf, Ind
1992–93...Cliff Robinson, Port

1993–94...Dell Curry, Cha
1994–95...Anthony Mason, NY
1995–96...Tony Kukoc, Chi
1996–97...John Starks, NY
1997–98...Danny Manning, Phx
1998–99...Darrell Armstrong, Orl
1999–00...Rodney Rogers, Phx
2000–01...Aaron McKie, Phil
2001–02...Corliss Williamson, Det
2002–03...Bobby Jackson, Sac
2003–04...Antawn Jamison, Dal

2004–05...Ben Gordon, Chi
2005–06...Mike Miller, Mem
2006–07...Leandro Barbosa, Phx
2007–08...Manu Ginobli, SA
2008–09...Jason Terry, Dal
2009–10...Jamal Crawford, Atl
2010–11...Lamar Odom, LAL
2011–12...James Harden, OKC
2012–13...J.R. Smith, NY

J. Walter Kennedy Citizenship Award

1974–75...Wes Unseld, Wash	1987–88...Alex English, Den	2000–01...Dikembe Mutombo, Phi
1975–76...Slick Watts, Sea	1988–89...Thurl Bailey, Utah	2001–02...Alonzo Mourning, Mia
1976–77...Dave Bing, Wash	1989–90...Glenn (Doc) Rivers, Atl	2002–03...David Robinson, SA
1977–78...Bob Lanier, Det	1990–91...Kevin Johnson, Phx	2003–04...Reggie Miller, Ind
1978–79...Calvin Murphy, Hou	1991–92...Magic Johnson, LAL	2004–05...Eric Snow, Clev
1979–80...Austin Carr, Cle	1992–93...Terry Porter, Port	2005–06...Kevin Garnett, Min
1980–81...Mike Glenn, NY	1993–94...Joe Dumars, Det	2006–07...Luol Deng, Chi
1981–82...Kent Benson, Det	1994–95...Joe O'Toole, Atl	2007–08...Grant Hill, Phx
1982–83...Julius Erving, Phi	1995–96...Chris Dudley, Port	2008–09...Dikembe Mutombo, Hou
1983–84...Frank Layden, Utah	1996–97...P.J. Brown, Mia	2009–10...Samuel Dalembert, Phi
1984–85...Dan Issel, Den	1997–98...Steve Smith, Atl	2010–11...Ron Artest, LAL
1985–86...Michael Cooper, LAL	1998–99...Brian Grant, Port	2011–12...Pau Gasol, LAL
........Rory Sparrow, NY	1999–00...Vlade Divac, Sac	2012–13...Kenneth Faried, Den
1986–87...Isiah Thomas, Det		

Most Improved Player

1985–86...Alvin Robertson, SA	1995–96.....Gheorghe Muresan, Wash	2005–06...Boris Diaw, Phx
1986–87...Dale Ellis, Sea	1996–97...Isaac Austin, Mia	2006–07...Monta Ellis, GS
1987–88...Kevin Duckworth, Port	1997–98...Alan Henderson, Atl	2007–08...Hedo Turkoglu, Orl
1988–89...Kevin Johnson, Phx	1998–99...Darrell Armstrong, Orl	2008–09...Danny Granger, Ind
1989–90...Rony Seikaly, Mia	1999–00...Jalen Rose, Ind	2009–10...Aaron Brooks, Hou
1990–91...Scott Skiles, Orl	2000–01...Tracy McGrady, Orl	2010–11...Kevin Love, Minn
1991–92...Pervis Ellison, Wash	2001–02...Jermaine O'Neal, Ind	2011–12...Ryan Anderson, Orl
1992–93...Mahmoud Abdul-Rauf, Den	2002–03...Gilbert Arenas, GS	2012–13...Paul George, Ind
1993–94...Don MacLean, Wash	2003–04...Zach Randolph, Port	
1994–95...Dana Barros, Phi	2004–05...Bobby Simmons, LAC	

Executive of the Year

1972–73...Joe Axelson, KC-Oma	1986–87...Stan Kasten, Atl	2000–01...Geoff Petrie, Sac
1973–74...Eddie Donovan, Buf	1987–88...Jerry Krause, Chi	2001–02...Rod Thorn, NJ
1974–75...Dick Vertlieb, GS	1988–89...Jerry Colangelo, Phx	2002–03...Joe Dumars, Det
1975–76...Jerry Colangelo, Phx	1989–90...Bob Bass, SA	2003–04...Jerry West, Mem
1976–77...Ray Patterson, Hou	1990–91...Bucky Buckwalter, Port	2004–05...Bryan Colangelo, Phx
1977–78...Angelo Drossos, SA	1991–92...Wayne Embry, Clev	2005–06...Elgin Baylor, LAC
1978–79...Bob Ferry, Wash	1992–93...Jerry Colangelo, Phx	2006–07...Bryan Colangelo, Tor
1979–80...Red Auerbach, Bos	1993–94...Bob Whitsitt, Sea	2007–08...Danny Ainge, Bos
1980–81...Jerry Colangelo, Phx	1994–95...Jerry West, LAL	2008–09...Mark Warkentien, Den
1981–82...Bob Ferry, Wash	1995–96...Jerry Krause, Chi	2009–10...John Hammond, Mil
1982–83...Zollie Volchok, Sea	1996–97...Bob Bass, Cha	2010–11...Gar Forman, Chi
1983–84...Frank Layden, Utah	1997–98...Wayne Embry, Clev	........Pat Riley, Mia
1984–85...Vince Boryla, Den	1998–99...Geoff Petrie, Sac	2011–12...Larry Bird, Ind
1985–86...Stan Kasten, Atl	1999–00...John Gabriel, Orl	2012–13...Masai Ujiri, Den

NBA Alltime Individual Leaders

Scoring

MOST POINTS, CAREER

	Pts	Avg
Kareem Abdul-Jabbar	38,387	24.6
Karl Malone	36,928	25.0
Michael Jordan	32,292	30.1
*Kobe Bryant	31,617	25.5
Wilt Chamberlain	31,419	30.1
Shaquille O'Neal	28,596	23.7
Moses Malone	27,409	20.6
Elvin Hayes	27,313	21.0
Hakeem Olajuwon	26,946	21.8
Oscar Robertson	26,710	25.7

*Active in 2012–13.

HIGHEST SCORING AVERAGE, CAREER

Michael Jordan	30.1	1,072 games
Wilt Chamberlain	30.1	1,045 games
*LeBron James	27.6	765 games
Elgin Baylor	27.4	846 games
Jerry West	27.0	932 games
Allen Iverson	26.7	914 games
*Kevin Durant	26.6	461 games
Bob Pettit	26.4	792 games
George Gervin	26.2	791 games
Oscar Robertson	25.7	1,040 games

*Active in 2012–13. Note: Minimum 400 games.

MOST POINTS, SEASON

Wilt Chamberlain, Phil	4,029	1961–62
Wilt Chamberlain, SF	3,586	1962–63
Michael Jordan, Chi	3,041	1986–87
Wilt Chamberlain, Phil	3,033	1960–61
Wilt Chamberlain, SF	2,948	1963–64
Michael Jordan, Chi	2,868	1987–88
Kobe Bryant, LA	2,832	2005–06
Bob McAdoo, Buff	2,831	1974–75
Kareem Abdul-Jabbar, Mil	2,822	1971–72
Rick Barry, SF	2,775	1966–67
Michael Jordan, Chi	2,753	1989–90

HIGHEST SCORING AVERAGE, SEASON

Wilt Chamberlain, Phil	50.4	1961–62
Wilt Chamberlain, SF	44.8	1962–63
Wilt Chamberlain, Phil	38.4	1960–61
Wilt Chamberlain, Phil	37.6	1959–60
Michael Jordan, Chi	37.1	1986–87
Wilt Chamberlain, SF	36.9	1963–64
Rick Barry, SF	35.6	1966–67
Kobe Bryant, LA	35.4	2005–06
Michael Jordan, Chi	35.0	1987–88
Kareem Abdul-Jabbar, LA	34.8	1971–72
Elgin Baylor, LA	34.8	1960–61

Note: Minimum 70 games.

Scoring (Cont.)

MOST POINTS, SINGLE GAME

	Player, Team	Opp	Date
100	Wilt Chamberlain, Phil	NY	3/2/62
81	Kobe Bryant, LAL	Tor	1/22/06
78	Wilt Chamberlain, Phil	LAL	12/8/61
73	Wilt Chamberlain, Phil	Chi	1/13/62
73	Wilt Chamberlain, SF	NY	11/16/62
73	David Thompson, Den	Det	4/9/78
72	Wilt Chamberlain, SF	LAL	11/3/62
71	David Robinson, SA	LAC	4/24/94
71	Elgin Baylor, LAL	NY	11/15/60
70	Wilt Chamberlain, SF	Syr	3/10/63

Field-Goal Percentage

Highest FG Percentage, Career: .599—Artis Gilmore

Highest FG Percentage, Season: .727—Wilt Chamberlain, LA Lakers, 1972–73 (426/586)

Free Throws

HIGHEST FREE-THROW PERCENTAGE, CAREER

*Steve Nash	.904
Mark Price	.904
Rick Barry	.900
*Peja Stojakovic	.895
*Chauncey Billups	.894
*Ray Allen	.894

Note: Minimum 1200 free throws made. *Active 2012–13.

HIGHEST FREE-THROW PERCENTAGE, SEASON

Jose Calderon, Tor	.981	2008–09
Calvin Murphy, Hou	.958	1980–81
Mahmoud Abdul-Rauf, Den	.956	1993–94
Ray Allen, Bos	.952	2008–09
Jeff Hornacek, Utah	.950	1999–00

MOST FREE THROWS MADE, CAREER

	No.	Yrs	Pct
Karl Malone	9,787	19	.742
Moses Malone	8,531	19	.769
*Kobe Bryant	7,932	17	.838
Oscar Robertson	7,694	14	.838
Michael Jordan	7,327	15	.835

Three-Point Field Goals

Most Three-Point Field Goals, Career: 2,857—Ray Allen*

Highest Three-Point Field-Goal Percentage, Career: .454—Steve Kerr

Most Three-Point Field Goals, Season: 272—Stephen Curry, Golden State, 2012–13

Highest Three-Point Field-Goal Percentage, Season: .536—Kyle Korver, Utah, 2009–10

Most Three-Point Field Goals, Game: 12—Kobe Bryant, LA Lakers vs Seattle, 1/7/03; Donyell Marshall, Toronto vs. Philadelphia, 3/13/05

Note: First season of three-point field goal: 1979–80.

*Active 2012–13.

Steals

Most Steals, Career: 3,265—John Stockton

Most Steals, Season: 301—Alvin Robertson, San Antonio, 1985–86

Most Steals, Game: 11—Kendall Gill, New Jersey vs Miami, 4/3/99; Larry Kenon, San Antonio vs Kansas City, 12/26/76

Rebounds

MOST REBOUNDS, CAREER

	No.	Yrs	Avg
Wilt Chamberlain	23,924	14	22.9
Bill Russell	21,620	13	22.5
Kareem Abdul-Jabbar	17,440	20	11.2
Elvin Hayes	16,279	16	12.5
Moses Malone	16,212	19	12.2
Karl Malone	14,968	19	10.1
Robert Parish	14,715	21	9.1
Nate Thurmond	14,464	14	15.0
Walt Bellamy	14,241	14	13.7
*Kevin Garnett	13,843	18	10.5

*Active 2012–13.

MOST REBOUNDS, SEASON

Wilt Chamberlain, Phil	2,149	1960–61
Wilt Chamberlain, Phil	2,052	1961–62
Wilt Chamberlain, Phil	1,957	1966–67
Wilt Chamberlain, Phil	1,952	1967–68
Wilt Chamberlain, SF	1,946	1962–63
Wilt Chamberlain, Phil	1,943	1965–66
Wilt Chamberlain, Phil	1,941	1959–60
Bill Russell, Bos	1,930	1963–64
Bill Russell, Bos	1,878	1964–65
Bill Russell, Bos	1,868	1960–61

MOST REBOUNDS, GAME

	Player, Team	Opp	Date
55	Wilt Chamberlain, Phil	Bos	11/24/60
51	Bill Russell, Bos	Syr	02/05/60
49	Bill Russell, Bos	Phil	11/16/57
49	Bill Russell, Bos	Det	03/11/65
45	Wilt Chamberlain, Phil	Syr	02/06/60
45	Wilt Chamberlain, Phil	LA	01/21/61

Assists

MOST ASSISTS, CAREER

John Stockton	15,806
*Jason Kidd	12,091
Mark Jackson	10,334
*Steve Nash	10,249
Magic Johnson	10,141

*Active in 2012–13.

MOST ASSISTS, SEASON

John Stockton, Utah	1,164	1990–91
John Stockton, Utah	1,134	1989–90
John Stockton, Utah	1,128	1987–88
John Stockton, Utah	1,126	1991–92
Isiah Thomas, Det	1,123	1984–85

MOST ASSISTS, GAME: 30—Scott Skiles, Orlando vs Denver, 12/30/90

Blocked Shots

MOST BLOCKED SHOTS, CAREER

Hakeem Olajuwon	3,830
Dikembe Mutombo	3,289
Kareem Abdul-Jabbar	3,189
Mark Eaton	3,064
David Robinson	2,954

MOST BLOCKED SHOTS, SEASON

Mark Eaton, Utah	456	1984–85
Manute Bol, Wash	397	1985–86
Elmore Smith, LAL	393	1973–74
Hakeem Olajuwon, Hou	376	1989–90
Mark Eaton, Utah	369	1985–86

MOST BLOCKED SHOTS, GAME: 17—Elmore Smith, LA Lakers vs Portland, 10/28/73

Scoring

MOST POINTS, CAREER

	Pts	App.	Avg
Michael Jordan	5,987	13	33.4
Kareem Abdul-Jabbar	5,762	18	24.3
*Kobe Bryant	5,640	15	25.6
Shaquille O'Neal	5,250	17	24.3
Karl Malone	4,761	19	24.7
*Tim Duncan	4,614	15	21.9
Jerry West	4,457	13	29.1
Larry Bird	3,897	12	23.8
*LeBron James	3,871	8	28.1
John Havlicek	3,776	13	22.0
Hakeem Olajuwon	3,755	15	25.9
Magic Johnson	3,701	13	19.5
Scottie Pippen	3,642	16	17.5
Elgin Baylor	3,623	12	27.0
Wilt Chamberlain	3,607	13	22.5

*Active 2012–13.

†HIGHEST SCORING AVERAGE, CAREER

	Avg	Games
Michael Jordan	33.4	179
Allen Iverson	29.7	71
Jerry West	29.1	153
*Kevin Durant	28.6	54
*LeBron James	28.05	138
Elgin Baylor	27.0	134
George Gervin	27.0	59
*Dirk Nowitzki	25.95	128
Hakeem Olajuwon	25.9	145
*Carmelo Anthony	25.65	66
*Kobe Bryant	25.6	220
Bob Pettit	25.5	88
Dominique Wilkins	25.4	55
Rick Barry	24.8	74
Karl Malone	24.7	193

†Minimum of 25 games. *Active 2012–13.

MOST POINTS, GAME

	Player, Team	Opp	Date
†63	Michael Jordan, Chi	Bos	4/20/86
61	Elgin Baylor, LAL	Bos	4/14/62
56	Wilt Chamberlain, Phil	Syr	3/22/62
56	Michael Jordan, Chi	Mia	4/29/92
56	Charles Barkley, Phx	GS	5/4/94
55	Rick Barry, SF	Phil	4/18/67
55	Michael Jordan, Chi	Cle	5/1/88
55	Michael Jordan, Chi	Phx	6/16/93
55	Michael Jordan, Chi	Was	4/27/97
55	Allen Iverson, Phi	NO	4/20/03

†Double overtime game.

John Stockton	19
Karl Malone	19
Kareem Abdul-Jabbar	18
Shaquille O'Neal	17
*Jason Kidd	17
Robert Horry	16
Robert Parish	16
Scottie Pippen	16
Terry Porter	16

Rebounds

MOST REBOUNDS, CAREER

	No.	App.	Avg
Bill Russell	4,104	13	24.9
Wilt Chamberlain	3,913	13	24.5
*Tim Duncan	2,522	15	12.0
Shaquille O'Neal	2,508	17	11.6
Kareem Abdul-Jabbar	2,481	18	10.5
Karl Malone	2,062	19	10.7

*Active 2012–13.

MOST REBOUNDS, GAME

	Player, Team	Opp	Date
41	Wilt Chamberlain, Phil	Bos	4/5/67
40	Bill Russell, Bos	Phil	3/23/58
40	Bill Russell, Bos	StL	3/29/60
†40	Bill Russell, Bos	LA	4/18/62

†Overtime game. Three tied at 39.

Assists

MOST ASSISTS, CAREER

	No.	Games
Magic Johnson	2,346	190
John Stockton	1,839	182
*Jason Kidd	1,263	158
Larry Bird	1,062	164
*Steve Nash	1,061	120
Scottie Pippen	1,048	208
*Kobe Bryant	1,040	220

*Active 2012–13.

MOST ASSISTS, GAME

	Player, Team	Opp	Date
24	Magic Johnson, LAL	Phx	5/15/84
24	John Stockton, Utah	LAL	5/17/88
23	Magic Johnson, LAL	Port	5/3/85
23	John Stockton, Utah	Port	4/25/96
23	Steve Nash, Phx	LAL	4/24/07

Games played

Robert Horry	244
Kareem Abdul-Jabbar	237
*Derek Fisher	240
*Kobe Bryant	220
Shaquille O'Neal	216
*Tim Duncan	211
Scottie Pippen	208
Danny Ainge	193
Karl Malone	193
Magic Johnson	190

*Active 2012–13.

Appearances

John Stockton	19
Karl Malone	19
Kareem Abdul-Jabbar	18
Shaquille O'Neal	17
*Jason Kidd	17
Robert Horry	16
Robert Parish	16
Scottie Pippen	16
Terry Porter	16

Dolph Schayes	15
Clyde Drexler	15
Jerome Kersey	15
Hakeem Olajuwon	15
Tree Rollins	15
*Kobe Bryant	15
*Derek Fisher	15
*Tim Duncan	15

*Active 2012–13.

Scoring

1946–47	Joe Fulks, Phil	1389	1980–81	Adrian Dantley, Utah	30.7
1947–48	Max Zaslofsky, Chi	1007	1981–82	George Gervin, SA	32.3
1948–49	George Mikan, Min	1698	1982–83	Alex English, Den	28.4
1949–50	George Mikan, Min	1865	1983–84	Adrian Dantley, Utah	30.6
1950–51	George Mikan, Min	1932	1984–85	Bernard King, NY	32.9
1951–52	Paul Arizin, Phil	1674	1985–86	Dominique Wilkins, Atl	30.3
1952–53	Neil Johnston, Phil	1564	1986–87	Michael Jordan, Chi	37.1
1953–54	Neil Johnston, Phil	1759	1987–88	Michael Jordan, Chi	35.0
1954–55	Neil Johnston, Phil	1631	1988–89	Michael Jordan, Chi	32.5
1955–56	Bob Pettit, StL	1849	1989–90	Michael Jordan, Chi	33.6
1956–57	Paul Arizin, Phil	1817	1990–91	Michael Jordan, Chi	31.5
1957–58	George Yardley, Det	2001	1991–92	Michael Jordan, Chi	30.1
1958–59	Bob Pettit, StL	2105	1992–93	Michael Jordan, Chi	32.6
1959–60	Wilt Chamberlain, Phil	2707	1993–94	David Robinson, SA	29.8
1960–61	Wilt Chamberlain, Phil	3033	1994–95	Shaquille O'Neal, Orl	29.3
1961–62	Wilt Chamberlain, Phil	4029	1995–96	Michael Jordan, Chi	30.4
1962–63	Wilt Chamberlain, SF	3586	1996–97	Michael Jordan, Chi	29.6
1963–64	Wilt Chamberlain, SF	2948	1997–98	Michael Jordan, Chi	28.7
1964–65	Wilt Chamberlain, SF-Phil	2534	1998–99	Allen Iverson, Phil	26.8
1965–66	Wilt Chamberlain, Phil	2649	1999–00	Shaquille O'Neal, LAL	29.7
1966–67	Rick Barry, SF	2775	2000–01	Allen Iverson, Phil	31.1
1967–68	Dave Bing, Det	2142	2001–02	Allen Iverson, Phil	31.4
1968–69	Elvin Hayes, SD	2327	2002–03	Tracy McGrady, Orl	32.1
1969–70	Jerry West, LAL	*31.2	2003–04	Tracy McGrady, Orl	28.0
1970–71	Kareem Abdul-Jabbar, Mil	31.7	2004–05	Allen Iverson, Phil	30.7
1971–72	Kareem Abdul-Jabbar, Mil	34.8	2005–06	Kobe Bryant, LAL	35.4
1972–73	Nate Archibald, KC-Oma	34.0	2006–07	Kobe Bryant, LAL	31.6
1973–74	Bob McAdoo, Buff	30.6	2007–08	LeBron James, Cle	30.0
1974–75	Bob McAdoo, Buff	34.5	2008–09	Dwyane Wade, Mia	30.2
1975–76	Bob McAdoo, Buff	31.1	2009–10	Kevin Durant, OKC	30.1
1976–77	Pete Maravich, NO	31.1	2010–11	Kevin Durant, OKC	27.7
1977–78	George Gervin, SA	27.2	2011–12	Kevin Durant, OKC	28.0
1978–79	George Gervin, SA	29.6	2012–13	Carmelo Anthony, NY	28.7
1979–80	George Gervin, SA	33.1			

*Based on per game average since 1969–70.

Rebounding

1950–51	Dolph Schayes, Syr	1080	1982–83	Moses Malone, Phil	15.3
1951–52	Larry Foust, FW	880	1983–84	Moses Malone, Phil	13.4
	Mel Hutchins, Mil	880	1984–85	Moses Malone, Phil	13.1
1952–53	George Mikan, Min	1007	1985–86	Bill Laimbeer, Det	13.1
1953–54	Harry Gallatin, NY	1098	1986–87	Charles Barkley, Phil	14.6
1954–55	Neil Johnston, Phil	1085	1987–88	Michael Cage, LAC	13.0
1955–56	Bob Pettit, StL	1164	1988–89	Hakeem Olajuwon, Hou	13.5
1956–57	Maurice Stokes, Roch	1256	1989–90	Hakeem Olajuwon, Hou	14.0
1957–58	Bill Russell, Bos	1564	1990–91	David Robinson, SA	13.0
1958–59	Bill Russell, Bos	1612	1991–92	Dennis Rodman, Det	18.7
1959–60	Wilt Chamberlain, Phil	1941	1992–93	Dennis Rodman, Det	18.3
1960–61	Wilt Chamberlain, Phil	2149	1993–94	Dennis Rodman, SA	17.3
1961–62	Wilt Chamberlain, Phil	2052	1994–95	Dennis Rodman, SA	16.8
1962–63	Wilt Chamberlain, SF	1946	1995–96	Dennis Rodman, Chi	14.9
1963–64	Bill Russell, Bos	1930	1996–97	Dennis Rodman, Chi	16.1
1964–65	Bill Russell, Bos	1878	1997–98	Dennis Rodman, Chi	15.0
1965–66	Wilt Chamberlain, Phil	1943	1998–99	Chris Webber, Sac	13.0
1966–67	Wilt Chamberlain, Phil	1957	1999–00	Dikembe Mutombo, Atl	14.1
1967–68	Wilt Chamberlain, Phil	1952	2000–01	Dikembe Mutombo, Atl	13.5
1968–69	Wilt Chamberlain, LAL	1712	2001–02	Ben Wallace, Det	13.0
1969–70	Elvin Hayes, SD	*16.9	2002–03	Ben Wallace, Det	15.4
1970–71	Wilt Chamberlain, LAL	18.2	2003–04	Kevin Garnett, Min	13.9
1971–72	Wilt Chamberlain, LAL	19.2	2004–05	Kevin Garnett, Min	13.5
1972–73	Wilt Chamberlain, LAL	18.6	2005–06	Kevin Garnett, Min	12.7
1973–74	Elvin Hayes, Capital (Wash.)	18.1	2006–07	Kevin Garnett, Min	12.8
1974–75	Wes Unseld, Wash	14.8	2007–08	Dwight Howard, Orl	14.2
1975–76	Kareem Abdul-Jabbar, LAL	16.9	2008–09	Dwight Howard, Orl	13.8
1976–77	Bill Walton, Port	14.4	2009–10	Dwight Howard, Orl	12.7
1977–78	Len Robinson, NO	15.7	2010–11	Kevin Love, Min	15.2
1978–79	Moses Malone, Hou	17.6	2011–12	Dwight Howard, Orl	14.5
1979–80	Swen Nater, SD	15.0	2012–13	Dwight Howard, LAL	12.4
1980–81	Moses Malone, Hou	14.8			
1981–82	Moses Malone, Hou	14.7			

*Based on per game average since 1969–70.

Assists

1946–47	Ernie Calverly, Prov	202
1947–48	Howie Dallmar, Phil	120
1948–49	Bob Davies, Roch	321
1949–50	Dick McGuire, NY	386
1950–51	Andy Phillip, Phil	414
1951–52	Andy Phillip, Phil	539
1952–53	Bob Cousy, Bos	547
1953–54	Bob Cousy, Bos	518
1954–55	Bob Cousy, Bos	557
1955–56	Bob Cousy, Bos	642
1956–57	Bob Cousy, Bos	478
1957–58	Bob Cousy, Bos	463
1958–59	Bob Cousy, Bos	557
1959–60	Bob Cousy, Bos	715
1960–61	Oscar Robertson, Cin	690
1961–62	Oscar Robertson, Cin	899
1962–63	Guy Rodgers, SF	825
1963–64	Oscar Robertson, Cin	868
1964–65	Oscar Robertson, Cin	861
1965–66	Oscar Robertson, Cin	847
1966–67	Guy Rodgers, Chi	908
1967–68	Wilt Chamberlain, Phil	702
1968–69	Oscar Robertson, Cin	772
1969–70	Lenny Wilkens, Sea	*9.1
1970–71	Norm Van Lier, Cin	10.1
1971–72	Jerry West, LAL	9.7
1972–73	Nate Archibald, KC-Oma	11.4
1973–74	Ernie DiGregorio, Buf	8.2
1974–75	Kevin Porter, Wash	8.0
1975–76	Don Watts, Sea	8.1
1976–77	Don Buse, Ind	8.5
1977–78	Kevin Porter, NJ-Det	10.2
1978–79	Kevin Porter, Det	13.4
1979–80	Micheal Ray Richardson, NY	10.1
1980–81	Kevin Porter, Wash	9.1
1981–82	Johnny Moore, SA	9.6
1982–83	Magic Johnson, LAL	10.5
1983–84	Magic Johnson, LAL	13.1
1984–85	Isiah Thomas, Det	13.9
1985–86	Magic Johnson, LAL	12.6
1986–87	Magic Johnson, LAL	12.2
1987–88	John Stockton, Utah	13.8
1988–89	John Stockton, Utah	13.6
1989–90	John Stockton, Utah	14.5
1990–91	John Stockton, Utah	14.2
1991–92	John Stockton, Utah	13.7
1992–93	John Stockton, Utah	12.0
1993–94	John Stockton, Utah	12.6
1994–95	John Stockton, Utah	12.3
1995–96	John Stockton, Utah	11.2
1996–97	Mark Jackson, Ind	11.4
1997–98	Rod Strickland, Wash	10.5
1998–99	Jason Kidd, Phx	10.8
1999–00	Jason Kidd, Phx	10.1
2000–01	Jason Kidd, Phx	9.8
2001–02	Andre Miller, Cle	10.9
2002–03	Jason Kidd, NJ	8.9
2003–04	Jason Kidd, NJ	9.2
2004–05	Steve Nash, Phx	11.5
2005–06	Steve Nash, Phx	10.5
2006–07	Steve Nash, Phx	11.6
2007–08	Chris Paul, NO	11.6
2008–09	Chris Paul, NO	11.0
2009–10	Steve Nash, Phx	11.0
2010–11	Steve Nash, Phx	11.4
2011–12	Rajon Rondo, Bos	11.7
2012–13	Rajon Rondo, Bos	11.1

*Based on per game average since 1969–70.

Free-Throw Percentage

1946–47	Fred Scolari, Wash	81.1
1947–48	Bob Feerick, Wash	78.8
1948–49	Bob Feerick, Wash	85.9
1949–50	Max Zaslofsky, Chi	84.3
1950–51	Joe Fulks, Phil	85.5
1951–52	Bob Wanzer, Roch	90.4
1952–53	Bill Sharman, Bos	85.0
1953–54	Bill Sharman, Bos	84.4
1954–55	Bill Sharman, Bos	89.7
1955–56	Bill Sharman, Bos	86.7
1956–57	Bill Sharman, Bos	90.5
1957–58	Dolph Schayes, Syr	90.4
1958–59	Bill Sharman, Bos	93.2
1959–60	Dolph Schayes, Syr	89.3
1960–61	Bill Sharman, Bos	92.1
1961–62	Dolph Schayes, Syr	89.7
1962–63	Larry Costello, Syr	88.1
1963–64	Oscar Robertson, Cin	85.3
1964–65	Larry Costello, Phil	87.7
1965–66	Larry Siegfried, Bos	88.1
1966–67	Adrian Smith, Cin	90.3
1967–68	Oscar Robertson, Cin	87.3
1968–69	Larry Siegfried, Bos	86.4
1969–70	Flynn Robinson, Mil	89.8
1970–71	Chet Walker, Chi	85.9
1971–72	Jack Marin, Balt	89.4
1972–73	Rick Barry, GS	90.2
1973–74	Ernie DiGregorio, Buf	90.2
1974–75	Rick Barry, GS	90.4
1975–76	Rick Barry, GS	92.3
1976–77	Ernie DiGregorio, Buf	94.5
1977–78	Rick Barry, GS	92.4
1978–79	Rick Barry, Hou	94.7
1979–80	Rick Barry, Hou	93.5
1980–81	Calvin Murphy, Hou	95.8
1981–82	Kyle Macy, Phx	89.9
1982–83	Calvin Murphy, Hou	92.0
1983–84	Larry Bird, Bos	88.8
1984–85	Kyle Macy, Phx	90.7
1985–86	Larry Bird, Bos	89.6
1986–87	Larry Bird, Bos	91.0
1987–88	Jack Sikma, Mil	92.2
1988–89	Magic Johnson, LAL	91.1
1989–90	Larry Bird, Bos	93.0
1990–91	Reggie Miller, Ind	91.8
1991–92	Mark Price, Clev	94.7
1992–93	Mark Price, Clev	94.8
1993–94	Mahmoud Abdul-Rauf, Den	95.6
1994–95	Spud Webb, Sac	93.4
1995–96	Mahmoud Abdul-Rauf, Den	93.0
1996–97	Mark Price, GS	90.6
1997–98	Chris Mullin, Ind	93.9
1998–99	Reggie Miller, Ind	91.5
1999–00	Jeff Hornacek, Utah	95.0
2000–01	Reggie Miller, Ind	92.8
2001–02	Reggie Miller, Ind	91.1
2002–03	Allan Houston, NY	91.9
2003–04	Peja Stojakovic, Sac	92.7
2004–05	Reggie Miller, Ind	93.3
2005–06	Steve Nash, Phx	92.1
2006–07	Kyle Korver, Phil	91.4
2007–08	Peja Stojakovic, NO	92.9
2008–09	Jose Calderon, Tor	98.1
2009–10	Steve Nash, Phx	93.8
2010–11	Stephen Curry, GS	93.4
2011–12	Jamal Crawford, Por	92.7
2012–13	Kevin Durant, OKC	90.5

Field-Goal Percentage

1946–47	Bob Feerick, Wash	40.1	1980–81	Artis Gilmore, Chi	67.0
1947–48	Bob Feerick, Wash	34.0	1981–82	Artis Gilmore, Chi	65.2
1948–49	Arnie Risen, Roch	42.3	1982–83	Artis Gilmore, SA	62.6
1949–50	Alex Groza, Ind	47.8	1983–84	Artis Gilmore, SA	63.1
1950–51	Alex Groza, Ind	47.0	1984–85	James Donaldson, LAC	63.7
1951–52	Paul Arizin, Phil	44.8	1985–86	Steve Johnson, SA	63.2
1952–53	Neil Johnston, Phil	45.2	1986–87	Kevin McHale, Bos	60.4
1953–54	Ed Macauley, Bos	48.6	1987–88	Kevin McHale, Bos	60.4
1954–55	Larry Foust, FW	48.7	1988–89	Dennis Rodman, Det	59.5
1955–56	Neil Johnston, Phil	45.7	1989–90	Mark West, Phx	62.5
1956–57	Neil Johnston, Phil	44.7	1990–91	Buck Williams, Port	60.2
1957–58	Jack Twyman, Cin	45.2	1991–92	Buck Williams, Port	60.4
1958–59	Ken Sears, NY	49.0	1992–93	Cedric Ceballos, Phx	57.6
1959–60	Ken Sears, NY	47.7	1993–94	Shaquille O'Neal, Orl	59.9
1960–61	Wilt Chamberlain, Phil	50.9	1994–95	Chris Gatling, GS	63.3
1961–62	Walt Bellamy, Chi	51.9	1995–96	Gheorghe Muresan, Wash	58.4
1962–63	Wilt Chamberlain, SF	52.8	1996–97	Gheorghe Muresan, Wash	60.4
1963–64	Jerry Lucas, Cin	52.7	1997–98	Shaquille O'Neal, LAL	58.4
1964–65	Wilt Chamberlain, SF-Phil	51.0	1998–99	Shaquille O'Neal, LAL	57.6
1965–66	Wilt Chamberlain, Phil	54.0	1999–00	Shaquille O'Neal, LAL	57.4
1966–67	Wilt Chamberlain, Phil	68.3	2000–01	Shaquille O'Neal, LAL	57.2
1967–68	Wilt Chamberlain, Phil	59.5	2001–02	Shaquille O'Neal, LAL	57.9
1968–69	Wilt Chamberlain, LAL	58.3	2002–03	Eddy Curry, Chi	58.5
1969–70	Johnny Green, Cin	55.9	2003–04	Shaquille O'Neal, LAL	58.4
1970–71	Johnny Green, Cin	58.7	2004–05	Shaquille O'Neal, Mia	60.1
1971–72	Wilt Chamberlain, LAL	64.9	2005–06	Shaquille O'Neal, Mia	60.0
1972–73	Wilt Chamberlain, LAL	72.7	2006–07	Mikki Moore, NJ	60.9
1973–74	Bob McAdoo, Buf	54.7	2007–08	Andris Biedrins, GS	62.6
1974–75	Don Nelson, Bos	53.9	2008–09	Erick Dampier, Dal	65.0
1975–76	Wes Unseld, Wash	56.1	2009–10	Erick Dampier, Dal	62.4
1976–77	Kareem Abdul-Jabbar, LAL	57.9	2010–11	Nene Hilario, Den	61.5
1977–78	Bobby Jones, Den	57.8	2011–12	Dwight Howard, Orl	57.3
1978–79	Cedric Maxwell, Bos	58.4	2012–13	DeAndre Jordan, LAC	64.3
1979–80	Cedric Maxwell, Bos	60.9			

Three-Point Field-Goal Percentage

1979–80	Fred Brown, Sea	44.3	1996–97	Glen Rice, Cha	47.0
1980–81	Brian Taylor, SD	38.3	1997–98	Dale Ellis, Sea	46.0
1981–82	Campy Russell, NY	43.9	1998–99	Dell Curry, Cha	47.6
1982–83	Mike Dunleavy, SA	34.5	1999–00	Hubert Davis, Dal	49.1
1983–84	Darrell Griffith, Utah	36.1	2000–01	Brent Barry, Sea	47.6
1984–85	Byron Scott, LAL	43.3	2001–02	Steve Smith, SA	47.2
1985–86	Craig Hodges, Mil	45.1	2002–03	Bruce Bowen, SA	44.1
1986–87	Kiki Vandeweghe, Port	48.1	2003–04	Anthony Peeler, Sac	48.2
1987–88	Craig Hodges, Mil-Phx	49.1	2004–05	Fred Hoiberg, Min	48.3
1988–89	Jon Sundvold, Mia	52.2	2005–06	Richard Hamilton, Det	45.8
1989–90	Steve Kerr, Clev	50.7	2006–07	Jason Kapono, Mia	51.4
1990–91	Jim Les, Sac	46.1	2007–08	Jason Kapono, Tor	48.3
1991–92	Dana Barros, Sea	44.6	2008–09	Anthony Morrow, GS	46.7
1992–93	Chris Mullin, GS	45.1	2009–10	Mike Miller, Wash	48.0
1993–94	Tracy Murray, Port	45.9	2010–11	Matt Bonner, SA	45.7
1994–95	Steve Kerr, Chi	52.4	2011–12	Steve Novak, NY	47.2
1995–96	Tim Legler, Wash	52.2	2012–13	Jose Calderon, Det/Tor	46.1

Steals

1973–74	Larry Steele, Port	2.68	1986–87	Alvin Robertson, SA	3.21
1974–75	Rick Barry, GS	2.85	1987–88	Michael Jordan, Chi	3.16
1975–76	Don Watts, Sea	3.18	1988–89	John Stockton, Utah	3.21
1976–77	Don Buse, Ind	3.47	1989–90	Michael Jordan, Chi	2.77
1977–78	Ron Lee, Phx	2.74	1990–91	Alvin Robertson, Mil	3.04
1978–79	M.L. Carr, Det	2.46	1991–92	John Stockton, Utah	2.98
1979–80	Micheal Ray Richardson, NY	3.23	1992–93	Michael Jordan, Chi	2.83
1980–81	Magic Johnson, LAL	3.43	1993–94	Nate McMillan, Sea	2.96
1981–82	Magic Johnson, LAL	2.67	1994–95	Scottie Pippen, Chi	2.94
1982–83	Micheal Ray Richardson, GS-NJ	2.84	1995–96	Gary Payton, Sea	2.85
1983–84	Rickey Green, Utah	2.65	1996–97	Mookie Blaylock, Atl	2.72
1984–85	Micheal Ray Richardson, NJ	2.96	1997–98	Mookie Blaylock, Atl	2.61
1985–86	Alvin Robertson, SA	3.67	1998–99	Kendall Gill, NJ	2.68

Steals (Cont.)

1999–00	Eddie Jones, Cha	2.67	2006–07	Baron Davis, GS	2.14
2000–01	Allen Iverson, Phil	2.51	2007–08	Chris Paul, NO	2.71
2001–02	Allen Iverson, Phil	2.80	2008–09	Chris Paul, NO	2.77
2002–03	Allen Iverson, Phil	2.74	2009–10	Rajon Rondo, Bos	2.33
2003–04	Baron Davis, NO	2.36	2010–11	Chris Paul, NO	2.35
2004–05	Larry Hughes, Wash	2.89	2011–12	Chris Paul, LAC	2.53
2005–06	Gerald Wallace, Cha	2.51	2012–13	Chris Paul, LAC	2.41

Blocked Shots

1973–74	Elmore Smith, LAL	4.85	1993–94	Dikembe Mutombo, Den	4.10
1974–75	Kareem Abdul-Jabbar, Mil	3.26	1994–95	Dikembe Mutombo, Den	3.91
1975–76	Kareem Abdul-Jabbar, LAL	4.12	1995–96	Dikembe Mutombo, Den	4.49
1976–77	Bill Walton, Port	3.25	1996–97	Shawn Bradley, NJ	3.40
1977–78	George Johnson, NJ	3.38	1997–98	Marcus Camby, Tor	3.65
1978–79	Kareem Abdul-Jabbar, LAL	3.95	1998–99	Alonzo Mourning, Mia	3.91
1979–80	Kareem Abdul-Jabbar, LAL	3.41	1999–00	Alonzo Mourning, Mia	3.72
1980–81	George Johnson, SA	3.39	2000–01	Theo Ratliff, Phil/Atl	3.74
1981–82	George Johnson, SA	3.12	2001–02	Ben Wallace, Det	3.48
1982–83	Wayne Rollins, Atl	4.29	2002–03	Theo Ratliff, Atl	3.23
1983–84	Mark Eaton, Utah	4.28	2003–04	Theo Ratliff, Port	3.61
1984–85	Mark Eaton, Utah	5.56	2004–05	Andrei Kirilenko, Utah	3.32
1985–86	Manute Bol, Wash	4.96	2005–06	Marcus Camby, Den	3.29
1986–87	Mark Eaton, Utah	4.06	2006–07	Marcus Camby, Den	3.30
1987–88	Mark Eaton, Utah	3.71	2007–08	Marcus Camby, Den	3.61
1988–89	Manute Bol, GS	4.31	2008–09	Dwight Howard, Orl	2.92
1989–90	Hakeem Olajuwon, Hou	4.59	2009–10	Dwight Howard, Orl	2.78
1990–91	Hakeem Olajuwon, Hou	3.95	2010–11	Andrew Bogut, Mil	2.58
1991–92	David Robinson, SA	4.49	2011–12	Serge Ibaka, OKC	3.65
1992–93	Hakeem Olajuwon, Hou	4.17	2012–13	Serge Ibaka, OKC	3.03

NBA All-Star Game Results

Year	Result	Site	Winning Coach	Most Valuable Player
1951	East 111, West 94	Boston	Joe Lapchick	Ed Macauley, Bos
1952	East 108, West 91	Boston	Al Cervi	Paul Arizin, Phil
1953	West 79, East 75	Ft Wayne	John Kundla	George Mikan, Min
1954	East 98, West 93 (OT)	New York	Joe Lapchick	Bob Cousy, Bos
1955	East 100, West 91	New York	Al Cervi	Bill Sharman, Bos
1956	West 108, East 94	Rochester	Charley Eckman	Bob Pettit, StL
1957	East 109, West 97	Boston	Red Auerbach	Bob Cousy, Bos
1958	East 130, West 118	St Louis	Red Auerbach	Bob Pettit, StL
1959	West 124, East 108	Detroit	Ed Macauley	B. Pettit, StL/ E. Baylor, Min
1960	East 125, West 115	Philadelphia	Red Auerbach	Wilt Chamberlain, Phil
1961	West 153, East 131	Syracuse	Paul Seymour	Oscar Robertson, Cin
1962	West 150, East 130	St Louis	Fred Schaus	Bob Pettit, StL
1963	East 115, West 108	Los Angeles	Red Auerbach	Bill Russell, Bos
1964	East 111, West 107	Boston	Red Auerbach	Oscar Robertson, Cin
1965	East 124, West 123	St Louis	Red Auerbach	Jerry Lucas, Cin
1966	East 137, West 94	Cincinnati	Red Auerbach	Adrian Smith, Cin
1967	West 135, East 120	San Francisco	Fred Schaus	Rick Barry, SF
1968	East 144, West 124	New York	Alex Hannum	Hal Greer, Phil
1969	East 123, West 112	Baltimore	Gene Shue	Oscar Robertson, Cin
1970	East 142, West 135	Philadelphia	Red Holzman	Willis Reed, NY
1971	West 108, East 107	San Diego	Larry Costello	Lenny Wilkens, Sea
1972	West 112, East 110	Los Angeles	Bill Sharman	Jerry West, LA
1973	East 104, West 84	Chicago	Tom Heinsohn	Dave Cowens, Bos
1974	West 134, East 123	Seattle	Larry Costello	Bob Lanier, Det
1975	East 108, West 102	Phoenix	K.C. Jones	Walt Frazier, NY
1976	East 123, West 109	Philadelphia	Tom Heinsohn	Dave Bing, Wash
1977	West 125, East 124	Milwaukee	Larry Brown	Julius Erving, Phil
1978	East 133, West 125	Atlanta	Billy Cunningham	Randy Smith, Buff
1979	West 134, East 129	Detroit	Lenny Wilkens	David Thompson, Den
1980	East 144, West 135 (OT)	Washington	Billy Cunningham	George Gervin, SA
1981	East 123, West 120	Cleveland	Billy Cunningham	Nate Archibald, Bos
1982	East 120, West 118	New Jersey	Bill Fitch	Larry Bird, Bos
1983	East 132, West 123	Los Angeles	Billy Cunningham	Julius Erving, Phil
1984	East 154, West 145 (OT)	Denver	K.C. Jones	Isiah Thomas, Det
1985	West 140, East 129	Indiana	Pat Riley	Ralph Sampson, Hou

Year	Result	Site	Winning Coach	Most Valuable Player
1986	East 139, West 132	Dallas	K.C. Jones	Isiah Thomas, Det
1987	West 154, East 149 (OT)	Seattle	Pat Riley	Tom Chambers, Sea
1988	East 138, West 133	Chicago	Mike Fratello	Michael Jordan, Chi
1989	West 143, East 134	Houston	Pat Riley	Karl Malone, Utah
1990	East 130, West 113	Miami	Chuck Daly	Magic Johnson, LAL
1991	East 116, West 114	Charlotte	Chris Ford	Charles Barkley, Phil
1992	West 153, East 113	Orlando	Don Nelson	Magic Johnson, LAL
1993	West 135, East 132	Salt Lake City	Paul Westphal	K. Malone/J. Stockton, Utah
1994	East 127, West 118	Minneapolis	Lenny Wilkens	Scottie Pippen, Chi
1995	West 139, East 112	Phoenix	Paul Westphal	Mitch Richmond, Sac
1996	East 129, West 118	San Antonio	Phil Jackson	Michael Jordan, Chi
1997	East 132, West 120	Cleveland	Doug Collins	Glen Rice, Cha
1998	East 135, West 114	New York	Larry Bird	Michael Jordan, Chi
1999	Cancelled due to lockout.			
2000	West 137, East 126	Oakland	Phil Jackson	S. O'Neal, LAL/T. Duncan, SA
2001	East 111, West 110	Washington	Larry Brown	Allen Iverson, Phi
2002	West 135, East 120	Philadelphia	Don Nelson	Kobe Bryant, LAL
2003	West 155, East 145 (2OT)	Atlanta	Rick Adelman	Kevin Garnett, Min
2004	West 136, East 132	Los Angeles	Flip Saunders	Shaquille O'Neal, LAL
2005	East 125, West 115	Denver	Stan Van Gundy	Allen Iverson, Phi
2006	East 122, West 120	Houston	Flip Saunders	LeBron James, Cle
2007	West 153, East 132	Las Vegas	Mike D'Antoni	Kobe Bryant, LAL
2008	East 134, West 128	New Orleans	Doc Rivers	LeBron James, Cle
2009	West 146, East 119	Phoenix	Phil Jackson	K. Bryant, LAL/S. O'Neal, Phx
2010	East 141, West 139	Dallas	Stan Van Gundy	Dwyane Wade, Mia
2011	West 148, East 143	Los Angeles	Gregg Popovich	Kobe Bryant, LAL
2012	West 152, East 149	Orlando	Scott Brooks	Kevin Durant, OKC
2013	West 143, East 138	Houston	Gregg Popovich	Chris Paul, LAC

Members of the Basketball Hall of Fame

Contributors

Senda Abbott (1984)
Don Barksdale (2012)
Clair F. Bee (1967)
Danny Biasone (2000)
Hubie Brown (2005)
Walter A. Brown (1965)
John W. Bunn (1964)
Jerry Buss (2010)
Jerry Colangelo (2004)
William Davidson (2008)
Bob Douglas (1971)
Al Duer (1981)
Wayne Embry (1999)
Clifford Fagan (1983)
Harry A. Fisher (1973)
Larry Fleisher (1991)
Dave Gavitt (2006)
Edward Gottlieb (1971)
Russ Granik (2013)
Luther H. Gulick (1959)

Lester Harrison (1979)
Chick Hearn (2003)
E.B. Henderson (2013)
Ferenc Hepp (1980)
Edward J. Hickox (1959)
Paul D. (Tony) Hinkle (1965)
Ned Irish (1964)
R. William Jones (1964)
J. Walter Kennedy (1980)
Phil Knight (2012)
Meadowlark Lemon (2003)
Emil S. Liston (1974)
Earl Lloyd (2003)
Bill Mokray (1965)
Ralph Morgan (1959)
Frank Morgenweck (1962)
James Naismith (1959)
C.M. Newton (2000)
John J. O'Brien (1961)
Larry O'Brien (1991)

Harold G. Olsen (1959)
Maurice Podoloff (1973)
H.V. Porter (1960)
William A. Reid (1963)
Elmer Ripley (1972)
Lynn W. St. John (1962)
Tom (Satch) Sanders (2011)
Abe Saperstein (1970)
Arthur A. Schabinger (1961)
Amos Alonzo Stagg (1959)
Boris Stankovic (1991)
Edward Steitz (1983)
Chuck Taylor (1968)
Bertha F. Teague (1984)
Oswald Tower (1959)
Arthur L. Trester (1961)
Dick Vitale (2008)
Clifford Wells (1971)
Lou Wilke (1982)
Fred Zollner (1999)

Players

Kareem Abdul-Jabbar (1995)
Nate (Tiny) Archibald (1991)
Paul J. Arizin (1977)
Charles Barkley (2006)
Thomas B. Barlow (1980)
Rick Barry (1987)
Elgin Baylor (1976)
John Beckman (1972)
Walt Bellamy (1993)
Sergei Belov (1992)
Dave Bing (1990)
Larry Bird (1998)
Carol Blazejowski (1994)
Bennie Borgmann (1961)

Bill Bradley (1982)
Joseph Brennan (1974)
Roger Brown (2013)
Al Cervi (1984)
Wilt Chamberlain (1978)
Charles (Tarzan) Cooper (1976)
Cynthia Cooper (2010)
Kresimir Cosic (1996)
Bob Cousy (1970)
Dave Cowens (1991)
Joan Crawford (1997)
Billy Cunningham (1986)
Denise Curry (1997)
Drazen Dalipagic (2004)

Mel Daniels (2012)
Adrian Dantley (2008)
Bob Davies (1969)
Forrest S. DeBernardi (1961)
Dave DeBusschere (1982)
H.G. (Dutch) Dehnert (1968)
Anne Donovan (1995)
Clyde Drexler (2004)
Joe Dumars (2006)
Teresa Edwards (2011)
Paul Endacott (1971)
Alex English (1997)
Julius Erving (1993)
Patrick Ewing (2008)

Players *(Cont.)*

Harold (Bud) Foster (1964)
Walter (Clyde) Frazier (1987)
Max (Marty) Friedman (1971)
Joe Fulks (1977)
Lauren (Laddie) Gale (1976)
Harry (the Horse) Gallatin (1991)
William Gates (1989)
George Gervin (1996)
Artis Gilmore (2011)
Tom Gola (1975)
Gail Goodrich (1996)
Hal Greer (1981)
Robert (Ace) Gruenig (1963)
Richard Guerin (2013)
Clifford O. Hagan (1977)
Victor Hanson (1960)
Lusia Harris-Stewart (1992)
John Havlicek (1983)
Connie Hawkins (1992)
Elvin Hayes (1990)
Marques Haynes (1998)
Tom Heinsohn (1986)
Nat Holman (1964)
Robert J. Houbregs (1987)
Bailey Howell (1997)
Chuck Hyatt (1959)
Dan Issel (1993)
Harry (Buddy) Jeannette (1994)
Dennis Johnson (2010)
Earvin (Magic) Johnson (2002)
Gus Johnson (2010)
William C. Johnson (1976)
D. Neil Johnston (1990)
K.C. Jones (1989)
Sam Jones (1983)
Michael Jordan (2009)
Bernard King (2013)
Edward (Moose) Krause (1975)
Bob Kurland (1961)
Bob Lanier (1992)
Joe Lapchick (1966)

Nancy Lieberman-Cline (1996)
Clyde Lovellette (1988)
Jerry Lucas (1979)
Angelo (Hank) Luisetti (1959)
C. Edward Macauley (1960)
Karl Malone (2010)
Moses Malone (2001)
Peter P. Maravich (1987)
Hortencia Marcari (2005)
Slater Martin (1981)
Bob McAdoo (2000)
Katrina McClain (2012)
Branch McCracken (1960)
Jack McCracken (1962)
Bobby McDermott (1988)
Dick McGuire (1993)
Kevin McHale (1999)
Dino Meneghin (2003)
Ann Meyers (1993)
George L. Mikan (1959)
Vern Mikkelsen (1995)
Cheryl Miller (1995)
Reggie Miller (2012)
Earl Monroe (1990)
Chris Mullin (2011)
Calvin Murphy (1993)
Charles (Stretch) Murphy (1960)
Hakeem Olajuwon (2008)
H.O. (Pat) Page (1962)
Robert Parish (2003)
Gary Payton (2013)
Maciel (Ubiratan) Pereira (2010)
Drazen Petrovic (2002)
Bob Pettit (1970)
Andy Phillip (1961)
Scottie Pippen (2010)
Jim Pollard (1977)
Frank Ramsey (1981)
Willis Reed (1981)
Arnie Risen (1998)
Oscar Robertson (1979)

David Robinson (2009)
Dennis Rodman (2011)
John S. Roosma (1961)
Bill Russell (1974)
John (Honey) Russell (1964)
Arvydas Sabonis (2011)
Ralph Sampson (2012)
Adolph Schayes (1972)
Ernest J. Schmidt (1973)
Oscar Schmidt (2013)
John J. Schommer (1959)
Barney Sedran (1962)
Uljana Semjonova (1993)
Bill Sharman (1975)
Dawn Staley (2013)
Christian Steinmetz (1961)
John Stockton (2009)
Maurice Stokes (2004)
Reece (Goose) Tatum (2011)
Isiah Thomas (2000)
David Thompson (1996)
John A. (Cat) Thompson (1962)
Nate Thurmond (1984)
Jack Twyman (1982)
Wes Unseld (1988)
Robert (Fuzzy) Vandivier (1974)
Edward A. Wachter (1961)
Chet Walker (2012)
Bill Walton (1993)
Robert F. Wanzer (1987)
Jerry West (1979)
Nera White (1992)
Lenny Wilkens (1989)
Jamaal Wilkes (2012)
Dominique Wilkins (2006)
Lynette Woodard (2004)
John R. Wooden (1960)
James Worthy (2003)
George (Bird) Yardley (1996)

Coaches

Lidia Alexeeva (2012)
Forest C. (Phog) Allen (1959)
Harold Anderson (1984)
Red Auerbach (1968)
Geno Auriemma (2006)
Leon Barmore (2003)
Sam Barry (1978)
Ernest A. Blood (1960)
Jim Boeheim (2005)
Larry Brown (2002)
Jim Calhoun (2005)
Howard G. Cann (1967)
H. Clifford Carlson (1959)
Lou Carnesecca (1992)
Ben Carnevale (1969)
Pete Carril (1997)
Everett Case (1981)
Van Chancellor (2007)
John Chaney (2001)
Jody Conradt (1998)
Denny Crum (1994)
Chuck Daly (1994)
Everett S. Dean (1966)
Antonio Diaz-Miguel (1997)
Edgar A. Diddle (1971)

Bruce Drake (1972)
Pedro Ferrandiz (2007)
Sandro Gamba (2006)
Clarence Gaines (1981)
Jack Gardner (1983)
Amory T. (Slats) Gill (1967)
Aleksandr Gomelsky (1995)
Sue Gunter (2005)
Alex Hannum (1998)
Marv Harshman (1984)
Don Haskins (1997)
Sylvia Hatchell (2013)
Edgar S. Hickey (1978)
Howard A. Hobson (1965)
Red Holzman (1986)
Bob Hurley Sr. (2010)
Hank Iba (1968)
Phil Jackson (2007)
Alvin F. (Doggie) Julian (1967)
Frank W. Keaney (1960)
George E. Keogan (1961)
Bob Knight (1991)
Mike Krzyzewski (2001)
John Kundla (1995)
Ward L. Lambert (1960)
Guy V. Lewis (2013)

Harry Litwack (1975)
Kenneth D. Loeffler (1964)
A.C. (Dutch) Lonborg (1972)
John B. McLendon (1978)
Arad A. McCutchan (1980)
Herb Magee (2011)
Al McGuire (1992)
Frank McGuire (1976)
Walter E. Meanwell (1959)
Raymond J. Meyer (1978)
Ralph Miller (1988)
Billie Moore (1999)
Don Nelson (2012)
Peter F. Newell (1978)
Aleksandar Nikolic (1998)
Mirko Novosel (2007)
Lute Olson (2002)
Rick Pitino (2013)
Jack Ramsay (1992)
Pat Riley (2008)
Cesare Rubini (1994)
Adolph F. Rupp (1968)
Cathy Rush (2008)
Leonard D. Sachs (1961)
Bill Sharman (2004)
Everett F. Shelton (1979)

Note: Year of election in parentheses.

Coaches (Cont.)

Jerry Sloan (2009)
Dean Smith (1982)
C. Vivian Stringer (2009)
Pat Summitt (2000)
Jerry Tarkanian (2013)
Fred R. Taylor (1985)

John Thompson (1999)
Tara VanDerveer (2011)
Margaret Wade (1984)
Stanley H. Watts (1985)
Lenny Wilkens (1998)
Roy Williams (2007)

Tex Winter (2011)
John R. Wooden (1972)
Morgan Wooten (2000)
Phil Woolpert (1992)
Kay Yow (2002)

Referees

James E. Enright (1978)
George T. Hepbron (1960)
George Hoyt (1961)
Matthew P. Kennedy (1959)
Lloyd Leith (1982)
Zigmund J. Mihalik (1985)
Hank Nichols (2012)

John P. Nucatola (1977)
Ernest C. Quigley (1961)
Marvin Rudolph (2007)
J. Dallas Shirley (1979)
Earl Strom (1995)
David Tobey (1961)
David H. Walsh (1961)

Teams

1960 USA Olympic Team (2010)
1966 Texas Western (2007)
1992 USA Olympic "Dream" Team (2010)
All American Redheads (2012)
Buffalo Germans (1961)
First Team (1959)
Harlem Globetrotters (2002)
New York Renaissance (1963)
Original Celtics (1959)

Note: Year of election in parentheses.

American Basketball Association (ABA)

Champions

Year	Champion	Series	Runner-up	Winning Coach
1968	Pittsburgh Pipers	4–3	New Orleans Bucs	Vince Cazetta
1969	Oakland Oaks	4–1	Indiana Pacers	Alex Hannum
1970	Indiana Pacers	4–2	Los Angeles Stars	Bob Leonard
1971	Utah Stars	4–3	Kentucky Colonels	Bill Sharman
1972	Indiana Pacers	4–2	New York Nets	Bob Leonard
1973	Indiana Pacers	4–3	Kentucky Colonels	Bob Leonard
1974	New York Nets	4–1	Utah Stars	Kevin Loughery
1975	Kentucky Colonels	4–1	Indiana Pacers	Hubie Brown
1976	New York Nets	4–2	Denver Nuggets	Kevin Loughery

ABA Postseason Awards

Most Valuable Player

1967–68 ....Connie Hawkins, Pitt
1968–69 ....Mel Daniels, Ind
1969–70 ....Spencer Haywood, Den
1970–71 ....Mel Daniels, Ind
1971–72 ....Artis Gilmore, Ken
1972–73 ....Billy Cunningham, Car
1973–74 ....Julius Erving, NY
1974–75 ....Julius Erving, NY
George McGinnis, Ind
1975–76 ....Julius Erving, NY

Rookie of the Year

1967–68 ....Mel Daniels, Minn
1968–69 ....Warren Armstrong, Oak
1969–70 ....Spencer Haywood, Den
1970–71 ....Dan Issel, Ken
Charlie Scott, Vir
1971–72 ....Artis Gilmore, Ken
1972–73 ....Brian Taylor, NY
1973–74 ....Swen Nater, SA
1974–75 ....Marvin Barnes, StL
1975–76 ....David Thompson, Den

Coach of the Year

1967–68 ....Vince Cazetta, Pitt
1968–69 ....Alex Hannum, Oak
1969–70 ....Joe Belmont, Den
Bill Sharman, LA
1970–71 ....Al Bianchi, Vir
1971–72 ....Tom Nissalke, Dal
1972–73 ....Larry Brown, Car
1973–74 ....Babe McCarthy, Ken
Joe Mullaney, Utah
1974–75 ....Larry Brown, Den
1975–76 ....Larry Brown, Den

ABA Season Leaders

Scoring

	GP	Pts	Avg
1967–68...Connie Hawkins, Pitt	70	1875	26.8
1968–69...Rick Barry, Oak	35	1190	34.0
1969–70...Spencer Haywood, Den	84	2519	30.0
1970–71...Dan Issel, Ken	83	2480	29.9
1971–72...Charlie Scott, Vir	79	2637	33.4
1972–73...Julius Erving, Vir	71	2268	31.9
1973–74...Julius Erving, NY	84	2299	27.4
1974–75...George McGinnis, Ind	79	2353	29.8
1975–76...Julius Erving, NY	84	2462	29.3

Rebounds

1967–68................Mel Daniels, Minn	15.6
1968–69................Mel Daniels, Ind	16.5
1969–70................Spencer Haywood, Den	19.5
1970–71................Mel Daniels, Ind	18.0
1971–72................Artis Gilmore, Ken	17.8
1972–73................Artis Gilmore, Ken	17.6
1973–74................Artis Gilmore, Ken	18.3
1974–75................Swen Nater, SA	16.4
1975–76................Artis Gilmore, Ken	15.5

Assists

1967–68................Larry Brown, NO	6.5
1968–69................Larry Brown, Oak	7.1
1969–70................Larry Brown, Wash	7.1
1970–71................Bill Melchionni, NY	8.3
1971–72................Bill Melchionni, NY	8.4
1972–73................Bill Melchionni, NY	7.4
1973–74................Al Smith, Den	8.2
1974–75................Mack Calvin, Den	7.7
1975–76................Don Buse, Ind	8.2

Steals

1973–74................Ted McClain, Car	2.98
1974–75................Brian Taylor, NY	2.80
1975–76................Don Buse, Ind	4.12

Blocked Shots

1973–74................Caldwell Jones, SD	4.00
1974–75................Caldwell Jones, SD	3.24
1975–76................Billy Paultz, SA	3.05

World Championship of Basketball

Year	Winner	Runner-Up	Score	Site
1950	Argentina	United States	†	Buenos Aires
1954	United States	Brazil	†	Rio de Janeiro
1959	Brazil	United States	†	Santiago, Chile
1963	Brazil	Yugoslavia	†	Rio de Janeiro
1967	Soviet Union	Yugoslavia	†	Montevideo, Uruguay
1970	Yugoslavia	Brazil	†	Ljubljana, Yugoslavia
1974	Soviet Union	Yugoslavia	†	San Juan
1978	Yugoslavia	Soviet Union	82–81 (OT)	Manila
1982	Soviet Union	United States	95–94	Cali, Colombia
1986	United States	Soviet Union	87–85	Madrid
1990	Yugoslavia	Soviet Union	92–75	Buenos Aires
*1994	United States	Russia	137–91	Toronto
†1998	Yugoslavia	Russia	64–62	Athens
2002	Yugoslavia	Argentina	84–77 (OT)	Indianapolis
2006	Spain	Greece	70–47	Saitama, Japan
2010	United States	Turkey	81–64	Istanbul, Turkey

*U.S. professionals began competing in 1994. †In 1998, a labor dispute resulted in a boycott of the World Championship by NBA stars; the U.S. roster was filled by members of the CBA and European professional leagues and college players.
†Result determined by overall record in final round of competition.

Luke Hancock and Peyton Siva jumped for joy—literally—after Louisville's 82–76 win over Michigan for the NCAA title

College Basketball

Winning For Ware

Inspired by a fallen teammate, the Louisville Cardinals gutted out one win after another, including a tense and entertaining victory over Michigan in the title game

BY B.J. SCHECTER

IN EVERY SEASON THERE ARE defining moments that are etched in our minds, events that transcend the box score and overshadow anything that has occurred before and after the event. When one looks back on the 2012–13 college basketball season, the first thing to come to mind will not be Louisville's epic championship game victory over Michigan, or the Cardinals' hard-fought win over hardscrabble Wichita State in the national semifinal. It will be the unforgettable image of Louisville reserve guard Kevin Ware lying on the floor, writhing in pain, his right leg protruding through his skin.

It was early in the first half of the Midwest Regional final against Duke in Indianapolis when Ware sprinted after a loose ball in front of the Louisville bench and leaped in an effort to save it. He landed at a bad angle and his leg snapped as he screamed in pain. Ware's coaches and teammates watched in horror (Coach Rick Pitino later admitted he nearly threw up)— as did millions of viewers at home when CBS showed the replay of the gruesome event—and immediately the Cardinals became emotional. "No!" screamed forward Chane Behanan, Ware's best friend on the team. Star guard Russ Smith began crying uncontrollably and forward Luke Hancock said, "The whole crowd turned white."

Ware's mother, Lisa Junior, was watching the game with a group of people at a friend's house outside of Atlanta when she saw the replay and completely "lost it." Feeling helpless she imagined the worst and wanted nothing more than to rush to her son's side. The feeling got worse as the minutes dragged on until Ware's girlfriend, Brittany Kelly, who was at the game and came down to the court, called from the ambulance and said that Kevin was okay and would likely need surgery that night to repair a broken tibia.

Out on the court, things were more frantic as Louisville players and coaches tried to process what had just happened. As the Cardinals grew more and more emotional, Hancock rushed to Ware's side, covered his leg and told him he was going to be fine. As soon as the initial shock wore off, Ware called his teammates over. Smith and guard Peyton Siva held Ware's hand as everyone gathered around their fallen teammate.

"Just go win this game for me," Ware said. "Don't worry about me. I'm fine. Just go win this game."

At the time Ware was wheeled off the

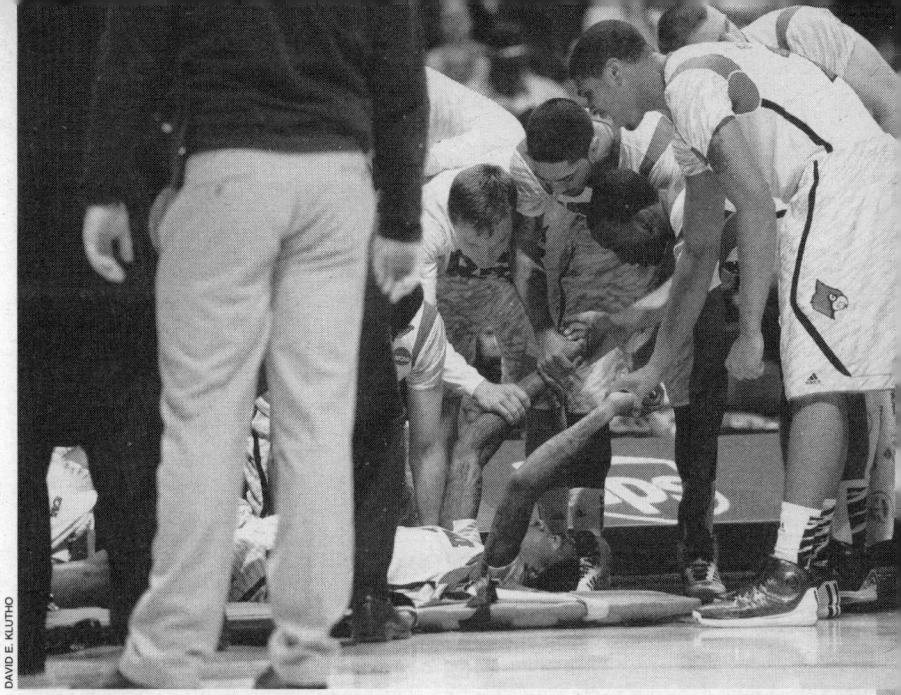

"Just go win this game," Ware told his stunned teammates after his gruesome injury; his team-first example inspired the Cardinals throughout their remarkable run.

court, Louisville led by a single point and the Cardinals sleepwalked through the rest of the half and somehow took a 35–32 lead into the break. "I think we were still in such shock," said Hancock. Pitino tried to calm the team down in the locker room, telling them if they let up for a second "then Kevin Ware doesn't mean how much he means to us."

Louisville came out in the second half with a purpose—to win the game for Ware and get him back home to Atlanta for the Final Four—and blew Duke off the floor, outscoring the Blue Devils 50–31 in the final 20 minutes. As the Cardinals prepared to cut down the nets, Pitino grabbed the microphone and addressed the crowd: "For about two minutes, can we all start chanting Kevin?" he said.

The fans happily obliged, and the Cardinals made sure that the net and Midwest Regional championship trophy were wait-ing for Ware in his hospital room when he came out of surgery at about 10 p.m. that night. In the jubilant locker room, the Cardinals marveled at Ware's toughness and his ability to put his teammates first even in the face of excruciating pain. Pitino credited Ware with calming everyone down and said Ware's I'm-fine-win-the-game-for-me speech was the difference between winning and losing.

"I don't think we could have gathered ourselves—I know we couldn't have—if Kevin didn't do that," said Pitino.

Heading into the Final Four, the Cardinals became the nation's darlings. Ware instantly became a household name and took calls from Oprah and Michelle Obama, and in the ultimate paradox, Louisville became the favorite and loveable underdog at the same time.

Meanwhile, Pitino was in the midst of an incredible run. The day after he returned from Indianapolis, he received a call informing him that he was selected to the Naismith Basketball Hall of Fame. While he was on the phone, he received a text from his son Richard telling him that he had

DAVID E. KLUTHO

Roanoke, Va., to Atlanta anyway to provide his son some extra pep during warmups. "I kind of choked up because he gets exhausted just sitting there," Luke said, "and he had his head down and didn't look at me."

Louisville quickly took control in the second half behind guards Smith and Siva and a reenergized Behanan, who took control inside, grabbed seven offensive rebounds and made several big hustle plays down the stretch. "I saw fear in their eyes and I kept going after them," Behanan said.

The Louisville women put together their own impressive run, knocking off Brittney Griner and Baylor in the Sweet 16 and making it to the national title game. The Cardinal women were true Cinderellas and scrapped, clawed and played at a frenetic pace much like Pitino's squad. The day after Louisville defeated Michigan, 82–76, the Cardinal women faced powerhouse UConn in the final. Pitino made the trip and tried to impart some of his magic, but to no avail. UConn had too much talent, and bolstered by 6'4" freshman center Breanna Stewart's 23 points, the Huskies cruised to a 93–60 victory to earn their eighth national title.

Despite the defeat, the season still belonged to Louisville. Only one team cut down the nets at the end, but both the Cardinal men and women captivated the nation with heart and determination. Back in Atlanta after the basket was lowered so Ware could snip a piece of the net, Pitino gathered his family at the edge of the court. Amidst a raucous celebration around them, they came together, interlocked arms and shared a private moment. A few minutes later, Pitino emerged all smiles, his eyes a little red. As much as he's accomplished in his illustrious career, the 60-year-old coach knew he may never experience a season like this again.

accepted the head coaching job at the University of Minnesota. "I was looking around for lightning," Pitino said.

Then as Louisville was mounting a comeback against Wichita State, one of the thoroughbred horses Pitino co-owns, Goldencents, won the Santa Anita Derby and qualified for the Kentucky Derby. "One day I hope to get lucky like Coach P," Smith would say later after Louisville held off Wichita State, 72–68.

Louisville would need everything in its arsenal—luck, talent, perseverance—to beat Michigan in the national championship game. The young Wolverines, led by national player of the year Trey Burke, were supremely talented and were athletic and disciplined enough to hang with any team. In one of the best title games in the last decade, both teams traded punches before Michigan jumped out to a 12-point lead midway through the first half.

But the lead didn't last for long as Hancock singlehandedly brought Louisville back with 14 straight points to cut the Michigan lead to one at the half. It was quite a year for Hancock, who came to Louisville after transferring from George Mason and became a reliable sharpshooter off the bench. Hancock entered the Michigan game with a heavy heart as his father, Bill, was battling terminal prostate cancer that had spread to his bones and sapped all his energy. But Bill made the trip from

NCAA Men's Championship Game Box Score

Michigan 76

	Min	FG M-A	FT M-A	Reb O-T	A	PF	TP
G. Robinson III	38	3-4	6-8	1-2	2	1	12
M. McGary	29	3-6	0-0	2-6	1	4	6
T. Burke	26	7-11	7-9	1-4	3	4	24
T. Hardaway	35	5-13	2-4	0-5	4	0	12
N. Stauskas	19	1-2	0-0	0-2	2	3	3
S. Albrecht	28	6-9	1-2	0-1	0	1	17
J. Horford	5	0-0	0-0	2-2	0	1	0
C. LeVert	12	0-0	0-0	1-3	0	1	0
J. Morgan	8	0-2	2-2	1-1	0	0	2
Totals		**25-48**	**18-25**	**8-26**	**12**	**15**	**76**

Percentages: FG-.521, FT-.720. 3-Point Goals: 8–18, .444 (G. Robinson 0-1, T. Burke 3-5, T. Hardaway 0-4, N. Stauskas 1-2, S. Albrecht 4-5, C. LeVert 0-1). Team Rebounds: 1. Blocked Shots: 2 (M. McGary, T. Burke). Turnovers: 12 (M. McGary 1, T. Burke 4, T. Hardaway 2, N. Stauskas 1, S. Albrecht 3, C. LeVert 1). Steals: 3 (M. McGary 1, N. Stauskas 1, C. LeVert 1). Technical Fouls: None.

Halftime: Michigan 38, Louisville 37.

Final Four Most Outstanding Player: Luke Hancock, Louisville.

Louisville 82

	Min	FG M-A	FT M-A	Reb O-T	A	PF	TP
C. Behanan	28	6-12	3-4	7-12	1	2	15
G. Dieng	37	4-6	0-0	5-8	6	4	8
W. Blackshear	19	3-5	0-0	0-1	1	3	8
R. Smith	32	3-16	2-3	1-1	2	4	9
P. Siva	36	6-15	6-6	0-6	5	3	18
L. Hancock	30	5-6	7-10	0-1	3	4	22
T. Henderson	3	0-0	0-0	0-0	0	1	0
M.I. Harrell	12	1-1	0-0	0-0	0	1	2
S. Van Treese	3	0-0	0-0	2-2	0	0	0
Totals		**28-61**	**18-23**	**15-31**	**18**	**22**	**82**

Percentages: FG-.459, FT-.783. 3-Point Goals: 8–16, .500 (W. Blackshear 2-3, R. Smith 1-6, P. Siva 0-2, L. Hancock 5-5). Team Rebounds: 1. Blocked Shots: 3 (G. Dieng 3). Turnovers: 9 (C. Behanan 2, G. Dieng 2, R. Smith 3, P. Siva 2). Steals: 9 (C. Behanan 1, G. Dieng 1, W. Blackshear 1, P. Siva 4, L. Hancock 2). Technical Fouls: None.

Officials: John Cahill, John Higgins, Tony Greene. **A:** 74,326.

Final ESPN/*USA Today* Top 25 Coaches Poll

1. Louisville (31)	34-5	
2. Michigan	31-7	
3. Syracuse	30-10	
4. Wichita State	30-9	
5. Duke	30-6	
6. Ohio State	29-8	
7. Indiana	29-7	
8. Kansas	31-6	
9. Florida	29-8	
10. Miami (FL)	29-7	
11. Marquette	26-9	
12. Gonzaga	32-3	
13. Michigan State	27-9	
14. Arizona	27-8	
15. Oregon	28-9	
16. Saint Louis	28-7	
17. Georgetown	25-7	
18. Memphis	31-5	
19. New Mexico	29-6	
20. Kansas State	27-8	
21. Creighton	28-8	
22. Wisconsin	23-12	
23. Virginia Commonwealth	27-9	
24. La Salle	24-10	
25. Florida Gulf Coast	26-11	

Note: First-place votes in parenthesis

National Invitation Tournament Scores

First round: Maryland 86, Niagara 70; St. John's 63, St. Joseph's 61; Louisiana Tech 71, Florida State 66; Robert Morris 59, Kentucky 57; Alabama 62, Northeastern 43; Virginia 67, Norfolk State 56; Denver 61, Ohio 57; BYU 90, Washington 79; Stanford 58, Stephen F. Austin 57; Iowa 68, Indiana State 52; Providence 75, Charlotte 66; Stony Brook 71, Massachusetts 58; Mercer 75, Tennessee 67; Baylor 112, Long Beach State 66; Southern Miss 78, Charleston Southern 71; Arizona State 83, Detroit 68.
Second round: Maryland 62, Denver 52; Baylor 89, Arizona State 86; Iowa 75, Stony Brook 63; Alabama 66, Stanford 54; Virginia 68, St. John's 50; Providence 77, Robert Morris 68; BYU 90, Mercer 71; Southern Miss 63, Louisiana Tech 52.
Quarterfinals: Maryland 58, Alabama 57; Iowa 75, Virginia 65; BYU 79, Southern Miss 62; Baylor 79, Providence 68
Semifinals: Baylor 76, BYU 70; Iowa 71, Maryland 60.
Championship Game: Baylor 74, Iowa 54.

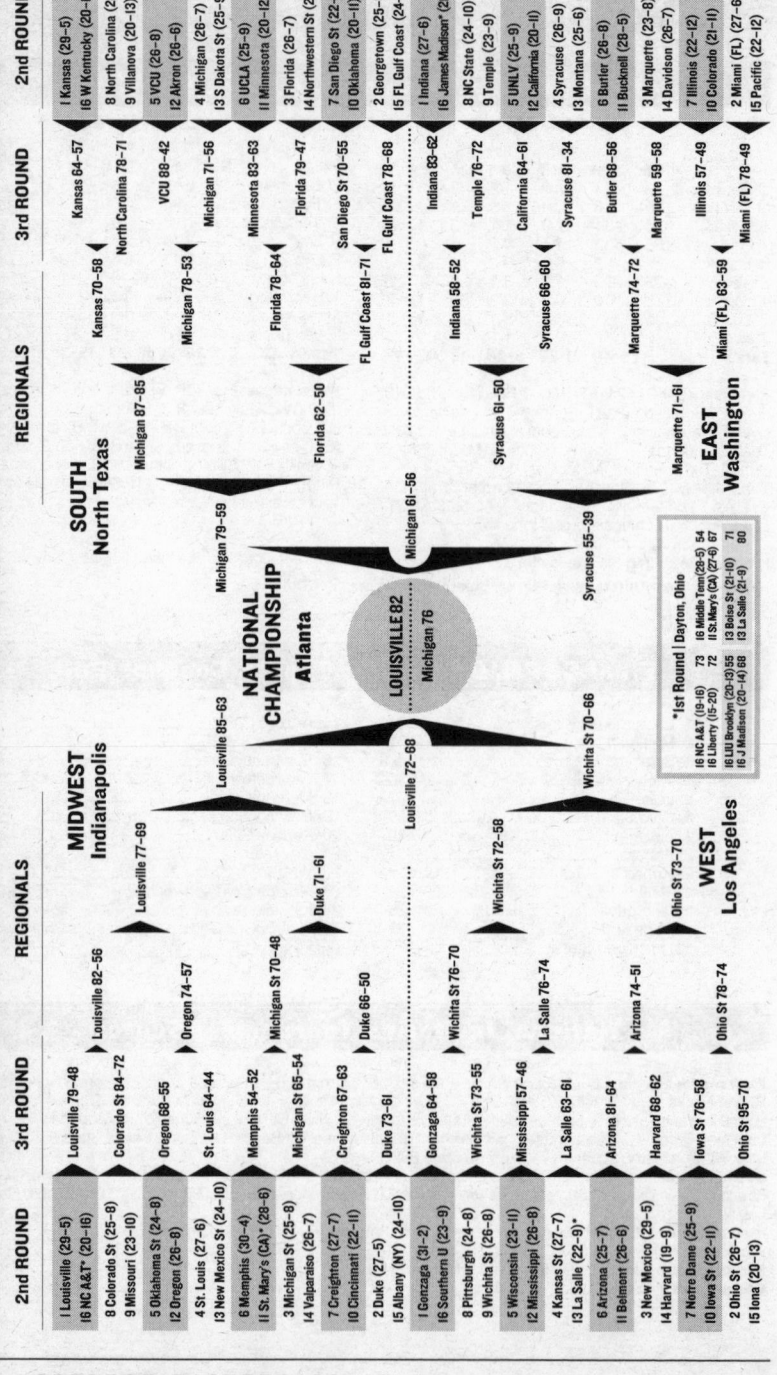

2nd ROUND

1 Louisville (29–5)
16 NC A&T* (20–16)

8 Colorado St (25–8)
9 Missouri (23–10)

5 Oklahoma St (24–8)
12 Oregon (26–8)

4 St. Louis (27–6)
13 New Mexico St (24–10)

6 Memphis (30–4)
11 St. Mary's (CA)* (28–6)

3 Michigan St (25–8)
14 Valparaiso (26–7)

7 Creighton (27–7)
10 Cincinnati (22–11)

2 Duke (27–5)
15 Albany (NY) (24–10)

1 Gonzaga (31–2)
16 Southern U (23–9)

8 Pittsburgh (24–8)
9 Wichita St (26–8)

5 Wisconsin (23–11)
12 Mississippi (26–8)

4 Kansas St (27–7)
13 La Salle (22–9)*

6 Arizona (25–7)
11 Belmont (26–6)

3 New Mexico (29–5)
14 Harvard (19–9)

7 Notre Dame (25–9)
10 Iowa St (22–11)

2 Ohio St (26–7)
15 Iona (20–13)

3rd ROUND

Louisville 79–48

Colorado St 84–72

Oregon 68–55

St. Louis 64–44

Memphis 54–52

Michigan St 65–54

Creighton 67–63

Duke 73–61

Gonzaga 64–58

Wichita St 73–55

Mississippi 57–46

La Salle 63–61

Arizona 81–64

Harvard 68–62

Iowa St 76–58

Ohio St 95–70

REGIONALS

MIDWEST
Indianapolis

Louisville 82–56

Oregon 74–57

Michigan St 70–48

Duke 66–50

WEST
Los Angeles

Wichita St 76–70

La Salle 76–74

Arizona 74–51

Ohio St 78–74

Louisville 77–69

Duke 71–61

Wichita St 72–58

Ohio St 73–70

Louisville 85–63

Michigan 79–59

NATIONAL
CHAMPIONSHIP
Atlanta

LOUISVILLE 82

Michigan 76

Louisville 72–68

Wichita St 70–66

Michigan 61–56

Syracuse 55–39

SOUTH
North Texas

Michigan 87–85

Florida 62–50

EAST
Washington

Syracuse 61–50

Marquette 71–61

REGIONALS

Kansas 70–58

Michigan 78–53

Florida 78–64

FL Gulf Coast 81–71

Indiana 58–52

Syracuse 66–60

Butler 68–56

Marquette 59–58

Miami (FL) 63–59

3rd ROUND

Kansas 64–57

North Carolina 78–71

VCU 88–42

Michigan 71–56

Minnesota 83–63

Florida 79–47

San Diego St 70–55

FL Gulf Coast 78–68

Indiana 83–62

Temple 76–72

California 64–61

Syracuse 81–34

Butler 68–56

Marquette 74–72

Illinois 57–49

Miami (FL) 78–49

2nd ROUND

1 Kansas (29–5)
16 W Kentucky (20–15)

8 North Carolina (24–10)
9 Villanova (20–13)

5 VCU (26–8)
12 Akron (26–6)

4 Michigan (26–7)
13 S Dakota St (25–9)

6 UCLA (25–9)
11 Minnesota (20–12)

3 Florida (26–7)
14 Northwestern St (23–8)

7 San Diego St (22–10)
10 Oklahoma (20–11)

2 Georgetown (25–6)
15 FL Gulf Coast (24–10)

1 Indiana (27–6)
16 James Madison* (21–14)

8 NC State (24–10)
9 Temple (23–9)

5 UNLV (25–9)
12 California (20–11)

4 Syracuse (26–9)
13 Montana (25–6)

6 Butler (26–8)
11 Bucknell (28–5)

3 Marquette (23–8)
14 Davidson (26–7)

7 Illinois (22–12)
10 Colorado (21–11)

2 Miami (FL) (27–6)
15 Pacific (22–12)

*1st Round | Dayton, Ohio

16 NC A&T (19–16)	73	16 Middle Tenn (28–5) 54
16 Liberty (15–20)	72	11 St. Mary's (CA) (27–6) 67
16 LIU Brooklyn (20–13) 55		13 Boise St (21–10) 71
16 J. Madison (20–14) 68		13 La Salle (21–9) 80

America East

	Conference			All Games		
	W	L	Pct	W	L	Pct
Stony Brook	14	2	.875	25	8	.758
Vermont	11	5	.688	21	12	.636
Boston University	11	5	.688	17	13	.567
Hartford	10	6	.625	17	14	.548
Albany	9	7	.563	24	11	.686
Maine	6	10	.375	11	19	.367
New Hampshire	5	11	.313	9	20	.310
UMBC	5	11	.313	8	23	.258
Binghamton	1	15	.063	3	27	.100

Atlantic Coast

	Conference			All Games		
	W	L	Pct	W	L	Pct
Miami (FL)	15	3	.833	29	7	.806
Duke	14	4	.778	30	6	.833
North Carolina	12	6	.667	25	11	.694
North Carolina St	11	7	.611	24	11	.686
Virginia	11	7	.611	23	12	.657
Florida State	9	9	.500	18	16	.529
Maryland	8	10	.444	25	13	.658
Boston College	7	11	.389	16	17	.485
Georgia Tech	6	12	.333	16	15	.516
Wake Forest	6	12	.333	13	18	.419
Clemson	5	13	.278	13	18	.419
Virginia Tech	4	14	.222	13	19	.406

Atlantic Sun

	Conference			All Games		
	W	L	Pct	W	L	Pct
Mercer	14	4	.778	24	12	.667
FGCU	13	5	.722	26	11	.703
Stetson	11	7	.611	15	16	.484
USC Upstate	9	9	.500	16	17	.485
Jacksonville	9	9	.500	14	18	.438
Northern Kentucky	9	9	.500	11	16	.407
North Florida	8	10	.444	13	19	.406
East Tennessee St	8	10	.444	10	22	.313
Lipscomb	7	11	.389	12	18	.400
Kennesaw State	2	16	.111	3	27	.100

Atlantic 10

	Conference			All Games		
	W	L	Pct	W	L	Pct
Saint Louis	13	3	.813	28	7	.800
VCU	12	4	.750	27	9	.750
Butler	11	5	.688	27	9	.750
Temple	11	5	.688	24	10	.706
La Salle	11	5	.688	24	10	.706
Massachusetts	9	7	.563	21	12	.636
Xavier	9	7	.563	17	14	.548
Charlotte	8	8	.500	21	12	.636
Saint Joseph's	8	8	.500	18	14	.563
Richmond	8	8	.500	19	15	.559
Dayton	7	9	.438	17	14	.548
St. Bonaventure	7	9	.438	14	15	.483
George Washington	7	9	.438	13	17	.433
Rhode Island	3	13	.188	8	21	.276
Fordham	3	13	.188	7	24	.226
Duquesne	1	15	.063	8	22	.267

Note: Standings based on regular-season conference play only; overall records include all tournament play.

Big East

	Conference			All Games		
	W	L	Pct	W	L	Pct
Louisville	14	4	.778	35	5	.875
Georgetown	14	4	.778	25	7	.781
Marquette	14	4	.778	26	9	.743
Pittsburgh	12	6	.667	24	9	.727
Syracuse	11	7	.611	30	10	.750
Notre Dame	11	7	.611	25	10	.714
Connecticut	10	8	.556	20	10	.667
Villanova	10	8	.556	20	14	.588
Cincinnati	9	9	.500	22	12	.647
Providence	9	9	.500	19	15	.559
St. John's	8	10	.444	17	16	.515
Rutgers	5	13	.278	15	16	.484
Seton Hall	3	15	.167	15	18	.455
South Florida	3	15	.167	12	19	.387
DePaul	2	16	.111	11	21	.344

Big Sky

	Conference			All Games		
	W	L	Pct	W	L	Pct
Montana	19	1	.950	25	7	.781
Weber State	18	2	.900	30	7	.811
North Dakota	12	8	.600	16	17	.485
Montana State	10	10	.500	13	17	.433
Northern Colorado	10	10	.500	13	18	.419
Sacramento State	8	12	.400	14	15	.483
Southern Utah	8	12	.400	11-	20	.355
Northern Arizona	8	12	.400	11	21	.344
Eastern Washington	7	13	.350	10	21	.323
Portland State	5	15	.250	8	20	.286
Idaho State	5	15	.250	6	24	.200

Big South

	Conference			All Games		
NORTH	W	L	Pct	W	L	Pct
High Point	12	4	.750	17	14	.548
VMI	8	8	.500	14	17	.452
Radford	7	9	.438	13	19	.406
Campbell	7	9	.438	13	20	.394
Liberty	6	10	.375	15	21	.417
Longwood	4	12	.250	8	25	.242
SOUTH						
Charleston Southern	12	4	.750	19	13	.594
Gardner-Webb	11	5	.688	21	13	.618
UNC Asheville	10	6	.625	16	16	.500
Coastal Carolina	9	7	.563	14	15	.483
Winthrop	6	10	.375	14	17	.452
Presbyterian	4	12	.250	8	24	.250

Big 10

	Conference			All Games		
	W	L	Pct	W	L	Pct
Indiana	14	4	.778	29	7	.806
Ohio State	13	5	.722	29	8	.784
Michigan State	13	5	.722	27	9	.750
Michigan	12	6	.667	31	8	.795
Wisconsin	12	6	.667	23	12	.657
Iowa	9	9	.500	25	13	.658
Illinois	8	10	.444	23	13	.639
Minnesota	8	10	.444	21	13	.618
Purdue	8	10	.444	16	18	.471
Nebraska	5	13	.278	15	18	.455
Northwestern	4	14	.222	13	19	.406
Penn State	2	16	.111	10	21	.323

Big 12

	Conference			All Games		
	W	L	Pct	W	L	Pct
Kansas	14	4	.778	31	6	.838
Kansas State	14	4	.778	27	8	.771
Oklahoma State	13	5	.722	24	9	.727
Iowa State	11	7	.611	23	12	.657
Oklahoma	11	7	.611	20	12	.625
Baylor	9	9	.500	23	14	.622
Texas	7	11	.389	16	18	.471
West Virginia	6	12	.333	13	19	.406
Texas Tech	3	15	.167	11	20	.355
TCU	2	16	.111	11	21	.344

Big West

	Conference			All Games		
	W	L	Pct	W	L	Pct
Long Beach State	14	4	.778	19	14	.576
Pacific	13	5	.722	22	13	.629
Cal Poly	12	6	.667	18	14	.563
UC Irvine	11	7	.611	21	16	.568
Hawaii	10	8	.556	17	15	.531
UC Davis	9	9	.500	14	17	.452
UC Santa Barbara	7	11	.389	11	20	.355
Cal State Fullerton	6	12	.333	14	18	.438
Cal State Northridge	5	13	.278	14	17	.452
UC Riverside	3	15	.167	6	25	.194

Colonial

	Conference			All Games		
	W	L	Pct	W	L	Pct
Northeastern	14	4	.778	20	13	.606
Towson	13	5	.722	18	13	.581
Delaware	13	5	.722	19	14	.576
James Madison	11	7	.611	21	15	.583
George Mason	10	8	.556	22	16	.579
Georgia State	10	8	.556	15	16	.484
Drexel	9	9	.500	13	18	.419
William & Mary	7	11	.389	13	17	.433
UNCW	5	13	.278	10	20	.333
Hofstra	4	14	.222	7	25	.219
Old Dominion	3	15	.167	5	25	.167

Conference USA

	Conference			All Games		
	W	L	Pct	W	L	Pct
Memphis	16	0	1.000	31	5	.861
Southern Miss	12	4	.750	27	10	.730
UTEP	10	6	.625	18	14	.563
East Carolina	9	7	.563	23	12	.657
UCF	9	7	.563	20	11	.645
Tulsa	8	8	.500	17	16	.515
Houston	7	9	.438	20	13	.606
UAB	7	9	.438	16	17	.485
Tulane	6	10	.375	20	15	.571
Marshall	6	10	.375	13	19	.406
SMU	5	11	.313	15	17	.469
Rice	1	15	.063	5	26	.161

**No automatic bid for conference tournament winner.
†Does not hold end-of-season conference tournament.

Great West**

	Conference			All Games		
	W	L	Pct	W	L	Pct
NJIT	6	2	.750	16	13	.552
Texas-Pan American	5	3	.625	16	16	.500
Houston Baptist	3	5	.375	14	17	.452
Utah Valley	3	5	.375	14	18	.438
Chicago State	3	5	.375	11	22	.333

Horizon League

	Conference			All Games		
	W	L	Pct	W	L	Pct
Valparaiso	13	3	.813	26	8	.765
Detroit	12	4	.750	20	13	.606
Wright State	10	6	.625	23	13	.639
Green Bay	10	6	.625	18	16	.529
Youngstown State	7	9	.438	18	16	.529
UIC	7	9	.438	18	16	.529
Loyola Chicago	5	11	.313	15	16	.484
Cleveland State	5	11	.313	14	18	.438
Milwaukee	3	13	.188	8	24	.250

Ivy League†

	Conference			All Games		
	W	L	Pct	W	L	Pct
Harvard	11	3	.786	20	10	.667
Princeton	10	4	.714	17	11	.607
Yale	8	6	.571	14	17	.452
Brown	7	7	.500	13	15	.464
Penn	6	8	.429	9	22	.290
Cornell	5	9	.357	13	18	.419
Dartmouth	5	9	.357	9	19	.321
Columbia	4	10	.286	12	16	.429

Metro Atlantic

	Conference			All Games		
	W	L	Pct	W	L	Pct
Niagara	13	5	.722	19	14	.576
Loyola Maryland	12	6	.667	23	12	.657
Rider	12	6	.667	19	15	.559
Iona	11	7	.611	20	14	.588
Canisius	11	7	.611	20	14	.588
Fairfield	9	9	.500	19	16	.543
Manhattan	9	9	.500	14	18	.438
Marist	6	12	.333	10	21	.323
Siena	4	14	.222	8	24	.250
Saint Peter's	3	15	.167	9	21	.300

Mid-American

	Conference			All Games		
EAST	W	L	Pct	W	L	Pct
Akron	14	2	.875	26	7	.788
Ohio	14	2	.875	24	10	.706
Kent State	9	7	.563	21	14	.600
Buffalo	7	9	.438	14	20	.412
Bowling Green	7	9	.438	13	19	.406
Miami (OH)	3	13	.188	9	22	.290
WEST						
Western Michigan	10	6	.625	22	13	.629
Toledo	10	6	.625	15	13	.536
Ball State	8	8	.500	15	15	.500
Eastern Michigan	7	9	.438	16	18	.471
Central Michigan	4	12	.250	11	20	.355
Northern Illinois	3	13	.188	5	25	.167

Mid-Eastern Athletic

	Conference			All Games		
	W	L	Pct	W	L	Pct
Norfolk State	16	0	1.000	21	12	.636
NC Central	15	1	.938	22	9	.710
Savannah State	11	5	.688	19	15	.559
Hampton	11	5	.688	14	17	.452
Morgan State	10	6	.625	17	15	.531
North Carolina A&T	8	8	.500	20	17	.541
Delaware State	8	8	.500	15	18	.455
Bethune-Cookman	7	9	.438	14	20	.412
Florida A&M	5	11	.313	8	23	.258
Coppin State	5	11	.313	8	24	.250
Howard	4	12	.250	7	24	.226
SC State	2	14	.125	6	24	.200
MD Eastern Shore	2	14	.125	2	26	.071

Ohio Valley

	Conference			All Games		
EAST	W	L	Pct	W	L	Pct
Belmont	14	2	.875	26	7	.788
Eastern Kentucky	12	4	.750	25	10	.714
Tennessee State	11	5	.688	18	15	.545
Jacksonville State	8	8	.500	17	11	.607
Morehead State	8	8	.500	15	18	.455
Tennessee Tech	5	11	.313	12	17	.414
WEST	W	L	Pct	W	L	Pct
Murray State	10	6	.625	21	10	.677
SE Missouri State	8	8	.500	17	16	.515
Eastern Illinois	6	10	.375	11	21	.344
SIUE	5	11	.313	9	18	.333
UT Martin	5	11	.313	9	21	.300
Austin Peay	4	12	.250	8	23	.258

Missouri Valley

	Conference			All Games		
	W	L	Pct	W	L	Pct
Creighton	13	5	.722	28	8	.778
Wichita State	12	6	.667	30	9	.769
UNI	11	7	.611	21	15	.583
Evansville	10	8	.556	21	15	.583
Indiana State	9	9	.500	18	15	.545
Illinois State	8	10	.444	18	15	.545
Bradley	7	11	.389	18	17	.514
Drake	7	11	.389	15	17	.469
Missouri State	7	11	.389	11	22	.333
Southern Illinois	6	12	.333	14	17	.452

Pac 12

	Conference			All Games		
	W	L	Pct	W	L	Pct
UCLA	13	5	.722	25	10	.714
Arizona	12	6	.667	27	8	.771
Oregon	12	6	.667	28	9	.757
California	12	6	.667	21	12	.636
Colorado	10	8	.556	21	12	.636
Arizona State	9	9	.500	22	13	.629
Stanford	9	9	.500	19	15	.559
Washington	9	9	.500	18	16	.529
USC	9	9	.500	14	18	.438
Utah	5	13	.278	15	18	.455
Oregon State	4	14	.222	14	18	.438
Washington State	4	14	.222	13	19	.406

Mountain West

	Conference			All Games		
	W	L	Pct	W	L	Pct
New Mexico	13	3	.813	29	6	.829
Colorado State	11	5	.688	26	9	.743
UNLV	10	6	.625	25	10	.714
San Diego State	9	7	.563	23	11	.676
Boise State	9	7	.563	21	11	.656
Air Force	8	8	.500	18	14	.563
Fresno State	5	11	.313	11	19	.367
Wyoming	4	12	.250	20	14	.588
Nevada	3	13	.188	12	19	.387

Patriot League

	Conference			All Games		
	W	L	Pct	W	L	Pct
Bucknell	12	2	.857	28	6	.824
Lehigh	10	4	.714	21	10	.677
Lafayette	10	4	.714	19	15	.559
Army	8	6	.571	16	15	.516
Colgate	5	9	.357	11	21	.344
American University	5	9	.357	10	20	.333
Holy Cross	4	10	.286	12	18	.400
Navy	2	12	.143	8	23	.258

Northeast

	Conference			All Games		
	W	L	Pct	W	L	Pct
Robert Morris	14	4	.778	24	11	.686
Bryant	12	6	.667	19	12	.613
Wagner	12	6	.667	19	12	.613
LIU Brooklyn	12	6	.667	20	14	.588
Mount St. Mary's	11	7	.611	18	14	.563
Quinnipiac	11	7	.611	15	16	.484
Central CT State	9	9	.500	13	17	.433
St. Francis Brooklyn	8	10	.444	12	18	.400
Sacred Heart	7	11	.389	9	20	.310
Monmouth	5	13	.278	10	21	.323
Saint Francis U	5	13	.278	5	24	.172
Fairleigh Dickinson	2	16	.111	7	24	.226

Southeastern

	Conference			All Games		
	W	L	Pct	W	L	Pct
Florida	14	4	.778	29	8	.784
Ole Miss	12	6	.667	27	9	.750
Alabama	12	6	.667	23	13	.639
Kentucky	12	6	.667	21	12	.636
Missouri	11	7	.611	23	11	.676
Tennessee	11	7	.611	20	13	.606
Arkansas	10	8	.556	19	13	.594
LSU	9	9	.500	19	12	.613
Georgia	9	9	.500	15	17	.469
Vanderbilt	8	10	.444	16	17	.485
Texas A&M	7	11	.389	18	15	.545
South Carolina	4	14	.222	14	18	.438
Mississippi State	4	14	.222	10	22	.313
Auburn	3	15	.167	9	23	.281

Southern

NORTH	Conference			All Games		
	W	L	Pct	W	L	Pct
Elon	13	5	.722	21	12	.636
Appalachian State	10	8	.556	15	16	.484
Western Carolina	9	9	.500	14	19	.424
Samford	9	9	.500	11	21	.344
Chattanooga	8	10	.444	13	19	.406
UNC Greensboro	6	12	.333	9	22	.290
SOUTH						
Davidson	17	1	.944	26	8	.765
Charleston	14	4	.778	24	11	.686
Georgia Southern	7	11	.389	14	19	.424
Wofford	7	11	.389	13	19	.406
Citadel	5	13	.278	8	22	.267
Furman	3	15	.167	7	24	.226

Southland

	Conference			All Games		
	W	L	Pct	W	L	Pct
Stephen F. Austin	16	2	.889	27	5	.844
Northwestern State	15	3	.833	23	9	.719
Oral Roberts	13	5	.722	20	15	.571
SE Louisiana	10	8	.556	13	18	.419
Sam Houston State	8	10	.444	17	17	.500
Nicholls	8	10	.444	9	21	.300
McNeese State	7	11	.389	14	17	.452
Central Arkansas	7	11	.389	13	17	.433
TX A&M-Corp. Christi	5	13	.278	6	23	.207
Lamar	1	17	.056	3	28	.097

Southwestern Athletic

	Conference			All Games		
	W	L	Pct	W	L	Pct
Texas Southern	16	2	.889	17	14	.548
Southern University	15	3	.833	23	10	.697
UAPB	15	3	.833	16	14	.533
Jackson State	9	9	.500	11	18	.379
Prairie View A&M	8	10	.444	15	19	.441
Alabama State	8	10	.444	10	22	.313
Alcorn State	8	10	.444	10	24	.294
Alabama A&M	6	12	.333	11	20	.355
Miss Valley State	5	13	.278	5	23	.179
Grambling State	0	18	.000	0	28	.000

Summit League

	Conference			All Games		
	W	L	Pct	W	L	Pct
SD State	13	3	.813	25	10	.714
Western Illinois	13	3	.813	22	9	.710
North Dakota State	12	4	.750	24	10	.706
Oakland	10	6	.625	16	17	.485
IPFW	7	9	.438	16	17	.485
Nebraska Omaha	6	10	.375	11	20	.355
South Dakota	5	11	.313	10	20	.333
UMKC	5	11	.313	8	24	.250
IUPUI	1	15	.063	6	26	.188

Sun Belt

EAST	Conference			All Games		
	W	L	Pct	W	L	Pct
Middle Tennessee	19	1	.950	28	6	.824
South Alabama	14	6	.700	17	13	.567
FIU	11	9	.550	18	14	.563
Western Kentucky	10	10	.500	20	16	.556
Florida Atlantic	9	11	.450	14	18	.438
Troy	6	14	.300	12	21	.364
WEST						
Arkansas State	12	8	.600	19	12	.613
Arkansas-Little Rock	11	9	.550	17	15	.531
Louisiana-Lafayette	8	12	.400	13	20	.394
North Texas	7	13	.350	12	20	.375
Louisiana-Monroe	3	17	.150	4	23	.148

West Coast

	Conference			All Games		
	W	L	Pct	W	L	Pct
Gonzaga	16	0	1.000	32	3	.914
Saint Mary's	14	2	.875	28	7	.800
BYU	10	6	.625	24	12	.667
Santa Clara	9	7	.563	26	12	.684
San Francisco	7	9	.438	15	16	.484
San Diego	7	9	.438	16	18	.471
Pepperdine	4	12	.250	12	18	.400
Portland	4	12	.250	11	21	.344
Loyola Marymount	1	15	.063	11	23	.324

Western Athletic

	Conference			All Games		
	W	L	Pct	W	L	Pct
Louisiana Tech	16	2	.889	27	7	.794
Denver	16	2	.889	22	10	.688
New Mexico State	14	4	.778	24	11	.686
Utah State	11	7	.611	21	10	.677
UT Arlington	11	7	.611	19	14	.576
Idaho	7	11	.389	12	18	.400
Texas State	5	13	.278	12	22	.353
UTSA	3	14	.176	10	22	.313
San Jose State	3	14	.176	9	20	.310
Seattle	3	15	.167	8	22	.267

Independents

	All Games		
	W	L	Pct
CSU Bakersfield	14	16	.467
New Orleans	8	18	.308

Scoring

Player and Team	Class	GP	FG	3FG	FT	Pts	Avg
Erick Green, Virginia Tech	Sr.	32	261	61	218	801	25.0
Doug McDermott, Creighton	Jr.	36	284	77	189	834	23.2
Lamont Jones, Iona	Sr.	34	246	56	221	769	22.6
Nate Wolters, South Dakota St.	Sr.	33	242	64	187	735	22.3
Travis Bader, Oakland	Jr.	33	206	139	179	730	22.1
Isaiah Canaan, Murray St.	Sr.	31	215	94	152	676	21.8
Tyler Haws, BYU	So.	36	276	43	185	780	21.7
Kyle Vinales, Central Conn. St.	So.	30	229	80	111	649	21.6
Shane Gibson, Sacred Heart	Sr.	29	212	87	115	626	21.6
Stan Okoye, VMI	Sr.	31	236	59	135	666	21.5
Greg Gantt, Fla. Atlantic	Sr.	32	235	84	123	677	21.2
Khaliff Wyatt, Temple	Sr.	34	209	75	204	697	20.5
Corey Hawkins, UC Davis	So.	28	183	48	155	569	20.3
Anthony Ireland, Loyola Marymount	Jr.	34	228	65	167	688	20.2
Colt Ryan, Evansville	Sr.	34	219	63	184	685	20.1
Marshall Henderson, Ole Miss	Jr.	36	209	138	166	722	20.1
Fred Hunter, Nicholls St.	Sr.	27	186	16	149	537	19.9
Devon Saddler, Delaware	Jr.	33	216	56	168	656	19.9
Deshaun Thomas, Ohio St.	Jr.	37	260	72	141	733	19.8
Pierre Jackson, Baylor	Sr.	36	216	88	192	712	19.8
Frank Gaines, IPFW	Sr.	32	198	55	181	632	19.8
Bryce Cotton, Providence	Jr.	32	195	98	142	630	19.7
Augustine Rubit, South Alabama	Jr.	30	192	0	198	582	19.4
Jud Dillard, Tennessee Tech	Sr.	29	182	36	160	560	19.3
Kevin Foster, Santa Clara	Sr.	38	241	120	130	732	19.3

FIELD-GOAL PERCENTAGE

	Class	GP	FG	FGA	Pct
Taylor Smith, Stephen F. Austin	Sr.	32	211	304	69.4
Marshall Bjorklund, ND State	Jr.	34	170	255	66.7
Kelly Olynyk, Gonzaga	Jr.	32	215	342	62.9
T.J. Warren, North Carolina St	Fr.	35	186	299	62.2
Jameel Warney, Stony Brook	Fr.	33	165	267	61.8
Cory Jefferson, Baylor	Jr.	37	191	313	61.0
Mason Plumlee, Duke	Sr.	36	221	369	59.9
Victor Oladipo, Indiana	Jr.	36	182	304	59.9
Colton Iverson, Colorado St	Sr.	35	183	307	59.6
Kyle Barone, Idaho	Sr.	30	178	299	59.5

Note: Minimum 5 made per game.

REBOUNDS

	Class	GP	Reb	Avg
O.D. Anosike, Siena	Sr.	32	364	11.4
Andre Roberson, Colorado	Jr.	31	347	11.2
Jerrelle Benimon, Towson	Jr.	31	346	11.2
Mike Muscala, Bucknell	Sr.	34	378	11.1
Richard Howell, North Carolina St	Sr.	35	380	10.9
Alan Williams, UC Santa Barbara	So.	28	300	10.7
Jamelle Hagins, Delaware	Sr.	33	353	10.7
Josh Davis, Tulane	Jr.	35	374	10.7
Eric Moreland, Oregon St.	So.	29	307	10.6
Augustine Rubit, South Alabama	Jr.	30	315	10.5
Keith Rendleman, UNC Wilmington	Sr.	30	314	10.5

FREE-THROW PERCENTAGE

	Class	GP	FT	FTA	Pct
Nik Cochran, Davidson	Sr.	34	116	124	93.5
Keith Hornsby, UNC Asheville	So.	30	99	107	92.5
Austin Morgan, Yale	Sr.	31	93	102	91.2
Holton Hunsaker, Utah Valley	Jr.	32	104	115	90.4
Travis Smith, Mercer	Sr.	36	114	127	89.8
Wes Eikmeier, Colorado St	Sr.	35	96	107	89.7
Colt Ryan, Evansville	Sr.	34	184	206	89.3
Kevin Dillard, Dayton	Sr.	31	140	157	89.2
Johnny Dee, San Diego	So.	34	87	98	88.8
Lamont Jones, Iona	Sr.	34	221	249	88.8

Note: Minimum 2.5 made per game.

ASSISTS

	Class	GP	Ast	Avg
Jason Brickman, LIU Brooklyn	Jr.	34	289	8.5
Phil Gaetano, Sacred Heart	So.	28	222	7.9
Chaz Williams, Massachusetts	Jr.	33	242	7.3
Larry Drew II, UCLA	Sr.	35	256	7.3
Michael Carter-Williams, Syracuse	So.	40	292	7.3
Lorenzo Brown, North Carolina St	Jr.	33	239	7.2
Miguel Paul, East Carolina	Sr.	33	236	7.2
D.J. Cooper, Ohio	Sr.	34	242	7.1
Pierre Jackson, Baylor	Sr.	36	255	7.1
Phil Pressey, Missouri	Jr.	34	240	7.1

*Includes games played in tournaments.

THREE-POINT FIELD-GOAL PERCENTAGE

	Class	GP	3FG	3FGA	Avg
Tyrus McGee, Iowa St.	Sr.	35	96	207	46.4
Ryan Sypkens, UC Davis	Jr.	29	106	230	46.1
Ian Clark, Belmont	Sr.	33	102	222	45.9
Scott Bamforth, Weber St.	Sr.	37	103	226	45.6
Malcolm Miller, Southern U.	Jr.	33	90	199	45.2
Jeff Elorriaga, Boise St.	Jr.	29	84	188	44.7
Marc Sonnen, UNI	Sr.	36	96	215	44.7
Sammy Yeager, Cal St-Fullerton	Sr.	25	66	148	44.6
Connor Hill, Idaho	So.	30	87	196	44.4

Note: Minimum 2.5 made per game

BLOCKED SHOTS

	Class	GP	BS	Avg
Chris Obekpa, St. John's (NY)	Fr.	33	133	4.03
Jeff Withey, Kansas	Sr.	37	146	3.95
Zeke Marshall, Akron	Sr.	33	122	3.70
Jordan Bachynski, Arizona St	Jr.	35	120	3.43
Chris Horton, Austin Peay	Fr.	31	100	3.23
Fred Sturdivant, Texas Southern	Sr.	31	99	3.19
Damian Eargle, Youngstown St	Sr.	32	102	3.19
D.J. Covington, VMI	Jr.	31	93	3.00
D.J. Cunningham, UNC Asheville	Jr.	31	93	3.00
Rhamel Brown, Manhattan	Jr.	32	95	2.97

THREE-POINT FIELD GOALS MADE PER GAME

	Class	GP	3FG	Avg
Travis Bader, Oakland	Jr.	33	139	4.21
Omar Strong, Texas Southern	Sr.	31	120	3.87
Marshall Henderson, Ole Miss	Jr.	36	138	3.83
Ryan Sypkens, UC Davis	Jr.	29	106	3.66
Parker Smith, North Florida	Sr.	32	116	3.63
Rotnei Clarke, Butler	Sr.	33	115	3.48
Troy Daniels, VCU	Sr.	36	124	3.44
Sean Armand, Iona	Jr.	34	112	3.29
Kevin Foster, Santa Clara	Sr.	38	120	3.16
Marcus Thornton, William & Mary	So.	30	93	3.10

STEALS

	Class	GP	Stl	Avg
Duke Mondy, Oakland	Jr.	33	100	3.03
Marcus Smart, Oklahoma St.	Fr.	33	99	3.00
Anthony Hickey, LSU	So.	29	85	2.93
Michael Carter-Williams, Syracuse	So.	40	111	2.78
Bernard Thompson, FGCU	So.	37	102	2.76
Briante Weber, VCU	So.	36	98	2.72
Matt Hunter, Central Conn. St.	Jr.	30	78	2.60
Pierria Henry, Charlotte	So.	33	84	2.55
Dyricus Simms-Edwards, Bradley	Sr.	35	86	2.46
Lazabian Jackson, Ark.-Pine Bluff	Sr.	30	73	2.43
Darius Theus, VCU	Sr.	35	85	2.43

Single-Game Highs

POINTS

53.........Nate Wolters, South Dakota St, February 7, 2013 (vs. IPFW)
47.........Travis Bader, Oakland, January 24, 2013 (vs IUPUI)
46.........Kendall Williams, New Mexico, February 23, 2013 (vs Colorado St)
45.........Michael Lyons, Air Force, February 16, 2013 (vs Colorado St)
44.........Christian Williams, Jackson St, February 23, 2013 (vs Mississippi Valley)
44.........Sam Prescott, Mt. St. Mary's, February 14, 2013 (vs Bryant)

REBOUNDS

25...........Earl Brown, Saint Francis (PA), January 3, 2013 (vs Central CT St)
23...........Jamelle Hagins, Delaware, November 28, 2012 (vs Lafayette)
22...........Aaron Anderson, Kennesaw St, March 2, 2013 (vs FGCU)
Four tied with 21.

ASSISTS

19.........Phil Pressey, Missouri, December 28, 2012 (vs UCLA)
17.........D.J. Cooper, Ohio, January 5, 2013 (vs Marshall)
17.........Neil Watson, Southern Miss., January 3, 2013 (vs Dillard)
16.........Pierre Jackson, Baylor, March 22, 2013 (vs Arizona St)
16.........Michael Carter-Williams, Syracuse, December 8, 2012 (vs Monmouth)

THREE-POINT FIELD GOALS

11.........Travis Bader, Oakland, January 24, 2013 (vs IUPUI)
11.........Troy Daniels, VCU, January 2, 2013 (vs East Tenn. St)
Five tied with 10.

STEALS

10.........Briante Weber, VCU, November 9, 2012 (vs FGCU)
9...........Isaiah Sykes, UCF, February 26, 2013 (vs Ga. Southwestern)
9...........Briante Weber, VCU, January 9, 2013 (vs Dayton)
9...........Tim Huskisson, Northern Colo., December 8, 2012 (vs Wichita St)
9...........Luke Martinez, Wyoming, December 4, 2012 (vs Illinois St)

BLOCKED SHOTS

12.........Nerlens Noel, Kentucky, January 29, 2013 (vs Ole Miss)
12.........Jordan Bachynski, Arizona St, December 8, 2012, (vs Cal St Northridge)
12.........Jeff Withey, Kansas, November 26, 2012 (vs San Jose St)
11.........Chris Obekpa, St. John's (NY), December 8, 2012 (vs Fordham)
Three tied with 10.

SCORING OFFENSE

	GP	W	L	Pts	Avg
Iona	34	20	14	2733	80.4
Northwestern St	32	23	9	2559	80.0
Iowa St.	35	23	12	2779	79.4
LIU Brooklyn	34	20	14	2677	78.7
Indiana	36	29	7	2831	78.6
VMI	31	14	17	2423	78.2
Houston	33	20	13	2578	78.1
Detroit	33	20	13	2568	77.8
North Carolina St	35	24	11	2708	77.4
Ole Miss	36	27	9	2779	77.2

SCORING DEFENSE

	GP	W	L	Pts	Avg
Stephen F. Austin	32	27	5	1639	51:2
Western Ill.	31	22	9	1663	53.6
Florida	37	29	8	2012	54.4
Savannah St	34	19	15	1887	55.5
Virginia	35	23	12	1945	55.6
Denver	32	22	10	1790	55.9
Wisconsin	35	23	12	1958	55.9
Pittsburgh	33	24	9	1847	56.0
North Dakota St	34	24	10	1906	56.1
Georgetown	32	25	7	1806	56.4

SCORING MARGIN

	GP	Off	Def	Mar
Gonzaga	35	77.0	59.9	17.2
Florida	37	71.4	54.4	17.0
Indiana	36	78.6	62.1	16.5
Louisville	40	74.5	58.8	15.7
Weber St.	37	75.7	61.5	14.2
Stephen F. Austin	32	64.8	51.2	13.6
Kansas	37	75.2	61.9	13.2
Pittsburgh	33	69.2	56.0	13.2
Middle Tenn	34	70.7	58.1	12.7
VCU	36	76.9	64.5	12.4

FIELD-GOAL PERCENTAGE

	GP	FGM	FGA	Pct
Weber St.	37	990	1957	50.6
Creighton	36	942	1882	50.1
Gonzaga	35	961	1934	49.7
North Carolina St.	35	985	1987	49.6
Belmont	33	906	1844	49.1
Valparaiso	34	823	1699	48.4
Michigan	39	1093	2260	48.4
Indiana	36	951	1972	48.2
Kansas	37	985	2049	48.1
Denver	32	739	1540	48.0
Bryant	31	812	1693	48.0
LIU Brooklyn	34	915	1908	48.0

FIELD-GOAL PERCENTAGE DEFENSE

	GP	Opp FG	Opp FGA	Opp Pct
Kansas	37	788	2183	36.1
Southern U.	33	658	1795	36.7
Syracuse	40	794	2154	36.9
Bucknell	34	703	1864	37.7
Georgetown	32	623	1649	37.8
Stony Brook	33	681	1802	37.8
Stephen F. Austin	32	588	1546	38.0
NJIT	29	628	1647	38.1
Florida	37	725	1897	38.2
Texas	34	739	1926	38.4

FREE-THROW PERCENTAGE

	GP	FTM	FTA	Pct
Davidson	34	560	704	79.5
Iona	34	538	689	78.1
South Dakota	30	463	593	78.1
Eastern Ky.	35	503	645	78.0
Montana	32	499	651	76.7
St. Bonaventure	29	481	630	76.3
South Dakota St.	35	478	627	76.2
Toledo	28	440	578	76.1
Creighton	36	489	644	75.9
Cal St. Fullerton	32	475	627	75.8

THREE-POINT FIELD GOALS MADE PER GAME

	GP	3FG	Avg
Iowa St.	35	346	9.9
Charleston So.	32	297	9.3
Canisius	34	313	9.2
VMI	31	282	9.1
Texas Southern	31	277	8.9
Eastern Ky.	35	307	8.8
Drake	32	279	8.7
Robert Morris	35	300	8.6
Mount St. Mary's	32	274	8.6
Creighton	36	307	8.5
Eastern Wash.	31	264	8.5
Air Force	32	272	8.5
Belmont	33	279	8.5

REBOUNDING MARGIN

	GP	Reb	Opp Reb	Margin Avg
Colorado St.	35	1400	984	11.9
Quinnipiac	31	1306	985	10.4
Utah St.	31	1162	880	9.1
Missouri	34	1386	1093	8.6
Maryland	38	1534	1209	8.6
St. Mary's (CA)	35	1295	1000	8.4
Wichita St.	39	1497	1190	7.9
Minnesota	34	1308	1048	7.6
Gonzaga	35	1310	1045	7.6
Michigan St.	36	1361	1089	7.6

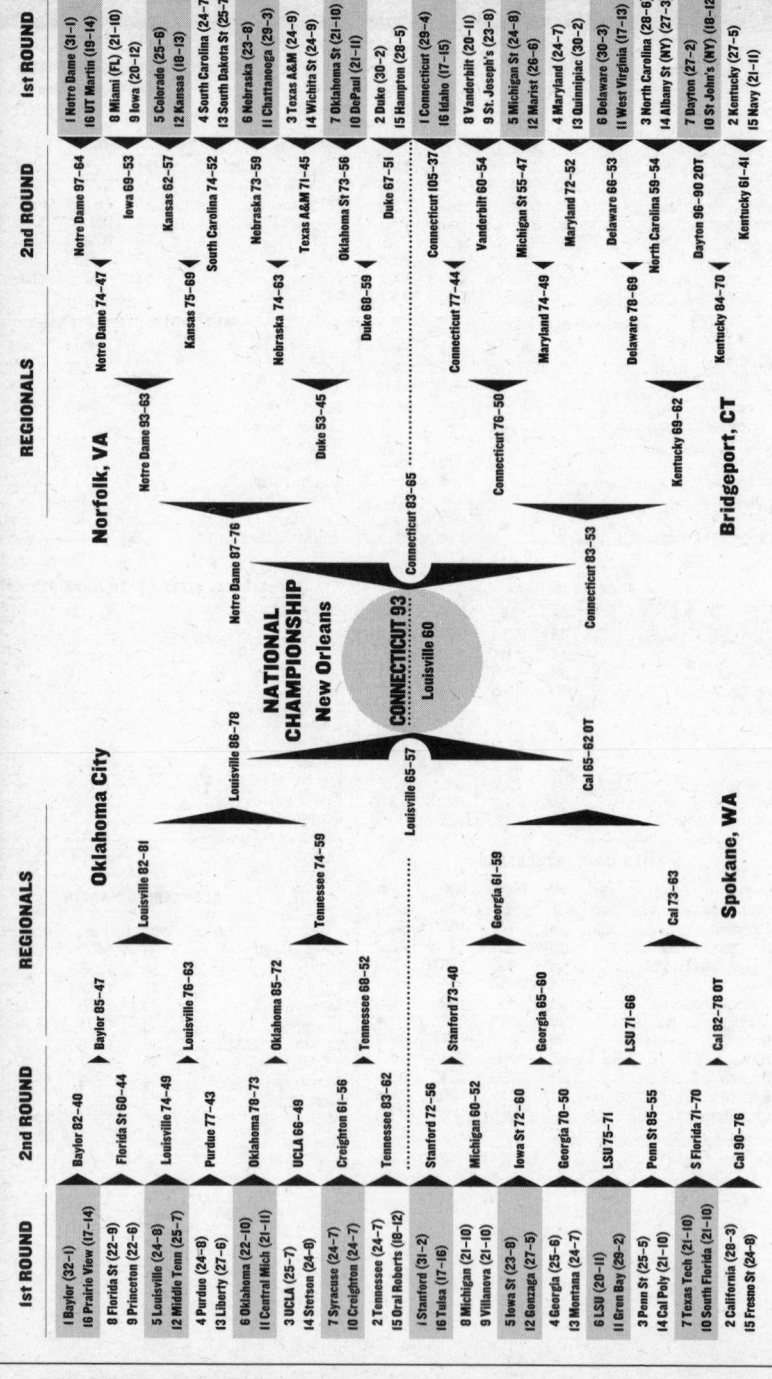

2013 NCAA Basketball Women's Division I Tournament

NATIONAL CHAMPIONSHIP
New Orleans

CONNECTICUT 93
Louisville 60

Oklahoma City

1st ROUND
- 1 Baylor (32–1)
- 16 Prairie View (17–14)
- 8 Florida St (22–9)
- 9 Princeton (22–6)
- 5 Louisville (24–8)
- 12 Middle Tenn (25–7)
- 4 Purdue (24–8)
- 13 Liberty (27–6)
- 6 Oklahoma (22–10)
- 11 Central Mich (21–11)
- 3 UCLA (25–7)
- 14 Stetson (24–8)
- 7 Syracuse (24–7)
- 10 Creighton (24–7)
- 2 Tennessee (24–7)
- 15 Oral Roberts (18–12)

2nd ROUND
- Baylor 82–40
- Florida St 60–44
- Louisville 74–49
- Purdue 77–43
- Oklahoma 78–73
- UCLA 66–49
- Creighton 61–56
- Tennessee 83–62

REGIONALS
- Baylor 85–47
- Louisville 76–63
- Oklahoma 85–72
- Tennessee 68–52
- Louisville 82–81
- Tennessee 74–59
- Louisville 86–78

Louisville 65–57

Spokane, WA

1st ROUND
- 1 Stanford (31–2)
- 16 Tulsa (17–16)
- 8 Michigan (21–10)
- 9 Villanova (21–10)
- 5 Iowa St (23–8)
- 12 Gonzaga (27–5)
- 4 Georgia (25–6)
- 13 Montana (24–7)
- 6 LSU (20–11)
- 11 Gren Bay (29–2)
- 3 Penn St (25–5)
- 14 Cal Poly (21–10)
- 7 Texas Tech (21–10)
- 10 South Florida (21–10)
- 2 California (28–3)
- 15 Fresno St (24–8)

2nd ROUND
- Stanford 72–56
- Michigan 60–52
- Iowa St 72–60
- Georgia 70–50
- LSU 75–71
- Penn St 85–55
- S Florida 71–70
- Cal 90–76

REGIONALS
- Stanford 73–40
- Georgia 65–60
- LSU 71–66
- Cal 82–78 OT
- Georgia 61–59
- Cal 73–63
- Cal 65–62 OT

Norfolk, VA

1st ROUND
- 1 Notre Dame (31–1)
- 16 UT Martin (19–14)
- 8 Miami (FL) (21–10)
- 9 Iowa (20–12)
- 5 Colorado (25–6)
- 12 Kansas (18–13)
- 4 South Carolina (24–7)
- 13 South Dakota St (25–7)
- 6 Nebraska (23–8)
- 11 Chattanooga (29–3)
- 3 Texas A&M (24–9)
- 14 Wichita St (24–9)
- 7 Oklahoma St (21–10)
- 10 DePaul (21–11)
- 2 Duke (30–2)
- 15 Hampton (28–5)

2nd ROUND
- Notre Dame 97–64
- Iowa 69–53
- Kansas 62–57
- South Carolina 74–52
- Nebraska 73–59
- Texas A&M 71–45
- Oklahoma St 73–56
- Duke 67–51

REGIONALS
- Notre Dame 74–47
- Kansas 75–69
- Nebraska 74–63
- Duke 68–59
- Notre Dame 93–63
- Duke 53–45
- Notre Dame 87–76

Connecticut 83–65

Bridgeport, CT

1st ROUND
- 1 Connecticut (29–4)
- 16 Idaho (17–15)
- 8 Vanderbilt (20–11)
- 9 St. Joseph's (23–8)
- 5 Michigan St (24–8)
- 12 Marist (26–6)
- 4 Maryland (24–7)
- 13 Quinnipiac (30–2)
- 6 Delaware (30–3)
- 11 West Virginia (17–13)
- 3 North Carolina (28–6)
- 14 Albany St (NY) (27–3)
- 7 Dayton (27–2)
- 10 St John's (NY) (18–12)
- 2 Kentucky (27–5)
- 15 Navy (21–11)

2nd ROUND
- Connecticut 105–37
- Vanderbilt 60–54
- Michigan St 55–47
- Maryland 72–52
- Delaware 66–53
- North Carolina 59–54
- Dayton 96–90 2OT
- Kentucky 61–41

REGIONALS
- Connecticut 77–44
- Maryland 74–49
- Delaware 78–69
- Kentucky 84–70
- Connecticut 76–50
- Kentucky 69–62
- Connecticut 83–53

Louisville 60

	Min	FG M-A	FT M-A	Reb O-T	A	PF	TP
S. Hammond	30	6-16	2-2	3-5	1	2	15
S. Schimmel	37	3-15	2-2	0-4	3	1	9
A. Slaughter	37	4-8	0-0	1-4	1	3	9
B. Smith	26	1-4	5-6	0-4	6	0	7
S. Vails	15	4-7	0-0	0-2	0	0	8
M. Deines	10	0-1	0-0	0-0	0	0	0
S. Harper	4	0-1	0-0	0-1	0	0	0
M. Reid	15	2-4	0-0	1-4	1	2	5
J. Schimmel	21	3-6	0-0	0-0	1	4	7
C. Walton	5	0-0	0-0	0-0	0	0	0
Totals		23-62	9-10	8-28	13	12	60

Percentages: FG-.371, FT-.900, 3-pt goals: 5–23, .217 (S. Hammond 1-3, S. Schimmel 1-8, A. Slaughter 1-4, B. Smith 0-1, S. Vails 0-1, M. Deines 0-1, S. Harper 0-1, M. Reid 1-2, J. Schimmel 1-2). Blocked shots: 4 (S. Hammond 2, A. Slaughter 1, B. Smith 1). Turnovers: 17 (S. Hammond 1, S. Schimmel 3, A. Slaughter 5, B. Smith 6, M. Deines 1, J. Schimmel 1). Steals: 10 (S. Hammond 2, S. Schimmel 1, A. Slaughter 4, B. Smith 1, S. Vails 1, J. Schimmel 1). Technical Fouls: None.

Halftime: Connecticut 48, Louisville 29.

Final Four Most Outstanding Player: Breanna Stewart, Connecticut.

Connecticut 93

	Min	FG M-A	FT M-A	Reb O-T	A	PF	TP
S. Dolson	26	4-7	4-4	3-6	5	0	12
C. Doty	13	0-1	0-0	0-0	0	1	0
K. Faris	33	6-11	0-0	1-9	6	2	16
K. Mosq.-Lewis	35	6-12	1-1	2-9	2	0	18
B. Stewart	30	9-15	2-5	3-9	3	0	23
H. Buck	3	1-2	0-0	0-0	1	1	2
B. Hartley	24	5-8	2-2	0-2	4	4	13
M. Jefferson	14	1-2	1-2	0-0	3	2	3
K. Stokes	4	0-0	0-0	0-1	0	1	0
M. Tuck	18	3-8	0-0	3-7	0	0	6
Totals		35-66	10-14	13-44	24	11	93

Percentages: FG-.530, FT-.714, 3-pt goals: 13–26, .500 (S. Dolson 0-1, C. Doty 0-1, K. Faris 4-7, K. Mosqueda-Lewis 5-8, B. Stewart 3-3, B. Hartley 1-2, M. Jefferson 0-1, M. Tuck 0-3). Blocked shots: 7 (S. Dolson 2, K. Faris 1, K. Mosqueda-Lewis 1, B. Stewart 3). Turnovers: 17 (S. Dolson 2, K. Faris 3, K. Mosqueda-Lewis 2, B. Stewart 1, B. Hartley 3, M. Jefferson 2, M. Tuck 4). Steals: 13 (S. Dolson 2, C. Doty 2, K. Faris 2, B. Stewart 3, H. Buck 1, B. Hartley 3). Technical Fouls: None.

Officials: Brenda Pantoja, Lisa Mattingly, Denise Brooks.

A: 17,545.

SCORING

Player and Team	Class	GP	TFG	3FG	FT	Pts	Avg
Jerica Coley, FIU	Jr.	32	299	34	208	840	26.3
Elena Delle Donne, Delaware	Sr.	30	271	52	187	781	26.0
Brittney Griner, Baylor	Sr.	36	355	0	148	858	23.8
Sugar Rodgers, Georgetown	Sr.	31	236	89	150	711	22.9
Jasmine Newsome, UT Martin	Jr.	34	264	75	167	770	22.6
Heather Butler, UT Martin	Jr.	34	249	105	159	762	22.4
Chiney Ogwumike, Stanford	Jr.	36	317	1	170	805	22.4
Shalonda Winton, Cleveland St	Sr.	30	202	52	203	659	22.0
Jasmine Grice, Florida A&M	Jr.	30	265	48	74	652	21.7
Diamond Ford, Texas St	Sr.	30	234	63	113	644	21.5
Tayler Hill, Ohio St	Sr.	30	189	64	192	634	21.1
Brittany Chambers, Kansas St	Sr.	37	273	117	115	778	21.0
Shareta Brown, Detroit	So.	34	241	13	219	714	21.0
Rachel Banham, Minnesota	So.	32	235	56	137	663	20.7
Alexis Govan, Western Kentucky	So.	33	253	27	138	671	20.3
Maggie Lucas, Penn St	Jr.	32	210	98	126	644	20.1
Devyn Christensen, Utah St	Sr.	32	213	107	110	643	20.1
Brandi Brown, Youngstown St	Sr.	33	241	53	127	662	20.1
Saadia Doyle, Howard	Sr.	32	207	8	215	637	19.9
Ta'Rea Cunnigan, San Jose St	So.	30	188	40	178	594	19.8
Megan Herbert, Central Arkansas	Sr.	30	195	27	176	593	19.8
Dequesha McClanahan, Winthrop	Jr.	33	237	43	135	652	19.8
Ebony Rowe, Middle Tennessee	Jr.	33	248	0	154	650	19.7
Kim Demmings, Wright St	So.	29	202	55	108	567	19.6
Hollie Mershon, Drexel	Sr.	38	259	81	142	741	19.5

FIELD-GOAL PERCENTAGE

Player and Team	Class	GP	FG	FGA	Pct
Brittney Griner, Baylor	Sr.	36	355	585	60.7
Stefanie Dolson, Connecticut	Jr.	38	213	359	59.3
Shareta Brown, Detroit	So.	34	241	407	59.2
Chiney Ogwumike, Stanford	Jr.	36	317	541	58.6
Temi Fagbenle, Harvard	So.	29	149	258	57.8
Kelsey Bone, Texas A&M	Jr.	35	244	431	56.6
Kacie Sowell, Seattle	Sr.	30	195	351	55.6
Carolyn Davis, Kansas	Sr.	34	212	383	55.4
Tianna Hawkins, Maryland	Sr.	34	257	473	54.3
Molly Schlemer, Cal Poly	Jr.	32	187	345	54.2

Note: Minimum 5 made per game.

REBOUNDS

Player and Team	Class	GP	Reb	Avg
Artemis Spanou, Robert Morris	Jr.	29	451	15.6
Sammie Jensen, Utah Valley	Sr.	28	394	14.1
Cheyenne Parker, High Point	Jr.	30	396	13.2
Naana Ankoma-Mensa, Bryant	Jr.	30	389	13.0
Chiney Ogwumike, Stanford	Jr.	36	466	12.9
S. Thomas, Sam Houston St	Sr.	33	410	12.4
Jillian Alleyne, Oregon	Fr.	31	370	11.9
E. Livermore, Fairleigh Dickinson	So.	29	344	11.9
Amanda Dowe, Charlotte	Sr.	32	374	11.7
Megan Herbert, Central Ark.	Sr.	30	346	11.5

FREE-THROW PERCENTAGE

Player and Team	Class	GP	FT	FTA	Pct
Jacqui Kalin, UNI	Sr.	34	169	177	95.5
Jaime Printy, Iowa	Sr.	34	135	146	92.5
Devyn Christensen, Utah St	Sr.	32	110	119	92.4
Elena Delle Donne, Delaware	Sr.	30	187	203	92.1
Samantha Heck, Evansville	Sr.	30	84	92	91.3
Liz Donohoe, Oklahoma St	So.	33	113	124	91.1
G. Washington, Sacred Heart	So.	33	101	111	91.0
Ali Ford, Elon	Sr.	33	89	98	90.8
Maggie Lucas, Penn St	Jr.	32	126	140	90.0
Rachel Banham, Minnesota	So.	32	137	153	89.5

Note: Minimum 2.5 made per game.

ASSISTS

Player and Team	Class	GP	Ast	Avg
Kacie Cassell, Akron	Jr.	33	259	7.8
Haley Steed, BYU	Sr.	34	254	7.5
Nikki Moody, Iowa St	So.	32	238	7.4
Sharnea Boykin, Mercer	Jr.	32	236	7.4
Angel Goodrich, Kansas	Sr.	34	245	7.2
Ericka Norman, Sacred Heart	Jr.	33	229	6.9
Chelsea Hopkins, San Diego St	Sr.	34	232	6.8
Jaci Bigham, Oral Roberts	Sr.	31	209	6.7
Ny Hammonds, Charlotte	Jr.	31	209	6.7
Andreana Thomas, Hofstra	So.	31	206	6.6
Jamierra Faulkner, Southern Miss.	Jr.	31	205	6.6

THREE-POINT FIELD-GOAL PERCENTAGE

Player and Team	Class	GP	3FG	3FGA	Pct
K. Mosqueda-Lewis, Connecticut	So.	38	118	240	49.2
Karlee Taylor, Presbyterian	Jr.	30	85	176	48.3
Tricia Liston, Duke	Jr.	36	80	172	46.5
Maggie Lucas, Penn St	Jr.	32	98	212	46.2
Taelor Karr, Gonzaga	Sr.	33	69	158	43.7
Jasmine Dale, Gardner-Webb	Jr.	24	55	129	42.6
Chantell Alford, Boston U.	Sr.	30	81	191	42.4
Damika Martinez, Iona	So.	33	79	187	42.2
A'Dia Mathies, Kentucky	Sr.	36	73	173	42.2
Kaitlyn Mileto, Wyoming	So.	32	70	167	41.9

Note: Minimum 2.0 made per game.

BLOCKED SHOTS

Player and Team	Class	GP	BS	Avg
Cheyenne Parker, High Point	Jr.	30	133	4.43
Brittney Griner, Baylor	Sr.	36	149	4.14
Latricia Lovings, TCU	Jr.	30	109	3.63
Megan Kritscher, Sacramento St	Sr.	31	111	3.58
Danielle Fiacco, Lafayette	Jr.	29	101	3.48
Schaquilla Nunn, Winthrop	Fr.	30	97	3.23
Sabrina Jeridore, Iona	Jr.	33	102	3.09
Elizabeth Williams, Duke	So.	36	107	2.97
Kayla Alexander, Syracuse	Sr.	32	94	2.94
S. Aleksandravicius, Davidson	Sr.	35	102	2.91

NCAA Men's Division II Individual Leaders

SCORING

Player and Team	Class	GP	TFG	3FG	FT	Pts	Avg
Tyshawn Good, Belmont Abbey	Sr.	32	279	64	242	864	27.0
Trevin Parks, Johnson C. Smith	Sr.	27	194	71	215	674	25.0
Ali Haidar, Michigan Tech	Sr.	30	271	14	187	743	24.8
Joe Graessle, Tiffin	Jr.	28	244	74	129	691	24.7
Tyshawn Patterson, North Greenville	Sr.	27	218	58	154	648	24.0
Aric Miller, Armstrong	Sr.	27	207	51	176	641	23.7
Byron Westmorland, Bowie St.	Sr.	29	211	103	153	678	23.4
Chad Moore, Shepherd	Sr.	27	220	9	168	617	22.9
Mark McLaughlin, Central Washington	Jr.	28	214	28	183	639	22.8
Micah Fraction, Kutztown	Sr.	28	180	57	219	636	22.7
Mitch Stahl, Oakland City	Sr.	28	220	11	180	631	22.5
Gerald Boston, Barton	Sr.	31	207	55	215	684	22.1
Nick Novak, Pitt.-Johnstown	Sr.	28	232	15	135	614	21.9
Nick Fox, Dallas Baptist	Sr.	26	204	26	125	559	21.5
Kelsey Williams, West Va. Wesleyan	Sr.	26	222	4	110	558	21.5

REBOUNDS

Player and Team	Class	GP	Reb	Avg
Garret Kerr, U Sciences	So.	26	322	12.4
Khouraichi Thiam, Mars Hill	Sr.	24	291	12.1
Eric Anderson, New Haven	So.	29	349	12.0
Dominykas Milka, Saint Rose	Jr.	29	338	11.7
Elijah Obade, Millersville	Sr.	30	334	11.1
Argelix Gil, Concordia (NY)	Sr.	28	307	11.0
Kelsey Williams, West Va. Wesleyan	Sr.	26	283	10.9
Brandon Morton, Oakland City	So.	28	300	10.7
Antoine Obery, Felician	Sr.	27	282	10.4
Kevin Kotzur, St. Mary's (TX)	Sr.	31	323	10.4

ASSISTS

Player and Team	Class	GP	Ast	Avg
Dino Mallios, St. Anselm	Jr.	29	210	7.2
Craig Nicholson, Fort Hays St	Fr.	28	192	6.9
Ben Siefert, Wheeling Jesuit	Sr.	29	190	6.6
D'Angelo Boyce, Augusta St	So.	27	176	6.5
Preston Guot, Southwest Baptist	So.	27	175	6.5
Re'Mon Nelson, S.C. Aiken	Sr.	33	209	6.3
D'Quan Lynch, Davis & Elkins	Sr.	25	158	6.3
Jake Wilcox, Post	Sr.	27	170	6.3
Brandon Lockhart, Drury	Sr.	35	215	6.1
Chris Tanzy, North Georgia	Jr.	21	128	6.1
Mike Gabbard, Erskine	Jr.	27	164	6.1

FIELD-GOAL PERCENTAGE

Player and Team	Class	GP	FG	FGA	Pct
Dazmond Starke, Ky. Wesleyan	Sr.	27	166	247	67.2
Kevin Kotzur, St. Mary's (TX)	Sr.	31	239	365	65.5
Emilio Parks, Johnson C. Smith	Jr.	27	166	254	65.4
Dermaine Smith, Lander	So.	25	131	204	64.2
Deandre Medlock, BYU-Hawaii	Jr.	28	164	256	64.1
Peter Alexis, Philadelphia U.	Fr.	29	185	291	63.6
Zach Roddenberry, Harding	Sr.	32	197	314	62.7
Zimmy Nwogbo, Cedarville	Sr.	30	191	305	62.6
Zach Robbins, Dixie St	So.	29	160	257	62.3
Will Bowles, Northwood (MI)	Jr.	27	138	222	62.2

Note: Minimum 5 made per game.

FREE-THROW PERCENTAGE

Player and Team	Class	GP	FT	FTA	Pct
Jonathan Hawkins, NW Nazarene	Sr.	26	80	85	94.1
Amry Shelby, Wayne St (NE)	Sr.	27	87	93	93.5
Austin Armga, Michigan Tech	Sr.	25	85	92	92.4
Vance Hall, Bellarmine	Jr.	32	96	105	91.4
Michael Weber, Mo.-St. Louis	Jr.	27	85	93	91.4
Chandler Hash, Anderson (SC)	Jr.	28	116	127	91.3
Riley Thomas, Lake Erie	Jr.	27	74	82	90.2
Gerald Boston, Barton	Sr.	31	215	240	89.6
Ryan Arel, Colorado St-Pueblo	Sr.	29	75	84	89.3
Seth Evans, Fla. Southern	Sr.	33	123	138	89.1

Note: Minimum 2.5 made per game.

SCORING

Player and Team	Class	GP	TFG	3FG	FT	Pts	Avg
Bianca Simmons, UMass Lowell	Sr.	27	281	53	147	762	28.2
Hillary Southworth, West Liberty	Jr.	29	253	63	131	700	24.1
Kari Daugherty, Ashland	Sr.	29	249	28	118	644	22.2
Ashley Watts, Paine	So.	28	184	71	132	571	20.4
April Thomas, Albany St (GA)	So.	26	184	84	72	524	20.2
Bria Jackson, Queens (NY)	Sr.	26	161	59	139	520	20.0
Monica Williams, Ouachita Baptist	Sr.	25	168	24	136	496	19.8
Drameka Griggs, Clayton St	Sr.	33	244	25	139	652	19.8
Keuna Flax, Central Mo.	Jr.	23	148	25	131	452	19.7
Tessondra Williams, Cal St L.A.	Sr.	32	200	46	173	619	19.3
Ginny Mills, Glenville St	Jr.	31	202	122	63	589	19.0
Lisa Petty, Humboldt St	Sr.	28	188	55	101	532	19.0
Teisha King, Tex. Permian Basin	Sr.	29	200	17	131	548	18.9
Kira Harvey, Lynn	Sr.	28	154	71	150	529	18.9
Ashle Freeman, Virginia Union	So.	27	193	28	94	508	18.8

REBOUNDS

Player and Team	Class	GP	Reb	Avg
Kiara Wright, Tarleton St	Jr.	29	406	14.0
Kari Daugherty, Ashland	Sr.	29	399	13.8
Hannah Heeter, Clarion	So.	25	332	13.3
N. Raincock-Ekunwe, Simon Fraser	Sr.	31	385	12.4
Courtney English, Miles	Sr.	27	332	12.3
Tori Arnao, Philadelphia U	Fr.	24	293	12.2
Carly Boag, Minot St	Jr.	27	319	11.8
Johnna Brown, Dixie St	Jr.	27	317	11.7
Kiara Johnson, Paine	Fr.	22	254	11.5
Destiny Smith, Henderson St	Sr.	27	308	11.4

ASSISTS

Player and Team	Class	GP	Ast	Avg
Sade Jackson, Adelphi	Jr.	28	203	7.3
Bobbi Knudsen, Mont. St Billings	Jr.	29	178	6.1
Mary Louise Dixon, Stonehill	Jr.	29	174	6.0
Sasha King, Alaska Anchorage	Sr.	23	136	5.9
Brittany Hill, S.C. Aiken	Jr.	30	176	5.9
Sierra West, Wis.-Parkside	Sr.	31	176	5.7
Stephanie Wagner, Concord	So.	27	152	5.6
Trena Moore-Smith, Montevallo	Sr.	29	160	5.5
Fernanda Mansilla, Post	Jr.	26	143	5.5
Bianca Simmons, UMass Lowell	Sr.	27	146	5.4
Kellie Rhoney, Pfeiffer	Sr.	32	172	5.4

NCAA Women's Division II Individual Leaders *(Cont.)*

FIELD-GOAL PERCENTAGE

Player and Team	Class	GP	FG	FGA	Pct
N. Raincock-Ekunwe, Simon Fraser	Sr.	31	207	318	65.1
Kiara Wright, Tarleton St	Jr.	29	189	311	60.8
Megan Fogt, Hillsdale	So.	25	147	250	58.8
Britt Harris, Western Wash	Sr.	33	185	315	58.7
Destiny Smith, Henderson St	Sr.	27	135	233	57.9
Danielle Wilson, Dowling	Sr.	33	227	400	56.8
Daiva Gerbec, Ashland	Sr.	37	217	388	55.9
Shuanda Ashford, Fayetteville St	Sr.	29	169	303	55.8
Carly Boag, Minot St	Jr.	27	190	341	55.7
Ali Wilkinson, Minn. St. Mankato	Sr.	32	191	346	55.2

Note: Minimum 5 FG per game.

FREE-THROW PERCENTAGE

Player and Team	Class	GP	FT	FTA	Pct
Sam Price, St. Cloud St	Jr.	28	97	104	93.3
Peyton Adamson, Tarleton St	Jr.	29	120	133	90.2
Taylor Lewis, Northeastern St	Sr.	27	71	79	89.9
Erin Chambers, Simon Fraser	So.	31	88	98	89.8
Tia Williams, Limestone	Sr.	31	123	137	89.8
Stephanie Kelly, Tiffin	Sr.	26	79	88	89.8
Bailey Welch, Southeastern Okla.	Sr.	27	155	173	89.6
Sam Hoyt, Michigan Tech	Sr.	30	102	114	89.5
Chelsie Luke, Northwest Nazarene	Jr.	29	76	85	89.4
Morgan Zabel, Minn. St Moorhead	Sr.	28	108	121	89.3

Note: Minimum 2.5 made per game.

NCAA Men's Division III Individual Leaders

SCORING

Player and Team	Class	GP	TFG	3FG	FT	Pts	Avg
Brandon Givens, N.C. Wesleyan	Sr.	27	207	38	272	724	26.8
Christian Jackson, Frostburg St	Sr.	26	224	44	178	670	25.8
Colton Hunt, Randolph	Sr.	28	223	49	183	678	24.2
Justin Pierce, Averett	Sr.	26	219	39	150	627	24.1
Taylor Koth, Ripon	Sr.	24	187	20	181	575	24.0
Nathan Roeder, North Central (MN)	Sr.	28	213	56	178	660	23.6
Darius Watson, Albertus Magnus	Jr.	28	239	48	127	653	23.3
John DiBartolomeo, Rochester (NY)	Sr.	27	181	60	188	610	22.6
AJ Matthews, Farmingdale St	Sr.	25	198	0	168	564	22.6
Joshua Ford, Mitchell	Jr.	26	237	9	97	580	22.3
Taeshon Johnson, Southern Vt.	Sr.	24	204	8	118	534	22.3
Jake Schwarz, Lakeland	Sr.	28	221	73	106	621	22.2
Ryan Sheehan, Nichols	Jr.	25	201	52	100	554	22.2
Tony Vails, York (NY)	Sr.	26	191	24	167	573	22.0
Sedale Jones, Curry	Sr.	29	208	49	173	638	22.0

REBOUNDS

Player and Team	Class	GP	Reb	Avg
AJ Matthews, Farmingdale St	Sr.	25	367	14.7
Winston Douglas, Medgar Evers	Sr.	26	349	13.4
Mike Marvin, Penn St-Abington	So.	26	330	12.7
Peterson Bernard, Newbury	Sr.	26	321	12.3
Dane Jobst, Worcester St	Jr.	26	314	12.1
Jack Bramswig, Manhattanville	Jr.	25	289	11.6
David Louison, St. Joseph's (Brkln)	So.	29	334	11.5
James Lazarcik, Beloit	Jr.	23	261	11.3
Anthonly DiLoreto, Crown (MN)	Jr.	26	289	11.1

Four tied with 11.0.

ASSISTS

Player and Team	Class	GP	Ast	Avg
Jerald Williams, Lycoming	Sr.	27	268	9.9
Bryan Hurley, Bowdoin	So.	24	200	8.3
Jason Rosenberg, Rowan	Jr.	26	199	7.7
Sean Rossi, Ithaca	Sr.	30	214	7.1
Andy Winters, Ohio Wesleyan	Sr.	29	204	7.0
Paul Dail, CCNY	Sr.	26	177	6.8
Isaiah Boxell, Ozarks (AR)	Sr.	24	158	6.6
Kwahmere Gredic, Rust	Jr.	24	156	6.5
Chris Shovlin, Wilkes	Jr.	21	135	6.4
Erik Olson, Wis.-Stout	Sr.	27	167	6.2

FIELD-GOAL PERCENTAGE

Player and Team	Class	GP	FG	FGA	Pct
James Lazarcik, Beloit	Jr.	23	159	235	67.7
Kevin McMahon, SUNY Cortland	Jr.	29	150	227	66.1
K. Williamson, Hampden-Sydney	Jr.	26	148	225	65.8
Joshua Ford, Mitchell	Jr.	26	237	369	64.2
Matt Lorello, Geneva	Sr.	26	190	298	63.8
Peter Kaasila, Amherst	Sr.	32	181	285	63.5
Zac Richards, Birmingham-So.	Sr.	27	151	238	63.4
Clayton Whitlock, MacMurray	So.	25	138	218	63.3
Peter Lynch, Middlebury	Sr.	28	171	272	62.9
Mark Lessen, Eureka	Sr.	24	192	307	62.5

Note: Minimum 5 made per game.

FREE-THROW PERCENTAGE

Player and Team	Class	GP	FT	FTA	Pct
John Henault, Endicott	So.	25	65	69	94.2
Angel Ortiz, Lasell	So.	21	63	69	91.3
Aaron Stefanov, Hiram	Jr.	23	81	89	91.0
J. DiBartolomeo, Rochester (NY)	Sr.	27	188	207	90.8
Tim Harwood, Salisbury	Jr.	27	80	89	89.9
Nate Vernon, Rochester (NY)	Jr.	27	76	85	89.4
Zach Peterson, Wis.-River Falls	Jr.	25	65	73	89.0
Chris Barsanti, Dickinson	Sr.	28	72	81	88.9
Aaron Toomey, Amherst	Jr.	32	135	152	88.8
Sean Rossi, Ithaca	Sr.	30	78	88	88.6

Note: Minimum 2.5 made per game.

SCORING

Player and Team	Class	GP	TFG	3FG	FT	Pts	Avg
Ashley Montecchio, Rosemont	Sr.	26	217	29	184	647	24.9
Mollie Whiting, Dubuque	Sr.	28	262	35	108	667	23.8
Aliah Curry, Norwich	So.	25	170	72	163	575	23.0
Deanna Purcell, Rivier	So.	25	196	45	128	565	22.6
Kate Nielsen, Simpson	Sr.	29	218	36	176	648	22.3
Bianca Richburg, Greensboro	Sr.	24	196	37	104	533	22.2
Caty Eeten, Eureka	Jr.	25	179	33	164	555	22.2
Makenzie Brandon, Occidental	Sr.	25	206	7	123	542	21.7
Elizabeth Coyne, Rosemont	So.	26	199	2	154	554	21.3
Ashley Roser, Wells	Jr.	26	199	4	149	551	21.2
Vanessa Bosques, Daniel Webster	Sr.	27	196	82	98	572	21.2
Emily Mehr, Minn.-Morris	Sr.	21	167	40	69	443	21.1
Lauren Avant, Rhodes	Jr.	25	179	20	139	517	20.7
Sarah Wetmore, Rensselaer	Sr.	25	168	39	137	512	20.5
Judy Mundt, Crown (MN)	Sr.	22	150	44	105	449	20.4

REBOUNDS

Player and Team	Class	GP	Reb	Avg
Ashley Roser, Wells	Jr.	26	433	16.7
Tytravia Riley, Bard	Fr.	25	380	15.2
Alyson Caiazzo, Manhattanville	So.	24	360	15.0
Catherine O'Connell, Newbury	Sr.	26	389	15.0
Rebecca Yoshor, Yeshiva	Jr.	19	281	14.8
Sarah Collins, Babson	Sr.	29	401	13.8
Jamecia Forsythe, John Jay	Jr.	26	352	13.5
Hayley Zophin, Nichols	Sr.	25	316	12.6
Meaghan O'Keefe, Worcester St	Sr.	26	328	12.6
Heather Fuller, Wesley	Sr.	24	299	12.5

ASSISTS

Player and Team	Class	GP	Ast	Avg
Katlin Michaels, King's (PA)	Sr.	27	197	7.3
Haley Ooms, Becker	Jr.	27	187	6.9
Aja Wallpher, York (PA)	Jr.	26	180	6.9
Kylie Yoshimura, Dallas	Sr.	26	167	6.4
Taylor Greene, DeSales	Sr.	26	161	6.2
Cailin Bullett, Colby-Sawyer	Sr.	29	177	6.1
Kaitlyn Birrell, Salve Regina	Sr.	28	159	5.7
Shea Smith, Ferrum	Jr.	27	151	5.6
Stephanie Kuzmanic, Carthage	Jr.	29	162	5.6
Jen Ashton, Westfield St	So.	30	166	5.5
Emily Grabiak, Catholic	Jr.	29	160	5.5
Kelsey Campbell, Olivet	Jr.	26	143	5.5
Sarah Johnson, Rhodes	So.	28	153	5.5

FIELD-GOAL PERCENTAGE

Player and Team	Class	GP	FG	FGA	Pct
Anecia Richardson, Trinity (TX)	Fr.	28	165	276	59.8
Kelecia Harris, Albright	Fr.	23	134	225	59.6
Lindsey Kelly, Nazareth	Fr.	25	161	276	58.3
Megan Boutilette, Bridgewater St	Jr.	27	142	244	58.2
Carissa Verkaik, Calvin	Sr.	27	211	364	58.0
Kelsey Shoemake, Eureka	So.	25	130	226	57.5
Jacole Hairston, Ferrum	So.	29	158	276	57.2
Emily Peel, Carnegie Mellon	Sr.	25	138	242	57.0
Fiona McMahon, Elmhurst	So.	24	125	222	56.3
Marla Willard, Monmouth (IL)	Jr.	24	130	236	55.1

Note: Minimum 5 made per game.

FREE-THROW PERCENTAGE

Player and Team	Class	GP	FT	FTA	Pct
Maureen Hirt, Kenyon	Jr.	28	84	91	92.3
Kelly Muffley, Thiel	Sr.	25	82	89	92.1
Kara McDuffee, St. Lawrence	So.	28	79	88	89.8
Shannon Allan, Lynchburg	So.	28	84	95	88.4
Mallory Shanahan, Neb. Wesleyan	Sr.	25	84	95	88.4
Connie Urmanski, Wis.-Superior	Sr.	27	68	77	88.3
Katie Budz, Dominican (IL)	Jr.	25	102	116	87.9
Megan Musashi, La Verne	Jr.	20	58	66	87.9
Lauren McNanna, Beloit	Jr.	23	140	160	87.5
Megan Koepnick, Luther	So.	26	80	92	87.0

Note: Minimum 2.5 made per game.

NCAA Men's Division I Championship Results

NCAA Final Four Results

Year	Winner	Score	Runner-up	Third Place	Fourth Place	Winning Coach
1939	Oregon	46–33	Ohio St	*Villanova	*Villanova	Howard Hobson
1940	Indiana	60–42	Kansas	*Duquesne	*USC	Branch McCracken
1941	Wisconsin	39–34	Washington St	*Pittsburgh	*Arkansas	Harold Foster
1942	Stanford	53–38	Dartmouth	*Colorado	*Kentucky	Everett Dean
1943	Wyoming	46–34	Georgetown	*Texas	*DePaul	Everett Shelton
1944	Utah	42–40 (OT)	Dartmouth	*Iowa St	*Ohio St	Vadal Peterson
1945	Oklahoma St	49–45	NYU	*Arkansas	*Ohio St	Hank Iba
1946	Oklahoma St	43–40	North Carolina	Ohio St	California	Hank Iba
1947	Holy Cross	58–47	Oklahoma	Texas	CCNY	Alvin Julian
1948	Kentucky	58–42	Baylor	Holy Cross	Kansas St	Adolph Rupp
1949	Kentucky	46–36	Oklahoma St	Illinois	Oregon St	Adolph Rupp
1950	CCNY	71–68	Bradley	North Carolina St	Baylor	Nat Holman
1951	Kentucky	68–58	Kansas St	Illinois	Oklahoma St	Adolph Rupp
1952	Kansas	80–63	St. John's (N.Y.)	Illinois	Santa Clara	Forrest Allen
1953	Indiana	69–68	Kansas	Washington	LSU	Branch McCracken
1954	La Salle	92–76	Bradley	Penn St	USC	Kenneth Loeffler
1955	San Francisco	77–63	La Salle	Colorado	Iowa	Phil Woolpert
1956	San Francisco	83–71	Iowa	Temple	SMU	Phil Woolpert
1957	North Carolina	54–53 (3OT)	Kansas	San Francisco	Michigan St	Frank McGuire
1958	Kentucky	84–72	Seattle	Temple	Kansas St	Adolph Rupp
1959	California	71–70	West Virginia	Cincinnati	Louisville	Pete Newell
1960	Ohio St	75–55	California	Cincinnati	NYU	Fred Taylor
1961	Cincinnati	70–65 (OT)	Ohio St	Vacated‡	Utah	Edwin Jucker
1962	Cincinnati	71–59	Ohio St	Wake Forest	UCLA	Edwin Jucker
1963	Loyola (Ill.)	60–58 (OT)	Cincinnati	Duke	Oregon St	George Ireland
1964	UCLA	98–83	Duke	Michigan	Kansas St	John Wooden
1965	UCLA	91–80	Michigan	Princeton	Wichita St	John Wooden
1966	UTEP	72–65	Kentucky	Duke	Utah	Don Haskins
1967	UCLA	79–64	Dayton	Houston	North Carolina	John Wooden
1968	UCLA	78–55	North Carolina	Ohio St	Houston	John Wooden
1969	UCLA	92–72	Purdue	Drake	North Carolina	John Wooden
1970	UCLA	80–69	Jacksonville	New Mexico St	St. Bonaventure	John Wooden
1971	UCLA	68–62	Vacated‡	Vacated‡	Kansas	John Wooden
1972	UCLA	81–76	Florida St	North Carolina	Louisville	John Wooden
1973	UCLA	87–66	Memphis St	Indiana	Providence	John Wooden
1974	North Carolina St	76–64	Marquette	UCLA	Kansas	Norm Sloan
1975	UCLA	92–85	Kentucky	Louisville	Syracuse	John Wooden
1976	Indiana	86–68	Michigan	UCLA	Rutgers	Bob Knight
1977	Marquette	67–59	North Carolina	UNLV	UNC-Charlotte	Al McGuire
1978	Kentucky	94–88	Duke	Arkansas	Notre Dame	Joe Hall
1979	Michigan St	75–64	Indiana St	DePaul	Penn	Jud Heathcote
1980	Louisville	59–54	Vacated‡	Purdue	Iowa	Denny Crum
1981	Indiana	63–50	North Carolina	Virginia	LSU	Bob Knight
1982	North Carolina	63–62	Georgetown	*Houston	*Louisville	Dean Smith
1983	North Carolina St	54–52	Houston	*Georgia	*Louisville	Jim Valvano
1984	Georgetown	84–75	Houston	*Kentucky	*Virginia	John Thompson
1985	Villanova	66–64	Georgetown	St. John's (N.Y.)	Vacated‡	Rollie Massimino
1986	Louisville	72–69	Duke	*Kansas	*LSU	Denny Crum
1987	Indiana	74–73	Syracuse	*UNLV	*Providence	Bob Knight
1988	Kansas	83–79	Oklahoma	*Arizona	*Duke	Larry Brown
1989	Michigan	80–79 (OT)	Seton Hall	*Duke	*Illinois	Steve Fisher
1990	UNLV	103–73	Duke	*Arkansas	*Georgia Tech	Jerry Tarkanian
1991	Duke	72–65	Kansas	*UNLV	*North Carolina	Mike Krzyzewski
1992	Duke	71–51	Michigan	*Cincinnati	*Indiana	Mike Krzyzewski
1993	North Carolina	77–71	Michigan	*Kansas	*Kentucky	Dean Smith
1994	Arkansas	76–72	Duke	*Arizona	*Florida	Nolan Richardson
1995	UCLA	89–78	Arkansas	*North Carolina	*Oklahoma St	Jim Harrick
1996	Kentucky	76–67	Syracuse	Vacated‡	Mississippi St	Rick Pitino
1997	Arizona	84–79 (OT)	Kentucky	Vacated‡	*North Carolina	Lute Olson
1998	Kentucky	78–69	Utah	*Stanford	*North Carolina	Tubby Smith
1999	Connecticut	77–74	Duke	*Michigan St	*Ohio St	Jim Calhoun
2000	Michigan St	89–76	Florida	*Wisconsin	*North Carolina	Tom Izzo
2001	Duke	82–72	Arizona	*Maryland	*Michigan St	Mike Krzyzewski

NCAA Final Four Results (Cont.)

Year	Winner	Score	Runner-up	Third Place	Fourth Place	Winning Coach
2002	Maryland	64–52	Indiana	*Kansas	*Oklahoma	Gary Williams
2003	Syracuse	81–78	Kansas	*Marquette	*Texas	Jim Boeheim
2004	Connecticut	82–73	Georgia Tech	*Oklahoma St	*Duke	Jim Calhoun
2005	North Carolina	75-70	Illinois	*Louisville	*Michigan St	Roy Williams
2006	Florida	73-57	UCLA	*George Mason	*LSU	Billy Donovan
2007	Florida	84–75	Ohio St	*UCLA	*Georgetown	Billy Donovan
2008	Kansas	75–68 (OT)	Vacated‡	*UCLA	*North Carolina	Bill Self
2009	North Carolina	89–72	Michigan St	*Villanova	*Connecticut	Roy Williams
2010	Duke	61–59	Butler	*West Virginia	*Michigan St	Mike Krzyzewski
2011	Connecticut	53–41	Butler	*Kentucky	*VCU	Jim Calhoun
2012	Kentucky	67–59	Kansas	*Ohio State	*Louisville	John Calipari
2013	Louisville	82–76	Michigan	*Syracuse	*Wichita State	Rick Pitino

*Tied for third place. ‡Student-athletes representing St. Joseph's (Pa.) in 1961, Villanova in 1971, Western Kentucky in 1971, UCLA in 1980, Memphis State in 1985, Massachusetts in 1996, Minnesota in 1997 and Memphis in 2008 were declared ineligible subsequent to the tournament. Under NCAA rules, the teams' and ineligible student-athletes' records were deleted, and the teams' places in the standings were vacated.

NCAA Final Four Most Outstanding Players

Year	Winner, School	GP	Field Goals		3-Pt FG		Free Throws		Reb	Ast	Stl	BS	Avg
			FGM	Pct	FGA	FGM	FTM	Pct					
1939	None selected												
1940	Marv Huffman, Indiana	2	7	—	—	—	4	—	—	—	—	—	9.0
1941	John Kotz, Wisconsin	2	8	—	—	—	6	—	—	—	—	—	11.0
1942	Howard Dallmar, Stanford	2	8	—	—	—	4	66.7	—	—	—	—	10.0
1943	Ken Sailors, Wyoming	2	10	—	—	—	8	72.7	—	—	—	—	14.0
1944	Arnie Ferrin, Utah	2	11	—	—	—	6	—	—	—	—	—	14.0
1945	Bob Kurland, Oklahoma St	2	16	—	—	—	5	—	—	—	—	—	18.5
1946	Bob Kurland, Oklahoma St	2	21	—	—	—	10	66.7	—	—	—	—	26.0
1947	George Kaftan, Holy Cross	2	18	—	—	—	12	70.6	—	—	—	—	24.0
1948	Alex Groza, Kentucky	2	16	—	—	—	5	—	—	—	—	—	18.5
1949	Alex Groza, Kentucky	2	19	—	—	—	14	—	—	—	—	—	26.0
1950	Irwin Dambrot, CCNY	2	12	42.9	—	—	4	50.0	—	—	—	—	14.0
1951	None selected												
1952	Clyde Lovellette, Kansas	2	24	—	—	—	18	—	—	—	—	—	33.0
1953	*B.H. Horn, Kansas	2	17	—	—	—	17	—	—	—	—	—	25.5
1954	Tom Gola, La Salle	2	12	—	—	—	14	—	—	—	—	—	19.0
1955	Bill Russell, San Francisco	2	19	—	—	—	9	—	—	—	—	—	23.5
1956	*Hal Lear, Temple	2	32	—	—	—	16	—	—	—	—	—	40.0
1957	*Wilt Chamberlain, Kansas	2	18	51.4	—	—	19	70.4	25	—	—	—	32.5
1958	*Elgin Baylor, Seattle	2	18	34.0	—	—	12	75.0	41	—	—	—	24.0
1959	*Jerry West, West Virginia	2	22	66.7	—	—	22	68.8	25	—	—	—	33.0
1960	Jerry Lucas, Ohio St	2	16	66.7	—	—	3	100.0	23	—	—	—	17.5
1961	*Jerry Lucas, Ohio St	2	20	71.4	—	—	16	94.1	25	—	—	—	28.0
1962	Paul Hogue, Cincinnati	2	23	63.9	—	—	12	63.2	38	—	—	—	29.0
1963	Art Heyman, Duke	2	18	41.0	—	—	15	68.2	19	—	—	—	25.5
1964	Walt Hazzard, UCLA	2	11	55.0	—	—	8	66.7	10	—	—	—	15.0
1965	*Bill Bradley, Princeton	2	34	63.0	—	—	19	95.0	24	—	—	—	43.5
1966	*Jerry Chambers, Utah	2	25	53.2	—	—	20	83.3	35	—	—	—	35.0
1967	Lew Alcindor, UCLA	2	14	60.9	—	—	11	45.8	38	—	—	—	19.5
1968	Lew Alcindor, UCLA	2	22	62.9	—	—	9	90.0	34	—	—	—	26.5
1969	Lew Alcindor, UCLA	2	23	67.7	—	—	16	64.0	41	—	—	—	31.0
1970	Sidney Wicks, UCLA	2	15	71.4	—	—	9	60.0	34	—	—	—	19.5
1971	*†Howard Porter, Villanova	2	20	48.8	—	—	7	77.8	24	—	—	—	23.5
1972	Bill Walton, UCLA	2	20	69.0	—	—	17	73.9	41	—	—	—	28.5
1973	Bill Walton, UCLA	2	28	82.4	—	—	2	40.0	30	—	—	—	29.0
1974	David Thompson, NC St	2	19	51.4	—	—	11	78.6	17	—	—	—	24.5
1975	Richard Washington, UCLA	2	23	54.8	—	—	8	72.7	20	—	—	—	27.0
1976	Kent Benson, Indiana	2	17	50.0	—	—	7	63.6	18	—	—	—	20.5
1977	Butch Lee, Marquette	2	11	34.4	—	—	8	100.0	6	2	1	1	15.0
1978	Jack Givens, Kentucky	2	28	65.1	—	—	8	66.7	17	4	1	3	32.0
1979	Earvin Johnson, Michigan St	2	17	68.0	—	—	19	86.4	17	3	0	2	26.5
1980	Darrell Griffith, Louisville	2	23	62.2	—	—	11	68.8	7	15	0	2	28.5
1981	Isiah Thomas, Indiana	2	14	56.0	—	—	9	81.8	4	9	3	4	18.5
1982	James Worthy, North Carolina	2	20	74.1	—	—	2	28.6	8	9	0	4	21.0
1983	*Akeem Olajuwon, Houston	2	16	55.2	—	—	9	64.3	40	3	2	5	20.5
1984	Patrick Ewing, Georgetown	2	8	57.1	—	—	2	100.0	18	1	1	15	9.0
1985	Ed Pinckney, Villanova	2	8	57.1	—	—	12	75.0	15	6	3	0	14.0

*Not a member of the championship-winning team. †Record later vacated.

NCAA Final Four Most Outstanding Players *(Cont.)*

Year	Winner, School	GP	Field Goals		3-Pt FG		Free Throws		Reb	Ast	Stl	BS	Avg
			FGM	Pct	FGA	FGM	FTM	Pct					
1986	Pervis Ellison, Louisville	2	15	60.0	—	—	6	75.0	24	2	3	1	18.0
1987	Keith Smart, Indiana	2	14	63.6	1	0	7	77.8	7	7	0	2	17.5
1988	Danny Manning, Kansas	2	25	55.6	1	0	6	66.7	17	4	8	9	28.0
1989	Glen Rice, Michigan	2	24	49.0	16	7	4	100.0	16	1	0	3	29.5
1990	Anderson Hunt, UNLV	2	19	61.3	16	9	2	50.0	4	9	1	1	24.5
1991	Christian Laettner, Duke	2	12	54.5	1	1	21	91.3	17	2	1	2	23.0
1992	Bobby Hurley, Duke	2	10	41.7	12	7	8	80.0	3	11	0	3	17.5
1993	Donald Williams, North Carolina	2	15	65.2	14	10	10	100.0	4	2	2	0	25.0
1994	Corliss Williamson, Arkansas	2	21	50.0	0	0	10	71.4	21	8	4	3	26.0
1995	Ed O'Bannon, UCLA	2	16	45.7	8	3	10	76.9	25	3	7	1	22.5
1996	Tony Delk, Kentucky	2	15	41.7	16	8	6	54.6	9	2	3	2	22.0
1997	Miles Simon, Arizona	2	17	45.9	10	3	17	77.3	8	6	0	1	27.0
1998	Jeff Sheppard, Kentucky	2	16	55.2	10	4	7	77.8	10	7	4	0	21.5
1999	Richard Hamilton, Connecticut	2	20	51.3	7	3	8	72.7	12	4	2	1	25.5
2000	Mateen Cleaves, Michigan St	2	8	44.4	4	3	10	83.3	6	5	2	0	14.5
2001	Shane Battier, Duke	2	13	50.0	12	5	12	70.6	19	8	2	6	21.5
2002	Juan Dixon, Maryland	2	16	59.3	15	7	12	80.0	8	5	7	0	25.5
2003	Carmelo Anthony, Syracuse	2	19	54.3	9	6	9	81.1	24	8	4	0	26.5
2004	Emeka Okafor, Connecticut	2	17	65.4	0	0	8	53.3	22	2	1	4	21.0
2005	Sean May, North Carolina	2	19	65.5	0	0	10	71.4	17	5	1	2	24.0
2006	Joakim Noah, Florida	2	12	60.0	1	0	4	100.0	17	5	2	10	14.0
2007	Corey Brewer, Florida	2	9	47.3	13	7	7	87.5	10	2	3	5	16.0
2008	Mario Chalmers, Kansas	2	10	43.5	9	3	6	75.0	7	6	7	0	14.5
2009	Wayne Ellington, North Carolina	2	14	53.8	11	8	3	75.0	13	4	0	0	19.5
2010	Kyle Singler, Duke	2	15	34.1	10	6	4	100.0	18	7	3	2	20.0
2011	Kemba Walker, Connecticut	2	11	32.4	9	1	11	84.6	15	7	3	1	17.0
2012	Anthony Davis, Kentucky	2	8	44.4	0	0	8	66.6	30	7	4	11	12.0
2013	Luke Hancock, Louisville	2	11	73.3	10	8	12	70.6	5	5	4	0	21.0

Best NCAA Tournament Single-Game Scoring Performances

Player and Team	Year	Round	FG	3FG	FT	TP
Austin Carr, Notre Dame vs Ohio	1970	1st	25	—	11	61
Bill Bradley, Princeton vs Wichita St	1965	C*	22	—	14	58
Oscar Robertson, Cincinnati vs Arkansas	1958	C	21	—	14	56
Austin Carr, Notre Dame vs Kentucky	1970	2nd	22	—	8	52
Austin Carr, Notre Dame vs TCU	1971	1st	20	—	12	52
David Robinson, Navy vs Michigan	1987	1st	22	0	6	50
Elvin Hayes, Houston vs Loyola (Ill.)	1968	1st	20	—	9	49
Hal Lear, Temple vs SMU	1956	C*	17	—	14	48
Austin Carr, Notre Dame vs Houston	1971	C	17	—	13	47
Dave Corzine, DePaul vs Louisville	1978	2nd	18	—	10	46

C=regional third place; C*=third-place game.

NIT Championship Results

Year	Winner	Score	Runner-up	Year	Winner	Score	Runner-up
1938	Temple	60–36	Colorado	1958	Xavier (Ohio)	78–74 (OT)	Dayton
1939	Long Island U.	44–32	Loyola (Ill.)	1959	St. John's (N.Y.)	76–71 (OT)	Bradley
1940	Colorado	51–40	Duquesne	1960	Bradley	88–72	Providence
1941	Long Island U.	56–42	Ohio U	1961	Providence	62–59	St. Louis
1942	West Virginia	47–45	W. Kentucky	1962	Dayton	73–67	St. John's (N.Y.)
1943	St. John's (N.Y.)	48–27	Toledo	1963	Providence	81–66	Canisius
1944	St. John's (N.Y.)	47–39	DePaul	1964	Bradley	86–54	New Mexico
1945	DePaul	71–54	Bowling Green	1965	St. John's (N.Y.)	55–51	Villanova
1946	Kentucky	46–45	Rhode Island	1966	BYU	97–84	NYU
1947	Utah	49–45	Kentucky	1967	Southern Illinois	71–56	Marquette
1948	St. Louis	65–52	NYU	1968	Dayton	61–48	Kansas
1949	San Francisco	48–47	Loyola (Ill.)	1969	Temple	89–76	Boston College
1950	CCNY	69–61	Bradley	1970	Marquette	65–53	St. John's (N.Y.)
1951	BYU	62–43	Dayton	1971	North Carolina	84–66	Georgia Tech
1952	La Salle	75–64	Dayton	1972	Maryland	100–69	Niagara
1953	Seton Hall	58–46	St. John's (N.Y.)	1973	Virginia Tech	92–91 (OT)	Notre Dame
1954	Holy Cross	71–62	Duquesne	1974	Purdue	97–81	Utah
1955	Duquesne	70–58	Dayton	1975	Princeton	80–69	Providence
1956	Louisville	93–80	Dayton	1976	Kentucky	71–67	UNC-Charlotte
1957	Bradley	84–83	Memphis St	1977	St. Bonaventure	94–91	Houston

NIT Championship Results *(Cont.)*

Year	Winner	Score	Runner-up	Year	Winner	Score	Runner-up
1978	Texas	101–93	North Carolina St	1996	Nebraska	60–56	St. Joseph's
1979	Indiana	53–52	Purdue	1997	Michigan	82–73	Florida St
1980	Virginia	58–55	Minnesota	1998	Minnesota	79–72	Penn St
1981	Tulsa	86–84 (OT)	Syracuse	1999	California	61–60	Clemson
1982	Bradley	67–58	Purdue	2000	Wake Forest	71–61	Notre Dame
1983	Fresno St	69–60	DePaul	2001	Tulsa	79–60	Alabama
1984	Michigan	83–63	Notre Dame	2002	Memphis	72–62	South Carolina
1985	UCLA	65–62	Indiana	2003	St. John's	70–67	Georgetown
1986	Ohio St	73–63	Wyoming	2004	Michigan	62–55	Rutgers
1987	Southern Miss	84–80	La Salle	2005	South Carolina	60–57	Saint Joseph's
1988	Connecticut	72–67	Ohio St	2006	South Carolina	76–64	Michigan
1989	St. John's (N.Y.)	73–65	St. Louis	2007	West Virginia	78–73	Clemson
1990	Vanderbilt	74–72	St. Louis	2008	Ohio St	92–85	Massachusetts
1991	Stanford	78–72	Oklahoma	2009	Penn St	69–63	Baylor
1992	Virginia	81–76	Notre Dame	2010	Dayton	79–68	North Carolina
1993	Minnesota	62–61	Georgetown	2011	Wichita St	66–57	Alabama
1994	Villanova	80–73	Vanderbilt	2012	Stanford	75–51	Minnesota
1995	Virginia Tech	65–64 (OT)	Marquette	2013	Baylor	74–54	Iowa

NCAA Men's Division I Season Leaders

Scoring Average

Year	Player and Team	Ht	Class	GP	FG	3FG	FT	Pts	Avg
1949	Murray Wier, Iowa	5-9	Sr.	19	152	—	95	399	21.0
1950	Tony Lavelli, Yale	6-3	Sr.	30	228	—	215	671	22.4
1951	Paul Arizin, Villanova	6-3	Sr.	29	260	—	215	735	25.3
1952	Bill Mlkvy, Temple	6-4	Sr.	25	303	—	125	731	29.2
1953	Clyde Lovellette, Kansas	6-9	Sr.	28	315	—	165	795	28.4
1954	Frank Selvy, Furman	6-3	Jr.	25	272	—	194	738	29.5
1955	Frank Selvy, Furman	6-3	Sr.	29	427	—	355	1209	41.7
1956	Darrell Floyd, Furman	6-1	Jr.	25	344	—	209	897	35.9
1957	Darrell Floyd, Furman	6-1	Sr.	28	339	—	268	946	33.8
1958	Grady Wallace, South Carolina	6-4	Sr.	29	336	—	234	906	31.2
1959	Oscar Robertson, Cincinnati	6-5	So.	28	352	—	280	984	35.1
1960	Oscar Robertson, Cincinnati	6-5	Jr.	30	331	—	316	978	32.6
1961	Oscar Robertson, Cincinnati	6-5	Sr.	30	369	—	273	1011	33.7
1962	Frank Burgess, Gonzaga	6-1	Sr.	26	304	—	234	842	32.4
1963	Billy McGill, Utah	6-9	Sr.	26	394	—	221	1009	38.8
1964	Nick Werkman, Seton Hall	6-3	Jr.	22	221	—	208	650	29.5
1965	Howard Komives, Bowling Green	6-1	Sr.	23	292	—	260	844	36.7
1966	Rick Barry, Miami (Fla.)	6-7	Sr.	26	340	—	293	973	37.4
1967	Dave Schellhase, Purdue	6-4	Sr.	24	284	—	213	781	32.5
1968	Jim Walker, Providence	6-3	Sr.	28	323	—	205	851	30.4
1969	Pete Maravich, LSU	6-5	So.	26	432	—	274	1138	43.8
1970	Pete Maravich, LSU	6-5	Jr.	26	433	—	282	1148	44.2
1971	Pete Maravich, LSU	6-5	Sr.	31	522	—	337	1381	44.5
1972	Johnny Neumann, Mississippi	6-6	So.	23	366	—	191	923	40.1
1973	Dwight Lamar, SW Louisiana	6-1	Jr.	29	429	—	196	1054	36.3
1974	William Averitt, Pepperdine	6-1	Sr.	25	352	—	144	848	33.9
1975	Larry Fogle, Canisius	6-5	So.	25	326	—	183	835	33.4
1976	Bob McCurdy, Richmond	6-7	Sr.	26	321	—	213	855	32.9
1977	Marshall Rodgers, Tex.-Pan American	6-2	Sr.	25	361	—	197	919	36.8
1978	Freeman Williams, Portland St	6-4	Jr.	26	417	—	176	1010	38.8
1979	Freeman Williams, Portland St	6-4	Sr.	27	410	—	149	969	35.9
1990	Lawrence Butler, Idaho St	6-3	Sr.	27	310	—	192	812	30.1
1981	Tony Murphy, Southern-Birmingham	6-3	Sr.	29	377	—	178	932	32.1
1982	Zam Fredrick, South Carolina	6-2	Sr.	27	300	—	181	781	28.9
1983	Harry Kelly, Texas Southern	6-7	Jr.	29	336	—	190	862	29.7
1984	Harry Kelly, Texas Southern	6-7	Sr.	29	333	—	169	835	28.8
1985	Joe Jakubick, Akron	6-5	Sr.	27	304	—	206	814	30.1
1986	Xavier McDaniel, Wichita St	6-8	Sr.	31	351	—	142	844	27.2
1987	Terrance Bailey, Wagner	6-2	Jr.	29	321	—	212	854	29.4
1988	Kevin Houston, Army	5-11	Sr.	29	311	63	268	953	32.9
1989	Hersey Hawkins, Bradley	6-3	Sr.	31	377	87	284	1125	36.3
1990	Hank Gathers, Loyola Marymount	6-7	Jr.	31	419	0	177	1015	32.7
1991	Bo Kimble, Loyola Marymount	6-5	Sr.	32	404	92	231	1131	35.3

Scoring Average *(Cont.)*

Year	Player and Team	Ht	Class	GP	FG	3FG	FT	Pts	Avg
1992	Kevin Bradshaw, U.S. Int'l	6-6	Sr.	28	358	60	278	1054	37.6
1993	Brett Roberts, Morehead St	6-8	Sr.	29	278	66	193	815	28.1
1994	Greg Guy, Tex.-Pan American	6-1	Jr.	19	189	67	111	556	29.3
1995	Glenn Robinson, Purdue	6-8	Jr.	34	368	79	215	1030	30.3
1996	Kurt Thomas, TCU	6-9	Sr.	27	288	3	202	781	28.9
1997	Kevin Granger, Texas Southern	6-3	Sr.	24	194	30	230	648	27.0
1998	Charles Jones, LIU-Brooklyn	6-3	Jr.	30	338	109	118	903	30.1
1999	Charles Jones, LIU-Brooklyn	6-3	Sr.	30	326	116	101	869	29.0
2000	Alvin Young, Niagara	6-3	Sr.	29	253	65	157	728	25.1
2001	Courtney Alexander, Fresno St	6-6	Sr.	27	252	58	107	669	24.8
2002	Ronnie McCollum, Centenary	6-4	Sr.	27	244	85	214	787	29.1
2003	Jason Conley, Virginia Military Institute	6-5	Fr.	28	285	79	171	820	29.3
2004	Ruben Douglas, New Mexico	6-5	Sr.	28	218	94	253	783	28.0
2005	Keydren Clark, St. Peter's	5-9	So.	29	233	112	197	775	26.7
2006	Keydren Clark, St. Peter's	5-9	Jr.	28	230	109	152	721	25.8
2007	Adam Morrison, Gonzaga	6-8	Jr.	33	306	74	240	926	28.1
2008	Reggie Williams, Virginia Military Institute	6-5	Jr.	33	338	76	176	928	28.1
2009	Stephen Curry, Davidson	6-3	Jr.	34	312	130	220	974	28.6
2010	Aubrey Coleman, Houston	6-4	Sr.	35	305	51	235	896	25.6
2011	Jimmer Fredette, BYU	6-2	Sr.	37	346	124	252	1068	28.9
2012	Reggie Hamilton, Oakland	5-11	Sr.	36	281	118	262	942	26.2
2013	Erick Green, Virginia Tech	6-4	Sr.	32	261	61	218	801	25.0

Rebounds

Year	Player and Team	Ht	Class	GP	Reb	Avg
1952	Ernie Beck, Pennsylvania	6-4	So.	27	556	20.6
1953	Bill Hannon, Army	6-3	So.	17	355	20.9
1954	Ed Conlin, Fordham	6-5	So.	26	612	23.5
1955	Art Quimby, Connecticut	6-5	Jr.	26	588	22.6
1956	Charlie Slack, Marshall	6-5	Jr.	21	538	25.6
1957	Joe Holup, George Washington	6-6	Sr.	26	604	†.256
1958	Elgin Baylor, Seattle	6-6	Jr.	25	508	†.235
1959	Alex Ellis, Niagara	6-5	Sr.	25	536	†.262
1960	Leroy Wright, Pacific	6-8	Jr.	26	652	†.238
1961	Leroy Wright, Pacific	6-8	Sr.	17	380	†.234
1961	Jerry Lucas, Ohio St	6-8	Jr.	27	470	†.198
1963	Jerry Lucas, Ohio St	6-8	Sr.	28	499	†.211
1964	Paul Silas, Creighton	6-7	Sr.	27	557	20.6
1965	Bob Pelkington, Xavier (Ohio)	6-7	Sr.	26	567	21.8
1966	Toby Kimball, Connecticut	6-8	Sr.	23	483	21.0
1967	Jim Ware, Oklahoma City	6-8	Sr.	29	607	20.9
1968	Dick Cunningham, Murray St	6-10	Jr.	22	479	21.8
1969	Neal Walk, Florida	6-10	Jr.	25	494	19.8
1970	Spencer Haywood, Detroit	6-8	So.	22	472	21.5
1971	Artis Gilmore, Jacksonville	7-2	Jr.	28	621	22.2
1972	Artis Gilmore, Jacksonville	7-2	Sr.	26	603	23.2
1973	Kermit Washington, American	6-8	Jr.	23	455	19.8
1974	Kermit Washington, American	6-8	Sr.	22	439	20.0
1975	Marvin Barnes, Providence	6-9	Sr.	32	597	18.7
1976	John Irving, Hofstra	6-9	So.	21	323	15.4
1977	Sam Pellom, Buffalo	6-8	So.	26	420	16.2
1978	Glenn Mosley, Seton Hall	6-8	Sr.	29	473	16.3
1979	Ken Williams, North Texas St	6-7	Sr.	28	411	14.7
1980	Monti Davis, Tennessee St	6-7	Jr.	26	421	16.2
1981	Larry Smith, Alcorn St	6-8	Sr.	26	392	15.1
1982	Darryl Watson, Miss. Valley St	6-7	Sr.	27	379	14.0
1983	LaSalle Thompson, Texas	6-10	Jr.	27	365	13.5
1984	Xavier McDaniel, Wichita St	6-7	So.	28	403	14.4
1985	Akeem Olajuwon, Houston	7-0	Jr.	37	500	13.5
1986	Xavier McDaniel, Wichita St	6-8	Sr	31	460	14.8
1987	David Robinson, Navy	6-11	Jr.	35	455	13.0
1988	Jerome Lane, Pittsburgh	6-6	So.	33	444	13.5
1989	Kenny Miller, Loyola (Ill.)	6-9	Fr.	29	395	13.6
1990	Hank Gathers, Loyola Marymount	6-7	Jr.	31	426	13.7
1991	Anthony Bonner, St. Louis	6-8	Sr.	33	456	13.8
1992	Shaquille O'Neal, LSU	7-1	So.	28	411	14.7

Rebounds (Cont.)

Year	Player and Team	Ht	Class	GP	Reb	Avg
1993	Popeye Jones, Murray St	6-8	Sr.	30	431	14.4
1994	Warren Kidd, Middle Tenn. St	6-9	Sr.	26	386	14.8
1995	Jerome Lambert, Baylor	6-8	Jr.	24	355	14.8
1996	Kurt Thomas, TCU	6-9	Sr.	27	393	14.6
1997	Marcus Mann, Miss. Valley St	6-8	Sr.	29	394	13.6
1998	Tim Duncan, Wake Forest	6-11	Sr.	31	457	14.7
1999	Ryan Perryman, Dayton	6-7	Sr.	33	412	12.5
2000	Ian McGinnis, Dartmouth	6-8	So.	26	317	12.2
2001	Darren Phillips, Fairfield	6-7	Sr.	29	405	14.0
2002	Chris Marcus, Western Kentucky	7-1	Jr.	31	374	12.1
2003	Jeremy Bishop, Quinnipiac	6-6	J..	29	347	12.0
2004	Brandon Hunter, Ohio	6-7	Sr.	30	378	12.6
2005	Paul Millsap, Louisiana Tech	6-7	Fr.	30	374	12.5
2006	Paul Millsap, Louisiana Tech	6-8	So.	29	360	12.4
2007	Paul Millsap, Louisiana Tech	6-8	Jr.	33	438	13.3
2008	Rashad Jones-Jennings, Ark.-Little Rock	6-8	Sr.	30	392	13.3
2009	Blake Griffin, Oklahoma	6-10	So.	35	504	14.4
2010	Artsiom Parakhouski, Radford	6-11	Sr.	31	414	13.4
2011	Kenneth Faried, Morehead St	6-8	Sr.	35	508	14.5
2012	O.D. Anosike, Siena	6-8	Jr.	31	388	12.5
2013	O.D. Anosike, Siena	6-8	Sr.	32	364	11.4

†From 1956–1962, title was based on highest individual recoveries out of total by both teams in all games.

Assists

Year	Player and Team	Class	GP	Ast	Avg
1985	Craig Lathen, Ill.-Chicago	Jr.	29	274	9.45
1986	Rob Weingard, Hofstra	Sr.	24	228	9.50
1987	Mark Jackson, St. John's (N.Y.)	Jr.	36	328	9.11
1988	Avery Johnson, Southern-Birm.	Jr.	31	333	10.74
1989	Avery Johnson, Southern-Birm.	Sr.	30	399	13.30
1990	Glenn Williams, Holy Cross	Sr.	28	278	9.93
1991	Todd Lehmann, Drexel	Sr.	28	260	9.29
1992	Chris Corchiani, North Carolina St	Sr.	31	299	9.65
1993	Van Usher, Tennessee Tech	Sr.	29	254	8.76
1994	Sam Crawford, New Mexico St	Sr.	34	310	9.12
1995	Jason Kidd, California	So.	30	272	9.06
1996	Nelson Haggerty, Baylor	Sr.	28	284	10.10
1997	Raimonds Miglinieks, UC-Irvine	Sr.	27	230	8.52
1998	Kenny Mitchell, Dartmouth	Sr.	26	203	7.81
1999	Ahlon Lewis, Arizona St	Sr.	32	294	9.19
2000	Doug Gottlieb, Oklahoma St	Jr.	34	299	8.79
2001	Mark Dickel, UNLV	Sr.	31	280	9.03
2002	Markus Carr, CSU-Northridge	Jr.	32	286	8.94
2003	T.J. Ford, Texas	Fr.	33	273	8.27
2004	Martell Bailey, Ill.-Chicago	Jr.	30	244	8.13
2005	Greg Davis, Troy St	Sr.	31	256	8.26
2006	Damitrius Coleman, Mercer	Jr.	28	224	8.00
	Will Funn, Portland St	Sr.	28	224	8.00
2007	Jared Jordan, Marist	Jr.	29	247	8.52
2008	Jared Jordan, Marist	Sr.	31	274	8.83
2009	Johnathon Jones, Oakland	Jr.	36	290	8.06
2010	Ronald Moore, Siena	Sr.	34	261	7.68
2011	Aaron Johnson, UAB	Sr.	31	239	7.71
2012	Scott Machado, Iona	Sr.	33	327	9.90
2013	Jason Brickman, LIU Brooklyn	Jr.	34	289	8.50

Blocked Shots

Year	Player and Team	Class	GP	BS	Avg
1986	David Robinson, Navy	Jr.	35	207	5.91
1987	David Robinson, Navy	Sr.	32	144	4.50
1988	Rodney Blake, St. Joseph's (Pa.)	Sr.	29	116	4.00
1989	Alonzo Mourning, Georgetown	Fr.	34	169	4.97
1990	Kenny Green, Rhode Island	Sr.	26	124	4.77
1991	Shawn Bradley, BYU	Fr.	34	177	5.21
1992	Shaquille O'Neal, LSU	Jr.	30	157	5.23
1993	Theo Ratliff, Wyoming	Jr.	28	124	4.43
1994	Grady Livingston, Howard	Jr.	26	115	4.42
1995	Keith Closs, Central Conn. St	Fr.	26	139	5.35
1996	Keith Closs, Central Conn. St	So.	28	178	6.36
1997	Adonal Foyle, Colgate	Jr.	28	180	6.43
1998	Jerome James, Florida A&M	Sr.	27	125	4.63
1999	Tarvis Williams, Hampton	So.	27	135	5.00
2000	Ken Johnson, Ohio St	Sr.	30	161	5.37
2001	Tarvis Williams, Hampton	Sr	32	147	4.59
2002	Wojciech Myrda, La.-Monroe	Sr.	32	172	5.38
2003	Emeka Okafor, Connecticut	So.	33	156	4.73
2004	Anwar Ferguson, Houston	Sr.	27	111	4.11
2005	Deng Gai, Fairfield	Sr.	30	165	5.50
2006	Shawn James, Northeastern	So.	30	196	6.53
2007	Mickell Gladness, Ala.-A&M	Jr.	30	188	6.26
2008	Jarvis Varnado, Mississippi St	So.	34	157	4.62
2009	Jarvis Varnado, Mississippi St	Jr.	36	170	4.72
2010	Hassan Whiteside, Marshall	Fr.	34	182	5.35
2011	William Mosley, Northwestern St	Jr.	32	156	4.88
2012	Anthony Davis, Kentucky	Fr.	40	186	4.65
2013	Chris Obekpa, St. John's (NY)	Fr.	33	133	4.03

Steals

Year	Player and Team	Class	GP	Stl	Avg
1987	Darron Brittman, Chicago St	Sr.	28	139	4.96
1988	Tony Fairley, Charleston South.	Sr.	28	114	4.07
1989	Aldwin Ware, Florida A&M	Sr.	29	142	4.90
1990	Kenny Robertson, Cleveland St	Jr.	28	111	3.96
1991	Ronn McMahon, E. Washington	Sr.	29	130	4.48
1992	Van Usher, Tennessee Tech	Jr.	28	104	3.71
1993	Victor Snipes, NE Illinois	So.	25	86	3.44
1994	Jason Kidd, California	Fr.	29	110	3.80
1995	Shawn Griggs, SW Louisiana	Sr.	30	120	4.00
1996	Roderick Anderson, Texas	Sr.	30	101	3.37
1997	Pointer Williams, McNeese St	Sr.	27	118	4.37
1998	Joel Hoover, Md.-Eastern Shore	Fr.	28	90	3.21
1999	Bonzi Wells, Ball St	Sr.	29	103	3.55
2000	Shawnta Rogers, George Wash.	Sr.	29	103	3.55
2001	Carl Williams, Liberty	Sr.	28	107	3.82
2002	Greedy Daniels, TCU	Jr.	25	108	4.32
2003	Desmond Cambridge, Ala. A&M	Sr.	29	160	5.52
2004	Alexis McMillan, Stetson	Sr.	22	87	3.95
2005	Marques Green, St. Bonaventure	Sr.	27	107	3.96
2006	Obie Trotter, Alabama A&M	Jr.	32	125	3.91
2007	Tim Smith, East Tennessee St	Sr.	28	95	3.39
2008	Travis Holmes, Virg. Mil. Inst.	So.	33	111	3.36
2009	Chavis Holmes, Virg. Mil. Inst.	Sr.	31	105	3.39
2010	Jay Threatt, Delaware St	So.	29	82	2.83
2011	Anthony Nelson, Niagara	Sr.	29	98	3.38
2012	Fuquan Edwin, Seton Hall	So.	34	102	3.00
2013	Duke Mondy, Oakland	Jr.	33	100	3.03

Single Game Records

SCORING HIGHS VS DIVISION I OPPONENT

Pts	Player and Team vs Opponent	Date
72	Kevin Bradshaw, U.S. Int'l vs Loyola Marymount	1-5-91
69	Pete Maravich, LSU vs Alabama	2-7-70
68	Calvin Murphy, Niagara vs Syracuse	12-7-68
66	Jay Handlan, Washington & Lee vs Furman	2-17-51
66	Pete Maravich, LSU vs Tulane	2-10-69
66	Anthony Roberts, Oral Roberts vs North Carolina A&T	2-19-77
65	Anthony Roberts, Oral Roberts vs Oregon	3-9-77
65	Scott Haffner, Evansville vs Dayton	2-18-89
64	Pete Maravich, LSU vs Kentucky	2-21-70
63	Johnny Neumann, Mississippi vs LSU	1-30-71
63	Hersey Hawkins, Bradley vs Detroit	2-22-88

SCORING HIGHS VS NON-DIVISION I OPPONENT

Pts	Player and Team vs Opponent	Date
100	Frank Selvy, Furman vs Newberry	2-13-54
85	Paul Arizin, Villanova vs Philadelphia NAMC	2-12-49
81	Freeman Williams, Portland St vs Rocky Mountain	2-3-78
73	Bill Mlkvy, Temple vs Wilkes	3-3-51
71	Freeman Williams, Portland St vs South Oregon	2-9-77

REBOUNDING HIGHS ALL-TIME

Reb	Player and Team vs Opponent	Date
51	Bill Chambers, William & Mary vs Virginia	2-14-53
43	Charlie Slack, Marshall vs Morris Harvey	1-12-54
42	Tom Heinsohn, Holy Cross vs Boston College	3-1-55
40	Art Quimby, Connecticut vs Boston University	1-11-55
39	Maurice Stokes, St. Francis (Pa.) vs John Carroll	1-28-55
39	Dave DeBusschere, Detroit vs C. Michigan	1-30-60
39	Keith Swagerty, Pacific vs UC-Santa Barbara	3-5-65

REBOUNDING HIGHS SINCE 1973*

Reb	Player and Team vs Opponent	Date
35	Larry Abney, Fresno St vs SMU	2-17-00
34	David Vaughn, Oral Roberts vs Brandeis	1-8-73
32	Jervaughn Scales, Southern-Birm. vs Grambling	2-7-94
32	Durand Macklin, LSU vs Tulane	11-26-76
31	Jim Bradley, Northern Illinois vs UW-Milwaukee	2-19-73
31	Calvin Natt, NE Louisiana vs Georgia Southern	12-29-76

ASSISTS

Asst	Player and Team vs Opponent	Date
22	Tony Fairley, Baptist vs Armstrong St	2-9-87
22	Avery Johnson, Southern-Birm. vs Texas Southern	1-25-88
22	Sherman Douglas, Syracuse vs Providence	1-28-89
21	Kelvin Scarborough, New Mexico vs Hawaii	2-13-87
21	Anthony Manuel, Bradley vs UC-Irvine	12-19-87
21	Avery Johnson, Southern-Birm. vs Alabama St	1-16-88

STEALS

Stl	Player and Team vs Opponent	Date
13	Mookie Blaylock, Oklahoma vs Centenary	12-12-87
13	Mookie Blaylock, Oklahoma vs Loyola Marymount	12-17-88
12	Kenny Robertson, Cleveland St vs Wagner	12-3-88
12	Terry Evans, Oklahoma vs Florida A&M	1-27-93
12	Richard Duncan, Middle Tenn. St vs Eastern Kentucky	2-20-99
12	Greedy Daniels, Texas Christian vs Ark.–Pine Bluff	12-30-00
12	Jehiel Lewis, Navy vs Bucknell	1-12-02
12	Carldell Johnson, Ala.-Birmingham vs. South Carolina St	11-27-05

BLOCKED SHOTS

BS	Player and Team vs Opponent	Date
16	Mickell Gladness, Alabama A&M vs Texas Southern	2-24-07
14	David Robinson, Navy vs UNC–Wilmington	1-4-86
14	Shawn Bradley, BYU vs Eastern Kentucky	12-7-90
14	Roy Rogers, Alabama vs Georgia	2-10-96
14	Loren Woods, Arizona vs Oregon	2-3-00
14	Darrius Garrett, Richmond vs Massachusetts	1-13-10

Eleven players tied with 13

Single Season Records

POINTS

Player and Team	Year	GP	FG	3FG	FT	Pts
Pete Maravich, LSU	1970	31	522	—	337	1381
Elvin Hayes, Houston	1968	33	519	—	176	1214
Frank Selvy, Furman	1954	29	427	—	355	1209
Pete Maravich, LSU	1969	26	433	—	282	1148
Pete Maravich, LSU	1968	26	432	—	274	1138
Bo Kimble, Loyola Marymount	1990	32	404	92	231	1131
Hersey Hawkins, Bradley	1988	31	377	87	284	1125
Austin Carr, Notre Dame	1970	29	444	—	218	1106
Austin Carr, Notre Dame	1971	29	430	—	241	1101
Otis Birdsong, Houston	1977	36	452	—	186	1090

SCORING AVERAGE

Player and Team	Year	GP	FG	FT	Pts	Avg
Pete Maravich, LSU	1970	31	522	337	1381	44.5
Pete Maravich, LSU	1969	26	433	282	1148	44.2
Pete Maravich, LSU	1968	26	432	274	1138	43.8
Frank Selvy, Furman	1954	29	427	355	1209	41.7
Johnny Neumann, Mississippi	1971	23	366	191	923	40.1
Freeman Williams, Portland St	1977	26	417	176	1010	38.8
Billy McGill, Utah	1962	26	394	221	1009	38.8
Calvin Murphy, Niagara	1968	24	337	242	916	38.2
Austin Carr, Notre Dame	1970	29	444	218	1106	38.1
Austin Carr, Notre Dame	1971	29	430	241	1101	38.0

REBOUNDS

Player and Team	Year	GP	Reb	Player and Team	Year	GP	Reb
Walt Dukes, Seton Hall	1953	33	734	Artis Gilmore, Jacksonville	1970	28	621
Leroy Wright, Pacific	1959	26	652	Tom Gola, La Salle	1955	31	618
Tom Gola, La Salle	1954	30	652	Ed Conlin, Fordham	1953	26	612
Charlie Tyra, Louisville	1956	29	645	Art Quimby, Connecticut	1955	25	611
Paul Silas, Creighton	1964	29	631	Bill Russell, San Francisco	1956	29	609
Elvin Hayes, Houston	1968	33	624	Jim Ware, Oklahoma City	1966	29	607

REBOUND AVERAGE

Player and Team	Year	GP	Reb	Avg
Charlie Slack, Marshall	1955	21	538	25.6
Leroy Wright, Pacific	1959	26	652	25.1
Art Quimby, Connecticut	1955	25	611	24.4
Charlie Slack, Marshall	1956	22	520	23.6
Ed Conlin, Fordham	1953	26	612	23.5

REBOUND AVERAGE SINCE 1973*

Player and Team	Year	GP	Reb	Avg
Kermit Washington, American	1973	22	439	20.0
Marvin Barnes, Providence	1973	30	571	19.0
Marvin Barnes, Providence	1974	32	597	18.7
Pete Padgett, Nev.-Reno	1973	26	462	17.8
Jim Bradley, Northern Illinois	1973	24	426	17.8

ASSISTS

Player and Team	Year	GP	Asst	Player and Team	Year	GP	Asst
Mark Wade, UNLV	1987	38	406	Mark Jackson, St. John's (N.Y.)	1986	32	328
Avery Johnson, Southern-Birm	1988	30	399	Scott Machado, Iona	2012	33	327
Anthony Manuel, Bradley	1988	31	373	Sherman Douglas, Syracuse	1989	38	326
Kendall Marshall, North Carolina	2012	36	351	Sam Crawford, New Mex. St.	1993	34	310
Avery Johnson, Southern-Birm	1987	31	333	Greg Anthony, UNLV	1991	35	310
				Reid Gettys, Houston	1984	37	309

ASSIST AVERAGE

Player and Team	Year	GP	Asst	Avg	Player and Team	Year	GP	Asst	Avg
Avery Johnson, Southern-Birm.	1988	30	399	13.3	Scott Machado, Iona	2012	33	327	9.9
Anthony Manuel, Bradley	1988	31	373	12.0	Kendall Marshall, North Carolina	2012	36	351	9.75
Avery Johnson, Southern-Birm.	1987	31	333	10.7	Chris Corchiani, North Carolina St.	1991	31	299	9.6
Mark Wade, UNLV	1987	38	406	10.7	Tony Fairley, Charleston South.†	1987	28	270	9.6
Nelson Haggerty, Baylor	1995	28	284	10.1	Tyrone Bogues, Wake Forest	1987	29	276	9.5
Glenn Williams, Holy Cross	1989	28	278	9.9	Ron Weingard, Hofstra	1985	24	228	9.5

*Freshmen became eligible for varsity play in 1973. †Formerly Baptist College.

Single Season Records *(Cont.)*

FIELD-GOAL PERCENTAGE

Player and Team	Year	GP	FG	FGA	Pct
Steve Johnson, Oregon St	1981	28	235	315	74.6
Dwayne Davis, Florida	1989	33	179	248	72.2
Keith Walker, Utica	1985	27	154	216	71.3
Steve Johnson, Oregon St	1980	30	211	297	71.0
Adam Mark, Belmont	2002	26	150	212	70.8
Oliver Miller, Arkansas	1991	38	254	361	70.4
Alan Williams, Princeton	1987	25	163	232	70.3
Mark McNamara, California	1982	27	231	329	70.2
Warren Kidd, Middle Tennessee St	1991	30	173	247	70.0
Pete Freeman, Akron	1991	28	175	250	70.0

Based on qualifiers for NCAA annual championship.

FREE-THROW PERCENTAGE

Player and Team	Year	GP	FT	FTA	Pct
Blake Ahearn, SW Missouri St†	2004	33	117	120	97.5
Ryan Toolson, Utah Valley St.	2006	29	96	99	97.0
Derek Raivio, Gonzaga	2006	33	146	152	96.1
Craig Collins, Penn St	1985	27	94	98	95.9
A.J. Graves, Butler	2006	32	137	143	95.8
J.J. Redick, Duke	2004	37	143	150	95.3
Steve Drabyn, Belmont	2003	29	78	82	95.1
Donald Sims, Appalachian St	2009	37	175	184	95.1
Rod Foster, UCLA	1982	27	95	100	95.0
Clay McKnight, Pacific	2000	24	74	78	94.9
Matt Logie, Lehigh	2003	28	91	96	94.8

THREE-POINT FIELD-GOAL PERCENTAGE

Player and Team	Year	GP	3FG	3FGA	Pct
Glenn Tropf, Holy Cross	1988	29	52	82	63.4
Sean Wightman, Western Michigan	1992	30	48	76	63.2
Keith Jennings, East Tennessee St	1991	33	84	142	59.2
Dave Calloway, Monmouth (N.J.)	1989	28	48	82	58.5
Steve Kerr, Arizona	1988	38	114	199	57.3
Reginald Jones, Prairie View	1987	28	64	112	57.1
Jim Cantamessa, Siena	1998	29	66	117	56.4
Joel Tribelhorn, Colorado St	1989	33	76	135	56.3
Mike Joseph, Bucknell	1988	28	65	116	56.0
Brian Jackson, Evansville	1995	27	53	95	55.8

Based on qualifiers for annual championship.

STEALS

Player and Team	Year	GP	Stl
Desmond Cambridge, Alabama A&M	2002	29	160
Mookie Blaylock, Oklahoma	1988	39	150
Aldwin Ware, Florida A&M	1988	29	142
Darron Brittman, Chicago St	1986	28	139
John Linehan, Providence	2002	31	139

BLOCKED SHOTS

Player and Team	Year	GP	BS
David Robinson, Navy	1986	35	207
Shawn James, Northeastern	2005	30	196
Mickell Gladness, Alabama A&M	2006	30	188
Anthony Davis, Kentucky	2012	40	186
Hassan Whiteside, Marshall	2010	34	182

STEAL AVERAGE

Player and Team	Year	GP	Stl	Avg
D. Cambridge, Alabama A&M	2002	29	160	5.52
Darron Brittman, Chicago St	1986	28	139	4.96
Aldwin Ware, Florida A&M	1988	29	142	4.90
John Linehan, Providence	2002	31	139	4.48
Ronn McMahon, E. Washington	1990	29	130	4.48

BLOCKED-SHOT AVERAGE

Player and Team	Year	GP	BS	Avg
Shawn James, Northeastern	2005	30	196	6.53
Adonal Foyle, Colgate	1997	28	180	6.43
Keith Closs, Central Conn. St	1996	28	178	6.36
Mickell Gladness, Alabama A&M	2006	30	188	6.26
David Robinson, Navy	1986	35	207	5.91

†Southwest Missouri State changed name to Missouri State after 2004–05 season.
Based on qualifiers for annual championship.

Career Records

POINTS

Player and Team	Ht	Final Year	GP	FG	3FG*	FT	Pts
Pete Maravich, LSU	6-5	1970	83	1387	—	893	3667
Freeman Williams, Portland St.	6-4	1978	106	1369	—	511	3249
Lionel Simmons, La Salle	6-7	1990	131	1244	56	673	3217
Alphonso Ford, Mississippi Valley St	6-2	1993	109	1121	333	590	3165
Harry Kelly, Texas Southern	6-7	1983	110	1234	—	598	3066
Keydren Clark, St. Peter's	5-9	2006	118	967	435	689	3058
Hersey Hawkins, Bradley	6-3	1988	125	1100	118	690	3008
Oscar Robertson, Cincinnati	6-5	1960	88	1052	—	869	2973
Danny Manning, Kansas	6-10	1988	147	1216	10	509	2951
Alfredrick Hughes, Loyola (Ill.)	6-5	1985	120	1226	—	462	2914
Elvin Hayes, Houston	6-8	1968	93	1215	—	454	2884
Tyler Hansbrough, North Carolina	6-9	2009	142	939	12	982	2872
Larry Bird, Indiana St.	6-9	1979	94	1154	—	542	2850
Otis Birdsong, Houston	6-4	1977	116	1176	—	480	2832
Kevin Bradshaw, Bethune-Cookman, U.S. Int'l.	6-6	1991	111	1027	132	618	2804
Allan Houston, Tennessee	6-6	1993	128	902	346	651	2801
J.J. Redick, Duke	6-4	2006	139	825	457	662	2769
Hank Gathers, USC, Loyola Marymount	6-7	1990	117	1127	0	469	2723
Reggie Lewis, Northeastern	6-7	1987	122	1043	30 (1)	592	2708
Daren Queenan, Lehigh	6-5	1988	118	1024	29	626	2703

*Listed is the number of three-pointers scored since it became the national rule in 1987; the number in the parentheses is number scored prior to 1987—these counted as three points in the game but counted as two-pointers in the national rankings. The three-pointers in the parentheses are not included in total points.

SCORING AVERAGE

Player and Team	Final Year	GP	FG	FT	Pts	Avg
Pete Maravich, LSU	1968	83	1387	893	3667	44.2
Austin Carr, Notre Dame	1971	74	1017	526	2560	34.6
Oscar Robertson, Cincinnati	1960	88	1052	869	2973	33.8
Calvin Murphy, Niagara	1970	77	947	654	2548	33.1
Dwight Lamar, SW Louisiana	1973	57	768	326	1862	32.7
Frank Selvy, Furman	1954	78	922	694	2538	32.5
Rick Mount, Purdue	1970	72	910	503	2323	32.3
Darrell Floyd, Furman	1956	71	868	545	2281	32.1
Nick Werkman, Seton Hall	1964	71	812	649	2273	32.0
Willie Humes, Idaho St.	1971	48	565	380	1510	31.5
William Averitt, Pepperdine	1973	49	615	311	1541	31.4
Elgin Baylor, Coll. of Idaho, Seattle	1958	80	956	588	2500	31.3
Elvin Hayes, Houston	1968	93	1215	454	2884	31.0
Freeman Williams, Portland St.	1978	106	1369	511	3249	30.7
Larry Bird, Indiana St.	1979	94	1154	542	2850	30.3

Career Records *(Cont.)*

REBOUNDS ALL-TIME

Player and Team	Final Year	GP	Reb
Tom Gola, La Salle	1955	118	2201
Joe Holup, George Washington	1956	104	2030
Charlie Slack, Marshall	1956	88	1916
Ed Conlin, Fordham	1955	102	1884
Dickie Hemric, Wake Forest	1955	104	1802

REBOUNDS SINCE 1973*

Player and Team	Final Year	GP	Reb
Kenneth Faried, Morehead St	2011	136	1673
Tim Duncan, Wake Forest	1997	128	1570
Derrick Coleman, Syracuse	1990	143	1537
Malik Rose, Drexel	1996	120	1514
Ralph Sampson, Virginia	1983	132	1511

ASSISTS

Player and Team	Final Year	GP	Asst
Bobby Hurley, Duke	1993	140	1076
Chris Corchiani, North Carolina St	1991	124	1038
Ed Cota, North Carolina	2000	138	1030
Keith Jennings, East Tennessee St	1991	127	983
Steve Blake, Maryland	2003	138	972

FIELD-GOAL PERCENTAGE

Player and Team	Final Year	FG	FGA	Pct
Steve Johnson, Oregon St	1981	828	1222	67.8
Michael Bradley, Kentucky/Villanova	2001	441	651	67.7
Murray Brown, Florida St	1980	566	847	66.8
Lee Campbell, SW Missouri St	1990	411	618	66.5
Warren Kidd, Middle Tennessee St	1993	496	747	66.4

Note: Minimum 400 field goals and 4 FG made per game.

FREE-THROW PERCENTAGE

Player and Team	Final Year	FT	FTA	Pct
Blake Ahearn, Missouri St	2007	435	460	94.6
Derek Raivio, Gonzaga	2007	343	370	92.7
Gary Buchanan, Villanova	2003	324	355	91.3
J.J. Redick, Duke	2006	662	726	91.2
Greg Starrick, Kentucky/Southern Illinois	1972	341	375	90.9

Note: Minimum 300 free throws made.

*Freshmen became eligible for varsity play in 1973.

Career Records *(Cont.)*

THREE-POINT FIELD GOALS MADE

Player and Team	Final Year	GP	3FG
J.J. Redick, Duke	2006	139	457
David Holston, Chicago St	2009	119	450
Keydren Clark, St. Peter's	2006	118	435
Chris Lofton, Tennessee	2008	128	431
Kevin Foster, Santa Clara	2013	133	431

THREE-POINT FIELD-GOAL PERCENTAGE

Player and Team	Final Year	3FG	3FGA	Pct
Tony Bennett, UW–Green Bay	1992	290	584	49.7
Stephen Sir, San Diego St/Northern Ariz.	2007	323	689	46.9
David Olson, Eastern Illinois	1992	262	562	46.6
Jaycee Carroll, Utah St	2008	369	793	46.5
Ross Land, Northern Arizona	2000	308	664	46.4

Note: Minimum 200 3-point field goals and 2.0 3-point field goals per game.

STEALS

Player and Team	Final Year	GP	Stl
John Linehan, Providence	2002	122	385
Eric Murdock, Providence	1991	117	376
Pepe Sanchez, Temple	2000	116	365
Cookie Belcher, Nebraska	2001	131	353
Kevin Braswell, Georgetown	2002	128	349

BLOCKED SHOTS

Player and Team	Final Year	GP	BS
Jarvis Varnado, Mississipi St	2010	141	564
Wojciech Myrda, La.-Monroe	2002	115	535
Adonal Foyle, Colgate	1997	87	492
Tim Duncan, Wake Forest	1997	128	481
William Mosley, Northwestern St	2012	124	460
Alonzo Mourning, Georgetown	1992	120	453

NCAA Men's Division I Team Leaders

Division I Team Alltime Wins

Team	First Year	Yrs	W	L
Kentucky	1903	110	2111	661
Kansas	1899	115	2101	812
North Carolina	1911	103	2090	745
Duke	1906	108	2001	840
Syracuse	1901	112	1874	832
Temple	1895	117	1814	992
St. John's (N.Y.)	1908	106	1754	931
UCLA	1920	94	1753	779
Notre Dame	1898	108	1748	949
Indiana	1901	113	1719	966
Pennsylvania	1897	113	1706	1020
Louisville	1912	99	1696	869
Illinois	1906	108	1690	910
Brigham Young	1903	111	1690	1026
Utah	1909	105	1685	936
Washington	1896	111	1683	1095

Division I Alltime Winning Percentage

Team	First Year	Yrs	W	L	Pct
Kentucky	1903	110	2111	661	.762
North Carolina	1911	103	2090	745	.737
Kansas	1899	115	2101	812	.721
UNLVTK	1959	54	1133	456	.713
Duke	1906	108	2001	840	.704
Syracuse	1901	112	1874	832	.693
UCLA	1920	94	1753	779	.692
Western Kentucky	1915	94	1675	844	.665
Louisville	1912	99	1696	869	.661
St. John's (N.Y.)	1908	106	1754	931	.653
Illinois	1906	108	1690	910	.650
Notre Dame	1898	108	1748	949	.648
Temple	1895	117	1814	992	.646
Arizona	1905	108	1645	900	.646
Utah	1909	105	1685	936	.643
Murray St	1926	88	1501	835	.643

Note: Minimum of 25 years in Division I.

NCAA Men's Division I Winning Streaks

Longest—Full Season

Team	Games	Years	Ended by
UCLA	88	1971–74	Notre Dame (71–70)
San Francisco	60	1955–57	Illinois (62–33)
UCLA	47	1966–68	Houston (71–69)
UNLV	45	1990–91	Duke (79–77)
Texas	44	1913–17	Rice (24–18)
Seton Hall	43	1939–41	LIU-Brooklyn (49–26)
LIU-Brooklyn	43	1935–37	Stanford (45–31)
UCLA	41	1968–69	USC (46–44)
Marquette	39	1970–71	Ohio St (60–59)
Cincinnati	37	1962–63	Wichita St (65–64)
North Carolina	37	1957–58	West Virginia (75–64)

Longest—Regular Season

Team	Games	Years	Ended by
UCLA	76	1971–74	Notre Dame (71–70)
Indiana	57	1975–77	Toledo (59–57)
Marquette	56	1970–72	Detroit (70–49)
Kentucky	54	1952–55	Georgia Tech (59–58)
San Francisco	51	1955–57	Illinois (62–33)
Pennsylvania	48	1970–72	Temple (57–52)
Ohio State	47	1960–62	Wisconsin (86–67)
Texas	44	1913–17	Rice (24–18)
UCLA	43	1966–68	Houston (71–69)
LIU-Brooklyn	43	1935–37	Stanford (45–31)
Seton Hall	42	1939–41	LIU-Brooklyn (49–26)

Longest—Home Court

Team	Games	Years	Team	Games	Years
Kentucky	129	1943–55	Lamar	80	1978–84
St. Bonaventure	99	1948–61	Long Beach St	75	1968–74
UCLA	98	1970–76	UNLV	72	1974–78
Cincinnati	86	1957–64	Arizona	71	1987–92
Marquette	81	1967–73	Kansas	69	2008–11
Arizona	81	1945–51	Cincinnati	68	1972–78

Active Coaches*

WINS

Coach and Team	W
Mike Krzyzewski, Duke	.957
Jim Boeheim, Syracuse	.920
Bob Huggins, West Virginia	.723
Roy Williams, North Carolina	.700
Bo Ryan, Wisconsin	.674
Jerry Slocum, Youngstown St	.673
Rick Byrd, Belmont	.663
Rick Pitino, Louisville	.661
Mike Montgomery, California	.656
Cliff Ellis, Coastal Carolina	.647

Note: Minimum 5 years as a Division I head coach; includes record at 4-year colleges only.

WINNING PERCENTAGE

Coach and Team	Yrs	W	L	Pct
Mark Few, Gonzaga	14	374	93	.801
Roy Williams, North Carolina	25	700	180	.795
Brad Stevens, Butler	6	166	49	.772
Thad Matta, Ohio St	13	352	104	.772
Mike Krzyzewski, Duke	38	957	297	.763
John Calipari, Kentucky	21	526	164	.762
Dave Rose, BYU	8	209	66	.760
Bo Ryan, Wisconsin	29	674	216	.757
Bill Self, Kansas	20	507	164	.756
Jamie Dixon, Pittsburgh	10	262	86	.753
Jim Boeheim, Syracuse	37	920	314	.746

Note: Minimum 5 years as a Division I head coach; includes record at 4-year colleges only.

Alltime Winningest Men's Division I Coaches

WINS

Coach	W
*Mike Krzyzewski (Army, Duke)	.957
*Jim Boeheim (Syracuse)	.920
Bob Knight (Army, Indiana, Texas Tech)	.902
Dean Smith (North Carolina)	.879
Adolph Rupp (Kentucky)	.876
Jim Calhoun (Northeastern, Connecticut)	.873
Jim Phelan (Mt. St. Mary's)	.830
Eddie Sutton (Creighton, Arkansas, Kentucky, Oklahoma St)	.804
Lefty Driesell (Davidson, Maryland, James Madison, Georgia St)	.786
Lute Olson (Long Beach St, Iowa, Arizona)	.780
Lou Henson (Hardin-Simmons, New Mexico St, Illinois, New Mexico St)	.779
Ed Diddle (Western Kentucky)	.759
Henry Iba (NW Missouri St, Colorado, Oklahoma St)	.755
Phog Allen (Baker, Kansas, Haskell, Central Missouri St, Kansas)	.746
John Chaney (Cheyney St, Temple)	.741
Jerry Tarkanian (Long Beach St, UNLV, Fresno St)	.729
Norm Stewart (Northern Iowa, Missouri)	.729
Ray Meyer (DePaul)	.724
*Bob Huggins (Walsh, Akron, Cincinnati, Kansas St, West Virginia)	.723
Don Haskins (Oklahoma St, UTEP)	.719
*Roy Williams (Kansas, North Carolina)	.700
Denny Crum (UCLA, Louisville)	.675
*Bo Ryan (UW-Platteville, Milwaukee, Wisconsin)	.674
*Jerry Slocum, (Nyack, Geneva, Gannon, Youngstown St	.673
Gary Williams (American, Boston College, Ohio St, Maryland)	.668
John Wooden (Indiana St, UCLA)	.664

Note: Minimum 10 head coaching seasons in Division I.

*Active in 2012–13.

Alltime Winningest Men's Division I Coaches *(Cont.)*

WINNING PERCENTAGE

Coach (Team, Years)	Yrs	W	L	Pct
Clair Bee (Rider 1929–31, LIU-Brooklyn 1932–45, 1946–51)	21	412	87	.826
Adolph Rupp (Kentucky 1931–72)	41	876	190	.822
John Wooden (Indiana St 1946–48, UCLA 1948–75)	29	664	162	.804
*Mark Few (Gonzaga 1999–)	14	374	93	.801
John Kresse (College of Charleston 1980–2002)	23	560	143	.797
*Roy Williams (Kansas 1989–2003, North Carolina 2003–)	25	700	180	.795
Jerry Tarkanian (Long Beach St 1969–73, UNLV 1974–92, Fresno St 1995–2002)	31	729	201	.784
Francis Schmidt (Tulsa 1916–17, Arkansas 1924–29, TCU 1930–34)	17	258	72	.782
Dean Smith (North Carolina 1962–97)	36	879	254	.776
*Thad Matta (Butler 2001, Xavier 2002–04, Ohio St 2005–)	13	352	104	.772
Jack Ramsay (St. Joseph's [Pa.] 1956–66)	11	231	71	.765
Frank Keaney (Rhode Island 1921–48)	28	401	124	.764
George Keogan (St. Louis 1916, Allegheny 1919, Valparaiso 1920–21, Notre Dame 1924–43)	27	414	127	.764
*Mike Krzyzewski (Army 1976–80, Duke 1981–)	38	957	297	.763
*John Calipari (Massachusetts 1989–96, Memphis 2001–09, Kentucky 2009–)	21	526	164	.762
Bruce Pearl (UW-Milwaukee 2001–05, Tennessee 2005–11)	19	462	145	.761
Vic Bubas (Duke 1960–69)	10	213	67	.761
Harry Fisher (Columbia 1907–16, Army 1922–23, 1925)	16	189	60	.759
*Bo Ryan (UW-Platteville 1984–99, UW-Milwaukee 1999–2001, Wisconsin 2001–)	29	674	216	.757
Fred Bennion (Brigham Young 1909–10, Utah 1911-14, Montana St 1915-19)	11	95	31	.756
*Bill Self (Oral Roberts 1993–97, Tulsa 1997–2000, Illinois 2000–03, Kansas 2003–)	20	507	164	.756
Jamie Dixon, (Pittsburgh 2003–)	10	262	86	.753
Charles (Chick) Davies (Duquesne 1925–43, 1947–48)	21	314	106	.748
Ray Mears (Wittenberg 1957–62, Tennessee 1963–77)	21	399	135	.747
Edward McNichol (Penn 1921-30)	10	186	63	.747
*Jim Boeheim (Syracuse 1977–)	37	920	314	.746

*Active in 2012–13. Note: Minimum 10 years head coaching in Division I.

NCAA Women's Division I Winningest Coaches

Alltime Winningest Women's Division I Coaches

WINNING PERCENTAGE

Coach (Team, Years)	Yrs	W	L	Pct
Leon Barmore (Louisiana Tech 1983–02)	20	576	87	.869
*Geno Auriemma (Connecticut 1986–)	28	839	133	.863
Pat Summitt (Tennessee 1975–2012)	38	1098	208	.841
*Kim Mulkey (Baylor 2001–)	13	372	81	.821
*Tara VanDerveer (Idaho 1979-80, Ohio St 1981–85, Stanford 1986–95, 1997–)	34	894	203	.815
Bill Sheahan (Mt. St. Mary's 1982–98)	17	372	104	.782
*Brian Giorgis (Marist 2003–)	11	277	80	.776
*Wes Moore (Maryville 1988–93, Francis Marion 1996–98, Chattanooga 1999–2013)	24	558	169	.768
*Robin Selvig (Montana 1979–)	35	798	255	.758
*Carey Green (Liberty 1999–)	14	337	110	.754

Note: Minimum 10 head coaching seasons in Division I.

*Active in 2012–13.

Alltime Winningest Women's Division I Coaches

	W
Pat Summitt (Tennessee)	1,098
*Sylvia Hatchell (Francis Marion, North Carolina)	908
*C. Vivian Stringer (Cheyney St, Iowa, Rutgers)	901
Jody Conradt (Sam Houston St, Tex.-Arlington, Texas)	900
*Tara VanDerveer (Idaho, Ohio St, Stanford)	894
*Geno Auriemma (Connecticut)	839
*Andy Landers (Georgia)	823
*Robin Selvig (Montana)	798
*Jim Foster (St. Joseph's, Vanderbilt, Ohio St)	765
Debbie Ryan (Virginia)	739
Kay Yow (Elon, North Carolina St)	737

Note: Minimum 10 head coaching seasons in Division I.

*Active in 2012–13.

NCAA Women's Division I Championship Results

Year	Winner	Score	Runner-up	Winning Coach
1982	Louisiana Tech	76–62	Cheyney	Sonja Hogg/Leon Barmore
1983	USC	69–67	Louisiana Tech	Linda Sharp
1984	USC	72–61	Tennessee	Linda Sharp
1985	Old Dominion	70–65	Georgia	Marianne Stanley
1986	Texas	97–81	USC	Jody Conradt
1987	Tennessee	67–44	Louisiana Tech	Pat Summitt
1988	Louisiana Tech	56–54	Auburn	Leon Barmore
1989	Tennessee	76–60	Auburn	Pat Summitt
1990	Stanford	88–81	Auburn	Tara VanDerveer
1991	Tennessee	70–67 (OT)	Virginia	Pat Summitt
1992	Stanford	78–62	Western Kentucky	Tara VanDerveer
1993	Texas Tech	84–82	Ohio State	Marsha Sharp
1994	North Carolina	60–59	Louisiana Tech	Sylvia Hatchell
1995	Connecticut	70–64	Tennessee	Geno Auriemma
1996	Tennessee	83–65	Georgia	Pat Summitt
1997	Tennessee	68–59	Old Dominion	Pat Summitt
1998	Tennessee	93–75	Louisiana Tech	Pat Summitt
1999	Purdue	62–45	Duke	Carolyn Peck
2000	Connecticut	71–52	Tennessee	Geno Auriemma
2001	Notre Dame	68–66	Purdue	Muffet McGraw
2002	Connecticut	82–70	Oklahoma	Geno Auriemma
2003	Connecticut	73–68	Tennessee	Geno Auriemma
2004	Connecticut	70–61	Tennessee	Geno Auriemma
2005	Baylor	84–62	Michigan St	Kim Mulkey-Robinson
2006	Maryland	78–75	Duke	Brenda Frese
2007	Tennessee	59–46	Rutgers	Pat Summitt
2008	Tennessee	64–48	Stanford	Pat Summitt
2009	Connecticut	76–54	Louisville	Geno Auriemma
2010	Connecticut	53–47	Stanford	Geno Auriemma
2011	Texas A&M	76–70	Notre Dame	Gary Blair
2012	Baylor	80–61	Notre Dame	Kim Mulkey
2013	Connecticut	93–60	Louisville	Geno Auriemma

NCAA Women's Division I Alltime Individual Leaders

Single Game Records

SCORING HIGHS

Pts	Player and Team vs Opponent	Year
60	Cindy Brown, Long Beach St vs San Jose St	1987
58	Kim Perrot, SW Louisiana vs SE Louisiana	1990
58	Lorri Bauman, Drake vs SW Missouri St*	1984
56	Jackie Stiles, SW Missouri St vs Evansville	2000
55	Patricia Hoskins, Mississippi Valley St vs Southern-Birm.	1989
55	Patricia Hoskins, Mississippi Valley St vs Alabama St	1989
54	Anjinea Hopson, Grambling vs Jackson St	1994
54	Mary Lowry, Baylor vs Texas	1994
54	Wanda Ford, Drake vs SW Missouri St*	1986
54	Elena Delle Donne, Delaware vs James Madison	2010
54	Briana Williams, Mercer vs. S.C. Upstate	2012

Three tied with 53.

REBOUNDS

Reb	Player and Team vs Opponent	Year
40	Deborah Temple, Delta St vs UAB	1983
37	Rosina Pearson, Bethune-Cookman vs Florida Memorial	1985
33	Maureen Formico, Pepperdine vs Loyola (Calif.)	1985
32	Lachelle Lyles, Southeast Missouri St vs Tennessee St	2006
31	Darlene Beale, Howard vs South Carolina St	1987
30	Cindy Bonforte, Wagner vs Queens (N.Y.)	1983
30	Kayone Hankins, New Orleans vs. Nicholls St	1994
30	Wanda Ford, Drake vs Eastern Illinois	1985
30	Jennifer Butler, Massachusetts vs Florida	2003

Three tied with 29.

*School changed name to Missouri State after 2004–05 season.

Single Game Records *(Cont.)*
ASSISTS

Asst	Player and Team vs Opponent	Year
23	Michelle Burden, Kent St vs Ball St	1991
22	Shawn Monday, Tennessee Tech vs Morehead St	1988
22	Veronica Pettry, Loyola (Ill.) vs Detroit	1989
22	Tine Freil, Pacific vs Wichita St	1991
21	Tine Freil, Pacific vs Fresno St	1992
21	Amy Bauer, Wisconsin vs Detroit	1989
21	Neacole Hall, Alabama St vs Southern-Birm.	1989

Six tied with 20.

Single Season Records
POINTS

Player and Team	Year	GP	FG	3FG	FT	Pts
Jackie Stiles, SW Missouri St*	2001	35	365	65	267	1062
Cindy Brown, Long Beach St	1987	35	362	—	250	974
Genia Miller, CSU-Fullerton	1991	33	376	0	217	969
Sheryl Swoopes, Texas Tech	1993	34	356	32	211	955
Alysha Clark, Middle Tennessee St	2009	34	343	12	237	935
Amber Holt, Middle Tennessee	2008	34	352	20	206	930
Brittney Griner, Baylor	2012	40	358	1	212	929
Elena Delle Donne, Delaware	2012	33	325	52	225	927
Andrea Congreaves, Mercer	1992	28	353	77	142	925
Wanda Ford, Drake	1986	30	390	—	139	919
Chamique Holdsclaw, Tennessee	1998	39	370	9	166	915
Andrea Riley, Oklahoma St	2010	34	296	78	239	909

SCORING AVERAGE

Player and Team	Year	GP	FG	3FG	FT	Pts	Avg
Patricia Hoskins, Mississippi Valley St	1989	27	345	13	205	908	33.6
Andrea Congreaves, Mercer	1992	28	353	77	142	925	33.0
Deborah Temple, Delta St	1984	28	373	—	127	873	31.2
Andrea Congreaves, Mercer	1993	26	302	51	150	805	31.0
Wanda Ford, Drake	1986	30	390	—	139	919	30.6
Anucha Browne, Northwestern	1985	28	341	—	173	855	30.5
LeChandra LeDay, Grambling	1988	28	334	36	146	850	30.4
Jackie Stiles, SW Missouri St*	2001	35	365	65	267	1062	30.3
Kim Perrot, SW Louisiana	1990	28	308	95	128	839	30.0
Tina Hutchinson, San Diego St	1984	30	383	—	132	898	29.9
Jan Jensen, Drake	1991	30	358	6	166	888	29.6
Sandra Hodge, New Orleans	1984	19	240	—	81	561	29.5
Genia Miller, CSU-Fullerton	1991	33	376	0	217	969	29.4
Barbara Kennedy, Clemson	1982	31	392	—	124	908	29.3
LaTaunya Pollard, Long Beach St	1983	31	376	—	155	907	29.3

REBOUNDS

Player and Team	Year	GP	Reb	Player and Team	Year	GP	Reb
Courtney Paris, Oklahoma	2006	36	539	Anne Donovan, Old Dominion	1983	35	504
Wanda Ford, Drake	1985	30	534	Courtney Paris, Oklahoma	2009	37	503
Lachelle Lyles, SE Missouri St.	2006	30	517	Darlene Jones, Miss Valley St.	1983	31	487
Courtney Paris, Oklahoma	2007	33	526	Melanie Simpson, Okla. City	1982	37	481
Wanda Ford, Drake	1986	30	506	R. Pearson, Beth.-Cookman	1985	26	480

REBOUND AVERAGE

Player and Team	Year	GP	Reb	Avg
Rosina Pearson, Bethune-Cookman	1985	26	480	18.5
Wanda Ford, Drake	1985	30	534	17.8
Katie Beck, East Tennessee St	1988	25	441	17.6
DeShawne Blocker, East Tennessee St	1994	26	450	17.3
Lachelle Lyles, SE Missouri St.	2006	31	527	17.0
Patricia Hoskins, Mississippi Valley St	1987	28	476	17.0
Wanda Ford, Drake	1986	30	506	16.9
Patricia Hoskins, Mississippi Valley St	1989	27	440	16.3
Joy Kellogg, Oklahoma City	1984	23	373	16.2
Deborah Mitchell, Mississippi Coll.	1983	28	447	16.0
Courtney Paris, Oklahoma	2007	33	526	15.9

*School changed name to Missouri State after 2004–05 season

Single Season Records *(Cont.)*

FIELD-GOAL PERCENTAGE

Player and Team	Year	GP	FG	FGA	Pct
Myndee Larsen, Southern Utah	1998	28	249	344	72.4
Chantelle Anderson, Vanderbilt	2001	34	292	404	72.3
Deneka Knowles, SE Louisiana	1996	26	199	276	72.1
Crystal Langhorne, Maryland	2006	32	202	280	72.1
Barbara Farris, Tulane	1998	27	151	210	71.9
Renay Adams, Tennessee Tech	1991	30	185	258	71.7
Carolyn Swords, Boston College	2011	33	240	336	71.4
Regina Days, Georgia Southern	1986	27	234	332	70.5
Kim Wood, UW-Green Bay	1994	27	188	271	69.4
Kelly Lyons, Old Dominion	1990	31	308	444	69.4

Based on NCAA qualifiers for annual championship.

FREE-THROW PERCENTAGE

Player and Team	Year	GP	FT	FTA	Pct
Adrienne Squire, Penn St	2006	29	80	83	96.4
Shanna Zolman, Tennessee	2004	35	88	92	95.7
Jacqui Kalin, UNI	2013	34	169	177	95.5
Ginny Doyle, Richmond	1992	29	96	101	95.0
Jill Marano, La Salle	2003	29	88	93	94.6
Sue Bird, Connecticut	2002	39	98	104	94.2
Paula Corder-King, SE Missouri St	1999	28	111	118	94.1
Abby Oliver, Richmond	2012	32	106	113	93.8
Kandi Brown, Morehead St	2003	28	104	111	93.7
Linda Cyborski, Delaware	1991	29	74	79	93.7
Kandi Brown, Morehead St	2002	29	74	79	93.7

Based on NCAA qualifiers for annual championship.

Career

POINTS

Player and Team	Yrs	GP	Pts
Jackie Stiles, SW Missouri St*	1997–01	129	3393
Brittney Griner, Baylor	2009–13	148	3,283
Patricia Hoskins, Mississippi Valley St	1985–89	110	3122
Lorri Bauman, Drake	1981–84	120	3115
Maya Moore, Connecticut	2007–11	154	3036
Chamique Holdsclaw, Tennessee	1995–99	148	3025
Cheryl Miller, USC	1983–86	128	3018
Cindy Blodgett, Maine	1994–98	118	3005
LaToya Thomas, Mississippi St	1999–2003	125	2981
Valorie Whiteside, Appalachian St	1984–88	116	2944
Kelly Mazzante, Penn St	2000–04	133	2919

SCORING AVERAGE

Player and Team	Yrs	GP	FG	3FG	FT	Pts	Avg
Patricia Hoskins, Mississippi Valley St	1985–89	110	1196	24	706	3122	28.4
Sandra Hodge, New Orleans	1981–84	107	1194	—	472	2860	26.7
Jackie Stiles, SW Missouri St*	1997–01	129°	1160	221	852	3393	26.3
Lorri Bauman, Drake	1981–84	120	1104	—	907	3115	26.0
Andrea Congreaves, Mercer	1989–93	108	1107	153	429	2796	25.9
Cindy Blodgett, Maine	1994–98	118	1055	219	676	3005	25.5
Valorie Whiteside, Appalachian St	1984–88	116	1153	0	638	2944	25.4
Joyce Walker, LSU	1981–84	117	1259	—	388	2906	24.8
Tarcha Hollis, Grambling	1989–91	84	891	3	246	2031	24.2
Korie Hlede, Duquesne	1994–98	109	1045	162	379	2631	24.1
Karen Pelphrey, Marshall	1983–86	114	1175	—	396	2746	24.1
Erma Jones, Bethune-Cookman	1982–84	87	961	—	173	2095	24.1

*School changed name to Missouri State after 2004–05 season

Year	Winner	Score	Runner-up	Third Place	Fourth Place
1957	Wheaton (Ill.)	89–65	Kentucky Wesleyan	Mt. St. Mary's (Md.)	CSU-Los Angeles
1958	South Dakota	75–53	St. Michael's	Evansville	Wheaton (Ill.)
1959	Evansville	83–67	SW Missouri St	North Carolina A&T	CSU-Los Angeles
1960	Evansville	90–69	Chapman	Kentucky Wesleyan	Cornell College
1961	Wittenberg	42–38	SE Missouri St	South Dakota St	Mt. St. Mary's (Md.)
1962	Mt. St. Mary's (Md.)	58–57 (OT)	CSU-Sacramento	Southern Illinois	Nebraska Wesleyan
1963	South Dakota St	44–42	Wittenberg	Oglethorpe	Southern Illinois
1964	Evansville	72–59	Akron	North Carolina A&T	Northern Iowa
1965	Evansville	85–82 (OT)	Southern Illinois	North Dakota	St. Michael's
1966	Kentucky Wesleyan	54–51	Southern Illinois	Akron	North Dakota
1967	Winston-Salem	77–74	SW Missouri St	Kentucky Wesleyan	Illinois St
1968	Kentucky Wesleyan	63–52	Indiana St	Trinity (Tex.)	Ashland
1969	Kentucky Wesleyan	75–71	SW Missouri St	†Vacated	Ashland
1970	Philadelphia Textile	76–65	Tennessee St	UC-Riverside	Buffalo St
1971	Evansville	97–82	Old Dominion	†Vacated	Kentucky Wesleyan
1972	Roanoke	84–72	Akron	Tennessee St	Eastern Mich
1973	Kentucky Wesleyan	78–76 (OT)	Tennessee St	Assumption	Brockport St
1974	Morgan St	67–52	SW Missouri St	Assumption	New Orleans
1975	Old Dominion	76–74	New Orleans	Assumption	Tenn.-Chattanooga
1976	Puget Sound	83–74	Tenn.-Chattanooga	Eastern Illinois	Old Dominion
1977	Tenn.-Chattanooga	71–62	Randolph-Macon	North Alabama	Sacred Heart
1978	Cheyney	47–40	UW-Green Bay	Eastern Illinois	Central Florida
1979	North Alabama	64–50	UW-Green Bay	Cheyney	Bridgeport
1980	Virginia Union	80–74	New York Tech	Florida Southern	North Alabama
1981	Florida Southern	73–68	Mt. St. Mary's (Md.)	Cal Poly-SLO	UW-Green Bay
1982	District of Columbia	73–63	Florida Southern	Kentucky Wesleyan	CSU-Bakersfield
1983	Wright St	92–73	District of Columbia	*CSU-Bakersfield	*Morningside
1984	Central Missouri St	81–77	St. Augustine's	*Kentucky Wesleyan	*N Alabama
1985	Jacksonville St	74–73	South Dakota St	*Kentucky Wesleyan	*Mt. St. Mary's (Md.)
1986	Sacred Heart	93–87	SE Missouri St	*Cheyney	*Florida Southern
1987	Kentucky Wesleyan	92–74	Gannon	*Delta St	*Eastern Montana
1988	Lowell	75–72	Ak.-Anchorage	Florida Southern	Troy St
1989	North Carolina Central	73–46	SE Missouri St	UC-Riverside	Jacksonville St
1990	Kentucky Wesleyan	93–79	CSU-Bakersfield	North Dakota	Morehouse
1991	North Alabama	79–72	Bridgeport (Conn.)	*CSU-Bakersfield	*Virginia Union
1992	Virginia Union	100–75	Bridgeport (Conn.)	*CSU-Bakersfield	*California (Pa.)
1993	CSU-Bakersfield	85–72	Troy St (Ala.)	*New Hampshire Coll	*Wayne St (Mich.)
1994	CSU-Bakersfield	92–86	Southern Indiana	*New Hampshire Coll	*Washburn
1995	Southern Indiana	71–63	UC–Riverside	*Norfolk St	*Indiana (Pa.)
1996	Fort Hays St	70–63	Northern Kentucky	*California (Pa.)	*Virginia Union
1997	CSU-Bakersfield	57–56	Northern Kentucky	*Lynn	*Salem-Teikyo
1998	UC-Davis	83–77	Kentucky Wesleyan	*St. Rose	*Virginia Union
1999	Kentucky Wesleyan	75–60	Metropolitan St	*Truman St	*Florida Southern
2000	Metropolitan St	97–79	Kentucky Wesleyan	*Missouri Southern	*Seattle Pacific
2001	Kentucky Wesleyan	72–63	Washburn	*Western Washington	*Tampa
2002	Metropolitan St	80–72	Kentucky Wesleyan	*Shaw	*Indiana (Pa.)
2003	Northeastern St (Okla.)	75–64	†Vacated	*Bowie St	*Queens (N.Y.)
2004	Kennesaw St	84–59	Southern Indiana	*Humboldt St	*Metropolitan St
2005	Virginia Union	63–58	Bryant	*Lynn	*Tarleton St
2006	Winona St (Minn.)	73–61	Virginia Union	*Seattle Pacific	*Stonehill
2007	Barton	77–75	Winona St (Minn.)	*CSU-San Bernardino	*Central Missouri
2008	Winona St (Minn.)	87–76	Augusta St	*Bentley	*Ak.-Anchorage
2009	Findlay	56–53 (OT)	Cal Poly.-Pomona	*Augusta St	*Central Missouri
2010	Cal Poly	65–53	Indiana Univ. (Pa.)	*Bentley	*St. Cloud St
2011	Bellarmine	71–68	BYU-Hawaii	*Minnesota St-Mankato	*West Liberty
2012	Western Washington	72–65	Montevallo	*Stonehill	*Bellarmine
2013	Drury	74–73	Metro St	*Western Washington	*West Liberty

*Indicates tied for third. †Student-athletes representing American International in 1969, Southwestern Louisiana in 1971, and Kentucky Wesleyan in 2003 were declared ineligible subsequent to the tournament. Under NCAA rules, the teams' and ineligible student-athletes' records were deleted, and the teams' places in the final standings were vacated.

SINGLE-GAME SCORING HIGHS

Pts	Player and Team vs Opponent	Date
113	Bevo Francis, Rio Grande vs Hillsdale	1954
84	Bevo Francis, Rio Grande vs Alliance	1954
82	Bevo Francis, Rio Grande vs Bluffton	1954
80	Paul Crissman, USC vs Pacific Christian	1966
77	William English, Winston-Salem vs Fayetteville St	1968

Single Season Records
SCORING AVERAGE

Player and Team	Year	GP	FG	FT	Pts	Avg
Bevo Francis, Rio Grande	1954	27	444	367	1255	46.5
Earl Glass, Mississippi Industrial	1963	19	322	171	815	42.9
Earl Monroe, Winston-Salem	1967	32	509	311	1329	41.5
John Rinka, Kenyon	1970	23	354	234	942	41.0
Willie Shaw, Lane	1964	18	303	121	727	40.4

REBOUND AVERAGE

Player and Team	Year	GP	Reb	Avg
Tom Hart, Middlebury	1955	22	649	29.5
Tom Hart, Middlebury	1956	21	620	29.5
Frank Stronczek, American Int'l	1966	26	717	27.6
R.C. Owens, College of Idaho	1954	25	677	27.1
Maurice Stokes, St. Francis (Pa.)	1954	26	689	26.5

ASSISTS

Player and Team	Year	GP	Asst
Steve Ray, Bridgeport	1989	32	400
Steve Ray, Bridgeport	1990	33	385
Tony Smith, Pfeiffer	1992	35	349
Luke Cooper, Alaska Anchorage	2008	35	310
Rob Paternostro, New Hamp. Coll.	1995	33	309
Jim Ferrer, Bentley	1989	31	309

ASSIST AVERAGE

Player and Team	Year	GP	Asst	Avg
Steve Ray, Bridgeport	1989	32	400	12.5
Steve Ray, Bridgeport	1990	33	385	11.7
Demetri Beekman, Assumption	1993	23	264	11.5
Ernest Jenkins, N.M.-Highlands	1995	27	291	10.8
Brian Gregory, Oakland	1989	28	300	10.7
Zack Whiting, Chaminade	2007	27	289	10.7

FIELD-GOAL PERCENTAGE

Player and Team	Year	Pct
Garret Siler, Augusta St	2009	78.9
Garret Siler, Augusta St	2008	76.2
Todd Linder, Tampa	1987	75.2
Maurice Stafford, North Alabama	1984	75.0
Matthew Cornegay, Tuskegee	1982	74.8

FREE-THROW PERCENTAGE

Player and Team	Year	Pct
Paul Cluxton, Northern Kentucky	1997	100.0
Jake Linton, Saint Martin's	2008	96.4
Ashton Brown, Tex. A&M-Kingsville	2012	96.1
Tomas Rimkus, Pace	1997	95.6
C.J. Cowgill, Chaminade	2001	95.0

Career Records
POINTS

Player and Team	Yrs	Pts
Travis Grant, Kentucky St	1969–72	4045
Bob Hopkins, Grambling	1953–56	3759
Tony Smith, Pfeiffer	1989–92	3350
Earnest Lee, Clark Atlanta	1984–87	3298
Joe Miller, Alderson-Broaddus	1954–57	3294

CAREER SCORING AVERAGE

Player and Team	Yrs	GP	Pts	Avg
Travis Grant, Kentucky St	1969–72	121	4045	33.4
John Rinka, Kenyon	1967–70	99	3251	32.8
Florindo Vieira, Quinnipiac	1954–57	69	2263	32.8
Willie Shaw, Lane	1961–64	76	2379	31.3
Mike Davis, Virginia Union	1966–69	89	2758	31.0

Note: Minimum 1,400 points.

REBOUND AVERAGE

Player and Team	Yrs	GP	Reb	Avg
Tom Hart, Middlebury	1953, 55–56	63	1738	27.6
Maurice Stokes, St. Francis (Pa.)	1953–55	72	1812	25.2
Frank Stronczek, American Int'l	1965–67	62	1549	25.0
Bill Thieben, Hofstra	1954–56	76	1837	24.2
Hank Brown, Lowell Tech	1965–67	49	1129	23.0

Note: Minimum 800 rebounds.

Career Records *(Cont.)*

ASSISTS

Player and Team	Yrs	Asst
Demetri Beekman, Assumption	1990–93	1044
Adam Kaufman, Edinboro	1998–01	936
Rob Paternostro, New Hamp. Coll.	1992–95	919
Luke Cooper, Alaska-Anchorage	2005–08	880
Josh Magette, Ala.-Huntsville	2009–12	878

ASSIST AVERAGE

Player and Team	Yrs	GP	Asst	Avg
Steve Ray, Bridgeport	1989-90	65	785	12.1
Demetri Beekman, Assumption	1990-93	119	1044	8.8
D.J. Ferguson, Flagler	2009–11	79	679	8.6
Ernest Jenkins, N.M.-Highlands	1992-95	84	699	8.3
Zack Whiting, Chaminade	2004–07	86	703	8.2

Note: Minimum 550 Assists.

FIELD-GOAL PERCENTAGE

Player and Team	Yrs	Pct
Garrett Siler, Augusta St	2006–09	74.5
Todd Linder, Tampa	1984–87	70.8
Tom Schurfranz, Bellarmine	1989–92	70.2
Chad Scott, California (Pa.)	1991–94	70.0
Ed Phillips, Alabama A&M	1968–71	68.9

Note: Minimum 400 FGM.

FREE-THROW PERCENTAGE

Player and Team	Yrs	Pct
Paul Cluxton, Northern Kentucky	1994–97	93.5
Jake Linton, St. Martin's	2006–09	92.4
Kent Andrews, McNeese St	1967-69	91.6
Kyle Caiola, Findlay	2011–12	91.2
Nathan Hyde, Findlay	2008–11	90.1

Note: Minimum 250 FTM.

NCAA Men's Division III Championship Results

Year	Winner	Score	Runner-up	Third Place	Fourth Place
1975	LeMoyne-Owen	57–54	Glassboro St	Augustana (Ill.)	Brockport St
1976	Scranton	60–57	Wittenberg	Augustana (Ill.)	Plattsburgh St
1977	Wittenberg	79–66	Oneonta St	Scranton	Hamline
1978	North Park	69–57	Widener	Albion	Stony Brook
1979	North Park	66–62	Potsdam St	Franklin & Marshall	Centre
1980	North Park	83–76	Upsala	Wittenberg	Longwood
1981	Potsdam St	67–65 (OT)	Augustana (Ill.)	Ursinus	Otterbein
1982	Wabash	83–62	Potsdam St	Brooklyn	CSU-Stanislaus
1983	Scranton	64–63	Wittenberg	Roanoke	UW–Whitewater
1984	UW–Whitewater	103–86	Clark (Mass.)	DePauw	Upsala
1985	North Park	72–71	Potsdam St	Nebraska Wesleyan	Widener
1986	Potsdam St	76–73	LeMoyne-Owen	Nebraska Wesleyan	Jersey City St
1987	North Park	106–100	Clark (Mass.)	Wittenberg	Stockton St
1988	Ohio Wesleyan	92–70	Scranton	Nebraska Wesleyan	Hartwick
1989	UW–Whitewater	94–86	Trenton St	Southern Maine	Centre
1990	Rochester	43–42	DePauw	Washington (Md.)	Calvin
1991	UW–Platteville	81–74	Franklin & Marshall	Otterbein	Ramapo (N.J.)
1992	Calvin	62–49	Rochester	UW–Platteville	Jersey City St
1993	Ohio Northern	71–68	Augustana	Mass.–Dartmouth	Rowan
1994	Lebanon Valley Coll	66–59 (OT)	NYU	Wittenberg	St. Thomas (Minn.)
1995	UW–Platteville	69–55	Manchester	Rowan	Trinity (Conn.)
1996	Rowan	100–93	Hope (Mich.)	Illinois Wesleyan	Franklin & Marshall
1997	Illinois Wesleyan	89–86	Nebraska Wesleyan	Williams	Alvernia
1998	UW–Platteville	69–56	Hope (Mich.)	Williams	Wilkes
1999	UW–Platteville	76–75 (2 OT)	Hampden-Sydney	William Paterson	Connecticut Coll.
2000	Calvin	79–74	UW-Eau Claire	Salem St	Franklin & Marshall
2001	Catholic	76–62	William Paterson	Illinois Wesleyan	Ohio Northern
2002	Otterbein	102–83	Elizabethtown	Carthage	Rochester
2003	Williams	67–65	Gustavus Adolphus	Wooster	Hampden Sydney
2004	UW–Stevens Point	84–82	Williams	John Carroll	Amherst
2005	UW–Stevens Point	73–49	Rochester	Calvin	York
2006	Virginia Wesleyan	59–56	Wittenberg	Illinois Wesleyan	Amherst
2007	Amherst	80–67	Virginia Wesleyan	Washington (Mo.)	Wooster
2008	Washington-St. Louis	90–86	Amherst	Hope	Ursinus
2009	Washington-St. Louis	61–52	Richard Stockton	Guilford	Franklin & Marshall
2010	UW-Stevens Point	78–73	Williams	*Guilford	*Randolph Macon
2011	St. Thomas (MN)	78–54	Wooster	*Middlebury	*Williams
2012	Wisconsin-Whitewater	63–60	Cabrini	*Illinois Wesleyan	*MIT
2013	Amherst	87–70	Mary Hardin-Baylor	N Central (Ill.)	St. Thomas (Minn.)

*Indicates tied for third. In 2010, the NCAA eliminated the consolation game to determine third place.

SINGLE-GAME SCORING HIGHS

Pts	Player and Team vs Opponent	Year
138	Jack Taylor, Grinnell vs. Faith Baptist Bible	2012
89	Griffin Lentsch, Grinnell vs. Principia	2012
77	Jeff Clement, Grinnell vs Illinois College	1998
69	Sami Wylie, Lincoln (Pa.) vs Ohio St-Marion	2007
69	Steve Diekmann, Grinnell vs Simpson	1995
64	Tim Russell, Albertus Magnus	2005
63	Ryan Hodges, Cal-Lutheran	2005
63	Joe DeRoche, Thomas vs St. Joseph's (Me.)	1988
62	Shannon Lilly, Bishop vs Southwest Assembly of God	1983
62	Nick Pelotte, Plymouth St	2005
62	Kyle Myrick, Lincoln (Pa.) vs. Penn St.-Abington	2006

Three tied at 61.

Single Season Records

SCORING AVERAGE

Player and Team	Year	GP	FG	FT	Pts	Avg
Steve Diekmann, Grinnell	1995	20	223	162	745	37.3
Rickey Sutton, Lyndon St	1976	14	207	93	507	36.2
Shannon Lilly, Bishop	1983	26	345	218	908	34.9
Dana Wilson, Husson	1974	20	288	122	698	34.9
Rickey Sutton, Lyndon St	1977	16	223	112	558	34.9

REBOUND AVERAGE

Player and Team	Year	GP	Reb	Avg
Joe Manley, Bowie St	1976	29	579	20.0
Fred Petty, New Hampshire Coll.	1974	22	436	19.8
Larry Williams, Pratt	1977	24	457	19.0
Larry Parker, Plattsburgh St	1975	23	430	18.7
Charles Greer, Thomas	1977	17	318	18.7

ASSISTS

Player and Team	Year	GP	Asst
Robert James, Kean	1989	29	391
Tennyson Whitted, Ramapo	2002	29	319
Ricky Spicer, UW-Whitewater	1989	31	295
Joe Marcotte, New Jersey Tech	1995	30	292
Andre Bolton, Chris. Newport	1996	30	289

ASSIST AVERAGE

Player and Team	Year	GP	Asst	Avg
Robert James, Kean	1989	29	391	13.5
Albert Kirchner, Mt. St. Vincent	1990	24	267	11.1
Tennyson Whitted, Ramapo	2002	29	319	11.0
Ron Torgalski, Hamilton	1989	26	275	10.6
David Arsenault, Grinnell	2008	21	219	10.4

FIELD-GOAL PERCENTAGE

Player and Team	Year	Pct
Travis Weiss, St. John's (Minn.)	1994	76.6
Brian Schmitting, Ripon	2006	76.3
Pete Metzelaars, Wabash	1982	75.3
Tony Rychlec, Mass. Maritime	1981	74.9
Tony Rychlec, Mass. Maritime	1982	73.1

FREE-THROW PERCENTAGE

Player and Team	Year	Pct
Korey Coon, Illinois Wesleyan	2000	96.3
Ryan Martin, Keene St	2011	96.1
Ryan Junghans, Hood	2008	95.9
Nick Wilkins, Coe	2003	95.7
Chanse Young, Manchester	1998	95.6

Career Records

POINTS

Player and Team	Yrs	Pts
Andre Foreman, Salisbury St	1989–92	2940
Willie Chandler, Misericordia	2000–03	2898
John Grotberg, Grinnell	2006–09	2848
Lamonte Thomas, Johnson & Wales (R.I.)	2009–12	2740
Lamont Strothers, Chris. Newport	1988–91	2709

SCORING AVERAGE

Player and Team	Yrs	GP	Avg
Dwain Govan, Bishop	1974–75	55	32.8
Dave Russell, Shepherd	1974–75	60	30.6
Kyle Myrick, Lincoln (Pa.)	2005–06	57	30.2
Rickey Sutton, Lyndon St	1976–79	80	29.7
John Grotberg, Grinnell	2006–09	96	29.7

Note: Minimum 1,400 points.

REBOUND AVERAGE

Player and Team	Yrs	GP	Reb	Avg
Larry Parker, Plattsburgh St	1975–78	85	1482	17.4
*Charles Greer, Thomas	1975–77	58	926	16.0
Willie Parr, LeMoyne-Owen	1974–76	76	1182	15.6
Michael Smith, Hamilton	1989–92	107	1632	15.2
Dave Kufeld, Yeshiva	1977–80	81	1222	15.1

Note: Minimum 800 rebounds.

ASSIST AVERAGE

Player and Team	Yrs	Avg
David Arsenault, Grinnell	2006–09	9.4
Phil Dixon, Shenandoah	1993–96	8.6
Tennyson Whitted, Ramapo	2000–03	8.5
Sean Rossi, Ithaca	2010–13	8.5
Steve Artis, Chris. Newport	1990–93	8.1

Note: Minimum 550 assists.

Hockey

The Chicago Blackhawks surrounded the coveted Cup after their hard-fought six-game final series victory over the Boston Bruins

Old-School Classic

The Blackhawks and Bruins—two teams from the NHL Original Six—staged a Stanley Cup for the ages and erased the bad taste from a season-shortening lockout

BY MARK BEECH

GARY BETTMAN AND DONALD Fehr couldn't have come up with a better ending to the lockout-shortened 2013 season—the season that almost wasn't—if they had hired a Hollywood screenwriter. At times, right up until the two men ended the impasse on Jan. 6, the commissioner of the NHL and the head of the players' union had seemed to be doing their level best to ensure that the league's third work stoppage in less than 20 years went on forever. It didn't, of course, and as Blackhawks third-line center Andrew Shaw bellowed happy profanities while taking a lap around the TD Garden ice, with blood gushing from a gash in his cheek and the Stanley Cup raised over his head, every fan could be grateful. Hockey was back, and in many ways the game had never been better.

Shaw's victory lap was the culmination of a frantic, 48-game regular season, a grueling playoff drive and an Original Six Cup finals that was a triumph not only for Chicago but also for the game itself. The Blackhawks' six-game victory over the ruggedly brilliant Bruins featured some of most compelling and competitive hockey in recent memory—including the decisive contest, in which Brian Bickell and Dave Bol-land scored last-minute goals just 17 seconds apart to lift Chicago to a scintillating 3–2 win. The two clubs hooked up for more than 435 minutes of action, including a cuticle-shredding triple-overtime opener in the Windy City. Neither team ever led a game by more than two goals, and Boston center Patrice Bergeron embodied the warrior spirit of the NHL postseason, playing Game 6 with a broken rib, torn rib cartilage, a punctured lung and a separated shoulder. Jaromir Jagr, the Bruins' 41-year-old winger, said it best after Boston's 2–1 overtime win in Game 2: "If you have a bad heart, you might get a heart attack.... For young people it's pretty exciting to watch. Old people, don't watch it."

Jagr's warning was offered in jest, of course, but it's worth noting that at least by NHL standards, plenty of people did watch. Games on NBC and the NBC SportsNetwork averaged 5.4 million viewers, the most in nearly 20 years. "It's only fitting," said Blackhawks winger Patrick Sharp after Chicago's 6–5 overitme victory in Game 4, "that two of the oldest teams would give people a series for the history books."

The Blackhawks won their second Stanley Cup since 2010 after a magical run through the abbreviated regular season.

Stanley Cup MVP Kane scored off this rebound to put the Blackhawks up 2–0 in Chicago's pivotal 3–1 win in Game 5.

They started the year 21-0-3. Coupled with a six-game run at the end of the 2011–2012 season (3-0-3), the start meant that Chicago earned at least one point—i.e., did not lose a regular-season game in regulation—in 30 straight matches, second only to the 1979–80 Flyers. "The Miami Heat can win 15, 16 games in a row," said Patrick Kane, the Blackhawks star right wing and an avowed fan of LeBron James, "but how many teams can really win an NBA title? Three? Four? I mean, the Kings won the Cup as an eight seed [in 2012]. In our league, if the 30th team beats the first team one night, it's not such a big deal. No game is a gimme."

Kane, who scored seven goals—including two game-winners—in his last eight post-season games, skated away with the Conn Smythe Trophy as the playoff MVP. The Bruins bruising forecheck was designed to force Chicago to the wings whenever the Blackhawks entered the offensive zone, but time and again the speedy Kane blew the scheme apart by carrying the puck through the middle himself. His work was an exten-

sion of the all-around game that he had flashed during the regular season, when he led Chicago in points (55, fifth best in the NHL) and assists (32), and tied center Jonathan Toews for the team lead in goals (23). "Patrick has the puck more than he's had in the past," Blackhawks coach Joel Quenneville said in March. "Every offensive situation is a chance to score, because he's not giving up on plays. A lot of times he's the first guy back, so I can trust him in more situations."

"My game," said Kane, "looks different now."

Also looking different this year than in the recent past was Capitals winger Alex Ovechkin. The season had begun slowly for the Great Eight, who had no goals and just one assist through Washington's first three games. From 2007–08 to '09–10, Ovechkin had won two Hart trophies as league MVP and scored 50 or more goals three times.

ADAM HUNGER

Ovechkin answered the critics with an MVP season, leading the league in goals, power-play goals and shots.

But his numbers had dropped in each of the last two seasons, to 32 and 38 goals, respectively. There were mutterings around the league that his days as a dominant offensive force were over.

But with the help of first-year coach Adam Oates, Ovechkin proved his legion of vociferous doubters wrong. Oates, himself a Hall of Fame center, moved Ovechkin, who is right-handed, from the left wing to the right. "I wanted my best player to have the puck more," said Oates. "And I felt playing on his off side, there's only so many times he can get the puck. I thought on the [right] side, I could double the opportunities he could get touching the puck." Ovechkin led the NHL in goals (32), power-play goals (16) and shots (220), and won his third Hart Trophy. He also led the Capitals into the playoffs. "This guy is better than he's ever been," said Washington GM George McPhee last spring. "Better than when he scored 65 [in 2007–08]. Better than he was in his Calder season, because he is a more complete player."

Also making his mark on the NHL was a player who entered the league with Ovechkin back in 2005–06: Sidney Crosby. Sid the Kid had his season cut short by a broken jaw after he was hit in the face by a puck during a game against the Islanders on March 30. Up to that point, however, he was widely acknowledged to be playing the best two way hockey of his life. In 36 games, Crosby averaged 1.56 points and was +26. He was out of the lineup for almost a month before somebody finally passed him for the lead in the scoring race. "How complete he is, that is what separates him," said Pittsburgh teammate Matt Niskanen. "That and his drive. Lots of guys work hard, but he works harder. Lots of guys can skate fast, and lots of guys can stickhandle really well. He can do both at the same time and at a very high level."

Crosby, Ovechkin, the Blackhawks and the game itself—the NHL's abbreviated season was full of comeback success stories. The trick for the league going forward will be to build momentum, perhaps by finding a way to goose its declining scoring average (which has dropped every season since the last lockout in 2004–05). It must also avoid any further labor strife: As everybody saw in 2013, hockey is better when it's on the ice.

FOR THE RECORD • 2012–2013

2012–13 NHL Final Regular Season Standings

Western Conference

CENTRAL DIVISION

	GP	W	L	OTL	Pts	GF	GA
‡Chicago	48	36	7	5	77	155	102
*St. Louis	48	29	17	2	60	129	115
*Detroit	48	24	16	8	56	124	115
Columbus	48	24	17	7	55	120	119
Nashville	48	16	23	9	41	111	139

NORTHWEST DIVISION

	GP	W	L	OTL	Pts	GF	GA
†Vancouver	48	26	15	7	59	127	121
*Minnesota	48	26	19	3	55	122	127
Edmonton	48	19	22	7	45	125	134
Calgary	48	19	25	4	42	128	160
Colorado	48	16	25	7	39	116	152

PACIFIC DIVISION

	GP	W	L	OTL	Pts	GF	GA
†Anaheim	48	30	12	6	66	140	118
*Los Angeles	48	27	16	5	59	133	118
*San Jose	48	25	16	7	57	124	116
Phoenix	48	21	18	9	51	125	131
Dallas	48	22	22	4	48	130	142

OTL=overtime loss; worth 1 pt.

Eastern Conference

NORTHEAST DIVISION

	GP	W	L	OTL	Pts	GF	GA
†Montreal	48	29	14	5	63	149	126
*Boston	48	28	14	6	62	131	109
*Toronto	48	26	17	5	57	145	133
*Ottawa	48	25	17	6	56	116	104
Buffalo	48	21	21	6	48	125	143

ATLANTIC DIVISION

	GP	W	L	OTL	Pts	GF	GA
‡Pittsburgh	48	36	12	0	72	165	119
*NY Rangers	48	26	18	4	56	130	112
*NY Islanders	48	24	17	7	55	139	139
Philadelphia	48	23	22	3	49	133	141
New Jersey	48	19	19	10	48	112	129

SOUTHEAST DIVISION

	GP	W	L	OTL	Pts	GF	GA
†Washington	48	27	18	3	57	149	130
Winnipeg	48	24	21	3	51	128	144
Carolina	48	19	25	4	42	128	160
Tampa Bay	48	18	26	4	40	148	150
Florida	48	15	27	6	36	112	171

‡Conference winner. †Division winner. *Playoff team.

2013 Stanley Cup Playoffs

WESTERN CONFERENCE | **EASTERN CONFERENCE**

QUARTERFINALS — SEMIFINALS — CONFERENCE FINAL | CONFERENCE FINAL — SEMIFINALS — QUARTERFINALS

STANLEY CUP — CHICAGO (4–2)

Western Conference:
- 1-Chicago
- 8-Minnesota
- Chicago (4–1)
- 2-Anaheim
- 7-Detroit
- Detroit (4–3)
- Chicago (4–3)
- Chicago (4–1)
- 3-Vancouver
- 6-San Jose
- San Jose (4–0)
- 4-St. Louis
- 5-Los Angeles
- Los Angeles (4–2)
- Los Angeles (4–3)

Eastern Conference:
- Pittsburgh-1
- NY Islanders-8
- Pittsburgh (4–2)
- Montreal-2
- Ottawa-7
- Ottawa (4–1)
- Pittsburgh (4–1)
- Boston (4–0)
- Washington-3
- NY Rangers-6
- NY Rangers (4–3)
- Boston (4–1)
- Boston (4–3)
- Boston-4
- Toronto-5

Note: Playoff teams are re-seeded after quarterfinals

Stanley Cup Playoff Results

Conference Quarterfinals

EASTERN CONFERENCE

Game 1	NY Islanders	0	at Pittsburgh	5
Game 2	NY Islanders	4	at Pittsburgh	3
Game 3	Pittsburgh	5	at NY Islanders	4*

*Overtime game.

Game 4	Pittsburgh	4	at NY Islanders	6
Game 5	NY Islanders	0	at Pittsburgh	4
Game 6	Pittsburgh	4	at NY Islanders	3*

Pittsburgh won series 4–2.

Conference Quarterfinals *(Cont.)*

EASTERN CONFERENCE *(CONT.)*

Game 1	Ottawa	4	at Montreal	2
Game 2	Ottawa	1	at Montreal	3
Game 3	Montreal	1	at Ottawa	6
Game 4	Montreal	2	at Ottawa	3*
Game 5	Ottawa	6	at Montreal	1

Ottawa won series 4–1.

Game 1	NY Rangers	1	at Washington	3
Game 2	NY Rangers	0	at Washington	1*
Game 3	Washington	3	at NY Rangers	4
Game 4	Washington	3	at NY Rangers	4
Game 5	NY Rangers	1	at Washington	2*

Game 6	Washington	0	at NY Rangers	1
Game 7	NY Rangers	5	at Washington	0

NY Rangers won series 4–3.

Game 1	Toronto	1	at Boston	4
Game 2	Toronto	4	at Boston	2
Game 3	Boston	5	at Toronto	2
Game 4	Boston	4	at Toronto	3*
Game 5	Toronto	2	at Boston	1
Game 6	Boston	1	at Toronto	2
Game 7	Toronto	4	at Boston	5*

Boston won series 4–3.

WESTERN CONFERENCE

Game 1	Minnesota	1	at Chicago	2*
Game 2	Minnesota	2	at Chicago	5
Game 3	Chicago	2	at Minnesota	3*
Game 4	Chicago	3	at Minnesota	0
Game 5	Minnesota	1	at Chicago	5

Chicago won series 4–1.

Game 1	Detroit	1	at Anaheim	3
Game 2	Detroit	5	at Anaheim	4*
Game 3	Anaheim	4	at Detroit	0
Game 4	Anaheim	2	at Detroit	3*
Game 5	Detroit	2	at Anaheim	3*
Game 6	Anaheim	3	at Detroit	4*
Game 7	Detroit	3	at Anaheim	2

Detroit won series 4–3.

Game 1	San Jose	3	at Vancouver	1
Game 2	San Jose	3	at Vancouver	2*
Game 3	Vancouver	2	at San Jose	5
Game 4	Vancouver	3	at San Jose	4*

San Jose won series 4–0.

Game 1	Los Angeles	1	at St. Louis	2*
Game 2	Los Angeles	1	at St. Louis	2
Game 3	St. Louis	0	at Los Angeles	4
Game 4	St. Louis	3	at Los Angeles	4
Game 5	Los Angeles	3	at St. Louis	2*
Game 6	St. Louis	1	at Los Angeles	2

Los Angeles won series 4–2.

Conference Semifinals

EASTERN CONFERENCE

Game 1	Washington	1	at Pittsburgh	4
Game 2	Washington	3	at Pittsburgh	4
Game 3	Pittsburgh	1	at Washington	2**
Game 4	Pittsburgh	7	at Washington	3
Game 5	Washington	2	at Pittsburgh	6

Pittsburgh won series 4–1.

Game 1	NY Rangers	2	at Boston	3*
Game 2	NY Rangers	2	at Boston	5
Game 3	Boston	2	at NY Rangers	1
Game 4	Boston	3	at NY Rangers	4*
Game 5	NY Rangers	1	at Boston	3

Boston won series 4–1.

WESTERN CONFERENCE

Game 1	San Jose	0	at Los Angeles	2
Game 2	San Jose	3	at Los Angeles	4
Game 3	Los Angeles	1	at San Jose	2*
Game 4	Los Angeles	1	at San Jose	2
Game 5	San Jose	0	at Los Angeles	3
Game 6	Los Angeles	1	at San Jose	2
Game 7	San Jose	1	at Los Angeles	2

Los Angeles won series 4–3.

Game 1	Detroit	1	at Chicago	4
Game 2	Detroit	4	at Chicago	1
Game 3	Chicago	1	at Detroit	3
Game 4	Chicago	0	at Detroit	2
Game 5	Detroit	1	at Chicago	4
Game 6	Chicago	4	at Detroit	3
Game 7	Detroit	1	at Chicago	2*

Chicago won series 4–3.

Eastern Conference Finals

Game 1	Boston	3	at Pittsburgh	0
Game 2	Boston	6	at Pittsburgh	1
Game 3	Pittsburgh	1	at Boston	2**
Game 4	Pittsburgh	0	at Boston	1

Boston won series 4–0.

Western Conference Finals

Game 1	Los Angeles	1	at Chicago	2
Game 2	Los Angeles	2	at Chicago	4
Game 3	Chicago	1	at Los Angeles	3
Game 4	Chicago	3	at Los Angeles	2
Game 5	Los Angeles	3	at Chicago	4**

Chicago won series 4–1.

Stanley Cup Final

Game 1	Boston	3	at Chicago	4***
Game 2	Boston	2	at Chicago	1*
Game 3	Chicago	0	at Boston	2

Game 4	Chicago	6	at Boston	5*
Game 5	Boston	1	at Chicago	3
Game 6	Chicago	3	at Boston	2

Chicago won series 4–2.

*Overtime game. **Double overtime game. ***Triple overtime game.

Stanley Cup Final Box Scores

Game 1

```
Boston ..............1   1   1   0   0   0——3
Chicago ...........0   1   2   0   0   1——4
```

FIRST PERIOD
Scoring: Boston 1, Lucic (Horton, Krejci), 13:11.

SECOND PERIOD
Scoring: Boston 1, Lucic (Krejci), 0:51; Chicago 1, Saad (Hossa). Penalties: Boston 3, Horton (interference), 7:37, Bench (too many men on ice), 8:20, Chara (high-sticking), 12:53.

THIRD PERIOD
Scoring: Boston 1, Bergeron (Seguin, Lucic), 6:09; Chicago 2, Bolland (Shaw), 8:00, Oduya (Kruger, Frolik), 12:14. Penalties: Chicago 1, Frolik (tripping), 5:51.

FIRST OVERTIME
Penalties: Chicago 1, Bench (too many men on ice), 12:08.

SECOND OVERTIME
Penalties: Chicago 1, Bench (too many men on ice), 19:07.

THIRD OVERTIME
Scoring: Chicago 1, Shaw (Bolland, Rozsival), 12:08.

Shots on goal: Bos 11–6–8–12–10–7—54; Chi 8–16–15–8–10–6—63.

Power-play opportunities: Bos 1–3, Chi 0–3.

Goalies: Bos, Rask (63 shots, 59 saves); Chi, Crawford (54 shots, 51 saves).

Referees: Rooney, Watson. Linesmen: Heyer, Murphy

A: 22,110.

Game 2

```
Boston ...........................0   1   0   1——2
Chicago ..........................1   0   0   0——1
```

FIRST PERIOD
Scoring: Chicago, 1, Sharp (Kane, Handzus), 11:22. Penalties: Boston 1, Ference (tripping), 6:51.

SECOND PERIOD
Scoring: Boston 1, Kelly (Paille), 14:58. Penalites: Chicago 2, Bolland (tripping), 1:19, Oduya (tripping), 19:14; Boston 2, Boychuk (holding), 8:15, Seidenberg (tripping), 17:11.

THIRD PERIOD
Scoring and Penalties: None.

OVERTIME
Scoring: Boston 1, Paille (Seguin, McQuaid), 13:48.

Shots on goal: Bos 4–8–8–8—28; Chi 19–4–5–6—34.

Power-play opportunities: Bos 0–2, Chi 0–3.

Goalies: Bos, Rask (34 shots, 33 saves); Chi, Crawford (28 shots, 26 saves).

Referees: O'Halloran, McCauley. Linesmen: Sharrers, Racicot

A: 22,154.

Game 3

```
Chicago .......................................0   0   0——0
Boston ..........................................0   2   0——2
```

FIRST PERIOD
Penalties: Boston 2, Daugavins (roughing), 9:57, Thornton (roughing), 14:15.

SECOND PERIOD
Scoring: Boston 2, Paille (Kelly, Seguin), 2:13, Bergeron (Jagr, Chara), 14:05. Penalites: Chicago 3, Bolland (cross checking), 12:00, Hjammarsson (tripping), 13:50, Bolland (tripping), 19:00.

THIRD PERIOD
Penalties: Boston 5, McQuaid (tripping), 7:56, Krejci (hooking), 15:55, Chara (double roughing), 19:48, Marchand (fighting), 19:48. Chicago 3, Bolland (tripping), 13:55, Bickell (roughing), 19:48, Shaw (fighting), 19:48.

Shots on goal: Chi 10–8–10—28; Bos 11–15–9—35.

Power-play opportunities: Chi 0–5, Bos 1–5.

Goalies: Chi, Crawford (35 shots, 33 saves). Bos, Rask (28 shots, 28 saves).

Referees: Rooney, Watson. Linesmen: Heyer, Murphy

A: 17,565.

Game 4

```
Chicago............................I   3   I   I——6
Boston ............................I   2   2   0——5
```

FIRST PERIOD

Scoring: Chicago 1, Handzus (Saad), 6:48. Boston 1, Peverley (Ference), 14:43. Penalties: Chicago 4, Oduya (interference), 5:15, Keith (hooking), 12:45, Shaw (roughing), 12:45, Keith (tripping), 18:58. Boston 2, Kelly (roughing), 12:45, Horton (slashing), 18:16.

SECOND PERIOD

Scoring: Chicago 3, Toews (Rozsival), 6:33, Kane (Bickell, Rozsival), 8:41, Kruger (Frolik, Bolland), 15:32. Boston 2, Lucic (Chara), 14:43, Bergeron (Chara, Jagr), 17:22. Penalties: Boston 1, Bench (too many men on ice), 9:58. Chicago 1, Kane (hooking), 16:24.

THIRD PERIOD

Scoring: Boston 2, Bergeron (Jagr), 2:05, Boychuk (Horton, Krejci), 12:14. Chicago 1, Sharp (Hossa, Keith), 11:19. Penalties: Chicago 1, Toews (high-sticking), 8:51. Boston 2, Jagr (high-sticking), 9:13, Krejci (hooking), 10:20.

OVERTIME

Scoring: Chicago 1, Seabrook (Bickell, Kane), 9:51.

Shots on goal: Chi 12–13–16–6—47; Bos 9–11–8–5—33.

Power-play opportunities: Chi 1–4, Bos 2–5.

Goalies: Chi, Crawford (33 shots, 28 saves), Bos, Rask (47 shots, 41 saves).

Referees: O'Halloran, McCauley. Linesmen: Racicot, Sharrers.

A: 17,565.

Game 5

```
Boston ..................................0   0   I——I
Chicago.................................I   I   I——3
```

FIRST PERIOD

Scoring: Chicago 1, Kane (Oduya, Toews), 17:27. Penalties: Chicago 1, Sharp (roughing), 17:56. Boston 1, Boychuk (roughing), 17:56.

SECOND PERIOD

Scoring: Chicago 1, Kane (Bickell, Toews), 5:13. Penalties: Boston 3, Horton (hooking), 0:49, Seidenberg (boarding), 5:59, McQuaid (roughing), 15:20; Chicago 1, Handzus (diving), 0:49.

THIRD PERIOD

Scoring: Boston 1, Chara (Krejci, Lucic), 3:40; Chicago 1, Bolland (Frolik), 19:46.

Shots on goal: Bos 11–5–9—25; Chi 8–11–13—32.

Power-play opportunities: Bos 0–0, Chi 0–2.

Goalies: Bos, Rask (31 shots, 29 saves). Chi, Crawford (25 shots, 24 saves).

Referees: Watson, Rooney. Linesmen: Heyer, Murphy.

A: 22,274.

Game 6

```
Chicago ......................................0   I   2——3
Boston ........................................I   0   I——2
```

FIRST PERIOD

Scoring: Boston 1, Kelly (Seguin, Paille), 7:19. Penalties: Chicago 2, Oduya (hooking), 10:40, Rozsival (high-sticking), 18:25.

SECOND PERIOD

Scoring: Chicago 1, Toews, 4:24. Penalties: Chicago 2, Shaw (roughing), 2:24, Seabrook (tripping), 5:12; Boston 1, Seguin (hooking), 13:57.

THIRD PERIOD

Scoring: Boston 1, Lucic (Krejci), 12:11; Chicago 2, Bickell (Toews, Keith), 18:44, Bolland (Frolik, Oduya), 19:01. Penalties: Boston 1, Kelly (high-sticking), 14:21.

Shots on goal: Chi 6–9–16—31; Bos 12–6–7–25.

Power-play opportunities: Chi 0–2, Bos 0–4.

Goalies : Chi, Crawford (25 shots, 23 saves), Bos, Rask (31 shots, 28 saves).

Referees: O'Halloran, McCauley. Linesmen: Racicot, Sharrers.

A: 17,565.

Scoring

POINTS

Player and Team	GP	G	Ast	Pts	+/–	PM	Player and Team	GP	G	Ast	Pts	+/–	PM
David Krejci, Bos	22	9	17	26	+13	14	Patrice Bergeron, Bos	22	9	6	15	+2	13
Patrick Kane, Chi	23	9	10	19	+7	8	Sidney Crosby, Pit	14	7	8	15	-3	8
Milan Lucic, Bos	22	7	12	19	+12	14	Zdeno Chara, Bos	22	3	12	15	+7	20
Nathan Horton, Bos	22	7	12	19	+20	14	Jonathan Toews, Chi	23	3	11	14	+9	18
Bryan Bickell, Chi	23	9	8	17	+11	14	Slava Voynov, LA	18	6	7	13	+9	0
Patrick Sharp, Chi	23	10	6	16	+1	8	Jeff Carter, LA	18	6	7	13	+6	14
Marian Hossa, Chi	22	7	9	16	+8	2	Brad Marchand, Bos	22	4	9	13	+4	21
Evgeni Malkin, Pit	15	4	12	16	-2	26	Duncan Keith, Chi	22	2	11	13	+10	18
Kris Letang, Pit	15	3	13	16	+2	8	Five tied at 12 points.						

GOALS

Player and Team	GP	G
Patrick Sharp, Chi	23	10
David Krejci, Bos	22	9
Patrick Kane, Chi	23	9
Bryan Bickell, Chi	23	9
Patrice Bergeron, Bos	22	9
Milan Lucic, Bos	22	7
Nathan Horton, Bos	22	7
Marian Hossa, Chi	22	7
Sidney Crosby, Pit	14	7
Pascal Dupuis, Pit	15	7

SHORT-HANDED GOALS

Player and Team	GP	SH
Pascal Dupuis, Pit	15	2
Twelve players tied at 1.		

POWER PLAY GOALS

Player and Team	GP	PPG
Logan Couture, SJ	11	5
Patrice Bergeron, Bos	22	4
Marian Hossa, Chi	22	3
Joe Pavelski, SJ	11	3
Chris Kunitz, Pit	15	3
Daniel Alfredsson, Ott	10	3
Johan Franzen, Det	14	3
Torey Krug, Bos	15	

ASSISTS

Player and Team	GP	A
David Krejci, Bos	22	17
Kris Letang, Pit	15	13
Milan Lucic, Bos	22	12
Nathan Horton, Bos	22	12
Evgeni Malkin, Pit	15	12
Zdeno Chara, Bos	22	12

PLUS/MINUS

Player and Team	GP	+/–
Anze Kopitar, LA	20	+16
Nathan Horton, Bos	22	+20
David Krejci, Bos	22	+13
Milan Lucic, Bos	22	+12
Johnny Oduya, Chi	23	+12
Bryan Bickell, Chi	23	+11

Goaltending*

GOALS AGAINST AVERAGE

Player and Team	GP	W-L-OT	Avg
Corey Crawford, Chi	23	16-7-2	1.84
Jonathan Quick, LA	18	9-9-3	1.86
Antti Niemi, SJ	11	7-4-0	1.87
Tuukka Rask, Bos	22	14-8-3	1.88
Tomas Vokoun, Pit	11	6-5-2	2.01
Henrik Lundqvist, NYR	12	5-7-3	2.14
Braden Holtby, Was	7	3-4-0	2.22

*minimum of 400 minutes

SAVE PERCENTAGE

Player and Team	GP	W-L-OT	SA	GA	SV	SV%
Tuukka Rask, Bos	22	14-8-3	761	46	715	.940
Henrik Lundqvist, NYR	12	5-7-3	411	27	384	.934
Tomas Vokoun, Pit	11	6-5-2	345	23	322	.933
Corey Crawford, Chi	23	16-7-2	674	46	628	.932
Antti Niemi, SJ	11	7-4-0	298	21	277	.930
Jimmy Howard, Det	14	7-7-2	461	35	426	.924

NHL Awards

Award	Player and Team
Hart Trophy (MVP)	Alex Ovechkin, Was
Lindsay Award (NHLPA MOP)	Sidney Crosby, Pit
Calder Trophy (top rookie)	Jonathan Huberdeau, Fla
Vezina Trophy (top goaltender)	Sergei Bobrovsky, Col
Norris Trophy (top defenseman)	P.K. Subban, Mon
Lady Byng Trophy (for gentlemanly play)	Martin St. Louis, TB

Award	Player and Team
Adams Award (top coach)	Paul MacLean, Ott
Selke Trophy (top def. forward)	Jonathan Toews, Chi
Jennings Trophy (goaltender/s on club allowing fewest goals)	Corey Crawford/ Ray Emery, Chi
Art Ross Trophy (most points)	Martin St. Louis, TB
Conn Smythe Trophy (playoff MVP)	Patrick Kane, Chi

Individual 2012–13 Regular Season Leaders

Scoring

POINTS

Player and Team	GP	G	Ast	Pts	+/–	PIM	Player and Team	GP	G	Ast	Pts	+/–	PIM
Martin St. Louis, TB	48	17	43	60	0	14	Pavel Datsyuk, Det	47	15	34	49	21	14
Steven Stamkos, TB	48	29	28	57	-4	32	Mike Ribeiro, Wash	48	13	36	49	-4	53
Alex Ovechkin, Wash	48	32	24	56	2	36	Jonathan Toews, Chi	47	23	25	48	28	27
Sidney Crosby, Pit	36	15	41	56	26	16	Claude Giroux, Phi	48	13	35	48	-7	22
Patrick Kane, Chi	47	23	32	55	11	8	Henrik Zetterberg, Det	46	11	37	48	2	18
Eric Staal, Car	48	18	35	53	5	54	Nicklas Backstrom, Wash	48	8	40	48	8	20
Chris Kunitz, Pit	48	22	30	52	30	39	John Tavares, NYI	48	28	19	47	-2	18
Phil Kessel, Tor	48	20	32	52	-3	18	Jakub Voracek, Phi	48	22	24	46	-7	35
Taylor Hall, Edm	45	16	34	50	5	33	Andrew Ladd, Winn	48	18	28	46	10	22
Ryan Getzlaf, Ana	44	15	34	49	14	41	Henrik Sedin, Van	48	11	34	45	19	24

Scoring *(Cont.)*

GOALS

Player and Team	GP	G
Alex Ovechkin, Wash	48	32
Steven Stamkos, TB	48	29
John Tavares, NYI	48	28
Jeff Carter, LA	48	26
Patrick Kane, Chi	47	23
Jonathan Toews, Chi	47	23
Jiri Tlusty, Car	48	23
Chris Kunitz, Pit	48	22
Jakub Voracek, Phi	48	22
Rick Nash, NYR	44	21
Logan Couture, SJ	48	21
James Neal, Pit	40	21

ASSISTS

Player and Team	GP	Ast
Martin St. Louis, TB	48	43
Sidney Crosby, Pit	36	41
N. Backstrom, Wash	48	40
Henrik Zetterberg, Det	46	37
Mike Ribeiro, Wash	48	36

ASSISTS *(CONT.)*

Player and Team	GP	Ast
Eric Staal, Car	48	35
Claude Giroux, Phi	48	35
Four tied with 34 assists.		

PLUS/MINUS

Player and Team	GP	+/–
Pascal Dupuis, Pit	48	+31
Chris Kunitz, Pit	48	+30
Jonathan Toews, Chi	47	+28
Sidney Crosby, Pit	36	+26
Derek Stepan, NYR	48	+25
Patrice Bergeron, Bos	42	+24
Brad Marchand, Bos	45	+23
Tyler Seguin, Bos	48	+23
Pavel Datsyuk, Det	47	+21
Marian Hossa, Chi	40	+20

POWER PLAY GOALS

Player and Team	GP	PPG
Alex Ovechkin, Wash	48	16
Steven Stamkos, TB	48	10
John Tavares, NYI	48	9
Chris Kunitz, Pit	48	9
James Neal, Pit	40	9
Thomas Vanek, Buf	38	9

SHORT-HANDED GOALS

Player and Team	GP	SHG
Ilya Kovalchuk, NJ	37	4
Ryan Getzlaf, Ana	44	3
Gabriel Landeskog, Col	36	3
Nine tied with two goals.		

GAME-WINNING GOALS

Player and Team	GP	GW
Jeff Carter, LA	48	8
James Neal, Pit	40	6
Derek Stepan, NYR	48	6
Marian Hossa, Chi	40	6
Pavel Datsyuk, Det	47	6

Goaltending

GOALS AGAINST AVERAGE

Player and Team	GP	W-L-OTL	GA	GAA
Craig Anderson, Ott	24	12-9-2	40	1.69
Ray Emery, Chi	21	17-1-0	36	1.94
Corey Crawford, Chi	30	19-5-5	57	1.94
Tuukka Rask, Bos	36	19-10-5	70	2.00
Sergei Bobrovsky, Col	38	21-11-6	74	2.00
Henrik Lundqvist, NYR	43	24-16-3	88	2.05
Cory Schneider, Van	30	17-9-4	61	2.11
Jimmy Howard, Det	42	21-13-7	87	2.13
Jaroslav Halak, StL	16	6-5-1	29	2.14
Antti Niemi, SJ	43	24-12-6	93	2.16

WINS

Player and Team	GP	GAA	W	L	OTL
Antti Niemi, SJ	43	2.16	24	12	6
Henrik Lundqvist, NYR	43	2.05	24	16	3
Niklas Backstrom, Min	42	2.48	24	15	3
Evgeni Nabokov, NYI	41	2.50	23	11	7
Braden Holtby, Wash	36	2.58	23	12	1
Marc-Andre Fleury, Pit	33	2.39	23	8	0
Ondrej Pavelec, Winn	44	2.80	21	20	3
Jimmy Howard, Det	42	2.13	21	13	7
Carey Price, Mtl	39	2.59	21	13	4
Sergei Bobrovsky, Col	38	2.00	21	11	6

SAVE PERCENTAGE

Player and Team	GP	W-L-OTL	GA	SV	SV%
Craig Anderson, Ott	24	12-9-2	40	637	.941
Sergei Bobrovsky, Col	38	21-11-6	74	1010	.932
Tuukka Rask, Bos	36	19-10-5	70	910	.929
Cory Schneider, Van	30	17-9-4	61	774	.927
Henrik Lundqvist, NYR	43	24-16-3	88	1102	.926
Corey Crawford, Chi	30	19-5-5	57	712	.926

SHUTOUTS

Player and Team	GP	W-L-OTL	SO
Tukka Rask, Bos	36	19-10-5	5
Corey Schneider, Van	30	17-9-4	5
Jimmy Howard, Det	42	21-13-7	5
Pekka Rinne, Nash	43	15-16-8	5
Mike Smith, Phx	34	15-12-5	5

NHL Team-by-Team Statistical Leaders

Anaheim Ducks

SCORING

Player	GP	G	Ast	Pts	+/–	PM
Ryan Getzlaf, C	44	15	34	49	14	41
Corey Perry, RW	44	15	21	36	10	72
Bobby Ryan, RW	46	11	19	30	3	17
Saku Koivu, C	47	8	19	27	4	18
Francois Beauchemin, D	48	6	18	24	19	22
Teemu Selanne, RW	46	12	12	24	-10	28
Andrew Cogliano, C	48	13	10	23	14	6
Kyle Palmieri, RW	42	10	11	21	2	9
Daniel Winnik, C	48	6	13	19	13	16
Sheldon Souray, D	44	7	10	17	19	52
Matt Beleskey, LW	42	8	5	13	2	56
Nick Bonino, C	27	5	8	13	-3	8
Cam Fowler, D	37	1	10	11	-4	4
Emerson Etem, RW	38	3	7	10	7	9
*Ben Lovejoy, D	32	0	10	10	6	29
Luca Sbisa, D	41	1	7	8	0	23
*David Steckel, C	21	1	5	6	2	4

SCORING *(CONT.)*

Player	GP	G	Ast	Pts	+/–	PM
Bryan Allen, D	41	0	6	6	1	34
Toni Lydman, D	35	0	6	6	-1	12
Peter Holland, C	21	3	2	5	4	4
Radek Dvorak, RW	9	4	0	4	2	2
Patrick Maroon, LW	13	2	1	3	-1	10
Brad Staubitz, RW	15	1	1	2	0	41
Sami Vatanen, D	8	2	0	2	3	0
Brandon McMillan, C	6	0	1	1	-1	2
Peter Holland, C	4	1	0	1	0	2
Ryan O'Marra, C	9	0	1	1	-1	4

GOALTENDING

Player	GP	W	L	OT	TGA	GAA	SO
Viktor Fasth	25	15	6	2	52	2.18	4
Jonas Hiller	26	15	6	4	59	2.36	1

*Midseason trade

Boston Bruins

SCORING

Player	GP	G	Ast	Pts	+/-	PM
Brad Marchand, LW	45	18	18	36	23	27
David Krejci, C	47	10	23	33	1	20
Patrice Bergeron, C	42	10	22	32	24	18
Tyler Seguin, C	48	16	16	32	23	16
Milan Lucic, LW	46	7	20	27	8	75
Nathan Horton, RW	43	13	9	22	1	22
Zdeno Chara, D	48	7	12	19	14	70
Rich Peverley, C	47	6	12	18	-9	16
Daniel Paille, LW	46	10	7	17	3	8
Dennis Seidenberg, D	46	4	13	17	18	10
Dougie Hamilton, D	42	5	11	16	4	14
Gregory Campbell, C	48	4	9	13	2	41
Andrew Ference, D	48	4	9	13	9	35
*Jaromir Jagr, RW	11	2	7	9	3	2
Chris Kelly, C	34	3*	6	9	-8	16
Shawn Thornton, RW	45	3	4	7	1	60
Johnny Boychuk, D	44	1	5	6	5	12
Chris Bourque, LW	18	1	3	4	-6	6
Adam McQuaid, D	32	1	3	4	0	60
Jordan Caron, LW	17	1	2	3	1	4
Matt Bartkowski, D	11	0	2	2	0	6
Carl Soderberg, C	6	0	2	2	-2	6
*Wade Redden, D	6	1	1	2	0	0
Torey Krug, D	1	0	1	1	-1	0
*Kaspars Daugavins, LW	6	0	1	1	-1	0

GOALTENDING

Player	GP	W	L	OT	TGA	GAA	SO
Tuukka Rask	36	19	10	5	70	2.00	5
Anton Khudobin	14	9	4	1	31	2.32	1

Buffalo Sabres

SCORING

Player	GP	G	Ast	Pts	+/-	PM
Thomas Vanek, LW	38	20	21	41	-1	20
Cody Hodgson, C	48	15	19	34	-4	20
Tyler Ennis, LW	47	10	21	31	-14	16
*Jason Pominville, RW	37	10	15	25	1	8
Steve Ott, C	48	9	15	24	3	93
Christian Ehrhoff, D	47	5	17	22	6	34
Drew Stafford, RW	46	6	12	18	-16	21
Marcus Foligno, LW	47	5	13	18	-4	41
Jochen Hecht, C	47	5	9	14	6	18
Andrej Sekera, D	37	2	10	12	-2	4
Brian Flynn, RW	26	6	5	11	6	0
Nathan Gerbe, C	42	5	5	10	-3	14
Kevin Porter, C	31	4	5	9	-1	10
Tyler Myers, D	39	3	5	8	-8	32
*Jordan Leopold, D	24	2	6	8	-6	14
Mike Weber, D	42	1	6	7	3	70
Ville Leino, LW	8	2	4	6	0	6
Mark Pysyk, D	19	1	4	5	-7	0
Mikhail Grigorenko, C	25	1	4	5	-1	0
Alexander Sulzer, D	17	3	1	4	3	10
Adam Pardy, D	17	0	4	4	4	14
*Robyn Regehr, D	29	0	2	2	-4	21
Patrick Kaleta, RW	34	1	0	1	-4	67
*T.J. Brennan, D	10	1	0	1	-1	6
Luke Adam, C	4	1	0	1	1	2

GOALTENDING

Player	GP	W	L	OT	TGA	GAA	SO
Ryan Miller	40	17	17	5	108	2.81	0
Jhonas Enroth	12	4	4	1	27	2.60	1

Calgary Flames

SCORING

Player	GP	G	Ast	Pts	+/-	PM
Mike Cammalleri, LW	44	13	19	32	-15	25
Lee Stempniak, RW	47	9	23	32	2	12
Jiri Hudler, LW	42	10	17	27	-13	22
Alex Tanguay, LW	40	11	16	27	-13	22
Curtis Glencross, LW	40	15	11	26	-8	18
Matt Stajan, C	43	5	18	23	7	26
Jarome Iginla, RW	31	9	13	22	-7	22
Dennis Wideman, D	46	6	16	22	-9	12
Roman Cervenka, C	39	9	8	17	-13	14
Mikael Backlund, C	32	8	8	16	-6	29
*Jay Bouwmeester, D	33	6	9	15	-11	16
Mark Giordano, D	47	4	11	15	-7	40
T.J. Brodie, D	47	2	12	14	-9	8
Sven Baertschi, LW	20	3	7	10	0	6
Chris Butler, D	44	1	7	8	-10	19
Steve Begin, C	36	4	4	8	-2	22
*Blake Comeau, RW	33	4	3	7	-9	14
Roman Horak, C	20	2	5	7	-5	2
Tim Jackman, RW	42	1	4	5	-9	76

SCORING (CONT.)

Player	GP	G	Ast	Pts	+/-	PM
*Brian McGrattan, RW	19	3	0	3	-4	49
Mark Cundari, D	4	1	2	3	-2	2
Max Reinhart, C	11	1	2	3	-3	4
Cory Sarich, D	28	0	2	2	-8	16
Anton Babchuk, D	7	0	1	1	-1	0
Brett Carson, D	10	0	1	1	-1	0
Blair Jones, C	15	0	1	1	-6	10
Derek Smith, D	22	0	1	1	-5	10
Ben Hanowski, RW	5	1	0	1	0	0
Ben Street, RW	6	0	1	1	-1	0
Paul Byron, C	4	0	1	1	-2	2

GOALTENDING

Player	GP	W	L	OT	TGA	GAA	SO
Miikka Kiprusoff	24	8	14	2	77	3.44	0
Joey MacDonald	21	8	9	1	55	2.87	0
Leland Irving	6	2	1	1	15	3.33	0
Danny Taylor	2	1	1	0	6	3.00	0

*Mid-season trade

Carolina Hurricanes

SCORING

Player	GP	G	Ast	Pts	+/-	PM
Eric Staal, C	48	18	35	53	5	54
Alexander Semin, LW	44	13	31	44	14	46
Jiri Tlusty, C	48	23	15	38	15	18
Jordan Staal, C	48	10	21	31	-18	32
Jeff Skinner, C	42	13	11	24	-21	26
Joe Corvo, D	40	6	11	17	-3	14
Patrick Dwyer, RW	46	8	8	16	-7	12
Justin Faulk, D	38	5	10	15	1	15
*Jussi Jokinen, LW	33	6	5	11	-8	18
Jay Harrison, D	47	3	7	10	-10	51
Joni Pitkanen, D	22	1	8	9	2	12
Tuomo Ruutu, C	17	4	5	9	-6	8
Tim Gleason, D	42	0	9	9	-3	40
Riley Nash, C	32	4	5	9	-4	8
Jamie McBain, D	40	1	7	8	0	12
Bobby Sanguinetti, D	37	2	4	6	-6	4
Drayson Bowman, LW	37	3	2	5	-7	17
Kevin Westgarth, RW	31	2	2	4	1	45
Chad LaRose, RW	35	2	2	4	-8	29
*M. Bergeron, D	13	0	4	4	-7	5
Tim Brent, C	30	0	3	3	-3	8
Zac Dalpe, C	10	1	2	3	-7	0
Tim Wallace, RW	28	1	1	2	-9	17
Brett Bellemore, D	8	0	2	2	-2	7
Chris Terry, LW	3	1	0	1	0	0
Andreas Nodl, RW	8	0	1	1	-1	2
Jeremy Welsh, C	5	0	1	1	1	0

GOALTENDING

Player	GP	W	L	OT	TGA	GAA	SO
Justin Peters	19	4	11	1	55	3.46	1
Cam Ward	17	9	6	1	44	2.84	0
Dan Ellis	19	6	8	2	52	3.13	1

Chicago Blackhawks

SCORING

Player	GP	G	Ast	Pts	+/-	PM
Patrick Kane, RW	47	23	32	55	11	8
Jonathan Toews, C	47	23	25	48	28	27
Marian Hossa, RW	40	17	14	31	20	16
Duncan Keith, D	47	3	24	27	16	31
Brandon Saad, LW	46	10	17	27	17	12
Viktor Stalberg, LW	47	9	14	23	16	25
Bryan Bickell, LW	48	9	14	23	12	25
Brent Seabrook, D	47	8	12	20	12	23
Patrick Sharp, C	28	6	14	20	8	14
Nick Leddy, D	48	6	12	18	15	10
Andrew Shaw, C	48	9	6	15	6	38
Dave Bolland, C	35	7	7	14	-7	22
Marcus Kruger, C	47	4	9	13	3	24
Michal Rozsival, D	27	0	12	12	18	14
Johnny Oduya, D	48	3	9	12	12	10
Niklas Hjalmarsson, D	46	2	8	10	15	22
Michael Frolik, C	45	3	7	10	5	8
*Michal Handzus, C	11	1	5	6	7	4
Jimmy Hayes, RW	10	1	3	4	0	0
Daniel Carcillo, LW	23	2	1	3	1	11
Jamal Mayers, C	19	0	2	2	2	16
Jeremy Morin, LW	3	1	1	2	1	0
Sheldon Brookbank, D	26	1	0	1	-2	21
Ben Smith, RW	1	1	0	1	1	0

GOALTENDING

Player	GP	W	L	OT	TGA	GAA	SO
Corey Crawford	30	19	5	5	57	1.94	3
Ray Emery	21	17	1	0	36	1.94	3
Carter Hutton	1	0	1	0	3	3.06	0

Colorado Avalanche

SCORING

Player	GP	G	Ast	Pts	+/-	PM
P.A. Parenteau, RW	48	18	25	43	-11	38
Matt Duchene, C	47	17	26	43	-12	12
Paul Stastny, C	40	9	15	24	-7	14
Jamie McGinn, LW	47	11	11	22	-13	26
John Mitchell, C	47	10	10	20	5	18
Ryan O'Reilly, C	29	6	14	20	-3	4
G. Landeskog, LW	36	9	8	17	-4	22
Tyson Barrie, D	32	2	11	13	-11	10
Cody McLeod, LW	48	8	4	12	4	83
Milan Hejduk, RW	29	4	7	11	-7	0
Jan Hejda, D	46	1	9	10	-3	28
Aaron Palushaj, RW	25	2	7	9	-2	8
Chuck Kobasew, RW	37	5	4	9	6	21
David Jones, RW	33	3	6	9	-11	6
Matt Hunwick, D	43	0	6	6	4	16
Greg Zanon, D	44	0	6	6	-16	28
Mark Olver, C	32	4	2	6	-5	6

SCORING (*CONT.*)

Player	GP	G	Ast	Pts	+/-	PM
Patrick Bordeleau, LW	46	2	3	5	-7	70
Stefan Elliott, D	18	1	3	4	-3	2
Erik Johnson, D	31	0	4	4	-3	18
Shane O'Brien, D	28	0	4	4	0	60
*Ryan O'Byrne, D	34	1	3	4	-8	54
Ryan Wilson, D	12	0	3	3	4	8
Brad Malone, C	13	1	1	2	-7	16
D. Van der Gulik, RW	9	0	2	2	2	6
Steve Downie, RW	2	0	1	1	1	6
*Tomas Vincour, C	2	0	1	1	-1	2

GOALTENDING

Player	GP	W	L	OT	TGA	GAA	SO
Semyon Varlamov	35	11	21	3	98	3.02	3
J-S. Giguere	18	5	4	4	43	2.84	0
Sami Aittokallio	1	0	0	0	2	2.43	0

*Mid-season trade

Columbus Blue Jackets

SCORING

Player	GP	G	Ast	Pts	+/–	PM
Vinny Prospal, C	48	12	18	30	3	32
Mark Letestu, C	46	13	14	27	7	10
Fedor Tyutin, D	48	4	18	22	9	28
Brandon Dubinsky, C	29	2	18	20	2	76
Nick Foligno, LW	45	6	13	19	6	28
Jack Johnson, D	44	5	14	19	-5	12
*Derick Brassard, C	34	7	11	18	-2	16
R.J. Umberger, C	48	8	10	18	3	16
Artem Anisimov, C	35	11	7	18	-6	12
Cam Atkinson, RW	35	9	9	18	9	4
Matt Calvert, LW	42	9	7	16	-9	32
James Wisniewski, D	30	5	9	14	-1	15
Ryan Johansen, C	40	5	7	12	-7	12
Nikita Nikitin, D	38	3	6	9	2	17
Derek Dorsett, RW	24	3	6	9	-11	53
Derek MacKenzie, C	43	3	5	8	1	36
*Marian Gaborik, RW	12	3	5	8	5	6
Dalton Prout, D	28	1	6	7	15	25
Jared Boll, RW	43	2	4	6	1	100
*Blake Comeau, RW	9	2	3	5	5	6
Tim Erixon, D	31	0	5	5	4	14
Adrian Aucoin, D	36	0	4	4	-8	16
Colton Gillies, C	27	1	1	2	1	17
*John Moore, D	17	0	1	1	-5	2
Cody Goloubef, D	11	1	0	1	-3	0

GOALTENDING

Player	GP	W	L	OT	TGA	GAA	SO
Sergei Bobrovsky	38	21	11	6	74	2.00	4
*Steve Mason	13	3	6	1	35	2.95	0

Detroit Red Wings

SCORING

Player	GP	G	Ast	Pts	+/–	PM
Pavel Datsyuk, C	47	15	34	49	21	14
Henrik Zetterberg, C	46	11	37	48	7	18
Johan Franzen, LW	41	14	17	31	13	41
Niklas Kronwall, D	48	5	24	29	-5	44
Damien Brunner, D	44	12	14	26	-6	12
Valtteri Filppula, C	41	9	8	17	-4	6
Daniel Cleary, RW	48	9	6	15	-6	40
Jakub Kindl, D	41	4	9	13	15	28
Jonathan Ericsson, D	45	3	10	13	6	29
Justin Abdelkader, LW	48	10	3	13	6	34
Joakim Andersson, C	38	3	5	8	2	8
Brendan Smith, D	34	0	8	8	1	36
Cory Emmerton, C	48	5	3	8	-1	4
Patrick Eaves, RW	34	2	6	8	-1	4
Drew Miller, LW	44	4	4	8	-8	2
Jordin Tootoo, RW	42	3	5	8	0	78
Tomas Tatar, C	18	4	3	7	2	4
Gustav Nyquist, C	22	3	3	6	0	6
Brian Lashoff, D	31	1	4	5	-10	15
Ian White, D	25	2	2	4	5	4
Kyle Quincey, D	36	1	2	3	7	18
Todd Bertuzzi, RW	7	2	1	3	3	2
Danny DeKeyser, D	11	0	1	1	4	2
Carlo Colaiacovo, D	6	0	1	1	-4	2
Mikael Samuelsson, RW	4	0	1	1	-3	0

GOALTENDING

Player	GP	W	L	OT	TGA	GAA	SO
Jimmy Howard	42	21	13	7	87	2.13	5
Jonas Gustavsson	7	2	2	1	17	2.92	0
Petr Mrazek	2	1	1	0	4	2.01	0

*Mid-season trade

Dallas Stars

SCORING

Player	GP	G	Ast	Pts	+/–	PM
Jamie Benn, LW	41	12	21	33	-12	40
Ray Whitney, LW	32	11	18	29	1	4
Loui Eriksson, LW	48	12	17	29	-9	8
Alex Goligoski, D	47	3	24	27	4	18
*Jaromir Jagr, RW	34	14	12	26	-5	20
Cody Eakin, C	48	7	17	24	1	31
*Derek Roy, C	30	4	18	22	3	4
Vernon Fiddler, C	46	4	13	17	3	48
*Michael Ryder, RW	19	6	8	14	4	8
Antoine Roussel, LW	39	7	7	14	3	85
Stephane Robidas, D	48	1	12	13	2	56
Trevor Daley, D	44	4	9	13	1	14
Eric Nystrom, LW	48	7	4	11	-3	61
*Brenden Morrow, LW	29	6	5	11	-8	18
Ryan Garbutt, C	36	3	7	10	1	32
Reilly Smith, RW	37	3	6	9	0	8
Brenden Dillon, D	48	3	5	8	1	65
Alex Chiasson, RW	7	6	1	7	3	0
*Erik Cole, RW	28	6	1	7	-7	10
Jordie Benn, D	26	1	5	6	-4	10
Philip Larsen, D	32	2	3	5	-10	18
Aaron Rome, D	27	0	5	5	-2	18
*Tomas Vincour, C	15	2	1	3	0	2
Matt Fraser, LW	12	1	2	3	0	0
Jamie Oleksiak, D	16	0	2	2	-5	14
*Lane MacDermid, LW	6	2	0	2	1	9
Colton Sceviour, C	1	0	1	1	-1	0
Tom Wandell, C	18	1	0	1	0	4

GOALTENDING

Player	GP	W	L	OT	TGA	GAA	SO
Kari Lehtonen	36	15	14	3	88	2.66	1
Richard Bachman	13	6	5	0	33	3.25	0
Cristopher Nilstorp	5	1	3	1	15	3.09	0

Edmonton Oilers

SCORING

Player	GP	G	Ast	Pts	+/–	PM
Taylor Hall, LW	45	16	34	50	5	33
Sam Gagner, C	48	14	24	38	-6	23
Jordan Eberle, C	48	16	21	37	-4	16
Nail Yakupov, RW	48	17	14	31	-4	24
Justin Schultz, D	48	8	19	27	-17	8
R. Nugent-Hopkins, C	40	4	20	24	3	8
Ales Hemsky, RW	38	9	11	20	-6	16
Magnus Paajarvi, LW	42	9	7	16	-1	14
Ryan Smyth, LW	47	2	11	13	-5	40
Ryan Whitney, D	34	4	9	13	-7	23
Jeff Petry, D	48	3	9	12	1	29
Shawn Horcoff, C	31	7	5	12	8	24
Nick Schultz, D	48	1	8	9	-13	24
Lennart Petrell, C	35	3	6	9	-4	4
Ryan Jones, RW	27	2	5	7	0	17
Mark Fistric, D	25	0	6	6	6	32
Ladislav Smid, D	48	1	3	4	-1	55
Corey Potter, D	33	3	1	4	8	6
Eric Belanger, C	26	0	3	3	-1	10
Teemu Hartikainen, C	23	1	2	3	-8	6
Ben Eager, LW	14	1	1	2	-4	25
*Jerred Smithson, C	10	1	0	1	0	2
*Mike Brown, RW	27	1	0	1	-8	53
Anton Lander, C	11	0	1	1	-4	2

GOALTENDING

Player	GP	W	L	OT	TGA	GAA	SO
Devan Dubnyk	38	14	16	6	90	2.57	2
Nikolai Khabibulin	12	4	6	1	29	2.55	1

Florida Panthers

SCORING

Player	GP	G	Ast	Pts	+/−	PM
Tomas Fleischmann, C...48		12	23	35	-10	16
J. Huberdeau, C..........48		14	17	31	-15	18
Tomas Kopecky, C 47		15	12	27	-8	28
Brian Campbell, D 48		8	19	27	-22	12
Shawn Matthias, C.......48		14	7	21	-8	16
Marcel Goc, C 42		9	10	19	-6	8
Peter Mueller, RW........43		8	9	17	-11	18
Drew Shore, C 43		3	10	13	-10	14
Jack Skille, RW............40		3	9	12	-9	11
Filip Kuba, D...............44		1	9	10	-18	24
Dmitry Kulikov, D..........34		3	7	10	-5	22
*T.J. Brennan, D 19		2	7	9	-8	2
Mike Weaver, D 27		1	8	9	-3	8
*Jerred Smithson, C 35		2	3	5	-4	10
Alex Kovalev, RW 14		2	3	5	-1	6
Scottie Upshall, RW.....27		4	1	5	-8	25
Stephen Weiss, C 17		1	3	4	-13	25
Tyson Strachan, D.......38		0	4	4	-13	40
Erik Gudbranson, D.....32		0	4	4	-22	47
Kris Versteeg, C 10		2	2	4	-8	8
*Mike Santorelli, C 24		2	1	3	-7	2
George Parros, RW 39		1	1	2	-15	57
Ed Jovanovski, D..........6		0	1	1	-4	0
Colby Robak, D...........16		0	1	1	-1	17
Greg Rallo, RW............10		1	0	1	-5	2
Eric Selleck, LW...........2		0	1	1	2	17
Nick Bjugstad, C 11		1	0	1	-8	2

GOALTENDING

Player	GP	W	L	OT	TGA	GAA	SO
Jacob Markstrom.......23		8	14	1	68	3.22	0
Jose Theodore 15		4	6	3	42	3.29	0
Scott Clemmensen 19		3	7	2	53	3.67	0

Los Angeles Kings

SCORING

Player	GP	G	Ast	Pts	+/−	PM
Anze Kopitar, C.............47		10	32	42	14	16
Justin Williams, RW.......48		11	22	33	15	22
Jeff Carter, C................48		26	7	33	0	16
Mike Richards, C 48		12	20	32	-8	42
Dustin Brown, RW........46		18	11	29	6	22
Slava Voynov, D...........48		6	19	25	5	14
Drew Doughty, D 48		6	16	22	4	36
Jarret Stoll, C...............48		7	11	18	1	28
Jake Muzzin, D 45		7	9	16	16	35
Kyle Clifford, LW 48		7	7	14	1	51
Dustin Penner, LW 33		2	12	14	-2	18
Trevor Lewis, C............48		5	9	14	5	19
Rob Scuderi, D 48		1	11	12	-6	4
Dwight King, C 47		4	6	10	-3	11
Colin Fraser, C 34		2	5	7	-4	25
Brad Richardson, C 16		1	5	6	2	10
Jordan Nolan, C...........44		2	4	6	-5	46
Tyler Toffoli, C 10		2	3	5	3	2
Alec Martinez, D 27		1	4	5	-2	10
*Simon Gagne, LW 11		0	5	5	2	2
*Davis Drewiske, D 20		1	3	4	3	14
*Keaton Ellerby, D 35		0	3	3	5	16
*Robyn Regehr, D 12		0	2	2	0	2
Matt Greene, D 5		0	1	1	-1	8

GOALTENDING

Player	GP	W	L	OT	TGA	GAA	SO
Jonathan Quick..........37		18	13	4	87	2.45	1
Jonathan Bernier 14		9	3	1	24	1.87	1

Minnesota Wild

SCORING

Player	GP	G	Ast	Pts	+/−	PM
Zach Parise, LW 48		18	20	38	2	16
Mikko Koivu, C.............48		11	26	37	2	26
Ryan Suter, D 48		4	28	32	2	24
Devin Setoguchi, RW....48		13	14	27	5	20
Matt Cullen, C.............42		7	20	27	9	10
Dany Heatley, RW 36		11	10	21	-12	8
P.-M. Bouchard, RW......43		8	12	20	3	8
Jared Spurgeon, D.......39		5	10	15	1	4
Charlie Coyle, RW 37		8	6	14	3	28
Tom Gilbert, D 43		3	10	13	-11	18
Kyle Brodziak, C...........48		8	4	12	-18	20
Jonas Brodin, D...........45		2	9	11	3	10
Cal Clutterbuck, RW.....42		4	6	10	-5	27
Clayton Stoner, D 48		0	10	10	4	42
*Jason Pominville, RW..10		4	5	9	0	0

SCORING *(CONT.)*

Player	GP	G	Ast	Pts	+/−	PM
Torrey Mitchell, LW.......45		4	4	8	-8	21
Mikael Granlund, C.......27		2	6	8	-4	6
Jason Zucker, LW.........20		4	1	5	4	8
*Mike Rupp, LW............32		1	3	4	1	67
Justin Falk, D...............36		0	3	3	-9	40
Marco Scandella, D........6		1	0	1	-1	4
Brett Clark, D...............8		0	1	1	-9	0

GOALTENDING

Player	GP	W	L	OT	TGA	GAA	SO
Niklas Backstrom.......42		24	15	3	98	2.48	2
Josh Harding 5		1	1	0	10	3.24	1
Darcy Kuemper 6		1	2	0	10	2.08	0
Matt Hackett 1		0	1	0	5	5.07	0

*Mid-season trade

Montreal Canadiens
SCORING

Player	GP	G	Ast	Pts	+/−	PM
Max Pacioretty, LW	44	15	24	39	8	28
P.K. Subban, D	42	11	27	38	12	57
Tomas Plekanec, C	47	14	19	33	3	24
Andrei Markov, D	48	10	20	30	-9	14
Lars Eller, C	46	8	22	30	8	45
David Desharnais, C	48	10	18	28	-2	26
Brendan Gallagher, RW	44	15	13	28	10	33
Alex Galchenyuk, C	48	9	18	27	14	20
Brian Gionta, RW	48	14	12	26	3	8
*Michael Ryder, RW	27	10	11	21	-2	8
Brandon Prust, RW	38	5	9	14	11	110
Raphael Diaz, D	23	1	13	14	4	6
Rene Bourque, LW	27	7	6	13	-1	32
Alexei Emelin, D	38	3	9	12	2	33
Josh Gorges, D	48	2	7	9	4	15
Francis Bouillon, D	48	1	8	9	4	21
*Erik Cole, RW	19	3	3	6	1	10
Travis Moen, LW	45	2	4	6	-4	32
Colby Armstrong, RW	37	2	3	5	1	12
Tomas Kaberle, D	10	0	3	3	4	0
*Davis Drewiske, D	9	1	2	3	0	0
Gabriel Dumont, C	10	1	2	3	1	13
Jarred Tinordi, D	8	0	2	2	5	2
Yannick Weber, D	6	0	2	2	-1	2
Nathan Beaulieu, D	6	0	2	2	5	0
*Jeff Halpern, C	16	1	1	2	-3	2
Ryan White, C	26	1	0	1	1	67

GOALTENDING

Player	GP	W	L	OT	TGA	GAA	SO
Carey Price	39	21	13	4	97	2.59	3
Peter Budaj	13	8	1	1	25	2.28	1

New Jersey Devils
SCORING

Player	GP	G	Ast	Pts	+/−	PM
Patrik Elias, LW	48	14	22	36	5	22
Ilya Kovalchuk, RW	37	11	20	31	-6	18
David Clarkson, C	48	15	9	24	-6	78
Travis Zajac, C	48	7	13	20	-5	22
Marek Zidlicky, D	48	4	15	19	-12	38
Andy Greene, D	48	4	12	16	12	20
Adam Henrique, C	42	11	5	16	-3	16
Steve Bernier, RW	47	8	7	15	-7	17
Ryan Carter, C	44	6	9	15	-2	31
Stephen Gionta, RW	48	4	10	14	2	14
Andrei Loktionov, C	28	8	4	12	-2	4
Dainius Zubrus, RW	22	2	7	9	-3	12
*A Ponikarovsky, LW	30	2	5	7	1	8
Mark Fayne, D	31	1	5	6	6	16
Adam Larsson, D	37	0	6	6	4	12
*Steve Sullivan, C	9	2	3	5	-4	4
Anton Volchenkov, D	37	1	4	5	-1	37
Peter Harrold, D	23	2	3	5	-8	6
*Matt D'Agostini, RW	13	2	2	4	-1	6
Henrik Tallinder, D	25	1	3	4	0	10
Stefan Matteau, C	17	1	2	3	-1	6
Jacob Josefson, C	22	1	2	3	-10	2
*Bobby Butler, RW	14	1	1	2	-6	0
Bryce Salvador, D	39	0	2	2	-12	22
Tom Kostopoulos, RW	15	1	0	1	0	18

GOALTENDING

Player	GP	W	L	OT	TGA	GAA	SO
Martin Brodeur	29	13	9	7	65	2.22	2
Johan Hedberg	19	6	10	3	51	2.76	1

*Mid-season trade

Nashville Predators
SCORING

Player	GP	G	Ast	Pts	+/−	PM
Shea Weber, D	48	9	19	28	-2	48
David Legwand, C	48	12	13	25	-6	20
*Martin-Erat, LW	36	4	17	21	-7	26
Mike Fisher, C	38	10	11	21	6	27
Colin Wilson, C	25	7	12	19	1	4
Roman Josi, D	48	5	13	18	-7	8
Gabriel Bourque, LW	34	11	5	16	6	4
Sergei Kostitsyn, LW	46	3	12	15	-5	11
Patric Hornqvist, RW	24	4	10	14	-1	14
Kevin Klein, D	47	3	11	14	-1	9
Nick Spaling, C	47	9	4	13	-10	18
Craig Smith, C	44	4	8	12	-11	20
Matt Halischuk, RW	36	5	6	11	1	10
Richard Clune, LW	47	4	5	9	3	113
*Bobby Butler, RW	20	3	6	9	-2	4
Brandon Yip, RW	34	3	5	8	-3	26
Taylor Beck, LW	16	3	4	7	0	2
Victor Bartley, D	24	0	7	7	2	6
Jonathon Blum, D	35	1	6	7	-1	6
Ryan Ellis, D	32	2	4	6	-2	15
Paul Gaustad, C	23	2	3	5	-1	20
Chris Mueller, RW	18	2	3	5	-4	6
Daniel Bang, RW	8	0	2	2	-2	0
Filip Forsberg, C	5	0	1	1	-5	0
Joonas Rask, C	2	0	1	1	-1	0
Austin Watson, LW	6	1	0	1	-2	0
Kevin Henderson, LW	4	1	0	1	-1	0

GOALTENDING

Player	GP	W	L	OT	TGA	GAA	SO
Pekka Rinne	43	15	16	8	99	2.43	5
Chris Mason	11	1	7	1	29	3.73	0

New York Islanders
SCORING

Player	GP	G	Ast	Pts	+/−	PM
John Tavares, C	48	28	19	47	-2	18
Matt Moulson, LW	47	15	29	44	-3	4
Brad Boyes, C	48	10	25	35	-6	16
Frans Nielsen, C	48	6	23	29	-3	12
Mark Streit, D	48	6	21	27	-14	22
Kyle Okposo, RW	48	4	20	24	-2	38
Michael Grabner, RW	45	16	5	21	4	12
Josh Bailey, C	38	11	8	19	7	6
Colin McDonald, RW	45	7	10	17	-1	32
Casey Cizikas, C	45	6	9	15	0	14
Lubomir Visnovsky, D	35	3	11	14	12	20
Keith Aucoin, C	41	6	6	12	-1	4
Andrew MacDonald, D	48	3	9	12	-2	20
Matt Martin, LW	48	4	7	11	-2	63
Travis Hamonic, D	48	3	7	10	-8	28
David Ullstrom, LW	20	2	3	5	-2	6
Marty Reasoner, C	31	0	5	5	-3	4
Thomas Hickey, D	39	1	3	4	9	8
Brian Strait, D	19	0	4	4	4	10
Radek Martinek, D	13	3	0	3	-2	4
Matt Carkner, D	22	0	2	2	-2	46
Jesse Joensuu, LW	7	0	2	2	2	6
Anders Lee, C	2	1	1	2	-3	0
Joe Finley, D	16	0	1	1	-5	20

GOALTENDING

Player	GP	W	L	OT	TGA	GAA	SO
Evgeni Nabokov	41	23	11	7	103	2.50	3
Kevin Poulin	5	1	3	0	13	3.03	0
Rick DiPietro	3	0	3	0	12	4.10	0

New York Rangers
SCORING

Player	GP	G	Ast	Pts	+/-	PM
Derek Stepan, C	48	18	26	44	25	12
Rick Nash, LW	44	21	21	42	16	26
Brad Richards, C	46	11	23	34	8	14
Ryan Callahan, RW	45	16	15	31	9	12
Carl Hagelin, LW	48	10	14	24	10	18
Michael Del Zotto, D	46	3	18	21	6	18
Ryan McDonagh, D	47	4	15	19	13	22
*Marian Gaborik, RW	35	9	10	19	-8	8
Dan Girardi, D	46	2	12	14	-1	16
*Derick Brassard, C	13	5	6	11	3	0
Taylor Pyatt, LW	48	6	5	11	5	6
Marc Staal, D	21	2	9	11	4	14
Mats Zuccarello, RW	15	3	5	8	10	8
*Ryane Clowe, RW	12	3	5	8	5	14
Anton Stralman, D	48	4	3	7	14	16
*John Moore, D	13	1	5	6	9	5
Brian Boyle, C	38	2	3	5	-13	29
J.T. Miller, C	26	2	2	4	-7	8
Chris Kreider, LW	23	2	1	3	-1	6
Steve Eminger, D	35	0	3	3	9	8
Arron Asham, RW	27	2	0	2	2	50
*Jeff Halpern, C	30	0	1	1	-5	8
Kris Newbury, C	6	0	1	1	1	9
Benn Ferriero, C	4	0	1	1	0	0

GOALTENDING

Player	GP	W	L	OT	TGA	GAA	SO
Henrik Lundqvist	43	24	16	3	88	2.05	2
Martin Biron	6	2	2	1	13	2.32	0

Philadelphia Flyers
SCORING

Player	GP	G	Ast	Pts	+/-	PM
Claude Giroux, C	48	13	35	48	-7	22
Jakub Voracek, RW	48	22	24	46	-7	35
Wayne Simmonds, RW	45	15	17	32	-7	82
Kimmo Timonen, D	45	5	24	29	3	36
Brayden Schenn, C	47	8	18	26	-8	24
Matt Read, C	42	11	13	24	1	2
Danny Briere, C	34	6	10	16	-13	10
Sean Couturier, C	46	4	11	15	-8	10
Ruslan Fedotenko, LW	47	4	9	13	8	12
*Simon Gagne, LW	27	5	6	11	-3	6
Scott Hartnell, RW	32	8	3	11	-5	70
Luke Schenn, D	47	3	8	11	3	34
Maxime Talbot, C	35	5	5	10	2	23
Mike Knuble, RW	28	4	4	8	-4	20
Erik Gustafsson, D	27	3	5	8	-1	2
Bruno Gervais, D	37	1	5	6	-17	10
Braydon Coburn, D	33	1	4	5	-10	41
Kurtis Foster, D	23	1	4	5	0	25
Zac Rinaldo, C	32	3	2	5	-7	85
Tye McGinn, LW	18	3	2	5	0	19
Nicklas Grossmann, D	30	1	3	4	-1	21
Oliver Lauridsen, D	15	2	1	3	0	34
Brandon Manning, D	6	0	2	2	4	0
*Tom Sestito, LW	7	2	0	2	1	12
Andrej Meszaros, D	11	0	2	2	-9	2

GOALTENDING

Player	GP	W	L	OT	TGA	GAA	SO
Ilya Bryzgalov	40	19	17	3	107	2.79	1
Steve Mason	7	2	2	0	12	1.90	0
Brian Boucher	4	0	2	0	6	2.50	0
Michael Leighton	1	0	1	0	5	5.07	0

*Mid-season trade

Ottawa Senators
SCORING

Player	GP	G	Ast	Pts	+/-	PM
Kyle Turris, C	48	12	17	29	6	24
Sergei Gonchar, D	45	3	24	27	4	26
Daniel Alfredsson, RW	47	10	16	26	1	33
Mika Zibanejad, C	42	7	13	20	9	6
Jakob Silfverberg, LW	48	10	9	19	9	12
Colin Greening, C	47	8	11	19	5	11
Patrick Wiercioch, D	42	5	14	19	9	39
Zack Smith, C	48	4	11	15	-9	56
Erik Karlsson, D	17	6	8	14	8	8
Chris Phillips, D	48	5	9	14	-5	43
Milan Michalek, LW	23	4	10	14	8	17
Chris Neil, RW	48	4	8	12	0	144
Erik Condra, RW	48	4	8	12	3	34
Marc Methot, D	47	2	9	11	2	31
Andre Benoit, LW	33	3	7	10	-3	8
G. Latendresse, LW	27	6	4	10	-2	8
Eric Gryba, D	33	2	4	6	-3	26
Jim O'Brien, C	29	5	1	6	-2	8
*Cory Conacher, LW	12	2	3	5	6	4
Jason Spezza, C	5	2	3	5	3	2
Jean-Gabriel Pageau, C	9	2	2	4	3	0
Peter Regin, C	27	0	3	3	-4	8
*K. Daugavins, LW	19	1	2	3	-7	9
David Dziurzynski, C	12	2	0	2	-1	13
Stephane Da Costa, C	9	1	1	2	-3	0

GOALTENDING

Player	GP	W	L	OT	TGA	GAA	SO
Craig Anderson	24	12	9	2	40	1.69	3
Robin Lehner	12	5	3	4	27	2.20	0
*Ben Bishop	13	8	5	0	31	2.45	1

Phoenix Coyotes
SCORING

Player	GP	G	Ast	Pts	+/-	PM
Keith Yandle, D	48	10	20	30	4	54
Radim Vrbata, RW	34	12	16	28	6	14
Shane Doan, RW	48	13	14	27	6	37
Mikkel Boedker, RW	48	7	19	26	0	12
O. Ekman-Larsson, D	48	3	21	24	5	26
Martin Hanzal, C	39	11	12	23	2	24
Antoine Vermette, C	48	13	8	21	-3	36
David Moss, LW	45	5	15	20	3	21
Kyle Chipchura, C	46	5	9	14	1	50
Boyd Gordon, C	48	4	10	14	0	8
*Steve Sullivan, C	33	5	7	12	-8	20
*Raffi Torres, LW	28	5	7	12	-1	13
Derek Morris, D	39	0	11	11	-6	36
Lauri Korpikoski, C	36	6	5	11	-3	12
Rob Klinkhammer, LW	22	5	6	11	7	10
Michael Stone, D	40	5	4	9	2	16
Rostislav Klesla, D	38	2	6	8	0	22
*Matthew Lombardi, C	21	4	4	8	0	4
Paul Bissonnette, LW	28	0	6	6	2	36
David Schlemko, D	30	1	5	6	8	12
Nick Johnson, RW	17	4	2	6	3	0
Chris Conner, RW	12	1	1	2	3	2
Zbynek Michalek, D	34	0	2	2	4	14
David Rundblad, D	8	0	1	1	-5	0

GOALTENDING

Player	GP	W	L	OT	TGA	GAA	SO
Mike Smith	34	15	12	5	84	2.58	5
Jason LaBarbera	15	4	6	2	32	2.64	0
Chad Johnson	4	2	0	2	5	1.22	1

Pittsburgh Penguins

SCORING

Player	GP	G	Ast	Pts	+/-	PM
Sidney Crosby, C	36	15	41	56	26	16
Chris Kunitz, LW	48	22	30	52	30	39
Kris Letang, D	35	5	33	38	16	8
Pascal Dupuis, RW	48	20	18	38	31	26
James Neal, LW	40	21	15	36	5	26
Evgeni Malkin, C	31	9	24	33	5	36
Paul Martin, D	34	6	17	23	14	16
Matt Cooke, LW	48	8	13	21	-2	36
Brandon Sutter, C	48	11	8	19	3	4
*Beau Bennett, RW	26	3	11	14	7	6
*Brenden Morrow, LW	15	6	8	14	5	19
Matt Niskanen, D	40	4	10	14	4	12
Tyler Kennedy, C	46	6	5	11	-6	19
*Jussi Jokinen, LW	10	7	4	11	3	6
*Jarome Iginla, RW	13	5	6	11	2	9
Craig Adams, RW	48	3	6	9	-1	28
Brooks Orpik, D	46	0	8	8	17	32
Simon Despres, D	33	2	5	7	9	20
Dustin Jeffrey, C	24	3	3	6	1	2
Deryk Engelland, D	42	0	6	6	5	54
Joe Vitale, C	33	2	3	5	-7	17
Robert Bortuzzo, D	15	2	2	4	3	27
*Douglas Murray, D	14	1	2	3	-1	9
Tanner Glass, C	48	1	1	2	-11	62

GOALTENDING

Player	GP	W	L	OT	TGA	GAA	SO
Marc-Andre Fleury	33	23	8	0	74	2.39	1
Tomas Vokoun	20	13	4	0	42	2.45	3

San Jose Sharks

SCORING

Player	GP	G	Ast	Pts	+/-	PM
Joe Thornton, C	48	7	33	40	6	26
Logan Couture, C	48	21	16	37	7	4
Patrick Marleau, C	48	17	14	31	-2	24
Joe Pavelski, C	48	16	15	31	2	10
Brent Burns, D	30	9	11	20	0	20
Dan Boyle, D	46	7	13	20	3	27
Martin Havlat, LW	40	8	10	18	7	30
Scott Gomez, C	39	2	13	15	-10	22
T.J. Galiardi, LW	36	5	9	14	1	14
Tommy Wingels, C	42	5	8	13	-9	26
Matt Irwin, D	38	6	6	12	-1	10
*Ryane Clowe, RW	28	0	11	11	-4	79
M-E. Vlasic, D	48	3	4	7	5	29
Justin Braun, D	41	0	7	7	-5	6
Brad Stuart, D	48	0	6	6	4	25
*Raffi Torres, LW	11	2	4	6	1	4
James Sheppard, C	32	1	3	4	-9	12
Jason Demers, D	22	1	2	3	-4	10
Andrew Desjardins, C	42	2	1	3	-6	61
Adam Burish, RW	46	1	2	3	-7	25
*Douglas Murray, D	29	0	3	3	-8	26
Tim Kennedy, LW	13	2	0	2	-3	2
*Michal Handzus, C	28	1	1	2	-9	12
Matt Tennyson, D	4	0	2	2	2	2

GOALTENDING

Player	GP	W	L	OT	TGA	GAA	SO
Antti Niemi	43	24	12	6	93	2.16	4
Thomas Greiss	6	1	4	0	13	2.53	1
Alex Stalock	2	0	0	1	2	2.87	0

St. Louis Blues

SCORING

Player	GP	G	Ast	Pts	+/-	PM
Chris Stewart, RW	48	18	18	36	0	40
David Backes, C	48	6	22	28	5	62
Alexander Steen, LW	40	8	19	27	5	14
Patrik Berglund, C	48	17	8	25	-2	12
David Perron, LW	48	10	15	25	0	44
Alex Pietrangelo, D	47	5	19	24	10	10
Kevin Shattenkirk, D	48	5	18	23	2	20
Andy McDonald, C	37	7	14	21	-2	16
T.J. Oshie, RW	30	7	13	20	-5	15
V. Tarasenko, RW	38	8	11	19	1	10
Vladimir Sobotka, C	48	8	11	19	-4	35
Jaden Schwartz, C	45	7	6	13	-4	4
Barret Jackman, D	46	3	9	12	6	39
Chris Porter, C	29	2	6	8	5	0
Kris Russell, D	33	1	6	7	6	9
*Jay Bouwmeester, D	14	1	6	7	5	6

SCORING (CONT.)

Player	GP	G	Ast	Pts	+/-	PM
Adam Cracknell, RW	20	2	4	6	3	4
Roman Polak, D	48	1	5	6	-2	48
Ryan Reaves, RW	43	4	2	6	3	79
*Wade Redden, D	23	2	3	5	-2	11
*Jordan Leopold, D	15	0	2	2	-2	0
*Matt D'Agostini, RW	16	1	1	2	-4	2
Scott Nichol, C	30	1	0	1	-2	25
Ian Cole, D	15	0	1	1	-4	10
J. Langenbrunner, RW	4	0	1	1	1	0

GOALTENDING

Player	GP	W	L	OT	TGA	GAA	SO
Brian Elliott	24	14	8	1	49	2.28	3
Jaroslav Halak	16	6	5	1	29	2.14	3
Jake Allen	15	9	4	0	33	2.46	1

*Mid-season trade

Tampa Bay Lightning

SCORING

Player	GP	G	Ast	Pts	+/–	PM
Martin St. Louis, RW 48		17	43	60	0	14
Steven Stamkos, C 48		29	28	57	-4	32
Teddy Purcell, RW.......48		11	25	36	-1	12
Vincent Lecavalier, C...39		10	22	32	-5	29
*Cory Conacher, LW 35		9	15	24	-3	16
Matt Carle, D..............48		5	17	22	1	4
Benoit Pouliot, LW......34		8	12	20	8	15
Victor Hedman, D 44		4	16	20	1	31
Alex Killorn, C 38		7	12	19	-6	14
Sami Salo, D 46		2	15	17	5	16
Tom Pyatt, C 43		8	8	16	5	12
Nate Thompson, C......45		7	8	15	-2	17
Eric Brewer, D............48		4	8	12	3	30
Richard Panik, RW 25		5	4	9	-2	4
B.J. Crombeen, RW 44		1	7	8	4	112
Ryan Malone, LW........24		6	2	8	-3	22
Keith Aulie, D 45		2	5	7	1	60
Tyler Johnson, C.........14		3	3	6	3	4
Radko Gudas, D 22		2	3	5	3	38
*M-A. Bergeron, D 12		1	4	5	3	4
*Adam Hall, RW 20		0	4	4	3	23
Ondrej Palat, LW........14		2	2	4	5	0
Dana Tyrell, C 21		1	3	4	-3	4
P. Labrie, LW 19		2	1	3	2	30
Brett Connolly, RW.......5		1	0	1	-3	0
Brendan Mikkelson, D ..4		0	1	1	1	6

GOALTENDING

Player	GP	W	L	OT	TGA	GAA	SO
Anders Lindback 24		10	10	1	63	2.90	0
Mathieu Garon 18		5	9	2	44	2.90	0
*Ben Bishop................9		3	4	1	25	2.99	1
Cedric Desjardins 3		0	3	0	8	3.00	0

Toronto Maple Leafs

SCORING

Player	GP	G	Ast	Pts	+/–	PM
Phil Kessel, RW............48		20	32	52	-3	18
Nazem Kadri, C 48		18	26	44	15	23
J. van Riemsdyk, LW....48		18	14	32	-7	26
Cody Franson, D...........45		4	25	29	4	8
Dion Phaneuf, D...........48		9	19	28	-4	65
Tyler Bozak, C 46		12	16	28	-1	6
Nikolai Kulemin, LW.....48		7	16	23	-5	22
Clarke MacArthur, LW...40		8	12	20	3	26
Joffrey Lupul, RW 16		11	7	18	8	12
Jay McClement, C........48		8	9	17	0	11
Mikhail Grabovski, C....48		9	7	16	-10	24
Carl Gunnarsson, D.....37		1	14	15	5	14
Matt Frattin, RW..........25		7	6	13	6	4
John-Michael Liles, D...32		2	9	11	-1	4
Leo Komarov, C...........42		4	5	9	-1	18
Mike Kostka, D...........35		0	8	8	-7	27
Mark Fraser, D.............45		0	8	8	18	85
*Frazer McLaren, LW ...35		3	2	5	0	102
Colton Orr, RW.............44		1	3	4	4	155
Jake Gardiner, D 12		0	4	4	0	0
Korbinian Holzer, D 22		2	1	3	-12	28
*Ryan O'Byrne, D...........8		1	1	2	4	6
Ryan Hamilton, LW 10		0	2	2	1	0
*Mike Brown, RW 12		0	1	1	1	70
*David Steckel, C...........13		0	1	1	-2	0

GOALTENDING

Player	GP	W	L	OT	TGA	GAA	SO
James Reimer............33		19	8	5	76	2.46	4
Ben Scrivens..............20		7	9	0	46	2.69	2
Jussi Rynnas................1		0	0	0	0	0.00	0

Vancouver Canucks

SCORING

Player	GP	G	Ast	Pts	+/–	PM
Henrik Sedin, C............48		11	34	45	19	24
Daniel Sedin, LW 47		12	28	40	12	18
Jannik Hansen, RW.....47		10	17	27	12	8
Alex Burrows, C...........47		13	11	24	15	54
Dan Hamhuis, D 47		4	20	24	9	12
Alexander Edler, D 45		8	14	22	-5	37
Mason Raymond, LW ..46		10	12	22	2	16
Jason Garrison, D........47		8	8	16	18	28
Chris Higgins, LW........41		10	5	15	-4	10
Ryan Kesler, C............17		4	9	13	-5	12
Kevin Bieksa, D 36		6	6	12	6	48
Zack Kassian, RW 39		7	4	11	-7	51
Maxim Lapierre, C 48		4	6	10	-6	45
Jordan Schroeder, C ...31		3	6	9	0	4
Chris Tanev, D.............38		2	5	7	4	10

SCORING (CONT.)

Player	GP	G	Ast	Pts	+/–	PM
Dale Weise, RW...........40		3	3	6	-7	43
*Derek Roy, C..............12		3	3	6	1	2
Andrew Ebbett, C........28		1	5	6	-1	4
David Booth, LW..........12		1	2	3	-3	4
Cam Barker, D.............14		0	2	2	-3	4
Keith Ballard, D...........36		0	2	2	-2	29
Andrew Alberts, D 24		0	1	1	-7	32
*Aaron Volpatti, LW.....16		1	0	1	0	28
*Tom Sestito, LW 23		1	0	1	-3	53

GOALTENDING

Player	GP	W	L	OT	TGA	GAA	SO
Cory Schneider..........30		17	9	4	61	2.11	5
Roberto Luongo.........20		9	6	3	51	2.56	2

*Mid-season trade

Washington Capitals

SCORING

Player	GP	G	Ast	Pts	+/-	PM
Alex Ovechkin, LW	48	32	24	56	2	36
Mike Ribeiro, C	48	13	36	49	-4	53
Nicklas Backstrom, C	48	8	40	48	8	20
Troy Brouwer, RW	47	19	14	33	-5	28
Mike Green, D	35	12	14	26	-3	20
John Carlson, D	48	6	16	22	11	18
Marcus Johansson, C	34	6	16	22	3	4
Joel Ward, RW	39	8	12	20	7	12
Eric Fehr, RW	41	9	8	17	14	10
Mathieu Perreault, C	39	6	11	17	7	20
Jason Chimera, LW	47	3	11	14	-5	48
Wojtek Wolski, LW	27	4	5	9	1	6
Jack Hillen, D	23	3	6	9	9	14
Steven Oleksy, D	28	1	8	9	9	33
Jay Beagle, C	48	2	6	8	-1	14
Matt Hendricks, C	48	5	3	8	-6	73

SCORING (CONT.)

Player	GP	G	Ast	Pts	+/-	PM
Tomas Kundratek, D	25	1	6	7	-5	8
John Erskine, D	30	3	3	6	10	34
Karl Alzner, D	48	1	4	5	-6	14
Brooks Laich, C	9	1	3	4	2	6
*Martin Erat, LW	9	1	2	3	0	4
Jeff Schultz, D	26	0	3	3	-6	12
Joey Crabb, RW	26	2	0	2	-1	8
Tom Poti, D	16	0	2	2	-2	2
*Roman Hamrlik, D	4	0	1	1	-1	2
*Aaron Volpatti, LW	17	0	1	1	-2	7
Dmitry Orlov, D	5	0	1	1	5	0

GOALTENDING

Player	GP	W	L	OT	TGA	GAA	SO
Braden Holtby	36	23	12	1	90	2.58	4
Michal Neuvirth	13	4	5	2	33	2.74	0
Philipp Grubauer	2	0	1	0	5	3.57	0

Winnipeg Jets

SCORING

Player	GP	G	Ast	Pts	+/-	PM
Andrew Ladd, LW	48	18	28	46	10	22
Blake Wheeler, RW	48	19	22	41	-3	28
Evander Kane, LW	48	17	16	33	-3	80
Bryan Little, C	48	7	25	32	8	4
Dustin Byfuglien, D	43	8	20	28	-1	34
Nik Antropov, LW	40	6	12	18	6	16
Grant Clitsome, D	44	4	12	16	10	18
Tobias Enstrom, D	22	4	11	15	-8	8
Kyle Wellwood, C	39	6	9	15	0	2
Olli Jokinen, C	45	7	7	14	-19	14
Zach Bogosian, D	33	5	9	14	-5	29
Ron Hainsey, D	47	0	13	13	-8	10
Alex Burmistrov, C	44	4	6	10	0	14
Paul Postma, D	34	4	5	9	-5	6
James Wright, C	38	2	3	5	-5	31
Antti Miettinen, RW	22	3	2	5	-3	2

SCORING

Player	GP	G	Ast	Pts	+/-	PM
Chris Thorburn, RW	42	2	2	4	-5	70
Mark Stuart, D	42	2	2	4	5	53
*Eric Tangradi, LW	36	1	3	4	-4	22
Zach Redmond, D	8	1	3	4	0	12
Aaron Gagnon, C	10	3	0	3	2	2
Anthony Peluso, RW	5	0	2	2	1	14
Jim Slater, C	26	1	1	2	-3	19
*Alexei Ponikarovsky, LW	12	2	0	2	-2	6
Derek Meech, D	16	0	1	1	0	2
*Mike Santorelli, C	10	0	1	1	-5	0

GOALTENDING

Player	GP	W	L	OT	TGA	GAA	SO
Ondrej Pavelec	44	21	20	3	119	2.80	0
Al Montoya	7	3	1	0	17	2.90	1

2013 NHL Draft

First Round

The opening round of the 2013 NHL entry draft was held on June 30 in Newark, New Jersey.

Team	Selection	Position
1.......Colorado	Nathan MacKinnon	C
2.......Florida	Aleksander Barkov	C
3.......Tampa Bay	Jonathan Drouin	LW
4.......Nashville	Seth Jones	D
5.......Carolina	Elias Lindholm	C
6.......Calgary	Sean Monahan	C
7.......Edmonton	Darnell Nurse	D
8.......Buffalo	Rasmus Ristolainen	D
9.......Vancouver	Bo Horvat	C
(from New Jersey)		
10.....Dallas	Valeri Nichushkin	RW
11.....Philadelphia	Samuel Morin	D
12.....Phoenix	Max Domi	C/LW
13.....Winnipeg	Joshua Morrissey	D
14.....Columbus	Alexander Wennberg	C
15.....NY Islanders	Ryan Pulock	D
16.....Buffalo	Nikita Zadorov	D
(from Minnesota)		
17.....Ottawa	Curtis Lazar	C/RW
18.....San Jose	Mirco Mueller	D
(from Detroit)		
19.....Columbus	Kerby Rychel	LW
(from NY Rangers)		
20.....Detroit	Anthony Mantha	RW
(from San Jose)		
21.....Toronto	Frederik Gauthier	C
22.....Calgary	Emile Poirier	LW
(from St. Louis)		
23.....Washington	Andre Burakovsky	LW
24.....Vancouver	Hunter Shinkaruk	C/LW
25.....Montreal	Michael McCarron	RW
26.....Anaheim	Shea Theodore	D
27.....Columbus	Marko Dano	C
(from Los Angeles)		
28.....Calgary	Morgan Klimchuk	LW
(from Pittsburgh)		
29.....Dallas	Jason Dickinson	C
(from Boston)		
30.....Chicago	Ryan Hartman	RW

The Stanley Cup

Awarded annually to the team that wins the NHL's best-of-seven final-round playoffs. The Stanley Cup is the oldest trophy competed for by professional athletes in North America. It was donated in 1893 by Frederick Arthur, Lord Stanley of Preston.

Results

1892–93	Montreal A.A.A.
1893–94	Montreal A.A.A.
1894–95	Montreal Victorias
1895–96	Winnipeg Victorias (Feb)
1895–96	Montreal Victorias (Dec)
1896–97	Montreal Victorias
1897–98	Montreal Victorias
1898–99	Montreal Victorias (Feb)
1898–99	Montreal Shamrocks (Mar)
1899–1900	Montreal Shamrocks
1900–01	Winnipeg Victorias
1901–02	Winnipeg Victorias (Jan)
1901–02	Montreal A.A.A. (Mar)
1902–03	Montreal A.A.A. (Feb)
1902–03	Ottawa Silver Seven (Mar)
1903–04	Ottawa Silver Seven
1904–05	Ottawa Silver Seven
1905–06	Ottawa Silver Seven (Feb)
1905–06	Montreal Wanderers (Mar)
1906–07	Kenora Thistles (Jan)
1906–07	Montreal Wanderers (Mar)
1907–08	Montreal Wanderers
1908–09	Ottawa Senators
1909–10	Montreal Wanderers
1910–11	Ottawa Senators
1911–12	Quebec Bulldogs
1912–13	Quebec Bulldogs
1913–14	Toronto Blueshirts
1914–15	Vancouver Millionaires
1915–16	Montreal Canadiens
1916–17	Seattle Metropolitans

NHL WINNERS AND FINALISTS

Season	Champion	Finalist	GP in Final
1917–18	Toronto Arenas	Vancouver Millionaires	5
1918–19	No decision*	No decision*	5
1919–20	Ottawa Senators	Seattle Metropolitans	5
1920–21	Ottawa Senators	Vancouver Millionaires	5
1921–22	Toronto St. Pats	Vancouver Millionaires	5
1922–23	Ottawa Senators	Vancouver Maroons, Edmonton Eskimos	2, 4
1923–24	Montreal Canadiens	Vancouver Maroons, Calgary Tigers	2, 2
1924–25	Victoria Cougars	Montreal Canadiens	4
1925–26	Montreal Maroons	Victoria Cougars	4
1926–27	Ottawa Senators	Boston Bruins	4
1927–28	New York Rangers	Montreal Maroons	5
1928–29	Boston Bruins	New York Rangers	2
1929–30	Montreal Canadiens	Boston Bruins	2
1930–31	Montreal Canadiens	Chicago Blackhawks	5
1931–32	Toronto Maple Leafs	New York Rangers	3
1932–33	New York Rangers	Toronto Maple Leafs	4
1933–34	Chicago Blackhawks	Detroit Red Wings	4
1934–35	Montreal Maroons	Toronto Maple Leafs	3
1935–36	Detroit Red Wings	Toronto Maple Leafs	4
1936–37	Detroit Red Wings	New York Rangers	5
1937–38	Chicago Blackhawks	Toronto Maple Leafs	4
1938–39	Boston Bruins	Toronto Maple Leafs	5
1939–40	New York Rangers	Toronto Maple Leafs	6
1940–41	Boston Bruins	Detroit Red Wings	4
1941–42	Toronto Maple Leafs	Detroit Red Wings	7
1942–43	Detroit Red Wings	Boston Bruins	4
1943–44	Montreal Canadiens	Chicago Blackhawks	4
1944–45	Toronto Maple Leafs	Detroit Red Wings	7
1945–46	Montreal Canadiens	Boston Bruins	5
1946–47	Toronto Maple Leafs	Montreal Canadiens	6
1947–48	Toronto Maple Leafs	Detroit Red Wings	4
1948–49	Toronto Maple Leafs	Detroit Red Wings	4
1949–50	Detroit Red Wings	New York Rangers	7
1950–51	Toronto Maple Leafs	Montreal Canadiens	5
1951–52	Detroit Red Wings	Montreal Canadiens	4
1952–53	Montreal Canadiens	Boston Bruins	5
1953–54	Detroit Red Wings	Montreal Canadiens	7
1954–55	Detroit Red Wings	Montreal Canadiens	7

NHL WINNERS AND FINALISTS *(CONT.)*

Season	Champion	Finalist	GP in Final
1955–56	Montreal Canadiens	Detroit Red Wings	5
1956–57	Montreal Canadiens	Boston Bruins	5
1957–58	Montreal Canadiens	Boston Bruins	6
1958–59	Montreal Canadiens	Toronto Maple Leafs	5
1959–60	Montreal Canadiens	Toronto Maple Leafs	4
1960–61	Chicago Blackhawks	Detroit Red Wings	6
1961–62	Toronto Maple Leafs	Chicago Blackhawks	6
1962–63	Toronto Maple Leafs	Detroit Red Wings	5
1963–64	Toronto Maple Leafs	Detroit Red Wings	7
1964–65	Montreal Canadiens	Chicago Blackhawks	7
1965–66	Montreal Canadiens	Detroit Red Wings	6
1966–67	Toronto Maple Leafs	Montreal Canadiens	6
1967–68	Montreal Canadiens	St. Louis Blues	4
1968–69	Montreal Canadiens	St. Louis Blues	4
1969–70	Boston Bruins	St. Louis Blues	4
1970–71	Montreal Canadiens	Chicago Blackhawks	7
1971–72	Boston Bruins	New York Rangers	6
1972–73	Montreal Canadiens	Chicago Blackhawks	6
1973–74	Philadelphia Flyers	Boston Bruins	6
1974–75	Philadelphia Flyers	Buffalo Sabres	6
1975–76	Montreal Canadiens	Philadelphia Flyers	4
1976–77	Montreal Canadiens	Boston Bruins	4
1977–78	Montreal Canadiens	Boston Bruins	6
1978–79	Montreal Canadiens	New York Rangers	5
1979–80	New York Islanders	Philadelphia Flyers	6
1980–81	New York Islanders	Minnesota North Stars	5
1981–82	New York Islanders	Vancouver Canucks	4
1982–83	New York Islanders	Edmonton Oilers	4
1983–84	Edmonton Oilers	New York Islanders	5
1984–85	Edmonton Oilers	Philadelphia Flyers	5
1985–86	Montreal Canadiens	Calgary Flames	5
1986–87	Edmonton Oilers	Philadelphia Flyers	7
1987–88	Edmonton Oilers	Boston Bruins	4
1988–89	Calgary Flames	Montreal Canadiens	6
1989–90	Edmonton Oilers	Boston Bruins	5
1990–91	Pittsburgh Penguins	Minnesota North Stars	6
1991–92	Pittsburgh Penguins	Chicago Blackhawks	4
1992–93	Montreal Canadiens	Los Angeles Kings	5
1993–94	New York Rangers	Vancouver Canucks	7
1994–95	New Jersey Devils	Detroit Red Wings	4
1995–96	Colorado Avalanche	Florida Panthers	4
1996–97	Detroit Red Wings	Philadelphia Flyers	4
1997–98	Detroit Red Wings	Washington Capitals	4
1998–99	Dallas Stars	Buffalo Sabres	6
1999–2000	New Jersey Devils	Dallas Stars	6
2000–01	Colorado Avalanche	New Jersey Devils	7
2001–02	Detroit Red Wings	Carolina Hurricanes	5
2002–03	New Jersey Devils	Anaheim Mighty Ducks	7
2003–04	Tampa Bay Lightning	Calgary Flames	7
2004–05	No Stanley Cup due to season lockout		
2005–06	Carolina Hurricanes	Edmonton Oilers	7
2006–07	Anaheim Ducks	Ottawa Senators	5
2007–08	Detroit Red Wings	Pittsburgh Penguins	6
2008–09	Pittsburgh Penguins	Detroit Red Wings	7
2009–10	Chicago Blackhawks	Philadelphia Flyers	6
2010–11	Boston Bruins	Vancouver Canucks	7
2011–12	Los Angeles Kings	New Jersey Devils	6
2012–13	Chicago Blackhawks	Boston Bruins	6

*In 1919 the Montreal Canadiens traveled to meet Seattle, the PCHL champions. After five games had been played—the teams were tied at two wins and one tie—the series was called off by the local Department of Health because of the influenza epidemic and the death of Canadiens defenseman Joe Hall from influenza.

Conn Smythe Trophy

Awarded to the Most Valuable Player of the Stanley Cup playoffs, as selected by the Professional Hockey Writers Association. The trophy is named after the former coach, general manager, president and owner of the Toronto Maple Leafs.

1965	Jean Beliveau, Mtl	1990	Bill Ranford, Edm
1966	Roger Crozier, Det	1991	Mario Lemieux, Pit
1967	Dave Keon, Tor	1992	Mario Lemieux, Pit
1968	Glenn Hall, StL	1993	Patrick Roy, Mtl
1969	Serge Savard, Mtl	1994	Brian Leetch, NYR
1970	Bobby Orr, Bos	1995	Claude Lemieux, NJ
1971	Ken Dryden, Mtl	1996	Joe Sakic, Col
1972	Bobby Orr, Bos	1997	Mike Vernon, Det
1973	Yvan Cournoyer, Mtl	1998	Steve Yzerman, Det
1974	Bernie Parent, Phi	1999	Joe Nieuwendyk, Dal
1975	Bernie Parent, Phi	2000	Scott Stevens, NJ
1976	Reggie Leach, Phi	2001	Patrick Roy, Col
1977	Guy Lafleur, Mtl	2002	Nicklas Lidstrom, Det
1978	Larry Robinson, Mtl	2003	J.-S. Giguere, Ana
1979	Bob Gainey, Mtl	2004	Brad Richards, TB
1980	Bryan Trottier, NYI	2005	No Award–No Season
1981	Butch Goring, NYI	2006	Cam Ward, Car
1982	Mike Bossy, NYI	2007	Scott Niedermayer, Ana
1983	Bill Smith, NYI	2008	Henrik Zetterberg, Det
1984	Mark Messier, Edm	2009	Evgeni Malkin, Pit
1985	Wayne Gretzky, Edm	2010	Jonathan Toews, Chi
1986	Patrick Roy, Mtl	2011	Tim Thomas, Bos
1987	Ron Hextall, Phi	2012	Jonathan Quick, LA
1988	Wayne Gretzky, Edm	2013	Patrick Kane, Chi
1989	Al MacInnis, Cgy		

Alltime Stanley Cup Playoff Leaders

Points

	Playoff Seasons	GP	G	Ast	Pts		Playoff Seasons	GP	G	Ast	Pts
Wayne Gretzky, four teams	16	208	122	260	382	Jean Beliveau, Mtl	17	162	79	97	176
Mark Messier, Edm, NYR, Van	18	236	109	186	295	Sergei Fedorov, Det, Wsh	15	183	52	124	176
Jari Kurri, five teams	15	200	106	127	233	Denis Savard, Chi, Mtl	16	169	66	109	175
Glenn Anderson, four teams	15	225	93	121	214	Mario Lemieux, Pit	8	107	76	96	172
*Jaromir Jagr, six teams	17	202	78	121	199	Peter Forsberg, Que, Col, Phi	13	151	64	107	171
Paul Coffey, six teams	16	194	59	137	196	Denis Potvin, NYI	14	185	56	108	164
Brett Hull, four teams	19	202	103	87	190	Mike Bossy, NYI	10	129	85	75	160
Doug Gilmour, seven teams	18	182	60	128	188	Gordie Howe, Det, Hfd	20	157	68	92	160
Joe Sakic, Que, Col	13	172	84	104	188	Bobby Smith, Min, Mtl	13	184	64	96	160
Steve Yzerman, Det	20	196	70	115	185	Al MacInnis, Cgy, StL	19	177	39	121	160
Bryan Trottier, NYI, Pit	17	221	71	113	184	Claude Lemieux, six teams	18	234	80	77	157
Nicklas Lidstrom, Det	19	258	54	129	183	Adam Oates, six teams	15	163	42	114	156
Ray Bourque, Bos, Col	21	214	41	139	180						

Goals

	Playoff Seasons	GP	G		Playoff Seasons	GP	Ast
Wayne Gretzky, four teams	16	208	122	Wayne Gretzky, four teams	16	208	260
Mark Messier, Edm, NYR, Van	18	236	109	Mark Messier, Edm, NYR, Van	18	236	186
Jari Kurri, five teams	15	200	106	Ray Bourque, Bos, Col	21	214	139
Brett Hull, Cgy, StL, Dal, Det	19	202	103	Paul Coffey, six teams	16	194	137
Glenn Anderson, four teams	15	225	93	Nicklas Lidstrom, Det	19	258	129
Mike Bossy, NYI	10	129	85	Doug Gilmour, seven teams	18	182	128
Joe Sakic, Que, Col	13	172	84	Jari Kurri, five teams	15	200	127
Maurice Richard, Mtl	15	133	82	Sergei Fedorov, Det, Wsh	15	183	124
Claude Lemieux, six teams	18	234	80	Glenn Anderson, four teams	15	225	121
Jean Beliveau, Mtl	17	162	79	Al MacInnis, Cgy, StL	19	177	121
*Jaromir Jagr, six teams	17	202	78	*Jaromir Jagr, six teams	17	202	121
Mario Lemieux, Pitt	8	107	76	Larry Robinson, Mtl, LA	20	227	116
Dino Ciccarelli, Min, Wsh, Det	14	141	73	Steve Yzerman, Det	20	196	115
Esa Tikkanen, five teams	13	186	72	Lawrence Murphy, six teams	20	215	115
Bryan Trottier, NYI, Pit	17	221	71	Adam Oates, six teams	15	163	114
Steve Yzerman, Det	20	196	70	Bryan Trottier, NYI, Pit	17	221	113
Gordie Howe, Det, Hfd	20	157	68	Chris Chelios, Mtl, Chi, Det	24	266	113
Denis Savard, Chi, Mtl	16	169	66	Denis Savard, Chi, Mtl	16	169	109
Joe Nieuwendyk, Cgy, Dal, NJ, Tor	16	158	66	Denis Potvin, NYI	14	185	108
Four tied with 64.				Peter Forsberg, Que, Col, Phi	13	151	107
				Joe Sakic, Que, Col	13	172	104

*Active in 2012–13.

Alltime Stanley Cup Playoff Goaltending Leaders

WINS	W	L	Pct	SHUTOUTS	GP	W	SO
Patrick Roy, Mtl, Col	151	94	.616	*Martin Brodeur, NJ	205	113	24
*Martin Brodeur, NJ	113	91	.554	Patrick Roy, Mtl, Col	247	151	23
Grant Fuhr, five teams	92	50	.648	Curtis Joseph, four teams	133	63	16
Billy Smith, LA, NYI	88	36	.710	Chris Osgood, NYI, StL, Det	129	74	15
Ed Belfour, four teams	88	68	.564	**GOALS AGAINST AVG**			**Avg**
Ken Dryden, Mtl	80	32	.714	George Hainsworth, Mtl, Tor			1.93
Mike Vernon, four teams	77	56	.579	Turk Broda, Tor			1.98
Chris Osgood, NYI, StL, Det	74	49	.602	Dominik Hasek, Chi, Buf, Det			2.02
Jacques Plante, five teams	71	36	.663	*Martin Brodeur, NJ			2.02
Andy Moog, four teams	68	57	.544	*Jonathan Quick, LA			2.03
Dominik Hasek, Chi, Buf, Det	65	49	.570	Tim Thomas, Bos			2.07
Curtis Joseph, four teams	63	66	.488	*Jean-Sebastien Giguere, Ana			2.08
Tom Barrasso, Buf, Pit, Ott	61	54	.530	Chris Osgood, NYI, StL, Det			2.09
Turk Broda, Tor	60	39	.606	Note: At least 50 games played.			
*Active in 2012–13.				*Active in 2012–13.			

Alltime Stanley Cup Team Playoff Record, by Wins

TEAM	W	L	Pct	TEAM	W	L	Pct
Montreal	411	295	.582	Vancouver	99	124	.444
Detroit	320	284	.530	Calgary*	94	114	.452
Boston	290	302	.490	Washington	96	116	.453
Toronto	254	273	.482	San Jose	84	90	.483
Pittsburgh	231	206	.529	Los Angeles	94	126	.427
Chicago	234	247	.486	Carolina§	59	68	.465
Philadelphia	214	199	.518	Anaheim	58	47	.552
NY Rangers	213	233	.478	Ottawa	59	67	.468
Edmonton	152	99	.606	Tampa Bay	37	32	.536
Dallas#	148	149	.498	Phoenix††	41	78	.345
St. Louis	143	178	.445	Florida	16	22	.421
Colorado**	132	117	.530	Nashville	18	27	.400
NY Islanders	133	106	.556	Minnesota	11	18	.379
Buffalo	124	132	.484	Columbus	0	4	.000
New Jersey†	136	118	.535				

*Atlanta Flames 1972–80. †Colorado Rockies 1976–82, Kansas City Scouts 1974–76. #Minnesota North Stars 1967–93. **Quebec Nordiques 1979–95. ††Winnipeg Jets 1979–96. §Hartford Whalers 1979–97.

Stanley Cup Playoff Coaching Records

Coach	Team	Plf Seas.	Series	Series W	Series L	Games	Games W	Games L	T	Cups	Pct
Glen Sather	Edm	10	27	21	6	†126	89	37	0	4	.706
Toe Blake	Mtl	13	23	18	5	119	82	37	0	8	.689
Scott Bowman	Five teams	28	68	49	19	353	223	130	0	9	.632
Hap Day	Tor	9	14	10	4	80	49	31	0	5	.613
*Mike Babcock	Ana, Det	9	24	15	9	132	78	54	0	1	.590
Al Arbour	StL, NYI	16	42	30	12	209	123	86	0	4	.589
*Bob Hartley	Col, Atl, Cal	5	14	10	4	84	49	35	0	1	.583
Fred Shero	Phi, NYR	8	21	15	6	110	63	47	0	2	.573
*Randy Carlyle	Ana, Tor	10	12	7	5	69	39	30	0	1	.565
Lindy Ruff	Buf	8	18	10	8	101	57	44	0	0	.564
Jacques Demers	StL, Det, Mtl	8	18	11	7	98	55	43	0	1	.561

†Does not include suspended game, May 24, 1988. *Active in 2012–13.
Note: Coaches ranked by winning percentage. Minimum: 65 games.

The 10 Longest Overtime Games

Date	Result	OT	Scorer	Series	Series Winner
3-24-36	Det 1 vs Mtl M 0	116:30	Mud Bruneteau	SF	Det
4-3-33	Tor 1 vs Bos 0	104:46	Ken Doraty	SF	Tor
5-4-00	Phi 2 vs Pit 1	92:01	Keith Primeau	CSF	Phi
4-24-03	Ana 4 vs Dal 3	80:48	Petr Sykora	CSF	Ana
4-24-96	Pit 3 vs Wsh 2	79:15	Petr Nedved	CQF	Pit
4-11-07	Van 5 vs Dal 4	78:06	Henrik Sedin	CQF	Van
3-23-43	Tor 3 vs Det 2	70:18	Jack McLean	SF	Det
5-4-08	Dal 2 vs SJ 1	69:03	Brenden Morrow	CSF	Dal
3-28-30	Mtl 2 vs NYR 1	68:52	Gus Rivers	SF	Mtl
4-18-87	NYI 3 vs Wsh 2	68:47	Pat LaFontaine	DSF	NYI

Hart Memorial Trophy

Awarded annually "to the player adjudged to be the most valuable to his team." The original trophy was donated by Dr. David A. Hart, father of Cecil Hart, former manager-coach of the Montreal Canadiens. In the 1980s Wayne Gretzky won the award nine times.

Year	Winner	Key Statistics	Runner-Up
1924	Frank Nighbor, Ott	10 goals, 3 assists in 20 games	Sprague Cleghorn, Mtl
1925	Billy Burch, Ham	20 goals, 4 assists in 27 games	Howie Morenz, Mtl
1926	Nels Stewart, Mtl M	42 points in 36 games	Sprague Cleghorn, Mtl
1927	Herb Gardiner, Mtl	12 points in 44 games as defenseman	Bill Cook, NYR
1928	Howie Morenz, Mtl	33 goals, 18 assists	Roy Worters, Pitt
1929	Roy Worters, NYA	1.21 goals against, 13 shutouts	Ace Bailey, Tor
1930	Nels Stewart, Mtl M	39 goals, 16 assists	Lionel Hitchman, Bos
1931	Howie Morenz, Mtl	28 goals, 23 assists	Eddie Shore, Bos
1932	Howie Morenz, Mtl	24 goals, 25 assists	Ching Johnson, NYR
1933	Eddie Shore, Bos	27 assists in 48 games as defenseman	Bill Cook, NYR
1934	Aurel Joliat, Mtl	27 points	Lionel Conacher, Chi
1935	Eddie Shore, Bos	26 assists in 48 games as defenseman	Charlie Conacher, Tor
1936	Eddie Shore, Bos	16 assists in 46 games as defenseman	Hooley Smith, Mtl M
1937	Babe Siebert, Mtl	28 points	Lionel Conacher, Mtl M
1938	Eddie Shore, Bos	17 points in 47 games as defenseman	Paul Thompson, Chi
1939	Toe Blake, Mtl	led NHL in points (47)	Syl Apps, Tor
1940	Ebbie Goodfellow, Det	28 points	Syl Apps, Tor
1941	Bill Cowley, Bos	led NHL in assists (45) and points (62)	Dit Clapper, Bos
1942	Tom Anderson, Bos	41 points	Syl Apps, Tor
1943	Bill Cowley, Bos	led NHL in assists (45)	Doug Bentley, Chi
1944	Babe Pratt, Tor	57 points in 50 games	Bill Cowley, Bos
1945	Elmer Lach, Mtl	led NHL in assists (54) and points (80)	Maurice Richard, Mtl
1946	Max Bentley, Chi	61 points in 47 games	Gaye Stewart, Tor
1947	Maurice Richard, Mtl	led NHL in goals (45); 26 assists	Milt Schmidt, Bos
1948	Buddy O'Connor, NYR	60 points in 60 games	Frank Brimsek, Bos
1949	Sid Abel, Det	28 goals, 26 assists	Bill Durnan, Mtl
1950	Charlie Rayner, NYR	6 shutouts	Ted Kennedy, Tor
1951	Milt Schmidt, Bos	61 points in 62 games	Maurice Richard, Mtl
1952	Gordie Howe, Det	led NHL in goals (47) and points (86)	Elmer Lach, Mtl
1953	Gordie Howe, Det	led NHL in goals (49) and points (95)	Al Rollins, Chi
1954	Al Rollins, Chi	5 shutouts	Red Kelly, Det
1955	Ted Kennedy, Tor	52 points	Harry Lumley, Tor
1956	Jean Beliveau, Mtl	led NHL in goals (47) and points (88)	Tod Sloan, Tor
1957	Gordie Howe, Det	led NHL in goals (44) and points (89)	Jean Beliveau, Mtl
1958	Gordie Howe, Det	33 goals, 77 points in 64 games	Andy Bathgate, NYR
1959	Andy Bathgate, NYR	74 points in 70 games	Gordie Howe, Det
1960	Gordie Howe, Det	45 assists, 73 points	Bobby Hull, Chi
1961	Bernie Geoffrion, Mtl	50 goals, 95 points	Johnny Bower, Tor
1962	Jacques Plante, Mtl	42 wins, 2.37 goals against avg.	Doug Harvey, NYR
1963	Gordie Howe, Det	47 assists, 73 points	Stan Mikita, Chi
1964	Jean Beliveau, Mtl	50 assists, 78 points	Bobby Hull, Chi
1965	Bobby Hull, Chi	39 goals, 32 assists	Norm Ullman, Det
1966	Bobby Hull, Chi	led NHL in goals (54) and points (97)	Jean Beliveau, Mtl
1967	Stan Mikita, Chi	led NHL in assists (62) and points (97)	Ed Giacomin, NYR
1968	Stan Mikita, Chi	40 goals, 47 assists	Jean Beliveau, Mtl
1969	Phil Esposito, Bos	led NHL in assists (77) and points (126)	Jean Beliveau, Mtl
1970	Bobby Orr, Bos	led NHL in assists (87) and points (120)	Tony Esposito, Chi
1971	Bobby Orr, Bos	102 assists, 139 points	Phil Esposito, Bos
1972	Bobby Orr, Bos	80 assists, 117 points	Ken Dryden, Mtl
1973	Bobby Clarke, Phi	67 assists, 104 points	Phil Esposito, Bos
1974	Phil Esposito, Bos	led NHL in goals (68) and points (145)	Bernie Parent, Phi
1975	Bobby Clarke, Phi	89 assists, 116 points	Rogatien Vachon, LA
1976	Bobby Clarke, Phi	89 assists, 119 points	Denis Potvin, NYI
1977	Guy Lafleur, Mtl	led NHL in assists (80) and points (136)	Bobby Clarke, Phi
1978	Guy Lafleur, Mtl	led NHL in goals (60) and points (132)	Bryan Trottier, NYI
1979	Bryan Trottier, NYI	led NHL in assists (87) and points (134)	Guy Lafleur, Mtl
1980	Wayne Gretzky, Edm	51 goals, 86 assists	Marcel Dionne, LA
1981	Wayne Gretzky, Edm	led NHL in assists (109) and points (164)	Mike Liut, StL
1982	Wayne Gretzky, Edm	NHL-record 92 goals and 212 points	Bryan Trottier, NYI
1983	Wayne Gretzky, Edm	led NHL in goals (71) and points (196)	Pete Peeters, Bos
1984	Wayne Gretzky, Edm	led NHL in goals (87) and points (205)	Rod Langway, Wsh
1985	Wayne Gretzky, Edm	led NHL in goals (73) and points (208)	Dale Hawerchuk, Win
1986	Wayne Gretzky, Edm	NHL-record 163 assists and 215 points	Mario Lemieux, Pit
1987	Wayne Gretzky, Edm	led NHL in assists (121) and points (183)	Ray Bourque, Bos
1988	Mario Lemieux, Pit	led NHL in goals (70) and points (168)	Grant Fuhr, Edm

Hart Memorial Trophy *(Cont.)*

Year	Winner	Key Statistics	Runner-Up
1989	Wayne Gretzky, LA	114 assists, 168 points	Mario Lemieux, Pit
1990	Mark Messier, Edm	84 assists, 129 points	Ray Bourque, Bos
1991	Brett Hull, StL	led NHL in goals (86); 131 points	Wayne Gretzky, LA
1992	Mark Messier, NYR	72 assists, 107 points	Patrick Roy, Mtl
1993	Mario Lemieux, Pit	69 goals, 91 assists in 60 games	Doug Gilmour, Tor
1994	Sergei Fedorov, Det	56 goals, 64 assists	Dominik Hasek, Buf
1995	Eric Lindros, Phi	29 goals, 41 assists in 46 games	Jaromir Jagr, Pit
1996	Mario Lemieux, Pit	led NHL in goals (69) and points (161)	Mark Messier, NYR
1997	Dominik Hasek, Buf	5 shutouts, 2.27 goals against avg.	Paul Kariya, Ana
1998	Dominik Hasek, Buf	13 shutouts, 2.09 goals against avg.	Jaromir Jagr, Pit
1999	Jaromir Jagr, Pit	44 goals, 127 points	Alexei Yashin, Ott
2000	Chris Pronger, StL	62 points, +52 plus/minus rating	Jaromir Jagr, Pit
2001	Joe Sakic, Col	118 points, +45 plus/minus rating	Mario Lemieux, Pit
2002	Jose Theodore, Mtl	2.11 goals against avg./7 shutouts	Jarome Iginla, Cal
2003	Peter Forsberg, Col	77 assists, +52 plus/minus rating	Markus Naslund, Van
2004	Martin St. Louis, TB	94 points, +35 plus/minus rating	Jarome Iginla, Cal
2005	No Award/no Season.		
2006	Joe Thornton, Bos/SJ	29 goals, 96 assists; 125 points	Jaromir Jagr, NYR
2007	Sidney Crosby, Pit	36 goals, 84 assists; 120 points	Roberto Luongo, Van
2008	Alexander Ovechkin, Wsh	65 goals, 47 assists; 112 points	Evgeni Malkin, Pit
2009	Alexander Ovechkin, Wsh	56 goals, 54 assists; 110 points	Evgeni Malkin, Pit
2010	Henrik Sedin, Van	29 goals, 83 assists; 112 points	Sidney Crosby, Pit
2011	Corey Perry, Ana	50 goals, 48 assists; 98 points	Daniel Sedin, Van
2012	Evgeni Malkin, Pit	50 goals, 59 assists, 109 points	Steven Stamkos, TB
2013	Alex Ovechkin, Wsh	32 goals, 24 assists, 56 points in 48 g.	Sidney Crosby, Pit

Art Ross Trophy

Awarded annually "to the player who leads the league in scoring points at the end of the regular season." The trophy was presented to the NHL in 1947 by Arthur Howie Ross, former manager-coach of the Boston Bruins. The tie-breakers, in order, are: (1) most goals, (2) fewer games played, (3) first goal of the season. Bobby Orr is the only defenseman in NHL history to win this trophy, and he won it twice (1970 and 1975).

Year	Winner	Pts	Year	Winner	Pts
1919	Newsy Lalonde, Mtl	44	1955	Bernie Geoffrion, Mtl	75
1920	Joe Malone, Que	30	1956	Jean Beliveau, Mtl	88
1921	Newsy Lalonde, Mtl	48	1957	Gordie Howe, Det	89
1922	Punch Broadbent, Ott	41	1958	Dickie Moore, Mtl	84
1923	Babe Dye, Tor	46	1959	Dickie Moore, Mtl	96
1924	Cy Denneny, Ott	37	1960	Bobby Hull, Chi	81
1925	Babe Dye, Tor	23	1961	Bernie Geoffrion, Mtl	95
1926	Nels Stewart, Mtl M	44	1962	Bobby Hull, Chi	84
1927	Bill Cook, NYR	42	1963	Gordie Howe, Det	86
1928	Howie Morenz, Mtl	37	1964	Stan Mikita, Chi	89
1929	Ace Bailey, Tor	51	1965	Stan Mikita, Chi	87
1930	Cooney Weiland, Bos	32	1966	Bobby Hull, Chi	97
1931	Howie Morenz, Mtl	73	1967	Stan Mikita, Chi	97
1932	Harvey Jackson, Tor	51	1968	Stan Mikita, Chi	87
1933	Bill Cook, NYR	53	1969	Phil Esposito, Bos	126
1934	Charlie Conacher, Tor	50	1970	Bobby Orr, Bos	120
1935	Charlie Conacher, Tor	57	1971	Phil Esposito, Bos	152
1936	Sweeney Schriner, NYA	45	1972	Phil Esposito, Bos	133
1937	Sweeney Schriner, NYA	46	1973	Phil Esposito, Bos	130
1938	Gordie Drillon, Tor	52	1974	Phil Esposito, Bos	145
1939	Toe Blake, Mtl	47	1975	Bobby Orr, Bos	135
1940	Milt Schmidt, Bos	52	1976	Guy Lafleur, Mtl	125
1941	Bill Cowley, Bos	62	1977	Guy Lafleur, Mtl	136
1942	Bryan Hextall, NYR	56	1978	Guy Lafleur, Mtl	132
1943	Doug Bentley, Chi	73	1979	Bryan Trottier, NYI	134
1944	Herb Cain, Bos	82	1980	Marcel Dionne, LA	137
1945	Elmer Lach, Mtl	80	1981	Wayne Gretzky, Edm	164
1946	Max Bentley, Chi	61	1982	Wayne Gretzky, Edm	212
1947	Max Bentley, Chi	72	1983	Wayne Gretzky, Edm	196
1948	Elmer Lach, Mtl	61	1984	Wayne Gretzky, Edm	205
1949	Roy Conacher, Chi	68	1985	Wayne Gretzky, Edm	208
1950	Ted Lindsay, Det	78	1986	Wayne Gretzky, Edm	215
1951	Gordie Howe, Det	86	1987	Wayne Gretzky, Edm	183
1952	Gordie Howe, Det	86	1988	Mario Lemieux, Pit	168
1953	Gordie Howe, Det	95	1989	Mario Lemieux, Pit	199
1954	Gordie Howe, Det	81	1990	Wayne Gretzky, LA	142

Art Ross Trophy *(Cont.)*

Year	Winner	Pts	Year	Winner	Pts
1991	Wayne Gretzky, LA	163	2003	Peter Forsberg, Col	106
1992	Mario Lemieux, Pit	131	2004	Martin St. Louis, TB	94
1993	Mario Lemieux, Pit	160	2005	No award/no season	
1994	Wayne Gretzky, LA	130	2006	Joe Thornton, Bos/SJ	125
1995	Jaromir Jagr, Pit	70	2007	Sidney Crosby, Pit	120
1996	Mario Lemieux, Pit	161	2008	Alexander Ovechkin, Wsh	112
1997	Mario Lemieux, Pit	122	2009	Evgeni Malkin, Pit	113
1998	Jaromir Jagr, Pit	102	2010	Henrik Sedin, Van	112
1999	Jaromir Jagr, Pit	127	2011	Daniel Sedin, Van	104
2000	Jaromir Jagr, Pit	96	2012	Evgeni Malkin, Pit	109
2001	Jaromir Jagr, Pit	121	2013	Martin St. Louis, TB	60
2002	Jarome Iginla, Cgy	96			

Note: Listing includes scoring leaders prior to inception of Art Ross Trophy in 1947–48.

Lady Byng Memorial Trophy

Awarded annually "to the player adjudged to have exhibited the best type of sportsmanship and gentlemanly conduct combined with a high standard of playing ability."

1925..........Frank Nighbor, Ott	1955..........Sid Smith, Tor	1985..........Jari Kurri, Edm
1926..........Frank Nighbor, Ott	1956..........Earl Reibel, Det	1986..........Mike Bossy, NYI
1927..........Billy Burch, NYA	1957..........Andy Hebenton, NYR	1987..........Joe Mullen, Cgy
1928..........Frank Boucher, NYR	1958..........Camille Henry, NYR	1988..........Mats Naslund, Mtl
1929..........Frank Boucher, NYR	1959..........Alex Delvecchio, Det	1989..........Joe Mullen, Cgy
1930..........Frank Boucher, NYR	1960..........Don McKenney, Bos	1990..........Brett Hull, StL
1931..........Frank Boucher, NYR	1961..........Red Kelly, Tor	1991..........Wayne Gretzky, LA
1932..........Joe Primeau, Tor	1962..........Dave Keon, Tor	1992..........Wayne Gretzky, LA
1933..........Frank Boucher, NYR	1963..........Dave Keon, Tor	1993..........Pierre Turgeon, NYI
1934..........Frank Boucher, NYR	1964..........Ken Wharram, Chi	1994..........Wayne Gretzky, LA
1935..........Frank Boucher, NYR	1965..........Bobby Hull, Chi	1995..........Ron Francis, Pit
1936..........Doc Romnes, Chi	1966..........Alex Delvecchio, Det	1996..........Paul Kariya, Ana
1937..........Marty Barry, Det	1967..........Stan Mikita, Chi	1997..........Paul Kariya, Ana
1938..........Gordie Drillon, Tor	1968..........Stan Mikita, Chi	1998..........Ron Francis, Pit
1939..........Clint Smith, NYR	1969..........Alex Delvecchio, Det	1999..........Wayne Gretzky, NYR
1940..........Bobby Bauer, Bos	1970..........Phil Goyette, StL	2000..........Pavol Demitra, StL
1941..........Bobby Bauer, Bos	1971..........John Bucyk, Bos	2001..........Joe Sakic, Col
1942..........Syl Apps, Tor	1972..........Jean Ratelle, NYR	2002..........Ron Francis, Car
1943..........Max Bentley, Chi	1973..........Gilbert Perreault, Buf	2003..........Alexander Mogilny, Det
1944..........Clint Smith, Chi	1974..........John Bucyk, Bos	2004..........Brad Richards, TB
1945..........Billy Mosienko, Chi	1975..........Marcel Dionne, Det	2005..........No Award
1946..........Toe Blake, Mtl	1976..........Jean Ratelle, NYR-Bos	2006..........Pavel Datsyuk, Det
1947..........Bobby Bauer, Bos	1977..........Marcel Dionne, LA	2007..........Pavel Datsyuk, Det
1948..........Buddy O'Connor, NYR	1978..........Butch Goring, LA	2008..........Pavel Datsyuk, Det
1949..........Bill Quackenbush, Det	1979..........Bob MacMillan, Atl	2009..........Pavel Datsyuk, Det
1950..........Edgar Laprade, NYR	1980..........Wayne Gretzky, Edm	2010..........Martin St. Louis, TB
1951..........Red Kelly, Det	1981..........Rick Kehoe, Pit	2011..........Martin St. Louis, TB
1952..........Sid Smith, Tor	1982..........Rick Middleton, Bos	2012..........Brian Campbell, Fla
1953..........Red Kelly, Det	1983..........Mike Bossy, NYI	2013..........Martin St. Louis, TB
1954..........Red Kelly, Det	1984..........Mike Bossy, NYI	

James Norris Memorial Trophy

Awarded annually "to the defense player who demonstrates throughout the season the greatest all-around ability in the position." James Norris was the former owner-president of the Detroit Red Wings. Bobby Orr holds the record for most consecutive times winning the award (eight, 1968–1975).

1954.......Red Kelly, Det	1969.......Bobby Orr, Bos	1984.......Rod Langway, Wsh
1955.......Doug Harvey, Mtl	1970.......Bobby Orr, Bos	1985.......Paul Coffey, Edm
1956.......Doug Harvey, Mtl	1971.......Bobby Orr, Bos	1986.......Paul Coffey, Edm
1957.......Doug Harvey, Mtl	1972.......Bobby Orr, Bos	1987.......Ray Bourque, Bos
1958.......Doug Harvey, Mtl	1973.......Bobby Orr, Bos	1988.......Ray Bourque, Bos
1959.......Tom Johnson, Mtl	1974.......Bobby Orr, Bos	1989.......Chris Chelios, Mtl
1960.......Doug Harvey, Mtl	1975.......Bobby Orr, Bos	1990.......Ray Bourque, Bos
1961.......Doug Harvey, Mtl	1976.......Denis Potvin, NYI	1991.......Ray Bourque, Bos
1962.......Doug Harvey, NYR	1977.......Larry Robinson, Mtl	1992.......Brian Leetch, NYR
1963.......Pierre Pilote, Chi	1978.......Denis Potvin, NYI	1993.......Chris Chelios, Chi
1964.......Pierre Pilote, Chi	1979.......Denis Potvin, NYI	1994.......Ray Bourque, Bos
1965.......Pierre Pilote, Chi	1980.......Larry Robinson, Mtl	1995.......Paul Coffey, Det
1966.......Jacques Laperriere, Mtl	1981.......Randy Carlyle, Pit	1996.......Chris Chelios, Chi
1967.......Harry Howell, NYR	1982.......Doug Wilson, Chi	1997.......Brian Leetch, NYR
1968.......Bobby Orr, Bos	1983.......Rod Langway, Wsh	1998.......Rob Blake, LA

James Norris Memorial Trophy *(Cont.)*

1999 ....Al MacInnis, StL	2004 ......Scott Niedermayer, NJ	2009 ....Zdeno Chara, Bos
2000 ....Chris Pronger, StL	2005 ......No Award	2010 ....Duncan Keith, Chi
2001 ....Nicklas Lidstrom, Det	2006 ......Nicklas Lidstrom, Det	2011 ....Nicklas Lidstrom, Det
2002 ....Nicklas Lidstrom, Det	2007 ......Nicklas Lidstrom, Det	2012 ....Erik Karlsson, Ott
2003 ....Nicklas Lidstrom, Det	2008 ......Nicklas Lidstrom, Det	2013 .......P.K. Subban, Mon

Calder Memorial Trophy

Awarded annually "to the player selected as the most proficient in his first year of competition in the National Hockey League." Frank Calder was a former NHL president. Sergei Makarov, who won the award in 1989–90, was the oldest recipient of the trophy, at 31. Players are no longer eligible for the award if they are 26 or older as of September 15th of the season in question.

1933 ....Carl Voss, Det	1960 ....Bill Hay, Chi	1987 ....Luc Robitaille, LA
1934 ....Russ Blinko, Mtl M	1961 ....Dave Keon, Tor	1988 ....Joe Nieuwendyk, Cgy
1935 ....Dave Schriner, NYA	1962 ....Bobby Rousseau, Mtl	1989 ....Brian Leetch, NYR
1936 ....Mike Karakas, Chi	1963 ....Kent Douglas, Tor	1990 ....Sergei Makarov, Cgy
1937 ....Syl Apps, Tor	1964 ....Jacques Laperriere, Mtl	1991 ....Ed Belfour, Chi
1938 ....Cully Dahlstrom, Chi	1965 ....Roger Crozier, Det	1992 ....Pavel Bure, Van
1939 ....Frank Brimsek, Bos	1966 ....Brit Selby, Tor	1993 ....Teemu Selanne, Win
1940 ....Kilby MacDonald, NYR	1967 ....Bobby Orr, Bos	1994 ....Martin Brodeur, NJ
1941 ....Johnny Quilty, Mtl	1968 ....Derek Sanderson, Bos	1995 ....Peter Forsberg, Que
1942 ....Grant Warwick, NYR	1969 ....Danny Grant, Min	1996 ....Daniel Alfredsson, Ott
1943 ....Gaye Stewart, Tor	1970 ....Tony Esposito, Chi	1997 ....Bryan Berard, NYI
1944 ....Gus Bodnar, Tor	1971 ....Gilbert Perreault, Buf	1998 ....Sergei Samsonov, Bos
1945 ....Frank McCool, Tor	1972 ....Ken Dryden, Mtl	1999 ....Chris Drury, Col
1946 ....Edgar Laprade, NYR	1973 ....Steve Vickers, NYR	2000 ....Scott Gomez, NJ
1947 ....Howie Meeker, Tor	1974 ....Denis Potvin, NYI	2001 ....Evgeni Nabokov, SJ
1948 ....Jim McFadden, Det	1975 ....Eric Vail, Atl	2002 ....Dany Heatley, Atl
1949 ....Pentti Lund, NYR	1976 ....Bryan Trottier, NYI	2003 ....Barret Jackman, StL
1950 ....Jack Gelineau, Bos	1977 ....Willi Plett, Atl	2004 ....Andrew Raycroft, Bos
1951 ....Terry Sawchuk, Det	1978 ....Mike Bossy, NYI	2005 ....No Award
1952 ....Bernie Geoffrion, Mtl	1979 ....Bobby Smith, Min	2006........Alexander Ovechkin, Wsh
1953 ....Gump Worsley, NYR	1980 ......Ray Bourque, Bos	2007........Evgeni Malkin, Pit
1954 ....Camille Henry, NYR	1981 ....Peter Stastny, Que	2008........Patrick Kane, Chi
1955 ....Ed Litzenberger, Chi	1982 ....Dale Hawerchuk, Win	2009........Steve Mason, CBJ
1956 ....Glenn Hall, Det	1983 ....Steve Larmer, Chi	2010........Tyler Myers, Buf
1957 ....Larry Regan, Bos	1984 ....Tom Barrasso, Buf	2011........Jeff Skinner, Car
1958 ....Frank Mahovlich, Tor	1985 ....Mario Lemieux, Pit	2012........Gabriel Landeskog, Col
1959 ....Ralph Backstrom, Mtl	1986 ......Gary Suter, Cgy	2013........Jonathan Huberdeau, Fla

Vezina Trophy

Awarded annually "to the goalkeeper adjudged to be the best at his position." The trophy is named after Georges Vezina, an outstanding goalie for the Montreal Canadiens who collapsed during a game on November 28, 1925, and died four months later of tuberculosis. The general managers of the NHL teams vote on the award.

1927 ....George Hainsworth, Mtl	1953 ....Terry Sawchuk, Det	1973 ....Ken Dryden, Mtl
1928 ....George Hainsworth, Mtl	1954 ....Harry Lumley, Tor	1974 ....Bernie Parent, Phi
1929 ....George Hainsworth, Mtl	1955 ....Terry Sawchuk, Det	Tony Esposito, Chi
1930 ....Tiny Thompson, Bos	1956 ....Jacques Plante, Mtl	1975 ....Bernie Parent, Phi
1931 ....Roy Worters, NYA	1957 ....Jacques Plante, Mtl	1976 ....Ken Dryden, Mtl
1932 ....Charlie Gardiner, Chi	1958 ....Jacques Plante, Mtl	1977 ....Ken Dryden, Mtl
1933 ....Tiny Thompson, Bos	1959 ....Jacques Plante, Mtl	Michel Larocque, Mtl
1934 ....Charlie Gardiner, Chi	1960 ....Jacques Plante, Mtl	1978 ....Ken Dryden, Mtl
1935 ....Lorne Chabot, Chi	1961 ....Johnny Bower, Tor	Michel Larocque, Mtl
1936 ....Tiny Thompson, Bos	1962 ....Jacques Plante, Mtl	1979 ....Ken Dryden, Mtl
1937 ....Normie Smith, Det	1963 ....Glenn Hall, Chi	Michel Larocque, Mtl
1938 ....Tiny Thompson, Bos	1964 ....Charlie Hodge, Mtl	1980 ....Bob Sauve, Buf
1939 ....Frank Brimsek, Bos	1965 ....Terry Sawchuk, Tor	Don Edwards, Buf
1940 ....Dave Kerr, NYR	Johnny Bower, Tor	1981 ....Richard Sevigny, Mtl
1941 ....Turk Broda, Tor	1966 ....Gump Worsley, Mtl	Michel Larocque, Mtl
1942 ....Frank Brimsek, Bos	Charlie Hodge, Mtl	1982 ....Billy Smith, NYI
1943 ....Johnny Mowers, Det	1967 ....Glenn Hall, Chi	Denis Herron, Mtl
1944 ....Bill Durnan, Mtl	Denis DeJordy, Chi	1983 ....Pete Peeters, Bos
1945 ....Bill Durnan, Mtl	1968 ....Gump Worsley, Mtl	1984 ....Tom Barrasso, Buf
1946 ....Bill Durnan, Mtl	1969 ....Jacques Plante, StL	1985 ....Pelle Lindbergh, Phi
1947 ....Bill Durnan, Mtl	Glenn Hall, StL	1986 ....John Vanbiesbrouck, NYR
1948 ....Turk Broda, Tor	1970 ....Tony Esposito, Chi	1987 ....Ron Hextall, Phi
1949 ....Bill Durnan, Mtl	1971 ....Ed Giacomin, NYR	1988 ....Grant Fuhr, Edm
1950 ....Bill Durnan, Mtl	Gilles Villemure, NYR	1989 ....Patrick Roy, Mtl
1951 ....Al Rollins, Tor	1972 ....Tony Esposito, Chi	1990 ....Patrick Roy, Mtl
1952 ....Terry Sawchuk, Det	Gary Smith, Chi	1991 ....Ed Belfour, Chi

Vezina Trophy (Cont.)

1992 ....Patrick Roy, Mtl	2000 ....Olaf Kolzig, Wash	2008 ....Martin Brodeur, NJ
1993 ....Ed Belfour, Chi	2001 ....Dominik Hasek, Buf	2009 ....Tim Thomas, Bos
1994 ....Dominik Hasek, Buf	2002 ....Jose Theodore, Mtl	2010 ....Ryan Miller, Buf
1995 ....Dominik Hasek, Buf	2003 ....Martin Brodeur, NJ	2011 ....Tim Thomas, Bos
1996 ....Jim Carey, Wsh	2004 ....Martin Brodeur, NJ	2012 ....Henrik Lundqvist, NYR
1997 ....Dominik Hasek, Buf	2005 ....No Award	2013 ....Sergei Bobrovsky, Col
1998 ....Dominik Hasek, Buf	2006 ....Miikka Kiprusoff, Cgy	
1999 ....Dominik Hasek, Buf	2007 ....Martin Brodeur, NJ	

Selke Trophy

Awarded annually "to the forward who best excels in the defensive aspects of the game." The trophy is named after Frank J. Selke, the architect of the Montreal Canadians dynasty that won five consecutive Stanley Cups in the late '50s. The winner is selected by a vote of the Professional Hockey Writers Association.

1978........Bob Gainey, Mtl	1990......Rick Meagher, StL	2002........Michael Peca, NYI
1979........Bob Gainey, Mtl	1991......Dirk Graham, Chi	2003........Jere Lehtinen, Dal
1980........Bob Gainey, Mtl	1992......Guy Carbonneau, Mtl	2004........Kris Draper, Det
1981........Bob Gainey, Mtl	1993......Doug Gilmour, Tor	2005........No Award
1982........Steve Kasper, Bos	1994......Sergei Fedorov, Det	2006........Rod Brind'Amour, Car
1983........Bobby Clarke, Phi	1995......Ron Francis, Pit	2007........Rod Brind'Amour, Car
1984........Doug Jarvis, Wsh	1996......Sergei Fedorov, Det	2008........Pavel Datsyuk, Det
1985........Craig Ramsay, Buf	1997......Michael Peca, Buf	2009........Pavel Datsyuk, Det
1986........Troy Murray, Chi	1998......Jere Lehtinen, Dal	2010........Pavel Datsyuk, Det
1987........Dave Poulin, Phi	1999......Jere Lehtinen, Dal	2011........Ryan Kesler, Van
1988........Guy Carbonneau, Mtl	2000......Steve Yzerman, Det	2012........Patrice Bergeron, Bos
1989........Guy Carbonneau, Mtl	2001......John Madden, NJ	2013........Jonathan Toews, Chi

Adams Award

Awarded annually "to the NHL coach adjudged to have contributed the most to his team's success." The trophy is named in honor of Jack Adams, longtime coach and general manager of the Detroit Red Wings. The winner is selected by a vote of the National Hockey League Broadcasters' Association.

1974 .....Fred Shero, Phi	1988 .....Jacques Demers, Det	2002 .....Bob Francis, Phx
1975 .....Bob Pulford, LA	1989 .....Pat Burns, Mtl	2003 .....Jacques Lemaire, Min
1976 .....Don Cherry, Bos	1990 .....Bob Murdoch, Win	2004 .....John Tortorella, TB
1977 .....Scott Bowman, Mtl	1991 .....Brian Sutter, StL	2005 .....No Award
1978 .....Bobby Kromm, Det	1992 .....Pat Quinn, Van	2006 .....Lindy Ruff, Buf
1979 .....Al Arbour, NYI	1993 .....Pat Burns, Tor	2007 .....Alain Vigneault, Van
1980 .....Pat Quinn, Phi	1994 .....Jacques Lemaire, NJ	2008 .....Bruce Boudreau, Wsh
1981 .....Red Berenson, StL	1995 .....Marc Crawford, Que	2009 .....Claude Julien, Bos
1982 .....Tom Watt, Win	1996 .....Scotty Bowman, Det	2010 .....Dave Tippett, Phx
1983 .....Orval Tessier, Chi	1997 .....Ted Nolan, Buf	2011 .....Dan Bylsma, Pit
1984 .....Bryan Murray, Wsh	1998 .....Pat Burns, Bos	2012 .....Ken Hitchcock, StL
1985 .....Mike Keenan, Phi	1999 .....Jacques Martin, Ott	2013 .....Paul MacLean, Ott
1986 .....Glen Sather, Edm	2000 .....Joel Quenneville, StL	
1987 .....Jacques Demers, Det	2001 .....Bill Barber, Phi	

Career Records

Alltime Point Leaders

Player	Yrs	GP	G	A	Pts	Pts/game
Wayne Gretzky, Edm, LA, StL, NYR 20		1487	894	1963	2857	1.921
Mark Messier, Edm, NYR, Van 25		1756	694	1193	1887	1.074
Gordie Howe, Det, Hfd 26		1767	801	1049	1850	1.047
Ron Francis, Hfd, Pit, Car, Tor 23		1731	549	1249	1798	1.039
Marcel Dionne, Det, LA, NYR 18		1348	731	1040	1771	1.314
Steve Yzerman, Det 22		1514	692	1063	1755	1.159
Mario Lemieux, Pit 17		915	690	1033	1723	1.883
*Jaromir Jagr, six teams 19		1391	681	1007	1688	1.214
Joe Sakic, Que, Col 20		1378	625	1016	1641	1.191
Phil Esposito, Chi, Bos, NYR 18		1282	717	873	1590	1.240
Ray Bourque, Bos, Col 22		1612	410	1169	1579	.980
Mark Recchi, seven teams 23		1652	577	956	1533	.928
Paul Coffey, eight teams..............................21		1409	396	1135	1531	1.087
Stan Mikita, Chi 22		1394	541	926	1467	1.052
*Teemu Selanne, Win, Ana, SJ, Col, Ana 20		1387	675	755	1430	1.031

*Active in 2012–13.

Alltime Goal-Scoring Leaders

Player	Yrs	GP	G	G/game
Wayne Gretzky, Edm, LA, StL, NYR	20	1487	894	.601
Gordie Howe, Det, Hfd	26	1767	801	.453
Brett Hull, Cgy, StL, Dal, Det	19	1269	741	.584
Marcel Dionne, Det, LA, NYR	18	1348	731	.542
Phil Esposito, Chi, Bos, NYR	18	1282	717	.559
Mike Gartner, Wsh, Min, NYR, Tor, Phx	19	1432	708	.494
Mark Messier, Edm, NYR, Van	25	1756	694	.395
Steve Yzerman, Det.	22	1514	692	.457
Mario Lemieux, Pit	17	915	690	.754
*Jaromir Jagr, six teams	19	1391	681	.490
*Teemu Selanne, Win, Ana, SJ, Col, Ana	20	1387	675	.487
Luc Robitaille, LA, Pit, NYR, Det	19	1431	668	.467
Brendan Shanahan, NJ, StL, Hfd, Det, NYR	21	1524	656	.430
Dave Andreychuk, seven teams	23	1,639	640	.390
Joe Sakic, Que, Col	20	1,378	625	.454

Alltime Assist Leaders

Player	Yrs	GP	A	A/game
Wayne Gretzky, Edm, LA, StL, NYR	20	1487	1963	1.320
Ron Francis, Hfd, Pit, Car, Tor	23	1731	1249	.722
Mark Messier, Edm, NYR, Van	25	1756	1193	.679
Ray Bourque, Bos, Col	22	1612	1169	.725
Paul Coffey, eight teams	21	1409	1135	.806
Adam Oates, seven teams	22	1337	1079	.807
Steve Yzerman, Det	22	1514	1063	.702
Gordie Howe, Det, Hfd	26	1767	1049	.594
Marcel Dionne, Det, LA, NYR	18	1348	1040	.772
Mario Lemieux, Pit	17	915	1033	1.129

Alltime Penalty Minutes Leaders

Player	Yrs	GP	PIM	Min/game
Dave Williams, Tor, Van, Det, LA, Hfd	14	962	3966	4.12
Dale Hunter, Que, Wsh, Col	19	1407	3565	2.53
Tie Domi, Tor, NYR, Win	16	1020	3515	3.45
Marty McSorley, Pit, Edm, LA, NYR, SJ, Bos	17	961	3381	3.52
Bob Probert, Det, Chi	16	935	3300	3.53

Goaltending Records

ALLTIME GOALTENDING LEADERS, BY WINS

Goaltender	W	L	T	OT
*Martin Brodeur, NJ	669	380	105	43
Patrick Roy, Mtl, Col	551	315	131	0
Ed Belfour, five teams	484	320	111	14
Curtis Joseph, five teams	454	352	90	6
Terry Sawchuk, five teams	447	330	172	0
Jacques Plante, five teams	437	246	145	0
Tony Esposito, Mtl, Chi	423	306	151	0
Glenn Hall, Det, Chi, StL	407	326	163	0
Grant Fuhr, six teams	403	295	114	0
Chris Osgood, Det, NYI, StL, Det	401	216	66	29
Dominik Hasek, Chi, Buf, Ott, Det	389	223	82	13

*Active in 2012–13.

ACTIVE GOALTENDING LEADERS, BY WINS

Goaltender	W	L	T	OT
Martin Brodeur, NJ	669	380	105	43
Roberto Luongo, Van	348	289	33	53
Evgeni Nabokov, NYI	335	207	29	47
Nikolai Khabibulin, Chi	332	334	58	38
Miikka Kiprusoff, Cal	319	213	7	64
Tomas Vokoun, Pit	300	288	35	43
Henrik Lundqvist, NYR	276	171	0	57
Ryan Miller, Buf	269	164	1	53
Jean-Sebastien Giguere, Col	251	210	25	49
Marc-Andre Fleury, Pit	249	151	2	39
Martin Biron, NYR	230	190	25	27

ALLTIME SHUTOUT LEADERS

Goaltender	Team	Yrs	GP	SO
*Martin Brodeur	NJ	20	1220	121
Terry Sawchuk	Det, Bos, Tor, LA, NYR	21	971	103
George Hainsworth	Mtl, Tor	11	465	94
Glenn Hall	Det, Chi, StL	18	906	84
Jacques Plante	Mtl, NYR, StL, Tor, Bos	18	837	82
Tiny Thompson	Bos, Det	12	553	81
Alex Connell	Ott, Det, NYA, Mtl M	12	417	81
Dominik Hasek	Chi, Buf, Ott, Det	16	735	81
Tony Esposito	Mtl, Chi	16	886	76
Ed Belfour	Chi, SJ, Dal, Tor	17	963	76

ALLTIME GOALS AGAINST AVERAGE LEADERS (PRE-1950)

Goaltender	Team	Yrs	GP	GA	GAA
Alec Connell	Ott, Det, NYA, Mtl M	12	417	830	1.91
George Hainsworth	Mtl, Tor	11	465	937	1.93
Chuck Gardiner	Chi	7	316	664	2.02
Lorne Chabot	NYR, Tor, Mtl, Chi, Mtl M, NYA	11	411	860	2.04
Tiny Thompson	Bos, Det	12	553	1183	2.08

ALLTIME GOALS AGAINST AVERAGE LEADERS (POST-1950)

Goaltender	Team	Yrs	GP	GA	GAA
Dominik Hasek	Chi, Buf, Det, Ott	16	735	1572	2.20
*Martin Brodeur	NJ	20	1200	2668	2.23
Ken Dryden	Mtl	8	397	870	2.24
*Henrik Lundqvist	NYR	8	511	1134	2.25
Roman Turek	Dal, StL, Cgy	8	328	734	2.31
*Jonathan Quick	LA	6	286	646	2.32

*Active in 2012–13. Note: Minimum 200 games played. GAA equals goals against per 60 minutes played.

Alltime Coaching Leaders, by Regular Season Wins

Coach	Team	Seasons	W	L	T	OTL
Scotty Bowman	StL, Mtl, Buf, Pit, Det	30	1244	573	314	10
Al Arbour	StL, NYI	23	782	577	248	0
Dick Irvin	Chi, Tor, Mtl, Chi	27	692	527	230	0
Pat Quinn	Phi, LA, Van, Tor, Ed	20	684	528	154	34
Mike Keenan	Phi, Chi, NYR, StL, Van, Bos, Fla, Cgy	20	672	531	147	36
*Joel Quenneville	StL, Col, Chi	16	660	389	77	85
Ron Wilson	Ana, Wash, SJ, Tor	18	648	561	101	91
Bryan Murray	Wash, Det, Fla, Ana, Ott	17	620	465	131	23
Jacques Lemaire	Mtl, NJ, Min, NJ	17	617	458	124	63
Jacques Martin	StL, Ott, Fla, Mtl	17	613	481	119	81
*Ken Hitchcock	Dal, Phi, CBJ, StL	16	605	382	88	83
*Lindy Ruff	Buf	15	571	432	78	84
Marc Crawford	Que, Col, Van, LA, Dal	15	549	421	103	78
Billy Reay	Tor, Chi	16	542	385	175	0
*Barry Trotz	Nash	14	519	447	60	88

*Active in 2012–13.

Single-Season Records

Goals

Player	Season	GP	G	Player	Season	GP	G
Wayne Gretzky, Edm	1981–82	80	92	Wayne Gretzky, Edm	1982–83	80	71
Wayne Gretzky, Edm	1983–84	74	87	Brett Hull, StL	1991–92	73	70
Brett Hull, StL	1990–91	78	86	Mario Lemieux, Pit	1987–88	77	70
Mario Lemieux, Pit	1988–89	76	85	Bernie Nicholls, LA	1988–89	79	70
Alexander Mogilny, Buf	1992–93	77	76	Mario Lemieux, Pit	1992–93	60	69
Phil Esposito, Bos	1970–71	78	76	Mario Lemieux, Pit	1995–96	70	69
Teemu Selanne, Win	1992–93	84	76	Mike Bossy, NYI	1978–79	80	69
Wayne Gretzky, Edm	1984–85	80	73	Phil Esposito, Bos	1973–74	78	68
Brett Hull, StL	1989–90	80	72	Jari Kurri, Edm	1985–86	78	68
Jari Kurri, Edm	1984–85	73	71	Mike Bossy, NYI	1980–81	79	68

Assists

Player	Season	GP	Asst	Player	Season	GP	Asst
Wayne Gretzky, Edm	1985–86	80	163	Bobby Orr, Bos	1970–71	78	102
Wayne Gretzky, Edm	1984–85	80	135	Mario Lemieux, Pit	1987–88	77	98
Wayne Gretzky, Edm	1982–83	80	125	Adam Oates, Bos	1992–93	84	97
Wayne Gretzky, LA	1990–91	78	122	Joe Thornton, SJ	2005–06	81	96
Wayne Gretzky, Edm	1986–87	79	121	Doug Gilmour, Tor	1992–93	83	95
Wayne Gretzky, Edm	1981–82	80	120	Pat LaFontaine, Buf	1992–93	84	95
Wayne Gretzky, Edm	1983–84	74	118	Mario Lemieux, Pit	1985–86	79	93
Mario Lemieux, Pit	1988–89	76	114	Peter Stastny, Que	1981–82	80	93
Wayne Gretzky, LA	1988–89	78	114	Wayne Gretzky, LA	1993–94	81	92
Wayne Gretzky, Edm	1987–88	64	109	Mario Lemieux, Pit	1995–96	70	92
Wayne Gretzky, Edm	1980–81	80	109	Ron Francis, Pit	1995–96	77	92
Wayne Gretzky, LA	1989–90	73	102	Joe Thornton, SJ	2006–07	82	92

Points

Player	Season	G	Asst	Pts	Player	Season	G	Asst	Pts
Wayne Gretzky, Edm	1985–86	52	163	215	Wayne Gretzky, LA	1990–91	41	122	163
Wayne Gretzky, Edm	1981–82	92	120	212	Mario Lemieux, Pit	1995–96	69	92	161
Wayne Gretzky, Edm	1984–85	73	135	208	Mario Lemieux, Pit	1992–93	69	91	160
Wayne Gretzky, Edm	1983–84	87	118	205	Steve Yzerman, Det	1988–89	65	90	155
Mario Lemieux, Pit	1988–89	85	114	199	Phil Esposito, Bos	1970–71	76	76	152
Wayne Gretzky, Edm	1982–83	71	125	196	Bernie Nicholls, LA	1988–89	70	80	150
Wayne Gretzky, Edm	1986–87	62	121	183	Wayne Gretzky, Edm	1987–88	40	109	149
Mario Lemieux, Pit	1987–88	70	98	168	Jaromir Jagr, Pit	1995–96	62	87	149
Wayne Gretzky, LA	1988–89	54	114	168	Pat LaFontaine, Buf	1992–93	53	95	148
Wayne Gretzky, Edm	1980–81	55	109	164	Mike Bossy, NYI	1981–82	64	83	147

Points per Game

Player	Season	GP	Pts	Avg	Player	Season	GP	Pts	Avg
Wayne Gretzky, Edm	1983–84	74	205	2.77	Mario Lemieux, Pit	1987–88	77	168	2.18
Wayne Gretzky, Edm	1985–86	80	215	2.69	Wayne Gretzky, LA	1988–89	78	168	2.15
Mario Lemieux, Pit	1992–93	60	160	2.67	Wayne Gretzky, LA	1990–91	78	163	2.09
Wayne Gretzky, Edm	1981–82	80	212	2.65	Mario Lemieux, Pit	1989–90	59	123	2.08
Mario Lemieux, Pit	1988–89	76	199	2.62	Wayne Gretzky, Edm	1980–81	80	164	2.05
Wayne Gretzky, Edm	1984–85	80	208	2.60	Mario Lemieux, Pit	1991–92	64	131	2.05
Wayne Gretzky, Edm	1982–83	80	196	2.45	Bill Cowley, Bos	1943–44	36	71	1.97
Wayne Gretzky, Edm	1987–88	64	149	2.33	Phil Esposito, Bos	1970–71	78	152	1.95
Wayne Gretzky, Edm	1986–87	79	183	2.32	Wayne Gretzky, LA	1989–90	73	142	1.95
Mario Lemieux, Pitt	1995–96	70	161	2.30	Steve Yzerman, Det	1988–89	80	155	1.94

Note: Minimum 50 points in one season.

Goals per Game

Player	Season	GP	G	Avg
Joe Malone, Mtl	1917–18	20	44	2.20
Cy Denneny, Ott	1917–18	20	36	1.80
Newsy Lalonde, Mtl	1917–18	14	23	1.64
Joe Malone, Que	1919–20	24	39	1.63
Newsy Lalonde, Mtl	1919–20	23	36	1.57
Reg Noble, Tor	1917–18	20	30	1.50
Babe Dye, Ham-Tor	1920–21	24	35	1.46
Cy Denneny, Ott	1920–21	24	34	1.42
Joe Malone, Ham	1920–21	20	28	1.40
Newsy Lalonde, Mtl	1920–21	24	33	1.38

Note: Minimum 20 goals in one season.

Assists per Game

Player	Season	GP	Asst	Avg
Wayne Gretzky, Edm	1985–86	80	163	2.04
Wayne Gretzky, Edm	1987–88	64	109	1.70
Wayne Gretzky, Edm	1984–85	80	135	1.69
Wayne Gretzky, Edm	1983–84	74	118	1.59
Wayne Gretzky, Edm	1982–83	80	125	1.56
Wayne Gretzky, LA	1990–91	78	122	1.56
Wayne Gretzky, Edm	1986–87	79	121	1.53
Mario Lemieux, Pit	1992–93	60	91	1.52
Wayne Gretzky, Edm	1981–82	80	120	1.50
Mario Lemieux, Pit	1988–89	76	114	1.50

Note: Minimum 35 assists in one season.

Shutout Leaders

Player	Season	SO	Length of Schedule	Player	Season	SO	Length of Schedule
George Hainsworth, Mtl	1928–29	22	44	Chuck Gardiner, Chi	1930–31	12	44
Alec Connell, Ott	1925–26	15	36	Terry Sawchuk, Det	1951–52	12	70
Alec Connell, Ott	1927–28	15	44	Terry Sawchuk, Det	1953–54	12	70
Hal Winkler, Bos	1927–28	15	44	Terry Sawchuk, Det	1954–55	12	70
Tony Esposito, Chi	1969–70	15	76	Glenn Hall, Det	1955–56	12	70
George Hainsworth, Mtl	1926–27	14	44	Bernie Parent, Phi	1973–74	12	78
Clint Benedict, Mtl M	1926–27	13	44	Bernie Parent, Phi	1974–75	12	80
Alec Connell, Ott	1926–27	13	44	Martin Brodeur, NJ	2006–07	12	82
George Hainsworth, Mtl	1927–28	13	44	Lorne Chabot, NYR	1927–28	11	44
John Roach, NYR	1928–29	13	44	Harry Holmes, Det	1927–28	11	44
Roy Worters, NYA	1928–29	13	44	Roy Worters, Pit Pirates	1927–28	11	44
Harry Lumley, Tor	1953–54	13	70	Clint Benedict, Mtl M	1928–29	11	44
Dominik Hasek, Buf	1997–98	13	82	Lorne Chabot, Tor	1928–29	11	44
Tiny Thompson, Bos	1928–29	12	44	Joe Miller, Pit Pirates	1928–29	11	44

Shutout Leaders *(Cont.)*

	Season	SO	Length of Schedule		Season	SO	Length of Schedule
Tiny Thompson, Bos	1932–33	11	48	Gerry McNeil, Mtl	1952–53	10	70
Terry Sawchuck, Det	1950–51	11	70	Tony Esposito, Chi	1973–74	10	78
Dominik Hasek, Buf	2000–01	11	82	Ken Dryden, Mtl	1976–77	10	80
Martin Brodeur, NJ	2003–04	11	82	Martin Brodeur, NJ	1996–97	10	82
Henrik Lundqvist, NYR	2010–11	11	82	Martin Brodeur, NJ	1997–98	10	82
Lorne Chabot, NYR	1926–27	10	44	Byron Dafoe, Bos	1998–99	10	82
Clarence Dolson, Det	1928–29	10	44	Roman Cechmanek, Phi	2000–01	10	82
John Roach, Det	1932–33	10	48	Ed Belfour, Tor	2003–04	10	82
Chuck Gardiner, Chi	1933–34	10	48	Miikka Kiprusoff, Cgy	2005–06	10	82
Tiny Thompson, Bos	1935–36	10	48	Henrik Lundqvist, NYR	2007–08	10	82
Frank Brimsek, Bos	1938–39	10	48	Steve Mason, CBJ	2008–09	10	82
Bill Durnan, Mtl	1948–49	10	60	Jonathan Quick, LA	2011–12	10	82
Harry Lumley, Tor	1952–53	10	70				

Wins

	Season	Record*		Season	Record*
Martin Brodeur, NJ	2006–07	48–23	Martin Brodeur, NJ	1997–98	43–17–8
Roberto Luongo, Van	2006–07	47–22	Martin Brodeur, NJ	1999–00	43–20–8
Bernie Parent, Phi	1973–74	47–13–12	Martin Brodeur, NJ	2005–06	43–23
Evgeni Nabokov, SJ	2007–08	46–21	Pekka Rinne, Nash	2011–12	43–26
Miikka Kiprusoff, Cgy	2008–09	45–24	Ken Dryden, Mtl	1975–76	42–10–8
Martin Brodeur, NJ	2009–10	45–25	Mike Richter, NYR	1993–94	42–12–6
Terry Sawchuk, Det	1950–51	44–13–13	Jacques Plante, Mtl	1955–56	42–12–10
Bernie Parent, Phi	1974–75	44–14–9	Jacques Plante, Mtl	1961–62	42–14–14
Terry Sawchuk, Det	1951–52	44–14–12	Roman Turek, StL	1999–00	42–15–9
Evgeni Nabokov, SJ	2009–10	44–16	Martin Brodeur, NJ	2000–01	42–17–11
Martin Brodeur, NJ	2007–08	44–27	Miikka Kiprusoff, Cgy	2005–06	42–20
Tom Barrasso, Pit	1992–93	43–14–5	Ilya Bryzgalov, Phx	2009–10	42–20
Ed Belfour, Chi	1990–91	43–19–7	Marc-Andre Fleury, Pit	2011–12	42–21

*Starting with the 2005–06 season, ties were eliminated.

Goals Against Average

(PRE-1950)	Season	GP	GAA	(POST-1950)	Season	GP	GAA
George Hainsworth, Mtl	1928–29	44	0.92	Brian Elliott, StL	2011–12	38	1.56
George Hainsworth, Mtl	1927–28	44	1.05	Craig Anderson, Ott	2012–12	24	1.69
Alec Connell, Ott	1925–26	36	1.12	Miika Kiprusoff, Cal	2003–04	38	1.69
Tiny Thompson, Bos	1928–29	44	1.15	Marty Turco, Dal	2002–03	55	1.73
Roy Worters, NYA	1928–29	38	1.15	Tony Esposito, Chi	1971–72	48	1.77

Single-Game Records

Goals

	Date	G
Joe Malone, Que vs Tor	1-31-20	7
Newsy Lalonde, Mtl vs Tor	1-10-20	6
Joe Malone, Que vs Ott	3-10-20	6
Corb Denneny, Tor vs Ham	1-26-21	6
Cy Denneny, Ott vs Ham	3-7-21	6
Syd Howe, Det vs NYR	2-3-44	6
Red Berenson, StL vs Phi	11-7-68	6
Darryl Sittler, Tor vs Bos	2-7-76	6

Assists

	Date	A
Billy Taylor, Det vs Chi	3-16-47	7
Wayne Gretzky, Edm vs Wsh	2-15-80	7
Wayne Gretzky, Edm vs Chi	12-11-85	7
Wayne Gretzky, Edm vs Que	2-14-86	7

Note: 24 tied with 6.

Points

	Date	G	A	Pts
Darryl Sittler, Tor vs Bos	2-7-76	6	4	10
Maurice Richard, Mtl vs Det	12-28-44	5	3	8
Bert Olmstead, Mtl vs Chi	1-9-54	4	4	8
Tom Bladon, Phi vs Clev	12-11-77	4	4	8
Bryan Trottier, NYI vs NYR	12-23-78	5	3	8
Peter Stastny, Que vs Wsh	2-22-81	4	4	8
Anton Stastny, Que vs Wsh	2-22-81	3	5	8
Wayne Gretzky, Edm vs NJ	11-19-83	3	5	8
Wayne Gretzky, Edm vs Min	1-4-84	4	4	8
Paul Coffey, Edm vs Det	3-14-86	2	6	8
Mario Lemieux, Pit vs StL	10-15-88	2	6	8
Bernie Nicholls, LA vs Tor	12-1-88	2	6	8
Mario Lemieux, Pit vs NJ	12-31-88	5	3	8
Sam Gagner, Edm vs. Chi	2-2-12	4	4	8

Points

Season	Player and Club	Pts	Season	Player and Club	Pts
1917–18	Joe Malone, Mtl	44	1965–66	Bobby Hull, Chi	97
1918–19	Newsy Lalonde, Mtl	30	1966–67	Stan Mikita, Chi	97
1919–20	Joe Malone, Que	48	1967–68	Stan Mikita, Chi	87
1920–21	Newsy Lalonde, Mtl	41	1968–69	Phil Esposito, Bos	126
1921–22	Punch Broadbent, Ott	46	1969–70	Bobby Orr, Bos	120
1922–23	Babe Dye, Tor	37	1970–71	Phil Esposito, Bos	152
1923–24	Cy Denneny, Ott	23	1971–72	Phil Esposito, Bos	133
1924–25	Babe Dye, Tor	44	1972–73	Phil Esposito, Bos	130
1925–26	Nels Stewart, Mtl M	42	1973–74	Phil Esposito, Bos	145
1926–27	Bill Cook, NY	37	1974–75	Bobby Orr, Bos	135
1927–28	Howie Morenz, Mtl	51	1975–76	Guy Lafleur, Mtl	125
1928–29	Ace Bailey, Tor	32	1976–77	Guy Lafleur, Mtl	136
1929–30	Cooney Weiland, Bos	73	1977–78	Guy Lafleur, Mtl	132
1930–31	Howie Morenz, Mtl	51	1978–79	Bryan Trottier, NYI	134
1931–32	Harvey Jackson, Tor	53	1979–80	Marcel Dionne, LA	137
1932–33	Bill Cook, NY	50		Wayne Gretzky, Edm	137
1933–34	Charlie Conacher, Tor	52	1980–81	Wayne Gretzky, Edm	164
1934–35	Charlie Conacher, Tor	57	1981–82	Wayne Gretzky, Edm	212
1935–36	Sweeney Schriner, NYA	45	1982–83	Wayne Gretzky, Edm	196
1936–37	Sweeney Schriner, NYA	46	1983–84	Wayne Gretzky, Edm	205
1937–38	Gord Drillon, Tor	52	1984–85	Wayne Gretzky, Edm	208
1938–39	Hector Blake, Mtl	47	1985–86	Wayne Gretzky, Edm	215
1939–40	Milt Schmidt, Bos	52	1986–87	Wayne Gretzky, Edm	183
1940–41	Bill Cowley, Bos	62	1987–88	Mario Lemieux, Pit	168
1941–42	Bryan Hextall, NY	54	1988–89	Mario Lemieux, Pit	199
1942–43	Doug Bentley, Chi	73	1989–90	Wayne Gretzky, LA	142
1943–44	Herb Cain, Bos	82	1990–91	Wayne Gretzky, LA	163
1944–45	Elmer Lach, Mtl	80	1991–92	Mario Lemieux, Pit	131
1945–46	Max Bentley, Chi	61	1992–93	Mario Lemieux, Pit	160
1946–47	Max Bentley, Chi	72	1993–94	Wayne Gretzky, LA	130
1947–48	Elmer Lach, Mtl	61	1994–95	Jaromir Jagr, Pit	70
1948–49	Roy Conacher, Chi	68	1995–96	Mario Lemieux, Pit	161
1949–50	Ted Lindsay, Det	78	1996–97	Mario Lemieux, Pit	122
1950–51	Gordie Howe, Det	86	1997–98	Jaromir Jagr, Pit	102
1951–52	Gordie Howe, Det	86	1998–99	Jaromir Jagr, Pit	127
1952–53	Gordie Howe, Det	95	1999–00	Jaromir Jagr, Pit	96
1953–54	Gordie Howe, Det	81	2000–01	Jaromir Jagr, Pit	121
1954–55	Bernie Geoffrion, Mtl	75	2001–02	Jarome Iginla, Cgy	96
1955–56	Jean Beliveau, Mtl	88	2002–03	Peter Forsberg, Col	106
1956–57	Gordie Howe, Det	89	2003–04	Martin St. Louis, TB	94
1957–58	Dickie Moore, Mtl	84	2004–05	No season	
1958–59	Dickie Moore, Mtl	96	2005–06	Joe Thornton, Bos/SJ	125
1959–60	Bobby Hull, Chi	81	2006–07	Sidney Crosby, Pit	120
1960–61	Bernie Geoffrion, Mtl	95	2007–08	Alexander Ovechkin, Wsh	112
1961–62	Andy Bathgate, NY	84	2008–09	Evgeni Malkin, Pit	113
	Bobby Hull, Chi	84	2009–10	Henrik Sedin, Van	112
1962–63	Gordie Howe, Det	86	2010–11	Daniel Sedin, Van	104
1963–64	Stan Mikita, Chi	89	2011–12	Evgeni Malkin, Pit	109
1964–65	Stan Mikita, Chi	87	2012–13	Martin St. Louis, TB	60

Goals

Season	Player and Club	G	Season	Player and Club	G
1917–18	Joe Malone, Mtl	44	1930–31	Charlie Lonacher, Tor	* 31
1918–19	Odie Cleghorn, Mtl	23	1931–32	Charlie Conacher, Tor	34
1919–20	Joe Malone, Que	39		Bill Cook, NY	34
1920–21	Babe Dye, Ham-Tor	35	1932–33	Bill Cook, NY	28
1921–22	Punch Broadbent, Ott	32	1933–34	Charlie Conacher, Tor	32
1922–23	Babe Dye, Tor	26	1934–35	Charlie Conacher, Tor	36
1923–24	Cy Denneny, Ott	22	1935–36	Charlie Conacher, Tor	23
1924–25	Babe Dye, Tor	38		Bill Thoms, Tor	23
1925–26	Nels Stewart, Mtl	34	1936–37	Larry Aurie, Det	23
1926–27	Bill Cook, NY	33		Nels Stewart, Bos-NYA	23
1927–28	Howie Morenz, Mtl	33	1937–38	Gord Drillon, Tor	26
1928–29	Ace Bailey, Tor	22	1938–39	Roy Conacher, Bos	26
1929–30	Cooney Weiland, Bos	43	1939–40	Bryan Hextall, NY	24

Goals *(Cont.)*

Season	Player and Club	G
1940–41	Bryan Hextall, NY	26
1941–42	Lynn Patrick, NY	32
1942–43	Doug Bentley, Chi	33
1943–44	Doug Bentley, Chi	38
1944–45	Maurice Richard, Mtl	50
1945–46	Gaye Stewart, Tor	37
1946–47	Maurice Richard, Mtl	45
1947–48	Ted Lindsay, Det	33
1948–49	Sid Abel, Det	28
1949–50	Maurice Richard, Mtl	43
1950–51	Gordie Howe, Det	43
1951–52	Gordie Howe, Det	47
1952–53	Gordie Howe, Det	49
1953–54	Maurice Richard, Mtl	37
1954–55	Bernie Geoffrion, Mtl	38
	Maurice Richard, Mtl	38
1955–56	Jean Beliveau, Mtl	47
1956–57	Gordie Howe, Det	44
1957–58	Dickie Moore, Mtl	36
1958–59	Jean Beliveau, Mtl	45
1959–60	Bronco Horvath, Bos	39
	Bobby Hull, Chi	39
1960–61	Bernie Geoffrion, Mtl	50
1961–62	Bobby Hull, Chi	50
1962–63	Gordie Howe, Det	38
1963–64	Bobby Hull, Chi	43
1964–65	Norm Ullman, Det	42
1965–66	Bobby Hull, Chi	54
1966–67	Bobby Hull, Chi	52
1967–68	Bobby Hull, Chi	44
1968–69	Bobby Hull, Chi	58
1969–70	Phil Esposito, Bos	43
1970–71	Phil Esposito, Bos	76
1971–72	Phil Esposito, Bos	66
1972–73	Phil Esposito, Bos	55
1973–74	Phil Esposito, Bos	68
1974–75	Phil Esposito, Bos	61
1975–76	Guy Lafleur, Mtl	56
1976–77	Steve Shutt, Mtl	60
1977–78	Guy Lafleur, Mtl	60
1978–79	Mike Bossy, NYI	69
1979–80	Charlie Simmer, LA	56
	Blaine Stoughton, Hart	56
1980–81	Mike Bossy, NYI	68
1981–82	Wayne Gretzky, Edm	92
1982–83	Wayne Gretzky, Edm	71
1983–84	Wayne Gretzky, Edm	87
1984–85	Wayne Gretzky, Edm	73
1985–86	Jari Kurri, Edm	68
1986–87	Wayne Gretzky, Edm	62
1987–88	Mario Lemieux, Pit	70
1988–89	Mario Lemieux, Pit	85
1989–90	Brett Hull, StL	72
1990–91	Brett Hull, StL	86
1991–92	Brett Hull, StL	70
1992–93	Alexander Mogilny, Buf	76
	Teemu Selanne, Win	76
1993–94	Pavel Bure, Van	60
1994–95	Peter Bondra, Wsh	34
1995–96	Mario Lemieux, Pit	69
1996–97	Keith Tkachuk, Phx	52
1997–98	Peter Bondra, Wsh	52
	Teemu Selanne, Ana	52
1998–99	Teemu Selanne, Ana	47
1999–00	Pavel Bure, Fla	58
2000–01	Pavel Bure, Fla	59
2001–02	Jarome Iginla, Cgy	52
2002–03	Milan Hejduk, Col	50
2003–04	Jarome Iginla, Cgy	41
	Ilya Kovalchuk, Atl	41
	Rick Nash, CBJ	41
2004–05	No season	
2005–06	Jonathan Cheechoo, SJ	56
2006–07	Vincent Lecavalier, TB	52
2007–08	Alexander Ovechkin, Wsh	65
2008–09	Alexander Ovechkin, Wsh	56
2009–10	Sidney Crosby, Pit	51
	Steven Stamkos, TB	51
2010–11	Corey Perry, Ana	50
2011–12	Steven Stamkos, TB	60
2012–13	Alex Ovechkin, Wsh	32

Assists

Season	Player and Club	Asst
1917–18	statistic not kept	
1918–19	Newsy Lalonde, Mtl	9
1919–20	Corbett Denneny, Tor	12
1920–21	Louis Berlinquette, Mtl	9
1921–22	Punch Broadbench, Ott	14
1922–23	Babe Dye, Tor	11
1923–24	Billy Boucher, Mtl	6
1924–25	Cy Denneny, Ott	15
1925–26	Frank Nighbor, Ott	13
1926–27	Dick Irvin, Chi	18
1927–28	Howie Morenz, Mtl	18
1928–29	Frank Boucher, NY	16
1929–30	Frank Boucher, NY	36
1930–31	Joe Primeau, Tor	32
1931–32	Joe Primeau, Tor	37
1932–33	Frank Boucher, NY	28
1933–34	Joe Primeau, Tor	32
1934–35	Art Chapman, NYA	34
1935–36	Art Chapman, NYA	28
1936–37	Syl Apps, Tor	29
1937–38	Syl Apps, Tor	29
1938–39	Bill Cowley, Bos	34
1939–40	Milt Schmidt, Bos	30
1940–41	Bill Cowley, Bos	45
1941–42	Phil Watson, NY	37
1942–43	Bill Cowley, Bos	45
1943–44	Clint Smith, Chi	49
1944–45	Elmer Lach, Mtl	54
1945–46	Elmer Lach, Mtl	34
1946–47	Billy Taylor, Det	46
1947–48	Doug Bentley, Chi	37
1948–49	Doug Bentley, Chi	43
1949–50	Ted Lindsay, Det	55
1950–51	Gordie Howe, Det	43
	Ted Kennedy, Tor	43
1951–52	Elmer Lach, Mtl	50
1952–53	Gordie Howe, Det	46
1953–54	Gordie Howe, Det	48
1954–55	Bert Olmstead, Mtl	48
1955–56	Bert Olmstead, Mtl	56
1956–57	Ted Lindsay, Det	55
1957–58	Henri Richard, Mtl	52
1958–59	Dickie Moore, Mtl	55
1959–60	Bobby Hull, Chi	42
1960–61	Jean Beliveau, Mtl	58
1961–62	Andy Bathgate, NY	56

Assists *(Cont.)*

Season	Player and Club	Asst	Season	Player and Club	Asst
1962–63	Henri Richard, Mtl	50	1989–90	Wayne Gretzky, LA	102
1963–64	Andy Bathgate, NY-Tor	58	1990–91	Wayne Gretzky, LA	122
1964–65	Stan Mikita, Chi	59	1991–92	Wayne Gretzky, LA	90
1965–66	Jean Beliveau, Mtl	48	1992–93	Adam Oates, Bos	97
	Stan Mikita, Chi	48	1993–94	Wayne Gretzky, LA	92
	Bobby Rousseau, Mtl	48	1994–95	Ron Francis, Pit	48
1966–67	Stan Mikita, Chi	62	1995–96	Ron Francis, Pit	92
1967–68	Phil Esposito, Bos	49		Mario Lemieux, Pit	92
1968–69	Phil Esposito, Bos	77	1996–97	Mario Lemieux, Pit	72
1969–70	Bobby Orr, Bos	87	1997–98	Wayne Gretzky, NYR	67
1970–71	Bobby Orr, Bos	102		Jaromir Jagr, Pit	67
1971–72	Bobby Orr, Bos	80	1998–99	Jaromir Jagr, Pit	83
1972–73	Phil Esposito, Bos	75	1999–00	Mark Recchi, Phi	63
1973–74	Bobby Orr, Bos	90	2000–01	Jaromir Jagr, Pit	69
1974–75	Bobby Clarke, Phi	89		Adam Oates, Wsh	69
	Bobby Orr, Bos	89	2001–02	Adam Oates, Wsh	64
1975–76	Bobby Clarke, Phi	89	2002–03	Peter Forsberg, Col	77
1976–77	Guy Lafleur, Mtl	80	2003–04	Scott Gomez, NJ	56
1977–78	Bryan Trottier, NYI	77		Martin St. Louis, TB	56
1978–79	Bryan Trottier, NYI	87	2004–05	No season	
1979–80	Wayne Gretzky, Edm	86	2005–06	Joe Thornton, Bos/SJ	96
1980–81	Wayne Gretzky, Edm	109	2006–07	Joe Thornton, SJ	92
1981–82	Wayne Gretzky, Edm	120	2007–08	Joe Thornton, SJ	67
1982–83	Wayne Gretzky, Edm	125	2008–09	Evgeni Malkin, Pit	78
1983–84	Wayne Gretzky, Edm	118	2009–10	Henrik Sedin, Van	83
1984–85	Wayne Gretzky, Edm	135	2010–11	Henrik Sedin, Van	75
1985–86	Wayne Gretzky, Edm	163	2011–12	Henrik Sedin, Van	67
1986–87	Wayne Gretzky, Edm	121	2013–13	Martin St. Louis, TB	43
1987–88	Wayne Gretzky, Edm	109			
1988–89	Wayne Gretzky, LA	114			
	Mario Lemieux, Pit	114			

Goals Against Average

Season	Goaltender and Club	GP	Min	GA	SO	Avg
1917–18	Georges Vezina, Mtl	21	1282	84	1	3.93
1918–19	Clint Benedict, Ott	18	1113	53	2	2.86
1919–20	Clint Benedict, Ott	24	1444	64	5	2.66
1920–21	Clint Benedict, Ott	24	1457	75	2	3.09
1921–22	Clint Benedict, Ott	24	1508	84	2	3.34
1922–23	Clint Benedict, Ott	24	1478	54	4	2.18
1923–24	Georges Vezina, Mtl	24	1459	48	3	1.97
1924–25	Georges Vezina, Mtl	30	1860	56	5	1.81
1925–26	Alec Connell, Ott	36	2251	42	15	1.12
1926–27	Clint Benedict, Mtl M	43	2748	65	13	1.42
1927–28	George Hainsworth, Mtl	44	2730	48	13	1.05
1928–29	George Hainsworth, Mtl	44	2800	43	22	0.92
1929–30	Tiny Thompson, Bos	44	2680	98	3	2.19
1930–31	Roy Worters, NYA	44	2760	74	8	1.61
1931–32	Chuck Gardiner, Chi	48	2989	92	4	1.85
1932–33	Tiny Thompson, Bos	48	3000	88	11	1.76
1933–34	Wilf Cude, Det-Mtl	30	1920	47	5	1.47
1934–35	Lorne Chabot, Chi	48	2940	88	8	1.80
1935–36	Tiny Thompson, Bos	48	2930	82	10	1.68
1936–37	Normie Smith, Det	48	2980	102	6	2.05
1937–38	Tiny Thompson, Bos	48	2970	89	7	1.80
1938–39	Frank Brimsek, Bos	43	2610	68	10	1.56
1939–40	Dave Kerr, NYR	48	3000	77	8	1.54
1940–41	Turk Broda, Tor	48	2970	99	5	2.00
1941–42	Frank Brimsek, Bos	47	2930	115	3	2.35
1942–43	Johnny Mowers, Det	50	3010	124	6	2.47
1943–44	Bill Durnan, Mtl	50	3000	109	2	2.18
1944–45	Bill Durnan, Mtl	50	3000	121	1	2.42
1945–46	Bill Durnan, Mtl	40	2400	104	4	2.60
1946–47	Bill Durnan, Mtl	60	3600	138	4	2.30
1947–48	Turk Broda, Tor	60	3600	143	5	2.38
1948–49	Bill Durnan, Mtl	60	3600	126	10	2.10

Goals Against Average (Cont.)

Season	Goaltender and Club	GP	Min	GA	SO	Avg
1949–50	Bill Durnan, Mtl	64	3840	141	8	2.20
1950–51	Al Rollins, Tor	40	2367	70	5	1.77
1951–52	Terry Sawchuk, Det	70	4200	133	12	1.90
1952–53	Terry Sawchuk, Det	63	3780	120	9	1.90
1953–54	Harry Lumley, Tor	69	4140	128	13	1.86
1954–55	Harry Lumley, Tor	69	4140	134	8	1.94
1955–56	Jacques Plante, Mtl	64	3840	119	7	1.86
1956–57	Jacques Plante, Mtl	61	3660	122	9	2.00
1957–58	Jacques Plante, Mtl	57	3386	119	9	2.11
1958–59	Jacques Plante, Mtl	67	4000	144	9	2.16
1959–60	Jacques Plante, Mtl	69	4140	175	3	2.54
1960–61	Charlie Hodge, Mtl	30	1800	74	4	2.47
1961–62	Jacques Plante, Mtl	70	4200	166	4	2.37
1962–63	Don Simmons, Tor	28	1680	69	1	2.46
1963–64	Johnny Bower, Tor	51	3009	106	5	2.11
1964–65	Johnny Bower, Tor	34	2040	81	3	2.38
1965–66	Johnny Bower, Tor	35	1998	75	3	2.25
1966–67	Glenn Hall, Chi	32	1664	66	2	2.38
1967–68	Gump Worsley, Mtl	40	2213	73	6	1.98
1968–69	Jacques Plante, StL	37	2139	70	5	1.96
1969–70	Ernie Wakely, StL	30	1651	58	4	2.11
1970–71	Jacques Plante, Tor	40	2329	73	4	1.88
1971–72	Tony Esposito, Chi	48	2780	82	9	1.77
1972–73	Ken Dryden, Mtl	54	3165	119	6	2.26
1973–74	Bernie Parent, Phi	73	4314	136	12	1.89
1974–75	Bernie Parent, Phi	68	4041	137	12	2.03
1975–76	Ken Dryden, Mtl	62	3580	121	8	2.03
1976–77	Michel Larocque, Mtl	26	1525	53	4	2.09
1977–78	Ken Dryden, Mtl	52	3071	105	5	2.05
1978–79	Ken Dryden, Mtl	47	2814	108	5	2.30
1979–80	Bob Sauve, Buff	32	1880	74	4	2.36
1980–81	Richard Sevigny, Mtl	33	1777	71	2	2.40
1981–82	Denis Herron, Mtl	27	1547	68	3	2.64
1982–83	Pete Peeters, Bos	62	3611	142	8	2.36
1983–84	Pat Riggin, Wsh	41	2299	102	4	2.66
1984–85	Tom Barrasso, Buf	54	3248	144	5	2.66
1985–86	Bob Froese, Phi	51	2728	116	5	2.55
1986–87	Brian Hayward, Mtl	37	2178	102	1	2.81
1987–88	Pete Peeters, Wsh	35	1896	88	2	2.78
1988–89	Patrick Roy, Mtl	48	2744	113	4	2.47
1989–90	Mike Liut, Hfd-Wsh	37	2161	91	4	2.53
	Patrick Roy, Mtl	54	3173	134	3	2.53
1990–91	Ed Belfour, Chi	74	4127	170	4	2.47
1991–92	Patrick Roy, Mtl	67	3935	155	5	2.36
1992–93	Felix Potvin, Tor	48	2781	116	2	2.50
1993–94	Dominik Hasek, Buf	58	3358	109	7	1.95
1994–95	Dominik Hasek, Buf	41	2416	85	5	2.11
1995–96	Ron Hextall, Phi	53	3102	112	4	2.17
	Chris Osgood, Det	50	2932	106	5	2.17
1996–97	Martin Brodeur, NJ	67	3838	120	10	1.88
1997–98	Ed Belfour, Dal	61	3581	112	9	1.88
1998–99	Ron Tugnutt, Ott	43	2508	75	3	1.79
1999–00	Brian Boucher, Phi	35	2038	65	4	1.91
2000–01	Marty Turco, Dal	26	1266	40	3	1.90
2001–02	Patrick Roy, Col	63	3773	122	9	1.94
2002–03	Marty Turco, Dal	55	3202	92	7	1.72
2003–04	Miikka Kiprusoff, Cgy	38	2301	65	4	1.69
2004–05	No season					
2005–06	Miikka Kiprusoff, Cgy	74	4379	151	10	2.07
2006–07	Niklas Backstrom, Min	41	2226	73	5	1.97
2007–08	Chris Osgood, Det	43	2409	84	4	2.09
2008–09	Tim Thomas, Bos	54	3259	114	5	2.10
2009–10	Tuukka Rask, Bos	45	2562	84	5	1.97
2010–11	Tim Thomas, Bos	57	3364	112	9	2.00
2011–12	Brian Elliott, StL	38	2235	58	9	1.56
2012–13	Craig Anderson, Ott	24	1,420	40	3	1.69

Penalty Minutes

Season	Player and Club	GP	PIM	Season	Player and Club	GP	PIM
1918–19	Joe Hall, Mtl	17	135	1966–67	John Ferguson, Mtl	67	177
1919–20	Cully Wilson, Tor	23	79	1967–68	Barclay Plager, StL	49	153
1920–21	Bert Corbeau, Mtl	24	86	1968–69	Forbes Kennedy, Phi-Tor	77	219
1921–22	Sprague Cleghorn, Mtl	24	63	1969–70	Keith Magnuson, Chi	76	213
1922–23	Billy Boucher, Mtl	24	55	1970–71	Keith Magnuson, Chi	76	291
1923–24	Bert Corbeau, Tor	24	55	1971–72	Brian Watson, Pit	75	212
1924–25	Billy Boucher, Mtl	30	92	1972–73	Dave Schultz, Phi	76	259
1925–26	Bert Corbeau, Tor	36	121	1973–74	Dave Schultz, Phi	73	348
1926–27	Nels Stewart, Mtl M	44	133	1974–75	Dave Schultz, Phi	76	472
1927–28	Eddie Shore, Bos	44	165	1975–76	Steve Durbano, Pit-KC	69	370
1928–29	Red Dutton, Mtl M	44	139	1976–77	Dave Williams, Tor	77	338
1929–30	Joe Lamb, Ott	44	119	1977–78	Dave Schultz, LA-Pit	74	405
1930–31	Harvey Rockburn, Det	42	118	1978–79	Dave Williams, Tor	77	298
1931–32	Red Dutton, NYA	47	107	1979–80	Jimmy Mann, Win	72	287
1932–33	Red Horner, Tor	48	144	1980–81	Dave Williams, Van	77	343
1933–34	Red Horner, Tor	42	126	1981–82	Paul Baxter, Pit	76	409
1934–35	Red Horner, Tor	46	125	1982–83	Randy Holt, Wsh	70	275
1935–36	Red Horner, Tor	43	167	1983–84	Chris Nilan, Mtl	76	338
1936–37	Red Horner, Tor	48	124	1984–85	Chris Nilan, Mtl	77	358
1937–38	Red Horner, Tor	47	82	1985–86	Joey Kocur, Det	59	377
1938–39	Red Horner, Tor	48	85	1986–87	Tim Hunter, Cgy	73	361
1939–40	Red Horner, Tor	30	87	1987–88	Bob Probert, Det	74	398
1940–41	Jimmy Orlando, Det	48	99	1988–89	Tim Hunter, Cgy	75	375
1941–42	Pat Egan, Bklyn	48	124	1989–90	Basil McRae, Min	66	351
1942–43	Jimmy Orlando, Det	40	89	1990–91	Rob Ray, Buf	66	350
1943–44	Mike McMahon, Mtl	42	98	1991–92	Mike Peluso, Chi	63	408
1944–45	Pat Egan, Bos	48	86	1992–93	Marty McSorley, LA	81	399
1945–46	Jack Stewart, Det	47	73	1993–94	Tie Domi, Win	81	347
1946–47	Gus Mortson, Tor	60	133	1994–95	Enrico Ciccone, TB	41	225
1947–48	Bill Barilko, Tor	57	147	1995–96	Matthew Barnaby, Buf	73	335
1948–49	Bill Ezinicki, Tor	52	145	1996–97	Gino Odjick, Van	70	371
1949–50	Bill Ezinicki, Tor	67	144	1997–98	Donald Brashear, Van	77	372
1950–51	Gus Mortson, Tor	60	142	1998–99	Rob Ray, Buf	76	261
1951–52	Gus Kyle, Bos	69	127	1999–00	Denny Lambert, Atl	73	219
1952–53	Maurice Richard, Mtl	70	112	2000–01	Matthew Barnaby, TB	76	265
1953–54	Gus Mortson, Chi	68	132	2001–02	Peter Worrell, Fla	79	354
1954–55	Fern Flaman, Bos	70	150	2002–03	Jody Shelley, CBJ	68	249
1955–56	Lou Fontinato, NYR	70	202	2003–04	Sean Avery, LA	76	261
1956–57	Gus Mortson, Chi	70	147	2004–05	No season		
1957–58	Lou Fontinato, NYR	70	152	2005–06	Sean Avery, LA	75	257
1958–59	Ted Lindsay, Chi	70	184	2006–07	Ben Eager, Phi	63	233
1959–60	Carl Brewer, Tor	67	150	2007–08	Daniel Carcillo, Phx	57	324
1960–61	Pierre Pilote, Chi	70	165	2008–09	Daniel Carcillo, Phi	74	254
1961–62	Lou Fontinato, Mtl	54	167	2009–10	Zenon Konopka, TB	74	265
1962–63	Howie Young, Det	64	273	2010–11	Zenon Konopka, NYI	82	307
1963–64	Vic Hadfield, NYR	69	151	2011–12	Derek Dorsett, CBJ	77	235
1964–65	Carl Brewer, Tor	70	177	2012–13	Colton Orr, Tor	44	155
1965–66	Reggie Fleming, Bos-NYR	69	166				

NHL All-Star Game

First played in 1947, this game started before the regular season and was used to match the defending Stanley Cup champions against the league All-Stars from other teams. In 1966 the game was moved to midseason, although there was no game that year. The format changed to a inter-conference showdown in 1969. The Challenge Cup, a series between the NHL All-Stars and the Soviet Union, was played instead of the All-Star Game in 1979. Eight years later, Rendez-Vous '87, a two-game series matching the Soviet Union and the NHL All-Stars, replaced the All-Star Game. The 1995 NHL All-Star game was cancelled due to a labor dispute. The 1998 NHL All-Star game, billed as a preview to the 1998 Winter Olympics in Nagano, Japan, matched North Amercian–born All-Stars and All-Stars born elsewhere.

Results

Year	Site	Score	MVP	Attendance
1947	Toronto	All-Stars 4, Toronto 3	None named	14,169
1948	Chicago	All-Stars 3, Toronto 1	None named	12,794
1949	Toronto	All-Stars 3, Toronto 1	None named	13,541
1950	Detroit	Detroit 7, All-Stars 1	None named	9,166
1951	Toronto	1st team 2, 2nd team 2	None named	11,469
1952	Detroit	1st team 1, 2nd team 1	None named	10,680
1953	Montreal	All-Stars 3, Montreal 1	None named	14,153
1954	Detroit	All-Stars 2, Detroit 2	None named	10,689
1955	Detroit	Detroit 3, All-Stars 1	None named	10,111
1956	Montreal	All-Stars 1, Montreal 1	None named	13,095
1957	Montreal	All-Stars 5, Montreal 3	None named	13,003
1958	Montreal	Montreal 6, All-Stars 3	None named	13,989
1959	Montreal	Montreal 6, All-Stars 1	None named	13,818
1960	Montreal	All-Stars 2, Montreal 1	None named	13,949
1961	Chicago	All-Stars 3, Chicago 1	None named	14,534
1962	Toronto	Toronto 4, All-Stars 1	Eddie Shack, Tor	14,236
1963	Toronto	All-Stars 3, Toronto 3	Frank Mahovlich, Tor	14,034
1964	Toronto	All-Stars 3, Toronto 2	Jean Beliveau, Mtl	14,232
1965	Montreal	All-Stars 5, Montreal 2	Gordie Howe, Det	13,529
1967	Montreal	Montreal 3, All-Stars 0	Henri Richard, Mtl	14,284
1968	Toronto	Toronto 4, All-Stars 3	Bruce Gamble, Tor	15,753
1969	Montreal	East 3, West 3	Frank Mahovlich, Det	16,260
1970	St. Louis	East 4, West 1	Bobby Hull, Chi	16,587
1971	Boston	West 2, East 1	Bobby Hull, Chi	14,790
1972	Minnesota	East 3, West 2	Bobby Orr, Bos	15,423
1973	NY Rangers	East 5, West 4	Greg Polis, Pit	16,986
1974	Chicago	West 6, East 4	Garry Unger, StL	16,426
1975	Montreal	Wales 7, Campbell 1	Syl Apps Jr, Pit	16,080
1976	Philadelphia	Wales 7, Campbell 5	Pete Mahovlich, Mtl	16,436
1977	Vancouver	Wales 4, Campbell 3	Rick Martin, Buf	15,607
1978	Buffalo	Wales 3, Campbell 2 (OT)	Billy Smith, NYI	16,433
1980	Detroit	Wales 6, Campbell 3	Reg Leach, Phi	21,002
1981	Los Angeles	Campbell 4, Wales 1	Mike Liut, StL	15,761
1982	Washington	Wales 4, Campbell 2	Mike Bossy, NYI	18,130
1983	NY Islanders	Campbell 9, Wales 3	Wayne Gretzky, Edm	15,230
1984	New Jersey	Wales 7, Campbell 6	Don Maloney, NYR	18,939
1985	Calgary	Wales 6, Campbell 4	Mario Lemieux, Pit	16,825
1986	Hartford	Wales 4, Campbell 3 (OT)	Grant Fuhr, Edm	15,100
1988	St. Louis	Wales 6, Campbell 5 (OT)	Mario Lemieux, Pit	17,878
1989	Edmonton	Campbell 9, Wales 5	Wayne Gretzky, LA	17,503
1990	Pittsburgh	Wales 12, Campbell 7	Mario Lemieux, Pit	16,236
1991	Chicago	Campbell 11, Wales 5	Vincent Damphousse, Tor	18,472
1992	Philadelphia	Campbell 10, Wales 6	Brett Hull, StL	17,380
1993	Montreal	Wales 16, Campbell 6	Mike Gartner, NYR	17,137
1994	NY Rangers	East 9, West 8	Mike Richter, NYR	18,200
1996	Boston	East 5, West 4	Ray Bourque, Bos	17,565
1997	San Jose	East 11, West 7	Mark Recchi, Mtl	17,422
1998	Vancouver	North America 8, World 7	Teemu Selanne, Ana (World)	18,422
1999	Tampa Bay	North America 8, World 6	Wayne Gretzky, NYR (N. America)	19,758
2000	Toronto	World 9, North America 4	Pavel Bure, Fla (World)	19,300
2001	Denver	North America 14, World 12	Bill Guerin, Bos (North America)	18,646
2002	Los Angeles	World 8, North America 5	Eric Daze, Chi (North America)	18,118
2003	Sunrise, Fla.	West 6, East 5 (shootout)	Dany Heatley, Atl (East)	19,250
2004	St. Paul	East 6, West 4	Joe Sakic, Col (West)	19,434
2005	No game played (season lockout)			
2006	No game played (2006 Winter Olympics)			
2007	Dallas	West 12, East 9	Daniel Briere, Buf (East)	18,532
2008	Atlanta	East 8, West 7	Eric Staal, Car (East)	18,644

Results (Cont.)

Year	Site	Score	MVP	Attendance
2009	Montreal	East 12, West 11	Alexei Kovalev, Mtl (East)	21,273
2010	No game played (2010 Winter Olympics)			
2011	Raleigh	Team Lidstrom 11, Team Staal 10	Patrick Sharp, Chi (Team Staal)	18,680
2012	Ottawa	Team Chara 12, Team Alfredsson 9	Marian Gaborik, NYR (Team Chara)	20,510
2013	No game played due to lockout			

Hockey Hall of Fame

Located in Toronto, the Hockey Hall of Fame was officially opened on August 26, 1961. There are, at present, 375 members of the Hockey Hall of Fame—259 players, 101 "builders," and 15 on-ice officials. (One member, Alan Eagleson, resigned from the Hall March 25, 1998.) To be eligible, player and referee/linesman candidates should have been out of the game for three years, but the Hall's Board of Directors can make exceptions.

Players

Sid Abel (1969)
Jack Adams (1959)
Glenn Anderson (2008)
Charles (Syl) Apps (1961)
George Armstrong (1975)
Irvine (Ace) Bailey (1975)
Donald H. (Dan) Bain (1945)
Hobey Baker (1945)
Bill Barber (1990)
Marty Barry (1965)
Andy Bathgate (1978)
Bobby Bauer (1996)
Ed Belfour (2011)
Jean Beliveau (1972)
Clint Benedict (1965)
Douglas Bentley (1964)
Max Bentley (1966)
Hector (Toe) Blake (1966)
Leo Boivin (1986)
Dickie Boon (1952)
Mike Bossy (1991)
Emile (Butch) Bouchard (1966)
Frank Boucher (1958)
George (Buck) Boucher (1960)
Ray Bourque (2004)
Johnny Bower (1976)
Russell Bowie (1945)
Frank Brimsek (1966)
Harry L. (Punch) Broadbent (1962)
Walter (Turk) Broda (1967)
John Bucyk (1981)
Billy Burch (1974)
Pavel Bure (2012)
Harry Cameron (1962)
Gerry Cheevers (1985)
Chris Chelios (2013)
Dino Ciccarelli (2010)
Francis (King) Clancy (1958)
Aubrey (Dit) Clapper (1947)
Bobby Clarke (1987)
Sprague Cleghorn (1958)
Paul Coffey (2004)
Neil Colville (1967)
Charlie Conacher (1961)
Lionel Conacher (1994)

Roy Conacher (1998)
Alex Connell (1958)
Bill Cook (1952)
Fred (Bun) Cook (1995)
Arthur Coulter (1974)
Yvan Cournoyer (1982)
Bill Cowley (1968)
Samuel (Rusty) Crawford (1962)
Jack Darragh (1962)
Allan M. (Scotty) Davidson (1950)
Clarence (Hap) Day (1961)
Alex Delvecchio (1977)
Cy Denneny (1959)
Marcel Dionne (1992)
Gordie Drillon (1975)
Charles Drinkwater (1950)
Ken Dryden (1983)
Terrance (Dick) Duff (2006)
Woody Dumart (1992)
Thomas Dunderdale (1974)
Bill Durnan (1964)
Mervyn A. (Red) Dutton (1958)
Cecil (Babe) Dye (1970)
Phil Esposito (1984)
Tony Esposito (1988)
Arthur F. Farrell (1965)
Bernie Federko (2002)
Viacheslav Fetisov (2001)
Ferdinand (Fern) Flaman (1990)
Frank Foyston (1958)
Ron Francis (2007)
Frank Frederickson (1958)
Grant Fuhr (2003)
Bill Gadsby (1970)
Bob Gainey (1992)
Chuck Gardiner (1945)
Herb Gardiner (1958)
Jimmy Gardner (1962)
Mike Gartner (2001)
Bernie (Boom Boom) Geoffrion (1972)
Eddie Gerard (1945)
Ed Giacomin (1987)
Rod Gilbert (1982)
Clark Gillies (2002)
Doug Gilmour (2011)

Note: Year of election to the Hall of Fame is in parentheses after the member's name.

Players *(Cont.)*

Hamilton (Billy) Gilmour (1962)
Frank (Moose) Goheen (1952)
Ebenezer R. (Ebbie)
  Goodfellow (1963)
Michel Goulet (1998)
Cammi Granato (2010)
Mike Grant (1950)
Wilfred (Shorty) Green (1962)
Wayne Gretzky (1999)
Si Griffis (1950)
George Hainsworth (1961)
Glenn Hall (1975)
Joe Hall (1961)
Doug Harvey (1973)
Dale Hawerchuk (2001)
George Hay (1958)
Geraldine Heaney (2013)
William (Riley) Hern (1962)
Bryan Hextall (1969)
Harry (Hap) Holmes (1972)
Tom Hooper (1962)
George (Red) Horner (1965)
Miles (Tim) Horton (1977)
Gordie Howe (1972)
Mark Howe (2011)
Syd Howe (1965)
Harry Howell (1979)
Bobby Hull (1983)
Brett Hull (2009)
John (Bouse) Hutton (1962)
Harry M. Hyland (1962)
James (Dick) Irvin (1958)
Angela James (2010)
Harvey (Busher) Jackson (1971)
Ernest (Moose) Johnson (1952)
Ivan (Ching) Johnson (1958)
Tom Johnson (1970)
Aurel Joliat (1947)
Gordon (Duke) Keats (1958)
Leonard (Red) Kelly (1969)
Ted (Teeder) Kennedy (1966)
Dave Keon (1986)
Valeri Kharlamov (2005)
Jari Kurri (2001)
Elmer Lach (1966)
Guy Lafleur (1988)
Pat LaFontaine (2003)
Edouard (Newsy) Lalonde (1950)
Rod Langway (2002)
Jacques Laperriere (1987)
Guy Lapointe (1993)
Edgar Laprade (1993)
Igor Larionov (2008)
Jean (Jack) Laviolette (1962)
Brian Leetch (2009)
Hugh Lehman (1958)
Jacques Lemaire (1984)
Mario Lemieux (1997)
Percy LeSueur (1961)
Herbert A. Lewis (1989)
Ted Lindsay (1966)
Harry Lumley (1980)
Lanny McDonald (1992)

Frank McGee (1945)
Billy McGimsie (1962)
George McNamara (1958)
Al MacInnis (2007)
Duncan (Mickey) MacKay (1952)
Frank Mahovlich (1981)
Joe Malone (1950)
Sylvio Mantha (1960)
Jack Marshall (1965)
Fred G. (Steamer) Maxwell (1962)
Mark Messier (2007)
Stan Mikita (1983)
Dicky Moore (1974)
Patrick (Paddy) Moran (1958)
Howie Morenz (1945)
Billy Mosienko (1965)
Joe Mullen (2000)
Larry Murphy (2004)
Cam Neely (2005)
Scott Niedermayer (2013)
Joe Nieuwendyk (2011)
Frank Nighbor (1947)
Reg Noble (1962)
Adam Oates (2012)
Herbert (Buddy) O'Connor (1988)
Harry Oliver (1967)
Bert Olmstead (1985)
Bobby Orr (1979)
Bernie Parent (1984)
Brad Park (1988)
Lester Patrick (1947)
Lynn Patrick (1980)
Gilbert Perreault (1990)
Tommy Phillips (1945)
Pierre Pilote (1975)
Didier (Pit) Pitre (1962)
Jacques Plante (1978)
Denis Potvin (1991)
Walter (Babe) Pratt (1966)
Joe Primeau (1963)
Marcel Pronovost (1978)
Bob Pulford (1991)
Harvey Pulford (1945)
Hubert (Bill) Quackenbush (1976)
Frank Rankin (1961)
Jean Ratelle (1985)
Claude (Chuck) Rayner (1973)
Kenneth Reardon (1966)
Henri Richard (1979)
Maurice (Rocket) Richard (1961)
George Richardson (1950)
Gordon Roberts (1971)
Larry Robinson (1995)
Luc Robitaille (2009)
Art Ross (1945)
Patrick Roy (2006)
Blair Russel (1965)
Ernest Russell (1965)
Jack Ruttan (1962)
Joe Sakic (2012)
Borje Salming (1996)
Denis Savard (2000)
Serge Savard (1986)

Note: Year of election to the Hall of Fame is in parentheses after the member's name.

Players (Cont.)

Terry Sawchuk (1971)
Fred Scanlan (1965)
Milt Schmidt (1961)
Dave (Sweeney) Schriner (1962)
Earl Seibert (1963)
Oliver Seibert (1961)
Brendan Shanahan (2013)
Eddie Shore (1947)
Steve Shutt (1993)
Albert C. (Babe) Siebert (1964)
Harold (Bullet Joe) Simpson (1962)
Daryl Sittler (1989)
Alfred E. Smith (1962)
Billy Smith (1993)
Clint Smith (1991)
Reginald (Hooley) Smith (1972)
Thomas Smith (1973)
Allan Stanley (1981)
Russell (Barney) Stanley (1962)
Peter Stastny (1998)
Scott Stevens (2007)
John (Black Jack) Stewart (1964)
Nels Stewart (1962)

Bruce Stuart (1961)
Hod Stuart (1945)
Mats Sundin (2012)
Frederic (Cyclone) Taylor (O.B.E.) (1947)
Cecil R. (Tiny) Thompson (1959)
Vladislav Tretiak (1989)
Harry J. Trihey (1950)
Bryan Trottier (1997)
Norm Ullman (1982)
Georges Vezina (1945)
Jack Walker (1960)
Marty Walsh (1962)
Harry Watson (1994)
Harry E. Watson (1962)
Ralph (Cooney) Weiland (1971)
Harry Westwick (1962)
Fred Whitcroft (1962)
Gordon (Phat) Wilson (1962)
Lorne (Gump) Worsley (1980)
Roy Worters (1969)
Steve Yzerman (2009)

Builders

Charles Adams (1960)
Weston W. Adams (1972)
Thomas (Frank) Ahearn (1962)
John (Bunny) Ahearne (1977)
Montagu Allan (C.V.O.) (1945)
Keith Allen (1992)
Al Arbour (1996)
Harold Ballard (1977)
David Bauer (1989)
John Bickell (1978)
Scott Bowman (1991)
Herb Brooks (2006)
George V. Brown (1961)
Walter A. Brown (1962)
Frank Buckland (1975)
Walter L. Bush (2000)
Jack Butterfield (1980)
Frank Calder (1947)
Angus D. Campbell (1964)
Clarence Campbell (1966)
Joe Cattarinich (1977)
Ed Chynoweth (2008)
Murray Costello (2005)
Joseph (Leo) Dandurand (1963)
Jimmy Devellano (2010)
Francis Dilio (1964)
George S. Dudley (1958)
James A. Dunn (1968)
*Robert Alan Eagleson (1989–98)
Cliff Fletcher (2004)
Emile Francis (1982)
Jack Gibson (1976)
Tommy Gorman (1963)
Jim Gregory (2007)
Frank Griffiths (1993)

William Hanley (1986)
Charles Hay (1974)
James C. Hendy (1968)
Foster Hewitt (1965)
William Hewitt (1947)
Harley Hotchkiss (2006)
Fred J. Hume (1962)
Mike Ilitch (2003)
George (Punch) Imlach (1984)
Tommy Ivan (1974)
William M. Jennings (1975)
Bob Johnson (1992)
Gordon W. Juckes (1979)
John Kilpatrick (1960)
Brian Kilrea (2003)
Seymour Knox III (1993)
Lou Lamoriello (2009)
George Leader (1969)
Robert LeBel (1970)
Thomas F. Lockhart (1965)
Paul Loicq (1961)
Frederic McLaughlin (1963)
John Mariucci (1985)
Frank Mathers (1992)
John (Jake) Milford (1984)
Hartland Molson (1973)
Scotty Morrison (1999)
Msgr. Athol (Pere) Murray (1998)
Roger Neilson (2002)
Francis Nelson (1947)
Bruce A. Norris (1969)
James Norris, Sr. (1958)
James D. Norris (1962)
William M. Northey (1947)
John O'Brien (1962)

*Eagleson resigned from Hall March 25, 1998.
Note: Year of election to the Hall of Fame is in parentheses after the member's name.

Builders *(Cont.)*

Brian O'Neill (1994)
Fred Page (1993)
Craig Patrick (1996)
Frank Patrick (1958)
Allan W. Pickard (1958)
Rudy Pilous (1985)
Norman (Bud) Poile (1990)
Samuel Pollock (1978)
Donat Raymond (1958)
John Robertson (1947)
Claude C. Robinson (1947)
Philip D. Ross (1976)
Gunther Sabetzki (1995)
Glen Sather (1997)
Daryl (Doc) Seaman (2010)
Frank J. Selke (1960)

Fred Shero (2013)
Harry Sinden (1983)
Frank D. Smith (1962)
Conn Smythe (1958)
Edward M. Snider (1988)
Lord Stanley of Preston (1945)
James T. Sutherland (1947)
Anatoli V. Tarasov (1974)
Bill Torrey (1995)
Lloyd Turner (1958)
William Tutt (1978)
Carl Potter Voss (1974)
Fred C. Waghorn (1961)
Arthur Wirtz (1971)
Bill Wirtz (1976)
John A. Ziegler, Jr. (1987)

Referees/Linesmen

Neil Armstrong (1991)
John Ashley (1981)
William L. Chadwick (1964)
John D'Amico (1993)
Chaucer Elliott (1961)
George Hayes (1988)
Robert W. Hewitson (1963)
Fred J. (Mickey) Ion (1961)

Matt Pavelich (1987)
Mike Rodden (1962)
Ray Scapinello (2008)
J. Cooper Smeaton (1961)
Roy (Red) Storey (1967)
Frank Udvari (1973)
Andy Van Hellemond (1999)

Note: Year of election to the Hall of Fame is in parentheses after the member's name.

Olympics

An ice show in Sochi, Russia, celebrated the one-year countown to the beginning of the 2014 Winter Games there

Winter Worries

With mounting costs, a less than hospitable climate and rampant corruption at every turn, the Sochi Games may need the iron hand of Vladimir Putin to be successful

BY MERRELL NODEN

NO ONE KNEW WHAT TO think last spring when Robert Kraft, owner of the New England Patriots, began spreading the story that Vladimir Putin had stolen his Super Bowl ring back in 2005, when Kraft was visiting the Russian president as part of a delegation of businessmen. "I can kill someone with this ring," Putin had mused as he fingered the gaudy bauble. Eight year later, he shrugged off the accusation, claiming Kraft had given him the ring.

But even if Kraft's accusation is true, it is petty larceny compared to the thievery the five Olympic rings seem to have inspired in Sochi, Russia, which will host the 2014 Winter Games starting February 7. And once again, Russia's strongman president was fingered as the culprit.

The cost of the Games, originally estimated at $12 billion, has now risen to $51 billion, making this the most expensive Olympics in history, Winter or Summer. According to former deputy-prime-minister-turned-Kremlin-critic Boris Nemtsov, more than half the funding—an incredible $30 billion—has disappeared, stolen by Putin's cronies. Nemtsov called the Sochi preparations a "monstrous scam," alleging

that secrecy and a lack of competitive bidding meant that Putin's pals had been allowed to make off with billions.

It hardly counts as news to hear of corruption in Russia—or in IOC circles. Jean-Claude Killy, the chairman of the IOC coordination commission for the Sochi Games, did not exactly boost confidence in the organization's honesty when he allowed: "I don't recall an Olympics without corruption."

None of this was lost on ordinary Russians. One poll showed that 65% of them felt that government spending on the Games was being wasted, while another 19% thought it was "simply being stolen." In Sochi itself, citizens whose homes were razed or appropriated to make way for Olympic construction complained that they had not been adequately compensated for their loss.

It's not at all unusual for host cities to suffer bidder's remorse once the thrill of securing the Olympics has worn off and the real costs have begun to mount. Rio de Janeiro, host city for the 2016 Summer Games as well as key games in the 2014 World Cup, was experiencing similar sticker shock in late spring. In Rio, what began as a grass-roots protest against a hike in bus fares quickly morphed into a

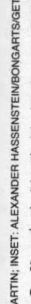
BOB MARTIN; INSET: ALEXANDER HASSENSTEIN/BONGARTS/GETTY IMAGES

general protest about national priorities that seemed to value fancy new stadiums over health care and education.

Sochi was always considered a risky choice. Never before has an Olympic site needed so much prepping. Virtually everything required for the Games—venues, infrastructure, a new airport terminal—had to be built from scratch. Russian billionaire Vladimir Potanin offered to build an entire ski resort from scratch. Bringing in all that construction material meant building two entirely new ports.

There were other, more fundamental worries. Standing on the eastern shore of the Black Sea, Sochi has a subtropical climate. It was Joseph Stalin's summer resort of choice, and palm trees still line its beach. A World Cup slopestyle event in early February 2012 had to be cancelled due to lack of snow, as nighttime temperatures fell to only 45 degrees. As a hedge against the possibility that the weather won't cooperate in providing snow, the Sochi organizing committee spent $8 million on seven on-site reservoirs to store

The subtropical climate in Sochi (above) makes the staging of winter events there risky; in spite of an offer from Potanin (inset) to build an entire ski resort, costs for the Games have skyrocketed.

450,000 cubic meters of the white stuff.

And then there is the critical issue of security. Sochi lies just west of Russia's six autonomous republics, one of which is Chechnya. In May of 2012 the Russian authorities announced that they had foiled a terror plot, hatched in the restive region. In April, when the Tsarneyev brothers detonated their bombs at the Boston Marathon, it was a painful reminder that at these Games security had to be taken seriously. When President Obama and Putin had their famously frosty meeting at the G8 summit they agreed on little except the need to cooperate on Olympic security.

The athletes certainly will do their part to make these Games special. And no one doubts that Putin will do everything in his power to ensure they run smoothly. In Russia, that is a pretty good insurance policy.

2012 Summer Games

TRACK AND FIELD
Men

100 METERS
1. ...Usain Bolt, Jamaica — 9.63 OR
2. ...Yohan Blake, Jamaica — 9.75
3. ...Justin Gatlin, United States — 9.79

200 METERS
1. ...Usain Bolt, Jamaica — 19.32
2. ...Yohan Blake, Jamaica — 19.44
3. ...Warren Weir, Jamaica — 19.84

400 METERS
1. ...Kirani James, Grenada — 43.94
2. ...Luguelin Santos, Dominican Rep. — 44.46
3. ...Lalonde Gordon, Trinidad and Tobago — 44.52

800 METERS
1. ...David Lekuta Rudisha, Kenya — 1:40.91 WR
2. ...Nijel Amos, Botswana — 1:41.73
3. ...Timothy Kitum, Kenya — 1:42.53

1,500 METERS
1. ...Taoufik Makhloufi, Algeria — 3:34.08
2. ...Leonel Manzano, United States — 3:34.79
3. ...Abdalaati Iguider, Morocco — 3:35.13

5,000 METERS
1. ...Mohamed Farah, Great Britain — 13:41.66
2. ...Dejen Gebremeskel, Ethiopia — 13:41.98
3. ...Thomas Pkemei Longosiwa, Kenya — 13:42.36

10,000 METERS
1. ...Mohamed Farah, Great Britain — 27:30.42
2. ...Galen Rupp, United States — 27:30.90
3. ...Tariku Bekele, Ethiopia — 27:31.43

MARATHON
1. ...Stephen Kiprotich, Uganda — 2:08:01
2. ...Abel Kirui, Kenya — 2:08:27
3. ...Wilson Kipsang Kiprotich, Kenya — 2:09:37

110-METER HURDLES
1. ...Aries Merritt, United States — 12.92
2. ...Jason Richardson, United States — 13.04
3. ...Hansle Parchment, Jamaica — 13.12

400-METER HURDLES
1. ...Felix Sanchez, Dominican Republic — 47.63
2. ...Michael Tinsley, United States — 47.91
3. ...Javier Culson, Puerto Rico — 48.10

3,000-METER STEEPLECHASE
1. ...Ezekiel Kemboi, Kenya — 8:18.56
2. ...Mahiedine Mekhissi-Benabbad, France — 8:19.08
3. ...Abel Kiprop Mutai, Kenya — 8:19.73

4 X 100-METER RELAY
1. ....Jamaica: (Y. Blake, U, Bolt, — 36.84 WR
N. Carter, M. Frater)
2. ...United States — 37.04
3. ...Trinidad and Tobago — 38.12

4 X 400-METER RELAY
1. ...Bahamas: (C. Brown, D. Pinder, — 2:56.72
M. Mathieu, R. Miller)
2. ...United States — 2:57.05
3. ...Trinidad and Tobago — 2:59.40

20-KILOMETER WALK
1. ...Ding Chen, China — 1:18:46 OR
2. ...Erick Barrondo, Guatemala — 1:18:57
3. ...Zhen Wang, China — 1:19:25

50-KILOMETER WALK
1. ...Sergey Kirdyapkin, Russia — 3:35:59 OR
2. ...Jared Tallent, Australia — 3:36:53
3. ...Tianfeng Si, China — 3:37:16

HIGH JUMP
1. ...Ivan Ukhov, Russia — 7 ft 9¾ in
2. ...Erik Kynard, United States — 7 ft 7¾ in
3. ...Derek Drouin, Canada — 7 ft 6¼ in

POLE VAULT
1. ...Renaud Lavillenie, France — 19 ft 7 in OR
2. ...Bjorn Otto, Germany — 19 ft 4¾ in
3. ...Raphael Holzdeppe, Germany — 19 ft 4¾ in

LONG JUMP
1. ...Greg Rutherford, Great Britain — 27 ft 3¼ in
2. ...Mitchell Watt, Australia — 26 ft 9¼ in
3. ...Will Claye, United States — 26 ft 7¾ in

TRIPLE JUMP
1. ...Christian Taylor, United States — 58 ft 5¼ in
2. ...Will Claye, United States — 57 ft 9¾ in
3. ...Fabrizio Donato, Italy — 57 ft 4¼ in

SHOT PUT
1. ...Tomasz Majewski, Poland — 71 ft 9¾ in
2. ...David Storl, Germany — 71 ft 8¾ in
3. ...Reese Hoffa, United States — 69 ft 7¾ in

DISCUS THROW
1. ...Robert Harting, Germany — 223 ft 11¾ in
2. ...Ehsan Hadadi, Iran — 223 ft 8¼ in
3. ...Gerd Kanter, Estonia — 223 ft 2¼ in

HAMMER THROW
1. ...Krisztian Pars, Hungary — 264 ft 4¾ in
2. ...Primoz Kozmus, Slovakia — 260 ft 4¾ in
3. ...Koji Murofushi, Japan — 258 ft 2¾ in

JAVELIN
1. ...Keshorn Walcott, Trinidad and Tobago — 277 ft 5¼ in
2. ...Oleksandr Pyatnytsya, Ukraine — 277 ft 3¼ in
3. ...Antti Ruuskanen, Finland — 275 ft 11¾ in

DECATHLON
    Pts
1. ...Ashton Eaton, United States — 8869
2. ...Trey Hardee, United States — 8671
3. ...Leonel Suarez, Cuba — 8523

TRACK AND FIELD
Women

100 METERS
1. ...Shelly-Ann Fraser-Pryce, Jamaica — 10.75
2. ...Carmelita Jeter, United States — 10.78
3. ...Veronica Campbell-Brown, Jamaica — 10.81

200 METERS
1. ...Allyson Felix, United States — 21.88
2. ....Shelly-Ann Fraser-Pryce, Jamaica — 22.09
3. ...Carmelita Jeter, United States — 22.14

Note: OR=Olympic Record. WR=World Record. EOR=Equals Olympic Record. EWR=Equals World Record.

TRACK AND FIELD (CONT.)
Women (Cont.)

400 METERS
1. ...Sanya Richards-Ross, United States 49.55
2. ....Christine Ohuruogu, Great Britain 49.70
3. .....DeeDee Trotter, United States 49.72

800 METERS
1. ...Mariya Savinova, Russia 1:56.19
2. ...Caster Semenya, South Africa 1:57.23
3. ...Ekaterina Poistogova, Russia 1:57.53

1,500 METERS
1. ...Asli Cakir Alptekin, Turkey 4:10.23
2. ...Gamze Bulut, Turkey 4:10.40
3. ...Maryam Yusuf Jamal, Bahrain 4:10.74

5,000 METERS
1. ...Meseret Defar, Ethiopia 15:04.25
2. ...Vivian Jepkemoi Cheruiyot, Kenya 15:04.73
3. ...Tirunesh Dibaba, Ethiopia 15:05.15

10,000 METERS
1. ...Tirunesh Dibaba, Ethiopia 30:20.75
2. ...Sally Jepkosgei Kipyego, Kenya 30:26.37
3. ...Vivian Jepkemoi Cheruiyot, Kenya 30:30.44

MARATHON
1. ...Tiki Gelana, Ethiopia 2:23:07 OR
2. .....Priscah Jeptoo, Kenya 2:23:12
3. .....Tatyana Petrova Arkhipova, Russia 2:23:29

100-METER HURDLES
1. ...Sally Pearson, Australia 12.35 OR
2. ...Dawn Harper, United States 12.37
3. ...Kellie Wells, United States 12.48

400-METER HURDLES
1. ...Natalya Antyukh, Russia 52.70
2. ...Lashinda Demus, United States 52.77
3. ...Zuzana Hejnova, Czech Republic 53.38

3,000-METER STEEPLECHASE
1. ...Yuliya Zaripova, Russia 9:06.72
2. ...Habiba Ghribi, Tunisia 9:08.37
3. ...Sofia Assefa, Ethiopia 9:09.84

4 X 100-METER RELAY
1. ...United States: (C. Jeter, T. Madison, 40.82 WR
A. Felix, B. Knight)
2. .....Jamaica 41.41
3. .....Ukraine 42.04

4 X 400-METER RELAY
1. ....United States: (A. Felix, F. McCorory 3:16.87
S. Richards-Ross, D. Trotter)
2. .....Russia 3:20.23
3. .....Jamaica 3:20.95

20-KILOMETER WALK
1. ...Elena Lashmanova, Russia 1:25:02 WR
2. ...Olga Kaniskina, Russia 1:25:09
3. ...Shenjie Qieyang, China 1:25:16

HIGH JUMP
1. ...Anna Chicherova, Russia 6 ft 8¾ in
2. ...Brigetta Barrett, United States 6 ft 7¼ in
3. ...Svetlana Shkolina, Russia 6 ft 7⅛ in

POLE VAULT
1. ...Jennifer Suhr, United States 15 ft 7 in
2. ...Yarisley Silva, Cuba 15 ft 7 in
3. ...Elena Isinbaeva, Russia 15 ft 5 in

LONG JUMP
1. ...Brittney Reese, United States .23 ft 4¼ in
2. ...Elena Sokolova, Russia 23 ft 2¼ in
3. ...Janay Deloach, United States 22 ft 7¼ in

TRIPLE JUMP
1. ...Olga Rypakova, Kazakhstan 49 ft 1¾ in
2. ...Caterine Ibarguen, Colombia 48 ft 6¾ in
3. ...Olha Saladuha, Ukraine 48 ft 6¼ in

SHOT PUT
1. ....Nadzeya Ostapchuk, Belarus 70 ft ⅞ in
2. ...Valerie Adams, New Zealand 67 ft 11 in
3. ...Evgeniia Kolodko, Russia 67 ft 2¼ in

DISCUS THROW
1. ...Sandra Perkovic, Croatia 226 ft 8¾ in
2. .....Darya Pishchalnikova, Russia 221 ft 7¾ in
3. .....Yanfeng Li, China 220 ft 6½ in

JAVELIN
1. ...Barbora Spotakova, Czech Republic 228 ft 2¼ in
2. ...Christina Obergfoll, Germany 213 ft 9⅜ in
3. .....Linda Stahl, Germany 212 ft 11½ in

HEPTATHLON Pts
1. ...Jessica Ennis, Great Britain 6955
2. ...Lilli Schwarzkopf, Germany 6649
3. ...Tatyana Chernova, Russia 6628

HAMMER THROW
1. ...Tatyana Lysenko, Russia 256 ft 6 in OR
2. ...Anita Wlodarczyk, Poland 254 ft 7⅛ in
3. ...Betty Heidler, Germany 253 ft ¼ in

INDIVIDUAL ARCHERY

Men
1. ...Jin Hyek Oh, South Korea
2. ...Takaharu Furukawa, Japan
3. ...Xiaoxiang Dai, China

Women
1. ...Bo Bae Ki, South Korea
2. ...Aida Roman, Mexico
3. ...Mariana Avitia, Mexico

TEAM ARCHERY

Men
1. .....Italy
2. .....United States
3. .....South Korea

Women
1. .....South Korea
2. .....China
3. .... Japan

Note: OR=Olympic Record. WR=World Record. EOR=Equals Olympic Record. EWR=Equals World Record.

BADMINTON

Men	**Women**	
SINGLES	**SINGLES**	**MIXED DOUBLES**

Men
SINGLES
1. ....Dan Lin, China
2. ....Chong Wei Lee, Malaysia
3. ....Long Chen, China

DOUBLES
1. ....Yun Cai/Haifeng Fu, China
2. ....Mathias Boe/Carsten Mogensen, Denmark
3. ......Yong Dae Lee/Jae Sung Chung, South Korea

Women
SINGLES
1. ....Xuerui Li, China
2. ....Yihan Wang, China
3. ....Saina Nehwal, India

DOUBLES
1. ......Qing Tian/Yunlei Zhao, China
2. ......Reika Kakiiwa/Mizuki Fujii, Japan
3. ......Nina Vislova/Valeria Sorokina, Russia

MIXED DOUBLES
1. ....Nan Zhang/Yunlei Zhao, China
2. ....Chen Xu/Jin Ma, China
3. ....Christinna Pedersen/Joachim Fischer, Denmark

BASKETBALL

Men

Final: United States 107, Spain 100
Russia (3rd)
United States: Kevin Durant, Chris Paul, Lebron James, Kobe Bryant, Carmelo Anthony, Kevin Love, Deron Williams, Russell Westbrook, Tyson Chandler, Andre Iguodala, Anthony Davis, James Harden

Women

Final: United States 86, France 50
Russia (3rd)
United States: Diana Taurasi, Maya Moore, Sue Bird, Candace Parker, Tina Charles, Lindsay Whalen, Tamika Catchings, Seimone Augustus, Sylvia Fowles, Angel McCoughtry, Asjha Jones, Swin Cash

BOXING – Men

LIGHT FLYWEIGHT (106 LB)
1. ......Shiming Zou, China
2. ....Kaeo Pongprayoon, Thailand
3. ....Paddy Barnes, Ireland
3. ....David Ayrapetyan, Russia

FLYWEIGHT (112 LB)
1. ......Robeisy Ramirez Carrazana, Cuba
2. ....Tugstsogt Nyambayar, Mongolia
3. ....Misha Aloian, Russia
3. ....Michael Conlan, Ireland

BANTAMWEIGHT (119 LB)
1. ....:..Luke Campbell, Great Britain
2. ....John Joe Nevin, Ireland
3. ....Satoshi Shimizu, Japan
3. ....Lazaro Alvarez Estrada, Cuba

LIGHTWEIGHT (132 LB)
1. ....Vasyl Lomachenko, Ukraine
2. ....Soonchul Han, South Korea
3. ....Evaldas Petrauskas, Lithuania
3. ....Yasnier Toledo Lopez, Cuba

LIGHT WELTERWEIGHT (139 LB)
1. ......Roniel Iglesias Sotolongo, Cuba
2. ....Denys Berinchyk, Ukraine
3. ....Munkh-Erdene Uranchimeg, Mongolia
3. ....Vincenzo Mangiacapre, Italy

WELTERWEIGHT (147 LB)
1. ......Serik Sapiyev, Kazakhstan
2. ....Freddie Evans, Great Britain
3. ....Taras Shelestyuk, Ukraine
3. ....Andrey Zamkovoy, Russia

MIDDLEWEIGHT (165 LB)
1. ......Serik Sapiyev, Kazakhstan
2. ....Esquiva Falcao Florentino, Brazil
3. ....Anthony Ogogo, Great Britain
3. ....Abbos Atoev, Uzbekistan

LIGHT HEAVYWEIGHT (178 LB)
1. ......Egor Mekhontcev, Russia
2. ....Adilbek Niyazymbetov, Kazakhstan
3. ....Yamaguchi Falcao Florentino, Brazil
3. ....Oleksandr Gvozdyk, Ukraine

HEAVYWEIGHT (201 LB)
1. ......Oleksandr Usyk, Ukraine
2. ....Clemente Russo, Italy
3. ....Tervel Pulev, Bulgaria
3. ....Teymur Mammadov, Azerbaijan

SUPERHEAVYWEIGHT (201+ LB)
1. ......Anthony Joshua, Great Britain
2. ....Roberto Cammarelle, Italy
3. ....Ivan Dychko, Kazakhstan
3.   Magomedrasul Medzhidov, Azerbaijan

Women

FLYWEIGHT (112 LB)
1. ......Nicola Adams, Great Britain
2. ....Cancan Ren, China
3. ....Chungneijang Mery Kom Hmangte, India
3. ....Marlen Esparza, United States

LIGHTWEIGHT (132 LB)
1. ......Katie Taylor, Ireland
2. ....Sofya Ochigava, Russia
3. ....Mavzuna Chorieva, Tajikistan
3. ....Adriana Araujo, Brazil

MIDDLEWEIGHT (165 LB)
1. ......Claressa Shields, United States
2. ....Nadezda Torlopova, Russia
3. ....Marina Volnova, Kazakhstan
3. ....Jinzi Li, China

CANOE/KAYAK
Men

CANOE SINGLES 200 METERS
1. ...Iurii Cheban, Ukraine — 42.291
2. ...Jevgenij Shuklin, Lithuania — 42.792
3. ...Ivan Shtyl, Russia — 42.853

CANOE SINGLES 1,000 METERS
1. ...Sebastian Brendel, Germany — 3:47.176
2. ...David Cal Figueroa, Spain — 3:48.053
3. ...Mark Oldershaw, Canada — 3:48.502

CANOE DOUBLES 1,000 METERS
1. ... K. Kuschela/P. Kretschmer, Germany 3:33.804
2. ...A. Bahdanovich/A. Bahdanovich, Belarus 3:35.206
3. ...I. Pervukhin/A. Korovashkov, Russia 3:36.414

CANOE SINGLE WHITEWATER SLALOM	**Pts**
1. ...Tony Estanguet, France	97.06
2. ...Sideris Tasiadis, Germany	98.09
3. ...Michal Martikan, Slovakia	98.31

CANOE DOUBLE WHITEWATER SLALOM	**Pts**
1. ...E. Stott/T. Baillie, Great Britain	106.41
2. ...R. Hounslow/D. Florence, Great Britain	106.77
3. ...P. Hochschorner/P. Hochschorner, Slovakia 108.28	

KAYAK SINGLES 200 METERS	
1. ...Ed Mckeever, Great Britain	36.246
2. ...Saul Craviotto Rivero, Spain	36.540
3. ...Mark de Jonge, Canada	36.657

CANOE/KAYAK *(CONT.)*

Men *(Cont.)*

KAYAK SINGLES 1,000 METERS
1. ...Eirik Veras Larsen, Norway — 3:26.462
2. ...Adam van Koeverden, Canada — 3:27.170
3. ...Max Hoff, Germany — 3:27.759

KAYAK DOUBLES 1,000 METERS
1. ...R. Kokeny/R. Dombi, Hungary — 3:09.646
2. ...E. Silva/F. Pimenta, Portugal — 3:09.699
3. ...A. Ihle/M. Hollstein, Germany — 3:10.117

KAYAK DOUBLES 200 METERS
1. ...A. Dyachenko/Y. Postrigay, Russia — 33.507
2. ...V. Makhneu/R. Piatrushenka, Belarus — 34.266
3. ...J. Schofield/L. Heath, Great Britain — 34.421

KAYAK FOURS 1,000 METERS
1. ...Australia — 2:55.085
2. ...Hungary — 2:55.699
3. ...Czech Republic — 2:55.850

KAYAK SINGLE WHITEWATER — Pts
1. ...Daniele Molmenti, Italy — 93.43
2. ...Vavrinec Hradilek, Czech Republic — 94.78
3. ...Hannes Aigner, Germany — 94.92

Women

KAYAK SINGLES 200 METERS
1. ...Lisa Carrington, New Zealand — 44.638
2. ...Inna Osypenko-Radomska, Ukraine — 45.053
3. ...Natasa Douchev-Janic, Hungary — 45.128

KAYAK SINGLES 500 METERS
1. ...Danuta Kozak, Hungary — 1:51.456
2. ...Inna Osypenko-Radomska, Ukraine — 1:52.685
3. ...Bridgitte Hartley, South Africa — 1:52.923

KAYAK DOUBLES 500 METERS
1. ...T. Dietze/F. Weber, Germany — 1:42.213
2. ...N. Douchev-Janic/K. Kovacs, Hungary — 1:43.278
3. ...B. Mikolajczyk/K. Naja,Poland — 1:44.000

KAYAK FOURS 500 METERS
1. ...Hungary — 1:30.827
2. ...Germany — 1:31.298
3. ...Belarus — 1:31.400

KAYAK SINGLE WHITEWATER — Pts
1. ...Emilie Fer, France — 105.90
2. ...Jessica Fox, Australia — 106.51
3. ...Maialen Chourraut, Spain — 106.87

CYCLING–Men

ROAD RACE
1. ...Alexandr Vinokurov, Kazakhstan — 5:45:57
2. ...Rigoberto Uran Uran, Colombia — 5:45:57
3. ...Alexander Kristoff, Norway — 5:46:05

INDIVIDUAL TIME TRIAL
1. ...Bradley Wiggins, Great Britain — 50:39.54
2. ...Tony Martin, Germany — 51:21.54
3. ...Christopher Froome, Great Britain — 51:47.87

TEAM PURSUIT
1. ...Great Britain: (E. Clancy, P. Kennaugh, 3:51.659
......S. Burke, G. Thomas)
2. ...Australia — 3:54.581
3. ...New Zealand — 3:55.952

SPRINT
1. ...Jason Kenny, Great Britain
2. ...Gregory Bauge, France
3. ...Shane Perkins, Australia

OMNIUM
1. ...Lasse Norman Hansen, Denmark — 27 pts
2. ...Bryan Coquard, France — 29 pts
3. ...Edward Clancy, Great Britain — 30 pts

KEIRIN
1. ...Chris Hoy, Great Britain
2. ...Maximilian Levy, Germany
3. ...Teun Mulder, Netherlands
3. ...Simon van Velthooven, New Zealand

TEAM SPRINT
1. ...Great Britain: (Hoy, Kenny, Hindes)42.600 WR
2. ...France — 43.013
3. ...Germany — 43.209

CROSS COUNTRY
1. ...Jaroslav Kulhavy, Czech Republic — 1:29:07
2. ...Nino Schurter, Switzerland — 1:29:08
3. ...Marco Aurelio Fontana, Italy — 1:29:32

BMX
1. ...Maris Strombergs, Latvia — 37.58 pts
2. ...Sam Willoughby, Australia — 37.93 pts
3. ...C. Mario Oquendo Zabala, Colombia — 38.25 pts

Women

INDIVIDUAL TIME TRIAL
1. ...Kristin Armstrong, United States — 37:34.82
2. ...Judith Arndt, Germany — 37:50.29
3. ...Olga Zabelinskaya, Russia — 37:57.35

OMNIUM
1. ...Laura Trott, Great Britain — 18 pts
2. ...Sarah Hammer, United States — 19 pts
3. ...Annette Edmondson, Australia — 24 pts

TEAM PURSUIT
1. ...Great Britain: (Rowsell, Trott, King) 3:14.051
2. ...United States — 3:19.727
3. ...Australia — 3:18.096

SPRINT
1. ...Anna Meares, Australia
2. ...Victoria Pendleton, Great Britain
3. ...Shuang Guo, China

TEAM SPRINT
1. ...Germany: (K. Vogel, M. Welte)
2. ...China
3. ...Australia

ROAD RACE
1. ...Marianne Vos, Netherlands — 3:35:29
2. ...Elizabeth Armitstead, Great Britain — 3:35:29
3. ...Olga Zabelinskaya, Russia — 3:35:31

CROSS COUNTRY
1. ...Julie Bresset, France — 1:30:52
2. ...Sabine Spitz, Germany — 1:31:54
3. ...Georgia Gould, United States — 1:32:00

KEIRIN
1. ...Victoria Pendleton, Great Britain
2. ...Shuang Guo, China
3. ...Wai Sze Lee, Hong Kong

BMX
1. ...Mariana Pajon, Colombia — 37.71 pts
2. ...Sarah Walker, New Zealand — 38.13 pts
3. ...Laura Smulders, Netherlands — 38.23 pts

Note: WR=World Record.

DIVING

Men

3-METER SPRINGBOARD	Pts
1. ....Ilya Zakharov, Russia	555.90
2. ....Kai Qin, China	541.75
3. ....Chong He, China	524.15

10-METER PLATFORM	Pts
1.........David Boudia, United States	568.65
2.........Bo Qiu, China	566.85
3..........Thomas Daley, Great Britain	556.95

Women

3-METER SPRINGBOARD	Pts
1. ....Minxia Wu, China	414.0
2. ....Zi He, China	379.2
3. ....Laura Sanchez Soto, Mexico	362.4

10-METER PLATFORM	Pts
1.........Ruolin Chen, China	422.3
2.........Brittany Broben, Australia	366.5
3.........Pandelela Rinong Pamg, Malaysia	359.2

EQUESTRIAN

TEAM EVENTING	Pen. Pts
1. ......Germany: (I. Klimke, D. Schrade, ...P. Thomsen)	133.7
2. ......Great Britain	138.2
3. ......New Zealand	144.4

INDIVIDUAL EVENTING	Pen. Pts
1. ......Michael Jung, Germany	40.6
2. ......Sara Algotsson Ostholt, Sweden	43.3
3. ......Sandra Auffarth, Germany	44.8

TEAM DRESSAGE	Pts
1. ......Great Britain: (C. Hester, ...L. Bechtolsheimer, C. Dujardin)	79.979
2. ......Germany	78.216
3. Netherlands	77.124

INDIVIDUAL DRESSAGE	Pts
1. ......Charlotte Dujardin, Great Britain	90.089
2. ......Adelinde Cornelissen, Netherlands	88.196
3. ......Laura Bechtolsheimer, Great Britain	84.339

TEAM JUMPING	Pen. Pts
1. ......Great Britain: (P. Charles, B. Maher, S. Brash, N. Skelton)	8
2. ......Netherlands	8
3. ......Saudi Arabia	14

INDIVIDUAL JUMPING	Pen. Pts
1. ......Steve Guerdat, Switzerland	0
2. ......Gerco Schroder, Netherlands	1
3. ......Cian O'Connor, Ireland	1

FENCING

Men

FOIL
1. ......Sheng Lei, China
2. ......A. Abouelkassem, Egypt
3. ....Byungchul Choi, South Korea

SABRE
1. ......Aron Szilagyi, Hungary
2. ......Diego Occhiuzzi, Italy
3. ......Nikolay Kovalev, Russia

ÉPÉE
1. ......Ruben Limardo Gascon, Venezuela
2. ......Bartosz Piasecki, Norway
3. ......Jinsun Jung, South Korea

TEAM SABRE
1.   South Korea: (J. Kim, W. Young Won, B. Gu)
2. ......Romania

TEAM FOIL
1.......Italy: (A. Cassara, A. Baldini,V. Aspromonte)
2.......Japan
3.......Germany

Women

FOIL
1......Elisa di Francisca, Italy
2.....Arianna Errigo, Italy
3......Valentina Vezzali, Italy

SABRE
1.....Jiyeon Kim, South Korea
2.....Sofya Velikaya, Russia
3......Olga Kharlan, Ukraine

ÉPÉE
1. ......Yana Shemyakina, Ukraine
2. ......Britta Heidemann, Germany
3. ......Yujie Sun, China

TEAM ÉPÉE
1. ......China: (Y. Sun, N. Li, X. Luo)
2. ......South Korea
3. ......United States

3. ......Italy

TEAM FOIL
1. ......Italy: (V. Vezzali, A. Errigo, ...E. di Francisca
2. ......Russia
3. ......South Korea

FIELD HOCKEY

Men

1. ....Germany
2. ....Netherlands
3. ....Australia

Women

1. ....Netherlands
2. ....Argentina
3. ....Great Britain

GYMNASTICS

Men

ALL-AROUND	Pts
1. ....Kohei Uchimura, Japan	92.690
2. ....Marcel Nguyen, Germany	91.031
3. ....Danell Leyva, United States	90.698

PARALLEL BARS	Pts
1. ....Zhe Feng, China	15.966
2. ....Marcel Nguyen, Germany	15.800
3. ....Hamilton Sabot, France	15.566

HORIZONTAL BAR	Pts
1. ....Epke Zonderland, Netherlands	16.533
2. ....Fabian Hambuchen, Germany	16.400
3. ....Kai Zou, China	16.366

VAULT	Pts
1. ....Hak Seon Yang, South Korea	16.533
2. ....Denis Ablyazin, Russia	16.399
3. ....Igor Radivilov, Ukraine	16.316

GYMNASTICS *(Cont.)*
Men *(Cont.)*

POMMEL HORSE Pts
1. ....Krisztian Berki, Hungary 16.066
2. ....Louis Smith, Great Britain 16.066
3. ....Max Whitlock, Great Britain 15.600

RINGS Pts
1. ....Arthur Nabarrete Zanetti, Brazil 15.900
2. ....Yibing Chen, China 15.800
3. ....Matteo Morandi, Italy 15.733

FLOOR EXERCISE Pts
1. ....Kai Zou, China 15.933
2. ....Kohei Uchimura, Japan 15.800
3. ....Denis Ablyazin, Russia 15.800

TEAM COMBINED EXERCISES
1. ....China: (C. Zhang, K. Zou, 275.997
   Y. Chen, Z. Feng)
2. ....Japan 271.952
3. ....Great Britain 271.711

Women

ALL-AROUND Pts
1. ....Gabrielle Douglas, United States 62.232
2. ....Victoria Komova, Russia 61.973
3. ....Aliya Mustafina, Russia 59.566

VAULT Pts
1. ....Sandra Raluca Izbasa, Romania 15.191
2. ....McKayla Maroney, United States 15.083
3. ....Maria Paseka, Russia 15.050

UNEVEN BARS Pts
1. ....Aliya Mustafina, Russia 16.133
2. ....Kexin He, China 15.933
3. ....Elizabeth Tweddle, Great Britain 15.916

BALANCE BEAM Pts
1. ....Linlin Deng, China 15.600
2. ....Lu Sui, China 15.500
3. ....Alexandra Raisman, United States 15.066

FLOOR EXERCISE Pts
1. ....Alexandra Raisman, United States 15.600
2. ....Catalina Ponor, Romania 15.200
3. ....Aliya Mustafina, Russia 14.900

TEAM COMBINED EXERCISES
1. ....United States: (J. Wieber, G. Douglas, 183.596
   K. Ross, A. Raisman, M. Maroney)
2. ....Russia 178.530
3. ....Romania 176.414

RHYTHMIC TEAM
1. ....Russia 57.000
2. ....Belarus 55.500
3. ....Italy 55.450

RHYTHMIC INDIVIDUAL ALL-AROUND
1. ....Evgeniya Kanaeva, Russia 116.900
2. ....Daria Dmitrieva, Russia 114.500
3. ....Liubou Charkashyna, Belarus 111.700

JUDO
Men

EXTRA-LIGHTWEIGHT
1. ....Arsen Galstyan, Russia
2. ....Hiroaki Hiraoka, Japan
3. ....Rishod Sobirov, Uzbekistan
3. ....Felipe Kitadai, Brazil

HALF-LIGHTWEIGHT
1. ....Lasha Shavdatuashvili, Georgia
2. ....Miklos Ungvari, Hungary
3. ....Jun-Ho Cho, South Korea
3. ....Masashi Ebinuma, Japan

LIGHTWEIGHT
1. ....Mansur Isaev, Russia
2. ....Riki Nakaya, Japan
3. ....Nyam-Ochir Sainjargal, Mongolia
3. ....Ugo Legrand, France

HALF-MIDDLEWEIGHT
1. ....Jae-Bum Kim, South Korea
2. ....Ole Bischof, Germany
3. ....Antoine Valois-Fortier, Canada
3. ....Ivan Nifontov, Russia

MIDDLEWEIGHT
1. ....Dae-Nam Song, South Korea
2. ....Asley Gonzalez, Cuba
3. ....Ilias Iliadis, Greece
3. ....Masashi Nishiyama, Japan

HALF-HEAVYWEIGHT
1. ....Tagir Khaibulaev, Russia
2. ....Tuvshinbayar Naidan, Mongolia
3. ....Dimitri Peters, Germany
3. ....Henk Grol, Netherlands

HEAVYWEIGHT
1. ....Teddy Riner, France
2. ....Alexander Mikhaylin, Russia
3. ....Rafael Silva, Brazil
3. ....Andreas Toelzer, Germany

Women

EXTRA-LIGHTWEIGHT
1. ....Sarah Menezes, Brazil
2. ....Alina Dumitru, Romania
3. ....Eva Csernoviczki, Hungary
3. ....Charline van Snick, Belgium

HALF-LIGHTWEIGHT
1. ....Kum Ae An, North Korea
2. ....Yanet Bermoy Acosta, Cuba
3. ....Priscilla Gneto, France
3. ....Rosalba Forciniti, Italy

LIGHTWEIGHT
1. ....Kaori Matsumoto, Japan
2. ....Corina Caprioriu, Romania
3. ....Marti Malloy, United States
3. ....Automne Pavia, France

HALF-MIDDLEWEIGHT
1. ....Urska Zolnir, Slovenia
2. ....Lili Xu, China
3. ....Gevrise Emane, France
3. ....Yoshie Ueno, Japan

MIDDLEWEIGHT
1. ....Lucie Decosse, France
2. ....Kerstin Thiele, Germany
3. ....Yuri Alvear, Colombia
3. ....Edith Bosch, Netherlands

HALF-HEAVYWEIGHT
1. ....Kayla Harrison, United States
2. ....Gemma Gibbons, Great Britain
3. ....Mayra Aguiar, Brazil
3. ....Audrey Tcheumeo, France

HEAVYWEIGHT
1. ....Idalys Ortiz, Cuba
2. ....Mika Sugimoto, Japan
3. ....Wen Tong, China
3. ....Karina Bryant, Great Britain

MODERN PENTATHLON

Men

1. ......David Svoboda, Czech Republic	5928
2. ......Zhongrong Cao, China	5904
3. ......Adam Marosi, Hungary	5836

Women

1. ......Laura Asadauskaite, Lithuania	5408
2. ......Samantha Murray, Great Britain	5356
3. ......Yane Marques, Brazil	5340

ROWING

Men

SINGLE SCULLS

1. ...Mahe Drysdale, New Zealand	6:57.82
2. ...Ondrej Synek, Czech Republic	6:59.37
3. ...Alan Campbell, Great Britain	7:03.28

DOUBLE SCULLS

1. ...N. Cohen/J. Sullivan, New Zealand	6:31.67
2. ...R. Battisti/A. Sartori, Italy	6:32.80
3. ...I. Cop/L. Spik, Slovenia	6:34.35

LIGHTWEIGHT DOUBLE SCULLS

1. ...R. Quist/M. Rasmussen, Denmark	6:37.17
2. ...M. Hunter/Z. Purchase, Great Britain	6:37.78
3. ...P. Taylor/S. Uru, New Zealand	6:40.86

QUADRUPLE SCULLS

1. ...Germany	5:42.48
2. ...Croatia	5:44.78
3. ...Australia	5:45.22

COXLESS PAIR

1. ...H. Bond/E. Murray, New Zealand	6:16.65
2. ...D. Mortelette/G. Chardin, France	6:21.11
3. ...W. Satch/G. Nash, Great Britain	6:21.77

COXLESS FOUR

1. ...Great Britain	6:03.97
2. ...Australia	6:05.19
3. ...United States	6:07.20

LIGHTWEIGHT COXLESS FOUR

1. ...South Africa	6:02.84
2. ...Great Britain	6:03.09
3. ...Denmark	6:03.16

EIGHT-OARS

1. ...Germany	5:48.75
2. ...Canada	5:49.98
3. ...Great Britain	5:51.18

Women

SINGLE SCULLS

1. ...Miroslava Knapkova, Czech Republic	7:54.37
2. ...Fie Udby Erichsen, Denmark	7:57.72
3. ...Kim Crow, Australia	7:58.04

DOUBLE SCULLS

1. ...K. Grainger/A. Watkins, Great Britain	6:55.82
2. ...B. Pratley/K. Crow, Australia	6:58.55
3. ...J. Michalska/M. Fularczyk, Poland	7:07.92

LIGHTWEIGHT DOUBLE SCULLS

1. ...S. Hosking/K. Copeland, Great Britain	7:09.30
2. ...W. Huang/D. Xu, China	7:11.93
3. ...A. Tsiavou/C. Giazitzidou, Greece	7:12.09

QUADRUPLE SCULLS

1. ...Ukraine	6:35.93
2. ...Germany	6:38.09
3. ...United States	6:40.63

COXLESS PAIR

1. ...H. Stanning/H. Glover, Great Britain	7:27.13
2. ...S. Tait/K. Hornsey, Australia	7:29.86
3. ...J. Haigh/R. Scown, New Zealand	7:30.19

EIGHT-OARS

1. ...United States	6:10.59
2. ...Canada	6:12.06
3. ...Netherlands	6:13.12

SHOOTING

Men

25M RAPID-FIRE PISTOL — Pts

1. ....Leuris Pupo, Cuba	34
2. ....Vijay Kumar, India	30
3. ....Feng Ding, China	27

50M FREE PISTOL — Pts

1. ....Jongoh Jin, South Korea	662.0
2. ....Young Rae Choi, South Korea	661.5
3. ....Zhiwei Wang, China	658.6

10M AIR PISTOL — Pts

1. ....Jongoh Jin, South Korea	688.2
2. ....Luca Tesconi, Italy	685.8
3. ....Andrija Zlatic, Serbia	685.2

50M FREE RIFLE, THREE-POSITION — Pts

1. ....Niccolo Campriani, Italy	1278.5
2. ....Jonghyun Kim, South Korea	1272.5
3. ....Matthew Emmons, United States	1271.3

50M FREE RIFLE, PRONE — Pts

1. ....Sergei Martynov, Belarus	705.5
2. ....Lionel Cox, Belgium	701.2
3. ....Rajmond Debevec, Slovenia	701.0

10M AIR RIFLE — Pts

1. ....Alin George Moldoveanu, Romania	702.1
2. ....Niccolo Campriani, Italy	701.5
3. ....Gagan Narang, India	701.1

SHOOTING (CONT.)

Men (Cont.)

TRAP	Pts
1. ....Giovanni Cernogoraz, Croatia	146
2. ....Massimo Fabbrizi, Italy	146
3. ....Fehaid Aldeehani, Kuwait	145

DOUBLE TRAP	Pts
1. ....Peter Robert Russell Wilson, Great Britain	188
2. ....Hakan Dahlby, Sweden	186
3. ....Vasily Mosin, Russia	185

SKEET	Pts
1. ....Vincent Hancock, United States	148
2. ....Anders Golding, Denmark	146
3. ....Nasser Al-Attiya, Qatar	144

Women

25M SPORT PISTOL	Pts
1. ......Jangmi Kim, South Korea	792.4
2. ......Ying Chen, China	791.4
3. ......Olena Kostevych, Ukraine	788.6

10M AIR PISTOL	Pts
1. ......Wenjun Guo, China	488.1
2. ......Celine Goberville, France	486.6
3. ......Olena Kostevych, Ukraine	486.6

50M STANDARD RIFLE, THREE-POSITION	Pts
1. ......Jamie Lynn Gray, United States	691.9
2. ......Ivana Maksimovic, Serbia	687.5
3. ......Adela Sykorova, Czech Republic	683.0

10M AIR RIFLE	Pts
1. ......Siling Yi, China	502.9
2. ......Sylwia Bogacka, Poland	502.2
3. ......Dan Yu, China	501.5

TRAP	Pts
1. ......Jessica Rossi, Italy	99
2. ......Zuzana Stefecekova, Slovakia	93
3. ......Delphine Reau, France	93

SKEET	Pts
1. ......Kimberly Rhode, United States	99
2. ......Ning Wei, China	91
3. ......Danka Bartekova, Slovakia	90

SOCCER

Men

1. ....Mexico
2. ....Brazil
3. ....South Korea

Women

1. ....United States
2. ....Japan
3. ....Canada

SWIMMING - Men

50-METER FREESTYLE	
1. ...Florent Manaudou, France	21.34
2. ...Cullen Jones, United States	21.54
3. ...Cesar Cielo, Brazil	21.59

100-METER FREESTYLE	
1. ...Nathan Adrian, United States	47.52
2. ...James Magnussen, Australia	47.53
3. ...Brent Hayden, Canada	47.80

200-METER FREESTYLE	
1. ...Yannick Agnel, France	1:43.14
2. ...Yang Sun, China	1:44.93
3. ...Taehwan Park, South Korea	1:44.93

400-METER FREESTYLE	
1. ...Yang Sun, China	3:40.14 OR
2. ...Taehwan Park, South Korea	3:42.06
3. ...Peter Vanderkaay, United States	3:44.69

1,500-METER FREESTYLE	
1. ...Yang Sun, China	14:31.02 WR
2. ...Ryan Cochrane, Canada	14:39.63
3. ...Oussama Mellouli, Tunisia	14:40.31

100-METER BACKSTROKE	
1. ...Matthew Grevers, United States	52.16 OR
2. ...Nick Thoman, United States	52.92
3. ...Ryosuke Irie, Japan	52.97

200-METER BACKSTROKE	
1. ...Tyler Clary, United States	1:53.41 OR
2. ...Ryosuke Irie, Japan	1:53.78
3. ...Ryan Lochte, United States	1:53.94

100-METER BREASTSTROKE	
1. ...Cameron van der Burgh, South Africa	58.46 WR
2. ...Christian Sprenger, Australia	58.93
3. ...Brendan Hansen, United States	59.49

200-METER BREASTSTROKE	
1. ...Daniel Gyurta, Hungary	2:07.28 WR
2. ...Michael Jamieson, Great Britain	2:07.43
3. ...Ryo Tateishi, Japan	2:08.29

100-METER BUTTERFLY	
1. ...Michael Phelps, United States	51.21
2. ...Chad le Clos, South Africa	51.44
3. ...Evgeny Korotyshkin, Russia	51.44

200-METER BUTTERFLY	
1. ...Chad le Clos, South Africa	1:52.96
2. ...Michael Phelps, United States	1:53.01
3. ...Takeshi Matsuda, Japan	1:53.21

200-METER INDIVIDUAL MEDLEY	
1. ...Michael Phelps, United States	1:54.27
2. ...Ryan Lochte, United States	1:54.90
3. ...Laszlo Cseh, Hungary	1:56.22

400-METER INDIVIDUAL MEDLEY	
1. ...Ryan Lochte, United States	4:05.18
2. ...Thiago Pereira, Brazil	4:08.86
3. ...Kosuke Hagino, Japan	4:08.94

4 X 100-METER MEDLEY RELAY	
1. ...United States: (M. Grevers, B. Hansen, M. Phelps, N. Adrian)	3:29.35
2. ...Japan	3:31.26
3. ...Australia	3:31.58

4 X 100-METER FREESTYLE RELAY	
1. ...France: (A. Leveaux, F. Gilot, C. Lefert, Y. Agnel)	3:09.93
2. ...United States	3:10.38
3. ...Russia	3:11.41

Note: OR=Olympic record. WR=world record. EOR=equals Olympic record. EWR=equals world record.

SWIMMING - Men (Cont.)

4 X 200-METER FREESTYLE RELAY

1. ...United States: (R. Lochte, C. Dwyer 6:59.70
   R. Berens, M. Phelps)
2. .....France   7:02.77
3. .....China   7:06.30

10 KM MARATHON

1. ...Oussama Mellouli, Tunisia   1:49:55.1
2. ...Thomas Lurz, Germany   1:49:58.5
3. ...Richard Weinberger, Canada   1:50:00.3

Women

50-METER FREESTYLE

1. ...Ranomi Kromowidjojo, Netherlands 24.05 OR
2. ...Aliaksandra Herasimenia, Belarus 24.28
3. ...Marleen Veldhuis, Netherlands   24.39

100-METER FREESTYLE

1. ...Ranomi Kromowidjojo, Netherlands 53.00 OR
2. ...Aliaksandra Herasimenia, Belarus 53.38
3. ...Yi Tang, China   53.44

200-METER FREESTYLE

1. ...Allison Schmitt, United States   1:53.61 OR
2. ...Camille Muffat, France   1:55.58
3. ...Bronte Barratt, Australia   1:55.81

400-METER FREESTYLE

1. ...Camille Muffat, France   4:01.45 OR
2. ...Allison Schmitt, United States   4:01.77
3. ...Rebecca Adlington, Great Britain 4:03.01

800-METER FREESTYLE

1. ...Katie Ledecky, United States   8:14.63
2. ...Mireia Belmonte Garcia, Spain   8:18.76
3. ...Rebecca Adlington, Great Britain 8:20.32

100-METER BACKSTROKE

1. ...Missy Franklin, United States   58.33
2. ...Emily Seebohm, Australia   58.68
3. ...Aya Terakawa, Japan   58.83

200-METER BACKSTROKE

1. ...Missy Franklin, United States   2:04.06 WR
2. ...Anastasia Zueva, Russia   2:05.92
3. ...Elizabeth Beisel, United States   2:06.55

100-METER BREASTSTROKE

1. ...Ruta Meilutyte, Lithuania   1:05.47
2. ...Rebecca Soni, United States   1:05.55
3. ...Satomi Suzuki, Japan   1:06.46

200-METER BREASTSTROKE

1. ...Rebecca Soni, United States   2:19.59 WR
2. ...Satomi Suzuki, Japan   2:20.72
3. ...Iuliia Efimova, Russia   2:20.92

100-METER BUTTERFLY

1. ...Dana Vollmer, United States   55.98 WR
2. ...Ying Lu, China   56.87
3. ...Alicia Coutts, Australia   56.94

200-METER BUTTERFLY

1. ...Liuyang Jiao, China   2:04.06 OR
2. ...Mireia Belmonte Garcia, Spain   2:05.25
3. ...Natsumi Hoshi, Japa   2:05.48

200-METER INDIVIDUAL MEDLEY

1. ...Shiwen Ye, China   2:07.57 OR
2. ...Alicia Coutts, Australia   2:08.15
3. ...Caitlin Leverenz, United States   2:08.95

400-METER INDIVIDUAL MEDLEY

1. ...Shiwen Ye, China   4:28.43 WR
2. ...Elizabeth Beisel, United States   4:31.27
3. ...Xuanxu Li, China   4:32.91

4 X 100-METER MEDLEY RELAY

1. ...United States: (M. Franklin, R. Soni, 3:52.05 WR
   D. Vollmer, A. Schmitt)
2. ...Australia   3:54.02
3. ...Japan   3:55.73

4 X 100-METER FREESTYLE RELAY

1. ...Australia: (A. Coutts, C. Campbell, 3:33.15 OR
   B. Elmslie, M. Schlanger)
2. ...Netherlands   3:33.79
3. ...United States   3:34.24

4 X 200-METER FREESTYLE RELAY

1. .....United States: (M. Franklin, D. Vollmer, 7:42.92 OR
   S. Vreeland, A. Schmitt)
2. .....Australia   7:44.41
3. .....France   7:47.49

10-KM MARATHON

1. ...Eva Risztov, Hungary   1:57:38.2
2. ...Haley Anderson, United States   1:57:38.6
3. ...Martina Grimaldi, Italy   1:57:41.8

SYNCHRONIZED DIVING

Men

3M SPRINGBOARD

		Pts
1.	..........K. Qin/Y. Luo, China	477.00
2.	..........I. Zakharov/E. Kuznetsov, Russia	459.63
3.	..........T. Dumais/K. Ipsen, United States	446.7

10M PLATFORM

		Pts
1.	..........Y. Cao/Y. Zhang, China	486.78
2.	..........G. Sanchez Sanchez/	468.90
	I. Garcia Navarro, Mexico	
3.	..........D. Boudia/N. Mccrory, United States	463.47

Women

3M SPRINGBOARD

		Pts
1.	..........Z. He/M. Wu, China	346.2
2.	...........A. Johnston/K. Bryant, United States	321.9
3.	..........E. Heymans/J. Abel, Canada	316.8

10M PLATFORM

		Pts
1.	..........H. Wang/R. Chen, China	368.40
2.	..........P. Espinosa Sanchez/	343.32
	A. Orozco Loza, Mexico	
3.	..........R. Filion/M. Benfeito, Canada	337.62

Note: OR=Olympic record. WR=world record. EOR=equals Olympic record. EWR=equals world record.

SYNCHRONIZED SWIMMING

DUET
1..........S. Romashina/N. Ishchenko, Russia
2..........O. Carbonell Ballestero/A. Fuentes Fache, Spain
3..........X. Huang/O. Liu, China

TEAM
1............................Russia
2............................China
3............................Spain

TABLE TENNIS

Men

SINGLES
1. ....Jike Zhang, China
2. ....Hao Wang, China
3. ....Dimitrij Ovtcharov, Germany

TEAM
1. ....China: (H. Wang, L. Ma, J. Zhang)
2. ....South Korea
3. ....Germany

Women

SINGLES
1. ....Xiaoxia Li, China
2. ....Ning Ding, China
3. ....Tianwei Feng, Singapore

TEAM
1. ....China: (X. Li, Y. Guo, N. Ding)
2. ....Japan
3. ....Singapore

TAEKWONDO

Men

FLYWEIGHT
1. ....Joel Gonzalez Bonilla, Spain
2. ....Daehoon Lee, South Korea
3. ....Alexey Denisenko, Russia
3. ....Oscar Munoz Oviedo, Colombia

FEATHERWEIGHT
1. ....Servet Tazegul, Turkey
2. ....Mohammad Bagheri Motamed, Iran
3. ....Rohullah Nikpah, Afghanistan
3. ....Terrence Jennings, United States

WELTERWEIGHT
1. ....S. Eduardo Crismanich, Argentina
2. ....Nicolas Garcia Hemme, Spain
3. ....Lutalo Muhammad, Great Britain
3. ....Mauro Sarmiento, Italy

HEAVYWEIGHT
1. ....Carlo Molfetta, Italy
2. ....Anthony Obame, Gabon
3. ....Xiaobo Liu, China
3. ....Robelis Despaigne, Cuba

Women

FLYWEIGHT
1. ....Jingyu Wu, China
2. ....Brigitte Yague Enrique, Spain
3. ....Chanatip Sonkham, Thailand
3. ....Lucija Zaninovic, Croatia

FEATHERWEIGHT
1. ....Jade Jones, Great Britain
2. ....Yuzhuo Hou, China
3. ....Marlene Harnois, France
3. ....Li-Cheng Tseng, Taiwan

WELTERWEIGHT
1. ....Kyung Seon Hwang, South Korea
2. ....Nur Tatar, Turkey
3. ....Paige McPherson, United States
3. ....Helena Fromm, Germany

HEAVYWEIGHT
1. ....Milica Mandic, Serbia
2. ....Anne-Caroline Graffe, France
3. ....Maria del Rosario Espinoza, Mexico
3. ....Anastasiia Baryshnikova, Russia

TEAM HANDBALL

Men
1. ....France
2. ....Sweden
3. ....Croatia

Women
1. ....Montenegro
2. ....Norway
3. ....Spain

TENNIS

Men

SINGLES
1..........Andy Murray, Great Britain
2..........Roger Federer, Switzerland
3..........Juan Martin del Potro, Argentina

DOUBLES
1...........Mike Bryan/Bob Bryan, United States
2...........Michael Llodra/Jo-Wilfried Tsonga, France
3...........Julien Benneteau/Richard Gasquet, France

Women

SINGLES
1..........Serena Williams, United States
2..........Maria Sharapova, Russia
3..........Victoria Azarenka, Belarus

DOUBLES
1..........Serena Willams/Venus Williams, United States
2..........Andrea Hlavackova/Lucie Hradecka, Czech Rep.
3..........Maria Kirilenko/Nadia Petrova, Russia

MIXED DOUBLES
1..........Max Mirnyi/Victoria Azarenka, Belarus
2..........Andy Murray/Laura Robson, Great Britain
3..........Mike Bryan/Lisa Raymond, United States

TRAMPOLINE

Men
1. ....Dong Dong, China   62.990
2. ....Dmitry Ushakov, Russia   61.769
3. ....Chunlong Lu, China   61.319

Women
1. ....Rosannagh Maclennan, Canada   57.305
2. ....Shanshan Huang, China   56.730
3. ....Wenna He, China   55.950

TRIATHLON

Men		Women	
1..........Alistair Brownlee, Great Britain	1:46:25	1..........Nicola Spirig, Switzerland	1:59:48.00
2..........Javier Gomez, Spain	1:46:36	2..........Lisa Norden, Sweden	1:59:48.00
3..........Jonathan Brownlee, Great Britain	1:46:56	3..........Erin Densham, Australia	1:59:50.00

VOLLEYBALL

Men	Women
1..........Russia	1..........Brazil
2..........Brazil	2..........United States
3..........Italy	3..........Japan

BEACH VOLLEYBALL

Men	Women
1. ...Jonas Reckermann/Julius Brink, Germany	1. ....Misty May-Treanor/Kerri Walsh Jennings, United States
2. ...Emanuel Rego/Alison Cerutti, Brazil	2. ...Jennifer Kessy/April Ross, United States
3. ...Janis Smedins/Martins Plavins, Latvia	3. ...Larissa Franca/Juliana Silva, Brazil

WATER POLO

Men	Women
1..........Croatia	1..........United States
2..........Italy	2..........Spain
3..........Serbia	3..........Australia

WEIGHTLIFTING - Men

123 POUNDS		187 POUNDS	
1..........Yun Chol Om, North Korea	644.60 lbs	1..........Adrian E. Zielinski, Poland	847.00 lbs
2..........Jingbiao Wu, China	635.80 lbs	2..........Apti Aukhadov, Russia	847.00 lbs
3..........Valentin Hristov, Azerbaijan	629.20 lbs	3..........Kianoush Rostami, Iran	836.00 lbs
137 POUNDS		**207 POUNDS**	
1..........Un Guk Kim, North Korea	719.40 lbs WR	1..........Ilya Ilyin, Kazakhstan	919.60 lbs WR
2..........Oscar Mosquera, Colombia	697.40 lbs	2..........Alexandr Ivanov, Russia	899.80 lbs
2..........Irawan Eko Yuli, Indonesia	697.40 lbs	3..........Anatoli Ciricu, Moldova	895.40 lbs
152 POUNDS		**231 POUNDS**	
1..........Qingfeng Lin, China	756.80 lbs	1..........Oleksiy Torokhtiy, Ukraine	906.40 lbs
2..........Triyatno, Indonesia	732.60 lbs	2..........Navab Nasirshelal, Iran	904.20 lbs
3..........R. Constantin Martin, Romania	730.40 lbs	3..........B. Wojciech Bonk, Poland	902.00 lbs
170 POUNDS		**231+ POUNDS**	
1..........Xiaojun Lu, China	833.80 lbs WR	1..........Behdad Salimikordasiabi, Iran	1,001.00 lbs
2..........Haojie Lu, China	792.00 lbs	2. ....S. Anoushiravani Hamlabad, Iran	987.80 lbs
3..........Ivan Cambar Rodriguez, Cuba	767.80 lbs	3...........Ruslan Albegov, Russia	985.60 lbs

Women

106 POUNDS		152 POUNDS	
1. ....Mingjuan Wang, China	451.00 lbs	1..........Jong Sim Rim, North Korea	574.20 lbs
2. ....Hiromi Miyake, Japan	433.40 lbs	2..........Roxana Daniela Cocos, Romania	563.20 lbs
3. ....Chun Hwa Ryang, North Korea	422.40 lbs	3..........Maryna Shkermankova, Belarus	563.20 lbs
117 POUNDS		**165 POUNDS**	
1. ....Zulfiya Chinshanlo, Kazakhstan	497.20 lbs OR	1. ....S. Podobedova, Kazakhstan	640.20 lbs
2. ....Shu-Ching Hsu, Taiwan	481.80 lbs	2. ....Natalya Zabolotnaya, Russia	640.20 lbs OR
3. ....Cristina Iovu, Moldova	481.80 lbs	3. ....Iryna Kulesha, Belarus	591.80 lbs
128 POUNDS		**165+ POUNDS**	
1. ....Xueying Li, China	541.2 lbs OR	1...............Lulu Zhou, China	732.60 lbs WR
2. ....Pimsiri Sirikaew, Thailand	519.20 lbs	2..........Tatiana Kashirina, Russia	730.40 lbs
3. ....Yuliya Kalina, Ukraine	517.00 lbs	3. ....Hripsime Khurshudyan, Armenia	646.80 lbs
139 POUNDS			
1...........Maiya Maneza, Kazakhstan	539 lbs OR		
2...........Svetlana Tsarukaeva, Russia	521.40 lbs		
3. ....Christine Girard, Canada	519.20 lbs		

Note: OR=Olympic Record. WR=World Record. EOR=Equals Olympic Record. EWR=Equals World Record.

FREESTYLE WRESTLING

MEN

121 POUNDS
1. ....Dzhamal Otarsultanov, Russia
2. ....Vladimer Khinchegashvili, Georgia
3. ....Shinichi Yumoto, Japan
3. ....Kyong Il Yang, North Korea

132 POUNDS
1. ....Toghrul Asgarov. Azerbaijan
2. ....Besik Kudukhov, Russia
3. ....Coleman Scott, United States
3. ....Yogeshwar Dutt, India

145.5 POUNDS
1. ....Tatsuhiro Yonemitsu, Japan
2. ....Sushil Kumar, India
3. ....Livan Lopez Azcuy, Cuba
3. ....Akzhurek Tanatarov, Kazakhstan

163 POUNDS
1. ....Jordan Ernest Burroughs, United States
2. ....Sadegh Saeed Goudarzi, Iran
3. ....Soslan Tigiev, Uzbekistan
3. ....Denis Tsargush, Russia

MEN (CONT.)

185 POUNDS
1. ....Sharif Sharifov, Azerbaijan
2. ....Jaime Yusept Espinal, Puerto Rico
3. ....Ehsan Naser Lashgari, Iran
3. ....Dato Marsagishvili, Georgia

211.5 POUNDS
1. ....Jacob Stephen Varner, United States
2. ....Valerii Andriitsev, Ukraine
3. ....George Gogshelidze, Georgia
3. ....Khetag Gazyumov, Azerbaijan

264.5 POUNDS
1. ....Artur Taymazov, Uzbekistan
2. ....Davit Modzmanashvili, Georgia
3. ....Bilyal Makhov, Russia
3. ....Komeil Ghasemi, Iran

WOMEN

106 POUNDS
1. ...Hitomi Obara, Japan
2. ...Mariya Stadnyk, Azerbaijan
3. ...Clarissa Chun, United States
3. ...Carol Huynh, Canada

121 POUNDS
1. ...Saori Yoshida, Japan
2. ...Tonya Lynn Verbeek, Canada
3. ...J. Renteria Castillo, Colombia
3. ...Yuliya Ratkevich, Azerbaijan

139 POUNDS
1. ...Kaori Icho, Japan
2. ...Ruixue Jing, China
3. ...B. Soronzonbold, Mongolia
3. ...Lubov Volosova, Russia

159 POUNDS
1. ...Natalia Vorobeva, Russia
2. ...Stanka Zlateva Hristova, Bulgaria
3. ...Guzel Manyurova, Kazakhstan
3. M. Unda Gonzalez de Audicana, Spain

GRECO-ROMAN WRESTLING

121 POUNDS
1. ....H. Mohammad Soryan Reihanpour, Iran
2. ....Rovshan Bayramov, Azerbaijan
3. ....Peter Modos, Hungary
3. ....Mingiyan Semenov, Russia

132 POUNDS
1. ....Omid Haji Noroozi, Iran
2. ....Revaz Lashkhi, Georgia
3. ....Ryutaro Matsumoto, Japan
3. ....Z. Kuramagomedov, Russia

145.5 POUNDS
1. ....Hyeonwoo Kim, South Korea
2. ....Tamas Lorincz, Hungary
3. ....Manuchar Tskhadaia, Georgia
3. ....Steeve Guenot, France

163 POUNDS
1. ....Roman Vlasov, Russia
2 ....Arsen Julfalakyan, Armenia
3. ....Emin Ahmadov, Azerbaijan
3. ....Aleksandr Kazakevic, Lithuania

185 POUNDS
1. ....Alan Khugaev, Russia
2. ....K. Mohamed Gaber Ebrahim, Egypt
3. ....Danyal Gajiyev, Kazakhstan
3. ....Damian Janikowski, Poland

211.5 POUNDS
1. ....Ghasem Gholamreza Rezaei, Iran
2. ....Rustam Totrov, Russia
3. ....Artur Aleksanyan, Armenia
3. ....Jimmy Lidberg, Sweden

264.5 POUNDS
1. ...Mijain Lopez Nunez, Cuba
2. ...Heiki Nabi, Estonia
3. ...Johan Euren, Sweden
3. ...Riza Kayaalp, Turkey

YACHTING

Men

470 - TWO-PERSON DINGHY
1. ....M. Page/M. Belcher, Australia
2. ....L. Patience/S. Bithell, Great Britain
3. ....L. Calabrese/J. de la Fuente, Argentina

FINN
1. ....Ben Ainslie, Great Britain
2. ....Jonas Hogh-Christensen, Denmark
3. ....Jonathan Lobert, France

ONE-PERSON DINGHY
1. ....Tom Slingsby, Australia
2. ....Pavlos Kontides, Cyprus
3. ....Rasmus Myrgren, Sweden

49ER SKIFF
1. ....I. Jensen/N. Outteridge, Australia
2. ....P. Burling/B. Tuke, New Zealand
3. ....P. Lang/A. Norregaard, Denmark

STAR
1. ....F. Loof/M. Salminen, Sweden
2. ....I. Percy/A. Simpson, Great Britain
3. ....B. Prada/R. Scheidt, Brazil

Men (Cont.)

RS:X - WINDSURFER
1. ....Dorian van Rijsselberge, Netherlands
2. ....Nick Dempsey, Great Britain
3. ....Przemyslaw Miarczynski, Poland

Women

ONE-PERSON DINGHY
1. ....Lijia Xu, China
2. ....Marit Bouwmeester, Netherlands
3. ....Evi Van Acker, Belgium

470 - TWO-PERSON DINGHY
1. ....O. Powrie/J. Aleh, New Zealand
2. ....S. Clark/H. Mills, Great Britain
3. ....L. Berkhout/L. Westerhof, Netherlands

KEEL
1. ....Spain
2. ....Australia
3. ....Finland

RS:X - WINDSURFER
1. ....Marina Alabau Neira, Spain
2. ....Tuuli Petaja, Finland
3. ....Zofia Noceti-Klepacka, Poland

Summer Olympic Games Locations and Dates

	Year	Site	Dates	Men	Women	Nations	Most Medals	US Medals
				COMPETITORS				
I	1896	Athens, Greece	Apr 6–15	311	0	13	Greece (10-19-18—47)	11-6-2—19 (2nd)
II	1900	Paris, France	May 20– Oct 28	1319	11	22	France (29-41-32—102)	20-14-19—53 (2nd)
III	1904	St Louis, United States	July 1– Nov 23	681	6	12	United States (80-86-72—238)	
—	1906	Athens, Greece	Apr 22– May 28	77	7	20	France (15-9-16—40)	12-6-5—23 (4th)
IV	1908	London, Great Britain	Apr 27– Oct 31	1999	36	23	Britain (56-50-39—145)	23-12-12—47 (2nd)
V	1912	Stockholm, Sweden	May 5– July 22	2490	57	28	Sweden (24-24-17—65)	23-19-19—61 (2nd)
VI	1916	Berlin, Germany	CANCELED BECAUSE OF WAR					
VII	1920	Antwerp, Belgium	Apr 20– Sep 12	2543	64	29	United States (41-27-28—96)	
VIII	1924	Paris, France	May 4– July 27	2956	136	44	United States (45-27-27—99)	
IX	1928	Amsterdam, Netherlands	May 17– Aug 12	2724	290	46	United States (22-18-16—56)	
X	1932	Los Angeles, United States	July 30– Aug 14	1281	127	37	United States (41-32-31—104)	
XI	1936	Berlin, Germany	Aug 1–16	3738	328	49	Germany (33-26-30—89)	24-20-12—56 (2nd)
XII	1940	Tokyo, Japan	CANCELED BECAUSE OF WAR					
XIII	1944	London, Great Britain	CANCELED BECAUSE OF WAR					
XIV	1948	London, Great Britain	July 29– Aug 14	3714	385	59	United States (38-27-19—84)	
XV	1952	Helsinki, Finland	July 19– Aug 3	4407	518	69	United States (40-19-17—76)	
XVI	1956	Melbourne, Australia*	Nov 22– Dec 8	2958	384	67	USSR (37-29-32—98)	32-25-17—74 (2nd)
XVII	1960	Rome, Italy	Aug 25– Sep 11	4738	610	83	USSR (43-29-31—103)	34-21-16—71 (2nd)
XVIII	1964	Tokyo, Japan	Oct 10–24	4457	683	93	United States (36-26-28—90)	
XIX	1968	Mexico City, Mexico	Oct 12–27	4750	781	112	United States (45-28-34—107)	
XX	1972	Munich, W Germany	Aug 26– Sep 10	5848	1299	122	USSR (50-27-22—99)	33-31-30—94 (2nd)
XXI	1976	Montreal, Canada	July 17– Aug 1	4834	1251	92†	USSR (49-41-35—125)	34-35-25—94 (3rd)
XXII	1980	Moscow, USSR	July 19– Aug 3	4265	1088	81‡	USSR (80-69-46—195)	Did not compete
XXIII	1984	Los Angeles, United States	July 28– Aug 12	5458	1620	141#	United States (83-61-30—174)	
XXIV	1988	Seoul, S Korea	Sep 17– Oct 2	7105	2476	160	USSR (55-31-46—132)	36-31-27—94 (3rd)
XXV	1992	Barcelona, Spain	July 25– Aug. 9	7555	3008	172	Unified Team (45-38-29—112)	37-34-37—108 (2nd)
XXVI	1996	Atlanta, United States	July 19– Aug 4	6984	3766	197	United States (44-32-25—101)	
XXVII	2000	Sydney, Australia	Sept 15– Oct 1	6862	4254	199	United States (39-25-33—97)	
XXVIII	2004	Athens, Greece	Aug 11– Aug 29	11,099 total		202	United States (35-39-29—103)	

	Year	Site	Dates	COMPETITORS Men	Women	Nations	Most Medals	US Medals
XXIX	2008	Beijing, China	Aug 8–Aug 24	11,028 total		204	United States (36-38-36—110)	
XXX	2012	London, England	July 27–August 12	10,903 total		205	United States (46-29-29—104)	

*The equestrian events were held in Stockholm, Sweden, June 10–17, 1956. †This figure includes Cameroon, Egypt, Morocco, and Tunisia, countries that boycotted the 1976 Olympics after some of their athletes had already competed. ‡The U.S. was among 65 countries that did not participate in the 1980 Summer Games in Moscow. #The USSR, East Germany, and 14 other countries did not participate in the 1984 Summer Games in Los Angeles.

Alltime Olympic Medal Winners

Summer

NATIONS

Nation	Gold	Silver	Bronze	Total	Nation	Gold	Silver	Bronze	Total
United States	990	765.5	679.5	2,435	East Germany (1956–88)	153	129	127	409
USSR (1952–1988)	440	357	325	1,122	Russia	119	140	135	394
Great Britain	238.5	276.5	280.5	796.5	Romania	87	104	123	314
Germany	208.5	253	256	717.5	Finland	101	83	115	299
(1896–1936, 1992–)					Canada	58	103	121	282
France	217	225	258	700	Poland	69	84	122	275
Italy	204	168	187	559	South Korea	93	82	91	266
China	219	153	129	501	Netherlands	76	83	107	266
Australia	137	170	180.5	487.5	Bulgaria	51	84	77	212
Sweden	141.5	164	172	477.5	Cuba	71	72	62	205
Hungary	162	145	170	477	West Germany (1952–88)	56	67	81	204
Japan	129	136	160	425	Denmark	42.5	66	72	180.5

INDIVIDUALS — OVERALL

Men

Athlete, Nation	Sport	G	S	B	Tot	Athlete, Nation	Sport	G	S	B	Tot
Michael Phelps, United States	Swim	18	2	2	22	Matt Biondi, United States	Swim	8	2	1	11
Nikolai Andrianov, USSR	Gym	7	5	3	15	Viktor Chukarin, USSR	Gym	7	3	1	11
Boris Shakhlin, USSR	Gym	7	4	2	13	Carl Osburn, United States	Shoot	5	4	2	11
Edoardo Mangiarotti, Italy	Fen	6	5	2	13	Ryan Lochte, United States	Swim	5	3	3	11
Takashi Ono, Japan	Gym	5	4	4	13	Ray Ewry, United States	Track	10	0	0	10
Paavo Nurmi, Finland	Track	9	3	0	12	Carl Lewis, United States	Track	9	1	0	10
Sawao Kato, Japan	Gym	8	3	1	12	Aladár Gerevich, Hungary	Fen	7	1	2	10
Alexei Nemov, Russia	Gym	4	2	6	12	Akinori Nakayama, Japan	Gym	6	2	2	10
Mark Spitz, United States	Swim	9	1	1	11	Vitaly Scherbo, UT/Belarus	Gym	6	0	4	10
						Aleksandr Dityatin, USSR	Gym	3	6	1	10

Women

Athlete, Nation	Sport	G	S	B	Tot	Athlete, Nation	Sport	G	S	B	Tot
Larissa Latynina, USSR	Gym	9	5	4	18	Dara Torres, United States	Swim	4	1	4	9
Jenny Thompson, United States	Swim	8	3	1	12	Nadia Comaneci, Romania	Gym	5	3	1	9
Natalie Coughlin, United States	Swim	3	4	5	12	Lyudmila Tourischeva, USSR	Gym	4	3	2	9
Vera Cáslavská, Czech	Gym	7	4	0	11	Valentina Vezzali, Italy	Fenc	6	1	2	9
Agnes Keleti, Hungary	Gym	5	3	2	10	Anky van Grunsven, Neth.	Eque	3	5	1	9
Polina Astaknova, USSR	Gym	5	2	3	10	Six tied with 8.					

INDIVIDUALS — GOLD

Men

Micheal Phelps, United States	18	Mark Spitz, United States	9	Boris Shakhlin, USSR	7
Ray Ewry, United States	10	Sawao Kato, Japan	8	Viktor Chukarin, USSR	7
Paavo Nurmi, Finland	9	Matt Biondi, United States	8	Aladár Gerevich, Hungary	7
Carl Lewis, United States	9	Nikolai Andrianov, USSR	7		

Women

Larissa Latynina, USSR	9	Krisztina Egerszegi, Hungary	5	Pat McCormick, United States	4
Jenny Thompson, U.S.	8	Kornelia Ender, E Germany	4	Bärbel Eckert Wöckel, E Ger.	4
Vera Cáslavská, Czech	7	Dawn Fraser, Australia	4	Amy Van Dyken, United States	4
Kristin Otto, E Germany	6	Lyudmila Tourischeva, USSR	4	Inge de Bruijn, Netherlands	4
Valentina Vezzali, Italy	6	Evelyn Ashford, United States	4	Yana Klochkova, Ukraine	4
Agnes Keleti, Hungary	5	Janet Evans, United States	4	Dara Torres, United States	4
Nadia Comaneci, Romania	5	Fanny Blankers-Koen, Neth.	4		
Polina Astaknova, USSR	5	Betty Cuthbert, Australia	4		

TRACK AND FIELD — Men

100 METERS

1896	Thomas Burke, United States	12.0
1900	Frank Jarvis, United States	11.0
1904	Archie Hahn, United States	11.0
1906	Archie Hahn, United States	11.2
1908	Reginald Walker, S Africa	10.8 OR
1912	Ralph Craig, United States	10.8
1920	Charles Paddock, United States	10.8
1924	Harold Abrahams, Great Britain	10.6 OR
1928	Percy Williams, Canada	10.8
1932	Eddie Tolan, United States	10.3 OR
1936	Jesse Owens, United States	10.3
1948	Harrison Dillard, United States	10.3
1952	Lindy Remigino, United States	10.4
1956	Bobby Morrow, United States	10.5
1960	Armin Hary, W Germany	10.2 OR
1964	Bob Hayes, United States	10.0 EWR
1968	Jim Hines, United States	9.95 WR
1972	Valery Borzov, USSR	10.14
1976	Hasely Crawford, Trinidad	10.06
1980	Allan Wells, Great Britain	10.25
1984	Carl Lewis, United States	9.99
1988	Carl Lewis, United States*	9.92 WR
1992	Linford Christie, Great Britain	9.96
1996	Donovan Bailey, Canada	9.84 WR
2000	Maurice Greene, United States	9.87
2004	Justin Gatlin, United States	9.85
2008	Usain Bolt, Jamaica	9.69 WR
2012	Usain Bolt, Jamaica	9.63 OR

*Ben Johnson, Canada, disqualified.

200 METERS

1900	John Walter Tewksbury, United States	22.2
1904	Archie Hahn, United States	21.6 OR
1906	Not held	
1908	Robert Kerr, Canada	22.6
1912	Ralph Craig, United States	21.7
1920	Allen Woodring, United States	22.0
1924	Jackson Scholz, United States	21.6
1928	Percy Williams, Canada	21.8
1932	Eddie Tolan, United States	21.2 OR
1936	Jesse Owens, United States	20.7 OR
1948	Mel Patton, United States	21.1
1952	Andrew Stanfield, United States	20.7
1956	Bobby Morrow, United States	20.6 OR
1960	Livio Berruti, Italy	20.5 EWR
1964	Henry Carr, United States	20.3 OR
1968	Tommie Smith, United States	19.83 WR
1972	Valery Borzov, USSR	20.00
1976	Donald Quarrie, Jamaica	20.23
1980	Pietro Mennea, Italy	20.19
1984	Carl Lewis, United States	19.80 OR
1988	Joe DeLoach, United States	19.75 OR
1992	Mike Marsh, United States	20.01
1996	Michael Johnson, United States	19.32 WR
2000	Konstadinos Kederis, Greece	20.09
2004	Shawn Crawford, United States	19.79
2008	Usain Bolt, Jamaica	19.30 WR
2012	Usain Bolt, Jamaica	19.32

400 METERS

1896	Thomas Burke, United States	54.2
1900	Maxey Long, United States	49.4 OR
1904	Harry Hillman, United States	49.2 OR
1906	Paul Pilgrim, United States	53.2
1908	Wyndham Halswelle, Great Britain	50.0
1912	Charles Reidpath, United States	48.2 OR
1920	Bevil Rudd, South Africa	49.6
1924	Eric Liddell, Great Britain	47.6 OR
1928	Ray Barbuti, United States	47.8
1932	William Carr, United States	46.2 WR

400 METERS *(Cont.)*

1936	Archie Williams, United States	46.5
1948	Arthur Wint, Jamaica	46.2
1952	George Rhoden, Jamaica	45.9
1956	Charles Jenkins, United States	46.7
1960	Otis Davis, United States	44.9 WR
1964	Michael Larrabee, United States	45.1
1968	Lee Evans, United States	43.86 WR
1972	Vincent Matthews, United States	44.66
1976	Alberto Juantorena, Cuba	44.26
1980	Viktor Markin, USSR	44.60
1984	Alonzo Babers, United States	44.27
1988	Steve Lewis, United States	43.87
1992	Quincy Watts, United States	43.50 OR
1996	Michael Johnson, United States	43.49 OR
2000	Michael Johnson, United States	43.84
2004	Jeremy Wariner, United States	44.00
2008	Lashawn Merritt, United States	43.75
2012	Kirani James, Grenada	43.94

800 METERS

1896	Edwin Flack, Australia	2:11
1900	Alfred Tysoe, Great Britain	2:01.2
1904	James Lightbody, United States	1:56 OR
1906	Paul Pilgrim, United States	2:01.5
1908	Mel Sheppard, United States	1:52.8 WR
1912	James Meredith, United States	1:51.9 WR
1920	Albert Hill, Great Britain	1:53.4
1924	Douglas Lowe, Great Britain	1:52.4
1928	Douglas Lowe, Great Britain	1:51.8 OR
1932	Thomas Hampson, Great Britain	1:49.8 WR
1936	John Woodruff, United States	1:52.9
1948	Mal Whitfield, United States	1:49.2 OR
1952	Mal Whitfield, United States	1:49.2 EOR
1956	Thomas Courtney, United States	1:47.7 OR
1960	Peter Snell, New Zealand	1:46.3 OR
1964	Peter Snell, New Zealand	1:45.1 OR
1968	Ralph Doubell, Australia	1:44.3 EWR
1972	Dave Wottle, United States	1:45.9
1976	Alberto Juantorena, Cuba	1:43.50 WR
1980	Steve Ovett, Great Britain	1:45.40
1984	Joaquim Cruz, Brazil	1:43.00 OR
1988	Paul Ereng, Kenya	1:43.45
1992	William Tanui, Kenya	1:43.66
1996	Vebjoern Rodal, Norway	1:42.58 OR
2000	Nils Schumann, Germany	1:45.08
2004	Yuriy Borzakovskiy, Russia	1:44.45
2008	Wilfred Kipkemboi Bungei, Kenya	1:44.65
2012	David Lekuta Rudisha, Kenya	1:40.91 WR

1,500 METERS

1896	Edwin Flack, Australia	4:33.2
1900	Charles Bennett, Great Britain	4:06.2 WR
1904	James Lightbody, United States	4:05.4 WR
1906	James Lightbody, United States	4:12.0
1908	Mel Sheppard, United States	4:03.4 OR
1912	Arnold Jackson, Great Britain	3:56.8 OR
1920	Albert Hill, Great Britain	4:01.8
1924	Paavo Nurmi, Finland	3:53.6 OR
1928	Harry Larva, Finland	3:53.2 OR
1932	Luigi Beccali, Italy	3:51.2 OR
1936	Jack Lovelock, New Zealand	3:47.8 WR
1948	Henri Eriksson, Sweden	3:49.8
1952	Josef Barthel, Luxemburg	3:45.1 OR
1956	Ron Delany, Ireland	3:41.2 OR
1960	Herb Elliott, Australia	3:35.6 WR
1964	Peter Snell, New Zealand	3:38.1
1968	Kipchoge Keino, Kenya	3:34.9 OR
1972	Pekkha Vasala, Finland	3:36.3
1976	John Walker, New Zealand	3:39.17
1980	Sebastian Coe, Great Britain	3:38.4
1984	Sebastian Coe, Great Britain	3:32.53 OR

Note: OR=Olympic Record. WR=World Record. EOR=Equals Olympic Record. EWR=Equals World Record. WB=World Best.

TRACK AND FIELD — Men *(Cont.)*

1,500 METERS *(Cont.)*

1988	Peter Rono, Kenya	3:35.96
1992	Fermin Cacho, Spain	3:40.12
1996	Noureddine Morceli, Algeria	3:35.78
2000	Noah Ngeni, Kenya	3:32.07 OR
2004	Hicham El Guerrouj, Morocco	3:34.18
2008	Rasheed Ramzi, Bahrain	3:32.94
2012	Taoufik Makhloufi, Algeria	3:34.08

5,000 METERS

1912	Hannes Kolehmainen, Finland	14:36.6 WR
1920	Joseph Guillemot, France	14:55.6
1924	Paavo Nurmi, Finland	14:31.2 OR
1928	Villie Ritola, Finland	14:38.0
1932	Lauri Lehtinen, Finland	14:30 OR
1936	Gunnar Höckert, Finland	14:22.2 OR
1948	Gaston Reiff, Belgium	14:17.6 OR
1952	Emil Zatopek, Czechoslovakia	14:06.6 OR
1956	Vladimir Kuts, USSR	13:39.6 OR
1960	Murray Halberg, New Zealand	13:43.4
1964	Bob Schul, United States	13:48.8
1968	Mohamed Gammoudi, Tunisia	14:05.0
1972	Lasse Viren, Finland	13:26.4 OR
1976	Lasse Viren, Finland	13:24.76
1980	Miruts Yifter, Ethiopia	13:21.0
1984	Said Aouita, Morocco	13:05.59 OR
1988	John Ngugi, Kenya	13:11.70
1992	Dieter Baumann, Germany	13:12.52
1996	Venuste Niyongabo, Burundi	13:07.96
2000	Millon Wolde, Ethiopia	13:35.49
2004	Hicham El Guerrouj, Morocco	13:14.39
2008	Kenenisa Bekele, Ethiopia	12:57.82OR
2012	Mohamed Farah, Great Britain	13:41.66

10,000 METERS

1912	Hannes Kolehmainen, Finland	31:20.8
1920	Paavo Nurmi, Finland	31:45.8
1924	Vilho (Ville) Ritola, Finland	30:23.2 WR
1928	Paavo Nurmi, Finland	30:18.8 OR
1932	Janusz Kusocinski, Poland	30:11.4 OR
1936	Ilmari Salminen, Finland	30:15.4
1948	Emil Zatopek, Czechoslovakia	29:59.6 OR
1952	Emil Zatopek, Czechoslovakia	29:17.0 OR
1956	Vladimir Kuts, USSR	28:45.6 OR
1960	Pyotr Bolotnikov, USSR	28:32.2 OR
1964	Billy Mills, United States	28:24.4 OR
1968	Naftali Temu, Kenya	29:27.4
1972	Lasse Viren, Finland	27:38.4 WR
1976	Lasse Viren, Finland	27:40.38
1980	Miruts Yifter, Ethiopia	27:42.7
1984	Alberto Cova, Italy	27:47.54
1988	Brahim Boutaib, Morocco	27:21.46 OR
1992	Khalid Skah, Morocco	27:46.70
1996	Haile Gebrselassie, Ethiopia	27:07.34 OR
2000	Haile Gebrselassie, Ethiopia	27:18.20
2004	Kenenisa Bekele, Ethiopia	27:05.10 OR
2008	Kenenisa Bekele, Ethiopia	27:01.17 OR
2012	Mohamed Farah, Great Britain	27:30.42

MARATHON

1896	Spiridon Louis, Greece	2:58:50
1900	Michel Theato, France	2:59:45
1904	Thomas Hicks, United States	3:28:53
1906	William Sherring, Canada	2:51:23.6
1908	John Hayes, United States	2:55:18.4 OR
1912	Kenneth McArthur, S Africa	2:36:54.8
1920	Hannes Kolehmainen, Finland	2:32:35.8 WB
1924	Albin Stenroos, Finland	2:41:22.6
1928	Boughera El Ouafi, France	2:32:57
1932	Juan Zabala, Argentina	2:31:36 OR
1936	Kijung Son, Japan (Korea)	2:29:19.2 OR
1948	Delfo Cabrera, Argentina	2:34:51.6
1952	Emil Zatopek, Czechoslovakia	2:23:03.2 OR
1956	Alain Mimoun O'Kacha, France	2:25:00.0
1960	Abebe Bikila, Ethiopia	2:15:16.2 WB

MARATHON *(Cont.)*

1964	Abebe Bikila, Ethiopia	2:12:11.2 WB
1968	Mamo Wolde, Ethiopia	2:20:26.4
1972	Frank Shorter, United States	2:12:19.8
1976	Waldemar Cierpinski, E Germ.	2:09:55 OR
1980	Waldemar Cierpinski, E Germ.	2:11:03.0
1984	Carlos Lopes, Portugal	2:09:21.0 OR
1988	Gelindo Bordin, Italy	2:10:32
1992	Hwang Young-Cho, S Korea	2:13:23
1996	Josia Thugwane, S Africa	2:12:36
2000	Gezahgne Abera, Ethiopia	2:10:11
2004	Stefano Baldini, Italy	2:10:55
2008	Samuel Kamau, Kenya	2:06:32 OR
2012	Stephen Kiprotich, Uganda	2:08.01

110-METER HURDLES

1896	Thomas Curtis, United States	17.6
1900	Alvin Kraenzlein, United States	15.4 OR
1904	Frederick Schule, United States	16.0
1906	Robert Leavitt, United States	16.2
1908	Forrest Smithson, United States	15.0 WR
1912	Frederick Kelly, United States	15.1
1920	Earl Thomson, Canada	14.8 WR
1924	Daniel Kinsey, United States	15.0
1928	Sydney Atkinson, S Africa	14.8
1932	George Saling, United States	14.6
1936	Forrest Towns, United States	14.2
1948	William Porter, United States	13.9 OR
1952	Harrison Dillard, United States	13.7 OR
1956	Lee Calhoun, United States	13.5 OR
1960	Lee Calhoun, United States	13.8
1964	Hayes Jones, United States	13.6
1968	Willie Davenport, United States	13.3 OR
1972	Rod Milburn, United States	13.24 EWR
1976	Guy Drut, France	13.30
1980	Thomas Munkelt, E Germany	13.39
1984	Roger Kingdom, United States	13.20 OR
1988	Roger Kingdom, United States	12.98 OR
1992	Mark McKoy, Canada	13.12
1996	Allen Johnson, United States	12.95 OR
2000	Anier Garcia, Cuba	13.00
2004	Xiang Liu, China	12.91 EWR
2008	Dayron Robles, Cuba	12.93
2012	Aries Merritt, United States	12.92

400-METER HURDLES

1900	John Walter Tewksbury, U.S.	57.6
1904	Harry Hillman, United States	53.0
1906	Not held	
1908	Charles Bacon, United States	55.0 WR
1912	Not held	
1920	Frank Loomis, United States	54.0 WR
1924	F. Morgan Taylor, United States	52.6
1928	David Burghley, Great Britain	53.4 OR
1932	Robert Tisdall, Ireland	51.7
1936	Glenn Hardin, United States	52.4
1948	Roy Cochran, United States	51.1 OR
1952	Charles Moore, United States	50.8 OR
1956	Glenn Davis, United States	50.1 EOR
1960	Glenn Davis, United States	49.3 EOR
1964	Rex Cawley, United States	49.6
1968	Dave Hemery, Great Britain	48.12 WR
1972	John Akii-Bua, Uganda	47.82 WR
1976	Edwin Moses, United States	47.64 WR
1980	Volker Beck, E Germany	48.70
1984	Edwin Moses, United States	47.75
1988	Andre Phillips, United States	47.19 OR
1992	Kevin Young, United States	46.78 WR
1996	Derrick Adkins, United States	47.54
2000	Angelo Taylor, United States	47.50
2004	Felix Sanchez, Dominican Rep	47.63
2008	Angelo Taylor, United States	47.25
2012	Felix Sanchez, Dominican Rep	47.63

TRACK AND FIELD — Men *(Cont.)*

3,000-METER STEEPLECHASE

1920	Percy Hodge, Great Britain	10:00.4 OR
1924	Vilho (Ville) Ritola, Finland	9:33.6 OR
1928	Toivo Loukola, Finland	9:21.8 WR
1932	Volmari Iso-Hollo, Finland	10:33.4*
1936	Volmari Iso-Hollo, Finland	9:03.8 WR
1948	Thore Sjöstrand, Sweden	9:04.6
1952	Horace Ashenfelter, U.S.	8:45.4 WR
1956	Chris Brasher, Great Britain	8:41.2 OR
1960	Zdzislaw Krzyszkowiak, Poland	8:34.2 OR
1964	Gaston Roelants, Belgium	8:30.8 OR
1968	Amos Biwott, Kenya	8:51
1972	Kipchoge Keino, Kenya	8:23.6 OR
1976	Anders Gärderud, Sweden	8:08.2 WR
1980	Bronislaw Malinowski, Poland	8:09.7
1984	Julius Korir, Kenya	8:11.8
1988	Julius Kariuki, Kenya	8:05.51 OR
1992	Matthew Birir, Kenya	8:08.84
1996	Joseph Keter, Kenya	8:07.12
2000	Reuben Kosgei, Kenya	8:21.43
2004	Ezekiel Kemboi, Kenya	8:05.81
2008	Brimin Kipruto, Kenya	8:10.34
2012	Ezekiel Kemboi, Kenya	8:18.56

*About 3,450 meters; extra lap by error.

4 X 100-METER RELAY

1912	Great Britain	42.4 OR
1920	United States	42.2 WR
1924	United States	41.0 EWR
1928	United States	41.0 EWR
1932	United States	40.0 EWR
1936	United States	39.8 WR
1948	United States	40.6
1952	United States	40.1
1956	United States	39.5 WR
1960	W Germany	39.5 EWR
1964	United States	39.0 WR
1968	United States	38.2 WR
1972	United States	38.19 EWR
1976	United States	38.33
1980	USSR	38.26
1984	United States	37.83 WR
1988	USSR	38.19
1992	United States	37.40 WR
1996	Canada	37.69
2000	United States	37.61
2004	Great Britain	38.07
2008	Jamaica	37.10 WR
2012	Jamaica	36.84 WR

4 X 400-METER RELAY

1908	United States	3:29.4
1912	United States	3:16.6 WR
1920	Great Britain	3:22.2
1924	United States	3:16.0 WR
1928	United States	3:14.2 WR
1932	United States	3:08.2 WR
1936	Great Britain	3:09.0
1948	United States	3:10.4 WR
1952	Jamaica	3:03.9 WR
1956	United States	3:04.8
1960	United States	3:02.2 WR
1964	United States	3:00.7 WR
1968	United States	2:56.16 WR
1972	Kenya	2:59.8
1976	United States	2:58.65
1980	USSR	3:01.1
1984	United States	2:57.91
1988	United States	2:56.16 EWR
1992	United States	2:55.74 WR
1996	United States	2:55.99
2000	United States	2:56.35

4 X 400-METER RELAY *(Cont.)*

2004	United States	2:55.91
2008	United States	2:55.39 OR
2012	Bahamas	2:56.72

20-KILOMETER WALK

1956	Leonid Spirin, USSR	1:31:27.4
1960	Vladimir Golubnichiy, USSR	1:33:07.2
1964	Kenneth Mathews, Great Britain	1:29:34.0 OR
1968	Vladimir Golubnichiy, USSR	1:33:58.4
1972	Peter Frenkel, E Germany	1:26:42.4 OR
1976	Daniel Bautista, Mexico	1:24:40.6 OR
1980	Maurizio Damilano, Italy	1:23:35.5 OR
1984	Ernesto Canto, Mexico	1:23:13.0 OR
1988	Jozef Pribilinec, Czechoslovakia	1:19:57.0 OR
1992	Daniel Plaza, Spain	1:21:45.0
1996	Jefferson Pérez, Ecuador	1:20:07
2000	Robert Korzeniowski, Poland	1:18:59 OR
2004	Ivano Brugnetti, Italy	1:19:40
2008	Valeriy Borchin, Russia	1:19:01
2012	Ding Chen, China	1:18.46 OR

50-KILOMETER WALK

1932	Thomas Green, Great Britain	4:50:10
1936	Harold Whitlock, Great Britain	4:30:41.4 OR
1948	John Ljunggren, Sweden	4:41:52
1952	Giuseppe Dordoni, Italy	4:28:07.8 OR
1956	Norman Read, New Zealand	4:30:42.8
1960	Donald Thompson, Great Britain	4:25:30 OR
1964	Abdon Parnich, Italy	4:11:12.4 OR
1968	Christoph Höhne, E Germany	4:20:13.6
1972	Bernd Kannenberg, W Germany	3:56:11.6 OR
1980	Hartwig Gauder, E Germany	3:49:24.0 OR
1984	Raul Gonzalez, Mexico	3:47:26.0 OR
1988	Viacheslav Ivanenko, USSR	3:38:29.0 OR
1992	Andrey Perlov, Unified Team	3:50:13
1996	Robert Korzeniowski, Poland	3:43:30
2000	Robert Korzeniowski, Poland	3:42:22 OR
2004	Robert Korzeniowski, Poland	3:38:46
2008	Alex Schwazer, Italy	3:37:09 OR
2012	Sergey Kirdyapkin, Russia	3:35.59 OR

HIGH JUMP

1896	Ellery Clark, United States	5 ft 11¼ in
1900	Irving Baxter, United States	6 ft 2¾ in OR
1904	Samuel Jones, United States	5 ft 11 in
1906	Cornelius Leahy, Great Britain/Ireland	5 ft 10 in
1908	Harry Porter, United States	6 ft 3 in OR
1912	Alma Richards, United States	6 ft 4 in OR
1920	Richmond Landon, United States	6 ft 4 in OR
1924	Harold Osborn, United States	6 ft 6 in OR
1928	Robert W. King, United States	6 ft 4½ in
1932	Duncan McNaughton, Canada	6 ft 5½ in
1936	Cornelius Johnson, United States	6 ft 8 in OR
1948	John L. Winter, Australia	6 ft 6 in
1952	Walter Davis, United States	6 ft 8½ in OR
1956	Charles Dumas, United States	6 ft 11½ in OR
1960	Robert Shavlakadze, USSR	7 ft 1 in OR
1964	Valery Brumel, USSR	7 ft 1¾ in OR
1968	Dick Fosbury, United States	7 ft 4¼ in OR
1972	Yuri Tarmak, USSR	7 ft 3¾ in
1976	Jacek Wszola, Poland	7 ft 4½ in OR
1980	Gerd Wessig, E Germany	7 ft 8¾ in WR
1984	Dietmar Mögenburg, W Ger	7 ft 8½ in
1988	Gennadiy Avdeyenko, USSR	7 ft 9¾ in OR
1992	Javier Sotomayor, Cuba	7 ft 8 in.
1996	Charles Austin, United States	7 ft 10 in OR
2000	Sergey Kliugin, Russia	7 ft 8¼ in

Note: OR=Olympic Record. WR=World Record. EOR=Equals Olympic Record. EWR=Equals World Record. WB=World Best.

TRACK AND FIELD — Men *(Cont.)*

HIGH JUMP *(Cont.)*

2004...Stefan Holm, Sweden	7 ft 8¾ in
2008...Andrey Silnov, Russia	7 ft 9 in
2012...Ivan Ukhov, Russia	7 ft 9¾ in

POLE VAULT

1896...William Hoyt, United States	10 ft 10 in
1900...Irving Baxter, United States	10 ft 10 in
1904...Charles Dvorak, United States	11 ft 5¾ in
1906...Fernand Gonder, France	11 ft 5¾ in
1908...Alfred Gilbert, United States	12 ft 2 in OR
Edward Cooke Jr., United States	
1912...Harry Babcock, United States	12 ft 11½ in OR
1920...Frank Foss, United States	13 ft 5 in WR
1924...Lee Barnes, United States	12 ft 11½ in
1928...Sabin Carr, United States	13 ft 9¼ in OR
1932...William Miller, United States	14 ft 1¾ in OR
1936...Earle Meadows, United States	14 ft 3¼ in OR
1948...Guinn Smith, United States	14 ft 1¼ in
1952...Robert Richards, United States	14 ft 11 in OR
1956...Robert Richards, United States	14 ft 11½ in OR
1960...Don Bragg, United States	15 ft 5 in OR
1964...Fred Hansen, United States	16 ft 8¾ in OR
1968...Bob Seagren, United States	17 ft 8½ in OR
1972...Wolfgang Nordwig, E Germany	18 ft ½ in OR
1976...Tadeusz Slusarski, Poland	18 ft ½ in EOR
1980...Wladyslaw Kozakiewicz, Pol	18 ft 11½ in WR
1984...Pierre Quinon, France	18 ft 10¼ in
1988...Sergei Bubka, USSR	19 ft 4¼ in OR
1992...Maksim Tarasov, Unified Team	19 ft ¼ in
1996...Jean Galfione, France	19 ft 5 ¼ in OR
2000...Nick Hysong, United States	19 ft 4¼ in
2004...Timothy Mack, United States	19 ft 6¼ in
2008...Steve Hooker, Australia	19 ft 6½ in OR
2012...Renaud Lavillenie, France	19 ft 7 in OR

LONG JUMP

1896...Ellery Clark, United States	20 ft 10 in
1900...Alvin Kraenzlein, United States	23 ft 6¾ in OR
1904...Meyer Prinstein, United States	24 ft 1 in OR
1906...Meyer Prinstein, United States	23 ft 7½ in
1908...Frank Irons, United States	24 ft 6½ in OR
1912...Albert Gutterson, United States	24 ft 11¼ in OR
1920...William Peterssen, Sweden	23 ft 5½ in
1924...DeHart Hubbard, United States	24 ft 5 in
1928...Edward B. Hamm, United States	25 ft 4½ in OR
1932...Edward Gordon, United States	25 ft ¾ in
1936...Jesse Owens, United States	26 ft 5½ in OR
1948...William Steele, United States	25 ft 8 in
1952...Jerome Biffle, United States	24 ft 10 in
1956...Gregory Bell, United States	25 ft 8¼ in
1960...Ralph Boston, United States	26 ft 7¾ in OR
1964...Lynn Davies, Great Britain	26 ft 5¾ in
1968...Bob Beamon, United States	29 ft 2½ in WR
1972...Randy Williams, United States	27 ft ½ in
1976...Arnie Robinson, United States	27 ft 4¾ in
1980...Lutz Dombrowski, E Germany	28 ft ¼ in
1984...Carl Lewis, United States	28 ft ¼ in
1988...Carl Lewis, United States	28 ft 7½ in
1992...Carl Lewis, United States	28 ft 5½ in
1996...Carl Lewis, United States	27 ft 10¾ in
2000...Ivan Pedrosa, Cuba	28 ft ¾ in
2004...Dwight Phillips, United States	28 ft 2¼ in
2008...Irving Jahir Saladino, Panama	27 ft 4¼ in
2012...Greg Rutherford, Great Britain	27 ft 3¼ in

TRIPLE JUMP

1896...James Connolly, United States	44 ft 11¾ in
1900...Meyer Prinstein, United States	47 ft 5¾ in OR
1904...Meyer Prinstein, United States	47 ft 1 in
1906...Peter O'Connor, GB/ Ire	46 ft 2¼ in

TRIPLE JUMP *(Cont.)*

1908...Timothy Ahearne, GB/ Ire	48 ft 11¼ in OR
1912...Gustaf Lindblom, Sweden	48 ft 5¼ in
1920...Vilho Tuulos, Finland	47 ft 7 in
1924...Anthony Winter, Australia	50 ft 11¼ in WR
1928...Mikio Oda, Japan	49 ft 11 in
1932...Chuhei Nambu, Japan	51 ft 7 in WR
1936...Naoto Tajima, Japan	52 ft 6 in WR
1948...Arne Ahman, Sweden	50 ft 6¼ in
1952...Adhemar da Silva, Brazil	53 ft 2¾ in WR
1956...Adhemar da Silva, Brazil	53 ft 7¾ in OR
1960...Jozef Schmidt, Poland	55 ft 2 in
1964...Jozef Schmidt, Poland	55 ft 3½ in OR
1968...Viktor Saneyev, USSR	57 ft ¾ in WR
1972...Viktor Saneyev, USSR	56 ft 11¾ in
1976...Viktor Saneyev, USSR	56 ft 8¾ in
1980...Jaak Uudmae, USSR	56 ft 11¼ in
1984...Al Joyner, United States	56 ft 7½ in
1988...Khristo Markov, Bulgaria	57 ft 9½ in OR
1992...Mike Conley, United States	59 ft 7½ in (w)
1996...Kenny Harrison, United States	59 ft 4 ¼ in OR
2000...Jonathon Edwards, G. Britain	58 ft 1¼ in
2004...Christian Olsson, Sweden	58 ft 4 ½ in
2008...Nelson Evora, Portugal	57 ft 11½ in
2012...Christian Taylor, United States	58 ft 5¼ in

SHOT PUT

1896...Robert Garrett, United States	36 ft 9¾ in
1900...Richard Sheldon, United States	46 ft 3¼ in OR
1904...Ralph Rose, United States	48 ft 7 in WR
1906...Martin Sheridan, United States	40 ft 5¼ in
1908...Ralph Rose, United States	46 ft 7½ in
1912...Pat McDonald, United States	50 ft 4 in OR
1920...Ville Porhola, Finland	48 ft 7¼ in
1924...Clarence Houser, United States	49 ft 2¼ in
1928...John Kuck, United States	52 ft ¾ in WR
1932...Leo Sexton, United States	52 ft 6 in OR
1936...Hans Woellke, Germany	53 ft 1¾ in OR
1948...Wilbur Thompson, United States	56 ft 2 in OR
1952...Parry O'Brien, United States	57 ft ½ in OR
1956...Parry O'Brien, United States	60 ft 11¼ in OR
1960...William Nieder, United States	64 ft 6¾ in OR
1964...Dallas Long, United States	66 ft 8½ in OR
1968...Randy Matson, United States	67 ft 4¾ in
1972...Wladyslaw Komar, Poland	69 ft 6 in OR
1976...Udo Beyer, E Germany	69 ft ¾ in
1980...Vladimir Kiselyov, USSR	70 ft ½ in OR
1984...Alessandro Andrei, Italy	69 ft 9 in
1988...Ulf Timmermann, E Germany	73 ft 8¾ in OR
1992...Mike Stulce, United States	71 ft 2½ in
1996...Randy Barnes, United States	70 ft 11 in
2000...Arsi Harju, Finland	69 ft 10¼ in
2004...Yuriy Bilonog, Ukraine	69 ft 5¼ in
2008...Tomasz Majewski, Poland	70 ft 6¾ in
2012...Tomasz Majewski, Poland	71 ft 9¾ in

DISCUS THROW

1896...Robert Garrett, United States	95 ft 7½ in
1900...Rudolf Bauer, Hungary	118 ft 3 in OR
1904...Martin Sheridan, United States	128 ft 10½ in OR
1906...Martin Sheridan, United States	136 ft
1908...Martin Sheridan, United States	134 ft 2 in OR
1912...Armas Taipele, Finland	148 ft 3 in OR
1920...Elmer Niklander, Finland	146 ft 7 in
1924...Clarence Houser, United States	151 ft 4 in OR
1928...Clarence Houser, United States	155 ft 3 in OR
1932...John Anderson, United States	162 ft 4 in OR
1936...Ken Carpenter, United States	165 ft 7 in OR
1948...Adolfo Consolini, Italy	173 ft 2 in OR
1952...Sim Iness, United States	180 ft 6 in OR
1956...Al Oerter, United States	184 ft 11 in OR

(w)-wind aided

Summer Games Champions (*Cont.*)

TRACK AND FIELD — Men (*Cont.*)

DISCUS (*Cont.*)

1960...Al Oerter, United States	194 ft 2 in OR
1964...Al Oerter, United States	200 ft 1 in OR
1968...Al Oerter, United States	212 ft 6 in OR
1972...Ludvik Danek, Czechoslovakia	211 ft 3 in
1976...Mac Wilkins, United States	221 ft 5 in OR
1980...Viktor Rashchupkin, USSR	218 ft 8 in
1984...Rolf Dannenberg, W Ger	218 ft 6 in
1988...Jürgen Schult, E Germany	225 ft 9 in OR
1992...Romas Ubartas, Lithuania	213 ft 8 in
1996...Lars Riedel, Germany	227 ft 8 in OR
2000...Virgilijus Alekna, Lithuania	227 ft 4 in
2004...Virgilijus Alekna, Lithuania	229 ft 3 in
2008...Gerd Kanter, Estonia	225 ft 9½ in
2012...Robert Harting, Germany	223 ft 11¾ in

HAMMER THROW

1900...John Flanagan, United States	163 ft 1 in
1904...John Flanagan, United States	168 ft 1 in OR
1906...Not held	
1908...John Flanagan, United States	170 ft 4 in OR
1912...Matt McGrath, United States	179 ft 7 in OR
1920...Pat Ryan, United States	173 ft 5 in
1924...Fred Tootell, United States	174 ft 10 in
1928...Patrick O'Callaghan, Ireland	168 ft 7 in
1932...Patrick O'Callaghan, Ireland	176 ft 11 in
1936...Karl Hein, Germany	185 ft 4 in OR
1948...Imre Nemeth, Hungary	183 ft 11 in
1952...Jozsef Csermak, Hungary	197 ft 11 in WR
1956...Harold Connolly, United States	207 ft 3 in OR
1960...Vasily Rudenkov, USSR	220 ft 2 in OR
1964...Romuald Klim, USSR	228 ft 10 in OR
1968...Gyula Zsivotsky, Hungary	240 ft 8 in OR
1972...Anatoli Bondarchuk, USSR	247 ft 8 in OR
1976...Yuri Sedykh, USSR	254 ft 4 in OR
1980...Yuri Sedykh, USSR	268 ft 4 in WR
1984...Juha Tiainen, Finland	256 ft 2 in
1988...Sergei Litvinov, USSR	278 ft 2 in OR
1992...Andrey Abduvaliyev, Unified Team	270 ft 9 in
1996...Balazs Kiss, Hungary	266 ft 6 in
2000...Szymon Ziolkowski, Poland	262 ft 6 in
2004...Adrian Zsolt, Hungary	272 fr 11 in
2008...Primoz Kozmus, Slovenia	269 ft 1 in
2012...Krisztian Pars, Hungary	264 ft 4¾ in

JAVELIN

1908...Erik Lemming, Sweden	179 ft 10 in
1912...Erik Lemming, Sweden	198 ft 11 in WR
1920...Jonni Myyrä, Finland	215 ft 10 in OR
1924...Jonni Myyrä, Finland	206 ft 6 in

JAVELIN (*Cont.*)

1928...Eric Lundkvist, Sweden	218 ft 6 in OR
1932...Matti Jarvinen, Finland	238 ft 6 in OR
1936...Gerhard Stöck, Germany	235 ft 8 in
1948...Kai Rautavaara, Finland	228 ft 10½ in
1952...Cy Young, United States	242 ft 1 in OR
1956...Egil Danielson, Norway	281 ft 2¼ in WR
1960...Viktor Tsibulenko, USSR	277 ft 8 in
1964...Pauli Nevala, Finland	271 ft 2 in
1968...Janis Lusis, USSR	295 ft 7 in OR
1972...Klaus Wolfermann, W Germany	296 ft 10 in OR
1976...Miklos Nemeth, Hungary	310 ft 4 in WR
1980...Dainis Kuta, USSR	299 ft 2⅜ in
1984...Arto Härkönen, Finland	284 ft 8 in
1988...Tapio Korjus, Finland	276 ft 6 in
1992...Jan Zelezny, Czechoslovakia	294 ft 2 in OR
1996...Jan Zelezny, Czech Republic	289 ft 3 in
2000...Jan Zelezny, Czech Republic	295 ft 9½ in OR
2004...Andreas Thorkildsen, Norway	283 ft 9 in
2008...Andreas Thorkildsen, Norway	297 ft 1¾ in OR
2012...Keshorn Walcott, Trinidad & Tobago	277 ft 5⅞ in

DECATHLON

	Pts
1904...Thomas Kiely, Ireland	6036
1912...Jim Thorpe, United States*	8412 WR
1920...Helge Lövland, Norway	6803
1924...Harold Osborn, United States	7711 WR
1928...Paavo Yrjölä, Finland	8053.29 WR
1932...James Bausch, United States	8462 WR
1936...Glenn Morris, United States	7900 WR
1948...Robert Mathias, United States	7139
1952...Robert Mathias, United States	7887 WR
1956...Milton Campbell, United States	7937 OR
1960...Rafer Johnson, United States	8392 OR
1964...Willi Holdorf, W Germany	7887
1968...Bill Toomey, United States	8193 OR
1972...Nikolai Avilov, USSR	8454 WR
1976...Bruce Jenner, United States	8617 WR
1980...Daley Thompson, Great Britain	8495
1984...Daley Thompson, Great Britain	8798 EWR
1988...Christian Schenk, E Germany	8488
1992...Robert Zmelik, Czechoslovakia	8611
1996...Dan O'Brien, United States	8824 OR
2000...Erki Nool, Estonia	8641
2004...Roman Seberle, Czech Rep	8893 OR
2008...Bryan Clay, United States	8791
2012...Ashton Eaton, United States	8869

*In 1913, Thorpe was disqualified for having played professional baseball in 1910. His record was restored in 1982.

TRACK AND FIELD — Women

100 METERS

1928....Elizabeth Robinson, United States	12.2 EWR
1932....Stella Walsh, Poland	11.9 EWR
1936....Helen Stephens, United States	11.5
1948....Francina Blankers-Koen, Neth	11.9
1952....Marjorie Jackson, Australia	11.5 EWR
1956....Betty Cuthbert, Australia	11.5 EWR
1960....Wilma Rudolph, United States	11.0
1964....Wyomia Tyus, United States	11.4
1968....Wyomia Tyus, United States	11.0 WR
1972....Renate Stecher, E Germany	11.07
1976....Annegret Richter, W Germany	11.08
1980....Lyudmila Kondratyeva, USSR	11.06
1984....Evelyn Ashford, United States	10.97 OR

100 METERS (*Cont.*)

1988....Florence Griffith Joyner, United States	10.54 WR
1992....Gail Devers, United States	10.82
1996....Gail Devers, United States	10.94
2000....Vacant*	
2004....Yuliya Nesterenko, Belarus	10.93
2008....Shelly-Ann Fraser, Jamaica	10.78
2012....Shelly-Ann Fraser-Pryce, Jamaica	10.75

200 METERS

1948....Francina Blankers-Koen, Neth	24.4
1952....Marjorie Jackson, Australia	23.7
1956....Betty Cuthbert, Australia	23.4 EOR
1960....Wilma Rudolph, United States	24.0

Note: OR=Olympic Record. WR=World Record. EOR=Equals Olympic Record. EWR=Equals World Record. WB=World Best.
*Marion Jones was stripped of her medals from the 2000 Olympics, no decision on replacing her victories has been made.

TRACK AND FIELD — Women (Cont.)

200 METERS (Cont.)

1964	Edith McGuire, United States	23.0 OR
1968	Irena Szewinska, Poland	22.5 WR
1972	Renate Stecher, E Germany	22.40 EWR
1976	Bärbel Eckert, E Germany	22.37 OR
1980	Bärbel Wöckel (Eckert), E Germ.	22.03 OR
1984	Valerie Brisco-Hooks, U.S.	21.81 OR
1988	Florence Griffith Joyner, U.S.	21.34 WR
1992	Gwen Torrence, United States	21.81
1996	Marie-José Pérec, France	22.12
2000	Vacant*	
2004	Veronica Campbell, Jamaica	22.05
2008	Veronica Campbell-Brown, Jamaica	21.74
2012	Allyson Felix, United States	21.88

400 METERS

1964	Betty Cuthbert, Australia	52.0 OR
1968	Colette Besson, France	52.0 EOR
1972	Monika Zehrt, E Germany	51.08 OR
1976	Irena Szewinska, Poland	49.29 WR
1980	Marita Koch, E Germany	48.88 OR
1984	Valerie Brisco-Hooks, U.S.	48.83 OR
1988	Olga Bryzgina, USSR	48.65 OR
1992	Marie-José Pérec, France	48.83
1996	Marie-José Pérec, France	48.25 OR
2000	Cathy Freeman, Australia	49.11
2004	T. Williams-Darling, Bahamas	49.41
2008	Christine Ohuruogu, Great Britain	49.62
2012	Sanya Richards-Ross, U. S.	49.55

800 METERS

1928	Lina Radke, Germany	2:16.8 WR
1932-56	Not held	
1960	Lyudmila Shevtsova, USSR	2:04.3 EWR
1964	Ann Packer, Great Britain	2:01.1 OR
1968	Madeline Manning, United States	2:00.9 OR
1972	Hildegard Falck, W Germany	1:58.55 OR
1976	Tatyana Kazankina, USSR	1:54.94 WR
1980	Nadezhda Olizarenko, USSR	1:53.42 WR
1984	Doina Melinte, Romania	1:57.6
1988	Sigrun Wodars, E Germany	1:56.10
1992	Ellen Van Langen, Netherlands	1:55.54
1996	Svetlana Masterkova, Russia	1:57.73
2000	Maria Mutola, Mozambique	1:56.15
2004	Kelly Holmes, Great Britain	1:56.38
2008	Pamela Jelimo, Kenya	1:54.87
2012	Mariya Savinova, Russia	1:56.19

1,500 METERS

1972	Lyudmila Bragina, USSR	4:01.4 WR
1976	Tatyana Kazankina, USSR	4:05.48
1980	Tatyana Kazankina, USSR	3:56.6 OR
1984	Gabriella Dorio, Italy	4:03.25
1988	Paula Ivan, Romania	3:53.96 OR
1992	Hassiba Boulmerka, Algeria	3:55.30
1996	Svetlana Masterkova, Russia	4:00.83
2000	Nouria Merah-Benida, Algeria	4:05.10
2004	Kelly Holmes, Great Britain	3:57.90
2008	Nancy Jebet Lagat, Kenya	4:00.23
2012	Asli Cakir Alptekin, Turkey	4:10.23

3,000 METERS

1984	Maricica Puica, Romania	8:35.96 OR
1988	Tatyana Samolenko, USSR	8:26.53 OR
1992	Elena Romanova, Unified Team	8:46.04

5,000 METERS

1996	Wang Junxia, China	14:57.88

5,000 METERS (Cont.)

2000	Gabriela Szabo, Romania	14:40.79 OR
2004	Meseret Defar, Ethiopia	14:45.65
2008	Tirunesh Dibaba Kenene, Ethiopia	15:41.40
2012	Meseret Defar, Ethiopia	15:04.25

10,000 METERS

1988	Olga Bondarenko, USSR	31:05.21 OR
1992	Derartu Tulu, Ethiopia	31:06.02
1996	Fernanda Ribeiro, Portugal	31:01.63 OR
2000	Derartu Tulu, Ethiopia	30:17.49 OR
2004	Huina Xing, China	30:24.36
2008	Tirunesh Dibaba Kenene, Ethiopia	29:54.66 OR
2012	Tirunesh Dibaba, Ethiopia	30:20.75

MARATHON

1984	Joan Benoit, United States	2:24:52 OR
1988	Rosa Mota, Portugal	2:25:40
1992	Valentin Yegorova, Unified Team	2:32:41
1996	Fatuma Roba, Ethiopia	2:26:05
2000	Naoko Takahashi, Japan	2:23:14 OR
2004	Noguchi Mizuki, Japan	2:26:20
2008	Constantina Tomescu Dita, Romania	2:26:44
2012	Tiki Gelana, Ethiopia	2:23:07 OR

80-METER HURDLES

1932	Babe Didrikson, United States	11.7 WR
1936	Trebisonda Valla, Italy	11.7
1948	Francina Blankers-Koen, Neth	11.2 OR
1952	Shirley Strickland, Australia	10.9 WR
1956	Shirley Strickland, Australia	10.7 OR
1960	Irina Press, USSR	10.8
1964	Karin Balzer, E Germany	10.5
1968	Maureen Caird, Australia	10.3 OR

100-METER HURDLES

1972	Annelie Ehrhardt, E Germany	12.59 WR *
1976	Johanna Schaller, E Germany	12.77
1980	Vera Komisova, USSR	12.56 OR
1984	Benita Fitzgerald-Brown, U.S.	12.84
1988	Yordanka Donkova, Bulgaria	12.38 OR
1992	Paraskevi Patoulidou, Greece	12.64
1996	Lyudmila Engqvist, Sweden	12.58
2000	Olga Shishigina, Kazakhstan	12.65
2004	Joanna Hayes, United States	12.37 OR
2008	Dawn Harper, United States	12.54
2012	Sally Pearson, Australia	12.35 OR

400-METER HURDLES

1984	Nawal el Moutawakel, Morocco	54.61 OR
1988	Debra Flintoff-King, Australia	53.17 OR
1992	Sally Gunnell, Great Britain	53.23
1996	Deon Hemmings, Jamaica	52.82 OR
2000	Irina Privalova, Russia	53.02
2004	Faní Halkiá, Greece	52.82
2008	Melaine Walker, Jamaica	52.64
2012	Natalya Antyukh, Russia	52.70

4 X 100-METER RELAY

1928	Canada	48.4 WR
1932	United States	46.9 WR
1936	United States	46.9
1948	Netherlands	47.5
1952	United States	45.9 WR
1956	Australia	44.5 WR
1960	United States	44.5
1964	Poland	43.6
1968	United States	42.8 WR
1972	W Germany	42.81 EWR
1976	E Germany	42.55 OR

Note: OR=Olympic Record; WR=World Record; EOR=Equals Olympic Record; EWR=Equals World Record; WB=World Best.
†Marion Jones was stripped of her medals from the 2000 Olympics, no decision on replacing her victories has been made.

TRACK AND FIELD — Women *(Cont.)*

4 X 100-METER RELAY *(Cont.)*

1980	E Germany	41.60 WR
1984	United States	41.65
1988	United States	41.98
1992	United States	42.11
1996	United States	41.95
2000	Bahamas	41.95
2004	Jamaica	41.73
2008	Russia	42.31
2012	United States	40.82 WR

4 X 400-METER RELAY

1972	E Germany	3:23 WR
1976	E Germany	3:19.23 WR
1980	USSR	3:20.02
1984	United States	3:18.29 OR
1988	USSR	3:15.18 WR
1992	Unified Team	3:20.20
1996	United States	3:20.91
2000	Vacant†	
2004	United States	3:19.01
2008	United States	3:18.54
2012	United States	3:16.87

10-KILOMETER WALK

1992	Chen Yueling, China	44:32
1996	Elena Nikolayeva, Russia	41:49 OR

20-KILOMETER WALK

2000	Liping Wang, China	1:29:05
2004	Athanasía Tsoumeléka, Greece	1:29:12
2008	Olga Kaniskina, Russia	1:26:31 OR
2012	Elena Lashmanova Russia	1:25:02 WR

HIGH JUMP

1928	Ethel Catherwood, Canada	5 ft 2½ in
1932	Jean Shiley, United States	5 ft 5¼ in WR
1936	Ibolya Csak, Hungary	5 ft 3 in
1948	Alice Coachman, United States	5 ft 6 in OR
1952	Esther Brand, South Africa	5 ft 5¾ in
1956	Mildred L. McDaniel, U.S.	5 ft 9¼ in WR
1960	Iolanda Balas, Romania	6 ft ¾ in OR
1964	Iolanda Balas, Romania	6 ft 2¾ in OR
1968	Miloslava Reskova, Czech.	5 ft 11½ in
1972	Ulrike Meyfarth, W. Germany	6 ft 3½ in EWR
1976	Rosemarie Ackermann, E Germ	6 ft 4 in OR
1980	Sara Simeoni, Italy	6 ft 5½ in OR
1984	Ulrike Meyfarth, W Germany	6 ft 7½ in OR
1988	Louise Ritter, United States	6 ft 8 in OR
1992	Heike Henkel, Germany	6 ft 7½ in
1996	Stefka Kostadinova, Bulgaria	6 ft 8¾ in OR
2000	Yelena Yelesina, Russia	6 ft 7 in
2004	Yelena Slesarenko, Russia	6 ft 9 in
2008	Tia Hellebaut, Belgium	6 ft 8¾ in
2012	Anna Chicherova, Russia	6 ft 8¾ in

POLE VAULT

2000	Stacy Dragila, United States	15 ft 1 in OR
2004	Yelena Isinbayeva, Russia	16 ft 1¼ in WR
2008	Yelena Isinbayeva, Russia	16 ft 6¾ in WR
2012	Jennifer Suhr, United States	15 ft 7 in

LONG JUMP

1948	Olga Gyarmati, Hungary	18 ft 8¼ in
1952	Yvette Williams, New Zealand	20 ft 5¾ in OR
1956	Elzbieta Krzeskinska, Poland	20 ft 10 in EWR
1960	Vyera Krepkina, USSR	20 ft 10¾ in OR
1964	Mary Rand, Great Britain	22 ft 2¼ in WR
1968	Viorica Viscopoleanu, Rom	22 ft 4½ in WR
1972	Heidemarie Rosendahl, W Ger	22 ft 3 in
1976	Angela Voigt, E Germany	22 ft ¾ in
1980	Tatyana Kolpakova, USSR	23 ft 2 in OR
1984	Anisoara Stanciu, Romania	22 ft 10 in

LONG JUMP *(Cont.)*

1988	Jackie Joyner-Kersee, U.S.	24 ft 3½ in OR
1992	Heike Drechsler, Germany	23 ft 5¼ in
1996	Chioma Ajunwa, Nigeria	23 ft 4½ in
2000	Heike Drechsler, Germany	22 ft 11¼ in
2004	Tatyana Lebedeva, Russia	23 ft 2½ in
2008	Maurren Higa Maggi, Brazil	23 ft 1 in
2012	Brittney Reese, United States	23 ft 4¼ in

TRIPLE JUMP

1996	Inessa Kravets, Ukraine	50 ft 3½ in
2000	Tereza Marinova, Bulgaria	49 ft 10½ in
2004	Francoise M. Etone, Cameroon	50 ft 2½ in
2008	Francoise M. Etone, Cameroon	50 ft 5 in OR
2012	Olga Rypakova, Kazakhstan	49 ft 1¾ in

SHOT PUT

1948	Micheline Ostermeyer, France	45 ft 1½ in
1952	Galina Zybina, USSR	50 ft 1¾ in WR
1956	Tamara Tyshkevich, USSR	54 ft 5 in OR
1960	Tamara Press, USSR	56 ft 10 in OR
1964	Tamara Press, USSR	59 ft 6¼ in OR
1968	Margitta Gummel, E Germany	64 ft 4 in WR
1972	Nadezhda Chizhova, USSR	69 ft WR
1976	Ivanka Hristova, Bulgaria	69 ft 5¼ in OR
1980	Ilona Slupianek, E Germany	73 ft 6¼ in OR
1984	Claudia Losch, W Germany	67 ft 2¼ in
1988	Natalya Lisovskaya, USSR	72 ft 11¾ in
1992	Svetlana Kriveleva, Unified Team	69 ft 1¼ in
1996	Astrid Kumbernuss, Germany	67 ft 5½ in
2000	Yanina Korolchik, Belarus	67 ft 5½ in
2004	Yumileidi Cumba Jay, Cuba	64 ft 3¼ in
2008	Valerie Vili, New Zealand	67 ft 5½ in
2012	Nadzeya Ostapchuk, Belarus	70 ft ⅞ in

DISCUS THROW

1928	Helena Konopacka, Poland	129 ft 11¾ in WR
1932	Lillian Copeland, United States	133 ft 2 in OR
1936	Gisela Mauermayer, Germany	156 ft 3 in OR
1948	Micheline Ostermeyer, France	137 ft 6 in
1952	Nina Romaschkova, USSR	168 ft 8 in OR
1956	Olga Fikotova, Czechoslovakia	176 ft 1 in OR
1960	Nina Ponomaryeva, USSR	180 ft 9 in OR
1964	Tamara Press, USSR	187 ft 10 in OR
1968	Lia Manoliu, Romania	191 ft 2 in OR
1972	Faina Melnik, USSR	218 ft 7 in OR
1976	Evelin Schlaak, E Germany	226 ft 4 in OR
1980	Evelin Jahl (Schlaak), E Germ.	229 ft 6 in OR
1984	Ria Stalman, Netherlands	214 ft 5 in
1988	Martina Hellmann, E Germany	237 ft 2 in OR
1992	Maritza Martén, Cuba	229 ft 10 in
1996	Ilke Wyludda, Germany	228 ft 6 in
2000	Ellina Zvereva, Belarus	224 ft 5 in
2004	Natalya Sadova, Russia	219 ft 10 in
2008	S. Brown-Trafton, United States	212 ft 4¾ in
2012	Sandra Perkovic, Croatia	226 ft 8¾ in

HAMMER THROW

2000	Kamila Skolimowska, Russia	233 ft 5 in OR
2004	Olga Kuzenkova, Russia	246 ft 1½ in OR
2008	Aksana Miankova, Belarus	250 ft 5½ in OR
2012	Tatyana Lysenko, Russia	256 ft 6 in OR

JAVELIN THROW

1932	Babe Didrikson, United States	143 ft 4 in OR
1936	Tilly Fleischer, Germany	148 ft 3 in OR
1948	Herma Bauma, Austria	149 ft 6 in
1952	Dana Zatopkova, Czechoslovakia	165 ft 7 in
1956	Inese Jaunzeme, USSR	176 ft 8 in
1960	Elvira Ozolina, USSR	183 ft 8 in OR
1964	Mihaela Penes, Romania	198 ft 7 in

TRACK AND FIELD — Women (Cont.)

JAVELIN (Cont.)

1968...Angela Nemeth, Hungary — 198 ft
1972...Ruth Fuchs, E Germany — 209 ft 7 in OR
1976...Ruth Fuchs, E Germany — 216 ft 4 in OR
1980...Maria Colon, Cuba — 224 ft 5 in OR
1984...Tessa Sanderson, Great Britain — 228 ft 2 in OR
1988...Petra Felke, E Germany — 245 ft OR
1992...Silke Renk, Germany — 224 ft 2 in
1996...Heli Rantanen, Finland — 222 ft 11 in
2000...Trine Hattestad, Norway — 226 ft ½ in OR
2004...Osleidys Menendez, Cuba — 234 ft 8 in OR
2008...B. Spotakova, Czech Republic — 234 ft 3¾in
2012...Barbora Spotakova, Czech Rep — 228 ft 2¼ in

PENTATHLON

		Pts
1964	Irina Press, USSR	5246 WR
1968	Ingrid Becker, W Germany	5098
1972	Mary Peters, Great Britain	4801 WR
1976	Siegrun Siegl, E Germany	4745
1980	Nadezhda Tkachenko, USSR	5083 WR

HEPTATHLON

		Pts
1984	Glynis Nunn, Australia	6390 OR
1988	Jackie Joyner-Kersee, U.S.	7291 WR
1992	Jackie Joyner-Kersee, U.S.	7044
1996	Ghada Shouaa, Syria	6780
2000	Denise Lewis, Great Britain	6584
2004	Carolina Kluft, Sweden	6952
2008	Natalia Dobrynska, Ukraine	6733
2012	Jessica Ennis, Great Britain	6955

BASKETBALL — Men

1936

Final: United States 19, Canada 8
United States: R. Bishop, J. Fortenberry, C. Knowles, J. Ragland, C. Shy, W. Wheatley, F. Johnson, S. Balter, J. Gibbons, F. Lubin, A. Mollner, D. Piper, D. Swanson, W. Schmidt

1948

Final: United States 65, France 21
United States: C. Barker, D. Barksdale, R. Beard, L. Beck, V. Boryla, G. Carpenter, A. Groza, W. Jones, B. Kurland, R. Lumpp, R. Pitts, J. Renick, B. Robinson, K. Rollins

1952

Final: United States 36, USSR 25
United States: C. Hoag, B. Hougland, M. Kelley, B. Kenney, C. Lovellette, M. Freiberger, V. Glasgow, F. McCabe, D. Pippen, H. Williams, R. Bontemps, B. Kurland, W. Lienhard, J. Keller

1956

Final: United States 89, USSR 55
United States: C. Cain, B. Hougland, K.C. Jones, B. Russell, J. Walsh, W. Evans, B. Haldorson, R. Tomsic, D. Boushka, G. Ford, B. Jeangerard, C. Darling

1960

Final: United States 90, Brazil 63
United States: J. Arnette, W. Bellamy, B. Boozer, T. Dischinger, J. Lucas, O. Robertson, A. Smith, B. Haldorson, D. Imhoff, A. Kelley, L. Lane, J. West

1964

Final: United States 73, USSR 59
United States: J. Barnes, B. Bradley, L. Brown, J. Caldwell, M. Counts, R. Davies, W. Hazzard, L. Jackson, J. McCaffrey, J. Mullins, J. Shipp, G. Wilson

1968

Final: United States 65, Yugoslavia 50
United States: J. Clawson, K. Spain, J. White, M. Barrett, S. Haywood, C. Scott, W. Hosket, C. Fowler, M. Silliman, G. Saulters, J. King, D. Dee

1972

Final: USSR 51, United States 50
United States: K. Davis, D. Collins, T. Henderson, M. Bantom, B. Jones, D. Jones, J. Forbes, J. Brewer, T. Burleson, T. McMillen, K. Joyce, E. Ratleff

1976

Final: United States 95, Yugoslavia 74
United States: P. Ford, S. Sheppard, A. Dantley, W. Davis, Q. Buckner, E. Grunfeld, K. Carr, S. May, M. Armstrong, T. La Garde, P. Hubbard, M. Kupchak

1980

Final: Yugoslavia 86, Italy 77
U.S. participated in boycott.

1984

Final: United States 96, Spain 65
United States: S. Alford, L. Wood, P. Ewing, V. Fleming, A. Robertson, M. Jordan, J. Kleine, J. Koncak, W. Tisdale, C. Mullin, S. Perkins, J. Turner

1988

Final: USSR 76, Yugoslavia 63
U.S. (3rd): M. Richmond, C. E. Smith, V. Coles, H. Hawkins, J. Grayer, C. D. Smith, W. Anderson, S. Augmon, D. Majerle, D. Manning, J.R. Reid, D. Robinson

1992

Final: United States 117, Croatia 85
United States: D. Robinson, C. Laettner, P. Ewing, L. Bird, S. Pippen, M. Jordan, C. Drexler, K. Malone, J. Stockton, C. Mullin, C. Barkley, E. Johnson

1996

Final: United States 95, Yugoslavia 69
United States: C. Barkley, A. Hardaway, G. Hill, K. Malone, R. Miller, H. Olajuwon, S. O'Neal, S. Pippen, M. Richmond, J. Stockton, D. Robinson, G. Payton

2000

Final: United States 85, France 75
United States: S. Abdur-Rahim, R. Allen, V. Baker, V. Carter, K. Garnett, T. Hardaway, A. Houston, J. Kidd, A. McDyess, A. Mourning, G. Payton, S. Smith

2004

Final: Argentina 84, Italy 69
U.S. (3rd): A. Iverson, L. James, T. Duncan, C. Anthony, D. Wade, R. Jefferson, L. Odom, S. Marbury, C. Boozer, E. Okafor, A. Stoudemire, S. Marion

2008

Final: United States 118, Spain 107
U.S.: C. Anthony, C. Boozer, C. Bosh, K. Bryant, D. Howard, L. James, J. Kidd, C. Paul, T. Prince, M. Redd, D. Wade, D. Williams

2012

Final: United States 107, Spain 100
U.S.: K. Durant, C, Paul, L. James, K. Bryant, C. Anthony, K. Love, D. Williams, R. Westbrook, T. Chandler, A. Iguodala, A. Davis, J. Harden

Summer Games Champions (Cont.)

BASKETBALL — Women

1976
Gold, USSR; Silver, United States*
United States: C. Brogdon, S. Rojcewicz, A. Meyers, L. Harris, N. Dunkle, C. Lewis, N. Lieberman, G. Marquis, P. Roberts, M. O'Connor, P. Head, J. Simpson

*In 1976 the women played a round-robin tournament, with the gold medal going to the team with the best record. The USSR won with a 5–0 record, and the USA, with a 3–2 record, was given the silver by virtue of a 95–79 victory over Bulgaria, which was also 3–2.

1980
Final: USSR 104, Bulgaria 73
U.S. participated in boycott.

1984
Final: United States 85, Korea 55
United States: T. Edwards, L. Henry, L. Woodard, A. Donovan, C. Boswell, C. Miller, J. Lawrence, C. Noble, K. Mulkey, D. Curry, P. McGee, C. Menken-Schaudt

1988
Final: United States 77, Yugoslavia 70
United States: T. Edwards, M. Ethridge, C. Brown, A. Donovan, T. Weatherspoon, B. Gordon, V. Bullett, A. Lloyd, K. McClain, J. Gillom, C. Cooper, S. McConnell

1992
Final: Unified Team 76, China 66
United States (3rd): T. Edwards, T. Weatherspoon, V. Bullett, K. McClain, C. Cooper, S. McConnell, D. Charles, C. Davis, T. Jackson, V. Orr, C. Jones, M. Dixon

1996
Final: United States 111, Brazil 87
United States: J. Azzi, R. Bolton, T. Edwards, L. Leslie, R. Lobo, K. McClain, N. McCray, C. McGhee, D. Staley, K. Steding, S. Swoopes, V. Lacey

2000
Final: United States 76, Australia 54
United States: R. Bolton-Holifield, T. Edwards, Y. Griffith, C. Holdsclaw, L. Leslie, N. McCray, D. Milton, K. Smith, D. Staley, S. Swoopes, N. Williams, K. Wolters

2004
Final: United States 74, Australia 63
United States: D. Staley, D. Taurasi, L. Leslie, S. Swoopes, T. Catchings, S. Bird, R. Riley, S. Johnson, K. Smith, Y. Griffith, S. Cash, T. Thompson

2008
Final: United States 92, Australia 65
United States: S. Augustus, S. Bird, S. Fowles, L. Leslie, D. Milton-Jones, C. Parker, C. Pondexter, T. Catchings, T. Thompson, D. Taurasi, K. Smith

2012
Final: United States 86, France 50
United States: D. Taurasi, M. Moore, S. Bird, C. Parker, T. Charles, L. Whalen, T. Catchings, S. Augustus, S. Fowles, A. McCoughtry, A. Jones, S. Cash

BOXING

LIGHT FLYWEIGHT (106 LB)
1968	Francisco Rodriguez, Venezuela
1972	Gyorgy Gedo, Hungary
1976	Jorge Hernandez, Cuba
1980	Shamil Sabyrov, USSR
1984	Paul Gonzalez, United States
1988	Ivailo Hristov, Bulgaria
1992	Rogelio Marcelo, Cuba
1996	Daniel Petrov, Bulgaria
2000	Brahim Asloum, France
2004	Yan Bhartelemy Varela, Cuba
2008	Shiming Zou, China
2012	Shiming Zou, China

FLYWEIGHT (112 LB)
1904	George Finnegan, United States
1920	Frank Di Gennara, United States
1924	Fidel LaBarba, United States
1928	Antal Kocsis, Hungary
1932	Istvan Enekes, Hungary
1936	Willi Kaiser, Germany
1948	Pascual Perez, Argentina
1952	Nathan Brooks, United States
1956	Terence Spinks, Great Britain
1960	Gyula Torok, Hungary
1964	Fernando Atzori, Italy
1968	Ricardo Delgado, Mexico
1972	Georgi Kostadinov, Bulgaria
1976	Leo Randolph, United States
1980	Peter Lessov, Bulgaria
1984	Steve McCrory, United States
1988	Kim Kwang Sun, S Korea
1992	Su Choi Chol, N Korea
1996	Maikro Romero, Cuba
2000	Wijan Ponlid, Thailand
2004	Yuriokis Toledano, Cuba

FLYWEIGHT (112 LB) (Cont.)
2008	Somit Jongjohor, Thailand
2012	Robeisy Ramirez Carrazana, Cuba

BANTAMWEIGHT (119 LB)
1904	Oliver Kirk, United States
1908	A. Henry Thomas, Great Britain
1920	Clarence Walker, S Africa
1924	William Smith, S Africa
1928	Vittorio Tamagnini, Italy
1932	Horace Gwynne, Canada
1936	Ulderico Sergo, Italy
1948	Tibor Csik, Hungary
1952	Pentti Hamalainen, Finland
1956	Wolfgang Behrendt, E Germany
1960	Oleg Grigoryev, USSR
1964	Takao Sakurai, Japan
1968	Valery Sokolov, USSR
1972	Orlando Martinez, Cuba
1976	Yong Jo Gu, N Korea
1980	Juan Hernandez, Cuba
1984	Maurizio Stecca, Italy
1988	Kennedy McKinney, United States
1992	Joel Casamayor, Cuba
1996	István Kovács, Hungary
2000	Guillermo Ortiz, Cuba
2004	Guillermo Ortiz, Cuba
2008	Badar-Uugan Enkhbat, Mongolia
2012	Luke Campbell, Great Britain

FEATHERWEIGHT (125 LB)
1904	Oliver Kirk, United States
1908	Richard Gunn, Great Britain
1920	Paul Fritsch, France
1924	John Fields, United States
1928	Lambertus van Klaveren, Netherlands
1932	Carmelo Robledo, Argentina

BOXING (Cont.)

FEATHERWEIGHT (125 LB) (Cont.)

1936	Oscar Casanovas, Argentina
1948	Ernesto Formenti, Italy
1952	Jan Zachara, Czechoslovakia
1956	Vladimir Safronov, USSR
1960	Francesco Musso, Italy
1964	Stanislav Stephashkin, USSR
1968	Antonio Roldan, Mexico
1972	Boris Kousnetsov, USSR
1976	Angel Herrera, Cuba
1980	Rudi Fink, E Germany
1984	Meldrick Taylor, United States
1988	Giovanni Parisi, Italy
1992	Andreas Tews, Germany
1996	Somluck Kamsing, Thailand
2000	Bekzat Sattarkhanox, Kazakhstan
2004	Alexei Tichtchenko, Russia
2008	Vasyl Lomachenko, Ukraine

LIGHTWEIGHT (132 LB)

1904	Harry Spanger, United States
1908	Frederick Grace, Great Britain
1920	Samuel Mosberg, United States
1924	Hans Nielsen, Denmark
1928	Carlo Orlandi, Italy
1932	Lawrence Stevens, S Africa
1936	Imre Harangi, Hungary
1948	Gerald Dreyer, S Africa
1952	Aureliano Bolognesi, Italy
1956	Richard McTaggart, Great Britain
1960	Kazimierz Pazdzior, Poland
1964	Jozef Grudzien, Poland
1968	Ronald Harris, United States
1972	Jan Szczepanski, Poland
1976	Howard Davis, United States
1980	Angel Herrera, Cuba
1984	Pernell Whitaker, United States
1988	Andreas Zuelow, E Germany
1992	Oscar De La Hoya, United States
1996	Hocine Soltani, Algeria
2000	Mario Mesa, Cuba
2004	Mario Mesa, Cuba
2008	Alexey Tishchenko, Russia
2012	Vasyl Lomachenko, Ukraine

LIGHT WELTERWEIGHT (139 LB)

1952	Charles Adkins, United States
1956	Vladimir Yengibaryan, USSR
1960	Bohumil Nemecek, Czechoslovakia
1964	Jerzy Kulej, Poland
1968	Jerzy Kulej, Poland
1972	Ray Seales, United States
1976	Ray Leonard, United States
1980	Patrizio Oliva, Italy
1984	Jerry Page, United States
1988	Viatcheslav Janovski, USSR
1992	Hector Vinent, Cuba
1996	Hector Vinent, Cuba
2000	Mahamadkadyz Abdullaev, Uzbekistan
2004	Manus Boonjumnong, Thailand
2008	Felix Diaz, Dominican Republic
2012	Roniel Iglesias Sotolongo, Cuba

WELTERWEIGHT (147 LB)

1904	Albert Young, United States
1920	Albert Schneider, Canada
1924	Jean Delarge, Belgium
1928	Edward Morgan, New Zealand
1932	Edward Flynn, United States
1936	Sten Suvio, Finland
1948	Julius Torma, Czechoslovakia
1952	Zygmunt Chychla, Poland
1956	Nicolae Linca, Romania

WELTERWEIGHT (147 LB) (Cont.)

1960	Giovanni Benvenuti, Italy
1964	Marian Kasprzyk, Poland
1968	Manfred Wolke, E Germany
1972	Emilio Correa, Cuba
1976	Jochen Bachfeld, E Germany
1980	Andres Aldama, Cuba
1984	Mark Breland, United States
1988	Robert Wangila, Kenya
1992	Michael Carruth, Ireland
1996	Oleg Saitov, Russia
2000	Oleg Saitov, Russia
2004	Bakhtiyar Artayev, Kazakhstan
2008	Bakhyt Sarsekbayev, Kazakhstan
2012	Serik Sapiyev, Kazakhstan

LIGHT MIDDLEWEIGHT (156 LB)

1952	Laszlo Papp, Hungary
1956	Laszlo Papp, Hungary
1960	Wilbert McClure, United States
1964	Boris Lagutin, USSR
1968	Boris Lagutin, USSR
1972	Dieter Kottysch, W Germany
1976	Jerzy Rybicki, Poland
1980	Armando Martinez, Cuba
1984	Frank Tate, United States
1988	Park Si-Hun, S Korea
1992	Juan Lemus, Cuba
1996	David Reid, United States
2000	Yermakhan Ibraimov, Kazakhstan

MIDDLEWEIGHT (165 LB)

1904	Charles Mayer, United States
1908	John Douglas, Great Britain
1920	Harry Mallin, Great Britain
1924	Harry Mallin, Great Britain
1928	Piero Toscani, Italy
1932	Carmen Barth, United States
1936	Jean Despeaux, France
1948	Laszlo Papp, Hungary
1952	Floyd Patterson, United States
1956	Gennady Schatkov, USSR
1960	Edward Crook, United States
1964	Valery Popenchenko, USSR
1968	Christopher Finnegan, Great Britain
1972	Vyacheslav Lemechev, USSR
1976	Michael Spinks, United States
1980	Jose Gomez, Cuba
1984	Shin Joon Sup, S Korea
1988	Henry Maske, E Germany
1992	Ariel Hernandez, Cuba
1996	Ariel Hernandez, Cuba
2000	Jorge Gutierrez, Cuba
2004	Gaydarbek Gaydarbekov, Russia
2008	James Degale, Great Britain
2012	Serik Sapiyev, Kazakhstan

LIGHT HEAVYWEIGHT (178 LB)

1920	Edward Eagan, United States
1924	Harry Mitchell, Great Britain
1928	Victor Avendano, Argentina
1932	David Carstens, S Africa
1936	Roger Michelot, France
1948	George Hunter, S Africa
1952	Norvel Lee, United States
1956	James Boyd, United States
1960	Cassius Clay, United States
1964	Cosimo Pinto, Italy
1968	Dan Poznyak, USSR
1972	Mate Parlov, Yugoslavia
1976	Leon Spinks, United States
1980	Slobodan Kacer, Yugoslavia

BOXING *(Cont.)*

LIGHT HEAVYWEIGHT (178 LB) *(Cont.)*

1984	Anton Josipovic, Yugoslavia
1988	Andrew Maynard, United States
1992	Torsten May, Germany
1996	Vassili Jirov, Kazakhstan
2000	Alexander Lebziak, Russia
2004	Andre Ward, United States
2008	Zhang Xiaoping, China
2012	Egor Mekhontcev, Russia

HEAVYWEIGHT*

1904	Samuel Berger, United States
1908	Albert Oldham, Great Britain
1920	Ronald Rawson, Great Britain
1924	Otto von Porat, Norway
1928	Arturo Rodriguez Jurado, Argentina
1932	Santiago Lovell, Argentina
1936	Herbert Runge, Germany
1948	Rafael Inglesias, Argentina
1952	H. Edward Sanders, United States
1956	T. Peter Rademacher, United States
1960	Franco De Piccoli, Italy
1964	Joe Frazier, United States
1968	George Foreman, United States
1972	Teofilo Stevenson, Cuba

HEAVYWEIGHT *(Cont.)*

1976	Teofilo Stevenson, Cuba
1980	Teofilo Stevenson, Cuba
1984	Henry Tillman, United States
1988	Ray Mercer, United States
1992	Félix Sávon, Cuba
1996	Félix Sávon, Cuba
2000	Félix Sávon, Cuba
2004	Odlanier Fonte, Cuba
2008	Rakhim Chakhiev, Russia
2012	Oleksandr Usyk, Ukraine

SUPERHEAVYWEIGHT (UNLIMITED)

1984	Tyrell Biggs, United States
1988	Lennox Lewis, Canada
1992	Roberto Balado, Cuba
1996	Vladimir Klitchko, Ukraine
2000	Audley Harrison, Great Britain
2004	Alexander Povetkin, Russia
2008	Roberto Cammarelle, Italy
2012	Anthony Joshua, Great Britain

*Until 1984 the heavyweight division was unlimited. With the addition of the super heavyweight division, a limit of 201 pounds was imposed.

SWIMMING — Men

50-METER FREESTYLE

1904	Zoltan Halmay, Hungary (50 yds)	28.0
1988	Matt Biondi, United States	22.14 WR
1992	Aleksandr Popov, Unified Team	22.30
1996	Aleksandr Popov, Russia	22.13
2000	Anthony Ervin, United States	21.98
	Gary Hall Jr, United States	21.98
2004	Gary Hall Jr, United States	21.93
2008	Cesar Cielo Filho, Brazil	21.30 OR
2012	Florent Manaudou, France	21.34

100-METER FREESTYLE

1896	Alfred Hajos, Hungary	1:22.2 OR
1904	Zoltan Halmay, Hungary (100 yds)	1:02.8
1906	Charles Daniels, United States	1:13.4
1908	Charles Daniels, United States	1:05.6 WR
1912	Duke Kahanamoku, United States	1:03.4
1920	Duke Kahanamoku, United States	1:00.4 WR
1924	John Weissmuller, United States	59.0 OR
1928	John Weissmuller, United States	58.6 OR
1932	Yasuji Miyazaki, Japan	58.2
1936	Ferenc Csik, Hungary	57.6
1948	Wally Ris, United States	57.3 OR
1952	Clarke Scholes, United States	57.4
1956	Jon Henricks, Australia	55.4 OR
1960	John Devitt, Australia	55.2 OR
1964	Don Schollander, United States	53.4 OR
1968	Mike Wenden, Australia	52.2 WR
1972	Mark Spitz, United States	51.22 WR
1976	Jim Montgomery, United States	49.99 WR
1980	Jörg Woithe, E Germany	50.40
1984	Rowdy Gaines, United States	49.80 OR
1988	Matt Biondi, United States	48.63 OR
1992	Aleksandr Popov, Unified Team	49.02
1996	Aleksandr Popov, Russia	48.74
2000	P. van den Hoogenband, Neth	48.30
2004	P. van den Hoogenband, Neth	48.17
2008	Alain Bernard, France	47.21 OR
2012	Nathan Adrian, United States	47.52

200-METER FREESTYLE

1900	Frederick Lane, Australia	2:25.2 OR
1904	Charles Daniels, United States	2:44.2
1968	Michael Wenden, Australia	1:55.2 OR

200-METER FREESTYLE *(CONT.)*

1972	Mark Spitz, United States	1:52.78 WR
1976	Bruce Furniss, United States	1:50.29 WR
1980	Sergei Kopliakov, USSR	1:49.81 OR
1984	Michael Gross, W Germany	1:47.44 WR
1988	Duncan Armstrong, Australia	1:47.25 WR
1992	Evgueni Sadovyi, Unified Team	1:46.70 OR
1996	Danyon Loader, New Zealand	1:47.63
2000	Pieter van den Hoogenband, Neth	1:45.35 EWR
2004	Ian Thorpe, Australia	1:44.71 OR
2008	Michael Phelps, United States	1:42.96 WR
2012	Yannick Agnel, France	1:43.14

400-METER FREESTYLE

1896	Paul Neumann, Austria (500 yds)	8:12.6
1904	Charles Daniels, U.S. (440 yds)	6:16.2
1906	Otto Scheff, Austria (440 yds)	6:23.8
1908	Henry Taylor, Great Britain	5:36.8
1912	George Hodgson, Canada	5:24.4
1920	Norman Ross, United States	5:26.8
1924	John Weissmuller, United States	5:04.2 OR
1928	Albert Zorilla, Argentina	5:01.6 OR
1932	Buster Crabbe, United States	4:48.4 OR
1936	Jack Medica, United States	4:44.5 OR
1948	William Smith, United States	4:41.0 OR
1952	Jean Boiteux, France	4:30.7 OR
1956	Murray Rose, Australia	4:27.3 OR
1960	Murray Rose, Australia	4:18.3 OR
1964	Don Schollander, United States	4:12.2 WR
1968	Mike Burton, United States	4:09.0 OR
1972	Brad Cooper, Australia	4:00.27 OR
1976	Brian Goodell, United States	3:51.93 WR
1980	Vladimir Salnikov, USSR	3:51.31 OR
1984	George DiCarlo, United States	3:51.23 OR
1988	Uwe Dassler, E Germany	3:46.95 WR
1992	Evgueni Sadovyi, Unified Team	3:45.00 WR
1996	Danyon Loader, New Zealand	3:47.97
2000	Ian Thorpe, Australia	3:40.59 WR
2004	Ian Thorpe, Australia	3:43.10
2008	Park Taehwan, South Korea	3:41.86
2012	Yang Sun, China	3:40.14 OR

SWIMMING— Men *(Cont.)*

1,500-METER FREESTLYE

1908	Henry Taylor, Great Britain	22:48.4 WR
1912	George Hodgson, Canada	22:00.0 WR
1920	Norman Ross, United States	22:23.2
1924	Andrew Charlton, Australia	20:06.6 WR
1928	Arne Borg, Sweden	19:51.8 OR
1932	Kusuo Kitamura, Japan	19:12.4 OR
1936	Noboru Terada, Japan	19:13.7
1948	James McLane, United States	19:18.5
1952	Ford Konno, United States	18:30.3 OR
1956	Murray Rose, Australia	17:58.9
1960	John Konrads, Australia	17:19.6 OR
1964	Robert Windle, Australia	17:01.7 OR
1968	Mike Burton, United States	16:38.9 OR
1972	Mike Burton, United States	15:52.58 OR
1976	Brian Goodell, United States	15:02.40 WR
1980	Vladimir Salnikov, USSR	14:58.27 WR
1984	Michael O'Brien, United States	15:05.20
1988	Vladimir Salnikov, USSR	15:00.40
1992	Kieren Perkins, Australia	14:43.48 WR
1996	Kieren Perkins, Australia	14:56.40
2000	Grant Hackett, Australia	14:48.33
2004	Grant Hackett, Australia	14:43.40 OR
2008	Ousama Mellouli, Tunisia	14:40.84 OR
2012	Yang Sun, China	14:31.02 WR

100-METER BACKSTROKE

1904	Walter Brack, Germany (100 yds)	1:16.8
1908	Arno Bieberstein, Germany	1:24.6 WR
1912	Harry Hebner, United States	1:21.2
1920	Warren Kealoha, United States	1:15.2
1924	Warren Kealoha, United States	1:13.2 OR
1928	George Kojac, United States	1:08.2 WR
1932	Masaji Kiyokawa, Japan	1:08.6
1936	Adolph Kiefer, United States	1:05.9 OR
1948	Allen Stack, United States	1:06.4
1952	Yoshi Oyakawa, United States	1:05.4 OR
1956	David Thiele, Australia	1:02.2 OR
1960	David Thiele, Australia	1:01.9 OR
1968	Roland Matthes, E Germany	58.7 OR
1972	Roland Matthes, E Germany	56.58 OR
1976	John Naber, United States	55.49 WR
1980	Bengt Baron, Sweden	56.33
1984	Rick Carey, United States	55.79
1988	Daichi Suzuki, Japan	55.05
1992	Mark Tewksbury, Canada	53.98 WR
1996	Jeff Rouse, United States	54.10
2000	Lenny Krayzelburg, United States	53.72 OR
2004	Aaron Peirsol, United States	54.06
2008	Aaron Peirsol, United States	52.54 WR
2012	Matthew Grevers, United States	52.16 OR

200-METER BACKSTROKE

1900	Ernst Hoppenberg, Germany	2:47.0
1964	Jed Graef, United States	2:10.3 WR
1968	Roland Matthes, E Germany	2:09.6 OR
1972	Roland Matthes, E Germany	2:02.82 EWR
1976	John Naber, United States	1:59.19 WR
1980	Sandor Wladar, Hungary	2:01.93
1984	Rick Carey, United States	2:00.23
1988	Igor Polianski, USSR	1:59.37
1992	Martin Lopez-Zubero, Spain	1:58.47 OR
1996	Brad Bridgewater, United States	1:58.54
2000	Lenny Krayzelburg, United States	1:56.76 OR
2004	Aaron Peirsol, United States	1:54.95 OR
2008	Ryan Lochte, United States	1:53.94 WR
2012	Tyler Clary, United States	1:53.41 OR

100-METER BREASTSTROKE

1968	Don McKenzie, United States	1:07.7 OR

100-METER BREASTSTROKE *(CONT.)*

1972	Nobutaka Taguchi, Japan	1:04.94 WR
1976	John Hencken, United States	1:03.11 WR
1980	Duncan Goodhew, Great Britain	1:03.44
1984	Steve Lundquist, United States	1:01.65 WR
1988	Adrian Moorhouse, Great Britain	1:02.04
1992	Nelson Diebel, United States	1:01.50 OR
1996	Fred DeBurghgraeve, Belgium	1:00.65
2000	Domenico Fioravanti, Italy	1:00.46 OR
2004	Kosuke Kitajima, Japan	1:00.08
2008	Kosuke Kitajima, Japan	58.91 WR
2012	Cameron van der Burgh, S. Africa	58.46 WR

200-METER BREASTSTROKE

1908	Frederick Holman, Great Britain	3:09.2 WR
1912	Walter Bathe, Germany	3:01.8 OR
1920	Haken Malmroth, Sweden	3:04.4
1924	Robert Skelton, United States	2:56.6
1928	Yoshiyuki Tsuruta, Japan	2:48.8 OR
1932	Yoshiyuki Tsuruta, Japan	2:45.4
1936	Tetsuo Hamuro, Japan	2:41.5 OR
1948	Joseph Verdeur, United States	2:39.3 OR
1952	John Davies, Australia	2:34.4 OR
1956	Masura Furukawa, Japan	2:34.7 OR
1960	William Mulliken, United States	2:37.4
1964	Ian O'Brien, Australia	2:27.8 WR
1968	Felipe Munoz, Mexico	2:28.7
1972	John Hencken, United States	2:21.55 WR
1976	David Wilkie, Great Britain	2:15.11 WR
1980	Robertas Zhulpa, USSR	2:15.85
1984	Victor Davis, Canada	2:13.34 WR
1988	Jozsef Szabo, Hungary	2:13.52
1992	Mike Barrowman, United States	2:10.16 WR
1996	Norbert Rózsa, Hungary	2:12.57
2000	Domenico Fioravanti, Italy	2:10.87
2004	Kosuke Kitajima, Japan	2:09.44 OR
2008	Kosuke Kitajima, Japan	2:07.64 OR
2012	Daniel Gyurta, Hungary	2:07.28 WR

100-METER BUTTERFLY

1968	Doug Russell, United States	55.9 OR
1972	Mark Spitz, United States	54.27 WR
1976	Matt Vogel, United States	54.35
1980	Pär Arvidsson, Sweden	54.92
1984	Michael Gross, W Germany	53.08 WR
1988	Anthony Nesty, Suriname	53.00 OR
1992	Pablo Morales, United States	53.32
1996	Denis Pankratov, Russia	52.27 WR
2000	Lars Froelander, Sweden	52.00
2004	Michael Phelps, United States	51.25 OR
2008	Michael Phelps, United States	50.58 OR
2012	Michael Phelps, United States	51.21

200-METER BUTTERFLY

1956	William Yorzyk, United States	2:19.3 OR
1960	Michael Troy, United States	2:12.8 WR
1964	Kevin Berry, Australia	2:06.6 WR
1968	Carl Robie, United States	2:08.7
1972	Mark Spitz, United States	2:00.70 WR
1976	Mike Bruner, United States	1:59.23 WR
1980	Sergei Fesenko, USSR	1:59.76
1984	Jon Sieben, Australia	1:57.04 WR
1988	Michael Gross, W Germany	1:56.94 OR
1992	Melvin Stewart, United States	1:56.26 OR
1996	Denis Pankratov, Russia	1:56.51
2000	Tom Malchow, United States	1:55.35 OR
2004	Michael Phelps, United States	1:54.04 OR
2008	Michael Phelps, United States	1:52.03 WR
2012	Chad le Clos, South Africa	1:52.96

Note: OR=Olympic Record. WR=World Record. EOR=Equals Olympic Record. EWR=Equals World Record. WB=World Best.

SWIMMING — Men (Cont.)

200-METER INDIVIDUAL MEDLEY

1968	Charles Hickcox, United States	2:12.0 OR
1972	Gunnar Larsson, Sweden	2:07.17 WR
1984	Alex Baumann, Canada	2:01.42 WR
1988	Tamas Darnyi, Hungary	2:00.17 WR
1992	Tamas Darnyi, Hungary	2:00.76
1996	Attila Czene, Hungary	1:59.91 OR
2000	Massimiliano Rosolino, Italy	1:58.98 OR
2004	Michael Phelps, United States	1:57.14 OR
2008	Michael Phelps, United States	1:54.23 WR
2012	Michael Phelps, United States	1:54.27

400-METER INDIVIDUAL MEDLEY

1964	Richard Roth, United States	4:45.4 WR
1968	Charles Hickcox, United States	4:48.4
1972	Gunnar Larsson, Sweden	4:31.98 OR
1976	Rod Strachan, United States	4:23.68 WR
1980	Aleksandr Sidorenko, USSR	4:22.89 OR
1984	Alex Baumann, Canada	4:17.41 WR
1988	Tamas Darnyi, Hungary	4:14.75 WR
1992	Tamas Darnyi, Hungary	4:14.23 OR
1996	Tom Dolan, United States	4:14.90
2000	Tom Dolan, United States	4:11.76 WR
2004	Michael Phelps, United States	4:08.26 WR
2008	Michael Phelps, United States	4:03.84 WR
2012	Ryan Lochte, United States	4:05.18

4 X 100-METER MEDLEY RELAY

1960	United States	4:05.4 WR
1964	United States	3:58.4 WR
1968	United States	3:54.9 WR
1972	United States	3:48.16 WR
1976	United States	3:42.22 WR
1980	Australia	3:45.70
1984	United States	3:39.30 WR
1988	United States	3:36.93 WR
1992	United States	3:36.93 EWR
1996	United States	3:34.84 WR
2000	United States	3:33.73 WR
2004	United States	3:30.68 WR
2008	United States	3:29.34 WR
2012	United States	3:29.35

4 X 100-METER FREESTYLE RELAY

1964	United States	3:32.2 WR
1968	United States	3:31.7 WR
1972	United States	3:26.42 WR
1984	United States	3:19.03 WR
1988	United States	3:16.53 WR
1992	United States	3:16.74
1996	United States	3:15.41 OR
2000	Australia	3:13.67 WR
2004	S Africa	3:13.17 WR
2008	United States	3:08.24 WR
2012	France	3:09.93

4 X 200-METER FREESTYLE RELAY

1906	Hungary (1,000 m)	16:52.4
1908	Great Britain	10:55.6
1912	Australia/New Zealand	10:11.6 WR
1920	United States	10:04.4 WR
1924	United States	9:53.4 WR
1928	United States	9:36.2 WR
1932	Japan	8:58.4 WR
1936	Japan	8:51.5 WR
1948	United States	8:46.0 WR
1952	United States	8:31.1 OR
1956	Australia	8:23.6 WR
1960	United States	8:10.2 WR
1964	United States	7:52.1 WR
1968	United States	7:52.33
1972	United States	7:35.78 WR
1976	United States	7:23.22 WR
1980	USSR	7:23.50
1984	United States	7:15.69 WR
1988	United States	7:12.51 WR
1992	Unified Team	7:11.95 WR
1996	United States	7:14.84
2000	Australia	7:07.05 WR
2004	United States	7:07.33
2008	United States	6:58.56 WR
2012	United States	6:59.70

10 KM MARATHON

2008	M. van der Weijden, Neth.	1:51:51.60
2012	Oussama Mellouli, Tunisia	1:49:55.1

SWIMMING — Women

50-METER FREESTYLE

1988	Kristin Otto, E Germany	25.49 OR
1992	Yang Wenyi, China	24.79 WR
1996	Amy Van Dyken, United States	24.87
2000	Inge de Bruijn, Netherlands	24.32 WR
2004	Inge de Bruijn, Netherlands	24.58
2008	Britta Steffen, Germany	24.06 OR
2012	Ranomi Kromowidjojo, Netherlands	24.05 OR

100-METER FREESTYLE

1912	Fanny Durack, Australia	1:22.2
1920	Ethelda Bleibtrey, United States	1:13.6 WR
1924	Ethel Lackie, United States	1:12.4
1928	Albina Osipowich, United States	1:11.0 OR
1932	Helene Madison, United States	1:06.8 OR
1936	Hendrika Mastenbroek, Neth	1:05.9 OR
1948	Greta Andersen, Denmark	1:06.3
1952	Katalin Szöke, Hungary	1:06.8
1956	Dawn Fraser, Australia	1:02.0 WR
1960	Dawn Fraser, Australia	1:01.2 OR
1964	Dawn Fraser, Australia	59.5 OR
1968	Jan Henne, United States	1:00.0
1972	Sandra Neilson, United States	58.59 OR
1976	Kornelia Ender, E Germany	55.65 WR
1980	Barbara Krause, E Germany	54.79 WR

100-METER FREESTYLE (CONT.)

1984	Carrie Steinseifer, United States	55.92
	Nancy Hogshead, United States	55.92
1988	Kristin Otto, E Germany	54.93
1992	Zhuang Yong, China	54.64 OR
1996	Le Jingyi, China	54.50 OR
2000	Inge de Bruijn, Netherlands	53.83 OR
2004	Jodie Henry, Australia	53.84
2008	Britta Steffen, Germany	53.12 OR
2012	Ranomi Kromowidjojo, Netherlands	53.00 OR

200-METER FREESTYLE

1968	Debbie Meyer, United States	2:10.5 OR
1972	Shane Gould, Australia	2:03.56 WR
1976	Kornelia Ender, E Germany	1:59.26 WR
1980	Barbara Krause, E Germany	1:58.33 OR
1984	Mary Wayte, United States	1:59.23
1988	Heike Friedrich, E Germany	1:57.65 OR
1992	Nicole Haislett, United States	1:57.90
1996	Claudia Poll, Costa Rica	1:58.16
2000	Susie O'Neill, Australia	1:58.24
2004	Camelia Potec, Romania	1:58.03
2008	Frederica Pellegrini, Italy	1:54.82 WR
2012	Allison Schmitt, United States	1:53.61 OR

Note: OR=Olympic Record. WR=World Record. EOR=Equals Olympic Record. EWR=Equals World Record. WB=World Best.

SWIMMING — Women *(Cont.)*

400-METER FREESTYLE

1924	Martha Norelius, United States	6:02.2 OR
1928	Martha Norelius, United States	5:42.8 WR
1932	Helene Madison, United States	5:28.5 WR
1936	Hendrika Mastenbroek, Neth	5:26.4 OR
1948	Ann Curtis, United States	5:17.8 OR
1952	Valeria Gyenge, Hungary	5:12.1 OR
1956	Lorraine Crapp, Australia	4:54.6 OR
1960	Chris von Saltza, United States	4:50.6 OR
1964	Virginia Duenkel, United States	4:43.3 OR
1968	Debbie Meyer, United States	4:31.8 OR
1972	Shane Gould, Australia	4:19.44 WR
1976	Petra Thümer, E Germany	4:09.89 WR
1980	Ines Diers, E Germany	4:08.76 WR
1984	Tiffany Cohen, United States	4:07.10 OR
1988	Janet Evans, United States	4:03.85 WR
1992	Dagmar Hase, Germany	4:07.18
1996	Michelle Smith, Ireland	4:07.25
2000	Brooke Bennett, United States	4:05.80
2004	Laure Manaudou, France	4:05.34
2008	Rebecca Adlington, Great Britain	4:03.22
2012	Camille Muffat, France	4:01.45 OR

800-METER FREESTYLE

1968	Debbie Meyer, United States	9:24.0 OR
1972	Keena Rothhammer, United States	8:53.68 WR
1976	Petra Thümer, E Germany	8:37.14 WR
1980	Michelle Ford, Australia	8:28.90 OR
1984	Tiffany Cohen, United States	8:24.95 OR
1988	Janet Evans, United States	8:20.20 OR
1992	Janet Evans, United States	8:25.52
1996	Brooke Bennett, United States	8:27.89
2000	Brooke Bennett, United States	8:19.67 OR
2004	Ai Shibata, Japan	8:24.54
2008	Rebecca Adlington, Great Britain	8:14.10 WR
2012	Katie Ledecky, United States	8:14.63

100-METER BACKSTROKE

1924	Sybil Bauer, United States	1:23.2 OR
1928	Marie Braun, Netherlands	1:22.0
1932	Eleanor Holm, United States	1:19.4
1936	Dina Senff, Netherlands	1:18.9
1948	Karen Harup, Denmark	1:14.4 OR
1952	Joan Harrison, South Africa	1:14.3
1956	Judy Grinham, Great Britain	1:12.9 OR
1960	Lynn Burke, United States	1:09.3 OR
1964	Cathy Ferguson, United States	1:07.7 WR
1968	Kaye Hall, United States	1:06.2 WR
1972	Melissa Belote, United States	1:05.78 OR
1976	Ulrike Richter, E Germany	1:01.83 OR
1980	Rica Reinisch, E Germany	1:00.86 WR
1984	Theresa Andrews, United States	1:02.55
1988	Kristin Otto, E Germany	1:00.89
1992	Krisztina Egerszegi, Hungary	1:00.68 OR
1996	Beth Botsford, United States	1:01.19
2000	Diana Iuliana Mocanu, Romania	1:00.21 OR
2004	Natalie Coughlin, United States	1:00.37
2008	Natalie Coughlin, United States	58.96
2012	Missy Franklin, United States	58.33

200-METER BACKSTROKE

1968	Pokey Watson, United States	2:24.8 OR
1972	Melissa Belote, United States	2:19.19 WR
1976	Ulrike Richter, E Germany	2:13.43 OR
1980	Rica Reinisch, E Germany	2:11.77 WR
1984	Jolanda De Rover, Netherlands	2:12.38
1988	Krisztina Egerszegi, Hungary	2:09.29 OR
1992	Krisztina Egerszegi, Hungary	2:07.06 OR
1996	Krisztina Egerszegi, Hungary	2:07.83
2000	Diana Iuliana Mocanu, Romania	2:08.16
2004	Kirsty Coventry, Zimbabwe	2:09.19

200-METER BACKSTROKE *(CONT.)*

2008	Kirsty Coventry, Zimbabwe	2:05.24 WR
2012	Missy Franklin, United States	1:58.33

100-METER BREASTSTROKE

1968	Djurdjica Bjedov, Yugoslavia	1:15.8 OR
1972	Catherine Carr, United States	1:13.58 WR
1976	Hannelore Anke, E Germany	1:11.16
1980	Ute Geweniger, E Germany	1:10.22
1984	Petra Van Staveren, Netherlands	1:09.88 OR
1988	Tania Dangalakova, Bulgaria	1:07.95 OR
1992	Elena Roudkovskaia, Unified Team	1:08.00
1996	Penelope Heyns, S Africa	1:07.73
2000	Megan Quann, United States	1:07.05
2004	Xue Juan Luo, China	1:06.64
2008	Liesel Jones, Australia	1:05.17 WR
2012	Ruta Meilutyte, Lithuania	1:05.47

200-METER BREASTSTROKE

1924	Lucy Morton, Great Britain	3:33.2 OR
1928	Hilde Schrader, Germany	3:12.6
1932	Clare Dennis, Australia	3:06.3 OR
1936	Hideko Maehata, Japan	3:03.6
1948	Petronella Van Vliet, Netherlands	2:57.2
1952	Eva Szekely, Hungary	2:51.7 OR
1956	Ursula Happe, W Germany	2:53.1 OR
1960	Anita Lonsbrough, Great Britain	2:49.5 WR
1964	Galina Prozumenshikova, USSR	2:46.4 OR
1968	Sharon Wichman, United States	2:44.4 OR
1972	Beverly Whitfield, Australia	2:41.71 OR
1976	Marina Koshevaia, USSR	2:33.35 WR
1980	Lina Kaciusyte, USSR	2:29.54 OR
1984	Anne Ottenbrite, Canada	2:30.38
1988	Silke Hoerner, E Germany	2:26.71 WR
1992	Kyoko Iwasaki, Japan	2:26.65 OR
1996	Penelope Heyns, S Africa	2:25.41 OR
2000	Agnes Kovacs, Hungary	2:24.35 OR
2004	Amanda Beard, United States	2:23.37 OR
2008	Rebecca Soni, United States	2:20.22 WR
2012	Rebecca Soni, United States	2:19.59 WR

100-METER BUTTERFLY

1956	Shelley Mann, United States	1:11.0 OR
1960	Carolyn Schuler, United States	1:09.5 OR
1964	Sharon Stouder, United States	1:04.7 WR
1968	Lynn McClements, Australia	1:05.5
1972	Mayumi Aoki, Japan	1:03.34 WR
1976	Kornelia Ender, E Germany	1:00.13 EWR
1980	Caren Metschuck, E Germany	1:00.42
1984	Mary T. Meagher, United States	59.26
1988	Kristin Otto, E Germany	59.00 OR
1992	Qian Hong, China	58.62 OR
1996	Amy Van Dyken, United States	59.13
2000	Inge de Bruijn, Netherlands	56.61 WR
2004	Petria Thomas, Australia	57.72
2008	Lisbeth Trickett, Australia	56.73
2012	Dana Vollmer, United States	55.98 WR

200-METER BUTTERFLY

1968	Ada Kok, Netherlands	2:24.7 OR
1972	Karen Moe, United States	2:15.57 WR
1976	Andrea Pollack, E Germany	2:11.41 OR
1980	Ines Geissler, E Germany	2:10.44 OR
1984	Mary T. Meagher, United States	2:06.90 OR
1988	Kathleen Nord, E Germany	2:09.51
1992	Summer Sanders, United States	2:08.67
1996	Susan O'Neill, Australia	2:07.76
2000	Misty Hyman, United States	2:05.88 OR
2004	Otylia Jedrzegczak, Poland	2:06.05
2008	Liu Zige, China	2:04.18 WR
2012	Liuyang Jiao, China	2:04.06 OR

Note: OR=Olympic Record. WR=World Record. EOR=Equals Olympic Record. EWR=Equals World Record. WB=World Best.

SWIMMING — Women *(Cont.)*

200-METER INDIVIDUAL MEDLEY

1968	Claudia Kolb, United States	2:24.7 OR
1972	Shane Gould, Australia	2:23.07 WR
1984	Tracy Caulkins, United States	2:12.64 OR
1988	Daniela Hunger, E Germany	2:12.59 OR
1992	Lin Li, China	2:11.65 WR
1996	Michelle Smith, Ireland	2:13.93
2000	Yana Klochkova, Ukraine	2:10.68 OR
2004	Yana Klochkova, Ukraine	2:11.14
2008	Stephanie Rice, Australia	2:08.45 WR
2012	Shiwen Ye, China	2:07.57 OR

400-METER INDIVIDUAL MEDLEY

1964	Donna de Varona, United States	5:18.7 OR
1968	Claudia Kolb, United States	5:08.5 OR
1972	Gail Neall, Australia	5:02.97 WR
1976	Ulrike Tauber, E Germany	4:42.77 WR
1980	Petra Schneider, E Germany	4:36.29 WR
1984	Tracy Caulkins, United States	4:39.24
1988	Janet Evans, United States	4:37.76
1992	Krisztina Egerszegi, Hungary	4:36.54
1996	Michelle Smith, Ireland	4:39.18
2000	Yana Klochkova, Ukraine	4:33.59 WR
2004	Yana Klochkova, Ukraine	4:34.83
2008	Stephanie Rice, Australia	4:29.45 WR
2012	Shiwen Ye, China	4:28.43 WR

4 X 100-METER MEDLEY RELAY

1960	United States	4:41.1 WR
1964	United States	4:33.9 WR
1968	United States	4:28.3 OR
1972	United States	4:20.75 WR
1976	E Germany	4:07.95 WR
1980	E Germany	4:06.67 WR
1984	United States	4:08.34
1988	E Germany	4:03.74 OR
1992	United States	4:02.54 WR
1996	United States	4:02.88
2000	United States	3:58:30 WR

4 X 100-METER MEDLEY RELAY *(CONT.)*

2004	Australia	3:57.32 WR
2008	Australia	3:52.69 WR
2012	United States	3:52.05 WR

4 X 100-METER FREESTYLE RELAY

1912	Great Britain	5:52.8 WR
1920	United States	5:11.6 WR
1924	United States	4:58.8 WR
1928	United States	4:47.6 WR
1932	United States	4:38.0 WR
1936	Netherlands	4:36.0 OR
1948	United States	4:29.2 OR
1952	Hungary	4:24.4 WR
1956	Australia	4:17.1 WR
1960	United States	4:08.9 WR
1964	United States	4:03.8 WR
1968	United States	4:02.5 OR
1972	United States	3:55.19 WR
1976	United States	3:44.82 WR
1980	E Germany	3:42.71 WR
1984	United States	3:43.43
1988	E Germany	3:40.63 OR
1992	United States	3:39.46 WR
1996	United States	3:39.29 OR
2000	United States	3:36.61 WR
2004	Australia	3:35.94 WR
2008	Netherlands	3:33.76 OR
2012	Australia	

4 X 200-METER FREESTYLE RELAY

1996	United States	7:59.87
2000	United States	7:57.80 OR
2004	United States	7:53.42 WR
2008	Australia	7:44.31 WR
2012	United States	3:33.15 OR

10 KM MARATHON

2008	Larisa Ilchenko, Russia	1:59:27.70
2012	Eva Risztov, Hungary	1:57:38.2

DIVING — Men

SPRINGBOARD		Pts
1908	Albert Zürner, Germany	85.5
1912	Paul Günther, Germany	79.23
1920	Louis Kuehn, United States	675.40
1924	Albert White, United States	97.46
1928	Pete DesJardins, United States	185.04
1932	Michael Galitzen, United States	161.38
1936	Richard Degener, United States	163.57
1948	Bruce Harlan, United States	163.64
1952	David Browning, United States	205.29
1956	Robert Clotworthy, United States	159.56
1960	Gary Tobian, United States	170.00
1964	Kenneth Sitzberger, United States	159.90
1968	Bernie Wrightson, United States	170.15
1972	Vladimir Vasin, USSR	594.09
1976	Phil Boggs, United States	619.05
1980	Aleksandr Portnov, USSR	905.02
1984	Greg Louganis, United States	754.41
1988	Greg Louganis, United States	730.80
1992	Mark Lenzi, United States	676.53
1996	Xiong Ni, China	701.46
2000	Xiong Ni, China	708.72
2004	Bo Peng, China	787.38
2008	He Chong, China	572.90
2012	Ilya Zakharov, Russia	555.90

PLATFORM		Pts
1904	George Sheldon, United States	12.66
1906	Gottlob Walz, Germany	156.0
1908	Hjalmar Johansson, Sweden	83.75
1912	Erik Adlerz, Sweden	73.94
1920	Clarence Pinkston, United States	100.67
1924	Albert White, United States	97.46
1928	Pete DesJardins, United States	98.74
1932	Harold Smith, United States	124.80
1936	Marshall Wayne, United States	113.58
1948	Sammy Lee, United States	130.05
1952	Sammy Lee, United States	156.28
1956	Joaquin Capilla, Mexico	152.44
1960	Robert Webster, United States	165.56
1964	Robert Webster, United States	148.58
1968	Klaus Dibiasi, Italy	164.18
1972	Klaus Dibiasi, Italy	504.12
1976	Klaus Dibiasi, Italy	600.51
1980	Falk Hoffmann, E Germany	835.65
1984	Greg Louganis, United States	710.91
1988	Greg Louganis, United States	638.61
1992	Sun Shuwei, China	677.31
1996	Dmitri Sautin, Russia	692.34
2000	Tian Liang, China	724.53
2004	Jia Hu, China	748.08
2008	Matthew Mitcham, Australia	537.95
2012	David Boudia, United States	568.65

DIVING — Women

SPRINGBOARD	Pts	PLATFORM	Pts
1920.....Aileen Riggin, United States	539.90	1912.....Greta Johansson, Sweden	39.90
1924.....Elizabeth Becker, United States	474.50	1920.....Stefani Fryland-Clausen, Denmark	34.60
1928.....Helen Meany, United States	78.62	1924.....Caroline Smith, United States	33.20
1932.....Georgia Coleman, United States	87.52	1928.....Elizabeth B. Pinkston, United States	31.60
1936.....Marjorie Gestring, United States	89.27	1932.....Dorothy Poynton, United States	40.26
1948.....Victoria Draves, United States	108.74	1936.....Dorothy Poynton Hill, United States	33.93
1952.....Patricia McCormick, United States	147.30	1948.....Victoria Draves, United States	68.87
1956.....Patricia McCormick, United States	142.36	1952.....Patricia McCormick, United States	79.37
1960.....Ingrid Krämer, E Germany	155.81	1956.....Patricia McCormick, United States	84.85
1964.....Ingrid Engel Krämer, E Germany	145.00	1960.....Ingrid Krämer, E Germany	91.28
1968.....Sue Gossick, United States	150.77	1964.....Lesley Bush, United States	99.80
1972.....Micki King, United States	450.03	1968.....Milena Duchkova, Czechoslovakia	109.59
1976.....Jennifer Chandler, United States	506.19	1972.....Ulrika Knape, Sweden	390.00
1980.....Irina Kalinina, USSR	725.91	1976.....Elena Vaytsekhovskaya, USSR	406.59
1984.....Sylvie Bernier, Canada	530.70	1980.....Martina Jäschke, E Germany	596.25
1988.....Gao Min, China	580.23	1984.....Zhou Jihong, China	435.51
1992.....Gao Min, China	572.40	1988.....Xu Yanmei, China	445.20
1996.....Mingxia Fu, China	547.68	1992.....Mingxia Fu, China	461.43
2000.....Mingxia Fu, China	609.42	1996.....Mingxia Fu, China	521.58
2004.....Guo Jingjing, China	633.15	2000.....Laura Wilkinson, United States	543.75
2008.....Guo Jingjing, China	415.35	2004.....Chantelle Newbery, Australia	590.31
2012.....Minxia Wu, China	414.00	2008.....Chen Ruoulin, China	447.70
		2012.....Chen Ruolin, China	422.3

GYMNASTICS — Men

ALL-AROUND	Pts	HORIZONTAL BAR *(CONT.)*	Pts
1900.....Gustave Sandras, France	302	1980.....Stoyan Deltchev, Bulgaria	19.825
1904.....Julius Lenhart, Austria	69.80	1984.....Shinji Morisue, Japan	20.00
1906.....Pierre Paysse, France	97	1988.....Vladimir Artemov, USSR	19.90
1908.....Alberto Braglia, Italy	317.0	1992.....Trent Dimas, United States	9.875
1912.....Alberto Braglia, Italy	135.0	1996.....Andreas Wecker, Germany	9.850
1920.....Giorgio Zampori, Italy	88.35	2000.....Alexei Nemov, Russia	9.787
1924.....Leon Stukelj, Yugoslavia	110.340	2004.....Igor Cassina, Italy	9.812
1928.....Georges Miez, Switzerland	247.500	2008.....Zou Kai, China	16.200
1932.....Romeo Neri, Italy	140.625	2012.....Epke Zonderland, Netherlands	16.533
1936.....Alfred Schwarzmann, Germany	113.100	PARALLEL BARS	Pts
1948.....Veikko Huhtanen, Finland	229.70	1896.....Alfred Flatow, Germany	—
1952.....Viktor Chukarin, USSR	115.70	1904.....George Eyser, United States	44
1956.....Viktor Chukarin, USSR	114.25	1924.....August Güttinger, Switzerland	21.63
1960.....Boris Shakhlin, USSR	115.95	1928.....Ladislav Vacha, Czechoslovakia	18.83
1964.....Yukio Endo, Japan	115.95	1932.....Romeo Neri, Italy	18.97
1968.....Sawao Kato, Japan	115.90	1936.....Konrad Frey, Germany	19.067
1972.....Sawao Kato, Japan	114.65	1948.....Michael Reusch, Switzerland	19.75
1976.....Nikolai Andrianov, USSR	116.65	1952.....Hans Eugster, Switzerland	19.65
1980.....Aleksandr Dityatin, USSR	118.65	1956.....Viktor Chukarin, USSR	19.20
1984.....Koji Gushiken, Japan	118.70	1960.....Boris Shakhlin, USSR	19.40
1988.....Vladimir Artemov, USSR	119.125	1964.....Yukio Endo, Japan	19.675
1992.....Vitaly Scherbo, Unified Team	59.025	1968.....Akinori Nakayama, Japan	19.475
1996.....Li Xiaoshuang, China	58.423	1972.....Sawao Kato, Japan	19.475
2000.....Alexei Nemov, Russia	58.474	1976.....Sawao Kato, Japan	19.675
2004.....Paul Hamm, United States	57.823	1980.....Aleksandr Tkachyov, USSR	19.775
2008.....Yang Wei, China	94.575	1984.....Bart Conner, United States	19.95
2012.....Kohei Uchimura, Japan	92.690	1988.....Vladimir Artemov, USSR	19.925
HORIZONTAL BAR	Pts	1992.....Vitaly Scherbo, Unified Team	9.900
1896.....Hermann Weingärtner, Germany	—	1996.....Rustan Sharipov, Ukraine	9.837
1904.....Anton Heida, United States	40	2000.....Li Xiaopeng, China	9.825
1924.....Leon Stukelj, Yugoslavia	19.73	2004.....Valeri Goncharov, Ukraine	9.787
1928.....Georges Miez, Switzerland	19.17	2008.....Li Xiaopeng, China	16.450
1932.....Dallas Bixler, United States	18.33	2012.....Zhe Feng, China	15.966
1936.....Aleksanteri Saarvala, Finland	19.367	VAULT	Pts
1948.....Josef Stalfer, Switzerland	19.85	1896.....Karl Schumann, Germany	—
1952.....Jack Günthard, Switzerland	19.55	1904.....George Eyser, United States	36
1956.....Takashi Ono, Japan	19.60	1924.....Frank Kriz, United States	9.98
1960.....Takashi Ono, Japan	19.60	1928.....Eugen Mack, Switzerland	9.58
1964.....Boris Shakhlin, USSR	19.625	1932.....Savino Guglielmetti, Italy	18.03
1968.....Akinori Nakayama, Japan	19.55	1936.....Alfred Schwarzmann, Germany	19.20
1972.....Mitsuo Tsukahara, Japan	19.725	1948.....Paavo Aaltonen, Finland	19.55
1976.....Mitsuo Tsukahara, Japan	19.675	1952.....Viktor Chukarin, USSR	19.20

GYMNASTICS — Men (Cont.)

VAULT (CONT.)

Year	Champion	Pts
1956	Helmut Bantz, Germany	18.85
1960	Takashi Ono, Japan	19.35
1964	Haruhiro Yamashita, Japan	19.60
1968	Mikhail Voronin, USSR	19.00
1972	Klaus Köste, E Germany	18.85
1976	Nikolai Andrianov, USSR	19.45
1980	Nikolai Andrianov, USSR	19.825
1984	Lou Yun, China	19.95
1988	Lou Yun, China	19.875
1992	Vitaly Scherbo, Unified Team	9.856
1996	Alexei Nemov, Russia	9.787
2000	Gervasio Deferr, Spain	9.712
2004	Gervasio Deferr, Spain	9.737
2008	Leszek Blanik, Poland	16.537
2012	Hak Seon Yang, South Korea	16.533

POMMEL HORSE

Year	Champion	Pts
1896	Louis Zutter, Switzerland	—
1904	Anton Heida, United States	42
1924	Josef Wilhelm, Switzerland	21.23
1928	Hermann Hänggi, Switzerland	19.75
1932	Istvan Pelle, Hungary	19.07
1936	Konrad Frey, Germany	19.333
1948	Paavo Aaltonen, Finland	19.35
1952	Viktor Chukarin, USSR	19.50
1956	Boris Shakhlin, USSR	19.25
1960	Eugen Ekman, Finland	19.375
1964	Miroslav Cerar, Yugoslavia	19.525
1968	Miroslav Cerar, Yugoslavia	19.325
1972	Viktor Klimenko, USSR	19.125
1976	Zoltan Magyar, Hungary	19.70
1980	Zoltan Magyar, Hungary	19.925
1984	Li Ning, China	19.95
1988	Dmitri Bilozerchev, USSR	19.95
1992	Vitaly Scherbo, Unified Team	9.925
1996	Donghua Li, Switzerland	9.875
2000	Marius Urzica, Romania	9.862
2004	Haibin Teng, China	9.837
2008	Xiao Qin, China	15.875
2012	Krisztian Berki, Hungary	16.066

RINGS

Year	Champion	Pts
1896	Ioannis Mitropoulos, Greece	—
1904	Hermann Glass, United States	45
1924	Francesco Martino, Italy	21.553
1928	Leon Stukelj, Yugoslavia	19.25
1932	George Gulack, United States	18.97
1936	Alois Hudec, Czechoslovakia	19.433
1948	Karl Frei, Switzerland	19.80
1952	Grant Shaginyan, USSR	19.75
1956	Albert Azaryan, USSR	19.35
1960	Albert Azaryan, USSR	19.725
1964	Takuji Haytta, Japan	19.475
1968	Akinori Nakayama, Japan	19.45
1972	Akinori Nakayama, Japan	19.35
1976	Nikolai Andrianov, USSR	19.65
1980	Aleksandr Dityatin, USSR	19.875

RINGS (CONT.)

Year	Champion	Pts
1984	Koji Gushiken, Japan	19.85
1988	Holger Behrendt, E Germany	19.925
1992	Vitaly Scherbo, Unified Team	9.937
1996	Yuri Chechi, Italy	9.887
2000	Szilveszter Csollany, Hungary	9.862
2004	Dimosthenis Tampakos, Greece	9.862
2008	Chen Yibing, China	16.600
2012	Arthur Nabarrete Zanetti, Brazil	15.900

FLOOR EXERCISE

Year	Champion	Pts
1932	Istvan Pelle, Hungary	9.60
1936	Georges Miez, Switzerland	18.666
1948	Ferenc Pataki, Hungary	19.35
1952	K. William Thoresson, Sweden	19.25
1956	Valentin Muratov, USSR	19.20
1960	Nobuyuki Aihara, Japan	19.45
1964	Franco Menichelli, Italy	19.45
1968	Sawao Kato, Japan	19.475
1972	Nikolai Andrianov, USSR	19.175
1976	Nikolai Andrianov, USSR	19.45
1980	Roland Brückner, E Germany	19.75
1984	Li Ning, China	19.925
1988	Sergei Kharkov, USSR	19.925
1992	Li Xiaoshuang, China	9.925
1996	Ioannis Melissanidis, Greece	9.850
2000	Igors Vihrovs, Latvia	9.812
2004	Kyle Shewfelt, Canada	9.787
2008	Kai Zou, China	16.050
2012	Kai Zou, China	15.933

TEAM COMBINED EXERCISES

Year	Champion	Pts
1904	Turngemeinde Philadelphia	374.43
1906	Norway	19.00
1908	Sweden	438
1912	Italy	265.75
1920	Italy	359.855
1924	Italy	839.058
1928	Switzerland	1718.625
1932	Italy	541.850
1936	Germany	657.430
1948	Finland	1358.30
1952	USSR	574.40
1956	USSR	568.25
1960	Japan	575.20
1964	Japan	577.95
1968	Japan	575.90
1972	Japan	571.25
1976	Japan	576.85
1980	USSR	598.60
1984	United States	591.40
1988	USSR	593.35
1992	Unified Team	585.45
1996	Russia	576.778
2000	China	231.919
2004	Japan	173.821
2008	China	286.125
2012	China	275.997

GYMNASTICS - Women

ALL-AROUND

	Pts
1952 .....Maria Gorokhovskaya, USSR	76.78
1956 .....Larissa Latynina, USSR	74.933
1960 .....Larissa Latynina, USSR	77.031
1964 .....Vera Caslavska, Czechoslovakia	77.564
1968 .....Vera Caslavska, Czechoslovakia	78.25
1972 .....Lyudmila Tousischeva, USSR	77.025
1976 .....Nadia Comaneci, Romania	79.275
1980 .....Yelena Davydova, USSR	79.15
1984 .....Mary Lou Retton, United States	79.175
1988 .....Yelena Shushunova, USSR	79.662
1992 .....Tatiana Gutsu, Unified Team	39.737
1996 .....Lilia Podkopayeva, Ukraine	39.255
2000 .....Simona Amanar, Romania	38.642
2004 .....Carly Patterson, United States	38.387
2008 .....Nastia Liukin, United States	63.325
2012 .....Gabrielle Douglas, United States	62.232

VAULT

	Pts
1952 .....Yekaterina Kalinchuk, USSR	19.20
1956 .....Larissa Latynina, USSR	18.833
1960 .....Margarita Nikolayeva, USSR	19.316
1964 .....Vera Caslavska, Czechoslovakia	19.483
1968 .....Vera Caslavska, Czechoslovakia	19.775
1972 .....Karin Janz, E Germany	19.525
1976 .....Nelli Kim, USSR	19.80
1980 .....Natalya Shaposhnikova, USSR	19.725
1984 .....Ecaterina Szabo, Romania	19.875
1988 .....Svetlana Boginskaya, USSR	19.905
1992 .....Henrietta Onodi, Hungary	9.925
Lavinia Milosovici, Romania	9.925
1996 .....Simona Amanar, Romania	9.825
2000 .....Yelena Zamolodtchikova, Russia	9.731
2004 .....Monica Rosu, Romania	9.656
2008 .....Un Jong Hong, North Korea	15.650
2012 .....Sandra Raluca Izbasa, Romania	15.191

UNEVEN BARS

	Pts
1952 .....Margit Korondi, Hungary	19.40
1956 .....Agnes Keleti, Hungary	18.966
1960 .....Polina Astakhova, USSR	19.616
1964 .....Polina Astakhova, USSR	19.332
1968 .....Vera Caslavska, Czechoslovakia	19.65
1972 .....Karin Janz, E Germany	19.675
1976 .....Nadia Comaneci, Romania	20.00
1980 .....Maxi Gnauck, E Germany	19.875
1984 .....Ma Yanhong, China	19.95
1988 .....Daniela Silivas, Romania	20.00
1992 .....Lu Li, China	10.00
1996 .....Svetlana Khorkina, Russia	9.850
2000 .....Svetlana Khorkina, Russia	9.862
2004 .....Emilie Lepennec, France	9.687
2008 .....He Kexin, China	16.725
2012 .....Aliya Mustafina, Russia	16.133

BALANCE BEAM

	Pts
1952 .....Nina Bocharova, USSR	19.22
1956 .....Agnes Keleti, Hungary	18.80
1960 .....Eva Bosakova, Czechoslovakia	19.283
1964 .....Vera Caslavska, Czechoslovakia	19.449
1968 .....Natalya Kuchinskaya, USSR	19.65
1972 .....Olga Korbut, USSR	19.40
1976 .....Nadia Comaneci, Romania	19.95
1980 .....Nadia Comaneci, Romania	19.80
1984 .....Simona Pauca, Romania	19.80
1988 .....Daniela Silivas, Romania	19.924
1992 .....Tatiana Lisenko, Unified Team	9.975
1996 .....Shannon Miller, United States	9.862
2000 .....Xuan Li, China	9.825

BALANCE BEAM *(CONT.)*

	Pts
2004 .....Catalina Ponor, Romania	9.787
2008 .....Shawn Johnson, United States	16.225
2012 .....Linlin Deng, China	15.600

FLOOR EXERCISE

	Pts
1952 .....Agnes Keleti, Hungary	19.36
1956 .....Agnes Keleti, Hungary	18.733
1960 .....Larissa Latynina, USSR	19.583
1964 .....Larissa Latynina, USSR	19.599
1968 .....Vera Caslavska, Czechoslovakia	19.675
1972 .....Olga Korbut, USSR	19.575
1976 .....Nelli Kim, USSR	19.85
1980 .....Nadia Comaneci, Romania	19.875
1984 .....Ecaterina Szabo, Romania	19.975
1988 .....Daniela Silivas, Romania	19.937
1992 .....Lavinia Milosovici, Romania	10.00
1996 .....Lilia Podkopayeva, Ukraine	9.887
2000 .....Yelena Zamolodtchikova, Russia	9.850
2004 .....Catalina Ponor, Romania	9.750
2008 .....Sandra Izbasa, Romania	15.650
2012 .....Alexandra Raisman, United States	15.600

TEAM COMBINED EXERCISES

	Pts
1928 .....The Netherlands	316.75
1932 .....Not held	
1936 .....Germany	506.50
1948 .....Czechoslovakia	445.45
1952 .....USSR	527.03
1956 .....USSR	444.800
1960 .....USSR	382.320
1964 .....USSR	280.890
1968 .....USSR	382.85
1972 .....USSR	380.50
1976 .....USSR	466.00
1980 .....USSR	394.90
1984 .....Romania	392.02
1988 .....USSR	395.475
1992 .....Unified Team	395.666
1996 .....United States	389.225
2000 .....Romania	154.608
2004 .....Romania	114.283
2008 .....China	188.900
2012 .....United States	183.596

RHYTHMIC ALL-AROUND

	Pts
1984 .....Lori Fung, Canada	57.95
1988 .....Marina Lobach, USSR	60.00
1992 .....A. Timoshenko, Unified Team	59.037
1996 .....E. Serebrianskaya, Ukraine	39.683
2000 .....Yulia Barsukova, Russia	39.632
2004 .....Alina Kabaeva, Russia	108.400
2008 .....Evgeniya Kanaeva, Russia	75.500
2012 .....Evgeniya Kanaeva, Russia	116.900

RHYTHMIC TEAM COMBINED EXERCISES

	Pts
1996 .....Spain	38.933
2000 .....Russia	39.500
2004 .....China	249.750
2008 .....Russia	35.550
2012 .....Russia	57.000

SOCCER

Men

1900 .....Great Britain	1936 .....Italy	1972 .....Poland	2000 .....Cameroon
1904 .....Canada	1948 .....Sweden	1976 .....E Germany	2004 .....Argentina
1908 .....Great Britain	1952 .....Hungary	1980 .....Czechoslovakia	2008 .....Argentina
1912 .....Great Britain	1956 .....USSR	1984 .....France	2012 .....Mexico
1920 .....Belgium	1960 .....Yugoslavia	1988 .....USSR	
1924 .....Uruguay	1964 .....Hungary	1992 .....Spain	
1928 .....Uruguay	1968 .....Hungary	1996 .....Nigeria	

Women

1996 ....United States	2008 ....United States
2000 ....Norway	2012 ....United States
2004 ....United States	

Tennis

With major titles on clay (French Open) and hard surfaces (U.S. Open, right), Rafael Nadal proved his enduring versatility

FOR THE RECORD • 2013

2013 Grand Slam Champions

Australian Open

Men's Singles

	Winner	Runner-up	Score
Quarterfinals	Novak Djokovic	Tomas Berdych	6–1, 4–6, 6–1, 6–4
	David Ferrer	Nicolas Almagro	4–6, 4–6, 7–5, 7–6 (7–4), 6–2
	Andy Murray	Jeremy Chardy	6–4, 6–1, 6–2
	Roger Federer	Jo-Wilfried Tsonga	7–6 (7–4), 4–6, 7–6 (7–4), 3–6, 6–3
Semifinals	Novak Djokovic	David Ferrer	6–2, 6–2, 6–1
	Andy Murray	Roger Federer	6-4, 6–7 (5–7), 6-3, 6-7 (2–7), 6-2
Final	Novak Djokovic	Andy Murray	6–7 (2–7), 7–6 (7–3), 6–3, 6-2

Women's Singles

	Winner	Runner-up	Score
Quarterfinals	Li Na	Agnieszka Radwanska	7–5, 6–3
	Maria Sharapova	Ekaterina Makarova	6–2, 6–2
	Victoria Azarenka	Svetlana Kuznetsova	7–5, 6–1
	Sloane Stephens	Serena Williams	3–6, 7–5, 6–4
Semifinals	Li Na	Maria Sharapova	6–2, 6–2
	Victoria Azarenka	Sloane Stephens	6–1, 6–4
Final	Victoria Azarenka	Li Na	4–6, 6–4, 6–3

Doubles

	Winner	Runner-up	Score
Men's Final	Bob Bryan/ Mike Bryan	Robin Haase/ Igor Sijsling	6–3, 6–4
Women's Final	Sara Errani/ Roberta Vinci	Ashleigh Barty/ Casey Dellacqua	6–2, 3–6, 6–2
Mixed Final	Jarmila Gajdosova/ Matthew Ebden	Lucie Hradecka/ Frantisek Cermak	6–3, 7–5

French Open

Men's Singles

	Winner	Runner-up	Score
Quarterfinals	Jo-Wilfried Tsonga	Roger Federer	7–5, 6–3, 6–3
	David Ferrer	Tommy Robredo	6–2, 6–1, 6–1
	Rafael Nadal	Stanislas Wawrinka	6–2, 6–3, 6–1
	Novak Djokovic	Tommy Haas	6–3, 7–6 (7–5), 7–5
Semifinals	David Ferrer	Jo-Wilfried Tsonga	6–1, 7–6 (7–3), 6–2
	Rafael Nadal	Novak Djokovic	6–4, 3–6, 6–1, 6–7 (3–7), 9–7
Final	Rafael Nadal	David Ferrer	6–3, 6–2, 6–3

Women's Singles

	Winner	Runner-up	Score
Quarterfinals	Sara Errani	Agnieszka Radwanska	6–4, 7–6 (8–6)
	Serena Williams	Svetlana Kuznetsova	6–1, 3–6, 6–3
	Maria Sharapova	Jelena Jankovic	0–6, 6–4, 6–3
	Victoria Azarenka	Maria Kirilenko	7–6 (7–3), 6–2
Semifinals	Serena Williams	Sara Errani	6–0, 6–1
	Maria Sharapova	Victoria Azarenka	6–1, 2–6, 6–4
Final	Serena Williams	Maria Sharapova	6–4, 6–4

Doubles

	Winner	Runner-Up	Score
Men's Final	Bob Bryan/ Mike Bryan	Michael Llodra/ Nicolas Mahut	6–4, 4–6, 7–6 (7–4)
Women's Final	Ekaterina Makarova/ Elena Vesnina	Sara Errani/ Roberta Vinci	7–5, 6–2
Mixed Final	Lucie Hradecka/ Frantisek Cermak	Kristina Mladenovic/ Daniel Nestor	1–6, 6–4, 1–0 (10–6)

Wimbledon

Men's Singles

	Winner	Runner-Up	Score
Quarterfinals	Andy Murray	Fernando Verdasco	4–6, 3–6, 6–1, 6–4, 7–5
	Jerzy Janowicz	Lukasz Kubot	7–5, 6–4, 6–4
	Juan Martin del Potro	David Ferrer	6–2, 6–4, 7–6 (7–5)
	Novak Djokovic	Tomas Berdych	7–6 (7–5), 6–4, 6–3
Semifinals	Andy Murray	Jerzy Janowicz	6–7 (2–7), 6–4, 6–4, 6–3
	Novak Djokovic	Juan Martin del Potro	7–5, 4–6, 7–6 (7–2), 6–7 (6–8), 6–3
Final	Andy Murray	Novak Djokovic	6–4, 7–5, 6–4

Women's Singles

	Winner	Runner-Up	Score
Quarterfinals	Kirsten Flipkens	Petra Kvitova	6–4, 3–6, 6–4
	Marion Bartoli	Sloane Stephens	6–4, 7–5
	Agnieszka Radwanska	Li Na	7–6 (7–5), 4–6, 6–2
	Sabine Lisicki	Kaia Kanepi	6–2, 6–3
Semifinals	Marion Bartoli	Kirsten Flipkens	6–1, 6–2
	Sabine Lisicki	Agnieszka Radwanska	6–4, 2–6, 9–7
Final	Marion Bartoli	Sabine Lisicki	6–1, 6–4

Doubles

	Winner	Runner-Up	Score
Men's Final	Bob Bryan/ Mike Bryan	Ivan Dodig/ Marcelo Melo	3–6, 6–3, 6–4, 6–4
Women's Final	Su-Wei Hsieh/ Peng Shuai	Ashleigh Barty/ Casey Dellacqua	7–6 (7–1), 6–1
Mixed Final	Daniel Nestor/ Kristina Mladenovic	Bruno Soares/ Lisa Raymond	5–7, 6–2, 8–6

U.S. Open

Men's Singles

	Winner	Runner-Up	Score
Quarterfinals	Novak Djokovic	Mikhail Youzhny	6–3, 6–2, 3–6, 6–0
	Stanislas Wawrinka	Andy Murray	6–4, 6–3, 6–2
	Richard Gasquet	David Ferrer	6–3, 6–1, 4–6, 2–6, 6–3
	Rafael Nadal	Tommy Robredo	6–0, 6–2, 6–2
Semifinals	Novak Djokovic	Stanislas Wawrinka	2–6, 7–6 (7–4), 3–6, 6–3, 6–4
	Rafael Nadal	Richard Gasquet	6–4, 7–6 (7–1), 6–2
Final	Rafael Nadal	Novak Djokovic	6–2, 3–6, 6–4, 6–1

Women's Singles

	Winner	Runner-Up	Score
Quarterfinals	Serena Williams	Carla Suarez Navarro	6–0, 6–0
	Li Na	Ekaterina Makarova	4–6, 7–6 (7–5), 6–2
	Flavia Pennetta	Roberta Vinci	6–4, 6–1
	Victoria Azarenka	Daniela Hantuchova	6–2, 6–3
Semifinals	Serena Williams	Li Na	6–0, 6–3
	Victoria Azarenka	Flavia Pennetta	6–4, 6–2
Final	Serena Williams	Victoria Azarenka	7–5, 6–7 (6–8), 6–1

Doubles

	Winner	Runner-Up	Score
Men's Final	Leander Paes/ Radek Stepanek	Alexander Peya/ Bruno Soares	6–1, 6–3
Women's Final	Andrea Hlavackova/ Lucie Hradecka	Ashleigh Barty/ Casey Dellacqua	6–7 (4–7), 6–1, 6–4
Mixed Final	Andrea Hlavackova/ Max Mirnyi	Abigail Spears/ Santiago Gonzalez	7–6 (7–5), 6–3

Major Tournament Results

Late 2012 ATP Tour Events

Date	Tournament	Site	Singles Winner	Surface	Prize Money
Oct 7	Shanghai Masters	Shanghai, China	Novak Djokovic	Outdoor Hard	$3,531,600
Oct 15	Stockholm Open	Stockholm, Sweden	Tomas Berdych	Indoor Hard	€486,750
Oct 15	Kremlin Cup	Moscow, Russia	Andreas Seppi	Indoor Hard	$673,150
Oct 15	Austria Trophy	Vienna, Austria	Juan Martin del Potro	Indoor Hard	€486,750
Oct 21	Valencia Open	Valencia, Spain	David Ferrer	Indoor Hard	€1,424,850
Oct 22	Swiss Indoor	Basel, Switzerland	Juan Martin del Potro	Indoor Hard	€1,404,300
Oct 29	Paris Masters	Paris, France	David Ferrer	Indoor Hard	€2,427,975
Nov 5	ATP World Tour Finals	London, England	Novak Djokovic	Indoor Hard	$5,500,000
Dec 30	Brisbane International	Brisbane, Australia	Andy Murray	Outdoor Hard	$436,630
Dec 31	Chennai Open	Chennai, India	Janko Tipsarevic	Outdoor Hard	$385,150
Dec 31	Qatar Open	Doha, Qatar	Richard Gasquet	Outdoor Hard	$1,054,720

2013 ATP Tour Events

Date	Tournament	Site	Singles Winner	Surface	Prize Money
Jan 7	Heineken Open	Auckland, New Zealand	David Ferrer	Outdoor Hard	$433,400
Jan 7	Sydney International	Sydney, Australia	Bernard Tomic	Outdoor Hard	$436,630
Jan 14	Australian Open	Melbourne, Australia	Novak Djokovic	Outdoor Hard	A$16,000,000
Feb 4	Sud de France Open	Montpellier, France	Richard Gasquet	Indoor Hard	€410,200
Feb 4	VTR Open	Vina Del Mar, Chile	Horacio Zeballos	Outdoor Clay	$410,200
Feb 4	Zagreb Indoors	Zagreb, Croatia	Marin Cilic	Indoor Hard	€410,200
Feb 11	ABN/AMRO	Rotterdam, Neth.	Juan Martin del Potro	Indoor Hard	€1,267,875
Feb 11	SAP Open	San Jose, California	Milos Raonic	Indoor Hard	$546,930
Feb 11	Brasil Open	Sao Paulo, Brazil	Rafael Nadal	Indoor Clay	$455,775
Feb 18	Copa Claro	Buenos Aires, Argentina	David Ferrer	Outdoor Clay	$493,670
Feb 18	Open 13	Marseille, France	Jo Wilfried Tsonga	Indoor Hard	€528,135
Feb 18	U.S. Nat'l Indoors	Memphis, Tenn.	Kei Nishikori	Indoor Hard	$1,212,750
Feb 25	Mexican Open	Acapulco, Mexico	Rafael Nadal	Outdoor Clay	$1,212,750
Feb 25	Delray Beach Int'l	Delray Beach, Fla.	Ernests Gulbis	Outdoor Hard	$455,775
Feb 25	Dubai Championships	Dubai, U.A.E.	Novak Djokovic	Outdoor Hard	$1,785,500
Mar 7	BNP Paribas Open	Indian Wells, Calif.	Rafael Nadal	Outdoor Hard	$5,191,943
Mar 20	Sony Open	Miami, Fla.	Andy Murray	Outdoor Hard	$4,330,625
Apr 8	Grand Prix Hassan II	Casablanca, Morocco	Tommy Robredo	Outdoor Clay	€410,200
Apr 8	U.S. Clay Champ'ship	Houston, Texas	John Isner	Outdoor Clay	$455,775
Apr 14	Monte Carlo Masters	Monte Carlo, Monaco	Novak Djokovic	Outdoor Clay	€2,646,495
Apr 22	Barcelona Open	Barcelona, Spain	Rafael Nadal	Outdoor Clay	€1,708,875
Apr 22	BRD Nastase Tiriac Tr.	Bucharest, Romania	Lukas Rosol	Outdoor Clay	€410,200
Apr 29	BMW Open	Munich, Germany	Tommy Haas	Outdoor Clay	€410,200
Apr 29	Portugal Open	Oeiras, Portugal	Stanislas Wawrinka	Outdoor Clay	€410,200
May 5	Madrid Open	Madrid, Spain	Rafael Nadal	Outdoor Clay	€3,368,265
May 12	Italia International	Rome, Italy	Rafael Nadal	Outdoor Clay	€2,646,495
May 19	Power Horse Cup	Dusseldorf, Germany	Juan Monaco	Outdoor Clay	€410,200
May 19	Nice Open	Nice, France	Albert Montanes	Outdoor Clay	€410,200
May 26	French Open	Paris, France	Rafael Nadal	Outdoor Clay	€7,984,000
June 10	Gerry Weber Open	Halle, Germany	Roger Federer	Outdoor Grass	€683,665
June 10	AEGON Championships	London, England	Andy Murray	Outdoor Grass	€683,665
June 16	Topshelf Open	's-Hertogenbosch, Netherlands	Nicolas Mahut	Outdoor Grass	€410,200
June 16	AEGON International	Eastbourne, England	Feliciano Lopez	Outdoor Grass	€468,460
June 24	Wimbledon	Wimbledon, England	Andy Murray	Outdoor Grass	£8,588,000
July 8	Swedish Open	Bastad, Sweden	Carlos Berlocq	Outdoor Clay	€433,770
July 8	Hall of Fame Champ's	Newport, R.I.	Nicolas Mahut	Outdoor Grass	$455,775
July 8	Mercedes Cup	Stuttgart, Germany	Fabio Fognini	Outdoor Clay	€410,200
July 15	German Open	Hamburg, Germany	Fabio Fognini	Outdoor Clay	€1,102,500
July 15	Claro Open Colombia	Bogota, Colombia	Ivo Karlovic	Outdoor Hard	$638,085
July 22	Atlanta Open	Atlanta, Georgia	John Isner	Outdoor Hard	$546,930
July 22	Swiss Open	Gstaad, Switzerland	Mikhail Youzhny	Outdoor Clay	€410,200
July 22	Croatia Open	Umag, Croatia	Tommy Robredo	Outdoor Clay	€410,200
July 28	Kitzbuhel Cup	Kitzbuhel, Austria	Marcel Granollers	Outdoor Clay	€410,200

2013 ATP Tour Events *(Cont.)**

Date	Tournament	Site	Singles Winner	Surface	Prize Money
July 29	Citi Open	Washington, D.C.	Juan Martin Del Potro	Outdoor Hard	$1,295,790
Aug 5	Rogers Cup	Montreal, Canada	Rafael Nadal	Outdoor Hard	$2,887,085
Aug 11	Western & Southern	Cincinnati, Ohio	Rafael Nadal	Outdoor Hard	$3,079,555
Aug 18	Winston-Salem Open	Winston-Salem, N.C.	Jurgen Melzer	Outdoor Hard	$575,250
Aug 26	U.S. Open	New York City	Rafael Nadal	Outdoor Hard	$13,052,000
Sept 16	Moselle Open	Metz, France	Gilles Simon	Indoor Hard	€410,200
Sept 16	St. Petersburg Open	St. Petersburg, Russia	Ernests Gulbis	Indoor Hard	$455,775

*Through Sept. 22, 2013

Late 2012 WTA Tour Events

Date	Tournament	Site	Singles Winner	Surface	Total Purse
Sept 23	Pan Pacific Open	Tokyo, Japan	Nadia Petrova	Outdoor Hard	$2,369.000
Sept 29	China Open	Bejing, China	Victoria Azarenka	Outdoor Hard	$4,500,000
Oct 8	Generali Ladies Open	Linz, Austria	Victoria Azarenka	Indoor Hard	$220,000
Oct 8	HP Japan Open	Osaka, Japan	Heather Watson	Indoor Hard	$220,000
Oct 15	BNP Luxembourg Open	Luxembourg	Venus Williams	Indoor Hard	$220,000
Oct 15	WTA Kremlin Cup	Moscow, Russia	Caroline Wozniacki	Indoor Hard	$721,000
Oct 23	WTA Championships	Itanbul, Turkey	Serena Williams	Indoor Hard	$4,900,000
Oct 30	Tourn. of Champions	Sofia, Bulgaria	Nadi Petrova		
Dec 30	Brisbane International	Brisbane, Australia	Serena Williams	Outdoor Hard	$1,000,000
Dec 31	ASB Classic	Auckland, New Zealand	Agnieszka Radwanska	Outdoor Hard	$220,000
Dec 31	Shenzen Open	Shenzen, China	Li Na	Outdoor Hard	$500,000

2013 WTA Tour Events

Date	Tournament	Site	Singles Winner	Surface	Total Purse
Jan 6	Apia International	Sydney, Australia	Agnieszka Radwanska	Outdoor Hard	$690,000
Jan 6	Hobart International	Hobart, Australia	Elena Vesnina	Outdoor Hard	$235,000
Jan 14	Australian Open	Melbourne, Australia	Victoria Azarenka	Outdoor Hard	A$16,000,000
Jan 28	GDF Suez Open	Paris, France	Mona Barthel	Indoor Hard	$690,000
Jan 28	Pattaya Open	Patttaya City, Thailand	Maria Kirilenko	Outdoor Hard	$235,000
Feb 11	Qatar Open	Doha, Qatar	Victoria Azarenka	Outdoor Hard	$2,369,000
Feb 11	Copa Bionaire	Cali, Colombia	L. Arruabarrena-Vecino	Outdoor Clay	$125,000
Feb 17	U.S. Nat'l Indoors	Memphis, Tenn	Marina Erakovic	Indoor Hard	$235,000
Feb 18	Copa Colsanitas	Bogota, Colombia	Jelena Jankovic	Outdor Clay	$235,000
Feb 18	Dubai Championships	Dubai, U.A.E.	Petra Kvitova	Outdoor Hard	$2,000,000
Feb 24	Brasil Cup	Florianopolis, Brazil	Monica Niculescu	Outdoor Clay	$235,000
Feb 25	Mexicano Open	Acapulco, Mexico	Sara Errani	Outdoor Clay	$235,000
Feb 25	Malaysian Open	Kuala Lumpur, Mal.	Karolina Pliskova	Outdoor Hard	$235,000
Mar 6	BNP Paribas Open	Indian Wells, Calif.	Maria Sharapova	Outdoor Hardi	$6,020,268
Mar 19	Sony Open	Miami, Florida	Serena Williams	Outdoor Hard	$5,185,625
Apr 1	Family Circle Cup	Charleston, S.C.	Serena Williams	Outdoor Clay	$795,707
Apr 1	Monterrey Open	Monterrey, Mexico	A. Pavlyuchenkova	Outdoor Hard	$235,000
Apr 8	Katowice Open	Katowice, Poland	Roberta Vinca	Indoor Clay	$235,000
Apr 22	Morocco Grand Prix	Marrakech, Morocco	Francesca Schiavone	Outdoor Clay	$235,000
Apr 22	Porsche Grand Prix	Stuttgart, Germany	Maria Sharapova	Indoor Clay	$740,000
Apr 29	Portugal Open	Oeiras, Portugal	A. Pavlyuchenkova	Outdoor Clay	$235,000
May 4	Madrid Open	Madrid, Spain	Serena Williams	Outdoor Clay	€4,033,254
May 13	d'Italia International	Rome, Italy	Serena Williams	Outdoor Clay	$2,369,000
May 20	Strasbourg International	Strasbourg, France	Alize Cornet	Outdoor Clay	$235,000
May 20	Brussels Open	Brussels, Belguim	Kaia Kanepi	Outdoor Clay	$690,000
May 26	French Open	Paris, France	Serena Williams	Outdoor Clay	€7,984,000
June 10	AEGON Classic	Birmingham, England	Daniela Hantuchova	Outdoor Grass	$235,000
June 10	Nurnberger Cup	Nurnberg, Germany	Simona Halep	Outdoor Clay	$235,000
June 16	Topshelf Open	's-Hertogenbosch, Neth.	Simona Halep	Outdoor Grass	$235,000
June 16	AEGON Int'l	Eastbourne, England	Elena Vesnina	Outdoor Grass	$690,000
June 24	Wimbledon	Wimbledon, England	Marion Bartoli	Outdoor Grass	£8,588,000
July 8	Hungarian Grand Prix	Budapest, Hungary	Simona Halep	Outdoor Clay	$235,000
July 8	Palermo International	Palermo, Italy	Roberta Vinci	Outdoor Clay	$235,000
July 15	Swedish Open	Bastad, Sweden	Serena Williams	Outdoor Clay	$235,000
June 15	Gastein International	Bad Gastein, Austria	Yvonne Meusburger	Outdoor Clay	$235,000
July 22	Baku Cup	Baku, Azerbaijan	Elina Svitolina	Outdoors Hard	$235,000
July 22	Bank of the West Classic	Stanford, Calif.	Dominika Cibulkova	Outdoor Hard	$795,707

2013 WTA Tour Events *(Cont.)**

Date	Tournament	Site	Singles Winner	Surface	Total Purse
July 29	Citi Open	Washington, D.C.	Magdalena Rybarikova	Outdoor Hard	$235,000
July 29	Southern California Open	Carlsbad, Calif.	Samantha Stosur	Outdoor Hard	$795,707
Aug 5	Suzhou Open	Suzhou, China	Shahar Peer	Outdoor Hard	$125,000
Aug 7	Rogers Cup	Montreal, Canada	Serena Williams	Outdoor Hard	$2,369,000
Aug 12	Western & Southern Open	Cincinnati, Ohio	Victoria Azarenka	Outdoor Hard	$2,369,000
Aug 18	New Haven Open	New Haven, Conn.	Simona Halep	Outdoor Hard	$690,000
Aug 26	U.S. Open	New York City	Serena Williams	Outdoor Hard	$13,052,000
Sept 9	Challenge Bell	Quebec City, Canada	Lucie Safarova	Indoor Hard	$235,000
Sept 9	Tashkent Open	Tashkent, Uzbekistan	Bojana Jovanovski	Outdoor Hard	$235,000
Sept 16	Guangzhou Open	Guangzhou, China	Shuai Zhang	Outdoor Hard	$500,000
Sept 16	Korea Open	Seoul, South Korea	Agnieszka Radwanska	Outdoor Hard	$500,000

*Through Sept. 22, 2013

2012 Final Season Singles Points Leaders

Men

Rank	Player	Country	Points	Events
1.	Novak Djokovic	SRB	12,920	18
2.	Roger Federer	SUI	10,265	21
3.	Andy Murray	GBR	8,000	20
4.	Rafael Nadal	ESP	6,690	18
5.	David Ferrer	ESP	6,505	25
6.	Tomas Berdych	CZE	4,680	24
7.	Juan Martin del Potro	ARG	4,480	23
8.	Jo-Wilfried Tsonga	FRA	3,490	26
9.	Janko Tipsarevic	SRB	2,990	28
10.	Richard Gasquet	FRA	2,515	23
11.	Nicolas Almagro	ESP	2,515	27

Note: Compiled by the ATP Tour, through the end of the 2012 season.

Women

Rank	Player	Country	Points
1	Victoria Azarenka	BLR	10595
2	Maria Sharapova	RUS	10045
3	Serena Williams	USA	9400
4	Agnieszka Radwanska	POL	7425
5	Angelique Kerber	GER	5550
6	Sara Errani	ITA	5100
7	Li Na	CHI	5095
8	Petra Kvitova	CZE	5085
9	Samantha Stosur	AUS	4135
10	Caroline Wozniacki	DEN	3765

Note: Compiled by the WTA, through the end of the 2012 season.

FOR THE RECORD • Year by Year

Grand Slam Tournaments

MEN

Australian Open Championships

Year	Winner	Finalist	Score
1905	Rodney Heath	A. H. Curtis	4–6, 6–3, 6–4, 6–4
1906	Tony Wilding	H. A. Parker	6–0, 6–4, 6–4
1907	Horace M. Rice	H. A. Parker	6–3, 6–4, 6–4
1908	Fred Alexander	A. W. Dunlop	3–6, 3–6, 6–0, 6–2, 6–3
1909	Tony Wilding	E. F. Parker	6–1, 7–5, 6–2
1910	Rodney Heath	Horace M. Rice	6–4, 6–3, 6–2
1911	Norman Brookes	Horace M. Rice	6–1, 6–2, 6–3
1912	J. Cecil Parke	A. E. Beamish	3–6, 6–3, 1–6, 6–1, 7–5
1913	E. F. Parker	H. A. Parker	2–6, 6–1, 6–2, 6–3
1914	Pat O'Hara Wood	G. L. Patterson	6–4, 6–3, 5–7, 6–1
1915	Francis G. Lowe	Horace M. Rice	4–6, 6–1, 6–1, 6–4
1916–18	No tournament		
1919	A. R. F. Kingscote	E. O. Pockley	6–4, 6–0, 6–3
1920	Pat O'Hara Wood	Ron Thomas	6–3, 4–6, 6–8, 6–1, 6–3
1921	Rhys H. Gemmell	A. Hedeman	7–5, 6–1, 6–4
1922	Pat O'Hara Wood	Gerald Patterson	6–0, 3–6, 3–6, 6–3, 6–2
1923	Pat O'Hara Wood	C. B. St John	6–1, 6–1, 6–3
1924	James Anderson	R. E. Schlesinger	6–3, 6–4, 3–6, 5–7, 6–3
1925	James Anderson	Gerald Patterson	11–9, 2–6, 6–2, 6–3
1926	John Hawkes	J. Willard	6–1, 6–3, 6–1
1927	Gerald Patterson	John Hawkes	3–6, 6–4, 3–6, 18–16, 6–3
1928	Jean Borotra	R. O. Cummings	6–4, 6–1, 4–6, 5–7, 6–3
1929	John C. Gregory	R. E. Schlesinger	6–2, 6–2, 5–7, 7–5
1930	Gar Moon	Harry C. Hopman	6–3, 6–1, 6–3
1931	Jack Crawford	Harry C. Hopman	6–4, 6–2, 2–6, 6–1
1932	Jack Crawford	Harry C. Hopman	4–6, 6–3, 3–6, 6–3, 6–1
1933	Jack Crawford	Keith Gledhill	2–6, 7–5, 6–3, 6–2
1934	Fred Perry	Jack Crawford	6–3, 7–5, 6–1
1935	Jack Crawford	Fred Perry	2–6, 6–4, 6–4, 6–4
1936	Adrian Quist	Jack Crawford	6–2, 6–3, 4–6, 3–6, 9–7
1937	Vivian B. McGrath	John Bromwich	6–3, 1–6, 6–0, 2–6, 6–1
1938	Don Budge	John Bromwich	6–4, 6–2, 6–1
1939	John Bromwich	Adrian Quist	6–4, 6–1, 6–3
1940	Adrian Quist	Jack Crawford	6–3, 6–1, 6–2
1941–45	No tournament		
1946	John Bromwich	Dinny Pails	5–7, 6–3, 7–5, 3–6, 6–2
1947	Dinny Pails	John Bromwich	4–6, 6–4, 3–6, 7–5, 8–6
1948	Adrian Quist	John Bromwich	6–4, 3–6, 6–3, 2–6, 6–3
1949	Frank Sedgman	Ken McGregor	6–3, 6–3, 6–2
1950	Frank Sedgman	Ken McGregor	6–3, 6–4, 4–6, 6–1
1951	Richard Savitt	Ken McGregor	6–3, 2–6, 6–3, 6–1
1952	Ken McGregor	Frank Sedgman	7–5, 12–10, 2–6, 6–2
1953	Ken Rosewall	Mervyn Rose	6–0, 6–3, 6–4
1954	Mervyn Rose	Rex Hartwig	6–2, 0–6, 6–4, 6–2
1955	Ken Rosewall	Lew Hoad	9–7, 6–4, 6–4
1956	Lew Hoad	Ken Rosewall	6–4, 3–6, 6–4, 7–5
1957	Ashley Cooper	Neale Fraser	6–3, 9–11, 6–4, 6–2
1958	Ashley Cooper	Mal Anderson	7–5, 6–3, 6–4
1959	Alex Olmedo	Neale Fraser	6–1, 6–2, 3–6, 6–3
1960	Rod Laver	Neale Fraser	5–7, 3–6, 6–3, 8–6, 8–6
1961	Roy Emerson	Rod Laver	1–6, 6–3, 7–5, 6–4
1962	Rod Laver	Roy Emerson	8–6, 0–6, 6–4, 6–4
1963	Roy Emerson	Ken Fletcher	6–3, 6–3, 6–1
1964	Roy Emerson	Fred Stolle	6–3, 6–4, 6–2
1965	Roy Emerson	Fred Stolle	7–9, 2–6, 6–4, 7–5, 6–1
1966	Roy Emerson	Arthur Ashe	6–4, 6–8, 6–2, 6–3
1967	Roy Emerson	Arthur Ashe	6–4, 6–1, 6–1
1968	Bill Bowrey	Juan Gisbert	7–5, 2–6, 9–7, 6–4

MEN *(Cont.)*

Australian Open Championships *(Cont.)*

Year	Winner	Finalist	Score
1969*	Rod Laver	Andres Gimeno	6–3, 6–4, 7–5
1970	Arthur Ashe	Dick Crealy	6–4, 9–7, 6–2
1971	Ken Rosewall	Arthur Ashe	6–1, 7–5, 6–3
1972	Ken Rosewall	Mal Anderson	7–6, 6–3, 7–5
1973	John Newcombe	Onny Parun	6–3, 6–7, 7–5, 6–1
1974	Jimmy Connors	Phil Dent	7–6, 6–4, 4–6, 6–3
1975	John Newcombe	Jimmy Connors	7–5, 3–6, 6–4, 7–5
1976	Mark Edmondson	John Newcombe	6–7, 6–3, 7–6, 6–1
1977 (Jan)	Roscoe Tanner	Guillermo Vilas	6–3, 6–3, 6–3
1977 (Dec)	Vitas Gerulaitis	John Lloyd	6–3, 7–6, 5–7, 3–6, 6–2
1978	Guillermo Vilas	John Marks	6–4, 6–4, 3–6, 6–3
1979	Guillermo Vilas	John Sadri	7–6, 6–3, 6–2
1980	Brian Teacher	Kim Warwick	7–5, 7–6, 6–3
1981	Johan Kriek	Steve Denton	6–2, 7–6, 6–7, 6–4
1982	Johan Kriek	Steve Denton	6–3, 6–3, 6–2
1983	Mats Wilander	Ivan Lendl	6–1, 6–4, 6–4
1984	Mats Wilander	Kevin Curren	6–7, 6–4, 7–6, 6–2
1985 (Dec)	Stefan Edberg	Mats Wilander	6–4, 6–3, 6–3
1987 (Jan)	Stefan Edberg	Pat Cash	6–3, 6–4, 3–6, 5–7, 6–3
1988	Mats Wilander	Pat Cash	6–3, 6–7, 3–6, 6–1, 8–6
1989	Ivan Lendl	Miloslav Mecir	6–2, 6–2, 6–2
1990	Ivan Lendl	Stefan Edberg	4–6, 7–6, 5–2, ret.
1991	Boris Becker	Ivan Lendl	1–6, 6–4, 6–4, 6–4
1992	Jim Courier	Stefan Edberg	6–3, 3–6, 6–4, 6–2
1993	Jim Courier	Stefan Edberg	6–2, 6–1, 2–6, 7–5
1994	Pete Sampras	Todd Martin	7–6, 6–4, 6–4
1995	Andre Agassi	Pete Sampras	4–6, 6–1, 7–6, 6–4
1996	Boris Becker	Michael Chang	6–2, 6–4, 2–6, 6–2
1997	Pete Sampras	Carlos Moya	6–2, 6–3, 6–3
1998	Petr Korda	Marcelo Ríos	6–2, 6–2, 6–2
1999	Yevgeny Kafelnikov	Thomas Enqvist	4–6, 6–0, 6–3, 7–6
2000	Andre Agassi	Yevgeny Kafelnikov	3–6, 6–3, 6–2, 6–4
2001	Andre Agassi	Arnaud Clement	6–4, 6–2, 6–2
2002	Thomas Johansson	Marat Safin	3–6, 6–4, 6–4, 7–6 (7-4)
2003	Andre Agassi	Rainer Schuettler	6–2, 6–2, 6–1
2004	Roger Federer	Marat Safin	7–6 (7–3), 6–4, 6–2
2005	Marat Safin	Lleyton Hewitt	1–6, 6–3, 6–4, 6–4
2006	Roger Federer	Marcos Baghdatis	5–7, 7–5, 6–0, 6–2
2007	Roger Federer	Fernando Gonzalez	7–6 (7–2), 6–4, 6–4
2008	Novak Djokovic	Jo-Wilfried Tsonga	4–6, 6–4, 6–3, 7–6 (7–2)
2009	Rafael Nadal	Roger Federer	7–5, 3–6, 7–6 (7–3), 3–6, 6–2
2010	Roger Federer	Andy Murray	6–3, 6–4, 7–6 (13–11)
2011	Novak Djokovic	Andy Murray	6–4, 6–2, 6–3
2012	Novak Djokovic	Rafael Nadal	5–7, 6–4, 6–2, 6–7 (5–7), 7–5
2013	Novak Djokovic	Andy Murray	6–7 (2–7), 7–6 (7–3), 6–3, 6–2

*Became Open (amateur and professional) in 1969.

MEN *(Cont.)*

French Championships

Year	Winner	Finalist	Score
1925†	Rene Lacoste	Jean Borotra	7–5, 6–1, 6–4
1926	Henri Cochet	Rene Lacoste	6–2, 6–4, 6–3
1927	Rene Lacoste	Bill Tilden	6–4, 4–6, 5–7, 6–3, 11–9
1928	Henri Cochet	Rene Lacoste	5–7, 6–3, 6–1, 6–3
1929	Rene Lacoste	Jean Borotra	6–3, 2–6, 6–0, 2–6, 8–6
1930	Henri Cochet	Bill Tilden	3–6, 8–6, 6–3, 6–1
1931	Jean Borotra	Claude Boussus	2–6, 6–4, 7–5, 6–4
1932	Henri Cochet	Giorgio de Stefani	6–0, 6–4, 4–6, 6–3
1933	Jack Crawford	Henri Cochet	8–6, 6–1, 6–3
1934	Gottfried von Cramm	Jack Crawford	6–4, 7–9, 3–6, 7–5, 6–3
1935	Fred Perry	Gottfried von Cramm	6–3, 3–6, 6–1, 6–3
1936	Gottfried von Cramm	Fred Perry	6–0, 2–6, 6–2, 2–6, 6–0
1937	Henner Henkel	Henry Austin	6–1, 6–4, 6–3
1938	Don Budge	Roderick Menzel	6–3, 6–2, 6–4
1939	Don McNeill	Bobby Riggs	7–5, 6–0, 6–3
1940	No tournament		
1941‡	Bernard Destremau	n/a	n/a
1942‡	Bernard Destremau	n/a	n/a
1943‡	Yvon Petra	n/a	n/a
1944‡	Yvon Petra	n/a	n/a
1945‡	Yvon Petra	Bernard Destremau	7–5, 6–4, 6–2
1946	Marcel Bernard	Jaroslav Drobny	3–6, 2–6, 6–1, 6–4, 6–3
1947	Joseph Asboth	Eric Sturgess	8–6, 7–5, 6–4
1948	Frank Parker	Jaroslav Drobny	6–4, 7–5, 5–7, 8–6
1949	Frank Parker	Budge Patty	6–3, 1–6, 6–1, 6–4
1950	Budge Patty	Jaroslav Drobny	6–1, 6–2, 3–6, 5–7, 7–5
1951	Jaroslav Drobny	Eric Sturgess	6–3, 6–3, 6–3
1952	Jaroslav Drobny	Frank Sedgman	6–2, 6–0, 3–6, 6–4
1953	Ken Rosewall	Vic Seixas	6–3, 6–4, 1–6, 6–2
1954	Tony Trabert	Arthur Larsen	6–4, 7–5, 6–1
1955	Tony Trabert	Sven Davidson	2–6, 6–1, 6–4, 6–2
1956	Lew Hoad	Sven Davidson	6–4, 8–6, 6–3
1957	Sven Davidson	Herbie Flam	6–3, 6–4, 6–4
1958	Mervyn Rose	Luis Ayala	6–3, 6–4, 6–4
1959	Nicola Pietrangeli	Ian Vermaak	3–6, 6–3, 6–4, 6–1
1960	Nicola Pietrangeli	Luis Ayala	3–6, 6–3, 6–4, 4–6, 6–3
1961	Manuel Santana	Nicola Pietrangeli	4–6, 6–1, 3–6, 6–0, 6–2
1962	Rod Laver	Roy Emerson	3–6, 2–6, 6–3, 9–7, 6–2
1963	Roy Emerson	Pierre Darmon	3–6, 6–1, 6–4, 6–4
1964	Manuel Santana	Nicola Pietrangeli	6–3, 6–1, 4–6, 7–5
1965	Fred Stolle	Tony Roche	3–6, 6–0, 6–2, 6–3
1966	Tony Roche	Istvan Gulyas	6–1, 6–4, 7–5
1967	Roy Emerson	Tony Roche	6–1, 6–4, 2–6, 6–2
1968*	Ken Rosewall	Rod Laver	6–3, 6–1, 2–6, 6–2
1969	Rod Laver	Ken Rosewall	6–4, 6–3, 6–4
1970	Jan Kodes	Zeljko Franulovic	6–2, 6–4, 6–0
1971	Jan Kodes	Ilie Nastase	8–6, 6–2, 2–6, 7–5
1972	Andres Gimeno	Patrick Proisy	4–6, 6–3, 6–1, 6–1
1973	Ilie Nastase	Nikki Pilic	6–3, 6–3, 6–0
1974	Bjorn Borg	Manuel Orantes	6–7, 6–0, 6–1, 6–1
1975	Bjorn Borg	Guillermo Vilas	6–2, 6–3, 6–4
1976	Adriano Panatta	Harold Solomon	6–1, 6–4, 4–6, 7–6
1977	Guillermo Vilas	Brian Gottfried	6–0, 6–3, 6–0
1978	Bjorn Borg	Guillermo Vilas	6–1, 6–1, 6–3
1979	Bjorn Borg	Victor Pecci	6–3, 6–1, 6–7, 6–4
1980	Bjorn Borg	Vitas Gerulaitis	6–4, 6–1, 6–2
1981	Bjorn Borg	Ivan Lendl	6–1, 4–6, 6–2, 3–6, 6–1
1982	Mats Wilander	Guillermo Vilas	1–6, 7–6, 6–0, 6–4
1983	Yannick Noah	Mats Wilander	6–2, 7–5, 7–6
1984	Ivan Lendl	John McEnroe	3–6, 2–6, 6–4, 7–5, 7–5
1985	Mats Wilander	Ivan Lendl	3–6, 6–4, 6–2, 6–2
1986	Ivan Lendl	Mikael Pernfors	6–3, 6–2, 6–4

†1925 was the first year that entries were accepted from all countries. ‡From 1941 to 1945 the event was called Tournoi de France and was closed to all foreigners. *Became Open (amateur and professional) in 1968, but restricted to only contract professionals in 1972.

MEN *(Cont.)*

French Championships *(Cont.)*

Year	Winner	Finalist	Score
1987	Ivan Lendl	Mats Wilander	7–5, 6–2, 3–6, 7–6
1988	Mats Wilander	Henri Leconte	7–5, 6–2, 6–1
1989	Michael Chang	Stefan Edberg	6–1, 3–6, 4–6, 6–4, 6–2
1990	Andres Gomez	Andre Agassi	6–3, 2–6, 6–4, 6–4
1991	Jim Courier	Andre Agassi	3–6, 6–4, 2–6, 6–1, 6–4
1992	Jim Courier	Petr Korda	7–5, 6–2, 6–1
1993	Sergi Bruguera	Jim Courier	6–4, 2–6, 6–2, 3–6, 6–3
1994	Sergi Bruguera	Alberto Berasategui	6–3, 7–5, 2–6, 6–1
1995	Thomas Muster	Michael Chang	7–5, 6–2, 6–4
1996	Yevgeny Kafelnikov	Michael Stich	7–6, 7–5, 7–6
1997	Gustavo Kuerten	Sergi Bruguera	6–3, 6–4, 6–2
1998	Carlos Moya	Alex Corretja	6–3, 7–5, 6–3
1999	Andre Agassi	Andrei Medvedev	1–6, 2–6, 6–4, 6–3, 6–4
2000	Gustavo Kuerten	Magnus Norman	6–2, 6–3, 2–6, 7–6
2001	Gustavo Kuerten	Alex Corretja	6–7, 7–5, 6–2, 6–0
2002	Albert Costa	Juan Carlos Ferrero	6–1, 6–0, 4–6, 6–3
2003	Juan Carlos Ferrero	Martin Verkerk	6–1, 6–3, 6–2
2004	Gaston Gaudio	Guillermo Coria	0–6, 3–6, 6–4, 6–1, 8–6
2005	Rafael Nadal	Mariano Puerta	6–7, 6–3, 6–1, 7–5
2006	Rafael Nadal	Roger Federer	1–6, 6–1, 6–4, 7–6
2007	Rafael Nadal	Roger Federer	6–3, 4–6, 6–3, 6–4
2008	Rafael Nadal	Roger Federer	6–1, 6–3, 6–0
2009	Roger Federer	Robin Soderling	6–1, 7–6 (7–1), 6–4
2010	Rafael Nadal	Robin Soderling	6–4, 6–2, 6–4
2011	Rafael Nadal	Roger Federer	7–5, 7–6 (7–3), 5–7, 6–1
2012	Rafael Nadal	Novak Djokovic	6–4, 6–3, 2–6, 7–5
2013	Rafael Nadal	David Ferrer	6–3, 6–2, 6–3

Wimbledon Championships

Year	Winner	Finalist	Score
1877	Spencer W. Gore	William C. Marshall	6–1, 6–2, 6–4
1878	P. Frank Hadow	Spencer W. Gore	7–5, 6–1, 9–7
1879	John T. Hartley	V. St. Leger Gould	6–2, 6–4, 6–2
1880	John T. Hartley	Herbert F. Lawford	6–0, 6–2, 2–6, 6–3
1881	William Renshaw	John T. Hartley	6–0, 6–2, 6–1
1882	William Renshaw	Ernest Renshaw	6–1, 2–6, 4–6, 6–2, 6–2
1883	William Renshaw	Ernest Renshaw	2–6, 6–3, 6–3, 4–6, 6–3
1884	William Renshaw	Herbert F. Lawford	6–0, 6–4, 9–7
1885	William Renshaw	Herbert F. Lawford	7–5, 6–2, 4–6, 7–5
1886	William Renshaw	Herbert F. Lawford	6–0, 5–7, 6–3, 6–4
1887	Herbert F. Lawford	Ernest Renshaw	1–6, 6–3, 3–6, 6–4, 6–4
1888	Ernest Renshaw	Herbert F. Lawford	6–3, 7–5, 6–0
1889	William Renshaw	Ernest Renshaw	6–4, 6–1, 3–6, 6–0
1890	William J. Hamilton	William Renshaw	6–8, 6–2, 3–6, 6–1, 6–1
1891	Wilfred Baddeley	Joshua Pim	6–4, 1–6, 7–5, 6–0
1892	Wilfred Baddeley	Joshua Pim	4–6, 6–3, 6–3, 6–2
1893	Joshua Pim	Wilfred Baddeley	3–6, 6–1, 6–3, 6–2
1894	Joshua Pim	Wilfred Baddeley	10–8, 6–2, 8–6
1895	Wilfred Baddeley	Wilberforce V. Eaves	4–6, 2–6, 8–6, 6–2, 6–3
1896	Harold S. Mahoney	Wilfred Baddeley	6–2, 6–8, 5–7, 8–6, 6–3
1897	Reggie F. Doherty	Harold S. Mahoney	6–4, 6–4, 6–3
1898	Reggie F. Doherty	H. Laurie Doherty	6–3, 6–3, 2–6, 5–7, 6–1
1899	Reggie F. Doherty	Arthur W. Gore	1–6, 4–6, 6–2, 6–3, 6–3
1900	Reggie F. Doherty	Sidney H. Smith	6–8, 6–3, 6–1, 6–2
1901	Arthur W. Gore	Reggie F. Doherty	4–6, 7–5, 6–4, 6–4
1902	H. Laurie Doherty	Arthur W. Gore	6–4, 6–3, 3–6, 6–0
1903	H. Laurie Doherty	Frank L. Riseley	7–5, 6–3, 6–0
1904	H. Laurie Doherty	Frank L. Riseley	6–1, 7–5, 8–6
1905	H. Laurie Doherty	Norman E. Brookes	8–6, 6–2, 6–4
1906	H. Laurie Doherty	Frank L. Riseley	6–4, 4–6, 6–2, 6–3
1907	Norman E. Brookes	Arthur W. Gore	6–4, 6–2, 6–2
1908	Arthur W. Gore	H. Roper Barrett	6–3, 6–2, 4–6, 3–6, 6–4
1909	Arthur W. Gore	M.J.G. Ritchie	6–8, 1–6, 6–2, 6–2, 6–2
1910	Anthony F. Wilding	Arthur W. Gore	6–4, 7–5, 4–6, 6–2
1911	Anthony F. Wilding	H. Roper Barrett	6–4, 4–6, 2–6, 6–2, ret.

Note: Prior to 1922 the tournament was run on a challenge-round system. The previous year's winner "stood out" of an All Comers event, which produced a challenger to play him for the title.

MEN *(Cont.)*

Wimbledon Championships *(Cont.)*

Year	Winner	Finalist	Score
1912	Anthony F. Wilding	Arthur W. Gore	6–4, 6–4, 4–6, 6–4
1913	Anthony F. Wilding	Maurice E. McLoughlin	8–6, 6–3, 10–8
1914	Norman E. Brookes	Anthony F. Wilding	6–4, 6–4, 7–5
1915–18	No tournament		
1919	Gerald L. Patterson	Norman E. Brookes	6–3, 7–5, 6–2
1920	Bill Tilden	Gerald L. Patterson	2–6, 6–3, 6–2, 6–4
1921	Bill Tilden	Brian I. C. Norton	4–6, 2–6, 6–1, 6–0, 7–5
1922	Gerald L. Patterson	Randolph Lycett	6–3, 6–4, 6–2
1923	Bill Johnston	Francis T. Hunter	6–0, 6–3, 6–1
1924	Jean Borotra	Rene Lacoste	6–1, 3–6, 6–1, 3–6, 6–4
1925	Rene Lacoste	Jean Borotra	6–3, 6–3, 4–6, 8–6
1926	Jean Borotra	Howard Kinsey	8–6, 6–1, 6–3
1927	Henri Cochet	Jean Borotra	4–6, 4–6, 6–3, 6–4, 7–5
1928	Rene Lacoste	Henri Cochet	6–1, 4–6, 6–4, 6–2
1929	Henri Cochet	Jean Borotra	6–4, 6–3, 6–4
1930	Bill Tilden	Wilmer Allison	6–3, 9–7, 6–4
1931	Sidney B. Wood Jr	Francis X. Shields	walkover
1932	Ellsworth Vines	Henry Austin	6–4, 6–2, 6–0
1933	Jack Crawford	Ellsworth Vines	4–6, 11–9, 6–2, 2–6, 6–4
1934	Fred Perry	Jack Crawford	6–3, 6–0, 7–5
1935	Fred Perry	Gottfried von Cramm	6–2, 6–4, 6–4
1936	Fred Perry	Gottfried von Cramm	6–1, 6–1, 6–0
1937	Don Budge	Gottfried von Cramm	6–3, 6–4, 6–2
1938	Don Budge	Henry Austin	6–1, 6–0, 6–3
1939	Bobby Riggs	Elwood Cooke	2–6, 8–6, 3–6, 6–3, 6–2
1940–45	No tournament		
1946	Yvon Petra	Geoff E. Brown	6–2, 6–4, 6–7 (7–9), 5–7, 6–4
1947	Jack Kramer	Tom P. Brown	6–1, 6–3, 6–2
1948	Bob Falkenburg	John Bromwich	7–5, 0–6, 6–2, 3–6, 7–5
1949	Ted Schroeder	Jaroslav Drobny	3–6, 6–0, 6–3, 4–6, 6–4
1950	Budge Patty	Frank Sedgman	6–1, 6–7 (8–10), 6–2, 6–3
1951	Dick Savitt	Ken McGregor	6–4, 6–4, 6–4
1952	Frank Sedgman	Jaroslav Drobny	4–6, 6–3, 6–2, 6–3
1953	Vic Seixas	Kurt Nielsen	9–7, 6–3, 6–4
1954	Jaroslav Drobny	Ken Rosewall	13–11, 4–6, 6–2, 9–7
1955	Tony Trabert	Kurt Nielsen	6–3, 7–5, 6–1
1956	Lew Hoad	Ken Rosewall	6–2, 4–6, 7–5, 6–4
1957	Lew Hoad	Ashley Cooper	6–2, 6–1, 6–2
1958	Ashley Cooper	Neale Fraser	3–6, 6–3, 6–4, 13–11
1959	Alex Olmedo	Rod Laver	6–4, 6–3, 6–4
1960	Neale Fraser	Rod Laver	6–4, 3–6, 9–7, 7–5
1961	Rod Laver	Chuck McKinley	6–3, 6–1, 6–4
1962	Rod Laver	Martin Mulligan	6–2, 6–2, 6–1
1963	Chuck McKinley	Fred Stolle	9–7, 6–1, 6–4
1964	Roy Emerson	Fred Stolle	6–4, 12–10, 4–6, 6–3
1965	Roy Emerson	Fred Stolle	6–2, 6–4, 6–4
1966	Manuel Santana	Dennis Ralston	6–4, 11–9, 6–4
1967	John Newcombe	Wilhelm Bungert	6–3, 6–1, 6–1
1968*	Rod Laver	Tony Roche	6–3, 6–4, 6–2
1969	Rod Laver	John Newcombe	6–4, 5–7, 6–4, 6–4
1970	John Newcombe	Ken Rosewall	5–7, 6–3, 6–2, 3–6, 6–1
1971	John Newcombe	Stan Smith	6–3, 5–7, 2–6, 6–4, 6–4
1972	Stan Smith	Ilie Nastase	4–6, 6–3, 6–3, 4–6, 7–5
1973	Jan Kodes	Alex Metreveli	6–1, 9–8, 6–3
1974	Jimmy Connors	Ken Rosewall	6–1, 6–1, 6–4
1975	Arthur Ashe	Jimmy Connors	6–1, 6–1, 5–7, 6–4
1976	Bjorn Borg	Ilie Nastase	6–4, 6–2, 9–7
1977	Bjorn Borg	Jimmy Connors	3–6, 6–2, 6–1, 5–7, 6–4
1978	Bjorn Borg	Jimmy Connors	6–2, 6–2, 6–3
1979	Bjorn Borg	Roscoe Tanner	6–7, 6–1, 3–6, 6–3, 6–4
1980	Bjorn Borg	John McEnroe	1–6, 7–5, 6–3, 6–7, 8–6
1981	John McEnroe	Bjorn Borg	4–6, 7–6, 7–6, 6–4
1982	Jimmy Connors	John McEnroe	3–6, 6–3, 6–7, 7–6, 6–4
1983	John McEnroe	Chris Lewis	6–2, 6–2, 6–2

Note: Prior to 1922 the tournament was run on a challenge-round system. The previous year's winner "stood out" of an All Comers event, which produced a challenger to play him for the title.

*Became Open (amateur and professional) in 1968, but restricted to only contract professionals in 1972.

MEN *(Cont.)*
Wimbledon Championships *(Cont.)*

Year	Winner	Finalist	Score
1984	John McEnroe	Jimmy Connors	6–1, 6–1, 6–2
1985	Boris Becker	Kevin Curren	6–3, 6–7, 7–6, 6–4
1986	Boris Becker	Ivan Lendl	6–4, 6–3, 7–5
1987	Pat Cash	Ivan Lendl	7–6, 6–2, 7–5
1988	Stefan Edberg	Boris Becker	4–6, 7–6, 6–4, 6–2
1989	Boris Becker	Stefan Edberg	6–0, 7–6, 6–4
1990	Stefan Edberg	Boris Becker	6–2, 6–2, 3–6, 3–6, 6–4
1991	Michael Stich	Boris Becker	6–4, 7–6, 6–4
1992	Andre Agassi	Goran Ivanisevic	6–7, 6–4, 6–4, 1–6, 6–4
1993	Pete Sampras	Jim Courier	7–6, 7–6, 3–6, 6–3
1994	Pete Sampras	Goran Ivanisevic	7–6, 7–6, 6–0
1995	Pete Sampras	Boris Becker	6–7, 6–2, 6–4, 6–2
1996	Richard Krajicek	MaliVai Washington	6–3, 6–4, 6–3
1997	Pete Sampras	Cedric Pioline	6–4, 6–2, 6–4
1998	Pete Sampras	Goran Ivanisevic	6–7, 7–6, 6–4, 3–6, 6–2
1999	Pete Sampras	Andre Agassi	6–3, 6–4, 7–5
2000	Pete Sampras	Patrick Rafter	6–7, 7–6, 6–4, 6–2
2001	Goran Ivanisevic	Patrick Rafter	6–3, 3–6, 6–3, 2–6, 9–7
2002	Lleyton Hewitt	David Nalbandian	6–1, 6–3, 6–2
2003	Roger Federer	Mark Philippoussis	7–6 (7-5), 6–2, 7–6 (7-3)
2004	Roger Federer	Andy Roddick	4–6, 7–5, 7–6 (7-3), 6–4
2005	Roger Federer	Andy Roddick	6–2, 7–6 (7-2), 6–4
2006	Roger Federer	Rafael Nadal	6–0, 7–6, (7–5), 6–7 (2–7), 6–3
2007	Roger Federer	Rafael Nadal	7–6 (9–7), 4–6, 7–6 (7–3), 2–6, 6–2
2008	Rafael Nadal	Roger Federer	6–4, 6–4, 6–7 (5–7), 6–7 (8–10) 9–7
2009	Roger Federer	Andy Roddick	5–7, 7–6 (8–6), 7–6 (7–5), 3–6, 16–14
2010	Rafael Nadal	Tomas Berdych	6–3, 7–5, 6–4
2011	Novak Djokovic	Rafael Nadal	6–4, 6–1, 1–6, 6–3
2012	Roger Federer	Andy Murray	4–6, 7–5, 6–3, 6–4
2013	Andy Murray	Novak Djokovic	6–4, 7–5, 6–4

United States Championships

Year	Winner	Finalist	Score
1881	Richard D. Sears	W.E. Glyn	6–0, 6–3, 6–2
1882	Richard D. Sears	C.M. Clark	6–1, 6–4, 6–0
1883	Richard D. Sears	James Dwight	6–2, 6–0, 9–7
1884	Richard D. Sears	H.A. Taylor	6–0, 1–6, 6–0, 6–2
1885	Richard D. Sears	G.M. Brinley	6–3, 4–6, 6–0, 6–3
1886	Richard D. Sears	R.L. Beeckman	4–6, 6–1, 6–3, 6–4
1887	Richard D. Sears	H.W. Slocum Jr	6–1, 6–3, 6–2
1888†	H. W. Slocum Jr	H.A. Taylor	6–4, 6–1, 6–0
1889	H. W. Slocum Jr	Q.A. Shaw	6–3, 6–1, 4–6, 6–2
1890	Oliver S. Campbell	H.W. Slocum Jr	6–2, 4–6, 6–3, 6–1
1891	Oliver S. Campbell	Clarence Hobart	2–6, 7–5, 7–9, 6–1, 6–2
1892	Oliver S. Campbell	Frederick H. Hovey	7–5, 3–6, 6–3, 7–5
1893†	Robert D. Wrenn	Frederick H. Hovey	6–4, 3–6, 6–4, 6–4
1894	Robert D. Wrenn	M.F. Goodbody	6–8, 6–1, 6–4, 6–4
1895	Frederick H. Hovey	Robert D. Wrenn	6–3, 6–2, 6–4
1896	Robert D. Wrenn	Frederick H. Hovey	7–5, 3–6, 6–0, 1–6, 6–1
1897	Robert D. Wrenn	Wilberforce V. Eaves	4–6, 8–6, 6–3, 2–6, 6–2
1898†	Malcolm D. Whitman	Dwight F. Davis	3–6, 6–2, 6–2, 6–1
1899	Malcolm D. Whitman	J. Parmly Paret	6–1, 6–2, 3–6, 7–5
1900	Malcolm D. Whitman	William A. Larned	6–4, 1–6, 6–2, 6–2
1901†	William A. Larned	Beals C. Wright	6–2, 6–8, 6–4, 6–4
1902	William A. Larned	Reggie F. Doherty	4–6, 6–2, 6–4, 8–6
1903	H. Laurie Doherty	William A. Larned	6–0, 6–3, 10–8
1904†	Holcombe Ward	William J. Clothier	10–8, 6–4, 9–7
1905	Beals C. Wright	Holcombe Ward	6–2, 6–1, 11–9
1906	William J. Clothier	Beals C. Wright	6–3, 6–0, 6–4
1907†	William A. Larned	Robert LeRoy	6–2, 6–2, 6–4
1908	William A. Larned	Beals C. Wright	6–1, 6–2, 8–6
1909	William A. Larned	William J. Clothier	6–1, 6–2, 5–7, 1–6, 6–1

† No challenge round played.

MEN (Cont.)
United States Championships (Cont.)

Year	Winner	Finalist	Score
1910	William A. Larned	Thomas C. Bundy	6–1, 5–7, 6–0, 6–8, 6–1
1911	William A. Larned	Maurice E. McLoughlin	6–4, 6–4, 6–2
1912‡	Maurice E. McLoughlin	Bill Johnson	3–6, 2–6, 6–2, 6–4, 6–2
1913	Maurice E. McLoughlin	Richard N. Williams	6–4, 5–7, 6–3, 6–1
1914	Richard N. Williams	Maurice E. McLoughlin	6–3, 8–6, 10–8
1915	Bill Johnston	Maurice E. McLoughlin	1–6, 6–0, 7–5, 10–8
1916	Richard N. Williams	Bill Johnston	4–6, 6–4, 0–6, 6–2, 6–4
1917#	R.L. Murray	N. W. Niles	5–7, 8–6, 6–3, 6–3
1918	R.L. Murray	Bill Tilden	6–3, 6–1, 7–5
1919	Bill Johnston	Bill Tilden	6–4, 6–4, 6–3
1920	Bill Tilden	Bill Johnston	6–1, 1–6, 7–5, 5–7, 6–3
1921	Bill Tilden	Wallace F. Johnson	6–1, 6–3, 6–1
1922	Bill Tilden	Bill Johnston	4–6, 3–6, 6–2, 6–3, 6–4
1923	Bill Tilden	Bill Johnston	6–4, 6–1, 6–4
1924	Bill Tilden	Bill Johnston	6–1, 9–7, 6–2
1925	Bill Tilden	Bill Johnston	4–6, 11–9, 6–3, 4–6, 6–3
1926	Rene Lacoste	Jean Borotra	6–4, 6–0, 6–4
1927	Rene Lacoste	Bill Tilden	11–9, 6–3, 11–9
1928	Henri Cochet	Francis T. Hunter	4–6, 6–4, 3–6, 7–5, 6–3
1929	Bill Tilden	Francis T. Hunter	3–6, 6–3, 4–6, 6–2, 6–4
1930	John H. Doeg	Francis X. Shields	10–8, 1–6, 6–4, 16–14
1931	Ellsworth Vines	George M. Lott Jr	7–9, 6–3, 9–7, 7–5
1932	Ellsworth Vines	Henri Cochet	6–4, 6–4, 6–4
1933	Fred Perry	Jack Crawford	6–3, 11–13, 4–6, 6–0, 6–1
1934	Fred Perry	Wilmer L. Allison	6–4, 6–3, 1–6, 8–6
1935	Wilmer L. Allison	Sidney B. Wood Jr	6–2, 6–2, 6–3
1936	Fred Perry	Don Budge	2–6, 6–2, 8–6, 1–6, 10–8
1937	Don Budge	Gottfried von Cramm	6–1, 7–9, 6–1, 3–6, 6–1
1938	Don Budge	Gene Mako	6–3, 6–8, 6–2, 6–1
1939	Bobby Riggs	Welby Van Horn	6–4, 6–2, 6–4
1940	Don McNeill	Bobby Riggs	4–6, 6–8, 6–3, 6–3, 7–5
1941	Bobby Riggs	Francis Kovacs II	5–7, 6–1, 6–3, 6–3
1942	Ted Schroeder	Frank Parker	8–6, 7–5, 3–6, 4–6, 6–2
1943	Joseph R. Hunt	Jack Kramer	6–3, 6–8, 10–8, 6–0
1944	Frank Parker	William F. Talbert	6–4, 3–6, 6–3, 6–3
1945	Frank Parker	William F. Talbert	14–12, 6–1, 6–2
1946	Jack Kramer	Tom P. Brown	9–7, 6–3, 6–0
1947	Jack Kramer	Frank Parker	4–6, 2–6, 6–1, 6–0, 6–3
1948	Pancho Gonzales	Eric W. Sturgess	6–2, 6–3, 14–12
1949	Pancho Gonzales	Ted Schroeder	16–18, 2–6, 6–1, 6–2, 6–4
1950	Arthur Larsen	Herbie Flam	6–3, 4–6, 5–7, 6–4, 6–3
1951	Frank Sedgman	Vic Seixas	6–4, 6–1, 6–1
1952	Frank Sedgman	Gardnar Mulloy	6–1, 6–2, 6–3
1953	Tony Trabert	Vic Seixas	6–3, 6–2, 6–3
1954	Vic Seixas	Rex Hartwig	3–6, 6–2, 6–4, 6–4
1955	Tony Trabert	Ken Rosewall	9–7, 6–3, 6–3
1956	Ken Rosewall	Lew Hoad	4–6, 6–2, 6–3, 6–3
1957	Mal Anderson	Ashley J. Cooper	10–8, 7–5, 6–4
1958	Ashley J. Cooper	Mal Anderson	6–2, 3–6, 4–6, 10–8, 8–6
1959	Neale Fraser	Alex Olmedo	6–3, 5–7, 6–2, 6–4
1960	Neale Fraser	Rod Laver	6–4, 6–4, 9–7
1961	Roy Emerson	Rod Laver	7–5, 6–3, 6–2
1962	Rod Laver	Roy Emerson	6–2, 6–4, 5–7, 6–4
1963	Rafael Osuna	Frank Froehling III	7–5, 6–4, 6–2
1964	Roy Emerson	Fred Stolle	6–4, 6–2, 6–4
1965	Manuel Santana	Cliff Drysdale	6–2, 7–9, 7–5, 6–1
1966	Fred Stolle	John Newcombe	4–6, 12–10, 6–3, 6–4
1967	John Newcombe	Clark Graebner	6–4, 6–4, 8–6
1968*	Arthur Ashe	Tom Okker	14–12, 5–7, 6–3, 3–6, 6–3
1968**	Arthur Ashe	Bob Lutz	4–6, 6–3, 8–10, 6–0, 6–4
1969	Rod Laver	Tony Roche	7–9, 6–1, 6–3, 6–2
1969**	Stan Smith	Bob Lutz	9–7, 6–3, 6–1
1970	Ken Rosewall	Tony Roche	2–6, 6–4, 7–6, 6–3
1971‡	Stan Smith	Jan Kodes	3–6, 6–3, 6–2, 7–6

#National Patriotic Tournament. *Became Open (amateur and professional) in 1968. **Amateur event held.
‡ Challenge round abolished.

MEN *(Cont.)*
United States Championships *(Cont.)*

Year	Winner	Finalist	Score
1972	Ilie Nastase	Arthur Ashe	3–6, 6–3, 6–7, 6–4, 6–3
1973	John Newcombe	Jan Kodes	6–4, 1–6, 4–6, 6–2, 6–3
1974	Jimmy Connors	Ken Rosewall	6–1, 6–0, 6–1
1975	Manuel Orantes	Jimmy Connors	6–4, 6–3, 6–3
1976	Jimmy Connors	Bjorn Borg	6–4, 3–6, 7–6, 6–4
1977	Guillermo Vilas	Jimmy Connors	2–6, 6–3, 7–6, 6–0
1978	Jimmy Connors	Bjorn Borg	6–4, 6–2, 6–2
1979	John McEnroe	Vitas Gerulaitis	7–5, 6–3, 6–3
1980	John McEnroe	Bjorn Borg	7–6, 6–1, 6–7, 5–7, 6–4
1981	John McEnroe	Bjorn Borg	4–6, 6–2, 6–4, 6–3
1982	Jimmy Connors	Ivan Lendl	6–3, 6–2, 4–6, 6–4
1983	Jimmy Connors	Ivan Lendl	6–3, 6–7, 7–5, 6–0
1984	John McEnroe	Ivan Lendl	6–3, 6–4, 6–1
1985	Ivan Lendl	John McEnroe	7–6, 6–3, 6–4
1986	Ivan Lendl	Miloslav Mecir	6–4, 6–2, 6–0
1987	Ivan Lendl	Mats Wilander	6–7, 6–0, 7–6, 6–4
1988	Mats Wilander	Ivan Lendl	6–4, 4–6, 6–3, 5–7, 6–4
1989	Boris Becker	Ivan Lendl	7–6, 1–6, 6–3, 7–6
1990	Pete Sampras	Andre Agassi	6–4, 6–3, 6–2
1991	Stefan Edberg	Jim Courier	6–2, 6–4, 6–0
1992	Stefan Edberg	Pete Sampras	3–6, 6–4, 7–6, 6–2
1993	Pete Sampras	Cedric Pioline	6–4, 6–4, 6–3
1994	Andre Agassi	Michael Stich	6–1, 7–6, 7–5
1995	Pete Sampras	Andre Agassi	6–4, 6–3, 4–6, 7–5
1996	Pete Sampras	Michael Chang	6–1, 6–4, 7–6
1997	Patrick Rafter	Greg Rusedski	6–3, 6–2, 4–6, 7–5
1998	Patrick Rafter	Mark Philippoussis	6–3, 3–6, 6–2, 6–0
1999	Andre Agassi	Todd Martin	6–4, 6–7, 6–7, 6–3, 6–2
2000	Marat Safin	Pete Sampras	6–4, 6–3, 6–3
2001	Lleyton Hewitt	Pete Sampras	7–6, 6–1, 6–1
2002	Pete Sampras	Andre Agassi	6–3, 6–4, 5–7, 6–4
2003	Andy Roddick	Juan Carlos Ferrero	6–3, 7–6 (7-2), 6–3
2004	Roger Federer	Lleyton Hewitt	6–0, 7–6 (7-3), 6–0
2005	Roger Federer	Andre Agassi	6–3, 2–6, 7–6 (7–1), 6–1
2006	Roger Federer	Andy Roddick	6–2, 4–6, 7–5, 6–1
2007	Roger Federer	Novak Djokovic	7–6 (7–4), 7–6 (7–2), 6–4
2008	Roger Federer	Andy Murray	6–2, 7–5, 6–2
2009	Juan Martin del Potro	Roger Federer	3–6, 7–6 (7–5), 4–6, 7–6 (7–4), 6–2
2010	Rafael Nadal	Novak Djokovic	6–4, 5–7, 6–4, 6–2
2011	Novak Djokovic	Rafael Nadal	6–2, 6–4, 6–7 (3–7), 6–1
2012	Andy Murray	Novak Djokovic	7–6 (12–10), 7–5, 2–6, 3–6, 6–2
2013	Rafael Nadal	Novak Djokovic	6–2, 3–6, 6–4, 6–1

WOMEN
Australian Championships

Year	Winner	Finalist	Score
1922	Margaret Molesworth	Esna Boyd	6–3, 10–8
1923	Margaret Molesworth	Esna Boyd	6–1, 7–5
1924	Sylvia Lance	Esna Boyd	6–3, 3–6, 6–4
1925	Daphne Akhurst	Esna Boyd	1–6, 8–6, 6–4
1926	Daphne Akhurst	Esna Boyd	6–1, 6–3
1927	Esna Boyd	Sylvia Harper	5–7, 6–1, 6–2
1928	Daphne Akhurst	Esna Boyd	7–5, 6–2
1929	Daphne Akhurst	Louise Bickerton	6–1, 5–7, 6–2
1930	Daphne Akhurst	Sylvia Harper	10–8, 2–6, 7–5
1931	Coral Buttsworth	Margorie Crawford	1–6, 6–3, 6–4
1932	Coral Buttsworth	Kathrine Le Messurier	9–7, 6–4
1933	Joan Hartigan	Coral Buttsworth	6–4, 6–3
1934	Joan Hartigan	Margaret Molesworth	6–1, 6–4
1935	Dorothy Round	Nancye Wynne Bolton	1–6, 6–1, 6–3
1936	Joan Hartigan	Nancye Wynne Bolton	6–4, 6–4
1937	Nancye Wynne Bolton	Emily Westacott	6–3, 5–7, 6–4
1938	Dorothy Bundy	D. Stevenson	6–3, 6–2
1939	Emily Westacott	Nell Hopman	6–1, 6–2
1940	Nancye Wynne Bolton	Thelma Coyne	5–7, 6–4, 6–0
1941–45	No tournament		
1946	Nancye Wynne Bolton	Joyce Fitch	6–4, 6–4
1947	Nancye Wynne Bolton	Nell Hopman	6–3, 6–2
1948	Nancye Wynne Bolton	Marie Toomey	6–3, 6–1
1949	Doris Hart	Nancye Wynne Bolton	6–3, 6–4
1950	Louise Brough	Doris Hart	6–4, 3–6, 6–4
1951	Nancye Wynne Bolton	Thelma Long	6–1, 7–5
1952	Thelma Long	H. Angwin	6–2, 6–3
1953	Maureen Connolly	Julia Sampson	6–3, 6–2
1954	Thelma Long	J. Staley	6–3, 6–4
1955	Beryl Penrose	Thelma Long	6–4, 6–3
1956	Mary Carter	Thelma Long	3–6, 6–2, 9–7
1957	Shirley Fry	Althea Gibson	6–3, 6–4
1958	Angela Mortimer	Lorraine Coghlan	6–3, 6–4
1959	Mary Carter-Reitano	Renee Schuurman	6–2, 6–3
1960	Margaret Smith	Jan Lehane	7–5, 6–2
1961	Margaret Smith	Jan Lehane	6–1, 6–4
1962	Margaret Smith	Jan Lehane	6–0, 6–2
1963	Margaret Smith	Jan Lehane	6–2, 6–2
1964	Margaret Smith	Lesley Turner	6–3, 6–2
1965	Margaret Smith	Maria Bueno	5–7, 6–4, 5–2, ret.
1966	Margaret Smith	Nancy Richey	Default
1967	Nancy Richey	Lesley Turner	6–1, 6–4
1968	Billie Jean King	Margaret Smith	6–1, 6–2
1969*	Margaret Smith Court	Billie Jean King	6–4, 6–1
1970	Margaret Smith Court	Kerry Melville Reid	6–3, 6–1
1971	Margaret Smith Court	Evonne Goolagong	2–6, 7–6, 7–5
1972	Virginia Wade	Evonne Goolagong	6–4, 6–4
1973	Margaret Smith Court	Evonne Goolagong	6–4, 7–5
1974	Evonne Goolagong	Chris Evert	7–6, 4–6, 6–0
1975	Evonne Goolagong	Martina Navratilova	6–3, 6–2
1976	Evonne Goolagong Cawley	Renata Tomanova	6–2, 6–2
1977 (Jan)	Kerry Melville Reid	Dianne Balestrat	7–5, 6–2
1977 (Dec)	Evonne Goolagong Cawley	Helen Gourlay	6–3, 6–0
1978	Chris O'Neil	Betsy Nagelsen	6–3, 7–6
1979	Barbara Jordan	Sharon Walsh	6–3, 6–3
1980	Hana Mandlikova	Wendy Turnbull	6–0, 7–5
1981	Martina Navratilova	Chris Evert Lloyd	6–7, 6–4, 7–5
1982	Chris Evert Lloyd	Martina Navratilova	6–3, 2–6, 6–3
1983	Martina Navratilova	Kathy Jordan	6–2, 7–6
1984	Chris Evert Lloyd	Helena Sukova	6–7, 6–1, 6–3
1985 (Dec)	Martina Navratilova	Chris Evert Lloyd	6–2, 4–6, 6–2
1987 (Jan)	Hana Mandlikova	Martina Navratilova	7–5, 7–6
1988	Steffi Graf	Chris Evert	6–1, 7–6
1989	Steffi Graf	Helena Sukova	6–4, 6–4
1990	Steffi Graf	Mary Joe Fernandez	6–3, 6–4
1991	Monica Seles	Jana Novotna	5–7, 6–3, 6–1

*Became Open (amateur and professional) in 1969.

WOMEN (Cont.)
Australian Championships (Cont.)

Year	Winner	Finalist	Score
1992	Monica Seles	Mary Joe Fernandez	6–2, 6–3
1993	Monica Seles	Steffi Graf	4–6, 6–3, 6–2
1994	Steffi Graf	Arantxa Sánchez Vicario	6–0, 6–2
1995	Mary Pierce	Arantxa Sánchez Vicario	6–3, 6–2
1996	Monica Seles	Anke Huber	6–4, 6–1
1997	Martina Hingis	Mary Pierce	6–2, 6–2
1998	Martina Hingis	Conchita Martinez	6–3, 6–3
1999	Martina Hingis	Amelie Mauresmo	6–2, 6–3
2000	Lindsay Davenport	Martina Hingis	6–1, 7–5
2001	Jennifer Capriati	Martina Hingis	6–4, 6–3
2002	Jennifer Capriati	Martina Hingis	4–6, 7–6 (9–7), 6–2
2003	Serena Williams	Venus Williams	7–6 (7-4), 3–6, 6–4
2004	Justine Henin-Hardenne	Kim Clijsters	6–3, 4–6, 6–3
2005	Serena Williams	Lindsay Davenport	2–6, 6–3, 6–0
2006	Amelie Mauresmo	Justine Henin-Hardenne	6–1, 2–0, ret.
2007	Serena Williams	Maria Sharapova	6–1, 6–2
2008	Maria Sharapova	Ana Ivanovic	7–5, 6–3
2009	Serena Williams	Dinara Safina	6–0, 6–3
2010	Serena Williams	Justine Henin	6–4, 3–6, 6–2
2011	Kim Clijsters	Li Na	3–6, 6–3, 6–3
2012	Victoria Azarenka	Maria Sharapova	6–3, 6–0
2013	Victoria Azarenka	Li Na	4–6, 6–4, 6–3

French Championships

Year	Winner	Finalist	Score
1925†	Suzanne Lenglen	Kathleen McKane	6–1, 6–2
1926	Suzanne Lenglen	Mary K. Browne	6–1, 6–0
1927	Kea Bouman	Irene Peacock	6–2, 6–4
1928	Helen Wills	Eileen Bennett	6–1, 6–2
1929	Helen Wills	Simone Mathieu	6–3, 6–4
1930	Helen Wills Moody	Helen Jacobs	6–2, 6–1
1931	Cilly Aussem	Betty Nuthall	8–6, 6–1
1932	Helen Wills Moody	Simone Mathieu	7–5, 6–1
1933	Margaret Scriven	Simone Mathieu	6–2, 4–6, 6–4
1934	Margaret Scriven	Helen Jacobs	7–5, 4–6, 6–1
1935	Hilde Sperling	Simone Mathieu	6–2, 6–1
1936	Hilde Sperling	Simone Mathieu	6–3, 6–4
1937	Hilde Sperling	Simone Mathieu	6–2, 6–4
1938	Simone Mathieu	Nelly Landry	6–0, 6–3
1939	Simone Mathieu	Jadwiga Jedrzejowska	6–3, 8–6
1940–45	No tournament		
1946	Margaret Osborne	Pauline Betz	1–6, 8–6, 7–5
1947	Patricia Todd	Doris Hart	6–3, 3–6, 6–4
1948	Nelly Landry	Shirley Fry	6–2, 0–6, 6–0
1949	Margaret Osborne duPont	Nelly Adamson	7–5, 6–2
1950	Doris Hart	Patricia Todd	6–4, 4–6, 6–2
1951	Shirley Fry	Doris Hart	6–3, 3–6, 6–3
1952	Doris Hart	Shirley Fry	6–4, 6–4
1953	Maureen Connolly	Doris Hart	6–2, 6–4
1954	Maureen Connolly	Ginette Bucaille	6–4, 6–1
1955	Angela Mortimer	Dorothy Knode	2–6, 7–5, 10–8
1956	Althea Gibson	Angela Mortimer	6–0, 12–10
1957	Shirley Bloomer	Dorothy Knode	6–1, 6–3
1958	Zsuzsi Kormoczi	Shirley Bloomer	6–4, 1–6, 6–2
1959	Christine Truman	Zsuzsi Kormoczi	6–4, 7–5
1960	Darlene Hard	Yola Ramirez	6–3, 6–4
1961	Ann Haydon	Yola Ramirez	6–2, 6–1
1962	Margaret Smith	Lesley Turner	6–3, 3–6, 7–5
1963	Lesley Turner	Ann Haydon Jones	2–6, 6–3, 7–5
1964	Margaret Smith	Maria Bueno	5–7, 6–1, 6–2
1965	Lesley Turner	Margaret Smith	6–3, 6–4
1966	Ann Jones	Nancy Richey	6–3, 6–1
1967	Francoise Durr	Lesley Turner	4–6, 6–3, 6–4
1968*	Nancy Richey	Ann Jones	5–7, 6–4, 6–1

†1925 was the first year that entries were accepted from all countries. *Became Open (amateur and professional) in 1968, but restricted to only contract professionals in 1972.

WOMEN (Cont.)
French Championships (Cont.)

Year	Winner	Finalist	Score
1969	Margaret Smith Court	Ann Jones	6–1, 4–6, 6–3
1970	Margaret Smith Court	Helga Niessen	6–2, 6–4
1971	Evonne Goolagong	Helen Gourlay	6–3, 7–5
1972	Billie Jean King	Evonne Goolagong	6–3, 6–3
1973	Margaret Smith Court	Chris Evert	6–7, 7–6, 6–4
1974	Chris Evert	Olga Morozova	6–1, 6–2
1975	Chris Evert	Martina Navratilova	2–6, 6–2, 6–1
1976	Sue Barker	Renata Tomanova	6–2, 0–6, 6–2
1977	Mima Jausovec	Florenza Mihai	6–2, 6–7, 6–1
1978	Virginia Ruzici	Mima Jausovec	6–2, 6–2
1979	Chris Evert Lloyd	Wendy Turnbull	6–2, 6–0
1980	Chris Evert Lloyd	Virginia Ruzici	6–0, 6–3
1981	Hana Mandlikova	Sylvia Hanika	6–2, 6–4
1982	Martina Navratilova	Andrea Jaeger	7–6, 6–1
1983	Chris Evert Lloyd	Mima Jausovec	6–1, 6–2
1984	Martina Navratilova	Chris Evert Lloyd	6–3, 6–1
1985	Chris Evert Lloyd	Martina Navratilova	6–3, 6–7, 7–5
1986	Chris Evert Lloyd	Martina Navratilova	2–6, 6–3, 6–3
1987	Steffi Graf	Martina Navratilova	6–4, 4–6, 8–6
1988	Steffi Graf	Natalia Zvereva	6–0, 6–0
1989	Arantxa Sánchez Vicario	Steffi Graf	7–6, 3–6, 7–5
1990	Monica Seles	Steffi Graf	7–6, 6–4
1991	Monica Seles	Arantxa Sánchez Vicario	6–3, 6–4
1992	Monica Seles	Steffi Graf	6–2, 3–6, 10–8
1993	Steffi Graf	Mary Joe Fernandez	4–6, 6–2, 6–4
1994	Arantxa Sánchez Vicario	Mary Pierce	6–4, 6–4
1995	Steffi Graf	Arantxa Sánchez Vicario	7–5, 4–6, 6–0
1996	Steffi Graf	Arantxa Sánchez Vicario	6–3, 6–7 (4–7), 10–8
1997	Iva Majoli	Martina Hingis	6–4, 6–2
1998	Arantxa Sánchez Vicario	Monica Seles	7–6 (7–5), 0–6, 6–2
1999	Steffi Graf	Martina Hingis	4–6, 7–5, 6–2
2000	Mary Pierce	Conchita Martinez	6–2, 7–5
2001	Jennifer Capriati	Kim Clijsters	1–6, 6–4, 12–10
2002	Serena Williams	Venus Williams	7–5, 6–3
2003	Justine Henin-Hardenne	Kim Clijsters	6–0, 6–4
2004	Anastasia Myskina	Elena Dementieva	6–1, 6–2
2005	Justine Henin-Hardenne	Mary Pierce	6–1, 6–1
2006	Justine Henin-Hardenne	Svetlana Kuznetsova	6–4, 6–4
2007	Justine Henin	Ana Ivanovic	6–1, 6–2
2008	Ana Ivanovic	Dinara Safina	6–4, 6–3
2009	Svetlana Kuznetsova	Dinara Safina	6–4, 6–2
2010	Francesca Schiavone	Samantha Stosur	6–4, 7–6 (7–2)
2011	Li Na	Francesca Schiavone	6–4, 7–6 (7–0)
2012	Maria Sharapova	Sara Errani	6–3, 6–2
2013	Serena Williams	Maria Sharapova	6–4, 6–4

Wimbledon Championships

Year	Winner	Finalist	Score
1884	Maud Watson	Lilian Watson	6–8, 6–3, 6–3
1885	Maud Watson	Blanche Bingley	6–1, 7–5
1886	Blanche Bingley	Maud Watson	6–3, 6–3
1887	Charlotte Dod	Blanche Bingley	6–2, 6–0
1888	Charlotte Dod	Blanche Bingley Hillyard	6–3, 6–3
1889	Blanche Bingley Hillyard	n/a	n/a
1890	Lena Rice	n/a	n/a
1891	Charlotte Dod	n/a	n/a
1892	Charlotte Dod	Blanche Bingley Hillyard	6–1, 6–1
1893	Charlotte Dod	Blanche Bingley Hillyard	6–8, 6–1, 6–4
1894	Blanche Bingley Hillyard	n/a	n/a
1895	Charlotte Cooper	n/a	n/a
1896	Charlotte Cooper	Mrs. W.H. Pickering	6–2, 6–3
1897	Blanche Bingley Hillyard	Charlotte Cooper	5–7, 7–5, 6–2
1898	Charlotte Cooper	n/a	n/a
1899	Blanche Bingley Hillyard	Charlotte Cooper	6–2, 6–3
1900	Blanche Bingley Hillyard	Charlotte Cooper	4–6, 6–4, 6–4
1901	Charlotte Cooper Sterry	Blanche Bingley Hillyard	6–2, 6–2
1902	Muriel Robb	Charlotte Cooper Sterry	7–5, 6–1

WOMEN (Cont.)

Wimbledon Championships (Cont.)

Year	Winner	Finalist	Score
1903	Dorothea Douglass	n/a	n/a
1904	Dorothea Douglass	Charlotte Cooper Sterry	6–0, 6–3
1905	May Sutton	Dorothea Douglass	6–3, 6–4
1906	Dorothea Douglass	May Sutton	6–3, 9–7
1907	May Sutton	Dorothea Douglass Lambert Chambers	6–1, 6–4
1908	Charlotte Cooper Sterry	n/a	n/a
1909	Dora Boothby	n/a	n/a
1910	Dorothea Douglass Lambert Chambers	Dora Boothby	6–2, 6–2
1911	Dorothea Douglass Lambert Chambers	Dora Boothby	6–0, 6–0
1912	Ethel Larcombe	n/a	n/a
1913	Dorothea Douglass Lambert Chambers	n/a	n/a
1914	Dorothea Douglass Lambert Chambers	Ethel Larcombe	7–5, 6–4
1915–18	No tournament		
1919	Suzanne Lenglen	Dorothea Douglass Lambert Chambers	10–8, 4–6, 9–7
1920	Suzanne Lenglen	Dorothea Douglass Lambert Chambers	6–3, 6–0
1921	Suzanne Lenglen	Elizabeth Ryan	6–2, 6–0
1922	Suzanne Lenglen	Molla Mallory	6–2, 6–0
1923	Suzanne Lenglen	Kathleen McKane	6–2, 6–2
1924	Kathleen McKane	Helen Wills	4–6, 6–4, 6–2
1925	Suzanne Lenglen	Joan Fry	6–2, 6–0
1926	Kathleen McKane Godfree	Lili de Alvarez	6–2, 4–6, 6–3
1927	Helen Wills	Lili de Alvarez	6–2, 6–4
1928	Helen Wills	Lili de Alvarez	6–2, 6–3
1929	Helen Wills	Helen Jacobs	6–1, 6–2
1930	Helen Wills Moody	Elizabeth Ryan	6–2, 6–2
1931	Cilly Aussem	Hilde Kranwinkel	7–5, 7–5
1932	Helen Wills Moody	Helen Jacobs	6–3, 6–1
1933	Helen Wills Moody	Dorothy Round	6–4, 6–8, 6–3
1934	Dorothy Round	Helen Jacobs	6–2, 5–7, 6–3
1935	Helen Wills Moody	Helen Jacobs	6–3, 3–6, 7–5
1936	Helen Jacobs	Hilde Kranwinkel Sperling	6–2, 4–6, 7–5
1937	Dorothy Round	Jadwiga Jedrzejowska	6–2, 2–6, 7–5
1938	Helen Wills Moody	Helen Jacobs	6–4, 6–0
1939	Alice Marble	Kay Stammers	6–2, 6–0
1940–45	No tournament		
1946	Pauline Betz	Louise Brough	6–2, 6–4
1947	Margaret Osborne	Doris Hart	6–2, 6–4
1948	Louise Brough	Doris Hart	6–3, 8–6
1949	Louise Brough	Margaret Osborne duPont	10–8, 1–6, 10–8
1950	Louise Brough	Margaret Osborne duPont	6–1, 3–6, 6–1
1951	Doris Hart	Shirley Fry	6–1, 6–0
1952	Maureen Connolly	Louise Brough	6–4, 6–3
1953	Maureen Connolly	Doris Hart	8–6, 7–5
1954	Maureen Connolly	Louise Brough	6–2, 7–5
1955	Louise Brough	Beverly Fleitz	7–5, 8–6
1956	Shirley Fry	Angela Buxton	6–3, 6–1
1957	Althea Gibson	Darlene Hard	6–3, 6–2
1958	Althea Gibson	Angela Mortimer	8–6, 6–2
1959	Maria Bueno	Darlene Hard	6–4, 6–3
1960	Maria Bueno	Sandra Reynolds	8–6, 6–0
1961	Angela Mortimer	Christine Truman	4–6, 6–4, 7–5
1962	Karen Hantze Susman	Vera Sukova	6–4, 6–4
1963	Margaret Smith	Billie Jean Moffitt	6–3, 6–4
1964	Maria Bueno	Margaret Smith	6–4, 7–9, 6–3
1965	Margaret Smith	Maria Bueno	6–4, 7–5
1966	Billie Jean King	Maria Bueno	6–3, 3–6, 6–1
1967	Billie Jean King	Ann Haydon Jones	6–3, 6–4

Note: Prior to 1922 the tournament was run on a challenge-round system. The previous year's winner "stood out" of an All-Comers event, which produced a challenger to play her for the title.

WOMEN (Cont.)
Wimbledon Championships (Cont.)

Year	Winner	Finalist	Score
1968*	Billie Jean King	Judy Tegart	9–7, 7–5
1969	Ann Haydon Jones	Billie Jean King	3–6, 6–3, 6–2
1970	Margaret Smith Court	Billie Jean King	14–12, 11–9
1971	Evonne Goolagong	Margaret Smith Court	6–4, 6–1
1972	Billie Jean King	Evonne Goolagong	6–3, 6–3
1973	Billie Jean King	Chris Evert	6–0, 7–5
1974	Chris Evert	Olga Morozova	6–0, 6–4
1975	Billie Jean King	Evonne Goolagong Cawley	6–0, 6–1
1976	Chris Evert	Evonne Goolagong Cawley	6–3, 4–6, 8–6
1977	Virginia Wade	Betty Stove	4–6, 6–3, 6–1
1978	Martina Navratilova	Chris Evert	2–6, 6–4, 7–5
1979	Martina Navratilova	Chris Evert Lloyd	6–4, 6–4
1980	Evonne Goolagong Cawley	Chris Evert Lloyd	6–1, 7–6
1981	Chris Evert Lloyd	Hana Mandlikova	6–2, 6–2
1982	Martina Navratilova	Chris Evert Lloyd	6–1, 3–6, 6–2
1983	Martina Navratilova	Andrea Jaeger	6–0, 6–3
1984	Martina Navratilova	Chris Evert Lloyd	7–6, 6–2
1985	Martina Navratilova	Chris Evert Lloyd	4–6, 6–3, 6–2
1986	Martina Navratilova	Hana Mandlikova	7–6, 6–3
1987	Martina Navratilova	Steffi Graf	7–5, 6–3
1988	Steffi Graf	Martina Navratilova	5–7, 6–2, 6–1
1989	Steffi Graf	Martina Navratilova	6–2, 6–7, 6–1
1990	Martina Navratilova	Zina Garrison	6–4, 6–1
1991	Steffi Graf	Gabriela Sabatini	6–4, 3–6, 8–6
1992	Steffi Graf	Monica Seles	6–2, 6–1
1993	Steffi Graf	Jana Novotna	7–6, 1–6, 6–4
1994	Conchita Martinez	Martina Navratilova	6–4, 3–6, 6–3
1995	Steffi Graf	Arantxa Sánchez Vicario	4–6, 6–1, 7–5
1996	Steffi Graf	Arantxa Sánchez Vicario	6–3, 7–5
1997	Martina Hingis	Jana Novotna	2–6, 6–3, 6–3
1998	Jana Novotna	Nathalie Tauziat	6–4, 7–6
1999	Lindsay Davenport	Steffi Graf	6–4, 7–5
2000	Venus Williams	Lindsay Davenport	6–3, 7–6
2001	Venus Williams	Justine Henin	6–1, 3–6, 6–0
2002	Serena Williams	Venus Williams	7–6 (7–4), 6–3
2003	Serena Williams	Venus Williams	4–6, 6–4, 6–2
2004	Maria Sharapova	Serena Williams	6–1, 6–4
2005	Venus Williams	Lindsay Davenport	4–6, 7–6 (7–4), 9–7
2006	Amelie Mauresmo	Justine Henin-Hardenne	2–6, 6–3, 6–4
2007	Venus Williams	Marion Bartoli	6–4, 6–1
2008	Venus Williams	Serena Williams	7–5, 6–4
2009	Serena Williams	Venus Williams	7–6 (7–3), 6–2
2010	Serena Williams	Vera Zvonareva	6–3, 6–2
2011	Petra Kvitova	Maria Sharapova	6–3, 6–4
2012	Serena Williams	Agnieszka Radwanska	6–1, 5–7, 6–2
2013	Marion Bartoli	Sabine Lisicki	6–1, 6–4

*Became Open (amateur and professional) in 1968, but restricted to only contract professionals in 1972.

United States Championships

Year	Winner	Finalist	Score
1887	Ellen Hansell	Laura Knight	6–1, 6–0
1888	Bertha L. Townsend	Ellen Hansell	6–3, 6–5
1889	Bertha L. Townsend	Louise Voorhes	7–5, 6–2
1890	Ellen C. Roosevelt	Bertha L. Townsend	6–2, 6–2
1891	Mabel Cahill	Ellen C. Roosevelt	6–4, 6–1, 4–6, 6–3
1892	Mabel Cahill	Elisabeth Moore	5–7, 6–3, 6–4, 4–6, 6–2
1893	Aline Terry	Alice Schultze	6–1, 6–3
1894	Helen Hellwig	Aline Terry	7–5, 3–6, 6–0, 3–6, 6–3
1895	Juliette Atkinson	Helen Hellwig	6–4, 6–2, 6–1
1896	Elisabeth Moore	Juliette Atkinson	6–4, 4–6, 6–2, 6–2
1897	Juliette Atkinson	Elisabeth Moore	6–3, 6–3, 4–6, 3–6, 6–3
1898	Juliette Atkinson	Marion Jones	6–3, 5–7, 6–4, 2–6, 7–5
1899	Marion Jones	Maud Banks	6–1, 6–1, 7–5
1900	Myrtle McAteer	Edith Parker	6–2, 6–2, 6–0
1901	Elisabeth Moore	Myrtle McAteer	6–4, 3–6, 7–5, 2–6, 6–2

WOMEN *(Cont.)*

United States Championships *(Cont.)*

Year*	Winner	Finalist	Score
1902*	Marion Jones	Elisabeth Moore	6–1, 1–0, ret.
1903	Elisabeth Moore	Marion Jones	7–5, 8–6
1904	May Sutton	Elisabeth Moore	6–1, 6–2
1905	Elisabeth Moore	Helen Homans	6–4, 5–7, 6–1
1906	Helen Homans	Maud Barger-Wallach	6–4, 6–3
1907	Evelyn Sears	Carrie Neely	6–3, 6–2
1908	Maud Barger–Wallach	Evelyn Sears	6–3, 1–6, 6–3
1909	Hazel Hotchkiss	Maud Barger–Wallach	6–0, 6–1
1910	Hazel Hotchkiss	Louise Hammond	6–4, 6–2
1911	Hazel Hotchkiss	Florence Sutton	8–10, 6–1, 9–7
1912†	Mary K. Browne	Eleanora Sears	6–4, 6–2
1913	Mary K. Browne	Dorothy Green	6–2, 7–5
1914	Mary K. Browne	Marie Wagner	6–2, 1–6, 6–1
1915	Molla Bjurstedt	Hazel Hotchkiss Wightman	4–6, 6–2, 6–0
1916	Molla Bjurstedt	Louise Hammond Raymond	6–0, 6–1
1917‡	Molla Bjurstedt	Marion Vanderhoef	4–6, 6–0, 6–2
1918	Molla Bjurstedt	Eleanor Goss	6–4, 6–3
1919	Hazel Hotchkiss Wightman	Marion Zinderstein	6–1, 6–2
1920	Molla Bjurstedt Mallory	Marion Zinderstein	6–3, 6–1
1921	Molla Bjurstedt Mallory	Mary K. Browne	4–6, 6–4, 6–2
1922	Molla Bjurstedt Mallory	Helen Wills	6–3, 6–1
1923	Helen Wills	Molla Bjurstedt Mallory	6–2, 6–1
1924	Helen Wills	Molla Bjurstedt Mallory	6–1, 6–3
1925	Helen Wills	Kathleen McKane	3–6, 6–0, 6–2
1926	Molla Bjurstedt Mallory	Elizabeth Ryan	4–6, 6–4, 9–7
1927	Helen Wills	Betty Nuthall	6–1, 6–4
1928	Helen Wills	Helen Jacobs	6–2, 6–1
1929	Helen Wills	Phoebe Holcroft Watson	6–4, 6–2
1930	Betty Nuthall	Anna McCune Harper	6–1, 6–4
1931	Helen Wills Moody	Eileen Whitingstall	6–4, 6–1
1932	Helen Jacobs	Carolin Babcock	6–2, 6–2
1933	Helen Jacobs	Helen Wills Moody	8–6, 3–6, 3–0, ret.
1934	Helen Jacobs	Sarah Palfrey	6–1, 6–4
1935	Helen Jacobs	Sarah Palfrey Fabyan	6–2, 6–4
1936	Alice Marble	Helen Jacobs	4–6, 6–3, 6–2
1937	Anita Lizana	Jadwiga Jedrzejowska	6–4, 6–2
1938	Alice Marble	Nancye Wynne	6–0, 6–3
1939	Alice Marble	Helen Jacobs	6–0, 8–10, 6–4
1940	Alice Marble	Helen Jacobs	6–2, 6–3
1941	Sarah Palfrey Cooke	Pauline Betz	7–5, 6–2
1942	Pauline Betz	Louise Brough	4–6, 6–1, 6–4
1943	Pauline Betz	Louise Brough	6–3, 5–7, 6–3
1944	Pauline Betz	Margaret Osborne	6–3, 8–6
1945	Sarah Palfrey Cooke	Pauline Betz	3–6, 8–6, 6–4
1946	Pauline Betz	Patricia Canning	11–9, 6–3
1947	Louise Brough	Margaret Osborne	8–6, 4–6, 6–1
1948	Margaret Osborne duPont	Louise Brough	4–6, 6–4, 15–13
1949	Margaret Osborne duPont	Doris Hart	6–4, 6–1
1950	Margaret Osborne duPont	Doris Hart	6–4, 6–3
1951	Maureen Connolly	Shirley Fry	6–3, 1–6, 6–4
1952	Maureen Connolly	Doris Hart	6–3, 7–5
1953	Maureen Connolly	Doris Hart	6–2, 6–4
1954	Doris Hart	Louise Brough	6–8, 6–1, 8–6
1955	Doris Hart	Patricia Ward	6–4, 6–2
1956	Shirley Fry	Althea Gibson	6–3, 6–4
1957	Althea Gibson	Louise Brough	6–3, 6–2
1958	Althea Gibson	Darlene Hard	3–6, 6–1, 6–2
1959	Maria Bueno	Christine Truman	6–1, 6–4
1960	Darlene Hard	Maria Bueno	6–4, 10–12, 6–4
1961	Darlene Hard	Ann Haydon	6–3, 6–4
1962	Margaret Smith	Darlene Hard	9–7, 6–4
1963	Maria Bueno	Margaret Smith	7–5, 6–4
1964	Maria Bueno	Carole Graebner	6–1, 6–0
1965	Margaret Smith	Billie Jean Moffitt	8–6, 7–5
1966	Maria Bueno	Nancy Richey	6–3, 6–1
1967	Billie Jean King	Ann Haydon Jones	11–9, 6–4

*Five-set final abolished. †Challenge round abolished. ‡National Patriotic Tournament.

WOMEN (Cont.)

United States Championships (Cont.)

Year	Winner	Finalist	Score
1968**	Virginia Wade	Billie Jean King	6–4, 6–4
1968#	Margaret Smith Court	Maria Bueno	6–2, 6–2
1969	Margaret Smith Court	Nancy Richey	6–2, 6–2
1969#	Margaret Smith Court	Virginia Wade	4–6, 6–3, 6–0
1970	Margaret Smith Court	Rosie Casals	6–2, 2–6, 6–1
1971	Billie Jean King	Rosie Casals	6–4, 7–6
1972	Billie Jean King	Kerry Melville	6–3, 7–5
1973	Margaret Smith Court	Evonne Goolagong	7–6, 5–7, 6–2
1974	Billie Jean King	Evonne Goolagong	3–6, 6–3, 7–5
1975	Chris Evert	Evonne Goolagong Cawley	5–7, 6–4, 6–2
1976	Chris Evert	Evonne Goolagong Cawley	6–3, 6–0
1977	Chris Evert	Wendy Turnbull	7–6, 6–2
1978	Chris Evert	Pam Shriver	7–6, 6–4
1979	Tracy Austin	Chris Evert Lloyd	6–4, 6–3
1980	Chris Evert Lloyd	Hana Mandlikova	5–7, 6–1, 6–1
1981	Tracy Austin	Martina Navratilova	1–6, 7–6, 7–6
1982	Chris Evert Lloyd	Hana Mandlikova	6–3, 6–1
1983	Martina Navratilova	Chris Evert Lloyd	6–1, 6–3
1984	Martina Navratilova	Chris Evert Lloyd	4–6, 6–4, 6–4
1985	Hana Mandlikova	Martina Navratilova	7–6, 1–6, 7–6
1986	Martina Navratilova	Helena Sukova	6–3, 6–2
1987	Martina Navratilova	Steffi Graf	7–6, 6–1
1988	Steffi Graf	Gabriela Sabatini	6–3, 3–6, 6–1
1989	Steffi Graf	Martina Navratilova	3–6, 6–4, 6–2
1990	Gabriela Sabatini	Steffi Graf	6–2, 7–6
1991	Monica Seles	Martina Navratilova	7–6, 6–1
1992	Monica Seles	Arantxa Sánchez Vicario	6–3, 6–2
1993	Steffi Graf	Helena Sukova	6–3, 6–3
1994	Arantxa Sánchez Vicario	Steffi Graf	1–6, 7–6, 6–4
1995	Steffi Graf	Monica Seles	7–6, 0–6, 6–3
1996	Steffi Graf	Monica Seles	7–5, 7–4
1997	Martina Hingis	Venus Williams	6–0, 6–4
1998	Lindsay Davenport	Martina Hingis	6–3, 7–5
1999	Serena Williams	Martina Hingis	6–3, 7–6
2000	Venus Williams	Lindsay Davenport	6–4, 7–5
2001	Venus Williams	Serena Williams	6–2, 6–4
2002	Serena Williams	Venus Williams	6–4, 6–3
2003	Justine Henin-Hardenne	Kim Clijsters	7–5, 6–1
2004	Svetlana Kuznetsova	Elena Dementieva	6–3, 7–5
2005	Kim Clijsters	Mary Pierce	6–3, 6–1
2006	Maria Sharapova	Justine Henin-Hardenne	6–4, 6–4
2007	Justine Henin	Svetlana Kuznetsova	6–1, 6–3
2008	Serena Williams	Jelena Jankovic	6–4, 7–5
2009	Kim Clijsters	Caroline Wozniacki	7–5, 6–3
2010	Kim Clijsters	Vera Zvonareva	6–2, 6–1
2011	Samantha Stosur	Serena Williams	6–2, 6–3
2012	Serena Williams	Victoria Azarenka	2–6, 6–2, 7–5
2013	Serena Williams	Victoria Azarenka	7–5, 6–7 (6–8), 6–1

**Became Open (amateur and professional) in 1968. #Amateur event held.

Single-Year Grand Slam Winners

Singles

Don Budge, 1938
Maureen Connolly, 1953
Rod Laver, 1962, 1969
Margaret Smith Court, 1970
Steffi Graf, 1988

Doubles

Frank Sedgman and Ken McGregor, 1951
Martina Navratilova and Pam Shriver, 1984
Maria Bueno and two partners, 1960
  Christine Truman (Australian),
  Darlene Hard (French, Wimbledon and U.S.)
Martina Hingis and two partners, 1998
  Mirjana Lucic (Australian),
  Jana Novotna (French, Wimbledon and U.S.)

Mixed Doubles

Margaret Smith and Ken Fletcher, 1963
Owen Davidson and two partners, 1967
  Lesley Turner (Australian),
  Billie Jean King (French, Wimbledon and U.S.)

Alltime Grand Slam Champions (Singles, Doubles, and Mixed Doubles)

MEN

Player	Aus. S-D-M	French S-D-M	Wim. S-D-M	U.S. S-D-M	Total
Roy Emerson	6-3-0	2-6-0	2-3-0	2-4-0	28
John Newcombe	2-5-0	0-3-0	3-6-0	2-3-1	25
Frank Sedgman	2-2-2	0-3-2	1-2-2	2-2-2	22
Todd Woodbridge	0-3-1	0-1-1	0-9-1	0-3-3	22
Bill Tilden	†	0-0-1	3-1-0	7-5-4	21
Rod Laver	3-4-0	2-1-1	4-1-2	2-0-0	20
John Bromwich	2-8-1	0-0-0	0-2-2	0-3-1	19
Jean Borotra	1-1-1	1-5-2	2-3-1	0-0-1	18
Fred Stolle	0-3-1	1-2-0	0-2-3	1-3-2	18
Ken Rosewall	4-3-0	2-2-0	0-2-0	2-2-1	18
Neale Fraser	0-3-1	0-3-0	1-2-0	2-3-3	18
Adrian Quist	3-10-0	0-1-0	0-2-0	0-1-0	17
John McEnroe	0-0-0	0-0-1	3-4-0	4-5-0	17
Jack Crawford	4-4-3	1-1-1	1-1-1	0-0-0	17
Mark Woodforde	0-2-2	0-1-1	0-6-1	0-3-1	17
*Roger Federer	4-0-0	1-0-0	7-0-0	5-0-0	17

†Did not compete.

WOMEN

Player	Aus. S-D-M	French S-D-M	Wim. S-D-M	U.S. S-D-M	Total
Margaret Smith Court	11-8-2	5-4-4	3-2-5	5-5-8	62
Martina Navratilova	3-8-1	2-7-2	9-7-4	4-9-3	59
Billie Jean King	1-0-1	1-1-2	6-10-4	4-5-4	39
Doris Hart	1-1-2	2-5-3	1-4-5	2-4-5	35
*Serena Williams	5-4-0	2-2-0	5-5-1	5-2-1	32
Helen Wills Moody	†	4-2-0	8-3-1	7-4-2	31
Louise Brough	1-1-0	0-3-0	4-5-4	1-8-3	30**
Margaret Osborne duPont	†	2-3-0	1-5-1	3-8-6	29**
Elizabeth Ryan	†	0-4-0	0-12-7	0-1-2	26
Steffi Graf	4-0-0	6-0-0	7-1-0	5-0-0	23
Pam Shriver	0-7-0	0-4-1	0-5-0	0-5-0	22
*Venus Williams	0-4-1	0-2-1	5-5-0	2-2-0	22
Chris Evert	2-0-0	7-2-0	3-1-0	6-0-0	21
Darlene Hard	†	1-3-2	0-4-3	2-6-0	21
Suzanne Lenglen	†	2-2-2#	6-6-3	0-0-0	21
Nancye Wynne Bolton	6-10-4	0-0-0	0-0-0	0-0-0	20

*Active player in 2012. †Did not compete. **From 1940–45, with competition in the U.S. Championships thinned due to war, Louise Brough won four doubles titles (1942–45) and one mixed doubles title (1942); and Margaret Osborne duPont won five doubles titles (1941–45) and three mixed doubles titles (1943–45).

Alltime Grand Slam Singles Champions

MEN

Player	Aus.	French	Wim.	U.S.	Total
*Roger Federer	4	1	7	5	17
Pete Sampras	2	0	7	5	14
*Rafael Nadal	1	8	2	2	13
Roy Emerson	6	2	2	2	12
Bjorn Borg	0	6	5	0	11
Rod Laver	3	2	4	2	11
Bill Tilden	†	0	3	7	10
Jimmy Connors	1	0	2	5	8
Ivan Lendl	2	3	0	3	8
Fred Perry	1	1	3	3	8
Ken Rosewall	4	2	0	2	8
Andre Agassi	4	1	1	2	8
Henri Cochet	†	4	2	1	7
Rene Lacoste	†	3	2	2	7
Bill Larned	†	†	0	7	7
John McEnroe	0	0	3	4	7
John Newcombe	2	0	3	2	7
Willie Renshaw	†	†	7	†	7
Dick Sears	†	†	0	7	7

WOMEN

Player	Aus.	French	Wim.	U.S.	Total
Margaret Smith Court	11	5	3	5	24
Steffi Graf	4	6	7	5	22
Helen Wills Moody	†	4	8	7	19
Chris Evert	2	7	3	6	18
Martina Navratilova	3	2	9	4	18
*Serena Williams	5	2	5	5	17
Billie Jean King	1	1	6	4	12
Maureen Connolly	1	2	3	3	9
Monica Seles	4	3	0	2	9
Suzanne Lenglen	†	2#	6	0	8
Molla Bjurstedt Mallory	†	†	0	8	8
Maria Bueno	0	0	3	4	7
Evonne Goolagong	4	1	2	0	7
Dorothea D.L. Chambers	†	†	7	0	7
Justine Henin	1	4	0	2	7
*Venus Williams	0	0	5	2	7
*Maria Sharapova	3	1	2	1	7

*Active player in 2012. †Did not compete. #Suzanne Lenglen won four singles titles at the French Championships before competition was opened to entries from all nations in 1925.

Golf

Phil Mickelson thrilled his legions of fans with a stirring final-round 66 to win the British Open for the first time in his storied career

BOB MARTIN

Men's Majors

The Masters
Augusta National GC (par 72; 7,445 yds);
Augusta, Ga., April 11–14, 2013

Player	Score	Earnings ($)
*Adam Scott	69-72-69-69--279	1,440,000
Angel Cabrera	71-69-69-70--279	864,000
Jason Day	70-68-73-70--281	544,000
Tiger Woods	70-73-70-70--283	352,000
Marc Leishman	66-73-72-72--283	352,000
Thorbjorn Olesen	78-70-68-68--284	278,000
Brandt Snedeker	70-70-69-75--284	278,000
Sergio Garcia	66-76-73-70--285	232,000
Lee Westwood	70-71-73-71--285	232,000
Matt Kuchar	68-75-69-73--285	232,000
John Huh	70-77-71-68--286	192,000
Tim Clark	70-76-67-73--286	192,000
David Toms	70-74-76-67--287	145,600
Ernie Els	71-74-73-69--287	145,600
Dustin Johnson	67-76-74-70--287	145,600
Fred Couples	68-71-77-71--287	145,600
Nick Watney	78-69-68-72--287	145,600
Henrik Stenson	75-71-73-69--288	116,000
Branden Grace	78-70-71-69--288	116,000
Bill Haas	71-72-74-72--289	89,920
Jason Dufner	72-69-75-73--289	89,920
Gonzalo Fdez-Castano	68-74-73-74--289	89,920
Bo Van Pelt	71-74-70-74--289	89,920
Steve Stricker	73-70-71-75--289	89,920

*Won in playoff.

U.S. Open
Merion GC (par 70; 6,996 yds);
Ardmore, Pa., June 13–16, 2013

Player	Score	Earnings ($)
Justin Rose	71-69-71-70--281	1,440,000
Jason Day	70-74-68-71--283	696,104
Phil Mickelson	67-72-70-74--283	696,104
Jason Dufner	74-71-73-67--285	291,406
Ernie Els	71-72-73-69--285	291,406
Billy Horschel	72-67-72-74--285	291,406
Hunter Mahan	72-69-69-75--285	291,406
Luke Donald	68-72-71-75--286	210,006
Steve Stricker	71-69-70-76--286	210,006
Hideki Matsuyama	71-75-74-67--287	168,530
Nicolas Colsaerts	69-72-74-72--287	168,530
Gonzalo Fdez-Castano	71-72-72-72--287	168,530
Rickie Fowler	70-76-67-74--287	168,530
Charl Schwartzel	70-71-69-78--288	144,444
Lee Westwood	70-77-69-73--289	132,453
John Senden	70-71-74-74--289	132,453
John Huh	71-73-75-71--290	115,591
Brandt Snedeker	74-74-70-72--290	115,591
David Lingmerth	74-71-71-74--290	115,591
Michael Kim	73-70-71-76--290	115,591

British Open
Muirfield GC (par 71; 7,192 yds);
East Lothian, Scotland, July 18–21, 2013

Player	Score	Earnings ($)
Phil Mickelson	69-74-72-66--281	1,442,826
Henrik Stenson	70-70-74-70--284	832,106
Ian Poulter	72-71-75-67--285	428,776
Adam Scott	71-72-70-72--285	428,776
Lee Westwood	72-68-70-75--285	428,776
Hideki Matsuyama	71-73-72-70--286	249,377
Zach Johnson	66-75-73-72--286	249,377
Tiger Woods	69-71-72-74--286	249,377
Francesco Molinari	69-74-72-72--287	175,582
Hunter Mahan	72-72-68-75--287	175,582
Brandt Snedeker	68-79-69-72--288	142,756
Angel Cabrera	69-72-73-74--288	142,756
Justin Leonard	74-70-74-71--289	121,381
Miguel Jimenez	68-71-77-73--289	121,381
Eduardo De La Riva	73-73-75-69--290	95,043
Harris English	74-71-75-70--290	95,043
Charl Schwartzel	75-68-76-71--290	95,043
Danny Willett	75-72-72-71--290	95,043
Matt Kuchar	74-73-72-71--290	95,043
Keegan Bradley	75-74-70-71--290	95,043

PGA Championship
Oak Hill CC (par 70; 7,163 yds);
Rochester, N.Y., August 8–11, 2013

Player	Score	Earnings ($)
Jason Dufner	68-63-71-68--270	1,445,000
Jim Furyk	65-68-68-71--272	865,000
Henrik Stenson	68-66-69-70--273	545,000
Jonas Blixt	68-70-66-70--274	385,000
Scott Piercy	67-71-72-65--275	304,000
Adam Scott	65-68-72-70--275	304,000
David Toms	71-69-69-67--276	259,000
Jason Day	67-71-72-67--277	206,250
Zach Johnson	69-70-70-68--277	206,250
Dustin Johnson	72-71-65-69--277	206,250
Rory McIlroy	69-71-67-70--277	206,250
Graeme McDowell	70-69-73-66--278	132,786
Boo Weekley	72-69-70-67--278	132,786
Marc Leishman	70-70-70-68--278	132,786
Roberto Castro	68-69-71-70--278	132,786
Marc Warren	74-67-68-69--278	132,786
Kevin Streelman	70-72-66-70--278	132,786
Steve Stricker	68-67-70-73--278	132,786
Keegan Bradley	69-72-72-66--279	93,167
Hideki Matsuyama	72-68-73-66--279	93,167
Rickie Fowler	70-68-72-69--279	93,167

PGA Tour Results

Late 2012 PGA Tour Events

Tournament	Final Round	Winner	Score/ Under Par	Earnings ($)
Justin Timberlake Shriners Open	Oct 7	Ryan Moore	260/-24	810,000
Frys.com Open	Oct 14	Jonas Blixt	268/-16	900,000
The McGladrey Classic	Oct 21	Tommy Gainey	264/-16	720,000
CIMB Classic	Oct 28	Nick Watney	262/-22	1,300,000
WGC–HSBC Champions	Nov 4	Ian Poulter	267/-21	1,200,000
Children's Miracle Network Classic	Nov 11	Charlie Beljan	272/-16	846,000
PGA TOUR Qualifying Tournament	Dec 3	Dong-hwan Lee	407/-25	50,000
Northwestern Mutual World Challenge	Dec 4	Graeme McDowell	271/-17	1,000,000

2013 PGA Tour Events

Tournament	Final Round	Winner	Score/ Under Par	Earnings ($)
Hyundai Tournament of Champions	Jan 8	Dustin Johnson	203/-16	1,140,000
Sony Open in Hawaii	Jan 13	Russell Henley	256/-24	1,008,000
Humana Challenge	Jan 20	Brian Gay*	263/-25	1,008,000
Farmers Insurance Open	Jan 28	Tiger Woods	274/-14	1,098,000
Waste Management Phoenix Open	Feb 3	Phil Mickelson	256/-28	1,116,000
AT&T Pebble Beach National Pro-Am	Feb 10	Brandt Snedeker	267/-19	1,170,000
Northern Trust Open	Feb 17	John Merrick*	273/-11	1,188,000
WGC–Accenture Match Play Champ.	Feb 24	Matt Kuchar	2 & 1	1,500,000
The Honda Classic	Mar 3	Michael Thompson	271 (-9)	1,080,000
WGC–Cadillac Championship	Mar 10	Tiger Woods	269/-19	1,500,000
Puerto Rico Open	Mar 10	Scott Brown	268/-20	630,000
Tampa Bay Championship	Mar 17	Kevin Streelman	274/-10	990,000
Arnold Palmer Invitational	Mar 25	Tiger Woods	275/-13	1,116,000
Shell Houston Open	Mar 31	D.A. Points	272/-16	1,116,000
Valero Texas Open	Apr 7	Martin Laird	274/-14	1,116,000
Masters Tournament	Apr 14	Adam Scott*	279/-9	1,440,000
RBC Heritage	Apr 21	Graeme McDowell*	275/-9	1,044,000
Zurich Classic of New Orleans	Apr 28	Billy Horschel	268/-20	1,188,000
Wells Fargo Championship	May 5	Derek Ernst*	280/-8	1,206,000
THE PLAYERS Championship	May 12	Tiger Woods	275/-13	1,710,000
Byron Nelson Championship	May 19	Sang-Moon Bae	267/-13	1,206,000
Crowne Plaza Invitational at Colonial	May 26	Boo Weekley	266/-14	1,152,000
The Memorial Tournament	Jun 2	Matt Kuchar	276/-12	1,116,000
FedEx St. Jude Classic	Jun 9	Harris English	268/-12	1,026,000
U.S. Open Golf Championship	Jun 16	Justin Rose	281/+1	1,440,000
Travelers Championship	Jun 23	Ken Duke*	268/-12	1,098,000
AT&T National	Jun 30	Bill Haas	272/-12	1,170,000
The Greenbrier Classic	Jul 7	Jonas Blixt	267/-13	1,134,000
John Deere Classic	Jul 14	Jordan Spieth*	265/-19	828,000
The Open Championship (British Open)	July 21	Phil Mickelson	281/-3	1,442,826
Sanderson Farms Championship	July 21	Woody Austin*	268/-20	540,000
Canadian Open	July 28	Brandt Snedeker	272/-16	1,008,000
#Reno-Tahoe Open	Aug 4	Gary Woodland	+44	540,000
WGC-Bridgestone Invitational	Aug 4	Tiger Woods	265/-15	1,500,000
PGA Championship	Aug 11	Jason Dufner	270/-10	1,445,000
Wyndham Championship	Aug 18	Patrick Reed*	266/-14	954,000
‡The Barclays	Aug 25	Adam Scott	273/-11	1,440,000
‡Deutsche Bank Championship	Sept 2	Henrik Stenson	262/-22	1,440,000
‡BMW Championship	Sept 16	Zach Johnson	268/-16	1,440,000
‡TOUR Championship	Sept 22	Henrik Stenson	267/-13	1,440,000

* Won in playoff. **Recognized as unofficial money event by the PGA Tour. ‡Part of four-tournament FedEx Cup playoffs, with size of field lowered with each successive event. #Modified Stableford scoring sytem.

2013 FedEx Cup Playoff Results

	Player	Points	Earnings ($)
1.	Henrik Stenson	4,750	10,000,000
2.	Tiger Woods	2,743	3,000,000
3.	Steve Stricker	2,650	2,000,000
4.	Adam Scott	2,278	1,500,000
5	Zach Johnson	2,238	1,000,000
6	Matt Kuchar	1,823	800,000
7	Jordan Spieth	1,690	700,000
8	Graham DeLaet	1,415	600,000
9	Phil Mickelson	1,313	550,000
10	Justin Rose	1,300	500,000

Women's Majors

Kraft Nabisco Championship
Mission Hills CC (par 72; 6,738 yds);
Rancho Mirage, Calif., April 4–7, 2013

Player	Score	Earnings ($)
Inbee Park	70-67-67-69--273	300,000
So Yeon Ryu	73-71-68-65--277	187,073
Suzann Pettersen	68-75-67-69--279	120,345
Caroline Hedwall	71-68-72-68--279	120,345
Haeji Kang	72-69-73-68--282	76,816
Karrie Webb	72-71-67-72--282	76,816
Giulia Sergas	70-69-76-68--283	44,980
Jiyai Shin	70-71-71-71--283	44,980
Hee Young Park	70-70-72-71--283	44,980
Anna Nordqvist	69-72-72-70--283	44,980
Catriona Matthew	72-73-70-68--283	44,980
Jodi Ewart Shadoff	68-72-74-69--283	44,980
Caroline Masson	70-73-71-70--284	29,156
Moriya Jutanugarn	70-72-72-70--284	29,156
Jennifer Johnson	72-71-73-68--284	29,156
Paula Creamer	74-68-69-73--284	29,156
Pornanong Phatlum	71-69-70-74--284	29,156
Hee Kyung Seo	72-70-71-71--284	29,156
Se Ri Pak	72-69-75-69--285	22,328
Angela Stanford	70-74-66-75--285	22,328
Karine Icher	72-70-68-75--285	22,328
Cristie Kerr	71-71-72-71--285	22,328
Jane Park	70-73-73-69--285	22,328
Ayako Uehara	72-72-70-71--285	22,328

LPGA Championship
Locust Hill CC (par 72; 6,534 yds);
Pittsford, N.Y., June 6–9, 2013

Player	Score	Earnings ($)
Inbee Park*	72-68-68-75--283	337,500
Catriona Matthew	71-71-73-68--283	206,304
Suzann Pettersen	72-73-74-65--284	132,716
Morgan Pressel	68-70-71-75--284	132,716
Jiyai Shin	68-73-69-75--285	72,288
Chella Choi	67-73-73-72--285	72,288
Amy Yang	71-70-74-70--285	72,288
Sun Young Yoo	73-69-70-73--285	72,288
Michelle Wie	76-68-71-71--286	46,121
Shanshan Feng	74-70-72-70--286	46,121
Na Yeon Choi	72-70-70-74--286	46,121
Caroline Masson	74-69-71-73--287	37,122
Anna Nordqvist	71-74-73-69--287	37,122
Cristie Kerr	75-72-70-70--287	37,122
Ai Miyazato	74-75-66-73--288	31,851
Kristy McPherson	73-72-69-74--288	31,851
a–Lydia Ko	77-70-73-69--289	—
Brittany Lincicome	69-73-77-70--289	29,367
Beatriz Recari	74-71-73-72--290	26,957
Jennifer Rosales	76-71-70-73--290	26,957
Yani Tseng	72-74-71-73--290	26,957

a–Amateur. *Won in playoff.

U.S. Women's Open
Sebonack GC (par 72; 6,821 yds);
Southampton, N.Y., June 27–30, 2013

Player	Score	Earnings ($)
Inbee Park	67-68-71-74--280	585,000
In-Kyung Kim	68-69-73-74--284	350,000
So Yeon Ryu	73-69-73-72--287	217,958
Angela Stanford	73-68-74-74--289	127,972
Paula Creamer	72-73-72-72--289	127,972
Jodi Ewart Shadoff	70-69-74-76--289	127,972
Brittany Lang	76-69-73-72--290	94,357
Jessica Korda	70-71-76-73--290	94,357
Shanshan Feng	71-75-75-70--291	79,711
Brittany Lincicome	72-72-74-73--291	79,711
Anna Nordqvist	68-74-77-73--292	69,432
Ai Miyazato	76-70-72-74--292	69,432
Lexi Thompson	75-69-76-73--293	61,477
Karrie Webb	73-73-73-74--293	61,477
Lindy Duncan	71-73-75-75--294	54,755
Catriona Matthew	70-75-74-75--294	54,755
Mariajo Uribe	70-76-76-73--295	47,784
Haeji Kang	71-73-77-74--295	47,784
Na Yeon Choi	71-77-72-75--295	47,784
Lizette Salas	68-72-82-74--296	37,920
Jennifer Rosales	70-76-76-74--296	37,920
Morgan Pressel	73-74-75-74--296	37,920
Karine Icher	70-72-77-77--296	37,920
Cristie Kerr	72-72-74-78--296	37,920

Women's British Open
Old Course, St. Andrews (par 72; 6,672 yds);
St. Andrews, Scotland, Aug 1–4, 2013

Player	Score	Earnings ($)
Stacy Lewis	67-72-69-72--280	402,584
Na Yeon Choi	67-67-75-73--282	198,296
Hee Young Park	70-69-70-73--282	198,296
Morgan Pressel	66-70-71-76--283	116,089
Suzann Pettersen	70-67-72-74--283	116,089
Lizette Salas	68-72-72-73--285	91,094
Mamiko Higa	70-69-72-75--286	78,318
Miki Saiki	69-66-74-77--286	78,318
Natalie Gulbis	71-72-74-70--287	64,432
Nicole Castrale	67-70-76-74--287	64,432
Pernilla Lindberg	68-73-73-74--288	46,991
Anna Nordqvist	70-74-72-72--288	46,991
Catriona Matthew	68-74-68-78--288	46,991
Meena Lee	71-69-70-78--288	46,991
Paula Creamer	68-72-72-76--288	46,991
Cristie Kerr	71-74-75-69--289	36,660
Ayako Uehara	69-74-70-77--290	31,772
Xi Yu Lin	72-68-73-77--290	31,772
So Yeon Ryu	69-70-73-78--290	31,772
Angela Stanford	69-70-76-75--290	31,772
Jenny Shin	69-71-74-76--290	31,772

The Evian Championship#†

**Evian Resort GC (par 71; 6,428 yds);
Evian-les-Bains, France, Sept 12–15, 2013**

Player	Score	Earnings ($)
Suzann Pettersen	66-69-68--203	487,500
a–Lydia Ko	68-67-70--205	—
Lexi Thompson	72-67-68--207	297,994
Se Ri Pak	66-71-71--208	191,700
So Yeon Ryu	71-66-71--208	191,700
Chella Choi	70-67-72--209	112,302
Stacy Lewis	69-67-73--209	112,302
Angela Stanford	69-71-69--209	112,302
Jennifer Johnson	70-70-70--210	76,681
Beatriz Recari	69-69-72--210	76,681
Lizette Salas	70-71-70--211	59,467
Shanshan Feng	70-72-69--211	59,467
Ilhee Lee	70-71-70--211	59,467
Rebecca Lee-Bentham	75-66-70--211	59,467
Karrie Webb	68-72-72--212	46,171
Cindy LaCrosse	73-70-69--212	46,171
Katherine Hull-Kirk	71-71-70--212	46,171
Ai Miyazato	75-68-69--212	46,171

Eight players tied at 213.

a–Amateur. #Added as fifth women's major in 2013.
†Shortened by rain.

LPGA Tour Results

Late 2012 LPGA Tour Events

Tournament	Final Round	Winner	Score/ Under Par	Earnings ($)
Sime Darby Malaysia	Oct 14	Inbee Park	269/-15	285,000
Hana Bank Championship	Oct 21	Suzann Pettersen*	205/-11	270,000
LPGA Taiwan Championship	Oct 28	Suzann Pettersen	269/-19	300,000
Mizuno Classic	Nov 4	Stacy Lewis	205/-11	180,000
Lorena Ochoa Invitational	Nov 11	Cristie Kerr	272/-16	200,000

2013 LPGA Tour Events#

Tournament	Final Round	Winner	Score/ Under Par	Earnings ($)
Australian Open	Feb 17	Jiyai Shin	274/-18	180,000
Honda Thailand	Feb 24	Inbee Park	276/-12	225,000
HSBC Champions	Mar 3	Stacy Lewis	273/-15	210,000
LPGA Founders Cup	Mar 17	Stacy Lewis	265/-23	225,000
KIA Classic	Mar 24	Beatriz Recari*	279/-9	255,000
Kraft Nabisco Championship	Apr 7	Inbee Park	273/-15	300,000
LPGA Lotte Championship	Apr 20	Suzann Pettersen*	269/-19	255,000
North Texas LPGA Shootout	Apr 28	Inbee Park	271/-13	195,000
Kingsmill Championship	May 5	Cristie Kerr*	272/-12	195,000
Mobil Bay LPGA Classic	May 19	Jennifer Johnson	267/-21	180,000
Bahamas Classic	May 26	Ilhee Lee	126/E	195,000
ShopRite Classic	June 2	Karrie Webb	209/-4	225,000
LPGA Championship	June 9	Inbee Park*	283/-5	337,500
NW Arkansas Championship	June 23	Inbee Park*	201/-12	300,000
U.S. Women's Open	June 30	Inbee Park	280/-8	585,000
Manulife Financial LPGA Classic	July 14	Hee Young Park*	258/-26	195,000
Marathon Classic	July 21	Beatriz Recari	267/-17	195,000
Women's British Open	Aug 4	Stacy Lewis	280/-8	402,584
Canadian Women's Open	Aug 25	Lydia Ko†	265/-15	—
Evian Championship	Sept 15	Suzann Pettersen	203/-10	487,500

#Through Sep. 22, 2013
* Won in playoff.
†Amateur

Late 2012 Champions Tour Events

Tournament	Final Round	Winner	Score/ Under Par	Earnings ($)
SAS Championship	Oct 7	Bernhard Langer	203/–13	315,000
Greater Hickory Classic at Rock Barn	Oct 14	Fred Funk	201/–15	240,000
AT&T Championship	Oct 28	David Frost	208/–8	277,500
Charles Schwab Cup Championship	Nov 4	Tom Lehman	258/–22	440,000

2013 Champions Tour Events

Tournament	Final Round	Winner	Score/ Under Par	Earnings ($)
Mitsubishi Electric Championship	Jan 20	John Cook*	199/-17	309,000
Allianz Championship	Feb 10	Rocco Mediate	199/-17	270,000
ACE Group Classic	Feb 17	Bernhard Langer	204/-12	240,000
Toshiba Classic	Mar 17	David Frost	194/-19	262,500
Mississippi Gulf Resort Classic	Mar 24	Michael Allen	205/-11	240,000
Greater Gwinnett Championship	Apr 21	Bernhard Langer	206/-10	270,000
Legends of Golf	Apr 28	Brad Faxon/Jeff Sluman	193/-23	230,000 each
Insperity Championship	May 5	Esteban Toledo*	210/-6	270,000
Senior PGA Championship	May 26	Kouki Idoki	273/-11	378,000
Principal Charity Classic	Jun 2	Russ Cochran	205/-11	262,500
Regions Tradition	Jun 9	David Frost	272/-16	330,000
Encompass Championship	Jun 23	Craig Stadler	203/-13	270,000
SENIOR PLAYERS Championship	Jun 30	Kenny Perry	261/-19	405,000
U.S. Senior Open Championship	July 14	Kenny Perry	267/-13	500,000
Senior British Open	July 28	Mark Wiebe*	271/-9	315,600
3M Championship	Aug 4	Tom Pernice Jr.	199/-17	262,500
Dick's Sporting Goods Open	Aug 18	Bart Bryant	200/-16	270,000
Boeing Classic	Aug 25	John Riegger	201/-15	300,000
Shaw Charity Classic	Sept 1	Rocco Mediate	191/-22	300,000
Montreal Championship	Sept 8	Esteban Toledo*	211/-5	240,000
Pacific Links Hawaii Championship	Sept 22	Mark Wiebe*	205/-11	270,000

* Won in playoff.

2013 U.S. Amateur Championships Results

Tournament	Final Round	Winner	Score	Runner-Up
Women's Amateur Public Links	June 22	Lauren Diaz-Yi	10 & 9	Doris Chen
Men's Amateur Public Links	July 20	Jordan Niebrugge	1 up	Michael Kim
Girls' Junior Amateur	July 27	Gabriella Then	2 &1	Lakareber Abe
Boys' Junior Amateur	July 27	Scottie Scheffler	3 & 2	Davis Riley
Women's Amateur	Aug 11	Emma Tally	2 & 1	Yueer Cindy Feng
Men's Amateur	Aug 18	Matthew Fitzpatrick	4 & 3	Oliver Goss
Senior Women's Amateur	Sept 26	Ellen Port	3 & 2	Susan Cohn
Senior Men's Amateur	Sept 26	Doug Hanzell	3 & 2	Pat O'Donnell
Men's Mid-Amateur	Oct 10	Michael McCoy	8 & 6	Bill Williamson
Women's Mid-Amateur	Oct 10	Julia Potter	19 holes	Margaret Shirley

2013 International

Tournament	Final Round	Winner	Score	Runner-Up
Solheim Cup	Aug 18	Great Britain & Ireland	18–10	United States
Walker Cup	Sept 8	United States	17–9	Great Britain & Ireland
President's CupTK	Oct 6	United States	18½–15½	International Tea,

PGA Tour Final 2012 Money Leaders

Name	Events	Best Finish	Scoring Average*	Money ($)
Rory McIlroy	16	1 (4)	68.87	8,047,952
Tiger Woods	19	1 (3)	68.90	6,133,158
Brandt Snedeker	22	1 (2)	69.84	4,989,739
Jason Dufner	22	1 (2)	69.46	4,869,304
Bubba Watson	19	1 (1)	69.64	4,644,997
Zach Johnson	25	1 (2)	69.82	4,504,244
Justin Rose	19	1 (1)	69.55	4,290,930
Phil Mickelson	22	1 (1)	70.03	4,203,821
Hunter Mahan	23	1 (2)	70.35	4,019,193
Keegan Bradley	25	1 (1)	69.98	3,910,658

*Adjusted for average score of field in tournaments entered.

LPGA Tour Final 2012 Money Leaders

Name	Events	Best Finish	Scoring Average	Money ($)
Inbee Park	24	1 (2)	69.64	2,287,080
Na Yeon Choi	22	1 (2)	70.12	1,981,834
Stacy Lewis	26	1 (4)	69.70	1,872,409
Yani Tseng	24	1 (3)	71.24	1,430,159
Ai Miyazato	23	1 (2)	70.97	1,334,977
So Yeon Ryu	24	1 (1)	70.55	1,282,673
Jiyai Shin	18	1 (2)	70.30	1,234,597
Azahara Muñoz	26	1 (1)	71.20	1,230,751
Suzann Pettersen	24	1 (2)	70.13	1,182,860
Shanshan Feng	19	1 (1)	70.87	1,101,147

Champions Tour Final 2012 Money Leaders

Name	Events	Best Finish	Scoring Average	Money ($)
Bernhard Langer	20	1 (2)	68.76	2,140,296
Tom Lehman	19	1 (2)	68.92	1,982,575
Michael Allen	22	1 (2)	69.57	1,686,488
Fred Funk	22	1 (2)	70.22	1,427,937
Jay Don Blake	24	1 (1)	70.15	1,378,180
Mark Calcavecchia	23	1 (1)	69.75	1,361,067
Jay Haas	21	1 (1)	69.94	1,234,571
Fred Couples	11	1 (2)	68.52	1,229,067
David Frost	24	1 (2)	70.42	1,189,740
John Cook	23	2 (2)	69.85	1,182,008

Men's Golf CAREER RECs UPDATED to 8/11/13

THE MAJOR TOURNAMENTS
The Masters

Year	Winner	Score	Runner-Up
1934	Horton Smith	284	Craig Wood
1935	Gene Sarazen* (144)	282	Craig Wood (149)
	(only 36-hole playoff)		
1936	Horton Smith	285	Harry Cooper
1937	Byron Nelson	283	Ralph Guldahl
1938	Henry Picard	285	Ralph Guldahl
			Harry Cooper
1939	Ralph Guldahl	279	Sam Snead
1940	Jimmy Demaret	280	Lloyd Mangrum
1941	Craig Wood	280	Byron Nelson
1942	Byron Nelson* (69)	280	Ben Hogan (70)
1943–45	No tournament		
1946	Herman Keiser	282	Ben Hogan
1947	Jimmy Demaret	281	Byron Nelson
			Frank Stranahan
1948	Claude Harmon	279	Cary Middlecoff
1949	Sam Snead	282	Johnny Bulla
			Lloyd Mangrum
1950	Jimmy Demaret	283	Jim Ferrier
1951	Ben Hogan	280	Skee Riegel
1952	Sam Snead	286	Jack Burke Jr..
1953	Ben Hogan	274	Ed Oliver Jr.
1954	Sam Snead* (70)	289	Ben Hogan (71)
1955	Cary Middlecoff	279	Ben Hogan
1956	Jack Burke Jr.	289	Ken Venturi
1957	Doug Ford	282	Sam Snead
1958	Arnold Palmer	284	Doug Ford
			Fred Hawkins
1959	Art Wall Jr.	284	Cary Middlecoff
1960	Arnold Palmer	282	Ken Venturi
1961	Gary Player	280	Charles R. Coe
			Arnold Palmer
1962	Arnold Palmer* (68)	280	Gary Player (71)
			D. Finsterwald (77)
1963	Jack Nicklaus	286	Tony Lema
1964	Arnold Palmer	276	Dave Marr
			Jack Nicklaus
1965	Jack Nicklaus	271	Arnold Palmer
			Gary Player
1966	Jack Nicklaus* (70)	288	Tommy Jacobs (72)
			Gay Brewer Jr. (78)
1967	Gay Brewer Jr.	280	Bobby Nichols
1968	Bob Goalby	277	Roberto DeVicenzo
1969	George Archer	281	Billy Casper
			George Knudson
			Tom Weiskopf
1970	Billy Casper* (69)	279	Gene Littler (74)
1971	Charles Coody	279	Johnny Miller
			Jack Nicklaus
1972	Jack Nicklaus	286	Bruce Crampton
			Bobby Mitchell
			Tom Weiskopf
1973	Tommy Aaron	283	J.C. Snead
1974	Gary Player	278	Tom Weiskopf
			Dave Stockton
1975	Jack Nicklaus	276	Johnny Miller
			Tom Weiskopf
1976	Ray Floyd	271	Ben Crenshaw
1977	Tom Watson	276	Jack Nicklaus
1978	Gary Player	277	Hubert Green
			Rod Funseth
			Tom Watson
1979	Fuzzy Zoeller* (4–3)†	280	Ed Sneed (4–4)
			Tom Watson (4–4)
1980	Seve Ballesteros	275	Gibby Gilbert
			Jack Newton
1981	Tom Watson	280	Johnny Miller
			Jack Nicklaus
1982	Craig Stadler* (4)	284	Dan Pohl (5)
1983	Seve Ballesteros	280	Ben Crenshaw
			Tom Kite
1984	Ben Crenshaw	277	Tom Watson
1985	Bernhard Langer	282	Curtis Strange
			Seve Ballesteros
			Ray Floyd
1986	Jack Nicklaus	279	Greg Norman
			Tom Kite
1987	Larry Mize* (4–3)	285	Greg Norman (4–4)
			Seve Ballesteros (5)
1988	Sandy Lyle	281	Mark Calcavecchia
1989	Nick Faldo* (5–3)	283	Scott Hoch (5–4)
1990	Nick Faldo* (4–4)	278	Ray Floyd (4–x)
1991	Ian Woosnam	277	José María
			Olazábal
1992	Fred Couples	275	Ray Floyd
1993	Bernhard Langer	277	Chip Beck
1994	José María Olazábal	279	Tom Lehman
1995	Ben Crenshaw	274	Davis Love III
1996	Nick Faldo	276	Greg Norman
1997	Tiger Woods	270	Tom Kite
1998	Mark O'Meara	279	David Duval
			Fred Couples
1999	José María Olazábal	280	Davis Love III
2000	Vijay Singh	278	Ernie Els
2001	Tiger Woods	272	David Duval
2002	Tiger Woods	276	Retief Goosen
2003	Mike Weir	281	Len Mattiace
2004	Phil Mickelson	279	Ernie Els
2005	Tiger Woods	276	Chris DiMarco
2006	Phil Mickelson	281	Tim Clark
2007	Zach Johnson	289	Tiger Woods
			Retief Goosen
			Rory Sabbatini
2008	Trevor Immelman	280	Tiger Woods
2009	Angel Cabrera	276	Chad Campbell
			Kenny Perry
2010	Phil Mickelson	272	Lee Westwood
2011	Charl Schwartzel	274	Jason Day
			Adam Scott
2012	Bubba Watson	278	Louis Oosthuizen
2013	Adam Scott	279	Angel Cabrera

*Winner in playoff. Playoff scores are in parentheses. †Playoff cut from 18 holes to sudden death.
Note: Played at Augusta National Golf Club, Augusta, GA.

United States Open Championship

Year	Winner	Score	Runner-Up	Site
1895	Horace Rawlins	†173	Willie Dunn	Newport GC, Newport, RI
1896	James Foulis	†152	Horace Rawlins	Shinnecock Hills GC, Southampton, NY
1897	Joe Lloyd	†162	Willie Anderson	Chicago GC, Wheaton, IL
1898	Fred Herd	328	Alex Smith	Myopia Hunt Club, Hamilton, MA
1899	Willie Smith	315	George Low	Baltimore CC, Baltimore, MD
			Val Fitzjohn	
			W.H. Way	
1900	Harry Vardon	313	John H. Taylor	Chicago GC, Wheaton, IL
1901	Willie Anderson* (85)	331	Alex Smith (86)	Myopia Hunt Club, Hamilton, MA
1902	Laurie Auchterlonie	307	Stewart Gardner	Garden City GC, Garden City, NY
1903	Willie Anderson* (82)	307	David Brown (84)	Baltusrol GC, Springfield, NJ
1904	Willie Anderson	303	Gil Nicholls	Glen View Club, Golf, IL
1905	Willie Anderson	314	Alex Smith	Myopia Hunt Club, Hamilton, MA
1906	Alex Smith	295	Willie Smith	Onwentsia Club, Lake Forest, IL
1907	Alex Ross	302	Gil Nicholls	Philadelphia Cricket Club, Chestnut Hill, PA
1908	Fred McLeod* (77)	322	Willie Smith (83)	Myopia Hunt Club, Hamilton, MA
1909	George Sargent	290	Tom McNamara	Englewood GC, Englewood, NJ
1910	Alex Smith* (71)	298	John McDermott (75)	Philadelphia Cricket Club, Chestnut Hill, PA
			Macdonald Smith (77)	
1911	John McDermott* (80)	307	Mike Brady (82)	Chicago GC, Wheaton, IL
			George Simpson (85)	
1912	John McDermott	294	Tom McNamara	CC of Buffalo, Buffalo, NY
1913	Francis Ouimet* (72)	304	Harry Vardon (77)	The Country Club, Brookline, MA
			Edward Ray (78)	
1914	Walter Hagen	290	Chick Evans	Midlothian CC, Blue Island, IL
1915	Jerry Travers	297	Tom McNamara	Baltusrol GC, Springfield, NJ
1916	Chick Evans	286	Jock Hutchison	Minikahda Club, Minneapolis. MN
1917–18	No tournament			
1919	Walter Hagen* (77)	301	Mike Brady (78)	Brae Burn CC, West Newton, MA
1920	Edward Ray	295	Harry Vardon	Inverness CC, Toledo, OH
			Jack Burke	
			Leo Diegel	
			Jock Hutchison	
1921	Jim Barnes	289	Walter Hagen	Columbia CC, Chevy Chase, MD
			Fred McLeod	
1922	Gene Sarazen	288	John L. Black	Skokie CC, Glencoe, IL
			Bobby Jones	
1923	Bobby Jones* (76)	296	Bobby Cruickshank (78)	Inwood CC, Inwood, NY
1924	Cyril Walker	297	Bobby Jones	Oakland Hills CC, Birmingham, MI
1925	W. MacFarlane* (75–72)	291	Bobby Jones (75–73)	Worcester CC, Worcester, MA
1926	Bobby Jones	293	Joe Turnesa	Scioto CC, Columbus, OH
1927	Tommy Armour* (76)	301	Harry Cooper (79)	Oakmont CC, Oakmont, PA
1928	Johnny Farrell* (143)	294	Bobby Jones (144)	Olympia Fields CC, Matteson, IL
1929	Bobby Jones* (141)	294	Al Espinosa (164)	Winged Foot GC, Mamaroneck, NY
1930	Bobby Jones	287	Macdonald Smith	Interlachen CC, Hopkins, MN
1931	Billy Burke* (149–148)	292	George Von Elm	Inverness Club, Toledo, OH
			(149–149)	
1932	Gene Sarazen	286	Phil Perkins	Fresh Meadows CC, Flushing, NY
			Bobby Cruickshank	
1933	Johnny Goodman	287	Ralph Guldahl	North Shore CC, Glenview, IL
1934	Olin Dutra	293	Gene Sarazen	Merion Cricket Club, Ardmore, PA
1935	Sam Parks Jr.	299	Jimmy Thompson	Oakmont CC, Oakmont, PA
1936	Tony Manero	282	Harry Cooper	Baltusrol GC (Upper Course), Springfield, NJ
1937	Ralph Guldahl	281	Sam Snead	Oakland Hills CC, Birmingham, MI
1938	Ralph Guldahl	284	Dick Metz	Cherry Hills CC, Denver, CO
1939	Byron Nelson* (68–70)	284	Craig Wood (68–73)	Philadelphia CC, Philadelphia, PA
			Denny Shute (76)	
1940	Lawson Little* (70)	287	Gene Sarazen (73)	Canterbury GC, Cleveland, OH
1941	Craig Wood	284	Denny Shute	Colonial Club, Fort Worth, TX
1942–45	No tournament			
1946	Lloyd Mangrum* (72–72)	284	Vic Ghezzi (72–73)	Canterbury GC, Cleveland, OH
			Byron Nelson (72–73)	
1947	Lew Worsham* (69)	282	Sam Snead (70)	St. Louis CC, Clayton, MO
1948	Ben Hogan	276	Jimmy Demaret	Riviera CC, Los Angeles, CA
1949	Cary Middlecoff	286	Sam Snead	Medinah CC, Medinah, IL
			Clayton Heafner	
1950	Ben Hogan* (69)	287	Lloyd Mangrum (73)	Merion GC, Ardmore, PA
			George Fazio (75)	

United States Open Championship (Cont.)

Year	Winner	Score	Runner-Up	Site
1951	Ben Hogan	287	Clayton Heafner	Oakland Hills CC, Birmingham, MI
1952	Julius Boros	281	Ed Oliver	Northwood CC, Dallas, TX
1953	Ben Hogan	283	Sam Snead	Oakmont CC, Oakmont, PA
1954	Ed Furgol	284	Gene Littler	Baltusrol GC (Lower Course), Springfield, NJ
1955	Jack Fleck* (69)	287	Ben Hogan (72)	Olympic Club (Lake Course), San Fran., CA
1956	Cary Middlecoff	281	Ben Hogan	Oak Hill CC, Rochester, NY
			Julius Boros	
1957	Dick Mayer* (72)	282	Cary Middlecoff (79)	Inverness Club, Toledo, OH
1958	Tommy Bolt	283	Gary Player	Southern Hills CC, Tulsa, OK
1959	Billy Casper	282	Bob Rosburg	Winged Foot GC, Mamaroneck, NY
1960	Arnold Palmer	280	Jack Nicklaus	Cherry Hills CC, Denver, CO
1961	Gene Littler	281	Bob Goalby	Oakland Hills CC, Birmingham, MI
			Doug Sanders	
1962	Jack Nicklaus* (71)	283	Arnold Palmer (74)	Oakmont CC, Oakmont, PA
1963	Julius Boros* (70)	293	Jacky Cupit (73)	The Country Club, Brookline, MA
			Arnold Palmer (76)	
1964	Ken Venturi	278	Tommy Jacobs	Congressional CC, Bethesda, MD
1965	Gary Player* (71)	282	Kel Nagle (74)	Bellerive CC, St. Louis, MO
1966	Billy Casper* (69)	278	Arnold Palmer (73)	Olympic Club (Lake Course), San Fran., CA
1967	Jack Nicklaus	275	Arnold Palmer	Baltusrol GC (Lower Course), Springfield, NJ
1968	Lee Trevino	275	Jack Nicklaus	Oak Hill CC, Rochester, NY
1969	Orville Moody	281	Deane Beman	Champions GC (Cypress Creek Course),
			Al Geiberger	Houston, TX
			Bob Rosburg	
1970	Tony Jacklin	281	Dave Hill	Hazeltine GC, Chaska, MN
1971	Lee Trevino* (68)	280	Jack Nicklaus (71)	Merion GC (East Course), Ardmore, PA
1972	Jack Nicklaus	290	Bruce Crampton	Pebble Beach GL, Pebble Beach, CA
1973	Johnny Miller	279	John Schlee	Oakmont CC, Oakmont, PA
1974	Hale Irwin	287	Forrest Fezler	Winged Foot GC, Mamaroneck, NY
1975	Lou Graham* (71)	287	John Mahaffey (73)	Medinah CC, Medinah, IL
1976	Jerry Pate	277	Tom Weiskopf	Atlanta Athletic Club, Duluth, GA
			Al Geiberger	
1977	Hubert Green	278	Lou Graham	Southern Hills CC, Tulsa, OK
1978	Andy North	285	Dave Stockton	Cherry Hills CC, Denver, CO
			J.C. Snead	
1979	Hale Irwin	284	Gary Player	Inverness Club, Toledo, OH
			Jerry Pate	
1980	Jack Nicklaus	272	Isao Aoki	Baltusrol GC (Lower Course), Springfield, NJ
1981	David Graham	273	George Burns	Merion GC, Ardmore, PA
			Bill Rogers	
1982	Tom Watson	282	Jack Nicklaus	Pebble Beach GL, Pebble Beach, CA
1983	Larry Nelson	280	Tom Watson	Oakmont CC, Oakmont, PA
1984	Fuzzy Zoeller* (67)	276	Greg Norman (75)	Winged Foot GC, Mamaroneck, NY
1985	Andy North	279	Dave Barr	Oakland Hills CC, Birmingham, MI
			T.C. Chen	
			Denis Watson	
1986	Ray Floyd	279	Lanny Wadkins	Shinnecock Hills GC, Southampton, NY
			Chip Beck	
1987	Scott Simpson	277	Tom Watson	Olympic Club (Lake Course), San Fran., CA
1988	Curtis Strange* (71)	278	Nick Faldo (75)	The Country Club, Brookline, MA
1989	Curtis Strange	278	Chip Beck	Oak Hill CC, Rochester, NY
			Mark McCumber	
			Ian Woosnam	
1990	Hale Irwin* (74) (3)	280	Mike Donald (74) (4)	Medinah CC, Medinah, IL
1991	Payne Stewart* (75)	282	Scott Simpson (77)	Hazeltine GC, Chaska, MN
1992	Tom Kite	285	Jeff Sluman	Pebble Beach GL, Pebble Beach, CA
1993	Lee Janzen	272	Payne Stewart	Baltusrol GC, Springfield, NJ
1994	Ernie Els* (74) (4-4)	279	Loren Roberts (74) (4-5)	Oakmont CC, Oakmont, PA
			Colin Montgomerie (78)	
1995	Corey Pavin	280	Greg Norman	Shinnecock Hills GC, Southampton, NY
1996	Steve Jones	278	Davis Love III	Oakland Hills CC, Birmingham, MI
			Tom Lehman	
1997	Ernie Els	276	Colin Montgomerie	Congressional CC, Bethesda, MD
1998	Lee Janzen	280	Payne Stewart	Olympic Club (Lake Course), San Fran., CA
1999	Payne Stewart	279	Phil Mickelson	Pinehurst Resort and CC, Pinehurst, NC
2000	Tiger Woods	272	Miguel Angel Jiménez	Pebble Beach GL, Pebble Beach, CA

United States Open Championship (Cont.)

Year	Winner	Score	Runner-Up	Site
			Ernie Els	
2001	Retief Goosen* (70)	276	Mark Brooks (72)	Southern Hills CC, Tulsa, OK
2002	Tiger Woods	277	Phil Mickelson	Bethpage State Park (Black), Farmingdale, NY
2003	Jim Furyk	272	Stephen Leaney	Olympia Fields CC, Olympia Fields, IL
2004	Retief Goosen	276	Phil Mickelson	Shinnecock Hills GC, Southampton, NY
2005	Michael Campbell	280	Tiger Woods	Pinehurst Resort and CC, Pinehurst, NC
2006	Geoff Ogilvy	285	Jim Furyk	Winged Foot GC, Mamaroneck, NY
			Colin Montgomerie	
			Phil Mickelson	
2007	Angel Cabrera	285	Jim Furyk	Oakmont CC, Oakmont, PA
			Tiger Woods	
2008	Tiger Woods* (71) (4)	283	Rocco Mediate (71) (5)	Torrey Pines GC (South), San Diego, CA
2009	Lucas Glover	276	Phil Mickelson	Bethpage State Park (Black), Farmingdale, NY
			David Duval	
			Ricky Barnes	
2010	Graeme McDowell	284	Gregory Havret	Pebble Beach GL, Pebble Beach, CA
2011	Rory McIlroy	268	Jason Day	Congressional CC, Bethesda, MD
2012	Webb Simpson	281	Michael Thompson	Olympic Club, San Francisco, CA
2013	Justin Rose	281	Jason Day	Merion GC, Ardmore, PA
			Phil Mickelson	

*Winner in playoff. Playoff scores are in parentheses. The 1990 and 2008 playoffs went to one hole of sudden death after an 18-hole playoff. In the 1994 playoff, Montgomerie was eliminated after 18 playoff holes, and Els beat Roberts on the 20th.
†Before 1898, 36 holes. From 1898 on, 72 holes.

The Open Championship (British Open)

Year	Winner	Score	Runner-Up	Site
1860†	Willie Park	174	Tom Morris Sr.	Prestwick, Scotland
1861‡	Tom Morris Sr.	163	Willie Park	Prestwick, Scotland
1862	Tom Morris Sr.	163	Willie Park	Prestwick, Scotland
1863	Willie Park	168	Tom Morris Sr.	Prestwick, Scotland
1864	Tom Morris Sr.	160	Andrew Strath	Prestwick, Scotland
1865	Andrew Strath	162	Willie Park	Prestwick, Scotland
1866	Willie Park	169	David Park	Prestwick, Scotland
1867	Tom Morris Sr.	170	Willie Park	Prestwick, Scotland
1868	Tom Morris Jr.	154	Tom Morris Sr.	Prestwick, Scotland
1869	Tom Morris Jr.	157	Tom Morris Sr.	Prestwick, Scotland
1870	Tom Morris Jr.	149	David Strath	Prestwick, Scotland
			Bob Kirk	
1871	No tournament			
1872	Tom Morris Jr.	166	David Strath	Prestwick, Scotland
1873	Tom Kidd	179	Jamie Anderson	St. Andrews, Scotland
1874	Mungo Park	159	No record	Musselburgh, Scotland
1875	Willie Park	166	Bob Martin	Prestwick, Scotland
1876	Bob Martin	176	David Strath#	St. Andrews, Scotland
1877	Jamie Anderson	160	Bob Pringle	Musselburgh, Scotland
1878	Jamie Anderson	157	Robert Kirk	Prestwick, Scotland
1879	Jamie Anderson	169	Andrew Kirkaldy	St. Andrews, Scotland
			James Allan	
1880	Robert Ferguson	162	No record	Musselburgh, Scotland
1881	Robert Ferguson	170	Jamie Anderson	Prestwick, Scotland
1882	Robert Ferguson	171	Willie Fernie	St. Andrews, Scotland
1883	Willie Fernie*	159	Robert Ferguson	Musselburgh, Scotland
1884	Jack Simpson	160	Douglas Rolland	Prestwick, Scotland
			Willie Fernie	
1885	Bob Martin	171	Archie Simpson	St. Andrews, Scotland
1886	David Brown	157	Willie Campbell	Musselburgh, Scotland
1887	Willie Park Jr.	161	Bob Martin	Prestwick, Scotland
1888	Jack Burns	171	Bernard Sayers	St. Andrews, Scotland
			David Anderson	
1889	Willie Park Jr.* (158)	155	Andrew Kirkaldy (163)	Musselburgh, Scotland
1890	John Ball	164	Willie Fernie	Prestwick, Scotland
1891	Hugh Kirkaldy	166	Andrew Kirkaldy	St. Andrews, Scotland
			Willie Fernie	
1892	Harold Hilton	**305	John Ball	Muirfield, Scotland
			Hugh Kirkaldy	
1893	William Auchterlonie	322	John E. Laidlay	Prestwick, Scotland

The Open Championship (British Open) *(Cont.)*

Year	Winner	Score	Runner-Up	Site
1894	John H. Taylor	326	Douglas Rolland	Royal St. George's, England
1895	John H. Taylor	322	Alexander Herd	St. Andrews, Scotland
1896	Harry Vardon* (157)	316	John H. Taylor (161)	Muirfield, Scotland
1897	Harold Hilton	314	James Braid	Royal Liverpool (Hoylake), England
1898	Harry Vardon	307	Willie Park Jr.	Prestwick, Scotland
1899	Harry Vardon	310	Jack White	Royal St. George's, England
1900	John H. Taylor	309	Harry Vardon	St. Andrews, Scotland
1901	James Braid	309	Harry Vardon	Muirfield, Scotland
1902	Alexander Herd	307	Harry Vardon	Royal Liverpool (Hoylake), England
1903	Harry Vardon	300	Tom Vardon	Prestwick, Scotland
1904	Jack White	296	John H. Taylor	Royal St. George's, England
1905	James Braid	318	John H. Taylor Rolland Jones	St. Andrews, Scotland
1906	James Braid	300	John H. Taylor	Muirfield, Scotland
1907	Arnaud Massy	312	John H. Taylor	Royal Liverpool (Hoylake), England
1908	James Braid	291	Tom Ball	Prestwick, Scotland
1909	John H. Taylor	295	James Braid Tom Ball	Deal, England
1910	James Braid	299	Alexander Herd	St. Andrews, Scotland
1911	Harry Vardon	303	Arnaud Massy	Royal St. George's, England
1912	Ted Ray	295	Harry Vardon	Muirfield, Scotland
1913	John H. Taylor	304	Ted Ray	Royal Liverpool (Hoylake), England
1914	Harry Vardon	306	John H. Taylor	Prestwick, Scotland
1915–19	No tournament			
1920	George Duncan	303	Alexander Herd	Deal, England
1921	Jock Hutchison* (150)	296	Roger Wethered (159)	St. Andrews, Scotland
1922	Walter Hagen	300	George Duncan Jim Barnes	Royal St. George's, England
1923	Arthur G. Havers	295	Walter Hagen	Troon, Scotland
1924	Walter Hagen	301	Ernest Whitcombe	Royal Liverpool (Hoylake), England
1925	Jim Barnes	300	Archie Compston Ted Ray	Prestwick, Scotland
1926	Bobby Jones	291	Al Watrous	Royal Lytham & St. Annes, England
1927	Bobby Jones	285	Aubrey Boomer	St. Andrews, Scotland
1928	Walter Hagen	292	Gene Sarazen	Royal St. George's, England
1929	Walter Hagen	292	Johnny Farrell	Muirfield, Scotland
1930	Bobby Jones	291	Macdonald Smith Leo Diegel	Royal Liverpool (Hoylake), England
1931	Tommy Armour	296	Jose Jurado	Carnoustie, Scotland
1932	Gene Sarazen	283	Macdonald Smith	Prince's, England
1933	Denny Shute* (149)	292	Craig Wood (154)	St. Andrews, Scotland
1934	Henry Cotton	283	Sidney F. Brews	Royal St. George's, England
1935	Alfred Perry	283	Alfred Padgham	Muirfield, Scotland
1936	Alfred Padgham	287	James Adams	Royal Liverpool (Hoylake), England
1937	Henry Cotton	290	Reginald A. Whitcombe	Carnoustie, Scotland
1938	Reginald A. Whitcombe	295	James Adams	Royal St. George's, England
1939	Richard Burton	290	Johnny Bulla	St. Andrews, Scotland
1940–45	No tournament			
1946	Sam Snead	290	Bobby Locke Johnny Bulla	St. Andrews, Scotland
1947	Fred Daly	293	Reginald W. Horne Frank Stranahan	Royal Liverpool (Hoylake), England
1948	Henry Cotton	294	Fred Daly	Muirfield, Scotland
1949	Bobby Locke* (135)	283	Harry Bradshaw (147)	Royal St. George's, England
1950	Bobby Locke	279	Roberto DeVicenzo	Troon, Scotland
1951	Max Faulkner	285	Tony Cerda	Portrush, Ireland
1952	Bobby Locke	287	Peter Thomson	Royal Lytham & St. Annes, England
1953	Ben Hogan	282	Frank Stranahan Dai Rees Peter Thomson Tony Cerda	Carnoustie, Scotland
1954	Peter Thomson	283	Sidney S. Scott Dai Rees Bobby Locke	Royal Birkdale, England
1955	Peter Thomson	281	John Fallon	St. Andrews, Scotland
1956	Peter Thomson	286	Flory Van Donck	Royal Liverpool (Hoylake), England
1957	Bobby Locke	279	Peter Thomson	St. Andrews, Scotland

The Open Championship (British Open) *(Cont.)*

Year	Winner	Score	Runner-Up	Site
1958	Peter Thomson* (139)	278	Dave Thomas (143)	Royal Lytham & St. Annes, England
1959	Gary Player	284	Fred Bullock	Muirfield, Scotland
			Flory Van Donck	
1960	Kel Nagle	278	Arnold Palmer	St. Andrews, Scotland
1961	Arnold Palmer	284	Dai Rees	Royal Birkdale, England
1962	Arnold Palmer	276	Kel Nagle	Troon, Scotland
1963	Bob Charles* (140)	277	Phil Rodgers (148)	Royal Lytham & St. Annes, England
1964	Tony Lema	279	Jack Nicklaus	St. Andrews, Scotland
1965	Peter Thomson	285	Brian Huggett	Royal Birkdale, England
			Christy O'Connor	
1966	Jack Nicklaus	282	Doug Sanders	Muirfield, Scotland
			Dave Thomas	
1967	Robert DeVicenzo	278	Jack Nicklaus	Royal Liverpool (Hoylake), England
1968	Gary Player	289	Jack Nicklaus	Carnoustie, Scotland
			Bob Charles	
1969	Tony Jacklin	280	Bob Charles	Royal Lytham & St. Annes, England
1970	Jack Nicklaus* (72)	283	Doug Sanders (73)	St. Andrews, Scotland
1971	Lee Trevino	278	Lu Liang Huan	Royal Birkdale, England
1972	Lee Trevino	278	Jack Nicklaus	Muirfield, Scotland
1973	Tom Weiskopf	276	Johnny Miller	Troon, Scotland
1974	Gary Player	282	Peter Oosterhuis	Royal Lytham & St. Annes, England
1975	Tom Watson* (71)	279	Jack Newton (72)	Carnoustie, Scotland
1976	Johnny Miller	279	Jack Nicklaus	Royal Birkdale, England
			Seve Ballesteros	
1977	Tom Watson	268	Jack Nicklaus	Turnberry, Scotland
1978	Jack Nicklaus	281	Ben Crenshaw	St. Andrews, Scotland
			Tom Kite	
			Ray Floyd	
			Simon Owen	
1979	Seve Ballesteros	283	Ben Crenshaw	Royal Lytham & St. Annes, England
			Jack Nicklaus	
1980	Tom Watson	271	Lee Trevino	Muirfield, Scotland
1981	Bill Rogers	276	Bernhard Langer	Royal St. George's, England
1982	Tom Watson	284	Nick Price	Troon, Scotland
			Peter Oosterhuis	
1983	Tom Watson	275	Andy Bean	Royal Birkdale, England
1984	Seve Ballesteros	276	Tom Watson	St. Andrews, Scotland
			Bernhard Langer	
1985	Sandy Lyle	282	Payne Stewart	Royal St. George's, England
1986	Greg Norman	280	Gordon Brand	Turnberry, Scotland
1987	Nick Faldo	279	Paul Azinger	Muirfield, Scotland
			Rodger Davis	
1988	Seve Ballesteros	273	Nick Price	Royal Lytham & St. Annes, England
1989††	Mark Calcavecchia* (4-3-3-3)	275	Wayne Grady (4-4-4-4)	Troon, Scotland
			Greg Norman (3-3-4-x)	
1990	Nick Faldo	270	Payne Stewart	St. Andrews, Scotland
			Mark McNulty	
1991	Ian Baker-Finch	272	Mike Harwood	Royal Birkdale, England
1992	Nick Faldo	272	John Cook	Muirfield, Scotland
1993	Greg Norman	267	Nick Faldo	Royal St. George's, England
1994	Nick Price	268	Jesper Parnevik	Turnberry, Scotland
1995	John Daly* (4-3-4-4)	282	C. Rocca (5-4-7-3)	St. Andrews, Scotland
1996	Tom Lehman	271	Mark McCumber	Royal Lytham & St. Annes, England
			Ernie Els	
1997	Justin Leonard	272	Jesper Parnevik	Troon, Scotland
			Darren Clarke	
1998	Mark O'Meara* (4-4-5-4)	280	Brian Watts (5-4-5-5)	Royal Birkdale, England
1999	Paul Lawrie* (5-4-3-3)	290	Jean Van de Velde (6-4-3-5)	Carnoustie, Scotland
			Justin Leonard (5-4-4-5)	
2000	Tiger Woods	269	Thomas Bjorn	St. Andrews, Scotland
			Ernie Els	
2001	David Duval	274	Niclas Fasth	Royal Lytham & St. Annes, England
2002	Ernie Els* (4-3-5-4-4)	278	Thommas Levet (4-2-5-5-5)	Muirfield, Scotland
2003	Ben Curtis	283	Vijay Singh	Royal St. George's, England
2004	Todd Hamilton* (4-4-3-4)	274	Ernie Els (4-4-4-4)	Troon, Scotland

The Open Championship (British Open) *(Cont.)*

Year	Winner	Score	Runner-Up	Site
2005	Tiger Woods	274	Colin Montgomerie	St. Andrews, Scotland
2006	Tiger Woods	270	Chris DiMarco	Royal Liverpool (Hoylake), England
2007	P. Harrington* (3-3-4-5)	277	Sergio Garcia (5-3-4-4)	Carnoustie, Scotland
2008	Padraig Harrington	283	Ian Poulter	Royal Birkdale, England
2009	Stewart Cink* (4-3-4-3)	278	Tom Watson (5-3-7-5)	Turnberry, Scotland
2010	Louis Oosthuizen	272	Lee Westwood	St. Andrews, Scotland
2011	Darren Clarke	275	Phil Mickelson	Royal St. George's, England
			Dustin Johnson	
2012	Ernie Els	273	Adam Scott	Royal Lytham & St. Annes, England
2013	Phil Mickelson	281	Henrik Stenson	Muirfield, Scotland

*Winner in playoff. †The first event was open only to professional golfers.
‡The second annual open was open to amateurs and pros. #Tied, but refused playoff.
**Championship extended from 36 to 72 holes. ††Playoff cut from 18 holes to 4 holes.

PGA Championship

Year	Winner	Score	Runner-Up	Site
1916	Jim Barnes	1 up	Jock Hutchison	Siwanoy CC, Bronxville, NY
1917–18	No tournament			
1919	Jim Barnes	6 & 5	Fred McLeod	Engineers CC, Roslyn, NY
1920	Jock Hutchison	1 up	J. Douglas Edgar	Flossmoor CC, Flossmoor, IL
1921	Walter Hagen	3 & 2	Jim Barnes	Inwood CC, Far Rockaway, NY
1922	Gene Sarazen	4 & 3	Emmet French	Oakmont CC, Oakmont, PA
1923	Gene Sarazen	1 up 38 holes	Walter Hagen	Pelham CC, Pelham, NY
1924	Walter Hagen	2 up	Jim Barnes	French Lick CC, French Lick, IN
1925	Walter Hagen	6 & 5	William Mehlhorn	Olympia Fields CC, Olympia Fields, IL
1926	Walter Hagen	5 & 3	Leo Diegel	Salisbury GC, Westbury, NY
1927	Walter Hagen	1 up	Joe Turnesa	Cedar Crest CC, Dallas, TX
1928	Leo Diegel	6 & 5	Al Espinosa	Five Farms CC, Baltimore, MD
1929	Leo Diegel	6 & 4	Johnny Farrell	Hillcrest CC, Los Angeles, CA
1930	Tommy Armour	1 up	Gene Sarazen	Fresh Meadow CC, Flushing, NY
1931	Tom Creavy	2 & 1	Denny Shute	Wannamoisett CC, Rumford, RI
1932	Olin Dutra	4 & 3	Frank Walsh	Keller GC, St. Paul, MN
1933	Gene Sarazen	5 & 4	Willie Goggin	Blue Mound CC, Milwaukee, WI
1934	Paul Runyan	1 up	Craig Wood	Park CC, Williamsville, NY
1935	Johnny Revolta	5 & 4	Tommy Armour	Twin Hills CC, Oklahoma City, OK
1936	Denny Shute	3 & 2	Jimmy Thomson	Pinehurst CC, Pinehurst, NC
1937	Denny Shute	1 up 37 holes	Harold McSpaden	Pittsburgh FC, Aspinwall, PA
1938	Paul Runyan	8 & 7	Sam Snead	Shawnee CC, Shawnee-on-Delaware, PA
1939	Henry Picard	1 up 37 holes	Byron Nelson	Pomonok CC, Flushing, NY
1940	Byron Nelson	1 up	Sam Snead	Hershey CC, Hershey, PA
1941	Vic Ghezzi	1 up 38 holes	Byron Nelson	Cherry Hills CC, Denver, CO
1942	Sam Snead	2 & 1	Jim Turnesa	Seaview CC, Atlantic City, NJ
1943	No tournament			
1944	Bob Hamilton	1 up	Byron Nelson	Manito G & CC, Spokane, WA
1945	Byron Nelson	4 & 3	Sam Byrd	Morraine CC, Dayton, OH
1946	Ben Hogan	6 & 4	Ed Oliver	Portland GC, Portland, OR
1947	Jim Ferrier	2 & 1	Chick Harbert	Plum Hollow CC, Detroit, MI
1948	Ben Hogan	7 & 6	Mike Turnesa	Norwood Hills CC, St. Louis, MO
1949	Sam Snead	3 & 2	Johnny Palmer	Hermitage CC, Richmond, VA
1950	Chandler Harper	4 & 3	Henry Williams Jr.	Scioto CC, Columbus, OH
1951	Sam Snead	7 & 6	Walter Burkemo	Oakmont CC, Oakmont, PA
1952	Jim Turnesa	1 up	Chick Harbert	Big Spring CC, Louisville, KY
1953	Walter Burkemo	2 & 1	Felice Torza	Birmingham CC, Birmingham, MI
1954	Chick Harbert	4 & 3	Walter Burkemo	Keller GC, St. Paul, MN
1955	Doug Ford	4 & 3	Cary Middlecoff	Meadowbrook CC, Detroit, MI
1956	Jack Burke	3 & 2	Ted Kroll	Blue Hill CC, Boston, MA
1957	Lionel Hebert	2 & 1	Dow Finsterwald	Miami Valley CC, Dayton, OH
1958#	Dow Finsterwald	276	Billy Casper	Llanerch CC, Havertown, PA
1959	Bob Rosburg	277	Jerry Barber	Minneapolis GC, St. Louis Park, MN
			Doug Sanders	

PGA Championship (Cont.)

Year	Winner	Score	Runner-Up	Site
1960	Jay Hebert	281	Jim Ferrier	Firestone CC, Akron, OH
1961	Jerry Barber* (67)	277	Don January (68)	Olympia Fields CC, Olympia Fields, IL
1962	Gary Player	278	Bob Goalby	Aronimink GC, Newton Square, PA
1963	Jack Nicklaus	279	Dave Ragan Jr.	Dallas Athletic Club, Dallas, TX
1964	Bobby Nichols	271	Jack Nicklaus Arnold Palmer	Columbus CC, Columbus, OH
1965	Dave Marr	280	Billy Casper Jack Nicklaus	Laurel Valley CC, Ligonier, PA
1966	Al Geiberger	280	Dudley Wysong	Firestone CC, Akron, OH
1967	Don January* (69)	281	Don Massengale (71)	Columbine CC, Littleton, CO
1968	Julius Boros	281	Bob Charles Arnold Palmer	Pecan Valley CC, San Antonio, TX
1969	Ray Floyd	276	Gary Player	NCR CC, Dayton, OH
1970	Dave Stockton	279	Arnold Palmer Bob Murphy	Southern Hills CC, Tulsa, OK
1971	Jack Nicklaus	281	Billy Casper	PGA Nat'l GC, Palm Beach Gardens, FL
1972	Gary Player	281	Tommy Aaron Jim Jamieson	Oakland Hills CC, Birmingham, MI
1973	Jack Nicklaus	277	Bruce Crampton	Canterbury GC, Cleveland, OH
1974	Lee Trevino	276	Jack Nicklaus	Tanglewood GC, Winston-Salem, NC
1975	Jack Nicklaus	276	Bruce Crampton	Firestone CC, Akron, OH
1976	Dave Stockton	281	Ray Floyd Don January	Congressional CC, Bethesda, MD
1977†	Lanny Wadkins* (4-4-4)	282	Gene Littler (4-4-5)	Pebble Beach GL, Pebble Beach, CA
1978	John Mahaffey* (4–3)	276	Jerry Pate (4–4) Tom Watson (4–5)	Oakmont CC, Oakmont, PA
1979	David Graham* (4-4-2)	272	Ben Crenshaw (4-4-4)	Oakland Hills CC, Birmingham, MI
1980	Jack Nicklaus	274	Andy Bean	Oak Hill CC, Rochester, NY
1981	Larry Nelson	273	Fuzzy Zoeller	Atlanta Athletic Club, Duluth, GA
1982	Raymond Floyd	272	Lanny Wadkins	Southern Hills CC, Tulsa, OK
1983	Hal Sutton	274	Jack Nicklaus	Riviera CC, Pacific Palisades, CA
1984	Lee Trevino	273	Gary Player Lanny Wadkins	Shoal Creek, Birmingham, AL
1985	Hubert Green	278	Lee Trevino	Cherry Hills CC, Denver, CO
1986	Bob Tway	276	Greg Norman	Inverness CC, Toledo, OH
1987	Larry Nelson* (4)	287	Lanny Wadkins (5)	PGA Natl GC, Palm Beach Gardens, FL
1988	Jeff Sluman	272	Paul Azinger	Oak Tree GC, Edmond, OK
1989	Payne Stewart	276	Mike Reid	Kemper Lakes GC, Hawthorn Woods, IL
1990	Wayne Grady	282	Fred Couples	Shoal Creek, Birmingham, AL
1991	John Daly	276	Bruce Lietzke	Crooked Stick GC, Carmel, IN
1992	Nick Price	278	Jim Gallagher Jr.	Bellerive CC, St. Louis, MO
1993	Paul Azinger* (4–4)	272	Greg Norman (4–5)	Inverness CC, Toledo, OH
1994	Nick Price	269	Corey Pavin	Southern Hills CC, Tulsa, OK
1995	Steve Elkington* (3)	267	Colin Montgomerie (4)	Riviera CC, Pacific Palisades, CA
1996	Mark Brooks* (3)	277	Kenny Perry (x)	Valhalla GC, Louisville, KY
1997	Davis Love III	269	Justin Leonard	Winged Foot GC, Mamaroneck, NY
1998	Vijay Singh	271	Steve Stricker	Sahalee CC, Redmond, WA
1999	Tiger Woods	277	Sergio Garcia	Medinah CC, Medinah, IL
2000‡	Tiger Woods* (3-4-5)	270	Bob May (4-4-x)	Valhalla GC, Louisville, KY
2001	David Toms	265	Phil Mickelson	Atlanta AC, Johns Creek, GA
2002	Rich Beem	278	Tiger Woods	Hazeltine National GC, Chaska, MN
2003	Shaun Micheel	276	Chad Campbell	Oak Hill CC, Rochester, NY
2004	Vijay Singh* (3-3-4)	280	Chris DiMarco (4-3-x) Justin Leonard (4-3-x)	Whistling Straits GC, Kohler, WI
2005	Phil Mickelson	276	Steve Elkington	Baltusrol GC, Springfield, NJ
2006	Tiger Woods	270	Shaun Micheel	Medinah CC, Medinah, IL
2007	Tiger Woods	272	Woody Austin	Southern Hills CC, Tulsa, OK
2008	Padraig Harrington	277	Sergio Garcia	Oakland Hills CC, Birmingham, MI
2009	Y.E. Yang	280	Tiger Woods	Hazeltine National GC, Chaska, MN
2010	Martin Kaymer* (4-2-5)	277	Bubba Watson (3-3-6)	Whistling Straits GC, Kohler, WI
2011	Keegan Bradley* (3-3-4)	272	Jason Dufner (4-4-3)	Atlanta AC, Johns Creek, GA
2012	Rory McIlroy	275	David Lynn	Kiawah Island Resort, Kiawah Island, SC
2013	Jason Dufner	270	Jim Furyk	Oak Hill CC, Rochester, NY

*Winner in playoff. †Playoff changed from 18 holes to sudden death. ‡ Playoff changed from sudden death to three-hole playoff. #Switched from match-play to stroke-play format in 1958.

THE PGA TOUR

Most Career Wins†

	Wins		Wins		Wins
Sam Snead	82	Billy Casper	51	Lloyd Mangrum	36
*Tiger Woods	79	Walter Hagen	44	*Vijay Singh	34
Jack Nicklaus	73	*Phil Mickelson	42	Horton Smith	32
Ben Hogan	64	Cary Middlecoff	40	Harry Cooper	31
Arnold Palmer	62	Gene Sarazen	39	Jimmy Demaret	31
Byron Nelson	52	Tom Watson	39	Leo Diegel	30

† Through 9/22/13. * Active player.

Alltime Major Championship Winners

	Masters	U.S. Open	British Open	PGA Champ.	U.S. Amateur	British Amateur	Total
Jack Nicklaus	6	4	3	5	2	0	20
*Tiger Woods	4	3	3	4	3	0	17
Bobby Jones	0	4	3	0	5	1	13
Walter Hagen	0	2	4	5	0	0	11
Ben Hogan	2	4	1	2	0	0	9
Gary Player	3	1	3	2	0	0	9
John Ball	0	0	1	0	0	8	9
Arnold Palmer	4	1	2	0	1	0	8
Tom Watson	2	1	5	0	0	0	8
Harold Hilton	0	0	2	0	1	4	7
Gene Sarazen	1	2	1	3	0	0	7
Sam Snead	3	0	1	3	0	0	7
Harry Vardon	0	1	6	0	0	0	7

*Active player.

Alltime Multiple Professional Major Winners

MASTERS		U.S. OPEN		BRITISH OPEN		PGA CHAMPIONSHIP	
Jack Nicklaus	6	Willie Anderson	4	Harry Vardon	6	Walter Hagen	5
Arnold Palmer	4	Ben Hogan	4	James Braid	5	Jack Nicklaus	5
*Tiger Woods	4	Bobby Jones	4	J.H. Taylor	5	*Tiger Woods	4
Jimmy Demaret	3	Jack Nicklaus	4	Peter Thomson	5	Gene Sarazen	3
Nick Faldo	3	Hale Irwin	3	Tom Watson	5	Sam Snead	3
*Phil Mickelson	3	*Tiger Woods	3	Walter Hagen	4	Jim Barnes	2
Gary Player	3	Julius Boros	2	Bobby Locke	4	Leo Diegel	2
Sam Snead	3	Billy Casper	2	Tom Morris Sr.	4	Raymond Floyd	2
Seve Ballesteros	2	*Ernie Els	2	Tom Morris Jr.	4	Ben Hogan	2
Ben Crenshaw	2	*Retief Goosen	2	Willie Park	4	Byron Nelson	2
Ben Hogan	2	Ralph Guldahl	2	Jamie Anderson	3	Larry Nelson	2
*Bernhard Langer	2	Walter Hagen	2	Seve Ballesteros	3	Gary Player	2
Byron Nelson	2	*Lee Janzen	2	Henry Cotton	3	Paul Runyan	2
*José María Olazábal	2	John McDermott	2	Nick Faldo	3	Denny Shute	2
Horton Smith	2	Cary Middlecoff	2	Robert Ferguson	3	*Vijay Singh	2
Tom Watson	2	Andy North	2	Bobby Jones	3	Dave Stockton	2
		Gene Sarazen	2	Jack Nicklaus	3	Lee Trevino	2
		Alex Smith	2	Gary Player	3		
		Payne Stewart	2	*Tiger Woods	3		
		Curtis Strange	2	*Ernie Els	2		
		Lee Trevino	2	*Padraig Harrington	2		
				Harold Hilton	2		
				Bob Martin	2		
				Greg Norman	2		
				Arnold Palmer	2		
				Willie Park Jr.	2		
				Lee Trevino	2		

*Active player.

THE PGA TOUR *(Cont.)*
Season Money Leaders

	Earnings ($)		Earnings ($)		Earnings ($)
1934 ...Paul Runyan	6,767.00	1961 ...Gary Player	64,540.45	1988 ...Curtis Strange	1,147,644.00
1935 ...Johnny Revolta	9,543.00	1962 ...Arnold Palmer	81,448.33	1989 ...Tom Kite	1,395,278.00
1936 ...Horton Smith	7,682.00	1963 ...Arnold Palmer	128,230.00	1990 ...Greg Norman	1,165,477.00
1937 ...Harry Cooper	14,138.69	1964 ...Jack Nicklaus	113,284.50	1991 ...Corey Pavin	979,430.00
1938 ...Sam Snead	19,534.49	1965 ...Jack Nicklaus	140,752.14	1992 ...Fred Couples	1,344,188.00
1939 ...Henry Picard	10,303.00	1966 ...Billy Casper	121,944.92	1993 ...Nick Price	1,478,557.00
1940 ...Ben Hogan	10,655.00	1967 ...Jack Nicklaus	188,998.08	1994 ...Nick Price	1,499,927.00
1941 ...Ben Hogan	18,358.00	1968 ...Billy Casper	205,168.67	1995 ...Greg Norman	1,654,959.00
1942 ...Ben Hogan	13,143.00	1969 ...Frank Beard	164,707.11	1996 ...Tom Lehman	1,780,159.00
1943 ...No statistics compiled		1970 ...Lee Trevino	157,037.63	1997 ...Tiger Woods	2,066,833.00
1944 ...Byron Nelson*	37,967.69	1971 ...Jack Nicklaus	244,490.50	1998 ...David Duval	2,591,031.00
1945 ...Byron Nelson*	63,335.66	1972 ...Jack Nicklaus	320,542.26	1999 ...Tiger Woods	6,616,585.00
1946 ...Ben Hogan	42,556.16	1973 ...Jack Nicklaus	308,362.10	2000 ...Tiger Woods	9,188,321.00
1947 ...Jimmy Demaret	27,936.83	1974 ...Johnny Miller	353,021.59	2001 ...Tiger Woods	5,687,777.00
1948 ...Ben Hogan	32,112.00	1975 ...Jack Nicklaus	298,149.17	2002 ...Tiger Woods	6,912,625.00
1949 ...Sam Snead	31,593.83	1976 ...Jack Nicklaus	266,438.57	2003 ...Vijay Singh	7,573,907.00
1950 ...Sam Snead	35,758.83	1977 ...Tom Watson	310,653.16	2004 ...Vijay Singh	10,905,166.00
1951 ...Lloyd Mangrum	26,088.83	1978 ...Tom Watson	362,428.93	2005 ...Tiger Woods	10,628,024.00
1952 ...Julius Boros	37,032.97	1979 ...Tom Watson	462,636.00	2006 ...Tiger Woods	9,941,563.00
1953 ...Lew Worsham	34,002.00	1980 ...Tom Watson	530,808.33	2007 ...Tiger Woods	10,867,052.00
1954 ...Bob Toski	65,819.81	1981 ...Tom Kite	375,698.84	2008 ...Vijay Singh	6,601,094.00
1955 ...Julius Boros	63,121.55	1982 ...Craig Stadler	446,462.00	2009 ...Tiger Woods	10,508,163.00
1956 ...Ted Kroll	72,835.83	1983 ...Hal Sutton	426,668.00	2010 ...Matt Kuchar	4,910,477.00
1957 ...Dick Mayer	65,835.00	1984 ...Tom Watson	476,260.00	2011 ...Luke Donald	6,683,214.00
1958 ...Arnold Palmer	42,607.50	1985 ...Curtis Strange	542,321.00	2012 ...Rory McIlroy	8,047,952.00
1959 ...Art Wall	53,167.60	1986 ...Greg Norman	653,296.00		
1960 ...Arnold Palmer	75,262.85	1987 ...Curtis Strange	925,941.00		

* War bonds. Note: Total money listed from 1968 through 1974. Official money listed from 1975 on.

Year-by-Year Statistical Leaders

SCORING AVERAGE			DRIVING DISTANCE	Yds		DRIVING ACCURACY	Pct./Fwy
1980	Lee Trevino	69.73	1980	Dan Pohl	274.3	1980	Mike Reid	79.5
1981	Tom Kite	69.80	1981	Dan Pohl	280.1	1981	Calvin Peete	81.9
1982	Tom Kite	70.21	1982	Bill Calfee	275.3	1982	Calvin Peete	84.6
1983	Raymond Floyd	70.61	1983	John McComish	277.4	1983	Calvin Peete	81.3
1984	Calvin Peete	70.56	1984	Bill Glasson	276.5	1984	Calvin Peete	77.5
1985	Don Pooley	70.36	1985	Andy Bean	278.2	1985	Calvin Peete	80.6
1986	Scott Hoch	70.08	1986	Davis Love III	285.7	1986	Calvin Peete	81.7
1987	David Frost	70.09	1987	John McComish	283.9	1987	Calvin Peete	83.0
1988	Greg Norman	69.38	1988	Steve Thomas	284.6	1988	Calvin Peete	82.5
1989	Payne Stewart	69.485†	1989	Ed Humenik	280.9	1989	Calvin Peete	82.6
1990	Greg Norman	69.10	1990	Tom Purtzer	279.6	1990	Calvin Peete	83.7
1991	Fred Couples	69.59	1991	John Daly	288.9	1991	Hale Irwin	78.3
1992	Fred Couples	69.38	1992	John Daly	283.4	1992	Doug Tewell	82.3
1993	Greg Norman	68.90	1993	John Daly	288.9	1993	Doug Tewell	82.5
1994	Greg Norman	68.81	1994	Davis Love III	283.8	1994	David Edwards	81.6
1995	Greg Norman	69.06	1995	John Daly	289.0	1995	Fred Funk	81.3
1996	Tom Lehman	69.32	1996	John Daly	288.8	1996	Fred Funk	78.7
1997	Nick Price	68.98	1997	John Daly	302.0	1997	Allen Doyle	80.8
1998	David Duval	69.13	1998	John Daly	299.4	1998	Bruce Fleisher	81.4
1999	Tiger Woods	68.43	1999	John Daly	305.6	1999	Fred Funk	80.2
2000	Tiger Woods	67.79	2000	John Daly	301.4	2000	Fred Funk	79.7
2001	Tiger Woods	68.81	2001	John Daly	306.7	2001	Joe Durant	81.1
2002	Tiger Woods	68.13	2002	John Daly	306.8	2002	Fred Funk	81.2
2003	Tiger Woods	68.41	2003	Hank Kuehne	321.4	2003	Fred Funk	77.9
2004	Vijay Singh	69.19	2004	Hank Kuehne	314.4	2004	Fred Funk	77.2
2005	Tiger Woods	68.66	2005	Scott Hend	318.9	2005	Jeff Hart	76.0
2006	Tiger Woods	68.11	2006	Bubba Watson	319.6	2006	Joe Durant	78.4
2007	Tiger Woods	67.79	2007	Bubba Watson	315.2	2007	Jose Coceres	75.5
2008	Sergio Garcia	69.12	2008	Bubba Watson	315.1	2008	Olin Browne	80.4
2009	Tiger Woods	68.05	2009	Robert Garrigus	312.3	2009	Joe Durant	74.8
2010	Matt Kuchar	69.61	2010	Robert Garrigus	315.5	2010	Omar Uresti	76.1
2011	Luke Donald	68.86	2011	J.B. Holmes	318.4	2011	Joe Durant	75.7
2012	Rory McIlroy	68.87	2012	Bubba Watson	315.5	2012	Joe Kelly	73.0

Note: Scoring avg. per round, with adjustments made for the field's course scoring average. †Carried to extra decimal place to determine winner.

Note: Average uses distance of two tee shots on a predetermined par-four or par-five hole (front & back).

Note: Percentage of fairways hit on number of par-four and par-five holes played; par-three holes excluded.

THE PGA TOUR (Cont.)

Year by Year Statistical Leaders (Cont.)

GREENS IN REGULATION

1980	Jack Nicklaus	72.1
1981	Calvin Peete	73.1
1982	Calvin Peete	72.4
1983	Calvin Peete	71.4
1984	Andy Bean	72.1
1985	John Mahaffey	71.9
1986	John Mahaffey	72.0
1987	Gil Morgan	73.3
1988	John Adams	73.9
1989	Bruce Lietzke	72.6
1990	Doug Tewell	70.9
1991	Bruce Lietzke	73.3
1992	Tim Simpson	74.0
1993	Fuzzy Zoeller	73.6
1994	Bill Glasson	73.0
1995	Lenny Clements	72.3
1996	Fred Couples	71.8
	Mark O'Meara	71.8
1997	Tom Lehman	72.7
1998	Hal Sutton	71.3
1999	Tiger Woods	71.4
2000	Tiger Woods	75.2
2001	Tom Lehman	74.5
2002	Tiger Woods	74.0
2003	Joe Durant	72.9
2004	Joe Durant	73.3
2005	Sergio Garcia	71.8
2006	Tiger Woods	74.2
2007	Tiger Woods	71.0
2008	Joe Durant	71.1
2009	John Senden	70.9
2010	John Senden	72.5
2011	Boo Weekley	71.7
2012	Justin Rose	70.3

Note: Average of greens reached in regulation out of total holes played; hole is considered hit in regulation if any part of the ball rests on the putting surface in two shots less than the hole's par—a par-5 hit in two shots is one green in regulation.

PUTTING

1980	Jerry Pate	28.81
1981	Alan Tapie	28.70
1982	Ben Crenshaw	28.65
1983	Morris Hatalsky	27.96
1984	Gary McCord	28.57
1985	Craig Stadler	28.627†
1986	Greg Norman	1.736
1987	Ben Crenshaw	1.743
1988	Don Pooley	1.729
1989	Steve Jones	1.734
1990	Larry Rinker	1.7467†
1991	Jay Don Blake	1.7326†
1992	Mark O'Meara	1.731
1993	David Frost	1.739
1994	Loren Roberts	1.737
1995	Jim Furyk	1.708
1996	Brad Faxon	1.709
1997	Don Pooley	1.718
1998	Rick Fehr	1.722
1999	Brad Faxon	1.723
2000	Brad Faxon	1.704
2001	David Frost	1.708
2002	Bob Heintz	1.682

PUTTING (Cont.)

2003	John Huston	1.713
2004	Stewart Cink	1.723
2005	Arjun Atwal	1.710
2006	Daniel Chopra	1.712
2007	Tim Clark	1.727
2008	Bob Tway	1.718
2009	Steve Stricker	1.726
2010	Brandt Snedeker	1.708
2011	Luke Donald	1.700
2012	Jonas Blixt	1.718

Note: Average number of putts taken per green in regulation; prior to 1986, based on average number of putts per 18 holes.

SAND SAVES

1980	Bob Eastwood	65.4
1981	Tom Watson	60.1
1982	Isao Aoki	60.2
1983	Isao Aoki	62.3
1984	Peter Oosterhuis	64.7
1985	Tom Purtzer	60.8
1986	Paul Azinger	63.8
1987	Paul Azinger	63.2
1988	Greg Powers	63.5
1989	Mike Sullivan	66.0
1990	Paul Azinger	67.2
1991	Ben Crenshaw	64.9
1992	Mitch Adcock	66.9
1993	Ken Green	64.4
1994	Corey Pavin	65.4
1995	Billy Mayfair	68.6
1996	Gary Rusnak	64.0
1997	Bob Estes	70.3
1998	Keith Fergus	71.0
1999	Jeff Sluman	67.3
2000	Fred Couples	67.0
2001	Franklin Langham	68.9
2002	J.M. Olazabal	64.9
2003	Stuart Appleby	62.1
2004	Dan Forsman	62.3
2005	Pat Perez	63.0
2006	Luke Donald	63.6
2007	Tim Clark	68.1
2008	Dudley Hart	63.7
2009	Luke Donald	64.4
2010	Luke Donald	66.4
2011	Brian Gay	63.4
2012	Jonas Blixt	65.4

Note: Percentage of up-and-down efforts from greenside bunkers only—fairway bunkers excluded.

EAGLES

1980	Dave Eichelberger	16
1981	Bruce Lietzke	12
1982	Tom Weiskopf	10
	J.C. Snead	10
	Andy Bean	10
1983	Chip Beck	15
1984	Gary Hallberg	15
1985	Larry Rinker	14
1986	Joey Sindelar	16
1987	Phil Blackmar	20
1988	Ken Green	21

EAGLES (Cont.)

1990	Lon Hinkle	14
	Duffy Waldorf	14
1990	Paul Azinger	14
1991	Andy Bean	15
1992	Dan Forsman	18
1993	Davis Love III	15
1994	Davis Love III	18
1995	Kelly Gibson	16
1996	Tom Watson	97.2
1997	Tiger Woods	104.1
1998	Davis Love III	83.3
1999	Vijay Singh	104.8
2000	Tiger Woods	72.0
2001	Phil Mickelson	73.8
2002	John Daly	78.4
2003	Tiger Woods	76.5
2004	Nick Price	90.0
2005	Brenden Pappas	70.6
2006	J.B. Holmes	72.9
2007	Chris Tidland	88.5
2008	Chad Campbell	105.8
2009	Bubba Watson	75.2
2010	Dustin Johnson	92.3
2011	Sunghoon Kang	75.6
2012	Bubba Watson	91.4

Note: Total of eagles scored 1980–1995. Since 1996 winner determined by number of holes played per eagle.

BIRDIES

1980	Andy Bean	388
1981	Vance Heafner	388
1982	Andy Bean	392
1983	Hal Sutton	399
1984	Mark O'Meara	419
1985	Joey Sindelar	411
1986	Joey Sindelar	415
1987	Dan Forsman	409
1988	Dan Forsman	465
1989	Ted Schulz	415
1990	Mike Donald	401
1991	Scott Hoch	446
1992	Jeff Sluman	417
1993	John Huston	426
1994	Brad Bryant	397
1995	Steve Lowery	410
1996	Fred Couples	4.20
1997	Tiger Woods	4.25
1998	David Duval	4.29
1999	Tiger Woods	4.46
2000	Tiger Woods	4.92
2001	Phil Mickelson	4.49
2002	Tiger Woods	4.47
2003	Vijay Singh	4.41
2004	Vijay Singh	4.40
2005	Tiger Woods	4.57
2006	Tiger Woods	4.65
2007	Tiger Woods	4.03
2008	Ryan Palmer	4.16
2009	Tiger Woods	4.15
2010	Tom Gillis	4.06
2011	Steve Stricker	4.28
2012	Rory McIlroy	4.20

Note: 1980–95: Total birdies. Since 1996, average number of birdies per round.

† Number carried to extra decimal place to determine winner.

THE PGA TOUR (Cont.)
Year-by-Year Statistical Leaders (Cont.)

ALL-AROUND

1987	Dan Pohl	170
1988	Payne Stewart	170
1989	Paul Azinger	250
1990	Paul Azinger	162
1991	Scott Hoch	283
1992	Fred Couples	256
1993	Gil Morgan	252
1994	Bob Estes	227
1995	Justin Leonard	323
1996	Fred Couples	214
1997	Bill Glasson	282

ALL-AROUND (Cont.)

1998	John Huston	151
1999	Tiger Woods	120
2000	Tiger Woods	113
2001	Phil Mickelson	174
2002	Phil Mickelson	259
2003	Tiger Woods	206
2004	Jeff Ogilvy	268
2005	Tiger Woods	265
2006	Tiger Woods	216
2007	Tiger Woods	240
2008	Pat Perez	323

ALL-AROUND (Cont.)

2009	Tiger Woods	151
2010	Matt Kuchar	270
2011	Webb Simpson	239
2012	Keegan Bradley	253

Note: Sum of the places of standing from the other statistical categories; the player with the number closest to zero leads.

PGA Player of the Year Award

1948	Ben Hogan
1949	Sam Snead
1950	Ben Hogan
1951	Ben Hogan
1952	Julius Boros
1953	Ben Hogan
1954	Ed Furgol
1955	Doug Ford
1956	Jack Burke
1957	Dick Mayer
1958	Dow Finsterwald
1959	Art Wall
1960	Arnold Palmer
1961	Jerry Barber
1962	Arnold Palmer
1963	Julius Boros
1964	Ken Venturi
1965	Dave Marr
1966	Billy Casper
1967	Jack Nicklaus
1968	Not awarded
1969	Orville Moody

1970	Billy Casper
1971	Lee Trevino
1972	Jack Nicklaus
1973	Jack Nicklaus
1974	Johnny Miller
1975	Jack Nicklaus
1976	Jack Nicklaus
1977	Tom Watson
1978	Tom Watson
1979	Tom Watson
1980	Tom Watson
1981	Bill Rogers
1982	Tom Watson
1983	Hal Sutton
1984	Tom Watson
1985	Lanny Wadkins
1986	Bob Tway
1987	Paul Azinger
1988	Curtis Strange
1989	Tom Kite
1990	Wayne Levi

1991	Fred Couples
1992	Fred Couples
1993	Nick Price
1994	Nick Price
1995	Greg Norman
1996	Tom Lehman
1997	Tiger Woods
1998	David Duval
1999	Tiger Woods
2000	Tiger Woods
2001	Tiger Woods
2002	Tiger Woods
2003	Tiger Woods
2004	Vijay Singh
2005	Tiger Woods
2006	Tiger Woods
2007	Tiger Woods
2008	Padraig Harrington
2009	Tiger Woods
2010	Jim Furyk
2011	Luke Donald
2012	Rory McIlroy

Vardon Trophy: Scoring Average

Year	Winner	Avg	Year	Winner	Avg	Year	Winner	Avg
1937	Harry Cooper	*500	1965	Billy Casper	70.85	1989	Greg Norman	69.49
1938	Sam Snead	520	1966	Billy Casper	70.27	1990	Greg Norman	69.10
1939	Byron Nelson	473	1967	Arnold Palmer	70.18	1991	Fred Couples	69.59
1940	Ben Hogan	423	1968	Billy Casper	69.82	1992	Fred Couples	69.38
1941	Ben Hogan	494	1969	Dave Hill	70.34	1993	Nick Price	69.11
1942–46	No award		1970	Lee Trevino	70.64	1994	Greg Norman	68.81
1947	Jimmy Demaret	69.90	1971	Lee Trevino	70.27	1995	Steve Elkington	69.62
1948	Ben Hogan	69.30	1972	Lee Trevino	70.89	1996	Tom Lehman	69.32
1949	Sam Snead	69.37	1973	Bruce Crampton	70.57	1997	Nick Price	68.98
1950	Sam Snead	69.23	1974	Lee Trevino	70.53	1998	David Duval	69.13
1951	Lloyd Mangrum	70.05	1975	Bruce Crampton	70.51	1999	Tiger Woods	68.43
1952	Jack Burke	70.54	1976	Don January	70.56	2000	Tiger Woods	67.79
1953	Lloyd Mangrum	70.22	1977	Tom Watson	70.32	2001	Tiger Woods	68.81
1954	E.J. Harrison	70.41	1978	Tom Watson	70.16	2002	Tiger Woods	68.13
1955	Sam Snead	69.86	1979	Tom Watson	70.27	2003	Tiger Woods	68.41
1956	Cary Middlecoff	70.35	1980	Lee Trevino	69.73	2004	Vijay Singh	68.84
1957	Dow Finsterwald	70.30	1981	Tom Kite	69.80	2005	Tiger Woods	68.66
1958	Bob Rosburg	70.11	1982	Tom Kite	70.21	2006	Jim Furyk	68.86
1959	Art Wall	70.35	1983	Raymond Floyd	70.61	2007	Tiger Woods	67.79
1960	Billy Casper	69.95	1984	Calvin Peete	70.56	2008	Sergio Garcia	69.12
1961	Arnold Palmer	69.85	1985	Don Pooley	70.36	2009	Tiger Woods	68.05
1962	Arnold Palmer	70.27	1986	Scott Hoch	70.08	2010	Matt Kuchar	69.61
1963	Billy Casper	70.58	1987	Don Pohl	70.25	2011	Luke Donald	68.86
1964	Arnold Palmer	70.01	1988	Chip Beck	69.46	2012	Rory McIlroy	68.87

*Point system used, 1937–41. NOTE: As of 1988, based on minimum of 60 rounds per year. Adjusted for average score of field in tournaments entered.

THE MAJOR TOURNAMENTS
LPGA Championship

Year	Winner	Score	Runner-Up	Site
1955	Beverly Hanson*	220	Louise Suggs	Orchard Ridge CC, Ft Wayne, IN
1956	Marlene Hagge*	291	Patty Berg	Forest Lake CC, Detroit, MI
1957	Louise Suggs	285	Wiffi Smith	Churchill Valley CC, Pittsburgh, PA
1958	Mickey Wright	288	Fay Crocker	Churchill Valley CC, Pittsburgh, PA
1959	Betsy Rawls	288	Patty Berg	Sheraton Hotel CC, French Lick, IN
1960	Mickey Wright	292	Louise Suggs	Sheraton Hotel CC, French Lick, IN
1961	Mickey Wright	287	Louise Suggs	Stardust CC, Las Vegas, NV
1962	Judy Kimball	282	Shirley Spork	Stardust CC, Las Vegas, NV
1963	Mickey Wright	294	Mary Lena Faulk Mary Mills Louise Suggs	Stardust CC, Las Vegas, NV
1964	Mary Mills	278	Mickey Wright	Stardust CC, Las Vegas, NV
1965	Sandra Haynie	279	Clifford A. Creed	Stardust CC, Las Vegas, NV
1966	Gloria Ehret	282	Mickey Wright	Stardust CC, Las Vegas, NV
1967	Kathy Whitworth	284	Shirley Englehorn	Pleasant Valley CC, Sutton, MA
1968	Sandra Post*	294	Kathy Whitworth	Pleasant Valley CC, Sutton, MA
1969	Betsy Rawls	293	Susie Berning Carol Mann	Concord GC, Kiameshia Lake, NY
1970	Shirley Englehorn*	285	Kathy Whitworth	Pleasant Valley CC, Sutton, MA
1971	Kathy Whitworth	288	Kathy Ahern	Pleasant Valley CC, Sutton, MA
1972	Kathy Ahern	293	Jane Blalock	Pleasant Valley CC, Sutton, MA
1973	Mary Mills	288	Betty Burfeindt	Pleasant Valley CC, Sutton, MA
1974	Sandra Haynie	288	JoAnne Carner	Pleasant Valley CC, Sutton, MA
1975	Kathy Whitworth	288	Sandra Haynie	Pine Ridge GC, Baltimore, MD
1976	Betty Burfeindt	287	Judy Rankin	Pine Ridge GC, Baltimore, MD
1977	Chako Higuchi	279	Pat Bradley Sandra Post Judy Rankin	Bay Tree Golf Plantation, N Myrtle Beach, SC
1978	Nancy Lopez	275	Amy Alcott	Jack Nicklaus GC, Kings Island, OH
1979	Donna Caponi	279	Jerilyn Britz	Jack Nicklaus GC, Kings Island, OH
1980	Sally Little	285	Jane Blalock	Jack Nicklaus GC, Kings Island, OH
1981	Donna Caponi	280	Jerilyn Britz Pat Meyers	Jack Nicklaus GC, Kings Island, OH
1982	Jan Stephenson	279	JoAnne Carner	Jack Nicklaus GC, Kings Island, OH
1983	Patty Sheehan	279	Sandra Haynie	Jack Nicklaus GC, Kings Island, OH
1984	Patty Sheehan	272	Beth Daniel Pat Bradley	Jack Nicklaus GC, Kings Island, OH
1985	Nancy Lopez	273	Alice Miller	Jack Nicklaus GC, Kings Island, OH
1986	Pat Bradley	277	Patty Sheehan	Jack Nicklaus GC, Kings Island, OH
1987	Jane Geddes	275	Betsy King	Jack Nicklaus GC, Kings Island, OH
1988	Sherri Turner	281	Amy Alcott	Jack Nicklaus GC, Kings Island, OH
1989	Nancy Lopez	274	Ayako Okamoto	Jack Nicklaus GC, Kings Island, OH
1990	Beth Daniel	280	Rosie Jones	Bethesda CC, Bethesda, MD
1991	Meg Mallon	274	Pat Bradley Ayako Okamoto	Bethesda CC, Bethesda, MD
1992	Betsy King	267	Karen Noble	Bethesda CC, Bethesda, MD
1993	Patty Sheehan	275	Lauri Merten	Bethesda CC, Bethesda, MD
1994	Laura Davies	279	Alice Ritzman	DuPont CC, Wilmington, DE
1995	Kelly Robbins	274	Laura Davies	DuPont CC, Wilmington, DE
1996	Laura Davies	213#	Julie Piers	DuPont CC, Wilmington, DE
1997	Chris Johnson*	281	Leta Lindley	DuPont CC, Wilmington, DE
1998	Se Ri Pak	273	Donna Andrews	DuPont CC, Wilmington, DE
1999	Juli Inkster	268	Liselotte Neumann	DuPont CC, Wilmington, DE
2000	Juli Inkster*	281	Stefania Croce	DuPont CC, Wilmington, DE
2001	Karrie Webb	270	Laura Diaz	DuPont CC, Wilmington, DE
2002	Se Ri Pak	279	Beth Daniel	DuPont CC, Wilmington, DE
2003	Annika Sorenstam*	278	Grace Park	DuPont CC, Wilmington, DE
2004	Annika Sorenstam	271	Shi Hyun Ahn	DuPont CC, Wilmington, DE
2005	Annika Sorenstam	277	Michelle Wie	Bulle Rock GC, Havre de Grace, MD
2006	Se Ri Pak*	280	Karrie Webb	Bulle Rock GC, Havre de Grace, MD
2007	Suzann Pettersen	274	Karrie Webb	Bulle Rock GC, Havre de Grace, MD
2008	Yani Tseng	276	Maria Hjorth	Bulle Rock GC, Havre de Grace, MD
2009	Anna Nordqvist	273	Lindsey Wright	Bulle Rock GC, Havre de Grace, MD
2010	Cristie Kerr	269	Song-Hee Kim	Bulle Rock GC, Havre de Grace, MD
2011	Yani Tseng	269	Morgan Pressel	Locust Hill CC, Pittsford, NY

*Won playoff. #Shortened due to rain.

LPGA Championship *(Cont.)*

Year	Winner	Score	Runner-Up	Site
2012........Shanshan Feng		282	Eun-Hee Ji	Locust Hill CC, Pittsford, NY
			Suzann Pettersen	
			Stacy Lewis	
			Mika Miyazato	
2013........Inbee Park*		283	Catriona Matthew	Locust Hill CC, Pittsford, NY

U.S. Women's Open

Year	Winner	Score	Runner-Up	Site
1946........Patty Berg		5 & 4	Betty Jameson	Spokane CC, Spokane, WA
1947........Betty Jameson		295	Sally Sessions	Starmount Forest CC, Greensboro, NC
			Polly Riley	
1948........Babe Zaharias		300	Betty Hicks	Atlantic City CC, Northfield, NJ
1949........Louise Suggs		291	Babe Zaharias	Prince George's G&CC, Landover, MD
1950........Babe Zaharias		291	Betsy Rawls	Rolling Hills CC, Wichita, KS
1951........Betsy Rawls		293	Louise Suggs	Druid Hills GC, Atlanta, GA
1952........Louise Suggs		284	Marlene Bauer	Bala GC, Philadelphia, PA
			Betty Jameson	
1953........Betsy Rawls* (71)		302	Jackie Pung (77)	CC of Rochester, Rochester, NY
1954........Babe Zaharias		291	Betty Hicks	Salem CC, Peabody, MA
1955........Fay Crocker		299	Mary Lena Faulk	Wichita CC, Wichita, KS
			Louise Suggs	
1956........Kathy Cornelius* (75)		302	Barbara McIntire (82)	Northland CC, Duluth, MN
1957........Betsy Rawls		299	Patty Berg	Winged Foot GC, Mamaroneck, NY
1958........Mickey Wright		290	Louise Suggs	Forest Lake CC, Detroit, MI
1959........Mickey Wright		287	Louise Suggs	Churchill Valley CC, Pittsburgh
1960........Betsy Rawls		292	Joyce Ziske	Worcester CC, Worcester, MA
1961........Mickey Wright		293	Betsy Rawls	Baltusrol GC (Lower Course), Springfield, NJ
1962........Murle Breer		301	Jo Ann Prentice	Dunes GC, Myrtle Beach, SC
			Ruth Jessen	
1963........Mary Mills		289	Sandra Haynie	Kenwood CC, Cincinnati,OH
			Louise Suggs	
1964........Mickey Wright* (70)		290	Ruth Jessen (72)	San Diego CC, Chula Vista, CA
1965........Carol Mann		290	Kathy Cornelius	Atlantic City CC, Northfield, NJ
1966........Sandra Spuzich		297	Carol Mann	Hazeltine Natl GC, Chaska, MN
1967........Catherine LaCoste		294	Susie Berning	The Homestead (Cascades Course),
			Beth Stone	Hot Springs, VA
1968........Susie Berning		289	Mickey Wright	Moslem Springs GC, Fleetwood, PA
1969........Donna Caponi		294	Peggy Wilson	Scenic Hills CC, Pensacola, FL
1970........Donna Caponi		287	Sandra Haynie	Muskogee CC, Muskogee, OK
			Sandra Spuzich	
1971........JoAnne Carner		288	Kathy Whitworth	Kahkwa CC, Erie, PA
1972........Susie Berning		299	Kathy Ahern	Winged Foot GC, Mamaroneck, NY
			Pam Barnett	
			Judy Rankin	
1973........Susie Berning		290	Gloria Ehret	CC of Rochester, Rochester, NY
			Shelley Hamlin	
1974........Sandra Haynie		295	Carol Mann	La Grange CC, La Grange, IL
			Beth Stone	
1975........Sandra Palmer		295	JoAnne Carner	Atlantic City CC, Northfield, NJ
			Sandra Post	
			Nancy Lopez	
1976........JoAnne Carner* (76)		292	Sandra Palmer (78)	Rolling Green CC, Springfield, PA
1977........Hollis Stacy		292	Nancy Lopez	Hazeltine Natl GC, Chaska, MN
1978........Hollis Stacy		289	JoAnne Carner	CC of Indianapolis, Indianapolis, IN
			Sally Little	
1979........Jerilyn Britz		284	Debbie Massey	Brooklawn CC, Fairfield, CT
			Sandra Palmer	
1980........Amy Alcott		280	Hollis Stacy	Richland CC, Nashville, TN
1981........Pat Bradley		279	Beth Daniel	La Grange CC, La Grange, IL
1982........Janet Anderson		283	Beth Daniel	Del Paso CC, Sacramento, CA
			Sandra Haynie	
			Donna White	
			JoAnne Carner	
1983........Jan Stephenson		290	JoAnne Carner	Cedar Ridge CC, Tulsa, OK
			Patty Sheehan	
1984........Hollis Stacy		290	Rosie Jones	Salem CC, Peabody, MA
1985........Kathy Baker		280	Judy Dickinson	Baltusrol GC (Upper Course), Springfield, NJ

U.S. Women's Open *(Cont.)*

Year	Winner	Score	Runner-Up	Site
1986	Jane Geddes* (71)	287	Sally Little (73)	NCR GC, Dayton, OH
1987	Laura Davies* (71)	285	Ayako Okamoto (73) JoAnne Carner (74)	Plainfield CC, Plainfield, NJ
1988	Liselotte Neumann	277	Patty Sheehan	Baltimore CC, Baltimore, MD
1989	Betsy King	278	Nancy Lopez	Indianwood G&CC, Lake Orion, MI
1990	Betsy King	284	Patty Sheehan	Atlanta Athletic Club, Duluth, GA
1991	Meg Mallon	283	Pat Bradley	Colonial Club, Fort Worth, TX
1992	Patty Sheehan* (72)	280	Juli Inkster	Oakmont CC, Oakmont, PA
1993	Lauri Merten	280	Donna Andrews Helen Alfredsson	Crooked Stick, Carmel, IN
1994	Patty Sheehan	277	Tammie Green	Indianwood G & CC, Lake Orion, MI
1995	Annika Sorenstam	278	Meg Mallon	The Broadmoor GC, Colorado Springs,CO
1996	Annika Sorenstam	272	Kris Tschetter	Pine Needles GC, Southern Pines, NC
1997	Alison Nicholas	274	Nancy Lopez	Pumpkin Ridge CC, North Plains, OR
1998	Se Ri Pak†	290	Jenny Chuasiriporn	Blackwolf Run Golf Resort, Kohler, WI
1999	Juli Inkster	272	Sherri Turner	Old Waverly GC, West Point, MS
2000	Karrie Webb	282	Cristie Kerr Meg Mallon	Merit GC, Libertyville, IL
2001	Karrie Webb	273	Se Ri Pak	Pine Needles GC, Southern Pines, NC
2002	Juli Inkster	276	Annika Sorenstam	Prairie Dunes CC, Hutchinson, KS
2003	Hilary Lunke*	283	Kelly Robbins	Pumpkin Ridge GC, North Plains, OR
2004	Meg Mallon	274	Annika Sorenstam	The Orchards GC, South Hadley, MA
2005	Birdie Kim	287	Brittany Lang Morgan Pressel	Cherry Hills CC, Cherry Hills Village, CO
2006	Annika Sorenstam*	284	Pat Hurst	Newport CC, Newport, RI
2007	Cristie Kerr	279	Angela Park Lorena Ochoa	Pine Needles GC, Southern Pines, NC
2008	Inbee Park	283	Helen Alfredsson	Interlachen CC, Edina, MN
2009	Eun-Hee Ji	284	Candie Kung	Saucon Valley CC-Old Course, Bethlehem, PA
2010	Paula Creamer	281	Na Yeon Choi	Oakmont CC, Oakmont, PA
2011	So Yeon Ryu*	281	Hee Kyung Seo	The Broadmoor GC, Colorado Springs, CO
2012	Na Yeon Choi	281	Amy Yang	Blackwolf Run Golf Resort, Kohler, WI
2013	Inbee Park	280	In-Kyung Kim	Sebonack CC, Southampton, NY

* Winner in playoff. † Winner on second hole of sudden death after 18-hole playoff ended in a tie.

Kraft Nabisco Championship

Year	Winner	Score	Runner-Up	Year	Winner	Score	Runner-Up
1972	Jane Blalock	213	Carol Mann Judy Rankin	1993	Helen Alfredsson	284	Amy Benz Tina Barrett Betsy King
1973	Mickey Wright	284	Joyce Kazmierski	1994	Donna Andrews	276	Laura Davies
1974	Jo Ann Prentice*	289	Jane Blalock Sandra Haynie	1995	Nanci Bowen	285	Susie Redman
1975	Sandra Palmer	283	Kathy McMullen	1996	Patti Sheehan	281	Kelly Robbins Meg Mallon Annika Sorenstam
1976	Judy Rankin	285	Betty Burfeindt				
1977	Kathy Whitworth	289	JoAnne Carner Sally Little	1997	Betsy King	276	Kris Tschetter
1978	Sandra Post*	283	Penny Pulz	1998	Pat Hurst	281	Helen Dobson
1979	Sandra Post	276	Nancy Lopez	1999	Dottie Pepper	269	Meg Mallon
1980	Donna Caponi	275	Amy Alcott	2000	Karrie Webb	274	Dottie Pepper
1981	Nancy Lopez	277	Carolyn Hill	2001	Annika Sorenstam	281	five players
1982	Sally Little	278	Hollis Stacy Sandra Haynie	2002	Annika Sorenstam	280	Liselotte Neumann
				2003	P. Meunier-Lebouc	281	Annika Sorenstam
1983	Amy Alcott	282	Beth Daniel Kathy Whitworth	2004	Grace Park	277	Aree Song
				2005	Annika Sorenstam	273	Rosie Jones
1984	Juli Inkster*	280	Pat Bradley	2006	Karrie Webb*	279	Lorena Ochoa
1985	Alice Miller	275	Jan Stephenson	2007	Morgan Pressel	285	Catriona Matthew Brittany Lincicome Suzann Pettersen
1986	Pat Bradley	280	Val Skinner				
1987	Betsy King*	283	Patty Sheehan				
1988	Amy Alcott	274	Colleen Walker	2008	Lorena Ochoa	277	Annika Sorenstam
1989	Juli Inkster	279	Tammie Green JoAnne Carner	2009	Brittany Lincicome	279	Kristy McPherson Cristie Kerr
1990	Betsy King	283	Kathy Postlewait Shirley Furlong	2010	Yani Tseng	275	Suzann Pettersen
				2011	Stacy Lewis	275	Yani Tseng
1991	Amy Alcott	273	Dottie Mochrie	2012	Sun Young Koo*	279	I.K. Kim
1992	Dottie Mochrie*	279	Juli Inkster	2013	Inbee Park	273	So Yeon Ryu

*Winner in sudden-death playoff. Note: Designated major in 1983; played at Mission Hills CC, Rancho Mirage, CA.

du Maurier Classic

Year	Winner	Score	Runner-Up	Site
1973	Jocelyne Bourassa*	214	Sandra Haynie	Montreal GC, Montreal
			Judy Rankin	
1974	Carole Jo Callison	208	JoAnne Carner	Candiac GC, Montreal
1975	JoAnne Carner*	214	Carol Mann	St. George's CC, Toronto
1976	Donna Caponi*	212	Judy Rankin	Cedar Brae G&CC, Toronto
1977	Judy Rankin	214	Pat Meyers	Lachute G & CC, Montreal
			Sandra Palmer	
1978	JoAnne Carner	278	Hollis Stacy	St. George's CC, Toronto
1979	Amy Alcott	285	Nancy Lopez	Richelieu Valley CC, Montreal
1980	Pat Bradley	277	JoAnne Carner	St. George's CC, Toronto
1981	Jan Stephenson	278	Nancy Lopez	Summerlea CC, Dorion, Quebec
			Pat Bradley	
1982	Sandra Haynie	280	Beth Daniel	St. George's CC, Toronto
1983	Hollis Stacy	277	JoAnne Carner	Beaconsfield GC, Montreal
			Alice Miller	
1984	Juli Inkster	279	Ayako Okamoto	St. George's G&CC, Toronto
1985	Pat Bradley	278	Jane Geddes	Beaconsfield CC, Montreal
1986	Pat Bradley*	276	Ayako Okamoto	Board of Trade CC, Toronto
1987	Jody Rosenthal	272	Ayako Okamoto	Islesmere GC, Laval, Quebec
1988	Sally Little	279	Laura Davies	Vancouver GC, Coquitlam, British Columbia
1989	Tammie Green	279	Pat Bradley	Beaconsfield GC, Montreal
			Betsy King	
1990	Cathy Johnston	276	Patty Sheehan	Westmount G & CC, Kitchener, Ontario
1991	Nancy Scranton	279	Debbie Massey	Vancouver GC, Coquitlam, British Columbia
1992	Sherri Steinhauer	277	Judy Dickinson	St. Charles CC, Winnipeg, Manitoba
1993	Brandie Burton	277	Betsy King	London Hunt and CC, London, Ontario
1994	Martha Nause	279	Michelle McGann	Ottawa Hunt and GC, Ottawa, Ontario
1995	Jenny Lidback	280	Liselotte Neumann	Beaconsfield GC, Pointe-Claire, Quebec
1996	Laura Davies	277	Nancy Lopez	Edmonton CC, Edmonton, Alberta
			Karrie Webb	
1997	Colleen Walker	278	Liselotte Neumann	Glen Abbey GC, Oakville, Ontario
1998	Brandie Burton	270	Annika Sorenstam	Essex G&CC, Windsor, Ontario
1999	Karrie Webb	277	Laura Davies	Priddis Greens G&CC, Calgary, Alberta
2000	Meg Mallon	282	Rosie Jones	Royal Ottawa GC, Aylmer, Quebec

*Winner in sudden-death playoff. Note: Designated major in 1979. Tournament discontinued in 2001.

Women's British Open

Year	Winner	Score	Runner-Up	Site
2001	Se Ri Pak	277	Mi Hyun Kim	Sunningdale GC, England
2002	Karrie Webb	273	Michelle Ellis	Turnberry GC, Scotland
			Paula Marti	
2003	Annika Sorenstam	278	Se Ri Pak	Royal Lytham & St. Annes, England
2004	Karen Stupples	269	Rachel Teske	Sunningdale GC, England
2005	Jeong Jang	272	Sophie Gustafson	Royal Birkdale CC, England
2006	Sherri Steinhauer	281	Cristie Kerr	Royal Lytham & St. Anne's, England
2007	Lorena Ochoa	287	Jee Young Lee	Old Course, St. Andrew's, Scotland
			Maria Hjorth	
2008	Jiyai Shin	270	Yani Tseng	Sunningdale GC, England
2009	Catriona Matthew	285	Karrie Webb	Royal Lytham & St. Annes, England
2010	Yani Tseng	277	Katherine Hull	Royal Birkdale CC, England
2011	Yani Tseng	272	Brittany Lang	Carnousie GL, Scotland
2012	Jiyai Shin	279	Inbee Park	Royal Liverpool GC, England
2013	Stacy Lewis	280	Hee Young Park	Old Course, St. Andrew's, Scotland

Note: Designated fourth major in 2001.

Evian Masters

Year	Winner	Score	Runner-Up	Site
2013	Suzann Pettersen	203	Lydia Ko	Evian Resort GC, Evian-les-Bains, France

Note: Designated fifth major in 2013.

THE LPGA TOUR
Most Career Wins†

	Wins		Wins		Wins
Kathy Whitworth	88	Sandra Haynie	42	*Juli Inkster	31
Mickey Wright	82	Babe Zaharias	41	Amy Alcott	29
Annika Sorenstam	72	*Karrie Webb	39	Jane Blalock	27
Patty Berg	60	Carol Mann	38	Lorena Ochoa	27
Louise Suggs	58	Patty Sheehan	35	Marlene Hagge	26
Betsy Rawls	55	Betsy King	34	Judy Rankin	26
Nancy Lopez	48	Beth Daniel	33	*Se Ri Pak	25
JoAnne Carner	43	Pat Bradley	31	Donna Caponi	24

†Through 9/22/13. *Active player.

Alltime Major Championship Winners

	LPGA	U.S. Open	Nabisco	Brit. Open	‡du Maurier	#Titleholders	†Western	U.S. Am	Brit. Am	Total
Patty Berg	0	1	0	0	0	7	7	1	0	16
Mickey Wright	4	4	0	0	0	2	3	0	0	13
Louise Suggs	1	2	0	0	0	4	4	1	1	13
Babe Zaharias	0	3	0	0	0	3	4	1	1	12
*Juli Inkster	2	2	2	0	1	0	0	3	0	10
Annika Sorenstam	3	3	3	1	0	0	0	0	0	10
Betsy Rawls	2	4	0	0	0	0	2	0	0	8
JoAnne Carner	0	2	0	0	0	0	0	5	0	7
*Karrie Webb	1	2	2	1	1	0	0	0	0	7
Kathy Whitworth	3	0	0	0	0	2	1	0	0	6
Pat Bradley	1	1	1	0	3	0	0	0	0	6
Patty Sheehan	3	2	1	0	0	0	0	0	0	6
Glenna Vare	0	0	0	0	0	0	0	6	0	6
Betsy King	1	2	3	0	0	0	0	0	0	6

*Active LPGA player.
#Major from 1937–1972. †Major from 1937–1967. ‡Major from 1979–2000.

Alltime Multiple Professional Major Winners

LPGA		U.S. OPEN		NABISCO/DINAH SHORE		WESTERN OPEN	
Mickey Wright	4	Betsy Rawls	4	Amy Alcott	3	Patty Berg	7
Nancy Lopez	3	Mickey Wright	4	Betsy King	3	Louise Suggs	4
Se Ri Pak	3	Susie Maxwell Berning	3	Annika Sorenstam	3	Babe Zaharias	4
Patty Sheehan	3	Hollis Stacy	3	*Juli Inkster	2	Mickey Wright	3
Annika Sorenstam	3	Babe Zaharias	3	*Karrie Webb	2	June Beebe	2
Kathy Whitworth	3	Annika Sorenstam	3			Opal Hill	2
Donna Caponi	2	JoAnne Carner	2	**TITLEHOLDERS**		Betty Jameson	2
Sandra Haynie	2	Donna Caponi	2	Patty Berg	7	Betsy Rawls	2
Mary Mills	2	Betsy King	2	Louise Suggs	4		
Betsy Rawls	2	Meg Mallon	2	Babe Zaharias	3	**DU MAURIER**	
Laura Davies	2	Patty Sheehan	2	Dorothy Kirby	2	Pat Bradley	3
*Juli Inkster	2	Louise Suggs	2	Marilynn Smith	2	Brandie Burton	2
*Yani Tseng	2	*Karrie Webb	2	Kathy Whitworth	2		
BRITISH OPEN		*Juli Inkster	2	Mickey Wright	2		
*Yani Tseng	2	*Inbee Park	2				
*Jiyai Shin	2						

*Active player.

THE LPGA TOUR *(Cont.)*

Season Money Leaders

	Earnings ($)		Earnings ($)		Earnings ($)
1950...Babe Zaharias	14,800	1971...Kathy Whitworth	41,181	1992...Dottie Mochrie	693,335
1951...Babe Zaharias	15,087	1972...Kathy Whitworth	65,063	1993...Betsy King	595,992
1952...Betsy Rawls	14,505	1973...Kathy Whitworth	82,864	1994...Laura Davies	687,201
1953...Louise Suggs	19,816	1974...JoAnne Carner	87,094	1995...Annika Sorenstam	666,533
1954...Patty Berg	16,011	1975...Sandra Palmer	76,374	1996...Karrie Webb	1,002,000
1955...Patty Berg	16,492	1976...Judy Rankin	150,734	1997...Annika Sorenstam	1,236,789
1956...Marlene Hagge	20,235	1977...Judy Rankin	122,890	1998...Annika Sorenstam	1,092,748
1957...Patty Berg	16,272	1978...Nancy Lopez	189,814	1999...Karrie Webb	1,591,959
1958...Beverly Hanson	12,639	1979...Nancy Lopez	197,489	2000...Karrie Webb	1,876,853
1959...Betsy Rawls	26,774	1980...Beth Daniel	231,000	2001...Annika Sorenstam	2,105,868
1960...Louise Suggs	16,892	1981...Beth Daniel	206,998	2002...Annika Sorenstam	2,863.904
1961...Mickey Wright	22,236	1982...JoAnne Carner	310,400	2003...Annika Sorenstam	2,029,506
1962...Mickey Wright	21,641	1983...JoAnne Carner	291,404	2004...Annika Sorenstam	2,544,707
1963...Mickey Wright	31,269	1984...Betsy King	266,771	2005...Annika Sorenstam	2,588,240
1964...Mickey Wright	29,800	1985...Nancy Lopez	416,472	2006...Lorena Ochoa	2,592,872
1965...Kathy Whitworth	28,658	1986...Pat Bradley	492,021	2007...Lorena Ochoa	4,364,994
1966...Kathy Whitworth	33,517	1987...Ayako Okamoto	466,034	2008...Lorena Ochoa	2,763,193
1967...Kathy Whitworth	32,937	1988...Sherri Turner	350,851	2009...Jiyai Shin	1,807,334
1968...Kathy Whitworth	48,379	1989...Betsy King	654,132	2010...Na Yeon Choi	1,871,166
1969...Carol Mann	49,152	1990...Beth Daniel	863,578	2011...Yani Tseng	2,921,713
1970...Kathy Whitworth	30,235	1991...Pat Bradley	763,118	2012...Inbee Park	2,287,080

LPGA Player of the Year

1966	Kathy Whitworth	1982	JoAnne Carner	1998	Annika Sorenstam
1967	Kathy Whitworth	1983	Patty Sheehan	1999	Karrie Webb
1968	Kathy Whitworth	1984	Betsy King	2000	Karrie Webb
1969	Kathy Whitworth	1985	Nancy Lopez	2001	Annika Sorenstam
1970	Sandra Haynie	1986	Pat Bradley	2002	Annika Sorenstam
1971	Kathy Whitworth	1987	Ayako Okamoto	2003	Annika Sorenstam
1972	Kathy Whitworth	1988	Nancy Lopez	2004	Annika Sorenstam
1973	Kathy Whitworth	1989	Betsy King	2005	Annika Sorenstam
1974	JoAnne Carner	1990	Beth Daniel	2006	Lorena Ochoa
1975	Sandra Palmer	1991	Pat Bradley	2007	Lorena Ochoa
1976	Judy Rankin	1992	Dottie Mochrie	2008	Lorena Ochoa
1977	Judy Rankin	1993	Betsy King	2009	Lorena Ochoa
1978	Nancy Lopez	1994	Beth Daniel	2010	Yani Tseng
1979	Nancy Lopez	1995	Annika Sorenstam	2011	Yani Tseng
1980	Beth Daniel	1996	Laura Davies	2012	Stacy Lewis
1981	JoAnne Carner	1997	Annika Sorenstam		

Vare Trophy: Best Scoring Average*

		Avg.			Avg.			Avg.
1953	Patty Berg	75.00	1973	Judy Rankin	73.08	1993	Nancy Lopez	70.83
1954	Babe Zaharias	75.48	1974	JoAnne Carner	72.87	1994	Beth Daniel	70.90
1955	Patty Berg	74.47	1975	JoAnne Carner	72.40	1995	Annika Sorenstam	71.00
1956	Patty Berg	74.57	1976	Judy Rankin	72.25	1996	Annika Sorenstam	70.47
1957	Louise Suggs	74.64	1977	Judy Rankin	72.16	1997	Karrie Webb	70.00
1958	Beverly Hanson	74.92	1978	Nancy Lopez	71.76	1998	Annika Sorenstam	69.99
1959	Betsy Rawls	74.03	1979	Nancy Lopez	71.20	1999	Karrie Webb	69.43
1960	Mickey Wright	73.25	1980	Amy Alcott	71.51	2000	Karrie Webb	70.05
1961	Mickey Wright	73.55	1981	JoAnne Carner	71.75	2001	Annika Sorenstam	69.42
1962	Mickey Wright	73.67	1982	JoAnne Carner	71.49	2002	Annika Sorenstam	68.70
1963	Mickey Wright	72.81	1983	JoAnne Carner	71.41	2003	Se Ri Pak	70.03
1964	Mickey Wright	72.46	1984	Patty Sheehan	71.40	2004	Grace Park	69.99
1965	Kathy Whitworth	72.61	1985	Nancy Lopez	70.73	2005	Annika Sorenstam	69.33
1966	Kathy Whitworth	72.60	1986	Pat Bradley	71.10	2006	Lorena Ochoa	69.23
1967	Kathy Whitworth	72.74	1987	Betsy King	71.14	2007	Lorena Ochoa	69.69
1968	Carol Mann	72.04	1988	Colleen Walker	71.26	2008	Lorena Ochoa	69.70
1969	Kathy Whitworth	72.38	1989	Beth Daniel	70.38	2009	Lorena Ochoa	70.16
1970	Kathy Whitworth	72.26	1990	Beth Daniel	70.54	2010	Na Yeon Choi	69.87
1971	Kathy Whitworth	72.88	1991	Pat Bradley	70.76	2011	Yani Tseng	69.66
1972	Kathy Whitworth	72.38	1992	Dottie Mochrie	70.80	2012	Inbee Park	70.21

*Must play 70 rounds or more to qualify; Annika Sorenstam compiled an average of 69.02 in 60 rounds in 2003.

U.S. Senior Open

Year	Winner	Score	Runner-Up	Site
1980	Roberto DeVicenzo	285	William C. Campbell	Winged Foot GC, Mamaroneck, NY
1981	Arnold Palmer* (70)	289	Bob Stone (74)	Oakland Hills CC, Birmingham, MI
			Billy Casper (77)	
1982	Miller Barber	282	Gene Littler, Dan Sikes, Jr.	Portland GC, Portland, OR
1983	Billy Casper* (75) (3)	288	Rod Funseth (75) (4)	Hazeltine GC, Chaska, MN
1984	Miller Barber	286	Arnold Palmer	Oak Hill CC, Rochester, NY
1985	Miller Barber	285	Roberto DeVicenzo	Edgewood Tahoe GC, Stateline, NV
1986	Dale Douglass	279	Gary Player	Scioto CC, Columbus, OH
1987	Gary Player	270	Doug Sanders	Brooklawn CC, Fairfield, CT
1988	Gary Player* (68)	288	Bob Charles (70)	Medinah CC, Medinah, IL
1989	Orville Moody	279	Frank Beard	Laurel Valley GC, Ligonier, PA
1990	Lee Trevino	275	Jack Nicklaus	Ridgewood CC, Paramus, NJ
1991	Jack Nicklaus* (65)	282	Chi Chi Rodriguez (69)	Oakland Hills CC, Birmingham, MI
1992	Larry Laoretti	275	Jim Colbert	Saucon Valley CC, Bethlehem, PA
1993	Jack Nicklaus	278	Tom Weiskopf	Cherry Hills CC, Englewood, CO
1994	Simon Hobday	274	Jim Albus	Pinehurst Resort & CC, Pinehurst, NC
1995	Tom Weiskopf	275	Jack Nicklaus	Congressional CC, Bethesda, MD
1996	Dave Stockton	277	Hale Irwin	Canterbury GC, Beachwood, OH
1997	Graham Marsh	280	Hale Irwin	Olympia Fields CC, Olympia Fields, IL
1998	Hale Irwin	285	Vicente Fernandez	Riviera CC, Pacific Palisades, CA
1999	Dave Eichelberger	281	Ed Dougherty	Des Moines G&CC, Des Moines, IA
2000	Hale Irwin	267	Bruce Fleisher	Saucon Valley CC, Bethlehem, PA
2001	Bruce Fleisher	280	Isao Aoki, Gil Morgan	Salem CC, Peabody, MA
2002	Don Pooley* (4-4-4-3-3)	274	Tom Watson (4-4-4-3-4)	Caves Valley GC, Owings Mill, MD
2003	Bruce Lietzke	277	Tom Watson	Inverness GC, Toledo, OH
2004	Peter Jacobsen	272	Hale Irwin	Bellerive CC, St. Louis, MO
2005	Allen Doyle	274	D.A. Weibring	NCR GC, Kettering, OH
			Loren Roberts	
2006	Allen Doyle	272	Tom Watson	Prairie Dunes CC, Hutchinson, KS
2007	Brad Bryant	282	Ben Crenshaw	Whistling Straits GC, Kohler, WI
2008	Eduardo Romero	274	Fred Funk	Broadmoor GC, Colorado Springs, CO
2009	Fred Funk	268	Joey Sindelar	Crooked Stick GC, Carmel, IN
2010	Bernhard Langer	272	Fred Couples	Sahalee GC, Sammamish, WA
2011	Olin Browne	269	Mark O'Meara	Inverness GC, Toledo, OH
2012	Roger Chapman	270	Fred Funk, Tom Lehman,	Indianwood G&CC, Lake Orion, MI
			Corey Pavin, Bernhard Langer	
2013	Kenny Perry	267	Fred Funk	Omaha CC, Omaha, NE

*Winner in playoff. Playoff scores are in parentheses. The 1983 playoff went to one hole of sudden death after an 18-hole playoff.

CHAMPIONS TOUR
Season Money Leaders

Year		Earnings ($)	Year		Earnings ($)	Year		Earnings ($)
1980	Don January	44,100	1991	Mike Hill	1,065,657	2002	Hale Irwin	3,028,304
1981	Miller Barber	83,136	1992	Lee Trevino	1,027,002	2003	Tom Watson	1,853,108
1982	Miller Barber	106,890	1993	Dave Stockton	1,175,944	2004	Craig Stadler	2,306,066
1983	Don January	237,571	1994	Dave Stockton	1,402,519	2005	Dana Quigley	2,170,258
1984	Don January	328,597	1995	Jim Colbert	1,444,386	2006	Jay Haas	2,420,227
1985	Peter Thomson	386,724	1996	Jim Colbert	1,627,890	2007	Jay Haas	2,581,001
1986	Bruce Crampton	454,299	1997	Hale Irwin	2,449,420	2008	Bernhard Langer	2,035,073
1987	Chi Chi Rodriguez	509,145	1998	Hale Irwin	2,861,945	2009	Bernhard Langer	2,164,451
1988	Bob Charles	533,929	1999	Bruce Fleisher	2,515,705	2010	Bernhard Langer	2,648,939
1989	Bob Charles	725,887	2000	Larry Nelson	2,708,005	2011	Tom Lehman	2,081,526
1990	Lee Trevino	1,190,518	2000	Larry Nelson	2,708,005	2012	Bernhard Langer	2,140,296
1990	Lee Trevino	1,190,518	2001	Allen Doyle	2,553,582			

Most Career Wins†

	Wins		Wins
*Hale Irwin	45	George Archer	19
Lee Trevino	29	Gary Player	19
Gil Morgan	25	Larry Nelson	19
Miller Barber	24	Bruce Fleisher	18
Bob Charles	23	Mike Hill	18
Don January	22	*Bernhard Langer	18
Chi Chi Rodriguez	22	*Jay Haas	16
Jim Colbert	20	Raymond Floyd	14
Bruce Crampton	20	Dave Stockton	14
		*Tom Watson	14

*Active player. †Through 9/22/13.

Ryder Cup Matches

Year	Results	Site
1927	United States 9½, Great Britain 2½	Worcester CC, Worcester, MA
1929	Great Britain 7, United States 5	Moortown GC, Leeds, England
1931	United States 9, Great Britain 3	Scioto CC, Columbus, OH
1933	Great Britain 6½, United States 5½	Southport and Ainsdale Courses, Southport, England
1935	United States 9, Great Britain 3	Ridgewood CC, Ridgewood, NJ
1937	United States 8, Great Britain 4	Southport and Ainsdale Courses, Southport, England
1939–1945	No tournament	
1947	United States 11, Great Britain 1	Portland GC, Portland, OR
1949	United States 7, Great Britain 5	Ganton GC, Scarborough, England
1951	United States 9½, Great Britain 2½	Pinehurst CC, Pinehurst, NC
1953	United States 6½, Great Britain 5½	Wentworth Club, Surrey, England
1955	United States 8, Great Britain 4	Thunderbird Ranch & CC, Palm Springs, CA
1957	Great Britain 7½, United States 4½	Lindrick GC, Yorkshire, England
1959	United States 8½, Great Britain 3½	Eldorado CC, Palm Desert, CA
1961	United States 14½, Great Britain 9½	Royal Lytham & St. Annes GC, St Anne's-on-the-Sea, England
1963	United States 23, Great Britain 9	East Lake CC, Atlanta, GA
1965	United States 19½, Great Britain 12½	Royal Birkdale GC, Southport, England
1967	United States 23½, Great Britain 8½	Champions GC, Houston, TX
1969	United States 16, Great Britain 16	Royal Birkdale GC, Southport, England
1971	United States 18½, Great Britain 13½	Old Warson CC, St. Louis, MO
1973	United States 19, Great Britain 13	Hon Co of Edinburgh Golfers, Muirfield, Scotland
1975	United States 21, Great Britain 11	Laurel Valley GC, Ligonier, PA
1977	United States 12½, Great Britain 7½	Royal Lytham & St. Annes GC, St. Annes-on-the-Sea, Eng.
1979	United States 17, Europe 11	Greenbrier CC, White Sulphur Springs, WV
1981	United States 18½, Europe 9½	Walton Heath GC, Surrey, England
1983	United States 14½, Europe 13½	PGA National GC, Palm Beach Gardens, FL
1985	Europe 16½, United States 11½	Belfry GC, Sutton Coldfield, England
1987	Europe 15, United States 13	Muirfield GC, Dublin, OH
1989	Europe 14, United States 14	Belfry GC, Sutton Coldfield, England
1991	United States 14½, Europe 13½	Ocean Course, Kiawah Island, SC
1993	United States 15, Europe 13	Belfry GC, Sutton Coldfield, England
1995	Europe 14½, United States 13½	Oak Hill CC, Rochester, NY
1997	Europe 14½, United States 13½	Valderrama GC, Sotogrande, Spain
1999	United States 14½, Europe 13½	The Country Club, Brookline, MA
2002	Europe 15½, Unites States 12½	Belfry GC, Sutton Coldfield, England
2004	Europe 18½, United States 9½	Oakland Hills CC, Bloomfield Hills, MI
2006	Europe 18½, United States 9½	The K Club, County Kildare, Ireland
2008	United States 16½, Europe 11½	Valhalla GC, Louisville, KY
2010	Europe 14½, United States 13½	Celtic Manor GC, Newport, Wales
2012	Europe 14½, United States 13½	Medinah CC, Medinah, IL

Team matches held every other year between U.S. professionals and those of Great Britain/Europe. Team members selected on basis of finishes in PGA and European tour events. Match in 2001 canceled due to 9/11 terrorist attacks.

Presidents Cup Matches

Year	Results	Site
1994	United States 20, International 12	Robert Trent Jones GC, Lake Manassas, VA
1996	United States 16½, International 15½	Robert Trent Jones GC, Lake Manassas, VA
1998	International 20½ United States 11½	Royal Melbourne GC, Melbourne, Australia
2000	United States 21½, International 10½	Robert Trent Jones GC, Lake Manassas, VA
2003	International 17, United States 17	Fan Court Hotel CC, George, South Africa
2005	United States 18½, International 15½	Robert Trent Jones GC, Lake Manassas, VA
2007	United States 19½, International 14½	Royal Montreal GC, Bizard, Quebec
2009	United States 19½, International 14½	Harding Park GC, San Francisco, CA
2011	United States 19, International 15	Royal Melbourne GC, Melbourne, Australia
2013	United States 18½, International 15½	Muirfield Village GC, Dublin, OH

A biennial event played in non-Ryder Cup years designed to provide non-European players with international team and match play.

Curtis Cup Matches

Year	Results	Site
1932	United States 5½, British Isles 3½	Wentworth GC, Wentworth, England
1934	United States 6½, British Isles 2½	Chevy Chase Club, Chevy Chase, MD
1936	United States 4½ British Isles 4½	King's Course, Gleneagles, Scotland
1938	United States 5½, British Isles 3½	Essex CC, Manchester, MA
1940–46	No tournament	
1948	United States 6½, British Isles 2½	Birkdale GC, Southport, England
1950	United States 7½, British Isles 1½	CC of Buffalo, Williamsville, NY
1952	British Isles 5, United States 4	Muirfield, Scotland
1954	United States 6, British Isles 3	Merion GC, Ardmore, PA
1956	British Isles 5, United States 4	Prince's GC, Sandwich Bay, England
1958	British Isles 4½, United States 4½	Brae Burn CC, West Newton, MA
1960	United States 6½, British Isles 2½	Lindrick GC, Worksop, England
1962	United States 8, British Isles 1	Broadmoor CG, Colorado Springs, CO
1964	United States 10½, British Isles 7½	Royal Porthcawl GC, Porthcawl, South Wales
1966	United States 13, British Isles 5	Va. Hot Springs G & TC, Hot Springs, VA
1968	United States 10½, British Isles 7½	Royal County Down GC, Newcastle, N. Ire.
1970	United States 11½, British Isles 6½	Brae Burn CC, West Newton, MA
1972	United States 10, British Isles 8	Western Gailes, Ayrshire, Scotland
1974	United States 13, British Isles 5	San Francisco GC, San Francisco, CA
1976	United States 11½, British Isles 6½	Royal Lytham & St. Annes GC, England
1978	United States 12, British Isles 6	Apawamis Club, Rye, NY
1980	United States 13, British Isles 5	St. Pierre G&CC, Chepstow, Wales
1982	United States 14½, British Isles 3½	Denver CC, Denver, CO
1984	United States 9½ British Isles 8½	Muirfield, Scotland
1986	British Isles 13, United States 5	Prairie Dunes CC, Hutchinson, KS
1988	British Isles 11, United States 7	Royal St. George's GC, Sandwich, England
1990	United States 14, British Isles 4	Somerset Hills CC, Bernardsville, NJ
1992	Great Britain/Ireland 10, United States 8	Royal Liverpool GC, Hoylake, England
1994	Great Britain/Ireland 9, United States 9	The Honors Course, Ooltewah, TN
1996	Great Britain/Ireland 11½, United States 6½	Killarney Golf & Fishing Club, Killarney, Ireland
1998	United States 10, Great Britain/Ireland 8	The Minikahda Club, Minneapolis, MN
2000	United States 10, Great Britain/Ireland 8	Ganton GC, North Yorkshire, England
2002	United States 11, Great Britain/Ireland 7	Fox Chapel GC, Pittsburgh, PA
2004	United States 10, Great Britain/Ireland 8	Formby GC, Merseyside, England
2006	United States 11½, Great Britain/Ireland 6½	Bandon Dunes GC, Bandon, OR
2008	United States 13, Great Britain/Ireland 7	Old Course, St. Andrews, Scotland
2010	United States 12½, Great Britain/Ireland 7½	Essex County Club, Manchester, MA
2012	Great Britain/Ireland 10½, United States 9½	Nairn GC, Nairn, Scotland

Women's amateur team competition every other year between the United States and Great Britain/Ireland. U.S. team members selected by USGA.

Solheim Cup Matches

Year	Results	Site
1990	United States 11½, Europe 4½	Lake Nona GC, Orlando, FL
1992	Europe 11½, United States 6½	Dalmahoy Hotel GC, Edinburgh, Scotland
1994	United States 13, Europe 7	The Greenbrier, White Sulphur Springs, WV
1996	United States 17, Europe 11	Marriott St Pierre Hotel & CC, Chepstow, Wales
1998	United States 16, Europe 12	Muirfield Village GC, Dublin, OH
2000	Europe 14½, United States, 11½	Loch Lomond GC, Luss, Scotland
2002	United States 15½, Europe 12½	Interlachen CC, Minneapolis, MN
2003	Europe 17½, United States 10½	Barseback G&CC, Malmo, Sweden
2005	United States 15½, Europe 12½	Crooked Stick GC, Carmel, IN
2007	United States 16, Europe 12	Halmstad GC, Halmstad, Sweden
2009	United States 16, Europe 12	Rich Harvest Farms GC, Sugar Grove, IL
2011	Europe 15, United States 13	Killeen Castle GC, Ireland
2013	Europe 18, United States 10	Colorado GC, Parker, CO

Women's team matches held every other year between U.S. professionals and those of Europe. Team members selected on the basis of finishes in LPGA and European tour events.

Soccer

Using his head: L.A.'s Omar Gonzalez led the Galaxy to a 3–1 win over Houston for the team's second consecutive MLS Cup title

2012 Major League Soccer

2012 Final Standings

WESTERN CONFERENCE

Team	GP	W	L	T	Pts	GF	GA
†San Jose	34	19	6	9	66	72	43
*Salt Lake	34	17	11	6	57	46	35
*Seattle	34	15	8	11	56	51	33
**Los Angeles	34	16	12	6	54	59	47
**Vancouver	34	11	13	10	43	35	41
Dallas	34	9	13	12	39	42	47
Colorado	34	11	19	4	37	44	50
Portland	34	8	16	10	34	34	56
Chivas USA	34	7	18	9	30	24	58

EASTERN CONFERENCE

Team	GP	W	L	T	Pts	GF	GA
†Kansas City	34	18	7	9	63	42	27
*D.C. United	34	17	10	7	58	53	43
*New York	34	16	9	9	57	57	46
**Chicago	34	17	11	6	57	46	41
**Houston	34	14	9	11	53	48	41
Columbus	34	15	12	7	52	44	44
Montreal	34	12	16	6	42	45	51
Philadelphia	34	10	18	6	36	37	45
New England	34	9	17	8	35	39	44
Toronto	34	5	21	8	23	36	62

Note: Three points for win; one point for tie. †Conference champion. *Qualified for playoffs. **Qualified for wild card play-in.

GOALS LEADERS

Player, Team	GP	G
Chris Wondolowski, SJ	32	27
Kenny Cooper, NY	33	18
Alvaro Saborio, SL	31	17
Robbie Keane, LA	28	16
Thierry Henry, NY	25	15
Eddie Johnson, SEA	28	14
Fredy Montero, SEA	33	13
Alan Gordon, SJ	23	13
Chris Pontius, DC	31	12
Will Bruin, HOU	32	12

ASSISTS LEADERS

Player, Team	GP	A
Graham Zusi, KC	32	15
Landon Donovan, LA	26	14
Martin Chavez, SJ	27	13
Mauro Rosales, SEA	27	13
Brad Davis, HOU	31	12
Dwayne De Rosario, DC	26	12
Thierry Henry, NY	25	12
Felipe Martins, MTL	30	10

Four tied with 9.

SAVES LEADERS

Player, Team	Saves	GAA
Andy Gruenebaum, CLB	124	1.26
Dan Kennedy, CHV	109	1.69
Sean Johnson, CHI	108	1.24
Matt Pickens, COL	107	1.54
Troy Perkins, MTL	101	1.40
Kevin Hartman, DAL	98	1.40
Zac MacMath, PHI	93	1.34
Matt Reis, NE	92	1.44
Bill Hamid, DC	88	1.03
Tally Hall, HOU	88	1.19

MLS Regular Season MVP: Chris Wondolowski, San Jose.

2012 MLS Playoffs

CONF. SEMIS (TWO LEGS)

San Jose	1	1—2
Los Angeles	0	3—3

Seattle	0	1—1
Salt Lake City	0	0—0

CONF. FINALS (TWO LEGS)

Los Angeles	3	1—4
Seattle	0	2—2

CONF. SEMIS (TWO LEGS)

Houston	2	1—3
Kansas City	0	0—0

D.C.	1	1—2
New York	1	0—1

CONF. FINALS (TWO LEGS)

Houston	3	1—4
D.C.	1	1—2

2012 MLS CUP (December 1, 2012 in Carson, California)

Houston	1	0—1
Los Angeles	0	3—3

FIRST HALF: Scoring: 1, Hou, Carr (Moffat), 44th minute.

SECOND HALF: Scoring: 3, LA, Gonzalez (Juninho, Franklin), 60th minute; Donovan, 65th minute; Keane, stoppage time.

Houston: Hall, Boswell, Sarkodie (Ching 77) , Ashe, Taylor, Moffat (Barnes 71), Clark, Davis, Garcia, Bruin, Carr (Kandji 59).

Los Angeles: Saunders, Franklin, Gonzalez, Dunivant, Meyer, Wilhelmsson (Buddle 74), Juninho (Stephens 76) , Beckham (Sarvas 89) , Magee, Keane, Donovan.

Attendance: 30,510. Referee: S. Petrescu. Asst. Referees: D. Belleau, D. Clark.

MLS Cup MVP: Omar Gonzalez, Los Angeles.

Group Stage

GROUP A						GROUP B						GROUP C				
Country	MP	W	L	D	Pts	Country	MP	W	L	D	Pts	Country	MP	W	L	D	Pts
*Germany	3	3	0	0	9	*England	3	2	0	1	7	*Sweden	3	3	0	0	9
*France	3	2	1	0	6	*Japan	3	2	1	0	6	*United States	3	2	1	0	6
Nigeria	3	1	2	0	3	Mexico	3	0	1	2	2	North Korea	3	0	2	1	1
Canada	3	0	3	0	0	New Zealand	3	0	2	1	1	Colombia	3	0	2	1	1

GROUP D					
Country	MP	W	L	D	Pts
*Brazil	3	3	0	0	9
*Australia	3	2	1	0	6
Norway	3	1	2	0	3
Equa. Guinea	3	0	3	0	0

*Moved on to quarterfinals.
Note: in group play, three points are awarded for a win, one for a tie.

Quarterfinals

Germany	0 0 0—0	Sweden	2 1—3	England	0 1 0—1 (3)	Brazil	0 1 1—2 (3)
Japan	0 0 1—1	Australia	1 0—1	France	0 1 0—1 (4)	U.S.	1 0 1—2 (5)
a.e.t.				a.e.t. (PSO)		a.e.t. (PSO)	

Semifinals

| Japan | 1 2—3 | France | 0 1—1 |
| Sweden | 1 0—1 | U.S. | 1 2—3 |

Third-Place Consolation Match

| Sweden | 1 1—2 |
| France | 0 1—1 |

2011 Women's World Cup Final

(July 17, 2011 in Frankfurt, Germany)

| Japan | 0 | | 1—— 2 (3) |
| United States | 0 | | 1—— 2 (1) |

FIRST HALF: Scoring: None.

SECOND HALF: Scoring: 1, United States, Morgan (Rapinoe), 69th minute; 1, Japan, Miyama, 81st minute.

EXTRA TIME: Scoring: 1, United States, Wambach (Morgan), 104th minute; 1, Japan, Sawa (Miyama), 117th minute.

PENALTY SHOOT-OUT: Scoring: 1, United States, Boxx (saved), Lloyd (missed), Heath (saved), Wambach (goal); 3, Japan: Miyama (goal), Nagasato (saved), Sakaguchi (goal), Kumagai (goal).

Japan: Kaihori, Kinga, Iwashimizu, Kumagai, Sakaguchi, Ando (Nagasato 66), Miyama, Kawasumi, Sawa, Ohno (Maruyama 66, Iwabuchi 119), Sameshima.

United States: Solo, Rampone, Le Peilbet, Boxx, O'Reilly, Lloyd, Krieger, Cheney (Morgan 46), Rapinoe (Heath 114), Buehler, Wambach.

Referee: Bibiana Steinhaus. Asst. Referees: Marina Wozniak, Katrin Rafalksi.

Final match attendance: 48,817.

2011 World Cup Golden Boot & Golden Ball Winner: Homare Sawa, Japan

The World Cup

Results—Men

Year	Champion	Score	Runner-Up	Winning Coach
1930	Uruguay	4–2	Argentina	Alberto Supicci
1934	Italy	2–1	Czechoslovakia	Vittorio Pozzo
1938	Italy	4–2	Hungary	Vittorio Pozzo
1950	Uruguay	2–1	Brazil	Juan Lopez
1954	West Germany	3–2	Hungary	Sepp Herberger
1958	Brazil	5–2	Sweden	Vicente Feola
1962	Brazil	3–1	Czechoslovakia	Aymore Moreira
1966	England	4–2	West Germany	Alf Ramsey
1970	Brazil	4–1	Italy	Mario Zagalo
1974	West Germany	2–1	Netherlands	Helmut Schoen
1978	Argentina	3–1	Netherlands	César Menotti
1982	Italy	3–1	West Germany	Enzo Bearzot
1986	Argentina	3–2	West Germany	Carlos Bilardo
1990	West Germany	1–0	Argentina	Franz Beckenbauer
1994	Brazil	0–0 (3–2)	Italy	Carlos Alberto Parreira
1998	France	3–0	Brazil	Aime Jacquet
2002	Brazil	2–0	Germany	Luis Felipe Scolari
2006	Italy	1–1 (5–3)	France	Marcello Lippi
2010	Spain	1–0 (2 OT)	Netherlands	Vicente Del Bosque

Alltime World Cup Wins

Nation	Matches	W	T	L	Goals For	Goals Against	Nation	Matches	W	T	L	Goals For	Goals Against
Brazil	97	67	15	15	210	89	Senegal	5	2	2	1	7	6
*Germany	99	60	19	20	206	119	Ukraine	5	2	1	2	5	7
Italy	80	44	21	15	126	78	Cote d'Ivoire	6	2	1	3	9	9
Argentina	70	37	13	20	123	79	East Germany	6	2	2	2	5	6
Spain	56	28	12	16	88	57	Norway	8	2	3	3	7	9
England	59	26	19	14	77	52	Algeria	9	2	2	5	6	12
France	54	25	11	18	96	70	South Africa	9	2	4	3	11	15
Netherlands	43	22	10	11	71	42	Australia	10	2	3	5	8	16
Uruguay	47	18	12	17	76	64	Ireland	13	2	8	3	10	10
†Russia	37	17	6	14	64	44	Morocco	13	2	4	7	12	17
Yugoslavia	37	17	6	14	60	46	Saudi Arabia	13	2	2	9	9	32
Sweden	46	16	13	17	74	71	Cuba	3	1	1	1	5	12
Poland	31	15	5	11	44	40	Jamaica	3	1	0	2	3	9
Hungary	32	15	3	14	87	58	Slovakia	3	1	1	1	4	5
Portugal	23	12	3	8	39	23	Wales	5	1	3	1	4	4
Austria	29	12	4	13	43	49	Greece	6	1	0	5	2	15
Czech Republic	33	12	5	16	47	48	Serbia	6	1	0	5	4	13
Mexico	49	12	13	24	52	87	Slovenia	6	1	1	4	5	10
Belgium	36	10	9	17	46	64	North Korea	7	1	1	5	6	21
Chile	29	9	6	14	34	45	Iran	9	1	2	6	6	17
Switzerland	29	9	6	14	38	51	Tunisia	12	1	4	7	8	17
Denmark	16	8	2	6	27	24	Angola	3	0	2	1	1	2
Romania	21	8	5	8	30	32	Israel	3	0	2	1	1	3
Paraguay	27	7	10	10	30	38	Indonesia	1	0	0	1	0	6
United States	29	7	5	17	32	57	Egypt	4	0	2	2	3	6
Croatia	13	6	2	5	15	11	Kuwait	3	0	1	2	2	6
Turkey	10	5	1	4	20	17	Trinidad and Tobago	3	0	1	2	0	4
South Korea	28	5	8	15	28	60	New Zealand	6	0	3	3	4	14
Ghana	9	4	2	3	9	10	Honduras	6	0	3	3	2	6
Japan	14	4	3	7	12	16	United Arab Emirates	3	0	0	3	2	11
Nigeria	14	4	2	8	17	21	Haiti	3	0	0	3	2	14
Peru	15	4	3	8	19	31	Iraq	3	0	0	3	1	4
Cameroon	20	4	7	9	17	34	Togo	3	0	0	3	1	6
Scotland	23	4	7	12	25	41	Canada	3	0	0	3	0	5
Ecuador	7	3	0	4	7	8	China	3	0	0	3	0	9
Costa Rica	10	3	1	6	12	21	Dem. Rep. of Congo	3	0	0	3	0	14
Colombia	13	3	2	8	14	22	Bolivia	6	0	1	5	1	20
Northern Ireland	13	3	5	5	13	23	El Salvador	6	0	0	6	1	22
Bulgaria	26	3	8	15	22	52							

*Includes West Germany 1950–90. †Includes USSR 1930–1990.
Note: Matches decided by penalty kicks are shown as drawn games.

World Cup Final Box Scores

URUGUAY 1930

| Uruguay | ....1 | 3 —4 |
| Argentina | ....2 | 0 —2 |

FIRST HALF: Scoring: 1, Uruguay, Dorado (12); 2, Argentina, Peucelle (20); 3, Argentina, Stabile (37).

SECOND HALF: Scoring: 4, Uruguay, Cea (57); 5, Uruguay, Iriarte (68); 6, Uruguay, Castro (89).

Argentina: Botosso, Della Toree, Paternoster, J. Evaristo, Monti, Suarez, Peucelle, Varallo, Stabile, Ferreira, M. Evaristo.

Uruguay: Ballesteros, Nasazzi, Mascheroni, Andrade, Fernandez, Gestido, Dorado, Scarone, Castro, Cea, Iriarte.

Referee: Langenus (Belgium).

ITALY 1934

| Italy | ....0 | 1 | 1—2 |
| Czechoslovakia | ......0 | 1 | 0—1 |

SECOND HALF: Scoring: 1, Czech., Puc (70); 2, Italy, Orsi (80).

OVERTIME: Scoring: 3, Italy, Schiavio (95).

Italy: Combi, Monzeglio, Allemandi, Ferraris Monti, Monti, Bertolini, Guaita, Meazza, Schiavio, Ferrari, Orsi.

Czechoslovakia: Planicka, Zenisek, Ctyroky, Kostalek, Cambal, Cambal, Krcil, Junek, Svoboda, Sobotka, Nejedly, Puc.

Referee: Eklind (Sweden).

FRANCE 1938

| Italy | ....3 | 1 —4 |
| Hungary | ....1 | 1 —2 |

FIRST HALF: Scoring: 1, Italy, Colaussi (5); 2, Hungary, Titkos (7); 3, Italy, Piola (16); 4, Italy, Piola (35).

SECOND HALF: Scoring: 5, Hungary, Sarosi (70); 6, Italy, Colaussi (82).

Italy: Olivieri, Foni, Rava, Serantoni, Andreolo, Locatelli, Biavati, Meazza, Piola, Ferrari, Colaussi.

Hungary: Szabo, Polger, Biro, Szalay, Szucs, Lazar, Sas, Vincze, Sarosi, Zsengeller, Titkos.

Referee: Capdeville (France).

BRAZIL 1950

| Uruguay | ....0 | 2 —2 |
| Brazil | ....0 | 1 —1 |

SECOND HALF: Scoring: 1, Brazil, Friaca (47); 2, Uruguay, Schiaffino (66); 3, Uruguay, Ghiggia (79).

Uruguay: Maspoli, Gonzales, Tejera, Gambretta, Varela, Andrade, Ghiggia, Perez, Miguez, Schiffiano, Moran.

Brazil: Barbosa, Augusto, Juvenal, Bauer, Banilo, Bigode, Friaca, Zizinho, Ademir, Jair, Chico.

Referee: Reader (England).

SWITZERLAND 1954

| West Germany | ......2 | 1 —3 |
| Hungary | ....2 | 2 —2 |

FIRST HALF: Scoring: 1, Hungary, Puskas (6); 2, Hungary, Czibor (8); 3, W Germany, Morlock (10); 4, W Germany, Rahn (18).

SECOND HALF: Scoring: 5, W Germany, Rahn (84).

West Germany: Turek, Posipal, Kohlmeyer, Eckel, Liebrich, Mai, Rahn, Morlock, O.Walter, F. Walter, Schaefer.

Hungary: Grosics, Buzansky, Lantos, Bozsik, Lorant, Zakarias, Czibor, Kocsis, Hidegkuti, Puskas, Toth.

Referee: Ling (England).

SWEDEN 1958

| Brazil | ....2 | 3 —5 |
| Sweden | ....1 | 1 —2 |

FIRST HALF: Scoring:1, Sweden, Liedholm (3); 2, Brazil, Vava (9); 3, Brazil, Vava (32).

SECOND HALF: Scoring: 4, Brazil, Pelé (55); 5, Brazil, Zagalo (68); 6, Sweden Simonsson (80); 7, Brazil, Pelé (90).

Brazil: Glymar, D. Santos, N. Santos, Zito, Bellini, Orlando, Garrincha, Didi, Vava, Pelé, Zagalo.

Sweden: Svensson, Bergmark, Axbom, Boerjesson, Gustavsson, Parling, Hamrin, Gren, Simonsson, Liedholm, Skoglund.

Referee: Guigue (France).

CHILE 1962

| Brazil | ....1 | 2 —3 |
| Czechoslovakia | .....1 | 0 —1 |

FIRST HALF: Scoring: 1, Czech., Masopust (15); 2, Brazil, Amarildo (17).

SECOND HALF: Scoring: 3, Brazil, Zito (68); 4, Brazil, Vava (77).

Brazil: Glymar, D. Santos, N. Santos, Zito, Mauro, Zozimo, Garrincha, Didi, Vava, Amarildo, Zagalo.

Czechoslovakia: Schroiff, Tichy, Novak, Pluskal, Popluhar, Masopust, Pospichal, Scherer, Kvasnak, Kadraba, Jelinek.

Referee: Latychev (USSR).

ENGLAND 1966

| England | ....1 | 1 | 2 —4 |
| West Germany | ....1 | 1 | 0 —2 |

FIRST HALF: Scoring: 1, W Germany, Haller (12); 2, England, Hurst (18).

SECOND HALF: Scoring: 3, England, Peters (78); 4, W. Germany, Weber (90).

EXTRA TIME: Scoring: 5, England, Hurst (101); 6, England, Hurst (120).

England: Banks, Cohen, Wilson, Stiles, J. Charlton, Moore, Ball, Hurst, Hunt, R. Charlton, Peters.

West Germany: Tilkowski, Hottges, Schmellinger, Beckenbauer, Schulz, Weber, Held, Haller, Seeler, Overath, Emmerich.

Referee: Dienst (Switzerland).

World Cup Final Box Scores *(Cont.)*

MEXICO 1970

| Brazil..........................l | 3 ——4 |
| Italy ....l | 0 ——l |

FIRST HALF: Scoring: 1, Brazil, Pelé (18); 2, Italy, Boninsegna (32).

SECOND HALF: Scoring: 3, Brazil, Gerson (65); 4, Brazil, Jairzinho (70); 5, Brazil, Alberto (86).

Brazil: Feliz, Alberto, Brito, Wilson, Piazza, Everaldo, Clodoaldo, Gerson, Jairzinho, Tostao, Pelé, Rivelino.

Italy: Albertosi, Burgnich, Cera, Rosato, Facchetti, Bertini (Juliano), Mazzola, De Sisti, Domenghini, Boninsegna (Rivera), Riva.

Referee: Glockner (E Germany).

WEST GERMANY 1974

| West Germany......2 | 0 ——2 |
| Netherlands............l | 0 ——l |

FIRST HALF: Scoring: 1, Netherlands, Neeskens, PK (1); 2, W Germany, Breitner, PK (26); 3, W Germany, Müller (44).

West Germany: Maier, Vogts, Beckenbauer, Schwarzenbeck, Breitner, Hoeness, Bonhof, Overath, Grabowski, Müller, Holzenbein.

Netherlands: Jongbloed, Suurbier, Rijsbergen (de Jong), Haan, Krol, Jansen, Neeskens, van Hanagem, Cruyff, Rensenbrink (van der Kerkhof).

Referee: Taylor (England).

ARGENTINA 1978

| Argentina ....l | 0 | 2 ——3 |
| Netherlands...........0 | l | 0 ——l |

FIRST HALF: Scoring: 1, Argentina, Kempes (38).

SECOND HALF: Scoring: 2, Netherlands, Nanninga (81).

EXTRA TIME: Scoring: 3, Arg., Kempes (104); 4, Arg., Bertoni (114).

Argentina: Fillol, Olguin, Galvan, Passarella, Tarantini, Ardiles (Larrosa), Gallego, Kempes, Bertoni, Luque, Ortiz (Houseman).

Netherlands: Jongbloed, Jansen (Suurbier), Krol, Brandts, Poortvliet, Neeskens, Haan, W. van der Kerkhoff, R. van der Kerkhoff, Rep (Nanninga), Rensenbrink.

Referee: Gonella (Italy).

SPAIN 1982

| Italy ....0 | 3 ——3 |
| West Germany......0 | l ——l |

SECOND HALF: Scoring: 1, Italy, Rossi (57); 2, Italy, Tardelli (68); 3, Italy, Altobelli (81); 4, W Germany, Breitner (83).

Italy: Zoff, Bergomi, Scirea, Collovati, Cabrini, Oriali, Gentile, Tardelli, Conti, Rossi, Graziani (Altobelli, Causio).

West Germany: Schumacher, Kaltz, Stielike, K. Foerster, B. Foerster, Dremmler (Hrubesch), Breitner, Briegel, Rummenigge (Müller), Fischcher (Littbarski).

Referee: Coelho (Brazil).

MEXICO 1986

| Argentina ....l | 2 ——3 |
| West Germany......0 | 2 ——2 |

FIRST HALF: Scoring: 1, Argentina, Brown (22).

SECOND HALF: Scoring: 2, Arg., Valdano (55); 3, W Germ., Rummenigge (73); 4, W Germ., Voller (81); 5, Arg., Burruchaga (83).

Argentina: Pumpido, Brown, Cuciuffo, Ruggeri, Olarticoecha, Bastista, Giusti, Burruchaga (Trobbiani 90), Enrique, Maradona, Valdona.

West Germany: Schumacher, Jakobs, Forster, Eder, Brehme, Matthaus, Berthold, Magath (Hoeness 62), Briegel, Rummenigge, Allofs (Voller 46).

Referee: Filho (Brazil).

ITALY 1990

| West Germany ....0 | l —— l |
| Argentina ....0 | 0 ——0 |

SECOND HALF: Scoring: 1, W Germany, Brehme, PK (84).

West Germany: Illgner, Brehme, Kohler, Augenthaler, Buchwald, Berthold (Reuter), Littbarski, Haessler, Mattaeus, Voeller, Klinsmann.

Argentina: Goychoechea, Lorenzo, Serrizuela, Sensini, Ruggeri (Monzon), Simon, Basualdo, Burruchag (Calderon), Maradona, Troglio, Dezottir.

Referee: Coelho (Brazil).

UNITED STATES 1994

| Italy ....0 | 0 | 0——0 |
| Brazil..........................0 | 0 | 0——0 |

Brazil won on penalty kicks, 3–2.

Scoring: None. Shootout goals: Italy—2: Albertini, Evani; Brazil—3: Romario, Branco, Dunga.

Italy: Pagliuca, Benarrivo, Maldini, Baresi, Mussi (Apolloni 35), Albertini, D. Baggio (Evani 95), Berti, Donadoni, Baggio, Massaro.

Brazil: Taffarel, Jorginho (Cafu 21), Branco, Aldair, Santos, Silva, Dunga, Zinho (Viola 106), Mazinho, Bebeto, Romario.

Referee: Puhl (Hungary).

FRANCE 1998

| Brazil ....0 | 0——0 |
| France..........................2 | l——3 |

FIRST HALF: Scoring: 1, France, Zidane (27); 2, France, Zidane (45).

SECOND HALF: Scoring: 3, France, Petit (90).

Brazil: Taffarel, Cafu, Aldair, Baiano, Carlos, Sampaio (Edmundo 74), Dunga, Rivaldo, Leonardo, (Denilson 46), Bebeto, Ronaldo.

France: Barthez, Lizarazu, Desailly, Thuram, Leboeuf, Djorkaeff (Vieira 75), Deschamps, Zidane, Petit, Karembeu (Boghossian 57), Guivarc'h (Dugarry 66).

Referee: Belqola (Morocco).

World Cup Final Box Scores *(Cont.)*

KOREA/JAPAN 2002

Brazil	0	2——2
Germany	0	0——0

SECOND HALF: Scoring: 1, Brazil, Ronaldo (67); 2, Brazil, Ronaldo (79).

Brazil: Marcos, Cafu, Lucio, Roque Junior, Edmilson, Carlos, Silva, Ronaldo (Denilson, 90), Rivaldo, Ronaldinho (Juninho, 85), Kleberson.

Germany: Kahn, Linke, Ramelow, Neuville, Hamann, Klose (Bierhoff, 74), Jeremies (Asamoah, 77), Bode (Ziege, 84), Schneider, Metzelder, Frings.

Referee: Collina (Italy).

GERMANY 2006

Italy	1	0	0——1
France	1	0	0——1

Italy won on penalty kicks, 5–3.

FIRST HALF: Scoring: 1, France, Zidane (7); 1, Italy, Materazzi (19).

SHOOTOUT GOALS: Italy—Pirlo, Materazzi, De Rossi, Del Piero, Grosso; France—Wiltord, Abidal, Sagnol.

Italy: Buffon, Zambrotta, Cannavaro, Materazzi, Grosso, Camoranesi (Del Piero 86), Pirlo, Gattuso, Perrotta (Iaquinta 61), Totti (De Rossi 61), Toni.

France: Barthez, Sagnol, Thuram, Gallas, Abidal, Ribery (Trezeguet 100), Vieira (Diarra 56), Makelele, Zidane, Malouda, Henry (Wiltord 107).

Referee: Elizondo (Argentina).

SOUTH AFRICA 2010

Spain	0	0	0	1——1
Netherlands	0	0	0	0——0

2ND EXTRA TIME: Scoring: 1, Spain, Iniesta (Fabregas), 116.

Spain: Casillas, Pique, Puyol, Iniesta, Pedro (Navas 60), Xavi, Capdevila, Fabregas (Alonso 87), Ramos, Busquets, Villa (Torres 105).

Netherlands: Stekelenburg, Van der Wiel, Heitinga, Mathijsen, Van Brommel, Robben, Sneijder, Kuyt (Elia 71), De Jong (Van der Vaart 99), Van Bronckhorst (Braafheid 105), Van Persie.

Referee: Webb (England).

Alltime Leaders

GOALS

Player, Nation	Tournaments	Goals	Player, Nation	Tournaments	Goals
Ronaldo, Brazil	1994, '98, 2002, '06	15	Teofilo Cubillas, Peru	1970, '78, '82	10
Gerd Müller, West Germany	1970, '74	14	Grzegorz Lato, Poland	1974, '78, '82	10
Miroslav Klose, Germany	2002, '06, '10	14	Ademir, Brazil	1950	9
Just Fontaine, France	1958	13	Eusebio, Portugal	1966	9
Pelé, Brazil	1958, '62, '66, '70	12	Jairzinho, Brazil	1970, '74	9
Sandor Kocsis, Hungary	1954	11	Paolo Rossi, Italy	1982, '86	9
Jurgen Klinsmann, Germany	1990, '94, '98	11	K.H. Rummenigge, W. Germany	1978, '82, '86	9
Helmut Rahn, West Germany	1954, '58	10	Uwe Seeler, West Germany	1958, '62, '66, '70	9
Gary Lineker, England	1986, '90	10	Vava, Brazil	1958, '62	9
Gabriel Batistuta, Argentina	1998, 2002	10	Christian Vieri, Italy	1998, 2002	9

LEADING SCORER, CUP BY CUP

Year	Player, Nation	Goals	Year	Player, Nation	Goals
1930	Guillermo Stabile, Argentina	8	1978	Mario Kempes, Argentina	6
1934	Oldrich Nejedly, Czechoslovakia	5	1982	Paolo Rossi, Italy	6
1938	Leonidas da Silva, Brazil	8	1986	Gary Lineker, England	6
1950	Ademir de Menenzes, Brazil	9	1990	Salvatore Schillaci, Italy	6
1954	Sandor Kocsis, Hungary	11	1994	Hristo Stoichkov, Bulgaria	6
1958	Just Fontaine, France	13		Oleg Salenko, Russia	
1962	Florian Albert, Hungary	4	1998	Davor Suker, Croatia	6
	Valentin Ivanov, USSR, Garrincha, Brazil,		2002	Ronaldo, Brazil	8
	Vava, Brazil, Drazan Jerkovic, Yugoslavia,		2006	Miroslav Klose, Germany	5
	Leonel Sanchez, Chile		2010	Thomas Mueller, Germany	5
1966	Eusebio Ferreira, Portugal	9		Diego Forlan, Uruguay	
1970	Gerd Müller, W Germany	10		Wesley Sneijder, Netherlands	
1974	Grzegorz Lato, Poland	7		David Villa, Spain	

Most Goals, Individual, One Game

Goals	Player, Nation	Score	Date
5	Oleg Salenko, Russia	Russia–Cameroon, 6–1	6-28-94
4	Ernest Wilimowski, Poland	Brazil–Poland, 6–5	6-5-38
4	Ademir, Brazil	Brazil–Sweden, 7–1	7-9-50
4	Sandor Kocsis, Hungary	Hungary–W Germany, 8–3	6-20-54
4	Just Fontaine, France	France–W Germany, 6–3	6-28-58
4	Eusebio, Portugal	Portugal–N Korea, 5–3	7-23-66
4	Emilio Butragueño, Spain	Spain–Denmark, 5–1	6-18-86

Note: In addition to the seven players above, 39 men have scored 42 World Cup hat tricks. Gerd Müller of West Germany, Sandor Kocsis of Hungary and Just Fontaine of France are the only men to score three or more World Cup goals twice. Geoff Hurst of England is the only man to have a hat trick in a final match (7-30-66 vs. West Germany).

Attendance and Goal Scoring, Year by Year

Year	Site	No. of Games	Goals	Goals/Game	Attendance	Avg. Att.
1930	Uruguay	18	70	3.89	434,500	24,139
1934	Italy	17	70	4.12	395,000	23,235
1938	France	18	84	4.67	483,000	26,833
1950	Brazil	22	88	4.00	1,337,000	60,773
1954	Switzerland	26	140	5.38	943,000	36,269
1958	Sweden	35	126	3.60	868,000	24,800
1962	Chile	32	89	2.78	776,000	24,250
1966	England	32	89	2.78	1,614,677	50,459
1970	Mexico	32	95	2.97	1,673,975	52,312
1974	W Germany	38	97	2.55	1,774,022	46,685
1978	Argentina	38	102	2.68	1,610,215	42,374
1982	Spain	52	146	2.80	1,856,277	35,698
1986	Mexico	52	132	2.54	2,441,731	46,956
1990	Italy	52	115	2.21	2,514,443	48,354
1994	United States	52	140	2.69	3,567,415	68,604
1998	France	64	171	2.67	2,775,400	43,366
2002	Korea/Japan	64	161	2.52	2,705,216	42,269
2006	Germany	64	147	2.23	3,353,655	52,400
2010	South Africa	64	145	2.27	3,178,856	49,670
Totals		**708**	**2,046**	**2.89**	**31,597,166**	**44,629**

Results—Women's World Cup

Year	Champion	Score	Runner-Up	Third Place	Fourth Place
1991	United States	2–1	Norway	Sweden	Germany
1995	Norway	2–0	Germany	United States	China
1999	United States	0–0 (5–4 PK)	China	Brazil	Norway
2003	Germany	2–1	Sweden	United States	Canada
2007	Germany	2–0	Brazil	United States	Norway
2011	Japan	2–2 (3–1 PK)	United States	Sweden	France

Major League Soccer Finals

MLS Cup Results

Year	Champion	Score	Runner-up	Regular Season MVP
1996	D.C. United	3–2 (OT)	Los Angeles	Carlos Valderrama, TB
1997	D.C. United	2–1	Colorado	Preki, KC
1998	Chicago	2–0	D.C. United	Marco Etcheverry, D.C.
1999	D.C. United	2–0	Los Angeles	Jason Kreis, Dal
2000	Kansas City	1–0	Chicago	Tony Meola, KC
2001	San Jose	2–1 (OT)	Los Angeles	Alex Pineda Chacon, Mia
2002	Los Angeles	1–0 (OT)	New England	Carlos Ruiz, LA
2003	San Jose	4–2	Chicago	Preki, KC
2004	D.C. United	3–2	Kansas City	Amado Guevara, NY
2005	Los Angeles	1–0 (OT)	New England	Taylor Twellman, NE
2006	Houston	1–1 (OT, 4-3 PKs)	New England	Christian Gomez, D.C.
2007	Houston	2–1	New England	Luciano Emilio, D.C.
2008	Columbus	3–1	New York	Guillermo Schelotto, Col
2009	Real Salt Lake	1–1 (OT, 5–4 PKs)	Los Angeles	Landon Donovan, LA
2010	Colorado	2–1 (OT)	FC Dallas	David Ferreira, Dal
2011	Los Angeles	1–0	Houston	Dwayne De Rosario, D.C.
2012	Los Angeles	3–1	Houston	Chris Wondolowski, SJ

United Soccer League (USL Pro) Finals

Year	Champion	Score	Runner-Up	Regular Season MVP
1991	San Francisco	1–3, 2–0 (1–0 PKs)	Albany	Jean Harbor, Maryland
1992	Colorado	1–0	Tampa Bay	Taifour Diane, Colorado
1993	Colorado	3–1 (OT)	Los Angeles	Taifour Diane, Colorado
1994	Montreal	1–0	Colorado	Paulinho, Los Angeles
1995	Seattle	1–2 (SO), 3–0, 2–1 (SO)	Atlanta	Peter Hattrup, Seattle
1996	Seattle	2–0	Rochester	Wolde Harris, Colorado
1997	Milwaukee	2–1 (SO)	Carolina	Doug Miller, Rochester
1998	Rochester	3–1	Minnesota	Mark Baena, Seattle
1999	Minnesota	2–1	Rochester	John Swallen, Minnesota
2000	Rochester	3–1	Minnesota	Vitalis Takawira, Milwaukee
2001	Rochester	2–0	Vancouver	Paul Conway, Charleston
2002	Milwaukee	2–1 (2 OT)	Richmond	Leighton O'Brien, Seattle
2003	Charleston	3–0	Minnesota	Thiago Martins, Pittsburgh
2004	Montreal	2–0	Seattle	Greg Sutton, Montreal
2005	Seattle	1–1 (4–3 on PKs)	Richmond	Jason Jordan, Vancouver
2006	Vancouver	3–0	Rochester	Joey Gjertsen, Vancouver
2007	Seattle	4–0	Atlanta	Sebastien Le Toux, Seattle
2008	Vancouver	2–1	Puerto Rico	Jonathan Steele, Puerto Rico
2009	Montreal	6–3 (two legs)	Vancouver	Cristian Arietta, Puerto Rico
2010	Puerto Rico	3–1 (two legs)	Carolina	Ryan Pore, Portland
2011	Orlando City	2–2 (3–2 PKs)	Harrisburg City	Yordany Alvarez, Orlando City
2012	Charleston	1–0	Wilmington	Kevin Molino, Orlando City
2013	Orlando City	7–4	Charlotte	Jose Angulo, Pittsburgh

Motor Sports

AL TIELEMANS

After 12 years of frustration and a race featuring a record number of lead changes, Tony Kanaan emerged as the popular winner of his first Indy 500

Indy Racing League

Indianapolis 500

Results of the 97th running of the Indianapolis 500 and fifth race of the 2013 Indy Racing League season. Held Sunday, May 26, 2013, at the 2.5-mile Indianapolis Motor Speedway in Indianapolis, Indiana. Distance, 500 miles; starters, 33; winning time of race, 2 hours, 40 minutes, 3.24181 seconds; average speed, 187.433 mph; margin of victory (under caution); caution flags, 5 for 21 laps; lead changes, 68 among 14 drivers.

TOP 10 FINISHERS

Pos.	Driver (start pos.)	Engine	Qual. Speed	Laps	Status
1	Tony Kanaan (12)	Chevrolet	226.949	200	running
2	Carlos Muñoz (2)	Chevrolet	228.342	200	running
3	Ryan Hunter-Reay (7)	Chevrolet	227.904	200	running
4	Marco Andretti (3)	Chevrolet	228.261	200	running
5	Justin Wilson (14)	Honda	226.370	200	running
6	Helio Castroneves (8)	Chevrolet	227.762	200	running
7	A. J. Allmendinger (5)	Chevrolet	228.099	200	running
8	Simon Pagenaud (21)	Honda	225.674	200	running
9	Charlie Kimball (19)	Honda	225.880	200	running
10	Ed Carpenter (1)	Chevrolet	228.762	200	running

2013 Indy Racing League Results

Date	Race	Winner (start pos.)	Engine	Avg. Speed
Mar 24	Grand Prix of St. Petersburg	James Hinchcliffe (4)	Chevrolet	83.539 mph
Apr 7	Indy Grand Prix of Alabama	Ryan Hunter-Reay (1)	Chevrolet	110.818 mph
Apr 21	Grand Prix of Long Beach	Takuma Sato (1)	Honda	85.763 mph
May 5	Sao Paulo Indy 300	James Hinchcliffe (5)	Chevrolet	88.070 mph
May 26	Indianapolis 500	Tony Kanaan (12)	Chevrolet	187.433 mph
June 1	Indy Dual in Detroit Race1	Mike Conway (2)	Honda	90.753 mph
June 2	Indy Dual in Detroit Race 2	Simon Pagenaud (6)	Honda	84.906 mph
Jun 8	Firestone 550	Helio Castroneves (6)	Chevrolet	177.257 mph
Jun 15	Milwaukee IndyFest	Ryan Hunter-Reay (4)	Chevrolet	136.848 mph
Jun 23	Iowa Corn Indy 250	James Hinchcliffe (2)	Chevrolet	148.559 mph
Jul 7	Pocono IndyCar 400	Scott Dixon (17)	Honda	192.864 mph
Jul 13	Indy Toronto Race 1	Scott Dixon (5)	Honda	88.370 mph
July 14	Indy Toronto Race 2	Scott Dixon (1)	Honda	94.177 mph
Aug 4	Indy 200 at Mid-Ohio	Charlie Kimball (5)	Honda	117.825 mph
Aug 25	Grand Prix of Sonoma	Will Power (3)	Chevrolet	86.401 mph
Sep 1	Grand Prix of Baltimore	Simon Pagenaud (3)	Honda	67.234 mph

2013 IRL Late-Season Standings†

Driver	Pts	Wins
Helio Castroneves	501	1
Scott Dixon	452	3
Simon Pagenaud	431	2
Marco Andretti	430	0
Ryan Hunter-Reay	427	2
Justin Wilson	393	0
Dario Franchitti	388	0
James Hinchcliffe	376	3
Will Power	371	1
Charlie Kimball	363	1

† Standings through Sept 22, 2013 (16 of 19 races).

Daytona 500

Results of the 55th Daytona 500. Held Sunday, February 24, 2013, at the 2.5-mile high-banked Daytona International Speedway. Distance, 500 miles; starters, 43; winning time of race, 3 hours, 8 minutes, 23 seconds; average speed, 159.25 mph; margin of victory, 0.129 seconds; caution flags, 6 for 24 laps; lead changes, 28 among 14 drivers.

TOP 10 FINISHERS

Pos.	Driver (start pos.)	Car	Laps	Winnings ($)
1	Jimmie Johnson (9)	Chevrolet	200	1,525,275
2	Dale Earnhardt Jr. (19)	Chevrolet	200	1,104,814
3	Mark Martin (14)	Toyota	200	817,013
4	Brad Keselowski (15)	Ford	200	707,855
5	Ryan Newman (34)	Chevrolet	200	572,771
6	Greg Biffle (5)	Ford	200	461,664
7	Regan Smith (40)	Chevrolet	200	411,822
8	Danica Patrick (1)	Chevrolet	200	357,464
9	Michael McDowell (38)	Ford	200	366,121
10	J.J. Yeley (41)	Chevrolet	200	338,738

2012 Sprint Chase for the Cup* Final Season Standings

Driver	Pts	Starts	Wins	Top 5	Top 10
Brad Keselowski	2400	36	5	13	23
Clint Bowyer	2361	36	3	10	23
Jimmie Johnson	2360	36	5	18	24
Kasey Kahne	2345	36	2	12	19
Greg Biffle	2332	36	2	12	21
Denny Hamlin	2329	36	5	14	17
Matt Kenseth	2324	36	3	13	19
Kevin Harvick	2321	36	1	5	14
Tony Stewart	2311	36	3	12	16
Jeff Gordon	2303	36	2	11	18
Martin Truex Jr.	2299	36	0	7	19
Dale Earnhardt Jr.	2245	34	1	10	20

2012 Sprint Cup* Final Season Driver Winnings

Driver	Winnings ($)
Jimmie Johnson	8,210,314
Matt Kenseth	7,536,232
Denny Hamlin	6,937,811
Tony Stewart	6,607,510
Kyle Busch	6,593,466
Brad Keselowski	6,231,925
Jeff Gordon	6,117,204
Kevin Harvick	5,796,991
Greg Biffle	5,690,323
Clint Bowyer	5,550,157
Ryan Newman	5,441,026
Carl Edwards	5,348,250

2013 Sprint Chase for the Cup Late-Season Standings†

Driver	Pts	Starts	Wins	Top 5	Top 10
Matt Kenseth	2149	29	7	8	16
Jimmie Johnson	2141	29	5	12	18
Kyle Busch	2137	29	4	14	18
Kevin Harvick	2110	29	2	7	15
Jeff Gordon	2110	29	0	6	14
Greg Biffle	2108	29	1	4	12
Ryan Newman	2101	29	1	6	14
Clint Bowyer	2098	29	0	8	15
Kurt Busch	2094	29	0	9	14
Dale Earnhardt Jr.	2092	29	0	6	16
Carl Edwards	2084	29	2	8	14
Joey Logano	2083	29	1	9	15

*Series name changed from Winston Cup to Nextel Cup after 2003 season, then to Sprint Cup beginning in 2008.
†2013 Sprint Chase for the Cup standings through September 29, 2013 (29 of 36 races).

2012-13 NASCAR Sprint Cup Results

Late 2012 Sprint Cup Series Results

Date	Track/Distance	Winner (start pos.)	Car	Laps	Winnings ($)
*Oct 7	Talladega 500	Matt Kenseth (15)	Ford	189	307,036
*Oct 13	Charlotte 500	Clint Bowyer (4)	Toyota	334	256,889
*Oct 21	Kansas 400	Matt Kenseth (12)	Ford	267	389,611
*Oct 28	Martinsville 500	Jimmie Johnson (1)	Chevrolet	500	202,511
*Nov 4	Texas 500	Jimmie Johnson (1)	Chevrolet	335	492,086
*Nov 11	Phoenix 500	Kevin Harvick (19)	Chevrolet	319	249,886
*Nov 18	Homestead/Miami 400	Jeff Gordon (15)	Chevrolet	267	334,161

2013 Sprint Cup Series Results†

Date	Track/Distance	Winner (start pos.)	Car	Laps	Winnings ($)
Feb 24	Daytona 500	Jimmie Johnson (9)	Chevrolet	200	1,525,275
Mar 3	Phoenix 500	Carl Edwards (15)	Ford	316	298,875
Mar 10	Las Vegas 400	Matt Kenseth (18)	Toyota	267	408,666
Mar 17	Bristol 500	Kasey Kahne (2)	Chevrolet	500	171,160
Mar 24	Fontana 400	Kyle Busch (4)	Toyota	200	334,233
Apr 7	Martinsville 500	Jimmie Johnson (1)	Chevrolet	500	214,471
Apr 13	Texas 500	Kyle Busch (1)	Toyota	334	550,858
Apr 21	Kansas 400	Matt Kenseth (1)	Toyota	267	263,816
Apr 27	Richmond 400	Kevin Harvick (17)	Chevrolet	406	242,511
May 5	Talladega 499	David Ragan (19)	Ford	192	378,308
May 11	Darlington 500	Matt Kenseth (7)	Toyota	367	314,866
May 26	Charlotte 600	Kevin Harvick (15)	Chevrolet	400	407,011
June 2	Dover 400	Tony Stewart (22)	Chevrolet	400	318,100
June 9	Pocono 400	Jimmie Johnson (1)	Chevrolet	160	244,436
June 16	Michigan 400	Greg Biffle (19)	Ford	200	240,460
June 23	Sonoma 350	Martin Truex Jr. (14)	Toyota	110	309,250
June 30	Kentucky 400	Matt Kenseth (16)	Toyota	267	200,451
July 6	Daytona 400	Jimmie Johnson (8)	Chevrolet	161	327,961
July 14	Loudon 301	Brian Vickers (13)	Toyota	302	214,075
July 28	Brickyard 400	Ryan Newman (1)	Chevrolet	160	423,033
Aug 4	Pocono 400	Kasey Kahne (18)	Chevrolet	160	208,500
Aug 11	Watkins Glen 355	Kyle Bush (5)	Toyota	90	236,658
Aug 18	Michigan 400	Joey Logano (1)	Ford	200	252,393
Aug 24	Bristol 500	Matt Kenseth (5)	Toyota	500	328,466
Sept 1	Atlanta 500	Kyle Bush (9)	Toyota	325	338,058
Sept 7	Richmond 400	Carl Edwards (26)	Ford	400	286,475
*Sept 15	Chicago 400	Matt Kenseth (10)	Toyota	267	334,891
*Sept 22	New Hampshire 300	Matt Kenseth (9)	Toyota	300	262,066
*Sept 29	Dover 400	Jimmie Johnson (8)	Chevrolet	400	243,836

† Through September 29, 2013.
* Part of 10-race Chase for the Cup.

Formula One Grand Prix Racing

Late 2012 Formula One Results

Grand Prix	Date	Winner	Team	Laps	Time
Japan	Oct 7	Sebastian Vettel	Red Bull Racing-Renault	53	1:28:56.242
Korea	Oct 14	Sebastian Vettel	Red Bull Racing-Renault	55	1:36:28.651
India	Oct 28	Sebastian Vettel	Red Bull Racing-Renault	60	1:31:10.744
Abu Dhabi	Nov 4	Kimi Räikkönen	Lotus-Renault	55	1:45:58.667
United States	Nov 18	Lewis Hamilton	McLaren-Mercedes	56	1:35:55.269
Brazil	Nov 25	Jenson Button	McLaren-Mercedes	71	1:45:22.656

2013 Formula One Results†

Grand Prix	Date	Winner	Team	Laps	Time
Australia	Mar 17	Kimi Räikkönen	Lotus-Renault	58	1:30:03.225
Malaysia	Mar 24	Sebastian Vettel	Red Bull Racing-Renault	56	1:38:56.681
China	Apr 14	Fernando Alonso	Ferrari	56	1:36:26.945
Bahrain	Apr 21	Sebastian Vettel	Red Bull Racing-Renault	57	1:36:00.498

†Through September 22, 2013.

2013 Formula One Results *(Cont.)*†

Grand Prix	Date	Winner	Team	Laps	Time
Spain	May 12	Fernando Alonso	Ferrari	66	1:39:16.596
Monaco	May 26	Nico Rosberg	Mercedes	78	2:17:52.056
Canada	June 9	Sebastian Vettel	Red Bull Racing-Renault	70	1:32:09.143
Great Britain	June 30	Nico Rosberg	Mercedes	52	1:32:59.456
Germany	July 7	Sebastian Vettel	Red Bull Racing-Renault	60	1:41:14.711
Hungary	July 28	Lewis Hamilton	Mercedes	70	1:42:29.445
Belgium	Aug 25	Sebastian Vettel	Red Bull Racing-Renault	44	1:23:42.196
Italy	Sept 8	Sebastian Vettel	Red Bull Racing-Renault	53	1:18:33.352
Singapore	Sept 22	Sebastian Vettel	Red Bull Racing-Renault	61	1:59:13.132

†Through September 22, 2013.

2012 World Championship Final Standings

Drivers compete in Grand Prix races for the title of World Driving Champion. Points are awarded for places 1–10 as follows: 25-18-15-12-10-8-6-4-2-1.

Driver	Country	Team	Pts
Sebastian Vettel	Germany	RBR-Renault	281
Fernando Alonso	Spain	Ferrari	278
Kimi Räikkönen	Finland	Lotus-Renault	207
Lewis Hamilton	Great Britain	McLaren-Mercedes	190
Jenson Button	Great Britain	McLaren-Mercedes	188
Mark Webber	Australia	RBR-Renault	179
Felipe Massa	Brazil	Ferrari	122
Romain Grosjean	France	Lotus-Renault	96
Nico Rosberg	Germany	Mercedes	93
Sergio Perez	Mexico	Sauber-Ferrari	66

Professional Sports Car Racing

The 24 Hours of Daytona

Held at the Daytona International Speedway on Jan 26–27, 2013, the 24 Hours of Daytona serves as the opening round of the Grand American Road Racing Association's season.

Place	Drivers	Engine/Chassis	Distance
1	C. Kimball, J. P. Montoya, S. Pruett, M. Rojas	BMW/Riley	709 laps
2	M. Angelelli, R. Hunter-Reay, J. Taylor	Chevy/Corvette DP	709 laps
3	A. J. Allmendinger, M. Ambrose, O. Negri, J. Pew, J. Wilson	Ford/Riley	709 laps
4	J. Barbosa, C. Fittipaldi, B Frisselle, M. Rockenfeller	Chevy/Corvette DP	708 laps
5	A. García, O. Gavin, R. Taylor, R. Westbrook	Chevy/Corvette DP	697 laps

2013 American Le Mans Series—P1 Class

Date	Race	Winners	Team
Mar 16	12 Hours of Sebring	Benoit Treluyer, Oliver Jarvis, Marcel Fassler	Audi Sport
April 20	Grand Prix of Long Beach	Lucas Luhr, Klaus Graf	Muscle Milk Pickett
May 11	Monterey Grand Prix	Lucas Luhr, Klaus Graf	Muscle Milk Pickett
July 6	Northeast Grand Prix	Lucas Luhr, Klaus Graf	Muscle Milk Pickett
July 21	Grand Prix of Mosport	Klaus Graf, Lucas Luhr	Muscle Milk Pickett
Aug 11	Road Race Showcase	Klaus Graf, Lucas Luhr	Muscle Milk Pickett
Aug 31	Baltimore Grand Prix	Klaus Graf, Lucas Luhr	Muscle Milk Pickett
Sept 21	Circuit of the Americas	Klaus Graf, Lucas Luhr	Muscle Milk Pickett

2013 American Le Mans Series—Prototype Challenge

Date	Race	Winners	Team
Mar 16	12 Hours of Sebring	David Ostella, David Cheng, Mike Guasch	Team Oreca
April 20	Grand Prix of Long Beach	Jonathan Bennett, Colin Braun	Core Autosport
May 11	Monterey Grand Prix	Michael Guasch, Luis Diaz	Level 5 Motorsports
July 6	Northeast Grand Prix	Bruno Junqueira, Duncan Ende	RSR Racing
July 21	Grand Prix of Mosport	Jonathan Bennett, Colin Braun	Core Autosport
Aug 11	Road Race Showcase	Bruno Junqueira, Duncan Ende	RSR Racing
Aug 31	Baltimore Grand Prix	Tristan Nunez, Charlie Shears	PT Motorsports
Sept 21	Circuit of the Americas	Kyle Marcelli, Chris Cumming	MS Racing

2013 American Le Mans Series—GT Class

Date	Race	Winners	Team
Mar 16	12 Hours of Sebring	O. Gavin, T. Milner, R. Westbrook	Corvette Racing
April 20	Grand Prix of Long Beach	Maxime Martin, Bill Auberlen	BMW Team RLL
May 11	Monterey Grand Prix	Jan Magnussen, Antonio Garcia	Corvette Racing
July 6	Northeast Grand Prix	Jorg Muller, Sean Edwards	BMW Team RLL
July 21	Grand Prix of Mosport	Oliver Gavin, Tommy Milner	Corvette Racing
Aug 11	Road Race Showcase	Dominik Farnbacher, Marc Goossens	SRT Motorsports
Aug 31	Baltimore Grand Prix	Jan Magnussen, Antonio Garcia	Corvette Racing
Sept 21	Circuit of the Americas	Jan Magnussen, Antonio Garcia	Corvette Racing

2013 American Le Mans Series—GT Challenge

Date	Race	Winners	Team
Mar 16	12 Hours of Sebring	J. Bleekemolen, D. von Moltke, C. MacNeil	Alex Job Racing
April 20	Grand Prix of Long Beach	Henrique Cisneros, Sean Edwards	NGT Motorsport
May 11	Monterey Grand Prix	Henrique Cisneros, Nick Tandy	NGT Motorsport
July 6	Northeast Grand Prix	Nelson Canache Jr., Spencer Pumpelly	Flying Lizard Motorsport
July 21	Grand Prix of Mosport	Cooper MacNeil, Jeroen Bleekemolen	Alex Job Racing
Aug 11	Road Race Showcase	Nelson Canache Jr., Spencer Pumpelly	Flying Lizard Motorsport
Aug 31	Baltimore Grand Prix	Seth Nieman, Dion von Moltke	Flying Lizard Motorsport
Sept 21	Circuit of the Americas	Ben Keating, Damien Faulkner	Green Hornet Racing

Final 2012 American Le Mans Series Championship Standings

P1 CLASS	Pts	P2 CLASS	Pts	PROTOTYPE CLASS	Pts
Klaus Graf	195	Christophe Bouchut	196	Alex Popow	185
Lucas Luhr	195	Scott Tucker	196	Jonathan Bennett	150
Chris Dyson	186	David Heinemeier Hansson	156	Colin Braun	150
Guy Smith	186	Martin Plowman	156	Bruno Junqueira	118
Eric Lux	87	Patrick Dempsey	53	Rudy Junco	81
Michael Marsal	74	Luis Diaz	51	Duncan Ende	80
				Henri Richard	80

GT CLASS	Pts	GTC CLASS	Pts
Oliver Gavin	146	Cooper MacNeil	161
Tommy Milner	146	Leh Keen	141
Johannes Van Overbeek	123	Damien Faulkner	116
Scott Sharp	123	Peter LeSaffre	116
Antonio Garcia	121	Spencer Pumpelly	116
Jan Magnussen	121	Chris Cumming	108

24 Hours of Le Mans

Held at Le Mans, France, on June 22–23, 2013, the 24 Hours of Le Mans is the most prestigious international event in endurance racing.

Place	Drivers	Team	Laps
1	Allan McNish, Tom Kristensen, Loïc Duval	Audi Sport Team Joest	348
2	Anthony Davidson, Stéphane Sarrazin, Sébastien Buemi	Toyota Racing	347
3	Marc Gené, Oliver Jarvis, Lucas di Grassi	Audi Sport Team Joest	347
4	Alexander Wurz, Nicolas Lapierre, Kazuki Nakajima	Toyota Racing	341
5	André Lotterer, Marcel Fässler, Benoît Tréluyer	Audi Sport Team Joest	338

Indianapolis 500

First held in 1911, the Indianapolis 500—200 laps of the 2.5-mile Indianapolis Motor Speedway Track (called the Brickyard in honor of its original pavement)—grew to become the most famous auto race in the world. Though the Memorial Day weekend event lost participants and prestige in the mid-1990s due to feuding in the world of U.S. open-wheel racing, it annually attracts crowds of over 100,000.

Year	Winner (start pos.)	Chassis-Engine	Avg speed	Pole Winner	Qual. Speed
1911	Ray Harroun (28)	Marmon-Marmon	74.590	Lewis Strang	First entered
1912	Joe Dawson (7)	National-National	78.720	Gil Anderson	First entered
1913	Jules Goux (7)	Peugeot-Peugeot	75.930	Caleb Bragg	Drew pole
1914	Rene Thomas (15)	Delage-Delage	82.470	Jean Chassagne	Drew pole
1915	Ralph DePalma (2)	Mercedes-Mercedes	89.840	Howard Wilcox	98.90
1916	Dario Resta (4)	Peugeot-Peugeot	84.000	John Aitken	96.69
1917–18	No race				
1919	Howard Wilcox (2)	Peugeot-Peugeot	88.050	Rene Thomas	104.78
1920	Gaston Chevrolet (6)	Frontenac-Frontenac	88.620	Ralph DePalma	99.15
1921	Tommy Milton (20)	Frontenac-Frontenac	89.620	Ralph DePalma	100.75
1922	Jimmy Murphy (1)	Duesenberg-Miller	94.480	Jimmy Murphy	100.50
1923	Tommy Milton (1)	Miller-Miller	90.950	Tommy Milton	108.17
1924	L.L. Corum	Duesenberg-Duesenberg	98.230	Jimmy Murphy	108.037
	Joe Boyer (21)				
1925	Peter DePaolo (2)	Duesenberg-Duesenberg	101.130	Leon Duray	113.196
1926	Frank Lockhart (20)	Miller-Miller	95.904	Earl Cooper	111.735
1927	George Souders (22)	Duesenberg-Duesenberg	97.545	Frank Lockhart	120.100
1928	Louis Meyer (13)	Miller-Miller	99.482	Leon Duray	122.391
1929	Ray Keech (6)	Miller-Miller	97.585	Cliff Woodbury	120.599
1930	Billy Arnold (1)	Summers-Miller	100.448	Billy Arnold	113.268
1931	Louis Schneider (13)	Stevens-Miller	96.629	Russ Snowberger	112.796
1932	Fred Frame (27)	Wetteroth-Miller	104.144	Lou Moore	117.363
1933	Louis Meyer (6)	Miller-Miller	104.162	Bill Cummings	118.524
1934	Bill Cummings (10)	Miller-Miller	104.863	Kelly Petillo	119.329
1935	Kelly Petillo (22)	Wetteroth-Offy	106.240	Rex Mays	120.736
1936	Louis Meyer (28)	Stevens-Miller	109.069	Rex Mays	119.664
1937	Wilbur Shaw (2)	Shaw-Offy	113.580	Bill Cummings	123.343
1938	Floyd Roberts (1)	Wetteroth-Miller	117.200	Floyd Roberts	125.681
1939	Wilbur Shaw (3)	Maserati-Maserati	115.035	Jimmy Snyder	130.138
1940	Wilbur Shaw (2)	Maserati-Maserati	114.277	Rex Mays	127.850
1941	Floyd Davis	Wetteroth-Offy	115.117	Mauri Rose	128.691
	Mauri Rose (17)				
1942–45	No race				
1946	George Robson (15)	Adams-Sparks	114.820	Cliff Bergere	126.471
1947	Mauri Rose (3)	Deidt-Offy	116.338	Ted Horn	126.564
1948	Mauri Rose (3)	Deidt-Offy	119.814	Rex Mays	130.577
1949	Bill Holland (4)	Deidt-Offy	121.327	Duke Nalon	132.939
1950	Johnnie Parsons (5)	Kurtis-Offy	124.002	Walt Faulkner	134.343
1951	Lee Wallard (2)	Kurtis-Offy	126.244	Duke Nalon	136.498
1952	Troy Ruttman (7)	Kuzma-Offy	128.922	Fred Agabashian	138.010
1953	Bill Vukovich (1)	KK500A-Offy	128.740	Bill Vukovich	138.392
1954	Bill Vukovich (19)	KK500A-Offy	130.840	Jack McGrath	141.033
1955	Bob Sweikert (14)	KK500C-Offy	128.209	Jerry Hoyt	140.045
1956	Pat Flaherty (1)	Watson-Offy	128.490	Pat Flaherty	145.596
1957	Sam Hanks (13)	Salih-Offy	135.601	Pat O'Connor	143.948
1958	Jim Bryan (7)	Salih-Offy	133.791	Dick Rathmann	145.974
1959	Rodger Ward (6)	Watson-Offy	135.857	Johnny Thomson	145.908
1960	Jim Rathmann (2)	Watson-Offy	138.767	Eddie Sachs	146.592
1961	A.J. Foyt (7)	Trevis-Offy	139.130	Eddie Sachs	147.481
1962	Rodger Ward (2)	Watson-Offy	140.293	Parnelli Jones	150.370
1963	Parnelli Jones (1)	Watson-Offy	143.137	Parnelli Jones	151.153
1964	A.J. Foyt (5)	Watson-Offy	147.350	Jim Clark	158.828
1965	Jim Clark (2)	Lotus-Ford	150.686	A.J. Foyt	161.233
1966	Graham Hill (15)	Lola-Ford	144.317	Mario Andretti	165.899
1967	A.J. Foyt (4)	Coyote-Ford	151.207	Mario Andretti	168.982
1968	Bobby Unser (3)	Eagle-Offy	152.882	Joe Leonard	171.559
1969	Mario Andretti (2)	Hawk-Ford	156.867	A.J. Foyt	170.568
1970	Al Unser (1)	PJ Colt-Ford	155.749	Al Unser	170.221
1971	Al Unser (5)	PJ Colt-Ford	157.735	Peter Revson	178.696
1972	Mark Donohue (3)	McLaren-Offy	162.962	Bobby Unser	195.940

Year	Winner (start pos.)	Chassis-Engine	Avg speed	Pole Winner	Qual. Speed
1973	Gordon Johncock (11)	Eagle-Offy	159.036	Johnny Rutherford	198.413
1974	Johnny Rutherford (25)	McLaren-Offy	158.589	A.J. Foyt	191.632
1975	Bobby Unser (3)	Racers Eagle-Offy	149.213	A.J. Foyt	193.976
1976	Johnny Rutherford (1)	McLaren-Offy	148.725	Johnny Rutherford	188.957
1977	A.J. Foyt (4)	Coyote-Ford	161.331	Tom Sneva	198.884
1978	Al Unser (5)	Lola-Cosworth	161.361	Tom Sneva	202.156
1979	Rick Mears (1)	Penske-Cosworth	158.899	Rick Mears	193.736
1980	Johnny Rutherford (1)	Chaparral-Coswoth	142.862	Johnny Rutherford	192.256
1981	Bobby Unser (1)	Penske-Cosworth	139.084	Bobby Unser	200.546
1982	Gordon Johncock (5)	Wildcat-Cosworth	162.026	Rick Mears	207.004
1983	Tom Sneva (4)	March-Cosworth	162.117	Teo Fabi	207.395
1984	Rick Mears (3)	March-Cosworth	163.612	Tom Sneva	210.029
1985	Danny Sullivan (8)	March-Cosworth	152.982	Pancho Carter	212.583
1986	Bobby Rahal (4)	March-Cosworth	170.722	Rick Mears	216.828
1987	Al Unser (20)	March-Cosworth	162.175	Mario Andretti	215.390
1988	Rick Mears (1)	Penske-Chevrolet	144.809	Rick Mears	219.198
1989	Emerson Fittipaldi (3)	Penske-Chevrolet	167.581	Rick Mears	223.885
1990	Arie Luyendyk (3)	Lola-Chevrolet	185.981	Emerson Fittipaldi	225.301
1991	Rick Mears (1)	Penske-Chevrolet	176.457	Rick Mears	224.113
1992	Al Unser Jr. (12)	Galmer-Chevrolet	134.477	Roberto Guerrero	232.482
1993	Emerson Fittipaldi (9)	Penske-Chevrolet	157.207	Arie Luyendyk	223.967
1994	Al Unser Jr. (1)	Penske-Mercedes	160.872	Al Unser Jr.	228.011
1995	Jacques Villeneuve (5)	Reynard-Ford	153.616	Scott Brayton	231.616
1996	Buddy Lazier (5)	Reynard-Ford	147.956	Tony Stewart	233.100†
1997	Arie Luyendyk (1)	G Force-Oldsmobile	145.827	Arie Luyendyk	231.468
1998	Eddie Cheever (17)	Dallara-Oldsmobile	145.155	Billy Boat	223.503
1999	Kenny Brack (8)	Dallara-Oldsmobile	153.176	Arie Luyendyk	225.179
2000	Juan Pablo Montoya (2)	G Force-Oldsmobile	167.607	Greg Ray	223.471
2001	Helio Castroneves (11)	Dallara-Oldsmobile	153.601	Scott Sharp	226.037
2002	Helio Castroneves (13)	Dallara-Chevrolet	166.499	Bruno Junqueira	231.342
2003	Gil de Ferran (10)	Panoz-Toyota	156.291	Helio Castroneves	231.725
2004	Buddy Rice (1)	G Force-Honda	138.518	Buddy Rice	222.024
2005	Dan Wheldon (16)	Dallara-Honda	157.603	Tony Kanaan	227.566
2006	Sam Hornish Jr. (1)	Dallara-Honda	157.085	Sam Hornish Jr.	228.985
2007	Dario Franchitti (3)	Dallara-Honda	151.744	Helio Castroneves	225.817
2008	Scott Dixon (1)	Dallara-Honda	143.567	Scott Dixon	226.366
2009	Helio Castroneves (1)	Dallara-Honda	150.138	Helio Castroneves	224.864
2010	Dario Franchitti (3)	Dallara-Honda	161.623	Helio Castroneves	227.970
2011	Dan Wheldon (6)	Dallara-Honda	170.265	Alex Tagliani	227.472
2012	Dario Franchitti (16)	Dallara-Honda	167.734	Ryan Briscoe	226.484
2013	Tony Kanaan (12)	Dallara-Chevrolet	187.433*	Ed Carpenter	228.762

*Track record, average winning speed. †Track record, qualifying speed.

Indianapolis 500 Rookie of the Year Award

1952 Art Cross	1974 Pancho Carter	1994 Jacques Villeneuve*
1953 Jimmy Daywalt	1975 Bill Puterbaugh	1995 Gil de Ferran*
1954 Larry Crockett	1976 Vern Schuppan	1996 Tony Stewart
1955 Al Herman	1977 Jerry Sneva	1997 Jeff Ward
1956 Bob Veith	1978 Rick Mears*	1998 Steve Knapp
1957 Don Edmunds	Larry Rice	1999 Robby McGehee
1958 George Amick	1979 Howdy Holmes	2000 Juan Pablo Montoya*
1959 Bobby Grim	1980 Tim Richmond	2001 Helio Castroneves*
1960 Jim Hurtubise	1981 Josele Garza	2002 Alex Barron
1961 Parnelli Jones*	1982 Jim Hickman	Tomas Scheckter
Bobby Marshman	1983 Teo Fabi	2003 Tora Tagaki
1962 Jimmy McElreath	1984 Michael Andretti	2004 Kosuke Matsuura
1963 Jim Clark*	Roberto Guerrero	2005 Danica Patrick
1964 Johnny White	1985 Arie Luyendyk*	2006 Marco Andretti
1965 Mario Andretti*	1986 Randy Lanier	2007 Phil Giebler
1966 Jackie Stewart	1987 Fabrizio Barbazza	2008 Ryan Hunter-Reay
1967 Denis Hulme	1988 Billy Vukovich III	2009 Alex Tagliani
1968 Billy Vukovich	1989 Bernard Jourdain	2010 Simona De Silvestro
1969 Mark Donohue*	Scott Pruett	2011 J.R. Hildebrand
1970 Donnie Allison	1990 Eddie Cheever*	2012 Rubens Barrichello
1971 Denny Zimmerman	1991 Jeff Andretti	2013 Carlos Muñoz
1972 Mike Hiss	1992 Lyn St. James	
1973 Graham McRae	1993 Nigel Mansell	

*Future winner of Indy 500.

Champ Car World Series Champions

From 1909 to 1955, this championship was awarded by the American Automobile Association (AAA), and from 1956 to 1979 by the United States Auto Club (USAC). During the 1979 season, Championship Auto Racing Teams (CART) split from the USAC and conducted the championship. Known as PPG CART World Series until 1998. Series name changed to Champ Car World Series for 2005 racing season. On Februray 22, 2008, the Champ Car World Series merged with the Indy Racing League.

1909 ....George Robertson	1942–45 ....No racing	1978 ....Tom Sneva
1910 ....Ray Harroun	1946 ....Ted Horn	1979 .............A.J. Foyt (USAC)
1911 ....Ralph Mulford	1947 ....Ted Horn	1979 ....Rick Mears (CART)
1912 ....Ralph DePalma	1948 ....Ted Horn	1980 ....Johnny Rutherford
1913 ....Earl Cooper	1949 ....Johnnie Parsons	1981 ....Rick Mears
1914 ....Ralph DePalma	1950 ....Henry Banks	1982 ....Rick Mears
1915 ....Earl Cooper	1951 ....Tony Bettenhausen	1983 ....Al Unser
1916 ....Dario Resta	1952 ....Chuck Stevenson	1984 ....Mario Andretti
1917 ....Earl Cooper	1953 ....Sam Hanks	1985 ....Al Unser
1918 ....Ralph Mulford	1954 ....Jimmy Bryan	1986 ....Bobby Rahal
1919 ....Howard Wilcox	1955 ....Bob Sweikert	1987 ....Bobby Rahal
1920 ....Tommy Milton	1956 ....Jimmy Bryan	1988 ....Danny Sullivan
1921 ....Tommy Milton	1957 ....Jimmy Bryan	1989 ....Emerson Fittipaldi
1922 ....Jimmy Murphy	1958 ....Tony Bettenhausen	1990 ....Al Unser Jr.
1923 ....Eddie Hearne	1959 ....Rodger Ward	1991 ....Michael Andretti
1924 ....Jimmy Murphy	1960 .............A.J. Foyt	1992 ....Bobby Rahal
1925 ....Peter DePaolo	1961 .............A.J. Foyt	1993 ....Nigel Mansell
1926 ....Harry Hartz	1962 ....Rodger Ward	1994 ....Al Unser Jr.
1927 ....Peter DePaolo	1963 .............A.J. Foyt	1995 ....Jacques Villeneuve
1928 ....Louis Meyer	1964 .............A.J. Foyt	1996 ....Jimmy Vasser
1929 ....Louis Meyer	1965 ....Mario Andretti	1997 ....Alex Zanardi
1930 ....Billy Arnold	1966 ....Mario Andretti	1998 ....Alex Zanardi
1931 ....Louis Schneider	1967 .............A.J. Foyt	1999 ....Juan Montoya
1932 ....Bob Carey	1968 ....Bobby Unser	2000 ....Gil de Ferran
1933 ....Louis Meyer	1969 ....Mario Andretti	2001 ....Gil de Ferran
1934 ....Bill Cummings	1970 ....Al Unser	2002 ....Cristiano da Matta
1935 ....Kelly Petillo	1971 ....Joe Leonard	2003 ....Paul Tracy
1936 ....Mauri Rose	1972 ....Joe Leonard	2004 ....Sebastian Bourdais
1937 ....Wilbur Shaw	1973 ....Roger McCluskey	2005 ....Sebastian Bourdais
1938 ....Floyd Roberts	1974 ....Bobby Unser	2006 ....Sebastian Bourdais
1939 ....Wilbur Shaw	1975 .............A.J. Foyt	2007 ....Sebastian Bourdais
1940 ....Rex Mays	1976 ....Gordon Johncock	
1941 ....Rex Mays	1977 ....Tom Sneva	

Alltime Champ Car* Leaders

WINS		POLE POSITIONS	
A.J. Foyt	67	Mario Andretti	67
Mario Andretti	52	A.J. Foyt	53
Michael Andretti	42	Bobby Unser	49
Al Unser	39	Rick Mears	40
Bobby Unser	35	Michael Andretti	32
Al Unser Jr	31	Sebastian Bourdais	28
Paul Tracy	31	Al Unser	27
Rick Mears	29	Paul Tracy	25
Sebastian Bourdais	29	Johnny Rutherford	23
Johnny Rutherford	27	Gordon Johncock	20
Rodger Ward	26	Rex Mays	19
Gordon Johncock	25	Danny Sullivan	19
Bobby Rahal	24	Bobby Rahal	18
Ralph DePalma	24	Emerson Fittipaldi	17
Tommy Milton	23	Gil de Ferran	16
Tony Bettenhausen	22	Tony Bettenhausen	14
Emerson Fittipaldi	22	Juan Pablo Montoya	14
Earl Cooper	20	Don Branson	14
Jimmy Bryan	19	Tom Sneva	14
Jimmy Murphy	19	Parnelli Jones	12
Danny Sullivan	17		
Ralph Mulford	17		

*Series known as CART prior to 2003 season

MAJOR EVENTS
Daytona 500

Year	Winner	Car	Avg. Speed	Pole Winner	Qual. Speed
1959	Lee Petty	Oldsmobile	135.520	Cotton Owens	143.198
1960	Junior Johnson	Chevrolet	124.740	Fireball Roberts	151.556
1961	Marvin Panch	Pontiac	149.601	Fireball Roberts	155.709
1962	Fireball Roberts	Pontiac	152.529	Fireball Roberts	156.995
1963	Tiny Lund	Ford	151.566	Johnny Rutherford	165.183
1964	Richard Petty	Plymouth	154.345	Paul Goldsmith	174.910
1965	Fred Lorenzen	Ford	141.539	Darel Dieringer	171.151
1966	Richard Petty	Plymouth	160.627	Richard Petty	175.165
1967	Mario Andretti	Ford	149.926	Curtis Turner	180.831
1968	Cale Yarborough	Mercury	143.251	Cale Yarborough	189.222
1969	Lee Roy Yarbrough	Ford	157.950	David Pearson	190.029
1970	Pete Hamilton	Plymouth	149.601	Cale Yarborough	194.015
1971	Richard Petty	Plymouth	144.462	A.J. Foyt	182.744
1972	A.J. Foyt	Mercury	161.550	Bobby Isaac	186.632
1973	Richard Petty	Dodge	157.205	Buddy Baker	185.662
1974	Richard Petty	Dodge	140.894	David Pearson	185.017
1975	Benny Parsons	Chevrolet	153.649	Donnie Allison	185.827
1976	David Pearson	Mercury	152.181	A.J. Foyt	185.943
1977	Cale Yarborough	Chevrolet	153.218	Donnie Allison	188.048
1978	Bobby Allison	Ford	159.730	Cale Yarborough	187.536
1979	Richard Petty	Oldsmobile	143.977	Buddy Baker	196.049
1980	Buddy Baker	Oldsmobile	177.602*	A.J. Foyt	195.020
1981	Richard Petty	Buick	169.651	Bobby Allison	194.624
1982	Bobby Allison	Buick	153.991	Benny Parsons	196.317
1983	Cale Yarborough	Pontiac	155.979	Ricky Rudd	198.864
1984	Cale Yarborough	Chevrolet	150.994	Cale Yarborough	201.848
1985	Bill Elliott	Ford	172.265	Bill Elliott	205.114
1986	Geoff Bodine	Chevrolet	148.124	Bill Elliott	205.039
1987	Bill Elliott	Ford	176.263	Bill Elliott	210.364†
1988	Bobby Allison	Buick	137.531	Ken Schrader	193.823
1989	Darrell Waltrip	Chevrolet	148.466	Ken Schrader	196.996
1990	Derrike Cope	Chevrolet	165.761	Ken Schrader	196.515
1991	Ernie Irvan	Chevrolet	148.148	Davey Allison	195.955
1992	Davey Allison	Ford	160.256	Sterling Marlin	192.213
1993	Dale Jarrett	Chevrolet	154.972	Kyle Petty	189.426
1994	Sterling Marlin	Chevrolet	156.931	Loy Allen Jr	190.158
1995	Sterling Marlin	Chevrolet	141.710	Dale Jarrett	193.498
1996	Dale Jarrett	Ford	154.308	Dale Earnhardt	189.510
1997	Jeff Gordon	Chevrolet	148.295	Mike Skinner	189.813
1998	Dale Earnhardt	Chevrolet	172.712	Bobby Labonte	192.415
1999	Jeff Gordon	Chevrolet	161.551	Jeff Gordon	195.067
2000	Dale Jarrett	Ford	155.669	Dale Jarrett	191.091
2001	Michael Waltrip	Chevrolet	161.783	Bill Elliott	183.570
2002	Ward Burton	Dodge	142.971	Jimmie Johnson	185.831
2003	Michael Waltrip	Chevrolet	133.870	Jeff Green	186.606
2004	Dale Earnhardt Jr.	Chevrolet	156.345	Greg Biffle	188.387
2005	Jeff Gordon	Chevrolet	135.173	Dale Jarrett	188.312
2006	Jimmie Johnson	Chevrolet	142.667	Jeff Burton	188.887
2007	Kevin Harvick	Chevrolet	149.335	David Gilliland	186.320
2008	Ryan Newman	Dodge	152.672	Jimmie Johnson	187.075
2009	Matt Kenseth	Ford	132.816	Martin Truex Jr.	188.001
2010	Jamie McMurray	Chevrolet	137.284	Mark Martin	191.188
2011	Trevor Bayne	Ford	130.326	Dale Earnhardt Jr.	186.089
2012	Matt Kenseth	Ford	140.256	Carl Edwards	194.738
2013	Jimmie Johnson	Chevrolet	159.250	Danica Patrick	196.434

Note: The Daytona 500, held annually in February, now opens the NASCAR season with 200 laps around the 2.5-mile high-banked Daytona International Speedway. Starting in 1988, cars racing at Daytona have used restrictor plates that curb power and acceleration. *Track record, winning speed. †Track record, qualifying speed.

Brickyard 400

Year	Winner	Car	Avg. Speed	Pole Winner	Qual. Speed
1994	Jeff Gordon	Chevrolet	131.977	Rick Mast	172.414
1995	Dale Earnhardt	Chevrolet	155.206	Jeff Gordon	172.536
1996	Dale Jarrett	Ford	139.508	Jeff Gordon	176.419
1997	Ricky Rudd	Ford	130.814	Ernie Irvan	177.736
1998	Jeff Gordon	Chevrolet	126.772	Ernie Irvan	179.394

Brickyard 400 (Cont.)

Year	Winner	Car	Avg. Speed	Pole Winner	Qual. Speed
1999	Dale Jarrett	Ford	148.194	Jeff Gordon	179.612
2000	Bobby Labonte	Pontiac	155.912*	Ricky Rudd	181.068
2001	Jeff Gordon	Chevrolet	130.790	Jimmy Spencer	179.666
2002	Bill Elliott	Dodge	125.033	Tony Stewart	182.960
2003	Kevin Harvick	Chevrolet	134.554	Kevin Harvick	184.343
2004	Jeff Gordon	Chevrolet	115.037	Casey Mears	186.293
2005	Tony Stewart	Chevrolet	148.782	Elliott Sadler	184.117
2006	Jimmie Johnson	Chevrolet	137.182	Jeff Burton	182.778
2007	Tony Stewart	Chevrolet	117.379	Reed Sorenson	184.207
2008	Jimmie Johnson	Chevrolet	115.117	Jimmie Johnson	181.763
2009	Jimmie Johnson	Chevrolet	145.882	Mark Martin	182.054
2010	Jamie McMurray	Chevrolet	136.054	Juan Pablo Montoya	182.278
2011	Paul Menard	Chevrolet	140.762	David Ragan	182.994
2012	Jimmie Johnson	Chevrolet	137.680	Denny Hamlin	182.763
2013	Ryan Newman	Chevrolet	153.485	Ryan Newman	187.531†

Note: Held at the 2.5-mile Indianapolis Motor Speedway.*Track record, winning speed. †Track record, qualifying speed.

Talladega 500

Year	Winner	Car	Avg. Speed	Pole Winner	Qual. Speed
1970	Pete Hamilton	Plymouth	152.321	Bobby Isaac	199.658
1971	Donnie Allison	Mercury	147.419	Donnie Allison	185.869
1972	David Pearson	Mercury	134.400	Bobby Isaac	192.428
1973	David Pearson	Mercury	131.956	Buddy Baker	193.435
1974	David Pearson	Mercury	130.220	David Pearson	186.086
1975	Buddy Baker	Ford	144.94	Buddy Baker	189.947
1976	Buddy Baker	Ford	169.887	Dave Marcis	189.197
1977	Darrell Waltrip	Chevrolet	164.887	A.J. Foyt	192.424
1978	Cale Yarborough	Oldsmobile	155.699	Cale Yarborough	191.904
1979	Bobby Allison	Ford	154.770	Darrell Waltrip	195.644
1980	Buddy Baker	Oldsmobile	170.481	David Pearson	197.704
1981	Bobby Allison	Buick	149.376	Bobby Allison	195.864
1982	Darrell Waltrip	Buick	156.697	Benny Parsons	200.176
1983	Richard Petty	Pontiac	135.936	Cale Yarborough	202.650
1984	Cale Yarborough	Chevrolet	172.988	Cale Yarborough	202.692
1985	Bill Elliott	Ford	186.288	Bill Elliott	209.398
1986	Bobby Allison	Buick	157.698	Bill Elliott	212.229
1987	Davey Allison	Ford	154.228	Bill Elliott	221.809†
1988	Phil Parsons	Oldsmobile	156.547	Davey Allison	198.969
1989	Davey Allison	Ford	155.869	Mark Martin	193.061
1990	Dale Earnhardt	Chevrolet	159.571	Bill Elliott	199.388
1991	Harry Gant	Oldsmobile	165.620	Ernie Irvan	195.186
1992	Davey Allison	Ford	167.609	Ernie Irvan	192.831
1993	Ernie Irvan	Chevrolet	155.412	Dale Earnhardt	192.355
1994	Dale Earnhardt	Chevrolet	157.478	Ernie Irvan	193.298
1995	Mark Martin	Ford	178.902	Terry Labonte	196.532
1996	Sterling Marlin	Chevrolet	149.999	Ernie Irvan	192.855
1997	Mark Martin	Ford	188.354*	John Andretti	193.627
1998	Dale Jarrett	Ford	159.318	Ken Schrader	196.153
1999	Dale Earnhardt	Chevrolet	166.632	Joe Nemechek	198.331
2000	Dale Earnhardt	Chevrolet	165.681	Joe Nemechek	190.279
2001	Dale Earnhardt Jr.	Chevrolet	164.185	Stacy Compton	185.240
2002	Dale Earnhardt Jr.	Chevrolet	183.665	qualifying cancelled	—
2003	Michael Waltrip	Chevrolet	156.045	Elliott Sadler	189.943
2004	Jeff Gordon	Chevrolet	129.396	Ricky Rudd	191.180
2005	Dale Jarrett	Ford	143.818	Elliott Sadler	189.260
2006	Brian Vickers	Chevrolet	157.602	David Gilliland	191.712
2007	Jeff Gordon	Chevrolet	143.438	Michael Waltrip	189.070
2008	Kyle Busch	Toyota	157.409	Joe Nemechek	187.396
2009	Brad Keselowski	Chevrolet	147.565	Juan Pablo Montoya	188.171
2010	Kevin Harvick	Chevrolet	150.590	qualifying cancelled	—
2011	Jimmie Johnson	Chevrolet	156.261	Jeff Gordon	178.248
2012	Brad Keselowski	Dodge	160.192	Jeff Gordon	191.623
2013	David Ragan	Ford	148.729	Carl Edwards	199.650

*Track record, winning speed. †Track record, qualifying speed.

Charlotte 600

Year	Winner	Car	Avg. Speed	Pole Winner
1960	Joe Lee Johnson	Chevrolet	107.752	Joe Lee Johnson
1961	David Pearson	Pontiac	111.634	Richard Petty
1962	Nelson Stacy	Ford	125.552	Fireball Roberts
1963	Fred Lorenzen	Ford	132.418	Junior Johnson
1964	Jim Paschal	Plymouth	125.772	Junior Johnson
1965	Fred Lorenzen	Ford	121.772	Fred Lorenzon
1966	Marvin Panch	Plymouth	135.042	Paul Goldsmith
1967	Jim Paschal	Plymouth	135.832	Cale Yarborough
1968	Buddy Baker	Dodge	104.207	Donnie Allison
1969	Lee Roy Yarbrough	Mercury	134.631	Donnie Allison
1970	Donnie Allison	Ford	129.680	Bobby Isaac
1971	Bobby Allison	Mercury	140.442	Charlie Glotzbach
1972	Buddy Baker	Dodge	142.255	Bobby Allison
1973	Buddy Baker	Dodge	134.890	Buddy Baker
1974	David Pearson	Mercury	135.720	David Pearson
1975	Richard Petty	Dodge	145.327	David Pearson
1976	David Pearson	Mercury	137.352	David Pearson
1977	Richard Petty	Dodge	137.636	David Pearson
1978	Darrell Waltrip	Chevrolet	138.355	David Pearson
1979	Darrell Waltrip	Chevrolet	136.674	Neil Bonnet
1980	Benny Parsons	Chevrolet	119.265	Cale Yarborough
1981	Bobby Allison	Buick	129.326	Neil Bonnett
1982	Neil Bonnett	Ford	130.508	David Pearson
1983	Neil Bonnett	Chevrolet	140.406	Buddy Baker
1984	Bobby Allison	Buick	129.233	Harry Gant
1985	Darrell Waltrip	Chevrolet	141.807	Bill Elliott
1986	Dale Earnhardt	Chevrolet	140.406	Geoff Bodine
1987	Kyle Petty	Ford	131.483	Bill Elliott
1988	Darrell Waltrip	Chevrolet	124.460	Davey Allison
1989	Darrell Waltrip	Chevrolet	144.077	Alan Kulwicki
1990	Rusty Wallace	Pontiac	137.650	Ken Schrader
1991	Davey Allison	Ford	138.951	Mark Martin
1992	Dale Earnhardt	Chevrolet	132.980	Bill Elliott
1993	Dale Earnhardt	Chevrolet	145.504	Ken Schrader
1994	Jeff Gordon	Chevrolet	139.445	Jeff Gordon
1995	Bobby Labonte	Chevrolet	151.952	Jeff Gordon
1996	Dale Jarrett	Ford	147.581	Jeff Gordon
1997	Jeff Gordon	Chevrolet	136.745	Jeff Gordon
1998	Jeff Gordon	Chevrolet	136.424	Jeff Gordon
1999	Jeff Burton	Ford	151.367	Bobby Labonte
2000	Matt Kenseth	Ford	142.640	Dale Earnhardt Jr
2001	Jeff Burton	Ford	138.107	Ryan Newman
2002	Mark Martin	Ford	137.729	Jimmie Johnson
2003	Jimmie Johnson	Chevrolet	126.198	Ryan Newman
2004	Jimmie Johnson	Chevrolet	142.763	Jimmie Johnson
2005	Jimmie Johnson	Chevrolet	114.698	Ryan Newman
2006	Kasey Kahne	Dodge	128.840	Scott Riggs
2007	Casey Mears	Chevrolet	130.222	Ryan Newman
2008	Kasey Kahne	Dodge	135.772	Kyle Busch
2009	David Reutimann	Toyota	120.899	Ryan Newman
2010	Kurt Busch	Dodge	144.966	Ryan Newman
2011	Kevin Harvick	Chevrolet	132.414	Brad Keselowski
2012	Kasey Kahne	Chevrolet	155.687*	Aric Almirola
2013	Kevin Harvick	Chevrolet	130.521	Denny Hamlin

Note: Held at the 1.5 mile high-banked Charlotte Motor Speedway on Memorial Day weekend.
*Track record, winning speed.

Darlington 500

Year	Winner	Car	Avg. Speed	Pole Winner
1950	Johnny Mantz	Plymouth	76.260	Wally Campbell
1951	Herb Thomas	Hudson	76.900	Marshall Teague
1952	Fonty Flock	Oldsmobile	74.510	Dick Rathman
1953	Buck Baker	Oldsmobile	92.780	Fonty Flock
1954	Herb Thomas	Hudson	94.930	Buck Baker
1955	Herb Thomas	Chevrolet	92.281	Tim Flock
1956	Curtis Turner	Ford	95.067	Buck Baker
1957	Speedy Thompson	Chevrolet	100.100	Paul Goldsmith
1958	Fireball Roberts	Chevrolet	102.590	Fireball Roberts
1959	Jim Reed	Chevrolet	111.836	Fireball Roberts
1960	Buck Baker	Pontiac	105.901	Cotton Owens
1961	Nelson Stacy	Ford	117.880	Fireball Roberts
1962	Larry Frank	Ford	117.965	Fireball Roberts
1963	Fireball Roberts	Ford	129.784	Fireball Roberts
1964	Buck Baker	Dodge	117.757	Richard Petty
1965	Ned Jarrett	Ford	115.924	Junior Johnson
1966	Darel Dieringer	Mercury	114.830	LeeRoy Yarbrough
1967	Richard Petty	Plymouth	131.933	David Pearson
1968	Cale Yarborough	Mercury	126.132	Charlie Glotzbach
1969	LeeRoy Yarbrough	Ford	105.612	Cale Yarborough
1970	Buddy Baker	Dodge	128.817	David Pearson
1971	Bobby Allison	Mercury	131.398	Bobby Allison
1972	Bobby Allison	Chevrolet	128.124	David Pearson
1973	Cale Yarborough	Chevrolet	134.033	David Pearson
1974	Cale Yarborough	Chevrolet	111.075	Richard Petty
1975	Bobby Allison	Matador	116.825	David Pearson
1976	David Pearson	Mercury	120.534	David Pearson
1977	David Pearson	Mercury	106.797	Darrell Waltrip
1978	Cale Yarborough	Oldsmobile	116.828	David Pearson
1979	David Pearson	Chevrolet	126.259	Bobby Allison
1980	Terry Labonte	Chevrolet	115.210	Darrell Waltrip
1981	Neil Bonnett	Ford	126.410	Harry Gant
1982	Cale Yarborough	Buick	126.703	David Pearson
1983	Bobby Allison	Buick	123.343	Neil Bonnett
1984	Harry Gant	Chevrolet	128.270	Harry Gant
1985	Bill Elliott	Ford	121.254	Bill Elliott
1986	Tim Richmond	Chevrolet	121.068	Tim Richmond
1987	Dale Earnhardt	Chevrolet	115.520	Davey Allison
1988	Bill Elliott	Ford	128.297	Bill Elliott
1989	Dale Earnhardt	Chevrolet	135.462	Alan Kulwicki
1990	Dale Earnhardt	Chevrolet	123.141	Dale Earnhardt
1991	Harry Gant	Oldsmobile	133.508	Davey Allison
1992	Darrell Waltrip	Chevrolet	129.114	Sterling Marlin
1993	Mark Martin	Ford	137.932	Ken Schrader
1994	Bill Elliott	Ford	127.915	Geoff Bodine
1995	Jeff Gordon	Chevrolet	121.231	John Andretti
1996	Jeff Gordon	Chevrolet	135.757	Dale Jarrett
1997	Jeff Gordon	Chevrolet	121.149	Bobby Labonte
1998	Jeff Gordon	Chevrolet	139.031	Dale Jarrett
1999	Jeff Burton	Ford	100.816	Kenny Irwin
2000	Bobby Labonte	Pontiac	108.275	Jeremy Mayfield
2001	Ward Burton	Dodge	122.773	Kurt Busch
2002	Jeff Gordon	Chevrolet	118.617	Sterling Marlin
2003	Terry Labonte	Chevrolet	120.744	Ryan Newman
2004	Jimmie Johnson	Chevrolet	125.044	Kurt Busch
2005	Greg Biffle	Ford	135.127	Kasey Kahne
2006	Greg Biffle	Ford	123.031	Kasey Kahne
2007	Jeff Gordon	Chevrolet	124.372	Clint Bowyer
2008	Kyle Busch	Toyota	140.350	Greg Biffle
2009	Mark Martin	Chevrolet	119.687	Matt Kenseth
2010	Denny Hamlin	Toyota	126.605	Jamie McMurray
2011	Regan Smith	Chevrolet	129.678	Kasey Kahne
2012	Jimmie Johnson	Chevrolet	133.802	Greg Biffle
2013	Matt Kenseth	Toyota	141.383*	Matt Kenseth

Note: Through 2004, results listed were for the Southern 500, traditionally the second race of the year at the 1.366-mile Darlington (S.C.) Raceway. Starting in 2005, Darlington only hosted one race a year, in May.
*Track record, winning speed.

Sprint Cup* NASCAR Champions

Year	Driver	Car	Wins	Poles	Winnings ($)
1949	Red Byron	Oldsmobile	2	1	5,800
1950	Bill Rexford	Oldsmobile	1	0	6,175
1951	Herb Thomas	Hudson	7	4	18,200
1952	Tim Flock	Hudson	8	4	20,210
1953	Herb Thomas	Hudson	11	10	27,300
1954	Lee Petty	Dodge	7	3	26,706
1955	Tim Flock	Chrysler	18	19	33,750
1956	Buck Baker	Chrysler	14	12	29,790
1957	Buck Baker	Chevrolet	10	5	24,712
1958	Lee Petty	Oldsmobile	7	4	20,600
1959	Lee Petty	Plymouth	10	2	45,570
1960	Rex White	Chevrolet	6	3	45,260
1961	Ned Jarrett	Chevrolet	1	4	27,285
1962	Joe Weatherly	Pontiac	9	6	56,110
1963	Joe Weatherly	Mercury	3	6	58,110
1964	Richard Petty	Plymouth	9	8	98,810
1965	Ned Jarrett	Ford	13	9	77,966
1966	David Pearson	Dodge	14	7	59,205
1967	Richard Petty	Plymouth	27	18	130,275
1968	David Pearson	Ford	16	12	118,824
1969	David Pearson	Ford	11	14	183,700
1970	Bobby Isaac	Dodge	11	13	121,470
1971	Richard Petty	Plymouth	21	9	309,225
1972	Richard Petty	Plymouth	8	3	227,015
1973	Benny Parsons	Chevrolet	1	0	114,345
1974	Richard Petty	Dodge	10	7	299,175
1975	Richard Petty	Dodge	13	3	378,865
1976	Cale Yarborough	Chevrolet	9	2	387,173
1977	Cale Yarborough	Chevrolet	9	3	477,499
1978	Cale Yarborough	Oldsmobile	10	8	530,751
1979	Richard Petty	Chevrolet	5	1	531,292
1980	Dale Earnhardt	Chevrolet	5	0	588,926
1981	Darrell Waltrip	Buick	12	11	693,342
1982	Darrell Waltrip	Buick	12	7	873,118
1983	Bobby Allison	Buick	6	0	828,355
1984	Terry Labonte	Chevrolet	2	2	713,010
1985	Darrell Waltrip	Chevrolet	3	4	1,318,735
1986	Dale Earnhardt	Chevrolet	5	1	1,783,880
1987	Dale Earnhardt	Chevrolet	11	1	2,099,243
1988	Bill Elliott	Ford	6	6	1,574,639
1989	Rusty Wallace	Pontiac	6	4	2,247,950
1990	Dale Earnhardt	Chevrolet	9	4	3,083,056
1991	Dale Earnhardt	Chevrolet	4	0	2,396,685
1992	Alan Kulwicki	Ford	2	6	2,322,561
1993	Dale Earnhardt	Chevrolet	6	2	3,353,789
1994	Dale Earnhardt	Chevrolet	4	2	3,400,733
1995	Jeff Gordon	Chevrolet	7	9	4,347,343
1996	Terry Labonte	Chevrolet	2	4	4,030,648
1997	Jeff Gordon	Chevrolet	10	1	4,201,227
1998	Jeff Gordon	Chevrolet	13	7	6,175,867
1999	Dale Jarrett	Ford	4	0	3,608,829
2000	Bobby Labonte	Pontiac	4	2	4,041,750
2001	Jeff Gordon	Chevrolet	6	8	6,649,076
2002	Tony Stewart	Pontiac	3	4	4,695,150
2003	Matt Kenseth	Ford	1	2	4,038,120
2004	Kurt Busch	Ford	3	1	4,200,330
2005	Tony Stewart	Chevrolet	5	3	6,987,530
2006	Jimmie Johnson	Chevrolet	5	1	8,909,140
2007	Jimmie Johnson	Chevrolet	10	4	7,646,420
2008	Jimmie Johnson	Chevrolet	7	6	7,354,860
2009	Jimmie Johnson	Chevrolet	7	4	7,339,630
2010	Jimmie Johnson	Chevrolet	6	2	7,264,780
2011	Tony Stewart/	Chevrolet	5	1	6,529,870
	Carl Edwards	Ford	1	3	8,485,990
2012	Brad Keselowski	Dodge	5	0	12,106,255

*Series name changed from Winston Cup after 2003 season, to Nextel Cup 2004–07, and then to Sprint Cup beginning in 2008.

Alltime NASCAR Leaders

WINS		WINS (CONT.)		POLE WINNERS		POLE WINNERS	
Richard Petty	200 ·	Rusty Wallace	55	Richard Petty	123	*Ryan Newman	51
David Pearson	105	Lee Petty	54	David Pearson	113	Bobby Isaac	49
*Jeff Gordon	87	Ned Jarrett	50	*Jeff Gordon	73	Junior Johnson	46
Bobby Allison	84	Junior Johnson	50	Cale Yarborough	69	Buck Baker	45
Darrell Waltrip	84	Herb Thomas	48	Darrell Waltrip	59	Herb Thomas	39
Cale Yarborough	83	*Tony Stewart	48	Bobby Allison	58	Buddy Baker	38
Dale Earnhardt	76	Buck Baker	46	*Mark Martin	56	Geoff Bodine	37
*Jimmie Johnson	64	Bill Elliott	44	Bill Elliott	55	Tim Flock	37

*Active drivers. Note: NASCAR wins leaders and pole position leaders through September 22, 2013.

Formula One Grand Prix Racing

World Driving Champions

Year	Winner	Car	Year	Winner	Car
1950	Guiseppe Farina, Italy	Alfa Romeo	1979	Jody Scheckter, S. Africa	Ferrari
1951	Juan-Manuel Fangio, Argentina	Alfa Romeo	1980	Alan Jones, Australia	Williams-Ford
1952	Alberto Ascari, Italy	Ferrari	1981	Nelson Piquet, Brazil	Brabham-Ford
1953	Alberto Ascari, Italy	Ferrari	1982	Keke Rosberg, Finland	Williams-Ford
1954	Juan-Manuel Fangio, Argentina	Maserati-Mercedes	1983	Nelson Piquet, Brazil	Brabham-BMW
1955	Juan-Manuel Fangio, Argentina	Mercedes	1984	Niki Lauda, Austria	McLaren-Porsche
			1985	Alain Prost, France	McLaren-Porsche
1956	Juan-Manuel Fangio, Argentina	Ferrari	1986	Alain Prost, France	McLaren-Porsche
			1987	Nelson Piquet, Brazil	Williams-Honda
1957	Juan-Manuel Fangio, Argentina	Maserati	1988	Ayrton Senna, Brazil	McLaren-Honda
			1989	Alain Prost, France	McLaren-Honda
1958	Mike Hawthorn, Grt. Britain	Ferrari	1990	Ayrton Senna, Brazil	McLaren-Honda
1959	Jack Brabham, Australia	Cooper-Climax	1991	Ayrton Senna, Brazil	McLaren-Honda
1960	Jack Brabham, Australia	Cooper-Climax	1992	Nigel Mansell, Great Britain	Williams-Renault
1961	Phil Hill, U.S.	Ferrari	1993	Alain Prost, France	Williams-Renault
1962	Graham Hill, Great Britain	BRM	1994	Michael Schumacher, Ger.	Benetton-Ford
1963	Jim Clark, Scotland	Lotus-Climax	1995	Michael Schumacher, Ger.	Benetton-Renault
1964	John Surtees, Great Britain	Ferrari	1996	Damon Hill, Great Britain	Williams-Renault
1965	Jim Clark, Scotland	Lotus-Climax	1997	Jacques Villeneuve, Can.	Williams-Renault
1966	Jack Brabham, Australia	Brabham-Repco	1998	Mika Hakkinen, Finland	McLaren-Mercedes
1967	Denny Hulme, New Zealand	Brabham-Repco	1999	Mika Hakkinen, Finland	McLaren-Mercedes
1968	Graham Hill, Great Britain	Lotus-Ford	2000	Michael Schumacher, Ger.	Ferrari
1969	Jackie Stewart, Scotland	Matra-Ford	2001	Michael Schumacher, Ger.	Ferrari
1970	Jochen Rindt, Austria*	Lotus-Ford	2002	Michael Schumacher, Ger.	Ferrari
1971	Jackie Stewart, Scotland	Tyrell-Ford	2003	Michael Schumacher, Ger.	Ferrari
1972	Emerson Fittipaldi, Brazil	Lotus-Ford	2004	Michael Schumacher, Ger.	Ferrari
1973	Jackie Stewart, Scotland	Tyrell-Ford	2005	Fernando Alonso, Spain	Renault
1974	Emerson Fittipaldi, Brazil	McLaren-Ford	2006	Fernando Alonso, Spain	Renault
1975	Niki Lauda, Austria	Ferrari	2007	Kimi Raikkonen, Finland	Ferrari
1976	James Hunt, Great Britain	McLaren-Ford	2008	Lewis Hamilton, Great Britain	McLaren-Mercedes
1977	Niki Lauda, Austria	Ferrari	2009	Jenson Button, Great Britain	Brawn-Mercedes
1978	Mario Andretti, U.S.	Lotus-Ford	2010	Sebastian Vettel, Germany	RBR-Renault
			2011	Sebastian Vettel, Germany	RBR-Renault
			2012	Sebastian Vettel, Germany	RBR-Renault

*The championship was awarded posthumously, after Rindt was killed during practice for the Italian Grand Prix.

Alltime F/1 Grand Prix Winners

Driver	Wins	Driver	Wins
Michael Schumacher, Germany	91	Jackie Stewart, Great Britain	27
Alain Prost, France	51	Jim Clark, Great Britain	25
Ayrton Senna, Brazil	41	Niki Lauda, Austria	25
*Sebastian Vettel, Germany	33	Juan-Manuel Fangio, Argentina	24
*Fernando Alonso, Spain	32	Nelson Piquet, Brazil	23
Nigel Mansell, Great Britain	31		

Alltime F/1 Grand Prix Pole Winners

Driver	Poles	Driver	Poles
Michael Schumacher, Germany	68	Nigel Mansell, Great Britain	32
Ayrton Senna, Brazil	65	*Lewis Hamilton, Great Britain	31
*Sebastian Vettel, Germany	41	Juan-Manuel Fangio, Argentina	29
Alain Prost, France	33	Mika Hakkinen, Finland	26
Jim Clark, Great Britain	33	Niki Lauda, Austria	24
		Nelson Piquet, Brazil	24

*Active driver in 2013. Note: Grand Prix winners and pole winners through September 22, 2013.

The 24 Hours of Daytona

Year	Winner	Car	Avg Speed	Distance
1962	Dan Gurney	Lotus 19-Class SP11	104.101 mph	3 hrs (312.42 mi)
1963	Pedro Rodriguez	Ferrari-Class 12	102.074 mph	3 hrs (308.61 mi)
1964	Pedro Rodriguez/Phil Hill	Ferrari 250 LM	98.230 mph	2,000 km
1965	Ken Miles/Lloyd Ruby	Ford	99.944 mph	2,000 km
1966	Ken Miles/Lloyd Ruby	Ford Mark II	108.020 mph	24 hrs (2,570.63 mi)
1967	Lorenzo Bandini/Chris Amon	Ferrari 330 P4	105.688 mph	24 hrs (2,537.46 mi)
1968	Vic Elford/Jochen Neerpasch	Porsche 907	106.697 mph	24 hrs (2,565.69 mi)
1969	Mark Donohue/Chuck Parsons	Chevy Lola	99.268 mph	24 hrs (2,383.75 mi)
1970	Pedro Rodriguez/Leo Kinnunen	Porsche 917	114.866 mph	24 hrs (2,758.44 mi)
1971	Pedro Rodriguez/Jackie Oliver	Porsche 917K	109.203 mph	24 hrs (2,621.28 mi)
1972*	Mario Andretti/Jacky Ickx	Ferrari 312/P	122.573 mph	6 hrs (738.24 mi)
1973	Peter Gregg/Hurley Haywood	Porsche Carrera	106.225 mph	24 hrs (2,552.7 mi)
1974	(No race)			
1975	Peter Gregg/Hurley Haywood	Porsche Carrera	108.531 mph	24 hrs (2,606.04 mi)
1976†	Peter Gregg/Brian Redman/ John Fitzpatrick	BMW CSL	104.040 mph	24 hrs (2,092.8 mi)
1977	John Graves/Hurley Haywood/ Dave Helmick	Porsche Carrera	108.801 mph	24 hrs (2,615 mi)
1978	Rolf Stommelen/ Antoine Hezemans/Peter Gregg	Porsche Turbo	108.743 mph	24 hrs (2,611.2 mi)
1979	Ted Field/Danny Ongais/ Hurley Haywood	Porsche Turbo	109.249 mph	24 hrs (2,626.56 mi)
1980	Volkert Meri/Rolf Stommelen/ Reinhold Joest	Porsche Turbo	114.303 mph	24 hrs (2,745.6 mi)
1981	Bob Garretson/Bobby Rahal/ Brian Redman	Porsche Turbo	113.153 mph	24 hrs (2,718.72 mi)
1982	John Paul Jr/John Paul Sr/ Rolf Stommelen	Porsche Turbo	114.794 mph	24 hrs (2,760.96 mi)
1983	Preston Henn/Bob Wollek/ Claude Ballot-Lena/A.J. Foyt	Porsche Turbo	98.781 mph	24 hrs (2,373.12 mi)
1984	Sarel van der Merwe/ Graham Duxbury/Tony Martin	Porsche March	103.119 mph	24 hrs (2,476.8 mi)
1985	A.J. Foyt/Bob Wollek/ Al Unser/Thierry Boutsen	Porsche 962	104.162 mph	24 hrs (2,502.68 mi)
1986	Al Holbert/Derek Bell/Al Unser Jr.	Porsche 962	105.484 mph	24 hrs (2,534.72 mi)
1987	Chip Robinson/Derek Bell/ Al Holbert/Al Unser Jr.	Porsche 962	111.599 mph	24 hrs (2,680.68 mi)
1988	Martin Brundle/John Nielsen/ Raul Boesel	Jaguar XJR-9	107.943 mph	24 hrs (2,591.68 mi)
1989	John Andretti/Derek Bell/ Bob Wollek	Porsche 962	92.009 mph	24 hrs (2,210.76 mi)
1990	Davy Jones/ Jan Lammers/ Andy Wallace	Jaguar XJR-12	112.857 mph	24 hrs (2,709.16 mi)
1991	Hurley Haywood/ John Winter/ Frank Jelinski/ Henri Pescarolo/ Bob Wollek	Porsche 962C	106.633 mph	24 hrs (2,559.64 mi)
1992	Massahiro Hasemi/ Kazuyoshi Hoshino/ Toshio Suzuki/ Anders Olofsson	Nissan R91CP	112.987 mph	24 hrs (2,712.72 mi)
1993	P.J. Jones/Mark Dismore/ Rocky Moran	Toyota Eagle MK III	103.537 mph	24 hrs (2,484.88 mi)
1994	Paul Gentilozzi/ Scott Pruett/ Butch Leitzinger/ Steve Millen	Nissan 300 ZX	104.80 mph	24 hrs (2,693.67 mi)
1995	Jurgen Lassig/ Christophe Buochut/ Giovanni Lavaggi/ Marco Werner	Porsche Spyder K8	102.28 mph	690 laps (2,456.4 mi)
1996	Wayne Taylor/ Scott Sharp/ Jim Pace	Oldsmobile Mark III	103.32 mph	697 laps (2,481.32 mi)
1997	Elliot Forbes-Robinson/ John Schneider/Rob Dyson/ John Paul Jr/Butch Leitzinger/James Weaver/Andy Wallace	Ford R & S MK III	102.292 mph	690 laps (2,456.4 mi)
1998	Arie Luyendyk/Didier Theys/ Mauro Baldi	Ferrari 333 SP	105.565 mph	711 laps (2,531.16 mi)
1999	Elliott Forbes-Robinson/ Butch Leitzinger/ Andy Wallace	Ford R & S MK III	104.9 mph	708 laps (2,520.48 mi)
2000	Olivier Beretta/Karl Wendlinger/ Dominique Dupuy	Dodge Viper	107.207 mph	723 laps (2,573.88 m)

*Race shortened due to fuel crisis. †Course lengthened from 3.81 miles to 3.84 miles.

The 24 Hours of Daytona *(Cont.)*

Year	Winner	Car	Avg. Speed	Distance
2001	Ron Fellows/Chris Kneifel/ Franck Freon/Johnny O'Connell	Corvette	97.293 mph	656 laps (2,335.360 mi)
2002	Didier Theys/Fredy Lienhard/ Max Papis/Mauro Baldi	Dallara-Judd (SRP)	106.143 mph	716 laps (2,548.96 mi)
2003	Kevin Buckler/Michael Schrom Timo Bernhard/Jorg Bergmeister	Porsche GT3 RS	114.068 mph (top speed)	694 laps (2,470.64 mi)
2004	Forest Barber/Terry Borcheller Andy Pilgrim/Christian Fittipaldi	Pontiac Doran	117.651 mph	526 laps (1,872.56 mi)
2005	Wayne Taylor/Max Angelelli Emmanuel Collard	Pontiac Riley	119.397 mph	710 laps (2,527.60 mi)
2006	Scott Dixon/Dan Wheldon Casey Mears	Lexus Riley	108.826 mph	734 laps (2,613.04 mi)
2007	Scott Pruett/Salvador Duran Juan Pablo Montoya	Lexus Riley	99.020 mph	668 laps (2,378.08 mi)
2008	Scott Pruett/Memo Rojas Juan Pablo Montoya/Dario Franchitti	Lexus Riley	103.057 mph	695 laps (2,474.20 mi)
2009	Darren Law/David Donohue Buddy Rice/Antonio Garcia	Porsche Riley	108.994 mph	735 laps (2,616.60 mi.)
2010	Terry Borcheller/Joao Barbosa Ryan Dalziel/Mike Rockenfeller	Porsche Riley	111.930 mph	755 laps (2,687.77 mi.)
2011	Joey Hand/Scott Pruett Graham Rahal/Memo Rojas	BMW Riley	106.877 mph	721 laps (2,566.76 mi.)
2012	John Pew, Oswaldo Negri Jr, AJ Allmendinger, Justin Wilson	Ford Riley	112.834 mph	761 laps (2,709.16 mi.)
2013	Charlie Kimball, J. P. Montoya, Scott Pruett, Memo Rojas	BMW Riley	105.122 mph	709 laps

World Sportscar Champions

Year	Winner	Car	Year	Winner	Car
1978	Peter Gregg	Porsche 935	1989	Geoff Brabham	Nissan GTP
1979	Peter Gregg	Porsche 935	1990	Geoff Brabham	Nissan GTP
1980	John Fitzpatrick	Porsche 935	1991	Geoff Brabham	Nissan NPT
1981	Brian Redman	Chevy Lola	1992	Juan Fangio II	Toyota EGL MKIII
1982	John Paul Jr	Chevy Lola	1993	Juan Fangio II	Toyota EGL MKIII
1983	Al Holbert	Chevy March	1994	Wayne Taylor	Mazda Kudzu
1984	Randy Lanier	Chevy March	1995	Fermin Velez	Ferrari 333 SP
1985	Al Holbert	Porsche 962	1996	Wayne Taylor	Mazda Kudzu
1986	Al Holbert	Porsche 962	1997	Butch Leitzinger	Ford R&S MKIII
1987	Chip Robinson	Porsche 962	1998	Butch Leitzinger	Ford R&S MKIII
1988	Geoff Brabham	Nissan GTP			

Year	PI	GTC	GT
1999	Elliott Forbes-Robinson	Olivier Beretta	Cort Wagner
2000	Allan McNish	Olivier Beretta	Sascha Maassen
2001	Emanuele Pirro	Terry Borcheller	Jörg Müller
2002	Tom Kristensen	Ron Fellows	Lucas Luhr
2003	Frank Biela/Marco Werner	Ron Fellows/John O'Connell	Sascha Maassen/L. Luhr
2004	Frank Biela/Emanuele Pirro	Oliver Gavin/Olivier Beretta	Patrick Long/Jorg Bergmeister
2005	Frank Biela/Emanuele Pirro	Oliver Gavin/Olivier Beretta	Patrick Long/Jorg Bergmeister
2006	R. Capello/A. McNish	Oliver Gavin/Olivier Beretta	Johannes van Overbeek
2007	R. Capello/A. McNish	Oliver Gavin/Olivier Beretta	Mika Salo/Jaime Melo
2008	Lucas Luhr/Marco Werner	Jan Magnussen/J. O'Connell	Jorg Bergmeister/Wolf Henzler
2009	David Brabham/Scott Sharp	Oliver Gavin/Olivier Beretta	Jorg Bergmeister/Patrick Long
2010	D. Brabham/Simon Pagenaud	Tim. Pappas/Jer. Bleekemolen	Jorg Bergmeister/Patrick Long
2011	Guy Smith/Chris Dyson	Timothy Pappas	Joey Hand/Dirk Mueller
2012	Klaus Graf/Lucas Luhr	Cooper MacNeil	Oliver Gavin/Tommy Milner

Year	Winning Drivers	Car
1923	André Lagache/ René Léonard	Chenard & Walker
1924	John Duff/Francis Clement	Bentley
1925	Gérard de Courcelles/ André Rossignol	La Lorraine
1926	Robert Bloch/ André Rossignol	La Lorraine
1927	J. Dudley Benjafield/ Sammy Davis	Bentley
1928	Woolf Barnato/Bernard Rubin	Bentley
1929	Woolf Barnato/ Sir Henry Birkin	Bentley Speed 6
1930	Woolf Barnato/Glen Kidston	Bentley Speed 6
1931	Earl Howe/ Sir Henry Birkin	Alfa Romeo 8C-2300 sc
1932	Raymond Sommer/ Luigi Chinetti	Alfa Romeo 8C-2300 sc
1933	Raymond Sommer/ Tazio Nuvolari	Alfa Romeo 8C-2300 sc
1934	Luigi Chinetti/ Philippe Etancelin	Alfa Romeo 8C-2300 sc
1935	John Hindmarsh/Louis Fontés	Lagonda M45R
1936	RACE CANCELLED	
1937	Jean-Pierre Wimille/Robert Benoist	Bugatti 57G sc
1938	Eugene Chaboud/Jean Tremoulet	Delahaye 135M
1939	Jean-Pierre Wimille/Pierre Veyron	Bugatti 57G sc
1940–48	RACES CANCELLED	
1949	Luigi Chinetti/Lord Selsdon	Ferrari 166MM
1950	Louis Rosier/Jean-Louis Rosier	Talbot-Lago
1951	Peter Walker/Peter Whitehead	Jaguar C
1952	Hermann Lang/Fritz Reiss	Mercedes-Benz 300 SL
1953	Tony Rolt/Duncan Hamilton	Jaguar C
1954	Froilan Gonzales/Maurice Trintignant	Ferrari 375
1955	Mike Hawthorn/Ivor Bueb	Jaguar D
1956	Ron Flockhart/Ninian Sanderson	Jaguar D
1957	Ron Flockhart/Ivor Bueb	Jaguar D
1958	Olivier Gendebien/Phil Hill	Ferrari 250 TR58
1959	Carroll Shelby/Roy Salvadori	Aston Martin DBR1
1960	Olivier Gendebien/Paul Frère	Ferrari 250 TR59/60
1961	Olivier Gendebien/Phil Hill	Ferrari 250 TR61
1962	Olivier Gendebien/Phil Hill	Ferrari 250P
1963	Lodovico Scarfiotti/ Lorenzo Bandini	Ferrari 250P
1964	Jean Guichet/Nino Vaccarella	Ferrari 275P
1965	Jochen Rindt/ Masten Gregory	Ferrari 250LM
1966	Chris Amon/Bruce McLaren	Ford Mk2
1967	Dan Gurney/A.J. Foyt	Ford Mk4
1968	Pedro Rodriguez/Lucien Bianchi	Ford GT40
1969	Jacky Ickx/Jackie Oliver	Ford GT40
1970	Hans Herrmann/Richard Attwood	Porsche 917
1971	Helmut Marko/Gijs van Lennep	Porsche 917
1972	Henri Pescarolo/Graham Hill	Matra-Simca MS670
1973	Henri Pescarolo/ Gérard Larrousse	Matra-Simca MS670B
1974	Henri Pescarolo/ Gérard Larrousse	Matra-Simca MS670B
1975	Jacky Ickx/Derek Bell	Mirage-Ford MB
1976	Jacky Ickx/Gijs van Lennep	Porsche 936
1977	Jacky Ickx/Jurgen Barth/ Hurley Haywood	Porsche 936
1978	Jean-Pierre Jaussaud/ Didier Pironi	Renault-Alpine A442
1979	Klaus Ludwig/ Bill Whittington/Don Whittington	Porsche 935
1980	Jean-Pierre Jaussaud/ Jean Rondeau	Rondeau-Ford M379B
1981	Jacky Ickx/Derek Bell	Porsche 936-81
1982	Jacky Ickx/Derek Bell	Porsche 956

Year	Winning Drivers	Car
1983	Vern Schuppan/ Hurley Haywood/Al Holbert	Porsche 956-83
1984	Klaus Ludwig/Henri Pescarolo	Porsche 956B
1985	Klaus Ludwig/ Paolo Barilla/John Winter	Porsche 956B
1986	Derek Bell/ Hans-Joachim Stuck/Al Holbert	Porsche 962C
1987	Derek Bell/ Hans-Joachim Stuck/Al Holbert	Porsche 962C
1988	Jan Lammers/ Johnny Dumfries/Andy Wallace	Jaguar XJR9LM
1989	Jochen Mass/ Manuel Reuter/Stanley Dickens	Sauber-Mercedes C9-88
1990	John Nielsen/ Price Cobb/Martin Brundle	TWR Jaguar XJR-12
1991	Volker Weidler/ Johnny Herbert/Bertrand Gachof	Mazda 787B
1992	Derek Warwick/ Yannick Dalmas/Mark Blundell	Peugeot 905B
1993	Geoff Brabham/ Christophe Bouchut/Eric Helary	Peugeot 905
1994	Yannick Dalmas/ Hurley Haywood/Mauro Baldi	Porsche 962
1995	Yannick Dalmas/ J.J. Lehto/Masanori Sekiya	McLaren BMW
1996	Manuel Reuter/ Davy Jones/Alexander Wurz	TWR Porsche
1997	Michele Alboreto/ Stefan Johansson/Tom Kristensen	TWR Porsche
1998	Allan McNish/ Laurent Aiello/Stephane Ortelli	Porsche GT One
1999	Yannick Dalmas/ Joachim Winkelhock/Pierluigi Martini	BMW V12 LMR
2000	Frank Biela/ Tom Kristensen/Emanuele Pirro	Audi R8
2001	Frank Biela/ Tom Kristensen/Emanuele Pirro	Audi R8
2002	Frank Biela/ Tom Kristensen/Emanuele Pirro	Audi R8
2003	Rinaldo Capello/ Tom Kristensen/Guy Smith	Bentley EXP Speed 8
2004	Rinaldo Capello/ Seiji Ara/Tom Kristensen	Audi R8
2005	J.J. Lehto/ Marco Werner/Tom Kristensen	Audi R8
2006	Frank Biela/ Emanuele Pirro/Marco Werner	Audi R10
2007	Frank Biela/ Emanuele Pirro/Marco Werner	Audi R10
2008	Rinaldo Capello/ Tom Kristensen/Allan McNish	Audi R10
2009	Marc Gene/ Alexander Wurz/David Brabham	Peugeot 908
2010	Timo Bernhard/ Romain Dumas/Mike Rockenfeller	Audi R15
2011	Marcel Fassler/Andre Lotterer/ Benoit Treluyer	Audi R18
2012	Marcel Fassler/Andre Lotterer/ Benoit Treluyer	Audi R18 e-tron quattro
2013	Allan McNish/Tom Kristensen/ Loïc Duval	Audi R18 e-tron quattro

Horse Racing

Jockey Joel Rosario
exulted in victory after
driving Orb through a stirring—
and muddy—stretch run at
the Kentucky Derby

BILL FRAKES

The Triple Crown

139th Kentucky Derby

May 4, 2013. Grade I, 3-year-olds; 11th race, Churchill Downs, Louisville. All: 126 lbs. Distance: 1¼ miles. Purse: $2,000,000 guaranteed. Track: sloppy. Off: 6:33 p.m. Winner: Orb (By Malibu Moon out of Lady Liberty by Unbridled); Times: 22.57, 45.33, 1:09.80, 1:36.16, 2:02.89. Won: driving. Breeder: Stuart Janney III & Phipps Stable (Kentucky).

Horse	Finish-PP	Margin	Trainer/Jockey
Orb	1–15	2½	Shug McGaughey/Joel Rosario
Golden Soul	2–3	1	Dallas Stewart/Miguel Mena
Revolutionary	3–2	hd	Todd Pletcher/Calvin Borel
Normandy Invasion	4–4	hd	Chad Brown/Javier Castellano
Mylute	5–5	6	Thomas Amoss/Rosie Napravnik
Oxbow	6–1	2	D. Wayne Lukas/Gary Stevens
Lines Of Battle	7–10	½	Aidan O'Brien/Ryan Moore
Will Take Charge	8–16	1	D. Wayne Lukas/Jon Court
Charming Kitten	9–14	hd	Todd Pletcher/Edgar Prado
Giant Finish	10–6	hd	Anthony Dutrow/Jose Espinoza
Overanalyze	11–8	hd	Todd Pletcher/Rafael Bejarano
Palace Malice	12–9	2	Todd Pletcher/Mike Smith
Java's War	13–18	nk	Kenneth McPeek/Julien Leparoux
Verrazano	14–13	6½	Todd Pletcher/John Velazquez
Itsmyluckyday	15–11	2	Edward Plesa/Elvis Trujillo
Frac Daddy	16–17	25¼	Kenneth McPeek/Victor Lebron
Goldencents	17–7	3¼	Doug O'Neill/Kevin Krigger
Vyjack	18–19	nk	Rudy Rodriguez/Garrett Gomez
Falling Sky	19–12		John Terranova/Luis Saez

138th Preakness Stakes

May 18, 2013. Grade I, 3-year-olds; 12th race, Pimlico Race Course, Baltimore. All: 126 lbs. Distance: 1³⁄₁₆ miles; Stakes value: $1,000,000. Track: fast. Off: 6:20 p.m. Winner: Oxbow (By Awesome Again out of Tizamazing by Cee's Tizzy); Times: 23.94, 48.60, 1:13.26, 1:38.14, 1:57.54. Won: driving. Breeder: Colts Neck Stables (Kentucky).

Horse	Finish-PP	Margin	Trainer/Jockey
Oxbow	1–6	1¾	D. Wayne Lukas/Gary Stevens
Itsmyluckyday	2–9	¹⁄₂	Edward Plesa/John Velazquez
Mylute	3–5	6¾	Thomas Amoss/Rosie Napravnik
Orb	4–1	½	Shug McGaughey/Joel Rosario
Goldencents	5–2	½	Doug O'Neill/Kevin Krigger
Departing	6–4	6	Albert Stall/B. Hernandez Jr.
Will Take Charge	7–7	16	D. Wayne Lukas/Mike Smith
Governor Charlie	8–8	15¼	Bob Baffert/Martin Garcia
Tinseltown Five	9–3	—	D. Wayne Lukas/Julien Leparoux

145th Belmont Stakes

June 8, 2013. Grade I, 3-year-olds; 11th race, Belmont Park, Elmont, NY. All: 126 lbs. Distance: 1½ miles. Stakes value: $1,000,000. Track: fast. Off: 6:38 p.m. Winner: Palace Malice (By Curlin out of Palace Rumor by Royal Anthem); Times: 23.11, 46.66, 1:10.95, 1:36.47, 2:03.12, 2:30.70. Won: driving. Breeder: W.S. Farish (Kentucky).

Horse	Finish-PP	Margin	Trainer/Jockey
Palace Malice	1–12	3¼	Todd Pletcher/Mike Smith
Oxbow	2–7	1¾	D. Wayne Lukas/Gary Stevens
Orb	3–5	1	Shug McGaughey/Joel Rosario
Incognito	4–6	½	Kiaran McLaughlin/Irad Ortiz
Revolutionary	5–9	2	Todd Pletcher/Javier Castellano
Unlimited Budget	6–13	no	Todd Pletcher/Rosie Napravnik
Overanalyze	7–3	1½	Todd Pletcher/John Velazquez
Vyjack	8–11	¾	Rudy Rodriguez/Julien Leparoux
Golden Soul	9–14	6¼	D. Stewart/Robby Albarado
Will Take Charge	10–10	18¼	D. Wayne Lukas/Jon Court
Giant Finish	11–4	14	Anthony Dutrow/Edgar Prado
Midnight Taboo	12–8	9¼	Todd Pletcher/Garrett Gomez
Freedom Child	13–2	5¼	Thomas Albertrani/Luis Saez
Frac Daddy	14–1	—	Kenneth McPeek/Alan Garcia

Grade I North American Stakes Races

Late 2012–2013*

Date	Race	Track	Distance	Winner	Jockey/Trainer	Purse ($)
Sep 29	Chandelier Stakes	Santa Anita	1 1/16 miles	Executiveprivilege	R. Bejarano/B. Baffert	250,000
Sep 29	Rodeo Drive Stakes	Santa Anita	1 1/4 miles	Marketing Mix	G. Gomez/T. Proctor	250,000
Sep 29	Zenyatta Stakes	Santa Anita	1 1/16 miles	Love and Pride	M. Garcia/T. Pletcher	250,000
Sep 29	Frontrunner Stakes	Santa Anita	1 1/16 miles	Power Broker	R. Bejarano/B. Baffert	250,000
Sep 29	Awesome Again Stakes	Santa Anita	1 1/8 miles	Game on Dude	R. Bejarano/B. Baffert	250,000
Sep 29	Jockey Club Gold Cup Invitational	Belmont Park	1 1/4 miles	Flat Out	J. Rosario/W. Mott	1,000,000
Sep 29	Joe Hirsch Turf Classic	Belmont Park	1 1/2 miles	Point Of Entry	J. Velazquez/C. McGaughey III	600,000
Sep 29	Flower Bowl Invitational	Belmont Park	1 1/4 miles	Nahrain	J. Velazquez/R. Varian	1,000,000
Sep 29	Beldame Stakes	Belmont Park	1 1/8 miles	Royal Delta	M. Smith/W. Mott	400,000
Sep 29	Vosburgh Stakes	Belmont Park	6 furlongs	The Lumber Guy	J. Velazquez/M. Hushion	400,000
Oct 5	Darley Alcibiades Stakes	Keeneland	1 1/16 miles	Spring In The Air	P. Husbands/M. Casse	400,000
Oct 6	Frizette Stakes	Belmont Park	1 mile	Dreaming Of Julia	J. Velazquez/T. Pletcher	400,000
Oct 6	Jamaica Handicap	Belmont Park	1 1/8 miles	King David	R. Napravnik/M. Maker	400,000
Oct 6	Santa Anita Sprint Champ.	Santa Anita	6 furlongs	Coil	M. Garcia/B. Baffert	250,000
Oct 6	Shadwell Turf Mile	Keeneland	1 mile	Wise Dan	J. Lezcano/C. Lopresti	750,000
Oct 6	Dixiana Breeders' Futurity	Keeneland	1 1/16 miles	Joha	R. Maragh/M. Maker	400,000
Oct 6	First Lady Stakes	Keeneland	1 mile	Tapitsfly	J. Lezcano/D. Romans	350,000
Oct 6	Champagne Stakes	Belmont Park	1 mile	Shanghai Bobby	R. Napravnik/T. Pletcher	400,000
Oct 7	Spinster Stakes	Keeneland	1 1/8 miles	In Lingerie	J. Velazquez/T. Pletcher	500,000
Oct 13	Queen Elizabeth II Challenge Cup	Keeneland	1 1/8 miles	Dayatthespa	J. Castellano/C. Brown	400,000
Oct 14	Canadian International Stakes	Woodbine	1 1/2 miles	Joshua Tree	L. Dettori/M. Botti	1,500,000
Oct 14	Nearctic Stakes	Woodbine	6 furlongs	Next Question	R. Dominguez/M. Trombetta	500,000
Oct 14	E.P. Taylor Stakes	Woodbine	1 1/4 miles	Siyouma	G. Mosse/F. Doumen	1,000,000
Nov 2	Breeders' Cup Juvenile Sprint	Santa Anita	6 furlongs	Hightail	R. Maragh/D. Lukas	500,000
Nov 2	Breeders' Cup Juvenile Fillies Turf	Santa Anita	1 mile	Flotilla	C. Lemaire/M. Delzangles	1,000,000
Nov 2	Breeders' Cup Juvenile Fillies	Santa Anita	1 1/16 miles	Beholder	G. Gomez/R. Mandella	2,000,000
Nov 2	Breeders' Cup Filly & Mare Turf	Santa Anita	1 1/4 miles	Zagora	J. Castellano/C. Brown	2,000,000
Nov 2	Breeders' Cup Ladies' Classic	Santa Anita	1 1/8 miles	Royal Delta	M. Smith/W. Mott	2,000,000
Nov 3	Breeders' Cup Juvenile Turf	Santa Anita	1 mile	George Vancouver	R. Moore/A. O'Brien	1,000,000
Nov 3	Breeders' Cup F & M Sprint	Santa Anita	7 furlongs	Groupie Doll	R. Maragh/W. Bradley	1,000,000
Nov 3	Breeders' Cup Sprint	Santa Anita	6 furlongs	Trinniberg	W. Martinez/S. Parbhoo	1,500,000
Nov 3	Breeders' Cup Turf Sprint	Santa Anita	6 1/2 furlongs	Mizdirection	M. Smith/M. Puype	1,000,000
Nov 3	Breeders' Cup Dirt Mile	Santa Anita	1 mile	Tapizar	C. Nakatani/S. Asmussen	1,000,000
Nov 3	Breeders' Cup Turf	Santa Anita	1 1/2 miles	Little Mike	R. Dominguez/D. Romans	3,000,000
Nov 3	Breeders' Cup Juvenile	Santa Anita	1 1/16 miles	Shanghai Bobby	R. Napravnik/T. Pletcher	2,000,000
Nov 3	Breeders' Cup Mile	Santa Anita	1 mile	Wise Dan	J. Velazquez/C. Lopresti	2,000,000
Nov 3	Breeders' Cup Classic	Santa Anita	1 1/4 miles	Fort Larned	B. Hernandez, Jr./I. Wilkes	5,000,000
Nov 23	Clark Handicap	Churchill Downs	1 1/8 miles	Shackleford	J. Castanon/D. Romans	400,000
Nov 24	Cigar Mile	Aqueduct	1 mile	Stay Thirsty	R. Dominguez/T. Pletcher	350,000
Nov 24	Gazelle Stakes	Aqueduct	1 1/8 miles	Dance Card	R. Dominguez/K. McLaughlin	350,000
Nov 25	The Matriarch	Hollywood Park	1 mile	Better Lucky	E. Castro/T. Albertrani	250,000
Nov 25	Hollywood Derby	Hollywood Park	1 1/4 miles	Unbridled Command	J. Castellano/T. Bush	250,000
Dec 08	Hollywood Starlet	Hollywood Park	1 1/16 miles	Pure Fun	G. Gomez/K. McPeek	500,000
Dec 15	CashCall Futurity	Hollywood Park	1 1/16 miles	Violence	J. Castellano/T. Pletcher	750,000
Dec 26	Malibu Stakes	Santa Anita	7 furlongs	Jimmy Creed	G. Gomez/R. Mandella	300,000
Dec 26	La Brea Stakes	Santa Anita	7 furlongs	Book Review	R. Bejarano/B. Baffert	300,000
Feb 9	Donn Handicap	Gulfstream Park	1 1/8 miles	Graydar	E. Prado/T. Pletcher	500,000
Feb 9	Gulfstream Park Turf Handicap	Gulfstream Park	1 1/8 miles	Point of Entry	J. Velazquez/C. McGaughey	300,000
Mar 2	Santa Anita Handicap	Santa Anita	1 1/4 miles	Game On Dude	M. Smith/B. Baffert	750,000
Mar 2	Frank E. Kilroe Mile	Santa Anita	1 mile	Suggestive Boy	J. Talamo/R. McAnally	300,000
Mar 2	Las Virgenes Stakes	Santa Anita	1 mile	Beholder	G. Gomez/R. Mandella	250,000
Mar 16	Santa Margarita Stakes	Santa Anita	1 1/8 miles	Joyful Victory	R. Napravnik/J. Jones	300,000
Mar 30	Florida Derby	Gulfstream Park	1 1/8 miles	Orb	J. Velazquez/C. McGaughey	1,000,000
Apr 6	Wood Memorial Stakes	Aqueduct	1 1/8 miles	Verrazano	J. Velazquez/T. Pletcher	1,000,000
Apr 6	Carter Handicap	Aqueduct	7 furlongs	Swagger Jack	I. Ortiz, Jr./M. Wolfson	400,000
Apr 6	Ashland Stakes	Keeneland	1 1/16 miles	Emollient	M. Smith/W. Mott	500,000
Apr 6	Santa Anita Derby	Santa Anita	1 1/8 miles	Goldencents	K. Krigger/D. O'Neill	750,000
Apr 6	Santa Anita Oaks	Santa Anita	1 1/16 miles	Beholder	G. Gomez/R. Mandella	300,000
Apr 12	Maker's 46 Mile Stakes	Keeneland	1 mile	Wise Dan	J. Lezcano/C. LoPresti	300,000

* Through September 22, 2013

Grade I North American Stakes Races (*Cont.)*

2013*

Date	Race	Track	Distance	Winner	Jockey/Trainer	Purse ($)
Apr 12	Apple Blossom Handicap	Oaklawn Park	1 1/16 miles	On Fire Baby	J. Johnson/G. Hartlage	500,000
Apr 13	Blue Grass Stakes	Keeneland	1⅛ miles	Java's War	J. Leparoux/K. McPeek	750,000
Apr 13	Jenny Wiley Stakes	Keeneland	1 1/16 miles	Centre Court	J. Leparoux/G. Arnold, II	300,000
Apr 13	Madison Stakes	Keeneland	7 furlongs	Last Full Measure	C. Nakatani/P. Oliver	300,000
Apr 13	Arkansas Derby	Oaklawn Park	1⅛ miles	Overanalyze	R. Bejarano/T. Pletcher	1,000,000
May 3	Kentucky Oaks	Churchill Downs	1⅛ miles	Princess of Slymar	M. Smith/T. Pletcher	1,000,000
May 4	Kentucky Derby	Churchill Downs	1¼ miles	Orb	J. Rosario/C. McGaughey III	2,000,000
May 4	Woodford Reserve Turf Classic	Churchill Downs	1⅛ miles4up	Wise Dan	J. Lezcano/C. LoPresti	500,000
May 4	Humana Distaff	Churchill Downs	7 furlongs	Aubby K	E. Prado/R. Nicks	300,000
May 18	Preakness Stakes	Pimlico	1 3/16 miles	Oxbow	G. Stevens/D. Lukas	1,000,000
May 27	Metropolitan Handicap	Belmont Park	1 mile	Sahara Sky	J. Rosario/J. Hollendorfer	750,000
May 27	Ogden Phipps Handicap	Belmont Park	1 1/16 miles	Tiz Miz Sue	J. Rocco, Jr./S. Hobby	400,000
May 27	Acorn Stakes	Belmont Park	1 mile	Midnight Lucky	R. Napravnik/B. Baffert	300,000
May 27	Gamely Stakes	Hollywood Park	1⅛ miles	Marketing Mix	G. Stevens/T. Proctor	250,000
Jun 8	Belmont Stakes	Belmont Park	1½miles	Palace Malice	M. Smith/T. Pletcher	1,000,000
Jun 8	Just a Game Stakes	Belmont Park	1 mile	Stephanie's Kitten	J. Velazquez/W. Catalano	500,000
Jun 8	Manhattan Handicap	Belmont Park	1¼ miles	Point of Entry	J. Velazquez/C. McGaughey III	500,000
Jun 15	Vanity Handicap	Hollywood Park	1⅛ miles	Byrama	G. Stevens/S. Callaghan	250,000
Jun 15	Stephen Foster Handicap	Churchill Downs	1⅛ miles	Fort Larned	B. Hernandez, Jr./I. Wilkes	500,000
Jun 22	Mother Goose Stakes	Belmont Park	1 1/16 miles	Close Hatches	J. Rosario/W. Mott	300,000
Jun 29	Shoemaker Mile Stakes	Hollywood Park	1 mile	Obviously	J. Talamo/M. Mitchell	300,000
Jun 29	Triple Bend Handicap	Hollywood Park	7 furlongs	Centralinteligence	V. Espinoza/R. Ellis	250,000
Jul 6	Hollywood Gold Cup	Hollywood Park	1¼ miles	Game on Dude	M. Smith/B. Baffert	500,000
Jul 6	United Nations Stakes	Monmouth Park	1⅜ miles	Big Blue Kitten	C. Brown/J. Bravo	500,000
Jul 6	Princess Rooney Handicap	Calder	6 furlongs	Starship Truffles	E. Zayas/M. Wolfson	350,000
Jul 13	American Oaks	Hollywood Park	1¼ miles	Emollient	M. Smith/W. Mott	350,000
Jul 13	Man O' War Stakes	Belmont Park	1⅜ miles	Boisterous	J. Velazquez/C. McGaughey III	600,000
Jul 20	Eddie Read Stakes	Del Mar	1⅛ miles	Jeranimo	R. Bejarano/M. Pender	300,000
Jul 20	Coaching Club American Oaks	Saratoga	1⅛ miles	Princess of Sylmar	J. Castellano/T. Pletcher	300,000
Jul 20	Delaware Handicap	Delaware Park	1¼ miles	Royal Delta	M. Smith/W. Mott	750,000
Jul 27	Diana Stakes	Saratoga	1⅛ miles	Laughing	J. Lezcano/A. Goldberg	600,000
Jul 27	Prioress Stakes	Saratoga	6 furlongs	Lighthouse Bay	J. Rocco, Jr/G. Weaver	300,000
Jul 28	Haskell Invitational	Monmouth Park	1⅛ miles	Verrazano	J. Velazquez/T. Pletcher	1,000,000
Jul 28	Molly Pitcher Stakes	Monmouth Park	1 1/16 miles	Joyful Victory	R. Napravnik/J. Jones	200,000
Jul 28	Bing Crosby Stakes	Del Mar	6 furlongs	Points Offthebench	M. Smith/T. Yakteen	300,000
Aug 3	Clement L. Hirsch Stakes	Del Mar	1 1/16 miles	Lady of Fifty	C. Nakatani/J. Hollendorfer	300,000
Aug 3	Whitney Invitational Handicap	Saratoga	1⅛ miles	Cross Traffic	J. Velazquez/T. Pletcher	750,000
Aug 4	Alfred G. Vanderbilt Handicap	Saratoga	6 furlongs	Justin Phillip	J. Velazquez/S. Asmussen	400,000
Aug 17	Secretariat Stakes	Arlington	1¼ miles	Admiral Kitten	R. Napravnik/M. Maker	500,000
Aug 17	Beverly D. Stakes	Arlington	1 3/16 miles	Dank	R.Moore/S. Stoute	750,000
Aug 17	Arlington Million Stakes	Arlington	1¼ miles	Real Solution	A. Garcia/C. Brown	1,000,000
Aug 17	Del Mar Oaks	Del Mar	1⅛ miles	Discreet Marq	J. Leparoux/C. Clement	300,000
Aug 17	Sword Dancer Invitational	Saratoga	1½ miles	Big Blue Kitten	J. Bravo/C. Brown	600,000
Aug 17	Alabama Stakes	Saratoga	1¼ miles	Princess of Sylmar	J. Castellano/T. Pletcher	600,000
Aug 23	Ballerina Stakes	Saratoga	7 furlongs	Dance to Bristol	X. Perez/O. Figgins, III	500,000
Aug 24	King's Bishop Stakes	Saratoga	7 furlongs	Capo Bostone	I. Ortiz, Jr./T. Pletcher	500,000
Aug 24	Test Stakes	Saratoga	7 furlongs	Sweet Lulu	J. Leparoux/J. Hollendorfer	500,000
Aug 24	Travers Stakes	Saratoga	1¼ miles	Will Take Charge	L. Saez/D. Lukas	1,000,000
Aug 25	Pacific Classic	Del Mar	1¼ miles	Game on Dude	M. Garcia/B. Baffert	1,000,000
Aug 25	Personal Ensign Stakes	Saratoga	1⅛ miles	Royal Delta	M. Smith/W. Mott	600,000
Aug 31	Del Mar Debutante	Del Mar	7 furlongs	She's A Tiger	G. Stevens/J. Bonde	300,000
Aug 31	Forego Stakes	Saratoga	7 furlongs	Strapping Groom	J. Alvarado/D. Jacobson	500,000
Aug 31	Woodward Stakes	Saratoga	1⅛ miles	Alpha	J. Velazquez/K. McLaughlin	750,000
Sept 1	Spinaway Stakes	Saratoga	7 furlongs	Sweet Reason	A. Solis/L. Gyarmati	300,000
Sept 2	Three Chimneys Hopeful Stakes	Saratoga	7 furlongs	Strong Mandate	J. Ortiz/D. Lukas	300,000
Sept 4	Del Mar Futurity	Del Mar	7 furlongs	Tamarando	J. Leparoux/J. Hollendorfer	300,000
Sept 14	Garden City Stakes	Belmont	1⅛ miles	Alterite	J. Velazquez/C. Brown	350,000
Sept 15	Woodbine Mile	Woodbine	1 mile	Wise Dan	J. Velazquez/C. LoPresti	1,000,000
Sept 15	Northern Dancer Turf	Woodbine	1½miles	Forte Del Marmi	E. Da Silva/R. Attfield	300,000
Sept 21	Cotillion Stakes	Parx	1 1/16 miles	Close Hatches	M. Smith/W. Mott	1,000,000

* Through September 22, 2013

FOR THE RECORD • Year by Year

THOROUGHBRED RACING

Kentucky Derby

Run at Churchill Downs, Louisville, KY, on the first Saturday in May.

Year	Winner (Margin)	Jockey	Second	Third	Time
1875	Aristides (1)	Oliver Lewis	Volcano	Verdigris	2:37¾
1876	Vagrant (2)	Bobby Swim	Creedmoor	Harry Hill	2:38¼
1877	Baden-Baden (2)	William Walker	Leonard	King William	2:38
1878	Day Star (2)	Jimmie Carter	Himyar	Leveler	2:37¼
1879	Lord Murphy (1)	Charlie Shauer	Falsetto	Strathmore	2:37
1880	Fonso (1)	George Lewis	Kimball	Bancroft	2:37½
1881	Hindoo (4)	Jimmy McLaughin	Lelex	Alfambra	2:40
1882	Apollo (½)	Babe Hurd	Runnymede	Bengal	2:40¼
1883	Leonatus (3)	Billy Donohue	Drake Carter	Lord Raglan	2:43
1884	Buchanan (2)	Isaac Murphy	Loftin	Audrain	2:40¼
1885	Joe Cotton (Neck)	Erskine Henderson	Bersan	Ten Booker	2:37¼
1886	Ben Ali (½)	Paul Duffy	Blue Wing	Free Knight	2:36½
1887	Montrose (2)	Isaac Lewis	Jim Gore	Jacobin	2:39¼
1888	MacBeth II (1)	George Covington	Gallifet	White	2:38¼
1889	Spokane (Nose)	Thomas Kiley	Proctor Knott	Once Again	2:34½
1890	Riley (2)	Isaac Murphy	Bill Letcher	Robespierre	2:45
1891	Kingman (1)	Isaac Murphy	Balgowan	High Tariff	2:52¼
1892	Azra (Nose)	Alonzo Clayton	Huron	Phil Dwyer	2:41½
1893	Lookout (5)	Eddie Kunze	Plutus	Boundless	2:39¼
1894	Chant (2)	Frank Goodale	Pearl Song	Sigurd	2:41
1895	Halma (3)	Soup Perkins	Basso	Laureate	2:37½
1896	Ben Brush (Nose)	Willie Simms	Ben Eder	Semper Ego	2:07¼
1897	Typhoon II (Head)	Buttons Garner	Ornament	Dr. Catlett	2:12½
1898	Plaudit (Neck)	Willie Simms	Lieber Karl	Isabey	2:09
1899	Manuel (2)	Fred Taral	Corsini	Mazo	2:12
1900	Lieut. Gibson (4)	Jimmy Boland	Florizar	Thrive	2:06¼
1901	His Eminence (2)	Jimmy Winkfield	Sannazarro	Driscoll	2:07¾
1902	Alan-a-Dale (Nose)	Jimmy Winkfield	Inventor	The Rival	2:08¾
1903	Judge Himes (¾)	Hal Booker	Early	Bourbon	2:09
1904	Elwood (½)	Frankie Prior	Ed Tierney	Brancas	2:08½
1905	Agile (3)	Jack Martin	Ram's Horn	Layson	2:10¾
1906	Sir Huon (2)	Roscoe Troxler	Lady Navarre	James Reddick	2:08⅕
1907	Pink Star (2)	Andy Minder	Zal	Ovelando	2:12⅗
1908	Stone Street (1)	Arthur Pickens	Sir Cleges	Dunvegan	2:15⅕
1909	Wintergreen (4)	Vincent Powers	Miami	Dr. Barkley	2:08⅕
1910	Donau (½)	Fred Herbert	Joe Morris	Fighting Bob	2:06⅖
1911	Meridian (¾)	George Archibald	Governor Gray	Colston	2:05
1912	Worth (Neck)	Carroll H. Schilling	Duval	Flamma	2:09⅖
1913	Donerail (½)	Roscoe Goose	Ten Point	Gowell	2:04⅘
1914	Old Rosebud (8)	John McCabe	Hodge	Bronzewing	2:03⅖
1915	Regret (2)	Joe Notter	Pebbles	Sharpshooter	2:05⅖
1916	George Smith (Neck)	Johnny Loftus	Star Hawk	Franklin	2:04
1917	Omar Khayyam (2)	Charles Borel	Ticket	Midway	2:04⅗
1918	Exterminator (1)	William Knapp	Escoba	Viva America	2:10⅘
1919	Sir Barton (5)	Johnny Loftus	Billy Kelly	Under Fire	2:09⅘
1920	Paul Jones (Head)	Ted Rice	Upset	On Watch	2:09
1921	Behave Yourself (Head)	Charles Thompson	Black Servant	Prudery	2:04⅕
1922	Morvich (½)	Albert Johnson	Bet Mosie	John Finn	2:04⅗
1923	Zev (1½)	Earl Sande	Martingale	Vigil	2:05⅖
1924	Black Gold (½)	John Mooney	Chilhowee	Beau Butler	2:05⅕
1925	Flying Ebony (1½)	Earl Sande	Captain Hal	Son of John	2:07⅗
1926	Bubbling Over (5)	Albert Johnson	Bagenbaggage	Rock Man	2:03⅗
1927	Whiskery (Head)	Linus McAtee	Osmond	Jock	2:06
1928	Reigh Count (3)	Chick Lang	Misstep	Toro	2:10⅖
1929	Clyde Van Dusen (2)	Linus McAtee	Naishapur	Panchio	2:10⅘
1930	Gallant Fox (2)	Earl Sande	Gallant Knight	Ned O.	2:07⅗
1931	Twenty Grand (4)	Charles Kurtsinger	Sweep All	Mate	2:01⅘
1932	Burgoo King (5)	Eugene James	Economic	Stepenfetchit	2:05⅕

Kentucky Derby *(Cont.)*

Year	Winner (Margin)	Jockey	Second	Third	Time
1933	Brokers Tip (Nose)	Don Meade	Head Play	Charley O.	2:06⅘
1934	Cavalcade (2½)	Mack Garner	Discovery	Agrarian	2:04
1935	Omaha (1½)	Willie Saunders	Roman Soldier	Whiskolo	2:05
1936	Bold Venture (Head)	Ira Hanford	Brevity	Indian Broom	2:03⅗
1937	War Admiral (1¾)	Charles Kurtsinger	Pompoon	Reaping Reward	2:03⅕
1938	Lawrin (1)	Eddie Arcaro	Dauber	Can't Wait	2:04⅘
1939	Johnstown (8)	James Stout	Challedon	Heather Broom	2:03⅗
1940	Gallahadion (1½)	Carroll Bierman	Bimelech	Dit	2:05
1941	Whirlaway (8)	Eddie Arcaro	Staretor	Market Wise	2:01⅖
1942	Shut Out (2½)	Wayne Wright	Alsab	Valdina Orphan	2:04⅖
1943	Count Fleet (3)	John Longden	Blue Swords	Slide Rule	2:04
1944	Pensive (4½)	Conn McCreary	Broadcloth	Stir Up	2:04⅕
1945	Hoop Jr. (6)	Eddie Arcaro	Pot o' Luck	Darby Dieppe	2:07
1946	Assault (8)	Warren Mehrtens	Spy Song	Hampden	2:06⅗
1947	Jet Pilot (Head)	Eric Guerin	Phalanx	Faultless	2:06⅘
1948	Citation (3½)	Eddie Arcaro	Coaltown	My Request	2:05⅖
1949	Ponder (3)	Steve Brooks	Capot	Palestinian	2:04⅕
1950	Middleground (1¼)	William Boland	Hill Prince	Mr. Trouble	2:01⅗
1951	Count Turf (4)	Conn McCreary	Royal Mustang	Ruhe	2:02⅗
1952	Hill Gail (2)	Eddie Arcaro	Sub Fleet	Blue Man	2:01⅗
1953	Dark Star (Head)	Hank Moreno	Native Dancer	Invigorator	2:02
1954	Determine (1½)	Ray York	Hasty Road	Hasseyampa	2:03
1955	Swaps (1½)	Bill Shoemaker	Nashua	Summer Tan	2:01⅘
1956	Needles (¾)	Dave Erb	Fabius	Come On Red	2:03⅖
1957	Iron Liege (Nose)	Bill Hartack	Gallant Man	Round Table	2:02⅕
1958	Tim Tam (½)	Ismael Valenzuela	Lincoln Road	Noureddin	2:05
1959	Tomy Lee (Nose)	Bill Shoemaker	Sword Dancer	First Landing	2:02⅕
1960	Venetian Way (3½)	Bill Hartack	Bally Ache	Victoria Park	2:02⅖
1961	Carry Back (¾)	John Sellers	Crozier	Bass Clef	2:04
1962	Decidedly (2¼)	Bill Hartack	Roman Line	Ridan	2:00⅖
1963	Chateaugay (1¼)	Braulio Baeza	Never Bend	Candy Spots	2:01⅘
1964	Northern Dancer (Neck)	Bill Hartack	Hill Rise	The Scoundrel	2:00
1965	Lucky Debonair (Neck)	Bill Shoemaker	Dapper Dan	Tom Rolfe	2:01⅕
1966	Kauai King (½)	Don Brumfield	Advocator	Blue Skyer	2:02
1967	Proud Clarion (1)	Bobby Ussery	Barbs Delight	Damascus	2:00⅗
1968	Forward Pass (Disq.)	Ismael Valenzuela	Francie's Hat	T.V. Commercial	2:02⅕
1969	Majestic Prince (Neck)	Bill Hartack	Arts and Letters	Dike	2:01⅘
1970	Dust Commander (5)	Mike Manganello	My Dad George	High Echelon	2:03⅖
1971	Canonero II (3¾)	Gustavo Avila	Jim French	Bold Reason	2:03⅕
1972	Riva Ridge (3¼)	Ron Turcotte	No Le Hace	Hold Your Peace	2:01⅘
1973	Secretariat (2½)	Ron Turcotte	Sham	Our Native	1:59⅖
1974	Cannonade (2¼)	Angel Cordero Jr.	Hudson County	Agitate	2:04
1975	Foolish Pleasure (1¾)	Jacinto Vasquez	Avatar	Diabolo	2:02
1976	Bold Forbes (1)	Angel Cordero Jr.	Honest Pleasure	Elocutionist	2:01⅗
1977	Seattle Slew (1¾)	Jean Cruguet	Run Dusty Run	Sanhedrin	2:02⅕
1978	Affirmed (1½)	Steve Cauthen	Alydar	Believe It	2:01⅕
1979	Spectacular Bid (2¾)	Ronald J. Franklin	General Assembly	Golden Act	2:02⅖
1980	Genuine Risk (1)	Jacinto Vasquez	Rumbo	Jaklin Klugman	2:02
1981	Pleasant Colony (¾)	Jorge Velasquez	Woodchopper	Partez	2:02
1982	Gato Del Sol (2½)	Eddie Delahoussaye	Laser Light	Reinvested	2:02⅕
1983	Sunny's Halo (2)	Eddie Delahoussaye	Desert Wine	Caveat	2:02⅕
1984	Swale (3¼)	Laffit Pincay Jr.	Coax Me Chad	At the Threshold	2:02⅖
1985	Spend A Buck (5)	Angel Cordero Jr.	Stephan's Odyssey	Chief's Crown	2:00⅕
1986	Ferdinand (2¼)	Bill Shoemaker	Bold Arrangement	Broad Brush	2:02⅘
1987	Alysheba (¾)	Chris McCarron	Bet Twice	Avies Copy	2:03⅖
1988	Winning Colors (Neck)	Gary Stevens	Forty Niner	Risen Star	2:02⅕
1989	Sunday Silence (2½)	Pat Valenzuela	Easy Goer	Awe Inspiring	2:05
1990	Unbridled (3½)	Craig Perret	Summer Squall	Pleasant Tap	2:02
1991	Strike the Gold (1¾)	Chris Antley	Best Pal	Mane Minister	2:03
1992	Lil E. Tee (1)	Pat Day	Casual Lies	Dance Floor	2:03
1993	Sea Hero (2½)	Jerry Bailey	Prairie Bayou	Wild Gale	2:02⅖
1994	Go for Gin (2½)	Chris McCarron	Strodes Creek	Blumin Affair	2:03⅗
1995	Thunder Gulch (2¼)	Gary Stevens	Tejano Run	Timber Country	2:01⅕

Kentucky Derby *(Cont.)*

Year	Winner (Margin)	Jockey	Second	Third	Time
1996	Grindstone (Nose)	Jerry Bailey	Cavonnier	Prince of Thieves	2:01
1997	Silver Charm (Head)	Gary Stevens	Captain Bodgit	Free House	2:02⅖
1998	Real Quiet (½)	Kent Desormeaux	Victory Gallop	Indian Charlie	2:02⅒
1999	Charismatic (Neck)	Chris Antley	Menifee	Cat Thief	2:03⅕
2000	Fusaichi Pegasus (1½)	Kent Desormeaux	Aptitude	Impeachment	2:01.12
2001	Monarchos (4¾)	Jorge Chavez	Invisible Ink	Congaree	1:59.97
2002	War Emblem (4)	Victor Espinoza	Proud Citizen	Perfect Drift	2:01.13
2003	Funny Cide (1¾)	Jose Santos	Empire Maker	Peace Rules	2:01.19
2004	Smarty Jones (2¾)	Stewart Elliott	Lion Heart	Imperialism	2:04.06
2005	Giacomo (½)	Mike Smith	Closing Argument	Afleet Alex	2:02.75
2006	Barbaro (1½)	Edgar Prado	Bluegrass Cat	Steppenwolfer	2:01.36
2007	Street Sense (2¼)	Calvin Borel	Hard Spun	Curlin	2:02.17
2008	Big Brown (4¾)	Kent Desormeaux	Eight Belles	Denis of Cork	2:01.82
2009	Mine That Bird (6¾)	Calvin Borel	Pioneer of the Nile	Musket Man	2:02.66
2010	Super Saver (2½)	Calvin Borel	Ice Box	Paddy O'Prado	2:04.45
2011	Animal Kingdom (2¾)	John Velazquez	Nehro	Mucho Macho Man	2:02.04
2012	I'll Have Another (1½)	Mario Gutierrez	Bodemeister	Dullahan	2:01.83
2013	Orb (2½)	Joel Rosario	Golden Soul	Revolutionary	2:02.89

Note: Distance: 1½ miles (1875–95), 1¼ miles (1896–present).

Preakness

Run at Pimlico Race Course, Baltimore, Md., two weeks after the Kentucky Derby.

Year	Winner (Margin)	Jockey	Second	Third	Time
1873	Survivor (10)	George Barbee	John Boulger	Artist	2:43
1874	Culpepper (¾)	William Donohue	King Amadeus	Scratch	2:56½
1875	Tom Ochiltree (2)	Lloyd Hughes	Viator	Bay Final	2:43½
1876	Shirley (4)	George Barbee	Rappahannock	Algerine	2:44¾
1877	Cloverbrook (4)	C. Holloway	Bombast	Lucifer	2:45½
1878	Duke of Magenta (6)	C. Holloway	Bayard	Albert	2:41¾
1879	Harold (3)	Lloyd Hughes	Jericho	Rochester	2:40½
1880	Grenada (¾)	Lloyd Hughes	Oden	Emily F.	2:40½
1881	Saunterer (½)	Tom Costello	Compensation	Baltic	2:40½
1882	Vanguard (Neck)	Tom Costello	Heck	Col Watson	2:44½
1883*	Jacobus (4)	George Barbee	Parnell		2:42½
1884*	Knight of Ellerslie (2)	S. Fisher	Welcher		2:39½
1885	Tecumseh (2)	Jim McLaughlin	Wickham	John C.	2:49
1886	The Bard (3)	S. Fisher	Eurus	Elkwood	2:45
1887	Dunboyne (1)	William Donohue	Mahoney	Raymond	2:39½
1888	Refund (3)	Fred Littlefield	Judge Murray	Glendale	2:49
1889*	Buddhist (8)	George Anderson	Japhet		2:17½
1890	Montague (3)	Willie Martin	Philosophy	Barrister	2:36¾
1894	Assignee (3)	Fred Taral	Potentate	Ed Kearney	1:49¼
1895	Belmar (1)	Fred Taral	April Fool	Sue Kittie	1:50½
1896	Margrave (1)	Henry Griffin	Hamilton II	Intermission	1:51
1897	Paul Kauvar (1½)	T. Thorpe	Elkins	On Deck	1:51¼
1898	Sly Fox (2)	Willie Simms	The Huguenot	Nuto	1:49⅗
1899	Half Time (1)	Richard Clawson	Filigrane	Lackland	1:47
1900	Hindus (Head)	Henry Spencer	Sarmation	Ten Candles	1:48⅖
1901	The Parader (2)	F. Landry	Sadie S.	Dr. Barlow	1:47⅕
1902	Old England (Nose)	L. Jackson	Major Daingerfield	Namtor	1:45⅘
1903	Flocarline (½)	William Gannon	Mackey Dwyer	Rightful	1:44⅘
1904	Bryn Mawr (1)	Gene Hildebrand	Wotan	Dolly Spanker	1:44⅕
1905	Cairngorm (Head)	Willie Davis	Kiamesha	Coy Maid	1:45⅘
1906	Whimsical (4)	Walter Miller	Content	Larabie	1:45
1907	Don Enrique (1)	George Mountain	Ethon	Zambesi	1:45⅖
1908	Royal Tourist (4)	Eddie Dugan	Live Wire	Robert Cooper	1:46⅖
1909	Effendi (1)	Willie Doyle	Fashion Plate	Hilltop	1:39⅘
1910	Layminster (½)	Roy Estep	Dalhousie	Sager	1:40⅗
1911	Watervale (1)	Eddie Dugan	Zeus	The Nigger	1:51

Preakness (Cont.)

Year	Winner (Margin)	Jockey	Second	Third	Time
1912	Colonel Holloway (5)	Clarence Turner	Bwana Tumbo	Tipsand	1:56⅗
1913	Buskin (Neck)	James Butwell	Kleburne	Barnegat	1:53⅖
1914	Holiday (¾)	Andy Schuttinger	Brave Cunarder	Defendum	1:53⅘
1915	Rhine Maiden (1½)	Douglas Hoffman	Half Rock	Runes	1:58
1916	Damrosch (1½)	Linus McAtee	Greenwood	Achievement	1:54⅘
1917	Kalitan (2)	Everett Haynes	Al M. Dick	Kentucky Boy	1:54⅖
1918*	War Cloud (¾)	Johnny Loftus	Sunny Slope	Lanius	1:53⅗
1918*	Jack Hare, Jr (2)	Charles Peak	The Porter	Kate Bright	1:53⅖
1919	Sir Barton (4)	Johnny Loftus	Eternal	Sweep On	1:53
1920	Man o' War (1½)	Clarence Kummer	Upset	Wildair	1:51⅗
1921	Broomspun (¾)	Frank Coltiletti	Polly Ann	Jeg	1:54⅕
1922	Pillory (Head)	Louis Morris	Hea	June Grass	1:51⅗
1923	Vigil (1¼)	Benny Marinelli	General Thatcher	Rialto	1:53⅗
1924	Nellie Morse (1½)	John Merimee	Transmute	Mad Play	1:57⅕
1925	Coventry (4)	Clarence Kummer	Backbone	Almadel	1:59
1926	Display (Head)	John Maiben	Blondin	Mars	1:59⅘
1927	Bostonian (½)	Whitey Abel	Sir Harry	Whiskery	2:01⅗
1928	Victorian (Nose)	Rymond Workman	Toro	Solace	2:00⅕
1929	Dr. Freeland (1)	Louis Schaefer	Minotaur	African	2:01⅗
1930	Gallant Fox (¾)	Earl Sande	Crack Brigade	Snowflake	2:00⅗
1931	Mate (1½)	Geirge Ellis	Twenty Grand	Ladder	1:59
1932	Burgoo King (Head)	Eugene James	Tick On	Boatswain	1:59⅘
1933	Head Play (4)	Charley Kurtsinger	Ladysman	Utopian	2:02
1934	High Quest (Nose)	Robert Jones	Cavalcade	Discovery	1:58⅕
1935	Omaha (6)	Willie Saunders	Firethorn	Psychic Bid	1:58⅖
1936	Bold Venture (Nose)	George Woolf	Granville	Jean Bart	1:59
1937	War Admiral (Head)	Charles Kurtsinger	Pompoon	Flying Scot	1:58⅖
1938	Dauber (7)	Maurice Peters	Cravat	Menow	1:59⅘
1939	Challedon (1¼)	George Seabo	Gilded Knight	Volitant	1:59⅘
1940	Bimelech (3)	Fred A. Smith	Mioland	Gallahadion	1:58⅗
1941	Whirlaway (5½)	Eddie Arcaro	King Cole	Our Boots	1:58⅘
1942	Alsab (1)	Basil James	Requested Sun Again	(dead heat for second)	1:57
1943	Count Fleet (8)	Johnny Longden	Blue Swords	Vincentive	1:57⅖
1944	Pensive (¾)	Conn McCreary	Platter	Stir Up	1:59⅕
1945	Polynesian (2½)	Wayne D. Wright	Hoop Jr.	Darby Dieppe	1:58⅘
1946	Assault (Neck)	Warren Mehrtens	Lord Boswell	Hampden	2:01⅖
1947	Faultless (1¼)	Doug Dodson	On Trust	Phalanx	1:59
1948	Citation (5½)	Eddie Arcaro	Vulcan's Forge	Boyard	2:02⅖
1949	Capot (Head)	Ted Atkinson	Palestinian	Noble Impulse	1:56
1950	Hill Prince (5)	Eddie Arcaro	Middleground	Dooley	1:59⅕
1951	Bold (7)	Eddie Arcaro	Counterpoint	Alerted	1:56⅖
1952	Blue Man (3½)	Conn McCreary	Jampol	One Count	1:57⅖
1953	Native Dancer (Neck)	Eric Guerin	Jamie K.	Royal Bay Gem	1:57⅘
1954	Hasty Road (Neck)	Johnny Adams	Correlation	Hasseyampa	1:57⅖
1955	Nashua (1)	Eddie Arcaro	Saratoga	Traffic Judge	1:54⅗
1956	Fabius (¾)	Bill Hartack	Needles	No Regrets	1:58⅖
1957	Bold Ruler (2)	Eddie Arcaro	Iron Liege	Inside Tract	1:56⅕
1958	Tim Tam (1½)	Ismael Valenzuela	Lincoln Road	Gone Fishin'	1:57⅕
1959	Royal Orbit (4)	William Harmatz	Sword Dancer	Dunce	1:57
1960	Bally Ache (4)	Bobby Ussery	Victoria Park	Celtic Ash	1:57⅗
1961	Carry Back (¾)	Johnny Sellers	Globemaster	Crozier	1:57⅗
1962	Greek Money (Nose)	John Rotz	Ridan	Roman Line	1:56⅕
1963	Candy Spots (3½)	Bill Shoemaker	Chateaugay	Never Bend	1:56⅕
1964	Northern Dancer (2¼)	Bill Hartack	The Scoundrel	Hill Rise	1:56⅘
1965	Tom Rolfe (Neck)	Ron Turcotte	Dapper Dan	Hail to All	1:56⅕
1966	Kauai King (1¾)	Don Brumfield	Stupendous	Amberoid	1:55⅖
1967	Damascus (2¼)	Bill Shoemaker	In Reality	Proud Clarion	1:55⅕
1968	Forward Pass (6)	Ismael Valenzuela	Out of the Way	Nodouble	1:56⅘
1969	Majestic Prince (Head)	Bill Hartack	Arts and Letters	Jay Ray	1:55⅗
1970	Personality (Neck)	Eddie Belmonte	My Dad George	Silent Screen	1:56⅕
1971	Canonero II (1½)	Gustavo Avila	Eastern Fleet	Jim French	1:54
1972	Bee Bee Bee (1¼)	Eldon Nelson	No Le Hace	Key to the Mint	1:55⅗
1973	Secretariat (2½)	Ron Turcotte	Sham	Our Native	1:54⅖

Preakness (*Cont.*)

Year	Winner (Margin)	Jockey	Second	Third	Time
1974	Little Current (7)	Miguel Rivera	Neapolitan Way	Cannonade	1:54⅗
1975	Master Derby (1)	Darrel McHargue	Foolish Pleasure	Diabolo	1:56⅖
1976	Elocutionist (3)	John Lively	Play the Red	Bold Forbes	1:55
1977	Seattle Slew (1½)	Jean Cruguet	Iron Constitution	Run Dusty Run	1:54⅖
1978	Affirmed (Neck)	Steve Cauthen	Alydar	Believe It	1:54⅖
1979	Spectacular Bid (5½)	Ron Franklin	Golden Act	Screen King	1:54⅕
1980	Codex (4¾)	Angel Cordero Jr.	Genuine Risk	Colonel Moran	1:54⅕
1981	Pleasant Colony (1)	Jorge Velasquez	Bold Ego	Paristo	1:54⅗
1982	Aloma's Ruler (½)	Jack Kaenel	Linkage	Cut Away	1:55⅖
1983	Deputed Testamony (2¾)	Donald Miller Jr.	Desert Wine	High Honors	1:55⅖
1984	Gate Dancer (1½)	Angel Cordero Jr.	Play On	Fight Over	1:53⅗
1985	Tank's Prospect (Head)	Pat Day	Chief's Crown	Eternal Prince	1:53⅖
1986	Snow Chief (4)	Alex Solis	Ferdinand	Broad Brush	1:54⅘
1987	Alysheba (½)	Chris McCarron	Bet Twice	Cryptoclearance	1:55⅘
1988	Risen Star (1¼)	E. Delahoussaye	Brian's Time	Winning Colors	1:56⅕
1989	Sunday Silence (Nose)	Pat Valenzuela	Easy Goer	Rock Point	1:53⅘
1990	Summer Squall (2¼)	Pat Day	Unbridled	Mister Frisky	1:53⅗
1991	Hansel (Head)	Jerry Bailey	Corporate Report	Mane Minister	1:54
1992	Pine Bluff (¾)	Chris McCarron	Alydeed	Casual Lies	1:55⅗
1993	Prairie Bayou (½)	Mike Smith	Cherokee Run	El Bakan	1:56⅗
1994	Tabasco Cat (¾)	Pat Day	Go For Gin	Concern	1:56⅖
1995	Timber Country (½)	Pat Day	Oliver's Twist	Thunder Gulch	1:54⅖
1996	Louis Quatorze (3¼)	Pat Day	Skip Away	Editor's Note	1:53⅖
1997	Silver Charm (Head)	Gary Stevens	Free House	Captain Bodgit	1:54⅖
1998	Real Quiet (2¼)	Kent Desormeaux	Victory Gallop	Classic Cat	1:54⅗
1999	Charismatic (1½)	Chris Antley	Menifee	Badge	1:55⅕
2000	Red Bullet (3¾)	Jerry Bailey	Fusaichi Pegasus	Impeachment	1:56.04
2001	Point Given (2¼)	Gary Stevens	A P Valentine	Congaree	1:55.51
2002	War Emblem (¾)	Victor Espinoza	Magic Weisner	Proud Citizen	1:56.36
2003	Funny Cide (9¾)	Jose Santos	Midway Road	Scrimshaw	1:55.61
2004	Smarty Jones (11½)	Stewart Elliott	Rock Hard Ten	Eddington	1:55.59
2005	Afleet Alex (7)	Jeremy Rose	Scrappy T	Giacomo	1:55.04
2006	Bernardini (5¼)	Javier Castellano	Sweetnorthernsaint	Hemingway's Key	1:54.65
2007	Curlin (Head)	Robby Albarado	Street Sense	Hard Spun	1:53.46
2008	Big Brown (5¼)	Kent Desormeaux	Macho Again	Icabad Crane	1:54.80
2009	Rachel Alexandra (1)	Calvin Borel	Mine That Bird	Musket Man	1:55.08
2010	Lookin at Lucky (1¾)	Martin Garcia	First Dude	Jackson Bend	1:55.47
2011	Shackleford (½)	Jesus Castanon	Animal Kingdom	Astrology	1:56.47
2012	I'll Have Another (Neck)	Mario Gutierrez	Bodemeister	Creative Cause	1:55.94
2013	Oxbow (1¾)	Gary Stevens	Itsmyluckyday	Mylute	1:57.54

*Preakness was a two-horse race in 1883, '84 and '89. It was not run 1891–1893; and in 1918, it was run in two divisions.

Note: Distance: 1½ miles (1873–88), 1¼ miles (1889), 1½ miles (1890), 1 1/16 miles (1894–1900), 1 mile and 70 yards (1901–1907), 1 1/16 miles (1908), 1 mile (1909–10), 1⅛ miles (1911–24), 1 3/16 miles (1925–present).

Belmont

Run at Belmont Park, Elmont, NY, three weeks after the Preakness Stakes. Held previously at two locations in the Bronx (NY): Jerome Park (1867–1889) and Morris Park (1890–1904).

Year	Winner (Margin)	Jockey	Second	Third	Time
1867	Ruthless (Head)	Gilbert Patrick	De Courcy	Rivoli	3:05
1868	General Duke (2)	Bobby Swim	Northumberland	Fannie Ludlow	3:02
1869	Fenian (Unknown)	C. Miller	Glenelg	Invercauld	3:04¼
1870	Kingfisher (½)	Edward Brown	Foster	Midday	2:59½
1871	Harry Bassett (3)	Walter Miller	Stockwood	By-the-Sea	2:56
1872	Joe Daniels (¾)	James Rowe	Meteor	Shylock	2:58¼
1873	Springbok (4)	James Rowe	Count d'Orsay	Strachino	3:01¾
1874	Saxon (Neck)	George Barbee	Grinstead	Aaron Pennington	2:39½
1875	Calvin (2)	Bobby Swim	Aristides	Milner	2:40¼
1876	Algerine (Head)	Billy Donahue	Fiddlestick	Barricade	2:40½

Belmont (Cont.)

Year	Winner (Margin)	Jockey	Second	Third	Time
1877	Cloverbrook (1)	C. Holloway	Loiterer	Baden-Baden	2:46
1878	Duke of Magenta (2)	Lloyd Hughes	Bramble	Sparta	2:43½
1879	Spendthrift (5)	George Evans	Monitor	Jericho	2:42¾
1880	Grenada (½)	Lloyd Hughes	Ferncliffe	Turenne	2:47
1881	Saunterer (Neck)	Tom Costello	Eole	Baltic	2:47
1882	Forester (5)	Jim McLaughlin	Babcock	Wyoming	2:43
1883	George Kinney (2)	Jim McLaughlin	Trombone	Renegade	2:42½
1884	Panique (½)	Jim McLaughlin	Knight of Ellerslie	Himalaya	2:42
1885	Tyrant (3½)	Paul Duffy	St. Augustine	Tecumseh	2:43
1886	Inspector B (1)	Jim McLaughlin	The Bard	Linden	2:41
1887*	Hanover (28-32)	Jim McLaughlin	Oneko		2:43½
1888*	Sir Dixon (12)	Jim McLaughlin	Prince Royal		2:40¼
1889	Eric (Head)	William Hayward	Diable	Zephyrus	2:47
1890	Burlington (1)	Pike Barnes	Devotee	Padishah	2:07¾
1891	Foxford (Neck)	Edward Garrison	Montana	Laurestan	2:08¾
1892*	Patron (Unknown)	William Hayward	Shellbark		2:17
1893	Comanche (Head)	Willie Simms	Dr. Rice	Rainbow	1:53¼
1894	Henry of Navarre (2-4)	Willie Simms	Prig	Assignee	1:56½
1895	Belmar (Head)	Fred Taral	Counter Tenor	Nanki Pooh	2:11½
1896	Hastings (Neck)	Henry Griffin	Handspring	Hamilton II	2:24½
1897	Scottish Chieftain (1)	Joe Scherrer	On Deck	Octagon	2:23¼
1898	Bowling Brook (8)	Fred Littlefield	Previous	Hamburg	2:32
1899	Jean Bereaud (Head)	Richard Clawson	Half Time	Glengar	2:23
1900	Ildrim (Head)	Nash Turner	Petrucio	Missionary	2:21½
1901	Commando (½)	Henry Spencer	The Parader	All Green	2:21
1902	Masterman (2)	John Bullmann	Ranald	King Hanover	2:22½
1903	Africander (2)	John Bullmann	Whorler	Red Knight	2:23⅕
1904	Delhi (3½)	George Odom	Graziallo	Rapid Water	2:06⅗
1905	Tanya (1/2)	Gene Hildebrand	Blandy	Hot Shot	2:08
1906	Burgomaster (4)	Lucien Lyne	The Quail	Accountant	2:20
1907	Peter Pan (1)	George Mountain	Superman	Frank Gill	Unknown
1908	Colin (Head)	Joe Notter	Fair Play	King James	Unknown
1909	Joe Madden (8)	Eddie Dugan	Wise Mason	Donald MacDonald	2:21⅗
1910*	Sweep (6)	James Butwell	Duke of Ormonde		2:22
1913	Prince Eugene (½)	Roscoe Troxler	Rock View	Flying Fairy	2:18
1914	Luke McLuke (8)	Merritt Buxton	Gainer	Charlestonian	2:20
1915	The Finn (4)	George Byrne	Half Rock	Pebbles	2:18⅖
1916	Friar Rock (3)	Everett Haynes	Spur	Churchill	2:22
1917	Hourless (10)	James Butwell	Skeptic	Wonderful	2:17⅘
1918	Johren (2)	Frank Robinson	War Cloud	Cum Sah	2:20⅖
1919	Sir Barton (5)	Johnny Loftus	Sweep On	Natural Bridge	2:17⅖
1920*	Man o' War (20)	Clarence Kummer	Donnacona		2:14⅕
1921	Grey Lag (3)	Earl Sande	Sporting Blood	Leonardo II	2:16⅘
1922	Pillory (2)	C. H. Miller	Snob II	Hea	2:18⅘
1923	Zev (1½)	Earl Sande	Chickvale	Rialto	2:19
1924	Mad Play (2)	Earl Sande	Mr. Mutt	Modest	2:18⅘
1925	American Flag (8)	Albert Johnson	Dangerous	Swope	2:16⅘
1926	Crusader (1)	Albert Johnson	Espino	Haste	2:32⅕
1927	Chance Shot (1½)	Earl Sande	Bois de Rose	Flambino	2:32⅖
1928	Vito (3)	Clarence Kummer	Genie	Diavolo	2:33⅕
1929	Blue Larkspur (¾)	Mack Garner	African	Jack High	2:32⅘
1930	Gallant Fox (3)	Earl Sande	Whichone	Questionnaire	2:31⅗
1931	Twenty Grand (10)	Charles Kurtsinger	Sun Meadow	Jamestown	2:29⅗
1932	Faireno (1½)	Tommy Malley	Osculator	Flag Pole	2:32⅘
1933	Hurryoff (1½)	Mack Garner	Nimbus	Union	2:32⅗
1934	Peace Chance (6)	Wayne D. Wright	High Quest	Good Goods	2:29⅕
1935	Omaha (1½)	Willie Saunders	Firethorn	Rosemont	2:30⅗
1936	Granville (Nose)	James Stout	Mr. Bones	Hollyrood	2:30
1937	War Admiral (3)	Charles Kurtsinger	Sceneshifter	Vamoose	2:28⅗
1938	Pasteurized (Neck)	James Stout	Dauber	Cravat	2:29⅖
1939	Johnstown (5)	James Stout	Belay	Gilded Knight	2:29⅗
1940	Bimelech (¾)	Fred A. Smith	Your Chance	Andy K	2:29⅗
1941	Whirlaway (2½)	Eddie Arcaro	Robert Morris	Yankee Chance	2:31
1942	Shut Out (2)	Eddie Arcaro	Alsab	Lochinvar	2:29⅕

Belmont *(Cont.)*

Year	Winner (Margin)	Jockey	Second	Third	Time
1943	Count Fleet (25)	Johnny Longden	Fairy Manhurst	Deseronto	2:28⅕
1944	Bounding Home (½)	Gayle Smith	Pensive	Bull Dandy	2:32⅕
1945	Pavot (5)	Eddie Arcaro	Wildlife	Jeep	2:30⅕
1946	Assault (3)	Warren Mehrtens	Natchez	Cable	2:30⅘
1947	Phalanx (5)	Ruperto Donoso	Tide Rips	Tailspin	2:29⅗
1948	Citation (8)	Eddie Arcaro	Better Self	Escadru	2:28⅕
1949	Capot (½)	Ted Atkinson	Ponder	Palestinian	2:30⅕
1950	Middleground (1)	William Boland	Lights Up	Mr. Trouble	2:28⅗
1951	Counterpoint (4)	David Gorman	Battlefield	Battle Morn	2:29
1952	One Count (2½)	Eddie Arcaro	Blue Man	Armageddon	2:30⅕
1953	Native Dancer (Neck)	Eric Guerin	Jamie K.	Royal Bay Gem	2:38⅗
1954	High Gun (Neck)	Eric Guerin	Fisherman	Limelight	2:30⅘
1955	Nashua (9)	Eddie Arcaro	Blazing Count	Portersville	2:29
1956	Needles (Neck)	David Erb	Career Boy	Fabius	2:29⅘
1957	Gallant Man (8)	Bill Shoemaker	Inside Tract	Bold Ruler	2:26⅗
1958	Cavan (6)	Pete Anderson	Tim Tam	Flamingo	2:30⅕
1959	Sword Dancer (¾)	Bill Shoemaker	Bagdad	Royal Orbit	2:28⅖
1960	Celtic Ash (5½)	Bill Hartack	Venetian Way	Disperse	2:29⅗
1961	Sherluck (2¼)	Braulio Baeza	Globemaster	Guadalcanal	2:29⅕
1962	Jaipur (Nose)	Bill Shoemaker	Admiral's Voyage	Crimson Satan	2:28⅘
1963	Chateaugay (2½)	Braulio Baeza	Candy Spots	Choker	2:30⅕
1964	Quadrangle (2)	Manuel Ycaza	Roman Brother	Northern Dancer	2:28⅖
1965	Hail to All (Neck)	John Sellers	Tom Rolfe	First Family	2:28⅖
1966	Amberold (2½)	William Boland	Buffle	Advocator	2:29⅗
1967	Damascus (2½)	Bill Shoemaker	Cool Reception	Gentleman James	2:28⅘
1968	Stage Door Johnny (1¼)	Hellodoro Gustines	Forward Pass	Call Me Prince	2:27⅕
1969	Arts and Letters (5½)	Braulio Baeza	Majestic Prince	Dike	2:28⅘
1970	High Echelon (¾)	John L. Rotz	Needles N Pins	Naskra	2:34
1971	Pass Catcher (¾)	Walter Blum	Jim French	Bold Reason	2:30⅖
1972	Riva Ridge (7)	Ron Turcotte	Ruritania	Cloudy Dawn	2:28
1973	Secretariat (31)	Ron Turcotte	Twice a Prince	My Gallant	2:24
1974	Little Current (7)	Miguel A. Rivera	Jolly Johu	Cannonade	2:29⅕
1975	Avatar (Neck)	Bill Shoemaker	Foolish Pleasure	Master Derby	2:28⅕
1976	Bold Forbes (Neck)	Angel Cordero Jr.	McKenzie Bridge	Great Contractor	2:29
1977	Seattle Slew (4)	Jean Cruguet	Run Dusty Run	Sanhedrin	2:29⅗
1978	Affirmed (Head)	Steve Cauthen	Alydar	Darby Creek Road	2:26⅘
1979	Coastal (3¼)	Ruben Hernandez	Golden Act	Spectacular Bid	2:28⅗
1980	Temperence Hill (2)	Eddie Maple	Genuine Risk	Rockhill Native	2:29⅘
1981	Summing (Neck)	George Martens	Highland Blade	Pleasant Colony	2:29
1982	Conquistador Cielo (14½)	Laffit Pincay Jr.	Gato Del Sol	Illuminate	2:28⅕
1983	Caveat (3½)	Laffit Pincay Jr.	Slew o'Gold	Barberstown	2:27⅘
1984	Swale (4)	Laffit Pincay Jr.	Pine Circle	Morning Bob	2:27⅕
1985	Creme Fraiche (½)	Eddie Maple	Stephan's Odyssey	Chief's Crown	2:27
1986	Danzig Connection (1¼)	Chris McCarron	Johns Treasure	Ferdinand	2:29⅘
1987	Bet Twice (14)	Craig Perret	Cryptoclearance	Gulch	2:28⅕
1988	Risen Star (14¾)	Eddie Delahoussaye	Kingpost	Brian's Time	2:26⅖
1989	Easy Goer (8)	Pat Day	Sunday Silence	Le Voyageur	2:26
1990	Go and Go (8¼)	Michael Kinane	Thirty Six Red	Baron de Vaux	2:27⅕
1991	Hansel (Head)	Jerry Bailey	Strike the Gold	Mane Minister	2:28
1992	A.P. Indy (¾)	Eddie Delahoussaye	My Memoirs	Pine Bluff	2:26
1993	Colonial Affair (2¼)	Julie Krone	Kissin Kris	Wild Gale	2:29⅘
1994	Tabasco Cat (2)	Pat Day	Go For Gin	Strodes Creek	2:26⅘
1995	Thunder Gulch (2)	Gary Stevens	Star Standard	Citadeed	2:32
1996	Editor's Note (1)	Rene Douglas	Skip Away	My Flag	2:28⅘
1997	Touch Gold (¾)	Chris McCarron	Silver Charm	Free House	2:28⅘
1998	Victory Gallop (Nose)	Gary Stevens	Real Quiet	Thomas Jo	2:28⅘
1999	Lemon Drop Kid (Head)	Jose Santos	Vision and Verse	Charismatic	2:27⅘
2000	Commendable (1½)	Pat Day	Aptitude	Unshaded	2:31.19
2001	Point Given (12¼)	Gary Stevens	A P Valentine	Monarchos	2:26.56
2002	Sarava (½)	Edgar Prado	Medaglia d'Oro	Sunday Break	2:29.71
2003	Empire Maker (¾)	Jerry Bailey	Ten Most Wanted	Funny Cide	2:28.26
2004	Birdstone (1)	Edgar Prado	Smarty Jones	Royal Assault	2:27.59

Belmont *(Cont.)*

Year	Winner (Margin)	Jockey	Second	Third	Time
2005	Afleet Alex (4¾)	Jeremy Rose	Andromeda's Hero	Nolan's Cat	2:28.75
2006	Jazil (1¼)	Fernando Jara	Bluegrass Cat	Sunriver	2:27.86
2007	Rags to Riches (Head)	John Velazquez	Curlin	Tiago	2:28.74
2008	Da' Tara (5¼)	Alan Garcia	Denis of Cork	Ready's Echo	2:29.65
2009	Summer Bird (2¾)	Kent Desormeaux	Dunkirk	Mine That Bird	2:27.54
2010	Drosselmeyer (1¾)	Mike Smith	Fly Down	First Dude	2:31.57
2011	Ruler On Ice (¾)	Jose Valdivia Jr.	Stay Thirsty	Brilliant Speed	2:30.88
2012	Union Rags (Neck)	John Velazquez	Paynter	Atigun	2:30.42
2013	Palace Malice (3¼)	Mike Smith	Oxbow	Orb	2:30.70

*Belmont was a two-horse race in 1887, '88, '92, 1910 and '20; and was not held in 1911–1912.
Note: Distance: 1 mile 5 furlongs (1867–89), 1¼ miles (1890–1905), 1⅜ miles (1906–25), 1½ miles (1926–present).

Triple Crown Winners

Year	Horse	Jockey	Owner	Trainer
1919	Sir Barton	John Loftus	J. K. L. Ross	H. G. Bedwell
1930	Gallant Fox	Earle Sande	Belair Stud	James Fitzsimmons
1935	Omaha	William Saunders	Belair Stud	James Fitzsimmons
1937	War Admiral	Charles Kurtsinger	Samuel D. Riddle	George Conway
1941	Whirlaway	Eddie Arcaro	Calumet Farm	Ben Jones
1943	Count Fleet	John Longden	Mrs. J. D. Hertz	Don Cameron
1946	Assault	Warren Mehrtens	King Ranch	Max Hirsch
1948	Citation	Eddie Arcaro	Calumet Farm	Jimmy Jones
1973	Secretariat	Ron Turcotte	Meadow Stable	Lucien Laurin
1977	Seattle Slew	Jean Cruguet	Karen L. Taylor	William H. Turner Jr.
1978	Affirmed	Steve Cauthen	Harbor View Farm	Laz Barrera

Boxing

**Heavyweight champion
Wladimir Klitschko scored a
sixth-round TKO over
Francesco Pianeta to retain his
WBA and IBF titles**

FOR THE RECORD • 2012—2013

Current World Champions†

Division	Weight Limit	WBA Champion	WBC Champion	IBF Champion
Heavyweight	None	Wladimir Klitschko	Vitali Klitschko	Wladimir Klitschko
Cruiserweight	200	Guillermo Jones	Krzysztof Wlodarczyk	Yoan Pablo Hernandez
Light Heavyweight	175	Beibut Shumenov	Adonis Stevenson	Bernard Hopkins
Super Middleweight	168	Andre Ward	Sakio Bika	Carl Froch
Middleweight	160	Gennady Golovkin	Sergio Gabriel Martinez	Darren Barker
Super Welterweight	154	Floyd Mayweather Jr.	Floyd Mayweather Jr.	Carlos Molina
Welterweight	147	Adrien Broner	Floyd Mayweather Jr.	Devon Alexander
Super Lightweight	140	Danny Garcia	Danny Garcia	Lamont Peterson
Lightweight	135	Richar Abril	Adrien Broner	Miguel Vazquez
Super Featherweight	130	Takashi Uchiyama	Takashi Miura	Argenis Mendez
Featherweight	126	Chris John	Jhonny Gonzalez	Evgeny Gradovich
Super Bantamweight	122	Guillermo Rigondeaux	Leo Santa Cruz	Kiko Martinez
Bantamweight	118	Anselmo Moreno	Shinsuke Yamanaka	Jamie McDonnell
Super Flyweight	115	Liborio Solis	Srisaket Sor Rungvisai	Juan Carlos Sanchez Jr.
Flyweight	112	Juan Francisco Estrada	Akira Yaegashi	Moruti Mthalane
Light Flyweight	108	Roman Gonzalez	Adrian Hernandez	John Riel Casimero
Strawweight	105	Ryo Miyazaki	Xiong Zhao Zhong	Katsunari Takayama

Note: WBA=World Boxing Association; WBC=World Boxing Council; IBF=International Boxing Federation. Champions as of September 29, 2013. †In divisions in which WBA has designated "super" champion and "regular" champion, list shows "super" champion only. Does not include "interim" title holders.

Title and Major Boxing Matches of Late 2012 and 2013**

Abbreviations: WBC=World Boxing Council; WBA= World Boxing Association; IBF=International Boxing Federation; KO=knockout; TKO=technical knockout; UD=unanimous decision; SD=split decision; MD=majority decision; TD=technical decision; DQ=disqualification; NC=no contest. Bouts from Oct. 1, 2012 to Oct. 1, 2013.

	Date	Winner	Loser	Result	Title/Org.	Site
HEAVYWEIGHT	Nov 10	Wladimir Klitschko	Mariusz Wach	UD	WBA, IBF	Moscow, Russia
	May 4	Wladimir Klitschko	Francesco Pianeta	TKO 6	WBA, IBF	Baden-Wurttemberg, Germany
	May 17	Alexander Povetkin	Andrzej Wawrzyk	TKO 3	WBA	Myakinino, Russia
	Oct 5	Wladimir Klitschko	Alexander Povetkin	UD	IBF	Moscow, Russia
CRUISERWEIGHT	Dec 17	Denis Lebedev	Santander Silgado	KO 4	WBA	Myakinino, Russia
	May 17	Guillermo Jones	Denis Lebedev	KO 11	WBA	Myakinino, Russia
	June 21	Krzysztof Wlodarczyk	Rakhim Chakhkiev	TKO 8	WBC	Moscow, Russia
LIGHT HEAVYWEIGHT	Mar 9	Bernard Hopkins	Tavoris Cloud	UD	IBF	Brooklyn, New York
	June 8	Adonis Stevenson	Chad Dawson	KO 1	WBC	Montreal, Canada
	Sept 28	Adonis Stevenson	Tavoris Cloud	RTD 7	WBC	Montreal, Canada
SUPER MIDDLEWEIGHT	Nov 10	Stanyslav Kashtanov	Server Yemurlayev	SD	WBA	Donetsk, Ukraine
	Nov 17	Carl Froch	Yusaf Mack	KO 3	IBF	Nottingham, U.K.
	Dec 8	Mikkel Kessler	Brian Magee	TKO 3	WBA	Herning, Denmark
	May 25	Carl Froch	Mikkel Kessler	UD	IBF	London, U.K.
	June 22	Sakio Bika	M. A. Periban	MD	WBC	Brooklyn, New York
	Aug 24	Stanyslav Kashtanov	Jaime Barboza	KO 10	WBA	Donetsk, Ukraine

**Does not include fights for "interim" titles or WBO title fights.

	Date	Winner	Loser	Result	Title/Org.	Site
MIDDLEWEIGHT	Nov 24	Martin Murray	Jorge Navarro	TKO 6	WBA	Manchester, U.K.
	Jan 19	Gennady Golovkin	Gabriel Rosado	TKO 7	WBA	New York, New York
	Jan 30	Daniel Geale	Anthony Mundine	UD	WBA	Sydney, Australia
	Mar 30	Gennady Golovkin	Nobuhiro Ishida	KO 3	WBA	Monte Carlo, Monaco
	April 27	Sergio Gabriel Martinez	Martin Murray	UD	WBC	Buenos Aires, Argentina
	June 29	Gennady Golovkin	Matthew Macklin	KO 3	WBA	Mashantucket, Connecticut
	Aug 17	Darren Barker	Daniel Geale	SD	IBF	Atlantic City, New Jersey
JR. MIDDLEWT. **(SUPER WELTER.)**	Dec 1	Austin Trout	Miguel Cotto	UD	WBA	New York, New York
	Feb 23	Ishe Smith	Cornelius Bundrage	MD	IBF	Detroit, Michigan
	Apr 20	Saul Alvarez	Austin Trout	UD 12	WBA, WBC	San Antonio, Texas
	June 8	Erislandy Lara	Alfredo Angulo	TKO 10	WBA	Carson, California
	Sep 14	Floyd Wayweather Jr.	Saul Alvarez	MD	WBA, WBC	Las Vegas, Nevada
	Sep 14	Carlos Molina	Ishe Smith	SD	IBF	Las Vegas, Nevada
WELTERWEIGHT	Oct 20	Devon Alexander	Randall Bailey	UD	IBF	Brooklyn, New York
	Oct 20	Paul Malignaggi	Pablo Cesar Cano	SD	WBA	Brooklyn, New York
	Nov 24	Robert Guerrero	Andre Berto	UD	WBC	Ontario, California
	May 4	Floyd Mayweather Jr.	Robert Guerrero	UD	WBC	Las Vegas, Nevada
	June 22	Adrien Broner	Paul Malignaggi	SD	WBA	Brooklyn, New York
	July 27	Keith Thurman	D. G. Chaves	KO 10	WBA	San Antonio, Texas
SUPER LIGHTWEIGHT (JUNIOR WELTERWEIGHT)	Oct 20	Danny Garcia	Erik Morales	KO 4	WBC, WBA	Brooklyn, New York
	Nov 30	Khabib Allakhverdiev	Joan Guzman	TD 8	WBA	Sunrise, Florida
	Dec 10	Lamont Peterson	Amir Khan	SD	IBF	Washington, D.C.
	Jan 26	L. M. Matthysse	Mike Dallas Jr	KO 1	WBC	Las Vegas, Nevada
	Feb 22	Lamont Peterson	Kendall Holt	TKO 8	IBF	Washington, D.C.
	Apr 27	Danny Garcia	Zab Judah	UD	WBC, WBA	Brooklyn, New York
	July 13	Khabib Allakhverdiev	Souleymane M'baye	TKO 11	WBA	Monte Carlo, Monaco
	Sep 14	Danny Garcia	L.M. Matthysse	UD	WBA, WBC	Las Vegas, Nevada
LIGHTWEIGHT	Oct 27	Miguel Vazquez	Marvin Quintero	SD	IBF	Verona, New York
	Nov 17	Adrien Broner	Antonio DeMarco	TKO 8	WBC	Atlantic City, New Jersey
	Dec 8	Miguel Vazquez	Mercito Gesta	UD	IBF	Las Vegas, Nevada
	March 2	Richar Abril	Sharif Bogere	UD	WBA	Las Vegas, Nevada
	Feb 16	Adrien Broner	Gavin Rees	TKO 5	WBC	Atlantic City, New Jersey
	June 8	Yuriorkis Gamboa	Darleys Perez	UD	WBA	Montreal, Canada
	July 27	Omar Figueroa	Nihito Arakawa	UD	WBC	San Antonio, Texas
SUPER FEATHERWEIGHT (JUNIOR LIGHTWEIGHT)	Oct 27	Gamaliel Diaz	Takahiro Ao	UD	WBC	Tokyo, Japan
	Dec 8	Yuriorkis Gamboa	Michael Farenas	UD	WBA	Las Vegas, Nevada
	Dec 31	Takashi Uchiyama	Bryan Vasquez	TKO 8	WBA	Tokyo, Japan
	Mar 9	Argenis Mendez	Juan Carlos Salgado	KO 4	IBF	Costa Mesa, California
	Apr 8	Takashi Miura	Gamaliel Diaz	TKO 9	WBC	Tokyo, Japan
	May 6	Takashi Uchiyama	Jaider Parra	KO 5	WBA	Tokyo, Japan
	Aug 17	Takashi Miura	Sergio Thompson	UD	WBC	Cancun, Mexico
	Aug 23	Argenis Mendez	Arash Usmanee	MD	IBF	Verona, New York
FEATHERWEIGHT	Nov 9	Chris John	Chonlatarn Piriyapinyo	UD	WBA	Singapore, Singapore
	Dec 8	Nicholas Walters	Daulis Prescott	TKO 7	WBA	Kingston, Jamaica
	Dec 8	Javier Fortuna	Patrick Hyland	UD	WBA	Las Vegas, Nevada
	Mar 1	Evgeny Gradovich	Billy Dib	SD	IBF	Mashantucket, Connecticut
	Apr 14	Chris John	Satoshi Hosono	TD 3	WBA	Jakarta, Indonesia
	Apr 19	Javier Fortuna	Miguel Zamudio	KO 1	WBA	Atlantic City, New Jersey
	May 4	Abner Mares	Daniel Ponce De Leon	TKO 9	WBC	Las Vegas, Nevada
	July 27	Evgeny Gradovich	M. J. Munoz	UD	IBF	Macao, China
	Aug 23	Jesus M. A. Cuellar	Claudio Marrero	UD	WBA	Verona, New York
	Aug 24	Jhonny Gonzalez	Abner Mares	KO 1	WBC	Carson, California

**Does not include fights for "interim" titles or WBO title fights.

	Date	Winner	Loser	Result	Title/Org.	Site
SUPER BANTAMWEIGHT (JUNIOR FEATHERWEIGHT)	Nov 10	Abner Mares	Anselmo Moreno	UD	WBC	Los Angeles, California
	Nov 24	Scott Quigg	Rendall Munroe	TKO 6	WBA	Manchester, United Kingdom
	Feb 16	Jhonatan Romero	Alejandro Lopez	SD	IBF	Tijuana, Mexico
	Apr 13	Guillermo Rigondeaux	Nonito Donaire	UD	WBA	New York, New York
	Apr 20	Victor Terrazas	Cristian Mijares	SD	WBC	Mexico City, Mexico
	Aug 10	Nehomar Cermeno	Oscar Escandon	SD	WBA	Panama City, Panama
	Aug 17	Kiko Martinez	Jhonatan Romero	TKO 6	IBF	Atlantic City, New Jersey
	Aug 24	Leo Santa Cruz	Victor Terrazas	TKO 3	WBC	Carson, California
	Oct 5	Scott Quigg	Yoandris Salinas	MDraw	WBA	London, United Kingdom
BANTAMWEIGHT	Nov 3	Roberto Vasquez	John Mark Apolinario	MD	WBA	Colon, Argentina
	Nov 3	Shinsuke Yamanaka	Tomas Rojas	KO 7	WBC	Miyagi, Japan
	Nov 10	Leo Santa Cruz	Victor Zaleta	TKO 9	IBF	Los Angeles, California
	Dec 4	Koki Kameda	Hugo Ruiz	SD	WBA	Osaka, Japan
	Dec 15	Leo Santa Cruz	Alberto Guevara	UD	IBF	Los Angeles, California
	Mar 16	Roberto Vasquez	John Mark Apolinario	SD	WBA	Panama City, Panama
	Apr 7	Koki Kameda	P. Kaiyanghadaogym	SD	WBA	Osaka, Japan
	Apr 8	Shinsuke Yamanaka	Malcolm Tunacao	TKO 12	WBC	Tokyo, Japan
	May 11	Jamie McDonnell	Julio Ceja	MD	IBF	Doncaster, United Kingdom
	July 23	Koki Kameda	John Mark Apolinario	UD	WBA	Tokyo, Japan
	Aug 10	Anselmo Moreno	William Urina	UD	WBA	Panama City, Panama
	Aug 12	Shinsuke Yamanaka	Jose Nieves	KO 1	WBC	Tokyo, Japan
SUPER FLYWEIGHT (JUNIOR BANTAMWEIGHT)	Sep 22	Juan Carlos Sanchez Jr	Rodel Mayol	KO 9	IBF	Sinaloa, Mexico
	Dec 31	Yota Sato	Ryo Akaho	UD	WBC	Tokyo, Japan
	Dec 31	Kohei Kono	Tepparith Kokietgym	KO 4	WBA	Tokyo, Japan
	May 3	Srisaket Sor Rungvisai	Yota Sato	TKO 8	WBC	Si Sa Ket, Thailand
	May 6	Liborio Solis	Kohei Kono	MD	WBA	Tokyo, Japan
	June 8	Juan Carlos Sanchez Jr	R. D. Sosa	UD	IBF	Las Vegas, Nevada
	Sep 3	Denkaosan Kaovichit	Nobuo Nashiro	SD	WBA	Nakhon Ratchasima, Thailand
	Sep 3	Daiki Kameda	Rodrigo Guerrero	UD	IBF	Kagawa, Japan
FLYWEIGHT	Nov 3	Toshiyuki Igarashi	N. D. Narvaes	MD	WBC	Miyagi, Japan
	Nov 10	Juan Carlos Reveco	Julian Rivera	UD	WBA	Mendoza, Argentina
	Nov 17	Brian Viloria	Hernan Marquez	TKO 10	WBA	Los Angeles, California
	Feb 27	Juan Carlos Reveco	Masayuki Kuroda	UD	WBA	Kawasaki, Japan
	Apr 6	Juan Francisco Estrada	Brian Viloria	SD	WBA	Macao, China
	Apr 8	Akira Yaegashi	Toshiyuki Igarashi	UD	WBC	Tokyo, Japan
	Apr 26	Kompayak Porpramook	Jean Piero Perez	TKO 6	WBA	Khon Kaen, Thailand
	June 22	Juan Carlos Reveco	Ulises Lara	TKO 8	WBA	Mendoza, Argentina
	July 27	Juan Francisco Estrada	Milan Melindo	UD	WBA	Macao China
	Aug 1	Koki Eto	K. Porpramook	UD	WBA	Bangkok, Thailand
	Aug 12	Akira Yaegashi	Oscar Blanquet	UD	WBC	Tokyo, Japan
LIGHT FLYWEIGHT (JUNIOR FLYWEIGHT)	Oct 6	Adrian Hernandez	K. Porpramook	TKO 6	WBC	Toluca, Mexico
	Nov 17	Roman Gonzalez	J. F. Estrada	UD	WBA	Los Angeles, California
	Dec 31	Kazuto Ioka	J. A. Rodriguez	TKO 6	WBA	Osaka, Japan
	Jan 12	Adrian Hernandez	Dirceu Cabarca	UD	WBC	Toluca, Mexico
	Mar 16	Alberto Rossel	Walter Tello	UD	WBA	Callao, Peru
	Mar 16	John Riel Casimero	Luis Alberto Rios	UD	IBF	Panama City, Panama
	May 8	Kazuto Ioka	Wisanu Kokietgym	KO 9	WBA	Osaka, Japan
	May 11	Adrian Hernandez	Yader Cardoza	UD	WBC	Toluca, Mexico
	Aug 31	Adrian Hernandez	Atsushi Kakutani	TKO 4	WBC	Mexico City, Mexico
	Sep 11	Kazuto Ioka	K. Sithmorseng	KO 7	WBA	Osaka, Japan
	Sep 11	Alberto Rossel	J. A. Zuniga	MD	WBA	Lima, Peru
STRAWWEIGHT (MINI FLYWT.) (MINIMUM WT.)	Oct 6	Jesus Silvestre	Takuya Mitamura	TKO 4	WBA	Nayarit, Mexico
	Nov 24	Xiong Zhao Zhong	J. M. Resendiz	UD	WBC	Kunming, China
	Dec 31	Ryo Miyazaki	P. Porpramook	SD	WBA	Osaka, Japan
	Mar 30	Katsunari Takayama	Mario Rodriguez	UD	IBF	Sinaloa, Mexico
	May 8	Ryo Miyazaki	Carlos Velarde	TKO 5	WBA	Osaka, Japan
	June 28	Xiong Zhao Zhong	Denver Cuello	MD	WBC	Dubai, United Arab Emirates
	Sep 11	Ryo Miyazaki	Jesus Silvestre	MD	WBA	Osaka, Japan

**Does not include fights for "interim" titles or WBO title fights.

World Champions**

Sanctioning bodies: the National Boxing Association (NBA), the New York State Athletic Commission (NY), the World Boxing Association (WBA), the World Boxing Council (WBC), and the International Boxing Federation (IBF).

Heavyweights (Weight: Unlimited)

Champion	Reign	Champion	Reign	Champion	Reign	Champion	Reign
John L. Sullivan*	1885–92	Muhammad Ali*	1964–70†	Trevor Berbick WBC	1986	Hasim Rahman* WBC/ IBF	2001–05
James J. Corbett*	1892–97	Ernie Terrell WBA	1965–67	Mike Tyson WBC	1986–87	Chris Byrd IBF	2002–06
Bob Fitzsimmons*	1897–99	Joe Frazier* NY	1968–70	James Smith WBA	1986–87	Roy Jones Jr. WBA	2003–05
James J. Jeffries*	1899–05†	Jimmy Ellis WBA	1968–70	Tony Tucker IBF	1987	Lennox Lewis* WBC	2001–04
Marvin Hart*	1905–06	Joe Frazier*	1970–73	Mike Tyson*	1987–90	John Ruiz, WBA	2003–05
Tommy Burns*	1906–08	George Foreman*	1973–74	Buster Douglas*	1990	Vitali Klitschko WBC	2004–05
Jack Johnson*	1908–15	Muhammad Ali*	1974–78	Evander Holyfield*	1990–92	Hasim Rahman WBC	2005–06
Jess Willard*	1915–19	Leon Spinks*	1978	Lennox Lewis WBC	1993–95	Nikolay Valuev WBA	2005–07
Jack Dempsey*	1919–26	Ken Norton WBC	1978	Riddick Bowe*	1992–93	Oleg Maskaev WBC	2006–08
Gene Tunney*	1926–28†	Larry Holmes WBC	1978–80	Evander Holyfield*	1993–94	Wladimir Klitschko. IBF/WBA	2006–
Max Schmeling*	1930–32	Muhammad Ali*	1978–79†	Michael Moorer*	1994	Ruslan Chagaev WBA	2007–08
Jack Sharkey*	1932–33	John Tate WBA	1979–80	George Foreman*	1994–95	Samuel Peter WBC	2008
Primo Carnera*	1933–34	Mike Weaver WBA	1980–82	Oliver McCall WBC	1995	Nikolai Valuev WBA	2008–09
Max Baer*	1934–35	Larry Holmes*	1980–85	Frank Bruno WBC	1995–96	Vitali Klitschko WBC	2008–
James J. Braddock*	1935–37	Michael Dokes WBA	1982–83	Bruce Seldon WBA	1995–96	David Haye WBA	2009–11
Joe Louis*	1937–49†	Gerrie Coetzee WBA	1983–84	Mike Tyson WBA	1996	Alexander Povetkin WBA	2011–13
Ezzard Charles*	1949–51	Tim Witherspoon WBC	1984	Michael Moorer IBF	1996–97		
Jersey Joe Walcott*	1951–52	Pinklon Thomas WBC	1984–86	Shannon Briggs*	1997–98		
Rocky Marciano*	1952–56†	Greg Page WBA	1984–85	Lennox Lewis* WBC	1997–01		
Floyd Patterson*	1956–59	Michael Spinks*	1985–87	E. Holyfield WBA, IBF	1996–99		
Ingemar Johansson*	1959–60	Tim Witherspoon WBA	1986	Lennox Lewis, IBF	1999–01		
Floyd Patterson*	1960–62			E. Holyfield WBA	2000–01		
Sonny Liston*	1962–64			John Ruiz WBA	2001–03		

Cruiserweights (Weight Limit: 200 pounds)

Champion	Reign	Champion	Reign	Champion	Reign	Champion	Reign
Marvin Camel* WBC	1980	Evander Holyfield*	1988†	Imamu Mayfield IBF	1997–98	David Haye WBC	2007–08
Carlos De Leon* WBC	1980–82	Toufik Belbouli WBA	1989	Fabrice Tiozzo WBA	1997–00	David Haye WBA	2007–08†
Ossie Ocasio WBA	1982–84	Robert Daniels WBA	1989–91	J.C. Gomez* WBC	1998–02†	Giacobbe Fragomeni WBC	2008–09
S.T. Gordon* WBC	1982–83	Carlos De Leon* WBC	1989–90	Arthur Williams IBF	1998–99	Tomasz Adamek IBF	2008–09†
Carlos De Leon* WBC	1983–85	Glenn McCrory IBF	1989–90	Vassiliy Girov* IBF	1999–03	Zsolt Erdei WBC	2009–10
Marvin Camel IBF	1983–84	Jeff Lampkin IBF	1990	Virgil Hill WBA	2000–02	Guillermo Jones WBA	2009–
Lee Roy Murphy IBF	1984–86	M. Duran* WBC	1990–91	Wayne Braithwaite WBC	2002–05	Kryzysztof Wlodarczyk WBC	2010–
Piet Crous WBA	1984–85	Bobby Czyz WBA	1991–92†	J.M. Mormeck WBA	2002–06	Steve Cunningham IBF	2010–11
Alfonso Ratliff* WBC	1985	Anaclet Wamba* WBC	1991–95†	James Toney* IBF	2003	Yoan Pablo Hernandez IBF	2011–
Dwight Braxton WBA	1985–86	James Pritchard IBF	1991	Melvin Davis IBF	2004–05		
Bernard Benton* WBC	1985–86	James Warring IBF	1991–92	J.M. Mormeck WBC	2005–06		
Carlos De Leon* WBC	1986–88	Alfred Cole IBF	1992–96	O'Neil Bell IBF	2005–06		
Evander Holyfield* WBA	1986–88	Orlin Norris WBA	1993–95	O'Neil Bell WBC/WBA	2006–07		
Ricky Parkey IBF	1986–87	Nate Miller WBA	1995–97	Steve Cunningham IBF	2006–08		
Evander Holyfield* WBA, IBF	1987–88	M. Dominguez* WBC	1996–98	J.M. Mormeck WBC/WBA	2007		
		A. Washington IBF	1996–97				
		Uriah Grant IBF	1997				

*Lineal champion.   †Champion relinquished title to retire or switch weight classes, or had title stripped by boxing organization.
**In case of WBA, includes both "super" and "regular" champions. Does not include interim or WBO title holders.

Light Heavyweights (Weight Limit: 175 pounds)

Champion	Reign	Champion	Reign	Champion	Reign	Champion	Reign
Jack Root*	1903	Dick Tiger*	1966–68	Virgil Hill* WBA	1987–91	Roy Jones Jr. WBC	2003
George Gardner*	1903	Bob Foster*	1968–74†	Pr Charles Williams		Glencoffe Johnson	
Bob Fitzsimmons*	1903–05	Vicente Rondon WBA	1971–72	IBF	1987–93	IBF	2004–05
Jack O'Brien*	1905–12†	John Conteh WBC	1974–77	Thomas Hearns WBC	1987†	Fabrice Tiozzo WBA	2004–05
Jack Dillon*	1914–16	Victor Galindez* WBA	1974–78	Donny Lalonde WBC	1987–88	Antonio Tarver* WBC	2004–05
Battling Levinsky*	1916–20	Miguel A. Cuello WBC	1977–78	Sugar Ray Leonard		Silvio Branco WBA	2005–07
Georges Carpentier*	1920–22	Mate Parlov WBC	1978	WBC	1988	Clinton Woods IBF	2005–08
Battling Siki*	1922–23	Mike Rossman*		Dennis Andries WBC	1989	Tomasz Adamek WBC	2005–07
Mike McTigue*	1923–25	WBA	1978–79	Jeff Harding WBC	1989–90	Stipe Drews WBA	2007
Paul Berlenbach*	1925–26	Marvin Johnson*		Dennis Andries WBC	1990–91	Chad Dawson WBC	2007–08
Jack Delaney*	1926–27†	WBC	1978–79	Thomas Hearns* WBA	1991–92		2008–09†
Jimmy Slattery NBA	1927	Victor Galindez*		Jeff Harding WBC	1991–94	Danny Green WBA	2007–08
Tommy Loughran*	1927–29†	WBA	1979	Iran Barkley* WBA	1992	Hugo Garay WBA	2008–09
Maxie Rosenbloom*	1930–34	M.S. Muhammad*		Virgil Hill* WBA	1992–97	Antonio Tarver IBF	2008
George Nichols NBA	1932	WBC	1979–81	Henry Maske IBF	1993–96	Adrian Diaconu WBC	2008–09
Bob Godwin NBA	1933	Marvin Johnson		Mike McCallum WBC	1994–95	Gabriel Campillo WBA	2009–10
Bob Olin*	1934–35	WBA	1979–80	Fabrice Tiozzo WBC	1995–96	Jean Pascal WBC	2009–11
John Henry Lewis*	1935–38†	E.M. Muhammad*		D. Michalczewski*		Tavoris Cloud IBF	2009–13
Melio Bettina	1939	WBA	1980–81	IBF	1997†	Beibut Shumenov	
Billy Conn*	1939–40†	Michael Spinks* WBA	1981–83	Roy Jones Jr.		WBA	2010–
Anton Christoforidis	1941	Dwight Qawi WBC	1981–83	WBC/WBA	1997–03	Bernard Hopkins	
Gus Lesnevich*	1941–48	Michael Spinks*	1983–85†	William Guthrie IBF	1997–98	WBC	2011
Freddie Mills*	1948–50	J. B. Williamson WBC	1985–86	Reggie Johnson IBF	1998–99	Chad Dawson WBC	2011–13
Joey Maxim*	1950–52	Slobodan Kacar IBF	1985–86	Roy Jones Jr.*	1999–03	Adonis Stevenson	
Archie Moore*	1952–62†	Marvin Johnson*		Bruno Girard WBA	2001–03	WBC	2013–
Harold Johnson NBA	1961	WBA	1986–87	Mehdi Sahnoune		Bernard Hopkins IBF	2013–
Harold Johnson*	1962–63	Dennis Andries WBC	1986–87	WBA	2003		
Willie Pastrano*	1963–65	Bobby Czyz IBF	1986–87	Silvio Branco WBA	2003–04		
Jose Torres*	1965–66	Leslie Stewart WBA	1987	Antonio Tarver			
				WBC/IBF	2003		

Super Middleweights (Weight Limit: 168 pounds)

Champion	Reign	Champion	Reign	Champion	Reign	Champion	Reign
Murray Sutherland*		James Toney IBF	1992–94	Glenn Catley WBC	2000–01	Joe Calzaghe, WBC	2007–08
IBF	1984	Michael Nunn* WBA	1992–94	Eric Lucas WBC	2000–03	Lucian Bute IBF	2007–12
Chong-Pal Park* IBF	1984–87	Steve Little* WBA	1994	Byron Mitchell WBA	2000–03	Joe Calzaghe WBA	2007–08
Chong-Pal Park* WBA	1987–88	Frank Liles* WBA	1994–99	Sven Ottke WBA	2003†	Carl Froch WBC	2008–10
G. Rocchigiani IBF	1988–89	Roy Jones Jr. IBF	1994–96	Anthony Mundine WBA	2003	Mikkel Kessler WBA	2008–09
F. Obelmejias* WBA	1988–89	Thulane Malinga WBC	1996	Markus Beyer WBC	2003–04	Andre Ward‡ WBA	2009–
Sugar Ray Leonard		V. Nardiello WBC	1996	Sven Ottke, IBF	2003–05	Mikkel Kessler WBC	2010†
WBC	1988–90†	Robin Reid WBC	1996–97	Cristian Sanavia WBC	2004	Carl Froch	2011
In-Chul Baek* WBA	1989–90	Charles Brewer IBF	1997–98	Manny Siaca, WBA	2004	Andre Ward WBC	2011–13†
Lindell Holmes IBF	1990–91	Thulane Malinga		Mikel Kessler WBA	2004–07	Carl Froch IBF	2012–
Chris Tiozzo* WBA	1990–91	WBC	1997–98	Markus Beyer WBC	2004–06	Sakio Bika WBC	2013–
Mauro Galvano WBC	1990–92	Richie Woodhall WBC	1998–99	Jeff Lacy IBF	2005	Carl Froch WBA	2013–
Victor Cordova* WBA	1991	Sven Ottke IBF	1998–03	Joe Calzaghe IBF	2006–07		
Darrin Van Horn IBF	1991–92	Byron Mitchell* WBA	1999–00	Mikkel Kessler WBC	2006–07		
Iran Barkley IBF	1992	Markus Beyer WBC	1999–00	Robert Stieglitz IBF	2007		
Nigel Benn WBC	1992–96	Bruno Girard* WBA	2000–01†	Alejandro Berrio IBF	2007		

Middleweights (Weight Limit: 160 pounds)

Champion	Reign	Champion	Reign	Champion	Reign	Champion	Reign
Jack Dempsey*	1884–91	George Chip*	1913–14	Marcel Thil*	1932–37	Billy Soose*	1941
Bob Fitzsimmons*	1891–97†	Al McCoy*	1914–17	Fred Apostoli*	1937–39	Tony Zale*	1941–47
Kid McCoy	1897–98	Mike O'Dowd*	1917–20	Al Hostak NBA	1938	Rocky Graziano*	1947–48
Tommy Ryan*	1898–07†	Johnny Wilson*	1920–23	Solly Krieger NBA	1938–39	Tony Zale*	1948
Stanley Ketchel*	1908	Harry Greb*	1923–26	Al Hostak NBA	1939–40	Marcel Cerdan*	1948–49
Billy Papke*	1908	Tiger Flowers*	1926	Ceferino Garcia*	1939–40	Jake La Motta*	1949–51
Stanley Ketchel*	1908–10†	Mickey Walker*	1926–31†	Ken Overlin*	1940–41	Sugar Ray Robinson*	1951
Frank Klaus*	1913	Gorilla Jones*	1931–32	Tony Zale NBA	1940–41	Randy Turpin*	1951

*Lineal champion. ‡ Super champion. †Champion relinquished title to retire or switch weight classes, or had title stripped by boxing organization.
**In case of WBA, includes both "super" and "regular" champions. Does not include interim or WBO title holders.

Middleweights (Weight Limit: 160 pounds)

Champion	Reign	Champion	Reign	Champion	Reign	Champion	Reign
Sugar Ray Robinson*	1951–52†	Rodrigo Valdez*	1977–78	Jorge Castro WBA	1994–95	Felix Sturm WBA	2006
Bobo Olson*	1953–55	Hugo Corro*	1978–79	Bernard Hopkins*		Javier Castillejo WBA	2006–07
Sugar Ray Robinson*	1955–57	Vito Antuofermo*	1979–80	IBF	1994–	Felix Sturm WBA	2007–
Gene Fullmer*	1957	Alan Minter*	1980	Shinji Takehara WBA	1995–96	Kelly Pavlik WBC	2007–10
Sugar Ray Robinson*	1957	Marvin Hagler*	1980–87	Jullian Jackson WBC	1995	Sebastian Sylvester	
Carmen Basilio*	1957–58	Sugar Ray Leonard*	1987†	Quincy Taylor WBC	1995–96	IBF	2009–11
Sugar Ray Robinson*	1958–60	Frank Tate IBF	1987–88	Keith Holmes WBC	1996–98	Sergio Gabriel Martinez	
Gene Fullmer NBA	1959–62	Sumbu Kalambay		William Joppy WBA	1996–97	WBC	2010–11†
Paul Pender*	1960–61	WBA	1987–89	J.C. Green WBA	1997	Sebastian Zbik WBC	2011
Terry Downes*	1961–62	Thomas Hearns*		William Joppy WBA	1998–01	Julio Cesar Chavez Jr.	
Paul Pender*	1962–63†	WBC	1987–88	Hassine Cherifi WBC	1998–99	WBC	2011–12
Dick Tiger WBA	1962–63	Iran Barkley* WBC	1988–89	Keith Holmes WBC	1999–00	Gennady Golovkin	
Dick Tiger*	1963	Michael Nunn IBF	1988–91	Felix Trinidad WBA	2001	WBA	2011–
Joey Giardello*	1963–65	Roberto Duran* WBC	1989–90†	William Joppy WBA	2001–03	Daniel Geale IBF	2011–13
Dick Tiger*	1965–66	Mike McCallum WBA	1989–91	Bernard Hopkins*		Sergio Gabriel Martinez	
Emile Griffith*	1966–67	Julian Jackson WBC	1990–93	WBC/IBF	2001–05	WBC	2012–
Nino Benvenuti*	1967	Michael Nunn* IBF	1991	Bernard Hopkins WBA	2003–05	Darren Barker IBF	2013–
Emile Griffith*	1967–68	James Toney* IBF	1991–93†	Jermain Taylor IBF	2005		
Nino Benvenuti*	1968–70	Reggie Johnson WBA	1992–94	Jermain Taylor WBA	2005–06		
Carlos Monzon*	1970–77†	Roy Jones Jr.* IBF	1993–95†	Jermain Taylor WBA*	2005–07		
Rodrigo Valdez WBC	1974–76	G. McClellan WBC	1993–95†	Arthur Abraham IBF	2005–09†		

Junior Middleweights (Weight Limit: 154 pounds)

Champion	Reign	Champion	Reign	Champion	Reign	Champion	Reign
Emile Griffith	1962–63	Roberto Duran WBA	1983–84	Terry Norris* WBC	1995–97	Oscar De La Hoya*	
Dennis Moyer*	1962–63	Mark Medal IBF	1984	Terry Norris* IBF	1995–96†	WBC	2006–07
Ralph Dupas*	1963	Thomas Hearns*	1984–86†	L. Boudouani WBA	1996–99	Cory Spinks IBF	2006–08
Sandro Mazzinghi*	1963–65	Mike McCallum*		Raul Marquez IBF	1997	Travis Simms WBA	2007
Nino Benvenuti*	1965–66	WBA	1984–87†	Keith Mullings* WBC	1997–99	Floyd Mayweather Jr.	
Ki-Soo Kim*	1966–68	Carlos Santos IBF	1984–86	Yori Boy Campas IBF	1997–98	WBC	2007
Sandro Mazzinghi*	1968	Buster Drayton IBF	1986–87	Fernando Vargas IBF	1998–00	Joachim Alcine WBA	2007–08
Freddie Little*	1969–70	Duane Thomas		F. Javier Castillejo*		Vernon Forrest WBC	2007–08
Carmelo Bossi*	1970–71	WBC	1986–87	WBC	1999–01	Sergio Mora WBC	2008
Koichi Wajima*	1971–74	Matthew Hilton IBF	1987–88	David Reid WBA	1999–00	Verno Phillips IBF*	2008†
Oscar Albarado*	1974–75	Lupe Aquino WBC	1987	Felix Trinidad WBA	2000–01	Daniel Santos WBA	2008–09
Koichi Wajima*	1975	Gianfranco Rosi		Felix Trinidad		Vernon Forrest	
Miguel de Oliveira WBC	1975–76	WBC	1987–88	WBA/IBF	2001†	WBC	2008–09
Jae-Do Yuh*	1975–76	Julian Jackson WBA	1987–90	Oscar De La Hoya*		Cory Spinks IBF	2009–10
Elisha Obed WBC	1975–76	Donald Curry WBC	1988–89	WBC	2001–03	Sergio Gabriel Martinez	
Koichi Wajima*	1976	Robert Hines IBF	1988–89	Fernando Vargas		WBC	2009–10†
Jose Duran*	1976	Darrin Van Horn IBF	1989	WBA	2001–02	Yuri Foreman WBA	2009–10
Eckhard Dagge WBC	1976–77	Rene Jacquot WBC	1989	Ronald Wright IBF†	2001–04	Miguel Cotto WBA‡	2010–12
Miguel Angel		John Mugabi* WBC	1989–90	Oscar De La Hoya*		Manny Pacquiao WBC	2010–11†
Castellini*	1976–77	Gianfranco Rosi IBF	1989–94	WBC/WBA	2002–03	Saul Alvarez WBC	2011–
Eddie Gazo*	1977–78	Terry Norris* WBC	1990–93	Shane Mosley* WBC	2003–04	Austin Trout WBA	2011–13
Rocky Mattioli WBC	1977–79	Gilbert Dele WBC	1991	Alejandro Garcia WBA	2003–05	Cornelius Bundrage	
Masashi Kudo*	1978–79	Vinny Pazienza		Ronald Wright		IBF	2011–13
Maurice Hope WBC	1979–81	WBA	1991–92	WBA/WBC	2004–05	Miguel Angel Cotto	
Ayub Kalule*	1979–81	Julio C. Vasquez WBA	1992–95	Verno Phillips IBF	2004–05	WBA	2011
Wilfred Benitez WBC	1981–82	Simon Brown* WBC	1993–94	Ricardo Mayora		Floyd Mayweather Jr.	
Sugar Ray Leonard*	1981–82†	Terry Norris* WBC	1994	WBC	2005–06	WBA‡	2012–
Tadashi Mihara WBA	1981–82	Vincent Pettway IBF	1994–95	Alex T. Garcia WBA	2005–06	Ishe Smith IBF	2013
Davey Moore WBA	1982–83	Luis Santana* WBC	1995–95	Roman Karmazin		Saul Alvarez WBC	2013
Thomas Hearns*		Paul Vaden IBF	1995	IBF	2005–06	Carlos Molina, IBF	2013–
WBC	1982–84	Carl Daniels WBA	1995	Jose A. Rivera WBA	2006–07	Floyd Mayweather Jr.	
						WBC	2013–

Welterweights (Weight Limit: 147 pounds)

Champion	Reign	Champion	Reign	Champion	Reign	Champion	Reign
Paddy Duffy*	1888–90†	Matty Matthews*	1900–01	Mike Sullivan*	1907–08†	Matt Wells*	1914–15
Billy Smith*	1892–94	Rube Ferns*	1901	Jimmy Gardner*	1908†	Mike Glover*	1915
Tommy Ryan*	1894–98†	Joe Walcott*	1901–04	Jimmy Clabby*	1910–11†	Jack Britton*	1915
Billy Smith*	1898–1900	The Dixie Kid*	1904–05†	Waldemar Holberg*	1914	Ted "Kid" Lewis*	1915–16
Rube Ferns*	1900	Honey Mellody*	1906–07	Tom McCormick*	1914	Jack Britton*	1916–17

*Lineal champion. ‡Super champion. †Champion relinquished title to retire or switch weight classes, or had title stripped by boxing organization.
**In case of WBA, includes both "super" and "regular" champions. Does not include interim or WBO title holders.

Welterweights (Weight Limit: 147 pounds)

Champion	Reign	Champion	Reign	Champion	Reign	Champion	Reign
Ted "Kid" Lewis*	1917–19	Emile Griffith*	1961	Mark Breland WBA	1989–90	Zab Judah WBA/WBC/IBF	2005–06
Jack Britton*	1919–22	Kid Paret*	1961–62	Marlon Starling*		Luis Collazo WBA	2006
Mickey Walker*	1922–26	Emile Griffith*	1962–63	WBC	1989–90	Ricky Hatton WBA	2006
Pete Latzo*	1926–27	Luis Rodriguez*	1963	Aaron Davis WBA	1990–91	Carlos Baldomir WBC	2006
Joe Dundee*	1927–29	Emile Griffith*	1963–66†	Maurice Blocker*		F. Mayweather, Jr. IBF	2006
Jackie Fields*	1929–30	Curtis Cokes*	1966–69	WBC	1990–91	Miguel Cotto WBA	2006–08
Young		Jose Napoles*	1969–70	Meldrick Taylor WBA	1991–92	F. Mayweather Jr.	
Jack Thompson*	1930	Billy Backus*	1970–71	Simon Brown* WBC	1991	WBC	2006–08
Tommy Freeman*	1930–31	Jose Napoles*	1971–75	Buddy McGirt* WBC	1991–93	Kermit Cintron IBF	2006–08
Young		Hedgemon Lewis NY	1972–73	Crisanto Espana		A. Margarito WBA	2008
Jack Thompson*	1931	Angel Espada WBA	1975–76	WBA	1992–94	Joshua Clottey IBF	2008–09†
Lou Brouillard*	1931–32	John H. Stracey*	1975–76	Felix Trinidad IBF	1993–00	Ant. Margarito WBA	2008–09
Jackie Fields*	1932–33	Carlos Palomino*	1976–79	Pernell Whitaker*		Andre Berto WBC	2008–11
Young Corbett III*	1933	Pipino Cuevas WBA	1976–80	WBC	1993–97	Shane Mosley WBA	2009
Jimmy McLarnin*	1933–34	Wilfredo Benitez*	1979	Ike Quartey WBA	1994–97†	Isaac Hlatshwayo IBF	2009
Barney Ross*	1934	Sugar Ray Leonard*	1979–80	Oscar De La Hoya*		Vyacheslav Senchenko	
Jimmy McLarnin*	1934–35	Roberto Duran*	1980	WBC	1997–99	WBA	2009–12
Barney Ross*	1935–38	Thomas Hearns		James Page WBA	1998–01	Dejan Zavec IBF	2009–11
Henry Armstrong*	1938–40	WBA	1980–81	Felix Trinidad*		Victor Ortz WBC	2011
Fritzie Zivic*	1940–41	Sugar Ray Leonard*	1980–82†	IBF/WBC	1999–00†	F. Mayweather Jr.	
Red Cochrane*	1941–46	Donald Curry* WBA	1983–85	Shane Mosley*		WBC	2011–
Marty Servo*	1946	Milton McCrory		WBC	2000–02	Andre Berto IBF	2011†
Sugar Ray		WBC	1983–85	Andrew Lewis WBA	2001–02	Randall Bailey IBF	2012–13
Robinson*	1946–51†	Donald Curry*	1985–86	Vernon Forrest IBF	2001	Paul Malignaggi WBA	2012–13
Johnny Bratton*	1951	Lloyd Honeyghan*	1986–87	Vernon Forrest* WBC	2001–03	Devon Alexander IBF	2013–
Kid Gavilan*	1951–54	Jorge Vaca* WBC	1987–88	Ricardo Mayorga		Adrien Broner WBA	2013–
Johnny Saxton*	1954–55	Mark Breland WBA	1987	WBA	2002		
Tony DeMarco*	1955	Marlon Starling		Michele Piccirillo IBF	2002–03		
Carmen Basilio*	1955–56	WBA	1987–88	Ricardo Mayorga*			
Johnny Saxton*	1956	Lloyd Honeyghan*		WBC	2003–05		
Carmen Basilio*	1956–57†	WBC	1988–89	Jose Rivera WBA	2003		
Virgil Akins*	1958	Tomas Molinares		Cory Spinks			
Don Jordan*	1958–60	WBA	1988–89	IBF, WBC, WBA	2003–05		
Kid Paret*	1960–61	Simon Brown IBF	1988–91				

Super Lightweights (Weight Limit: 140 pounds)

Champion	Reign	Champion	Reign	Champion	Reign	Champion	Reign
Pinkey Mitchell*	1922–25	Wilfred Benitez*	1976–79†	James McGirt IBF	1988	Kostya Tszyu WBC	1998–04
Red Herring	1925	M. Velasquez WBC	1976	Meldrick Taylor IBF	1988–90	Terronn Millett* IBF	1999–00
Mushy Callahan*	1926–30	S. Muangsurin WBC	1976–78	Julio César Chávez*		Zab Judah* IBF	2000–01
Jack (Kid) Berg*	1930–31	A. Cervantes WBA	1977–80	WBC	1989–94	Kostya Tszyu*†	
Tony Canzoneri*	1931–32	Sang-Hyun Kim WBC	1978–80	Julio César Chávez*		WBA	2001–03
Johnny Jadick*	1932–33	Saoul Mamby WBC	1980–82	IBF	1990–91	Kostya Tszyu* IBF	2003–05
Sammy Fuller	1932–33	Aaron Pryor* WBA	1980–83	Loreto Garza WBA	1990–91	Vivian Harris WBA	2003–05
Battling Shaw*	1933	Leroy Haley WBC	1982–83	Juan Coggi WBA	1991	Arturo Gatti WBC	2004–05
Tony Canzoneri*	1933	Aaron Pryor* IBF	1983–85†	Edwin Rosario WBA	1991–92	F. Mayweather Jr.	
Barney Ross*	1933–35†	Bruce Curry WBC	1983–84	Rafael Pineda IBF	1991–92	WBC	2005–06
Tippy Larkin*	1946	Johnny Bumphus		Akinobu Hiranaka		Carlos Maussa	
Carlos Ortiz*	1959–60	WBA	1984	WBA	1992	WBA	2005–06
Duilio Loi*	1960–62	Bill Costello WBC	1984–85	Pernell Whitaker IBF	1992–93†	Ricky Hatton IBF	2005–06
Eddie Perkins*	1962	Gene Hatcher WBA	1984–85	Charles Murray IBF	1993–94	Souleymane M'baye	
Duilio Loi*	1962–63†	Ubaldo Sacco WBA	1985–86	Juan Coggi WBA	1993–94	WBA	2006–07
Roberto Cruz WBA	1963	Lonnie Smith* WBC	1985–86	Jake Rodriguez IBF	1994–95	Juan Urango IBF	2006–07
Eddie Perkins*	1963–65	Patrizio Oliva WBA	1986–87	Frankie Randall* WBC	1994	Junior Witter WBC	2006–08
Carlos Hernandez*	1965–66	Gary Hinton IBF	1986	Frankie Randall WBA	1994–96	Gavin Rees WBC	2007–08
Sandro Lopopolo*	1966–67	Rene Arredondo*		Juan Coggi WBA	1996	Ricky Hatton IBF	2007
Paul Fujii*	1967–68	WBC	1986	Julio César Chávez*		Lovemore N'Dou	
Nicolino Loche*	1968–72	Tsuyoshi Hamada		WBC	1994–96	IBF	2007
Pedro Adigue WBC	1968–70	WBC	1986–87	Kostya Tszyu IBF	1995–97	Paul Malignaggi	
Bruno Arcari WBC	1970–74	Joe Louis Manley		Frankie Randall WBA	1996–97	IBF	2007–09†
Alfonso Frazer*	1972	IBF	1986–87	Oscar De La Hoya*		Timothy Bradley	
Antonio Cervantes*	1972–76	Terry Marsh IBF	1987	WBC	1996–97†	WBC	2008–09
Perico Fernandez		Juan Coggi WBA	1987–90	Khalid Rahilou WBA	1997–99	Andreas Kotelnik WBA	2008–09
WBC	1974–75	Rene Arredondo WBC	1987	Vincent Phillips* IBF	1997–99	Devon Alexander WBC	2009–11
S. Muangsurin WBC	1975–76	R. Mayweather* WBC	1987–89	Sharmba Mitchell WBA	1998–01		

*Lineal champion. †Champion relinquished title to retire or switch weight classes, or had title stripped by boxing organization.
**In case of WBA, includes both "super" and "regular" champions. Does not include interim or WBO title holders.

Super Lightweights (Cont.)

Champion	Reign	Champion	Reign	Champion	Reign	Champion	Reign
Amir Khan WBA‡	2009–	Marcos Maidana WBA	.2010	Erik Morales WBC	2011–12	Danny Garcia	
Juan Urango IBF	2009–10	Zab Judah IBF	.2011	Amir Khan WBA/IBF	2011	WBA/WBC	2012–
Devon Alexander IBF	2010†	Timothy Bradley WBC	.2011†	Lamont Peterson IBF	2011–		

Lightweights (Weight Limit: 135 pounds)

Champion	Reign	Champion	Reign	Champion	Reign	Champion	Reign
Jack McAuliffe*	1886–94†	Carlos Ortiz*	1962–65	Jose Luis Ramirez		Stefano Zoff WBA	1999
Kid Lavigne*	1896–99	Ismael Laguna*	1965	WBC	1987–88	Paul Spadafora IBF	1999–03
Frank Erne*	1899–1902	Carlos Ortiz*	1965–68	Vinny Pazienza IBF	1987–88	Gilbert Serrano WBA	1999–00
Joe Gans*	1902–04	Carlos Teo Cruz*	1968–69	Julio César Chávez*	1988–89†	T. Hatakeyama WBA	2000–01
Jimmy Britt*	1904–05	Mando Ramos*	1969–70	Greg Haugen IBF	1988–89	Jose Luis Castillo*	
Battling Nelson*	1905–06	Ismael Laguna*	1970	P. Whitaker*		WBC	2000–02
Joe Gans*	1906–08	Ken Buchanan*	1970–72	WBC/IBF	1989–90	Julien Lorcy WBA	2001
Battling Nelson*	1908–10	Roberto Duran*	1972–79†	Edwin Rosario WBA	1989–90	Raul Balbi WBA	2001
Ad Wolgast*	1910–12	Chango Carmona		Juan Nazario WBA	1990	F. Mayweather* WBC	2002–03
Willie Ritchie*	1912–14	WBC	1972	P. Whitaker*		Leonard Dorin WBA	2002–03
Freddie Welsh*	1915–17	Rodolfo Gonzalez		WBA/WBC	1990–92†	Javier Jauregui IBF	2003–04
Benny Leonard*	1917–25†	WBC	1972–74	Julio César Chávez		Julio Diaz IBF	2004–05
Jimmy Goodrich*	1925	Ishimatsu Suzuki		IBF	1990–91	Lakva Sim WBA	2004
Rocky Kansas*	1925–26	WBC	1974–76	Julio César Chávez		Juan Diaz WBA	2004–08
Sammy Mandell*	1926–30	Esteban DeJesus		WBC	1990–92	Jose Luis Castillo	
Al Singer*	1930	WBC	1976–78	Pernell Whitaker*		WBC	2004–05
Tony Canzoneri*	1930–33	Jim Watt WBC*	1979–81	IBF	1991–92†	Diego Corrales WBC	2005–06
Barney Ross*	1933–35†	Ernesto Espana		Edwin Rosario WBA	1991–92	Jesus Chavez IBF	2005–07
Tony Canzoneri*	1935–36	WBA	1979–80	Miguel Gonzalez		Joel Casamayor	
Lou Ambers*	1936–38	Hilmer Kenty WBA	1980–81	WBC	1992–95	WBC	2006–08
Henry Armstrong*	1938–39	Sean O'Grady WBA	1981	Joey Gamache		Julio Diaz IBF	2007
Lou Ambers*	1939–40	Claude Noel WBA	1981	WBA	1992–93	Juan Diaz	2007–08
Sammy Angott NBA	1940–41	Alexis Arguello*		Dingaan Thobela		David Diaz WBC	2008
Lew Jenkins*	1940–41	WBC	1981–82†	WBA	1993	Yusuke Kobori WBA	2008–09
Sammy Angott*	1941–42†	Arturo Frias WBA	1981–82	Fred Pendleton* IBF	1993–94	Nate Campbell IBF	2008–09†
Beau Jack* NY	1942–43	Ray Mancini* WBA	1982–84	Orzubek Nazarov		Manny Pacquiao	
Bob Montgomery*		Alexis Arguello	1982–83	WBA	1993–98	WBC	2008–09†
NY	1943	Edwin Rosario WBC	1983–84	Rafael Ruelas* IBF	1994–95	Juan Manual Marquez	
Sammy Angott NBA	1943–44	Choo Choo Brown		Oscar De La Hoya*		WBA	2009-12†
Beau Jack* NY	1943–44	IBF	1984	IBF	1995†	Edwin Valero WBC	2009–10†
Bob Montgomery*		L. Bramble* WBA	1984–86	Phillip Holiday IBF	1995–97	Miguel Vazquez IBF	2010–
NY	1944–47	Jose Luis Ramirez		Jean B. Mendy*		Humberto Soto WBC	2010–11
Juan Zurita NBA	1944–45	WBC	1984–85	WBC	1996–97	Miguel Acosta WBA	2010–11
Ike Williams*	1947–51	Harry Arroyo IBF	1984–85	Steve Johnston*		Brandon Rios WBA	2011†
James Carter*	1951–52	Jimmy Paul IBF	1985–86	WBC	1997–98	Antonio DeMarco WBC	2011–12
Lauro Salas*	1952	Hector Camacho		Shane Mosley IBF	1997–99†	Adrien Broner WBC	2012–
James Carter*	1952–54	WBC	1985–86	Jean B. Mendy WBA	1998–99	Richar Abril WBA	2013–
Paddy DeMarco*	1954	Greg Haugen IBF	1986–87	Cesar Bazan* WBC	1998–99		
James Carter*	1954–55	Edwin Rosario* WBA	1986–87	Steve Johnston*			
Wallace Smith*	1955–56	Julio César Chávez*		WBC	1999–00		
Joe Brown*	1956–58	WBA	1987–88	Julien Lorcy WBA	1999		

Super Featherweights (Weight Limit: 130 pounds)

Champion	Reign	Champion	Reign	Champion	Reign	Champion	Reign
Johnny Dundee*	1921–23	Hiroshi Kobayashi*	1967–71	Rafael Limon WBC	1980–81	Barry Michael IBF	1985–87
Jack Bernstein*	1923	Rene Barrientos WBC	1969–70	C. Boza-Edwards WBC	1981	Alfredo Layne* WBA	1986
Johnny Dundee*	1923–24	Yoshiaki Numata WBC	1970–71	Samuel Serrano*	1981–83	Brian Mitchell* WBA	1986–91†
Steve (Kid) Sullivan*	1924–25	Alfredo Marcano*	1971–72	R. Navarrete WBC	1981–82	Rocky Lockridge IBF	1987–88
Mike Ballerino*	1925	R. Arredondo WBC	1971–74	Rafael Limon WBC	1982	Azumah Nelson* WBC	1988–94
Tod Morgan*	1925–29	Ben Villaflor*	1972–73	Bobby Chacon WBC	1982–83	Tony Lopez IBF	1988–89
Benny Bass*	1929–31	Kuniaki Shibata*	1973	Roger Mayweather*	1983–84	Juan Molina IBF	1989–90
Kid Chocolate*	1931–33	Ben Villaflor*	1973–76	Hector Camacho WBC	1983–84	Tony Lopez IBF	1990–91
Frankie Klick*	1933–34†	Kuniaki Shibata WBC	1974–75	Rocky Lockridge*	1984–85	Joey Gamache WBA	1991
Sandy Saddler*	1949–50†	Alfredo Escalera WBC	1975–78	Hwan-Kil Yuh IBF	1984–85	Brian Mitchell IBF	1991
Harold Gomes*	1959–60	Samuel Serrano*	1976–80	Julio César Chávez WBC	1984–87	Genaro Hernandez WBA	1991–95
Gabriel (Flash) Elorde*	1960–67	Alexis Arguello WBC	1978–80	Lester Ellis IBF	1985	Juan Molina IBF	1991–95
Yoshiaki Numata*	1967	Yasutsune Uehara*	1980–81	Wilfredo Gomez*	1985–86	James Leija* WBC	1994

*Lineal champion. †Champion relinquished title to retire or switch weight classes, or had title stripped by boxing organization.
**In case of WBA, includes both "super" and "regular" champions. Does not include interim or WBO title holders.

Super Featherweights (Cont.)

Champion	Reign	Champion	Reign	Champion	Reign	Champion	Reign
Gabriel Ruelas* WBC	..1994–95	Steve Forbes IBF	......2000–02†	Gairy St. Clair IBF	2006	Vitaly Tajbert WBC	2010
Eddie Hopson IBF	1995	Acelino Freitas* WBA	..2002–04	Malcolm Klassen IBF...2006–07		Takahiro Aoh WBC	2010–12
Tracy Patterson IBF	1995	Y. Nantchachai WBA....2002–05		Mzonke Fana IBF	2007–08	Mzonke Fana IBF	......2010–11†
Azumah Nelson* WBC.1995–97		S. Singmanassak WBC .2002–03		J. M. Marquez WBC....2007–08		Juan Carlos Salgado	
Choi Yong-Soo WBA...1995–98		Jesus Chavez WBC.....2003–04		Manny Pacquiao WBC.......2008		IBF	.................:.....2011–13
Arturo Gatti IBF........1995–98†		Carlos Hernandez IBF..2003–04		Jorge Linares WBA......2008–09		Gamaliel Diaz WBC.....2012–13	
Genaro Hernandez* WBC.1997–98		Erik Morales WBC/IBF .2004–05		Cassius Baloyi IBF	2008–09	Takashi Miura WBC........2013–	
Roberto Garcia IBF......1998–99		Erik Morales IBF	2004–05	Humberto Soto WBC.2008–10†		Argenis Mendez IBF	2013–
F. Mayweather Jr.* WBC1998–01†		Marco A. Barrera WBC2005–07		Malcolm Klassen IBF	2009		
T. Hatakeyama WBA....1998–99		V. Mosquera WBA	2005–06	Juan Carlos Salgado IBF ..2009			
Lakva Sim WBA................1999		Robbie Peden IBF	2005	Juan Carlos Salgado			
Diego Corrales IBF......1999–01		Marco A. Barrera, IBF...2005–06		WBA	2009–10		
Jong Kwon Baek WBA...1999–00		Cassius Baloyi WBF	2006	Robert Guerrero IBF ..2009–10†			
Joel Casamayor WBA ...2000–02		Edwin Valero WBA	2006–08	Takashi Uchiyama WBA...2010–			

Featherweights (Weight Limit: 126 pounds)

Champion	Reign	Champion	Reign	Champion	Reign	Champion	Reign
Torpedo Billy Murphy*.........1890		Sandy Saddler*	1948–49	Jorge Paez IBF	1988–91	In Jin Chi WBC	2004–06
Young Griffo*	.............1890–92†	Willie Pep*	1949–50	Jeff Fenech WBC	......1988–90†	Valdemir Pereira IBF	2006
George Dixon*	1892–97	Sandy Saddler*	...........1950–57†	Marcos Villasana WBC...1990–91		Eric Aiken IBF	2006
Solly Smith*	1897–98	Kid Bassey*	1957–59	Paul Hodkinson WBC...1991–93		T. Koshimoto WBC	2006
Dave Sullivan*	1898	Davey Moore*	1959–63	Troy Dorsey IBF	1991	Rudolfo Lopez WBC	2006
George Dixon*	1898–1900	Sugar Ramos*	1963–64	Manuel Medina IBF	1991–93	Robert Guerrero IBF	2006
Terry McGovern*	1900–01	Vicente Saldivar*	........1964–67†	Yung Kyun Park* WBA.1991–93		Orlando Salido IBF	2006
Young Corbett II*	........1901–03†	Paul Rojas WBA	1968	Gregorio Vargas WBC........1993		In Jin Chi WBC	2006–07
Abe Attell*	1903–04	Jose Legra WBA	1968–69	Tom Johnson IBF	......1993–97†	Robert Guerrero IBF .2007–08†	
Tommy Sullivan*	........1904–05†	Shozo Saijyo WBA	1968–71	Eloy Rojas* WBA..........1993–96		Jorge Linares WBC	2007–08
Abe Attell*	1906–12	J. Famechon* WBC	1969–70	Kevin Kelley WBC	1993–95	Oscar Larios WBC.......2008–09	
Johnny Kilbane*	1912–23	Vicente Saldivar* WBC......1970		A. Gonzalez WBC	1995	Cristobal Cruz IBF	2008–10
Eugene Criqui*	1923	Kuniaki Shibata* WBC ...1970–72		Manuel Medina WBC.1995–99		Takahiro Aoh WBC	2009
Johnny Dundee*	.......1923–24†	Antonio Gomez WBA 1971–72		Luisito Espinosa WBC...1995–99		Elio Rojas WBC.........2009–10†	
"Kid" Kaplan*	............1925–26†	Jose Legra* WBC	1972–73	Wilfredo Vazquez* WBA.1996–98		Yuriorkis Gamboa	
Tony Canzoneri*	1927–28	Eder Jofre* WBC	........1973–74†	Hector Lizarraga IBF ...1997–98		WBA	................2009–11†
Andre Routis*	1928–29	Ruben Olivares WBA	1974	Naseem Hamed* WBA ....1998†		Hozumi Hasegawa WBC2010–11	
Battling Battalino*	......1929–32†	Bobby Chacon WBC	1974–75	Naseem Hamed*	1998–01	Orlando Salido IBF	.........2010†
Tommy Paul NBA	1932–33	Alexis Arguello* WBA..1974–76†		Freddy Norwood WBA..........1998		Yuriorkis Gamboa IBF...2010–11	
Kid Chocolate NY	......1932–33†	Ruben Olivares WBA	1975	Manuel Medina IBF	1998–99	Jhonny Gonzalez WBC 2011–12	
Freddie Miller NBA	1933–36	Poison Kotey WBC	1975–76	Antonio Cermeno WBA.1998–99		Jonathan Barros WBA.......2011	
Mike Beloise NY	1936–37	Danny Lopez* WBC	1976–80	Cesar Soto WBC	1999	Billy Dib IBF	2011–13
Petey Sarron NBA	1936–37	Rafael Ortega WBA	1977	Freddy Norwood WBA...1999–00		Celestino Caballero	
Maurice Holtzer	1937–38	Cecilio Lastra WBA	1977–78	Naseem Hamed* WBC ....1999†		WBA	................2011–12†
Henry Armstrong*	......1937–38†	Eusebio Pedroza* WBA ..1978–85		Paul Ingle IBF	1999–00	Chris John WBA	2012–
Joey Archibald* NY	1938–39	S. Sanchez* WBC	......1980–82†	Guty Espadas WBC.......2000–01		Daniel Ponce De Leon	
Leo Rodak NBA	1938–39	Juan LaPorte WBC	1982–84	Erik Morales WBC	2000–02	WBC	2012–13
Joey Archibald	1939–40	Wilfredo Gomez WBC...........1984		Derrick Gainer WBA....2000–03		Abner Mares WBC	2013
Petey Scalzo NBA	1940–41	Min-Keun Oh IBF	1984–85	Mbulelo Botile IBF	2001	Jhonny Gonzalez WBC 2013–	
Harry Jeffra*	1940–41	Azumah Nelson WBC ...1984–88		Frankie Toledo IBF	2001	Evgeni Gradovich IBF 2013–
Joey Archibald*	1941	Barry McGuigan* WBA ..1985–86		Manuel Medina IBF	2001–02		
Richie Lamos NBA	1941	Ki Young Chung IBF	1985–86	Marco A. Barrera*			
Chalky Wright*	1941–42	Steve Cruz* WBA	1986–87	WBA/WBC	2001–03		
Jackie Wilson NBA	1941–43	Antonio Rivera IBF	1986–88	Johnny Tapia IBF	2002		
Willie Pep*	1942–48	A. Esparragoza* WBA ...1987–91		Marco A. Barrera* WBC ...2002†			
Jackie Callura NBA	1943	Calvin Grove IBF	1988	Erik Morales WBC	2002–03		
Phil Terranova NBA	1943–44			Juan Marquez IBF.......2003–06			
Sal Bartolo NBA	1944–46			Chris John WBA‡	2003		

*Lineal champion. †Champion relinquished title to retire or switch weight classes, or had title stripped by boxing organization.
**In case of WBA, includes both "super" and "regular" champions. Does not include interim or WBO title holders.

Super Bantamweights (Weight Limit: 122 pounds)

Champion	Reign	Champion	Reign	Champion	Reign	Champion	Reign
Jack (Kid) Wolfe*	1922–23	Jeff Fenech* WBC	1987†	Daniel Zaragoza* WBC	1995–97	Israel Vazquez WBC	2007–08†
Carl Duane*	1923–24	Julio Gervacio WBA	1987–88	Erik Morales* WBC	1997–00†	Ricardo Cordoba WBA	2008–09
Rigoberto Riasco* WBC	1976	Daniel Zaragoza* WBC	1988–90	Enrique Sanchez WBA	1998	Toshiaki Nishioka WBC	2008–12
R. Kobayashi* WBC	1976	Jose Sanabria IBF	1988–89	Nestor Garza WBA	1998–00	Bernard Dunne WBA	2009
Dong-Kyun Yum* WBC	1976–77	B. Pinango WBA	1988	Benedict Ledwaba IBF	1999–01	Poon. Kratingdaenggym	
Wilfredo Gomez* WBC	1977–83†	J.J. Estrada WBA	1988–89	Clarence Adams WBA	2000–01†	WBA	2009–10
Soo-Hwan Hong WBA	1977–78	Fabrice Benichou IBF	1989–90	Willie Jorrin WBC	2000–02	Steve Molitor IBF	2010–11
Ricardo Cardona WBA	1978–80	Jesus Salud WBA	1989–90	Manny Pacquiao IBF	2001–04	Ryol Li Lee WBA	2010–11
Leo Randolph WBA	1980	Welcome Ncita IBF	1990–92	Yober Ortega WBA	2001–02	Akifumi Shimoda WBA	2011
Sergio Palma WBA	1980–82	Paul Banke* WBC	1990	Y. Sithyodthong WBA	2002	Rico Ramos WBA	2011–12
Leonardo Cruz WBA	1982–84	Luis Mendoza WBA	1990–91	Osamu Sato WBA	2002	Takalani Ndlovu IBF	2011–12
Jaime Garza* WBC	1983	Pedro Decima* WBC	1990–91	Salim Medjkoune WBA	2002–03	Guillermo Rigondeaux‡	
Bobby Berna IBF	1983–84	K. Hatanaka* WBC	1991	Oscar Larios WBC	2002–05	WBA	2012–
Loris Stecca WBA	1984	Daniel Zaragoza* WBC	1991–92	Mahyar Monshipour WBA	2003–06	Nonito Donaire IBF	2012–13†
Seung-Il Suh IBF	1984–85	Raul Perez WBA	1992	Israel Vazquez IBF	2004–05	Abner Mares WBC	2012–13†
Victor Callejas WBA	1984–86	Thiery Jacob* WBC	1992	Israel Vazquez WBC	2005–07	Jhonatan Romero IBF	2013
Juan Meza* WBC	1984–85	Tracy Patterson* WBC	1992–94	S. Sithchatchawal WBA	2006	Kiko Martinez IBF	2013–
Ji-Won Kim IBF	1985–86	Wilfredo Vasquez WBA	1992–95	C. Caballero WBA	2006–10†	Victor Terrazas WBC	2013
Lupe Pintor* WBC	1985–86	Kennedy McKinney IBF	1993–94	IBF	2008–09†	Leo Santa Cruz WBC	2013–
S. Payakaroon* WBC	1986–87	Vuyani Bungu IBF	1994–99†	Michael Hunter IBF	2006		
Seung-Hoon Lee IBF	1987–88	H. Acero* Sanchez WBC	1994–95	Steve Molitor IBF	2006–08		
Louie Espinoza WBA	1987	Antonio Cermeno WBA	1995–98†	Rafael Marquez WBC	2007		

Bantamweights (Weight Limit: 118 pounds)

Champion	Reign	Champion	Reign	Champion	Reign	Champion	Reign
Spider Kelly	1887	Sixto Escobar*	1936–37	Jeff Chandler*	1980–84	Nana Konadu* WBA	1996–98
Hughey Boyle	1887–88	Harry Jeffra*	1937–38	Albert Davila WBC	1983–85	S. Singmanassak	
Spider Kelly	1889	Sixto Escobar*	1938–39†	Richard Sandoval*	1984–86	WBC	1996–97
Chappie Moran	1889–90	Georgie Pace NBA	1939–40	Satoshi Shingaki IBF	1984–85	Tim Austin IBF	1997–03
George Dixon	1890–91	Lou Salica*	1940–42	Jeff Fenech IBF	1985	J.Tatsuyoshi WBC	1997–98
Pedlar Palmer	1895–99	Manuel Ortiz*	1942–47	Daniel Zaragoza WBC	1985	Johnny Tapia* WBA	1998–99
Terry McGovern*	1899–00†	Harold Dade*	1947	Miguel Lora WBC	1985–88	V. Sahaprom* WBC	1998–05
Harry Harris	1901	Manuel Ortiz*	1947–50	Gaby Canizales*	1986	Paulie Ayala* WBA	1999–01†
Harry Forbes*	1901–03	Vic Toweel*	1950–52	Bernardo Pinango*	1986–87†	Eidy Moya WBA	2001–02
Frankie Neil*	1903–04	Jimmy Carruthers*	1952–54†	W. Vasquez WBA	1987–88	Johnny Bredahl WBA	2002–05
Joe Bowker*	1904–05†	Robert Cohen*	1954–56	Kevin Seabrooks* IBF	1987–88	Rafael Marquez IBF	2003–07
Jimmy Walsh*	1905–06†	Paul Macias NBA	1955–57	Kaokor Galaxy WBA	1988	W. Sidorenko WBA	2005–08
Owen Moran	1907–08	Mario D'Agata*	1956–57	Moon Sung-Kil WBA	1988–89	H. Hasegawa WBC	2005–10
Monte Attell	1909–10	Alphonse Halimi*	1957–59	Kaokor Galaxy WBA	1989	Luis Perez IBF	2007
Frankie Conley	1910–11	Joe Becerra*	1959–60†	Raul Perez WBC	1988–91	Joseph Agbeko IBF	2007–09
Johnny Coulon*	1910–14	Eder Jofre*	1961–65	O. Canizales* IBF	1988–95†	Anselmo Moreno‡	
Kid Williams*	1914–17	Fighting Harada*	1965–68	Luisito Espinosa WBA	1989–91	WBA	2008–
Kewpie Ertle	1915	Lionel Rose*	1968–69	Israel Contreras WBA	1991–92	Yohnny Perez IBF	2009–10
Pete Herman*	1917–20	Ruben Olivares*	1969–70	Greg Richardson WBC	1991	Fernando Montiel WBC	2010–11
Joe Lynch*	1920–21	Chucho Castillo*	1970–71	J. Tatsuyoshi, WBC	1991–92	Joseph Agbeko IBF	2010–11
Pete Herman*	1921	Ruben Olivares*	1971–72	Eddie Cook WBA	1992–93	Koki Kameda WBA	2010–
Johnny Buff*	1921–22	Rafael Herrera*	1972	Victor Rabanales		Nonito Donaire WBC	2011–12
Joe Lynch*	1922–24	Enrique Pinder*	1972–73	WBC	1992–93	Abner Mares IBF	2011–12
Abe Goldstein*	1924	Romeo Anaya*	1973	Jung-Il Byun WBC	1993	Leo Santa Cruz IBF	2012–13†
Cannonball Martin*	1924–25	Arnold Taylor*	1973–74	Jorge Julio WBA	1993	Shinsuke Yamanaka	
Phil Rosenberg*	1925–27†	Rafael Herrera WBC	1973–74	Yasuei Yakushiji WBC	1993–95	WBC	2012–
Bud Taylor NBA	1927–28	Soo-Hwan Hong*	1974–75	Junior Jones WBA	1994	Jamie McDonnell IBF	2013–
Bushy Graham NY	1928–29	Rodolfo Martinez		John M. Johnson			
Panama Al Brown*	1929–35	WBC	1974–76	WBA	1994		
Sixto Escobar NBA	1934–35	Alfonso Zamora*	1975–77	D. Chuvatana WBA	1994–95		
Baltazar Sangchilli*	1935–36	Carlos Zarate* WBC	1976–79	V. Sahaprom* WBA	1995–96		
Lou Salica NBA	1935	Jorge Lujan	1977–80	W. McCullough WBC	1995–96		
Sixto Escobar NBA	1935–36	Lupe Pintor* WBC	1979–83†	Harold Mestre IBF	1995		
Tony Marino*	1936	Julian Solis	1980	Mbulelo Botile IBF	1995–97		

*Lineal champion. †Champion relinquished title to retire or switch weight classes, or had title stripped by boxing organization.
**In case of WBA, includes both "super" and "regular" champions. Does not include interim or WBO title holders.

Super Flyweights (Weight Limit: 115 pounds)

Champion	Reign
Rafael Orono* WBC	1980–81
Chul-Ho Kim* WBC	1981–82
Gustavo Ballas WBA	1981
Rafael Pedroza WBA	1981–82
Jiro Watanabe WBA	1982–84
Rafael Orono* WBC	1982–83
Payao Poontarat* WBC	1983–84
Joo-Do Chun IBF	1983–85
Jiro Watanabe*	1984–86
Kaosai Galaxy WBA	1984
Ellyas Pica IBF	1985–86
Cesar Polanco IBF	1986
Gilberto Roman* WBC	1986–87
Ellyas Pical IBF	1986
Santos Laciar* WBC	1987
Tae-Il Chang IBF	1987
Sugar Rojas* WBC	1987–88
Ellyas Pical IBF	1987–89
Giberto Roman* WBC	1988–89
Juan Polo Perez IBF	1989–90
Nana Konadu* WBC	1989–90
Sung-Kil Moon* WBC	1990–93
Robert Quiroga IBF	1990–93
Julio Borboa IBF	1993–94
Katsuya Onizuka WBA	1993–94
Jose Luis Bueno* WBC	1993–94
Lee Hyung-Chul WBA	1994–95
H. Kawashima* WBC	1994–97
Harold Grey IBF	1994–95
Alimi Goitia WBA	1995–96
Carlos Salazar IBF	1995–96
Yokthai Sith-Oar WBA	1996–97
Harold Grey IBF	1996
Danny Romero IBF	1996–97
Gerry Penalosa* WBC	1997–98
Johnny Tapia IBF	1997–99†
Satoshi Iida WBA	1997–98
In-Joo Cho* WBC	1998–00
Jesus Rojas WBA	1998–99
Mark Johnson IBF	1999–00
Hideki Todaka WBA	1999–00
Felix Machado IBF	2000–03
M. Tokuyama* WBC	2000–04
Leo Gamez WBA	2000–01
Celes Kobayashi WBA	2001–02
Alexander Munoz WBA	2002–05
Luis Alberto Perez IBF	2003–06
Katsushige Kawashima WBC	2004–05
M. Tokuyama WBA	2005–06
Jose M. Castillo WBA	2005–06
Nobuo Nashiro WBA	2006–08
Cristian Mijares WBC	2006–08
Dmitri Kirilov IBF	2007–08
Vic Darchinyan WBC, WBA	2008–10†
Vic Darchinyan IBF	2006–09†
Simphiwe Nonggayi IBF	2009–10
Juan Alberto Rosas, IBF	2010
Cristian Mijares IBF	2010–11†
Hugo Cazares WBA	2010–11
Tomas Rojas WBC	2010–11
Suriyan Sor Rungvisai WBC	2011–12
Tomonobu Shimizu, WBA	2011–12
Roberto Guerrero IBF	2011–12
Juan Carlos Sanchez Jr. IBF	2012–
Tepparith Kokietgym WBA	2012
Yota Sato WBC	2012–13
Kohei Kono WBA	2012–13
Liborio Solis WBA	2013–
Srisaket Sor Rungvisai WBC	2013–

Flyweights (Weight Limit: 112 pounds)

Champion	Reign
Sid Smith*	1913
Bill Ladbury*	1913–14
Percy Jones*	1914†
Joe Symonds*	1914–16
Jimmy Wilde*	1916–23
Pancho Villa*	1923–25†
Fidel La Barba*	1925–27†
Frenchy Belanger* NBA	1927–28
Izzy Schwartz NY	1927–29
Frankie Genaro* NBA	1928–29
Spider Pladner* NBA	1929
Frankie Genaro* NBA	1929–31
Midget Wolgast NY	1930–35
Young Perez* NBA	1931–32
Jackie Brown* NBA	1932–35
Benny Lynch*	1935–38†
Small Montana NY	1935–37
Peter Kane*	1938–43
Little Dado NY	1938–40
Jackie Paterson*	1943–48
Rinty Monaghan*	1948–50†
Terry Allen*	1950
Dado Marino*	1950–52
Yoshio Shirai*	1952–54
Pascual Perez*	1954–60
Pone Kingpetch*	1960–62
Masahiko Harada*	1962–63
Pone Kingpetch*	1963
Hiroyuki Ebihara*	1963–64
Pone Kingpetch*	1964–65
Salvatore Burrini*	1965–66
H. Accavallo WBA	1966–68
Walter McGowan*	1966
Chartchai Chionoi*	1966–69
Efren Torres*	1969–70
Hiroyuki Ebihara WBA	1969
B. Villacampo WBA	1969–70
Chartchai Chionoi*	1970
B. Chartvanchai WBA	1970
Masao Ohba WBA	1970–73
Erbito Salavarria*	1970–73†
B. Gonzalez WBA	1972
V. Borkorsor WBC	1972–73†
Venice Borkorsor*	1973†
Chartchai Chionoi WBA	1973–74
B. Gonzalez* WBA	1973–74
Shoji Oguma* WBC	1974–75
S. Hanagata WBA	1974–75
Miguel Canto* WBC	1975–79
Erbito Salavarria WBA	1975–76
Alfonso Lopez WBA	1976
G. Espadas WBA	1976–78
B. Gonzalez WBA	1978–79
Chan-Hee Park* WBC	1979–80
Luis Ibarra WBA	1979–80
Tae-Shik Kim WBA	1980
Shoji Oguma* WBC	1980–81
Peter Mathebula WBA	1980–81
Santos Laciar WBA	1981
Antonio Avelar* WBA	1981–82
Luis Ibarra WBA	1981
Juan Herrera WBA	1981–82
P. Cardona* WBC	1982
Santos Laciar WBA	1982–85
Freddie Castillo* WBC	1982
E. Mercedes* WBC	1982–83
Charlie Magri* WBC	1983
Frank Cedeno* WBC	1983–84
Soon-Chun Kwon IBF	1983–85
Koji Kobayashi* WBC	1984
Gabriel Bernal* WBC	1984
Sot Chitalada* WBC	1984–88
Hilario Zapate WBA	1985–87
Chong-Kwan Chung IBF	1985–86
Bi-Won Chung IBF	1986
Hi-Sup Shin IBF	1986–87
Dodie Penalosa IBF	1987
Fidel Bassa WBA	1987–89
Choi-Chang Ho IBF	1987–88
Rolando Bohol IBF	1988
Yong-Kang Kim* WBC	1988–89
Duke McKenzie IBF	1988–89
Sot Chitalada* WBC	1989–91
Dave McAuley IBF	1989–92
Jesus Rojas WBA	1989–90
Yul-Woo Lee WBA	1990
L. Tamakuma WBA	1990–91
M. Kittikasem* WBC	1991–92
Yong Kang Kim WBA	1991–92
Yuri Arbachakov* WBC	1992–97
Rodolfo Blanco IBF	1992–93
David Griman WBA	1992–94
P. Sithbangprachan IBF	1993–95
S.S. Ploenchit WBA	1994–96
Francisco Tejedor IBF	1995
Danny Romero IBF	1995–96
Mark Johnson IBF	1996–99†
Jose Bonilla WBA	1996–98
Chatchai Sasakul* WBC	1997–98
Hugo Soto WBA	1998–99
Manny Pacquiao* WBC	1998–99
Leo Gamez WBA	1999
Irene Pacheco IBF	1999–05
S. Pisnurachan WBA	1999–00
M. Sinsurat* WBC	1999–00
Malcolm Tunacao* WBC	2000–01
Eric Morel WBA	2000–03
P. Wonjongkam* WBC	2001–07
Lorenzo Parra WBA	2003–07
Vic Darchinyan IBF	2005–07
Takefumi Sakata WBA	2007–08
Daisuke Naito WBC	2007–09
Nonito Donaire IBF	2007–09†
Denkaosan Kaovichit WBA	2008–10
Koki Kameda WBC	2009–10
Moruti Mthalane IBF	2009–
Daiki Kameda WBA	2010–11†
Pongsaklek Wonjongkam WBC	2010–12
Luis Concepcion WBA	2011
Heman Marquez‡ WBA	2011–12
Sonny Boy Jaro WBC	2012
T. Igarashi WBC	2012–13
Brian Viloria‡ WBA	2012–13
Juan Francisco Estrada ‡ WBA	2013–
Juan Carlos Reveco	2012–
Akira Yaegashi WBC	2013–

*Lineal champion. †Champion relinquished title to retire or switch weight classes, or had title stripped by boxing organization.
**In case of WBA, includes both "super" and "regular" champions. Does not include interim or WBO title holders.

Light Flyweights (Weight Limit: 108 pounds)

Champion	Reign	Champion	Reign	Champion	Reign	Champion	Reign
Franco Udella WBC	1975	Joey Olivo WBA	1985	Carlos Murillo WBA	1996	Brahim Asloum WBA	2007–09†
Jaime Rios WBA	1975–76	Myung-Woo Yuh* WBA	1985–91	Keiji Yamaguchi WBA	1996	Giovanni Segura	
Luis Estaba* WBC	1975–78	Jum-Hwan Choi IBF	1986–88	Michael Carbajal IBF	1996–97	WBA‡	2009–10†
Juan Guzman WBA	1976	Tacy Macalos IBF	1988–89	Phichitchor Siriwat		Brian Viloria IBF	2009–10
Yoko Gushiken WBA	1976–81	German Torres WBC	1988–89	WBA	1996–00	Rodel Mayol WBC	2009–10
Freddy Castillo* WBC	1978	Yul-Woo Lee WBC	1989	Mauricio Pastrana IBF	1997–98†	Omar Nino Romero WBC	2010
Sor Vorasingh* WBC	1978	M. Kittikasem IBF	1989–90	Will Grigsby IBF	1998–99	Carlos Tamara IBF	2010
Sung-Jun Kim* WBC	1978–80	H. Gonzalez WBC	1989–90	Ricardo Lopez IBF	1999–02	Juan Carlos Reveco	
Shigeo Nakajima* WBC	1980	Michael Carbajal IBF	1990–94	Yo-Sam Choi* WBC	1999–02	WBA	2010–11
Hilario Zapata* WBC	1980–82	R. Pascua WBC	1990	Beibis Mendoza WBA	2000–01	Luis Alberto Lazarte IBF	2010–11
Pedro Flores WBA	1981	M. C. Castro WBC	1991	Rosendo Alvarez WBA	2001–05	Gilberto Keb Bass WBC	2010–11
Hwan-Jin Kim WBA	1981	H. Gonzalez WBC	1991–93	Jorge Arce* WBC	2002–05	Ulises Solis IBF	2011–12†
Katsuo Tokashiki WBA	1981–83	Hirokia Ioka* WBA	1991–92	Jose Burgos IBF	2003–05	Adrian Hernandez WBC	2011
Amado Urzua* WBC	1982	Myung-Woo Yuh* WBA	1993†	Brian Viloria WBC	2005–06	Roman Gonzalez WBA	2011–
Tadashi Tomori* WBC	1982	Michael Carbajal* WBC	1993–94	R. Vasquez WBA	2005–06	K. Porpramook WBC	2011–12
Hilario Zapata* WBC	1982–83	Leo Gamez WBA	1993–95	Will Grigsby IBF	2005–06	John Riel Casimero IBF	2012–
Jung-Koo Chang*		H. Gonzalez* WBC/IBF	1994–95	Koki Kameda WBA	2006–07	Adrian Hernandez WBC	2012–
WBC	1983–88†	Choi Hi-Yong WBA	1995–96	Omar Nino Rivero WBC	2006–07		
Lupe Madera WBA	1983–84	S. Sor Jaturong		Ulises Solis IBF	2006–09		
Dodie Penalosa IBF	1983–86	WBC/IBF	1995–96	Juan Carlos Reveco WBA	2007		
Francisco Quiroz WBA	1984–85	Saman Jaturong* WBC	1995–99	Edgar Sosa WBC	2007–09		

Strawweights (Weight Limit: 105 pounds)

Champion	Reign	Champion	Reign	Champion	Reign	Champion	Reign
Kyung-Yun Lee* IBF	1987	R.S. Voraphin IBF	1992–96	Miguel Barrera IBF	2002–03	Kwanthai Sithmorseng	
Hiroki Ioka* WBC	1987–88	Chana Porpaoin WBA	1993–95	Noel Arambulet WBA	2002–04	WBA	2010–11
Leo Gamez WBA	1988–89	Rosendo Alvarez WBA	1995–98	Edgar Cardenas IBF	2003	Nkosinathi Joyi IBF	2010–12
S. Sithnaruepol IBF	1988–89	R. Sor Vorapin IBF	1996–97	Daniel Reyes IBF	2003–05	Muhammad Rachman	
N. Kiatwanchai* WBC	1988–89	Zolani Petelo* IBF	1997–00†	Eagle Junlaphan WBC	2004	WBA	2011
Bong-Jun Kim WBA	1989–91	W. Chor Charoen WBC	1998–00	Isaac Bustos WBC	2004–05	Kazuto Ioka WBC	2011–12†
Nico Thomas IBF	1989	Chana Porpaoin WBA	1998–99†	Yukata Niida WBA	2004–08	Pornsawan Porpramook	
Eric Chavez IBF	1989–90	Songkram Popaoin WBA	1999	K. Takayama WBC	2005	WBA	2011
Jum-Hwan Choi* WBC	1989–90	Noel Arambulet WBA	1999–00	Eagle Junlaphan WBC	2005–07	Akira Yaegashi WBA	2011–12
Hideyuki Ohashi* WBC	1990	Jose Aguirre* WBC	2000–04	M. Rachman IBF	2005–07	Kazuto Ioka WBA	2012†
F. Lookmingkwan IBF	1990–92	Joma Gamboa WBA	2000	Florante Condes IBF	2007–08	Xiong Zhao Zhong WBC	2012–
Ricardo Lopez* WBC	1990–98†	Keitaro Hoshino WBA	2000–01	O. Sithsamerchai WBC	2007–11	Mario Rodriguez IBF	2012–13
Hi-Yong Choi WBA	1991–92	Chana Porpaoin WBA	2001	Roman Gonzalez		Ryo Miyazaki WBA	2012–
Manny Melchor IBF	1992	Roberto Leyva IBF	2001–02	WBA	2008–10†	Katsunari Takayama IBF	2013–
Hideyuki Ohashi WBA	1992–93	Yutaka Niida WBA	2001†	Raul Garcia IBF	2008–10		

*Lineal champion.   †Champion relinquished title to retire or switch weight classes, or had title stripped by boxing organization.
**In case of WBA, includes both "super" and "regular" champions. Does not include interim or WBO title holders.

Champion	Reign	Age*	Career	W-L-D (KO)	SD
John L. Sullivan	1885–92	26	1878–92	38-1-3 (33)	0
James J. Corbett	1892–97	26	1884–03	11-4-2 (7)	1
Bob Fitzsimmons	1897–99	33	1880–16	74-8-3 (67)	0
James J. Jeffries†	1899–05	24	1896–10	18-1-2 (15)	7
Marvin Hart	1905–06	28	1899–10	28-7-4 (19)	0
Tommy Burns	1906–08	24	1900–20	46-5-8 (37)	11
Jack Johnson	1908–15	30	1894–28	77-13-14 (48)	9
Jess Willard	1915–19	33	1911–23	23-6-1 (20)	1
Jack Dempsey	1919–26	24	1914–27	60-6-8 (50)	5
Gene Tunney†	1926–28	29	1915–28	61-1-1 (45)	2
Max Schmeling	1930–32	24	1924–48	56-10-4 (39)	1
Jack Sharkey	1932–33	29	1924–36	38-13-3 (14)	0
Primo Carnera	1933–34	26	1928–37	88-14-0 (69)	2
Max Baer	1934–35	25	1929–41	72-12-0 (53)	0
James J. Braddock	1935–37	29	1926–38	51-26-7 (26)	0
Joe Louis†	1937–49	23	1934–51	68-3-0 (54)	25
Ezzard Charles	1949–51	27	1940–59	96-25-1 (59)	8
Jersey Joe Walcott	1951–52	37	1930–53	53-18-1 (33)	1
Rocky Marciano†	1952–56	29	1947–56	49-0-0 (43)	6
Floyd Patterson	1956–59	21	1952–72	55-8-1 (40)	4
Ingemar Johansson	1959–60	26	1952–63	26-2-0 (17)	0
Floyd Patterson	1960–62	25	1952–72	55-8-1 (40)	2
Sonny Liston	1962–64	30	1953–70	50-4-0 (39)	1
Muhammad Ali	1964–71	22	1960–81	56-5-0 (37)	9
Joe Frazier	1971–73	27	1965–81	32-4-1 (27)	2
George Foreman	1973–74	24	1969–97	76-5-0 (68)	2
Muhammad Ali	1974–78	32	1960–81	56-5-0 (37)	10
Leon Spinks	1978	24	1977–95	26-17-3 (14)	0
Muhammad Ali†	1978–79	36	1960–81	56-5-0 (37)	0
Larry Holmes	1980–85	29	1973–2002	69-6-0 (44)	20
Michael Spinks	1985–88	29	1977–88	32-1-0 (21)	3
Mike Tyson	1988–90	21	1985–2005	49-4-0 (43)	2
Buster Douglas	1990	29	1981–99	38-6-1 (25)	0
Evander Holyfield	1990–92	28	1984–	38-5-2 (26)	3
Riddick Bowe	1992–93	25	1989–96	40-1-0 (32)	2
Evander Holyfield	1993–94	31	1984–94; 1995–	44-10-2 (29)	0
Michael Moorer	1994	26	1988–97	52-4-1 (40)	0
George Foreman	1994–97	45	1969–97	76-5-0 (68)	3
Shannon Briggs	1997–98	25	1992–00	32-3-1 (25)	0
Lennox Lewis	1998–01	32	1989–2004	41-2-1 (32)	5
Hasim Rahman	2001	28	1994–	50-7-2 (41)	0
Lennox Lewis†	2001–04	36	1989–2004	41-2-1 (32)	2
John Ruiz	2001–03	31	1992–2010	44-9-1 (30)	2
Chris Byrd	2002–06	35	1993–2009	41-5-1 (20)	3
Roy Jones, Jr.	2003	34	1989–	54-8-0 (40)	0
John Ruiz	2003–05	33	1992–2010	41-6-1 (28)	2
Vitali Klitschko†	2004–05	34	1996–2005; 2007–	44-2-0 (40)	1
Hasim Rahman	2005-06	33	1994–	50-7-2 (40)	1
Nikolay Valuev	2005–07 2008–09	32	1993–2009	50-2-0 (34)	1
Oleg Maskaev	2006–08	37	1993–2009	36-7-0 (27)	0
Wladimir Klitschko‡	2006–	33	1996–	58-3-0 (51)	0
Ruslan Chagaev	2007–08	28	2001–	29-2-1 (18)	1
Samuel Peter	2008	28	2004–11	34-5-0 (27)	0
Vitali Klitschko^	2008–	38	1996–2005; 2007–	44-2-0 (40)	1
Nikolay Valuev	2008–09	36	1993–2009	50-2-0 (34)	0
David Haye	2009–11	30	2002–	26-2-0 (24)	0
Alexander Povetkin	2011–	31	2005–	24-0-0 (16)	0

*Age when boxer won world championship.
† Boxer retired or relinquished world title.
‡ Maintains WBA Super Champion status
^ Boxer returned from retirement.

NCAA Sports

The UCLA Bruins celebrated their 8–0 victory over Mississippi State in the second and deciding game of the NCAA College World Series

NCAA Team Champions

Fall 2012

			Champion	Runner-Up
Cross-Country	**MEN**	Division I:	Oklahoma State	Wisconsin
		Division II:	Adams State	Colorado Mines
		Division III:	North Central (Ill.)	Haverford/Calvin (tie)
	WOMEN	Division I:	Oregon	Providence
		Division II:	Grand Valley State	Augustana (S.D.)
		Division III:	Johns Hopkins	Wartburg
Field Hockey	**WOMEN**	Division I:	Princeton	North Carolina
		Division II	West Chester	UMass-Lowell
		Division III:	Tufts	Montclair State
Football	**MEN**	FCS (I-AA):	North Dakota State	Sam Houston State
		Division II:	Valdosta State	Winston-Salem
		Division III:	Mount Union	St. Thomas (Minn.)
Soccer	**MEN**	Division I:	Indiana	Georgetown
		Division II:	Lynn	Saginaw Valley
		Division III:	Messiah	Ohio Northern
	WOMEN	Division I:	North Carolina	Penn State
		Division II:	West Florida	UC-San Diego
		Division III:	Messiah	Emory
Volleyball	**MEN**	Division I:	UC-Irvine	BYU
		Division III:	Springfield	Nazareth
WOMEN		Division I:	Texas	
			Oregon	
		Division II:	Concordia-St. Paul	Tampa
		Division III:	St. Thomas	Calvin
Water Polo	**MEN**		USC	UCLA
	WOMEN		Texas	Oregon

Winter 2012–13

			Champion	Runner-Up
Basketball	**MEN**	Division I:	Louisville	Michigan
		Division II:	Drury	Metro State
		Division III:	Amherst	Mary Hardin-Baylor
	WOMEN	Division I:	Connecticut	Louisville
		Division II:	Ashland	Dowling
		Division III:	DePauw	Wisconsin-Whitewater
Bowling	**WOMEN**		Nebraska	Vanderbilt
Fencing			Princeton	Notre Dame
Gymnastics	**MEN**		Michigan	Oklahoma
	WOMEN		Florida	Oklahoma
Ice Hockey	**MEN**	Division I:	Yale	Quinnipiac
		Division III:	Wisconsin-Eau Claire	Oswego State
	WOMEN	Division I:	Minnesota	Boston University
		Division III:	Elmira	Middlebury
Rifle			West Virginia	Kentucky
Skiing			Colorado	Utah
Swimming and Diving	**MEN**	Division I:	Michigan	California
		Division II:	Drury	Florida Southern
		Division III:	Kenyon	Denison
	WOMEN	Division I:	Georgia	California
		Division II:	Drury	Wayne St (Mich.)
		Division III:	Emory	Kenyon

Winter 2012-2013 *(Cont.)*

			Champion	Runner-Up
Indoor Track and Field	MEN	Division I:	Arkansas	Florida
		Division II:	St. Augustine	Ashland
		Division III:	UW-La Crosse	UW-Oshkosh
	WOMEN	Division I:	Oregon	Kansas
		Division II:	Academy of Art	Lincoln (Mo.)
		Division III:	UW-Oshkosh	Illinois College
Wrestling	MEN	Division I:	Penn St	Oklahoma State
		Division II:	Neb.-Kearney	St. Cloud State
		Division III:	Wartburg	Augsburg (Minn.)

Spring 2013

			Champion	Runner-Up
Baseball		Division I:	UCLA	Mississippi State
		Division II:	Tampa	Minn. St–Mankato
		Division III:	Linfield	Southern Maine
Golf	MEN	Division I:	Alabama	Illinois
		Division II:	Barry	Lynn
		Division III:	Texas-Tyler	Transylvania
	WOMEN	Division I:	Southern Cal	Duke
		Division II:	Lynn	Nova Southeastern
		Division III	Mary Hardin-Baylor	Texas-Tyler
Lacrosse	MEN	Division I:	Duke	Syracuse
		Division II:	Le Moyne	Mercyhurst
		Division III:	Stevenson	RIT
	WOMEN	Division I:	North Carolina	Maryland
		Division II	LIU Post	Limestone
		Division III:	Salisbury	Trinity (Conn.)
Rowing	WOMEN	Division I:	Ohio State	California
		Division II	Nova Southeastern	Barry
		Division III:	Williams	Bates
Softball		Division I:	Oklahoma	Tennessee
		Division II:	Central Oklahoma	Kutztown
		Division III:	Tufts	Cortland State
Tennis	MEN	Division I:	Virginia	UCLA
		Division II:	Barry	Armstrong Atlantic
		Division III:	Williams	Claremont-Mudd-Scripps
	WOMEN	Division I:	Stanford	Texas A&M
		Division II:	Armstrong Atlantic	BYU-Hawaii
		Division III:	Williams	Emory
Outdoor Track and Field	MEN	Division I:	Florida/Texas A&M (tie)	Arkansas
		Division II:	St. Augustine	Ashland
		Division III:	UW-La Crosse	UW-Eau Claire
	WOMEN	Division I:	Kansas	Texas A&M
		Division II:	Academy of Art	Johnson C. Smith
		Division III:	Wartburg	UW-Oshkosh

NCAA Division I Individual Champions

Fall 2012 – Cross Country

MEN

	Champion	Runner-Up
	Kennedy Kithuka, Texas Tech	Stephen Sambu, Arizona

WOMEN

	Champion	Runner-Up
	Betsy Saina, Iowa State	Abbey D'Agostino, Dartmouth

Winter 2012–13
Gymnastics

MEN

	Champion	Runner-Up
All-around	Sam Mikulak, Michigan	Adrian de los Angeles, Michigan
Vault	Fred Hartville, Illinois	Alec Robin, Oklahoma
Parallel bars	Sam Mikulak, Michigan	Syque Caesar, Michigan
Horizontal bar	Sam Mikulak, Michigan	Austin Phillips, Illinois
Floor exercise	Trevor Howard, Penn St	Eddie Penev, Stanford
Pommel horse	Michael Newburger, Ohio St	Ellis Mannon, Minnesota
Rings	Michael Squires, Oklahoma	Landon Funiciello, William & Mary

WOMEN

	Champion	Runner-Up
All-around	Bridget Sloan, Florida	Rheagan Courville, LSU
Balance beam	Bridget Sloan, Florida	Hanna Nordquist, Minnesota/ Katie Zurales, Michigan (tie)
Uneven bars	Alaina Johnson, Florida	Bridget Sloan, Florida/ Georgia Dabritz, Utah (tie)
Floor exercise	Joanna Sampson, Michigan	Diandra Milliner, Alabama
Vault	Diandra Milliner, Alabama/Rheagan Courville, LSU (tie)	

Skiing

MEN

	Champion	Runner-Up
Slalom	Joonas Rasanen, New Mexico	David Donaldson, Middlebury
Giant slalom	Jonathon Nordbotten, Vermont	Jeremy Elliot, Utah/ Oliver Coley, New Hampshire
10-kilometer classic	Rune Oedegaard, Colorado	Mats Resaland, New Mexico
20-kilometer free	Miles Havlick, Utah	Rune Oedegaard, Colorado

WOMEN

	Champion	Runner-Up
Slalom	Kristine Haugen, Denver	Kristina Riis-Johannessen, Vermont
Giant slalom	Kristine Haugen, Denver	Brooke Wales, Colorado
5-kilometer classic	Anja Gruber, Vermont	Mary O'Connell, Dartmouth
15-kilometer free	Joanne Reid, Colorado	Eliska Hajkova, Colorado

Wrestling

	Champion	Runner-Up
125 lb	Jesse Delgado, Illinois	Nicholas Megaludis, Penn St
133 lb	Logan Stieber, Ohio St	Tony Ramos, Iowa
141 lb	Kendric Maple, Oklahoma	Mitchell Port, Edinboro
149 lb	Jordan Oliver, Oklahoma St	Jason Chamberlain, Boise St
157 lb	Derek St. John, Iowa	Jason Welch, Northwestern
165 lb	Kyle Dake, Cornell	David Taylor, Penn St
174 lb	Chris Perry, Oklahoma St	Matthew Brown, Penn St
184 lb	Edward Ruth, Penn St	Robert Hamlin, Lehigh
197 lb	Dustin Kilgore, Kent St	Quentin Wright, Penn St
285 lb	Anthony Nelson, Minnesota	Michael McMullan, Northwestern

Swimming and Diving — Men

	Champion	Time	Runner-Up	Time
50-yd freestyle	Vlad Morozov, Southern Cal	18.63	Marce Chierighini, Auburn	18.99
100-yd freestyle	Vlad Morozov, Southern Cal	40.76*	Marce Chierighini, Auburn	41.51
200-yd freestyle	Jao De Lucca, Louisville	1:31.51	Dmitri Colupaev, Southern Cal	1:32.74
500-yd freestyle	Connor Jaeger, Michigan	4:10.84	Michael McBroom, Texas	4:11.39
1650-yd freestyle	Connor Jaeger, Michigan	14:27.18	Michael McBroom, Texas	14:32.75
100-yd backstroke	David Nolan, Stanford	44.99	Thomas Shields, California	45.21
200-yd backstroke	Andrew Teduits, Wisconsin	1:38.27	David Nolan, Stanford	1:39.31
100-yd breaststroke	Kevin Cordes, Arizona	50.74*a	Kevin Steel, Arizona	51.69
200-yd breaststroke	Kevin Cordes, Arizona	1:48.68*a	Carl Mickelson, Arizona	1:51.90
100-yd butterfly	Thomas Shields, California	44.59	Marcin Cieslak, Florida	45.35
200-yd butterfly	Thomas Shields, California	1:39.65a	Marcin Cieslak, Florida	1:40.62
200-yd IM	David Nolan, Stanford	1:41.21	Marcin Cieslak, Florida	1:41.45
400-yd IM	Chase Kalisz, Georgia	3:38.05	Michael Weiss, Wisconsin	3:39.61
200-yd free relay	Auburn	1:15.48	Southern Cal	1:16.49
400-yd free relay	Southern Cal	2:48.33	Michigan	2:50.18
800-yd free relay	Florida	6:13.27	Michigan	6:15.54
200-yd medley relay	Michigan	1:22.27*	California	1:23.17a
400-yd medley relay	Arizona	3:02.09	California	3:04.46
1-meter diving	Kristian Ipsen, Stanford	473.75	Nick McCrory, Duke	436.60
3-meter diving	Kristian Ipsen, Stanford	450.60	Nick McCrory, Duke	440.40
Platform	Nick McCrory, Duke	495.90	Kristian Ipsen, Stanford	452.90

*NCAA record. a-American record.

Winter 2012–13 *(Cont.)*
Swimming and Diving — Women

	Champion	Time/Pts	Runner-Up	Time/Pts
50-yd freestyle	Margo Greer, Arizona	21.73	Megan Romano, Georgia	21.88
100-yd freestyle	Margo Greer, Arizona	47.19	Megan Romano, Georgia	47.37
200-yd freestyle	Allison Schmitt, Georgia	1:41.85	Elizabeth Pelton, California	1:42.13
500-yd freestyle	Haley Anderson, Southern Cal	4:34.66	Amber McDermott, Georgia	4:34.86
1650-yd freestyle	Haley Anderson, Southern Cal	15:45.98	Sarah Henry, Texas A&M	15:46.41
100-yd backstroke	Rachel Bootsma, California	50.13	Sinead Russell, Florida	51.46
200-yd backstroke	Elizabeth Pelton, California	1:47.84*a	Dominique Bouchard, Missouri	1:50.06
100-yd breaststroke	Breeja Larson, Texas A&M	57.63	Kasey Carlson, Southern Cal	58.36
200-yd breaststroke	Laura Sogar, Texas	2:05.41	Haley Spencer, Minnesota	2:06.15
100-yd butterfly	Olivia Scott, Auburn	51.64	Rachel Bootsma, California	51.68
200-yd butterfly	Cammile Adams, Texas A&M	1:52.61	Lauren Harrington, Georgia	1:54.39
200-yd IM	Caitlin Leverenz, California	1:53.39	Elizabeth Pelton, California	1:53.82
400-yd IM	Elizabeth Beisel, Florida	4:00.49	Maya Dirado, Stanford	4:01.02
200-yd free relay	Tennessee	1:27.14	Georgia	1:27.38
400-yd free relay	Georgia	3:09.40*	Arizona	3:10.63a
800-yd free relay	Georgia	6:54.43	Arizona	6:57.26
200-yd medley relay	Tennessee	1:34.95	California	1:35.53
400-yd medley relay	Tennessee	3:28.51	Arizona	3:28.83
1-meter diving	Samantha Pickens, Arizona	348.45	Margaret Keefer, Minnesota	338.20
3-meter diving	Casey Matthews, Purdue	386.55	Hailey Casper, Arizona St	377.70
Platform	Haley Ishimatsu, Southern Cal	396.75	Victoria Lamp, Tennessee	328.60

*NCAA record. a-American record.

Indoor Track and Field — Men

	Champion	Time/Mark	Runner-Up	Time/Mark
60-meter dash	D'Angelo Cherry, Mississippi St	6.54	Marcus Rowland, Auburn	6.55
60-meter hurdles	Eddie Lovett, Florida	7.50	Wayne Davis II, Texas A&M	7.59
200-meter dash	Ameer Webb, Texas A&M	20.42	Anaso Jobodwana, Jackson St	20.47
400-meter dash	Errol Nolan, Houston	45.75	Mike Berry, Oregon	45.83
800-meter run	Elijah Greer, Oregon	1:47.13	Casimir Loxsom, Penn St	1:47.23
4x400-meter relay	Arkansas	3:03.50*	Florida	3:03.71
Mile run	Lawi Lalang, Arizona	3:54.74	Ryan Hill, North Carolina	3:55.25
3,000-meter run	Lawi Lalang, Arizona	7:45.94	Kemoy Campbell, Arkansas	7:46.95
5,000-meter run	Kennedy Kithuka, Texas Tech	13:25.38	Diego Estrada, Northern Arizona	13:30.24
Distance medley	Princeton	9:33.01	Penn St	9:34.00
High jump	Derek Drouin, Indiana	2.35m	Marcus Jackson, Mississippi St	2.29m
Pole vault	Andrew Irwin, Arkansas	5.70m	Jack Whitt, Oral Roberts	5.60m
Long jump	Marquis Dendy, Florida	8.28m	Damar Forbes, LSU	8.21m
Triple jump	Bryce Lamb, Texas Tech	16.96m	Omar Craddock, Florida	16.80m
Shot put	Jordan Clarke, Arizona St	20.50m	Kole Weldon, Texas Tech	20.02m
Weight throw	Alexander Ziegler, Virginia Tech	22.46m	Antonio James, Michigan St	22.25m
Heptathlon	Kevin Lazas, Arkansas	6,175 pts	Japheth Cato, Wisconsin	6,165 pts

Indoor Track and Field — Women

	Champion	Time/Mark	Runner-Up	Time/Mark
60-meter dash	Aurieyall Scott, Central Florida	7.13	English Gardner, Oregon	7.15
60-meter hurdles	Brianna Rollins, Clemson	7.79	Tiffani McReynolds, Baylor	7.96
200-meter dash	Kimberlyn Duncan, LSU	22.58	Aurieyall Scott, Central Florida	22.71
400-meter dash	Shaunae Miller, Georgia	50.88	Regina George, Arkansas	51.05
800-meter run	Natoya Goule, LSU	2:02.00	Laura Roesler, Oregon	2:02.32
4x400-meter relay	Oregon	3:30.22	Arkansas	3:30.35
Mile run	Emma Coburn, Colorado	4:29.91	Amanda Winslow, Florida St	4:31.08
3,000-meter run	Abbey D'Agostino, Dartmouth	9:01.08	Jordan Hasay, Oregon	9:06.61
5,000-meter run	Abbey D'Agostino, Dartmouth	15:28.11	Betsy Saina, Iowa St	15:33.66
Distance medley	Michigan	10:56.46	Villanova	10:57.96
High jump	Brigetta Barrett, Arizona	1.95m	Tynita Butts, East Carolina	1.90m
			Jeannelle Scheper, South Carolina	
Pole vault	Natalia Bartnovskaya, Kansas	§4.45m	Jade Riebold, Eastern Illinois	4.45m
Long jump	Andrea Geubelle, Kansas	§6.55m	Christabel Nettey, Arizona St	6.55m
Triple jump	Andrea Geubelle, Kansas	14.18m	Shanieka Thomas, San Diego St	13.82m
Shot Put	Tia Brooks, Oklahoma	19.22m*	Christina Hillman, Iowa St	17.69m
Weight throw	Felisha Johnson, Indiana St	23.52m	Beth Rohl, Michigan St	22.31m
Pentathlon	Erica Bougard, Mississippi St	4,399 pts	Keia Pinnick, Arizona St	4,327 pts

Rifle

	Champion	Pts	Runner-Up	Pts
Smallbore	Petra Zublasing, West Virginia	688.3	Henri Junghanel, Kentucky	687.8
Air rifle	Petra Zublasing, West Virginia	701.7	Sarah Scherer, Texas Christian	695.3

§-Final place determined by which athlete cleared height first. *Collegiate record.

Spring 2013

Golf

	Champion	Score	Runner-Up	Score
MEN	Max Homa, California	201	Six players, tied	204
WOMEN	Annie Park, Southern Cal	278	Lindy Duncan, Duke	284

Outdoor Track and Field

MEN

	Champion	Time/Mark	Runner-Up	Time/Mark
100-meter dash	Charles Silmon, Texas Christian	9.89	Dentarius Locke, Florida St	9.91
200-meter dash	Ameer Webb, Texas A&M	20.10	Isiah Young, Mississippi	20.17
400-meter dash	Bryshon Nellum, Southern Cal	44.73	Deon Lendore, Texas A&M	44.94
4x100-meter relay	Florida	38.53	Alabama	38.54
800-meter run	Elijah Greer, Oregon	1:46.58	Casimir Loxsom, Penn St	1:46.88
1,500-meter run	Mac Fleet, Oregon	3:50.25	Zach Perkins, Air Force	3:50.39
4x400-meter relay	Florida	3:01.34	Arkansas	3:02.89
5,000-meter run	Lawi Lalang, Arizona	13:35.19	Paul Chelimo, UNC-Greensboro	13:40.41
10,000-meter run	Lawi Lalang, Arizona	29:29.65	Paul Katam, UNC-Greensboro	29:41.27
110-meter hurdles	Wayne Davis II, Texas A&M	13.14	Eddie Lovett, Florida	13.32
400-meter hurdles	Reggie Wyatt, Southern Cal	48.58	Michael Stigler, Kansas	49.19
3,000-meter steeple	Anthony Rotich, UTEP	8:21.19	Henry Lelei, Texas A&M	8:23.16
High jump	Derek Drouin, Indiana	2.34m	Erik Kynard, Kansas St	2.31m
Pole vault	Sam Kendricks, Mississippi	5.70m	Jack Whitt, Oral Roberts	5.65m
Long jump	Damar Forbes, LSU	8.35m	Raymond Higgs, Arkansas	8.03m
Triple jump	Omar Craddock, Florida	16.92m	Manuel Ziegler, Memphis	16.48m
Shot put	Ryan Crouser, Texas	20.31m	Jordan Clarke, Arizona St	20.28m
Discus throw	Julian Wruck, UCLA	64.94m	Chad Wright, Nebraska	63.74m
Hammer throw	Tomas Kruzliak, Virginia Tech	69.26m	Remy Conaster, Southern Cal	68.30m
Javelin throw	Sam Humphreys, Texas A&M	77.95m	Tim Glover, Illinois St	75.44m
Decathlon	Johannes Hock, Texas	8,267 pts	Jeremy Taiwo, Washington	8,239 pts

WOMEN

	Champion	Time/Mark	Runner-Up	Time/Mark
100-meter dash	English Gardner, Oregon	10.96	Octavious Freeman, Central Florida	11.00
200-meter dash	Kimberlyn Duncan, LSU	22.04	Kamaria Brown, Texas A&M	22.21
400-meter dash	Ashley Spencer, Illinois	50.28	Shaunae Miller, Georgia	50.70
4x100-meter relay	Texas A&M	42.88	Central Florida	43.36
800-meter run	Natoya Goule, LSU	2:00.06	Laura Roesler, Oregon	2:00.98
1,500-meter run	Natalja Piliusina, Oklahoma St	4:13.25	Cory McGee, Florida	4:13.94
4x400-meter relay	Arkansas	3:27.09	Texas A&M	3:27.59
5,000-meter run	Abbey D'Agostino, Dartmouth	15:43.68	Betsy Saina, Iowa St	15:50.26
10,000-meter run	Betsy Saina, Iowa St	33:08.85	Aliphine Tuliamuk, Wichita State	33:14.12
100-meter hurdles	Brianna Rollins, Clemson	12.39	Kori Carter, Stanford	12.79
400-meter hurdles	Kori Carter, Stanford	53.21†	Georganne Moline, Arizona	53.72
3,000-meter steeple	Emma Coburn, Colorado	9:35.38	Colleen Quigley, Florida St	9:38.23
High jump	Brigetta Barrett, Arizona	1.95m	Courtney Anderson, South Florida	1.86m
Pole vault	Bethany Buell, South Dakota	4.45m†	Natalia Bartnovskaya, Kansas	4.40m
Long jump	Lorraine Ugen, Texas Christian	6.77m	Andrea Geubelle, Kansas	6.50m
Triple jump	Shanieka Thomas, San Diego St	14.14m	Andrea Geubelle, Kansas	13.63m
Shot put	Tia Brooks, Oklahoma	18.91m†	Brittany Smith, Illinois St	17.85m
Discus throw	Anna Jelmini, Arizona St	57.95m	Julie Labonte, Arizona	56.25m
Hammer throw	Chelsea Cassulo, Arizona St	69.12m	Brittany Smith, Illinois State	68.51m
Javelin throw	Freya Jones, Georgia	54.95m	Marija Vucenovic, Florida	54.76m
Heptathlon	Lindsay Vollmer, Kansas	6,086 pts	Makeba Alcide, Arkansas	6,050 pts

†NCAA meet record.

Tennis

		Champion	Score	Runner-Up
MEN	Singles	Blaz Rola, Ohio St	7–6 (8), 6–4	Jarmere Jenkins, Virginia
	Doubles	J. Jenkins/M. Styslinger, Virginia	3–6, 6–2, 6–4	C. Camillone/D. Holiner, Texas
WOMEN	Singles	Nicole Gibbs, Stanford	6–2, 6–4	Mary Weatherholt, Nebraska
	Doubles	K. Christian/S. Santamaria, S Cal	6–4, 6–3	R. Anderson/S. Morton, UCLA

DIVISION I

Year	Champion	Coach	Score	Runner-Up	Most Outstanding Player
1947	California*	Clint Evans	8–7	Yale	No award
1948	Southern Cal	Sam Barry	9–2	Yale	No award
1949	Texas*	Bibb Falk	10–3	Wake Forest	Charles Teague, Wake Forest, 2B
1950	Texas	Bibb Falk	3–0	Washington St	Ray VanCleef, Rutgers, CF
1951	Oklahoma*	Jack Baer	3–2	Tennnessee	Sidney Hatfield, Tennessee, P-1B
1952	Holy Cross	Jack Barry	8–4	Missouri	James O'Neill, Holy Cross, P
1953	Michigan	Ray Fisher	7–5	Texas	J.L. Smith, Texas, P
1954	Missouri	John (Hi) Simmons	4–1	Rollins	Tom Yewcic, Michigan St, C
1955	Wake Forest	Taylor Sanford	7–6	Western Michigan	Tom Borland, Oklahoma St, P
1956	Minnesota	Dick Siebert	12–1	Arizona	Jerry Thomas, Minnesota, P
1957	California*	George Wolfman	1–0	Penn St	Cal Emery, Penn St, P-1B
1958	Southern Cal	Rod Dedeaux	8–7†	Missouri	Bill Thom, Southern Cal, P
1959	Oklahoma St	Toby Greene	5–3	Arizona	Jim Dobson, Oklahoma St, 3B
1960	Minnesota	Dick Siebert	2–1‡	Southern Cal	John Erickson, Minnesota, 2B
1961	Southern Cal*	Rod Dedeaux	1–0	Oklahoma St	Littleton Fowler, Oklahoma St, P
1962	Michigan	Don Lund	5–4	Santa Clara	Bob Garibaldi, Santa Clara, P
1963	Southern Cal	Rod Dedeaux	5–2	Arizona	Bud Hollowell, Southern Cal, C
1964	Minnesota	Dick Siebert	5–1	Missouri	Joe Ferris, Maine, P
1965	Arizona St	Bobby Winkles	2–1#	Ohio St	Sal Bando, Arizona St, 3B
1966	Ohio St	Marty Karow	8–2	Oklahoma St	Steve Arlin, Ohio St, P
1967	Arizona St	Bobby Winkles	11–2	Houston	Ron Davini, Arizona St, C
1968	Southern Cal*	Rod Dedeaux	4–3	Southern Illinois	Bill Seinsoth, Southern Cal, 1B
1969	Arizona St	Bobby Winkles	10–1	Tulsa	John Dolinsek, Arizona St, LF
1970	Southern Cal	Rod Dedeaux	2–1	Florida St	Gene Ammann, Florida St, P
1971	Southern Cal	Rod Dedeaux	7–2	Southern Illinois	Jerry Tabb, Tulsa, 1B
1972	Southern Cal	Rod Dedeaux	1–0	Arizona St	Russ McQueen, Southern Cal, P
1973	Southern Cal*	Rod Dedeaux	4–3	Arizona St	Dave Winfield, Minnesota, P-OF
1974	Southern Cal	Rod Dedeaux	7–3	Miami (Fla.)	George Milke, Southern Cal, P
1975	Texas	Cliff Gustafson	5–1	S Carolina	Mickey Reichenbach, Texas, 1B
1976	Arizona	Jerry Kindall	7–1	Eastern Michigan	Steve Powers, Arizona, P-DH
1977	Arizona St	Jim Brock	2–1	S Carolina	Bob Horner, Arizona St, 3B
1978	Southern Cal*	Rod Dedeaux	10–3	Arizona St	Rod Boxberger, Southern Cal, P
1979	CSU–Fullerton	Augie Garrido	2–1	Arkansas	Tony Hudson, CSU–Fullerton, P
1980	Arizona	Jerry Kindall	5–3	Hawaii	Terry Francona, Arizona, LF
1981	Arizona St	Jim Brock	7–4	Oklahoma St	Stan Holmes, Arizona St, LF
1982	Miami (Fla.)*	Ron Fraser	9–3	Wichita St	Dan Smith, Miami (Fla.), P
1983	Texas*	Cliff Gustafson	4–3	Alabama	Calvin Schiraldi, Texas, P
1984	CSU–Fullerton	Augie Garrido	3–1	Texas	John Fishel, CSU–Fullerton, LF
1985	Miami (Fla.)	Ron Fraser	10–6	Texas	Greg Ellena, Miami (Fla.), DH
1986	Arizona	Jerry Kindall	10–2	Florida St	Mike Senne, Arizona, LF
1987	Stanford	Mark Marquess	9–5	Oklahoma St	Paul Carey, Stanford, RF
1988	Stanford	Mark Marquess	9–4	Arizona St	Lee Plemel, Stanford, P
1989	Wichita St	Gene Stephenson	5–3	Texas	Greg Brummett, Wichita St, P
1990	Georgia	Steve Webber	2–1	Oklahoma St	Mike Rebhan, Georgia, P
1991	LSU	Skip Bertman	6–3	Wichita St	Gary Hymel, LSU, C
1992	Pepperdine	Andy Lopez	3–2	CSU–Fullerton	Phil Nevin, CSU–Fullerton, 3B
1993	LSU	Skip Bertman	8–0	Wichita St	Todd Walker, LSU, 2B
1994	Oklahoma	Larry Cochell	13–5	Georgia Tech	Chip Glass, Oklahoma, CF
1995	CSU–Fullerton*	Augie Garrido	11–5	Southern Cal	Mark Kotsay, CSU–Fullerton, CF-P
1996	LSU*	Skip Bertman	9–8	Miami (Fla.)	Pat Burrell, Miami (Fla.), 3B
1997	LSU*	Skip Bertman	13–6	Alabama	Brandon Larson, LSU, SS
1998	Southern Cal	Mike Gillespie	21–14	Arizona St	Wes Rachels, Southern Cal, 2B
1999	Miami (Fla.)	Jim Morris	6–5	Florida St	Marshall McDougall, FSU 3B/2B
2000	LSU*	Skip Bertman	6–5	Stanford	Trey Hodges, LSU, P
2001	Miami (Fla.)*	Jim Morris	12–1	Stanford	Charlton Jimerson, Miami (Fla.), OF
2002	Texas	Augie Garrido	12–6	South Carolina	Huston Street, Texas, P
2003	Rice	Wayne Graham	14–2^	Stanford	John Hudgins, Stanford, P
2004	CSU–Fullerton	George Horton	3–2^	Texas	Jason Windsor, CSU–Fullerton
2005	Texas	Augie Garrido	6–2^	Florida	David Maroul, Texas

*Undefeated teams in College World Series play.
†12 innings.   ‡10 innings.   #15 innings.   ^Score of decisive game of best-of-three series.

DIVISION I *(CONT.)*

Year	Champion	Coach	Score	Runner-Up	Most Outstanding Player
2006 ....Oregon St	Pat Casey	3–2^	North Carolina	Jonah Nickerson, Oregon St, P
2007 ....Oregon St	Pat Casey	9–3^	North Carolina	Jorge Reyes, Oregon St, P
2008 ....Fresno St	Mike Batesole	6–1^	Georgia	Tommy Mendonca. Fresno St, 3B
2009 ....LSU	Paul Mainieri	11–4^	Texas	Jared Mitchell, LSU, OF
2010 ....South Carolina	Ray Tanner	2–1^†	UCLA	Jackie Bradley Jr., South Carolina, OF
2011 ....South Carolina	Ray Tanner	5–2^	Florida	Scott Wingo, South Carolina, 2B
2012 ...Arizona	Andy Lopez	4–1^	South Carolina	Robert Refsnyder, Arizona, OF
2013 ....UCLA	John Savage	8–0^	Mississippi St	Adam Plutko, UCLA, P

*Undefeated teams in College World Series play. †11 innings. ^Score of decisive game of best-of-three series.

DIVISION II

Year	Champion
1968 ....Chapman
1969 ....Illinois St
1970 ....CSU-Northridge
1971 ....Florida Southern
1972 ....Florida Southern
1973 ....UC–Irvine
1974 ....UC–Irvine
1975 ....Florida Southern
1976 ....Cal Poly–Pomona
1977 ....UC–Riverside
1978 ....Florida Southern
1979 ....Valdosta St
1980 ....Cal Poly–Pomona
1981 ....Florida Southern
1982 ....UC–Riverside
1983 ....Cal Poly–Pomona

Year	Champion
1984 ....CSU–Northridge
1985 ....Florida Southern
1986 ....Troy St
1987 ....Troy St
1988 ....Florida Southern
1989 ....Cal Poly–SLO
1990 ....Jacksonville St
1991 ....Jacksonville St
1992 ....Tampa
1993 ....Tampa
1994 ....Central Missouri St
1995 ....Florida Southern
1996 ....Kennesaw St
1997 ....CSU–Chico
1998 ....Tampa
1999 ....CSU–Chico

Year	Champion
2000 ....SE Oklahoma St
2001 ....St. Mary's (Tex.)
2002 ....Columbus St
2003 ....Central Missouri St
2004 ....Kennesaw St
2005 ....Florida Southern
2006 ....Tampa
2007 ....Tampa
2008 ....Mount Olive
2009 ....Lynn
2010 ....Southern Indiana
2011 ....West Florida
2012 ....West Chester
2013 ....Tampa

DIVISION III

Year	Champion
1976 ....CSU-Stanislaus
1977 ....CSU-Stanislaus
1978 ....Glassboro St
1979 ....Glassboro St
1980 ....Ithaca
1981 ....Marietta
1982 ....Eastern Connecticut St
1983 ....Marietta
1984 ....Ramapo
1985 ....UW-Oshkosh
1986 ....Marietta
1987 ....Montclair St
1988 ....Ithaca

Year	Champion
1989 ....N. Carolina Wesleyan
1990 ....Eastern Connecticut St
1991 ....Southern Maine
1992 ....William Paterson
1993 ....Montclair St
1994 ....UW-Oshkosh
1995 ....La Verne
1996 ....William Paterson
1997 ....Southern Maine
1998 ....Eastern Connecticut St
1999 ....N.Carolina Wesleyan
2000 ....Montclair St
2001 ....St. Thomas (Minn.)

Year	Champion
2002 ....Eastern Connecticut St
2003 ....Chapman
2004 ....UW-Stevens Pt
2005 ....Wisconsin
2006 ....Marietta
2007 ....Kean
2008 ....Trinity (Conn.)
2009 ....St. Thomas (Minn.)
2010 ....Illinois Wesleyan
2011 ....Marietta
2012 ....Marietta
2013 ....Linfield

Ice Hockey

Men

DIVISION I

Year	Champion	Coach	Score	Runner-Up	Most Outstanding Player
1948 ....Michigan	Vic Heyliger	8–4	Dartmouth	Joe Riley, Dartmouth, F
1949 ....Boston College	John Kelley	4–3	Dartmouth	Dick Desmond, Dartmouth, G
1950 ....Colorado College	Cheddy Thompson	13–4	Boston University	Ralph Bevins, Boston University, G
1951 ....Michigan	Vic Heyliger	7–1	Brown	Ed Whiston, Brown, G
1952 ....Michigan	Vic Heyliger	4–1	Colorado College	Kenneth Kinsley, Colorado Coll, G
1953 ....Michigan	Vic Heyliger	7–3	Minnesota	John Matchefts, Michigan, F
1954 ....RPI	Ned Harkness	5–4 (OT)	Minnesota	Abbie Moore, Rensselaer, F
1955 ....Michigan	Vic Heyliger	5–3	Colorado College	Philip Hilton, Colorado College, D
1956 ....Michigan	Vic Heyliger	7–5	Michigan Tech	Lorne Howes, Michigan, G
1957 ....Colorado College	Thomas Bedecki	13–6	Michigan	Bob McCusker, Colorado Coll, F
1958 ....Denver	Murray Armstrong	6–2	North Dakota	Murray Massier, Denver, F
1959 ....North Dakota	Bob May	4–3 (OT)	Michigan St	Reg Morelli, North Dakota, F
1960 ....Denver	Murray Armstrong	5–3	Michigan Tech	Lou Angotti, Michigan Tech, F
					Bob Marquis, Boston U, F
					Barry Urbanski, Boston U, G
1961 ....Denver	Murray Armstrong	12–2	St. Lawrence	Bill Masterton, Denver, F
1962 ....Michigan Tech	John MacInnes	7–1	Clarkson	Lou Angotti, Michigan Tech, F

Men *(Cont.)*
DIVISION I *(CONT.)*

Year	Champion	Coach	Score	Runner-Up	Most Outstanding Player
1963	North Dakota	Barney Thorndycraft	6–5	Denver	Al McLean, North Dakota, F
1964	Michigan	Allen Renfrew	6–3	Denver	Bob Gray, Michigan, G
1965	Michigan Tech	John MacInnes	8–2	Boston College	Gary Milroy, Michigan Tech, F
1966	Michigan St	Amo Bessone	6–1	Clarkson	Gaye Cooley, Michigan St, G
1967	Cornell	Ned Harkness	4–1	Boston University	Walt Stanowski, Cornell, D
1968	Denver	Murray Armstrong	4–0	North Dakota	Gerry Powers, Denver, G
1969	Denver	Murray Armstrong	4–3	Cornell	Keith Magnuson, Denver, D
1970	Cornell	Ned Harkness	6–4	Clarkson	Daniel Lodboa, Cornell, D
1971	Boston University	Jack Kelley	4–2	Minnesota	Dan Brady, Boston University, G
1972	Boston University	Jack Kelley	4–0	Cornell	Tim Regan, Boston University, G
1973	Wisconsin	Bob Johnson	4–2	Vacated	Dean Talafous, Wisconsin, F
1974	Minnesota	Herb Brooks	4–2	Michigan Tech	Brad Shelstad, Minnesota, G
1975	Michigan Tech	John MacInnes	6–1	Minnesota	Jim Warden, Michigan Tech, G
1976	Minnesota	Herb Brooks	6–4	Michigan Tech	Tom Vanelli, Minnesota, F
1977	Wisconsin	Bob Johnson	6–5 (OT)	Michigan	Julian Baretta, Wisconsin, G
1978	Boston University	Jack Parker	5–3	Boston College	Jack O'Callahan, Boston Univ, D
1979	Minnesota	Herb Brooks	4–3	North Dakota	Steve Janaszak, Minnesota, G
1980	North Dakota	John Gasparini	5–2	Northern Michigan	Doug Smail, North Dakota, F
1981	Wisconsin	Bob Johnson	6–3	Minnesota	Marc Behrend, Wisconsin, G
1982	North Dakota	John Gasparini	5–2	Wisconsin	Phil Sykes, North Dakota, F
1983	Wisconsin	Jeff Sauer	6–2	Harvard	Marc Behrend, Wisconsin, G
1984	Bowling Green	Jerry York	5–4 (OT)	Minn.–Duluth	Gary Kruzich, Bowling Green, G
1985	RPI	Mike Addesa	2–1	Providence	Chris Terreri, Providence, G
1986	Michigan St	Ron Mason	6–5	Harvard	Mike Donnelly, Michigan St, F
1987	North Dakota	John Gasparini	5–3	Michigan St	Tony Hrkac, North Dakota, F
1988	Lake Superior St	Frank Anzalone	4–3 (OT)	St. Lawrence	Bruce Hoffort, Lake Superior St, G
1989	Harvard	Bill Cleary	4–3 (OT)	Minnesota	Ted Donato, Harvard, F
1990	Wisconsin	Jeff Sauer	7–3	Colgate	Chris Tancill, Wisconsin, F
1991	Northern Michigan	Rick Comley	8–7 (3OT)	Boston University	Scott Beattie, Northern Michigan, F
1992	Lake Superior St	Jeff Jackson	4–2	Wisconsin	Paul Constantin, Lake Superior St, F
1993	Maine	Shawn Walsh	5–4	Lake Superior St	Jim Montgomery, Maine, F
1994	Lake Superior St	Jeff Jackson	9–1	Boston University	Sean Tallaire, Lake Superior St, F
1995	Boston University	Jack Parker	6–2	Maine	Chris O'Sullivan, Boston Univ, F
1996	Michigan	Red Berenson	3–2 (OT)	Colorado College	Brendan Morrison, Michigan, F
1997	North Dakota	Dean Blais	6–4	Boston University	Matt Henderson, North Dakota, F
1998	Michigan	Red Berenson	3–2 (OT)	Boston College	Marty Turco, Michigan, G
1999	Maine	Shawn Walsh	3–2 (OT)	New Hampshire	Alfie Michaud, Maine, G
2000	North Dakota	Dean Blais	4–2	Boston College	Lee Goren, North Dakota, F
2001	Boston College	Jerry York	3–2 (OT)	North Dakota	Chuck Kobasew, Boston College, F
2002	Minnesota	Don Lucia	4–3 (OT)	Maine	Grant Potulny, Minnesota, F
2003	Minnesota	Don Lucia	5–1	New Hampshire	Thomas Vanek, Minnesota, F
2004	Denver	George Gwozdecky	1–0	Maine	Adam Berkhoel, Denver, G
2005	Denver	George Gwozdecky	4–1	North Dakota	Peter Mannino, Denver
2006	Wisconsin	Mike Eaves	2–1	Boston College	Robbie Earl, Wisconsin, F
2007	Michigan St	Rick Comley	3–1	Boston College	Justin Abdelkader, Michigan St, F
2008	Boston College	Jerry York	4–1	Notre Dame	Nathan Gerbe, Boston College, F
2009	Boston University	Jack Parker	4–3 (OT)	Miami (Ohio)	Colby Cohen, Boston University, D
2010	Boston College	Jerry York	5–0	Wisconsin	Ben Smith, Boston College, F
2011	Minn.–Duluth	Scott Sandelin	3–2 (OT)	Michigan	J.T. Brown, Minn.–Duluth, F
2012	Boston College	Jerry York	4–1	Ferris St	Parker Milner, Boston College, G
2013	Yale	Keith Allain	4–0	Quinnipiac	Andrew Miller, Yale, F

DIVISION II *(Discontinued)*

Year	Champion	Coach	Score	Runner-Up
1978	Merrimack	Thom Lawler	12–2	Lake Forest
1979	Lowell	Bill Riley Jr	6–4	Mankato St
1980	Mankato St	Don Brose	5–2	Elmira
1981	Lowell	Bill Riley Jr	5–4	Plattsburgh St
1982	Lowell	Bill Riley Jr	6–1	Plattsburgh St
1983	RIT	Brian Mason	4–2	Bemidji St
1984	Bemidji St	R.H. (Bob) Peters	14–4*	Merrimack
1993	Bemidji St	R.H. (Bob) Peters	15–6*	Mercyhurst
1994	Bemidji St	R.H. (Bob) Peters	7–6*	Ala.–Huntsville
1995	Bemidji St	R.H. (Bob) Peters	11–6*	Mercyhurst
1996	Ala.–Huntsville	Doug Ross	10–1*	Bemidji St
1997	Bemidji St	R.H. (Bob) Peters	7–4*	Ala.–Huntsville
1998	Ala.–Huntsville	Doug Ross	11–4*	Bemidji St
1999	St. Michael's (Vt.)	Lou DiMasi	12–9*	New Hamp. Coll

*Two-game, total-goal series.

Men (Cont.)
DIVISION III

Year	Champion	Coach	Score	Runner-Up
1984	Babson	Bob Riley	8–0	Union (N.Y.)
1985	RIT	Bruce Delventhal	5–1	Bemidji St
1986	Bemidji St	R.H. (Bob) Peters	8–5	Vacated
1987	Vacated			Oswego St
1988	UW-River Falls	Rick Kozuback	7–1, 3–5, 3–0	Elmira
1989	UW-Stevens Point	Mark Mazzoleni	3–3, 3–2	RIT
1990	UW-Stevens Point	Mark Mazzoleni	10–1, 3–6, 1–0	Plattsburgh St
1991	UW-Stevens Point	Mark Mazzoleni	6–2	Mankato St
1992	Plattsburgh St	Bob Emery	7–3	UW-Stevens Point
1993	UW-Stevens Point	Joe Baldarotta	4–3	UW-River Falls
1994	UW-River Falls	Dean Talafous	6–4	UW-Superior
1995	Middlebury	Bill Beaney	1–0	Fredonia St
1996	Middlebury	Bill Beaney	3–2	RIT
1997	Middlebury	Bill Beaney	3–2	UW-Superior
1998	Middlebury	Bill Beaney	2–1	UW-Stevens Point
1999	Middlebury	Bill Beaney	5–0	UW-Superior
2000	Norwich	Michael McShane	2–1	St. Thomas (Minn.)
2001	Plattsburgh St	Bob Emery	6–2	RIT
2002	UW-Superior	Dan Stauber	3–2	Norwich
2003	Norwich	Michael McShane	2–1	Oswego St
2004	Middlebury	Bill Beaney	1–0	St. Norbert
2005	Middlebury	Bill Beaney	5–0	St. Thomas (Minn.)
2006	Middlebury	Bill Beaney	3–0	St. Norbert
2007	Oswego St	Ed Gosek	4–3	Middlebury
2008	St. Norbert	Tim Coghlin	2–0	Plattsburgh St
2009	Neumann	Dominick Dawes	4–1	Gustavus Adolphus
2010	Norwich	Michael McShane	2–1	St. Norbert
2011	St. Norbert	Tim Coghlin	4–3	Adrian
2012	St. Norbert	Tim Coghlin	4–1	Oswego St
2013	Wisconsin-Eau Claire	Matt Loen	5–3	Oswego St

Women - DIVISION I

Year	Champion	Coach	Score	Runner-Up
2001	Minn.-Duluth	Shannon Miller	4–2	St. Lawrence
2002	Minn.-Duluth	Shannon Miller	3–2	Brown
2003	Minn.-Duluth	Shannon Miller	4–3 (2 OT)	Harvard
2004	Minnesota	Laura Holldorson	6–2	Harvard
2005	Minnesota	Laura Holldorson	4–3	Harvard
2006	Wisconsin	Mark Johnson	3–0	Minnesota
2007	Wisconsin	Mark Johnson	4–1	Minnesota
2008	Minn.-Duluth	Shannon Miller	4–0	Wisconsin
2009	Wisconsin	Mark Johnson	5–0	Mercyhurst
2010	Minn.-Duluth	Shannon Miller	3–2 (3 OT)	Cornell
2011	Wisconsin	Mark Johnson	4–1	Boston Univ.
2012	Minnesota	Brad Frost	4–2	Wisconsin
2013	Minnesota	Brad Frost	6–3	Boston Univ.

Soccer

Men - DIVISION I

Year	Champion	Coach	Score	Runner-Up
1959	St. Louis	Bob Guelker	5–2	Bridgeport
1960	St. Louis	Bob Guelker	3–2	Maryland
1961	West Chester	Mel Lorback	2–0	St. Louis
1962	St. Louis	Bob Guelker	4–3	Maryland
1963	St. Louis	Bob Guelker	3–0	Navy
1964	Navy	F.H. Warner	1–0	Michigan St
1965	St. Louis	Bob Guelker	1–0	Michigan St
1966	San Francisco	Steve Negoesco	5–2	LIU–Brooklyn
1967	Michigan St	Gene Kenney	0–0	Game called due to
	St. Louis	Harry Keough		inclement weather
1968	Maryland	Doyle Royal	2–2 (2 OT)	
	Michigan St	Gene Kenney		
1969	St. Louis	Harry Keough	4–0	San Francisco
1970	St. Louis	Harry Keough	1–0	UCLA
1971	Vacated		3–2	St. Louis
1972	St. Louis	Harry Keough	4–2	UCLA

Men - DIVISION I *(CONT.)*

Year	Champion	Coach	Score	Runner-Up
1973	St. Louis	Harry Keough	2–1 (OT)	UCLA
1974	Howard	Lincoln Phillips	2–1 (4 OT)	St. Louis
1975	San Francisco	Steve Negoesco	4–0	SIU–Edwardsville
1976	San Francisco	Steve Negoesco	1–0	Indiana
1977	Hartwick	Jim Lennox	2–1	San Francisco
1978	Vacated		2–0	Indiana
1979	SIU–Edwardsville	Bob Guelker	3–2	Clemson
1980	San Francisco	Steve Negoesco	4–3 (OT)	Indiana
1981	Connecticut	Joe Morrone	2–1 (OT)	Alabama A&M
1982	Indiana	Jerry Yeagley	2–1 (8 OT)	Duke
1983	Indiana	Jerry Yeagley	1–0 (2 OT)	Columbia
1984	Clemson	I.M. Ibrahim	2–1	Indiana
1985	UCLA	Sigi Schmid	1–0 (8 OT)	American
1986	Duke	John Rennie	1–0	Akron
1987	Clemson	I.M. Ibrahim	2–0	San Diego St
1988	Indiana	Jerry Yeagley	1–0	Howard
1989	Santa Clara / Virginia	Steve Sampson / Bruce Arena	1–1 (2 OT)	
1990	UCLA	Sigi Schmid	1–0 (OT)	Rutgers
1991	Virginia	Bruce Arena	0–0* (3-1 PKs)	Santa Clara
1992	Virginia	Bruce Arena	2–0	San Diego
1993	Virginia	Bruce Arena	2–0	South Carolina
1994	Virginia	Bruce Arena	1–0	Indiana
1995	Wisconsin	Jim Launder	2–0	Duke
1996	St. John's (N.Y.)	Dave Masur	4–1	Florida International
1997	UCLA	Sigi Schmid	2–1	Virginia
1998	Indiana	Jerry Yeagley	3–1	Stanford
1999	Indiana	Jerry Yeagley	1–0	Santa Clara
2000	Connecticut	Ray Reid	2–0	Creighton
2001	North Carolina	Elmar Bolowich	2–0	Indiana
2002	UCLA	Tom Fitzgerald	1–0	Stanford
2003	Indiana	Jerry Yeagley	2–1	St. John's (N.Y.)
2004	Indiana	Jerry Yeagley	0–0 (3-2 PKs)	UC–Santa Barbara
2005	Maryland	Sasho Cirovski	1–0	New Mexico
2006	UC–Santa Barbara	Tim Vom Steeg	2–1	UCLA
2007	Wake Forest	Tony da Luz	2–0	Ohio St
2008	Maryland	Sasha Cirovski	1–0	North Carolina
2009	Virginia	George Gelnovatch	0–0 (3-2 PKs)	Akron
2010	Akron	Caleb Porter	1–0	Louisville
2011	North Carolina	Carlos Somoano	1–0	Charlotte
2012	Indiana	Todd Yeagley	1–0	Georgetown

*Under a rule passed in 1991, the NCAA determined that when a score is tied after regulation and overtime, and the championship is determined by penalty kicks, the official score will be 0–0.

Men - DIVISION II

Year	Champion	Year	Champion	Year	Champion
1972	SIU–Edwardsville	1986	Seattle Pacific	2000	Cal St–Dominguez Hills
1973	Missouri–St. Louis	1987	Southern Conn St	2001	Tampa
1974	Adelphi	1988	Florida Tech	2002	Sonoma St
1975	Baltimore	1989	New Hampshire College	2003	Lynn
1976	Loyola (Md.)	1990	Southern Conn St	2004	Seattle
1977	Alabama A&M	1991	Florida Tech	2005	Fort Lewis
1978	Seattle Pacific	1992	Southern Conn St	2006	Dowling (N.Y.)
1979	Alabama A&M	1993	Seattle Pacific	2007	Franklin Pierce
1980	Lock Haven	1994	Tampa	2008	Cal St–Dominguez Hills
1981	Tampa	1995	Southern Conn St	2009	Fort Lewis
1982	Florida International	1996	Grand Canyon	2010	Northern Kentucky
1983	Seattle Pacific	1997	CSU–Bakersfield	2011	Fort Lewis
1984	Florida International	1998	Southern Conn St	2012	Lynn
1985	Seattle Pacific	1999	Southern Conn St		

Men - DIVISION III

Year	Champion	Year	Champion	Year	Champion
1974	Brockport St	1980	Babson	1986	N.C.–Greensboro
1975	Babson	1981	Glassboro St	1987	N.C.–Greensboro
1976	Brandeis	1982	N.C.–Greensboro	1988	UC–San Diego
1977	Lock Haven	1983	N.C.–Greensboro	1989	Elizabethtown
1978	Lock Haven	1984	Wheaton (Ill.)	1990	Glassboro St
1979	Babson	1985	N.C.–Greensboro	1991	UC–San Diego

Men - DIVISION III (CONT.)

Year	Champion	Year	Champion	Year	Champion
1992.....Kean		1999.....St. Lawrence		2006.....Messiah	
1993.....UC–San Diego		2000.....Messiah		2007.....Middlebury	
1994.....Bethany (W.V.)		2001.....Richard Stockton		2008.....Messiah	
1995.....Williams		2002.....Messiah		2009.....Messiah	
1996.....The College of New Jersey*		2003.....Trinity (Tex.)		2010.....Messiah	
1997.....Wheaton (Ill.)		2004.....Messiah		2011.....Ohio Wesleyan	
1998.....Ohio Wesleyan		2005.....Messiah		2012.....Messiah	

Women - DIVISION I

Year	Champion	Coach	Score	Runner-Up
1982	North Carolina	Anson Dorrance	2–0	Central Florida
1983	North Carolina	Anson Dorrance	4–0	George Mason
1984	North Carolina	Anson Dorrance	2–0	Connecticut
1985	George Mason	Hank Leung	2–0	North Carolina
1986	North Carolina	Anson Dorrance	2–0	Colorado College
1987	North Carolina	Anson Dorrance	1–0	Massachusetts
1988	North Carolina	Anson Dorrance	4–1	North Carolina St
1989	North Carolina	Anson Dorrance	2–0	Colorado College
1990	North Carolina	Anson Dorrance	6–0	Connecticut
1991	North Carolina	Anson Dorrance	3–1	Wisconsin
1992	North Carolina	Anson Dorrance	9–1	Duke
1993	North Carolina	Anson Dorrance	6–0	George Mason
1994	North Carolina	Anson Dorrance	5–0	Notre Dame
1995	Notre Dame	Chris Petrucelli	1–0	Portland
1996	North Carolina	Anson Dorrance	1–0	Notre Dame
1997	North Carolina	Anson Dorrance	2–0	Connecticut
1998	Florida	Becky Burleigh	1–0	North Carolina
1999	North Carolina	Anson Dorrance	2–0	Notre Dame
2000	North Carolina	Anson Dorrance	2–1	UCLA
2001	Santa Clara	Jerry Smith	1–0	North Carolina
2002	Portland	Clive Charles	2–1	Santa Clara
2003	North Carolina	Anson Dorrance	6–0	Connecticut
2004	Notre Dame	Randy Waldrum	1–1 (OT 4–3)	UCLA
2005	Portland	Garrett Smith	4–0	UCLA
2006	North Carolina	Anson Dorrance	2–1	Notre Dame
2007	USC	Ali Khosroshahin	2–0	Florida St
2008	North Carolina	Anson Dorrance	2–1	Notre Dame
2009	North Carolina	Anson Dorrance	1–0	Stanford
2010	Notre Dame	Randy Waldrum	1–0	Stanford
2011	Stanford	Paul Ratcliffe	1–0	Duke
2012	North Carolina	Anson Dorrance	4–1	Penn St

Women - DIVISION II

Year	Champion	Year	Champion	Year	Champion
1988.....CSU–Hayward		1997.....Franklin Pierce		2006.....Metro St	
1989.....Barry		1998.....Lynn		2007.....Tampa	
1990.....Sonoma St		1999.....Franklin Pierce		2008.....Seattle Pacific	
1991.....CSU–Dominguez Hills		2000.....UC–San Diego		2009.....Grand Valley St	
1992.....Barry		2001.....UC–San Diego		2010.....Grand Valley St	
1993.....Barry		2002.....Christian Brothers		2011.....St. Rose	
1994.....Franklin Pierce		2003.....Kennesaw St		2012.....West Florida	
1995.....Franklin Pierce		2004.....Metro St			
1996.....Franklin Pierce		2005.....Nebraska-Omaha			

Women - DIVISION III

Year	Champion	Year	Champion	Year	Champion
1986 .....Rochester		1995 .....UC–San Diego		2004 .....Wheaton (Ill.)	
1987 .....Rochester		1996 .....UC–San Diego		2005 .....Messiah	
1988 .....William Smith		1997 .....UC–San Diego		2006 .....Wheaton (Ill.)	
1989 .....UC–San Diego		1998 .....Macalester		2007 .....Wheaton (Ill.)	
1990 .....Ithaca		1999 .....UC–San Diego		2008 .....Messiah	
1991 .....Ithaca		2000 .....The College of New Jersey*		2009 .....Messiah	
1992 .....Cortland St		2001 .....Ohio Wesleyan		2010 .....Hardin-Simmons	
1993 .....Trenton St		2002 .....Ohio Wesleyan		2011 .....Messiah	
1994 .....Trenton St		2003 .....Oneonta St		2012 .....Messiah	

*formerly Trenton St

IAN MCNICHOL/GETTY IMAGES

Track & Field

Usain Bolt continued to dominate at the World Championships in Moscow, winning both the 100- (right) and 200-meter dashes.

2012 Olympics

London, England July 27–August 12, 2012

Men

100 METERS

1. ..Usain Bolt, Jamaica	9.63 OR
2. ..Yohan Blake, Jamaica	9.75
3. ..Justin Gatlin, U.S.	9.79

200 METERS

1. ..Usain Bolt, Jamaica	19.32
2. ..Yohan Blake, Jamaica	19.44
3. ..Warren Weir, Jamaica	19.84

400 METERS

1. ..Kirani James, Grenada	43.94
2. ..Luguelin Santos, Dominican Rep.	44.46
3. ..Lalonde Gordon, Trinidad & Tobago	44.52

800 METERS

1....David Lekuta Rudisha, Kenya	1:40.91 WR
2. ..Nijel Amos, Botswana	1:41.73
3. ..Timothy Kitum, Kenya	1:42.53

1,500 METERS

1. ..Taoufik Makhloufi, Algeria	3:34.08
2. ..Leonel Manzano, U.S.	3:34.79
3. ..Abdalaati Iguider, Morocco	3:35.13

5,000 METERS

1. ..Mohamed Farah, G.B.	13:41.66
2. ..Dejen Gebremeskel, Ethiopia	13:41.98
3. ..Thomas P. Longosiwa, Kenya	13:42.36

10,000 METERS

1. ..Mohamed Farah, G.B.	27:30.42
2. ..Galen Rupp, United States	27:30.90
3. ..Tariku Bekele, Ethiopia	27:31.43

MARATHON

1. ..Stephen Kiprotich, Uganda	2:08:01
2. ..Abel Kirui, Kenya	2:08:27
3....Wilson Kipsang Kiprotich, Kenya	2:09:37

110-METER HURDLES

1. ..Aries Merritt, United States	12.92
2. ..Jason Richardson, United States	13.04
3. ..Hansle Parchment, Jamaica	13.12

400-METER HURDLES

1. .. Felix Sanchez, Dominican Republic	47.63
2. ..Michael Tinsley, United States	47.91
3. ..Javier Culson, Puerto Rico	48.10

3,000-METER STEEPLECHASE

1. ..Ezekiel Kemboi, Kenya	8:18.56
2. ..M. Mekhissi-Benabbad, France	8:19.08
3. ..Abel Kiprop Mutai, Kenya	8:19.73

4 X 100-METER RELAY

1 ...Jamaica (Y. Blake, U, Bolt, N. Carter, M. Frater)	36.84 WR
2. ..United States	37.04
3. ..Trinidad and Tobago	38.12

4 X 400-METER RELAY

1. ..Bahamas (C. Brown, D. Pinder M. Mathieu, R. Miller)	2:56.72
2. ..United States	2:57.05
3. ..Trinidad and Tobago	2:59.40

20-KILOMETER WALK

1. ..Ding Chen, China	1:18:46 OR
2. ..Erick Barrondo, Guatemala	1:18:57
3. ..Zhen Wang, China	1:19:25

50-KILOMETER WALK

1. ..Sergey Kirdyapkin, Russia	3:35:59 OR
2. ..Jared Tallent, Australia	3:36:53
3. ..Tianfeng Si, China	3:37:16

HIGH JUMP

1. ..Ivan Ukhov, Russia	7 ft 9¾ in
2. ..Erik Kynard, United States	7 ft 7¾ in
3. ..Derek Drouin, Canada	7 ft 6¼ in

POLE VAULT

1. ..Renaud Lavillenie, France	19 ft 7 in OR
2. ..Bjorn Otto, Germany	19 ft 4¾ in
3. ..Raphael Holzdeppe, Germany	19 ft 4¾ in

LONG JUMP

1. ..Greg Rutherford, G.B.	27 ft 3¼ in
2. ..Mitchell Watt, Australia	26 ft 9¼ in
3. ..Will Claye, United States	26 ft 7¾ in

TRIPLE JUMP

1. ..Christian Taylor, United States	58 ft 5¼ in
2. ..Will Claye, United States	57 ft 9¾ in
3. ..Fabrizio Donato, Italy	57 ft 4¼ in

SHOT PUT

1. ..Tomasz Majewski, Poland	71 ft 9¾ in
2. ..David Storl, Germany	71 ft 8⅝ in
3. ..Reese Hoffa, United States	69 ft 7¾ in

DISCUS THROW

1. ..Robert Harting, Germany	223 ft 11¾ in
2. ..Ehsan Hadadi, Iran	223 ft 8¼ in
3. ..Gerd Kanter, Estonia	223 ft 2¼ in

HAMMER THROW

1. ..Krisztian Pars, Hungary	264 ft 4¾ in
2. ..Primoz Kozmus, Slovakia	260 ft 4⅜ in
3. ..Koji Murofushi, Japan	258 ft 2¾ in

JAVELIN

1. ..Keshorn Walcott, Trin. and Tob.	277 ft 5⅞ in
2....Oleksandr Pyatnytsya, Ukraine	277 ft 3¼ in
3. ..Antti Ruuskanen, Finland	275 ft 11¾ in

DECATHLON

	Pts
1. ..Ashton Eaton, United States	8869
2. ..Trey Hardee, United States	8671
3. ..Leonel Suarez, Cuba	8523

Women

100 METERS

1. ..Shelly-Ann Fraser-Pryce, Jamaica	10.75
2. ..Carmelita Jeter, United States	10.78
3. ..Veronica Campbell-Brown, Jamaica	10.81

200 METERS

1. ..Allyson Felix, United States	21.88
2....Shelly-Ann Fraser-Pryce, Jamaica	22.09
3....Carmelita Jeter, United States	22.14

400 METERS

1. ..Sanya Richards-Ross, United States	49.55
2....Christine Ohuruogu, Great Britain	49.70
3....DeeDee Trotter, United States	49.72

800 METERS

1. ..Mariya Savinova, Russia	1:56.19
2. ..Caster Semenya, South Africa	1:57.23
3. ..Ekaterina Poistogova, Russia	1:57.53

1,500 METERS

1. ..Asli Cakir Alptekin, Turkey	4:10.23
2. ..Gamze Bulut, Turkey	4:10.40
3. ..Maryam Yusuf Jamal, Bahrain	4:10.74

5,000 METERS

1. ..Meseret Defar, Ethiopia	15:04.25
2....Vivian Jepkemoi Cheruiyot, Kenya	15:04.73
3. ..Tirunesh Dibaba, Ethiopia	15:05.15

10,000 METERS

1. ..Tirunesh Dibaba, Ethiopia	30:20.75
2....Sally Jepkosgei Kipyego, Kenya	30:26.37
3....Vivian Jepkemoi Cheruiyot, Kenya	30:30.44

MARATHON

1. ..Tiki Gelana, Ethiopia	2:23:07 OR
2. ..Priscah Jeptoo, Kenya	2:23:12
3....Tatyana Petrova Arkhipova, Russia	2:23:29

100-METER HURDLES

1. ..Sally Pearson, Australia	12.35 OR
2. ..Dawn Harper, United States	12.37
3. ..Kellie Wells, United States	12.48

400-METER HURDLES

1. ..Natalya Antyukh, Russia	52.70
2. ..Lashinda Demus, United States	52.77
3. ..Zuzana Hejnova, Czech Republic	53.38

3,000-METER STEEPLECHASE

1. ..Yuliya Zaripova, Russia	9:06.72
2. ..Habiba Ghribi, Tunisia	9:08.37
3. ..Sofia Assefa, Ethiopia	9:09.84

4 X 100-METER RELAY

1....United States (C. Jeter, T. Madison, A. Felix, B. Knight)	40.82 WR
2. ..Jamaica	41.41
3. ..Ukraine	42.04

Note: OR=Olympic Record. WR=World Record. EOR=Equals Olympic Record. EWR=Equals World Record.

London, England July 27–August 12, 2012
Women (*Cont.*)

4 X 400-METER RELAY
1....United States (A. Felix,F. McCrory, 3:16.87
   S. Richards-Ross, D. Trotter)
2. ..Russia   3:20.23
3. ..Jamaica   3:20.95

20-KILOMETER WALK
1. ..Elena Lashmanova Russia   1:25:02 WR
2. ..Olga Kaniskina, Russia   1:25:09
3. ..Shenjie Qieyang, China   1:25:16

HIGH JUMP
1. ..Anna Chicherova, Russia   6 ft 8¾ in
2. ..Brigetta Barrett, United States   6 ft 7⅛ in
3. ..Svetlana Shkolina, Russia   6 ft 7⅛ in

POLE VAULT
1. ..Jennifer Suhr, United States   15 ft 7 in
2. ..Yarisley Silva, Cuba   15 ft 7 in
3. ..Elena Isinbaeva, Russia   15 ft 5 in

LONG JUMP
1. ..Brittney Reese, United States 23 ft 4¼ in
2. ..Elena Sokolova, Russia   23 ft 2¼ in
3. ..Janay Deloach, United States 22 ft 7⅛ in

TRIPLE JUMP
1. ..Olga Rypakova, Kazakhstan   49 ft 1⅜ in
2....Caterine Ibarguen, Colombia   48 ft 6¾ in
3....Olha Saladuha, Ukraine   48 ft 6¼ in

SHOT PUT
1. ..Nadzeya Ostapchuk, Belarus   70 ft ⅛ in
2. ..Valerie Adams, New Zealand 67 ft 11 in
3. ..Evgeniia Kolodko, Russia   67 ft 2¼ in

DISCUS THROW
1. ..Sandra Perkovic, Croatia   226 ft 8¼ in
2....Darya Pishchalnikova, Russia   221 ft 7⅞ in
3. ..Yanfeng Li, China   220 ft 6½ in

HAMMER THROW
1. ..Tatyana Lysenko, Russia   256 ft 6 in OR
2. ..Anita Wlodarczyk, Poland   254 ft 7⅞ in
3. ..Betty Heidler, Germany   253 ft ¼ in

JAVELIN
1. ..Barbora Spotakova, Czech Rep. 228 ft 2¼ in
2....Christina Obergfoll, Germany   213 ft 9⅞ in
3....Linda Stahl, Germany   212 ft 11½ in

HEPTATHLON   Pts
1. ..Jessica Ennis, Great Britain   6955
2. ..Lilli Schwarzkopf, Germany   6649
3. ..Tatyana Chernova, Russia   6628

Note: OR=Olympic Record. WR=World Record. EOR=Equals Olympic Record. EWR=Equals World Record.

World and American Outdoor Records

As of September 13, 2013. World outdoor records are recognized by the International Amateur Athletics Federation (IAAF). American records recognized by U.S.A. Track & Field. (A) represents an American record, (W) represents a World record.

Men

Event	Mark	Record Holder	Date	Site
100 meters	9.58	Usain Bolt, Jamaica (W)	8-16-09	Berlin
	9.69	Tyson Gay (A)	9-20-09	Shanghai
200 meters	19.19	Usain Bolt, Jamaica (W)	8-20-09	Berlin
	19.32	Michael Johnson (A)	8-01-96	Atlanta
400 meters	43.18	Michael Johnson, U.S. (W,A)	8-26-99	Seville, Spain
800 meters	1:40.91	David Lekuta Rudisha, Kenya (W)	8-9-12	London
	1:42.60	Johnny Gray (A)	8-28-85	Koblenz, Germany
1,000 meters	2:11.96	Noah Ngeny, Kenya (W)	9-05-99	Rieti, Italy
	2:13.90	Rick Wohlhuter (A)	7-30-74	Oslo
1,500 meters	3:26.00	Hicham El Guerrouj, Morocco (W)	7-14-98	Rome
	3:29.30	Bernard Lagat (A)	8-28-05	Rieti, Italy
Mile	3:43.13	Hicham El Guerrouj, Morocco (W)	7-07-99	Rome
	3:46.91	Alan Webb (A)	7-21-07	Brasschaat, Belguim
2,000 meters	4:44.79	Hicham El Guerrouj, Morocco (W)	9-07-99	Berlin
	4:52.44	Jim Spivey (A)	9-15-87	Lausanne, Switzerland
3,000 meters	7:20.67	Daniel Komen, Kenya (W)	9-01-96	Rieti, Italy
	7:29.00	Bernard Lagat (A)	8-29-10	Rieti, Italy
3,000-m Steeplechase	7:53.63	Saif Saaeed Shaheen, Qatar (W)	9-03-04	Brussels
	8:06.81	Evan Jaeger (A)	7-20-12	Fontvielle, Monaco
5,000 meters	12:37.35	Kenenisa Bekele, Ethiopia (W)	5-31-04	Hengelo, Netherlands
	12:53.60	Bernard Lagat (A)	7-22-11	Fontvielle, Monaco
10,000 meters	26:17.53	Kenenisa Bekele, Ehtiopia (W)	8-26-05	Brussels
	26:48.00	Galen Rupp (A)	9-16-11	Brussels
Marathon	2:03:23	Wilson Kipsang, Kenya (W)	9-29-13	Berlin
	2:05:38	Khalid Khannouchi (A)	4-14-02	London
110-meter hurdles	12.80	Aries Merritt, United States (W, A)	9-7-12	Brussels
400-meter hurdles	46.78	Kevin Young, United States (W, A)	8-6-92	Barcelona
20-kilometer walk	1:17.16	Vladimir Kanaykin, Russia (W)	9-29-07	Saransk, Russia
	1:22:02	Tim Seaman (A)	5-23-04	Vallensbaek, Denmark
50-kilometer walk	3:34:14	Denis Nizhegorodov, Russia (W)	5-11-08	Cheboksary, Russia
	3:48:04	Curt Clausen (A)	5-2-99	Mezidon, France
4 x 100-meter relay	36.84	Jamaica (Nesta Carter, (W) Michael Prater, Yohan Blake, Usain Bolt)	8-11-12	London
	37.04	Trell Kimmons, Justin Gatlin, (A) Tyson Gay, Ryan Bailey	8-11-12	London

Men (*Cont.*)

4 x 200-meter relay	1:18.68	U.S. (Mike Marsh, Leroy Burrell, (W,A) 4-17-94 Floyd Heard, Carl Lewis)	Walnut, Calif.
4 x 400-meter relay	2:54.29	U.S. (Andrew Valmon, (W,A) 8-22-93 Quincy Watts, Butch Reynolds, Michael Johnson)	Stuttgart, Germany
4 x 800-meter relay	7:02.43	Kenya (Wilfred Bungei, (W) 8-25-06 William Yiampoy, Joseph Mutua, Ismael Kombich)	Brussels
	7:02.82	Jebreh Harris, Khadevis Robinson, (A) 8-25-06 Sam Burley, David Krummenacker	Brussels
4 x 1,500-meter relay	14:36.23	Kenya (W) 9-04-09 (William Biwoot Tanui, Gideon Gathimba, Geoffrey Kipkoech Rono, Augustine Kiprono Choge)	Brussels
	14:46.30	Dan Aldridge, Andy Clifford, (A) 6-24-79 Todd Harbour, Tom Duits	Bourges, France
High jump	2.45m	Javier Sotomayor, Cuba (W)	7-27-93	Salamanca, Spain
	2.40m	Charles Austin (A)	8-07-91	Zurich
Pole vault	6.14m	Sergei Bubka, Ukraine (W)	7-31-94	Sestriere, Italy
	6.04m	Brad Walker (A)	6-08-08	Eugene, Oregon
Long jump	8.95m	Mike Powell, United States (W, A)	8-30-91	Tokyo
Triple jump	18.29m	Jonathan Edwards, U.K. (W)	8-07-95	Göteborg, Sweden
	18.09m	Kenny Harrison (A)	7-27-96	Atlanta
Shot put	23.12m	Randy Barnes, United States (W, A)	5-20-90	Westwood, California
Discus throw	74.08m	Jürgen Schult, East Germany (W)	6-06-86	Neubrandenburg, Germany
	72.34m	Ben Plucknett (A)	7-07-81	Stockholm
Hammer throw	86.74m	Yuriy Syedikh, USSR (W)	8-30-86	Stuttgart, Germany
	82.52m	Lance Deal (A)	9-17-96	Milan
Javelin throw	98.48m	Jan Zelezny, Czech Republic (W)	5-25-96	Jena, Germany
	91.29m	Breaux Greer (A)	6-21-07	Indianapolis
Decathlon	9039 pts	Ashton Eaton, United States (W, A)	6-23-12	Eugene, Oregon

Note: The decathlon consists of 10 events: the 100 meters, long jump, shot put, high jump and 400 meters on the first day; the 110-meter hurdles, discus, pole vault, javelin and 1,500 meters on the second.

Women

Event	Mark	Record Holder	Date	Site
100 meters	10.49	Florence Griffith Joyner, U.S. (W, A)	7-16-88	Indianapolis
200 meters	21.34	Florence Griffith Joyner, U.S. (W, A)	9-29-88	Seoul
400 meters	47.60	Marita Koch, E Germany (W)	10-6-85	Canberra, Australia
	~48.70	Sanya Richards-Ross (A)	9-17-06	Athens
800 meters	1:53.28	Jarmila Kratochvílová, Czech. (W)	7-26-83	Munich
	1:56.40	Jearl Miles Clark (A)	8-11-99	Zurich
1,000 meters	2:28.98	Svetlana Masterkova, Russia (W)	8-23-96	Brussels
	2:31.80	Regina Jacobs (A)	7-03-99	Brunswick, Maine
1,500 meters	3:50.46	Yunxia Qu, China (W)	9-11-93	Beijing
	3:57.12	Mary Slaney (A)	7-26-83	Stockholm
Mile	4:12.56	Svetlana Masterkova, Russia (W)	8-14-96	Zurich
	4:16.71	Mary Slaney (A)	8-21-85	Zurich
2,000 meters	5:25.35	Sonia O'Sullivan, Ireland (W)	7-08-94	Edinburgh
	5:32.70	Mary Slaney (A)	8-03-84	Eugene, Oregon
3,000 meters	8:06.11	Junxia Wang, China (W)	9-13-93	Beijing
	8:25.83	Mary Slaney (A)	9-07-85	Rome
3,000-m Steeplechase	8:58.81	Gulnara Samitova-Galkina, Russia (W)	8-17-08	Beijing
	9:12.50	Jenny Simpson (A)	8-17-09	Berlin
5,000 meters	14:11.15	Tirunesh Dibaba, Ethiopia (W)	6-06-08	Oslo
	14:44.76	Molly Huddle (A)	8-27-10	Brussels
10,000 meters	29:31.78	Junxia Wang, China (W)	9-08-93	Beijing
	30:22.22	Shalane Flanagan (A)	8-15-08	Beijing
Marathon	2:15:25	Paula Radcliffe, Great Britain (W)	4-13-03	London
	2:19:36	Deena Kastor (A)	4-23-06	London
100-meter hurdles	12.21	Yordanka Donkova, Bulgaria (W)	8-20-88	Stara Zagora, Bulgaria
	12.26	Brianna Rollins (A)	6-22-13	Des Moines, Iowa
400-meter hurdles	52.34	Yuliya Pechonkina, Russia (W)	8-08-03	Tula, Russia
	52.47	Lashinda Demus (A)	9-01-11	Daegu, South Korea
20-kilometer walk	1:25:02	Yelena Lashmanova, Russia (W)	8-11-12	London
	1:31:51	Michelle Rohl (A)	5-13-00	Kenosha, Wisconsin
4 x 100-meter relay	40.82	United States (Tianna Madison, (W, A) 8-11-12 Allyson Felix, Bianca Knight, Carmelita Jeter)	London
4 x 200-meter relay	1:27.46	United States (LaTasha Jenkins, (W, A) 4-29-00 LaTasha Colander-Richardson, Nanceen Perry, Marion Jones)	Philadelphia

Women *(Cont.)*

4 x 400-meter relay........3:15.17	USSR (Tatyana Ledovskaya, (W) 10-01-88 Olga Nazarova, Maria Pinigina, Olga Bryzgina)		Seoul
3:15.51	Denean Howard, Diane Dixon, (A) 10-01-88 Valerie Brisco, Florence Griffith-Joyner		Seoul
4 x 800-meter relay........7:50.17	USSR (Nadezhda Olizarenko, (W) 8-05-84 Lyubov Gurina, Lyudmila Borisova, Irina Podyalovskaya)		Moscow
8:04.31	Lea Wallace, Brenda Martinez (A) 4-27-13 Ajee Wilson, Alysia Montano		Philadelphia
High jump 2.09m	Stefka Kostadinova, Bulgaria (W)	8-30-87	Rome
2.05m	Chaunte Lowe (A)	6-26-10	Des Moines, Iowa
Pole vault 5.06m	Yelena Isinbayeva, Russia (W)	8-28-09	Zurich
5.02m	Jenn Suhr (A)	3-01-13	Albuquerque, New Mexico
Long jump.......................7.52m	Galina Chistyakova, USSR (W)	6-11-88	St. Petersburg, Russia
7.49m	Jackie Joyner-Kersee (A)	7-31-94	Sestriere, Italy
Triple jump 15.50m	Inessa Kravets, Ukraine (W)	8-10-95	Göteborg, Sweden
14.45m	Tiombe Hurd (A)	7-11-04	Sacramento, Calif.
Shot put.........................22.63m	Natalya Lisovskaya, USSR (W)	6-07-87	Moscow
20.24m	Michelle Carter (A)	6-22-13	Des Moines, Idaho
Discus throw 76.80m	Gabriele Reinsch, East Germany (W)	7-09-88	Neubrandenburg, Germany
67.74m	Stephanie Brown-Trafton (A)	5-4-12	Wailuku, Hawaii
Hammer throw 79.42m	Betty Heidler, Germany (W)	5-21-11	Halle, Germany
75.73m	Amanda Bingson (A)	6-22-13	Des Moines, Idaho
Javelin throw................72.28m	Barbora Spotakova, Czech Rep. (W)	9-13-08	Stuttgart, Germany
66.67m	Kara Patterson (A)	6-25-10	Des Moines, Iowa
Heptathlon ....7291 pts	Jackie Joyner-Kersee, U.S. (W,A)	9-24-88	Seoul

Note: The heptathlon consists of 7 events: the 100-meter hurdles, high jump, shot put and 200 meters on the first day; the long jump, javelin and 800 meters on the second.

World and American Indoor Records

As of September 13, 2013. World Indoor records are recognized by the International Amateur Athletics Federation (IAAF). American indoor records are recognized by USA Track and Field. (A) represents an American record, (W) represents a World record.

Men

Event	Mark	Record Holder	Date	Site
50 meters 5.56		Donovan Bailey, Canada (W)	2-09-96	Reno, Nev.
	5.56	Maurice Greene (A)	2-13-99	Los Angeles
60 meters 6.39		Maurice Greene (W, A)	2-03-98	Madrid
	6.39	Maurice Greene (W, A)	3-03-01	Atlanta
200 meters 19.92		Frankie Fredericks, Namibia (W)	2-18-96	Liévin, France
	20.10	Wallace Spearmon (A)	3-11-05	Fayetteville, Ark.
400 meters 44.57		Kerron Clement (W, A)	3-12-05	Fayetteville, Ark.
800 meters 1:40.91		David Lekuta Rudisha, Kenya (W)	8-09-12	London
	1:45.00	Johnny Gray (A)	3-08-92	Sindelfingen, Germany
1,000 meters 2:14.96		Wilson Kipketer, Denmark (W)	2-20-00	Birmingham, England
	2:17.86	David Krummenacker (A)	1-27-02	Boston
1,500 meters 3:31.18		Hicham El Guerrouj, Morocco (W)	2-02-97	Stuttgart, Germany
	3:33.34	Bernard Lagat (A)	2-11-05	Fayetteville, Ark.
Mile.................................3:48.45		Hicham El Guerrouj, Morocco (W)	2-12-97	Ghent, Belgium
	3:49.89	Bernard Lagat (A)	2-11-05	Fayetteville, Ark.
3,000 meters 7:24.90		Daniel Komen, Kenya (W)	2-06-98	Budapest, Hungary
	7:30.16	Galen Rupp (A)	2-21-13	Stockholm, Sweden
5,000 meters 12:49.60		Kenenisa Bekele, Ethiopia (W)	2-20-04	Birmingham, England
	13:07.00	Lopez Lomong (A)	3-01-13	New York City
50-meter hurdles...................6.25		Mark McKoy, Canada (W)	3-05-86	Kobe, Japan
	6.35	Greg Foster (A)	1-31-87	Ottawa
	6.35	Greg Foster (A)	1-27-85	Rosemont, Illinois
60-meter hurdles...................7.30		Colin Jackson, Great Britain (W)	3-6-94	Sindelfingen, Germany
	7.36	Greg Foster (A)	1-16-87	Los Angeles
	7.36	Allen Johnson (A)	3-06-04	Budapest, Hungary
	7.36	Terrence Trammell (A)	3-14-10	Doha, Qatar
5,000-meter walk.............18:07.08		Mikhail Shchennikov, Russia (W)	2-14-95	Moscow
	19:15.88	Tim Seaman (A)	2-25-06	Boston

Men *(Cont.)*

Event	Mark	Record Holder	Date	Site
4 x 200-meter relay	1:22.11	United Kingdom (Linford Christie, (W) Darren Braithwaite, Ade Mafe, John Regis)	3-03-91	Glasgow
	1:22.71	National Team (A) (Thomas Jefferson, Raymond Pierre, Antonio McKay, Kevin Little)	3-03-91	Glasgow
4 x 400-meter relay	3:01.96	United States (W, A) (Kerron Clement, Wallace Spearmon Darold Williamson, Jeremy Wariner)	2-11-06	Fayetteville, Ark.
4 x 800-meter relay	7:13.94	United States (W, A) (Joey Woody, Karl Paranya, Rich Kenah, David Krummenacker)	2-06-00	Boston
High jump	2.43m	Javier Sotomayor, Cuba (W)	3-4-89	Budapest, Hungary
	2.40m	Hollis Conway (A)	3-10-91	Seville
Pole vault	6.15m	Sergei Bubka, Ukraine (W)	2-21-93	Donetsk, Ukraine
	6.02m	Jeff Hartwig (A)	3-10-02	Sindelfingen, Germany
Long jump	8.79m	Carl Lewis (W, A)	1-27-84	New York City
Triple jump	17.92m	Teddy Tamgho, France (W)	3-6-11	Paris
	17.76m	Mike Conley (A)	2-27-87	New York City
Shot put	22.66m	Randy Barnes (W, A)	1-20-89	Los Angeles
Weight throw*	25.86m	Lance Deal (A)	3-04-95	Atlanta
Pentathlon*	4478 pts	Steve Fritz, (A)	1-14-95	Lawrence, Kan.
Heptathlon	6645 pts	Ashton Eaton (W, A)	3-10-12	Istanbul

Women

Event	Mark	Record Holder	Date	Site
50 meters	5.96	Irina Privolova, Russia (W)	2-09-95	Madrid
	6.02	Gail Devers (A)	2-22-99	Liévin, France
55 meters*	6.56	Gwen Torrence (A)	3-14-87	Oklahoma City, Okla.
60 meters	6.92	Irina Privalova, Russia (W)	2-11-93	Madrid
	6.92	Irina Privalova, Russia (W)	2-09-95	Madrid
	6.95	Gail Devers (A)	3-12-93	Toronto
	6.95	Marion Jones (A)	3-07-98	Maebashi, Japan
200 meters	21.87	Merlene Ottey, Jamaica (W)	2-13-93	Liévin, France
	22.33	Gwen Torrence (A)	3-02-66	Atlanta
400 meters	49.59	Jarmila Kratochvilová, Czecho. (W)	3-07-82	Milan
	50.54	Francena McCorory (A)	3-13-10	Fayetteville, Ark.
800 meters	1:55.82	Jolanda Ceplak, Slovenia (W)	3-03-02	Vienna
	1:58.71	Nicole Teter (A)	3-02-02	New York City
1,000 meters	2:30.94	Maria Mutola, Mozambique (W)	2-25-99	Stockholm
	2:34.19	Jennifer Toomey (A)	2-20-04	Birmingham, England
1,500 meters	3:58.28	Yelena Soboleva, Russia (W)	2-18-06	Moscow
	3:59.98	Regina Jacobs, (A)	2-01-03	Boston
Mile	4:17.14	Doina Melinte, Romania (W)	2-09-90	East Rutherford, N.J.
	4:20.50	Mary Slaney (A)	2-19-82	San Diego
3,000 meters	8:23.72	Meseret Defar, Ethiopia (W)	2-03-07	Stuttgart, Germany
	8:33.25	Shalane Flanagan (A)	1-27-07	Boston
5,000 meters	14:24.37	Meseret Defar, Ethiopia (W)	2-18-09	Stockholm
	14:47.62	Shalane Flanagan (A)	2-07-09	Boston
50-meter hurdles	6.58	Cornelia Oschkenat, E Germany (W)	2-20-88	Berlin
	6.67	Jackie Joyner-Kersee (A)	2-10-95	Reno, Nev.
55-meter hurdles*	7.37	Jackie Joyner-Kersee (A)	2-03-89	New York City
60-meter hurdles	7.68	Susanna Kallur, Sweden (W)	2-20-08	Karlsruhe, Germany
	7.72	Lolo Jones (A)	3-13-10	Doha, Qatar
3,000-meter walk	11:40.33	Claudia Stef, Romania (W)	1-30-99	Bucharest, Romania
	12:20.79	Debbi Lawrence (A)	3-12-93	Toronto
4 x 200-meter relay	1:32.41	Russia (Y, Kondratyeva, (W) I. Khabarova, Y. Pechonkina, Y. Gushchina)	1-29-05	Glasgow
	1:33.24	Flirtisha Harris, Chryste Gaines, (A) Terri Dendy, Michele Collins	2-12-94	Glasgow
4 x 400-meter relay	3:23.37	Russia (Y. Gushchina, (W) O. Kotlyarova, O. Zaytseva, O. Krasnomovets)	1-28-06	Glasgow
	3:27.34	Debbie Dunn, DeeDee Trotter, (A) Natasha Hastings, Allyson Felix	3-14-10	Doha, Qatar
4 x 800-meter relay	8:06.24	Russia, (A. Bulanova, E. Martynova, (W) E. Kofanova, A. Balakshina)	2-18-11	Moscow
	8:28.41	Wisconsin (Sarah Renk, (A) Kim Sherman, Sue Gentes, Amy Wickus)	3-14-92	Indianapolis

*No recognized world record.

Women *(Cont.)*

Event	Mark	Record Holder	Date	Site
High jump	2.08m	Kajsa Bergqvist, Sweden (W)	2-4-06	
Arnstadt, Germany				
	2.02m	Chaunte Lowe (A)	2-26-12	Albuquerque, N.M.
Pole vault	5.02m	Jenn.Suhr (W, A)	3-01-13	Albuquerque, N.M.
Long jump	7.37m	Heike Drechsler, East Germany (W)	2-13-88	Vienna
	7.23m	Brittney Reese (A)	3-11-12	Istanbul
Triple jump	15.36m	Tatyana Lebedeva, Russia (W)	3-6-04	Budapest, Hungary
	14.23m	Sheila Hudson-Strudwick (A)	3-4-95	Atlanta
Shot put	22.50m	Helena Fibingerová, Czecho. (W)	2-19-77	Jablonec, Czecho.
	19.89m	Jillian Camarena-Williams (A)	2-11-12	Fayetteville, Ark.
Weight throw*	25.56m	Brittany Riley (A)	3-10-07	Fayetteville, Ark.
Pentathlon	5013 pts	Nataliya Dobrynska, Ukraine (W)	3-9-12	Istanbul
	4753 pts	DeDee Nathan (A)	3-05-99	Maebashi, Japan
	4753 pts	Hyleas Fountain (A)	3-13-10	Doha, Qatar

*No recognized world record.

World Track and Field Championships

Men

100 METERS

1983	Carl Lewis, United States	10.07
1987*	Carl Lewis, United States	9.93 WR
1991	Carl Lewis, United States	9.86 WR
1993	Linford Christie, Great Britain	9.87
1995	Donovan Bailey, Canada	9.97
1997	Maurice Greene, United States	9.86
1999	Maurice Greene, United States	9.80
2001	Maurice Greene, United States	9.82
2003	Kim Collins, St. Kitts & Nevis	10.07
2005	Justin Gatlin, United States	9.88
2007	Tyson Gay, United States	9.85
2009	Usain Bolt, Jamaica	9.58WR
2011	Yohan Blake, Jamaica	9.92
2013	Usain Bolt, Jamaica	9.77

200 METERS

1983	Calvin Smith, United States	20.14
1987	Calvin Smith, United States	20.16
1991	Michael Johnson, United States	20.01
1993	Frank Fredericks, Namibia	19.85
1995	Michael Johnson, United States	19.79
1997	Ato Boldon, Trinidad and Tobago	20.04
1999	Maurice Greene, United States	19.90
2001	Konstadínos Kedéris, Greece	20.04
2003	John Capel, United States	20.30
2005	Justin Gatlin, United States	20.04
2007	Tyson Gay, United States	19.76
2009	Usain Bolt, Jamaica	19.19WR
2011	Usain Bolt, Jamaica	19.40
2013	Usain Bolt, Jamaica	19.66

400 METERS

1983	Bert Cameron, Jamaica	45.05
1987	Thomas Schoenlebe, E Germany	44.33
1991	Antonio Pettigrew, United States	44.57
1993	Michael Johnson, United States	43.65
1995	Michael Johnson, United States	43.39
1997	Michael Johnson, United States	44.12
1999	Michael Johnson, United States	43.18 WR
2001	Avard Moncur, Bahamas	44.64
2003	Jerome Young, United States	44.50
2005	Jeremy Wariner, United States	43.93
2007	Jeremy Wariner, United States	43.45
2009	LaShawn Merritt, United States	44.06
2011	Kirani James, Grenada	44.60
2013	LaShawn Merritt, United States	43.74

800 METERS

1983	Willi Wulbeck, West Germany	1:43.65
1987	Billy Konchellah, Kenya	1:43.06
1991	Billy Konchellah, Kenya	1:43.99
1993	Paul Ruto, Kenya	1:44.71
1995	Wilson Kipketer, Denmark	1:45.08
1997	Wilson Kipketer, Denmark	1:43.38
1999	Wilson Kipketer, Denmark	1:43.30
2001	André Bucher, Switzerland	1:43.70
2003	Djabir Saïd-Guerni, Algeria	1:44.81
2005	Rashid Ramzi, Brunei	1:44.24
2007	Alfred Kirwa Yego	1:47.09
2009	Mbulaeni Mulaudzi, South Africa	1:45.29
2011	David Lekuta Rudisha, Kenya	1:43.91
2013	Mohammed Aman, Ethiopia	1:43.31

1,500 METERS

1983	Steve Cram, Great Britain	3:41.59
1987	Abdi Bile, Somalia	3:36.80
1991	Noureddine Morceli, Algeria	3:32.84
1993	Noureddine Morceli, Algeria	3:34.24
1995	Noureddine Morceli, Algeria	3:33.73
1997	Hicham El Guerrouj, Morocco	3:35.83
1999	Hicham El Guerrouj, Morocco	3:27.65
2001	Hicham El Guerrouj, Morocco	3:30.68
2003	Hicham El Guerrouj, Morocco	3:31.77
2005	Rashid Ramzi, Brunei	3:37.88
2007	Bernard Lagat, United States	3:34.77
2009	Yusuf Kamel, Bahrain	3:35.93
2011	Asbel Kiprop, Kenya	3:35.69
2013	Asbel Kiprop, Kenya	3:36.28

3,000-METER STEEPLECHASE

1983	Patriz Ilg, West Germany	8:15.06
1987	Francesco Panetta, Italy	8:08.57
1991	Moses Kiptanui, Kenya	8:12.59
1993	Moses Kiptanui, Kenya	8:06.36
1995	Moses Kiptanui, Kenya	8:04.16
1997	Wilson Boit Kipketer, Kenya	8:05.84
1999	Christopher Koskei, Kenya	8:11.76
2001	Reuben Kosgei, Kenya	8:15.16
2003	Saif Saaeed Shaheen, Qatar	8:04.39
2005	Saif Saaeed Shaheen, Qatar	8:13.31
2007	Brimin Kipruto, Kenya	8:13.82
2009	Ezekiel Kemboi, Kenya	8:00.43
2011	Ezekiel Kemboi, Kenya	8:14.85
2013	Ezekiel Kemboi, Kenya	8:06.01

WR=World record. *Ben Johnson, Canada, disqualified.

Men *(Cont.)*

5,000 METERS

1983	Eamonn Coghlan, Ireland	13:28.53
1987	Said Aouita, Morocco	13:26.44
1991	Yobes Ondieki, Kenya	13:14.45
1993	Ismael Kirui, Kenya	13:02.75
1995	Ismael Kirui, Kenya	13:16.77
1997	Daniel Komen, Kenya	13:07.38
1999	Salah Hissou, Morocco	12:58.13
2001	Richard Limo, Kenya	13:00.77
2003	Eliud Kipchoge, Kenya	12:52.79
2005	Benjamin Limo, Kenya	13:32.55
2007	Bernard Lagat, United States	13:45.87
2009	Kenenisa Bekele, Ethiopia	13:17.09
2011	Mohamed Farah, U.K.	13:23.36
2013	Mohamed Farah, U.K.	13:26.98

10,000 METERS

1983	Alberto Cova, Italy	28:01.04
1987	Paul Kipkoech, Kenya	27:38.63
1991	Moses Tanui, Kenya	27:38.74
1993	Haile Gebrselassie, Ethiopia	27:46.02
1995	Haile Gebrselassie, Ethiopia	27:12.95
1997	Haile Gebrselassie, Ethiopia	27:24.58
1999	Haile Gebrselassie, Ethiopia	27:57.27
2001	Charles Kamathi, Kenya	27:53.25
2003	Kenenisa Bekele, Ethiopia	26:49.57
2005	Kenenisa Bekele, Ethiopia	27:08.33
2007	Kenenisa Bekele, Ethiopia	27:05.90
2009	Kenenisa Bekele, Ethiopia	26:46.31
2011	Ibrahim Jeilan, Ethiopia	27:13.81
2013	Mohamed Farah, U.K.	27:21.71

MARATHON

1983	Rob de Castella, Australia	2:10:03
1987	Douglas Wakiihuri, Kenya	2:11:48
1991	Hiromi Taniguchi, Japan	2:14:57
1993	Mark Plaatjes, United States	2:13:57
1995	Martín Fiz, Spain	2:11:41
1997	Abel Anton, Spain	2:13:16
1999	Abel Anton, Spain	2:13:36
2001	Gezahegne Abera, Ethiopia	2:12:42
2003	Jaouad Gharib, Morocco	2:08.31
2005	Jaouad Gharib, Morocco	2:10:10
2007	Luke Kibet, Kenya	2:15:59
2009	Abel Kirui, Kenya	2:06.54
2011	Abel Kirui, Kenya	2:07:38
2013	Stephen Kiprotech, Uganda	2:09.51

110-METER HURDLES

1983	Greg Foster, United States	13.42
1987	Greg Foster, United States	13.21
1991	Greg Foster, United States	13.06
1993	Colin Jackson, Great Britain	12.91 WR
1995	Allen Johnson, United States	13.00
1997	Allen Johnson, United States	12.93
1999	Colin Jackson, Great Britain	13.04
2001	Allen Johnson, United States	13.04
2003	Allen Johnson, United States	13.12
2005	Ladji Doucoure, France	13:07
2007	Liu Xiang, China	12.95
2009	Ryan Brathwaite, Barbados	13.14
2011	Jason Richardson, United States	13.16
2013	David Oliver, United States	13.00

400-METER HURDLES

1983	Edwin Moses, United States	47.50
1987	Edwin Moses, United States	47.46
1991	Samuel Matete, Zambia	47.64
1993	Kevin Young, United States	47.18
1995	Derrick Adkins, United States	47.98
1997	Stéphane Diagana, France	47.70
1999	Fabrizio Mori, Italy	47.72
2001	Felix Sánchez, Dominican Rep.	47.49

400-METER HURDLES *(Cont.)*

2003	Felix Sánchez, Dominican Rep.	47.25
2005	Bershawn Jackson, United States	47.30
2007	Kerron Clement, United States	47.61
2009	Kerron Clement, United States	47.91
2011	David Greene, United Kingdom	48.26
2013	Jehue Gordon, Trinidad	47.69

20-KILOMETER WALK

1983	Ernesto Canto, Mexico	1:20:49
1987	Maurizio Damilano, Italy	1:20:45
1991	Maurizio Damilano, Italy	1:19:37
1993	Valentin Massana, Spain	1:22:31
1995	Michele Didoni, Italy	1:19:59
1997	Daniel Garcia, Mexico	1:21:43
1999	Ilya Markov, Russia	1:23:34
2001	Roman Rasskazov, Russia	1:20:31
2003	Jefferson Pérez, Ecuador	1:17.21 WR
2005	Jefferson Pérez, Ecuador	1:18:35
2007	Jefferson Pérez, Ecuador	1:22:20
2009	Valeriy Borchin, Russia	1:18.41
2011	Valeriy Borchin, Russia	1:19.56
2013	Aleksandr Ivanov, Russia	1:20.58

50-KILOMETER WALK

1983	Ronald Weigel, East Germany	3:43:08
1987	Hartwig Gauder, East Germany	3:40:53
1991	Aleksandr Potashov, USSR	3:53:09
1993	Jesus Angel Garcia, Spain	3:41:41
1995	Valentin Kononen, Finland	3:43:42
1997	Robert Korzeniowski, Poland	3:44:46
1999	German Skurygin, Russia	3:44:23
2001	Robert Korzeniowski, Poland	3:42:08
2003	R. Korzeniowski, Poland	3:36:03 WR
2005	S. Kirdyapkin, Russia	3:38:08
2007	Nathan Deakes, Australia	3:43:53
2009	Sergey Kirdyapkin, Russia	3:38.35
2011	Sergey Bakulin, Russia	3:41.24
2013	Robert Heffernan, Ireland	3:37.56

4 X 100-METER RELAY

1983	United States (E. King, W. Gault, C. Smith, C. Lewis)	37.86
1987	United States (L. McRae, L. McNeil, H. Glance, C. Lewis)	37.90
1991	United States (A. Cason, L. Burrell, D. Mitchell, C. Lewis)	37.50 WR
1993	United States (J. Drummond, A. Cason, D. Mitchell, L. Burrell)	37.48
1995	Canada (R. Esmie, G. Gilbert, B. Surin, D. Bailey)	38.31
1997	Canada (R. Esmie, G. Gilbert, B. Surin, D. Bailey)	37.86
1999	United States (J. Drummond, T. Montgomery, B. Lewis, M. Greene)	37.59
2001	United States (M. Grimes, B. Williams, D. Mitchell, T. Montgomery)	37.96
2003	United States (J. Capel, B. Williams, D. Patton, J. Johnson)	38.06
2005	Trinidad and Tobago (L. Doucoure, R. Pognon, E. De Lepine, D. Lueyi)	38.08
2007	United States (D. Patton, W. Spearmon, T. Gay, L. Dixon)	37.78
2009	Jamaica (S. Mullings, M. Frater, U. Bolt, A. Powell)	37.31
2011	Jamaica (N. Carter, M. Frater, Y. Blake, U. Bolt)	37.04 WR
2013	Jamaica (N. Carter, K. Bailey-Cole, N. Ashmeade, U. Bolt)	37.36

WR=World record.

Men *(Cont.)*

4 X 400-METER RELAY

1983	USSR (S. Lovachev, A. Troschilo,	3:00.79
	N. Chernyetski, V. Markin)	
1987	United States (D. Everett	2:57.29
	R. Haley, A. McKay,B. Reynolds)	
1991	Great Britain (R. Black,	2:57.53
	D. Redmond, J. Regis, K. Akabusi)	
1993	United States (A. Valmon,	2:54.29 WR
	Q. Watts, B. Reynolds, M. Johnson)	
1995	United States (M. Ramsey,	2:57.32
	D. Mills, B. Reynolds, M. Johnson)	
1997	United States (J. Young,	2:56.47
	A. Pettigrew, C. Jones, T. Washington)	
1999	United States (J. Davis,	2:56.45
	A. Pettigrew, A.Taylor, M. Johnson)	
2001	United States (L. Byrd,	2:57.54
	A. Pettigrew, D. Brew, A. Taylor)	
2003	United States (C. Harrison,	2:58.88
	T. Washington, D. Brew, J. Young)	
2005	United States (D. Brew,	2:56.91
	R. Andrew, D. Williamson, B. Wariner)	
2007	United States (L. Merritt,	2:55.56
	A. Taylor, D. Williamson, J. Wariner)	
2009	United States (A. Taylor,	2:57.86
	J. Wariner, K. Clement, L. Merritt)	
2011	United States (G. Nixon,	2:59.31
	B. Jackson, A. Taylor, L. Merritt)	
2013	United States (D. Verburg,	2:58.71
	T. McQuay, A. Hall, L. Merritt	

HIGH JUMP

1983	Gennadi Avdeyenko, USSR	2.32m
1987	Patrik Sjoberg, Sweden	2.38m
1991	Charles Austin, United States	2.38m
1993	Javier Sotomayor, Cuba	2.40mWR
1995	Troy Kemp, Bahamas	2.37m
1997	Javier Sotomayor, Cuba	2.37m
1999	Vyacheslav Voronin, Russia	2.37m
2001	Martin Buss, Germany	2.36m
2003	Jacques Freitag, South Africa	2.35m
2005	Yuriy Krymarenko,Ukraine	2.32m
2007	Donald Thoma, Bahamas	2.35m
2009	Yaroslav Rybakov, Russia	2.32m
2011	Jesse Williams, United States	2.35m
2013	Bohdan Bondarenko, Ukraine	2.41m

POLE VAULT

1983	Sergei Bubka, USSR	5.70m
1987	Sergei Bubka, USSR	5.85m
1991	Sergei Bubka, USSR	5.95m
1993	Sergei Bubka, Ukraine	6.00m
1995	Sergei Bubka, Ukraine	5.92m
1997	Sergei Bubka, Ukraine	6.01m
1999	Maksim Tarasov, Russia	6.02m
2001	Dmitri Markov, Australia	6.05mWR
2003	Guiseppe Gibilisco, Italy	5.90m
2005	Rens Blom, Netherlands	5.80m
2007	Brad Walker, United States	5.86m
2009	Steven Hooker, Australia	5.90m
2011	Pawel Wojciechowski, Poland	5.90m
2013	Raphael Holzdeppe, Germany	5.89m

LONG JUMP

1983	Carl Lewis, United States	8.55m
1987	Carl Lewis, United States	8.67m
1991	Mike Powell, United States	8.95mWR
1993	Mike Powell, United States	8.59m
1995	Iván Pedroso, Cuba	8.71m
1997	Iván Pedroso, Cuba	8.51m
1999	Iván Pedroso, Cuba	8.62m
2001	Iván Pedroso, Cuba	8.43m
2003	Dwight Phillips, United States	8.29m

LONG JUMP *(Cont.)*

2005	Dwight Phillips, United States	8.60m
2007	Irving Saladino, Panama	8.57m
2009	Dwight Phillips, United States	8.54m
2011	Dwight Phillips, United States	8.45m
2013	Aleksandr Menkov, Russia	8.56m

TRIPLE JUMP

1983	Zdzislaw Hoffmann, Poland	17.42m
1987	Hristo Markov, Bulgaria	17.92m
1991	Kenny Harrison, United States	17.78m
1993	Mike Conley, United States	17.86m
1995	Jonathan Edwards, G.B.	18.29m WR
1997	Yoelvis Quesada, Cuba	17.85m
1999	Charles Friedek, Germany	17.59m
2001	Jonathan Edwards, G. Britain	17.92m
2003	Christian Olsson, Sweden	17.72m
2005	Walter Davis, United States	17.57m
2007	Nelson Evora, Portugal	17.74m
2009	Phillips Idowu, United Kingdom	17.73m
2011	Christian Taylor, United States	17.96m
2013	Teddy Tamgho, France	18.04m

SHOT PUT

1983	Edward Sarul, Poland	21.39m
1987	Werner Günthör, Switz.	22.23mWR
1991	Werner Günthör, Switz.	21.67m
1993	Werner Günthör, Switz.	21.97m
1995	John Godina, United States	21.47m
1997	John Godina, United States	21.44m
1999	C.J. Hunter, United States	21.79m
2001	John Godina, United States	21.87m
2003	Andrei Mikahnevic, Bulgaria	21.69m
2005	Adam Nelson, United States	21.73m
2007	Reese Hoffa, United States	22.04m
2009	Christian Cantwell, United States	22.03m
2011	David Storl, Germany	21.78m
2013	David Storl, Germany	21.73m

DISCUS THROW

1983	Imrich Bugar, Czechoslovakia	67.72m
1987	Juergen Schult, East Germany	68.74m
1991	Lars Riedel, Germany	66.20m
1993	Lars Riedel, Germany	67.72m
1995	Lars Riedel, Germany	68.76m
1997	Lars Riedel, Germany	68.54m
1999	Anthony Washington, U.S.	69.08m
2001	Lars Riedel, Germany	69.72m
2003	Virgilijus Alekna, Lithuania	69.69m
2005	Virgilijus Alekna, Lithuania	70.17mWR
2007	Gerd Kanter, Estonia	68.94m
2009	Robert Harting, Germany	69.43m
2011	Robert Harting, Germany	68.97m
2013	Robert Harting, Germany	69.11m

HAMMER THROW

1983	Sergei Litvinov, USSR	82.68m
1987	Sergei Litvinov, USSR	83.06m
1991	Yuriy Sedykh, USSR	81.70m
1993	Andrei Abduvaliyev, Tajikistan	81.64m
1995	Andrey Abduvaliyev, Tajikistan	81.56m
1997	Heinz Weis, Germany	81.78m
1999	Karsten Kobs, Germany	80.24m
2001	Szymon Ziolkowski, Poland	83.38m
2003	Ivan Tikhon, Belarus	83.05m
2005	Ivan Tikhon, Belarus	83.89mWR
2007	Ivan Tikhon, Belarus	83.63m
2009	Primoz Kozmus, Slovenia	80.84m
2011	Koji Murofushi, Japan	81.24m
2013	Pawel Fajdek, Poland	81.97m

Men *(Cont.)*

JAVELIN

1983	Detlef Michel, East Germany	89.48m
1987	Seppo Räty, Finland	83.54m
1991	Kimmo Kinnunen, Finland	90.82m
1993	Jan Zelezny, Czech Rep.	85.98m
1995	Jan Zelezny, Czech Rep.	89.58m
1997	Marius Corbett, South Africa	88.40m
1999	Aki Parviainen, Finland	89.52m
2001	Jan Zelezny, Czech Rep.	92.80mWR
2003	Sergey Makarov, Russia	85.44m
2005	Andrus Varnik, Estonia	87.17m
2007	Tero Pitkämäki, Finland	90.33m
2009	Andreas Thorkildsen, Norway	89.59m
2011	Matthias de Zordo, Germany	86.27m
2013	Vitezslav Vesely, Czech Rep.	87.17m

DECATHLON

1983	Daley Thompson, Great Britain	8666 pts
1987	Torsten Voss, East Germany	8680 pts
1991	Dan O'Brien, United States	8812 pts
1993	Dan O'Brien, United States	8817 pts
1995	Dan O'Brien, United States	8695 pts
1997	Tomás Dvorák, Czech Rep.	8837 pts
1999	Tomás Dvorák, Czech Rep.	8744 pts
2001	Tomás Dvorák, Czech Rep.	8902 ptsWR
2003	Tom Pappas, United States	8750 pts
2005	Bryan Clay, United States	8732 pts
2007	Roman Sebrle, Czech Rep.	8676 pts
2009	Trey Hardee, United States	8790 pts
2011	Trey Hardee, United States	8607 pts
2013	Ashton Eaton, United States	8809 pts

Women

100 METERS

1983	Marlies Gohr, East Germany	10.97
1987	Silke Gladisch, East Germany	10.90
1991	Katrin Krabbe, Germany	10.99
1993	Gail Devers, United States	10.82
1995	Gwen Torrence, United States	10.85
1997	Marion Jones, United States	10.83
1999	Marion Jones, United States	10.70
2001	Zhanna Pintusevich-Block, Ukraine	10.82
2003	Kelli White, United States	10.85
2005	Lauryn Williams, United States	10.93
2007	Veronica Campbell, Jamaica	11.01
2009	Shelly-Ann Fraser, Jamaica	10.73
2011	Carmelita Jeter, United States	10.90
2013	Shelly-Ann Fraser-Pryce, Jamaica	10.71

200 METERS

1983	Marita Koch, East Germany	22.13
1987	Silke Gladisch, East Germany	21.74
1991	Katrin Krabbe, Germany	22.09
1993	Merlene Ottey, Jamaica	21.98
1995	Merlene Ottey, Jamaica	22.12
1997	Zhanna Pintusevich, Ukraine	22.32
1999	Inger Miller, United States	21.77
2001	Marion Jones, United States	22.39
2003	Kelli White, United States	22.05
2005	Allyson Felix, United States	22.16
2007	Allyson Felix, United States	21.81
2009	Allyson Felix, United States	22.02
2011	Veronica Campell-Brown, Jamaica	22.22
2013	Shelly-Ann Fraser-Pryce, Jamaica	22.17

400 METERS

1983	Jarmila Kratochvilova, Czech.	47.99
1987	Olga Bryzgina, USSR	49.38
1991	Marie-José Pérec, France	49.13
1993	Jearl Miles, United States	49.82
1995	Marie-José Pérec, France	49.28
1997	Cathy Freeman, Australia	49.77
1999	Cathy Freeman, Australia	49.67
2001	Amy Mbacke Thiam, Senegal	49.86
2003	Ana Guevara, Mexico	48.89
2005	Darling Williams, Bahamas	49.55
2007	Christine Ohuruogu, Great Britain	49.61
2009	Sanya Richards, United States	49.00
2011	Amantie Montsho, Botswana	49.56
2013	Christine Ohuruogu, Great Britain	49.41

800 METERS

1983	Jarmila Kratochvilova, Czech.	1:54.68
1987	Sigrun Wodars, East Germany	1:55.26
1991	Lilia Nurutdinova, USSR	1:57.50
1993	Maria Mutola, Mozambique	1:55.43
1995	Ana Quirot, Cuba	1:56.11
1997	Ana Quirot, Cuba	1:57.14
1999	Ludmila Formanová, Czech Rep.	1:56.68
2001	Maria Mutola, Mozambique	1:57.17
2003	Maria Mutola, Mozambique	1:59.89
2005	Zulia Calatayud, Cuba	1:58.82
2007	Janeth Jepkosgei, Kenya	1:56.04
2009	Caster Semenya, South Africa	1:55.45
2011	Mariya Savinova, Russia	1:55.87
2013	Eunice Jepkoech Sum, Kenya	1:57.38

1,500 METERS

1983	Mary Slaney, United States	4:00.90
1987	Tatyana Samolenko, USSR	3:58.56
1991	Hassiba Boulmerka, Algeria	4:02.21
1993	Dong Liu, China	4:00.50
1995	Hassiba Boulmerka, Algeria	4:02.42
1997	Carla Sacramento, Portugal	4:04.24
1999	Svetlana Masterkova, Russia	3:59.53
2001	Gabriela Szabo, Romania	4:00.57
2003	Tatyana Tomashova, Russia	3:58.52
2005	Tatyana Tomashova, Russia	4:00.35
2007	Maryam Yusuf Jamal, Bahrain	3:58.75
2009	Maryam Yusuf Jamal, Bahrain	4:03.74
2011	Jennifer Simpson, United States	4:05.40
2013	Abeba Aregawi, Sweden	4:02.67

3,000 METERS

1983	Mary Slaney, United States	8:34.62
1987	Tatyana Samolenko, USSR	8:38.73
1991	Tatyana Dorovskikh, USSR	8:35.82
1993	Qu Yunxia, China	8:28.71

3,000 METER STEEPLECHASE

2005	Docus Inzikuru, Uganda	9:18.24
2007	Yekaterina Volkova, Russia	9:06.57
2009	Marta Dominguez, Spain	9:07.32
2011	Yuliya Zaripova, Russia	9:07.03
2013	Milcah Chemos Cheywa, Kenya	9:11.65

5,000 METERS

1995	Sonia O'Sullivan, Ireland	14:46.47
1997	Gabriela Szabo, Romania	14:57.68
1999	Gabriela Szabo, Romania	14:41.82
2001	Olga Yegorova, Russia	15:03.39

WR=World record.

Women *(Cont.)*

5,000 METERS *(Cont.)*

2003	Tirunesh Dibaba, Ethiopia	14:51.72
2005	Tirunesh Dibaba, Ethiopia	14:38.59
2007	Meseret Defar, Ethiopia	14:57.91
2009	Vivian Cheruiyot, Kenya	14:57.97
2011	Vivian Cheruiyot, Kenya	14:55.36
2013	Meseret Defar, Ethiopia	14:50.19

10,000 METERS

1987	Ingrid Kristiansen, Norway	31:05.85
1991	Liz McColgan, Great Britain	31:14.31
1993	Wang Junxia, China	30:49:30
1995	Fernanda Ribeiro, Portugal	31:04.99
1997	Sally Barsosio, Kenya	31:32.92
1999	Gete Wami, Ethiopia	30:24.56
2001	Derartu Tulu, Ethiopia	31:48.81
2003	Berhane Adere, Ethiopia	30:04.18
2005	Tirunesh Dibaba, Ethiopia	30:24.02
2007	Tirunesh Dibaba, Ethiopia	31:55.41
2009	Linet Masai, Kenya	30:51.24
2011	Vivian Cheruiyot, Kenya	30:48.98
2013	Tirunesh Dibaba, Ethiopia	30:43.35

MARATHON

1983	Grete Waitz, Norway	2:28:09
1987	Rosa Mota, Portugal	2:25:17
1991	Wanda Panfil, Poland	2:29:53
1993	Junko Asari, Japan	2:30:03
1995	Manuela Machado, Portugal	2:25:39*
1997	Hiromi Suzuki, Japan	2:29:48
1999	Jong Song-Ok, North Korea	2:26:59
2001	Lidia Simon, Romania	2:26.01
2003	Catherine Ndereba, Kenya	2:23:55
2005	Paula Radcliffe, Great Britain	2:20:57
2007	Catherine Ndereba, Kenya	2:30:37
2009	Xue Bai, China	2:25.15
2011	Edna Kiplagat, Kenya	2:28.43
2013	Edna Kiplagat, Kenya	2:25.44

100-METER HURDLES

1983	Bettine Jahn, East Germany	12.35
1987	Ginka Zagorcheva, Bulgaria	12.34
1991	Lyudmila Narozhilenko, USSR	12.59
1993	Gail Devers, United States	12.46
1995	Gail Devers, United States	12.68
1997	Ludmila Engquist, Sweden	12.50
1999	Gail Devers, United States	12.37
2001	Anjanette Kirkland, United States	12.42
2003	Perdita Felicien, Canada	12.53
2005	Michelle Perry, United States	12:66
2007	Michelle Perry, United States	12.46
2009	Brigitte Foster-Hylton, Jamaica	12.51
2011	Sally Pearson, Australia	12.28
2013	Brianna Rollins, United States	12.44

400-METER HURDLES

1983	Yekaterina Fesenko, USSR	54.14
1987	Sabine Busch, East Germany	53.62
1991	Tatyana Ledovskaya, USSR	53.11
1993	Sally Gunnell, Great Britain	52.74WR
1995	Kim Batten, United States	52.61
1997	Nezha Bidouane, Morocco	52.97
1999	Daimi Pernia, Cuba	52.89
2001	Nezha Bidouane, Morocco	53.34
2003	Jana Pittman, Australia	53.22
2005	Yuliya Pechonkina, Russia	52.90
2007	Jana Rawlinson, Australia	53.31
2009	Melaine Walker, Jamaica	52.42
2011	Lashinda Demus, United States	52.47
2013	Zuzana Hejnova, Czech Rep.	52.83

20-KILOMETER WALK

1999	Hongyu Liu, China	1:30:50
2001	Olimpiada Ivanova, Russia	1:27:48
2003	Yelena Nikolayeva, Russia	1:26:52
2005	Olimpiada Ivanova, Russia	1:25:41
2007	Olga Kaniskina, Russia	1:30:09
2009	Olga Kaniskina, Russia	1:28.09
2011	Olga Kaniskina, Russia	1:29.42
2013	Elena Lashmanova, Russia	1:27.08

4 X 100-METER RELAY

1983	East Germany (S. Gladisch, M. Koch, I. Auerswald, M. Gohr)	41.76
1987	United States (A. Brown, D. Williams, F. Griffith, P. Marshall)	41.58
1991	Jamaica (D. Duhaney, J. Cuthbert, B. McDonald, M. Ottey)	41.94
1993	Russia (O. Bogoslovskaya, G. Malchugina, N. Voronova, I. Privalova)	41.49
1995	United States (C. Mondie-Milner, C. Guidry, C. Gaines, G. Torrence)	42.12
1997	United States (C. Gaines, M. Jones, I. Miller, G. Devers)	41.47
1999	Bahamas (S. Fynes, C. Sturrup, P. Davis-Thompson, D. Ferguson)	41.92
2001	United States (K. White, C. Gaines, I. Miller, M Jones)	41.71
2003	France (P. Girard, M. Hurtis S. Félix, C. Arron)	41.78
2005	United States, (A. Daigle-Bowen, M. Lee, M. Barber, L. Williams	41.78
2007	United States (L. Williams, A. Felix, M. Barber, T. Edwards)	41.98
2009	Jamaica (S. Facey, S. Fraser, A. Bailey, K. Stewart)	42.06
2011	United States (B. Knight, A. Felix, M. Myers, C. Jeter)	41.56
2013	Jamaica (C. Russell K. Stewart, S. Calvert, S. Fraser-Pryce)	41.29

4 X 400-METER RELAY

1983	East Germany (K. Walther, S. Busch, M. Koch, D. Rubsam)	3:19.73
1987	East Germany (D. Neubauer, K. Emmelmann, P. Müller, S. Busch)	3:18.63
1991	USSR (T. Ledovskaya, L. Dzhigalova, O. Nazarova, O. Bryzgina)	3:18.43
1993	United States (G. Torrence, M. Malone, N. Kaiser-Brown, J. Miles)	3:16.71
1995	United States (K. Graham, R. Stevens, C. Jones, J. Miles)	3:22.39
1997	Germany (A. Feller, U. Rohlander, A. Rucker, G. Breuer)	3:20.92
1999	Russia (T. Chebykina, S. Goncharenko, O. Kotylarova, N. Nazarova)	3:21.98
2001	Jamaica (S. Richards, C. Scott, D. Parris, L. Fenton)	3:20.65
2003	United States (M. Barber, D. Washington, J. Miles-Clark, S. Richards)	3:22.63
2005	Russia (Y. Pechonkina, O. Krasnomovets, N. Antyukh, S. Pospelova)	3:20.95
2007	United States (D. Trotter, A. Felix, M. Wineberg, S. Richards)	3:18.55
2009	United States (D. Dunn, A. Felix, L. Demus, S. Richards)	3:17.83
2011	United States (S. Richards-Ross, A. Felix, J. Beard, F. McCrory)	3:18.09
2013	Russia (Y. Gushchina T. Firova, K. Ryzhova, A. Krivoshapka	3:20.19

*400 meters short. WR=World Record.

Women *(Cont.)*

HIGH JUMP

1983	Tamara Bykova, USSR	2.01m
1987	Stefka Kostadinova, Bulgaria	2.09mWR
1991	Heike Henkel, Germany	2.05m
1993	Ioamnet Quintero, Cuba	1.99m
1995	Stefka Kostadinova, Bulgaria	2.01m
1997	Hanne Haugland, Norway	1.99m
1999	Inga Babakova, Ukraine	1.99m
2001	Hestrie Cloete, South Africa	2.00m
2003	Hestrie Cloete, South Africa	2.06m
2005	Kajsa Bergvist, Sweden	2.02m
2007	Blanka Vlasic, Croatia	2.05m
2009	Blanka Vlasic, Croatia	2.04m
2011	Anna Chicerova, Russia	2.03m
2013	Svetlana Shkolina, Russia	2.03m

POLE VAULT

1999	Stacy Dragila, United States	4.06mEWR
2001	Stacy Dragila, United States	4.75m
2003	Svetlana Feofanova, Russia	4.75m
2005	Yelena Isinbayeva, Russia	5.01mWR
2007	Yelena Isinbayeva, Russia	4.80m
2009	Anna Rogowska, Poland	4.75m
2011	Fabiana Murer, Brazil	4.85m
2013	Elena Isinbaeva, Russia	4.89m

LONG JUMP

1983	Heike Daute, East Germany	7.27m
1987	Jackie Joyner-Kersee, U.S.	7.36mWR
1991	Jackie Joyner-Kersee, U.S.	7.32m
1993	Heike Drechsler, Germany	7.11m
1995	Fiona May, Italy	6.98m
1997	Lyudmila Galkina, Russia	7.05m
1999	Niurka Montalvo, Spain	7.06m
2001	Fiona May, Italy	6.87m
2003	Eunice Barber, France	6.99m
2005	Tianna Madison, United States	6.89m
2007	Tatyana Lebedeva, Russia	7.03m
2009	Brittney Reese, United States	7.10m
2011	Brittney Reese, United States	6.82m
2013	Brittney Reese, United States	7.01m

TRIPLE JUMP

1993	Ana Biryukova, Russia	15.09m
1995	Inessa Kravets, Ukraine	15.50mWR
1997	S. Kasparkova, Czech Rep.	15.20m
1999	Paraskevi Tsiamita, Greece	14.88m
2001	Tatyana Lebedeva, Russia	15.25m
2003	Tatyana Lebedeva, Russia	15.18m
2005	Trecia Smith, Jamaica	15.11m
2007	Yargeris Savigne, Cuba	15.28m
2009	Yargeris Savigne, Cuba	14.95m
2011	Olha Saladuha, Ukraine	14.94m
2013	Caterine Ibarguen, Colombia	14.85m

SHOT PUT

1983	Helena Fibingerova, Czech.	21.05m
1987	Natalya Lisovskaya, USSR	21.24mWR
1991	Zhihong Huang, China	20.83m
1993	Zhihong Huang, China	20.57m
1995	Astrid Kumbernuss, Germany	21.22m
1997	Astrid Kumbernuss, Germany	20.71m
1999	Astrid Kumbernuss, Germany	19.85m
2001	Yanina Korolchik, Belarus	20.61m
2003	Svetlana Krivelyova, Russia	20.63m
2005	Nadezhda Ostapchuk, Russia	20.51m
2007	Valerie Vili, New Zealand	20.54m
2009	Valerie Vili, New Zealand	20.44m
2011	Valerie Adams, New Zealand	21.24m
2013	Valerie Adams, New Zealand	20.88m

HAMMER THROW

1999	Mihaela Melinte, Romania	75.20mWR
2001	Yipsi Moreno, Cuba	70.65m
2003	Yipsi Moreno, Cuba	70.30m
2005	Olga Kuzenkova, Russia	75.10m
2007	Betty Heidler, Germany	74.76m
2009	Anita Wlodarczyk, Poland	77.96mWR
2011	Tatyana Lysenko, Russia	77.13m
2013	Tatyana Lysenko, Russia	78.80m

JAVELIN

1983	Tiina Lillak, Finland	70.82m
1987	Fatima Whitbread, United Kingdom	76.64m
1991	Xu Demei, China	68.78m
1993	Trine Solberg-Hattestad, Norway	69.18m
1995	Natalya Shikolenko, Belarus	67.56m
1997	Trine Hattestad, Norway	68.78m
1999	Mirela Manjani-Tzelili, Greece	67.09m
2001	Osleidys Menendez, Cuba	69.53m
2003	Mirela Manjani, Greece	66.52m
2005	Osleidys Menendez, Cuba	71.70m
2007	Barbora Spotakova, Czech Rep.	67.07m
2009	Steffi Nerius, Germany	67.30m
2011	Maria Abakumova, Russia	71.99m
2013	Christine Obergfoll, Germany	69.05m

DISCUS THROW

1983	Martina Opitz, East Germany	68.94m
1987	Martina Hellmann, East Germany	71.62mWR
1991	Tsvetanka Khristova, Bulgaria	71.02m
1993	Olga Burova, Russia	67.40m
1995	Ellina Zvereva, Belarus	68.64m
1997	Beatrice Faumuina, New Zealand	66.82m
1999	Franka Dietzsch, Germany	68.14m
2001	Ellina Zvereva,, Belarus	67.10m
2003	Irina Yatchenko, Belarus	67.32m
2005	Franka Dietzsch, Germany	66.56m
2007	Franka Dietzsch, Germany	66.61m
2009	Dani Samuels, Australia	65.44m
2011	Yanfeng Li, China	66.52m
2013	Sandra Perkovic, Croatia	67.99m

HEPTATHLON

1983	Ramona Neubert, East Germany	6714 pts
1987	Jackie Joyner-Kersee, U.S.	7128 pts
1991	Sabine Braun, Germany	6672 pts
1993	Jackie Joyner-Kersee, U.S.	6831 pts
1995	Ghada Shouaa, Syria	6651 pts
1997	Sabine Braun, Germany	6739 pts
1999	Eunice Barber, France	6861 pts
2001	Yelena Prokhorova, Russia	6694 pts
2003	Carolina Kluft, Sweden	7001 pts
2005	Carolina Kluft, Sweden	6887 pts
2007	Carolina Kluft, Sweden	7032 pts
2009	Jessica Ennis, United Kingdom	6731 pts
2011	Tatyana Chernova, Russia	6880 pts
2013	Ganna Melnichenko, Ukraine	6586 pts

WR=World Record. EWR=Equals world record.

Great Britain's Chris Froome crossed the finish line arm-in-arm with his teammates in celebration of his dominant victory in the Tour de France

Miscellaneous Sports

Miscellaneous Sport Champions

Archery

2013 U.S. National Field Championships

	Winner (Recurve)	Winner (Compound)	Winner (Barebow)
MEN	Brady Ellison	Jess Broadwater	Ben Rogers
WOMEN	Heather Koehl	Jamie Van Natta	Rebecca Nelson-Harris

Bowling

		Money Winner ($)	Highest Average (pts.)
2012–13 PBA Tour TOUR LEADERS		Jason Belmonte ($169,386)	Wes Malott (229.50)
2012–13 PBA 50 (Senior Tour) TOUR LEADERS		Money Winner ($) Walter Ray Williams Jr. ($41,175)	Highest Average (pts.) Pete Weber (231.18)

Curling

2013 World Championships

	Winner	Runner-up
MEN	Sweden (8–6)	Canada
WOMEN	Scotland (6–5)	Sweden

2013 U.S. National Championships

	Winner (skip)	Runner-up (skip)
MEN	Washington (Clark)	Minnesota (George)
WOMEN	Wisconsin (Brown)	Minnesota (George)

Cycling

	Winner	Time
2013 TOUR DE FRANCE	Chris Froome, G.B.	83:56:40

Sled Dog Racing

	Winner	Time
2013 IDITAROD	Mitch Seavey	9 days, 7:39:56

Figure Skating

2013 ISU World Championships

	Winner	Country
MEN	Patrick Chan	Canada
WOMEN	Kim Yu-Na	South Korea
PAIRS	Tatiana Volosozhar/ Maxim Trankov	Russia
ICE DANCING	Meryl Davis/ Charlie White	United States

2013 U.S. Figure Skating Nat'l Championships

	Winner	Club
MEN	Max Aaron	Broadmoor SC
WOMEN	Ashley Wagner	SC of Wilmington
PAIRS	Marissa Casteli/ Simon Shnapir	SC of Boston/ SC of Boston
ICE DANCING	Meryl Davis/ Charlie White	Arctic FSC/ Detroit SC

Handball

2013 U.S. Three-Wall Nat'l Championships

	Winner	Runner-up
MEN	Sean Lenning	Nikolai Nahorniak
WOMEN	Megan Mehilos	Tracy Davis

Lacrosse

League	Winner (Score)	Runner-up
AMERICAN LACROSSE LEAGUE	NYAC (5–0)	Magerk's
NATIONAL LACROSSE LEAGUE	Rochester (11–10)	Washington
MAJOR LEAGUE LACROSSE	Chesapeake (10–9)	Charlotte

Little League Baseball

	Winner (Score)	Runner-up
WORLD SERIES CHAMPION	Tokyo, Japan (6–4)	Chula Vista, Calif.

Motor Boat Racing

American Power Boat Association	Winning Boat	Winning Driver
GOLD CUP CHAMPION (UNLIMITED)	95 Spirit of Qatar	Kip Brown

Polo

2013 U.S. Open U.S. POLO ASSOCIATION	Zacara (16–13)	Valiente

Rodeo

2012 PRCA World Champions	Winner(s)
ALL-AROUND	Trevor Brazile
SADDLE BRONC RIDING	Jesse Wright
BAREBACK RIDING	Kaycee Feild
BULL RIDING	Cody Teel
STEER WRESTLING	Luke Branquinho
STEER ROPING	Trevor Brazile
CALF TIE-DOWN ROPING	Tuf Cooper
TEAM ROPING (Header, Heeler)	Chad Masters, Jade Corkill

Rowing

2013 Intercollegiate Rowing Association	Winner	Runner-Up
MEN (VARSITY EIGHTS)	Washington	Harvard

Rugby

2013 Rugby Union	Winner	Runner-Up
COLLEGE PREMIER DIVISION	Life University	St. Mary's (Calif.)

2013 USA Rugby League	Winner	Runner-Up
U.S. CHAMPION	Philadelphia Fight	New Haven Warriors

Skiing

2013 FIS World Cup Season Points Champion	Men's Winner (Season)	Women's Winner (Season)
OVERALL	Marcel Hirscher, Aus.	Tina Maze, Slovenia
DOWNHILL	Aksel Lund Svindal, Nor.	Lindsey Vonn, U.S.
SLALOM	Marcel Hirscher, Aus	Mikaela Shiffrin, U.S.
GIANT SLALOM	Ted Ligety, U.S.	Tina Maze, Slovenia
SUPER G	Aksel Lund Svindal, Nor.	Tina Maze, Slovenia
COMBINED	Ivica Kostelic, Croatia/ Alexis Pinturault, France (tie)	Tina Maze, Slovenia

Softball

2013 U.S. ASA Championship	Major Fast Pitch Winner
MEN'S FAST PITCH MAJOR	Hill United Chiefs
WOMEN FAST PITCH MAJOR	Tournament cancelled

Speed Skating

2013 ISU World All-Around Champion	Winner
MEN	Sven Kramer, Netherlands
WOMEN	Ireen Wust, Netherlands

Squash

2012 U.S. Open Championship	Winner
MEN	Ramy Ashour
WOMEN	Nicol David

Triathlon

2012 Ironman World Championship	Winner	Time
MEN	Pete Jacobs	8:18:37
WOMEN	Leanda Cave	9:15.53

2013 Olympic-Distance Nat'l Championship	Winner	Time
MEN	Colin Riley	1:52:54
WOMEN	Heather Lendway	2:05:37

Volleyball

2013 U.S. Adult Championship (Open Div.)	Winner	Runner-Up
MEN	Team Florida Wave	Team Pineapple

Wrestling

2013 World Wrestling Championships

	Freestyle	Greco-Roman
121 LBS.	Hassan Rahimi, Iran	Won Chol Yun, N. Korea
132 LBS.	Bekhan Golgereev, Russia	Ivo Angelov, Bulgaria
145.5 LBS.	David Safaryan, Armenia	Han-Su Ryu, S. Korea
163 LBS.	Jordan Burroughs, United States	Hyeonwoo Kim, S. Korea
185 LBS.	Ibrahim Aldatov, Ukraine	Taleb Nematpour, Iran
211.5 LBS.	Reza Yazdani, Iran	Nikita Melnikov, Russia
264.5 LBS.	Khadshimourad Gatsalov, Russia	Amir Aziz Aliakbari, Iran
TEAM	Iran	Russia

2012–13 PBA TOUR RESULTS

Date	Event	Winner/s	Earnings ($)	Runner-Up
Nov 3–11	Cheetah Championship	Bill O'Neill	20,000	Mike Wolfe
Nov 4–11	WSOB Viper Open	Brad Angelo	20,000	Mika Koivuniemi
Nov 5–11	WSOB Chameleon Championship	Scott Norton	20,000	Jason Belmonte
Nov 6–11	PBA Scorpion Championship	Tom Daugherty	20,000	Osku Palermaa
Nov 7–11	PBA World Championship	Parker Bohn III	50,100	Jason Belmonte
Nov 7	WTBA World Bowling Tour Men's Final	Chris Barnes	20,000	Mika Koivuniemi
Nov 29–Dec.2	Round 1 Japan Cup Bowling	Mika Koivuniemi	71,152	Osku Palermaa
Jan 22–26	Carmen Salvino Classic	Andres Gomez	15,000	D.J. Archer
Jan 23–26	Mark Roth Classic	Michael Haugen Jr.	15,000	Scott Norton
Jan 24–26	Don Carter Classic	Jason Sterner	15,000	Wes Malott
Jan 25–27	Earl Anthony Players Champ.	Scott Norton	25,000	Sean Rash
Feb 18–24	USBC Masters	Jason Belmonte	50,000	Wes Malott
Jan 23–29	USBC Masters	Mike Fagan	50,000	Chris Barnes
Mar 26–31	PBA Tournament of Champions	Pete Weber	50,100	Jason Belmonte
May 19–June1	PBA Badger Open	Jack Peters	8,000	Josh Blanchard
May 22–June1	PBA Wolf Open	Chris Loschetter	8,000	Bill O'Neill
May 26–June 2	PBA Bear Open	Jason Belmonte	8,000	Chris Barnes
May 29–June 2	PBA Milwaukee Open	Chris Barnes	15,100	Norm Duke
June 2	King of the Swing	Norm Duke	10,000	Chris Barnes
July 21–27	U.S. Open	Wes Malott	50,000	Jason Belmonte

2013 SENIOR PBA TOUR RESULTS

Date	Event	Winner	Earnings ($)	Runner-Up
April 14–17	Suncoast Open	Bob Learn Jr.	7,500	Wayne Webb
Apr 20–23	Sun Bowl	Walter Ray Williams Jr.	7,850	Amleto Monacelli
April 28–May 1	Greater Birmingham Open	Tom Baker	7,600	Bryan Goebel
May 5–8	Miller High Life Classic	Lennie Boresch Jr.	7,500	Michael Henry
May 13–16	Dayton Classic	Randy Pedersen	7,500	Amleto Monacelli
June 2–7	Senior U.S. Open	Amleto Monacelli	14,000	Ron Mohr
June 9–14	USBC Senior Masters	Pete Weber	16,000	Lennie Boresch Jr.
June 16–19	Northern California Classic	Walter Ray Williams Jr.	8,000	Pete Thomas
Aug 5–8	South Shore Open	Walter Ray Williams Jr.	7,500	Mark Williams
Aug 18–21	Treasure Island Open	Pete Weber	7,500	Robert Harvey

TOUR LEADERS - PBA: 2012–13

MONEY LEADERS	Events	Earnings ($)	AVERAGE	Events	Average
Jason Belmonte	20	169,386.34	Wes Malott	13	229.50
Mika Koivuniemi	22	163,312.00	Jason Belmonte	20	229.21
Sean Rash	22	159,672.90	Rhino Page	12	227.23
Tommy Jones	19	122,180.00	Sean Rash	22	226.20
Wes Malott	13	113,258.54	Pete Weber	17	225.95

TOUR LEADERS - SENIOR PBA: 2012–13

MONEY LEADERS	Events	Earnings ($)	AVERAGE	Events	Average
Walter Ray Williams Jr	11	41,175.00	Walter Ray Williams Jr	9	233.41
Amleto Monacelli	8	29,850.00	Wayne Webb	7	229.85
Lennie Boresch Jr	10	28,350.00	Mike Edwards	4	228.71
Wayne Webb	11	25,375.00	Lennie Boresch Jr	8	228.66
Pete Weber	5	24,500.00	Bob Learn Jr	8	228.33

PBA CAREER STATISTICS

CAREER EARNINGS		CAREER TITLES	
*Walter Ray Williams Jr.	$4,471,513.44	*Walter Ray Williams Jr.	47
*Pete Weber	$3,667,265.69	Earl Anthony	43
*Norm Duke	$3,085,127.26	*Norm Duke	37
*Parker Bohn III	$2,897,088.21	*Pete Weber	37
Brian Voss	$2,477,062.88	Mark Roth	34
*Amleto Monacelli	$2,236,180.99	*Parker Bohn III	33
Mike Aulby	$2,097,520.33	Dick Weber	30
*Chris Barnes	$2,068,595.55	Mike Aulby	29
Tom Baker	$1,944,474.00	Don Johnson	26
Jason Couch	$1,763,711.83	Brian Voss	25

Note: Career leaders through Sep. 19, 2013. *Active in 2012–13 season.

Cycling

Tour de France Winners

Year	Winner	Time	Year	Winner	Time
1903	Maurice Garin, France	94 hrs, 33 min	1963	Jacques Anquetil, France	113 hrs, 30 min, 5 sec
1904	Henry Cornet, France	96 hrs, 5 min, 56 sec	1964	Jacques Anquetil, France	127 hrs, 9 min, 44 sec
1905	Louis Trousselier, France	110 hrs, 18 min, 58 sec	1965	Felice Gimondi, Italy	116 hrs, 42 min, 6 sec
1906	Rene Pottier, France	Not available	1966	Lucien Aimar, France	117 hrs, 34 min, 21 sec
1907	Lucien Petit-Breton, France	158 hrs, 54 min, 5 sec	1967	Roger Pingeon, France	136 hrs, 53 min, 50 sec
1908	Lucien Petit-Breton, France	Not available	1968	Jan Janssen, Netherlands	133 hrs, 49 min, 32 sec
1909	Francois Faber, Luxembourg	157 hrs, 1 min, 22 sec	1969	Eddy Merckx, Belgium	116 hrs, 16 min, 2 sec
1910	Octave Lapize, France	162 hrs, 41 min, 30 sec	1970	Eddy Merckx, Belgium	119 hrs, 31 min, 49 sec
1911	Gustave Garrigou, France	195 hrs, 37 min	1971	Eddy Merckx, Belgium	96 hrs, 45 min, 14 sec
1912	Odile Defraye, Belgium	190 hrs, 30 min, 28 sec	1972	Eddy Merckx, Belgium	108 hrs, 17 min, 18 sec
1913	Philippe Thys, Belgium	197 hrs, 54 min	1973	Luis Ocana, Spain	122 hrs, 25 min, 34 sec
1914	Philippe Thys, Belgium	200 hrs, 28 min, 48 sec	1974	Eddy Merckx, Belgium	116 hrs, 16 min, 58 sec
1915–18	NO RACE		1975	Bernard Thevenet, France	114 hrs, 35 min, 31 sec
1919	Firmin Lambot, Belgium	231 hrs, 7 min, 15 sec	1976	Lucien Van Impe, Belgium	116 hrs, 22 min, 23 sec
1920	Philippe Thys, Belgium	228 hrs, 36 min, 13 sec	1977	Bernard Thevenet, France	115 hrs, 38 min, 30 sec
1921	Leon Scieur, Belgium	221 hrs, 50 min, 26 sec	1978	Bernard Hinault, France	108 hrs, 18 min
1922	Firmin Lambot, Belgium	222 hrs, 8 min, 6 sec	1979	Bernard Hinault, France	103 hrs, 6 min, 50 sec
1923	Henri Pelissier, France	222 hrs, 15 min, 30 sec	1980	Joop Zoetemelk, Netherlands	109 hrs, 19 min, 14 sec
1924	Ottavio Bottechia, Italy	226 hrs, 18 min, 21 sec	1981	Bernard Hinault, France	96 hrs, 19 min, 38 sec
1925	Ottavio Bottechia, Italy	219 hrs, 10 min, 18 sec	1982	Bernard Hinault, France	92 hrs, 8 min, 46 sec
1926	Lucien Buysse, Belgium	238 hrs, 44 min, 25 sec	1983	Laurent Fignon, France	105 hrs, 7 min, 52 sec
1927	Nicolas Frantz, Luxembourg	198 hrs, 16 min, 42 sec	1984	Laurent Fignon, France	112 hrs, 3 min, 40 sec
1928	Nicolas Frantz, Luxembourg	192 hrs, 48 min, 58 sec	1985	Bernard Hinault, France	113 hrs, 24 min, 23 sec
1929	Maurice Dewaele, Belgium	186 hrs, 39 min, 16 sec	1986	Greg LeMond, United States	110 hrs, 35 min, 19 sec
1930	Andre Leducq, France	172 hrs, 12 min, 16 sec	1987	Stephen Roche, Ireland	115 hrs, 27 min, 42 sec
1931	Antonin Magne, France	177 hrs, 10 min, 3 sec	1988	Pedro Delgado, Spain	84 hrs, 27 min, 53 sec
1932	Andre Leducq, France	154 hrs, 12 min, 49 sec	1989	Greg LeMond, United States	87 hrs, 38 min, 35 sec
1933	Georges Speicher, France	147 hrs, 51 min, 37 sec	1990	Greg LeMond, United States	90 hrs, 43 min, 20 sec
1934	Antonin Magne, France	147 hrs, 13 min, 58 sec	1991	Miguel Induráin, Spain	101 hrs, 1 min, 20 sec
1935	Romain Maes, Belgium	141 hrs, 32 min	1992	Miguel Induráin, Spain	100 hrs, 49 min, 30 sec
1936	Sylvere Maes, Belgium	142 hrs, 47 min, 32 sec	1993	Miguel Induráin, Spain	95 hrs, 57 min, 9 sec
1937	Roger Lapebie, France	138 hrs, 58 min, 31 sec	1994	Miguel Induráin, Spain	103 hrs, 38 min, 38 sec
1938	Gino Bartali, Italy	148 hrs, 29 min, 12 sec	1995	Miguel Induráin, Spain	92 hrs, 44 min, 59 sec
1939	Sylvere Maes, Belgium	132 hrs, 3 min, 17 sec	1996	Bjarne Riis, Denmark	95 hrs, 57 min, 16 sec
1940–46	NO RACE		1997	Jan Ullrich, Germany	100 hrs, 30 min, 35 sec
1947	Jean Robic, France	148 hrs, 11 min, 25 sec	1998	Marco Pantani, Italy	92 hrs, 49 min, 46 sec
1948	Gino Bartali, Italy	147 hrs, 10 min, 36 sec	#1999	Lance Armstrong, United States	91 hrs, 32 min, 16 sec
1949	Fausto Coppi, Italy	149 hrs, 40 min, 49 sec	#2000	Lance Armstrong, United States	92 hrs, 33 min, 8 sec
1950	Ferdi Kubler, Switzerland	145 hrs, 36 min, 56 sec	#2001	Lance Armstrong, United States	86 hrs, 17 min, 28 sec
1951	Hugo Koblet, Switzerland	142 hrs, 20 min, 14 sec	#2002	Lance Armstrong, United States	82 hrs, 5 min, 12 sec
1952	Fausto Coppi, Italy	151 hrs, 57 min, 20 sec	#2003	Lance Armstrong, United States	83 hrs, 41 min, 12 sec
1953	Louison Bobet, France	129 hrs, 23 min, 25 sec	#2004	Lance Armstrong, United States	83 hrs, 36 min, 2 sec
1954	Louison Bobet, France	140 hrs, 6 min, 5 sec	#2005	Lance Armstrong, United States	82 hrs, 34 min, 1 sec
1955	Louison Bobet, France	130 hrs, 29 min, 26 sec	†2006	Oscar Pereiro, Spain	82 hrs, 48 min, 30 sec
1956	Roger Walkowiak, France	124 hrs, 1 min, 16 sec	2007	Alberto Contador, Spain	91 hrs, 26 sec
1957	Jacques Anquetil, France	129 hrs, 46 min, 11 sec	2008	Carlos Sastre, Spain	87 hrs, 52 min, 52 sec
1958	Charly Gaul, Luxembourg	116 hrs, 59 min, 5 sec	2009	Alberto Contador, Spain	85 hrs, 48 min, 35 sec
1959	Federico Bahamontes, Spain	123 hrs, 46 min, 45 sec	*2010	Alberto Contador, Spain	91 hrs, 58 min, 48 sec
1960	Gastone Nencini, Italy	112 hrs, 8 min, 42 sec	2011	Cadel Evans, Australia	86 hrs, 12 min, 22 sec
1961	Jacques Anquetil, France	122 hrs, 1 min, 33 sec	2012	Bradley Wiggins, Great Britain	87 hrs, 34 min, 47 sec
1962	Jacques Anquetil, France	114 hrs, 31 min, 54 sec	2013	Chris Froome, Great Britain	83 hrs, 56 min, 40 sec

†Floyd Landis, the initial winner, was officially stripped of his title on Sept. 20, 2007 by the ICU after a hearing affirmed that he had tested positive for using banned substances during Stage 17 of the 2006 Tour.

*Alberto Contador was stripped of his 2010 Tour de France title and suspended for two years after a test sample showed trace amounts of a performance-enhancing stimulant in one of that race's final stages.

#Lance Armstrong was stripped of all seven of his titles in 2012 and banned for life by the U.S. Anti-Doping Agency.

Figure Skating

WORLD CHAMPIONS
Women

1906 .....Madge Sayers-Cave, Great Britain	1951 .....Jeannette Altwegg, Great Britain	1984 .....Katarina Witt, E. Germany
1907 .....Madge Sayers-Cave, Great Britain	1952 .....Jacqueline duBief, France	1985 .....Katarina Witt, E. Germany
1908 .....Lily Kronberger, Hungary	1953 .....Tenley Albright, United States	1986 .....Debi Thomas, United States
1909 .....Lily Kronberger, Hungary	1954 .....Gundi Busch, W. Germany	1987 .....Katarina Witt, E. Germany
1910 .....Lily Kronberger, Hungary	1955 .....Tenley Albright, United States	1988 .....Katarina Witt, E. Germany
1911 .....Lily Kronberger, Hungary	1956 .....Carol Heiss, United States	1989 .....Midori Ito, Japan
1912 .....Opika von Meray Horvath, Hungary	1957 .....Carol Heiss, United States	1990 .....Jill Trenary, United States
1913 .....Opika von Meray Horvath, Hungary	1958 .....Carol Heiss, United States	1991 .....Kristi Yamaguchi, United States
1914 .....Opika von Meray Horvath, Hungary	1959 .....Carol Heiss, United States	1992 .....Kristi Yamaguchi, United States
1915–21 NO COMPETITION	1960 .....Carol Heiss, United States	1993 .....Oksana Baiul, Ukraine
1922 .....Herma Plank-Szabo, Austria	1961 .....NO COMPETITION	1994 .....Yuka Sato, Japan
1923 .....Herma Plank-Szabo, Austria	1962 .....Sjoukje Dijkstra, Netherlands	1995 .....Chen Lu, China
1924 .....Herma Plank-Szabo, Austria	1963 .....Sjoukje Dijkstra, Netherlands	1996 .....Michelle Kwan, United States
1925 .....Herma Jaross-Szabo, Austria	1964 .....Sjoukje Dijkstra, Netherlands	1997 .....Tara Lipinski, United States
1926 .....Herma Jaross-Szabo, Austria	1965 .....Petra Burka, Canada	1998 .....Michelle Kwan, United States
1927 .....Sonja Henie, Norway	1966 .....Peggy Fleming, United States	1999 .....Maria Butyrskaya, Russia
1928 .....Sonja Henie, Norway	1967 .....Peggy Fleming, United States	2000 .....Michelle Kwan, United States
1929 .....Sonja Henie, Norway	1968 .....Peggy Fleming, United States	2001 .....Michelle Kwan, United States
1930 .....Sonja Henie, Norway	1969 .....Gabriele Seyfert, E. Germany	2002 .....Irina Slutskaya, Russia
1931 .....Sonja Henie, Norway	1970 .....Gabriele Seyfert, E. Germany	2003 .....Michelle Kwan, United States
1932 .....Sonja Henie, Norway	1971 .....Beatrix Schuba, Austria	2004 .....Shizuka Arakawa, Japan
1933 .....Sonja Henie, Norway	1972 .....Beatrix Schuba, Austria	2005 .....Irina Slutskaya, Russia
1934 .....Sonja Henie, Norway	1973 .....Karen Magnussen, Canada	2006 .....Kimmie Meissner, United States
1935 .....Sonja Henie, Norway	1974 .....Christine Errath, E. Germany	2007 .....Miki Ando, Japan
1936 .....Sonja Henie, Norway	1975 .....Dianne DeLeeuw, Netherlands	2008 .....Mao Asada, Japan
1937 .....Cecilia Colledge, Great Britain	1976 .....Dorothy Hamill, United States	2009 .....Yu-Na Kim, South Korea
1938 .....Megan Taylor, Great Britain	1977 .....Linda Fratianne, United States	2010 .....Mao Asada, Japan
1939 .....Megan Taylor, Great Britain	1978 .....Annett Poetzsch, E. Germany	2011 .....Miki Ando, Japan
1940–46.NO COMPETITION	1979 .....Linda Fratianne, United States	2012 .....Carolina Kostner, Italy
1947 .....Barbara Ann Scott, Canada	1980 .....Annett Poetzsch, E. Germany	2013 .....Yu-Na Kim, South Korea
1948 .....Barbara Ann Scott, Canada	1981 .....Denise Biellmann, Switzerland	
1949 .....Alena Vrzanova, Czechoslovakia	1982 .....Elaine Zayak, United States	
1950 .....Alena Vrzanova, Czechoslovakia	1983 .....Rosalynn Sumners, United States	

Men

1896 .....Gilbert Fuchs, Germany	1928 .....Willy Bockl, Austria	1960 .....Alan Giletti, France
1897 .....Gustav Hugel, Austria	1929 .....Gillis Grafstrom, Sweden	1961 .....NO COMPETITION
1898 .....Henning Grenander, Sweden	1930 .....Karl Schafer, Austria	1962 .....Donald Jackson, Canada
1899 .....Gustav Hugel, Austria	1931 .....Karl Schafer, Austria	1963 .....Donald McPherson, Canada
1900 .....Gustav Hugel, Austria	1932 .....Karl Schafer, Austria	1964 .....Manfred Schneldorfer, W. Germany
1901 .....Ulrich Salchow, Sweden	1933 .....Karl Schafer, Austria	1965 .....Alain Calmat, France
1902 .....Ulrich Salchow, Sweden	1934 .....Karl Schafer, Austria	1966 .....Emmerich Danzer, Austria
1903 .....Ulrich Salchow, Sweden	1935 .....Karl Schafer, Austria	1967 .....Emmerich Danzer, Austria
1904 .....Ulrich Salchow, Sweden	1936 .....Karl Schafer, Austria	1968 .....Emmerich Danzer, Austria
1905 .....Ulrich Salchow, Sweden	1937 .....Felix Kaspar, Austria	1969 .....Tim Wood, United States
1906 .....Gilbert Fuchs, Germany	1938 .....Felix Kaspar, Austria	1970 .....Tim Wood, United States
1907 .....Ulrich Salchow, Sweden	1939 .....Graham Sharp, Great Britain	1971 .....Andrej Nepela, Czechoslovakia
1908 .....Ulrich Salchow, Sweden	1940–46..NO COMPETITION	1972 .....Andrej Nepela, Czechoslovakia
1909 .....Ulrich Salchow, Sweden	1947 .....Hans Gerschwiler, Switzerland	1973 .....Andrej Nepela, Czechoslovakia
1910 .....Ulrich Salchow, Sweden	1948 .....Dick Button, United States	1974 .....Jan Hoffmann, E. Germany
1911 .....Ulrich Salchow, Sweden	1949 .....Dick Button, United States	1975 .....Sergei Volkov, USSR
1912 .....Fritz Kachler, Austria	1950 .....Dick Button, United States	1976 .....John Curry, Great Britain
1913 .....Fritz Kachler, Austria	1951 .....Dick Button, United States	1977 .....Vladimir Kovalev, USSR
1914 .....Gosta Sandhal, Sweden	1952 .....Dick Button, United States	1978 .....Charles Tickner, United States
1915–21.NO COMPETITION	1953 .....Hayes Alan Jenkins, United States	1979 .....Vladimir Kovalev, USSR
1922 .....Gillis Grafstrom, Sweden	1954 .....Hayes Alan Jenkins, United States	1980 .....Jan Hoffmann, E. Germany
1923 .....Fritz Kachler, Austria	1955 .....Hayes Alan Jenkins, United States	1981 .....Scott Hamilton, United States
1924 .....Gillis Grafstrom, Sweden	1956 .....Hayes Alan Jenkins, United States	1982 .....Scott Hamilton, United States
1925 .....Willy Bockl, Austria	1957 .....David W. Jenkins, United States	1983 .....Scott Hamilton, United States
1926 .....Willy Bockl, Austria	1958 .....David W. Jenkins, United States	1984 .....Scott Hamilton, United States
1927 .....Willy Bockl, Austria	1959 .....David W. Jenkins, United States	1985 .....Aleksandr Fadeev, USSR

WORLD CHAMPIONS (Cont.)

Men (Cont.)

1986.....Brian Boitano, United States	1996.....Todd Eldredge, United States	2006.....Stephane Lambiel, Switzerland
1987.....Brian Orser, Canada	1997.....Elvis Stojko, Canada	2007.....Brian Joubert, France
1988.....Brian Boitano, United States	1998.....Alexei Yagudin, Russia	2008.....Jeffrey Buttle, Canada
1989.....Kurt Browning, Canada	1999.....Alexei Yagudin, Russia	2009.....Evan Lysacek, United States
1990.....Kurt Browning, Canada	2000.....Alexei Yagudin, Russia	2010.....Daisuke Takahaski, Japan
1991.....Kurt Browning, Canada	2001.....Evgeni Plushenko, Russia	2011.....Patrick Chan, Canada
1992.....Viktor Petrenko, CIS	2002.....Alexei Yagudin, Russia	2012.....Patrick Chan, Canada
1993.....Kurt Browning, Canada	2003.....Evgeni Plushenko, Russia	2013.....Patrick Chan, Canada
1994.....Elvis Stojko, Canada	2004.....Evgeni Plushenko, Russia	
1995.....Elvis Stojko, Canada	2005.....Stephane Lambiel, Switzerland	

Pairs

1908.....Anna Hubler, Heinrich Burger, Germany	1966.....Ljudmila Protopopov, Oleg Protopopov, USSR
1909.....Phyllis Johnson, James H. Johnson, Great Britain	1967.....Ljudmila Protopopov, Oleg Protopopov, USSR
1910.....Anna Hubler, Heinrich Burger, Germany	1968.....Ljudmila Protopopov, Oleg Protopopov, USSR
1911.....Ludowika Eilers, Walter Jakobsson, Germany/Finland	1969.....Irina Rodnina, Aleksey Ulanov, USSR
1912.....Phyllis Johnson, James H. Johnson, Great Britain	1970.....Irina Rodnina, Aleksey Ulanov, USSR
1913.....Helene Engelmann, Karl Majstrik, Germany	1971.....Irina Rodnina, Aleksey Ulanov, USSR
1914.....Ludowika Jakobsson-Eilers, Walter Jakobsson-Eilers, Finland	1972.....Irina Rodnina, Aleksey Ulanov, USSR
	1973.....Irina Rodnina, Aleksandr Zaytsev, USSR
1915–21 NO COMPETITION	1974.....Irina Rodnina, Aleksandr Zaytsev, USSR
1922.....Helene Engelmann, Alfred Berger, Germany	1975.....Irina Rodnina, Aleksandr Zaytsev, USSR
1923.....Ludowika Jakobsson-Eilers, Walter Jakobsson-Eilers, Finland	1976.....Irina Rodnina, Aleksandr Zaytsev, USSR
	1977.....Irina Rodnina, Aleksandr Zaytsev, USSR
1924.....Helene Engelmann, Alfred Berger, Germany	1978.....Irina Rodnina, Aleksandr Zaytsev, USSR
1925.....Herma Jaross-Szabo, Ludwig Wrede, Austria	1979.....Tai Babilonia, Randy Gardner, United States
1926.....Andree Joly, Pierre Brunet, France	1980.....Maria Cherkasova, Sergei Shakhrai, USSR
1927.....Herma Jaross-Szabo, Ludwig Wrede, Austria	1981.....Irina Vorobieva, Igor Lisovsky, USSR
1928.....Andree Joly, Pierre Brunet, France	1982.....Sabine Baess, Tassilio Thierbach, E. Germany
1929.....Lilly Scholz, Otto Kaiser, Austria	1983.....Elena Valova, Oleg Vasiliev, USSR
1930.....Andree Brunet-Joly, Pierre Brunet-Joly, France	1984.....Barbara Underhill, Paul Martini, Canada
1931.....Emilie Rotter, Laszlo Szollas, Hungary	1985.....Elena Valova, Oleg Vasiliev, USSR
1932.....Andree Brunet-Joly, Pierre Brunet-Joly, France	1986.....Ekaterina Gordeeva, Sergei Grinkov, USSR
1933.....Emilie Rotter, Laszlo Szollas, Hungary	1987.....Ekaterina Gordeeva, Sergei Grinkov, USSR
1934.....Emilie Rotter, Laszlo Szollas, Hungary	1988.....Elena Valova, Oleg Vasiliev, USSR
1935.....Emilie Rotter, Laszlo Szollas, Hungary	1989.....Ekaterina Gordeeva, Sergei Grinkov, USSR
1936.....Maxi Herber, Ernst Bajer, Germany	1990.....Ekaterina Gordeeva, Sergei Grinkov, USSR
1937.....Maxi Herber, Ernst Bajer, Germany	1991.....Natalia Mishkutienok, Artur Dmitriev, USSR
1938.....Maxi Herber, Ernst Bajer, Germany	1992.....Natalia Mishkutienok, Artur Dmitriev, CIS
1939.....Maxi Herber, Ernst Bajer, Germany	1993.....Isabelle Brasseur, Lloyd Eisler, Canada
1940–46 NO COMPETITION	1994.....Evgenia Shishkova, Vadim Naumov, Russia
1947.....Micheline Lannoy, Pierre Baugniet, Belgium	1995.....Radka Kovarikova, Rene Novotny, Czech Republic
1948.....Micheline Lannoy, Pierre Baugniet, Belgium	1996.....Marina Eltsova, Andrey Buskhov, Russia
1949.....Andrea Kekessy, Ede Kiraly, Hungary	1997.....Mandy Wötzel, Ingo Steuer, Germany
1950.....Karol Kennedy, Peter Kennedy, United States	1998.....Jenni Meno, Todd Sand, United States
1951.....Ria Baran, Paul Falk, W. Germany	1999.....Elena Berezhnaya, Anton Sikharulidze, Russia
1952.....Ria Baran Falk, Paul Falk, W. Germany	2000.....Maria Petrova, Aleksei Tikhonov, Russia
1953.....Jennifer Nicks, John Nicks, Great Britain	2001.....Jamie Salé, David Pelletier, Canada
1954.....Frances Dafoe, Norris Bowden, Canada	2002.....Xue Shen, Hongbo Zhao, China
1955.....Frances Dafoe, Norris Bowden, Canada	2003.....Xue Shen, Hongbo Zhao, China
1956.....Sissy Schwarz, Kurt Oppelt, Austria	2004.....Tatiana Totmianina, Maxim Marinin, Russia
1957.....Barbara Wagner, Robert Paul, Canada	2005.....Tatiana Totmianina, Maxim Marinin, Russia
1958.....Barbara Wagner, Robert Paul, Canada	2006.....Qing Pang, Jian Tong, China
1959.....Barbara Wagner, Robert Paul, Canada	2007.....Shen Xue, Zhao Hongbo, China
1960.....Barbara Wagner, Robert Paul, Canada	2008.....Aliona Savchenko, Robin Szolkowy, Germany
1961.....NO COMPETITION	2009.....Aliona Savchenko, Robin Szolkowy, Germany
1962.....Maria Jelinek, Otto Jelinek, Canada	2010.....Qin Pang, Jian Tong, China
1963.....Marika Kilius, Hans-Jurgen Baumler, W Germany	2011.....Aliona Savchenko, Robin Szolkowy, Germany
1964.....Marika Kilius, Hans-Jurgen Baumler, W Germany	2012.....Aliona Savchenko, Robin Szolkowy, Germany
1965.....Ljudmila Protopopov, Oleg Protopopov, USSR	2013.....Tatiana Volosozhar/Maxim Trankov, Russia

WORLD CHAMPIONS *(Cont.)*

Dance

1950 .....Lois Waring, Michael McGean, United States
1951 .....Jean Westwood, Lawrence Demmy, Great Britain
1952 .....Jean Westwood, Lawrence Demmy, Great Britain
1953 .....Jean Westwood, Lawrence Demmy, Great Britain
1954 .....Jean Westwood, Lawrence Demmy, Great Britain
1955 .....Jean Westwood, Lawrence Demmy, Great Britain
1956 ....Pamela Wieght, Paul Thomas, Great Britain
1957 ....June Markham, Courtney Jones, Great Britain
1958 ....June Markham, Courtney Jones, Doreen D. Denny,
         Courtney Jones, Great Britain
1960 ....Doreen D. Denny, Courtney Jones, Great Britain
1961 .....NO COMPETITION
1962 ....Eva Romanova, Pavel Roman, Czechoslovakia
1963 ....Eva Romanova, Pavel Roman, Czechoslovakia
1964 ....Eva Romanova, Pavel Roman, Czechoslovakia
1965 ....Eva Romanova, Pavel Roman, Czechoslovakia
1966 ....Diane Towler, Bernard Ford, Great Britain
1967 ....Diane Towler, Bernard Ford, Great Britain
1968 ....Diane Towler, Bernard Ford, Great Britain
1969 ....Diane Towler, Bernard Ford, Great Britain
1970 ....Ljudmila Pakhomova, Aleksandr Gorshkov, USSR
1971 ....Ljudmila Pakhomova, Aleksandr Gorshkov USSR
1972 ....Ljudmila Pakhomova, Aleksandr Gorshkov USSR
1973 ....Ljudmila Pakhomova, Aleksandr Gorshkov USSR
1974 ....Ljudmila Pakhomova, Aleksandr Gorshkov USSR
1975 ....Irina Moiseeva, Andreij Minenkov, USSR
1976 ....Ljudmila Pakhomova, Aleksandr Gorshkov USSR
1977 ....Irina Moiseeva, Andreij Minenkov, USSR
1978 ....Natalia Linichuk, Gennadi Karponosov, USSR
1979 ....Natalia Linichuk, Gennadi Karponosov, USSR
1980 ....Krisztina Regoeczy, Andras Sallai, Hungary
1981 .....Jayne Torvill, Christopher Dean, Great Britain
1982 ....Jayne Torvill, Christopher Dean, Great Britain

1983 ....Jayne Torvill, Christopher Dean, Great Britain
1984 ....Jayne Torvill, Christopher Dean, Great Britain
1985 .....Natalia Bestemianova, Andrei Bukin, USSR
1986 ....Natalia Bestemianova, Andrei Bukin, USSR
1987 ....Natalia Bestemianova, Andrei Bukin, USSR
1988 ....Natalia Bestemianova, Andrei Bukin, USSR
1989 ....Marina Klimova, Sergei Ponomarenko, USSR
1990 ....Marina Klimova, Sergei Ponomarenko, USSR
1991 .....Isabelle Duchesnay, Paul Duchesnay, France
1992 ....Marina Klimova, Sergei Ponomarenko, CIS
1993 .....Renee Roca, Gorsha Sur, United States
1994 ....Oksana Grishuk, Evgeny Platov, Russia
1995 ....Oksana Grishuk, Evgeny Platov, Russia
1996 ....Oksana Grishuk, Evgeny Platov, Russia
1997 ....Oksana Grishuk, Evgeny Platov, Russia
1998 ....Anjelika Krylova, Oleg Ovsyannikov, Russia
1999 ....Anjelika Krylova, Oleg Ovsyannikov, Russia
2000 ....Marina Anissina, Gwendal Peizerat, France
2001 ....Barbara Fusar Poli, Maurizio Margaglio, Italy
2002 ....Irina Lobacheva, Ilia Averbukh, Russia
2003 ....Shae-Lynn Bourne, Victor Kraatz, Canada
2004 ....Tatiana Navka, Roman Kostomarov, Russia
2005 ....Tatiana Navka, Roman Kostomarov, Russia
2006 ....Albena Denkova, Maxim Staviski, Bulgaria
2007 ....Albena Denkova ,Maxim Staviski, Bulgaria
2008 .....Isabelle Delobel, Olivier Schoenfelder, France
2009 ....Oksana Domnina, Maxim Shabalin, Russia
2010 .....Tessa Virtue, Scott Moir, Canada
2011 .....Meryl Davis, Charlie White, United States
2012 .....Tessa Virtue, Scott Moir, Canada
2013 .....Meryl Davis, Charlie White, United States

CHAMPIONS OF THE UNITED STATES

Women

The championships held in 1914, 1918, 1920 and 1921 under the auspices of the International Skating Union of America were open to Canadians, although the competitions were considered to be United States championships. Beginning in 1922, the championships have been held under the auspices of the United States Figure Skating Association.

1914 .....Theresa Weld, SC of Boston
1915-17..NO COMPETITION
1918 ....Rosemary S. Beresford,
         New York SC
1919 .....NO COMPETITION
1920 ....Theresa Weld, SC of Boston
1921 .....Theresa Weld Blanchard,
         SC of Boston
1922 ....Theresa Weld Blanchard,
         SC of Boston
1923 ....Theresa Weld Blanchard,
         SC of Boston
1924 .....Theresa Weld Blanchard,
         SC of Boston
1925 ....Beatrix Loughran, New York SC
1926 ....Beatrix Loughran, New York SC
1927 ....Beatrix Loughran, New York SC
1928 ....Maribel Y. Vinson, SC of Boston
1929 ....Maribel Y. Vinson, SC of Boston
1930 ....Maribel Y. Vinson, SC of Boston
1931 ....Maribel Y. Vinson, SC of Boston
1932 ....Maribel Y. Vinson, SC of Boston
1933 .....Maribel Y. Vinson, SC of Boston

1934 .....Suzanne Davis, SC of Boston
1935 .....Maribel Y. Vinson, SC of Boston
1936 .....Maribel Y. Vinson, SC of Boston
1937 .....Maribel Y. Vinson, SC of Boston
1938 .....Joan Tozzer, SC of Boston
1939 .....Joan Tozzer, SC of Boston
1940 .....Joan Tozzer, SC of Boston
1941 .....Jane Vaughn, Philadelphia
         SC & HS
1942 .....Jane Vaughn Sullivan,
         Philadelphia SC & HS
1943 .....Gretchen Van Zandt Merrill,
         SC of Boston
1944 .....Gretchen Van Zandt Merrill,
         SC of Boston
1945 ....Gretchen Van Zandt Merrill,
         SC of Boston
1946 ....Gretchen Van Zandt Merrill,
         SC of Boston
1947 ....Gretchen Van Zandt Merrill,
         SC of Boston
1948 .....Gretchen Van Zandt Merrill,
         SC of Boston

1949 ....Yvonne Claire Sherman,
         SC of New York
1950 ....Yvonne Claire Sherman,
         SC of New York
1951 .....Sonya Klopfer,
         Junior SC of New York
1952 ....Tenley E. Albright, SC of Boston
1953 ....Tenley E. Albright, SC of Boston
1954 ....Tenley E. Albright, SC of Boston
1955 ....Tenley E. Albright, SC of Boston
1956 ....Tenley E. Albright, SC of Boston
1957 ....Carol E. Heiss, SC of New York
1958 ....Carol E. Heiss, SC of New York
1959 ....Carol E. Heiss, SC of New York
1960 ....Carol E. Heiss, SC of New York
1961 ....Laurence R. Owen,
         SC of Boston
1962 ....Barbara Roles Pursley,
         Arctic Blades FSC
1963 ....Lorraine G. Hanlon,
         SC of Boston
1964 ....Peggy Fleming,
         Arctic Blades FSC

CHAMPIONS OF THE UNITED STATES (Cont.)
Women (Cont.)

1965.....Peggy Fleming,
     Arctic Blades FSC
1966.....Peggy Fleming,
     City of Colorado Springs
1967.....Peggy Fleming, Broadmoor SC
1968.....Peggy Fleming, Broadmoor SC
1969.....Janet Lynn, Wagon Wheel FSC
1970.....Janet Lynn, Wagon Wheel FSC
1971.....Janet Lynn, Wagon Wheel FSC
1972.....Janet Lynn, Wagon Wheel FSC
1973.....Janet Lynn, Wagon Wheel FSC
1974.....Dorothy Hamill, SC of New York
1975.....Dorothy Hamill, SC of New York
1976.....Dorothy Hamill, SC of New York
1977.....Linda Fratianne, Los Angeles FSC
1978.....Linda Fratianne, Los Angeles FSC
1979.....Linda Fratianne, Los Angeles FSC
1980.....Linda Fratianne, Los Angeles FSC
1981.....Elaine Zayak, SC of New York
1982.....Rosalynn Sumners, Seattle SC
1983.....Rosalynn Sumners, Seattle SC

1984.....Rosalynn Sumners, Seattle SC
1985.....Tiffany Chin, San Diego FSC
1986.....Debi Thomas, Los Angeles FSC
1987.....Jill Trenary, Broadmoor SC
1988.....Debi Thomas, Los Angeles FSC
1989.....Jill Trenary, Broadmoor SC
1990.....Jill Trenary, Broadmoor SC
1991.....Tonya Harding, Carousel FSC
1992.....Kristi Yamaguchi, St Moritz ISC
1993.....Nancy Kerrigan, Colonial FSC
1994.....Tonya Harding, Portland FSC
1995.....Nicole Bobek, Los Angeles FSC
1996.....Michelle Kwan, Los Angeles FSC
1997.....Tara Lipinski, Detroit SC
1998.....Michelle Kwan, Los Angeles FSC
1999.....Michelle Kwan, Los Angeles FSC
2000.....Michelle Kwan, Los Angeles FSC
2001.....Michelle Kwan, Los Angeles FSC
2002.....Michelle Kwan, Los Angeles FSC
2003.....Michelle Kwan, Los Angeles FSC

2004.....Michelle Kwan, Los Angeles FSC
2005.....Michelle Kwan, Los Angeles FSC
2006.....Sasha Cohen, Orange County FSC
2007....Kimmie Meissner,
     Univ. of Delaware FSC
2008.....Mirai Nagasu, Pasadena FSC
2009.....Alissa Czisny, Detroit SC
2010.....Rachael Flatt, Broadmoor SC
2011.....Alissa Czisny, Detroit SC
2012.....Ashley Wagner, SC of Wilmington
2013.....Ashley Wagner, SC of Wilmington

Men

1914.....Norman M. Scott,
     WC of Montreal
1915–17.NO COMPETITION
1918.....Nathaniel W. Niles, SC of Boston
1919.....NO COMPETITION
1920.....Sherwin C. Badger, SC of Boston
1921.....Sherwin C. Badger, SC of Boston
1922.....Sherwin C. Badger, SC of Boston
1923.....Sherwin C. Badger, SC of Boston
1924.....Sherwin C. Badger, SC of Boston
1925.....Nathaniel W. Niles, SC of Boston
1926.....Chris I. Christenson,
     Twin City FSC
1927.....Nathaniel W. Niles, SC of Boston
1928.....Roger F. Turner, SC of Boston
1929.....Roger F. Turner, SC of Boston
1930.....Roger F. Turner, SC of Boston
1931.....Roger F. Turner, SC of Boston
1932.....Roger F. Turner, SC of Boston
1933.....Roger F. Turner, SC of Boston
1934.....Roger F. Turner, SC of Boston
1935.....Robin H. Lee, SC of New York
1936.....Robin H. Lee, SC of New York
1937.....Robin H. Lee, SC of New York
1938.....Robin H. Lee, Chicago FSC
1939.....Robin H. Lee, St Paul FSC
1940.....Eugene Turner, Los Angeles FSC
1941.....Eugene Turner, Los Angeles FSC
1942.....Robert Specht, Chicago FSC
1943.....Arthur R. Vaughn Jr.,
     Phila. SC & HS
1944–45..NO COMPETITION
1946.....Dick Button,
     Philadelphia SC & HS
1947.....Dick Button,
     Philadelphia SC & HS
1948.....Dick Button,
     Philadelphia SC & HS
1949.....Dick Button,
     Philadelphia SC & HS
1950.....Dick Button, SC of Boston
1951.....Dick Button, SC of Boston

1952.....Dick Button, SC of Boston
1953....Hayes Alan Jenkins,
     Cleveland SC
1954.....Hayes Alan Jenkins,
     Broadmoor SC
1955.....Hayes Alan Jenkins,
     Broadmoor SC
1956.....Hayes Alan Jenkins,
     Broadmoor SC
1957.....David Jenkins, Broadmoor SC
1958.....David Jenkins, Broadmoor SC
1959.....David Jenkins, Broadmoor SC
1960.....David Jenkins, Broadmoor SC
1961.....Bradley R. Lord, SC of Boston
1962.....Monty Hoyt, Broadmoor SC
1963.....Thomas Litz, Hershey FSC
1964.....Scott Ethan Allen,
     SC of New York
1965.....Gary C. Visconti, Detroit SC
1966.....Scott Ethan Allen,
     SC of New York
1967.....Gary C. Visconti, Detroit SC
1968.....Tim Wood, Detroit SC
1969.....Tim Wood, Detroit SC
1970.....Tim Wood, City of
     Colorado Springs
1971.....John Misha Petkevich,
     Great Falls FSC
1972.....Kenneth Shelley,
     Arctic Blades FSC
1973.....Gordon McKellen Jr.,
     SC of Lake Placid
1974.....Gordon McKellen Jr.,
     SC of Lake Placid
1975.....Gordon McKellen Jr.,
     SC of Lake Placid
1976.....Terry Kubicka, Arctic Blades FSC
1977.....Charles Tickner, Denver FSC
1978.....Charles Tickner, Denver FSC
1979....Charles Tickner, Denver FSC
1980.....Charles Tickner, Denver FSC

1981.....Scott Hamilton,
     Philadelphia SC & HS
1982.....Scott Hamilton,
     Philadelphia SC & HS
1983.....Scott Hamilton,
     Philadelphia SC & HS
1984.....Scott Hamilton,
     Philadelphia SC & HS
1985.....Brian Boitano, Peninsula FSC
1986.....Brian Boitano, Peninsula FSC
1987.....Brian Boitano, Peninsula FSC
1988.....Brian Boitano, Peninsula FSC
1989.....Christopher Bowman,
     Los Angeles FSC
1990.....Todd Eldredge, Los Angeles FSC
1991.....Todd Eldredge, Los Angeles FSC
1992.....Christopher Bowman,
     Los Angeles FSC
1993.....Scott Davis, Broadmoor SC
1994.....Scott Davis, Broadmoor SC
1995.....Todd Eldredge, Detroit SC
1996.....Rudy Galindo, St Moritz ISC
1997.....Todd Eldredge, Detroit SC
1998.....Todd Eldredge, Detroit SC
1999.....Michael Weiss, Washington FSC
2000.....Michael Weiss, Washington FSC
2001.....Timothy Goebel, Winterhurst FSC
2002.....Todd Eldredge, Los Angeles FSC
2003.....Michael Weiss, Washington FSC
2004.....Johnny Weir, SC of New York
2005.....Johnny Weir, SC of New York
2006.....Johnny Weir, SC of New York
2007.....Evan Lysacek, DuPage FSC
2008.....Evan Lysacek, DuPage FSC
2009.....Jeremy Abbott, Broadmoor SC
2010.....Jeremy Abbott, Detroit SC
2011.....Ryan Bradley, Broadmoor SC
2012.....Jeremy Abbott, Detroit SC
2013.....Max Aaron, Broadmoor SC

CHAMPIONS OF THE UNITED STATES *(Cont.)*
Pairs

1914	Jeanne Chevalier, Norman M. Scott, WC of Montreal	
1915–17	NO COMPETITION	
1918	Theresa Weld, Nathaniel W. Niles, SC of Boston	
1919	No competition	
1920	Theresa Weld, Nathaniel W. Niles, SC of Boston	
1921	Theresa Weld Blanchard, Nathaniel W. Niles, SC of Boston	
1922	Theresa Weld Blanchard, Nathaniel W. Niles, SC of Boston	
1923	Theresa Weld Blanchard, Nathaniel W. Niles, SC of Boston	
1924	Theresa Weld Blanchard, Nathaniel W. Niles, SC of Boston	
1925	Theresa Weld Blanchard, Nathaniel W. Niles, SC of Boston	
1926	Theresa Weld Blanchard, Nathaniel W. Niles, SC of Boston	
1927	Theresa Weld Blanchard, Nathaniel W. Niles, SC of Boston	
1928	Maribel Y. Vinson, Thornton L. Coolidge, SC of Boston	
1929	Maribel Y. Vinson, Thornton L. Coolidge, SC of Boston	
1930	Beatrix Loughran, Sherwin C. Badger, SC of New York	
1931	Beatrix Loughran, Sherwin C. Badger, SC of New York	
1932	Beatrix Loughran, Sherwin C. Badger, SC of New York	
1933	Maribel Y. Vinson, George E. B. Hill, SC of SC of Boston	
1936	Maribel Y. Vinson, George E. B. Hill, SC of Boston	
1937	Maribel Y. Vinson, George E. B. Hill, SC of Boston	
1938	Joan Tozzer, M. Bernard Fox, SC of Boston	
1939	Joan Tozzer, M. Bernard Fox, SC of Boston	
1940	Joan Tozzer, M. Bernard Fox, SC of Boston	
1941	Donna Atwood, Eugene Turner, Mercury FSC/Los Angeles FSC	
1942	Doris Schubach, Walter Noffke, Springfield Ice Birds	
1943	Doris Schubach, Walter Noffke, Springfield Ice Birds	
1944	Doris Schubach, Walter Noffke, Springfield Ice Birds	
1945	Donna Jeanne Pospisil, Jean-Pierre Brunet, SC of New York	
1946	Donna Jeanne Pospisil, Jean-Pierre Brunet, SC of New York	
1947	Yvonne Claire Sherman, Robert J. Swenning, SC of New York	
1948	Karol Kennedy, Peter Kennedy, Seattle SC	
1949	Karol Kennedy, Peter Kennedy, Seattle SC	
1950	Karol Kennedy, Peter Kennedy, Broadmoor SC	
1951	Karol Kennedy, Peter Kennedy, Broadmoor SC	
1952	Karol Kennedy, Peter Kennedy, Broadmoor SC	
1953	Carole Ann Ormaca, Robin Greiner, SC of Fresno	
1954	Carole Ann Ormaca, Robin Greiner, SC of Fresno	
1955	Carole Ann Ormaca, Robin Greiner, St Moritz ISC	
1956	Carole Ann Ormaca, Robin Greiner, St Moritz ISC	
1957	Nancy Rouillard Ludington, Ronald Ludington, Commonwealth FSC/SC of Boston	
1958	Nancy Rouillard Ludington, Ronald Ludington, Commonwealth FSC/SC of Boston	
1959	Nancy Rouillard Ludington, Ronald Ludington, Commonwealth FSC	
1960	Nancy Rouillard Ludington, Ronald Ludington, Commonwealth FSC	
1961	Maribel Y. Owen, Dudley S. Richards, SC of Boston	
1962	Dorothyann Nelson, Pieter Kollen, Village of Lake Placid	
1963	Judianne Fotheringill, Jerry J. Fotheringill, Broadmoor SC	
1964	Judianne Fotheringill, Jerry J. Fotheringill, Broadmoor SC	
1965	Vivian Joseph, Ronald Joseph, Chicago FSC	
1966	Cynthia Kauffman, Ronald Kauffman, Seattle SC	
1967	Cynthia Kauffman, Ronald Kauffman, Seattle SC	
1968	Cynthia Kauffman, Ronald Kauffman, Seattle SC	
1969	Cynthia Kauffman, Ronald Kauffman, Seattle SC	
1970	Jo Jo Starbuck, Kenneth Shelley, Arctic Blades FSC	
1971	Jo Jo Starbuck, Kenneth Shelley, Arctic Blades FSC	
1972	Jo Jo Starbuck, Kenneth Shelley, Arctic Blades FSC	
1973	Melissa Militano, Mark Militano, SC of New York	
1974	Melissa Militano, Johnny Johns, SC of New York/Detroit SC	
1975	Melissa Militano, Johnny Johns, SC of New York/Detroit SC	
1976	Tai Babilonia, Randy Gardner, Los Angeles FSC	
1977	Tai Babilonia, Randy Gardner, Los Angeles FSC	
1978	Tai Babilonia, Randy Gardner, Los Angeles FSC/ Santa Monica FSC	
1979	Tai Babilonia, Randy Gardner, Los Angeles FSC/ Santa Monica FSC	
1980	Tai Babilonia, Randy Gardner, Los Angeles FSC/ Santa Monica FSC	
1981	Caitlin/Peter Carruthers, SC of Wilmington	
1982	Caitlin/Peter Carruthers, SC of Wilmington	
1983	Caitlin/Peter Carruthers, SC of Wilmington	
1984	Caitlin/Peter Carruthers, SC of Wilmington	
1985	Jill Watson, Peter Oppegard, Los Angeles FSC	
1986	Gillian Wachsman, Todd Waggoner, SC of Wilmington	
1987	Jill Watson, Peter Oppegard, Los Angeles FSC	
1988	Jill Watson, Peter Oppegard, Los Angeles FSC	
1989	Kristi Yamaguchi, Rudy Galindo, St Mortiz ISC	
1990	Kristi Yamaguchi, Rudy Galindo, St Mortiz ISC	
1991	Natasha Kuchiki, Todd Sand, Los Angeles FSC	
1992	Calla Urbanski, Rocky Marval, U of Delaware FSC/ SC of New York	
1993	Calla Urbanski, Rocky Marval, U of Delaware FSC/ SC of New York	
1994	Jenni Meno, Todd Sand, Winterhurst FSC/ Los Angeles FSC	
1995	Jenni Meno, Todd Sand, Winterhurst FSC/ Los Angeles FSC	
1996	Jenni Meno, Todd Sand, Winterhurst FSC/ Los Angeles FSC	
1997	Kyoko Ina, Jason Dungjen, SC of New York	
1998	Kyoko Ina, Jason Dungjen, SC of New York	
1999	Danielle Hartsell, Steve Hartsell, Detroit SC	
2000	Kyoko Ina, John Zimmerman, SC of New York/Birmingham FSC	
2001	Kyoko Ina, John Zimmerman, SC of New York/Birmingham FSC	
2002	Kyoko Ina, John Zimmerman, SC of New York/Birmingham FSC	
2003	Tiffany Scott, Philip Dulebohn, Colonial FSC/ Univ of Delaware FSC	
2004	Rena Inoue, John Baldwin, All Year FSC	
2005	Kathryn Orscher, Garrett Lucash, Charter Oak FSC	
2006	Rena Inoue, John Baldwin, All Year FSC	
2007	Brooke Castile, Benjamin Okolski, Arctic FSC	
2008	Keauna McLaughlin, Rockne Brubaker, Los Angeles FSC/ Broadmoor SC	
2009	Keauna McLaughlin, Rockne Brubaker, Los Angeles FSC/ Broadmoor SC	
2010	Caydee Denney, Jeremy Barrett, SW Florida FSC	
2011	Caitlin Yankowskas, John Coughlin, Broadmoor SC/Kansas City FSC	
2012	Caydee Denney, John Coughlin, Broadmoor SC/Kansas City FSC	
2013	Marissa Castelli, Simon Shnapir, SC of Boston	

CHAMPIONS OF THE UNITED STATES *(Cont.)*
Dance

1914	Waltz: Theresa Weld, Nathaniel W. Niles, SC of Boston
1915–19	NO COMPETITION
1920	Waltz: Theresa Weld, Nathaniel W. Niles, SC of Boston Fourteenstep: Gertrude Cheever Porter, Irving Brokaw, New York SC
1921	Waltz and Fourteenstep: Theresa Weld Blanchard, Nathaniel W. Niles, SC of Boston
1922	Waltz: Beatrix Loughran, Edward M. Howland, New York SC/ SC of Boston Fourteenstep: Theresa Weld Blanchard, Nathaniel W. Niles, SC of Boston
1923	Waltz: Mr. & Mrs. Henry W. Howe, New York SC Fourteenstep: Sydney Goode, James B. Greene, New York SC
1924	Waltz: Rosaline Dunn, Frederick Gabel, New York SC Fourteenstep: Sydney Goode, James B. Greene, New York SC
1925	Waltz and Fourteenstep: Virginia Slattery, Ferrier T. Martin, New York SC
1926	Waltz: Rosaline Dunn, Joseph K. Savage, New York SC Fourteenstep: Sydney Goode, James B. Greene, New York SC
1927	Waltz and Fourteenstep: Rosaline Dunn, Joseph K. Savage, New York SC
1928	Waltz: Rosaline Dunn, Joseph K. Savage, New York SC Fourteenstep: Ada Bauman Kelly, George T. Braakman, New York SC
1929	Waltz and Original Dance combined: Edith C. Secord, Joseph K. Savage, SC of New York
1930	Waltz: Edith C. Secord, Joseph K. Savage, SC of New York Original: Clara Rotch Frothingham, George E. B. Hill, SC of Boston
1931	Waltz: Edith C. Secord, Ferrier T. Martin, SC of New York Original: Theresa Weld Blanchard, Nathaniel W. Niles, SC of Boston
1932	Waltz: Edith C. Secord, Joseph K. Savage, SC of New York Original: Clara Rotch Frothingham, George E. B. Hill, SC of Boston
1933	Waltz: Ilse Twaroschk, Frederick F. Fleishmann, Brooklyn FSC Original: Suzanne Davis, Frederick Goodridge, SC of Boston
1934	Waltz: Nettie C. Prantel, Roy Hunt, SC of New York Original: Suzanne Davis, Frederick Goodridge, SC of Boston
1935	Waltz: Nettie C. Prantel, Roy Hunt, SC of New York
1936	Marjorie Parker, Joseph K. Savage, SC of New York

1937	Nettie C. Prantel, Harold Hartshorne, SC of New York
1938	Nettie C. Prantel, Harold Hartshorne, SC of New York
1939	Sandy Macdonald, Harold Hartshorne, SC of New York
1940	Sandy Macdonald, Harold Hartshorne, SC of New York
1941	Sandy Macdonald, Harold Hartshorne, SCNY
1942	Edith B. Whetstone, Alfred N. Richards, Jr, Philadelphia SC & HS
1943	Marcella May, James Lochead Jr., Skate & Ski Club
1944	Marcella May, James Lochead Jr., Skate & Ski Club
1945	Kathe Mehl Williams, Robert J. Swenning, SC of New York
1946	Anne Davies, Carleton C. Hoffner Jr., Washington FSC
1947	Lois Waring, Walter H. Bainbridge Jr., Baltimore FSC/Washigton FSC
1948	Lois Waring, Walter H. Bainbridge Jr., Baltimore FSC/Washington FSC
1949	Lois Waring, Walter H. Bainbridge Jr., Baltimore FSC/Washington FSC
1950	Lois Waring, Michael McGean, Baltimore FSC
1951	Carmel Bodel, Edward L. Bodel, St. Moritz ISC
1952	Lois Waring, Michael McGean, Baltimore FSC
1953	Carol Ann Peters, Daniel C. Ryan, Washington FSC
1954	Carmel Bodel, Edward L. Bodel, St Moritz ISC
1955	Carmel Bodel, Edward L. Bodel, St Moritz ISC
1956	Joan Zamboni, Roland Junso, Arctic Blades FSC
1957	Sharon McKenzie, Bert Wright, Los Angeles FSC
1958	Andree Anderson, Donald Jacoby, Buffalo SC
1959	Andree Anderson Jacoby, Donald Jacoby, Buffalo SC
1960	Margie Ackles, Charles W. Phillips Jr., Los Angeles FSC/Arctic Blades FSC
1961	Diane C. Sherbloom, Larry Pierce, Los Angeles FSC/ WC of Indianapolis
1962	Yvonne N. Littlefield, Peter F. Betts, Arctic Blades FSC/Paramount, CA
1963	Sally Schantz, Stanley Urban, SC of Boston/Buffalo SC
1964	Darlene Streich, Charles D. Fetter Jr., WC of Indianapolis
1965	Kristin Fortune, Dennis Sveum, Los Angeles FSC
1966	Kristin Fortune, Dennis Sveum, Los Angeles FSC
1967	Lorna Dyer, John Carrell, Broadmoor SC
1968	Judy Schwomeyer, James Sladky, WC of Indianapolis/Genesee FSC

1969	Judy Schwomeyer, James Sladky, WC of Indianapolis/Genesee FSC
1970	Judy Schwomeyer, James Sladky, WC of Indianapolis/Genesee FSC
1971	Judy Schwomeyer, James Sladky, WC of Indianapolis/Genesee FSC
1972	Judy Schwomeyer, James Sladky, WC of Indianapolis/Genesee FSC
1973	Mary Karen Campbell, Johnny Johns, Lansing SC/Detroit SC
1974	Colleen O'Connor, Jim Millns, Broadmoor SC/ City of Colorado Springs
1975	Colleen O'Connor, Jim Millns, Broadmoor SC
1976	Colleen O'Connor, Jim Millns, Broadmoor SC
1977	Judy Genovesi, Kent Weigle, SC of Hartford/Charter Oak FSC
1978	Stacey Smith, John Summers, SC of Wilmington
1979	Stacey Smith, John Summers, SC of Wilmington
1980	Stacey Smith, John Summers, SC of Wilmington
1981	Judy Blumberg, Michael Seibert, Broadmoor SC/ISC of Indianapolis
1982	Judy Blumberg, Michael Seibert, Broadmoor SC/ISC of Indianapolis
1983	Judy Blumberg, Michael Seibert, Pittsburgh FSC
1984	Judy Blumberg, Michael Seibert, Pittsburgh FSC
1985	Judy Blumberg, Michael Seibert, Pittsburgh FSC
1986	Renee Roca, Donald Adair, Genesee FSC/Academy FSC
1987	Suzanne Semanick, Scott Gregory, U of Delaware SC
1988	Suzanne Semanick, Scott Gregory, U of Delaware SC
1989	Susan Wynne, Joseph Druar, Broadmoor SC/Seattle SC
1990	Susan Wynne, Joseph Druar, Broadmoor SC/Seattle SC
1991	Elizabeth Punsalan, Jerod Swallow, Broadmoor SC
1992	April Sargent, Russ Witherby, Ogdensburg FSC/ U of Delaware FSC
1993	Renee Roca, Gorsha Sur, Broadmoor SC
1994	Elizabeth Punsalan, Jerod Swallow, Broadmoor SC/Detroit SC
1995	Renee Roca, Gorsha Sur, Broadmoor SC
1996	Elizabeth Punsalan, Jerod Swallow, Detroit SC
1997	Elizabeth Punsalan, Jerod Swallow, Detroit SC
1998	Elizabeth Punsalan, Jerod Swallow, Detroit SC
1999	Naomi Lang, Peter Tchernyshev, Detroit SC
2000	Naomi Lang, Peter Tchernyshev, Detroit SC

CHAMPIONS OF THE UNITED STATES *(CONT.)*
Dance *(Cont.)*

2001 Naomi Lang, Peter Tchernyshev, Detroit SC	2006 Tanith Belbin, Ben Agosto, Arctic FSC	2011 Meryl Davis, Charlie White, Arctic FSC/Detroit SC
2002 Naomi Lang, Peter Tchernyshev, American Academy FSC	2007 Tanith Belbin, Ben Agosto, Arctic FSC	2012 Meryl Davis, Charlie White, Arctic FSC/Detroit SC
2003 Naomi Lang, Peter Tchernyshev, American Academy FSC	2008 Tanith Belbin, Ben Agosto, Arctic FSC	2013 Meryl Davis, Charlie White, Arctic FSC/Detroit SC
2004 Tanith Belbin, Ben Agosto, Detroit SC	2009 Meryl Davis, Charlie White, Arctic FSC/Detroit SC	
2005 Tanith Belbin, Ben Agosto, Detroit SC	2010 Meryl Davis, Charlie White, Arctic FSC/Detroit SC	

Gymnastics

WORLD CHAMPIONS — Men

All-Around

Year	Champion, Nation
1903	Joseph Martinez, France
1905	Marcel Lalue, France
1907	Joseph Czada, Czechoslovakia
1909	Marcos Torres, France
1911	Ferdinand Steiner, Czechoslovakia
1913	Marcos Torres, France
1922	Peter Sumi, Yugoslavia
	F. Pechacek, Czechoslovakia
1926	Peter Sumi, Yugoslavia
1930	Josip Primozic, Yugoslavia
1934	Eugene Mack, Switzerland
1938	Jan Gajdos, Czechoslovakia
1950	Walter Lehmann, Switzerland
1954	Valentin Mouratov, USSR
	Victor Chukarin, USSR
1958	Boris Shaklin, USSR
1962	Yuri Titov, USSR
1966	Mikhail Voronin, USSR
1970	Eizo Kenmotsu, Japan
1974	Shigeru Kasamatsu, Japan
1978	Nikolai Andrianov, USSR
1979	Alexander Ditiatin, USSR
1981	Yuri Korolev, USSR
1983	Dimitri Bilozertchev, USSR
1985	Yuri Korolev, USSR
1987	Dimitri Bilozertchev, USSR
1989	Igor Korobchinsky, USSR
1991	Grigori Misutin, CIS
1993	Vitaly Scherbo, Belarus
1994	Ivan Ivankov, Belarus
1995	Li Xiaoshuang, China
1997	Ivan Ivankov, Belarus
1999	Nicolae Krukov, Russia
2001	Feng Jing, China
2003	Paul Hamm, United States
2005	Hiroyuki Tomita, Japan
2007	Yang Wei, China
2009	Kohei Uchimura, Japan
2011	Kohei Uchimura, Japan
2013	Kohei Uchimura, Japan

Pommel Horse

Year	Champion, Nation
1930	Josip Primozic, Yugoslavia
1934	Eugene Mack, Switzerland
1938	Michael Reusch, Switzerland
1950	Josef Stalder, Switzerland
1954	Grant Chaguinjan, USSR
1958	Boris Shaklin, USSR
1962	Miroslav Cerar, Yugoslavia
1966	Miroslav Cerar, Yugoslavia
1970	Miroslav Cerar, Yugoslavia
1974	Zoltan Magyar, Hungary
1978	Zoltan Magyar, Hungary
1979	Zoltan Magyar, Hungary
1981	Michael Mikolai, East Germany
1983	Dmitri Bilozertchev, USSR
1985	Valentin Moguilny, USSR
1987	Zsolt Borkai, Hungary
	Dmitri Bilozertchev, USSR
1989	Valentin Moguilny, USSR
1991	Valeri Belenki, USSR
1992	Pae Gil Su, North Korea
	Vitaly Scherbo, CIS
	Li Jing, China
1993	Pae Gil Su, North Korea
1994	Marius Urzica, Romania
1995	Li Donghua, Switzerland
1996	Pae Gil Su, North Korea
1997	Valeri Belenki, Germany
1999	Alexei Nemov, Russia
2001	Marius Urzica, Romania
2003	Teng Haibin, China
	Takehiro Kashima, Japan
2005	Qin Xiao, China
2007	Qin Xiao, China
2009	Hongtao Zhang, China
2011	Krisztian Berki, Hungary
2013	Kohei Kameyama, Japan

Floor Exercise

Year	Champion, Nation
1930	Josip Primozic, Yugoslavia
1934	Georges Miesz, Switzerland
1938	Jan Gajdos, Czechoslovakia
1950	Josef Stalder, Switzerland
1954	Valentin Mouratov, USSR
	Masao Takemoto, Japan
1958	Masao Takemoto, Japan
1962	Nobuyuki Aihara, Japan
	Yukio Endo, Japan
1966	Akinori Nakayama, Japan
1970	Akinori Nakayama, Japan
1974	Shigeru Kasamatsu, Japan
1978	Kurt Thomas, United States
1979	Kurt Thomas, United States
	Roland Brucker, E Germany
1981	Yuri Korolev, USSR,
	Li Yuejui, China
1983	Tong Fei, China
1985	Tong Fei, China
1987	Lou Yun, China
1989	Igor Korobchinsky, USSR
1991	Igor Korobchinsky, USSR
1992	gor Korobchinsky, CIS
1993	Grigori Misutin, Ukraine
1994	Vitaly Scherbo, Belarus
1995	Vitaly Scherbo, Belarus
1996	Vitaly Scherbo, Belarus
1997	Alexei Nemov, Russia
1999	Alexei Nemov, Russia
2001	Marian Dragulescu, Romania
2003	Paul Hamm, United States
	Jordan Jovtchev, Bulgaria
2005	Diego Hypolito, Brazil
2007	Zou Kai, China
2009	Marian Dragulescu, Romania
2011	Kohei Uchimura, Japan
2013	Kenzo Shirai, Japan

WORLD CHAMPIONS — Men *(Cont.)*

Rings

Year	Champion, Nation
1930	Emanuel Loffler, Czechoslovakia
1934	Alois Hudec, Czechoslovakia
1938	Alois Hudec, Czechoslovakia
1950	Walter Lehmann, Switzerland
1954	Albert Azarian, USSR
1958	Albert Azarian, USSR
1962	Yuri Titov, USSR
1966	Mikhail Voronin, USSR
1970	Akinori Nakayama, Japan
1974	N. Andrianov, USSR/D. Grecu, Rom.
1978	Nikolai Andrianov, USSR
1979	Alexander Ditiatin, USSR
1981	Alexander Ditiatin, USSR
1983	Dimitri Bilozertchev, USSR
1985	Li Ning, China, Yuri Korolev, USSR
1987	Yuri Korolev, USSR
1989	Andreas Aguilar, W Germany
1991	Grigory Misutin, USSR
1992	Vitaly Scherbo, CIS
1993	Yuri Chechi, Italy
1994	Yuri Chechi, Italy
1995	Yuri Chechi, Italy
1996	Yuri Chechi, Italy
1997	Yuri Chechi, Italy
1999	Zhen Dong, China
2001	Jordan Jovtchev, Bulgaria
2003	Jordan Jovtchev, Bulgaria/ Dimosthenis Tampakos, Greece
2005	Yuri Van Gelder, Netherlands
2007	Diego Hypolito, Brazil
2009	Mingyong Yan, China
2011	Yibing Chen, China
2013	Arthur Nabarrete Zanetti, Brazil

Parallel Bars

Year	Champion, Nation
1930	Josip Primozic, Yugoslavia
1934	Eugene Mack, Switzerland
1938	Michael Reusch, Switzerland
1950	Hans Eugster, Switzerland
1954	Victor Chukarin, USSR
1958	Boris Shaklin, USSR
1962	Miroslav Cerar, Yugoslavia
1966	Sergei Diamidov, USSR
1970	Akinori Nakayama, Japan
1974	Eizo Kenmotsu, Japan
1978	Eizo Kenmotsu, Japan
1979	Bart Conner, United States
1981	Koji Gushiken, Japan/ Alexandr Ditiatin, USSR
1983	Vladimir Artemov, USSR/ Lou Yun, China
1985	Sylvio Kroll, East Germany/ Valentin Moguilny, USSR
1987	Vladimir Artemov, USSR
1989	Li Jing, China Vladimir Artemov, USSR
1991	Li Jing, China
1992	Li Jin, China/Alexei Voropaev, CIS
1993	Vitaly Scherbo, Belarus
1994	Huang Liping, China
1995	Vitaly Scherbo, Belarus
1996	Rustam Sharipov, Ukraine
1997	Zhang Jinjing, China

Parallel Bar *(Cont.)*

Year	Champion, Nation
1999	Joo-Hyung Lee, South Korea
2001	Sean Townsend, United States
2003	Li Xiao-Peng, China
2005	Mitja Petkovsek, Slovenia
2007	Mitja Petkovsek, Slovenia
2009	Guanyin Yang, China
2011	Danell Leyva, United States
2013	Chaopan Lin, China

Horizontal Bar

Year	Champion, Nation
1930	Istvan Pelle, Hungary
1934	Ernst Winter, Germany
1938	Michael Reusch, Switzerland
1950	Paavo Aaltonen, Finland
1954	Valentin Mouratov, USSR
1958	Boris Shaklin, USSR
1962	Takashi Ono, Japan
1966	Akinori Nakayama, Japan
1970	Eizo Kenmotsu, Japan
1974	Eberhard Gienger, W Germany
1978	Shigeru Kasamatsu, Japan
1979	Kurt Thomas, United States
1981	Alexander Takchev, USSR
1983	Dimitri Bilozertchev, USSR
1985	Tong Fei, China
1987	Dimitri Bilozertchev, USSR
1989	Li Chunyang, China
1991	Li Chunyang, China/ R. Buechner, Germany
1992	Grigori Misutin, CIS
1993	Sergei Kharkov, Russia
1994	Vitaly Scherbo, Belarus
1995	Andreas Wecker, Germany
1996	Jesús Carballo, Spain
1997	Jani Tanskanen, Finland
1999	Jesus Carballo, Spain
2001	Vlasios Maras, Greece
2003	Takehiro Kashima, Japan
2005	Vlasios Maras, Greece
2007	Fabian Hambuechen, Germany
2009	Kai Zou, China
2011	Kai Zou, China
2013	Epke Zonderland, Netherlands

Vault

Year	Champion, Nation
1934	Eugene Mack, Switzerland
1938	Eugene Mack, Switzerland
1950	Ernst Gebendinger, Switzerland
1954	Leo Sotornik, Czechoslovakia
1958	Yuri Titov, USSR
1962	Premysel Krbec, Czechoslovakia
1966	Haruhiro Yamashita, Japan
1970	Mitsuo Tsukahara, Japan
1974	Shigeru Kasamatsu, Japan
1978	Junichi Shimizu, Japan
1979	Alexander Ditiatin, USSR
1981	Ralf-Peter Hemmann, East Germany
1983	Arthur Akopian, USSR
1985	Yuri Korolev, USSR

Vault *(Cont.)*

Year	Champion, Nation
1987	Lou Yun, China/ Sylvio Kroll, East Germany
1989	Joreg Behrend, East Germany
1991	Yoo Ok Youl, South Korea
1992	Yoo Ok Youl, South Korea
1993	Vitaly Scherbo, Belarus
1994	Vitaly Scherbo, Belarus
1995	Grigory Misutin, Ukraine/ Alexei Nemov, Russia
1996	Alexei Nemov, Russia
1997	Sergei Fedorchenko, Kazakhstan
1999	Li Xiao-Peng, China
2001	Marian Dragulescu, Romania
2003	Li Xiao-Peng, China
2005	Eichi Sekiguchi, Japan
2007	Leszek Blanik, Poland
2009	Marian Dragulescu, Romania
2011	Hak-seon Yang, South Korea
2013	Hak-seon Yang, South Korea

WORLD CHAMPIONS — Women

All-Around

Year	Champion, Nation
1934	Vlasta Dekanova, Czechoslovakia
1938	Vlasta Dekanova, Czechoslovakia
1950	Helena Rakoczy, Poland
1954	Galina Roudiko, USSR
1958	Larissa Latynina, USSR
1962	Larissa Latynina, USSR
1966	Vera Caslavska, Czechoslovakia
1970	Ludmilla Tourischeva, USSR
1974	Ludmilla Tourischeva, USSR
1978	Elena Mukhina, USSR
1979	Nelli Kim, USSR
1981	Olga Bicherova, USSR
1983	Natalia Yurchenko, USSR
1985	Elena Shoushounova, USSR/ Oksana Omeliantchik, USSR
1987	Aurelia Dobre, Romania
1989	Svetlana Bouguinskaia, USSR
1991	Kim Zmeskal, United States
1993	Shannon Miller, United States
1994	Shannon Miller, United States
1995	Lilia Podkopayeva, Ukraine
1997	Svetlana Khorkina, Russia
1999	Maria Olaru, Romania
2001	Svetlana Khorkina, Russia
2003	Svetlana Khorkina, Russia
2005	Chellsie Memmel, United States
2007	Shawn Johnson, United States
2009	Bridget Sloan, United States
2011	Jordyn Wieber, United States
2013	Simone Biles, United States

Floor Exercise

Year	Champion, Nation
1950	Helena Rakoczy, Poland
1954	Tamara Manina, USSR
1958	Eva Bosakava, Czechoslovakia
1962	Larissa Latynina, USSR
1966	Natalia Kuchinskaya, USSR
1970	Ludmilla Tourischeva, USSR
1974	Ludmilla Tourischeva, USSR
1978	Nelli Kim, USSR/ Elena Mukhina, USSR
1979	Emilia Eberle, Romania
1981	Natalia Ilenko, USSR
1983	Ecaterina Szabo, Romania
1985	Oksana Omeliantchik, USSR
1987	Elena Shoushounova, USSR/ Daniela Silivas, Romania
1989	Svetlana Bouguinskaia, USSR/ Daniela Silivas, Romania
1991	Cristina Bontas, Romania/ Oksana Tchusovitina, USSR
1992	Kim Zmeskal, United States
1993	Shannon Miller, United States
1994	Dina Kochetkova, Russia
1995	Gina Gogean, Romania
1996	Gina Gogean, Romania
1997	Gina Gogean, Romania
1999	Andreea Raducan, Romania
2001	Andreea Raducan, Romania
2003	Daiane Dos Santos, Brazil
2005	Nastia Liukin, United States
2007	Shawn Johnson, United States
2009	Elizabeth Tweddle, United Kingdom

Floor Exercise *(Cont.)*

Year	Champion, Nation
2011	Kseniia Afanaseva, Russia
2013	Simone Biles, United States

Uneven Bars

Year	Champion, Nation
1950	Gertchen Kolar, Austria/ Anna Pettersson, Sweden
1954	Agnes Keleti, Hungary
1958	Larissa Latynina, USSR
1962	Irina Pervuschina, USSR
1966	Natalia Kuchinskaya, USSR
1970	Karin Janz, East Germany
1974	Annelore Zinke, East Germany
1978	Marcia Frederick, United States
1979	Ma Yanhong, China/ Maxi Gnauck, East Germany
1981	Maxi Gnauck, East Germany
1983	Maxi Gnauck, East Germany
1985	Gabriele Fahnrich, East Germany
1987	Daniela Silivas, Romania/ Doerte Thuemmler, East Germany
1989	Fan Di, China/ Daniela Silivas, Romania
1991	Gwang Suk Kim, North Korea
1992	Lavinia Milosivici, Romania
1993	Shannon Miller, United States
1994	Luo Li, China
1995	Svetlana Khorkina, Russia
1996	Svetlana Khorkina, Russia
1997	Svetlana Khorkina, Russia
1999	Svetlana Khorkina, Russia
2001	Svetlana Khorkina, Russia
2003	Chellsie Memmel, United States Hollie Vise, United States
2005	Nastia Liukin, United States
2007	Ksenia Semenov, Russia
2009	Kexin He, China
2011	Viktoria Komova, Russia
2013	Jinnan Yao, China

Balance Beam

Year	Champion, Nation
1950	Helena Rakoczy, Poland
1954	Keiko Tanaka, Japan
1958	Larissa Latynina, USSR
1962	Eva Bosakova, Czech.
1966	Natalia Kuchinskaya, USSR
1970	Erika Zuchold, East Germany
1974	Ludmilla Tourischeva, USSR
1978	Nadia Comaneci, Romania
1979	Vera Cerna, Czechoslovakia
1981	Maxi Gnauck, East Germany
1983	Olga Mostepanova, USSR
1985	Daniela Silivas, Romania
1987	Aurelia Dobre, Romania
1989	Daniela Silivas, Romania
1991	Svetlana Boguinskaia, USSR
1992	Kim Zmeskal, United States
1993	Lavinia Milosovici, Romania
1994	Shannon Miller, United States
1995	Mo Huilan, China
1996	Dina Kochetkova, Russia
1997	Gina Gogean, Romania

Balance Beam *(Cont.)*

Year	Champion, Nation
1999	E. Zamolodchikova, Russia
2001	Andreea Raducan, Romania
2003	Fan Ye, China
2005	Nan Zhang, China
2007	Nastia Liukin, United States
2009	Linlin Deng, China
2011	Lu Sui, China
2013	Larisa Andreea Iordache, Romania

Vault

Year	Champion, Nation
1950	Helena Rakoczy, Poland
1954	Tamara Manina, USSR/ Anna Pettersson, Sweden
1958	Larissa Latynina, USSR
1962	Vera Caslavska, Czech.
1966	Vera Caslavska, Czech.
1970	Erika Zuchold, East Germany
1974	Olga Korbut, USSR
1978	Nelli Kim, USSR
1979	Dumitrita Turner, Romania
1981	Maxi Gnauck, East Germany
1983	Boriana Stoyanova, Bulgaria
1985	Elena Shoushounova, USSR
1987	Elena Shoushounova, USSR
1989	Olesia Durnik, USSR
1991	Lavinia Milosovici, Romania
1992	Henrietta Onodi, Hungary
1993	Elena Piskun, Belarus
1994	Gina Gogean, Romania
1995	Lilia Podkopayeva, Ukraine/ Simona Amanar, Romania
1996	Gina Gogean, Romania
1997	Simona Amanar, Romania
1999	Jie Ling, China
2001	Svetlana Khorkina, Russia
2003	Oksana Chusovitina, Uzbekistan
2005	Fei Cheng, China
2007	Fei Cheng, China
2009	Kayla Williams, United States
2011	McKayla Maroney, United States
2013	McKayla Maroney, United States

CHAMPIONS OF THE UNITED STATES — Men

All-Around

Year	Champion
1963	Art Shurlock
1964	Rusty Mitchell
1965	Rusty Mitchell
1966	Rusty Mitchell
1967	Katsuzoki Kanzaki
1968	Yoshi Hayasaki
1969	Steve Hug
1970	Makoto Sakamoto, Mas Watanabe
1971	Yoshi Takei
1972	Yoshi Takei
1973	Marshall Avener
1974	John Crosby
1975	Tom Beach, Bart Conner
1976	Kurt Thomas
1977	Kurt Thomas
1978	Kurt Thomas
1979	Bart Conner
1980	Peter Vidmar
1981	Jim Hartung
1982	Peter Vidmar
1983	Mitch Gaylord
1984	Mitch Gaylord
1985	Brian Babcock
1986	Tim Daggett
1987	Scott Johnson
1988	Dan Hayden
1989	Tim Ryan
1990	John Roethlisberger
1991	Chris Waller
1992	John Roethlisberger
1993	John Roethlisberger
1994	Scott Keswick
1995	John Roethlisberger
1996	Blaine Wilson
1997	Blaine Wilson
1998	Blaine Wilson
1999	Blaine Wilson
2000	Blaine Wilson
2001	Sean Townsend
2002	Paul Hamm
2003	Paul Hamm
2004	Paul Hamm
2005	Todd Thornton
2006	Alexander Artemev
2007	David Durante
2008	David Sender
2009	Jonathan Horton
2010	Jonathan Horton
2011	Danell Leyva
2012	John Orozco
2013	Sam Mikulak

Floor Exercise

Year	Champion
1963	Tom Seward
1964	Rusty Mitchell
1965	Rusty Mitchell
1966	Dan Millman
1967	Katsuzoki Kanzaki, Ron Aure
1968	Katsuzoki Kanzaki
1969	Steve Hug, Dave Thor
1970	Makoto Sakamoto
1971	John Crosby
1972	Yoshi Takei

Floor Exercise *(Cont.)*

Year	Champion
1973	John Crosby
1974	John Crosby
1975	Peter Korman
1977	Ron Galimore
1978	Kurt Thomas
1979	Ron Galimore
1980	Ron Galimore
1981	Jim Hartung
1982	Jim Hartung
1983	Mitch Gaylord
1984	Peter Vidmar
1985	Mark Oates
1986	Robert Sundstrom
1987	John Sweeney
1988	Mark Oates, Charles Lakes
1989	Mike Racanelli
1990	Bob Stelter
1991	Mike Racanelli
1992	Gregg Curtis
1993	Kerry Huston
1994	Jeremy Killen
1995	Daniel Stover
1996	Jay Thornton
1997	Jason Gatson
1998	Jason Gatson
1999	Jason Gatson
2000	Blaine Wilson
2001	Sean Townsend
2002	Morgan Hamm
2003	Morgan Hamm
2004	Paul Hamm
2005	Guillermo Alvarez
2006	Jonathan Horton
2007	Paul Hamm
2008	Morgan Hamm
2009	Steven Legendre
2010	Joshua Dixon
2011	Jacob Dalton
2012	Jacob Dalton
2013	Steven Legendre

Pommel Horse

Year	Champion
1963	Larry Spiegel
1964	Sam Bailie
1965	Jack Ryan
1966	Jack Ryan
1967	Paul Mayer, Dave Doty
1968	Katsuoki Kanzaki
1969	Dave Thor
1970	Mas Watanabe
1971	Leonard Caling
1972	Sadao Hamada
1973	Marshall Avener
1974	Marshall Avener
1975	Bart Conner
1977	Gene Whelan
1978	Jim Hartung
1979	Bart Conner
1980	Jim Hartung
1981	Jim Hartung
1982	Jim Hartung
1983	Bart Conner
1984	Tim Daggett
1985	Phil Cahoy

Pommel Horse *(Cont.)*

Year	Champion
1986	Phil Cahoy
1987	Tim Daggett
1988	Kevin Davis
1989	Kevin Davis
1990	Patrick Kirksey
1991	Chris Waller
1992	Chris Waller
1993	Chris Waller
1994	Mihai Begiu
1995	Mark Sohn
1996	Josh Stein
1997	John Roethlisberger
1998	John Roethlisberger
1999	John Roethlisberger
2000	John Roethlisberger
2001	Brett McClure
2002	Paul Hamm
2003	Paul Hamm
2004	Brett McClure
2005	Yewki Tomita
2006	Alexander Artemev
2007	Alexander Artemev
2008	Yewki Tomita
2009	Luke Stannard
2010	Daniel Ribiero
2011	Alexander Naddour
2012	Alexander Naddour
2013	Alexander Naddour

Rings

Year	Champion
1963	Art Shurlock
1964	Glen Gailis
1965	Glen Gailis
1966	Glen Gailis
1967	Fred Dennis, Don Hatch
1968	Yoshi Hayasaki
1969	Fred Dennis, Bob Emery
1970	Makoto Sakamoto
1971	Yoshi Takei
1972	Yoshi Takei
1973	Jim Ivicek
1974	Tom Weeder
1975	Tom Beach
1977	Kurt Thomas
1978	Mike Silverstein
1979	Bart Conner
1980	Jim Hartung
1981	Jim Hartung
1982	Jim Hartung, Peter Vidmar
1983	Mitch Gaylord
1984	Jim Hartung
1985	Dan Hayden
1986	Dan Hayden
1987	Scott Johnson
1988	Dan Hayden
1989	Scott Keswick
1990	Scott Keswick
1991	Scott Keswick
1992	Tim Ryan
1993	John Roethlisberger
1994	Scott Keswick
1995	Paul O'Neill
1996	Kip Simons
1997	Blaine Wilson

Rings *(Cont.)*

Year	Champion
1998	Jeff Johnson
1999	Blaine Wilson
2000	Blaine Wilson
2001	Sean Townsend
2002	Blaine Wilson
2003	Blaine Wilson
2004	Raj Bhavsar
2005	Sean Golden
2006	Kevin Tan
2007	Kevin Tan
2008	Kevin Tan
2009	Jonathan Horton
2010	Brandon Wynn
2011	Brandon Wynn
2012	Jonathan Horton
2013	Brandon Wynn

Vault

Year	Champion
1963	Art Shurlock
1964	Gary Hery
1965	Brent Williams
1966	Dan Millman
1967	Jack Kenan, Sid Jensen
1968	Rich Scorza
1969	Dave Butzman
1970	Makoto Sakamoto
1971	Gary Morava
1972	Mike Kelley
1973	Gary Morava
1974	John Crosby
1975	Tom Beach
1977	Ron Galimore
1978	Jim Hartung
1979	Ron Galimore
1980	Ron Galimore
1981	Ron Galimore
1982	Jim Hartung, Jim Mikus
1983	Chris Reigel
1984	Chris Reigel
1985	Scott Johnson, Mark Oates
1986	Scott Wilbanks
1987	John Sweeney
1988	John Sweeney, Bill Paul
1989	Bill Roth
1990	Lance Ringnald
1991	Scott Keswick
1992	Trent Dimas
1993	Bill Roth
1994	Keith Wiley
1995	David St. Pierre
1996	Blaine Wilson
1997	Blaine Wilson
1998	Brent Klaus
1999	Guard Young
2000	Blaine Wilson
2001	Jason Furr
2002	Paul Hamm
2003	Raj Bhavsar
2004	David Sender
2005	Sean Golden
2006	David Sender
2007	Sean Golden
2008	David Sender
2009	Jake Dalton

CHAMPIONS OF THE UNITED STATES - Men *(Cont.)*

Vault *(Cont.)*

Year	Champion
2010	Steven Legendre
2011	Jacob Dalton
2012	Sean Senters, Jacob Dalton
2013	Sean Senters, Eddie Penev

Parallel Bars

Year	Champion
1963	Tom Seward
1964	Rusty Mitchell
1965	Glen Gailis
1966	Ray Hadley
1967	Katsuzoki Kanzaki, Tom Goldsborough
1968	Yoshi Hayasaki
1969	Steve Hug
1970	Makoto Sakamoto
1971	Brent Simmons
1972	Yoshi Takei
1973	Marshall Avener
1974	Jim Ivicek
1975	Bart Conner
1977	Kurt Thomas
1978	Bart Conner
1979	Bart Conner
1980	Phil Cahoy, Larry Gerard
1981	Bart Conner
1982	Peter Vidmar
1983	Mitch Gaylord

Parallel Bars *(Cont.)*

Year	Champion
1984	Peter Vidmar, Mitch Gaylord, Tim Daggett
1985	Tim Daggett
1986	Tim Daggett
1987	Scott Johnson
1988	D. Hayden, K. Davis
1989	Conrad Voorsanger
1990	Trent Dimas
1991	Scott Keswick
1992	Jair Lynch
1993	Chainey Umphrey
1994	Steve McCain
1995	John Roethlisberger
1996	Jair Lynch
1997	Blaine Wilson
1998	Blaine Wilson
1999	Jason Gatson
2000	Trent Wells
2001	Sean Townsend
2002	Sean Townsend
2003	Jason Gatson
2004	Alexander Artemev
2005	D.J. Bucher
2006	Alexander Artemev
2007	David Durante
2008	Justin Spring
2009	Tim McNeill
2010	Danell Leyva
2011	Danell Leyva
2012	Danell Leyva
2013	Sam Mikulak

Horizontal Bar

Year	Champion
1963	Art Shurlock
1964	Glen Gailis
1965	Rusty Mitchell
1966	Katsuzoki Kanzaki
1967	Katsuzoki Kanzaki, Jerry Fontana
1968	Yoshi Hayasaki
1969	Rich Grisby
1970	Makoto Sakamoto
1971	Yoshi Takei
1972	Tom Lindner
1973	John Crosby
1974	Brent Simmons
1975	Tom Beach
1977	Kurt Thomas
1978	Kurt Thomas
1979	Yoichi Tomita
1980	Jim Hartung
1981	Bart Conner
1982	Mitch Gaylord
1983	Mario McCutcheon
1983	Mario McCutcheon
1984	Peter Vidmar, Tim Daggett, Mitch Gaylord
1985	Dan Hayden
1986	D. Hayden, D. Moriel
1987	David Moriel

Horiz. Bar *(Cont.)*

Year	Champion
1988	Dan Hayden
1989	Tim Ryan
1990	Trent Dimas, Lance Ringnald
1991	Lance Ringnald
1992	Jair Lynch
1993	Steve McCain
1994	Scott Keswick
1995	John Roethlisberger
1996	Bill Roth
1997	Douglas Stibel
1998	Jason Gatson
1999	Jamie Natalie
2000	Trent Wells, Jamie Natalie
2001	Daniel Diaz-Luong
2002	Blaine Wilson
2003	Paul Hamm
2004	Paul Hamm
2005	D.J. Bucher
2006	Chris Brooks
2007	Justin Spring
2008	Joseph Hagerty
2009	Jonathan Horton
2010	Chris Brooks
2011	Danell Leyva
2012	Danell Leyva
2013	Sam Mikulak

CHAMPIONS OF THE UNITED STATES — Women

All-Around

Year	Champion
1963	Donna Schanezer
1965	Gail Daley
1966	Donna Schanezer
1968	Linda Scott
1969	Joyce Tanac Schroeder
1970	Cathy Rigby
1971	Joan Moore Gnat, Linda Metheny Mulvihill
1972	Joan Moore Gnat, Cathy Rigby
1973	Joan Moore Gnat
1974	Joan Moore Gnat
1975	Tammy Manville
1976	Denise Cheshire
1977	Donna Turnbow
1978	Kathy Johnson
1979	Leslie Pyfer
1980	Julianne McNamara
1981	Tracee Talavera
1982	Tracee Talavera
1983	Dianne Durham
1984	Mary Lou Retton
1985	Sabrina Mar
1986	Jennifer Sey
1987	Kristie Phillips
1988	Phoebe Mills
1989	Brandy Johnson
1990	Kim Zmeskal
1991	Kim Zmeskal

All-Around *(Cont.)*

Year	Champion
1992	Kim Zmeskal
1993	Shannon Miller
1994	Dominique Dawes
1995	Dominique Moceanu
1996	Shannon Miller
1997	Vanessa Atler, Kristy Powell
1998	Kristen Maloney
1999	Kristen Maloney
2000	Elise Ray
2001	Tasha Schwikert
2002	Tasha Schwikert
2003	Courtney Kupets
2004	Courtney Kupets, Carly Patterson
2005	Nastia Liukin
2006	Nastia Liukin
2007	Shawn Johnson
2008	Shawn Johnson
2009	Bridget Sloan
2010	Rebecca Bross
2011	Jordyn Wieber
2012	Jordyn Wieber
2013	Simone Biles

Vault

Year	Champion
1963	Donna Schanezer
1965	Gail Daley
1966	Donna Schanezer
1968	Terry Spencer

Vault *(Cont.)*

Year	Champion
1969	Joyce Tanac Schroeder, Cleo Carver
1970	Cathy Rigby
1971	Joan Moore Gnat, Adele Gleaves
1972	Cindy Eastwood
1973	Roxanne Pierce Mancha
1974	Dianne Dunbar
1975	Kolleen Casey
1976	Debbie Wilcox
1977	Lisa Cawthron
1978	Rhonda Schwandt, Sharon Shapiro
1979	Christa Canary
1980	J. McNamara, B. Kline
1981	Kim Neal
1982	Yumi Mordre
1983	Dianne Durham
1984	Mary Lou Retton
1985	Yolanda Mavity
1986	Joyce Wilborn
1987	Rhonda Faehn
1988	Rhonda Faehn
1989	Brandy Johnson
1990	Brandy Johnson
1991	Kerri Strug
1992	Kerri Strug
1993	Dominique Dawes
1994	Dominique Dawes
1995	Shannon Miller
1996	Dominique Dawes
1997	Vanessa Atler

CHAMPIONS OF THE UNITED STATES— Women *(Cont.)*

Vault *(Cont.)*

Year	Champion
1998	Dominique Moceanu
1999	Vanessa Atler
2000	Kristen Maloney
2001	Mohini Bhardwaj
2002	Elizabeth Tricase
2003	Annia Hatch
2004	Liz Tricase
2005	Alicia Sacramone
2006	Alicia Sacramone
2007	Alicia Sacramone
2008	Alicia Sacramone
2009	Kayla Williams
2010	Alicia Sacramone
2011	McKayla Maroney
2012	Alicia Sacramone
2013	McKayla Maroney

Uneven Bars

Year	Champion
1963	Donna Schanezer
1965	Irene Haworth
1966	Donna Schanezer
1968	Linda Scott
1969	Joyce Tanac Schroeder, Lisa Nelson
1970	Roxanne Pierce Mancha
1971	Joan Moore Gnat
1972	Cathy Rigby
1973	Roxanne Pierce Mancha
1974	Diane Dunbar
1975	Leslie Wolfsberger
1976	Leslie Wolfsberger
1977	Donna Turnbow
1978	Marcia Frederick
1979	Marcia Frederick
1980	Marcia Frederick
1981	Julianne McNamara
1982	Marie Roethlisberger
1983	Julianne McNamara
1984	Julianne McNamara
1985	Sabrina Mar
1986	Marie Roethlisberger
1987	Melissa Marlowe
1988	Chelle Stack
1989	Chelle Stack
1990	Sandy Woolsey
1991	Elisabeth Crandall
1992	Dominique Dawes
1993	Shannon Miller
1994	Dominique Dawes
1995	Dominique Dawes
1996	Dominique Dawes
1997	Kristy Powell
1998	Elise Ray
1999	Jamie Dantzscher, Jennie Thompson
2000	Elise Ray
2001	Katie Heenan
2002	Tasha Schwikert
2003	Katie Heenan
2004	Courtney Kupets
2005	Nastia Liukin
2006	Nastia Liukin
2007	Nastia Liukin

Uneven Bars *(Cont.)*

Year	Champion
2008	Nastia Liukin
2009	Bridget Sloan
2010	Rebecca Bross
2011	Jordyn Wieber
2012	Gabrielle Douglas
2013	Kyla Ross

Balance Beam

Year	Champion
1963	Leissa Krol
1965	Gail Daley
1966	Irene Haworth, Linda Scott
1968	Linda Scott
1969	Lonna Woodward
1970	Joyce Tanac Schroeder
1971	Linda Metheny Mulvihill
1972	Kim Chace
1973	Nancy Thies Marshall
1974	Joan Moore Gnat
1975	Kyle Gayner
1976	Carrie Englert
1977	Donna Turnbow
1978	Christa Canary
1979	Heidi Anderson
1980	Kelly Garrison-Steves
1981	Tracee Talavera
1982	Julianne McNamara
1983	Dianne Durham
1984	Pam Bileck, Tracee Talavera
1986	Angie Denkins
1987	Kristie Phillips
1985	Kelly Garrison-Steves
1988	Kelly Garrison-Steves
1989	Brandy Johnson
1990	Betty Okino
1991	Shannon Miller
1992	Kerri Strug, Kim Zmeskal
1993	Dominique Dawes
1994	Dominique Dawes
1995	Doni Thompson, Monica Flammer
1996	Dominique Dawes
1997	Kendall Beck
1998	Dominique Moceanu
1999	Vanessa Atler
2000	Alyssa Beckerman, Amy Chow
2001	Tasha Schwikert
2002	Tasha Schwikert
2003	Hollie Vise
2004	Courtney Kupets
2005	Nastia Liukin
2006	Nastia Liukin
2007	Shawn Johnson
2008	Nastia Liukin
2009	Ivana Hong
2010	Rebecca Bross
2011	Alicia Sacramone
2012	Aly Raisman
2013	Kyla Ross

Floor Exercise

Year	Champion
1963	Donna Schanezer
1965	Gail Daley
1966	Donna Schanezer
1968	Linda Scott
1970	Cathy Rigby
1971	Joan Moore Gnat, Linda Metheny Mulvihill
1972	Joan Moore Gnat
1973	Joan Moore Gnat
1974	Joan Moore Gnat
1975	Kathy Howard
1976	Carrie Englert
1977	Kathy Johnson
1978	Kathy Johnson
1979	Heidi Anderson
1980	Beth Kline
1981	Michelle Goodwin
1982	Amy Koopman
1983	Dianne Durham
1984	Mary Lou Retton
1985	Sabrina Mar
1986	Yolanda Mavity
1987	Kristie Phillips
1988	Phoebe Mills
1989	Brandy Johnson
1990	Brandy Johnson
1991	Kim Zmeskal, Dominique Dawes
1992	Kim Zmeskal
1993	Shannon Miller
1994	Dominique Dawes
1995	Dominique Dawes
1996	Dominique Dawes
1997	Lindsay Wing
1998	Vanessa Atler
1999	Elise Ray
2000	Kristen Maloney
2001	Tabitha Yim
2002	Tasha Schwikert
2003	Ashley Postell
2004	Carly Patterson
2005	Alicia Sacramone
2006	Alicia Sacramone, Randi Stageberg
2007	Shawn Johnson
2008	Shawn Johnson
2009	Bridget Sloan
2010	Mattie Larson
2011	Jordyn Wieber
2012	Aly Raisman
2013	McKayla Maroney

Skiing World Cup Season Title Holders

Men – OVERALL

1967	Jean-Claude Killy, France
1968	Jean-Claude Killy, France
1969	Karl Schranz, Austria
1970	Karl Schranz, Austria
1971	Gustavo Thoeni, Italy
1972	Gustavo Thoeni, Italy
1973	Gustavo Thoeni, Italy
1974	Piero Gros, Italy
1975	Gustavo Thoeni, Italy
1976	Ingemar Stenmark, Sweden
1977	Ingemar Stenmark, Sweden
1978	Ingemar Stenmark, Sweden
1979	Peter Lüscher, Switzerland
1980	Andreas Wenzel, Liechtenstein
1981	Phil Mahre, United States
1982	Phil Mahre, United States
1983	Phil Mahre, United States
1984	Pirmin Zurbriggen, Switzerland
1985	Marc Girardelli, Luxembourg
1986	Marc Girardelli, Luxembourg
1987	Pirmin Zurbriggen, Switzerland
1988	Pirmin Zurbriggen, Switzerland
1989	Marc Girardelli, Luxembourg
1990	Pirmin Zurbriggen, Switzerland
1991	Marc Girardelli, Luxembourg
1992	Paul Accola, Switzerland
1993	Marc Girardelli, Luxembourg
1994	Kjetil André Aamodt, Norway
1995	Alberto Tomba, Italy
1996	Lasse Kjus, Norway
1997	Luc Alphand, France
1998	Hermann Maier, Austria
1999	Lasse Kjus, Norway
2000	Hermann Maier, Austria
2001	Hermann Maier, Austria
2002	Stephan Eberharter, Austria
2003	Stephan Eberharter, Austria
2004	Hermann Maier, Austria
2005	Bode Miller, United States
2006	Benjamin Raich, Austria
2007	Aksel Lund Svindal, Norway
2008	Bode Miller, United States
2009	Aksel Lund Svindal, Norway
2010	Carlo Janka, Switzerland
2011	Ivica Kostelic, Croatia
2012	Marcel Hirscher, Austria
2013	Marcel Hirscher, Austria

Women – OVERALL

1967	Nancy Greene, Canada
1968	Nancy Greene, Canada
1969	Gertrud Gabl, Austria
1970	Michèle Jacot, France
1971	Annemarie Pröll, Austria
1972	Annemarie Pröll, Austria
1973	Annemarie Pröll, Austria
1974	Annemarie Moser-Pröll, Austria
1975	Annemarie Moser-Pröll, Austria
1976	Rosi Mitermaier, West Germany
1977	Lise-Marie Morerod, Switzerland
1978	Hanni Wenzel, Liechtenstein
1979	Annemarie Moser-Pröll, Austria
1980	Hanni Wenzel, Liechtenstein
1981	Marie-Thérèse Nadig, Switzerland
1982	Erika Hess, Switzerland
1983	Tamara McKinney, United States
1984	Erika Hess, Switzerland
1985	Michela Figini, Switzerland
1986	Maria Walliser, Switzerland
1987	Maria Walliser, Switzerland
1988	Michela Figini, Switzerland
1989	Vreni Schneider, Switzerland
1990	Petra Kronberger, Austria
1991	Petra Kronberger, Austria
1992	Petra Kronberger, Austria
1993	Anita Wachter, Austria
1994	Vreni Schneider, Switzerland
1995	Vreni Schneider, Switzerland
1996	Katja Seizinger, Germany
1997	Pernilla Wiberg, Sweden
1998	Katja Seizinger, Germany
1999	Alexandra Meissnitzer, Austria
2000	Renate Goetschl, Austria
2001	Janica Kostelic, Croatia
2002	Michaela Dorfmeister, Austria
2003	Janica Kostelic, Croatia
2004	Anja Paerson, Sweden
2005	Anja Paerson, Sweden
2006	Janica Kostelic, Croatia
2007	Nicole Hosp, Austria
2008	Lindsey Vonn, United States
2009	Lindsey Vonn, United States
2010	Lindsey Vonn, United States
2011	Maria Hoefl-Riesch, Germany
2012	Lindsay Vonn, United States
2013	Tina Maze, Slovenia

United States National Champions

1983
FREESTYLE
105.5	Rich Salamone
114.5	Joe Gonzales
125.5	Joe Corso
136.5	Rich Dellagatta*
149.5	Bill Hugent
163	Lee Kemp
180.5	Chris Campbell
198	Pete Bush
220	Greg Gibson
Hvy	Bruce Baumgartner
Team	Sunkist Kids

GRECO-ROMAN
105.5	T.J. Jones
114.5	Mark Fuller
125.5	Rob Hermann
136.5	Dan Mello
149.5	Jim Martinez
163	James Andre
180.5	Steve Goss
198	Steve Fraser*
220	Dennis Koslowski
Hvy	No champion
Team	Minn. Wrestling Club

1984
FREESTYLE
105.5	Rich Salamone
114.5	Charlie Heard
125.5	Joe Corso
136.5	Rich Dellagatta*
149.5	Andre Metzger
163	Dave Schultz*
180.5	Mark Schultz
198	Steve Fraser
220	Harold Smith
Hvy	Bruce Baumgartner
Team	Sunkist Kids

GRECO-ROMAN
105.5	T.J. Jones
114.5	Mark Fuller
136.5	Dan Mello
149.5	Jim Martinez*
163	John Matthews
180.5	Tom Press
198	Mike Houck
220	No champion
Hvy	No champion
Team	Adirondack 3-Style, Wash.

1985
FREESTYLE
105.5	Tim Vanni
114.5	Jim Martin
125.5	Charlie Heard
136.5	Darryl Burley
149.5	Bill Nugent*
163	Kenny Monday
180.5	Mike Sheets
198	Mark Schultz
220	Greg Gibson
286	Bruce Baumgartner
Team	Sunkist Kids

1985 (Cont.)
GRECO-ROMAN
105.5	T.J. Jones
114.5	Mark Fuller
125.5	Eric Seward*
136.5	Buddy Lee
149.5	Jim Martinez
163	David Butler
180.5	Chris Catallo
198	Mike Houck
220	Greg Gibson
286	Dennis Koslowski
Team	U.S. Marine Corps

1986
FREESTYLE
105.5	Rich Salamone
114.5	Joe Gonzales
125.5	Kevin Darkus
136.5	John Smith
149.5	Andre Metzger*
163	Dave Schultz
180.5	Mark Schultz
198	Jim Scherr
220	Dan Severn
286	Bruce Baumgartner
Team	Sunkist Kids (Div. I)
	Hawkeye Wrestling
	Club (Div. II)

GRECO-ROMAN
105.5	Eric Wetzel
114.5	Shawn Sheldon
125.5	Anthony Amado
136.5	Frank Famiano
149.5	Jim Martinez
163	David Butler*
180.5	Darryl Gholar
198	Derrick Waldroup
220	Dennis Koslowski
286	Duane Koslowski
Team	U.S. Marine Corps (Div. I)
	U.S. Navy (Div. II)

1987
FREESTYLE
105.5	Takashi Irie
114.5	Mitsuru Sato
125.5	Barry Davis
136.5	Takumi Adachi
149.5	Andre Metzger
163	Dave Schultz*
180.5	Mark Schultz
198	Jim Scherr
220	Bill Scherr
286	Bruce Baumgartner
Team	Sunkist Kids (Div. I)
	Team Foxcatcher (Div. II)

GRECO-ROMAN
105.5	Eric Wetzel
114.5	Shawn Sheldon
125.5	Eric Seward
136.5	Frank Famiano
149.5	Jim Martinez
163	David Butler
180.5	Chris Catallo
198	Derrick Waldroup*

1987 (Cont.)
GRECO-ROMAN (CONT.)
220	Dennis Koslowski
286	Duane Koslowski
Team	U.S. Marine Corp (Div. I)
	U.S. Army (Div. II)

1988
FREESTYLE
105.5	Tim Vanni
114.5	Joe Gonzales
125.5	Kevin Darkus
136.5	John Smith*
149.5	Nate Carr
163	Kenny Monday
180.5	Dave Schultz
198	Melvin Douglas III
220	Bill Scherr
286	Bruce Baumgartner
Team	Sunkist Kids (Div. I)
	Team Foxcatcher (Div. II)

GRECO-ROMAN
105.5	T.J. Jones
114.5	Shawn Sheldon
125.5	Gogi Parseghian*
136.5	Dalen Wasmund
149.5	Craig Pollard
163	Tony Thomas
180.5	Darryl Gholar
198	Mike Carolan
220	Dennis Koslowski
286	Duane Koslowski
Team	U.S. Marine Corps (Div. I)
	Sunkist Kids (Div. II)

1989
FREESTYLE
105.5	Tim Vanni
114.5	Zeke Jones
125.5	Brad Penrith
136.5	John Smith
149.5	Nate Carr
163	Rob Koll
180.5	Rico Chiapparelli
198	Jim Scherr*
220	Bill Scherr
286	Bruce Baumgartner
Team	Sunkist Kids (Div. I)
	Team Foxcatcher (Div. II)

GRECO-ROMAN
105.5	Lew Dorrance
114.5	Mark Fuller
125.5	Gogi Parseghian
136.5	Isaac Anderson
149.5	Andy Seras*
163	David Butler
180.5	John Morgan
198	Michial Foy
220	Steve Lawson
286	Craig Pittman
Team	USMC (Div. I)
	Jets USA (Div. II)

*Outstanding wrestler.

United States National Champions (Cont.)

1990
FREESTYLE
105.5 ......Rob Eiter
114.5 ......Zeke Jones
125,5 ......Joe Melchiore
136.5 ......John Smith
149.5 ......Nate Carr
163 ....Rob Koll
180.5 ......Royce Alger
198 ....Chris Campbell*
220 ....Bill Scherr
286 ....Bruce Baumgartner
Team ......Sunkist Kids (Div. I)
Team Foxcatcher (Div. II)

GRECO-ROMAN
105.5 ......Lew Dorrance
114.5 ......Sam Henson
125.5 ......Mark Pustelnik
136.5 ......Isaac Anderson
149.5 ......Andy Seras
163 ....David Butler
180.5 ......Derrick Waldroup
198 ....Randy Couture*
220 ....Chris Tironi
286 ....Matt Ghaffari
Team ......Jets USA (Div. I)
California Jets (Div. II)

1991
FREESTYLE
105.5 ......Tim Vanni
114.5 ......Zeke Jones
125.5 ......Brad Penrith
136.5 ......John Smith*
149.5 ......Townsend Saunders
163 ....Kenny Monday
180.5 ......Kevin Jackson
198 ....Chris Campbell
220 ....Mark Coleman
286 ....Bruce Baumgartner
Team ......Sunkist Kids (Div. I)
Jets USA (Div. II)

GRECO-ROMAN
105.5 ......Eric Wetzel
114.5 ......Shawn Sheldon
125.5 ......Frank Famiano
136.5 ......Buddy Lee
149.5 ......Andy Seras
163 ....Gordy Morgan
180.5 ......John Morgan*
198 ....Michial Foy
220 ....Dennis Koslowski
286 ....Craig Pittman
Team ......Jets USA (Div. I)
Sunkist Kids (Div. II)

1992
FREESTYLE
105.5 ......Rob Eiter
114.5 ......Jack Griffin
125.5 ......Kendall Cross*
136.5 ......John Fisher
149.5 ......Matt Demaray
163 ....Greg Elinsky
180.5 ......Royce Alger
198 ....Dan Chaid
220 ....Bill Scherr

1992 (Cont.)
FREESTYLE (CONT.)
286 ....Bruce Baumgartner
Team ......Sunkist Kids (Div. I)
Team Foxcatcher (Div. II)

GRECO-ROMAN
105.5 ......Eric Wetzel
114.5 ......Mark Fuller
125.5 ......Dennis Hall
136.5 ......Buddy Lee*
149.5 ......Rodney Smith
163 ....Travis West
180.5 ......John Morgan
198 ....Michial Foy
220 ....Dennis Koslowski
286 ....Matt Ghaffari
Team ......N.Y. Athletic Club (Div. I)
Sunkist Kids (Div. II)

1993
FREESTYLE
105.5 ......Rob Eiter
114.5 ......Zeke Jones
125.5 ......Brad Penrith
136.5 ......Tom Brands
149.5 ......Matt Demaray
163 ....Dave Schultz*
180.5 ......Kevin Jackson
198 ....Melvin Douglas
220 ....Kirk Trost
286 ....Bruce Baumgartner
Team ......Sunkist Kids (Div. I)
Team Foxcatcher (Div. II)

GRECO-ROMAN
105.5 ......Eric Wetzel
114.5 ......Shawn Sheldon
125.5 ......Dennis Hall*
136.5 ......Shon Lewis
149.5 ......Andy Seras
163 ....Gordy Morgan
180.5 ......Dan Henderson
198 ....Randy Couture
220 ....James Johnson
286 ....Matt Ghaffari
Team ......N.Y. Athletic Club (Div. I)
Sunkist Kids (Div. II)

1994
FREESTYLE
105.5 ......Tim Vanni
114.5 ......Zeke Jones
125.5 ......Terry Brands
136.5 ......Tom Brands
149.5 ......Matt Demaray
163 ....Dave Schultz
180.5 ......Royce Alger
198 ....Melvin Douglas
220 ....Mark Kerr
286 ....Bruce Baumgartner*
Team ......Sunkist Kids (Div. I)
Team Foxcatcher (Div. II)

GRECO-ROMAN
105.5 ......Isaac Ramaswamy
114.5 ......Shawn Sheldon
125.5 ......Dennis Hall
136.5 ......Shon Lewis
149.5 ......Andy Seras*

1994 (Cont.)
GRECO-ROMAN (CONT.)
163 ....Gordy Morgan
180.5 ......Dan Henderson
198 ....Derrick Waldroup
220 ....James Johnson
286 ....Matt Ghaffari
Team ......Armed Forces (Div. I)
N.Y. Athletic Club (Div. II)

1995
FREESTYLE
105.5 ......Tim Vanni
114.5 ......Zeke Jones
125.5 ......Terry Brands
136.5 ......Tom Brands
149.5 ......Matt Demaray
163 ....Dave Schultz
180.5 ......Royce Alger
198 ....Melvin Douglas
220 ....Mark Kerr
286 ....Bruce Baumgartner*
Team ......Sunkist Kids (Div. I)
Team Foxcatcher (Div. II)

GRECO-ROMAN
105.5 ......Isaac Ramaswamy
114.5 ......Shawn Sheldon
125.5 ......Dennis Hall
136.5 ......Shon Lewis
149.5 ......Andy Seras*
163 ....Gordy Morgan
180.5 ......Dan Henderson
198 ....Derrick Waldroup
220 ....James Johnson
286 ....Matt Ghaffari
Team ......Armed Forces (Div. I)
N.Y. Athletic Club (Div. II)

1996
FREESTYLE
105.5 ......Rob Eiter
114.5 ......Lou Rosselli
125.5 ......Kendall Cross*
136.5 ......Tom Brands
149.5 ......Matt Demaray
163 ....Dave Schultz
180.5 ......Kevin Jackson
198 ....Melvin Douglas
220 ....Kurt Angle
286 ....Bruce Baumgartner
Team ......Sunkist Kids (Div. I)
Team Foxcatcher (Div. II)

GRECO-ROMAN
105.5 ......Isaac Ramaswamy
114.5 ......Shawn Sheldon
125.5 ......Dennis Hall*
136.5 ......Van Fronhofer
149.5 ......Heath Sims
163 ....Matt Lindland
180.5 ......Marty Morgan
198 ....Michial Foy
220 ....James Johnson
286 ....Rulon Gardner
Team ......Armed Forces (Div. I)
Sunkist Kids (Div. II)

*Outstanding wrestler.

United States National Champions (Cont.)

1997

FREESTYLE

110 ....Kanamti Soloman
119 ....Zeke Jones
127.75 .....Terry Brands
138.75 .....Carl Kolat
152 ....Lincoln McIlravy*
167.5 ....Dan St. John
187.25 .....Les Gutches
213.75 .....Melvin Douglas
275.5 ....Tom Erikson
Team ....Sunkist Kids (Div. I)
　　　　　N.Y. Athletic Club (Div. II)

GRECO-ROMAN

110 ....Mark Yanagihara
119 ....Broderick Lee
127.75 .....Dennis Hall
138.75 .....Kevin Bracken
152 ....Chris Saba
167.5 ....Miguel Spencer
187.25 .....Dan Henderson
213.75 .....Randy Couture*
275.5 ....Rulon Gardner
Team ....Armed Forces (Div. I)
　　　　　N.Y. Athletic Club (Div. II)

1998

FREESTYLE

119 ....Sam Henson
127.75 .....Tony Purler
138.75 .....Shawn Charles
152 ....Lincoln McIlravy
167.5 ....Steve Marianetti
187.25 .....Les Gutches*
213.75 .....Melvin Douglas
286 ....Tolly Thompson
Team ....Sunkist Kids (Div. I)
　　　　　N.Y. Athletic Club (Div. II)

GRECO-ROMAN

119 ....Shawn Sheldon
127.75 .....Dennis Hall
138.75 .....Shon Lewis
152 ....Chris Saba
167.5 ....Matt Lindland
187.25 .....Dan Niebuhr*
213.75 .....Jason Klohs
286 ....Matt Ghaffari
Team ....Armed Forces (Div. I)
　　　　　Sunkist Kids (Div. II)

1999

FREESTYLE

119 ....Lou Rosselli
127.75 .....Terry Brands
138.75 .....Cary Kolat
152 ....Lincoln McIlravy
167.5 ....Joe Williams
187.25 .....Les Gutches
213.75 .....Dominic Black
286 ....Stephen Neal*
Team ....Sunkist Kids (Div. I)
　　　　　N.Y. Athletic Club (Div. II)

GRECO-ROMAN

119 ....Steven Mays
127.75 .....Dennis Hall
138.75 .....Glen Nieradka
152 ....David Zuniga
167.5 ....Matt Lindland
187.25 .....Quincey Clark

1999 (Cont.)

GRECO-ROMAN (CONT.)

213.75 .....Randy Couture
286 ....Dremiel Byers*
Team ....Minnesota Storm (Div. I)
　　　　　Sunkist Kids (Div. II)

2000

FREESTYLE

119 ....Sammie Henson
127.75 .....Keyy Boumans
138.75 .....Cary Kolat
152 ....Lincoln McIlravy
167.5 ....Brandon Slay*
187.25 .....Les Gutches
213.75 .....Melvin Douglas
286 ....Kerry McCoy
Team ....Sunkist Kids (Div. I)
　　　　　New York A.C. (Div. II)

GRECO-ROMAN

119 ....Brandon Paulson
127.75 .....Dennis Hall
138.75 .....Kevin Bracken
152 ....Heath Sims
167.5 ....Matt Lindland
187.25 .....Quincey Clark*
213.75 .....Jason Gleasman
286 ....Rulon Gardner
Team ....Armed Forces (Div. I)
　　　　　Sunkist Kids (Div. II)

2001

FREESTYLE

119 ....Eric Akin
127.75 .....Eric Guerrero
138.75 .....Bill Zadick
152 ....Ramico Blackmon
167.5 ....Joe Williams
187.25 .....Cael Sanderson*
213.75 .....Dominic Black
286 ....Kerry McCoy
Team ....Sunkist Kids (Div. I)
　　　　　New York A.C. (Div. II)

GRECO-ROMAN

119 ....Jeff Cervone
127.75 .....Dennis Hall
138.75 .....Kevin Bracken
152 ....Marcel Cooper
167.5 ....Keith Sieracki
187.25 .....Matt Lindland*
213.75 .....Garrett Lowney
286 ....Rulon Gardner
Team .......U.S. Army (Div. I)
　　　　　Sunkist Kids (Div. II)

2002

FREESTYLE

121 ....Teague Moore
132 ....Eric Guerrero
145.5 ....Bill Zadick
163 ....Joe Williams*
185 ....Cael Sanderson
211.5 ....Tim Hartung
264.5 ....Kerry McCoy
Team ....Sunkist Kids (Div. I)
　　　　　New York A.C. (Div. II)

GRECO-ROMAN

121 ....Brandon Paulson
132 ....Glenn Nieradka*

2002 (Cont.)

GRECO-ROMAN (CONT.)

145.5 ....Kevin Bracken
163 ....Keith Sieracki
185 ....Ethan Bosch
211.75 .....Garrett Lowney
264.5 ....Dremiel Byers
Team .......U.S. Army (Div. I)
　　　　　New York A.C. (Div. II)

2003

FREESTYLE

121 ....Stephen Abas
132 ....Eric Guerrero*
145.5 ....Chris Bono
163 ....Joe Williams
185 ....Cael Sanderson
211.5 ....Daniel Cormier
264.5 ....Kerry McCoy
Team ....Sunkist Kids (Div. I)
　　　　　Gator WC (Div. II)

GRECO-ROMAN

121 ....Brandon Paulson
132 ....James Gruenwald*
145.5 ....Kevin Bracken
163 ....Keith Sieracki
185 ....Brad Vering
211.5 ....Garrett Lowney
264.5 ....Dremiel Byers
Team .......U.S. Army (Div. I)
　　　　　Air Force (Div. II)

2004

FREESTYLE

121 ....Stephen Abbas
132 ....Eric Guerrero
145.5 ....Jamill Kelly
163 ....Joe Williams
185 ....Lee Fullhart*
211.5 ....Daniel Cormier
264.5 ....Kerry McCoy
Team ....Sunkist Kids (Div. I)
　　　　　Gator WC (Div. II)

GRECO-ROMAN

121 ....Brandon Paulson
132 ....James Gruenwald
145.5 ....Faruk Sahin
163 ....Darryl Christian
185 ....Brad Vering
211.5 ....Justin Ruiz
264.5 ....Dremiel Byers*
Team ....New York A.C. (Div. I)
　　　　　Air Force (Div. II)

2005

FREESTYLE

121 ....Sam Henson
132 ....Michael Lightner*
145.5 ....Chris Bono
163 ....Joe Williams
185 ....Mo Lawal
211.5 ....Daniel Cormier
264.5 ....Tolly Thompson
Team ....Sunkist Kids (Div. I)
　　　　　Gator WC (Div. II)

GRECO-ROMAN

121 ....Sam Hazewinkel
132 ....Joseph Warren
145.5 ....Harry Lester

*Outstanding wrestler.

United States National Champions

2005 *(Cont.)*
GRECO-ROMAN *(CONT.)*
163 ....Darryl Christian
185 ....Brad Vering
211.5 ....Justin Ruiz
264.5 ....Dremiel Byers*
Team ....New York A.C. (Div.I)
　　　　　Air Force (Div. II)

2006
FREESTYLE
121 ....Henry Cejudo
132 ....Zach Roberson
145.5 ....Chris Bono
163 ....Donny Pritzlaff*
185 ....Mo Lawal
211.5 ....Daniel Cormier
264.5 ....Tolly Thompson
Team ....Sunkist Kids (Div. I)
　　　　　Gator WC (Div. II)

GRECO-ROMAN
121 ....Lindsey Durlacher
132 ....Joseph Warren
145.5 ....Marcel Cooper
163 .........T.C. Dantzler
185 ....Jacob Clark*
211.5 ....Justin Ruiz
264.5 ....Dremiel Byers
Team .......U.S. Army (Div. I)
　　　　　New York A.C. (Div. II)

2007
FREESTYLE
121 ....Henry Cejudo
132 ....Nate Gallick*
145.5 ....Chris Bono
163 ....Joe Heskett
185 ....Joe Williams
211.5 ....Daniel Cormier
264.5 ....Tommy Rowlands
Team ....Sunkist Kids (Div. I)
　　　　　Gator WC (Div. II)

GRECO-ROMAN
121 ....Sam Hazewinkel*
132 ....Joseph Warren
145.5 ....Glenn Garrison
163 .........T.C. Dantzler
185 ....Brad Vering
211.5 ....Justin Ruiz
264.5 ....Russ Davie
Team .......U.S. Army (Div. I)
　　　　　New York A.C. (Div. II)

2008
FREESTYLE
121 ....Matt Azevedo*
132 ....Shawn Bunch
145.5 ....Doug Schwab
163 ....Ben Askren
185 ....Mo Lawal
211.5 ....Daniel Cormier
264.5 ....Tommy Rowlands
Team ....Sunkist Kids (Div. I)
　　　　　New York A.C. (Div. II)

2008 *(Cont.)*
GRECO-ROMAN
121 ....Spencer Mango*
132 ....Jim Gruenwald
145.5 ....Mark Rial
163 .........T.C. Dantzler
185 ....Brad Ahearn
211.5 ....Justin Ruiz
264.5 ....Dremiel Byers
Team .......U.S. Army (Div. I)
　　　　　New York A.C. (Div. II)

2009
FREESTYLE
121 ....Nick Simmons
132 ....Mike Zadick
145.5 ....Trent Paulson
163 ....Travis Paulson
185 ....Jake Herbert*
211.5 ....Jake Varner
264.5 ....Steve Mocco
Team ....Sunkist Kids (Div. I)
　　　　　Gator WC (Div. II)

GRECO-ROMAN
121 ....Jermaine Hodge
132 ....Joe Betterman
145.5 ....Faruk Sahin
163 ....Harry Lester*
185 .........T.C. Dantzler
211.5 ....Brad Ahearn
264.5 ....Dremiel Byers
Team .......U.S. Army (Div. I)
　　　　　Sunkist Kids (Div. II)

2010
FREESTYLE
121 ....Obe Blanc
132 ....Shawn Bunch
145.5 ....Jared Frayer
163 ....Andrew Howe*
185 ....Jake Herbert
211.5 .......J.D. Bergman
264.5 ....Les Sigman
Team ....New York A.C. (Div. I)
　　　　　Gator WC (Div. II)

GRECO-ROMAN
121 ....Spenser Mango
132 ....Nathan Piasecki
145.5 ....Glenn Garrison
163 ....Jake Fisher
185 ....Cheney Haight*
211.5 ....Justin Ruiz
264.5 ....Brandon Rupp
Team .......U.S. Army (Div. I)
　　　　　Sunkist Kids (Div. II)

2011
FREESTYLE
121 ....Sam Hazewinkel
132 ....Reece Humphrey
145.5 ....Teyon Ware*
163 ....Jordan Burroughs
185 ....Jake Herbert
211.5 ....Jake Varner
264.5 ....Tervel Dlagnev
Team ....New York A.C.

2011 *(Cont.)*
GRECO-ROMAN
121 ....Spenser Mango*
132 ....Joe Betterman
145.5 ....Justin Lester
163 ....Ben Provisor
185 ....Jordan Holm
211.5 ....Justin Ruiz
264.5 ....Dremiel Byers
Team .......U.S. Army (Div. I)
　　　　　Sunkist Kids (Div. II)

2012
FREESTYLE
121 ....Nick Simmons
132 ....Coleman Scott
145.5 ....Jared Frayer
163 ....Jordan Burroughs
185 ....Travis Paulson
211.5 ....Jake Varner
264.5 ....Tervel Dlagnev
Team ....Sunkist

GRECO-ROMAN
121 ....Spenser Mango
132 ....Ellis Coleman
145.5 ....Justin Lester
163 ....Ben Provisor
185 ....Chas Betts
211.5 .......R.C. Johnson
264.5 ....Dremiel Byers
Team .......U.S. Army

2013
FREESTYLE
121 ....Obe Blanc
132 ....Reece Humphrey*
145.5 ....Kellen Russell
163 ....Jordan Burroughs
185 ....Keith Gavin
211.5 .......J.D. Bergman
264.5 ....Dom Bradley
Team ....New York A.C. (Div. I)
　　　　　Sunkist Kids (Div. II)

GRECO-ROMAN
121 ....Spenser Mango
132 ....Joseph Betterman
145.5 ....Ellis Coleman
163 ....Ben Provisor
185 ....Jordan Holm
211.5 ....John Wechter
264.5 ....David Arendt Jr.
Team .......U.S. Army (Div. I)
　　　　　Minnesota Storm (Div. II)

*Outstanding wrestler.

2014 MAJOR EVENTS

JANUARY

NHL Winter Classic	Jan 1
Major College BCS Bowl Games	Jan 1–3
NFL Wild-Card Playoffs	Jan 4–5
BCS Championship Game	Jan 6
NFL Divisional Playoffs	Jan 11–12
Australian Open	Jan 13–26
NFL Conference Championships	Jan 19
Millrose Games	Jan 24
NFL Pro Bowl	Jan 26

FEBRUARY

Super Bowl XLVIII	Feb 2
MLB Spring Training begins (voluntary)	*Feb 8*
NBA All-Star Game	Feb 16
Daytona 500	Feb 23
MLB Spring Training begins (mandatory)	*Feb 24*

MARCH

March Madness begins	Mar 18
NCAA Women's Hockey Frozen Four	Mar 21 & 23
MLB Opening Day (in Australia)	Mar 22
World Figure Skating Championships	Mar 24–30

APRIL

Kraft Nabisco Championship (Golf)	Apr 3–6
NCAA Men's Basketball Final Four semifinals	April 5
NCAA Women's B-ball Final Four & Champ.	Apr 6 & 8
NCAA Men's Basketball Championship Game	Apr 7
NCAA Men's Hockey Frozen Four & Champ.	Apr 10 & 12
The Masters	Apr 10–13
NHL Playoffs begin	Apr 16
NBA Playoffs begin	Apr 19
Boston Marathon	Apr 21

MAY

Kentucky Derby	May 3
NFL Draft	May 8–10
The Players Championship (Golf)	May 8–11
Preakness Stakes	May 17
NASCAR Sprint Cup All-Star Race	May 17
NBA Draft Lottery	May 20
UEFA Champions League Final (Soccer)	May 24
Indianapolis 500	May 25
French Open	May 26–June 8
NHL Stanley Cup Final begins	*May 26*

JUNE

MLB First-Year Player Draft	June 5
NBA Finals begin	*June 5*
Belmont Stakes	June 7
U.S. Open (Golf)	June 12–15
College World Series	June 14–25
U.S. Women's Open (Golf)	June 19–22
Wimbledon	June 23–July 6
NBA Draft	June 26
NHL Entry Draft	June 27–28

JULY

Tour de France	July 5–27
Women's British Open (Golf)	July 10–13
MLB All-Star Game	July 15
Men's British Open	July 17–20
Brickyard 400	July 27

AUGUST

NFL Hall of Fame Induction	Aug 3
PGA Championship	Aug 7–10
LPGA Championship	Aug 14–17
Little League World Series	Aug 14–23
U.S. Open (Tennis)	Aug 25–Sept 7
College Football Season begins	Aug 30

SEPTEMBER

NFL Season begins	*Sept 4*
NASCAR Chase for the Cup begins	*Sept 7*
PGA TOUR Championship	Sept 11–14
Ryder Cup	Sept 23–28
MLB Wild-Card Games	*Sept 30–Oct 1*

OCTOBER

MLB Divisional Series begin	*Oct 2*
NHL Season begins	*Oct 2*
MLB League Championship Series begin	*Oct 10*
World Series begins	*Oct 22*
NBA Regular Season begins	*Oct 21*
WTA Tournament of Champions	*Oct 27–Nov 3*

NOVEMBER

Breeders' Cup	Nov 1–2
New York Marathon	Nov 2
ATP World Tour Finals (Tennis)	Nov 3–10
NASCAR Chase for the Cup ends	*Nov 9*
Davis Cup Final (Tennis)	Nov 21–23

DECEMBER

MLS Cup	*Dec 1*
Major Conf. Championships (Coll. Football)	Dec 6
World Swimming Championships	Dec 3–7
Heisman Trophy Presentation	Dec 15
College Football Bowl Games begin	*Dec 20*

Italics indicate approximate date